Civilization of the
Ancient Mediterranean

GREECE AND ROME

Civilization of the Ancient Mediterranean

GREECE AND ROME

EDITED BY

Michael Grant and Rachel Kitzinger

VOLUME III

CHARLES SCRIBNER'S SONS
MACMILLAN LIBRARY REFERENCE
New York

Simon & Schuster Macmillan and Prentice Hall International
LONDON · MEXICO CITY · NEW DELHI · SINGAPORE · SYDNEY · TORONTO

Library of Congress Cataloging-in-Publication Data

Civilization of the ancient Mediterranean.
Includes bibliographies and index.
1. Civilization, Classical.   I. Grant, Michael,
1914–   . II. Kitzinger, Rachel, 1948–
DE59.C55   1987   938   87–23465
ISBN 0–684–17594–0 (set)

ISBN 0–684–18864–3 (vol. 1)
ISBN 0–684–18865–1 (vol. 2)
ISBN 0–684–18866–X (vol. 3)

Charles Scribner's Sons
An Imprint of Simon & Schuster Macmillan
1633 Broadway, New York, NY 10019-6785

9 11 13 15 17 19   Q/C   20 18 16 14 12 10 8

Printed in the United States of America

The paper in this book meets the guidelines for permanence and
durability of the Committee on Production Guidelines for Book
Longevity of the Council on Library Resources.

Contents

VOLUME I

Chronological Table · xvii

Introduction · xxv

HISTORY

Historical Summary of Greece
A. R. Burn · 3

Historical Summary of Rome
Arther Ferrill · 45

LAND AND SEA

Land and Sea
J. Donald Hughes · 89

CONTENTS

POPULATION

Races and Physical Types in the Classical World
Peyton Randolph Helm · 137

Early Greek Migrations
Ronald A. Crossland · 155

Late Roman Migrations
E. A. Thompson · 171

Languages and Dialects
David Langslow · 183

AGRICULTURE AND FOOD

Farming and Animal Husbandry
K. D. White · 211

Foodstuffs, Cooking, and Drugs
Don R. Brothwell · 247

TECHNOLOGY

Theories of Progress and Evolution
G. E. R. Lloyd · 265

Greek Building Techniques
J. J. Coulton · 277

Roman Building Techniques
James E. Packer · 299

Engineering
John G. Landels · 323

CONTENTS

Transportation
Lionel Casson · 353

Crafts and Craftsmen
Alison Burford · 367

Calendars and Time-Telling
Alan E. Samuel · 389

Alphabets and Writing
Rachel Kitzinger · 397

Book Production
Susan A. Stephens · 421

GOVERNMENT AND SOCIETY

Greek Forms of Government
Oswyn Murray · 439

Alternative Paths: Greek Monarchy and Federalism
Michael Grant · 487

Roman Forms of Government
E. Stuart Staveley · 495

Greek Class Structures and Relations
Stanley M. Burstein · 529

Roman Class Structures and Relations
Richard P. Saller · 549

Slavery
Thomas E. J. Wiedemann · 575

CONTENTS

Greek Law

Douglas M. MacDowell · 589

Roman Law

Alan Watson · 607

Greek Administration

Chester G. Starr · 631

Roman Administration

John Ferguson · 649

Interstate Relations

Shalom Perlman · 667

Wars and Military Science: Greece

J. K. Anderson · 679

Wars and Military Science: Rome

Graham Webster · 703

VOLUME II

ECONOMICS

Greek Trade, Industry, and Labor

M. M. Austin · 723

Roman Trade, Industry, and Labor

Keith Hopkins · 753

Mines and Quarries

John F. Healy · 779

Greek Taxation

Robert J. Littman · 795

Roman Taxation
Brent D. Shaw · 809

Insurance and Banking
Wesley E. Thompson · 829

Piracy
Lionel Casson · 837

RELIGION

Divinities
John Ferguson · 847

Myths and Cosmologies
Michael Simpson · 861

Magic
John Ferguson · 881

Greek Cults
Susan Guettel Cole · 887

Roman Cults
John Ferguson · 909

Greek Priesthoods
Judy Ann Turner · 925

Roman Priesthoods
Mary Beard · 933

Divination and Oracles: Greece
John Pollard · 941

Divination and Oracles: Rome
John Ferguson · 951

CONTENTS

Sacrifice and Ritual: Greece
Michael H. Jameson · *959*

Sacrifice and Ritual: Rome
John A. North · *981*

The Afterlife: Greece
Emily Vermeule · *987*

The Afterlife: Rome
John A. North · *997*

Ruler Worship
J. Rufus Fears · *1009*

Judaism
Seth Schwartz · *1027*

Christianity
Helmut Koester and Vasiliki Limberis · *1047*

PRIVATE AND SOCIAL LIFE

Greek Education and Rhetoric
Carolyn Dewald · *1077*

Roman Education and Rhetoric
Cecil W. Wooten · *1109*

Folklore
William F. Hansen · *1121*

Athletics
David C. Young · *1131*

Greek Spectacles and Festivals
Robert Garland · *1143*

CONTENTS

Roman Games
John H. Humphrey · 1153

Greek Associations, Symposia, and Clubs
Nicholas R. E. Fisher · 1167

Roman Associations, Dinner Parties, and Clubs
Nicholas R. E. Fisher · 1199

Medicine
John Scarborough · 1227

Greek Attitudes Toward Sex
Jeffrey Henderson · 1249

Roman Attitudes Toward Sex
Judith P. Hallett · 1265

Images of the Individual
Peter Walcot · 1279

Prostitution
Werner A. Krenkel · 1291

VOLUME III

WOMEN AND FAMILY LIFE

Women in Greece
Helene P. Foley · 1301

Women in Rome
Sheila K. Dickison · 1319

Greek Marriage
Sarah B. Pomeroy · 1333

CONTENTS

Roman Marriage

Susan Treggiari · 1343

Birth Control, Childbirth, and Early Childhood

Valerie French · 1355

Houses

Alexander Gordon McKay · 1363

Clothing and Ornament

Larissa Bonfante and Eva Jaunzems · 1385

LITERARY AND PERFORMING ARTS

Epic Poetry

Bryan Hainsworth · 1417

Greek Lyric and Elegiac Poetry

Joseph Russo · 1437

Roman Lyric and Elegiac Poetry

Gordon Williams · 1455

Bucolic Poetry

David M. Halperin · 1467

Drama

Peter D. Arnott · 1477

Epigrams and Satire

J. P. Sullivan · 1495

Music and Dance

Edward Kerr Borthwick · 1505

Literary Criticism

Frederick T. Griffiths · 1515

Greek Historiography and Biography
Stephen Usher · 1525

Roman Historiography and Biography
Ronald Mellor · 1541

The Novel
John J. Winkler · 1563

Letter Writing
Robert Glenn Ussher · 1573

PHILOSOPHY

Greek Philosophy
G. E. R. Lloyd · 1585

Roman Philosophical Movements
Elizabeth Asmis · 1637

THE VISUAL ARTS

Greek Architecture
J. J. Coulton · 1653

Roman Architecture
Roger Ling · 1671

Urban Planning
Thomas D. Boyd · 1691

Greek Sculpture and Gems
Jerome J. Pollitt · 1701

Roman Sculpture and Gems
Richard Brilliant · 1727

Greek Painting and Mosaic

Jerome J. Pollitt · 1749

Roman Painting and Mosaic

Roger Ling · 1771

Coins

R. A. G. Carson · 1795

EPILOGUE

The Progress of Classical Scholarship

R. R. Bolgar · 1819

Maps · 1833
List of Contributors · 1845
Index · 1851

Civilization of the
Ancient Mediterranean

GREECE AND ROME

WOMEN AND FAMILY LIFE

Women in Greece

HELENE P. FOLEY

ALTHOUGH WOMEN IN FACT play virtually no public role other than a religious one in the political and social life of ancient Greece, they dominate the imaginative life of Greek men to a degree almost unparalleled in the Western tradition. Poetry in particular endows its female characters with an extraordinary spectrum of views from conventional to iconoclastic. These ubiquitous fictional women range from wise to foolish, pure to corrupt, strong to subservient. They may endanger male order, life, and sanity, or become sources of heroic salvation. Virtually none of our literary sources—the writings of poets, historians, philosophers, medical writers, orators, or popular moralists—or even nonliterary sources—inscriptions, the fine arts, or papyrus letters and documents—offers or even pretends to offer an objective view of women. Even a prose writer, like the classical historian and popular philosopher Xenophon, in his treatise *Household Management (Oeconomicus)* gives an idealized and prescriptive rather than realistic picture of life inside the *oikos* (household). Many texts deal only obliquely with women and no full biography of any woman's life exists. The atti-tudes expressed in different sources and kinds of sources or at different historical periods frequently contradict each other and represent almost entirely the views of upper-class citizen males. We have only fragments of literature or papyrus letters by women as evidence of an alternative perspective. Yet the very visibility and ambiguity attributed by Greek men to their otherwise silent women makes the problem of the Greek attitude toward women and its influence on later Western tradition a particularly important one.

The sheer multiplicity of sources and the contradictions among them require in a brief treatment of this problem the establishment of severe limits. A fully adequate study would be entitled "Greek Conceptions of the Feminine" in order to include attitudes to female divinities as well as to mortal women, and would examine shifts in attitudes from Homer to late antiquity. This essay confines itself to Greek attitudes toward women represented in written sources from Homer to the end of the classical period, with occasional references to the Hellenistic world to report important contrasts or continuities. The rationale for establishing these limits is twofold. First, until the spread of Greek culture by Alexander and his successors, we are dealing largely with Greek culture in Asia Minor, southern Italy, mainland Greece, and the islands in between; in the Hellenistic period Greek culture becomes international, and the collapse of the Greek city-states and increased contact with the rest of the Mediterranean world, especially Egypt and later Italy, shatter an earlier cultural coherence. Second, relatively little work has been done on conceptions of women in the postclassical period, and to begin such analysis here would be to engage in sheer speculation.

The essay will be divided into two parts. The first part summarizes Greek male attitudes throughout the designated period to woman's role inside and outside the household, as well as to her mind, body, and moral capacity. The second part offers first a summary of some of the possible socioeconomic reasons for these conceptions of women, and then an explanation of the variety of ways that Greek writers used the female—in a fashion that bore little relation to the lives of actual women—to understand, express, criticize, and experiment with the problems and contradictions of their culture. In general, Greek attitudes toward woman seemed to vary with women's actual social status; sexual dimorphism was greater and the conception of women more negative where the division between public and domestic spheres was most articulated, and where women lived isolated from one another in individual households.

WOMEN'S ROLE IN THE HOUSEHOLD

The ideals concerning women's role in the household remain relatively fixed from Homer onward. Most important, a wife was to create legitimate heirs for her husband's household. Unless engaged in religious activities, wives were to remain almost exclusively inside the house—and in fifth-century Athens, even confined within their own women's quarters—to guard and manage the household, to care for small children and servants, and to supervise weaving and cooking. For Homer, each sex has a mutually beneficial function to perform in society. As Hector says to his wife, Andromache, about the sexual division of labor: "But returning to the house, attend to your work, the loom and the distaff, and bid your handmaidens to do so also; but the men will have charge of the fighting, all of those from Ilium, but I more than others" (*Iliad* 6.490–493). Yet public and private worlds are less remote in Homeric epics than in later periods. Inside the household, queens in the *Odyssey* receive or question guests at their husband's side, present gifts, tell stories of their own, and even—at least in the utopia of Phaeacia—adjudicate quarrels among favorites (7.73–74). They establish reputations in their own right for beauty, chastity, or intelligence. Not only mortal women but also goddesses weave, hence woman's task of weaving is viewed as something beyond mere labor; like a poet, Helen (*Iliad* 3.125–128) represents on her web the battles fought for her at Troy; Penelope unravels her web to deceive the suitors for many years. All types of Greek poetry use weaving as a metaphor to describe the poetic process.

Like Homer, Xenophon in *Household Management* justifies and idealizes the sexual division of labor as natural and as a source of dignity and pride for women. Women's work, he argues, is best done in a sheltered and protected environment, in which the wife acts as a queen bee (*hegemon melitta*) in her own separate sphere, whereas man's outdoor agricultural labor prepares him for his other duties in war and politics. Xenophon even goes so far as to propose that a wife be educated for her important role and learn to imitate her husband's ability to deal rationally with all aspects of his environment. The ideal wife will understand that her own interests are best served by serving those of an affectionate husband; her domestic routine should include, like the male routine, some form of moderate exercise to maintain health; she should learn from her husband's example how to adjudicate fairly in household matters. The prescriptive tone of *Household Management*, however, suggests that Xenophon's—and, reputedly, the famous hetaera Aspasia's—interest in the wife's domestic role was unusual and not the rule. In *Household Management* (3.12) Socrates' interlocutor Critobolus admits that in fact there is almost no one with whom he converses less than his wife.

Greek epitaphs movingly praise the Athenian wife for her role as wife and mother, and vase paintings show in the late fifth century a growing interest in idealizing domestic subjects. The historian Herodotus, in part because of his anthropological concern with all aspects of culture rather than simply with the political sphere, gives considerable attention to the often positive influence of women in the household on history. He mentions how captured Carian women from Asia Minor transmit native customs to their daughters from one generation to the next; and that the Lydian king Candaules' wife takes justified revenge on her husband for allowing her to be seen nude by another man (*Histories* 1.146; 1.8–11). But Herodotus draws his examples largely from outside the Greek world of the classical era. Unlike Xenophon, most Attic prose writers, reflecting an increased gap between public and private life in classical Athens, prefer not to dwell on women and the private sphere. In his famous funeral oration (Thucydides, *History of the Peloponnesian War* 2.46), Pericles asserts that the virtuous widow lacks a reputation for either good or evil.

Later orators also praise women for their silence and invisibility, and avoid mentioning the names of living respectable women. In one court case, a man's sister and nieces are said to be embarrassed even to be seen by close male relatives (Lysias, *Against Simon* 6). In another, entering a married man's house in his absence earns great opprobrium (Demosthenes, *Against Euergus* 47). Most Athenian sources express dismay at the degree to which Spartan women made public appearances, exercised like men, and displayed their wealth. As to women's creativity, the Parthenon frieze honored women for their weaving of a peplos (an embroidered ceremonial robe) for Athena at the panathenaic festival, and in fiction, Aristophanes' Lysistrata uses weaving imagery to describe her plan to unite Greece in peace (*Lysistrata* 567 ff.); but only in the epitaphs of girls who died unwed does the domestic weaving of individual Athenian women receive the recognition accorded to Helen's or Penelope's webs. Indeed, in Attic drama weaving and clothing made by women more frequently serve an anticultural function. Clytemnestra entraps Agamemnon in the "nets" of her weaving, and Deianira destroys her husband, Heracles, with a poisoned garment.

Aristotle's analysis of the relative importance of household and state in the *Politics* seems to typify the classical view on the relative merits of male and female life. For Aristotle, the household is a more primitive and natural form of social organization than the polis. By being confined to the household and its hierarchies, women cannot live a fully human life, which consists in the free, rational, and public pursuit of happiness, moral excellence, and philosophical contemplation.

The archaic misogynistic poetry of Hesiod, Semonides of Amorgos, and others offers the most negative view of woman's domestic role. Women are a necessary evil, required for the reproduction of children. Apart from this function, Hesiod, for example, describes woman as a drone who wastes a man's substance, both sexually and economically, and apparently makes no other contribution to the household whatsoever. Although his *Works and Days* makes private life its central subject, weaving and cooking by women are never mentioned. Instead, the farmer himself is described as stitching together goat hides to ward off the winter's cold (540–543).

WOMEN'S ACTIVITIES OUTSIDE THE HOUSEHOLD

In many Greek cities individual aristocratic women apparently had an informal influence on politics; but until the Hellenistic period, when queens and other female office-holders were in a position to demand public recognition of their deeds, only the Homeric epics viewed women as able to make even a minor contribution to political life. Clytemnestra in Aeschylus' *Agamemnon* (259–260) is said to exercise authority legitimately in the absence of her husband; but, since the queen monstrously abuses her power by killing her husband, committing adultery, disenfranchising her son, and establishing a tyranny, this example from the mythic past serves finally to make the case against allowing such sovereignty to classical women. Like many tragic heroes, Creon in Sophocles' *Antigone* (672–678) associates civic anarchy with yielding to a woman's will. In the Hellenistic period and later, inscriptions record appreciation for economic contributions to the state by women; previously they rarely had their own property to dispense. Women poets are praised, although sometimes rather condescendingly, provided they refrain from competing with men, as Myrtis supposedly did with Pindar (Corinna, frag. 664 Page, *Poetae Melici Graeci*). Sappho was designated the tenth Muse.

Remarkably, women at all periods in the Greek world played an important role in religion, as priestesses, as mourners at funerals, and as participants in weddings and a large variety of festivals. Some festivals were confined to women, some to citizens of both sexes, and some, such as the Eleusinian Mysteries, were open to all people who spoke Greek. Prose texts rarely mention or express attitudes to women's role in religion, while poetic texts often emphasize it. Poets voice approval when women act in public cults or perform ritual activities that serve the benefit of the whole city. In *Iliad* 6, Hector returns to the city to exhort his mother to pray with other Trojan women for the favor of Athena. Aristophanes' Lysistrata, who is associated in a thinly disguised fashion with the contemporary priestess of Athena Polias Lysimache, receives little mockery, in contrast to her sex-mad colleagues, for her plan to bring peace to Greece in the Peloponnesian War. The female chorus of the *Lysistrata* (638–647) appeals for a male hearing on the grounds of the religious education they received as virgins from the state. A fragment from Euripides' *Captive Melanippe* (Page, *Select Papyri* III, 113–114) praises women's important role in religion, and uses it as evidence to counter the Greek misogynist tradition:

> Men's blame and denigration of women twangs an idle bowstring. As I will show, they are better than men. . . . They care for the house and preserve within merchandise brought over the sea. Without a wife, no home is clean and prosperous. As to religious matters, here I rest my claim that we play the most important role. Women interpret Apollo's mind at his oracles, and, at the holy seat of Dodona near the sacred oak, woman presents the will of Zeus to all Greeks who desire it. They conduct rites for the Fates and the nameless goddesses. These are not holy for men to perform, but flourish in the hands of women. Given women's righteous role in divine matters, how is it appropriate for the female race to be abused?

Yet even such highly legitimate religious observances can provoke suspicion. Aeschylus' Eteocles chastises the chorus of women in the first scene of the *Seven Against Thebes* for upsetting the besieged city with their hysterical public prayers to the gods. (And, as many writers remark, festivals offer as well a dangerous opportunity for women to meet men and begin clandestine affairs.)

Other female religious activities consistently evoke more ambivalent attitudes. Women's dominant role in funerals, and in secret and chthonic rites, associated them with the dangerous, the unknown, the polluting. At the Thesmophoria, a three-day women's fertility festival, women in Athens left their homes to camp out on the slope of the Pnyx Hill to the southwest of the Agora (normally the meeting place of the exclusively male ecclesia, or general assembly). Imitating a precivilized way of life, they slept on mats of osier in makeshift huts and cured meat in the sun. To promote fertility, the women descended into underground pits to bring up the remains of pigs that had been earlier left to rot, mixed them with cakes baked in the shape of sexual symbols, and shouted ritual obscenities. Such all-female cults were financed by men and given priority in the civic calendar. At the same time, the secret, aggressive, and primitive nature of the rites reinforced male fear of female autonomy. Aristophanes' *Women at the Thesmophoria* shows a typical ambivalence to women's rites. In this play the women are plotting to take revenge on Euripides for his misogyny, yet their own behavior justifies the poet's reputed suspicions; elsewhere in the works of Aristophanes women also use religious rites as an occasion to hatch plots or as an excuse to challenge men.

Dionysiac cults reinforced the cultural stereotype of women as irrational and closer to nature than men. Evidence for the actual nature of these cults is virtually nonexistent before the Hellenistic period. Yet typical Dionysiac myths, such as that represented in Euripides' *The Bacchants* (*Bacchae*) stress the dangers inherent in women's departure from the confines of the household and their conventional sexual role as well as female susceptibility to ecstatic trances; such stories tend to close with maddened women destroying male relatives or children.

Attic sources imply that women's extensive participation in religion was tolerated as a form of compensation for their lack of access to other aspects of public life. Aeschylus' trilogy about the Danaids (*The Suppliants*, *The Egyptians*, and *The Daughters of Danaus*) may have concluded with the establishment of the Thesmophoria in Greece in compensation for women's acceptance of subordination in marriage. In Aeschylus' *Eumenides*, the Erinyes (Furies), spirits of revenge who represent the female side in the trial of Orestes, are offered and accept a cult that promotes fertility to compensate their failure, in this instance, to avenge intrafamilial murder.

A portion of a Pythagorean treatise on women's role from the second or third century B.C. (Thesleff, pp. 151–154) shows little change in attitude from the classical period. A virtuous woman should above all be clean and chaste; she should leave the house only by day and be well chaperoned; she should sacrifice in accordance with her means to the principal deity of the community on behalf of herself, her husband, and her household; and she should refuse to participate in secret or Cybeline cults that promote drunkenness and ecstasy.

WOMEN'S BODIES AND MINDS

The Homeric poems view anatomical differences between the sexes largely in relation to the division of roles between them. Woman's physical capacities and her role in reproduction confine her to the world of peace and the household. The ideal husband and wife have the same mind (*Odyssey* 6.180–185), and Homeric women consistently show rationality and intelligence. From the fifth century onward, however, most writers assume that woman's nature dooms her to a considerably more subordinate role in the culture. Throughout his ethical, political, and biological works (*History of Animals, On the Parts of Animals,* and *Generation of Animals*), Aristotle views the female anatomy and generative capacity as linked with mental, emotional, and moral capacities. Both Aristotle and the medical texts agree that woman's body is more porous than man's. For Aristotle, her blood, like that of old and sick people, is thicker than that of the male, her teeth are fewer and less effective, her muscles weaker, her brain smaller and with fewer sutures to allow it to breathe. Females are the products of a weaker sperm; the female fetus moves later and causes a more difficult pregnancy. After birth, she develops more quickly than the male, a sign of her lesser perfection. The cooler temperature of the female ensures that her menses provide only the matter out of which the human fetus develops; male heat concocts blood into sperm and gives the male seed the exclusive generating power. When the sperm fails to prevail fully over the menses, a "natural mutilation" or female child is produced. Contemporary popular literature confirms Aristotle's view of conception; woman is the earth, the furrow for a man actively to plow. Aristotle recommends that the pregnant woman, as nurturer of the child, avoid physical and rational activity (*Politics* 7.12.1335b17–19). As a deformed or incomplete male, the woman has a deliberative faculty, but it is "without authority" (*akuros*) (*Politics* 1.13.1260b28–31); she is unable fully to control her emotions and appetites; less capable of shame than a man, she tends by nature to lie and deceive (*History of Animals* 9.1.608b16–17). Xenophon in the *Household Management* similarly finds the domestic role natural to woman because she is weaker, less courageous, and more affectionate to children than a man.

The medical writers in the Hippocratic corpus also find an intimate connection between women's mental and physical health. The healthy adult woman is pregnant, menstruating, or lactating (although these natural processes can also lead to disease or death). Dysmenorrheal women, virgins, and widows are subject to a variety of mental and physical disorders. The womb, when it is not weighted with child or wet with semen, can migrate to various parts of the body, causing in the woman hysterical symptoms, a lust for wandering, or even madness; repellent fumigations must be applied at the mouth, or sweet pessaries used at the entrance to the vagina to entice the womb back into place (Hippocratic *Diseases of Women* and *Nature of Women*). Before menstruation, virgins may experience suffocation and depression from the pressure of the unreleased menstrual blood. They may choke themselves or leap spontaneously into wells. In this case, doctors propose marriage and intercourse as the appropriate cure (Hippocratic *On Virgins*). Women's unstable and penetrable bodies make them, in the popular view, more susceptible not only to erotic desire, but also to madness, prophecy, demonic possession, and pain. As the chorus of women laments in Euripides' *Hippolytus* (161–162), woman's body dooms her to helplessness by its *dustropos harmonia* (ill-turned unity).

Misogynist writers of the archaic period even went so far as to attribute to women a separate origin from men. Hesiod's first woman, Pandora, was created to bring about the fall of men, who earlier lived as lesser gods, into mortality and disease. Pandora is a deceitful imitation of an immortal goddess, whose enticing exterior conceals a deceptive and unreliable interior. Classical

Athens, by worshiping Pandora alongside Ericthonius, a mythical king born spontaneously from the earth, seems to have preserved Hesiod's myth of a separate race of women. For Semonides of Amorgos, different tribes of women descend from an animal (such as weasel women, pig women, or horse women), the sea, or earth, and reflect the characteristics of their origin. Zeus "made women's minds separately"; their appetites are ill controlled. Only the sexless bee woman, who devotes herself to a family isolated from outside influences, transcends the subcultural nature of her sex. Tragic heroes like Hippolytus or Jason are prone to wish angrily for a different method of procreating children (Euripides, *Hippolytus* 616–624; *Medea* 573–574), and the entire misogynist tradition emphasizes the dangerous effects of the company of women on women. Female gossip stimulates erotic fantasy and idle behavior, and groups of women are especially prone to Dionysiac possession.

Women had frequent contact with sources of pollution, as with the dead bodies that it was their task to prepare for burial and lament. There is little direct evidence that women's own bodies were viewed as a source of pollution until the fourth century B.C., when inscriptions begin to prohibit women from participating in cults, for example, after intercourse, parturition, or the miscarriage of a fully formed fetus. Earlier, Hesiod recommends not using a woman's bathwater (*Works and Days* 753–754), and Aeschylus' fearsome Furies drip blood as they pursue Orestes. In Aristotle's *On Dreams* (459b–460a), a menstruating woman can cloud the surface of a mirror into which she looks. In what may represent a deliberate contrast, the medical texts seem to view all aspects of the normal reproductive cycle of women as healthy, and recommend intercourse during menstruation as the best time for conceiving children.

Male writers appropriate birth, like weaving, as a metaphor for creativity; but male "births" are spiritual rather than physical. Plato's philosopher becomes a midwife for a soul pregnant with ideas (*Theaetetus* 149a ff.; *Symposium* 206c ff.). Hesiod's Zeus in the *Theogony* (886 ff.) confirms his control of the universe by appropriating the birth process for himself. After swallowing the goddess Metis, he gives birth to Athena from his head.

Views of woman's moral capacity seem to vary with the attitude toward her mind and body. Homeric women reason and make their own moral judgments in areas appropriate to their own sphere; war and poetry must be left to men (*Iliad* 6.492–493; *Odyssey* 1.346–359). Penelope's protection of her chastity and her fight to preserve her marriage with Odysseus are a matter of conscious choice; Princess Nausicaa in the *Odyssey* makes a careful assessment of how to treat the stranger Odysseus in the light of cultural expectations about the moral behavior appropriate to young women. In Homer women are generally viewed as morally responsible, and can thus, like men, be praised or blamed for their acts. In the Homeric *Hymn to Demeter,* the young daughters of Celeus win the disguised Demeter's admiration for their understanding of how to treat old women. Although Helen's adultery brings her no explicit blame, except from herself, because she was under the influence of the goddess Aphrodite, men are also subject to divinely imposed misjudgments. In *Iliad* 2 the gods inflict on Agamemnon a temporary blindness (*ate*); Zeus sends a false dream to Agamemnon to deceive him into thinking that he is about to take Troy without Achilles.

Both the archaic misogynists and classical literature tend to view women as less rational and morally capable than men. Semonides' fox woman cannot distinguish good from bad; his sea woman "thinks two things," whimsically changing from pleasant to hostile regardless of circumstances. From Semonides to Aristotle, women are considered to fall victim to their appetites, their innate tendency to overeat, drink, desire, and deceive. Even when they know what is right, like Euripides' Phaedra, they fail finally to pursue it (*Hippolytus* 380–383). Women's preeminent virtue is a passive *sophrosune*, the capacity for self-control, and especially sexual self-control. For Aristotle, woman's moral capacity derives from her function in life: "All things derive their essential characters from their function and capacity" (*Politics* 1.2.1253a23–24). Confined to the private world, she may make decisions about housework; but in other matters she preserves a modest silence, obeying her husband because, like a child, she lacks sufficient rationality to make an independent moral choice. A wife loves her husband more than he does her, for friendship, too, must accord with the virtue of each party (*Nicomachean Ethics* 8.7). Wills made under the undue influence of madness, senility, alcohol, drugs, or a woman could be declared invalid (Isaeus, *On the Estate of Menecles* 2).

Before marriage a girl was not formally educated, except by participation in religious rites, but "tamed" like a domestic animal. Xenophon in the *Household Management* urges a husband to train his young wife in domestic management; if young girls received informal training in such matters at home—as they probably did—neither Xenophon nor others chose to mention it. Such views implicitly justify women's status in classical Athens, their legal and economic minority, their lack of formal education and even literacy. Aristotle also blames rich Spartan women, who had more social and economic autonomy, for their city's decline (*Politics* 2.9.1269b–1270a); shaped by their exclusion from public life, Spartan women are accused of using their wealth to win attention—financing victories in horse races at

Olympia, for example—or to gratify private desires, rather than to support the public good.

As Euripides' Medea laments, women are fundamentally incapable of doing good (*Medea* 407–409), or indeed of *acting* outside the domestic world in any positive fashion. Any nonreligious public action taken by a woman as an individual violates the silence, invisibility, and moral dependence appropriate to a virtuous wife. Greek men are virtuous when they receive public recognition for their moral acts, when they can confer benefits on friends and harm enemies. As possessions of men, women lack the resources independently to confer benefits (although Medea can do so with magic); they are reduced merely to devious modes of revenge, which win them no real honor but confirm their fundamental unreliability and duplicity. Attic tragedy celebrates female excellence (*arete*) publicly only in cases where heroines such as Antigone, Alcestis, and Iphigenia voluntarily sacrifice themselves to save city, family, or nation. And many of these heroines go to their deaths asserting that their own lives are of less worth than those of men (for example, *Iphigenia in Aulis* 1392–1394).

Nevertheless, there are many signs that such assumptions about women's nature and moral capacities were being questioned or at least partially revised in the late fifth and early fourth centuries. Socrates apparently made a point of arguing that the virtue of a man and a woman were the same (Plato, *Meno* 72A–73C). Despite a generally low opinion of his female contemporaries, Plato in the *Republic* views women's lesser physical capacity as unrelated to their mental and moral potential, and argues that some women of the guardian class will rule as philosopher kings. He suggests that all irrational human behavior is due first and foremost to lack of knowledge and inadequate training, but that women are further crippled by their confinement to private life in the family. Sophocles' *Women of Trachis* shows that even the most virtuous wife has insufficient knowledge of the world to make correct moral judgments. Deianira, in attempting to win back Heracles' love from a young concubine, mistakenly gives him a robe smeared with a fatal poison that she believes to be a love potion. She innocently accepts as true and benevolent the deceptive instructions of the dying Nessus, the centaur who has just tried to rape her. As a virtuous wife, she fails to have the knowledge of eros necessary to avoid her fatal error.

In the seventh century, Sappho makes Helen a deliberate agent in her own adultery. No attempt is made to exonerate her, but rather Sappho's poem shows that all humans pursue what they perceive to be most beautiful: "Some say that a troop of horsemen, some of foot soldiers, some a fleet of ships is the most beautiful thing on the dark earth; but I say that it is whatever one loves" (frag. 16 Lobel and Page). The case of Helen reminds Sappho of "absent Anactoria, whose beloved step and brilliant glance I would prefer to see than Lydian chariots and men in arms." The male preference for war is by implication as much a product of a subjective yet amoral desire as the woman's erotic preference for an individual; the public is no better than the private. In the classical period, Euripides similarly revises myths about women to question masculine ideals. In *Helen*, his heroine is no longer the passive victim of eros, persuasion, or divinity, as in the Sophist Gorgias' *Encomium on Helen*, but, as in Stesichorus, she is a virtuous wife who has preserved her chastity in Egypt while the Trojan War was being fought absurdly for a phantom. The chorus in Euripides' *Medea* (410–430) sees Jason's treachery as confirming what women have always known, if history had allowed them a poetic voice to express their views: men as well as women break oaths and deliberately deceive the families who depend on them. Medea's later action in killing her children to take revenge on Jason, however, undercuts the chorus' optimism that Medea's story will reverse sexual stereotypes.

Among other female characters, Jocasta in Euripides' *Phoenician Women* and Aristophanes' Lysistrata represent the voices of reason and the public good in the face of masculine irrationality, loss of political perspective, and devotion to self-interest. In Aristophanes' *Assemblywomen* women take over the government to save the state from men who have become so obsessed with private gain and private affairs, and hence feminized, that they are unable to keep the public interest in view. In these cases the sexual reversal offers not so much a defense of women, who often continue in these very plays to exhibit stereotypical feminine behavior, as an exposure of men's vulnerability to weaknesses more often associated with women. Men here use women to express those sides of reality that they prefer to see as alien to their own "godlike," rational, and public selves: the vulnerability of the mind and body, the painful division between the inner and outer, between the public and private selves.

The Hellenistic period, which confirmed a growing late-fifth-century interest in the private over the public self, in Dionysus and Aphrodite above other Olympian deities, continued to expand in its literature on this theme of the fundamentally androgynous nature of human irrationality, and to use sex-role reversal to criticize traditional cultural stereotypes. Medea, as the erotic heroine of the *Voyage of the Argonauts,* an epic by Apollonius Rhodius, not only outshines the antihero Jason, but also acts for him. While Jason allows others to accomplish his quest for him, Medea's decisive wrestling with the anguish produced by desire and divided loyalties comes to seem a far more enthralling and heroic struggle.

THEORIES EXPLAINING THE GREEK CONCEPTION OF WOMEN

Social, historical, and economic factors can provide a partial explanation for both the constant features and the variations in the archaic and classical views of Greek women: the political and economic organization of the society, marriage and family patterns, the social class of the writer, and the changing relations between state and household, public and private worlds.

The aristocratic viewpoints depicted in the Homeric epics and the lyric poems of later archaic aristocrats emphasize women's positive contribution to their societies and their inclusion in them. This poetry celebrates female beauty, fertility, intelligence, dancing, weaving, or creative management of the domestic world. The necessary absence of the husband in war gives to the wife's role in the household a public as well as a private importance. The *Odyssey* romantically celebrates the relation between husband and wife, makes domestic life a valuable goal, and treats both spouses as heroic. Penelope is repeatedly described with similes—a cornered lion, a good king, a swimmer who has reached land against all hope—that associate her with her husband. Odysseus is once compared to a female victim of war (*Odyssey* 8.521–531) and undergoes with the goddess Calypso the feminine experience of anonymous isolation and sexual subservience. These implied role reversals serve to emphasize the common humanity of man and wife over their differences, to reduce the distance between public and private worlds, and to make clear that an intelligent and sympathetic wife is an asset to a good king, and even necessary to his survival.

Similarly, whereas the misogynist tradition expresses strong ambivalence toward group activities by women, the maiden songs of the Spartan poet Alcman and the poetry of Sappho glorify and romanticize the initiatory experiences of young women. Perhaps Spartan society chose to celebrate women publicly because, as Plutarch remarks, children belonged less to their parents than to the whole society, which put the highest priority on producing superior warriors; indeed, wives could be lent to produce children for other men (hence the claim that adultery did not exist in Sparta) and women were exempt from weaving and participated in gymnastics and music in order to prepare themselves for bearing and rearing children (Plutarch, *Parallel Lives,* "Lycurgus" 14–16; Plato, *Laws* 7.806a).

The archaic misogynist tradition prominent in Hesiod, Semonides, and iambic poetry reflects different social and economic conditions. In *Works and Days* Hesiod represents himself as a "middle-class" farmer engaged in labor-intensive agriculture on a small farm and struggling to exist in an unstable world where the *basileis,* or petty kings, prove corrupt and self-aggrandizing. Slave women, not wives, are said to assist in this essential agricultural work (*Works and Days* 405–406). Although Hesiod needs a wife to produce heirs for his household, from an economic point of view she is represented as a luxury. In a similar vein, Semonides particularly denigrates the lazy sow woman, or the aristocratic mare woman, who do not work, and celebrates the bee woman, who by implication works continually. Although the danger of female adultery played an important role in epic, Hesiod and Semonides seem particularly concerned with controlling female sexuality. Marriages in the epics were largely exogamous, provided a dowry over which the husband had full control, and allowed the Homeric king to make political alliances. Kings could, moreover, produce legitimate heirs from concubines. Hesiod recommends marrying the daughter of a neighbor (*Works and Days* 699–701); he apparently expects to receive little benefit from this arrangement beyond the opportunity to judge the wife's potential for chastity and good behavior before the marriage. As in classical Athens, the need to produce a legitimate heir for the household, a consciousness of family honor, and the development of endogamous marriage patterns seem to be accompanied by a growing fear of adultery and by the social seclusion and denigration of women. Hence adulterous women in Athens were to be divorced and excluded from participation in religious festivals.

As Jean-Pierre Vernant (1969) has emphasized, however, Greek marriage patterns contributed to male anxiety about women at all periods in the Greek world. The wife, brought into the household at a young age to marry a considerably older man and often tied to her natal family by a dowry or other legal obligations, occupied a precarious mediating position between two households, and was unlikely to be fully trusted by either. (As an *epikleros,* or heiress, an Attic woman was required to marry the next of kin on her father's side—even if she was already married—in order to produce a male heir for her father's *oikos.*) Indeed, the role of the chaste yet fertile wife is both paradoxical and inherently threatening. Greek writers from Homer to Xenophon continually stress the need for the wife to treat her husband's interests as her own. Xenophon recommends educating the wife to this point of view, a measure that implies that this perspective on the woman's dowry was far from common. Euripides' Andromache, in *Andromache* (224–225), advises Hermione not to rely on her father, Menelaus, but to serve her husband, Neoptolemus, devotedly; she herself even went so far as to nurse Hector's bastards. Women in Attic tragedy are far more likely to express strong allegiance to their natal families than to their husbands. They lament their role as dependent strangers in an alien household, who are ex-pected to acquiesce to social isolation, painful childbearing, and an unknown spouse without complaint (Euripides' *Medea* 230–251; Sophocles' *Tereus,* frag. 583 Radt).

The Homeric *Hymn to Demeter* deals with the pain caused by the separation of mother from daughter occasioned by Hades' rape of Persephone, and Greek literature often treats marriage as a kind of symbolic death for the woman. Women's religious cults celebrated the myth of Demeter and Persephone, and women's own poetry in the ancient world (as well as papyrus letters from Egypt) seems to have been especially concerned with the theme of separation, whether of two women, of a daughter and her natal family, or of husband and wife. Sappho dwells on the pains of pursuing a reluctant or inaccessible beloved, consoles women in her circle over the loss of a beloved girl, or unites them imaginatively with a remote love. Erinna, too, laments in her poem *The Distaff* the loss of a beloved friend, first to marriage and then to early death. Women from Penelope to the real-life wives writing letters in Hellenistic and Roman Egypt emphasize the difficulties posed by the absence of a spouse. Beginning with Andromache in *Iliad* 6, fictional women stress their utter dependence on husband or family, their helplessness in the aftermath of war.

Attic democracy, in attempting to equalize wealth and legal capacity for all citizens and to ensure maximum attention to the interests of the city, curbed the influence of the aristocratic family with land reform and with the legal control and isolation of the *oikos,* and reduced in power those local communities that had mediated between the interests of household and state. As part of this effort, Solon's laws placed new restrictions on the lives of women. By reinforcing the separation between family and state and between public and private life, Attic democracy further divided the lives of men and women and enhanced a view of sexual difference disadvantageous to women that served to explain and justify their new social structure. As Friedrich Engels argued, societies consistently value the public over the private; labor that visibly contributes to the public good is viewed as superior to that which supports the survival of an individual household. Attic women, silent and invisible in their women's quarters, produced clothing and heirs for the household, while men spent a considerably higher proportion of their time contributing in multiple ways—military, political, economic, and artistic—to the good of the polis. While the aristocratic wife in the archaic period could through her husband have some positive effect on the public life of her society and win her own reputation for virtue, the Attic wife lived isolated from politics (if not from public religion) and hence from most sources of social prestige. Demosthenes' coldly functional remark about women in Athens (Demosthenes, *Against Neaira* 59.118–222), that wives served to produce legitimate heirs and guard the household, concubines (*hetairai*) to provide pleasure, and prostitutes to serve the daily needs of the body, encapsulates the difference between the Attic marriage and the respectful and often affectionate aristocratic marriage idealized in Homeric epic.

The sociologist Philip Slater (1968) has suggested that the Attic family pattern enhanced hostility between the sexes. The wife, angered by her social isolation, alternately expressed her hostility to her son and overwhelmed him with her own frustrated ambition. The father's frequent absences, Slater believes, made him an inaccessible role model; hence the son turned to competition and romance with his male peers, but failed to acquire a mature male identity. Misogynistic myths reflected both the male child's fear of female hostility and engulfment and an intense dependence on the powerful maternal figure. Slater's evidence is drawn largely from poetic sources and is too selective, since, for example, the Oedipus myth emphasizes the hostility of the father, rather than the mother, to his sons, and other texts suggest that fathers were considerably closer to their infants than he allows. He imposes his own contemporary biases about homosexuality, generalizes inappropriately from American suburban marriages to the classical context, and focuses too narrowly on family concerns. For drama used private life to explore public issues, and Greek poets consciously shaped their representation of family life to this end. However controversial, Slater's work has nevertheless raised important questions about powerful women and misogynist themes in Greek tragedy. And certainly the encouragement of homosexuality, narcissism, and prolonged bachelorhood in the early life of Attic men must have had a profound effect on the emotional relations between husband and wife.

The international culture and kingdoms of the Hellenistic world allowed increasing prestige to private life. Few people had access to public power, whether male or female. Due in part to the influence of other Mediterranean cultures, the economic and legal position of Greek women outside Athens improved, although access to office or financial independence meant considerably less. With this new relation between public and private worlds, misogynistic literature became rare, and although women continued to be thought less rational than men, there was a growing interest in female psychology and in heterosexual love.

Finally, however, it should be emphasized that genre and the overall agenda of a work of art may be as important in determining the attitude toward women in a given literary text as socioeconomic considerations. Internal evidence suggests that epic and much Hellenistic literature were directed particularly at an aristocratic and Panhellenic audience that included women on some occasions. Epic aims above all to praise and idealize the world it represents, and often suppresses aspects of the inherited tradition to this end. At the same time, it does not shy away from dealing with important cultural problems. The *Iliad* turns to women to stress the devastating effects of war on private life and to provide a motive for war. The *Odyssey* attempts to confront the relation between nature and culture, and to explore and justify the cultural order. In his journey Odysseus confronts both male and female deities and monsters, and societies that organize culture differently from his own. The poem celebrates family life on Ithaca but enlarges, through its exploration of sex roles, our understanding of the necessity and meaning of the sexual division of labor particular to Odysseus' own island. In *Odyssey* 11 the Phaeacian queen Arete shows her own appreciation of Odysseus' tale by urging her countrymen to give him gifts. In Ithaca, Penelope alone hears the full story of Odysseus' journey.

Similarly, Hellenistic literature produced in the court of the Ptolemies often aimed to retain royal patronage, including that of the reigning queen. In Theocritus' *Idylls* (15), the poet flatters queen Arsinoë II by showing the awed reaction of a group of Alexandrian housewives to a festival of Adonis that she has organized for women. Hesiod in *Works and Days,* on the other hand, establishes for himself a male audience that includes his own brother Perses and kings who are willing to be receptive to his advice. As a farmer, the poet aims to escape from a fallen world, an iron age, through virtue and the accumulation of wealth. Woman plays a negative role in this scenario through her association with the fall into culture that condemned man to agriculture, marriage, and sacrifice. In the Golden Age, before the creation of woman, men did not work to eat and communicated directly with the gods. To regain this age would be to return to a world without women. Hence Hesiod has a poetic motive for ignoring women's work.

Prose sources have different aims and biases. Thucydides, by emphasizing political and economic causes for historical events, shows no interest in women and the private world. Orators often idealize family life, both to defend their own cause or to denigrate the deviant behavior of an opponent. Medical writers aim to prevent women from seeking cures in religious cults, and hence they may have ignored some popular views about women's nature and diseases in favor of "scientific" explanation; furthermore, by emphasizing disease, they deprive us of information and views on normal pregnancy and birth. Philosophers examine and justify or question the status quo. Aristotle relies in the *Politics* 1 on his representation of the natural hierarchies of the household in order to win his hearers to the view that a constitutional monarchy is the ideal and "natural" government for a city-state. Plato's interest in changing women's role derives not from a concern for women's rights, but from a desire to root out private interest from the ruling class.

Greek literature as a whole, but especially Attic drama and postclassical literature outside Athens, frequently represents women characters who act and speak in ways unavailable to them in life. Forcefully intelligent, they assert their views in public, criticize their lot, challenge their men, and act in the political sphere denied to them in life. Tragedy in particular violates the norms for women expressed by Attic prose writers because its plots focus on cultural crisis and on an aristocratic culture foreign to contemporary democracy. In Aeschylus' *Agamemnon,* Clytemnestra, using powerful public rhetoric, usurps power in Argos after killing her husband. Sophocles' Antigone defies a state decree and buries her brother. Aristophanes' Praxagora takes over the assembly for women. Hellenistic literature, too, delights in removing the restrictions that confine women in ordinary life. Simaetha in Theocritus' *Idylls* 2 pursues her man and concludes her affair without getting pregnant. Later, women in the Greek novel miraculously preserve their chastity in a series of adventures through time and space that no real woman could have imagined. Clearly, to understand the Greek conception of women we must assume that male writers created female characters to think with, and to argue out symbolically the tensions and contradictions of their culture.

Attic drama, for example, uses the battle between the sexes to express tensions between past and present, public and private, and family and state that were also central to Attic democracy. Democratic ideology, which served to reinforce the subordination of private to public life, made it difficult for poets to express allegiance to the household through male characters. Creon shows inadequate leadership in refusing to sacrifice his son for the state in Euripides' *The Phoenician Women,* for example; in contrast, tragedy consistently views with some sympathy Clytemnestra's hostile reaction to Agamemnon's sacrifice of her daughter Iphigenia in order to inaugurate the Trojan War. Antigone wins the support of gods and the people for upholding the interests of the family against Creon, whose narrow view of the state cannot meet the needs of the private world. Lysistrata argues for the women who cannot marry because of the Peloponnesian War. These female intruders into the public sphere seek to redress male violation of private interests. Through them, drama criticizes the male world for violating cultural norms or failing to balance public and private interests. At the same time, by allowing the private world to invade the public world, tragic women multiply rather than resolve tragic disasters. Ill suited for a public role, they often abandon the positive causes for which they initially stood to pursue power, desire, revenge, or self-interest. Indeed, the utopian literature of both drama and philosophy uses women to demonstrate the dangers inherent in a life devoted to private concerns. Aristophanes' *Assemblywomen* and Plato's *Republic* seek to restore public life by bringing women out of the household and by eliminating private property for the ruling class altogether.

Female characters in drama do not always represent private interests, however. Both Lysistrata and Euripides' Iphigenia claim to serve the common interests of all Greece; Jocasta in *The Phoenician Women* and Praxithea in Euripides' lost *Erechtheus* argue for the polis. Because woman has no stake in political life and power, she can be used to represent a disinterested view. Because she acts in public religious cult to promote fertility for the city, she can stand for peace. Because she is not fully a citizen of any polis, she can stand for Panhellenic ideals. And because, as medical texts remark, it is her nature to bleed like a sacrificial animal, she can become the sacrifice necessary to preserve her society in times of crisis or unite it in war.

Greek thinking, especially in myth, tended to be organized around polarities. The Pythagorean table of opposites associated the male with the limited, right, light, and good, and female with the unlimited, left, darkness, and bad (Aristotle, *Metaphysics* 1.5.986 a3). Medical and philosophical texts asserted that male children were engendered from the right testicle, female from the left; male children develop on the right side of the womb, female on the left side. Ethnographic literature makes the sexual polarity the key element in its analysis of culture. In Egypt (Herodotus, *Histories* 2.35–36), a reversal of sex roles ensures an overall reversal of Greek culture. Here women trade while men weave; women carry burdens on their shoulders, men carry them on their heads; women urinate standing, men sitting;

daughters, not sons, must support their fathers; Egyptians also write from right to left, not left to right, and live with rather than separately from animals. Herodotus views Egypt as a civilization past its prime; by contrast, he often characterizes primitive and remote cultures by a more liberated role for women accompanied by promiscuity, communism, and a pastoral economy.

As a result of thinking in polarities, Greek writers frequently represent or associate women with what male culture has categorized as other: nature as opposed to culture, the barbaric, the supernatural, the irrational, the hidden and deceptive, inner space, anarchy, and lack of freedom. Women often endanger the male-controlled institutions that are central to the definition of Greek culture—marriage, sacrifice, and agriculture—through adultery, perversion of ritual, and waste of household resources. Poetic texts both question and reassert these cultural stereotypes. Of all Greek literature, Aeschylus' *Oresteia* most inclusively associates the female with all that is alien to Greek culture. The trilogy opens with a female challenge to the male order and in the final play achieves justice in large part by establishing control over the feminine on both divine and human levels. In the *Agamemnon,* the rebellious queen Clytemnestra, bitter over the sacrifice of her daughter Iphigenia, lures her husband to destruction in the inner rooms of the palace by tempting him to step on purple tapestries sacred to the gods and by using duplicitous rhetoric. She disrupts the marriage rites of society by choosing and feminizing her new partner Aegisthus, misuses Agamemnon's wealth to establish a tyranny, and finally turns against her own children. The imagery of the trilogy associates female power and "justice" with the monstrous and anarchic, with the perversion of the social and natural world, with diseases of the mind or body.

Women in the *Oresteia* consistently have special access to the divine world, and their abuse of these powers again serves to emphasize the dangers of allowing women to act independently of men. Clytemnestra shows prophetic power in her "beacon speech," but perverts religious rites in her murder of Agamemnon. In *The Libation Bearers,* she can no longer make ritual serve her own ends. Her daughter Electra and the chorus of women refuse to carry out her plan to propitiate Agamemnon's spirit with libations, and instead unite with Orestes to pray for the dead king's help in taking revenge on the queen and the usurping Aegisthus and in restoring his son to his inheritance. In the *Agamemnon* the prophetess Cassandra, by refusing Apollo's addresses, has lost the ability to win belief for her prophecies, and appears to the male chorus irrational. The final play of the trilogy, however, opens with a speech by Apollo's prophetess at Delphi. Anticipating the resolution of the trilogy, the Pythian Priestess uses her prophetic powers only to serve voluntarily the will of the male god.

In the *Eumenides,* the otherness of woman and her misuse of power ultimately serve to justify her exclusion from public life. Clytemnestra's cause is represented by the dark, fearful, polluting, archaic, and virginal Furies and associated with Theseus' defeat of the Amazons, mythical warrior women who kill male children and live independently from the male. Apollo justifies Orestes' matricide by claiming, like Aristotle, that the father, as inseminator, is the only true parent. The mother is merely the receptacle in which the child is nurtured. Athena supports this argument by referring to the myth of her own birth from the head of Zeus; an androgynous and virginal daughter, she, like all good women in Greek literature, serves first and foremost the interests of the male in both public and family life. Justice is taken from the hands of the female Furies and placed in the hands of a masculine jury. By implication the Furies win for the female an exclusion from the rational political sphere and, by agreeing to accept marriage sacrifices, confirm women's subordination to the male in marriage; the interests of family and state now stand separated. Like the women of Athens, the Furies receive in compensation for the loss of their earlier privileges the opportunity to serve the city in cult. From a dark and hidden position underground they will promote fertility and protect the society from intrafamilial strife.

As was remarked earlier, male writers also explore through female experience those sides of their own life that society categorizes as inappropriate to the masculine. In *The Bacchants,* Euripides' Pentheus, mistakenly associating Dionysiac irrationality with the feminine, fails to see it as a part of his own nature, and the chorus links the Dionysiac with the behavior of the (male) democratic masses. In this play, Euripides seems to look back to epic and to anticipate Hellenistic literature in showing the dangers of categorizing nature, and by association the female and the barbarian, as fundamentally alien to Greek culture, rather than as something to be incorporated creatively within it. The Homeric epics view dead bodies as feminized in their vulnerability. Hector fears to be stripped of his armor and lie naked like a girl, pierced by a sharp weapon, with his dead body softer and hence more feminine to handle (*Iliad* 22.126, 373). Other heroes, such as Heracles in Sophocles' *Women of Trachis* (1083), view their experience of physical suffering as feminine. Some plays, such as Euripides' *Iphigenia in Tauris* or *Helen,* view positively women's ability to deceive in order to save. Indeed, as paradigmatic sufferers and victims, and as mediators between divine and human worlds, women stand by nature close to the heart of the tragic experience, which opens its protagonists to knowledge of the dangerous unknown hidden in the human psyche, in nature, in the divine.

The Eleusinian Mysteries were built around the story of Persephone's rape by Hades and the anguished separation of Demeter from her daughter. In the Homeric *Hymn to Demeter,* after being temporarily subject to mortal experience and mortal limits, these goddesses promise in their rites to mitigate the bleak view of death and the afterlife that Olympian religion had offered in epic. In her own person Persephone links the worlds of men, gods, and the dead. Here above all Attic religion accepted female experience as a model for and source of salvation. For Athenians, the alien woman was not only a being to be tamed and controlled, but also a representative of what must be included in masculine culture, which could not in the end survive simply on the rational, the open, the public, the competitive, and the egalitarian.

BIBLIOGRAPHY

SOURCES

The only collection of primary sources is Mary R. Lefkowitz and Maureen B. Fant, *Women's Life in Greece and Rome: A Source Book in Translation* (1982), which contains a useful selection from the medical texts. Other sources mentioned in this essay are: E. Littré, *Oeuvres complètes d'Hippocrate,* 10 vols. (1839–1861); E. Lobel and D. L. Page, *Poetarum Lesbiorum Fragmenta* (1955); Denys L. Page, ed., *Select Papyri* III (1941), and *Poetae Melici Graeci* (1962); Stefan L. Radt, ed., *Tragicorum Graecorum Fragmenta* IV (1977); Holgar Thesleff, ed., *The Pythagorean Texts of the Hellenistic Period* (1965).

STUDIES: GENERAL

Averil Cameron and Amelie Kuhrt, eds., *Images of Women in Antiquity* (1983); Claude Calame, *Les choeurs de jeunes filles en Grèce archaïque,* 2 vols.

(1977); Page DuBois, *Centaurs and Amazons* (1982); Friedrich Engels, *The Origin of the Family, Private Property and the State,* A. West, trans., Eleanor B. Leacock, ed., (1972); Helene P. Foley, ed., *Reflections of Women in Antiquity* (1981); Sarah C. Humphreys, *The Family, Woman, and Death* (1983); Mary R. Lefkowitz, *Heroines and Hysterics* (1981); Susan M. Okin, *Women in Western Political Thought* (1979); John Peradotto and J. P. Sullivan, eds., *Women in the Ancient World: The Arethusa Papers* (1984); Sarah B. Pomeroy, *Goddesses, Whores, Wives, and Slaves: Women in Classical Antiquity* (1975); Michelle Rosaldo and Louise Lamphere, *Woman, Culture, and Society* (1974); Philip Slater, *The Glory of Hera: Greek Mythology and the Greek Family* (1968).

STUDIES: SPECIALIZED

Marylin B. Arthur, "Early Greece: The Origins of the Western Attitude Towards Women," in *Arethusa,* **6** (1973), "Review Essay: Classics," in *Signs,* **2** (1976), "The Liberated Women of the Classical Era," in Renate Bridenthal and Claudia Koonz, eds., *Becoming Visible* (1977), and "The Divided World of Iliad VI," in Helene R. Foley, ed., *Reflections on Women in Antiquity* (1981); A. L. T. Bergren, "Language and the Female in Early Greek Thought," in *Arethusa,* **16** (1983); William J. Booth, "Politics and the Household: A Commentary on Aristotle's *Politics* Book One," in *History of Political Thought,* **2** (1981); Maryanne Cline Horowitz, "Aristotle and Woman," in *Journal of the History of Biology,* **9** (1976).

Carolyn J. Dewald, "Women and Culture in Herodotus' *Histories,*" in *Women's Studies,* **8** (1981); Helene P. Foley, " 'Reverse Similes' and Sex Roles in the *Odyssey,*" in *Arethusa,* **11** (1978), "The Conception of Women in Athenian Drama," in Helene P. Foley, ed., *Reflections of Women in Antiquity* (1981), and "The 'Female Intruder' Reconsidered: Women in Aristophanes' *Lysistrata* and *Ecclesiazusae,*" in *Classical Philology,* **77** (1982); John Gould, "Law, Custom and Myth: Aspects of the Social Position of Women in Classical Athens," in *Journal of Hellenic Studies,* **100** (1980); Roger Just, "The Conception of Women in Classical Antiquity," in *Journal of the Anthropological Society of Oxford,* **6** (1975).

Helen King, "Bound to Bleed: Artemis and Greek Women," in Averil Cameron and Amelie Kuhrt, eds., *Images of Women in Antiquity* (1983); Nicole Loraux, "Sur la race des femmes et quelques-unes de ses tribus," in *Arethusa,* **11** (1978), and "Le lit, la guerre," in *L'Homme,* **21** (1981); Ruth Padel, "Women: Model for Possession for Greek Daemons," in Averil Cameron and Amelie Kuhrt, eds., *Images of Women in Antiquity* (1983); Sarah B. Pomeroy, "Selected Bibliography on Women in Antiquity," in John Peradotto and J. P. Sullivan, eds., *Women in the Ancient World: The Arethusa Papers* (1984); Suzanne Said, "Woman and the Female in the Biological Treatises of Aristotle," in *Skrifter Udgivet af Institut for Klassiske Studier* (1982); Linda S. Sussman, "Workers and Drones; Labor, Idleness and Gender Definition in Hesiod's Beehive," in *Arethusa,* **11** (1978).

Jean-Pierre Vernant, "Hestia-Hermes: The Religious Expression of Space and Movement Among the Greeks," H. Piat, trans., in *Social Science Information,* **8** (1969); Jack Winkler, "Gardens of Nymphs: Public and Private in Sappho's Lyrics," in Helene P. Foley, ed., *Reflections of Women in Antiquity* (1981); Froma Zeitlin, "The Dynamics of Misogyny: Myth and Mythmaking in the *Oresteia,*" in *Arethusa,* **11** (1978), and "Cultic Models of the Female: Rites of Dionysus and Demeter," in *Arethusa,* **15** (1982).

Women in Rome

SHEILA K. DICKISON

THE CONFINED AND NARROW LIFE of an upper-class wife of fifth-century B.C. Athens and the life of a comparable Roman woman of the first century B.C. are not simply centuries but worlds apart. The Romans themselves recognized how very differently their wives lived. Cornelius Nepos wrote in *Lives of the Famous Men* (preface 6–7).

> For what Roman is ashamed to take his wife to a dinner party? Or whose wife is not prominent at home or not involved in society? In Greece things are far different. For neither is a wife invited to a dinner party, except of relatives, nor does she pass her life except in the inner part of the house, which is called the women's quarters, where a man is not welcome, save for a close relation.

Not only the dinner parties but also the streets, colonnades, theater, amphitheater, and circus provided Roman women with opportunities for public visibility that suggest a relatively unrestricted life-style.

That conclusion is borne out in this essay, which examines the lives of upper-class Roman women focusing on the following concerns: female spheres of activity, spheres of influence, and ideals of behavior that the Romans held appropriate for a woman to display. The study focuses on the last century of the Roman Republic and the first century of the empire, although evidence from earlier and later periods are occasionally used for purposes of illustration.

SPHERES OF ACTIVITY

Whether Roman *matronae* (married women with or without children) had always been allowed the freedom of movement indicated in Nepos' first-century B.C. remarks is difficult to tell. Certainly Romans liked to believe that at an earlier time husbands exercised strict control over their wives' activities in public. Examples of marital severity from the moralist Valerius Maximus (first century A.D.) include a husband who divorced his wife because he learned that she had gone outdoors with her head uncovered, another because he saw her having a private conversation in public with a freedwoman of dubious reputation, and another because she dared to go to the games without his knowledge (*Memorable Deeds and Sayings* 6.3.10–12).

These edifying examples of early Roman behavior also seem to imply that even in those days Romans did not view a woman's world as bound exclusively by the domestic sphere. A passage from Livy (*History of Rome* 34.7.8–9) on the debate to repeal the Lex Oppia, an emergency measure that limited women's use of expensive goods, makes an important distinction between the male and female worlds: "No offices, no priesthoods, no triumphs, no symbols of office, no gifts, no spoils of war can come to them [women]; elegance of appearance, jewelry, clothes, these are the badges of honor of women; in these they rejoice and pride themselves; these our ancestors called the woman's world." The meaning of the passage turns on the pun in the word *mundus* (elegance, world). As the male and female worlds are different, so do the insignia of these worlds differ. Men's badges of honor record their offices and military triumphs; women's insignia are their clothing, jewelry, and elegant appearance. An important implication is that the contrast between the two worlds is based not on a spatial division (men act in the public sphere, women in the domestic one), but on a distinction based on kinds of activity.

Because Roman women do not tell us directly about their lives or their reaction to society's expectations of them it will be necessary to examine sources that do so only indirectly. In order to show the many kinds of activities in which a Roman woman might engage in the late first century B.C., let us look at the biography of a woman as revealed in funerary inscriptions. In the so-called *Laudatio Turiae* (Dessau, *Inscriptiones Latinae Selectae* 8393) a husband's tribute to his departed wife (Wistrand [1976], pp. 19–29) reviews at length more than forty years of a very happy (although childless) mar-

riage in which, according to the husband, the wife time and time again displayed remarkable courage and loyalty in the face of great danger. (Her identity is in doubt; the inscription dates to the end of the first century B.C.)

Although Roman epitaphs are given to distortions of truth and framed in conventional language, the text of this inscription provides details that show the range of public activities some women could perform. As a young woman, not yet married, the woman of the inscription brought the murderers of her parents to justice without aid from her fiancé or brother-in-law, who were both abroad. Then she managed to thwart attempts by relatives to deprive her and her sister of their inheritance from their father. When her husband was proscribed (*ca.* 43 B.C.), she helped him escape and managed the estate while he was away. In exile she supplied him with servants, money, and provisions without being detected. In the period of civil disturbance she successfully defended their home against a band of plunderers. When Octavian (the future Augustus) pardoned her husband, she forced Lepidus, who was in Rome, to keep Octavian's word. In this encounter she suffered humiliation and even physical abuse but prevailed. When peace was restored, the couple was able to lead a quiet and happy life, marred only by their failure to have children. When the wife proposed divorce so the husband could have children with another wife, the husband angrily refused. To his great sorrow, she predeceased him.

This Roman woman's actions do not seem atypical, when compared to what is known about other women of the same period. Terentia, Cicero's first wife of many years, is an example of a woman of independent action in certain public areas. She brought to her marriage financial resources of her own and, from Cicero's letters, appears to have managed (with the help of a freedman) a considerable financial empire. Her properties included high-rent apartment houses in Rome, valuable farmland, forestland, and holdings of *ager publicus* (public land). Cicero's eventual suspicion of financial misdealings on her part suggests the extent to which she acted independently of him. According to Roman law, a woman, even if independent "in her own power" (*sui iuris*), nonetheless needed a *tutor* or male guardian to perform certain legal acts. The sources unfortunately do not reveal if legal restrictions in any way interfered with Terentia's ability to manage her own affairs.

Appropriate public activities for women were those that raised little or no disapproval from male authority figures. The financial doings of a Terentia or the comparable acts of the brave wife from the funerary inscription fit this category of activities. Certainly by the time of the late republic women *sui iuris* probably were able to act independently, despite the need for a guardian to authorize certain legal acts. For some women even that necessity was removed by Augustan and subsequent legislation.

State religion was one area in which Roman women played an acknowledged public role from very early times. The most visible women were the college of Vestal Virgins who during their thirty years of service performed important ritual obligations, including the onerous task of keeping the sacred flame alive in the temple of Vesta as a guarantee of Rome's survival. The well-being of the state was thought to depend on the Vestals' careful performance of their sacred duties, and they were required to remain chaste during their years of service.

Wives of certain public priests (*flaminicae*), such as the wife of the flamen Dialis, were closely associated with their husbands in the observance of ritual and taboo. As their contribution to the maintenance of the peace of the gods (*pax deorum*), married women held their own twice-yearly festivals in honor of the Bona Dea, a Roman goddess worshiped exclusively by women. Married women also appear prominently in onetime religious events of importance to the state: the bringing of the Magna Mater (Cybele) to Rome in 204 B.C. and the secular games (*ludi saeculares*) in 17 B.C.

On occasion Roman women also gathered in public for other than religious purposes. Probably the most famous example of a female demonstration was the gathering in 195 B.C. to urge the repeal of the *Lex Oppia*, sumptuary legislation that closely affected women. The long discussion assigned in Livy (34.1–8) to the episode and the carefully balanced opposing speeches that he gives to Cato and the tribune suggest that Romans had ambivalent feelings about such actions on the part of women. Certainly there were precedents for group political action going back to the myth of the Sabine women but in every case these examples involve a patriotic act on behalf of the state.

A female activity that bordered on the unacceptable was public speechmaking. Valerius Maximus preserves the names of three women who pleaded cases either in the courts or in the Forum Romanum; his introduction to their stories (*Memorable Deeds and Sayings* 8.3) is revealing: "We ought not pass over in silence those women whom the circumstance of their nature and the modesty of their sex were not able to prevent from speaking in the Forum or in the courts." The first speaker got herself acquitted on her one appearance in court and earned the nickname "Androgyne" (mannish woman) because "she bore a man's courage under a woman's appearance." The second was roundly condemned for making a habit of bringing suits to court in which she represented herself. The third was Hortensia, daughter of the great republican orator Quintus Hortensius. When no man would take the women's case, she spoke before Octavian, Mark Antony, and Lepidus against a tribute imposed on women (in 42 B.C.). Appian's version of the speech also makes the point that the women had first made a delegation to the wives of the triumvirs, but on being repulsed by Fulvia, the wife of Antony, they were forced to come to address the triumvirs themselves (*Civil Wars* 4.32–34). These anecdotes make it clear that only under unusual circumstances did a woman speak in public and even then she ran the risk of incurring a negative reaction.

Two areas that did not allow female participation were public and military service, the very areas that the Roman aristocrat used to define his own ideal of *virtus.* Agrippina, mother of Nero, for a time exercised power that Tacitus (*Annals* 12.7.10) described as "an almost masculine despotism," and she brazenly claimed partnership in the empire won by her ancestors, when she sat with Claudius before the praetorian standards (12.37.6). But rule by a woman was abhorrent to the Romans, and in the end she remained only the daughter of a general and the sister, wife, and mother of an emperor (12.42.3).

Military service was the exclusive domain of men. For a woman even to witness military maneuvers was considered improper; to sit before standards on a public occasion was shocking behavior. Fulvia's command of legions during the Perusine War (41 B.C.) drew charges of "unwomanly" behavior from Plutarch and Dio Cassius. So strong was the taboo on women in the military that it is not until the reign of Marcus Aurelius that an empress (his wife, the younger Faustina) is described by the title *mater castrorum* (mother of the camps).

Although Roman women were able to move about freely in public and take part in certain public activities, Roman custom and tradition (*mos maiorum*) defined their major obligation as the home (*domus*). A well-run home allowed the husband to concentrate on public concerns, politics, and the military (*fora, exercitus*); it also provided him with a place of rest from the heavy strain of public duties (Tacitus, *Annals* 12.5.5; Columella, 12, preface 7). The mistress of the house had two traditional duties, "to manage the house and look after the children" (Tacitus, *Dialogue on Orators* [*Dialogus*] 28.4). The spindle and distaff were her time-honored symbols, and the bride or her attendants carried them in the procession when she was married and came into the house. Woolmaking, moreover, was a conventional reason for praise in married Roman women's epitaphs.

The house as woman's domain is illustrated by the marriage hymn of Catullus (poem 61). Celebrating the marriage of Manlius Torquatus (praetor of 49 B.C.?), the poem incorporates the Roman wedding ritual into a hymn to Hymen, the god of marriage. The bride is very closely associated with the house: "Call to her home the mistress of the house" (31), sings the chorus. As the bride and her procession near her new home, the chorus continues, "See how powerful and prosperous your husband's house is for you! Allow it to be at your service" (152–154). At the poem's close husband and wife are urged to enjoy themselves and soon produce children—a son who looks like his father and proves by his resemblance to his mother her unblemished reputation. As this and other ancient evidence indicates, woman was guardian (*custos*) of the house, protector not only of its physical contents but also of the well-being of its inhabitants. Thus was echoed on the private level what the Vestal Virgins celebrated on the public.

SPHERES OF INFLUENCE

A woman's influence stemmed from her position as mistress of the house, and as an important member of a family she played several roles. As a mother, to begin with, she served as a model of behavior for her daughters. Sources also suggest that mothers sometimes exercised considerable influence in choosing their daughters' husbands and in agreeing to divorces, although legally this right rested with the paterfamilias (the male head of household). Since marriages between families of the aristocracy kept power within the group and also served as a means of cementing political alliances, a mother's involvement in matters of marriage and divorce must also have given her some informal influence in political decision-making.

Roman sources are eloquent on the subject of a mother's influence over her son, and some mothers apparently compensated for their own lack of power by exercising it through their sons. As Seneca the Younger noted in *On Consolation* (14.2), they are "ambitious through their sons" because "women are not allowed to hold office." Generally, though, their influence was viewed as a force for the good. Since upper-class women were often highly cultured, if not formally educated, it is not surprising that a mother exercised direct influence on her son's life. Tacitus (*Dialogus* 28) claims that in the good old days, when a mother reared her son herself rather than turning him over to a hired nursemaid, she was able to fire his enthusiasm and mold his youth to ensure distinction in whatever field he found of interest: the army, law, or public speaking. A good example was Cornelia, mother of the Gracchi, said to be well versed in Greek and Latin literature. In fact the eloquence of her writing style in extant letters caused Cicero to remark (*Brutus* 58), "It seems that her sons were not so much nurtured in their mother's lap as in the purity of her language." Cicero clearly considered it important for an orator to have heard language that was well spoken at home when he was a child.

The Romans did not think it advisable to educate women too thoroughly. When in

On Consolation to Helvia (17.4) Seneca the Younger recommends *liberalia studia* to his mother to console her in his exile, he regrets that his father did not allow her to acquire a complete knowledge of these studies:

> Would that my father, the best of men, had not given in to the practice of our ancestors and had wanted you to be well versed in the teachings of philosophy, rather than merely introduced to it. . . . But he did not allow you to indulge in studies on account of those women who use learning not as a means toward wisdom but provide themselves with it for the purpose of display.

As to a mother's political influence once her son became politically powerful, Roman myth held up Veturia and Volumnia, mother and wife of the legendary Coriolanus, as examples. They changed Coriolanus' mind when he threatened to march on Rome at the head of an army of the Volsci in 491 B.C. (Livy, 2.40). In historical times female members of ruling families are said to have exercised power through sons or husbands or other male connections. Servilia, mother of Brutus (Caesar's assassin), is typically cited as the example of a woman who, as Ronald Syme (1939) puts it, exercised from behind the scenes "power beyond the reach of many a senator." A recent discussion by T. W. Hillard (1983) of a mother's power (*materna auctoritas*) shows that Servilia's numerous family connections alone placed her in the highest reaches of Roman society and politics. At various stages in her life, she was half-sister of Cato, mistress of Caesar, wife of Decimus Junius Silanus (consul in 63/62 B.C.), mother-in-law of Marcus Aemilius Lepidus (triumvir), Publius Servilius Isauricus (consul in 48 B.C.), and Cassius Longinus the tyrannicide, and sister-in-law to Lucius Licinius Lucullus (consul in 74 B.C.) and Lucius Domitius Ahenobarbus (consul in 54 B.C.). But these connections cannot entirely account for Servilia's reputation among contemporaries as a forceful individual. A woman of "high intelligence and great energy," as Cicero called her, she was someone who mattered (*Brutus* 1.18).

In the period after Caesar's murder Cicero's letters provide a fascinating glimpse of Servilia as an active and informed participant in family councils. In *Letters to Atticus* (15.11) (June 44 B.C.), for example, he describes a meeting at which Servilia, Junia Tertia (Tertulla, half-sister of Brutus and wife of Cassius), and Porcia (wife of Brutus) were present with a large number of men to discuss what was to be done about the grain commission proposed for Brutus and Cassius. Servilia apparently disagreed sharply with Cicero's assessment of what should have been done prior to their meeting. She promised to see that the humiliating commission was removed from the jurisdiction of a senatorial decree already passed. In a following letter (15.12) Cicero again mentions that she would see to the removal of the commission. This behind-the-scene glimpse reveals the female assertiveness for which Roman women were evidently already known. But although we know that Servilia's advice was greatly valued by Brutus, it may be impossible to assess her large impact on Roman political life. Roman sources make it clear that allegations of female influence could be damaging to male politicians, and thus evidence for political influence by women is not always reliable.

Evidence is clearer in the case of Fulvia, who was a political force in her own right not only during her marriage to Mark Antony but also for the fifteen or so years before 45 B.C. She was the visible and moving force behind events in the Second Triumvirate when she joined Antony's brother, Lucius Antonius, against Octavian. Modern scholarship now also traces to some extent her influence on the careers of her first two husbands, Publius Clodius and Gaius Scrib-

onius Curio, influence perhaps extending even to their legislative programs and alliance with Caesar.

Personal wealth or important family connections partially explain on an individual basis the impact of a Servilia or a Fulvia. Judith Hallett's recent study (1984) has sought a systematic explanation for the personal and public power that some upper-class Roman women yielded despite legal restrictions on women and their exclusion from an official role in politics. She finds that women's influence relates to the roles they played within the Roman family, whether daughter, sister, or mother. The important role ascribed to daughters, a phenomenon peculiar to the Romans, appears to be crucial to understanding the special status upper-class women enjoyed within Roman society.

In general, however, Roman women seem to have viewed themselves and been viewed by others in the light of their relationships with male family members: the great Cornelia, for example, spurred her sons to action by saying that the Romans still called her the mother-in-law of Scipio Aemilianus rather than the mother of the Gracchi (Plutarch, *Parallel Lives,* "Tiberius Gracchus" 8). When women did exercise power, not surprisingly it was on behalf of a male member of the family who could act in the political sphere. Unfortunately this kind of activity does not always leave traces in the sources (Fulvia's early career is an example). What evidence that does exist suggests that within the confines of the family a Roman politician generally did not react negatively to female interest or participation in political discussion and activity.

It was quite a different matter for a Roman woman to display power in public or usurp male prerogatives in the political or military arena. Here, she shows up in satire as a dry-breasted, poker-faced creature who dashes boldly all over town, barging into male meetings, and giving advice to generals in uniform (Juvenal, *Satires* 6.398–412). Fulvia's public actions in the Perusine War earned her violent sexual abuse and caused her to be described as a woman "who had nothing womanly about her except her body" (Velleius Paterculus, *Roman Histories* 2.74.2). Plutarch (*Parallel Lives*, "Antony" 10) claims that, unlike other women, Fulvia was not born for spinning or housewifery or even to rule a husband at home: she wanted to rule a husband with political power or who was at least a general.

All this goes to suggest that Romans reacted harshly to women exercising or attempting to exercise power in public. In the last analysis, Tacitus' version of Agrippina's attempt to display publicly her joint power with Nero (A.D. 54) speaks eloquently about how the Romans viewed a public act of power on the part of a woman. "When some Armenian legates were pleading a case in front of Nero," he wrote (*Annals* 13.5), "[Agrippina] was preparing to ascend the emperor's tribunal and sit beside him. Although all the others were transfixed with fear, Seneca urged the emperor to go to meet his mother. With this show of filial duty a scandal was averted." From Dio Cassius (*Roman History* 61.35), it seems that the emperor and his mother did not go back onto the tribunal but to save face before the foreigners the rest of the embassy was heard elsewhere.

IDEALS OF BEHAVIOR

The aristocratic ideal for men found its expression in public action. An early epitaph sums up the characteristics of a successful life as "office, reputation and *virtus*, glory and natural talent" (*Corpus Inscriptionum Latinarum* 1.2.10). Donald Earl (1967) defines the central concept of *virtus* as "the gaining of preeminent *gloria* by the winning of pub-

lic office and the participation in public life and by using these methods to achieve great deeds in the service of the state" (p. 35).

The qualities held up for women to emulate are the domestic virtues (*domestica bona*), those that "married women who care for their good name cultivate" (Wistrand, 1976, pp. 20–21). The *Laudatio Turiae* epitaph mentioned earlier lists many of these virtues when it enumerates the "domestic virtues of chastity, deference, graciousness, good nature, industry in woolworking, religious devotion without superstition, sobriety of dress, modesty of appearance, . . . affection for relatives, devotion to the family" (Wistrand, *ibid.*). Only fertility (*fecunditas*) is missing from the list, suggesting that this Roman lady was unable to bear children.

What *virtus* represented to men, *pudicitia* was to women (Livy, 10.23.7–8). The ideal of *pudicitia* finds its most vivid expression in Livy, whose early history is peopled with individuals embodying virtues that he believed made Rome great. The parallel stories of Verginia and Lucretia (Lucrece) are austere models of behavior for a woman, corresponding to the two distinct and important stages of her life, the virginal and the matronal. As a young girl she is chaste (*pudica*), if she remains physically pure (*intacta*) until her marriage. The *matrona* exhibits the same virtue by remaining sexually faithful to her husband.

Let us begin with the Lucretia story (Livy, 1.57–59) because it appears to have been the older of the two stories and the one on which the Verginia story is based. When, during a legendary siege of Ardea in Latium, the officers were discussing whose wife was the most virtuous, it was decided to visit each home by surprise; Lucretia, late at night, was found at home with her maidservants spinning; the other wives were spending time together at an extravagant dinner party. There was no doubt that Lucretia had won the contest in womanly virtue.

Her beauty and proven chastity (*castitas*) filled Sextus Tarquinius, son of the last king of Rome, with lust and he decided to violate her. Returning a few days later, he found her virtue unassailable until he threatened to kill her and a slave in order to make it look as if she had been caught in adultery; she surrendered to him. The unhappy woman then sent for her father and husband and begged them to promise vengeance. She refused to be consoled on the grounds that she was innocent. With the words, "Although I absolve myself of the crime, I do not free myself from the punishment; no unchaste woman shall live after this, using Lucretia as an example" (Livy, 1.58.10), she killed herself. Vengeance on Tarquin led to the overthrow of the monarchy and the establishment of the republic (*ca.* 509 B.C.).

Verginia is the *exemplum pudicitiae* for the unmarried girl (Livy, 2.44–49). A beautiful girl of plebeian origins, Verginia caught the attention of the arrogant Appius Claudius, one of the decemvirs (the ten patricians who were commissioned to draw up a code of laws). After she rebuffed his attentions, he determined to debauch her and had one of his dependents claim her as his slave. When neither her fiancé nor her uncle was able to reclaim her, they called her father back to Rome from the field. Sitting as judge in the case, Appius had her declared his slave (and therefore legally his to abuse). When all seemed lost, her father asked for a moment alone with his daughter and leading her over to shops in the Forum Romanum, he snatched a knife from a butcher's shop and stabbed her in the heart. She died near the shrine of Venus Cloacina (the Purifier). Her father acted, as Valerius Maximus (6.1.2) explains, because "he preferred to be the murderer of a chaste daughter than the father of a dishonored one." Indignation at her treatment at the hands of Appius Claudius subsequently led to the overthrow of the decemvirs and a return to consular government

(449 B.C.). Although other uplifting stories of female chastity are mentioned by Roman writers, these two examples are noteworthy for the uncompromising nature of the ideal: a woman's virtue is more precious than life itself. It is also significant that both stories relate the preservation of female chastity to the very well-being of the Roman state.

The consequences of unchaste behavior are bluntly illustrated in Horace's *Odes* (3.6.16–20) where the disasters that have befallen the Roman state are attributed to a lack of chastity among its women: "Generations, fertile in sin, first polluted marriages and families and homes; drawn off from this source, disaster flowed out over the whole country and people." The three stanzas that follow provide a contemporary example of the corruption of women. The young girl, still a virgin, delights in improper dances and entertainment and even before marriage dreams of adultery. After marriage the same woman seeks younger lovers with her husband's full knowledge; he will profit from her pleasure because some of her lovers are business connections. Not from a marriage such as this was the virtuous youth of the past born who helped make Rome great. That youth's mother was upright (*severa*). The poem ends on a very pessimistic note as the poet decries the decline of morals, for which he sees no end in sight.

If there is a positive side to the virtue of *pudicitia*, it is in the wife's active expression of loyalty and devotion to her husband. In this respect *pudicitia* is the equivalent of fidelity (*fides*). Humble or extraordinary actions alike might earn a woman praise for being loyal. The wife of the great Scipio Africanus the Elder, for example, shows *fides* to her husband by overlooking the fact that he had a young slave for a mistress because she did not want the conqueror of the Carthaginians to be humiliated by having his wife lodge a complaint against him (Valerius Maximus, 6.7.1). The supreme example of *fides* is surely Arria, whose husband, Caecina Paetus, was ordered by the emperor Claudius to put an end to his life. When he hesitated, Arria took the dagger, stabbed herself, and set an example, saying, "Paetus, it doesn't hurt." A moving letter of Pliny the Younger (*Letters* 3.16) provides still other examples of Arria's heroic behavior, which he had learned from her granddaughter.

Before leaving *pudicitia,* we need to examine a special aspect of that virtue which the Romans singled out for highest praise, the condition of having had only one husband: "Those women who had been content with only one marriage were honored with the crown of chastity" (Valerius Maximus, 2.1.3). Not many upper-class women will have achieved that ideal in a society where women married very young, husbands often died in the prime of life, and divorce was frequent.

The Romans expected a wife to display obedience or deference (*obsequium*) to her husband. It is probable that the Roman marriage ceremony contained a ritual formula in it that instructed the bride to practice submission (to be *morigera*) to the will of her husband. The importance attached to this virtue is best understood from Roman reaction to the shrewish and domineering wife, the opposite of the ideal; the bossy wife, a frequent target of Roman humor, is one of the most prominent and repulsive types in Satire Six of Juvenal.

The other Roman ideals for women can be summed up briefly together since they all relate to the general concept of *pudor* (decency, propriety). In addition to the virtues enumerated on the Roman lady's epitaph above, the roughly contemporary *Laudatio Murdiae* refers to "modesty, goodness, industry in woolworking, careful attention to duties, loyalty" (Dessau, *Inscriptiones Latinae Selectae* 8394). How these ideals translated into actual behavior is charmingly seen in the younger Pliny's description (*Letters* 4.19)

of his third wife, Calpurnia, who, although accomplished in her own right, subordinated her talents to the total devotion of her husband:

> She is highly intelligent, incomparably temperate. Her love for me is a sure sign of her chastity. She adds to these qualities a fondness for literature, which she has derived from her affection for me. She has my books, she reads them over and over again, she even learns them by heart. With what concern is she moved when I am about to start a case; how great her pleasure when I have finished it. She posts messengers to bring her news about the approval and the applause I have earned, about the outcome of the trial I have received. When I recite, she sits nearby concealed by a curtain and hears our praises with the greediest of ears. She sings my verses and even sets them to the lyre with no master but love as her teacher, the best instructor of all.

Even though the sources depict striking cases of women who ignored these ideals and moralists who decry their disappearance, there is a good deal of evidence to indicate that they persisted into late antiquity. As early as the comic dramatist Plautus, Alcmena, the archetypal matron in *Amphitryon* (839–842), claims these virtues as her dowry when she defends her unjustly maligned reputation, saying to her husband, "I do not consider that my dowry is that which is usually called a dowry but chastity and propriety and self-control, a fear of the gods, love of parents, a good relationship with my relatives, deference to you." These are the same virtues that the prominent pagan Vettius Agorius Praetextatus praises in his wife, Paulina, in an epitaph dated A.D. 384: "Conscious of truth and chastity, dedicated to the temples and a friend of the gods, preferring her husband to herself and Rome to her husband, modest, loyal, pure of mind and body, kind to all" (Dessau, *Inscriptiones Latinae Selectae* 1259).

A good proof of the survival of these

ideals is the criticism of behavior across all periods that does not measure up to these standards. Since *pudicitia* is the main virtue for women, a concern with lack of chastity among women is to be expected, the more so as the Romans believed—as the stories of Lucretia and Verginia bear out—that a direct relationship existed between the well-being of the state and the purity of its women. This interest in female chastity may help explain the Roman preoccupation with adultery.

As evidence to show that Romans would have recognized *pudicitia* as an important virtue for upper-class women, even if some women disregarded the ideal, let us look at Cicero's *In Defense of Caelius* (*Pro Caelio*), given in 56 B.C. In this case Cicero is defending Caelius on a charge of breaching the peace: there were five separate counts against him, one of which was that he tried to poison Clodia (a former lover of Marcus Caelius Rufus, and the sister of Publius Clodius Pulcher), who was clearly behind the charges with a view to destroying Caelius' public career. The case for the defense was shaky and in order to bolster it Cicero turned his powers of invective against Clodia. To discredit her it was necessary to show how divergent her life-style was from that expected of a *matrona* (she was a widow) of the upper class. From the very beginning, Clodia's *pudicitia* is questioned. What kind of relationship, Cicero asks, does she have with Caelius, a young man, not her husband? Is he a kinsman, relative by marriage, friend of her husband? Since he is none of these, the implication is obvious. Details of her profligate life are piled up: every aspect of her behavior (bearing, dress, companions, ardor of her looks, looseness of her speech, location of her activities) suggests that she is not a *matrona* but a *meretrix* (prostitute) of the most shameless kind. At the height of his attack on her reputation, Cicero asks, "If some young man has perhaps been with this woman, would you consider this man an adulterer or a lover? Would you think that he wanted to assault her chastity or satisfy his passion?" (20.49). So important does Cicero try to make the issue of Clodia's character that he finally claims that his case rests on her propriety or lack of it: "Please give us our means and method of defense. Either your modest behavior will disprove that Caelius has acted in an improper manner or your indecent behavior provide to him and others a good opportunity to defend themselves" (20.50). Cicero's depiction of Clodia may have had some truth in it but the picture is drawn in such an exaggerated manner that the audience can only conclude that she did not live up to the behavior expected of a woman of her class. In discrediting Clodia's reputation, Cicero bolsters the case of his client.

The impact of Sallust's portrait of the aristocratic and cultured Sempronia, who was a follower of Catiline in his conspiracy against Rome (63 B.C.), also depends on a recognition that *pudicitia* was a major female virtue: "There was nothing of less value to her than her modesty and chastity; it would be difficult to decide whether she was less sparing of her money or her reputation" (*The Conspiracy of Catiline* 25). One of the ways in which Tacitus (*Annals* 12.7) makes his case against Agrippina is to depict her as a woman who would compromise her *pudicitia* for power: "In public Agrippina appeared austere and often arrogant; her life at home was chaste, unless it was useful in her quest for power."

Impudicitia (lack of chastity) is also a major theme in Juvenal's Satire Six, a diatribe of over 650 lines railing against the misbehavior of upper-class Roman women, especially married women. In the two prologues of the poem (1–20; 286–300) the satirist contends that the goddess Pudicitia has not been seen in Rome since the end of the Golden Age when life was rude but virtuous. With the arrival of wealth and foreign influence Pudicitia had been superseded by Luxuria (excess). As if to underline the total repudiation of *pudicitia,* the ultimate indignity to the ideal is described: wives in their nightly revels urinate on the old altar of the deity (306–313).

As one of the ways of illustrating the lack of chastity in Rome the narrator tries to dissuade a certain Postumus from marrying. Why would anyone wish to marry when adultery is an ancient and long-established practice at Rome? You wish to produce an heir, he asks? How can you be sure the child will be your own? In Rome women fancy actors, flute players, gladiators, almost anyone but their husbands. Eppia, "a senator's wife," runs off to Egypt with a broken-down gladiator. Even the imperial ladies are not immune; Claudius' wife prefers to put on a disguise and ply her trade in a low-class brothel.

To make his case against wives the satirist also uses *pudicitia* in a broader than sexual sense to mean *pudor* (moderation or propriety). Any behavior on the part of women that displays lack of moderation is subject to criticism. Juvenal is especially offended by women who violate the traditional virtues of compliancy and obedience. Case after case is cited of women who are cruel, abusive, domineering, who rule their husbands or succession of husbands like a kingdom; for example, "She issues orders to her husband but then soon leaves this domain" (6.224). Worse than the woman who runs off with the gladiator is the one who aspires to be a gladiator herself and thus is involved with exercises, equipment, ointments, and the like (6.246–276). No impropriety great or small escapes Juvenal's notice. Even the proverbially ideal wife Cornelia, mother of the Gracchi, receives criticism for her immodest *superbia* (arrogance) on account of her family and ancestors (6.161–166).

In the second part of the poem the satirist develops the theme of *luxuria* (excess). The perversion of traditional religion is one of the major excesses in which women indulge: the rites of the Bona Dea are polluted by sexual contests; the auspices are taken and Janus and Vesta consulted, with offerings of cakes and wine, as to whether a lyre player will win a prize; other women consult about a comedian or a tragic actor. Foreign deities are frequented—Bellona and his crown of eunuchs, Io, Isis, Anubis, Osiris. Soothsayers and astrologers (especially the most disreputable sort) are asked by married women how long their husbands will live. No action, however, is taken without consulting the appropriate seer; the Roman matron even becomes an expert herself. Charms and spells are sought that a wife may use to drive a husband mad. Perversion of religion is the clearest proof of a total breakdown in morality, marked first by *impudicitia* and then whole-scale *luxuria* on the part of Roman women. Rome has destroyed itself.

Obviously the exaggerated rantings of a satirist (and master rhetorician) such as Juvenal cannot be taken at face value as evidence for a society's view about women. What does emerge from Juvenal is that his major theme of female behavior as a symptom of society's decline has close parallels with the moralizing of Sallust, Livy, Tacitus, and other Roman historians. All mark the last stages of the decline with the preeminence of *luxuria,* best defined as female behavior diametrically opposed to what the ideal prescribes—the behavior of women out of control, women who act like men.

This essay began by stating that Roman women of the upper class led publicly visible lives that suggest a relatively unrestricted life-style. That conclusion, however, should now be qualified. What were the restrictions on a woman's life that made it different from a man's? If there is a dominant theme running through Roman stereotypes of women, it is that of *infirmitas* or *imbecillitas* (weakness), *impotentia* (lack of control), or *luxuria* (tendency to excess) (Livy, 34.1–7; Tacitus, *Annals* 3.33–34). Wherever control over them is relaxed, they burst into vicious behavior—the most flagrant example of which is meddling in men's business. Unlike the Greeks, however, the Romans did not keep upper-class women confined to the home or severely prescribe the public activities in which they might participate.

Roman restraints were of a different kind. The Romans, for example, could claim that it was this need for control that was the basis for the lifelong legal authority exercised over women (except for Vestal Virgins and women *sui iuris* exempted under Augustan and subsequent legislation). Even the non-*manus* form of marriage, which left the woman under the control of her father or nearest male agnate (kinsman on her father's side) rather than her husband, did not necessarily weaken authority over her.

Roman ideals of behavior also contain the idea of limitation and control: *pudicitia* and *pudor* (chastity and propriety), preeminent virtues for women, depend on restraint of body and mind. Significantly the Roman system of religion and morality ties the idea of female virtue to the well-being of the state. Unchaste behavior has far-reaching and disastrous consequences, as the civil wars of the last century B.C. suggested. Augustus' moral and marriage legislation is in part a response to this system of beliefs.

Roman custom and tradition (*mos maiorum*), a powerful force in the Roman value system, also set limits on what activities were appropriate for women in the public sphere. Although over time women enjoyed a wider range of activities, the political and military remained off limits. A conservative Roman might, however, insist that the unthinkable had already happened: "Women were once controlled by the Oppian and other laws," Tacitus complains (*Annals* 3.33), "but these

bonds have been shaken off so that they now rule everywhere, at home, in the courts, and now even in the army." A woman who ventures into male activities is deemed a "monstrous thing" (*monstrum*), words fraught with connotations of supernatural horror.

There were obviously some women who chose not to live within the confines set for them by tradition and the law. Is it an accident that the majority of these women flourished in the last generation of the Roman Republic in the very period that upper-class men were asserting their rights as individuals against the greater good of the state?

More telling about Roman society than the women we see in the sources is the fact that Roman women do not speak across the centuries in their own voices. For that reason it is appropriate to conclude with a poem that sensitively explores the differences between the male and female worlds. Propertius' elegy (*Elegies* 4.11) is a funeral *laudatio* put in the mouth of the deceased herself. Cornelia, member of a noble house with close connections to the emperor Augustus, dies young (*ca.* 16 B.C.), leaving a husband, Paullus Aemilius Lepidus, and three children (two sons and a daughter of about six). As the poem opens, Cornelia's shadow addresses her husband and then pleads the case for her own life before the judges of the underworld. Even if a literary fiction (a male poet's conception of a woman's life), the poem presents a unique glimpse into a woman's feelings.

She first presents some facts from her life. She was born into a household that was noble on both sides, but it was especially distinguished by the ancestors on her father's side. Life for her began only when the toga *praetexta* (the purple-bordered robe worn by freeborn children) was laid aside on her wedding day, and in essence, as Cornelia remarks, her life passed between "the marriage and the funeral torch" (46). During that time she served her husband faithfully and bore three children (two of them sons), thus earning for herself special privileges (61). She also believes she has been a good sister and a good daughter. In short, she has earned the supreme honor a woman can earn, the praise of her children now and in the years to come. In Cornelia's words, "This is the final reward, the reward of a triumph for a woman, when her reputation among her children honors the cold pyre" (71–72, Laurence Richardson, trans. [1977]).

The speaker reveals what has been important to her in her short life: as a member of her class she is conscious of her family's past and the high standards set for her. As a woman she is concerned with having lived up to the ideals that her family and society expected of her: chastity (here of a special kind, since she has been married only once), fecundity (she did not die leaving a barren house), and affection and devotion to her family (*pietas*). She touchingly expresses in this poem a love for her children, whom she has had to leave prematurely.

Propertius artfully captures the differences between the male and female worlds by contrasting men's public triumphs and women's private ones. He refers to the victory triumphs awarded the family's male members ("triumphal chariots of the ancestors, glory from ancestral trophies, inscriptions attesting to the family past, spoils of war") and contrasts them with women's triumphs, which are marked by passive and private signs: the *praetexta* put aside on the wedding day, the wreath adorning the ritual hairstyle of the bride, the torches of the wedding procession. The *fama* (glory or reputation) won by each is clearly different: men win public recognition for their achievements and thereby add to the family glory; women receive their reward after death from the recognition that they have lived up to their family's expectations.

BIBLIOGRAPHY

SOURCES

Catullus, *The Poems*, Kenneth Quinn, ed. (1970); Cicero, *In Defense of Caelius*, vol. 8, J. H. Freese, trans. (1958); *Corpus Inscriptionum Latinarum* (1863-); Marcel Durry, ed., *Éloge funèbre d'une matrone romaine* [*Laudatio Turiae*] (1950); Horace, *Odes*, C. E. Bennett, trans. (1914; rev. ed. 1927); Hermann Dessau, *Inscriptiones Latinae Selectae* (1892–1916); Mary R. Lefkowitz and Maureen B. Fant, eds., *Women's Life in Greece and Rome: A Source Book in Translation* (1982); Plautus, *Amphitryon* I, Paul Nixon, trans. (1916); Pliny the Younger, *Letters and Panegyricus*, Betty Radice, trans., 2 vols. (1969); Plutarch, *The Roman Questions of Plutarch*, Herbert J. Rose, trans. (1924; repr. 1974); Propertius, *Elegies I–IV*, Lawrence Richardson, Jr., ed. (1977); Seneca, *De Consolatione ad Helviam* (*On Consolation to Helvia*), John W. Basore, trans. (1932); Eric Wistrand, ed. and trans., *The So-Called Laudatio Turiae* (1976).

STUDIES

F. E. Adcock, "Women in Roman Life and Letters," in *Greece and Rome*, 14 (1945); Thomas W. Africa, "The Mask of an Assassin: A Psychohistorical Study of M. Junius Brutus," in *Journal of Interdisciplinary History*, 8 (1978); William S. Anderson, "Juvenal 6: A Problem in Structure," in *Classical Philology*, 51 (1965); Charles L. Babcock, "The Early Career of Fulvia," in *American Journal of Philology*, 86 (1965); J. P. V. D. Balsdon, *Roman Women* (1962); Mary Beard, "The Sexual Status of Vestal Virgins," in *Journal of Roman Studies*, 70 (1980); Edward E. Best Jr., "Cicero, Livy and Educated Roman Women," in *Classical Journal*, 65 (1970); Teresa Carp, "Two Matrons of the Late Republic," in Helene Foley, ed., *Reflections of Women in Antiquity* (1982); John Crook, *Law and Life of Rome* (1967).

Sheila K. Dickison, "Abortion in Antiquity: A Review Article," in *Arethusa*, 6 (1973), "Women in Antiquity: A Review Article," in *Helios*, 4 (1976), "Claudius: Saturnalicius Princeps," in *Latomus*, 36 (1977), and "Postscript to Women in

Antiquity," in *Helios,* **6** (1978); Ian Donaldson, *The Rapes of Lucretia* (1982); Donald Earl, *The Moral and Political Tradition of Rome* (1967); Moses I. Finley, "The Silent Women of Rome," in his *Aspects of Antiquity* (1960); Linda Frey, Marsha Frey, and Joanne Schneider, eds., *Women in Western European History: A Select Chronological, Geographical, and Topical Bibliography from Antiquity to the French Revolution,* I (1982); Ernestine Friedl, "The Position of Women: Appearance and Reality," in *Anthropological Quarterly,* **40** (1967).

Karl Galinsky, "Augustus' Legislation on Morals and Marriage," in *Philologus,* **125** (1981); Katherine A. Geffcken, *Comedy in the Pro Caelio* (1973); John Gould, "Law, Custom and Myth: Aspects of the Social Position of Women in Classical Athens," in *Journal of Hellenic Studies,* **100** (1980); Judith P. Hallett, "The Role of Women in Roman Elegy: Counter-Cultural Feminism," in *Arethusa,* **6** (1973), "Perusinae Glandes and the Changing Image of Augustus," in *American Journal of Ancient History,* **2** (1977), and *Fathers and Daughters in Roman Society* (1984); T. W. Hillard, "*Materna Auctoritas:* The Political Influence of Roman Matronae," in *Classicum,* **9** (1983); Keith Hopkins, "The Age of Roman Girls at Marriage," in *Population Studies,* **18** (1965), and "Contraception in the Roman Empire," in *Comparative Studies in Society and History,* **8** (1965); Nicholas Horsfall, "Some Problems in the 'Laudatio Turiae'," in *Bulletin of the Institute of Classical Studies, University of London,* **30** (1983).

Natalie Kampen, *Image and Status: Roman Working Women in Ostia* (1981); Richmond Lattimore, "Themes in Greek and Latin Epitaphs," in *Illinois Studies in Language and Literature,* **28** (1942); Mary R. Lefkowitz, "Wives and Husbands," in *Greece and Rome,* 2d series, **30** (1983); John H. W. G. Liebeschuetz, *Continuity and Change in Roman Religion* (1979); Marjorie Lightman and William Zeisel, "Univira: An Example of Continuity and Change in Roman Society," in *Church History,* **46**

(1977); Saara Lilja, *The Roman Elegists' Attitude to Women* (1965); Ramsey MacMullen, "Women in Public in the Roman Empire," in *Historia,* **29** (1980); Anthony J. Marshall, "Roman Women and the Provinces," in *Ancient Society,* **6** (1975), and "Tacitus and the Governor's Lady," in *Greece and Rome,* 2d series, **22** (1975); H. G. Mullens, "The Women of the Caesars," in *Greece and Rome,* **11** (1942); Helen North, *Sophrosyne: Self-Knowledge and Self-Restraint in Greek Literature* (1966); Robert E. A. Palmer, "Roman Shrines of Female Chastity from the Caste Struggle to the Papacy of Innocent I," in *Rivista storica dell' antichità,* **4** (1974); T. E. V. Pearce, "The Role of the Wife as *Custos* in Ancient Rome," in *Eranos,* **72** (1974); Jane E. Phillips, "Roman Mothers and the Lives of Their Adult Daughters," in *Helios,* **6** (1978); Sarah B. Pomeroy, *Goddesses, Whores, Wives, and Slaves: Women in Classical Antiquity* (1975), "The Relationship of the Married Woman to Her Blood Relatives in Rome," in *Ancient Society,* **7** (1976), and "Selected Bibliography on Women in Antiquity," in John Peradotto and J. P. Sullivan, eds., *Women in the Ancient World* (1984).

Amy Richlin, "Approaches to the Sources on Adultery at Rome," in Helene Foley, ed., *Reflections on Women in Antiquity* (1982); Linda W. Rutland, "Women as Makers of Kings in Tacitus' *Annals,*" in *Classical World,* **72** (1978); David M. Schaps, *Economic Rights of Women in Ancient Greece* (1979); S. E. Smethurst, "Women in Livy's *History,*" in *Greece and Rome,* **19** (1950); Ronald Syme, *The Roman Revolution* (1939); Patrick G. Walsh, *Livy: His Historical Aims and Methods* (1961); Alan Watson, *The Law of Succession in the Later Roman Republic* (1971), *Roman Private Law Around 200 B.C.* (1971), and *Rome of the XII Tables* (1975); Elizabeth Lyding Will, "Women in Pompeii," in *Archaeology,* **32** (1979); Gordon Williams, "Some Aspects of Roman Marriage Ceremonies and Ideals," in *Journal of Roman Studies,* **48** (1958).

Greek Marriage

SARAH B. POMEROY

MARRIAGE WAS A FUNDAMENTAL INSTITUTION in Greek society and evidence for it is pervasive in written sources and in the visual arts. Practices varied according to geographical region and social and economic class and changed over time. However, several features remained constant: marriage was normally monogamous and patriarchal, the married couple consisted of a male and female, and the bride was accompanied by a dowry rather than purchased by the groom.

MARRIAGE IN HOMERIC EPIC

Because epics were composed over a period of several hundred years and tell of the activities of a wide range of societies, both Greek and non-Greek, they provide evidence for a variety of marriage patterns. Matrilocal marriage—in which the couple lived in the wife's home—and patrilocal marriage—in which the couple lived in the husband's home—coexisted within the same city and even within one family. Clytemnestra and Helen were born in Sparta; Agamemnon and Menelaus in Mycenae. Clytemnestra's marriage to Agamemnon was patrilocal, while Menelaus' marriage to Helen was matrilocal. The succession to the throne at Sparta was matrilineal; thus Menelaus became king of Sparta as a consequence of his marriage. Agamemnon's succession was patrilineal; he inherited the throne directly from his father, Atreus. The pattern shifted when Aegisthus became king of Mycenae by marrying Clytemnestra and Helen went to Troy as the wife of Paris. Neither Clytemnestra nor Helen formally divorced her previous husband; thus, although they were considered to be the wives of Aegisthus and Paris, respectively, these marriages were bigamous. Polygyny—marriage of one man to more than one woman—appeared at Troy, but only in the household of the great king. Priam had fifty sons and twelve daughters. His chief wife, Hecuba, was the mother of nineteen of his sons; the rest were born from other wives.

Matrilocal marriage with matrilineal succession was often preceded by a prenuptial contest. The suitor had to prove by military prowess that he deserved to be incorporated into the bride's kingdom and to succeed her father as ruler. Thus, in his quasi courtship of Nausicaa (which did not, however, culminate in marriage), Odysseus defeated the young men of Scheria in athletic competition (*Odyssey* 8.19). He reasserted his right to be Penelope's husband and king of Ithaca by defeating the suitors in the contest of the bow (*Odyssey* 21). The bride was awarded to the victor of a prenuptial contest. A related pattern of taking a wife is marriage by capture. At Troy Achilles captured and enslaved Briseis. Yet he promised that he would marry her when they returned to Greece. Two other patterns, exogamy and endogamy—marriage outside and within a given social group, respectively—appear in epic. For example, the Greek Helen married the barbarian Paris; in contrast, Arete married her uncle Alcinous.

Some form of dowry system was in force in Greece at all times. Because suitors in patrilocal marriage offered gifts (*hedna*) to the father of the bride, scholars formerly believed that the bride-price system prevailed and that bridegrooms purchased wives. However, the exchange of gifts, like the exchange of the brides themselves, was common between friends and allies and served to create social bonds. In patrilocal marriages brides in Homeric epic brought with them slaves, as did Penelope, and valuable clothing, as did Helen.

Following a pattern that was repeated in later Greek societies, husbands and wives occupied separate spheres. Although women in epic were not secluded, they were expected to remain indoors and busy themselves with tasks appropriate for women. When Hector finds Andromache standing on the wall of Troy, he admonishes her that war is the business of men and sends her back home to her weaving. The roles of male and female were complementary, but wives were more dependent on husbands than husbands were on wives. All women except slaves were destined for marriage and the marital relationship was the most important one in a woman's life. Andromache declares that Hector is father, brother, and husband to her, and experiences his death as total devastation. Odysseus, indeed, states that nothing is better than when a husband and wife have a harmonious marriage (*Odyssey* 6.182–184), but he made the statement to a nubile Nausicaa. What marriage was to women, war and related activities were to men. Wives were not absolutely essential to men, for women's work could be performed by slaves. Even in the area of human reproduction wives did not exercise a monopoly. Menelaus intended that Megapenthes, his son by a slave woman, would inherit his throne, although his legitimate wife, Helen, had borne him a daughter.

Epic portrays marriage in heroic society for the most part, although the marriages of commoners are depicted in the city at peace on the Shield of Achilles (*Iliad* 18.491–496). Nocturnal wedding processions in which brides are being led to their new homes are accompanied by a marriage song (*hymenaios*) and by dancers and musicians playing flutes and lyres. These components were also standard in wedding processions of later periods.

MARRIAGE IN ARCHAIC POETRY

Hesiod was the first to write about the benefits and liabilities of marriage. He recommends that a man marry at about the age of thirty so that he can produce an heir to inherit his possessions and have a woman to nurse him in old age. He should choose a wife from the neighborhood. She should be a virgin, but mature (around eighteen). Still, she should be young enough for her husband to be able to teach her careful ways. Such a wife is the greatest boon for a man, her opposite the greatest bane (*Theogony*

603–612; *Works and Days* 373–375, 695–705).

The latter type appears in Hesiod's description of Pandora, the first mortal woman and wife. Pandora was created as a punishment for men; she was deceptive and mercenary and her beauty served to ensnare them. Much of the misogyny of Hesiod and later archaic poets such as Semonides derived from their view that women like Pandora were consumers, drones, and takers of gifts. They could diminish a man's honor by making him a cuckold and a laughingstock among his peers. The good wife, in contrast, was like a worker bee. She caused her husband's property to increase and was not interested in sex (Semonides, frag. 7.83–93 Diehl).

The *Homeric Hymn to Demeter* gives a picture of marriage from the perspective of a bride, Persephone, and her mother, Demeter. Other females, both mortal and divine, are prominent in the *Hymn*. The myth describes the rape of Persephone by Hades, Demeter's search for her daughter, and the final compromise whereby Persephone was to spend part of each year as a daughter in the world above with her mother and the remaining time as a wife in the underworld with Hades. Many features of the story are reminiscent of human marriage. The marriage was arranged by the males who were the bride's closest relatives: her father, Zeus, and her paternal uncle, Hades.

The perils of endogamy for a bride are dramatized when Persephone calls in vain upon her father to aid her. The mother, who was ignorant of the arrangement, had been reluctant to permit her daughter to marry, and was devastated by her loss. Persephone, a younger version of her mother, was nubile and mature, but unwilling to wed. Eventually she received a separate identity and honor through marriage. The reunification with the mother, of course, did not occur in human life.

Sappho also gives voice to sorrow at the recurrent departure of girls upon marriage. One of Sappho's nine books of poetry is devoted to songs sung at weddings (*epithalamia*). In them the groom is variously described as charming, handsome, and loving, but he is tall as the indomitable Ares. A veritable giant guards the door of the wedding chamber (*thalamos*), perhaps to guarantee privacy to the married couple.

MARRIAGE IN SPARTA

The legendary lawgiver Lycurgus is said to have given the Spartans their regulations for marriage. Because the historical sources for the Spartan constitution are much later than its supposed creation and emanate from non-Spartan authors who often use archaic Sparta as a basis for criticism of other societies and who emphasize differences between Spartans and other Greeks, much of the testimony is contradictory and difficult to interpret.

The ideal Spartan society was composed of citizens who were equals (*homoioi*). Social structure was communal: men ate and, until the age of thirty, slept with their army units. No one needed to possess private property, for every Spartan was granted a land allotment (*kleros*) at birth. Domestic and agricultural labor was performed by Helots. Thus the motives for marriage found elsewhere in Greece—for example, acquisition of a wife with a large dowry, the wish to perpetuate one's family and produce an heir to one's property, companionship, and a person of the opposite sex to perform gender-specific labor—were lacking for men at Sparta.

Human propagation in such a system could be a problem, and indeed Spartan history was plagued by diminishing population. The so-called Lycurgan regulations for men included incentives for marriage and penalties for celibacy. Erotic reactions were stimulated by the sight of partially clothed women, while bachelors were subjected to ridicule and peer pressure. The cooperation of women was encouraged by allowing them to marry at the relatively late age of eighteen to twenty and by a physical education that strengthened their bodies for childbirth. Thus they entered marriage when they were mature and without undue fear of childbirth.

Furthermore, certain features of Spartan society made marriage less formidable for women than it was elsewhere in Greece. The Spartans were endogamous and xenophobic and therefore did not marry off their women to foreigners. Women were not secluded, but in fact mingled with unmarried men. Since men and women were the same age when they married for the first time, husband and wife were probably not total strangers to each other. Finally, in the early stages of marriage, the bride remained in her own home. Only a rite of transvestism in which the bride's hair was cut and she was dressed in man's clothing marked her passage to her new status. The fact that Spartan women suffered a minimum amount of dislocation in marriage and also married men who were unlikely to have been dominating or intimidating must have contributed to their celebrated self-confidence.

Spartan marriage customs were anomalous among the Greeks. The Spartan customs of marriage by capture, in which nubile people were confined in a dark room and men chose spouses at random (followed by marriage of the entire cohort), secret trial marriage to establish whether a couple was fertile, and wife-lending for purposes of procreation must be viewed in terms of the lack of personal motives for marriage mentioned above and the communal need to foster human reproduction.

Spartan society changed over time and acquired features found even in its antithesis, Athenian society. In reality private property in addition to the *kleroi* had existed even in archaic Sparta, so that there was a hierarchical class structure. Dowries (some of which were constituted of vast amounts of land), marriages motivated by the wish to acquire or consolidate wealth, the *oikos* (meaning family, including people and their property) system, women wealthy enough to own horses that were victorious at Panhellenic festivals, and wealthy "heiresses" (*epikleroi*)—fatherless, brotherless women who transmitted their father's property to their children, who thus became heirs to their grandfather's *oikos*—all were found despite their conflict with the communal social structure. Vestiges of the "Lycurgan" system remained, so that Xenophon (*Spartan Constitution* 1.7–9) suggested that the reason for wife-lending was that Spartan women wished to produce heirs for more than one lineage so that they could control more than one household and men wished to obtain for their sons brothers who would inherit from a different father.

MARRIAGE IN GORTYN

In several respects, marriage at Gortyn, Crete, resembled marriage at Sparta. Gortyn, like Sparta, was Dorian, and communal life was emphasized for men. The Code of Gortyn, a series of laws inscribed in the fifth century B.C. but recording legislation of the archaic period, gives evidence for social status, marriage, inheritance, and other aspects of family law.

The *oikos* system was in force, but the law did not protect *oikoi* to the extent that it did at Athens. The *patroïoikos* was analogous to the *epikleros*. In order to keep her inheritance intact she was obliged to marry her next of kin, precedence being given to her oldest paternal uncle, then to her other uncles in order of age, followed by her paternal cousins, starting with the oldest. However, if she relinquished her claim to the bulk of her father's property and let his kin take it, she could marry whom she pleased and her father's *oikos* would die out. The *patroïoikos* was to marry at twelve, but it is not known if this age was normal for all brides. The grooms were as young as at Sparta. Regulations on adultery prescribing various penalties if the act took place at the home of the wife's father, brother, or husband, indicate that the wife did not move to her husband's house until she was old enough to manage the household.

Divorce regulations recognized communal property. The wife took not only what she had brought as dowry, but also half the household produce and a portion of the textiles she had woven. Divorce could be initiated by either spouse. If the husband was responsible he paid a small fine. In divorce, freeborn children belonged to their father. There was less concern with women's chastity than there was at Athens; at Gortyn adultery, seduction, and rape were civil rather than criminal offenses, and the penalties were monetary.

Gortyn was unusual among Greek cities in recognizing marriages of slaves and between people of unequal social status. A relationship between a free man and an unfree woman was not recognized as marriage, but a male slave could marry a free woman. If the marriage had been matrilocal a child took the mother's status; if, on the other hand, the mother moved to the father's house, the child was a slave like its father. Perhaps in the former case the purpose of the marriage was to provide an heir to a family that lacked a son.

MARRIAGE AT ATHENS

There is a larger quantity and a wider variety of evidence for marriage at Athens than for any other city in the Greek world. Written sources range from prose texts, especially private orations and prescriptive works like Xenophon's *Household Management* (*Oeconomicus*) to dramatic poetry and funerary epigrams. Artistic sources, especially black-figure and red-figure vases and funerary stelae, depict weddings and married life. In the archaic and early classical period, Athenian marriage was more exogamous than in later times. Megacles and Miltiades were married to foreign women and their sons Cleisthenes and Cimon (like Themistocles) were not held in low esteem because of their mothers. With the establishment of the empire after the Persian wars, men of the lower classes, including sailors and cleruchs, were presented with opportunities to marry foreign brides.

The exchange of women, like the exchange of gifts in Homeric epic, served to create alliances between families. Such alliances between Athenians and foreigners posed potential threats to the stability of the democracy. As the Cleisthenic reforms had created tribes that unified Athenians through fictitious relationships, so the exchange of women within the citizen body could weave a network of genuine kinship relations. Moreover, the competition with foreign fathers who may have been willing to give daughters large dowries in order to gain a son-in-law who was a citizen of the hegemoneous city would have made it more difficult for Athenian fathers to find husbands for their daughters.

The Periclean citizenship law of 451/450 B.C., which required that citizens be born of parents who were both citizens, imposed a highly endogamous pattern. Marriages between first cousins or uncles and nieces were not uncommon. Such marriages prevented a family's wealth from being dissipated, and they strengthened kinship ties. Incest regulations outlawed unions only between ascendants and descendants, full siblings, and half-siblings born of the same mother. The

Athenian citizenship law was adopted as a model by other Greek cities. Plutarch (*Roman Questions* 108) observed that Roman marriage was exogamous, and remarked that endogamy put women at a disadvantage in the power structure of the family.

A marriage was arranged by men, the bridegroom and the father or other guardian (*kyrios*) of the bride. The betrothal (*engye*) was the prerequisite for a legal marriage. The *engye* involved agreeing to a marriage contract in which the size and contents of the dowry were specified. The dowry passed from the father to the bridegroom, and had to be returned if the marriage was dissolved and the woman was returned. Since women were barred from owning land at Athens, land could not be part of a dowry. However, fathers pledged their own land as surety for dowries. *Horoi* (boundary) inscriptions recording such pledges have been excavated in Attica.

Although the provision of a dowry was not compulsory for legal marriage, except in the case of the *epikleros thessa,* discussed later, it was uncertain whether a man would be willing to marry a woman without one. The need to dower a daughter might persuade a father that it was kinder to expose a newborn girl rather than raise her. There was no place for respectable spinsters in Athenian society. Preventing a woman from marrying was tantamount to a crime. The unequal sex ratio created by the exposure of female infants among the freeborn meant that a man might be found who would accept a dowerless girl, but the lack of a dowry might lead to insinuations that a relationship was something less than full-fledged marriage. In fact, some dowerless women were given away by their *kyrioi* to be concubines according to terms stipulated in a written contract. Wealthier relatives and friends might contribute dowries, and at times the state itself dowered the daughters of patriots.

Several years might intervene between the *engye* and the giving away of the bride (*ek-dosis*) or wedding (*gamos*) proper. During this time the groom supported his future bride with the interest from the dowry reckoned at 18 percent. Women generally married at about fourteen or fifteen, and men at about thirty years of age.

Marriage was one of a series of major events in a man's life, but it was the single most important event for a woman and it changed her life dramatically. Ritualized activities in the presence of other women helped her to make the transition to her new status. Before they married, young girls participated in the cult of Artemis at Brauron. The central myth was the sacrifice of the virgin Iphigenia to Artemis. The blood of the animals that were substituted for human victims associated the ritual with menarche. The cult at Brauron remained central in the lives of married women. Mothers dedicated statues of their children to Artemis, and the clothes and unfinished weaving of women who had died in childbirth were offered to Iphigenia. Athenian vases depict both divine and mortal marriages. Marriages by capture—for example, the conquest of Thetis by Peleus and the rape of Persephone by Hades—were common among portrayals of the immortals.

A human bride is often the focus of attention on vases depicting marriage. For her the rite consists of leaving her father's house, a transitional procession to her bridegroom's house, and finally incorporation into her new home. The bride's preparations are frequently shown on vases. Some portrayals of women bathing may represent the prenuptial bath. Water for this bath was brought from Enneakrounos-Kallirrhoe in loutrophoroi. (Vases of this shape were also used to mark the graves of those who died unwed.) The dressing of the bride is also common on vases. Despite the abundant visual and written evidence, there is no full extant description of an Athenian wedding. Although customs and the order of events may have varied, the normal wedding would have included sacrifices performed by the fathers of the bride and groom. Deities who were honored included Zeus, Hera, Apollo, Artemis, Athena, Peitho, the Moirai, and local divinities.

A banquet was held at the home of the bride or the groom. Women were present at the banquet, although they sat separately, and they were particularly prominent in the wedding procession. Since marriages were patrilocal, the procession started at the home of the bride and ended at the home of the groom. It took place at night, by torchlight; one of the torchbearers was the mother of the bride, who traditionally lighted her torch from her own hearth fire. One purpose of such processions was to assure that there were numerous witnesses to the marriage. The music of flutes and lyres and the singing of marriage hymns (*hymenaioi*) served to draw attention to the group. The bride and groom either rode in a chariot or walked. Vases depict the bridegroom holding the bride's wrist firmly, an indication that he will be the dominant figure in the marriage. She usually has a shy demeanor, appropriately enough since the groom is a virtual stranger. But the vase painters often include Erotes (Eros figures) in marriage scenes, and the groom looks at his bride with love.

The groom's mother welcomed the bride at the door of the bridegroom's home. Other features of the wedding ceremony included showering nuts and dried fruits (symbols of fertility) upon the newly married couple, and the offering of a basket of bread by a boy with two living parents (the *pais amphithales*). The bride, whose face perhaps had never been seen by the groom, unveiled herself before him using a ritual gesture (*anakalypteria*) alluding to sexuality. She ate the first food that her husband provided for her in her new home, a quince, a fruit that symbolized fertility. The groom's mother or another older female relative then led the couple to the wedding chamber (*thalamos*).

The day after the consummation of the wedding, presents were exchanged, and soon afterward the groom announced his wedding to his phratry with a celebration (*gamelia*).

The purpose of marriage was to create legitimate children. In the verbal formula of betrothal, the bride's father gave her to the groom for his begetting of legitimate children. According to pseudo-Demosthenes (59.122), wives were distinguished from other women with whom men might associate because only they could produce legitimate children, both boys who could be presented to the phratry and deme, and girls who could be given in marriage as the husband's own. Moreover, only the wife served as trustworthy guardian of the household.

The word *oikos* refers to both family and household. Since the *oikoi* were fundamental units of the state, marriage was both a public and a private institution. Athenian law regulated nuptiality and sexual intercourse as well as the citizenship of children. The sexual code reflected concern that through a woman's extramarital intercourse a child of a man who was not an Athenian citizen might be insinuated into the ranks of citizens. A father was required to sell into slavery an unmarried daughter who had lost her virginity; a husband was required to divorce a wife who had been seduced or raped and was permitted to kill the seducer.

Despite the possible previous homosexual experience of the husband, the youth of the bride, and the disparity in age of the married couple, comedy, prose texts (e.g., Xenophon, *Symposium*) and vase painting indicate that married couples enjoyed sexual intercourse. Of course the authors and painters were all men, but the vases were purchased by men for women. Male children were most valued, for many reasons including the practical one that the law obliged them to support their parents in old age. The production of a son tied a woman more closely to her husband's lineage. A widow might remain in her late husband's house if she had produced a son. Her children would inherit her dowry. Pregnant widows were under the care of the archon, as were orphans. If a childless woman became a widow, she returned with her dowry to her natal family, who often found another husband for her.

A married woman was actually only lent to a husband for the production of legitimate children for his *oikos*. Her family retained the right to reclaim her services to produce its own children. If a father died without leaving a male heir, his daughter was required to perpetuate his *oikos*. Such a girl was called *epikleros* ("heiress," or literally attached to [her father's] property). Although she never truly owned the property, it went with her to her husband and finally to their child, who was his grandfather's legal heir. The father's nearest male relative had the right to marry the *epikleros*, even if both were already married to other spouses. If the nearest male relative did not exercise his right, then the obligation passed to more distant relatives. The order of succession to the hand of the *epikleros* was the same order in which the kinsmen would have succeeded to the father's estate if there had not been any *epikleros*, starting with brothers of the deceased. In the case of a woman of the lowest property class (*epikleros thessa*) the male relatives were obliged to furnish a dowry so that marriage to her would be attractive to one of them.

In addition to family, *oikos* refers to household. Demographic factors, including short life spans, precluded the existence of large multigenerational families, but there were households with large numbers of slaves, dependent orphans, the husband's children from previous marriages, and perhaps his widowed mother and unmarried siblings. The sexes occupied separate quarters. Men and women played complementary roles in the domestic economy. Men's work was largely performed out of doors, women's indoors. Vases rarely depict married life after

the wedding, but there are some scenes of women caring for male babies. More commonly women are shown spinning, or involved in some other stage of textile manufacture.

The emotional component of marriage is more difficult to assess. The polarities of male and female could lead to complementariness or conflict. A double standard of sexual conduct was in force throughout Greek antiquity, and the proximity of slave women made extramarital relationships accessible to men without a great deal of wealth. Yet a wife, even a young one, might object to a husband's involvement with a household slave (Lysias, 1.12; pseudo-Demosthenes, 59.22) or to a husband's bringing prostitutes into the house (Andocides, 4.14). A wife could exercise some informal power in the home through scolding (pseudo-Demosthenes, 59.111) or withholding of sexual favors (Aristophanes, *Lysistrata*). A husband could divorce a wife merely by expelling her from the house. A wife, in contrast, needed to obtain the approval of the archon, and would have to find a man who was willing to help her obtain it.

In addition to the laws, the myth-based literature makes it clear that the wife was at a disadvantage in marriage. According to myth, Cecrops, the first king of Athens, invented marriage as a punishment for women, who had previously enjoyed equal political power with men. Medea points out that men can leave the house if they are unsatisfied with married life, but that for women there is no substitute for marriage (Euripides, *Medea* 244–247). The gynecological works in the Hippocratic corpus discuss the illnesses generated by prolonged virginity, sterility, and widowhood. Marriage and sexual intercourse are common remedies.

Marriage among metics (resident aliens) at Athens apparently was similar to that of citizens, for Aristotle (*Constitution of Athens* 58.3) refers to estates (*kleroi*) and "heiresses" (*epikleroi*). There is little information about marriage in Greek states other than Athens before the Hellenistic period, but it is likely that the Athenian pattern was standard. According to Demosthenes (24.210), many Greek states adopted the laws of Athens as their own.

MARRIAGE IN PLATO'S *REPUBLIC*

Marriage among the upper classes in the communal utopian society described by Plato in the *Republic* was the antithesis of the Athenian institution. The ruling classes had neither private property nor *oikoi*. Group marriage was practiced, though incest was avoided. Women did not engage in the marital rites until, like Spartans, they were mature enough to bear children without risk to their health. The parentage of children was not divulged, but children were raised in common by the state. Gender roles were nearly androgynous.

MARRIAGE IN THE HELLENISTIC WORLD

Marriage changed over time. The marital relationship was affected by modifications in gender roles and by the relationship of the bride and groom to their larger kinship groups. This change is most apparent in the Hellenistic world beyond Athens, but the earliest traces appear in Athenian vase paintings of the last part of the fifth century. Portrayals of the married couple emphasize a romantic union, rather than the bride's departure from her father's house in an ostentatious wedding procession. The groom is more youthful than on earlier pottery. Falling in love as a motive for marriage appears a century later in Athenian New Comedy.

The changes in marriage in the Hellenistic Greek world were profound. Some Macedonian monarchs were polygamous. Others practiced brother-sister marriage. The first marriage of full siblings was that of Ptolemy II and Arsinoë II (*ca.* 276–275 B.C.). Such a marriage made the Philadelphoi more than mortal, for their only predecessors were Greek and Egyptian divinities, and perhaps some pharaohs. The geographical extent of the Hellenistic world brought Greeks into contact with other peoples and resulted in exogamy, ranging from marriages between Greeks of different ethnic backgrounds to mixed marriages between Greeks and non-Greeks. Migration meant that marriages were concluded simply and efficiently. The earliest extant Greek marriage contract (*Elephantine Papyri* 1) dates from 311/310 B.C. The contract, as always, stipulates the size and composition of the dowry and the conditions for its return, but the sexual code and proper relationship of the married couple are also described. The couple refer to themselves in the first person plural and the contract foresees a change in domicile. Owing to such moves, kinship bonds were weakened, but affective ties between husband and wife were strengthened. Aphrodite reigned as goddess of marriage.

Hellenistic states were not founded on the *oikos* system. Hence marriage became a private matter, and the necessity for daughters to serve as *epikleroi* disappeared. The wife is not lent to the husband for purposes of reproduction; in fact, except for provisions for the disposition of the dowry after a wife's death, children are not mentioned in marriage contracts. Instead, a married couple can declare that they have come together to "share a common life" (*Giessen Papyri* 1.2; *Berliner Griechische Urkunden* 4.1052).

Women's status in marital law improved. In the *Elephantine Papyri* 1, the mother of the bride joins the father in giving away the bride. The first extant example of a bride giving herself is dated to 173 B.C. (*Giessen Papyri* 1.2). The bride who gives herself away does so with her father acting as legal guardian. Although the woman is still being given—albeit by herself—Greek marriage has certainly evolved from the marriage by capture found in earlier times. The average age of women's marriage seems to have been a little higher than it was in classical Athens. Divorce could proceed from either spouse, and it was not necessary to obtain the approval of a magistrate. Divorce documents and receipts for the return of dowry are found among the papyri. The form of marriage known as "unwritten" does not appear in Egypt before the Roman period.

Continuity as well as change characterized marriage in the Hellenistic world. Misogyny continued to exist, and some philosophers, notably Cynics and Epicureans, were outspoken in their hostility to marriage. Marriage contracts as well as literary works show that marriage was still an unequal partnership, but less unequal than it had been previously. Despite the existence of a dowry, the husband is viewed as the provider. A double standard in sexual conduct remained in force, although the Hellenistic husband had less leeway than his classical predecessors. Plutarch in the *Lives* and *Moralia,* but particularly in *Advice to the Bride and Groom,* and philosophical treatises, including Neopythagorean writings by women authors, advise a wife to tolerate a husband's infidelities while the husband, on his part, is not to insult the wife with evidence of them. Women should be modest and remain indoors, not because they are secluded, but because their responsibilities are there. Yet wives and husbands should share intellectual pursuits and pleasures. Like Xenophon, Plutarch advises the husband to be the wife's teacher, but he is not to teach her home economics, but rather the liberal arts, notably philosophy, astronomy, and geometry. He writes that the marriage of those who merely sleep in the same bed is of separate people who cohabit but do not really live together, that of those who marry for dowry or for children is of persons joined together, but the marriage of a couple in love is an intimate union (*Moralia* 142).

BIBLIOGRAPHY

Walter Erdmann, "Die Ehe im alten Griechenland," in *Münchener Beiträge zur Papyrusforschung der antiken Rechtsgeschichte,* **20** (1934); Helene P. Foley, ed., *Reflections of Women in Antiquity* (1981); Alick R. W. Harrison, *The Law of Athens: The Family and Property* (1968); Walter K. Lacey, *The Family in Classical Greece* (1968); Geoffrey E. R. Lloyd, *Science, Folklore and Ideology* (1983); Edgar Lobel and Denys Page, *Poetarum Lesbiorum Fragmenta* (1963); J. Modrzejewski, "La structure juridique du mariage grec," in *Scritti in onore di Orsolina Montevecchi* (1981); Orsolina Montevecchi, *La papirologia* (1973); William L. Odom, "A Study of Plutarch: The Position of Greek Women in the First Century after Christ," Ph. D. diss., University of Virginia, Charlottesville (1961); Sarah B. Pomeroy, *Goddesses, Whores, Wives, and Slaves: Women in Classical Antiquity* (1975), "Charities for Greek Women," in *Mnemosyne,* **35** (1982), "Selected Bibliography on Women in Classical Antiquity," in *Women in the Ancient World: The Arethusa Papers,* John Peradotto and J. P. Sullivan, eds. (1984), and *Women in Hellenistic Egypt from Alexander to Cleopatra* (1984); David M. Schaps, *Economic Rights of Women in Ancient Greece* (1979); Robert F. Sutton, "The Interaction Between Men and Women Portrayed on Attic Red-Figure Pottery," Ph.D. diss., University of North Carolina, Chapel Hill (1981); Helmut Thierfelder, *Die Geschwisterehe im Hellenistisch-Römischen Ägypten* (1960); Claude Vatin, *Recherches sur le mariage et la condition de la femme mariée à l'époque hellénistique* (1970); R. F. Willets, ed., *The Law Code of Gortyn* (1967); Hans Julius Wolff, *Written and Unwritten Marriage in Hellenistic and Postclassical Roman Law* (1939), and "Marriage Law and Family Organization in Ancient Athens: A Study in the Interrelation of Public and Private Law in the Greek City," in *Traditio,* **2** (1944).

Roman Marriage

SUSAN TREGGIARI

SOURCES ON THE LEGAL RULES and social norms that affected marriage in ancient Roman times are scattered and often hard to interpret. In outline it is possible to discern a gradual liberalization as patriarchalism diminished, until a high point of freedom for both sexes is reached in the late republic. This is followed by normative legislation and growing juristic standardization in the principate, until Constantine revolutionized the state's view of marriage in order to bring it more into line with Christian ideas. There are many excellent detailed modern accounts of the various areas with which Roman lawyers concerned themselves. How marriage worked in practice is a subject that has been comparatively neglected. The focus here is on the social reality of marriage in its developed form from about 100 B.C. to about A.D. 200.

"Marriage is the joining together of a male and a woman, and a partnership in all of life, a sharing in divine and human law." This is the definition of the lawyer Modestinus in the third century A.D. (*Digest* 23.2.1).

All his themes can be traced earlier. Marriage was considered a natural development of animal behavior: "Because the urge to reproduce is an instinct common to all animals, society originally consists of the pair, next of the pair with their children, then one house and all things in common. This is the beginning of the city and the seedbed of the state" (Cicero, *On Duty* [*De Officiis*] 1.54). It was part of natural law (*Digest* 1.1.1.3, Ulpian). Its stated purpose was the acquisition of children, who would inherit their father's rights in the state. The state therefore encouraged and sometimes compelled marriage. Early censors asked each registrant if he were married (Aulus Gellius 4.3.2, cf. 4.20.3–4; Cicero, *On Oratory* 2.260). Augustan legislation penalizing the unmarried remained in force until the empire became Christian. It was regarded as a normal duty for citizens of both sexes to marry and produce children. A major and peculiar exception is provided by the (possibly Augustan) ban on marriage of lower ranks in the army, a minor exception by the Vestal Virgins.

MANUS

Originally, there are said to have been three ways of being married, by "use" (*usus*), by a religious ceremony (*confarreatio*), and by purchase (*coemptio*) (Boethius, *Commentary on Cicero's Topics* 3.14; Servius, *Commentary on Vergil's Georgics* 1.31). The fullest discussion is in Gaius' *Institutes* (second century A.D.), where he correctly regards these as three ways in which a woman might enter her husband's control (*manus*). This control was analogous to a father's power over his legitimate children (*patria potestas*). *Manus* meant that the wife became a member of her husband's family, "in the position of a daughter," who would succeed (equally with his children) to his property if he were intestate; that all of her property became his on marriage; and that he had power to divorce and perhaps to kill her (although no execution of a wife is securely attested). On marriage, she gave up her rights and obligations in her family of birth, emerging from *patria potestas* or guardianship.

Confarreatio, an archaic sacrament practicable only for the upper class (Gaius, *Institutes* [hereafter Gaius] 1.112; Ulpian, *Tituli ex Corpore Ulpiani* [hereafter *Tit. Ulp.*] 9; Servius, *Commentary on Vergil's Georgics* 1.31, cf. *Commentary on Vergil's Aeneid* 4.103, 374) had become very rare by the early principate (Tacitus, *Annals* 4.16; Gaius, 1.136) but probably survived until pagan sacrifice was abolished in A.D. 394. *Coemptio* was marked by an imaginary sale of the woman to the man, analogous to a legal ceremony used for other sales (Gaius, 1.113, 123; Cicero, *On Oratory* 1.237; *Topics* 14). Gaius speaks of *coemptio* as if it was still alive in his day, but it probably disappeared during the third century A.D. *Usus*, which perhaps developed from *coemptio*, was simpler: "By *usus* a woman came into the control of her husband if she continued married to him for a

full year" (Gaius, 1.111; cf. Servius, *On Vergil's Georgics* 1.31). Although *confarreatio* and *coemptio* conferred *manus* at once and we cannot distinguish marriage ceremony from rituals associated with *manus*, no ceremony is known to mark the beginning of *usus*, and *manus* came about automatically unless the woman broke it by absenting herself for three nights. *Usus* fell into disuse, probably in the first century B.C., and was obsolete by Gaius' time. This was perhaps because, if *manus* were needed, it was simpler and safer to achieve it by *coemptio*. Marriage without *manus*, "free marriage," was occurring by the fifth century B.C. (Gaius, 1.111); since it produced no alteration in the woman's legal status, no legal forms are attested. A *filiafamilias* remained a member of her original family; a woman whose paterfamilias was dead or had freed her remained independent. Although marriage with *manus* was frequent down to the third century, it was relatively uncommon by the time of Cicero (Cicero, *For Flaccus* 84). But the Augustan legislation took it into account (*Comparison of the Law of Moses and of the Romans* [hereafter *Coll.*] 4.2.3; 4.7) and Gaius devoted a good deal of attention to it (1.49, 108 ff., 136 ff., 162; 3.83 ff.).

The growth of free marriage should not be identified with a gradual liberation of women. The reasons were complex. Consideration of property no doubt dominated in the upper class; the choice may have been made through negotiation and compromise between the families. The early strictness of the husband's control was gradually modified. For example, by the late republic upon divorce the wife could reclaim her property as she could reclaim dowry in free marriage (Cicero, *Topics* 23); she could also divorce the husband and compel him to break the *manus* (Gaius, 1.137a). A wife *in manu* had the advantage of being recognized as a relation, and heir on intestacy, of husband and children. It might also happen that a husband's control was milder than that of a paterfamilias. Conversely, continuing to belong to her original family might give other financial advantages and allow the father to intervene against the husband.

The increase in free marriages (in which the woman was often independent because her father had died or freed her) coincides with an increased freedom for both sexes, which had developed by the time at which our sources become informative, about 70 B.C. The view detailed by second- and third-century A.D. jurists that marriage depends essentially on consent and intention is already present (e.g., Cicero, *On Oratory* 1.183).

CONSENT

"A marriage cannot exist unless everyone consents, that is, those who come together and those under whose control they are" (*Digest* 23.2.2, Paul; cf. 23.1.11, *Tit. Ulp.* 5.2.2), that is, the couple and their patresfamilias, if any. It was consent and not physical union that made the relationship a marriage (*Digest* 50.17.30, Ulpian), the "mind of those who came together," not a contract (Quintilian, *Education of an Orator* 5.11.32), their will, not a wedding (Quintilian, *Declamations* 12.22). These passages concentrate on the initiation of marriage: the consent, implied or expressed (usually by one or more of the signs rejected here as inessential) at the wedding. During the marriage, the continuing consent of the two partners is sometimes expressed by jurists in phrases such as *affectio maritalis*, roughly, the intention to be in the married state with someone, the acceptance of the other as a legal partner. "If a wife and husband have lived apart for a long time, but each has honored the marriage . . . I think that gifts between them

are invalid, on the grounds that the marriage is still in existence, for it is not cohabitation which makes a marriage, but *maritalis affectio*" (*Digest* 24.1.32.13, Ulpian). Or a couple might be living in concubinage and begin to treat each other as husband and wife, with *maritalis honor et affectio;* they thus become married (*Digest* 39.5.31 *pr.,* cf. *Justinian Codex* 5.27.11. *pr.*). The difference between a wife and a concubine was in choice and intention (*Sententiae Pauli* [hereafter *Pauli Sent.*] 2.20.1; *Digest* 25.7.4, Paul). Questions about the status of a relationship might arise only after one or both of the partners was dead, when it would have to be deduced from their manner of life or from consideration of whether marriage would have been legal. Usually a respectable freeborn woman would be assumed to be wife (*Digest* 23.2.24). The emphasis on continued consent by both explains why withdrawal of consent permitted unilateral divorce.

CAPACITY

Consent was essential in the developed law. Capacity for marriage involved age, lack of close relationship, and in general the right of two specific persons to marry each other (*conubium*). The legal minimum age for a girl was twelve, probably fixed, by some lawyers at least, before Augustus. A girl married before her twelfth birthday did not become a legal wife until that birthday: fairly frequent mention of this in the jurists suggests that such marriages did occur. Legal writers tend to equate or associate the legal minimum age for girls with their sexual maturity (*Digest* 24.1.65; 36.2.30), although medical writers put menarche, which is not the same as the completion of puberty, between thirteen and fourteen. This estimate of the average proves nothing about the maturity of individual girls who married at or even below the legal age, and there is some evidence that physical maturity was desired in a bride (e.g., Vergil, *Aeneid* 7.52–53; Ovid, *Metamorphoses* 11.301–302). But girls married young by modern Western standards.

Although there is evidence that marriage for girls appeared urgent at some time in their mid teens, it is hard to generalize about the exact age or degree of maturity that suggested to those responsible for establishing them that "the age of the girls began to press" (Tacitus, *Annals* 6.15.1; cf. Terence, *Phormio* 570–571; *The Brothers* [*Adelphi*] 672–674). Upper-class girls are rarely attested as unmarried in their late teens; those who are had probably been delayed by an unsuccessful engagement or had waited for a fiancé to reach the right age. Thus the younger daughter of Mark Antony and Octavia, Antonia, born in 36 B.C., did not marry Livia's son Drusus until the year 16, when she was nineteen or twenty and he two years older. Those whose relative wealth or position made them attractive to eligible men were often probably "preempted" young by betrothal or marriage. Vipsania Agrippina, daughter of Marcus Agrippa and the heiress Attica, was betrothed to Octavian's stepson Tiberius when she was scarcely one year old (Nepos, *Atticus* 19.4). Emperors manipulating dynasties organized the marriages of key women relatively early.

The minimum legal age of marriage for boys is assumed to be the age at which they were freed from guardianship, on which jurists disagreed; it was either fourteen or puberty, or both. The question is of chiefly academic interest, since it was rare for anyone to raise the possibility of a boy marrying under age (*Digest* 12.4.8; Quintilian, *Declamations* 279), and it seems clear that it was considered usual for a boy to marry only after he had put on the plain white toga of adulthood (*toga virilis*) at about sixteen or seventeen, and even then after an interval (Apuleius, *Apology* 70, 73). Precocious mar-

riage for dynastic reasons is attested: Nero, the elder son of Germanicus, married Julia, daughter of Germanicus' adoptive brother Drusus, soon after he took the *toga virilis* in A.D. 20 (Tacitus, *Annals* 2.43.3; 3.29.4), and the future emperor Nero, born 15 December A.D. 37, took the *toga virilis* in 51 and married his adoptive sister Octavia, aged about thirteen, in 53, when he was only sixteen (*ibid.* 12.58.1). Marriage for less important men of the imperial house and for their senatorial contemporaries seems ideally to have taken place at twenty-one or twenty-two. The motive was the seniority offered to fathers by Augustus' laws: each child reduced the minimum age for a particular office by one year. Men in general must have been more affected by family and financial circumstances; for example, independent patresfamilias or only sons may have married younger. It must have been of great significance for the relationship of husband and wife in first marriages not only that the bride was usually so young, but that she was probably at least five years younger than he was. The effect was intensified when a young girl married a man who had been married before.

Apart from age, there were other legal requirements. Marriage between ascendant and descendant, between brother and sister, or with a sibling's child (until Claudius legalized marriages between a man and his brother's daughter) were considered incestuous and null. A man might not marry his aunt, stepmother, stepdaughter, mother-in-law, or daughter-in-law, nor a woman the equivalent male relatives. For a marriage valid in Roman law, it was necessary for both parties to have *conubium*. Roman citizens normally had this right with each other and with certain Latins and foreigners if the right had been conferred. There was no *conubium* with other noncitizens. Later laws modified the general right: for instance, ordinary soldiers could not marry during service, a rule in force at least from the time of Claudius (probably from Augustus) to that of Septimius Severus. Augustus introduced restrictions on intermarriage between certain categories. The presence of *conubium* ensured that the children were legitimate and took their father's citizenship (Gaius, 1.55–96). If a citizen married a noncitizen with whom he or she did not have *conubium,* the union might be valid for the foreign tribe or city but was invalid in Roman law. This would mean that the children were illegitimate and took their mother's status, but the Minucian law (passed in the first century B.C.) modified this rule, removing the privilege of children of a Roman woman who had married a foreigner with whom she did not have *conubium.* Although by natural law such children would be illegitimate but Roman, the law ruled that they should take the citizenship of the "inferior" (that is, non-Roman) parent (Gaius 1.78). The extension of Roman citizenship increased the number of people with whom the Romans could intermarry legally, but down to the Decree of Caracalla the problem of mixed-status marriages must have been relatively common.

Modern scholars disagree about the legal position of couples who entered on a marriage for which they lacked *conubium.* The texts seem to indicate that they were in a sense married: the marriage was not completely null, but *matrimonium iniustum*—a marriage "unjust," meaning invalid, under Roman law. The couple regarded themselves as married, but their union did not bring about all the effects of valid civil law marriage. *Matrimonium iniustum* had some recognition: there was dowry and divorce (Cicero, *Topics* 20), and Ulpian even claims that a husband could prosecute his *iniusta uxor* for adultery (*Digest* 48.5.14.1: he quotes Homer's line, "for not only the sons of Atreus love their wives"). But rights of succession of a "valid" husband or wife, privileges of the Augustan legislation, legitimacy

of children, and *patria potestas* did not follow (*Digest* 34.9.13; 38.11.1 *pr.*; *Tit. Ulp.* 5.8).

ENGAGEMENT

Within the pool of potential husbands and wives delimited by the rules on *conubium,* considerations of social class, wealth, age, similarity of outlook and background, looks, ability, breeding potential, and character further circumscribed choice. Among the senatorial aristocracy, and probably among Romans in general if Plautus' representation of betrothals indicates what was acceptable, virgins were not expected to take a leading role in their own engagements. Theoretically, a daughter, probably even a *filiafamilias,* could refuse her father's choice if he was unsuitable (*Digest* 23.1.12.1), and this may sometimes have happened, for example, if her mother prompted her. The woman's consent was, in classical law, essential for both engagement and marriage (*Digest* 23.1.7.1; 23.1.11). Similarly, a *filiusfamilias* might be ordered to marry, but his consent was needed. The consent of a paterfamilias was required for the marriage of his son or daughter, but might in some circumstances be presumed. By the first century B.C. betrothal was not actionable. The engaged couple were fiancé and fiancée (*sponsus* and *sponsa*) and the words used for relations by marriage could begin to be used. Negotiations about dowry would begin or continue.

DOWRY

Dowry (*dos*) was property (such as land or slaves) or money or a combination of these, handed over to the husband in recognition of the fact that he was responsible for the proper support of his wife (*Digest* 23.3.56.1). If a woman entered her husband's control, all her property became his as dowry (Cicero, *Topics* 23). A poorer woman marrying a social superior might wish to give all her property as dowry (*Vatican Fragment* 115; cf. *Digest* 23.3.72 *pr.*), for the amount depended on a delicate calculation of the position of both partners. But usually families tried to strike a mean between what they could afford and what their status dictated (*Digest* 23.3.60; 23.3.69.4; 32.43). The figure of one million sesterces is mentioned in the early principate as ample (Tacitus, *Annals* 2.86.2; Martial 11.23.3–4; Juvenal, *Satires* 6.137) but this had already been exceeded by the two daughters of Scipio Africanus with about 1,200,000 (Polybius, 32.13). Apuleius got a "moderate" 300,000 sesterces with his wealthy Tripolitanian widow (Apuleius, *Apology* 91–92); a woman "marrying" a marine in Egypt took him only some clothes and perhaps 802 drachmas (Riccobono, ed., *Sources of Roman Law Before Justinian* [*Fontes Iuris Romani Anteiustiniani*], 2d ed., 3.20). Dowry was essential: a girl marrying without it might seem to be a concubine (Plautus, *Three-Coin Day* [*Trinummus*] 689–691); even slave women tried to give a quasi dowry (*Digest* 23.3.39 *pr.*). Women with no or inadequate dowry would find it hard to marry, at least in their own class (Plautus, *The Gold Pot* [*Aulularia*] 191; *Persa* 387–389; Seneca the Elder, *Controversiae* 7.6.18). Dowry might come from the bride's father, mother or other relative, from herself, from an outsider, or even from the husband, as might happen if a rich man wanted to marry a dowerless girl but to secure her position. For dowry was meant to guarantee that the woman would have enough to live on or to remarry if the marriage ended. This is made clear by the insistence of jurists that "it is in the state's interest for women to have their dowries safe, since because of them they are able to marry" (*Digest* 23.3.2; cf. 24.3.1). Dowry might be a major part of the property that a daughter could expect; she was pro-

vided for on marriage and her father might take this into account when he made his will, or she might relinquish her inheritance and be satisfied with her dowry.

Dotal property could be transferred to the husband before or after the wedding (*Pauli Sent.* 2.21b.1). The parties could make special agreements (*pacta dotalia*); otherwise, it was customary for the dowry to be paid in three annual installments, beginning a year after the marriage (Polybius, 32.13). If the dowry came from a male ascendant, it reverted to him if she died, except that the husband kept one-fifth for each child (*Digest* 23.3.5; 23.3.6; 24.3.10 *pr.*; *Tit. Ulp.* 6.4). All other dowry was recoverable only by agreement (*Tit. Ulp.* 6.3; 6.5).

If the marriage ended in the death of the husband or in divorce, the wife (from *ca.* 230 B.C.) or her paterfamilias with her consent could sue for the restoration of her dowry (by the *actio rei uxoriae*) in which praetors emphasized equity (Cicero, *Topics* 66; *On Duty* 3.61). By the late republic an innocent divorcing husband who could prove his wife's adultery could keep one-sixth of the dowry, or one-eighth for lesser faults such as unauthorized drinking (*Tit. Ulp.* 6.9; 6.12). If the wife or her paterfamilias were responsible for divorcing a husband who had committed no fault, then he could keep one-sixth of the dowry for each of up to three children, but if he were responsible he kept nothing (Cicero, *Topics* 19; *Tit. Ulp.* 6.10). The husband guilty of a major fault had to repay the dowry immediately; if the fault was minor, he had six months (*Tit. Ulp.* 6.13). Otherwise he could pay cash in three annual installments, although nonliquid property (such as farms) had to be restored at once (*Tit. Ulp.* 6.8; *Digest* 23.4.19). The difficulties caused by payment and repayment of dowry installments (*pensiones*) for men chronically short of ready money can be seen in several of Cicero's letters. Some deal with the payment of his second installment to Dolabella, due 1 July 48 B.C. (*Letters to Atticus* 11.2.2; 11.3.1; 11.4a); when the third installment was due in 47 Cicero debated whether a divorce would not be better and whether it would suit Tullia if she or Dolabella initiated it (*ibid.* 11.25.3; 11.23.3). Other letters reveal anxiety about getting Dolabella to pay installments after the divorce (*ibid.* 12.8; 16.3.5; 16.15.2; *Letters to Friends* 6.18.5), or Cicero's own problems in repaying Terentia in 45 (*Letters to Atticus* 12.12.1) and on 1 January 43 (*ibid.* 16.15.5; *Letters to Friends* 16.24.1). Husbands were allowed to charge certain expenses against the dowry (*Tit. Ulp.* 6.14–17; *Digest* 25.1).

PROPERTY

Married women might have their own property apart from dowry: if they were *filiaefamilias,* this was *peculium* and technically belonged to their paterfamilias; if they were independent, they would normally need a guardian to help them administer it. It was acceptable for the husband to act as guardian, or for a wife to be involved in the administration of her husband's business or property. But gifts between husband and wife (*donatio inter virum et uxorem*) were by custom (e.g., *Digest* 24.1.1) illegal if they were of a sort that enriched the recipient (small birthday presents and the like were legal; *Digest* 24.1.31.8), for fear that "in their reciprocal love each should despoil himself in turn by extravagant giving" (*Digest* 24.1.1). Spouses managed to circumvent this rule. Inheritance was also restricted. A wife *in manu* had the same rights as his children to the estate of her intestate husband, but other wives and husbands could claim on intestacy only after blood relations (*Tit. Ulp.* 28.7). If the dead husband had made a will, a wife's right to inherit in the late republic was restricted by the general rules about women, but the Papian and Poppaean law of A.D. 9 allowed a childless husband of age twenty-five to sixty or a wife of twenty to fifty to take only one-tenth of a bequest from the other. The existence of one living child allowed them to take the whole, and children who died or children of a previous marriage allowed them to take fractions (*Tit. Ulp.* 15, 16). This produced the striking anomaly that a man could leave more to a mistress than to a childless wife (Quintilian, *Education of an Orator* 8.5.19). But the law could be partly circumvented by leaving a legacy in trust or by leaving the spouse a usufruct of one-third of the property (*Tit. Ulp.* 15.3; *Oxyrhynchus Papyri* 17.2089). A house and annual income could thus be assured. If the spouse had the right to inherit as much as the testator wanted, a variety of dispositions would be possible: he or she could be either the sole or joint heir or receive a legacy. Augustus left one-third of his private property to Livia and two-thirds to his adoptive son Tiberius.

WEDDINGS

Ceremonies marked entry into the married state. Modern handbooks conflate from a variety of sources, such as epithalamiums and antiquarian writings, a detailed account of the "standard" wedding, which assumes that no ritual was ever omitted and that the entire citizenry could afford it. Among the more important components are the taking of auspices (Cicero, *On Divination* 1.28), sacrifice (Servius, *Commentary on Vergil's Aeneid* 3.136), dinner at the bride's house (Plautus, *Aulularia* 294 f.; Juvenal, *Satires* 2.119 f.), a torchlit procession of the bride (wearing a flame-colored veil) to the house of the bridegroom (*deductio in domum mariti*), the singing of obscene songs and the throwing of nuts to the crowd (to encourage fertility; Catullus 61, 62), the lifting of the bride across the threshold by her attendants (Plutarch, *Moralia: Roman Questions* 29; *Parallel Lives,* "Romulus" 15.5), the sacramental offering to her of fire and water (Plutarch, *Roman Questions* 1; *Digest* 24.1.66.1). Perhaps only in *coemptio* and *confarreatio,* the bridegroom asked the bride her name and she replied, "Where you are Gaius, I am Gaia" (Plutarch, *Roman Questions* 30; Anon., *On Names* 7; cf. Cicero, *In Defense of Murena* 27; Quintilian, *Education of an Orator* 1.7.28). We have no full and precise description of an actual wedding, although both Catullus (61) and Tacitus (*Annals* 11.27), give vivid sketches. Presumably the lower classes celebrated as well as they could. For everyone, much was optional: it is hard to believe that all virgin brides parted their hair with a spear as Ovid prescribes (*The Roman Calendar* [*Fasti*] 2.436). When the Stoic Cato remarried his ex-wife Marcia in 49 B.C., Lucan alleges (2.352–379) that "the mere agreement, laws without vain pomp, please them. The gods are admitted as witnesses to the rites. . . . They are joined without speaking and content themselves with only Brutus as augur. . . . Nor did they try the union of their former bed."

The generalization that widows and divorcees had quieter weddings is unwarranted (Plutarch, *Roman Questions* 105 notwithstanding) although some might have done so to avoid expense (Apuleius, *Apology* 87–88). The wealthy gave parties, inviting acquaintances and eminent people (Pliny, *Letters* 1.9.2; Plutarch, *Parallel Lives,* "Antony" 9.3), despite legislators' attempts to fix maximum expenditure on weddings (Gellius, 2.24.7) and on the drinking party held next day at the bridegroom's house. Neighbors might expect a handout (Apuleius, *Apology* 88).

ROLES

Further rituals were prescribed for the day after the wedding, when the bride took over her duties as materfamilias and matrona. As a *matrona,* she had a role in public worship (again most relevant to the upper classes) and a position of respect and responsibility in the household, where she had charge of the keys and domestic staff. In poorer families, the wife seems often to have worked alongside a craftsman or shopkeeper husband, or to have had independent employment, for example, as a market-woman. Lower-class housewives must also have cleaned, cooked, carried water, and shopped.

Ideally, husband and wife could expect of each other devotion, support, and sharing; not just children, but life in common, companionship, and love (Musonius Rufus, 13–14). A wife entered a partnership of life with her husband (Quintilian, *Declamations* 247); she was a partner in good and bad fortune (Lucan 2.346–347; Tacitus, *Annals* 3.34.8; 12.5.5; Plutarch, *Parallel Lives,* "Brutus" 13.7, *Roman Questions* 1; Quintilian, *op. cit.* 257); ideally, spouses shared their property (Cicero, *On Duty* 1.54; Columella, *On Country Matters* [*De Re Rustica*] 12.8; Quintilian, *op. cit.* 247). The emphasis is on the wife as partner since she on marriage took her husband's status (Polybius, 32.12; *Digest* 1.9.1 *pr.;* 1.9.8; 1.9.12; *Vatican Fragment* 104). Gaius Sallust remarks disapprovingly of wives in polygamous cultures, "none of them has the position of a partner; all are held equally cheap" (*Jugurthine War* 80.7). In Ovid, the idea of equal partnership in sexual and marital union is strong (e.g., *Tristia* 2.161; 5.14.28; *Letters from Pontus* 3.1.73). Duty to share misfortune was taken very seriously. Ovid praises his wife's heroism when he was exiled (*Tristia* 1.6; 5.14); wives are praised for joining their husbands in suicide forced by the emperor or incurable disease (Tacitus, *Annals* 6.29.7; 15.63–64; Pliny, *Letters* 6.24) or for accompanying them into exile (Pliny, *Letters* 7.19.4). Less dramatically, they supported them when old and ill (*ibid.* 8.18.8–9). Lack of evidence on self-sacrificing husbands can in part be attributed to emphasis on women's virtues as wifely and to the scarcity of detailed eulogies by women.

Both partners owed compliance or consideration, reverence, and dutifulness (*obsequium, reverentia, pietas*). Legal consequences followed, for example, prohibition of defaming or penal actions against the spouse. Adultery by the wife was the classic example of violation (*Digest* 48.5.30 *pr.*), because it threatened the legitimacy of children and love for the husband (cf. Pliny, *Letters* 4.19.2). A husband who killed a wife taken in adultery could claim justification before Augustus' law (Gellius, 10.23.5); the offense was grounds for divorce and partial retention of dowry; Augustus obliged a husband who detected his wife's adultery to divorce her. A husband's extramarital intercourse was defined as fornication, generally condoned if with slaves and prostitutes, unless so blatant as to insult the wife (*Justinian Codex* 5.17.8.2), although wives were expected to resent their husbands' mistresses (*paelices*). Moralists sometimes condemned a husband's extramarital sex (Seneca the Younger, *Letters* 95.37) or even all extramarital intercourse (Musonius Rufus, 12) or demanded that he set an example (*Digest* 48.5.14.5). Some deprecated passion toward a wife because it degraded her to the level of a mistress (Seneca the Younger, *Marriage* frag. 4).

But, although much love poetry addresses mistresses, strongly affectionate language is used by Cicero to Terentia as he imagines her night and day (*Letters to Friends* 14.2) and by Ovid to his third wife, using classic themes of the absent lover as well as allusions to conjugal duty (*Tristia* 3.3); Pliny rereads his absent wife's letters, imagines her, and visits her empty room (*Letters* 6.4; 6.7; 7.5). Emotional investment in a spouse may have been conditioned by relatively high chances of widowhood and low life expectancy. Praise was due to widows who refused to remarry; their chastity was proclaimed on tombs and celebrated by edifying anecdotes. When Octavia asked Marcella the Elder if she was glad she had married, she replied, "So much so that I don't want to do it again" (Seneca, *Marriage* frag. 27). A man was expected to feel the loss of a wife (Pliny, *Letters* 8.5). The ideal was monogamy: "Happy three times over—and more—are those whom love holds in an unbroken bond and, not ripped away by cruel complaints, will release only at their death" (Horace, *Odes* 1.13.17–20). Epitaphs attest the ideal, for example, that of a freed couple, who respected each other and lived in harmony for sixty years; they built a tomb so that they would have a bedroom in which to be buried together (*Corpus Inscriptionum Latinarum* 6.33087). A harmonious marriage was too valuable to be disturbed by outsiders (*Digest* 43.30.1.5; *Pauli Sent.* 5.6.15). Alongside idealization of marriage and of the good wife with her domestic virtues, there was a strong misogynist tradition (e.g., Lucilius 26.678–680; Juvenal, *Satires* 6; Jerome, *Against Iovinianus* 1.47–48). On balance, epitaphs tell us more about individuals than do satirists.

Motherhood was among the chief wifely virtues (e.g., *Corpus Inscriptionum Latinarum* 1 [2d ed.] 1211). Women such as Cornelia, who had twelve children, three of whom grew up, and Agrippina the Elder, who reared six out of nine, were praised for their fecundity; notable fathers included Metellus Macedonicus, with six (Pliny, *Natural History* 7.57–60). But most literary and epigraphic data suggest low reproductivity. Augustus' law set three children as a goal. Reasons for the population problem need further research. Contraception was practiced but would have been of limited efficacy for fertile couples; the incidence of abortion, surgical or chemical, is hard to determine from medical or moralizing sources. Exposure of babies may have been a more usual solution for the poor who were unable or the rich who were unwilling to rear them.

DIVORCE

By the end of the republic, divorce was simple, informal, and relatively common. It could be achieved by consent of both or by the unilateral action of either, except, perhaps, for wives *in manu,* although they could divorce at least by the time of Gaius (1.137a). *Filiaefamilias* divorced without reference to their fathers (cf. especially *Digest* 24.3.66.2). As late as Justinian I, a paterfamilias could compel the divorce of his child for serious reasons, although second-century emperors set limits to his power to make the couple separate or to reclaim the dowry (*Digest* 43.30.1.5; *Pauli Sent.* 2.19.2; 5.6.15; *Vatican Fragment* 116; *Justinian Codex* 5.17.5 *pr.*). Informality in the late republic went so far that it was argued that a husband might divorce his wife without telling her (Cicero, *On Oratory* 1.183–184, 238), but a verbal declaration, for example, "Keep your things for yourself" (Plautus, *Amphitruo* 928; *Three-Coin Day* 266; Cicero, *Philippics* 2.69), was expected, although revocable if uttered in anger (*Digest* 24.2.3; 50.17.48). A verbal declaration continued to be used in the second century A.D. (*Digest* 24.2.2.1), but it was safe to make it before witnesses, to write, or to send an agent to make the declaration (*nuntium remittere;* Cicero, *On Oratory* 1.183; *Topics* 19; *Letters to Friends* 14.13). It was probably the Julian law on adultery, that stated, "No divorce is ratified unless seven adult Roman citizens are called in [as witnesses], apart from the freedman of the person making the divorce" (*Digest* 24.2.9). This formality was necessary to protect the husband who was divorcing his wife for adultery, but probably not for other unilateral and bilateral divorces.

Upper-class men seem to have divorced easily, often in order to remarry more advantageously. Octavian is an example. It is less clear if women could divorce without scandal (cf. Cicero, *Letters to Friends* 8.7.2)

and remarry easily if they were divorced on moral grounds or when old. Nor is anything known about divorce among the lower classes. Divorce may have become less acceptable after the Julio-Claudian period. It must often have caused suffering (*Digest* 23.3.29.1), but could be by mutual consent, "for it often happens, that because of a priesthood or even sterility or old age or illness or military service a marriage cannot conveniently be maintained, and so it is dissolved with good feeling" (*Digest* 24.1.60–62).

AUGUSTAN LEGISLATION

Augustus' laws, meant to encourage marriage, were a thorough attack on the principle that it was largely outside the scope of law. In the Julian law on the marriage of social classes of 18 B.C. and the Papian and Poppaean law of A.D. 9, he prohibited intermarriage of senators and their sons, sons' sons, or grandsons and their daughters, sons' daughters, and sons' sons' daughters with ex-slaves, actors or actresses, or children of actors or actresses, and prohibited marriage of freeborn citizens with procuresses, women freed by procurers, actresses, women taken in adultery or condemned in the criminal courts, and, presumably, prostitutes. But since (if we can trust Dio Chrysostom, 54.16.2) there was a shortage of wellborn (perhaps meaning freeborn) women, he encouraged intermarriage with ex-slaves for nonsenatorial Romans. Incentives and penalties (for men unmarried between the ages of twenty-five and sixty, and women between twenty and fifty) affected chiefly the wealthier classes. Children gave various privileges. The right of husband and wife to inherit from one another was improved. An unmarried person was debarred from taking under wills (except of kin up to the sixth degree), although he had one hundred days' grace if he wished to marry, and engaged men qualified for two years; women had two years in which to remarry after the husband's death and eighteen months after divorce. Childless persons could only inherit half.

These laws do not seem to have increased the birthrate or enabled senatorial families to continue. Nor did Augustus' attempt to curb the perceived permissiveness of society, the Julian law on adultery (?18 B.C.), make marriage more sacred or improve sexual morality. This made adultery (sexual intercourse outside marriage by a married woman) and other heterosexual or homosexual fornication (*stuprum*) a crime. The penalties, including banishment, confiscation of half a woman's dowry and one-third of her property and of half the lover's property, were severe and affected the husband too. They encouraged prosecution by informers (who were rewarded by a percentage), attempts to shield wives (dangerous, because the law prescribed similar penalties for conniving husbands), and collusive prosecutions by a woman's husband or kinsmen (hoping to prove her innocent). A handful of notorious cases in which adultery was a makeweight charge against eminent Julio-Claudian women (of whom Octavia cannot be the only innocent victim) and the continued interest of emperors and lawyers (which suggests that it was a live issue) do not prove how pervasive the threat of the law was to the upper classes. Social change and the example of moral reaction set by post-Julio-Claudian emperors probably had more effect on marital fidelity.

CONCUBINAGE AND UNION WITH SLAVES

Concubinatus and *contubernium*, two extralegal, paramarital types of relationship, deserve mention. Concubinage (*concubinatus*) was a relatively stable, recognized union in which a man kept a woman, often his social inferior, whom he did not wish to regard as his wife. It was appropriate for men who were below or above the age for marriage, particularly for men who had produced enough legitimate children, for instance, Vespasian, who had as his *concubina* the freedwoman Antonia Caenis, whom he could not, as a senator, legally marry. Much more common was *contubernium*, which involved a large class of people who could not legally marry, the slaves. "There is no *conubium* with slaves" (*Tit. Ulp.* 5.5). Unions that involved at least one slave were *contubernia*. *Contubernales* wished to regard each other as husband and wife and often give each other that title on their epitaphs. If the bar to their legal marriage was removed by manumission, and they stayed together, they automatically were validly married and subsequent children were legitimate.

BIBLIOGRAPHY

J. P. V. D. Balsdon, *Roman Women; Their History and Habits* (1962, rev. ed. 1974); P. A. Brunt, *Italian Manpower 225 B.C.–A.D. 14* (1971); Brian Campbell, "The Marriage of Soldiers under the Empire," in *Journal of Roman Studies*, **68** (1978); Gillian Clark, "Roman Women," in *Greece and Rome*, **28** (1981); Percy E. Corbett, *The Roman Law of Marriage* (1930); John A. Crook, *Law and Life of Rome* (1967); Pal Csillag, *The Augustan Laws on Family Relations* (1976); Sheila Dickison, "Abortion in Antiquity," in *Arethusa*, **6** (1973); William Warde Fowler, *Social Life at Rome in the Age of Cicero* (1908); J. Gaudemet, "Iustum matrimonium," in *Revue international des droits de l'antiquité*, **2** (1949); Jasper Griffin, "Augustan Poetry and the Life of Luxury," in *Journal of Roman Studies*, **66** (1976).

Keith Hopkins, "The Age of Roman Girls at Marriage," in *Population Studies*, **18** (1965), "Contraception in the Roman Empire," in *Comparative Studies in Society and History*, **8** (1965), "On the

Probable Age Structure of the Roman Population," in *Population Studies,* **20** (1966), and *Death and Renewal* (1983); Michel Humbert, *Le remariage à Rome: étude d'histoire juridique et sociale* (1972); I. Kajanto, "On Divorce Among the Common People of Rome," in *Revue des études latines,* **47** bis (1969); G. MacCormack, *"Coemptio* and Marriage by Purchase," in *Bullettino dell'Istituto di Diritto Romano,* **20** (1978); T. E. V. Pearce, "The Role of the Wife as *Custos* in Ancient Rome," in *Eranos,* **72** (1974).

Beryl Rawson, "Roman Concubinage and Other *de facto* Marriages," in *Transactions of the American Philological Association,* **104** (1974); J. A. C. Thomas, "Lex Julia de adulteriis coercendis," in *Études maqueron* (1970); Susan Treggiari, "Lower-class Women in the Roman Economy," in *Florilegium,* **1** (1979), "Consent to Roman Marriage: Some Aspects of Law and Reality," in *Classical Views,* n.s. **1** (1982), and "Women as Property in the Early Roman Empire," in *Women and the Law: The Social Historical Perspective* II, D. Kelly Weisberg, ed. (1982); Robert Villers, *"Manus* et mariage," in *The Irish Jurist,* **4** (1969); Edoardo Volterra, "Matrimonio: Diritto Romano," in *Enciclopedia del Diritto* (1975).

Alan Watson, *The Law of Persons in the Later Roman Republic* (1967), *The Law of the Ancient Romans* (1970), *Roman Private Law around 200 B.C.* (1971), and *Rome of the Twelve Tables: Persons and Property* (1975); Gordon Williams, "Some Aspects of Roman Marriage Ceremonies and Ideals," in *Journal of Roman Studies,* **48** (1958), and "Poetry in the Moral Climate of Augustan Rome," in *Journal of Roman Studies,* **52** (1962); T. Peter Wiseman, *New Men in the Roman Senate 139 B.C.–A.D. 14* (1971).

Birth Control, Childbirth, and Early Childhood

VALERIE FRENCH

PROCREATION AND CHILD REARING were the predominant occupations of women in antiquity. But because the extant sources describing birth control, childbirth, and early childhood were almost entirely composed by men, a male bias inevitably colors these descriptions. The extant works of few writers treat procreation and child rearing in any systematic fashion; nonetheless, the ancient philosophers, medical writers, biographers, and essayists present enough material to reconstruct a fairly detailed picture of the activities so crucial to the perpetuation of both family and culture.

BIRTH CONTROL

By and large, ancient families were small, with two or perhaps three children that survived to early adulthood. The tendency to limit family size seems to have been constant over time and across socioeconomic strata. The motivations for limiting the number of children, however, probably varied over time and according to the family's economic status. Among the wealthy, limits were desired to avoid both dissipating the family's estate among too many heirs and providing too many dowries. For the poor, too many children were often simply too expensive to raise. Efforts to limit the size of families, however, should not be construed as evidence that Greeks and Romans did not care about children; the overwhelming majority of discussions and remarks about children in the extant sources display considerable knowledge of and affection for youngsters.

Family size was a privately, not publicly determined matter. Although the philosophical treatises of Plato and Aristotle give considerable attention to family planning, only rarely did the state actually try to set policy. The Romans in particular recognized the problems that overly small families caused—a failure of the upper classes to reproduce themselves and a lack of manpower for the legions. They believed that Romulus' "laws" required families to raise all boys and at least one girl. With the Lex Papia Poppaea, Augustus tried to increase family size by rewarding the parents of three or more children and by punishing childlessness and bachelorhood among the upper classes; his laws were reenacted several times in succeeding centuries. In the second century A.D., an alimentary system was introduced to provide subsidies for the children of the poor, partly, as Pliny the Younger suggests, to improve the birthrates of the poor and thereby increase potential recruits for the legions. The Augustan laws provoked great opposition and the *alimenta* became a financial burden. Neither seems to have had much impact on family size.

Parents had available three methods for family planning: contraception, abortion, and exposure or infanticide. We cannot hazard even an educated guess about which of these methods was the most frequently employed. Reasonably effective but by no means foolproof contraceptive techniques were certainly known as early as the fifth century B.C. Vaginal suppositories (a plug of wool alone or treated with olive oil, resin, alum, or white lead) and spermicides (cedar gum, olive oil, vinegar, or brine solutions) are described in the medical treatises. The less effective rhythm method was also known, but coitus interruptus does not seem to have been employed. Along with these more or less effective means of contraception, there was a gamut of ineffective techniques—including amulets, holding one's breath, sneezing, and charms.

Despite the ready availability of cheap and reasonably effective contraceptives, literary sources do not often refer to them. It is likely that except for well-educated and highly experienced physicians such as Soranus (second century A.D.), people did not know how to tell effective from ineffective methods of contraception and thus had little confidence in their efficacy. Moreover, people generally may have drawn no clear distinction between contraception and abortion; thus it is possible that the many references to abortion mask a fairly widespread use of contraceptives.

No matter how prevalent the use of contraceptives was, there surely must have been countless unwanted pregnancies. Abortion was apparently a common solution. Although the Hippocratic oath proscribed a physician's use of abortifacients, and some writers beginning in the period of the Roman Empire (notably Philo Judaeus and Musonius Rufus) and, of course, the Christians condemned abortion as murder, most medical treatises describe methods of abortion; and most extant authors seem to accept the practice at least as a necessary evil. No state passed laws against abortion until the early third century A.D.

Techniques of abortion ranged from jumping seven times so that the heels touched the buttocks to toxic potions to insertion of sticks or rods into the uterus. The effective techniques carried considerable risk. The dangers of abortion no doubt account for the often negative attitude of the pagan literary sources. It is worth noting that the Romans condemned most violently the motives of women who underwent abortions—desire to preserve their figures and robbing the father of a potential child—and not the act of abortion itself.

When contraception and abortion failed, parents of an unwanted child sometimes resorted to exposure and infanticide. By leaving the infant in a conspicuous place, clothed and with some kind of birth token (usually a piece of jewelry), parents seemed to try to protect themselves against the pain of the act by indulging in the hope that someone else would rear their child. The right of a father to expose an unwanted baby was almost unquestioned. Among Greek cities, only Thebes and Ephesus ever outlawed the practice, and it was not until A.D. 374 that Roman law made infanticide a capital offense.

There is no way to determine how often parents took this extreme action. Although it is fairly well accepted that deformed and sickly babies were strangled at birth or left in a temple or on a hillside, it is by no means clear that exposure of healthy children was in any sense routine. There is a strong probability that girls were more often exposed than were boys, but at what rate is unknown. Estimates range from 10 to upward of 20 percent. It seems likely that rates of infanticide varied over time and according to economic and social conditions. Exposure seems to have been more common among the poor and more prevalent in the East after the fourth century and in the West after the first century B.C.

CHILDBIRTH

Although the birth of a child usually marked one of the great events within a family, it carried with it a significant risk of death or serious illness for both mother and child. Ancient perinatal and neonatal mortality (immediately before and after birth) could have been as high as 5 to 8 percent, judging from statistics in modern communities that do not employ antisepsis in obstetrical care. Maternal mortality may have been as high as 2.5 percent. As an event of such importance and potential danger, childbirth was the special concern of many gods and goddesses. The Greeks looked to Artemis, Athena, and especially Eileithyia, whose special concern childbirth was; the Romans looked to her counterpart Juno Lucina, the Carmentes, and the Parcae or Fates.

Obstetrical practices ranged from unsophisticated and crude folk traditions to highly skilled and knowledgeable medicine. The former is well described in Pliny the Elder's *Natural History,* the latter in Soranus' *Gynecology.* Pliny was chiefly concerned with ways to hasten and ease labor and to bring away the placenta, but his recommendations were not likely to have been effective. The presence in the delivery room of hyenas' feet, snake sloughs, canine placentas, sticks, and vulture feathers must have significantly increased the risk of infection. And parturients who drank potions with powdered

sow's dung, sow's milk, goose semen, root of vervain, scordotis, dittany leaves, or earthworms are not likely to have fared better for it.

Drawn from a reservoir of folk medicine, Pliny's prescriptions probably reflect the kind of obstetrical care received by the vast majority of women. Although a highly educated and affluent man, Pliny did not make light of these treatments or doubt their efficacy. It seems probable, therefore, that these practices were not confined to the lower socioeconomic strata but were employed among the upper classes as well. Although the prescriptions were of dubious value, the personal care given the mother was emotionally supportive. The parturient was at home and attended by close relatives and a midwife, all encouraging her. For normal, uncomplicated deliveries, this type of folk medicine was probably adequate.

With Soranus (physician under Trajan and Hadrian, A.D. 98–138) we find surprisingly modern obstetrical practices. His treatise was not an anomaly in ancient medicine; rather it seems to be a part of a chain of obstetrical literature stretching from the Hippocratic corpus of the fourth century B.C. to the medical encyclopedists of the Byzantine period. Although most of this tradition has been lost, it was once extensive and shows both interest in and considerable knowledge of obstetrics.

The first desideratum, according to Soranus, was a highly competent midwife: literate, intelligent, hard-working, of good character and health, of sympathetic disposition, and not superstitious. Some midwives were well trained and conversant with the large body of medical literature on obstetrics and gynecology. In the eastern end of the Mediterranean, some women advanced beyond the profession of midwife to that of obstetrician. In the East, at least, obstetrical care was a profession in which respectable women could earn a living. In the Roman West, however, midwives seem to have been of mainly servile origin, judging from the few epitaphs that survive.

Soranus gives a detailed description of the most sophisticated obstetrical care then available. Delivery should take place in a room of moderate size and temperature in which there were two beds, one hard (for use during labor) and one soft (for rest after delivery). The midwife was to see that there were adequate supplies of fresh olive oil, warm water, ointments, sea sponges, bandages to swaddle the baby, a pillow, and aromatic substances such as pennyroyal, lemons, or quinces for the parturient to inhale (presumably to revive her if necessary). The midwife was also to bring a birthing chair.

The midwife was to encourage dilation in the early stage of labor by gently massaging the cervix. At the second stage, the parturient was moved to the birthing chair. (The time for this stage is reduced by about 50 percent if the parturient is seated instead of supine.) Assisted by three other women, the midwife superintended delivery. There is no indication that anything like an episiotomy (cutting the outlet of the vagina to facilitate childbirth) was performed. The parturient was expected to do the work of expelling the infant from the womb, but the assistants might press gently on her abdomen; the midwife instructed her on breathing and pushing during contractions. In a normal, headfirst delivery, the midwife eased the baby's head and shoulders out, gently pulled out the rest of the body, tended to the umbilical cord, and removed the placenta.

Soranus' treatise includes a lengthy discussion of difficult deliveries and detailed instructions for handling a wide variety of complications. Although the obstetrical procedures are basically sound (at least according to contemporary theory), many otherwise healthy fetuses probably died during a difficult labor and delivery.

The midwife, and occasionally an obstetrician, supervised not only the birth but also the postnatal care of the mother and the newborn baby. Again Soranus' prescriptions strike a modern note and Pliny's reflect folk treatments. Intumescence seems to have been a common problem; and Soranus tells how to stop lactation in women who did not intend to nurse their infants themselves.

Once the baby had been safely delivered, the midwife carefully inspected it for any congenital defects; apparently the midwife made the initial determination of whether the baby was healthy and fit to rear. The newborn was cleansed soon after delivery. Greeks tended to bathe the baby in cold water, except the Spartans, who used wine. Pliny reports the use of brine and urine. Soranus rejected all these, recommending instead sprinkling the infant with a fine powdery substance such as salt or natron and then rinsing with warm water.

After the immediate needs of the mother and child had been attended to, the baby was presented to the father. In classical Sparta, a board of elders decided whether to rear the newborn. In most societies, however, this was the father's decision. In Rome, the father signaled his intention to rear the child by lifting it up from the ground. Both the Greeks and the Romans celebrated a more elaborate ritual about a week after the child's birth (Gk. *amphidromion*, Lat. *dies lustricus*) at which the child was given a name and formally accepted into the family.

In Athens, male children were officially registered in their phratries or kinship groups on the third day of the festival of the Apaturia after their births. According to Roman tradition, parents presented a coin at the temple of Juno Lucina so that the kings could keep track of how many children were born each year. The tradition is patently unhistorical but does reflect the care Romans took to keep population records. By the period of the empire citizen children were registered with the state within a month of their births and were issued birth certificates.

EARLY CHILDHOOD

Just as the male voice prevails in the literary sources, so also it dominated the households of antiquity. The Romans especially embraced paternal authority with the principle of the *patria potestas*. Although the patriarchal tradition sometimes succumbed to the dynamics of family life (as with fifth-century B.C. statesman Themistocles' jest that his little son was the most powerful person in Greece because the Greeks were ruled by the Athenians, the Athenians were ruled by him, he was ruled by his wife, and his wife was ruled by the boy), it appears that fathers directed and were often closely involved in the rearing of their young children.

Fatherly attention to their small offspring is almost necessarily implied in the literary sources, for they reveal considerable and detailed knowledge of the characteristics and needs of young children. Aeschylus can write of the difficulty of determining what a little baby wants (*Libation Bearers* 753–757); Aristophanes' hapless hero Strepsiades tends his son's toilet training and understands his baby talk (*Clouds* 1381–1385); Euripides can portray the child's fear of abandonment (*Alcestis* 406–415); Horace recognizes the balkiness of two-year-olds (*Satires* 2.3.258–259); Fronto knows that one of a baby's first words is likely to be "da"— "give me"—(*Letters to Friends* 1.12).

References to children abound in many of the extant ancient writers. Early childhood was clearly seen as a distinctive stage of life, young children having special characteristics and needs. Both Greeks and Romans saw children as unformed and capable of being molded (impressionable, amoral, ignorant, gullible); as helpless and weak; as easily frightened; as cheerful, playful, and affectionate; as unruly and willful; as imitative; and as asexual and innocent. Romans also described the young child as naturally competitive and curious. Just as the pre-school child had special characteristics, so also it had special needs. Again both Greeks and Romans believed that small children needed play, special food and clothing, love and physical affection, protection, and mild discipline. Seldom did either Greek or Roman authors describe child rearing in a decidedly negative tone or young children as a bother.

Early childhood was not seen as a unitary stage of life. Five authors—Plato, Aristotle, Quintilian, Augustine, and Macrobius—present what are essentially theories of physiological and psychological development in early childhood. These implicit theories of developmental psychology are remarkably similar to contemporary models and probably reflect commonly held views and expectations about the general pattern of growth of small children. Although these five writers alone describe stages of development from birth to school age (about seven), many other authors' remarks about children reveal their awareness of stages of development.

Infancy lasted to the second or third year, until the child learned to talk and was weaned. The baby's inability to communicate its needs and wishes seems to have been the most frustrating aspect of this stage for both Greeks and Romans; toilet training does not seem to have been an issue. Plato and Aristotle saw two more stages between infants and school-age children: the first when the child was mostly still in the company of adults and the second when the child began to establish relations with peers. Quintilian and Augustine described only one stage between infancy and school age, ignoring the transition the child makes into the world of other children.

Both Plato (*Laws* 789E–795E) and Aristotle (*Politics* 1336a–b; 1338b) advocated a regimen that was protective, attentive, and free from harsh discipline for children up to the age of six or seven. Both certainly subscribed to the adage that as the twig is bent, so the tree is inclined—a correlate of the view of the child as moldable and impressionable. Plato's prescripts aimed at gently but firmly accustoming the child to follow the rules of the community and suppressing innovative play. Aristotle's advice emphasized physical development and protection from the base influences of the adult society.

Quintilian (*Education of an Orator* 1.1.5–36) was chiefly concerned about raising boys to be excellent orators, and his developmental scheme stressed speech and education. Like Plato and Aristotle, he saw early childhood as a crucial phase of life; he advocated mild treatment, good examples of adult behavior, and the stimulation of play and praise. Augustine (*Confessions* 1.6–1.9) based his description of a child's growth on his recollections of his own childhood, displaying a remarkable empathy for the difficulties of learning to speak and communicate. Macrobius (*Commentary on the Dream of Scipio* 67–70) dealt exclusively with stages of physiological development and schematized the maturation process based on the number seven.

Surprisingly, there seems to have been little difference in the treatment advocated for boys and girls as young children. Small boys were probably allowed to run about less fully clothed than girls, but until they were of school age, specific and conscious gender differentiation was likely to have been minimal.

The generally nurturing and mild treatment of children up to school age recommended by most Greek and Roman writers seems also to have been practiced in Sparta. Piecing together the evidence about early childhood in Xenophon's *Constitution of the Lacedaemonians* and in Plutarch's "Lycurgus" in *Parallel Lives* and in his *Moralia,* we can safely infer that, until the end of the fifth century, Spartan mothers devoted themselves to their small children and that the

harsh discipline of the Spartan educational system was not enforced until boys entered the state-managed education system (*agoge*) at about the age of seven.

Medical writers also recognized infancy and early childhood as distinctive phases of life with their own distinctive problems and special requirements for treatment. From Hippocrates to the Byzantine encyclopedists, medical treatises contained much information about and special treatments for the diseases and conditions of childhood. The Hippocratic corpus had one section that focused specifically on a pediatric problem—dentition; but otherwise, discussion of pediatrics was scattered throughout these writings. It was not until Aulus Cornelius Celsus' work of the first century A.D. that a medical writer flatly stated the principle that children should not be treated as adults, and not until Soranus that pediatrics were grouped together in a single, extended treatment. Although we hear of no pediatricians per se, it is clear that pediatrics was a distinct area of medicine.

The medical writers report a host of childhood ailments—gangrene, meningitis, diarrhea, aphthae (thrush), mumps, rickets, cholera, anthrax, diphtheria, epilepsy, dermatitis, tonsilitis, and tetanus. Most writers included advice on special dietary needs and exercise. From Hippocrates on, doctors recognized that diseases run different courses in children. For example, Hippocrates noted that fevers bring convulsions in children, that children die more quickly than adults from head wounds, and that spare diets are not good for children. Moreover, the medical treatises also distinguish between the ailments of infancy and those of young childhood. In the second century A.D., Galen compiled a catalog of congenital abnormalities.

Both Greeks and Romans tended to emphasize the role of nurture in their discussions of child rearing. But they were not oblivious to the natural differences among children. Plutarch often mentioned characteristics that his subjects had as children that set them apart from their peers; he also noted radical differences in the personalities or dispositions of brothers. Suetonius too recognized differences among children in his *Lives of the Twelve Caesars;* but more than Plutarch, Suetonius tried to connect his subjects' childhood experiences to their adult personalities, sometimes contending that early traumas produced abnormal, undesirable adult behavior.

Biographers were not alone in seeing differences among children and variety in their natural aptitudes. Plato feared children who showed innovation in their play. Aristotle recommended tailoring a child's education to attend to its particular needs, as did Quintilian. It was generally believed that somehow the children of the aristocracy were by nature superior to other children and that children tended to inherit personality traits and abilities from their ancestors.

That adults attended to the special needs of children is amply attested by material evidence. Excavations all over the Mediterranean area and from the archaic through the late periods have unearthed a wide variety of childhood paraphernalia—bassinets, cradles, feeding bottles, potty chairs (only in Athens), jewelry, and many kinds of toys. The range of toys available is impressive: rattles; dolls made of terra-cotta, bone, wood, ivory, and papyrus—some with articulated limbs and real hair; miniature pots, tools, and furniture; wooden pull-toys in the shape of animals; balls, tops, marbles, and hoops. Reliefs depict children with such pets as dogs, rabbits, birds, and cats; they also portray them playing games with dice, knucklebones, and balls and show them busy with small carts, scooters, and wagons.

The material evidence for the accoutrements of early childhood is paralleled by numerous remarks in the literary sources about children's toys and games. The literary sources also reveal a rich tradition of children's stories, from the delightful country mouse and city mouse tales of Horace to scary tales of demons and monsters that prey on children. Most philosophers, however, decried the baleful effects of horror stories on young minds.

Children also had their own special divinities. Artemis was the special protectress of young Greek children. The Romans looked to over a dozen gods and goddesses: three presided over a baby's eating and drinking (Educa, Potina, and Rumilia); three more over its walking (Abeona, Adeona, and Statulinus); and one each over its sleeping, speaking, fearfulness, crying, and growth of bones (Cunina, Fabulinus, Paventia, Vagitanus, and Ossipaga). This array of protective deities clearly shows the Romans' awareness of the difficulties and dangers of childhood.

Although young children seem to have been of concern and interest throughout antiquity, the nature and degree of parental involvement with child rearing does appear to have changed over time, especially among the upper classes. In Greece to the end of the fifth century and in Rome to the beginning of the second century B.C., the child's mother and father directly provided most of the daily care and training. Even the redoubtable Cato the Elder came home daily from the Forum Romanum to superintend his small son's bath. But with the introduction of imperial wealth in Athens, Sparta, and Rome, more and more of the child care was turned over to nurses and *paidagogoi,* at least among the families that could afford them.

The effects of the increasing reliance on outsiders, often slaves, for child care are difficult to determine. In fourth-century Sparta, it appears that with the loss of maternal inculcation of traditional values, it became impossible to sustain the traditional Spartan way of life in the adult community.

Both fourth-century Athenians and late republican and imperial Romans lamented the decay of ancestral discipline; but few suggested a link between contemporary early child care practices and the passing of the old ways.

As child care became less and less the central concern of upper-class mothers, child abuse increased, particularly for those unfortunates who were "rescued" from exposure and sold as slaves to be used as household drudges, as child prostitutes in brothels, or as deliberately maimed street beggars. However, not all foundlings were treated so brutally; many funerary epitaphs were set up by grateful foster children to honor their surrogate parents.

Recent efforts to paint ancient childhood in grisly hues are undoubtedly overdrawn. A naturally high infant and child mortality, infanticide, and some horrendous child abuse surely existed. But generally both Greeks and Romans valued their young children, took steps to protect and nurture them, and frequently delighted in their childish antics. Moreover, with the Romans, we find the beginning of the use of the child as a symbol of innocence or purity. Cicero contended that nature's plan can be seen most clearly in children, portending an important theme of later Christian thought.

The parental love and affection for young children that existed in classical antiquity is perhaps most eloquently expressed in a letter sent by Plutarch to his wife to console her after the death of their two-year-old daughter, Timoxena (*Moralia* 608C; 608E):

> Our affection for children so young has, furthermore, a poignancy all its own; the delight that it gives is quite pure and free from all anger and reproach. . . . Just as she was herself the most delightful thing in the world to embrace, to see, to hear, so too must the thought of her live with us and be our companion, bringing with it joy in greater measure, nay in many times greater measure, than it brings sorrow (Philip H. De Lacy and Benedict Einarson, trans. [1959]).

BIBLIOGRAPHY

SOURCES

Plutarch, *Moralia,* Philip M. De Lacy and Benedict Einarson, trans., vol. 7 (1959).

STUDIES

Sheila Dickison, "Abortion in Antiquity," in *Arethusa,* **6** (1973); Donald Engels, "The Problem of Female Infanticide in the Greco-Roman World," in *Classical Philology,* **75** (1980); Emiel Eyben, "Family Planning in Graeco-Roman Antiquity," in *Ancient Society,* **11/12** (1981/1982); Valerie French, "History of the Child's Influence: Ancient Mediterranean Civilizations," in *Child Effects on Adults,* Richard Q. Bell and Lawrence V. Harper, eds. (1977), and "Midwives and Maternity Care in the Roman World," in *Helios,* **13** (1986); Mark Golden, "Aspects of Childhood in Classical Athens," Ph.D. diss., University of Toronto (1981), and "Demography and the Exposure of Girls at Athens," in *Phoenix* (Toronto), **35** (1981).

W. V. Harris, "The Theoretical Possibility of Infanticide in the Graeco-Roman World," in *Classical Quarterly,* n.s. **32** (1982); Keith Hopkins, "Contraception in the Roman Empire," in *Comparative Studies in Society and History,* **8** (1965–1966); Werner A. Krenkel, "Familienplanung und Familienpolitik in der Antike," in *Würzburger Jahrbücher für die Altertumswissenschaft,* **4** (1978); Sarah B. Pomeroy, "Infanticide in Hellenistic Greece," in *Images of Women in Antiquity,* A. Cameron and A. Kuhrt, eds. (1983); Anthony Preus, "Biomedical Techniques for Influencing Reproduction in the Fourth Century B.C.," in *Arethusa,* **8** (1975); Georges Raepsaet, "Les motivations de la natalité à Athènes aux Ve let IVe siècles avant notre ère," in *Acta Classica,* **40** (1971); George F. Still, *History of Paediatrics* (1931).

Houses

ALEXANDER GORDON McKAY

EARLY GREEK HOUSES

Greek housing of the archaic period, judging by literary references and meager finds, was generally inferior and certainly unpretentious. Even during the fifth century Thucydides suggests (*History of the Peloponnesian War* 2.14) that country living was preferable to the crowded conditions of the city, and recent study of farmhouse and cottage remains at Vari and near Mount Aigaleos, both in western Attica, confirms the historian's generalization. The latter country place, the short-lived Dema house (422–413 B.C.) shown in figure 1, is a simple but durable construction with stone foundation walls, a mud-brick and timber frame, tile roofing, earthen floors, and an impressive 72-foot by 52-foot (22 m × 16 m) frontage. The *andron* (men's dining room) could conveniently accommodate seven dining couches, and the kitchen was no doubt flanked by cooking or bathing facilities. Braziers served cooking and heating needs. Storerooms and workrooms downstairs were complemented by bedrooms upstairs that opened onto a gallery corresponding with the portico or veranda element (*pastas*) on the ground level. Furnishings were sparse but guaranteed a measure of comfort.

The archaeological remains of Athens have yielded few insights into early urban home life. Although the Persian destruction of 480–479 B.C. was extensive, the loss for posterity was neither irreparable nor serious. Athenian housing never measured up to the standards of elegance of the acropolis program or the civic square (agora) buildings. "Violet-crowned" Athens (Pindar, frag. 76) was a crowded warren of tortuous, shadowy alleys. Excavation, however, has disclosed a not unattractive residential and industrial area to the southwest of the agora and on the slopes of the Areopagus hill. Most of the units appear to have belonged to artisans who plied their trades at home or worked in shops nearby. The dwellings generally reflect the uniform modesty of residential life in Periclean Athens (460–430 B.C.): simple, single-story homes, devoid of mosaic floors, painted walls, kitchen facilities, and toilets. Simon the Cobbler, based on a triangular site at the southwest corner of the agora, conversed with Pericles

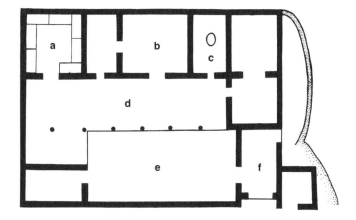

Figure 1. The Dema house in Attica, 422–413 B.C., as reconstructed by J. E. Jones: (*top*) plan showing (*a*) *andron;* (*b*) kitchen; (*c*) hearth; (*d*) *pastas* colonnade; (*e*) courtyard; (*f*) vestibule; (*bottom*) view from southeast showing pent roofed porch. *Reproduced from* ANNUAL OF THE BRITISH SCHOOL AT ATHENS 57 (1962). BY PERMISSION OF THE BRITISH SCHOOL AT ATHENS

and Socrates in an establishment that measured 42 feet by 49 feet (13 m × 15 m), with a modest 18-foot by 21-foot (5.5 m × 6.5 m) courtyard in its northeast corner.

The town and country houses already cited adhere rather closely to the pronouncements of Xenophon (*Household Management*

[*Oeconomicus*] 9.2–4, E. C. Marchant, trans. [1923]) when reporting to Socrates a tour of inspection that he and his young bride made of their residence:

[The house] contains few elaborate decorations, Socrates; but the rooms are designed simply with the object of providing as convenient receptacles as possible for the things that are to fill them, and thus each room invited just what was suited to it. Thus the storeroom by the security of its position called for the most valuable blankets and utensils, the dry covered rooms for the corn, the cool for the wine, the well-lit for those works of art and vessels that need light. I showed her decorated living rooms for the family that are cool in summer and warm in winter. I showed her that the whole house fronts south, so that it was obvious that it is sunny in winter and shady in summer.

Normally Greek householders favored structural forms with a horizontal emphasis: low chests, cabinets, tables, wall benches and the like, with simple color emphasis derived from floor coverings or pillow covers. The depictions of dining parties (symposia) on Attic vases generally show cups and floral wreaths hanging from wall brackets, thereby serving utilitarian and decorative designs simultaneously. It is a fact that evidence for formal interior decoration in Athenian and Greek houses generally before the Hellenistic period is limited, although Alcibiades certainly enlisted the perspective painter Agatharchus to decorate what seems to be his dining room, and Zeuxis was commissioned by the Macedonian king Archelaus to decorate his palace in Pella.

Provision for drainage and waste removal was generally primitive, but more determined and effective measures appear in a third-century limestone house located between the Athenian Areopagus and the hill of the Pnyx: it contained a toilet that emptied into a drain under the adjoining street. A drainage channel in the *andron* suggests too that the floor must have been washed frequently, perhaps as a consequence of symposiasts' boisterousness, perhaps also as a means of cooling the chamber on sultry evenings.

HOUSE STYLE AT OLYNTHUS

The most abundant evidence for classical Greek houses derives from excavations at the orthogonally planned town site of Olynthus in the Chalcidic peninsula, about thirty-six miles southeast of Thessalonica (Salonika). Although workshops and the modest dwellings of workers clustered around the market square, the majority of the town-house plans responded to the seven broad north-south thoroughfares and twenty-two narrower east-west cross streets. Each block was bisected by a narrow alley, two yards wide, that was closed at either end, and each house in a half-block of five houses was based on a module that was indistinguishable in size from its neighbors; all shared a common two-story roof line. However, beneath the roof the individual was free to divide his dwelling space according to his personal preference. Houses commonly had a 60-foot (18 m) frontage with a common bonding wall in front and rear. Sometimes part of a ground floor might be partitioned off to allow the owner to install a shop that could be sold or leased to outsiders.

Building materials at Olynthus were simple and conventional. Sun-dried brick, or adobe, provided the architect or interior designers with a medium that was considerably more malleable than burnt brick or stone. Living quarters were usually located in the northern half of the house in a roofed transverse block, normally two stories high, fronted by a colonnade (*pastas*) on the lower floor and a gallery above. The *pastas* basic unit, which might vary from 10 to 13 feet (3–4 m) in width, offered access to rooms on the northern side and resembled a long room itself, open to the sky, with a colonnade opening onto the court. The rectangular court, often paved with cobblestones, might accommodate an open-air altar dedicated to Zeus Herkeios, the divine protector of the household. The dining room followed the classic pattern on a fairly intimate scale. The host and his guests would recline on couches arranged around the sides of the room in such a way that they could recline facing inward on their left elbows. The first couch would then fill the space between the entry and the corner of the room; on the other side of the door the corresponding place would usually be occupied by the last couch and the foot of the preceding one. The host usually reclined to the left of the entrance, with the place of honor reserved on the right of the entry. Normally the *andron* was designed to accommodate four single dining couches, each 6.5 feet (2 m) long. Often a low platform appears alongside the dado, suggesting the aforementioned arrangements. The walls were sometimes painted red, with a white dado, and the floor was either paved or covered with mosaic.

Most of the middle-class house designs at Olynthus contain a large oblong room (*oikos*) with a hearth as permanent furnishing. The *oikos* was clearly the most important working and living area in the house. Floors were generally earthen and the plastered walls were left plain. Bathrooms might contain a terra-cotta hip bath and sometimes a terra-cotta basin fixed to the wall, with facilities for drainage. Sometimes the bathroom floor was lime-cemented, sometimes tiled; its location, near the *oikos* hearth and the kitchen, ensured warmth. Kitchen appointments were rudimentary. The flue over the fireplace of a typical Olynthian kitchen was usually large; to guard against heat loss, and probably to safeguard the interior against the inrush of cold Macedonian winds, the roof was furnished with a diminutive vent. The kitchen floor was of earth, flag, or cobblestone. Bedrooms were usually located on the second floor and upstairs heating was supplied either by portable stoves and braziers or by means of the kitchen flue, which had its counterpart upstairs. Apart from the *andron* there was no segregation of sexes; no apartment was set aside for the exclusive use of women involved with weaving, spinning, and other household chores. Wooden ceilings, on both the ground and upstairs floors, were left unplastered.

In general, Olynthian houses had to conform to plots of common dimension, 58 feet (18 m) square, but there are exceptions. The

Figure 2. The Villa of Good Fortune at Olynthus (Macedonia), fourth century B.C.: (*top*) restored plan showing (*a*) *andron;* (*b*) kitchen; (*c*) flue; (*d*) reception room; (*e*) anteroom; (*f*) *pastas* colonnade; (*g*) storage room; (*h*) open-air altar; (*i*) workroom; (*bottom*) reconstructed view from southeast showing main entrance. *Reproduced from David M. Robinson and J. Walter Graham,* THE HELLENIC HOUSE, EXCAVATIONS AT OLYNTHUS SERIES *VIII* © 1938 BY THE JOHNS HOPKINS PRESS

Villa of Good Fortune (fig. 2) certainly departed from the norm. Although the plan of the house (it may be a hostel) follows standards generally encountered in the community, there are noteworthy deviations in the lavish use of mosaic floors and in the storage facilities. Finds of straw, olive pits, and pine bark suggest that resinated wine was stored on the property, along with olive oil and grain. There were ten upstairs rooms on both the north and south sides catering to children and servants, and no doubt duplicating rooms on the ground-floor level. The nearby House of the Comedian rejected the usual *pastas* design for an oblong peristyle court with a mosaic catch basin for rainwater. The latter featured a mosaic frieze of hunting scenes and likely housed a sculpture base at its center. The walls were painted in a tricolor scheme varying from wall to wall: sometimes white, yellow, and red; at other times white, black, and red. The entire city was razed by Philip II in 348 B.C. with a resolution and fury that only Vesuvius rivaled in centuries to come.

HOUSES OF PRIENE, MORGANTINA, AND DELOS

The Olynthian house plan was not universal, however, or even common. Hellenistic houses of the nobility at Pella are far different in style, but the basic components of the Olynthian house do recur, suggesting that the paratactic plan favored by the northern architects, in which houses were built as connected modules, did become common. The *pastas* plan recurs at Morgantina (Serra Orlando), in central Sicily, in third- and second-century B.C. Delos, and at Seuthopolis in Thrace (now Kazanlak in Bulgaria).

The house patterns of Priene (Turunçlar, Turkey), on the other hand, were more reminiscent of the Mycenaean megaron or central "baronial" hall than they were of Olyn-

thian or Attic designs. Priene in Asia Minor and Olynthus in northern Greece were both model communities in the sense that they followed the Hippodamian patterns of town planning developed first in the populous centers of Asia Minor. Residential blocks at Priene, almost in defiance of its hillside situation, favored the same modular pattern as Olynthus. But the houses also sought formality and monumentality in their design. Fourth-century examples preferred a long narrow entranceway, often to one side, that led into a courtyard on the north side, with rooms opening off it (fig. 3). The portico had two columns *in antis* (columns whose pilasters did not conform with the order used elsewhere in the building and were placed at the ends) and led into the inner salon. The porch usually towered over the rest of the house. Sleeping accommodations, offices, kitchen, and storage spaces were arranged around the court, which provided ventilation and light for the interior. Dining rooms generally accommodated three couches, and the walls were decorated in the panel or encrustation style. Mosaic floors were not unusual. Later housing, during the third and second centuries, was marked by advances: the basic court matured into a peristyle—an area contained on all sides by a row of columns—and there are indications that the spirit of individualism, rampant during Hellenistic times, had invaded the house interiors, the privacy of which reflected new pretensions.

Vitruvius' remarks on Hellenistic housing as background to his dictates for decorous Roman house forms shed light on the character and style of house forms and accommodation at Priene and elsewhere (*The Ten Books on Architecture* 6.7.3, Morris Hicky Morgan, trans. [1914]):

There are [also] ampler sets of apartments with more sumptuous peristyles, surrounded by four colonnades of equal height, or else the

with polished stucco in relief and plain, and with coffered ceilings of woodwork; off the colonnades that face the north they have Cyzicene [style] dining rooms and picture galleries; to the east, libraries; exedrae [lounges] to the west; and to the south, large square rooms of such generous dimensions that four sets of dining couches can easily be arranged in them, with plenty of room for serving and for the amusements.

Vitruvius clearly singles out the hallmarks of Hellenistic high living. No two residences at Priene were the same, and none seems to adhere to the implied monumentality and formalism of the Vitruvian description.

Morgantina, near Piazza Armerina, Sicily, has yielded two outstanding houses of Hellenistic date: the House of the Official (*ca.* 250 B.C.) and the House of the Arched Cistern (*ca.* 250–200 B.C.). The House of the Official has twenty-four rooms on the ground floor. Even more attractive is the House of Ganymede overlooking the stepped civic center. The house incorporates a large peristyle 56 foot (17 m) long with a simply contrived mosaic flooring. The mosaic depicting Ganymede appears in a small room opening off the peristyle.

House architecture on the islands of the Cyclades has probably changed little over the centuries. Whitewashed facades with wooden staircases plunging recklessly from creaky balconies to cobblestone streets below—the picturesque elements of contemporary Mykonos, Naxos, and Thera (Santorini) today—almost surely provide the same visual experience as their ancient counterparts. Delos, in the central Aegean, offers a varied house repertoire (fig. 4). Many of the Hellenistic houses recall old-style Athenian houses and some continue to favor the *pastas* style; but peristyle mansions, constructed in island marble, are more common. Amplitude and elegance, as well as monumentality, are the keynotes of the

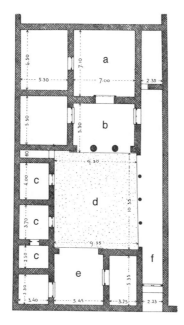

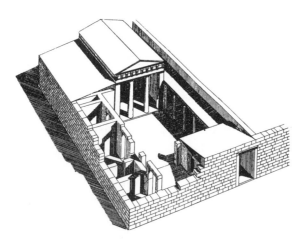

Figure 3. House No. 33 at Priene (Asia Minor), late fourth century B.C.: (*top*) plan showing (*a*) main room; (*b*) *prostas* porch; (*c*) rooms for servants and storage; (*d*) courtyard; (*e*) sitting room (*exedra*); (*f*) entrance way; (*bottom*) reconstructed view showing elevation of *prostas* porch. *Reproduced from Theodor Wiegand and Hans Schrader,* PRIENE (1904). THE NEW YORK PUBLIC LIBRARY

one which faces the south has higher columns than the others. A peristyle that has one such higher colonnade is called a Rhodian peristyle. Such apartments have fine entrance courts with imposing front doors of their own; the colonnades of the peristyles are decorated

Delian magnates' homes. Upper rooms normally face onto a gallery with columns or piers supported by the peristyle underneath. Roofs were designed to drain rainwater into a courtyard basin, and so to the underground cistern for household needs. Delos, like Neapolitan Capreae (Capri), had no available water supply, so rainwater had to be husbanded carefully. Bathing facilities, common at Olynthus, were a rarity on Delos; latrines were usually located in a cubicle off the main hall and emptied into a service drain beneath the adjacent street. Unlike the householders of Priene, where pretensions masked pedestrian designs, Delian householders often leased separate rooms in their facades as shops, particularly if they were located on main traffic arteries, and the proprietors of these lived in lofts above their businesses. (Delos, in Hellenistic times, emerged as a great market.) Occasionally, too, houses were subdivided to accommodate a number of tenants, both transient and permanent. In such instances the homeowner probably retained the ground floor, so as to enjoy the peristyle and its amenities, while leasing the entire second story.

The scale of Delian houses is often startling, and registers a marked deviation from the patterned dimensions of communities like Olynthus or Priene. Lake House, for example, absorbed an entire city block; the House of the Diadumenos, located in the opulent Sacred Lake quarter, has a peristyle court that surpasses the entire ground area of many houses. Their scale and sumptuous character suggest that the architects may have been indebted to grander models in Athens, perhaps in Macedonian centers; links with Asiatic Greece, although influential in earlier times, were virtually nonexistent by the mid second century B.C., by which time Athens had acquired Delos. At any rate, the peristyle house types of Delos reappear at almost every site where Hellenistic Greeks established themselves, from

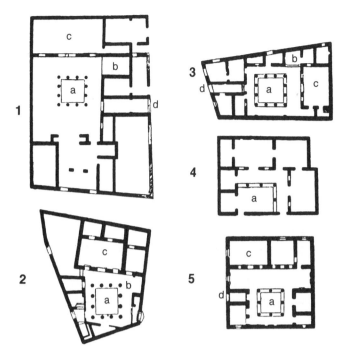

Figure 4. Hellenistic houses at Delos, second century B.C.: (1) House of the Diadumenos; (2) House of the Sacred Lake; (3) House of the Trident; (4) House of the Inopus; (5) Hill House. Plans showing (a) courtyard; (b) sitting room (*exedra*); (c) main room; (d) entrance. *Reproduced from W. B. Dinsmoor,* THE ARCHITECTURE OF ANCIENT GREECE © 1975 BY W.W. NORTON & CO.

Dura-Europos on the Euphrates to Olbia in southern Russia, and to Glanum (St. Rémy) in southern France.

INTERIOR DECORATION AND FURNISHING

The overall impression from literary allusions and from archaeological finds is that Greeks lived modestly, even those of high station. When Alcibiades, Socrates' student, a blithe spirit with a flair for the grand gesture, lost his home to the democratic confiscators and auctioneers in 415 B.C., the epigraphical inventory of his household furnishings revealed his stylish pretensions to all. His interior walls, for example, were decorated with panel pictures (*pinakes*) or terra-cotta plaques. Their subject matter can be reconstructed from the known repertoire of late-fifth-century masters, who favored mythical scenes, heroic subject matter, portraits, athletes, and obscene topics. Alcibiades' establishment was by no means characteristic. More modest homes were content with walls covered with smooth limestone stucco, sometimes painted red and yellow. Floors were usually hard-packed earth, durable by nature and cool in summer, and enlivened with rugs, carpets, sheepskins, and reed mats according to the house owner's desires and status. The more important rooms in upper-class residences used cement paving with mosaic insets (*emblemata*). But the privacy of the household remained paramount; it was reflected in the simple character of the exterior, the paucity of windows, and the desire to downplay the portals and interior vistas—a style far removed from the patterns of living and housing in Rome and in the cities of Pompeii and Herculaneum.

Household furnishings, in both quantity and style, seem sparse and surprisingly simple to modern tastes. The average interior would accommodate formal chairs, sometimes with backs and armrests, easy chairs with curving backs, four-legged backless stools, folding stools with crossed legs, and benches that doubled as settee and step stool. Beds and dining couches were wooden, with interlacings of fiber and leather. Mattress covers, bedspreads, cushions, rugs, and tapestries, often richly woven or dyed solid colors, enhanced the interiors. Small rectangular tables, three-legged for better stability on the uneven clay floors, were the normal adjuncts to dining from couches; they were portable and easily stacked when not in use. Lighting was fairly primitive. Lampstands consisted of tripods or wall brackets with projections from which the clay or bronze oil lamps could be sus-

pended by chains or leather thongs; sometimes lamps perched on standing rings of metal or terra-cotta. Chests, boxes, and smaller containers were household staples; cupboards were nonexistent until Hellenistic times, when collections of objets d'art and libraries became more common.

Apart from the foregoing, the average household would also own braziers, bronze caldrons for cooking, glazed ware cups, bowls, plates, jars, and containers, ranging from storage amphorae to saltcellars. Kitchens would house sieves, graters, ladles, pestles, meat hooks, and cutlery, along with the traditional braziers. Hardware, such as door knockers, was often elegant, and bronze decorations in the shape of nail heads, decorative disks, and key plates were often deployed richly over the surfaces of doors and wooden chests to enhance their appearance. Front doors, which normally opened inward, were simply constructed with vertical boards held together by crosspieces. Some of the houses at Olynthus have single and double doors alongside one another: one for pedestrians, the other for carts and animals. Hinges were found at Olynthus, somewhat unexpectedly, since doors traditionally hung on vertical pivots of wood, tipped with bronze at the base, that were set into bronze or stone sockets in the threshold and lintel. Doors were normally not part of the interior arrangements except perhaps at entries into deliberately restricted areas or storage rooms. Curtains, made of either simple linen or colorful dyed materials, might hang at the entry to bedrooms. While no serious impediment to circulation of persons or ventilation, door curtains provided a degree of privacy and a deterrent to flies.

Mosaic floor coverings abound on Delos, in Morgantina, Pella, and elsewhere throughout the Hellenistic period. Pella, for example, birthplace of Alexander the Great and Macedonian capital from the late fifth century to the Roman conquest (168 B.C.), has yielded two "official" residences with splendid pebble mosaics dating to about 300 B.C. One mansion features a youthful Dionysus riding a panther; the other provides a scene of Greeks battling Amazons, a Helen and Theseus, and two men engaged in a stag hunt, perhaps Alexander and Krateros—a masterpiece signed by the artist Gnosis (see fig. 14 in GREEK PAINTING AND MOSAIC). Palatitsa, nearby, has produced a magnificent floral mosaic in the same style. Olynthian and Delian houses are sometimes embellished with geometric and pictorial pebble mosaics that complement the schematic arrangement of painted blocks of color or marble veneer, commonly in the men's dining room. Pebble mosaics were gradually superseded by more diminutive marble, glass, and stone versions of astonishing dexterity and color gradation (*opus tessellatum*).

Sculpture was also often a complement to wealthier Hellenistic homes. Three of the Delian mansions, those of Dionysus, Diadumenos, and Hermes, owe their modern names to sculptures found in their porticoes. The House of Cleopatra also lodged life-size portraits of the owners in the bay of a door on the west side of the peristyle. The sculptural finds in the Delian House of Hermes compare most closely with the repertoires found in the Villa of the Papyri (outside Herculaneum) and in the Pompeian House of the Vettii, both mansions that aped Hellenistic models.

Hellenistic interiors differed vastly from their somewhat ascetic forebears. Unquestionably they sought to reflect elements of the lordly homes of their owners' Seleucid, Attalid, or Ptolemaic rulers. These were the mansions encountered by the Roman officials, generals, and traders who paraded through the Hellenistic kingdoms and palaces during the third century B.C. and later. It was such mansions as these, with their reflecting pools and luxuriant gardens, with aviaries, orchards, and plantations, with colorful mosaics spread like oriental rugs and tapestries over their floors, that aroused the envy and competitive spirit of Romans during the final centuries of the republican era.

ETRUSCAN HOUSES

The Etruscans settled in Tuscany and Umbria initially but later expanded into the hinterland of Greek settlements along the Neapolitan shoreline. Whatever their origins, whether they were immigrants from Asia Minor or aboriginal to Italy, they had abundant inspiration and tangible models for their house forms in the contemporary designs of the western Greeks, in southern Italy and Sicily, and in the native styles, the so-called Villanovan patterns, of their northern habitat. Their underground tomb forms, at Caere (Cerveteri) and elsewhere, and their transformation of Rome during the benevolent tyranny of the Tarquins offer impressive testimony to their mastery of tufa masonry and to their prodigious carpentry. Archaic houses at Veii, near Rome, and the Regia itself, in the Roman Forum, show the fundamental plan favored by the Etruscans: a rectangular design with a shallow antechamber and a deep back room where the hearth was installed. Orvieto's "Crocefisso del Tufo" tomb sector offers additional insight into the organized character of Etruscan city streets, with houselike tombs aligned scrupulously along streets that intersect at right angles; their close juxtaposition may also reflect a preference for strip-housing in their populous communities. Houses at Marzabotto (thought to be ancient Misa), an Etruscan industrial town in the Apennines, fifteen miles south of Felsina (Bononia, Bologna), rest on stone foundations, with superimposed timber or timber-framed construction. They tend to favor a paved central courtyard with living quarters arranged somewhat haphazardly around it. The yard frequently contained a well or cistern and had provision for drainage into the street conduit. Designed as semidetached town houses, the Marzabotto residences often incorporated small rectangular rooms that opened directly onto the street or sidewalk, serving no doubt as dwellings, shops, and workshops for the working community. The pebbled courtyards offered outdoor accommodation for household services, such as laundry or cooking, and space for the wagon and mules required by the householder with farming properties outside the confines of the residential community.

The houses of Marzabotto, when associated with the triadic temple design and tomb forms of the Etruscans, offer strong support for the conjecture that the house based on the atrium, a large reception hall, was an Etruscan innovation. The central hall and the axial plan are evidently basic components of both houses and temples, suggesting that the courtyard with its well was eventually transformed into a living space with a vaulted cistern underground that was designed to serve the needs of households in an expanding community. Recently excavated houses at Ansedonia (Cosa), eighty-five miles northwest of Rome, adopt the atrium pattern after 273 B.C. The Tomb of the Volumnii, at Umbrian Perusia (Perugia), dating to the second half of the second century B.C., has a layout reminiscent of atrium houses such as the House of the Surgeon at Pompeii. Although the doorway and entrance passage of normal housing have been replaced by a staircase that leads down into the tomb interior, the main rooms are clearly grouped around a central hall, or atrium, with a beamed ridged roof. The main room of the interior, with a richly coffered ceiling, lies opposite the doorway in the characteristic atrium house pattern.

However, Etruscan house patterns were by no means restricted to a center hall plan. Tomb facades, cut into the rocks of Blera (Bieda), Axia (Castel d'Asso), Orgola (Norchia), San Giovenale, and Manturanum (San Giuliano), all overlooking the Marta River and its tributaries, offer a varied assembly of house (and temple) forms. Some are gabled buildings with a single central portal; others are two-storied, with a colonnaded loggia over the entry like the later terrace housing on the southern slopes of Pompeii. Ash urns in the shape of buildings are another priceless source for information about Etruscan house designs. A second-century B.C. example from Clusium (Chiusi) reproduces a rectangular building, with a projecting pitch roof and an arched entrance on the short side. The lower part of the house reveals rusticated masonry with a wooden upper story, possibly even a second-floor gallery with pilasters. Another ash urn from Clusium reflects a fourth-century manor house set on a high podium and provided with wide eaves and a ceiling aperture (compluvium) on the low pyramidal roof. The repertoire continues to expand with recent finds at Spina, at the mouth of the Po River, where residents lived like later Venetians in houses built on piles.

Tomb interiors at Caere and tomb paintings, particularly at Tarquinii (Tarquinia), offer additional insights into Etruscan house decoration and furnishing. Although the paintings have to be interpreted cautiously, since the subject matter frequently derives from outdoor rituals and wakes celebrating the occupant's death, they do contain valuable clues to the Etruscan taste for luxury and refinement.

Armchairs, footstools with carved and rectangular legs, folding stools, benches, couches, and banqueting tables are standard furnishings in the tomb paintings. Toilet chests, household containers, bronze candelabras, tripods, incense burners, and braziers, some mounted on wheels, are also frequent tomb finds. The Tomb of the Painted Stuccoes at Caere is a mortuary chapel of considerable scale with richly diverse stucco renderings of household objects framing the niches and supporting columns of the interior.

ROMAN TOWN HOUSES

The traditional Roman town house (*domus*) favored a one-story design with an entrance hall (*vestibulum*) and corridor (*fauces*) closest to the street leading into the large reception hall (atrium), a shadowy high-ceilinged space with a series of rooms symmetrically ordered around its outer edges (fig. 5). A central basin (*impluvium*) set into the atrium floor was designed to catch the rain that entered through a skylight (*compluvium*) immediately above the basin. The water then fed into cisterns beneath the house, and a wellhead set into the atrium floor provided access to it. The principal salon (*tablinum*) usually faced the front door and occupied the far end of the atrium. It served, as circumstances required, as repository of the family archives (*tabulae*) and as dayroom or dining area. Another element appeared during the second century: a peristyle (*peristylium*), indebted to Hellenistic models on Delos and elsewhere and to patterns of gymnasia; the peristyle was basically a garden or green space surrounded by a cloisterlike colonnade. This addition ushered in new units with diverse functions: dining rooms (*triclinia*) for spring and summer, reception rooms (*oeci*), and relaxation rooms (*diaetae*). Early *domus* interiors, basically cavernous and austere, were brightened considerably by the natural light that came from the market (fruit and vegetable) garden (*hortus*) or peristyle garden behind.

Pompeii and Herculaneum offer a rich repertoire of house forms extending from

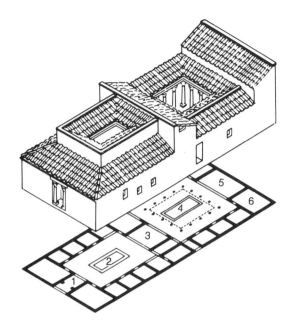

Figure 5. Isometric drawing showing atrium and peristyle layout of a Pompeian house, *ca.* late third century B.C. to A.D. 79: (*1*) entrance passage; (*2*) atrium with central floor basin (*impluvium*) and corresponding skylight (*compluvium*) in roof above; (*3*) main salon (*tablinum*); (*4*) peristyle garden; (*5*) reception room (*oecus*); (*6*) dining room (*triclinium*). *Reproduced from Eugenio La Rocca and Mariette and Arnold de Vos,* GUIDA ARCHEOLOGICA DI POMPEI © 1976 ARNOLDO MONDADORI EDITORE, MILAN

the late third century B.C. to A.D. 79, the year of the eruption of Mount Vesuvius. Older homes, such as the House of the Surgeon in Pompeii and the Samnite House in Herculaneum, were subjected to frequent remodelings as their owners aspired to more conspicuous, more attractive interiors and more pretentious reception areas. Vitruvius comments on the propriety of housing for the different classes during the final decades of the republican era (*The Ten Books on Architecture* 6.5.2, Morgan, trans.):

For capitalists and farmers of the revenue, somewhat comfortable and showy apartments must be constructed, secure against robbery; for advocates and public speakers, handsomer and more roomy, to accommodate meetings;

for men of rank who, from holding offices and magistracies, have social obligations to their fellow-citizens, lofty entrance courts in regal style, and most spacious atria and peristyles, with plantations and walks of some extent in them, appropriate to their dignity. They need also libraries, picture galleries, and basilicas, finished in a style similar to that of great public buildings, since public councils as well as private law suits and hearings before arbitrators are very often held in the houses of such men.

Not all dwellings conformed to the atrium or peristyle layout; simpler dwellings might contain several shops with rear rooms, with confined living quarters provided by small rooms arranged around a larger central salon. Some of the larger houses, of which the Pompeian House of the Faun (*ca.* 150–100 B.C.) was the first, might incorporate a private bath system (*balneum*); otherwise, house dwellers resorted to sponge bathing at home or paid for the sophisticated routines and services of the city baths (*thermae*). (There were three public baths inside the fortifications of Pompeii by A.D. 79.) Bedrooms (*cubicula*) were often arranged in sequential order on the ground floor or above; servants tended to occupy quarters near the service area of the house. The House of the Faun (fig. 6) has two large peristyles; the second garden space accommodated a stage for recitations, mimes, and pantomimes. The reception room (*oecus*) in the first peristyle, closer to the atrium, displayed the well-known mosaic of the Battle of Alexander and Darius (see fig. 15 in GREEK PAINTING AND MOSAIC), with Nilotic scenes and theatrical masks as complements. The domestic wing, to the right of the entrance and beyond a second colonnaded (tetrastyle) atrium, contained the bathing room and kitchen, both served by the same furnace. The servants' quarters are darker and more confined.

Traditional atria with the characteristic catch basin and underground cistern per-

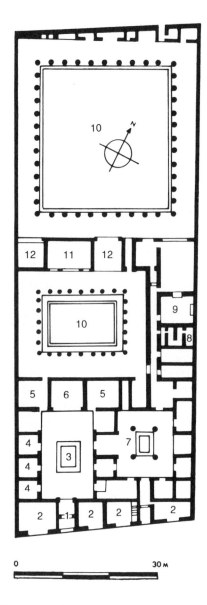

Figure 6. House of the Faun at Pompeii, *ca.* 150–100 B.C., plan: (*1*) entrance passage; (*2*) storefront shops (*tabernae*); (*3*) atrium with *impluvium;* (*4*) bedrooms (*cubicula*); (*5*) dining rooms (*triclinia*); (*6*) main salon (*tablinum*); (*7*) tetrastyle atrium; (*8*) private bath (*balneum*); (*9*) kitchen; (*10*) peristyle gardens; (*11*) reception room (*oecus*); (*12*) summer dining rooms. *Reproduced from Frank Sear,* ROMAN ARCHITECTURE (1982). BY PERMISSION OF CORNELL UNIVERSITY PRESS

sisted in Pompeian housing even after the advent of the Augustan aqueduct (Acqua Serino), but the welcome, more lavish provision of water soon altered the design and aesthetic of Pompeian life-styles. Houses were designed or adapted then to enjoy garden or orchard amenities; windows were enlarged, and walls were expanded by means of the new illusionistic style of mural art. Houses were sometimes terraced out over the old city walls in both Pompeii and Herculaneum to gain panoramic views of the sea or the mountains. The House of the Mosaic Atrium and the House of the Stags are both splendid examples of the new-style housing at Herculaneum. And the roads that led out of Pompeii, together with the hills around Herculaneum, were prized terrain for extensive suburban residences. The Villa of the Mysteries outside Pompeii, for example, located its central room (*tablinum*) where the occupants could enjoy a sea view. The increasing scale of mansions in Campania is apparent in the sixty-room complex of the Villa of the Mysteries and its well-regulated spread over more than an acre of ground.

The Augustan peace brought prosperity and fresh demands for manufactured goods in the Campanian towns. House properties responded to the need for new markets by supplying new outlets; bakers, cleaning establishments, condiment factories, and perfume and jewelry shops were let increasingly into the facades and interiors of the older homes. Emancipated slaves usually managed them for their patrician or freedman patrons. The bustling commercial and industrial activity probably induced the older families to leave town, to retreat to their farms and plantations, thereby enabling the newly enriched freedmen to buy up, subdivide, and convert the older mansions into commercial properties, hotels, and rooming houses. The Villa of the Mysteries certainly became a baker's establishment, and in ever-increasing numbers town houses were revised to accommodate upper stories, balconies, and upstairs windows facing onto the streets and sidewalks. The Pompeian House of the Vettii, the lavishly decorated property

of two freedmen brothers, both commercial magnates during Flavian times (A.D. 69–96), follows new dictates and expedients: the atrium now served only as anteroom to the peristyle; the *tablinum* evaporated, and the gloomy interiors of yore were replaced with agreeably ventilated sun-drenched spaces. The House of Loreius Tiburtinus in Pompeii, originally atrium-styled, was redesigned to accommodate an ornamental canal across its width, with another even more impressive watercourse issuing from a cascade in the domestic quarter and running the length of the landscaped garden.

ROMAN VILLAS

Town houses of the Julio-Claudian and Flavian eras clearly responded to the pattern of the developed rustic and maritime villas. *Villae rusticae* also responded imitatively to town house designs, but with large-scale agricultural properties as appendages. Although managed generally by overseers (*vilici*), rustic villas also offered lodging for the owners of the property. Tenant farmers and owners of small country properties were at the lower end of the rustic social scale, with the more extensive, highly productive, and expensively furnished villa properties of aristocrats, members of the imperial court, and wealthy freedmen at the other end.

Horace's Sabine farm, onetime property of Maecenas, located about ten miles northeast of Tibur (Tivoli), according to his own self-effacing comments a modest establishment ("modus non ita magnus; villula; agellus; angulus ille"—not of particularly large size; a little farm; a little field; that quiet corner), has been revealed (if rightly identified) to be a villa of considerable scale. The house proper, perched on the upper level, contains twelve rooms, with a central atrium and peristyle; the garden, on the lower level, covers an area of 2,900 square yards (2,425 m²). The villa proper may also have had an upper residential story with windows overlooking the Digentia (Licenza) River, the hill towns of Licenza and Civitella, and the landscaped garden. A bathhouse is an adjunct on the west side of the garden estate. Five families of free peasants (*coloni*) were tenants on Horace's estate, and eight slaves saw to his needs while he was in residence.

Platform villas elsewhere in Latium, and in Campania, embraced by productive properties, competed with the splendor and luxuries of hillside maritime properties like those excavated recently at Stabiae (Castellammare di Stabia) and at Oplontis (Torre Annunziata), both in the vicinity of Pompeii. These expansive complexes, with their array of porticoes, their landscaped gardens replete with statuary and fountains, and their plantations often of unexpected scale and complexity, are reflected repeatedly in the mural paintings of the time. Appearances notwithstanding, the villas of rich men were often highly productive properties, self-supporting and commercially venturesome, producing flowers, fruits, grapes, olives, birds, and fish. The Villa of San Rocco, in northern Campania near Francolise, includes a peristyle villa and an oil-producing plant. *Villae rusticae* at Boscoreale, near Pompeii, normally combine residences with a winery or oil press, threshing areas, and open-air wine storage facilities. Recent excavations in Lucania, at San Giovanni di Ruoti, and elsewhere testify eloquently to the continuing industrial and productive character of Roman farms in wine-making and oil-processing into late Roman times.

Imperial villas, like those of Augustus and Tiberius on Capreae (Capri), the Villa Jovis high above the sea on an almost inaccessible promontory, the Villa of Damecuta and the Palazzo a Mare (both porticoed villas strung along the shoreline), Tiberius' villa at Spelunca (Sperlonga), and the multilevel palace at Baiae (Baia)—product of a massive con-

version during the third century A.D.—all illustrate the capabilities, ingenuity, and skills of architects and designers in providing privacy, intimate gardens and sunny exposures, and porticoed walks (*ambulationes*), together with nymphaea, baths, and swimming pools, for wealthy owners. Nero's Golden House (*Domus Aurea*), constructed in the years after the Great Fire of Rome in A.D. 64, was an enormous urban villa in the center of the city, a complex of polygonal shapes, domical rooms, and spatial effects hitherto untried on the grand scale (see fig. 3 in ROMAN ARCHITECTURE). Nero's longing for "a contrived solitude of woods and vistas and open pastures" (Tacitus, *Annals* 15.42) was triumphantly satisfied by his architect and engineer, Severus and Celer, and in a remarkably short span of time. The Villa of Hadrian at Tibur and the late Roman villa at Piazza Armerina (fig. 7) in Sicily, near the ancient town of Philosophiana, are again simply magnified versions of the mature country house forms that had originated in republican times. The Sicilian villa (*ca.* A.D. 300–325), with its extensive polychrome mosaic floors, its peristyle audience hall, baths, dramatic dining room, and glistening corridors, offers a layout and elegance that may be indebted to North African models but that also recalls Hadrian's extravaganza at Tibur.

Gardens have been painstakingly studied and restored in recent times. Wall paintings, somewhat unexpectedly, shed valuable light on the recently recovered accessories of the villa and town house gardens: statuary, colonnade murals, fountains, pools, and aviaries. Pliny the Younger's account of his villas (*Letters* 2.17; 5.6) helps in the reconstruction of formal planting, with box hedges and low shrubbery; so too does modern analysis of pollens and seeds and other vestiges of the original fruits and plants as they emerge from the volcanic ash and overlay.

The House of Gaius Julius Polybius at Pompeii has yielded traces of five trees in its

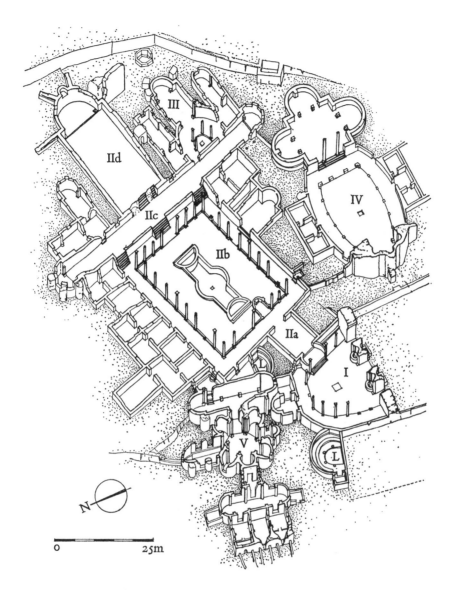

Figure 7. Late Roman villa at Piazza Armerina in Sicily, *ca.* A.D. 300–325, axonometric drawing: (*I*) entrance forecourt; (*IIa*) vestibule; (*IIb*) peristyle garden with fountain pool flanked by living quarters; (*IIc*) transverse corridor; (*IId*) apsidal audience hall; (*III*) private wing with two bedrooms and miniature courtyard; (*IV*) ceremonial wing with trilobed *triclinium* and oval, porticoed forecourt; (*V*) bath suite. *Reproduced from Axel Boëthius and J. B. Ward-Perkins,* ETRUSCAN AND ROMAN ARCHITECTURE © 1970 BY THE ESTATE OF AXEL BOËTHIUS AND J. B. WARD-PERKINS

peristyle: fig trees, probably forty years old, fruit trees (either cherry or pear), and a young olive tree. Lemon or citron trees probably also grew against the garden wall, adding their fragrance and color to the shaded orchard space. Apparently property with green space attached—private home, tenement (*insula*), or hostel—used that space either for alfresco dining and drinking or for productive ends, and sometimes for both. Homegrown fruits, vegetables, and flowers, so often the complement to dinner parties and symposia, were practically omnipresent in both Pompeii and Herculaneum.

Oleander, flowering ivy and myrtle, viburnum, roses, Madonna lilies, violas (stocks?), and flowering fruit trees, such as the pear, peach, lemon, and pomegranate, were visible testimony to the productivity of the Campania Felix, fruitful Campania.

OSTIAN APARTMENT HOUSES

Multiple housing units and multistoried apartment blocks appear in Rome during the third century B.C. However, the first practical illustrations of what became a housing revolution in the late republic and early empire have survived not in Rome but in the port city of Ostia on the Tiber. The big housing blocks that tower over the excavations of Ostia today were originally the outgrowth of strip-housing and of shopping rows with upstairs apartments. But the more sophisticated versions of post-Neronian times, particularly from the reigns of Trajan and Hadrian (A.D. 98–138), tend to adhere to a standard plan (fig. 8). The basic pattern consists of a long central corridor room (*medianum*) with windows drawing light from the street, garden, or inner court, and with rooms opening on three sides. Bedrooms (*cubicula*) appear on the inner

side, removed from the direct light and street noise; two larger, better appointed rooms (*exedrae*) dominate the extremities of the *medianum*. This plan, with minor variations, predominates, but there are many variations that favor more luxurious layouts.

Constructed in brick and concrete, with wooden raftering and occasionally concrete vaults, the Ostian apartment blocks sometimes attain four or five stories. They were designed to provide reasonably sound, secure lodging for both middle-class and upper-class citizenry. The lower classes (*humiliores*) tended to live in shops (*tabernae*) or in less attractive tenements where what was once single accommodation had been subdivided into two or three cramped units by means of partitions. Examples of lower-class housing appear in the apartment block of the Charioteers and the House of Themistocles. Overcrowding and squalid conditions with minimal amenities were inescapable aspects of living for penurious Romans. The more prosperous middle class, although they might have to share a single apartment block with the poor, would find accommodation in apartments (*cenacula*) that adhered to the basic *medianum* plan but with added features. The dayrooms at either end of the *medianum* were generally

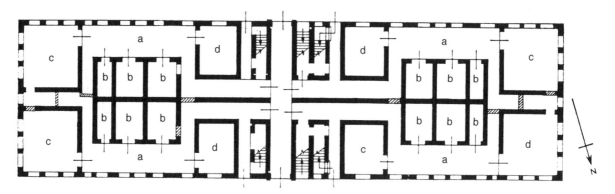

Figure 8. Garden houses at Ostia, A.D. 117–138, plan showing one of a pair of identical apartment blocks containing four separate units situated around a central park: (*a*) central corridor room (*medianum*); (*b*) bedrooms (*cubicula*); (*c–d*) sitting rooms (*exedrae*). *Reproduced from Russell Meiggs,* ROMAN OSTIA © 1960 BY OXFORD UNIVERSITY PRESS

well lighted; some were even two-storied, with a double range of windows. Bedrooms sometimes opened onto garden courts, and internal mezzanines sometimes crop up in apartments over the entire lower floor area.

Garden house complexes (fig. 8) for upper-class residents appear in Hadrianic times. A continuous line of exterior buildings rises around and above a central park in that most attractive design, with shops and apartments alternating, usually at the ground-floor level. Smaller complexes, the Casette Tipo units, might comprise three or four ground-floor apartments, without mezzanines, but with a second story above. These were reasonable alternatives to the general run of tenement accommodation and offered the exceptional dividend of latrines at the ground-floor level. Apartments in commercial blocks were another possibility for persons who sought or favored accommodation in bath buildings, grain storage warehouses, or barracks.

Seneca the Younger's letter on the agonies of residing over a bathing establishment is a graphic portrayal of rooming-house hazards (*Letters* 56.1–5, Richard M. Gummere, trans. [1917]):

> I have lodgings right over a bathing establishment. So picture to yourself the assortment of sounds. . . . When your strenuous gentleman, for example, is exercising himself by flourishing leaden weights; when he is working hard, or else pretends to be working hard, I can hear him grunt; and whenever he releases his imprisoned breath, I can hear him panting in wheezy and high-pitched tones. Or perhaps I notice some lazy fellow, content with a cheap rubdown, and hear the crack of the pummeling hand on his shoulder, varying in sound according as the hand is laid on flat or hollow. Then, perhaps, a professional comes along, shouting out the score; that is the finishing touch. Add to this the arresting of an occasional roysterer or pickpocket, the racket of the man who always likes to hear his own voice

> in the bathroom, or the enthusiast who plunges into the swimming-tank with unconscionable noise and splashing. . . . Imagine the hair-plucker with his penetrating, shrill voice,—for purposes of advertisement—continually giving it vent and never holding his tongue except when he is plucking the armpits and making his victim yell instead. Then the cake-seller with his varied cries, the sausageman, the confectioner, and all the vendors of food hawking their wares, each with his own distinctive intonation. . . . Among the sounds that din round me without distracting, I include passing carriages, a machinist in the same block, a saw-sharpener near by, or some fellow who is demonstrating with little pipes and flutes at the Trickling Fountain [*meta sudans*], shouting rather than singing.

The aftermath of the holocaust in Rome in A.D. 64 introduced new safety measures into Rome's urban renewal and into Ostia subsequently. Legislation thereafter required house owners and apartment dwellers to ensure that water was available for emergencies; communal walls were generally outlawed; and porticoes had to be built in front of apartment blocks (*insulae*) and private houses to guarantee against the spread of fires from falling house and tenement walls. Suetonius (*Lives of the Twelve Caesars,* "Nero" 16) states that fire fighters could work more effectively against fires in upper stories from the balcony level, but the hazard of flaming timber and debris falling into the streets was of much greater concern. The porticoes, with their overhead balconies, provided added stability to the highrise, multistoried blocks, and afforded a protected exit for refugees in extreme conditions. The use of braziers (*foculi*) and occasionally fireplaces (*foci*) in the apartment units was a constant menace. Juvenal's classic description (*Satires* 3.193–202, G. G. Ramsay, trans. [1918]) suggests that the jerry-built blocks that dated from pre-Neronian times, or were cheap replacements after Nero's death (A.D. 68)—soaring, rickety tenements with timber walls containing reed and stucco latticework—were still in place:

> Here we inhabit a city supported for the most part by slender props: for that is how the bailiff holds up the tottering house, patches up gaping cracks in the old wall, bidding the inmates sleep at ease under a roof ready to tumble about their ears. No, no, I must live where there are no fires, no nightly alarms. Ucalegon [Vergil, *Aeneid* 2.311] below is already shouting for water and shifting his chattels; smoke is pouring out of your third-floor attic, but you know nothing of it; for if the alarm begins in the ground-floor, the last man to burn will be he who has nothing to shelter him from the rain but the tiles, where the gentle doves lay their eggs.

The height of apartment blocks was a matter of concern to the more paternalistic emperors; Augustus limited the height of buildings to 70 feet (21 m), Trajan to 60 feet (18 m). But these regulations related only to the facades of buildings; it was the builder's responsibility to determine the height of sectors that did not face onto the street or sidewalk. On the average, Ostian apartment blocks attained four stories; the Serapis apartment block, which soared five stories, had porticoes surrounding its inside courtyard.

Furnishings in general in the Ostian apartment blocks were simple, the basic materials of any time or place. The *medianum*, sometimes used as a communal kitchen and dining area in lower-class tenements (cf. Mark 14:15; Luke 22:12), was alternative accommodation to the customary kitchen unit in middle-class apartments. On other occasions the *medianum* might be handsomely decorated to suit the tastes and the decorum of local councillors and affluent traders who used that central room as reception and entertainment area. The bright and airy character of the *medianum* undoubtedly made it the center of activity in the apartment unit. The lower classes, shopkeepers and tradesmen, tended to live behind or above their working space and with few amenities beyond the necessities for themselves and their families. Floor mosaics, laid over rafters, and wall paintings brightened middle-class interiors, extended their horizons, and alleviated their confinement.

Bedrooms, opening off the *medianum* in the common plan, were usually designed to accommodate two beds, end to end, along one wall. Slaves—and many of the luxury-class apartments would have housed a staff of retainers—were lodged at the mezzanine level or, in less roomy circumstances, in the narrow quarters under a flight of stairs, or informally in vestibules and doorways. No doubt their duties, as janitor, domestic, butler, cook, or tutor, would dictate their living conditions.

The House of Diana in Ostia has shops on the ground level along with access portals to staircases that served the upper floors. Apartments at the mezzanine level offered small one- and two-room units (*cellae*) with some common rooms where the garret residents could assemble for meals and social intercourse. The mezzanine dwellers were probably shopkeepers or servants attached to upstairs apartments. The apartment block of the Charioteers offered similar accommodation, but with a courtyard providing ventilation and lighting for rooms on the north and west sides. A water cistern in the central court served the needs of the tenants; lavatories and kitchens were limited, however, and above the first floor they may have been nonexistent. Drainpipes and cesspools served to empty the chamber pots that were the normal recourse throughout the city.

Building restrictions and fire protection measures notwithstanding, the style of living was static; in many respects it survives today in the older sectors of Rome, such as Trastevere, and in the cities of Bologna, Arezzo, and Siena. Shopkeepers cluttered the streets with wares that tumbled from the storefronts or refreshment stands that characterized practically every apartment block frontage (fig. 9). Water had to be drawn from public fountains and lugged upstairs for domestic uses; cooking was done on charcoal braziers or rude stoves. Lighting came from oil lamps, and heating was a matter of braziers, portable but hazardous in the extreme.

Bathing facilities were found in private and public baths distributed generously throughout Ostia and Rome. Bars and restaurants offered rush service snacks, hot and cold beverages, and finger foods, and provided neighborhood meeting places for the local population. Balconies served as outlets for young and old, and deliveries to the upper floors of apartment blocks were no doubt commonly drawn up by rope and baskets or other containers from the street level to balconies and streetside windows for

the sake of convenience. The noise factor, Seneca's complaint, particularly at night when deliveries were normally made, was an inescapable torment. Martial's experience in a tenement near the Quirinal Hill accents the limitations and the agonies of living on the fourth floor in a metropolitan tenement, with the constant menace of kitchen fires, in a waterless apartment that was liable to drafts and noise pollution (*Epigrams* 1.108, 117; 8.14, 67).

OSTIAN TOWN HOUSES

Ostia remained a visibly prosperous, expanding center until the third century A.D. Thereafter, with the decline in trading activity, the service personnel chose to live at Portus, which eventually succeeded Ostia as the Tiber-mouth harbor. During the depressed times of the late empire Ostia suffered a major decline in apartment block occupancy and a considerable reduction in

Figure 9. Ostian apartment block (*insula*), second century A.D., reconstruction of facade showing storefront shops (*tabernae*) including a cookhouse (*thermopolium*) on the ground level and balconies above. *Reproduced from Axel Boëthius and J. B. Ward-Perkins,* ETRUSCAN AND ROMAN ARCHITECTURE © 1970 BY THE ESTATE OF AXEL BOËTHIUS AND J. B. WARD-PERKINS

property values. Patricians, displaced during the boom period by the inroads of merchants, middlemen service personnel, warehouse operators, shippers, and the like, returned with their large support staffs. They generally constructed new houses that provided them with ample space and expensive interior decoration. The House of Cupid and Psyche and the House of the Nymphaeum are typical examples of late imperial houses in Ostia. Both may be dated around A.D. 300. The former assimilates the *medianum* plan to luxury-style living with a nymphaeum (fountain) garden opening off the corridor, after the pattern of earlier forms where the *medianum* faced onto the street or a garden court. The rooms to the left of the corridor have floors and walls of polychrome marble; the sitting room (*exedra*), at the far end, has marble-lined walls and marble flooring. A second story rose over the smaller rooms on the left. The open garden features a row of five round-headed fountain niches lined with marble and glass mosaic. But the decline of the city was inevitable, and the apartment blocks were gradually evacuated; some were razed, others simply subsided into disrepair. Eventually the one-time opulent town houses and baths were left deserted and malaria ended the life span of ancient Ostia sometime in the ninth century A.D.

BIBLIOGRAPHY

SOURCES

Juvenal, *Satires*, G. G. Ramsay, trans. (1918; repr. 1969); W. Kendrick Pritchett and D. A. Amyx, "The Attic Stelai," in *Hesperia*, **22** (1953), **25** (1956), and **27** (1958); Seneca, *Ad Lucilium Epistulae Morales* (*Letters to Lucilius*), Richard M. Gummere, trans. 3 vols. (1917–1925); Vitruvius, *The Ten Books on Architecture*, Morris Hicky Morgan, trans. (1914; repr. 1960); Xenophon, *House-hold Management* (*Oeconomicus*), E. C. Marchant, trans. (1923; repr. 1968).

STUDIES

Greek and Hellenistic

J. Walter Graham, "Origins and Interrelations of the Greek House and the Roman House," in *Phoenix*, **20** (1966), and "Houses of Classical Athens," in *Phoenix*, **28** (1974); John Ellis Jones *et al.*, "The Dema House in Attica," in *Annual of the British School at Athens*, **57** (1962), "Town and Country Houses in Attica in Classical Times," in *Miscellanea Graeca* (Ghent), **1** (1975), and "Berlin Conference on 'Living in the Classical City,'" in *Liverpool Classical Monthly*, **8** (1983); Paul McKendrick, *The Greek Stones Speak*, 2d ed. (1981); Gisela M. A. Richter, *The Furniture of the Greeks, Etruscans, and Romans* (1966); Bertha C. Rider, *Ancient Greek Houses* (1916; repr. 1984); David M. Robinson, J. Walter Graham, *et al.*, *Excavations at Olynthus*, 14 pts. (1929–1952); Brian A. Sparkes and Lucy Talcott, *Pots and Pans of Classical Athens* (1958); J. Travlos, *Pictorial Dictionary of Ancient Athens* (1971); Thomas B. L. Webster, *Everyday Life in Classical Athens* (1969); Richard E. Wycherley, *How the Greeks Built Cities*, 2d ed. (1962), and *The Stones of Athens* (1978).

Etruscan Houses

Luisa Banti, *The Etruscan Cities and Their Culture*, Erika Bizzarri, trans. (1978); Axel Boëthius and John B. Ward-Perkins, *Etruscan and Roman Architecture* (1970); Alexander G. McKay, *Houses, Villas, and Palaces in the Roman World* (1975); Gisela M. A. Richter, *op. cit.;* Mario Torelli, *Etruria* (1980).

Roman Houses and Villas; Roman and Ostian Apartment Blocks

S. Aurigemma, *Villa Adriana* (1962); John P. V. D. Balsdon, *Life and Leisure in Ancient Rome* (1969); Boëthius and Ward-Perkins, *op. cit.;* Frank E. Brown, *Cosa: The Making of a Roman City* (1980); R. C. Carrington, "Studies in the Campanian 'Villae Rusticae,' " in *Journal of Roman Studies,* **21** (1931); Gilbert Charles-Picard, *Roman Painting* (1970); Matteo della Corte, *Case ed abitanti di Pompei,* 3d ed. (1965); M. Aylwin Cotton, *The Late Republican Villa at Posto, Francolise* (1979); John H. D'Arms, *Romans on the Bay of Naples* (1970), and *Commerce and Social Standing in Ancient Rome* (1981); Joseph J. Deiss, *Herculaneum, Italy's Buried Treasure* (1966); Katherine M. D. Dunbabin, *The Mosaics of Roman North Africa* (1978); Robert Etienne, *La vie quotidienne à Pompéi,* 2d rev. ed. (1977).

S. Ferraio, *Stabiae: le ville et l'antiquarium* (1981); Alfonso de Franciscis, "La villa romana di Oplontis," in *Parola del Passato,* **153** (1973), and *The Pompeian Wall Paintings in the Roman Villa of Oplontis,* Rosemary Kunisch, trans. (1975); Bruce W. Frier, *Landlords and Tenants in Imperial Rome* (1980); Michael Grant, *Cities of Vesuvius: Pompeii and Herculaneum* (1971); Gustav Hermansen, *Ostia, Aspects of Roman City Life* (1981); Wilhelmina Jashemski, *The Gardens of Pompeii, Herculaneum, and the Villas Destroyed by Vesuvius* (1979); Theodor Kraus, *Pompeii and Herculaneum,* Robert Erich Wolf, trans. (1975); Eugenio La Rocca, Mariette De Vos, and Arnold De Vos, *Guida archeologica di Pompei* (1976); Alexander G. McKay, *op. cit.,* and *Ancient Campania,* 2 vols. (1972); Paul MacKendrick, *The Mute Stones Speak,* 2d ed. (1983); Amedeo Maiuri, *L'Ultima fase edilizia di Pompei* (1942), and *Herculaneum and the Villa of the Papyri* (196[3]); August Mau, *Pompeii, Its Life and Art,* Francis W. Kelsey, trans., rev. ed. (repr. 1982); Russell Meiggs, *Roman Ostia,* 2d ed. (1973).

James E. Packer, "Housing and Population in Imperial Ostia and Rome," in *Journal of Roman Studies,* **57** (1967), *The Insulae of Imperial Ostia,* Memoirs of the American Academy in Rome, **31** (1971), and "Middle and Lower Class Housing in Pompeii and Herculaneum," in *Neue Forschungen in Pompeji,* Bernard Andreae, ed. (1975); Kenneth S. Painter, ed., *Roman Villas in Italy: Recent Excavation and Research,* British Museum, Department of Greek and Roman Antiquities, no. 24 (1980); John Percival, *The Roman Villa* (1976); Jeremy Rossiter, *Roman Farm Building in Italy,* British Archaeological Reports, International Series, **52** (1978), and "Wine and Oil Processing at Roman Farms in Italy," in *Phoenix,* **35** (1981); Frank Sear, *Roman Architecture* (1982).

Adrian N. Sherwin-White, *The Letters of Pliny* (1966); Alastair M. Small, "San Giovanni di Ruoti," in Painter, *op. cit.;* Alastair M. Small and R. J. Buck, "The Topography of Roman Villas in Basilicata," in *Studi in onore di D. Adamesteanu: attività àrcheologica in Basilicata 1964–77* (1980); Helen H. Tanzer, *The Villas of Pliny the Younger* (1924); John B. Ward-Perkins, "Nero's Golden House," in *Antiquity,* **30** (1956), and *Roman Architecture* (1977); John B. Ward-Perkins and Amanda Claridge, *Pompeii A.D. 79,* 2 vols. (1978); Roger J. A. Wilson, *Piazza Armerina* (1983).

Clothing and Ornament

LARISSA BONFANTE AND EVA JAUNZEMS

THERE IS ABUNDANT EVIDENCE about the appearance and costumes of the ancient Greeks, Etruscans, and Romans: their clothes, jewelry, make-up, hairstyles, shoes, hats, and other accessories. It would be impossible to do justice to all this evidence here, or to deal with the great variety of garments and costumes, their connotations, and the changes that occurred over more than twelve hundred years in the various geographical areas. Yet certain patterns can be discerned.

One characteristic of ancient fashion is that it changed less rapidly than fashions do today. We can, however, divide the history of Greek, Etruscan, and Roman dress into chronological units. For the Greeks and Etruscans, who were contemporaries, these are, broadly speaking, the following: (1) the Orientalizing and archaic periods, 800–500 B.C., (2) the classical period, 500–300 B.C., (3) the Hellenistic period, 300–30 B.C. The Roman period, over a thousand years long, can be divided as follows: (1) Italic, under Etruscan influence, 600–400 B.C., (2) the early Roman period, 400–100 B.C., (3) the late republic to early empire, 100 B.C.–A.D.

250, (4) the late Roman period, A.D. 250–600.

A word must be said about the sources of information about ancient dress: artistic representations, literature, and actual remains. Of the three types of evidence, the third is practically negligible. The fragments of fabrics that have survived include bits of Etruscan linen; linen cloth from Egypt; plaid-woven wool from the northern peat bogs; silk, wool, and leather from the Roman soldiers' camp at Dura-Europos on the Euphrates; and decorated Coptic textiles. More will be made available by careful excavation and from scientific analyses that can detect the imprint left by a textile on a bronze object. Clothes and textiles were often left as gifts in the sanctuaries of the gods. Inventory lists of temple treasuries at Athens and elsewhere have been found describing such gifts; and thousands of loom weights have been excavated in sanctuaries, graves, and habitation sites. In contrast to the meager finds of cloth and garments, archaeology has provided a fairly accurate picture of the jewelry used in various periods, because precious objects were often placed in the tomb with the deceased, where they were later found by archaeologists or tomb robbers.

Literary evidence is valuable because it yields names of garments, sometimes with descriptions and often the connotations of a special costume, dress, or fashion. Only rarely does it give any idea of what these articles of clothing looked like. For this we must rely on the visual evidence of ancient art. Yet here too there are difficulties. We have to interpret these pictures and learn how to read them in order to understand the shapes of the garments represented. What is often shown is not how people really looked, but what they wanted to look like, or how the artists thought they should look. In each case we must distinguish fashions, garments and outfits actually worn and familiar to the artist, from artistic conventions, stylizations used by the artist that can obscure the actual appearance of garments or accessories. We also must distinguish special costumes not used in daily life or used only in special circumstances, such as theatrical dress, mythological attributes, priestly habits, and antique or archaic fashions worn or depicted for special effect.

Real garments in antiquity were fundamentally different from ours. They were never cut, fitted, and sewn from a number of pieces. An ancient Greek, Etruscan, or Roman garment consisted rather of a piece of cloth woven to fit the wearer's size and draped loosely on the body. Because such garments were draped and not tailored, they were often multipurpose. A cloak might double as a blanket, like a Mexican poncho. There were no pockets: coins were kept in the mouth, although a handkerchief might well be tucked into the folds of a robe or mantle. Pins, brooches, belts, and even buttons could be used to hold a garment in place. Occasionally the sides of the cloth were sewn up into a seam. The change from draped garments to the fitted long sleeves and trousers characteristic of our way of

dressing marked the end of classical antiquity. The sleeved, tightly fitting *camisia*, the ancestor of our modern shirt or chemise, first described by St. Jerome about 395 A.D. (*Epistles* 64.11), took the place of the loose, flowing tunic; and soon men everywhere wore the *bracae* or trousers that had for so long been the sign of a barbarian.

Artistic evidence is our richest and clearest source of information on ancient dress since the majority of Greek, Etruscan, and Roman sculpture, decorated vases, and paintings represent clothed human figures. But such evidence must be used with care, for there was a real distinction between the actual garment or fashion as worn and the artistic conventions with which it was represented in any particular period. The prevailing artistic style of a period affected the representation of clothing. There were also powerful traditions, some with religious roots, that governed the representation of gods and heroes, who were often represented with standard attributes including archaic dress. Moreover, artists sometimes copied other artistic representations, rather than real costumes drawn from life and familiar to them.

In the following discussion, the conventional modern archaeological terminology is used; the reader should be aware, however, that although fashions changed in the course of time, the terminology used to describe them often did not. The meaning of *peplos*, for example, changed significantly between the eighth and the fifth centuries B.C.

GREEK DRESS

Material and Fabrics

Wool, the material most used by the Greeks for warm clothing, was provided by sheep, which were reared throughout the Greek world from the Neolithic period on. In Asia Minor goats were also raised, and their hair used for rough fabrics. Lighter linen garments were produced from spun flax, a craft no doubt learned from Egypt or from the Near East where linen was the most common textile material. During the eighth and seventh centuries B.C., Phoenician traders brought linen and elaborately decorated textiles to Greece, along with other products of the Orient. It has been suggested that the rich patterns of Corinthian pottery reflect these weavings. Silk was also imported from the East, first as finished garments, then as cocoons from which thread was spun. It was certainly known in Greece by the time of Alexander (356–323 B.C.), and perhaps earlier, for in the late fifth century Aeschylus mentions a diaphanous fabric that could have been either silk or a very fine linen (*Persians* [*Persae*] 125). Later, mulberry trees were planted on the island of Kos, where a native silk industry developed to supply the tastes of Hellenistic ladies.

The Greeks obtained their dyes from both vegetable and animal sources. Most highly prized was the purple Tyrian dye obtained from two species of sea snails, *purpura* and *murex brandaris,* native to the Syro-Phoenician coast. Violet could also be obtained from the kermes worm, a scaled insect similar to the Mexican cochineal insect; red from madder (*rubia tinctoria*); and yellow, a color particularly popular with women, from saffron (*crocus sativa*). Raw fibers were either used in their natural colors or dyed before they were spun. Homer's description of garments as "silvery" or "shining like the sun" could refer to the brilliance of the colors of dyed wool, or to the oiled, shiny linen threads. Whereas wool is easily dyed, linen is not.

Preparation of Fabrics

In Greece textiles for clothing were almost always manufactured at home, as were the necessary blankets, pillows, and spreads. The women of each household were proud of their skill in producing garments of soft texture that, when draped, fell in full, richly varied folds. They invented their own patterns and techniques and taught them to their daughters and maidservants.

The process of wool preparation is illustrated in a number of vase paintings, and is described at some length in Aristophanes' *Lysistrata* (567–569; 571–587). First the raw wool was washed and the matted fibers pulled apart with the fingers; next the women would rub and card it to produce a loose mass of tow yarn. They did this over their knees, sitting with feet propped on a footstool called a donkey (*onos*) and protecting their knees with a tubular device (*epinetron*) of terra-cotta that was sometimes decorated with scenes of woolworking. The wool was oiled to make it supple.

The tow yarn was then wound around a distaff. The spinner pulled out a length of tow, twisted it, and fastened it to a hook on a spindle that she held in her left hand. A weight called a whorl was attached to the bottom of the spindle. When the spindle was released and set spinning, it pulled the tow taut and twisted it into yarn. The spinner continued to feed tow from the distaff into the growing length of yarn until, drawn downward by the weight of the whorl, the spindle reached the floor. Then the yarn was wound up around the spindle and the process was repeated. By controlling the rate of the spin with her hand, the spinner could control the texture and strength of the yarn. As soon as a full skein was completed, it was removed from the spindle and placed in a wool basket.

Weaving was done on an upright loom with two sturdy side posts joined together by horizontal crossbeams to form a frame (fig. 1). The balls of wool that were to form the warp of the fabric were fastened to the uppermost beam and the thread from each ball hung straight down in such a way that it could be lengthened at will. The warps were held taut by loom weights, usually made of clay. A second upper beam could be turned to roll up the finished weaving. Cloth was produced by passing weft threads wound around a shuttle between the vertical warp threads in such a way that some passed over the warps and others under the warps. A simple one-on-one tabby weave was achieved by passing the weft over the odd warps and under the even ones, or vice versa. To simplify this process alternate warp threads were placed in front of a horizontal crossbeam near the base of the loom. Each of the warps that hung behind this crossbeam was attached by a loop of string to a movable heddle rod that the weaver could pull forward or release to create the proper shed or opening between the warp threads for each pass of the shuttle. The new weft row was pushed into place with a kind of comb or spatula. At each edge the shuttle was turned back and pulled through the warp once more, this time with the position of the warps reversed, thus producing a reinforced edge called the selvage at the vertical sides of the weaving. At the ends of the warps fringes could be braided after the fabric was removed from the loom.

Homer's description of Circe and Calypso weaving shows that the weaver stood before the loom or walked back and forth in front of it. Penelope, however, sits on a stool in front of the shroud that she is weaving for Laertes and that she repeatedly unravels in order to stall her unwanted suitors. She is probably seated because she is practicing a more intricate kind of weaving. Patterns such as stripes, checks, and plaids could be produced by using different colors of yarns, and by devising more complex arrangements of sheds. The most intricate floral and animal patterns were no doubt created by tapestry weaving, a process that required the weaver to work different-colored weft threads into place by hand. The Greeks also liked to mix different textures of yarn; the combination of a strong, tightly spun warp and a lighter, thinner weft, for example, produced a loose weave that gave an elegant fall to the finished garment.

The vertical, warp-weighted loom was the only type used in the classical world until the Roman imperial period when a loom with warp stretched between two beams was introduced. The two-beam loom was used for weaving both wool and linen, and perhaps even for silk. In addition to weaving, the Greeks also produced clothing by knitting; the process of feltmaking was known and used for caps and other types of sturdy outerwear; and leatherworking was practiced to produce shoes and belts.

The manufacture of textiles remained

Figure 1. Diagram of a warp-weighted loom: (*a*) upright side posts; (*b*) crossbeam; (*c*) heddle rod; (*d*) shed rod; (*e*) supports for the heddle rod; (*f*) crotches for the crossbeam; (*g*) hole for nailing the upright to a wall or beam; (*h*) front warp thread; (*i*) back warp thread; (*k*) chained spacing cord; (*l*) loom weights. *Reproduced from Marta Hoffmann,* THE WARP-WEIGHTED LOOM © 1974 BY THE NORWEGIAN RESEARCH COUNCIL FOR SCIENCE AND THE HUMANITIES

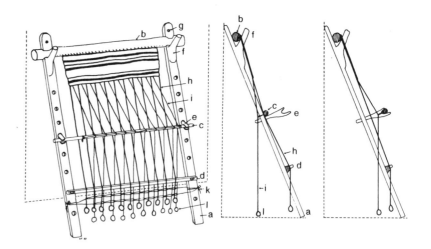

principally a woman's household industry until the Romans organized textile production on a larger scale in the conquered Greek provinces and in other parts of their empire. Certain crafts connected with the production of clothing and ornaments, however, were already practiced by professionals, who were men in the Greek period. They included shoemakers, jewelers, and the fullers whose task it was to finish cloth and to clean and press soiled garments.

The Principal Greek Garments:
Peplos, Chiton, Himation, Chlamys

The basic form of all Greek clothing was a rectangle. When a piece of weaving left the loom it was essentially a finished garment, woven to measure and requiring no tailoring. Fitting was achieved by draping the garment and securing it with the aid of brooches, fibulae (fasteners similar to safety pins), buttons, stitching, and belts. Much of

the beauty and creativity of Greek dress both in art and, one must assume, in life, lay in the elegant patterns of folds that could be achieved by artfully draping a finely woven fabric.

The chief garments of women were the peplos and the long chiton that was worn sometimes under the peplos and sometimes alone. The peplos (fig. 2) was a rectangle measuring in width as much as twice the distance between the wearer's elbows when she stood with arms outstretched, at most six and a half feet (two meters). Its length was the wearer's height from her neck to her feet, plus an overfold that varied in length and could be adjusted. The total length was at most ten feet (three meters). The peplos was folded in half and placed around the wearer's body with the fold under the left arm. It was secured with two pins at the shoulders, a belt at the waist, and sometimes a second belt over the overfold.

The term *chiton* is commonly used to de-

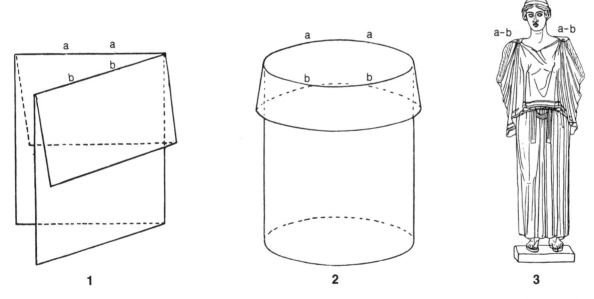

1   **2**   **3**

Figure 2. The draping of the peplos: (*1*) a large rectangular piece of cloth is folded over itself (overfold) and then folded in half to form the front and back of the garment; (*2*) two pins joining points (*a* and *b*) along the upper edge of the fold secure the peplos on the shoulders; openings are left along the top for armholes; (*3*) a peplos of the classical period (fifth century B.C.). *Reproduced from Margarete Bieber,* GRIECHISCHE KLEIDUNG *(1928).* THE NEW YORK PUBLIC LIBRARY

scribe both a woman's and a man's garment of slightly different construction. Both were made of one or two pieces of fabric sewn together along their selvages to form a tube, and lacked the open side and overfold of the peplos. The man's chiton was narrower than the woman's and had openings left in the sides for armholes (fig. 3a). Unlike the woman's, it could be long (for older men, musicians, and charioteers) or short (for young men and slaves). The woman's was long and was pinned or sewn in two or more places along the shoulders in such a way as to form armholes or even, if the tube were wide enough, to produce the appearance of sleeves (fig. 3b).

Men wore a cloak called a himation, sometimes alone, sometimes over their chiton. The himation was worn loosely draped over one shoulder and wrapped around the hips. Women also wore the himation as a cloak, sometimes pulling it around the head to leave only the face exposed. A shorter, less encumbering cloak for men called a chlamys was pinned on one shoulder; it was typically worn by younger men, particularly by horsemen and travelers (see fig. 7 in GREEK PAINTING AND MOSAIC).

Although extremely simple in their basic

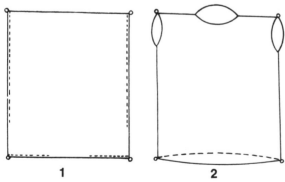

Figure 3a. The draping of the man's chiton: (*1*) one or two pieces of cloth are sewn together almost to the top; (*2*) armholes are left open along the side seams; the shoulders are sewn together at the top, leaving an opening for the head. *Reproduced from Margarete Bieber,* GRIECHISCHE KLEIDUNG *(1928).* THE NEW YORK PUBLIC LIBRARY

shapes, the chiton and peplos could be worn —and represented—in a great variety of ways. Through the use of belts various configurations of folds could be produced; a full fold pulled out over the belt was called a *kolpos.*

These are the principal garments worn by the ancient Greeks during the major portion of their history. Because they were so simple in design they were often multipurpose. Either a peplos or a himation could, as we have seen, double as a blanket. Changes over time were less radical than changes of fashion today, but they are nonetheless apparent, particularly in art, and will be considered in the discussions of each historical period. (The Homeric era will be discussed separately because it presents special problems.)

The first useful representations of costume appear on the artistic monuments of the Orientalizing period (ninth through seventh centuries B.C.), mostly statues, relief sculpture, and vase paintings. In the archaic period (sixth century B.C.), life-size statues of beautiful young men and women, *kouroi* and *korai,* were dedicated at sanctuaries and used as funeral monuments. The best-known series comes from the Athenian Acropolis. The *kouroi* are usually nude; many *korai* wear a characteristic late archaic woman's costume that consists of a linen chiton and an obliquely draped mantle. During the Orientalizing and archaic periods bright colors and rich patterns were favored. Belts, pins and brooches, and hair ornaments seem also to have been especially varied and luxurious.

During the classical period of the fifth and fourth centuries B.C. clothing developed a simplicity of outline and decoration. This is particularly to be noted in monuments from Athens, some of which now begin to show scenes of everyday life: votive reliefs, grave reliefs, and statues of marble, bronze, and terra-cotta. Ornament is restricted mostly to

Figure 3b. The draping of the woman's chiton: (*1*) one or two pieces of cloth are sewn together to form a tube; (*2–3*) the upper edges are brought together at two or more points by sewing or pinning; openings are left for the arms and for the head along the upper edge; (*4*) female figure wearing the wide Ionic chiton of fine linen under a himation with woven decorations, from a red-figure vase in the British Museum. *Diagrams reproduced from Margarete Bieber, GRIECHISCHE KLEIDUNG* (1928). THE NEW YORK PUBLIC LIBRARY. DRAWING COURTESY OF NANCY DE GRUMMOND, CLASSICS, FLORIDA STATE UNIVERSITY

bands along the seams and hems. Men's garments are usually undecorated.

In the Hellenistic period the Greeks came once again into contact with the luxury of the Near East, as a result of Alexander's conquest of the Persian Empire and lands farther east, and of the foundation of eastern kingdoms by his successors, the Ptolemies in Egypt, the Seleucids in Syria, and the Attalids in Pergamum. New forms were imported, such as the rounded Macedonian chlamys, which the Ptolemies brought to Greece, and new textiles: cotton from Egypt and silk from India and China. Sculpture and painting provide illustrations; valuable for this period are the abundant terra-cotta statuettes showing men, women, and children in realistic pose and dress.

Homeric Dress

The poems of Homer are important for a study of Greek dress not only because they provide the first references in literature to Greek costumes and ornaments, introducing terms such as *peplos* and *chiton* that became standard elements of the vocabulary of Greek dress, but also because they show the importance of costume and the textile arts to the emerging Hellenistic culture. What the poems cannot do is tell us what the garments looked like. Attempts to connect garments mentioned by Homer with styles represented on the monuments, or with actual objects that have come down to us from either his period, the eighth century B.C., or from the Mycenaean age four to eight centuries earlier that he writes about, have been largely unconvincing. Scenes of dressing and descriptions of costumes are regularly formulaic, and there is no way of knowing whether the poet's material is relevant to his own day or is a borrowing of older conventions. The evidence Homer does provide is, however, of great value to the philologist and to the student interested in the role of costume in social life.

The task of producing garments for the Homeric household fell to both noblewomen and slave women. In the household of the Phaeacian king Alcinous there are fifty slave women whose tasks are to grind grain, to weave, and to spin (*Odyssey* 7.105); Alcinous' wife Arete spins purple yarn (6.306), and his daughter Nausicaa does the household laundry, a chore that requires an expedition to a riverbank (6.57–98). The Phaeacian episode may still reflect some aspects of the Mycenaean palace society of the Bronze Age, for Linear B tablets found at Pylos provide evidence of a developed linen industry carried out by a large number of workers, under what may have been near factory conditions. Such, perhaps, was the work of Alcinous' slave women. That his noble wife and daughter were also involved in the production and care of textiles reflects the prestige that the textile crafts had achieved and were to retain throughout antiquity. Weaving is done not only by noble ladies such as Arete, Helen (*Iliad* 3.125–128; *Odyssey* 15.105), Andromache (*Iliad* 22.440–441), and Penelope (*Odyssey* 2.93–110), but also by goddesses such as Circe (*Odyssey* 10.220–223) and Calypso (*Odyssey* 5.62), and most importantly by Athena (*Iliad* 5.733–737; 14.178–179), who was the patroness of the craft.

An abundance of beautiful clothing and textiles was a mark of social standing. Clothing also showed that an individual belonged to a cultural group. Honored guests were presented with clothing by their hosts to signify their acceptance into the household. When Nausicaa finds the shipwrecked Odysseus near the river, for example, she orders her handmaidens to give him food and drink, to bathe him, and to provide him with a chiton and a *pharos* (cloak) (*Odyssey* 6.214). When he arrives at the palace the queen asks him where he got his clothing, for she immediately recognizes it as her own work (7.234). In the scene of recognition in Aeschylus' *Libation Bearers* (*Choephoroi* 231), too, Electra recognizes Orestes, despite his absence of several years, because he is wearing a garment that she wove for him. Both stories suggest an ethnographic parallel with groups such as the Scottish clans who use distinct patterns of weaving as symbols of group allegiance.

At a later point in the Phaeacian episode, when Odysseus has made his identity known to the king and is about to depart, he is presented with a gift of twelve newly washed tunics, twelve mantles, and twelve talents of gold, one from each of the twelve Phaeacian rulers (*Odyssey* 8.390–393), and a thirteenth from Alcinous' own household (8.441). The conjunction of precious metal and textiles as gifts (*Odyssey* 15.104–129) suggests that in the Homeric economy they were of comparable worth. The custom of giving a new peplos to Athena is at least as old as the Homeric epics (*Odyssey* 6.289–295), and the annual giving of the peplos to the goddess at the panathenaic festival must go back to an ancient custom of offering valuables to the gods.

The principal garment of men in the Homeric poems, the chiton, was worn next to the skin. It was usually a short garment, sometimes secured with a belt. Long trailing chitons are worn by the Ionians (*Iliad* 13.685; *Homeric Hymn to Apollo* 147), and the war tunic that Athena borrows from Zeus is surely also a long chiton (*Iliad* 5.736; 8.387). The word *chiton* is Semitic in origin, but it had entered the Greek language by the end of the Bronze Age, for the Linear B tablets contain the form *ki-to*, and also the word *ri-no* for linen (Gk. *linon*).

Over the chiton a thick woolen cloak called a *chlaina* was worn for protection against the elements. The *chlaina* of aristocrats was purple. It was wrapped around the body and fastened with a *perone*, a type of pin or brooch that could be quite elaborate in design: Odysseus' is of gold with double clasps and decorated with a hound attacking a fawn (*Odyssey* 19.226–231). This cloak was in form probably a simple woven rectangle, like the later chlamys and himation, for the word *chlaina* is also used for bedding. Another word that signifies a cloak when used for men's garments is *pharos*, which occurs in Linear B as *pa-wo*. Like the *chlaina*, it was worn by men over the chiton (*Iliad* 2.43). Women wore it next to their skin and fastened it with a belt (*Odyssey* 5.230–231; 10.543–544). The color, when it is indicated, is purple for men, silver-white for women.

The *zoma* is a garment worn in Homer's *Iliad* only by men, generally when engaged in vigorous activities such as warfare (4.187, 216), boxing (23.683), or wrestling (23.710). It was a kind of loincloth or binding for the thighs and genitals. However, a garment worn by Odysseus is called a *zoma* in one passage (*Odyssey* 14.482) and later a chiton (14.489), suggesting that it was a piece of cloth that could be worn in several different ways. The Homeric man's belt, called a *zoster*, was normally made of metal, or perhaps of cloth or leather covered with metal plates. Agamemnon's was silver (*Iliad* 11.237), Menelaus' had golden clasps (4.132–133). The *zoster* that Ajax gave to Hector was certainly of cloth, for it was dyed violet (*Iliad* 7.305).

The principal garment for women in the Homeric epics is a full-length gown secured with a belt and with several pins or brooches —twelve in the case of the garment given to Penelope by Antinous (*Odyssey* 18.292–294). Analogy to later costumes suggests that it was an untailored rectangular piece of cloth draped and fastened rather loosely like the classical peplos or chiton. The names used for this garment, almost certainly synonymous, are *peplos*, a reduplicated form from the same stem as the noun "fold" and the verb "to fold," and *heanos*, a substantive noun that occurs in Linear B as *we-a-no* and is related to the adjective *heanoos*, meaning "fine" or "light," that is sometimes used to modify *peplos*. The substantive *heanos* refers to a peplos as we might refer to a woman's silk gown as her "silk."

The garment was colored and therefore was probably made of wool, for linen does not readily retain dyes. The finer peploi and *heanoi* were decorated with patterns, probably woven into the fabric (*Iliad* 6.294; 14.179; *Odyssey* 15.107; 8.293; *Homeric Hymn to Aphrodite* 87). Over their gowns women wore a veil called a *kredemnon* or *kaluptre*, regularly described as "shining." It covered the hair and was long enough to be drawn before the face to conceal it modestly (*Odyssey* 16.416; 18.210; 21.165). Mourning women tore off their veils in anguish (*Iliad* 22.406, 470; Homeric *Hymn to Demeter* 42).

Women girdled themselves with a *zone*, a term in later literature used also of men's belts but in Homer reserved for women's. Like the *zoster*, the *zone* was made of metal or decorated with metal. Calypso (*Odyssey* 5.231–232) and Circe (10.544–545) both fasten a golden *zone* around their *pharos*; Hera's *zone* has golden tassels. The two words for footwear in the epics are *hypodemata*, derived from the verb "to bind," and *pedila,* which are also bound onto the feet. Both terms refer to leather sandals with straps. The gods when they travel over the sea wear golden sandals (*Iliad* 24.340–341; *Odyssey* 1.96–97; 5.44–45).

The Geometric Period ("Dark Age")

The recent discovery of burials connected with a tenth-century hero in Lefkandi, Euboea, has revealed something about the dress actually worn in this early period. The cremated remains of a warrior were wrapped in a remarkably well-preserved piece of linen cloth with looped fringes (one of the rare known examples of textiles from Greece). Alongside was the skeleton of a woman, whose jewelry included a decorated gold lunate neckpiece and similarly made disk-shaped breast covers. Her garment was fastened by pins of bronze and gilt iron.

Otherwise we know little of the dress of this period. The stick figures of Geometric vase painting distinguish between men, variously shown armed or naked, and women, wearing long dresses with cross-hatched decoration that represents an ornamented wool fabric, perhaps of plaid or checkered pattern. A mantle or poncho slung across a man's shoulder is similarly decorated. The nudity of some figures on the vases may be an artistic device to identify the figure as male or female. Bronze statuettes of the same period are shown in realistic poses, but they show few details of dress: they wear hats and little else.

The Orientalizing and Archaic Periods

Evidence for clothing in the three centuries from 800 to 500 B.C. comes from life-size sculptures and from vase paintings. Artistic representations show two principal types of female dresses, the chiton and the peplos. The earlier of the two is the chiton, which is the garment shown on the earliest Greek statues of the so-called Daedalic style, such as the goddess in Auxerre (see fig. 2 in GREEK SCULPTURE AND GEMS) and the Nikandre statue (so called after the woman who dedicated the image on Delos). The chiton worn by these early figures is a simple narrow, tight-fitting garment, belted at the waist, sometimes worn with a short shawl draped symmetrically over both shoulders. Nikandre is one of the earliest examples of the class of standing marble statues known as *korai,* of which one of the best-known series is from the Athenian Acropolis. All beautifully dressed, they reflect the costume of fashionable ladies from 650 to 480 B.C. Chronological as well as regional distinctions account for many of the differences in the way they are represented by sculptors.

The typical dress of the later *korai* was the so-called Ionic chiton, a fuller garment whose crinkly texture and fine folds suggest linen. *Korai* from the Ionian cities of Asia Minor in the early sixth century B.C. (*ca.* 575 B.C.) were shown wearing this garment. It soon became the typical costume of the *korai* of Athens. Typical of Samos and Miletos in the early sixth century B.C. is a veil, a transparent, light, oblong piece of cloth, folded double lengthwise, worn over the head and falling in two layers over the back. One layer is pulled forward and tucked under the belt over the left hip. Attic *korai* more often followed another Ionian fashion, wearing a heavier mantle (himation) draped under the left arm and pinned over the right shoulder, forming an elegant and pleasing fall of stylized folds (see fig. 13 in CRAFTS AND CRAFTS-MEN). Although variously represented as wavy or spiral locks, the hairstyle of all the *korai* was basically the same: long tresses falling down the back and over the breasts in front.

Another woman's garment associated with the archaic period is the heavy, probably woolen, peplos with overfold that is fastened with long pins. One of its earliest appearances in art occurs on the François vase (see fig. 3 in GREEK PAINTING AND MOSAIC) where it is worn by goddesses and by other mythological females. Here it is brilliantly decorated with animal friezes. On other vases of the period mortal women are shown wearing peploi less elaborately decorated. The François vase also represents the garments worn by gods and men in the archaic period: young men wear short, dark-colored (therefore woolen) belted chitons, with decorated seams and arm openings. Older men have long, white chitons with dark, frequently decorated, mantles. For evidence on the normal costume of men during this period we rely principally on vase paintings. Attic *kouroi* are shown naked, as athletes, citizens, and soldiers; East Greek *kouroi*, however, wear mantles draped over their left shoulders. The simple narrower robe of the Daedalic statues, the so-called Doric chiton, was associated with the Peloponnese, the Ionian chiton and diagonally draped himation with East Greece. Athens changed from one to the other.

The change to the Ionic fashion took place gradually. Soon after 550 B.C. the East Greek convention of thin grooves and ridges in sculpture was generally adopted to repre-sent the crinkly texture of the full, fine linen chiton. The fashion was fully adopted by about 530 B.C. with the beginning of the red-figure style in vase painting, which reveled in the stylized representation of its fine folds and full transparent skirts, the swallowtail pattern of the mantle, and the elegant gesture of ladies holding out their long, trailing dresses at the side. Like the softer, clinging chitons, this style emphasized the soft, natural forms of the human body, which were sometimes shown beneath the cloth, almost as though the garments were made of transparent fabrics.

According to Thucydides (1.6) it was the Athenians who first of the mainland Greeks adopted in real life the luxury and refinement of the Ionian style of dress. Certainly the shift did not occur overnight; it was several decades before the Ionian style was commonly worn. But once accepted in Athens, and to an even greater degree in the Etruscan cities, it lasted well into the fifth century. Thucydides assures us that not long before his own time, the mid fifth century, older men from aristocratic families still wore the long Ionian robes, and tied up their long hair in the *krobylos* hairstyle, a kind of bun fastened with golden "grasshopper" pins (1.6; Aristophanes, *Knights* 1321–1334; *Clouds* 984–986).

The Greeks' northern and eastern neighbors, often represented in sculpture and painting, were clearly recognizable in real life by their dress as well as their language. These peoples, whom the Greeks called barbarians, included both real peoples such as the Phrygians, Trojans, Scythians, Persians, and Medes, living out near the borders of the civilized world, and legendary peoples such as the Amazons. Many were represented wearing warm, often plaid-patterned garments as a protection against the cold. For the northern tribes, and the Persians and Medes, who rode on horseback, leather pants were practical (Herodotus 1.71). On the great staircase of the Apadana (the audience hall) in Persepolis (*ca.* 500 B.C.) we see in the procession tribute-bearers bringing sleeved coats and pants, no doubt made of leather. Only the nobility wore the long-sleeved jacket, or *kandys,* evidently by this time a status symbol, slung over the shoulders. A curious detail of the Persian costume is that the sleeves were not only empty, but sewn closed, probably to show the king they hid no weapons. A splendid gold pectoral in Kiev shows two Scythians (from southern Russia) with needle and thread, making a sleeved fur jacket. A Phrygian hat with lappets that could be tied under the chin completed the outfit. In Athens in the fifth century the police force, which was made up of public slaves, usually Scythian, adopted this colorful costume as their uniform, including the bow and quiver. This was the costume worn on stage by the Scythian policeman in Aristophanes' *Women at the Thesmophoria,* and by Heracles, doubling as a policeman, on the famous vase by the "Berlin painter" of the satyrs' attempted rape of Hera.

Several items of non-Greek dress were borrowed at various times as exotic fashionable or practical attire, as in the case of the warm, gaily patterned wool mantle of the Thracians, worn by travelers, which could double as a blanket or sleeping bag along the way, and the wide-brimmed traveling hat (*petasos*), which was of Thessalian origin and worn by Hermes. The simple narrow-brimmed felt or leather hat (*pilos*) was worn by workers, or by Hephaestus as god of the forge.

Gods are shown wearing the same costumes as men, with special accessories serving as attributes to identify them. On the François vase, as elsewhere in art, Hera modestly holds her veil before her in the gesture of the wife; Athena was often armed, and wore the peplos with a snake-edged aegis; Hermes has his traveling hat; Apollo and Artemis, the archers, their bows and arrows.

The Classical Period

With the end of the Persian War (480 B.C.) came a reaction against the earlier aristocratic style, imported foreign luxuries, and artificial, complicated garments and drapery. The Severe style that emerges in art (480–450 B.C.), thoughtful, solemn, and slow, coincides with a change in fashion. Men wore short hair and short chitons. In Athens women rolled up their hair in a more practical fashion and once again adopted the woolen Doric peplos, which they had given up fifty or sixty years earlier. The men of Athens laid aside their long linen chitons and gold hair ornaments, as the sign of a way of life in which it was hard to distinguish between rich and poor (Thucydides, 1.6.4). Everything became more simple and democratic. Foreign elements were eliminated: only Orientals and servant girls wore garments with long, narrow sleeves attached.

The heavy folds of the women's woolen peplos were favored by the artists of the Severe style (see fig. 5 in GREEK SCULPTURE AND GEMS). The peplos was worn either alone or over a thin chiton, which became all but hidden by the heavier woolen garment. The peplos was folded over for about a third of its length to create the overfold; it was then draped around the body below the armpits, loosely gathered and fastened over both shoulders by long pins or brooches. The vertical opening, usually on the right side, could either be closed or left open. Young girls usually wore it open; they also wore a long overfold that could be let out as they grew. The peplos could be belted in various ways. If a mantle was worn over the peplos, it hung down much farther than the archaic himation and was draped in a different way.

In the classical period proper (450–430 B.C.), the representation of costumes changed more than the costumes themselves. On the Parthenon frieze there is a good deal of subtle variation in the costumes represented, but the differences are understated (see fig. 8 in GREEK SCULPTURE AND GEMS). The frieze itself represents the procession of the panathenaic festival, when a new garment was presented to the olive-wood statue of Athena Polias, presumably to be worn by the statue for the four-year interval between festivals. According to all the sources this was a richly decorated peplos (*Inscriptiones Graecae* I,2.8011; Plato, *Euthyphro* 6o; Euripides, *Hecuba* 468; Aristotle, *Constitution of Athens* 49.3; 60.1), woven by Athenian noblewomen and carried up to the Acropolis, after having been displayed as a sail on the mast of a wheeled ship that was drawn to the base of the Acropolis. The fact that it could serve as a sail is evidence that this peplos was a simple rectangular piece of fabric, and this is confirmed by the picture of the peplos being handed to a priestess on the east side of the Parthenon frieze.

In this context it may be wise to note that although the term *peplos* was applied by the Greeks to the simple rectangular garment with overfold that is worn by Athena and other Greek women, the term is by no means restricted to this use. The peploi worn by the Great King and the Persian elders in Aeschylus' *Persians* (468, 1030, 1060) and by the Armenian king Tigranes (Xenophon, *Education of Cyrus* 3.1.13), could not be the simple woolen garment we have described. Nor was *peplos* the only term by which this garment was called. Herodotus, in a story about a shift from Doric to Ionian fashion (5.87), states that the Athenian women killed the lone returning soldier (from a military expedition against Aegina) with the pins from their himatia; from the context, however, it appears he meant the garment we call a peplos. The death-bringing garment that Deianira sends to Herakles is called both a chiton and a peplos (Sophocles, *Women of Trachis* 602, 612, 758). *Peplos* probably had some connotation similar to our word "robe" (as did, perhaps, *chiton* and *himation*). The simplicity in the form of these garments was matched by a flexibility in the vocabulary applied to them.

In democratic Greek society, persons of all social standings and professions could, generally speaking, wear whatever they preferred and could afford. Certain garments, however, were deemed more appropriate for some people than others. The regular costume of gods and mature men was the himation, draped over the left shoulder, under the right arm, and back over the left shoulder to fall in front. It left the right arm and shoulder bare (see fig. 14 in GREEK SCULPTURE AND GEMS). Elderly men and women wore long chitons, younger men short ones. For warriors, horsemen, and travelers, a short chlamys pinned over the shoulder was more practical than a loosely draped mantle. Children's clothing was not belted and was provided with a large overfold so that it could be lengthened as the child grew. Philosophers wore the *tribon,* a rough, threadbare cloak of dark color, and generally neglected their appearance and let their beards grow.

Certain special costumes—as distinct from normal dress—were developed and in time became set in their final forms: tragic and comic costumes, sports costumes, divine and priestly dress, attributes of non-Greeks and of mythological figures, and costumes of professions. Some of these characteristic habits, virtual uniforms, have survived to our own day together with their original connotations. Priests wore long, free-flowing chitons or robes that were not belted; charioteers and musicians the same robe but belted. Actors in tragedy covered their arms with long sleeves just as they covered their faces with masks so that they could play a variety of roles. Because they represented kings and queens, their costumes were woven with rich patterns. Active persons such as craftsmen, farmers, and shepherds, as well as poor people and slaves, wore narrow chitons, sometimes fastened only on the left, leaving the right shoulder bare. But there was no legally sanctioned standard dress. When not appearing nude, young men taking part in the panathenaic procession wore a variety of garments; they dressed in short chitons, or short cavalrymen's cloaks pinned at the shoulder or throat, with wide petasoi (traveling hats), or even fox-skin caps. There was no uniform for the young riders who took part in the military review, or *dokimasia.*

In the late fifth century B.C. we note the occasional appearance of the sleeved Persian jacket (*kandys*) on women and small children. This adoption of a barbarian fashion may have been due, it has been suggested, to the influence of Euripides' *Medea* (431 B.C.). But during the Peloponnesian War (431–404 B.C.) and its immediate aftermath, vase paintings show more effeminate figures, richer garments, pretty postures, and delicately curved lines. The "Meidias painter," who was enormously influential, specialized in rich swirling draperies, elaborate hairstyles, and soft, luxurious figures. Clinging, transparent drapery was represented on sculpture as well as in painting. There was obviously what amounted to a new fashion; whether the Athenians were conscious of this or not is unclear.

Fourth-century representations of dress, mostly from outside Athens, show that the costumes of this period are still classical—simple basic forms, arranged in a variety of ways. The delicate, lighter fabrics of the women's chitons fall in fine folds, contrasting with the heavy drapery of the himation. The mantle sometimes falls in back from the shoulders. The belt divides the garment more evenly.

The Hellenistic Period

In the Hellenistic period (300 to 30 B.C.), luxury comes back, along with variety. Richly colored and patterned fabrics, sometimes decorated with embroidery after the Near Eastern fashion, were worn at the royal courts, especially at Alexandria and Pergamum. Silk was now used. From Alexandria came a new women's fashion: a narrow, sleeveless chiton tied in a high-waisted manner with a narrow belt that was just below the breasts in front, much like the nineteenth-century empire style (see fig. 5 in CRAFTS AND CRAFTSMEN). The chiton was made of fine linen, but was not as full as the Ionian chiton of the sixth century. It had a long overfall and was simply pinned once at each shoulder, giving a sleeveless effect. The earliest figures wearing such dresses date from about 275 B.C. During this period artistic devices such as the dramatic billowing drapery worn by gods and giants on the Altar of Pergamum are developed simultaneously with realistic details as in the colorful blue, pink, and gold garments, the mantles, and the sun hats worn by the fashionable ladies represented in terra-cotta Tanagra statuettes. The new style made women look more slender, as did a new costume, a pinned robe made of a costly wool weave called a *peronatris.* It was attached at the shoulders with fibulae, and was worn over the chiton. Another novelty was a chlamys with rounded "Macedonian" edges.

Hairstyles, jewelry, and footwear in this period were all rich and colorful and carefully represented. Men now affected the full-haired, clean-shaven style of the young Alexander. A favorite hairstyle of women was achieved by combing the hair back and dividing it by a number of parts, creating a "melon" effect. Women wore a great deal of jewelry: Herakles' knots as bracelets and garters, and a new type of body jewelry, gold chains crossing the breasts in front over the chiton and fastened with a rosette or brooch. The latter is shown on statues of the nude Aphrodite.

The adoption of barbarian dress encouraged by Alexander in the East shocked the Greeks back home perhaps more than any other feature of Alexander's reign, except his adoption of the Persian-derived ritual salute of the monarch (*proskynesis*). The so-called Macedonian *kausia,* a pancake-shaped felt hat represented on coins and terra-cotta figures of the Hellenistic period, has been shown to be identical with a cap still worn today by men in Afghanistan. It came to the Mediterranean as a campaign hat worn by Alexander and veterans of his campaigns in India.

ETRUSCAN DRESS

During the Greek Orientalizing period, the people of the region now called Tuscany developed their own civilization in close contact with Greek and Near Eastern culture. From the figures represented in their art, from about 800 to 100 B.C., it appears that their clothes conformed in general to the prevailing Greek fashions—Orientalizing, archaic, classical, and Hellenistic—but there were always differences. In the Orientalizing period, the mineral resources of the Etruscans brought them great wealth; this is reflected in the dress of the period, particularly the gold jewelry, decorated with gaudy granulation or filigree in the south (Caere, modern Cerveteri, and the Latin city of Praeneste, now Palestrina), and using the more refined *pulviscolo* (dusting) technique in the north (Vetulonia). They doubtless learned these advanced techniques, as well as the use of a variety of hats and many garments to signify high status (nudity was adopted only as an artistic convention) from the Near East, possibly by way of the Phoenicians.

Etruscan athletes and young men wore short pants (*perizoma*); older men wore a long linen chiton with a heavy woolen mantle (himation or *chlaina*) pinned at the shoulder with a fibula or brooch. The short chiton was worn less frequently than in Greece or in the East; a three-quarter chiton, more

eastern than Greek, was often used instead. Men wore their hair bobbed, in the Greek Daedalic style. Women wore the usual long chiton, but over it they wore a long mantle covering only the back, and a long back braid. Hats, worn more frequently than in Greece, included the simple Greek *pilos* and the petasos, as well as pointed or sugar-loaf "oriental" models. Women wore these as well as the men. In general, throughout their history Etruscan women are distinguished by dressing more like men than in Greece; they also were represented wearing more outer garments, perhaps because they participated more in public life.

Orientalizing styles of art and dress lasted longer in Etruria than in Greece. By the mid sixth century B.C., many Ionian elements had been adopted, probably by way of Greek colonies in southern Italy and Sicily. In art the thin linen Ionian tunic or chiton replaced the earlier straight woolen chiton, although a fine chiton with many folds had already been known in the seventh century B.C. The peplos with overfold was never adopted as a real garment in Etruria, although it was occasionally represented on statuettes of Athena. Pointed shoes in the Ionian style became the rage for both men and women between 550 and about 475 B.C.; after this date they were used as attributes of female divinities. Typical for women was the high chignon (*tutulus*), often covered by a veil or the Greek kerchief (*mitra*). Men wore their hair in long ringlets, and either the rectangular himation or the rounded *tebenna,* the forerunner of the Roman toga. On the Apollo from Veii, a purple-bordered *tebenna* covers a fine chiton (fig. 4). The *trabea,* a short version of this rounded mantle, worn in Rome at the time of Tarquinius Superbus (*ca.* 534–510 B.C.), the last king of Rome, was adopted as Roman religious dress.

From about 450 to 300 B.C. Etruscan garments conformed more closely to Greek dress, but certain local features gave them a

Figure 4. Apollo from Veii, wearing a chiton (tunic) and purple-bordered *tebenna*, terra-cotta, *ca.* 515 B.C. ROME, MUSEO NAZIONALE DI VILLA GIULIA. *ALINARI/ART RESOURCE*

distinctive appearance: a reluctance to show male nudity, the rounded *tebenna* of the men, a special chiton with tassel for important ladies, heavier garments, and more accessories such as shoes, hats, and rich jewelry. The latter included bronze or gold locket-shaped pendants (*bullae*) worn by Etruscan and Latin women on necklaces and by men —for whom they evidently were a mark of honor—on bracelets on the upper arm. The legend of Tarpeia, who betrayed Rome to the Sabines, asking in return for what they carried on their left arms (Livy, *History of Rome* 1.11) may be connected with the tradition of wearing these gold bracelets with pendant *bullae* of Italic style. Perhaps the rings with *bullae* worn on the arms by grown men may have been necklaces when they were boys. In the fifth century B.C. the Etruscans borrowed from their northern neighbors, the Celts, the twisted necklace or torque, which was for them a badge of honor. Necklaces, both beaded and hung with huge pendants, were worn, the latter by men as well as women. The shape of earrings is a useful criterion for dating; they were huge in the seventh century B.C., barrel-shaped in the sixth, formed like clusters of grapes in the fifth and fourth, then pendant drops like those characteristic of sculpture from Taras (Tarentum, Taranto) and Latium of the fourth and third centuries B.C.

In general the fashions of the Hellenistic period contrasted with the heavily clothed look of the previous century, but the third century B.C. still favored accessories; jewelry and shoes were worn as much by naked as by dressed figures of both sexes. Countless figures of Etruscan nymphs wear only slippers and a torque or necklace; a fashionable nudity prevailed for male and female figures from Greek mythology. Women's chitons were belted high, at the breasts, as in Greece; body jewelry or double straps were often worn. Long, loose hair was in vogue for both men and women. Women also wore their hair bound up with a diadem or kerchief, or loosely tied, often with a loose topknot. By the end of this period Etruria had been absorbed by the Romans, and the *tebenna* had become the toga, worn by all Romans or Italians, including the Etruscans, as a mark of Roman citizenship.

ROMAN DRESS

Despite the great changes that took place during the course of a thousand years of Roman dress, we can nevertheless list two basic differences between Greek and Roman dress. First, Greek patterns were basically simple, Roman patterns complicated. Greek garments were based on a rectangular pattern—exceptions such as the rounded Hellenistic chlamys were rare. The Romans used a variety of forms aside from the rectangle; there were polygonal, rounded, elliptical, and cross-shaped patterns, with separate pieces or curved edges. Furthermore, although Greek garments were always woven in one piece, some Roman clothes, for example tunics, were often made up of separate parts, fitted and stitched together.

The second difference is that Greek dress expressed the choices of the individual. It varied with the mood or intent of the wearer; he or she decided when to put on party clothes or a traveling outfit. Roman dress was specialized for different functions. It was bad form to wear anything but the proper formal dinner attire, the *synthesis,* at a party. At different ages, people wore different clothes: a young girl wore a toga, a woman did not. An upper-class boy wore a *toga praetexta* (a white toga with purple bands along the borders), and changed it for a *toga pura* (a white toga) when he came of age. Decoration on Greek and Etruscan clothes was purely ornamental; on Roman garments it was symbolic. Roman dress marked the social class of the wearer. A citizen wore toga and shoes; a senator, a consul, a knight, or a priest was recognized by his special garb.

Materials and Fabrics

The Romans used the same raw materials for their clothing as the Greeks. Throughout Italy herds of sheep were kept for their wool.

White, gray, brown, and black breeds were reared. An especially fine wool was produced in the southern Italian Greek colony of Taras, which from 272 B.C. was Roman, under the name of Tarentum (now Taranto). Linen and silk were imported in great quantities for the clothing of the luxury-loving Romans of the imperial period. Herdsmen and country people contented themselves with coarse weaves, made of wool or goat's hair. In parts of the empire fabrics were even made from the hair of beavers, hares, and camels. The Romans imported much more, both raw materials and finished textiles, than the Greeks. In fact it has been noted that Italy contributed little in the way of either textile output or technical ideas. The two major textile-producing centers in the Roman world lay at opposite ends of the empire, in northern Gaul and Syria.

The Etruscans who ruled central Italy in the first centuries of the first millennium B.C. —and Rome until about 510 B.C.—probably introduced linen garments. Cotton was brought to Italy from Egypt after the Asiatic wars, about 190 B.C. Especially popular in the late imperial and Byzantine periods, silk (*serica*) was obtained from China and India— in part as raw silk, but also as thread and as finished textiles. The Parthian banners of the army that defeated Crassus' army at Carrhae (Altıbaşak, Haran) in 53 B.C. were of silk. Although rare, silk was an object of trade from the earliest times, known even to the prehistoric communities of northern Europe.

Preparation of Fabrics, Manufacture and Distribution

Roman clothing of the Republican period was still made by women working at home. By the end of the republic cloth could be bought at the market. Augustus not only insisted on wearing homemade clothes but encouraged traditional household crafts along with traditional customs and home and family virtues. As usual, Roman religious conservatism preserved older traditions; the wife of the high priest of Jupiter long continued to weave his official robe (*laena*) with her own hands. When home production could no longer fulfill the needs of the enormous population and the armies of the empire, textile factories came into being. Aside from the vertical loom of the Greeks and the Egyptian horizontal loom, both of which were used by the Romans, new types of looms were developed, especially for the complicated tapestry weaving of rich patterns that came into use in the later period.

Textile factories were established in lands of Asia Minor when they were taken over by the Romans. In Laodicea ad Lycum (Denizli) in Phrygia and Selge (Serik) in Pisidia, for example, the sleeved tunic (*dalmatica*) and the hooded cloak (*birrus*) were manufactured. In Tyre in Phoenicia imperial factories were set up to produce purple dye. In Rome and in all the large cities of the empire there were workshops and factories for mass production and distribution, where cloaks were prepared and distributed to the garrisons in Mediolanum (Milan), Lugdunum (Lyons), Nemetacum (Arras), and Vienna (Vienne). There were also specialty shops, some in Rome, that sold only purple garments (*taberna purpurea*). Byzantium was the center of the silk trade.

The Romans began to manufacture clothing on a considerable scale. Many workers specialized, limiting themselves to only one of the many steps involved in the production of textiles. Weavers of wool (*lanarii*) were distinguished from weavers of linen (*linteones*). Among the dyers (*infectores*), those who worked with purple (*purpurarii*) were especially esteemed. The art of embroidery was indigenous to Phrygia and embroiderers were perhaps brought thence to Rome, which would explain why embroiderers were called *phrygiones*. Male embroiderers (*seg-*

mentarii) worked the patterns of the rectangular, triangular, and circular trimmings that were woven into or stitched onto late Roman clothing. *Strophiarii* prepared women's chestbands; *ornatrices* prepared ornaments. Among the workers who produced clothing (*vestifici*), the Romans distinguished between those who worked fine garments (*tenuarii*), rain cloaks (*paenularii*), soldiers' cloaks (*sagarii*), and trousers (*bracarii*). Tailors (*sartores*) were perhaps the same workers as those who made slaves' clothing from rags (*centonarii*). Many workers—fullers, for example—sold their services or products directly to the consumer, and others to merchants, who were likewise specialized.

Dyeing and Decoration

Along with the garments themselves, the Romans adopted the colors of oriental, Egyptian, Etruscan, and Greek clothing. These colors, however, were used by wearers according to their station in life. Purple in particular was used for decorative borders and stripes denoting class distinctions. A toga dyed entirely with the true purple obtained from the purple snail (*murex*) was reserved for emperors. The *toga praetexta* was worn by senators and other high officials. Boys of noble families wore both the *toga praetexta* and a tunic with stripes. When they left school, they would exchange the *toga praetexta* for the *toga pura* or *toga virilis*. The term *candidate* derives from the *toga candida*, a white robe that was worn by young men when they stood for public office. Dark-colored wool was worn by agricultural workers, shepherds, slaves, and other poor people. Dark colors were also worn for mourning. Women wore garments of many colors. As in Greece, yellow obtained from the crocus seems to have been favored. Brides wore a flame-colored, red-orange veil (*flammeum*).

The decoration of Roman clothing often had symbolic meaning. Wide stripes indicated a higher station than narrow ones. A senator could wear a tunic with wide vertical stripes (*tunica laticlavia*), while a knight wore a tunic with narrower stripes (*tunica angusticlavia*). (Later, under the empire, the privilege of wearing the *tunica laticlavia* was extended.) The stripes descended vertically from the shoulders, sometimes all the way to the bottom seam. Although usually woven in, they sometimes were prepared on a tapestry loom and sewn on or set into the fabric. Decorative stripes became progressively richer and more varied: geometric, floral, and figural motifs were used in combination, woven with white, yellow, brown, black, red, blue, and violet yarns. These stripes and the round and square trimmings that were attached to tunics in later times made these undergarments stiff (fig. 5). The Romans, like Near Easterners, eventually also sewed metal ornaments onto their garments, which further stiffened them. Such ornaments have been found at Kerch (ancient Panticapaeum) in southern Russia, and in Etruria.

The Form of Garments

The Romans themselves distinguished between an undergarment that was put on (*indutus*) and a draped outer garment (*amictus*), a mantle or cloak. Each type changed in the course of time, but we might start by describing the garments involved. The basic undergarment, made of linen, was a pair of trunks or a loincloth, the equivalent of the Greek *perizoma*. Worn by both men and women from the earliest days to the end of the empire, it was called a *subligar, subligaculum,* or *cinctus,* as it was wrapped and tied about the body; or it was called a *campestre* because it was worn in the exercise grounds at the Campus Martius. It became visible only when someone stripped naked, as did manual laborers, athletes, gladiators, and soldiers at the exercise ground. Con-

Figure 5. High Roman official wearing decorated *tunica manicata* and cloak (*paludamentum*). Detail from the Great Hunt mosaic in the villa at Piazza Armerina in Sicily, *ca.* A.D. 320–360. *ALINARI/ART RESOURCE*

servative families that clung to the old ways wore nothing else under the toga; *cincuti Cethegi*, Horace (*Art of Poetry* 50) calls them, implying that they were old-fashioned.

The tunic—the Latin word comes from the Greek *chiton*—resembled in shape the Greek archaic chiton, with openings for the arms at the sides rather than at the top edge (see fig. 11 in ROMAN SCULPTURE AND GEMS). Usually of wool, it was made of two pieces, seamed at the sides, and was long enough to reach from the neck to the calves; it could be shortened by pulling it up from the belt.

Sleeved tunics (*manicatae*) and longer tunics (*talares*) that reached to the heels were known in the late republic, but were considered effeminate; they did not become common until the third century A.D. (Augustine, *On Christian Doctrine* 3.2). In the house, or at work, a Roman citizen wore the tunic alone; but during the republic and early empire he never appeared in public without the toga.

The woman's tunic, sometimes made of linen, was longer than that of the men, had no stripes (*clavi*), and was generally fuller and looser. Women wore, in addition to the *subligar*, a brassiere (*strophium*). It was made of linen, or leather, and supported, bound, and shaped the breasts. The *strophium*, represented on numerous works of Roman art, is also mentioned in erotic literature (e.g., the mention in *Palatine Anthology* 5.13, of an older woman so youthful-looking she needs no brassiere). People who suffered from the cold could wear an extra tunic, or long underwear reaching just below the knee. Such knee breeches were worn by soldiers on the northern campaigns pictured on the Column of Trajan in Rome (see fig. 8 in ROMAN SCULPTURE AND GEMS), probably indicating a military use of the full-length trousers (*bracae*) worn by Celts. More common for civilians were the knee-trousers (*feminalia*) Augustus wore for extra warmth (Suetonius, *Lives of the Twelve Caesars*, "Augustus" 82), also called bandages (*fasciae*) or leggings (*tibialia*).

The most traditional and important outer garment was the toga, a half ellipse with one straight and one oblong side; this shape could be easily finished on the loom in one piece (fig. 6). During most of Roman history, a Roman who did not wear the toga ran the risk of being taken for a workman or a slave. Wearing the toga, together with the shoes (*calcei*), was the equivalent of saying, "Civis romanus sum" (I am a citizen of Rome). Yet it was not always so. The Romans themselves remembered a time when the toga

was worn by both men and women—not just men—and served as an all-purpose cover, a dress by day and a blanket by night. The shape of the toga and the manner of draping it distinguished it from the rectangular Greek himation, as the monuments show. Several anecdotes also illustrate this difference, and its connotations. It was by means of their dress that the Roman inhabitants of Asia were picked out by their assassins in 88 B.C. (Athenaeus, *The Learned Banquet* 5.213). Augustus once ordered an exchange of togas and himatia to symbolize understanding between Greeks and Romans (Suetonius, *Lives of the Twelve Caesars*, "Augustus" 98). The Romans were *gens togata*, "the toga-wearing people," by Vergil's definition (*Aeneid* 1.282).

The rectangular Greek himation was also worn in Rome, where it was called the pallium. Pallium and sandals constituted the dress of Greeks, philosophers, Greek gods like Aesculapius (Asklepios), and Romans when at home or when the occasion did not require them to wear the formal toga. The plays of Plautus and Terence, set in Greece, were called *fabulae palliatae*, because the actors dressed as Greeks. Eventually the pallium was taken over as the mantle of the Christians, as we hear from Tertullian, who

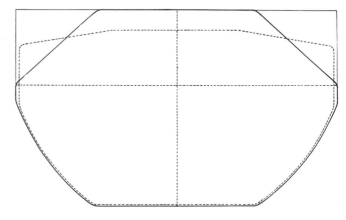

Figure 6. Diagram of the toga on the Ara Pacis. *Reproduced from Lillian M. Wilson,* THE CLOTHING OF THE ANCIENT ROMANS © 1938 BY THE JOHNS HOPKINS PRESS

wrote a treatise on the subject, *On the Robe.* Women normally wore the feminine equivalent, the palla. Custom dictated that the male toga on a woman was the sign of a prostitute. Children, however, wore the toga, at least until the time of Augustus, as can be seen on several monuments. There was no difference between boys and girls in this respect. It was also the custom for married women to cover their heads in public, in Rome as in Greece. A patrician once divorced his wife because she had gone to the Forum bareheaded (Valerius Maximus, 6.3.10). The veil, made of linen, was the sign of a lady.

There were specialized mantles and cloaks designed to fit more closely than the draping of pallium or toga would allow. The military cloaks worn by officers (*paludamenta*) and soldiers (*saga*) corresponded to the Greek chlamys, but were generally somewhat longer (see fig. 13 in ROMAN SCULPTURE AND GEMS). Several cloaks designed to be worn in bad weather were either polygonal or rounded. A light rain mantle (*lacerna*) had a rounded lower border. A heavy stiff wool cape (*birrus*), woven in one piece with a hood (*cucullus*), was fastened at the neck with a fibula. A thick cape (*paenula*) was woven as a circle that fit around the neck, covered the entire body including the arms, and was fastened in the middle of the front. It was regularly provided with a hood.

Changes in Fashion

Certain Roman fashions changed rapidly, especially in certain periods; others, fossilized as ritual fashions, lasted with little or no change over surprisingly long periods of time. For the earliest period of Roman history (600–400 B.C.), when the Latin speakers of Rome were only one of many varied groups of early Italians, the evidence provided by archaeology and by such later scholarly classical authors as Servius, Varro, and Suetonius yield information about fashion changes. Since the Augustan restoration laid great stress on ritual garments from this early period, they are featured prominently in the art and literature of Augustus' time.

Republican Roman (400–100 B.C.) dress can be reconstructed from contemporary monuments such as the third-century triumphal paintings from the tomb of a noble Roman on the Esquiline, and from contemporary authors such as Plautus and Terence. The dress of non-Romans, especially Celts (called Gauls by the Romans) and Carthaginians, was known to the Romans.

In the late republic and early empire (100 B.C.–A.D. 250) the dress of a wide variety of groups and social classes is illustrated on contemporary monuments (funerary reliefs, paintings from Pompeii and Dura-Europos); costumes and ritual dress of priests, vestals, magistrates, and emperors appear on historical reliefs and portrait statues. Contemporary authors from Livy to Plutarch and Tertullian record and comment on Roman ways of dressing and what they meant.

The late empire (A.D. 250–600) sees many changes, as illustrated in the art and implied by legal and other writings of the period. The official toga is transformed and, at the same time, replaced by the pallium and *paenula,* which become the normal dress of the middle class. The long-sleeved tunic and the long trousers of the barbarians also come into common usage at this time. The gap between normal dress and special costumes becomes wider: Byzantine mosaics in Ravenna dating from this period illustrate the splendid clothing and ornament of the emperors and their court. Earlier everyday Roman garments became fossilized as liturgical dress by the church. Classical garments continue to be represented in art. Figures in theatrical dress, with masks and scarves, decorate fourth-century manuscripts of the plays of Terence. Changes earlier described by Tertullian (*On the Robe*) now became more pronounced: people in the first century B.C. chose their dress so that their appearance would show their religious stand in the complex world they inhabited.

The developments in clothing in each of these periods may now be discussed in detail. The earliest shepherds and farmers who lived in the Iron Age at the site of Rome, in the hills and groves by the Tiber, dressed—as a later age imagined—in animal-skin pants or loincloths like those long preserved as ritual dress by the primitive Lupercalian priesthood, dating back to Rome's rural past. Men and women covered themselves with warm mantles, doubling as blankets, woven from the wool of their sheep, which they fastened with bronze fibulae or brooches; some of these fibulae have been found in Villanovan burials. Women and men both wore high belts of bronze over leather backings, shaped like willow leaves. When the men left their fields to go to war they wore their *perizoma*-like loincloths, tied and belted, and a type of Villanovan helmet, of bronze or leather, with a point or apex much like that of the priests pictured on the Ara Pacis (Augustus' "Altar of Peace").

Soon Rome's Etruscan and Latin neighbors at Praeneste, Veii, and Cerveteri had developed rich cities and were importing luxury items from abroad: amber from the Baltic by way of northern Italy, gold and ivory from the East, styles and fashions from the Greeks. They were weaving their own fine linen. At Decima, near Rome, a woman was buried in a robe sewn with carved amber and glass beads, wearing a gold and amber pectoral and gold spiral hair-rings.

During the sixth century B.C. Rome was, according to tradition, ruled by Etruscan kings. Although Etruscan influence touched neither their language nor their religion, it changed outward signs of civilization: writing, monumental temples, and styles of dress. Among the distinctive features of Roman dress that derive from Etruscan fash-

ion are complicated patterns with separate pieces stitched together or rounded edges, a tendency to wear more clothes than the Greeks did, covering a greater part of the body, and wearing more outer garments and accessories—mantles, tunics, shoes, hats, jewelry. Etruscan influence is clearest in certain garments denoting civil rank, magistracies, or priesthoods, and the costume connected with the institution of the triumph. The attributes of the Salian priesthood, who wore a military costume—a short mantle (*trabea*), helmetlike cap, wide bronze belt, and short tunic (Livy, 20.4)—during special processions and feast days in Rome go back to this time or shortly after. So do other priestly attributes (the headdress of the priest's wife, for example).

By their own definition, the Romans were distinguished from non-Italian peoples as the *gens togata*. The rounded toga contrasted with the rectangular pallium and constituted the visible mark of a Roman citizen. The garment and the name by which Greek authors referred to it, *tebenna*, were Etruscan in origin. Special types of togas were also Etruscan, the *toga praetexta* with purple border, for example, which in Roman times became a symbol of rank or office. Boys of the nobility also wore it, together with an amulet (*bulla*). Closest in form to the original *tebenna* was the Roman *trabea*. According to tradition, it too had been the custom of early kings. It was purple and scarlet, with a purple border, fastened with a fibula. The feature that most resembled the Etruscan *tebenna* was its length: the *trabea*, worn by knights on horseback, was considerably shorter than the toga.

The Romans' claim that their shoes (*calcei*) were derived from early Etruscan footwear is confirmed by archaic Etruscan monuments, which show that the laced, pointed shoe, worn with the rounded mantle (*tebenna*), was a purely local style in Etruria just after 550 B.C. The shoes of the typical Etruscan *togatus* of this period, as well as of the figures on the Ara Pacis (late first century B.C.), are all high boots reaching up to mid calf, with horizontal straps above the ankle; only the point has been lost in the later models.

The manner of draping a toga or mantle in what the Romans called the *cinctus Gabinus* (girding in the manner of the town of Gabii) is illustrated on Etruscan representations of active figures from this period. Literary sources connect the *cinctus Gabinus* with an ancient war costume—the ancient Latins wore no armor, but simply wrapped their mantles about themselves when they went to war; the army was thus said to be girded (*praecincta*). In this later period the *cinctus Gabinus* and ritual veiling of the head were distinguishing features of the garb of those performing or assisting at sacrifices. Etruscan influence affected the costume and accessories used in the most prestigious honor a Roman could be awarded, the triumph: the dress and insignia of the triumphator or triumphing general—the *toga purpurea, tunica palmata* (presumably a tunic with a border one handspan wide), and golden *bullae*—the chariot, and other traditional paraphernalia.

Between the fifth and third centuries B.C. Celts settled in Italy, where they became a familiar sight to Etruscans and Romans. Their warriors were often represented in art as naked, wearing only a belt and a twisted necklace or torque. The Roman Titus Manlius Torquatus reputedly gained his surname from the collar he took from a Celt he had killed in combat. These northerners wore practical clothes of leather, fur, or heavy wool. Roman sources give detailed descriptions of their appearance. They were tall and had long hair or blond, bleached, bristly hair that they treated with a special soap to make it stand out straight. They were horsemen, and wore fitted pants, fitted shirts, or *chemises,* and heavy wool mantles or capes, many with hoods.

Because it was convenient to have their wealth portable, they wore a great deal of gold, especially in the form of the collars or torques so often represented on the men. Torques are found mostly in women's graves: apparently this mark of honor was passed on from father to son or leader to leader, rather than buried with its owner; but a man's widow was permitted to take his collar with her to her grave. So impressed were the Romans with the appearance of the Celts that they eventually named the areas where they settled according to their dress: Gallia Bracata, or "pants-wearing Gaul," was southern Gaul, Narbonensis; the rest was Gallia Comata, "long-haired Gaul." They later borrowed from the Celts many of their practical garments, and the Celtic words for mantle, cape, drape, breeches, and chemise, as well as beaver fur, came into Latin at this time; our modern forms are little different from the original words.

The Carthaginians were also recognized by their barbarian dress: they wore neither mantle nor toga, but only an unbelted tunic, ankle-length, with long, wide sleeves, and were so portrayed by Plautus in his play *The Little Carthaginian.* Artistic representations on stelae show that the men's tunics were sometimes belted, and that the women had adopted a Greek style of dress by the third century B.C. (According to Tertullian [*On the Robe* 1], old-fashioned Carthaginians *ca.* A.D. 200 wore a straight, narrow mantle fastened with fibulae.) Priests were splendidly dressed in purple, with wide, fringed bands. Carthaginian textiles were famous. Much use was made of jewelry: both men and women wore heavy necklaces, nose rings, and earrings, as both artistic representations and archaeological finds show.

The Romans of the republic resisted such oriental luxury. Judas Maccabaeus in 167 B.C. registered his surprise at seeing that the powerful Roman senators wore neither diadems nor purple, the established Hellenistic signs of royalty (1 *Maccabees* 8:14); and King Prusias II of Bithynia (182–149 B.C.) removed his diadem and purple garments as a sign of submission and put on the cap and clothes of a Roman freedman when a Roman senatorial embassy visited him (Diodorus Siculus, *Histories* 31.15.2). Sumptuary measures restricting luxury dress enacted in 215 B.C. in the course of the Second Punic War (218–201 B.C.) forbade women to own more than half an ounce of gold or to wear multicolored clothes; the debate on the Oppian law as recorded by Livy (34.1–8) includes the vigorous defense of the women, which led to its repeal (195 B.C.), and records the general use of colored textiles and gold to display status.

Inevitably, Hellenistic luxury was added to native rituals, in particular the triumphs. Those accorded to Scipio Africanus in 201 B.C. (Appian, *Roman History* 8.66) and to Lucius Aemilius Paullus Macedonicus in 167 B.C. (Plutarch, *Parallel Lives*, "Aemilius Paullus" 34) are typical of the new type of triumph, in which unheard-of splendor and enormous personal prestige were bestowed on the victorious generals. The old triumphal *toga purpurea* and *tunica palmata* now seemed old-fashioned and plain and were replaced by more elaborate dress, the *toga picta*, decorated with designs in gold threads, and a newly styled *tunica palmata*, which was now decorated with palm branches. We can turn to the triumphal portrait of Vel Saties in the François tomb from Vulci to see the effect of the purple *toga picta* (although what he wears is a rectangular himation, not a toga); for at this time the clothes of the Etruscans and the Romans influenced each other in connotations and symbolism. The bronze statue of the Orator (*Arringatore*), made around 100 B.C., wears the official, formal dress uniform of a Roman magistrate in the republic: the *toga praetexta* and a striped tunic (*clavus*), gold ring, and heavy shoes with laces (fig. 7). But the toga is worn in the short, Etruscan style.

The period of the late republic and early

Figure 7. Bronze statue of Aulus Metellus, called the "Orator" (Arringatore), wearing a shorter version of the Roman toga, derived from the *tebenna, ca.* 100 B.C. FLORENCE, MUSEO ARCHEOLOGICO INV. NR. 249. *ALINARI*

empire sees the crystallization and stabilization of real fashions and of the ritual garments of priests, Vestal Virgins, and magistrates, now illustrated on historical reliefs and official statues. The triumphal insignia and costume become the exclusive property of the emperor, starting with Augustus. Despite repeated attempts on the part of several emperors to regulate the use of the expensive, "royal" sea purple from Tyre, unrestricted private use of purple so increased that there was a huge demand for purple throughout the first and second centuries A.D. The Christians soon joined Roman moralists in denouncing this conspicuous consumption: Tertullian called it the devil's pomp, for purple was associated with the garments of pagan priests and gods; and he ranted against women who used it. Most clothesmakers probably used inferior, imitation purple dyes, rather than the expensive sea purple from the *murex.* In the second century purple became increasingly associated with the imperial insignia. Not only the triumphal purple *toga picta,* an exclusively imperial dress worn on special occasions, but also the general's purple cloak became symbols of imperial sovereignty.

Until the time of Augustus small girls wore togas; on the Ara Pacis, little Domitia, granddaughter of Mark Antony, wears the same Augustan type as her brother Gnaeus Domitius Ahenobarbus and cousin Germanicus (fig. 8). Women wore the rectangular palla, which remained unchanged in form although there were surely changing fashions in color, cloth, and decoration. Funerary reliefs of couples show clearly the difference between the husband's rounded toga and the wife's rectangular mantle, draped over her head. Women could vary their appearance by means of wigs. These came in different shapes; portrait statues, for example that of Caracalla's wife, Plautilla, in the Louvre, had removable hair, so that the statue could be kept fashionable by changing the style of wig. Yellow was by far the favorite color; blond hair was imported from Gaul, Germany, or Britain. Even as early as about 500 B.C., Etruscan ladies with blond hair had been portrayed at banquets in tomb paintings: they either dyed their hair or wore wigs. Messalina's wig was blond. Old women realized that they could turn black and white hair blond, which they thought was more attractive; they could even turn white hair black (Tertullian, *On Women's Appearance* 10).

The toga acquired its fixed form in the time of Augustus, as the prescribed dress for magistrates during their terms of public office. It was draped over the left shoulder, across the back and under the right arm and thrown across the breast and over the left shoulder so that the end hung down the back. A section was folded over, to form a deep hollow (*sinus*). By reaching under the fold across the breast, the wearer could partially draw up the portion hanging in front (*umbo*) and drape it over the fold, making it fairly secure. The straight edge hung in back to the ankles, although not so far down as in front.

In the first century A.D., Quintilian gives orators explicit instructions on how to arrange and wear their togas. The fashion continued to develop in the direction of a more securely draped toga. In the Flavian period, toward the end of the first century A.D., the *umbo* became a large sacklike bulge. In the Antonine period, one hundred years later, it was replaced by a bundle of folds on the left shoulder, used to secure the end of the *sinus.* The *sinus* became fuller and larger and by the third century A.D. it was made into a heavy folded band, a characteristic of portraits of this date. This band, which ran from the right underarm to the left shoulder, gave the costume stability and firmness, but turned it into something formal and static, no longer classically draped.

The traditional toga, which was by now becoming more and more unusual in daily life, became for the Antonines an indispensable attribute. Marcus Aurelius was shown wearing a toga even on his equestrian statue in Rome. Augustus, one hundred and fifty years earlier, had worn it to emphasize his priestly and civic functions. For official statues such as that of Prima Porta, he preferred to portray himself in military costume (see

Figure 8. Procession of the members of the Imperial family: (*left to right*) Agrippa wears a toga draped to form a semicircular overfold (*sinus*) drawn up over the head; the Empress Livia wears a palla draped to cover her head with a long-sleeved tunic (*stola*) showing underneath; Antonia wears her palla off the head and looks back toward her husband, Drusus, who wears a short tunic under a cloak (probably a *paludamentum*); children in the foreground wear togas draped identically to those worn by the adult men. Detail from the marble frieze on the south side of the Ara Pacis Augustae (Altar of Augustan Peace) in Rome, 13–9 B.C. *FOTOTECA UNIONE, ROME*

fig. 4 in ROMAN SCULPTURE AND GEMS). The tunic, which in the republican period had been relatively narrow, became wider during the empire; this was especially true for the tunic of the priest's assistant (*camillus*). Two stripes down the sides of the tunic are shown on bronze statues.

In the late empire costumes diverged sharply for different groups and different classes. The middle class from which the early Christian community arose wore the Roman tunics and pallia whose forms had been borrowed from the Greeks. Tertullian, who was converted to Christianity about A.D. 190, says of the pallium, in his *On the Robe*:

All teachers of literature, rhetoric and mathematics, all grammarians, sophists, doctors, poets, musicians, astronomers, and soothsayers dressed in this costume. Within its four corners, all of the liberal arts were clothed. Today, though, the pallium has become even more precious than these wisdoms, for it clothes Christians.

Classical Roman dress survived in the costumes of the Christian Copts in Egypt and of the Byzantine culture. Many of these late costumes also became the formal vestments of the Christian clergy. New forms of professional dress developed. In addition to wool and linen, silk was increasingly used for the clothing of prominent persons. Gold, woven and appliquéd, was reserved for the emperors and the highest officials. Increasingly, each station had its strictly prescribed textiles, colors, and forms. The arts of tapestry weaving, gold brocade, and colorful embroidery, which were developed at this point, lived on in the Middle Ages.

A protective mantle with a hood (*paenula*) had long been worn directly over the tunic by private citizens of all classes, men and women. It was fastened in front like a modern raincoat; part of it could be thrown back to free the arm for action. Soldiers, especially centurions, wore it as an off-duty mantle, not part of their uniform. During the course of the empire, the *paenula* came to take the place of the toga as the normal outdoor dress of Roman citizens; by the fourth century A.D. this custom was officially recognized and even high-ranking personages could wear it inside the boundaries of Rome. Finally, the *paenula* was adopted as the dress typical of the church. The bishops in the mosaics of Ravenna are portrayed in the full splendor of their purple *paenulae.*

At Ravenna, too, the resplendent Byzantine mosaics in the church of San Vitale show the dazzling, rigidly codified costumes of the emperor and empress, Justinian and Theodora, and their court. Justinian wears, under a cloak fastened with a gem-studded brooch, a long-sleeved white tunic with stripes; he and Theodora both wear jeweled crowns. The women's mantles, made of richly patterned fabrics, are draped about them and over the tops of their tunics. A special long tunic with wide sleeves, woven from the wool of Dalmatian sheep, the *dalmatica,* which had developed in the second century, was taken over as a Christian liturgical vestment. Although the sleeves were longer, they were still woven on.

The toga, abandoned as the dress of Roman citizens, long remained the symbol of the emperor and of the pagan magistrates of the senatorial aristocracy of Rome. After Constantine the Great moved to Byzantium, destined to be the new capital of the Roman Empire, the fashion for the imperial toga changed again. From the fourth to the sixth century A.D., it became even shorter and was worn over a long tunic. The stiff folded band now circled the entire upper torso. In the fifth and sixth centuries this fashion was again superseded by a new form with a second folded band laid over the left shoulder and firmly attached to the original band, which ensured a secure fit for the toga. The toga, which was worn over two tunics, was richly decorated with embroidery and with ornaments, some of metal. Once again—this time through Byzantium—oriental luxury had reached the Romans.

A documented example of the use of extravagant dress to show disaffection, reminiscent of some modern groups, is the dress code of the circus factions under Justinian. The revolutionists, in order to look different from other Romans, let their mustaches and beards grow in the Persian fashion. Shaving their hair off the front part of their heads, they let it grow long and wild behind; this fashion, as well as that of their shoes and accessories, they copied from the Huns. Their richly decorated, expensive clothes included a tunic with outrageously wide sleeves, tight at the wrists, which flapped in the breezes when they clapped or waved their arms in the hippodrome, according to Procopius (*Anecdota* 7). This was a showy, rebellious use of barbarian fashion. In contrast, a pagan classical revival at Rome in the late fourth century touched all aspects of culture: art, literature, the Roman ways of life, with praetors presiding at games as in the early days of the empire.

Two attempts at legislation give us some insight into the kinds of dress people wore, the economic and social situation that governed their choices, and the central government's concern. The first, Diocletian's edict on maximum prices (A.D. 301), listing a wide variety of goods and services from food and textiles to salaries for Greek teachers, is a precious source for the relative prices of garments, ranging from the utilitarian to the outrageously luxurious, and of textiles—

silks, wools, purple, gold, and the like. One hundred years later, the emperor Honorius established severe penalties—exile and confiscation of property—for the wearing of certain barbarian fashions within the city of Rome. Prohibited were certain styles of boots and trousers (*tzangae* and *bracae*) and a mantle called a *raga.* In A.D. 416 after Alaric's sack of Rome, a desperate imperial order tried to stem the tide by forbidding the wearing of long hair or leather garments.

It was too late. In the sixth century John the Lydian describes the official dress for the Fathers, or Patricians, in Constantinople: russet-colored double-folded mantles (chlamydes), which come down from the shoulders to the knees, girt up with golden brooches, with a purple stripe down the middle; *paragaudas,* tunics with sleeves; white leggings, covering the whole leg, foot and all; and black sandals. Frescoes from Bulgaria show a fourth-century official being brought these same symbolic garments: the trousers, the pinned cloak with characteristic colored patches, and jeweled military belt. Fitted pants, shirts with sleeves, and hooded mantles eventually take the place of the loose flowing classical garments. In our own dress we are the heirs of the Celts and the Germans, not the Greeks and Romans, for we too wear fitted pants and sleeves, and gloves, and shoes instead of sandals, and raincoats with hoods.

BIBLIOGRAPHY

SOURCES

Unless otherwise specified, all editions of classical texts mentioned are those of the Loeb Classical Library. Ancient texts that are specifically informative on details of clothing include: Sextus Pompeius Festus, W. M. Lindsay, trans. and ed. (1913), a late-second-century A.D. scholar who epitomized Verrius Flaccus, *De Significatu Verborum* (*On the Meaning of the Words*), and was himself epitomized in the eighth century by Paulus Diaconus (a later edition by Lindsay in *Glossaria Latina* **4** includes additional Festus material); John the Lydian, *On the Magistracy* (*De Magistratibus*), T. F. Carney, ed. and trans. (1971); Tertullian, *On the Robe* (*De Pallio*).

STUDIES

András Alföldi, *Der frührömische Reiteradel und seine Ehrenabzeichen* (1952), and *Die monarchische Repräsentation im römischen Kaiserreiche* (1970); Margarete Bieber, *Griechische Kleidung* (1928), *The History of the Greek and Roman Theater,* 2d. ed. (1961), *Entwicklungsgeschichte der griechischen Tracht,* 2d ed. (1967), and "Charakter und Unterschiede der griechischen und römischen Kleidung," in *Archäologischer Anzeiger* (1973); Horst Blanck, *Einführung in das Privatleben der Griechen und Römer* (1976); Larissa Bonfante, "Roman Costumes: A Glossary and Some Etruscan Derivations," in Hildegard Temporini, ed., *Aufstieg und Niedergang der römischen Welt,* I, pt. 4 (1973), *Etruscan Dress* (1975), and "Daily Life," in Nancy T. de Grummond, ed., *A Guide to Etruscan Mirrors* (1982); Peter R. Brown, *The World of Late Antiquity: A.D. 150–750* (1971); Dorothy Burnham, *Warp and Weft, A Dictionary of Textile Terms* (1981); Herbert A. Cahn, "Dokimasia," in *Revue archéologique* (1973).

Charles Daremberg and Edmund Saglio, *Dictionnaire des antiquités grecques et romaines* (1873–1919); Richard Delbrück, *Die Consulardiptychen und verwandte Denkmäler* (1929); *I Galli e l'Italia,* exhibit catalog (1978); Bernard Goldman, "Origin of the Persian Robe," in *Iranica Antiqua,* **4** (1964), and "The Dura Synagogue Costumes and Parthian Art," in Joseph Guttmann, ed., *The Dura-Europos Synagogue, a Reevaluation (1932–1972)* (1973); A. S. F. Gow, "Notes on the *Persae* of Aeschylus," in *Journal of Hellenic Studies,* **48** (1928); Milton N. Grass, "The Origins of the Art of Knitting," in *Archaeology,* **8** (1955); Bernard Grillet, *Les femmes et les fards dans l'antiquité grecque* (1975); Elsa Gullberg and Paul Åström, *The Thread of Ariadne, A Study of Ancient Greek Dress* (1970).

Marta Hoffmann, *The Warp-Weighted Loom* (1964); Jacques Heurgon, *Daily Life of the Etruscans,* James Kirkup, trans. (1964); Reynold Higgins, *Greek and Roman Jewellery,* 2d ed. (1980), includes Etruscan jewelry; Hans-Jürgen Hundt, "Grabefunde aus Hallstatt: Webkunst und Tracht in der Hallstattzeit," in *Krieger und Salzherren: Austellungskatalog,* Römisch-Germanisches Zentralmuseum, Mainz, **4** (1970); Ian Jenkins and Sue Bird, *Spinning and Weaving in Ancient Greece* (n.d. [*ca.* 1980]); Bonnie M. Kingsley, "The Cap That Survived Alexander," in *American Journal of Archaeology,* **85** (1981); Frank Kolb, "Römische Mäntel: *Paenula, Lacerna, Mandye,*" in *Romische Mitteilungen des Deutschen Archäologischen Instituts,* **80** (1973).

Tullia Linders, *Studies in the Treasure Records of Artemis Brauronia Found in Athens* (1972); Helen L. Lorimer, *Homer and the Monuments* (1950); Spyridon Marinatos, *Kleidung, Haar- und Barttracht: Archaeologia Homerica,* **1** (1967), to be read in light of a review by Anthony M. Snodgrass, *Gnomon,* **41** (1969); Henri Irénée Marrou, *Décadence romaine ou antiquité tardive?: III-VI siècle* (1977); Walter O. Moeller, *The Wool Trade of Ancient Pompeii* (1976); Yvette Morizot, "A propos de la représentation sculptée des vêtements dans l'art grec," in *Revue des études anciennes,* **76** (1974); Walter Muller, *Daedalus and Thespis: The Contributions of Ancient Dramatic Poets to Our Knowledge of the Arts and Crafts of Greece,* 3 vols. (1929–1932); José Luis Murga, "Tres leyes de Honorio sobre el modo de vestir los Romanos," in *Studia et Documenta Historia et Juris,* Pontificium Institutum Utriusque Iuris, **29** (1973); Ugo Enrico Paoli,

Rome: Its People, Life, and Customs, R. D. Macnaughten, trans. (1963); Marie-Thérèse Picard-Schmitter, "Recherches sur les métiers à tisser antiques: à propos de la frise du Forum de Nerva à Rome," in *Latomus,* **24** (1965); M. Popham, E. Touloupa and L. H. Sackett, *Lefkandi* I, British School at Athens, Supplement 2 (1980), and "The Hero of Lefkandi," in *Antiquity,* **56** (1982).

Meyer Reinhold, *History of Purple as a Status Symbol in Antiquity* (1970), reviewed by P. Bruneau in *Revue des études grecques,* **85** (1972); Emeline Hill Richardson, "The Etruscan Origins of Early Roman Sculpture," in *Memoirs of the American Academy in Rome,* **21** (1953), and *The Etruscans* (1964); Emeline Hill Richardson and Laurence Richardson, Jr., "*Ad Cohibendum Bracchium Toga:* An Archaeological Examination of Cicero, *Pro Caelio* 5.11," in *Yale Classical Studies,* **19** (1966); Gisela Marie Richter, *Korai: Archaic Greek Maidens* (1968); Martin Robertson, *A History of Greek Art* (1975), and *The Parthenon Frieze* (1975); Detlef Rössler, "Gab es Modetendenzen in der griechischen Tracht am Ende des 5. und im 4. Jahrhundert v.u.Z.?" in E. Welskopf, ed., *Hellenische Poleis,* III (1974); Paolo Rovesti, *Alla ricerca dei cosmetici perduti* (1975).

Laura Stone, *Costume in Aristophanic Comedy,* rev. ed. (1981); Alan J. B. Wace, "Weaving or Embroidery?" in *American Journal of Archaeology,* **52** (1948); John Peter Wild, *Textile Manufacture in the Northern Roman Provinces* (1970); Josef Wilpert, *Die Gewandung der Christen in den ersten Jahrhunderten* (1898); Lillian May Wilson, *The Roman Toga* (1924), and *The Clothing of the Ancient Romans* (1938).

LITERARY AND PERFORMING ARTS

Epic Poetry

BRYAN HAINSWORTH

THE EPIC WAS GENERALLY REGARDED by antiquity as the highest form of literary art; it was certainly the longest lived. Epic poetry emerged, mature and perfected, out of literary prehistory in the eighth century B.C.; more than eleven hundred years later its recognizable descendants, the poems of Claudian and Nonnus, added some distinction to the last decades of the Roman Empire.

For the ancients an epic poet (*epopoios*) was simply one who composed hexameter verses (*epe*). It was implicit, and not always necessary, that the poem would be of a certain length, that it would be predominantly narrative and serious in tone, and that it would be concerned with the deeds of heroes, or sometimes with the heroic deeds of gods. Within such a form many different ideas of the nature of poetry could be accommodated, according to the fashion of the age. In the history of the classical epic there are seven chapters: prehistoric origins (?–*ca.* 700 B.C.); Greek primary epic and its offshoots (*ca.* 700–400 B.C.); Hellenistic literary epic and derivative forms (*ca.* 400–30 B.C.); early Roman epic (*ca.* 250–60 B.C.);

Neoteric and Augustan epic (*ca.* 60 B.C.–A.D. 20); Roman rhetorical epic (*ca.* A.D. 50–100); and the epic of the Greek revival (*ca.* A.D. 100–450).

Literary movements, however, are always untidy; they overlap and coexist; they have forerunners and afterlives. The order of the schema is something imposed, and reflects a judgment as to which concept of the epic poem was dominant rather than universally accepted.

PREHISTORIC ORIGINS

Narrative verse is an art that occurred almost everywhere among people who, to civilized eyes, might seem to have had little other claim to culture. The Byzantines observed it among the Huns; the Romans in the second century B.C. reported it among their ancestors, and later noted it among the Germans. Its origins in Greece, the only place where what may pass for evidence is available, are without doubt very old. Early Greek narrative verse set its stories in the late second millennium B.C.; its language

1417

sometimes described the material world of that period; its meter and diction, some have argued, derived from an even remoter Indo-European past.

Narrative verse, however, is not yet epic. It is put to many uses and it lacks literary form. In Greece, it seems to have been used to tell tales about gods as well as heroes, about culture heroes as well as heroes of war, and to preserve folktale and peasant lore as well as legends of battle and exploration. It is so elsewhere. In short, in the absence of more sophisticated means, narrative verse is an important vehicle for the transmission of culture, especially in such relatively static and isolated societies as that of the Greeks in the Dark Age (ca. 1100–700 B.C.). In these circumstances, there is more to be learned about narrative verse by comparative methods, which aim to discover general principles of form and development, than from history in the normal sense. So the student of the Greek art of song (*aoide*) uses the results of those who have studied contemporary traditions of heroic poetry, and to good effect. But an unspoken assumption underlies this approach—that *aoide* was a native growth, unaffected by external influences. This assumption is almost certainly correct, but it is easy to see that *aoide* might have developed otherwise.

The Greeks of the second millennium had developed a high culture that was in contact with most parts of the eastern Mediterranean, but Greece lay at the edge of the civilized world. The focus of civilization was well to the east, outside the Mediterranean basin, in Mesopotamia, where the culture of Sumer had merged into that of Akkad. Mesopotamian culture diffused into Asia Minor and was spread by trade and conquest into Syria and beyond. Sumerians and Akkadians had, of course, their narrative poetry: moreover, with the aid of a literate priesthood, they had developed it very considerably in scale and purpose. The stories

of Enmerkar and Lugalbanda are already epics. The content may be heavy with folktale, but the background is historical and the color is heroic. These elements are also found in the Sumerian fragments of the *Epic of Gilgamesh*. But when *Gilgamesh* became current in Akkad in the early second millennium B.C., the heroic color was tinged with the tragic. The poem was made to express a religious and moral standpoint. This function accounts for its preservation, just as it does in the more obvious cases of the Babylonian epics of the creation (*Enuma Eliš*) and the flood (*Atra Ḫasīs*). Narrative poetry in the service of religion was an aspect of Mesopotamian culture wherever it was diffused. It has been found among the Hittites of Asia Minor (*Song of Ullikummi*) and the Canaanites of the Syrian coast (*Keret, Aqhat, Baal*). But to arrive in Greece, Mesopotamian culture (Egyptian culture hardly matters here) had to pass over several hundred miles of open sea, through staging posts in Cyprus and Rhodes and in the ships of merchants whose first interest was not the diffusion of culture. Some ideas passed, including some of literary importance such as battles in heaven and successions of gods, but no literary forms, at least none that survived the debacle of the Mycenaean (Bronze Age) culture toward the end of the second millennium B.C.

In this way Greek narrative poetry avoided the entanglement of religion and developed, or retained, a strongly heroic color. Greek had its folktales (the story of Bellerophon, *Iliad* 6.144 ff., is an almost pure example), its novellae (the story of Jason and the Argonauts), and its legends of superhuman deliverers (Heracles and Theseus), but these took second place. What distinguishes the heroic is a realistic quality, a historical background, and a characteristic tone. The hero, not by magic or trickery but by strength, valor, and will, strives for the glory of some mighty exploit. One infers from the massive fortifications of Mycenae, Tiryns, and other Bronze Age sites that the mighty exploits that *aoide* celebrated were likely to have been those of war and, within that context, sieges. No doubt many songs were composed—modern parallels bear witness to the astonishing fecundity of a vigorous tradition of heroic narrative song. When the Mycenaean Age, the heroic age of Greece, was overtaken by catastrophe in the twelfth century B.C., many of the survivors colonized the Asiatic shore of the Aegean. They took their heroic songs with them. However, whether from the shock of disaster or obscurer causes, in the new environment the repertoire of heroic legends was closed. No more contemporary exploits were celebrated, and what was preserved became centered on two legends: the deeds of the heroes whom "war and bitter strife destroyed, some before seven-gated Thebes in the land of Cadmus fighting for the flocks of Oedipus, some when war had brought them in their ships to Troy over the great gulf of the sea for fair-haired Helen's sake" (Hesiod, *Works and Days* 161–165).

In classical times three poems devoted to the tale of Thebes were known, and seven to that of Troy, but this way of breaking the saga into convenient parts has no special authority. From the picture of the bard drawn in *Odyssey* 8, the Dark Age poet seems to have been the entertainer of the aristocracy. He sang at their bidding, on subjects of their choosing, and ceased at their command. It was not a situation that would encourage elaborate formal structure. In the event, Demodocus, the bard of *Odyssey* 8, had perhaps an hour or less, but, like Odysseus himself in *Odyssey* 9–12, he might very well have had all night. In these circumstances his strategy was to rely on his knowledge of the whole saga of Troy, to take up the story "at some point" (*Odyssey* 8.500), and to add episode to episode as long as the interest of the audience required. This style of composition, called parataxis, is very common wherever heroic poetry is sung. And, like his modern counterparts, Demodocus literally sang, accompanying himself on the lyre. He was blind and is represented as having the whole tale in mind. But it would be hasty to assume that only simple memory was involved in performance. The poet was complimented on the quality of his composition, not on his skill as a performer. Modern research suggests that when narrative poetry is sung in illiterate societies, composition and performance are essentially simultaneous. The song is recreated as the singer proceeds. Demodocus needed to know the roll of heroes, their homes and relations, their special exploits, the detail of the heroic world, and, above all, the special language and diction in which heroic poetry was composed. Armed with this skill and knowledge, and well rehearsed, he took up the tale wherever the Muse or his patrons prompted, and did not falter. There was something uncanny about it and, as usual when confronted by the inexplicable, the Greeks attributed the bard's skill to a god: it was the gift of the Muse. Modern scholars have described the *Kunstsprache*—the elaborate poetic language, the masses of formulae, the ingenious ways in which they are adapted to the needs of the moment, the type-scenes, the repeated theme and topics that appear at every level of narrative, and even traditional plots.

GREEK PRIMARY EPIC AND ITS OFFSHOOTS

The craft of narrative poetry, though fascinating, is often a finite chapter in literary history. It is created in an environment of illiteracy. Literacy renders its techniques redundant and introduces more sophisticated literary forms, often with the prestige of foreign origin. If *aoide* did not die in Greece, it was due to the genius of the poet (or poets) who created out of the background of traditional heroic poetry the two "Homeric" epics, the *Iliad* and the *Odyssey*. The uncertainty of the genesis of these works and of their purpose, occasion, and audience have permitted the airing of many radical proposals, usually founded on the assumption that the present monumental epic form is secondary, perhaps no earlier than from the sixth century B.C. For the literary historian, however, the simplest assumption is the conservative one: that we have the epics more or less as they were created, and that they were in existence by the late eighth century B.C. Good arguments support this position, which was also the belief of the Greeks themselves (except that they tended to exaggerate the poems' antiquity), and the assumption on which they permitted the epic to influence their later literature.

For the conditions described in *Odyssey* 8, both the *Iliad* and the *Odyssey* (fourteen and twelve thousand verses respectively) are inordinately large, each demanding at a minimum twenty-four hours of reciting time. It is not easy to imagine the circumstances that called for, or even permitted, such scale. Some have sought to associate them with the religious festivals (*panegyreis*), such as occurred in the archaic period on the island of Delos in honor of Apollo. But the Homeric epics are secular poems, and would have been recited at such festivals chiefly because the poet had seized the opportunity of an audience at leisure. Other opportunities were provided by the obsequies of the great aristocrats, where contests in the arts (*mousike*) supplemented the traditional athletic events from the late eighth century B.C. (Hesiod, *Works and Days* 654). It is indeed likely enough that the scale of the Homeric epic is an expression of the willfulness of genius, and there is a strong indication in the stories that surround the "edi-

tion" of the poems made at the command of the Athenian tyrant Peisistratos (560–528 B.C.) that the integrity of the poems was difficult to maintain in practice before the classical period.

The scale of the *Iliad* and the *Odyssey*, however, repays a closer look. Although the poet begins from a certain point in the Trojan saga, he treats a very small segment of time—in the case of the *Iliad*, the events of forty days or so out of two decades or more. In itself this short period neither entails nor is entailed by any unity of action. Nevertheless both epics show a strong formal sense. They set the scene with a book of concise and rapid narrative, creating an expectation of the next key event, but they relax and digress before the expectation is fulfilled. They repeat this pattern, and then move quickly to climax. Two books of aftermath follow to make explicit what more sophisticated artists might have wished to leave to implication. The *Iliad*, with a simple linear plot, has the better natural balance. The *Odyssey* has its longueurs, but is notable for an effective use of a developed flashback technique, by which the events of several years are recounted—but as a digression, not as part of a long paratactic narrative.

Such consciousness of form is not common in the history of epic poetry, where the long linear narrative is the rule. Much more influential was the canonical shape given by Homer to many traditional ornaments and devices. Henceforth it was impossible, apart from two or three unimportant exceptions, for an epic poet, Greek or Roman, to employ any metrical form but the dactylic hexameter. The famous measure founded its rhythm on an alternation of long and short syllables: in Greek, stress was of no consequence until the very end of antiquity; Latin sought a clash of verse and speech accent at the beginning and middle of the verse, and a coincidence at the end. The basic foot was the dactyl ($- \smile \smile$), repeated six times except that the last foot was shortened to two syllables. Most important, however, two short syllables were counted the equivalent of one long, so that spondees (– –) might be substituted for dactyls. This happens regularly in the first four feet, but rarely in the fifth. Since the last syllable in any long verse form is indifferent as to quantity, it follows that there are sixteen common variants of the hexameter. No classical epic therefore need be rhythmically monotonous. A long verse like the hexameter tends to fall into shorter sections, called cola, which make for smooth reading. The articulation into cola tended to become stricter in the Hellenistic and Roman periods.

For Greek epic Homer also defined the form of language. The *Kunstsprache* itself, created by and for an oral tradition of verse making, soon broke down in detail, but its underlying dialect of Greek, the Ionic, and many of its archaic forms remained in use. Homer revealed also the enormous utility of direct speech for vividness and characterization. Over half of the *Iliad* is in *oratio recta,* and even in the books of action the proportion is over 30 percent. Later epicists have between 30 and 40 percent, except for the unimaginative Quintus of Smyrna, in whose work direct speech sinks below a quarter. Various Homeric devices became almost indispensable: catalogs of heroes, prophetic dreams, visits to the underworld, descriptions of shields or clothing with pictorial ornament, funeral games, and, above all, gods to initiate the action and guide its course. A special legacy was that of the extended simile. The Homeric hero did not advance to battle merely "like a lion," he went (*Iliad* 12.299 ff.)

like a mountain-bred lion, who for a long time has been starved of meat, and his proud heart urges him to go for the flocks and get inside the well-built fold. And should he find the herdsmen there guarding their flock with spears and dogs, he has no thought to leave the fold without attacking but leaps in and seizes his prey or else is himself wounded among the foremost by a dart from some swift hand.

The Homeric poems themselves are quite opaque as to their creator's profounder intentions. They flaunt no religious, ethnic, political, or social claims (which is not to say they could not be made to support such ends). By one of those convenient antitheses of literary criticism, the critical treatise *On the Sublime* (*De Sublimitate,* first century A.D., attributed to "Longinus") compares the *Iliad* to tragedy, the *Odyssey* to comedy. Indeed, the dominant note of the *Iliad* is that of a homily upon heroism, the glory and the cost, whereas the *Odyssey*—which is fundamentally a folktale—exploits the appeal of the romantic, of crafty success and virtue triumphant.

How the Homeric poems were preserved after the death of their creator is a mystery. Perhaps it was made possible by a change in the mode of performance from the seventh century B.C. The singers (*aoidoi*) were superseded by reciters (*rhapsodoi*) who declaimed, rather than sang, poems composed by others. Those who presided over festivals—the Panathenaea at Athens is best documented—found them an attractive addition to the program. Such presentations would have tended to fix the text, and that in its turn put the tradition of the Trojan saga on a special footing. The *Iliad* and the *Odyssey* became the foci around which lesser poets (the names of Stasinus, Arctinus, Lesches, and Eugammon are reported) in the seventh and sixth centuries constructed the "Trojan Cycle" as we know it: a *Cypria* to introduce it, an *Aethiopis* to recount the death of Achilles, a *Little Iliad* to relate several stories, including that of the Wooden Horse, a *Sack of Ilium* (*Iliu Persis*) to describe the fall of Troy, *Homecomings* (*Nostoi*) to tell of the dismal aftermath, and a *Story of Telegonus (Telegonia) to end the saga with the death of Odysseus. (Throughout this essay an asterisk preceding a name denotes an author whose work is not extant or is known only through fragments, or such a work itself.) It is unjust to criticize the quality of work about which so little is known directly, but the reputation of the cycle in antiquity was low, and the fragments reveal an interest in romantic and miraculous episodes that would have contrasted sharply with the austerity of the *Iliad*'s heroic tone. The cycle's chief contribution to literature was its content, a quarry for those genres such as tragedy that used the saga for subject matter.

The impulse to complete a theme, a part of which a poet of genius had treated definitively, affected a genre that the Greeks did not sharply distinguish from the epic, the didactic poetry of Hesiod and his "school." The Muses of Hesiod know how to "speak truth" (*Theogony* 28), where "truth" turns out to mean "traditional knowledge" about gods in the *Theogony,* and about work and social behavior in *Works and Days.* To the school belong various *catalogs that extend the genealogies of gods to the genealogies of their descendants, the heroes and heroines of legend. These formless catalogs would have been dull reading for anyone to whom their contents had not represented priceless information. In the sixth century B.C. this tradition threw up the *Shield of Heracles,* a short narrative poem of Heracles' battle with Cycnus in the guise of a description, after *Iliad* 18, of the hero's shield.

With Hesiod, Greek literature renews its contacts with outside currents. In the plastic arts of the seventh century B.C. there is a strong "orientalizing" influence, and it would have been surprising if literature had received no new impulses. The myth of the succession of gods in heaven (*Theogony* 154–210; 453–506) has parallels in Mesopotamia and among the Hurrians, Hittites, and Phoe-

nicians; so too the myth of the ages of man's decline (*Works and Days* 106–201). The genre itself of Hesiod's work, wisdom literature, is one well entrenched from the earliest times not only in the Levant (*Instructions of Suruppak,* Sumerian, *ca.* 2500 B.C.) but also in Egypt from at least the time of the Middle Kingdom. The original time of these contacts is problematic, but if they were very old they could hardly fail to be reinforced when horizons widened again in the late eighth century B.C.

Didactic poetry overtly assumes a function that other genres perform by indirection or, more usually, have thrust upon them: moral admonition and practical instruction. The Homeric epic presently found itself cast in this role. It was just as well, for kings and their courts disappeared from Greece in the course of the seventh century B.C., and changing audiences brought new attitudes. If the old poems (after suitable interpretation) had not seemed to reflect these attitudes they would not have survived. As it was, they became deeply revered. Vase painters depicted children learning their letters from epic scrolls. Some boys even learned Homer by heart (Xenophon, *Symposium* 3.5). Homer as the "Bible of the Greeks" received its most extreme, and not altogether serious, exposition in Plato's dialogue *Ion,* about a fifth-century B.C. rhapsode who, to the philosopher's amusement, presented Homer as the accomplished expert in every branch of human knowledge from medicine to military tactics. However, the underlying attitude that the function of poetry was utilitarian was widespread and shared by Plato himself.

An effect of this attitude was a willingness to accept Homer even as a political authority, to legitimize territorial claims or simply to promote the self-esteem of city-states. But what of those cities that Homer had unaccountably overlooked, like Corinth, or neglected, like Athens? Patriotic poets rushed in to fill the gap, *Eumelus (? late eighth century B.C.) for Corinth, *Asius (? sixth century B.C.) for Samos and Boeotia. These poets did not dare to break the convention of the heroic age; their aim was to establish the place of their patrons in that age. This sometimes required a bold handling of existing myth. Thus, Eumelus appears to have invented the equation of the unknown epic city of Ephyre with Corinth and so usurped its mythology. Asius, a genealogical poet, was no less reckless in the invention of eponymous heroines and suppositious offspring. The Athenians were more fortunate in having a heroic mythology of their own, that of Theseus. The late sixth century B.C., when there was a marked revival in the popularity of Theseus, may have seen the composition of a *Theseid, an epic of unknown authorship and probably of little merit (Aristotle, *Poetics* 8).

It is not an exception to this tendency to canonize the epic genre that there existed an early comic narrative poem, *Margites, starring an antihero of that name ("Tun-belly," akin to "greedy" [*margos*]), and some other narrative light pieces (*paegnia*). Archaic Greece had a tradition of "blame poetry," known to us from Archilochus and Hipponax, and religion sanctioned many occasions on which abusive and obscene lampooning allowed the unmentionable to be spoken. Margites was the archetypal village imbecile, the antithesis of Achilles and Odysseus. Another comic piece, still extant, is the *Battle of the Frogs and Mice* (*Batrachomyomachia*), a literary parody of no remarkable brilliance. One Pigres (? fifth century B.C.) was sometimes said to be the author.

Narrative poets were also attracted to stories about gods. The battles of Zeus with his monstrous opponents—Titans, Giants, Typhon—held a permanent fascination. There was an early *Battle of the Titans* (*Titanomachia*), and the theme was still being ex-

ploited by Claudian and Nonnus in the fifth century A.D. Short narratives about gods, however, formed a separate class, called *Homeric Hymns* (*hymnoi*, seventh and sixth centuries B.C.), although identical in diction and technique with the epic.

Societies that put their faith in a book, as the Greeks did in Homer, must eventually face the problem that society evolves but the book, of course, does not. This problem confronted the Greeks at about the turn of the sixth and fifth centuries B.C. The philosophers Xenophanes and Heraclitus attacked the traditional epic and didactic poets, especially for their low conception of the divine. "Everything that is shameful among men, theft, lechery, and deceit, Homer and Hesiod attribute to the gods" (Xenophanes frag. 11 Diels). The defense took refuge in allegory, and suggested that the gods of the epic were really dramatic personifications of natural forces. This kind of exegesis is almost indelible. In Hellenistic times it achieved a certain respectability in the hands of Stoic philosophers, and again in the hands of the Neoplatonist Porphyry (*ca.* A.D. 232–305), but the major critics of antiquity rightly found it beneath notice.

HELLENISTIC LITERARY EPIC AND DERIVATIVE FORMS

The latest names in the primary tradition of epic poetry are those of *Pisander (late sixth century B.C.) and *Panyassis (mid fifth century B.C.), both celebrants of Heracles. The next epicist of note, *Antimachus of Colophon (*ca.* 400 B.C.), was a poet of a different character. The poets of the primary tradition had necessarily been craftsmen in verse; they were masters of traditional lore and of the traditional poetic speech. Many were doubtless little more. Antimachus, however, was a literary artist: for him the literary tradition was not a craft, but a corpus of masterpieces for imitation and emulation. A scholar, he was one of the first "editors" of the Homeric text. The late classical and Hellenistic epochs would not have found this combination of activities remarkable. The idea of the "mad" poet, seized by divine possession, was now past: erudition, soberly acquired, and intellectual qualities generally were becoming necessary features of good verse. But they were not yet sufficient qualities: Plato is reported to have admired Antimachus, which argues that he also had a certain moral force. His chief productions were a *Thebais, an epic in twenty-four books, and an anthology of elegies, *Lyde. What we know of these works has come down because they figured, especially the Lyde, in fierce literary polemic in the third century B.C. Conventional opinion held Antimachus in high repute: elegant epigrams celebrated both his epic and elegiac talents. But in an important respect Antimachus fell short; he lacked something that ought to go with learning—care. It was to this lack of care that the poet-critic Callimachus (ca. 305–240 B.C.) chiefly objected: Antimachus was sloppy. But the critic did not stop there: sloppiness was the concomitant of length. Antimachus was too ambitious; he challenged Homer, the unassailable pinnacle of poetic achievement, when Hesiod would have been a better mentor. He chose bad models like the *Nanno (an elegy) of Mimnermus, and it all led to bombast and pretension.

This dispute was about means and not ends, and some of its assumptions had been anticipated in Aristotle's Poetics. That powerful, difficult, and wayward work concluded with the judgment that the epic was a genre innately flawed. It was not merely that tragedy had everything that epic had, plus the histrionic qualities of the stage, but tragedy was also naturally more direct and more concentrated even when divorced from its presentation. It thus more effectively conveyed the appropriate aesthetic pleasure. This judgment is passed upon the best epic, that of Homer, which Aristotle thought very good indeed. Most epics, for him, were nonstarters. They had no "plot" to speak of, and plot was fundamental (Poetics 23). By "plot" Aristotle meant the logical articulation of the parts into the whole, into a single story with recognizable beginning, middle, and end. A congeries of incidents was not a plot, but that was precisely what the Heracleads, Theseids, cyclic poems, and the rest were. With that contemptuous dismissal Aristotle focused his attention on Homer, what epic ought to be. The epic, we learn, was free from tragedy's restrictions on length (5). The reference is probably not to mere bulk but to extension of plot. The epic simply had a larger canvas. The literary dogmatists of seventeenth-century France formalized this point in the dictum that the action of tragedy was limited to one day, that of epic to one year. But there were practical limits. Homer did not choose to relate the whole Trojan War or the whole career of Odysseus. If he had, it would not have been easy for the reader to comprehend the action, or not to be overwhelmed by its complexity. "As it is, [Homer] picks out one portion of the story"—that constituted the plot—"and uses many other parts as 'episodes' . . . with which he intersperses his poem" (23). By "episodes" Aristotle referred to the undoubted fact that Homeric epic repeatedly set up open-ended situations that could be filled with a series of paratactically arranged scenes before the plot was again advanced.

The Poetics has been immensely influential on Renaissance and modern criticism, but its impact on its own age was largely limited to committed Aristotelians. However, its own age had an impact on the Poetics: one observes the tendency to emphasize the importance of technical excellences and to minimize the moral and social effects of literature. There is an interest in minutiae

(25), and in the status of the various genres in the hierarchy of literature and the mode appropriate to each. The scholar-poets of the Hellenistic age turned these tendencies into something of a cult. They were encouraged by Ptolemy II's foundation at Alexandria of the Museum (a sort of literary and scientific research institute) and Library in the early third century B.C., and later by similar facilities at Pergamum. Such poets did not necessarily share Aristotle's theoretical objections to epic. For them Homer was *ho poietes,* the poet par excellence. A relief in the British Museum (BM 2191) depicts his apotheosis. On the mundane level he was studied, edited, corrected, and commented upon. Some of this scholarship, sadly attenuated, survives in the scholia, the marginal notes found in the best medieval manuscripts of Homer. It gives some indication of the specific qualities that the age expected of the art of an epic poet. He must be careful about the arrangement of his material so that, for example, developments are properly anticipated; he must be graphic in his narrative, avoid monotony, ensure that his detail is not illogical or unconvincing; and above all he must show regard for the decency, dignity, and order appropriate to the prime genre of literature.

Naturally not all these students of Homer held Callimachus' view that Homericizing epic was bound to be overpretentious, or shared his restraint. There is extant from Callimachus' own lifetime a full-scale epic, an *Argonautica,* by one of the librarians of Alexandria, Apollonius of Rhodes (*ca.* 295–230? B.C.). A sensitive scholar, Apollonius possessed a fine visual and psychological imagination. Nor is there any lack of care in the execution of his poem. Readers who do not share his prejudices would probably complain that there was too much, that the erudite mastery of the arcane Homeric *Kunstsprache* sometimes descends to pedantic polemics on abstruse points of scholar-

ship, and that the obsession with detail permitted neglect of the whole. For the *Argonautica,* like the epics detested by Aristotle, is a paratactic string of episodes culminating in a long bathetic sequence after the natural climax, Jason's winning of the Golden Fleece. It seems that Callimachus had reason on his side, but not because mere size entailed bad workmanship—Apollonius had refuted that. It is rather that the moral force required to sustain an epic was incompatible with the literary ethos of the Hellenistic age.

Whether they sensed it or not, Apollonius' contemporaries had found an answer to this problem: to compose epyllia (epic fragments). The prime example was the *Hecale* of Callimachus himself. True to his own spirit, Callimachus chose an uncommon subject, Theseus and the bull of Marathon. That sort of exploit was the usual prerogative of Heracles. This heroic, narrative episode was set within a description of Theseus' lodging with Hecale, the young prince with the peasant crone, on his way to and from Marathon. It was a very successful recipe. Simple examples of epyllia are extant among the *Idylls* of Theocritus (*ca.* 300–260? B.C.), and the genre was taken up in the next generation by *Euphorion, who was to become influential in certain Roman circles two centuries later. The epyllion freed the poet from the need for grand vision and sustained interest, and permitted indulgence of the artistic inclinations of his own age. It never fell wholly out of fashion.

But to whom were Hellenistic epyllia, or indeed epics, addressed? In the hands of *aoidoi* and *rhapsodoi* the old epic poetry had reached almost everyone, high and low. In the fifth century B.C. choral lyric poetry and tragedy had reached mass audiences. In the Hellenistic age the dispersal of Greek culture meant that literature was more a matter of books and reading. Books and reading meant an educated audience. A gulf opened between polite literature, based on archaic and classical models, and popular culture, the mime and the music hall. The former literally spoke a different language. A fragment of the comic poet Strato (frag. 1) introduces a desperate citizen whose cook (a profession notorious in comedy for arrogance and temperament) will communicate with him only in the epic *Kunstsprache,* until he is forced to have recourse to a Homeric dictionary to order a meal. From this time forward serious literature was the province of highly educated men and of the social classes that had the leisure for that sort of education.

These qualifications did not narrow audiences to a tiny handful of citizens. The Hellenistic age had great respect for the classical culture, and the arts were the lubricant of its social and even its public life. An ambassador, according to a decree of Cnossos (*Inscriptiones Creticae* 1.8.11), made political capital out of his ability to "sing to the lyre the poems of Timotheus and Polydius and others of our ancient poets as befits an educated man." Original compositions also gained recognition. Even quite small towns had their festivals and offered prizes for epic compositions. From inscriptions we know of the Charitesia (Festival of the Graces) at Orchomenus (*Inscriptiones Graecae* 7.3195–3197) and of the Amphiaraia (Festival of Amphiaraus) at Oropus (*Inscriptiones Graecae* 7.416–420), both in Boeotia. No titles are listed, but no doubt the competitors knew what was expected, or expedient. Chaleon, a township in Locris, was quite frank: the community honored Aristodama, a "poetess of *epe*" (hexameter verses), and her brother Dionysius "in order that all who visit the temple may know that the city of Chaleon is concerned to pay tribute to those who choose to speak or write about the god" and because Aristodama had made mention of "forebears of our community" (*Inscriptiones Graecae,* 2d. ed., 9.1.740.).

The genre of these pieces, most of which must have died with their authors, would have been the "geographical epyllion," whose most respectable exponent was the Homeric scholar Rhianus (*ca.* 275–200? B.C.). He made his subject matter out of the myths and history of a city or region, composing *Messeniaka, *Akhaika, *Eliaka,* and *Thessalika.* A subclass of this genre was "foundation stories," such as *Foundation of Rhodes (Ktisis Rhodou)* by Apollonius, who also wrote about Caunus, Alexandria, Naucratis, and Canopus.

Grander epic was never out of fashion either, in spite of Callimachus. The age saw at least two more *Argonauticas,* several *Heracleads* (one by Rhianus), yet more *Thebaids,* and (an omen for the future) at least two *Bacchicas* or *Dionysiads.* An interest in exploits performed in distant places, especially distant Asiatic places, was natural after the conquests of Alexander the Great. Monarchy, the normal Hellenistic polity, encouraged the hopes of panegyrists. Some rose to the bait, but in general Greek convention was too strong for the idea of a new heroic age to take firm root; in Rome, however, the soil was virgin.

EARLY ROMAN EPIC

Ptolemy III Euergetes, the last patron of Callimachus and Apollonius, died in 221 B.C. The following year began that period of fifty-three years in the course of which, according to the historian Polybius, the Romans made themselves masters of the world. The historian attributed the Romans' triumphs to their command of statecraft and the arts of war. In all other respects the Romans were a primitive people, and were usually happy to admit it. After all, primitive people preserved primitive virtue, and the heroic virtues that carried Rome through the wars with Carthage and Macedonia made the epoch a sort of Roman heroic age. Latin literature fitly began with a translation of Homer, an *Odyssey,* the work of the Tarentine slave Livius Andronicus (*ca.* 280–205 B.C.). He thoroughly Latinized the Greek, and used a native verse form, the Saturnian. His contemporary Naevius (*ca.* 270?–201 B.C.) used the same meter for a historical epic on contemporary events, the *Punic War* (*Bellum Punicum,* describing the First Punic War, 264–241 B.C.), originally a continuous narrative but later divided into seven books, and it might have seemed that the culture of Greece was about to give Rome no more than the example of epic poetry for emulation. But Naevius left no successors. Quintus Ennius (239–169 B.C.), who for most later Romans was the ancient poet par excellence, forced Latin into the Homeric meter. But again he chose a historical theme, and of the most ambitious kind: the *Annales,* in eighteen books, recounted the story of Rome from the landing of Aeneas to the poet's own day. Ennius (frag. 6) saw himself as the Roman Homer, and perhaps not just in a literary sense—he affected a belief in reincarnation. Even scholarly opinion conceded that the main events of the Trojan saga were historical, and was prepared to make Homer a near contemporary. Perhaps Ennius thought of Homer as the poetic historian of his nation's achievements, and of himself in a similar role. Some Greek poets had cast themselves as historians, but without much impact. Choerilus (of Samos, *ca.* 400 B.C.) composed a respectable account of the invasion of Greece by Xerxes, 480–479 B.C. (*Persica*), and another *Choerilus (of Iasos, *ca.* 330 B.C.) celebrated the victories of Alexander in a work that became a byword for badness. They were followed by a long string of mediocre eulogists of Hellenistic kings. Since all this work is lost and was probably short-lived, its rightful place in literary history is elusive. What posterity condemns may be

influential in its own time; nor of course were the Romans of 200 B.C. well placed to be judges of Greek literature. For them Greek poetry was uniformly prestigious. They observed contemporary mythological epicists and historical epicists, and a mighty father of literature in the background. Ennius was all three, a Roman Homer celebrating his country's mythical past and glorious present.

A historical epic using the conventions of mythological epic has certain problems to surmount. Homer's world was heavily populated by gods; so too was that of Apollonius. Hellenistic readers may not have believed literally in such beings, any more than modern audiences believe in the ghost of Hamlet's father, but they were credible in their context—myth. The early history of Rome could be justly put into that category, and divine machinery could enhance the grandeur of the foundation of the city. But the convention could seem fatuous if introduced for the benefit of contemporary politicians. Ennius had critics as well as emulators. The satirist Gaius Lucilius (*ca.* 180–102 B.C.) was the first of many to find fault with the pioneer's clumsy verses. Ennius could not help his versification, but some of Lucilius' criticism had a fairer basis. The first book of the *Satires* contained a parody of the council of the gods (*concilium deorum*), a venerable epic theme, as can be seen in *Odyssey* 1.26 ff. and 5.1 ff.

NEOTERIC AND AUGUSTAN EPIC

Such criticisms usually fall on deaf ears, and Ennius continued to be the father of Latin literature, admired by Lucretius, echoed by Vergil, still quoted by Seneca the Younger. Of his emulators, nothing need be said of *Hostius (*ca.* 129 B.C.) or *Furius (*ca.* 100 B.C.), who wrote on contemporary wars. Both were friends of prominent statesmen, and may be suspected of eulogy. But Ennius had followers among the aristocracy itself, among men of taste and learning. They included the great orators of the first century B.C., Hortensius and Cicero. The combination of professions, orator and poet, is startling and worth examination. Cicero composed three epics, *Marius (on the great populist general, 157–86 B.C.), *On His Times (De Temporibus Suis), and *On His Consulship (De Consulatu Suo). Their success was limited. Wits suggested they were responsible for his exile. Some lines, such as "Cedant arma togae, concedat laurea laudi" (Let arms yield to the toga, the victor's laurel give way to civic praise) dogged him all his life. But in 54 B.C., undeterred, he was thinking of finishing off something on Caesar's conquest of Gaul (Letters to His Brother Quintus [Ad Quintum Fratrem] 3.8), if not too busy. At the same time he was contemplating with malicious relish an insertion into On My Times: Apollo prophesying the humiliations of Piso and Gabinius (Letters to His Brother Quintus 3.1). Not much hint here of the poetical impulse. Literary education had reduced the composition of hexameters to a polite accomplishment, a recreation for the jaded public man, who could toss off an epic poem with the same ease and with the same talents as a public address. It was a fatal facility—Hortensius was credited with 50,000 verses—and not conducive to a serious consideration of the aesthetic problems of a contemporary epic in Homeric dress. Yet it is possible to take these products of their authors' leisure hours too seriously. They have an ephemeral air, like much late Hellenistic production.

Practice, however, improved versification and with passing years Ennius began to look more and more uncouth—"hirsute" is Ovid's favorite description—and not just due to archaism. His genius could not conceal his lack of art. And suddenly the lack became important. In 62 B.C., pleading in

defense of the poet Archias, Cicero had spoken a noble elogium on the old Roman poetry and the moral and social ideals that created it. It might almost have been its obituary. Within a year or two the "New Poets," or Neoterics, were beginning to dominate the literary scene: Catullus, Calvus, Cinna, and many lesser figures. Their gospel was that of Callimachus, although at first their prime model was Euphorion, whose morbid taste for tales of unnatural and incestuous love had been popularized by the Greek pundit Parthenius. Naturally this school of thought eschewed epic, especially historical epic, deriding the sad example of Volusius' *Annales, which Catullus suggested might be more useful in the privy than the library. But they admitted epyllion: Catullus' Peleus and Thetis is extant, and we know of Calvus' *Io and Cinna's *Smyrna. An interesting literary career is that of the opportunistic Varro Atacinus. In 58 or 57 B.C. he produced the *War Against the Sequani (Bellum Sequanicum), a historical epic of the old type in praise (one assumes) of Julius Caesar's first campaign in Gaul. Perhaps it did not go down too well even with its hero, no mean judge of literature. Varro's next venture was a mythological epic, the *Argonautae, translated or adapted from Apollonius' poem. Subsequently he joined the vogue for amatory elegiac verse, and finally allied himself to the Callimacheans with a number of learned didactic pieces. This rapid change in the outlook of the Roman intelligentsia in the 50s B.C. left the middle-aged, like Cicero, puzzled and indignant. He saw a pleasure-seeking, apolitical younger generation, corrupted by Greek morals, worshiping cleverness and erudition. Such young men had no use for the example of Ennius, in style or in values.

In this way the Neoterics effected a second and thorough Hellenization of Latin poetry, turning it in fact into a continuation of the best age of Alexandria. For a generation no respectable poet essayed the epic; the best repudiated it (Vergil, *Eclogues* 6.3 ff.). But new ideas take time to become orthodoxy, and meanwhile they may be overtaken by events. The events in this case were a revolution in political affairs and the establishment—whatever fair words were used to conceal it—of an emperor in place of the free magistrates of the republic. The rise of Octavian (styled "Augustus" from 28 B.C.) was abetted by the learned and subtle Maecenas, whose pleasure it was, in the intervals of political intrigue, to patronize needy men of poetic talent. Horace, Vergil, and Propertius, all victims of the civil wars, enjoyed his favor. What was his return? One must not discount the mere entertainment value of a salon. His whole troupe went with Maecenas to Brundisium in 37 B.C. for negotiations with Marcus Antonius—but not as diplomats. Tiberius' staff in the East in 20 B.C. was a party of poets, vying with each other in the epic and lyric modes, and to entertain, or keep, a man of letters or two was a mark of good breeding. But it has often appeared that there was something more sinister to the patronage of Maecenas. His protégés have seemed too fulsome in their praises of the new dictator, as if the chorus were orchestrated by one skilled in the molding of opinion. One doubts if much orchestration was required in the circumstances.

It is the literary, not the political historian, who should find the patronage of Maecenas alarming. His master, Octavian, had annexed the military glory of Julius Caesar by inheritance and after the destruction of Antonius in 30 B.C. had begun to present himself as the new Romulus, the second founder of Rome. This was something fit to be extolled in epic verse: Ennius updated, as it were, with the famous laudation of Romulus in the *Annales* appropriately rededicated. If Maecenas, even without the smallest ulterior motive, had not mentioned such an infallible subject to his entourage he would have failed as a patron. Of course, they knew better, and developed what is almost a minor genre, the refusal (*recusatio*): "My metier is the poetry of love; my genius is not equal to so lofty a theme; 'X' [or 'you'] will attempt it." Naturally there were those who succumbed to blandishment. *Varius, lifelong friend of Vergil and his literary executor, was one, although his forte was tragedy. We do not know what his patrons thought of his effort. Maecenas at least was no ignoramus, though some thought his taste depraved (Seneca, *Epistles* 114.4); but in the background was the emperor whose unreconstructed views on literature are recorded by the biographer Suetonius (*Lives of the Twelve Caesars,* "Augustus" 89):

> In reading the writers of both tongues [Latin and Greek] there was nothing he looked for so carefully as for precepts and examples instructive in public or in private life, and these he would frequently copy out word for word and send to his household or to his army commanders and provincial governors whenever any needed admonition (J. C. Rolfe, trans., vol. 1 [1914]).

It was an attitude Cicero would have understood.

"Omne tulit punctum qui miscuit utile dulci" (He has gained every point who has joined what is profitable with what is attractive, *Art of Poetry* [*Ars Poetica*] 343). The typical Horatian compromise illustrates the dilemma of the best Augustan poets. The Neoterics were better in theory than in practice. For behind the elegant facades, epyllia on mythological motifs were trivial and escapist. But grand epics on mythological themes were artificial and dull, epics on historical themes were artificial, sycophantic, and dull. What kind of literature was relevant to a people emerging from a generation of deep political crisis? Hellenistic models, which avoided any kind of moral commitment on the part of the author, were inadequate. Horace sought earlier, classical models. Vergil after the *Eclogues* moved in the same direction. In the epic genre this road leads back beyond Ennius and Antimachus to Homer himself. Was a second Homer possible after all?

Vergil took up the challenge, but not lightly or quickly. He worked on the *Aeneid* for a decade, and left it unrevised at his death in 19 B.C. Of its emotive and moral powers, which derive from the genius of the poet, nothing can be said here, but the *Aeneid* is also a startling instance of artistic skill. In the most general way the comments of Horace on the epic (*Art of Poetry* 129 ff.) are apposite to Vergil: the selection of a story with beginning and climax, the immediate engagement of the reader, the blending of fact and fiction, the unity of style, and epic elevation and decorum. Ultimately this is Aristotelian, at last having impact on poetic practice. But the *Aeneid* is more than Homericizing in form and technique; incorporating an astonishing quantity of Homeric thematic material by a remarkable feat of compression into twelve books, it is both a Roman *Odyssey* and a Roman *Iliad*.

Vergil put his epic into the mythological age. Doubtless this was a necessary condition for success: it admitted at once and without any breach of decorum the Homeric form, content, and color. But within the outward form were developed the Roman aims of Ennius. A few devices—divine prophecy, the underworld, the hero's shield—permitted a grand (and of course highly selective) vision of the rise of the Roman people to universal dominion, achieved and preserved by the Roman virtues of piety and courage, justice and mercy (the public virtues, as it happened, of Augustus). It is the same theme as that proclaimed contemporaneously in Livy's *History*.

The trick was played outstandingly well, but it could be played only once; there could

not be a second, and original, Roman Homer. For once the literary world seems to have had the sense not to try the impossible. Ovid's *Metamorphoses* (A.D. 8) proves the point. The work is epic in scale (fifteen books) but in no other respect. Essentially it is an anthology of short unconnected narrative pieces. Narrative verse brings with it some epic devices, seldom taken seriously by Ovid. The *Metamorphoses,* although clearly Ovid's bid for fame, does not challenge the *Aeneid.* For the Greek precedent we should look to Callimachus' *Causes* (*Aitia*), not to Homer or even to Apollonius. For poets less imaginative than Ovid the fact that the *Aeneid* was sui generis meant that the traditional genres could continue unabated. Thebes, Theseus, and the wars of Rome inspired a dozen minor poets before the death of Augustus in A.D. 14 (listed by Ovid, *Letters from Pontus* [*Epistulae ex Ponto*] 4.16). *Cornelius Severus even had a place in Quintilian's reading list eighty years later.

ROMAN RHETORICAL EPIC

In A.D. 8 Ovid was exiled. For the first time in the literary history of Greece and Rome a major and serious poet had been suppressed, in part at least for his poetry. From this moment literature flourished, when it did, by the favor of absolute and unpredictable governments. In such circumstances the epic, whether historical (with the right subject) or mythological, had certain attractions. It was safe, protected by its prestige and its political irrelevance, suitable for the discreetly retired and the unambitious. Relevance too often required an attitude of sycophancy toward reigning emperors and vindictive malice toward their predecessors.

It is also necessary to consider the increasing dominance of the literary education by oratory. By the end of the first century A.D. in Quintilian's time the two have become synonymous. The taste for a declamatory style, which infected most genres of literature in the first century of the Roman Empire, is not unconnected with changes in the art of publication. The Augustan and earlier writers did not advertise themselves. They often affect to address a friend or patron, as if a book were a private letter. Patrons, of course, were favored with prepublication readings by their protégés. From the 30s B.C. we begin to hear of shameless authors reciting publicly. The practice soon became general, by the end of the first century A.D. reaching the proportions of a social evil (Juvenal, *Satires* 1.1 ff.; Pliny, *Letters* 1.13). Naturally, when publication took the form of an address to a public meeting, authors veered toward a style that a public meeting would applaud. What was applauded was the well-turned phrase and the smart antithesis. It is usual to deplore this development, for rhetoric is out of fashion. Certainly in the epic genre the effect was ultimately terminal, not because rhetoric tended to mistake a debating point for an argument and tried to astonish rather than involve its audience, but because it cast its mantle of approbation over the ornaments of the epic poem, over the descriptions and speeches, to the neglect of the art of narrative—which, after all, is the essence of the epic style.

Most rhetorical of first-century epicists was Lucan (Marcus Annaeus Lucanus, A.D. 39–65). The *Civil War* (*De Bello Civili*, sometimes called *Pharsalia* in modern works) is in ten books and incomplete; twelve books were probably intended. The title refers to the conflict of Julius Caesar and Pompeius Magnus a century before the poet's time. It was this conflict that had destroyed the free republic, yet its political color in Lucan's time was a peculiar shade of gray. The Romans always experienced feelings of guilt about their civil wars; Augustus, and subsequent emperors at their inaugurations, had pretended to restore the free state; Nero,

Lucan's emperor, was of the house of the Caesars in the male line only by adoptions in two generations, and his natural family, the Domitii, had been staunch Pompeians. If Lucan was hostile to Caesar, and he was, there is no reason to suppose that this was politically dissident: Vergil himself had not been exactly complimentary. But a personal animus developed between emperor and poet, Lucan was forbidden to recite, and in the later books of the *Civil War* a sharper tone is apparent. The conflict becomes the death struggle of liberty against tyranny. Fittingly, Lucan was implicated in Piso's attempted coup d'état in A.D. 65 and suffered the inevitable penalty of a forced suicide.

With such a theme it is a wonder that Lucan does not stand beside Vergil. His poem abounds in startling descriptions, memorable epigrams, and many tense, pointed speeches. Yet it is a question how far this is poetry. Quintilian thought not; "a better example for orators than poets" (*Education of an Orator* [*Institutio Oratoria*] 10.1 90). The tone is unvaried, the verse monotonous, and the taste for the gruesome and horrific unappealing. But one great innovation stands to Lucan's credit: he has no gods. The defeated are consoled, if at all, with the bleak dogmas of the Stoic philosophy.

How is a historical poem to be a poem and not a history? Aristotle had said that poetry dealt with universals and history with particulars (*Poetics* 9). What could this mean in practice? Lucan's contemporary Petronius glanced at the problem in his novella, *Satyricon* (118 ff.). History should be left to the historians, the poet should use the apparatus of poetry (including gods) and the grand manner and should simplify the story to accommodate declamatory topics. An essay of nearly 300 lines illustrates the method: a loosely linked series of declamations on ambition, luxury, fortune, and the career of Caesar cast in a highly unhistorical form.

Not surprisingly this has been thought a parody of the *Civil War*.

When the establishment of the Flavian dynasty (A.D. 70) forced him into retirement, Silius Italicus, most despised of Roman epicists, began the composition of his unfinished *Punic War* (*Punica*), relating the Second or Hannibalic war of 218–201 B.C. Seventeen books were finished. Silius was a competent versifier and a fervent admirer of Vergil. Yet the scale of epic needs an ego to match, and Silius was utterly conventional. He worked "maiore cura quam ingenio" (with more care than talent), as his contemporary Pliny the Younger put it (*Letters* 3.7). But then Pliny never spoke ill of a writer. He even rejoiced (*Letters* 8.4) when a friend announced a project on Trajan's Dacian war:

> Where could you have found a subject so new, so full of events, so extensive and poetical? Or such wondrous material yet perfectly true? You will tell of rivers diverted or bridged for the first time, of camps pitched on mountain crags, of a king ever resolute driven from palace and even from life itself, and of the double triumph won over that unconquered nation (Betty Radice, trans. [1969]).

This is a fair catalog of the historical epicist's inspirations. Flavian taste also ran to the mythological epic, not always uncritically. Cordus' *Theseid* was immortalized by Juvenal (*Satires* 1.1), who—by this point beyond endurance—found himself more familiar with centaurs and Argonauts than a man might be with his own household. Two epics and a substantial fragment of this genre survive, the *Argonautica* of Valerius Flaccus (*ca.* A.D. 80) and the *Thebaid* of Statius (A.D. 45–96) with the two books of the *Achilleid*.

Flaccus probably intended twelve books, but died before the eighth was completed. His method was the same as that of Apollonius: a linear narrative from the departure of the Argo from Iolkos to (presumably) her return. He was thus bound to the familiar series of adventures, although Flaccus avoids being too obviously dependent on the Greek. The route of the Argo's return from Colchis was less canonical and would have given some scope to the imagination.

Statius was a writer of altogether greater weight. Naturally, the *Thebaid* shows no originality in content, but Statius avoids the error of beginning at the very beginning, and is thus not committed to the whole saga of the house of Laius. He begins with the blinding of Oedipus—a scene of horror irresistible to the taste of the age—and takes the story to the death of Antigone and the obsequies of Polynices. The poem is well finished, having taken twelve years to compose, and it is easy to understand the high reputation in which it was held during medieval and Renaissance times. Statius observed the standard epic length of twelve books. In style the *Thebaid* and *Achilleid* are declamatory, although not so fiercely rhetorical as Lucan. They show, however, the same tendency toward episodic treatment, as if the epic were slipping from a whole toward a connected string of epyllia.

None of these writers dared challenge Vergil openly, although heavily dependent on him for thought and diction. For Vergil had rapidly achieved at Rome the position Homer held in Greece, well ahead of any rival. This was the judgment of Quintilian (*Education of an Orator* 10.1.86), but later commentators went further in their praise of his skill and erudition, turning him into the all-knowing genius of literature. The fruits of this criticism may be read in Macrobius' *Saturnalia* 4–6. It created a mold that the epic genre badly needed to break if it was to revitalize itself.

THE EPIC OF THE GREEK REVIVAL

The civil wars of the Romans, which led to the burning of the Library at Alexandria in

47 B.C., marked the nadir of Greek culture in antiquity. But Greek survived, although as an artificial, classicizing language, and from the latter half of the first century A.D., reasserted with considerable success its ancient claims as the language of learning and culture. Epic poetry, however, languished for lack of any revivifying ideas. The second century A.D. produced another romance of the Argonauts, the so-called *Orphic Argonautica;* it is seldom read. Finds of papyri bear witness to the continuing production of encomiastic historical poems. In mythology the Trojan War still seemed worthy of attention. Perhaps Vergil's noble treatment of the end of Troy in *Aeneid* 2, insofar as the Greeks allowed themselves to think of Latin literature, seemed to expose the weaknesses of the old cyclic poem, if it still existed.

Two poets of the fourth century A.D. tried to mend matters, Tryphiodorus (also referred to as "Triphiodorus" in papyri and inscriptions) in a short *Sack of Troy (Iliupersis)* of 691 verses, and Quintus of Smyrna in the fourteen books of his *Posthomerica* that bridged the interval between the *Iliad* and the *Odyssey.* Tryphiodorus also executed an **Odyssey omitting letters.* Since the books of the Homeric poems were known by the twenty-four letters of the Greek alphabet, his idea was to rewrite the poem omitting the corresponding letter—not a poetic notion. There was also an **Iliad omitting letters* by one Nestor. Such pedantic jokes demonstrate very forcefully that, being composed in what was virtually a dead language, "poetry" had fallen firmly into the hands of grammarians. Quintus, for example, was soaked in the language of Homer, but neither he nor Tryphiodorus was a poet.

A more promising topic than the saga of Troy, however, had been in the course of development—the myth of Dionysus, god of ecstasy and intoxication. Dionysus represented exoticism and sensuality. Unlike most of the old mythology, the matter of Dionysus could also represent at the literary level some of the religious impulses of an age that was turning to the mysteries of Mithraism, Christianity, and the cults of Hermes Trismegistos. As a conqueror of Asia, Dionysus could absorb some of the romance and allure of another ancient conqueror, Alexander—ancient, because six centuries had elapsed since Alexander passed the Hellespont. In the time of the emperor Diocletian (A.D. 284–305) one Soterichus wrote an **Epic of Bassareus [Dionysus] (Bassarica)* in four books. Papyrus fragments show that this effort was not unique. These works mentioned the conquest of India by Dionysus and his army of maenads, a campaign (if that is the word) that forms the main substance of the last great epic of antiquity, the *Epic of Dionysus (Dionysiaca)* of Nonnus of Panopolis (fifth century A.D.) in forty-eight books. Nonnus was a master of language and verse, both admirably correct, yet not uncritically so. His hexameter favors, as appropriate to Dionysiac ecstasy, a fast, bounding, dactylic rhythm; but it also incorporates an interesting concession to the accentual character of contemporary spoken Greek. He sought to avoid a harsh clash of verse accent and speech accent at the verse end, where meter should be clearest.

It is a question how far Nonnus could assume a familiarity with the theme of the Indian war in his audience. In order to begin in medias res in Homeric fashion he would have had to make just such an assumption. Instead he began at the very beginning, with the primeval chaos, and ended with the admission of Dionysus, youngest of the gods, to Olympus. The main theme is thus long delayed, and the preliminaries and sequel to it weave in an encyclopedia of mythology. It is vain to look for an Aristotelian plot, but any deficiencies in that direction Nonnus makes up in exuberance. "Exuberance" also describes his diction. The style is torrential, another Dionysiac touch, but the richness inevitably cloys for lack of variety. Indeed by a severe standard the *Epic of Dionysus* would be called romance rather than epic. As a god, Dionysus does not risk failure in his conflicts with men, and since there is no risk, there cannot be true heroism in his exploits. Like the Greek novella of the late empire, the *Epic of Dionysus* appeals to a taste for the exotic, the sensual, and the miraculous, but does it in the grand manner.

The minor epic genres continued in use in late antiquity. Two epyllia are extant, the *Rape of Helen* by Colluthos (*ca.* A.D. 500), a dull piece, and the pleasing *Hero and Leander* of Musaeus (*ca.* A.D. 450). The young Claudian, another poet of Egypt, served his apprenticeship in this tradition of classicizing verse. He wrote foundation stories and a *Gigantomachia,* popular themes of which Nonnus also made striking use. But Claudian soon moved to richer pastures in Italy, becoming panegyrist and propagandist to the imperial court of Honorius at Ravenna. His mastery of the Latin language is remarkable, but even more so, for a Greek, is his mastery of the Latin stylistic tradition perfected by Lucan and Statius. As court poet Claudian's function was to eulogize the chief luminary of Honorius' circle, the romanized barbarian Stilicho, and to satirize his enemies. Panegyric (and invective, which is simply an inversion of panegyric) had long since been reduced to an art. One described the birth and education of the subject, compared him favorably with others, and recounted his deeds. In part then panegyric was a narrative genre. Since the epic in the later Latin tradition contained much formal description and declamation, the difference between Claudian's historical epics, which have diagnostic titles—*War Against Gildo* (*De Bello Gildonico*) and *War Against the Getae* (*De Bello Getico*)—and his panegyrics is slight. The tendency for narrative to dissolve into a series of tableaux, already marked in Lucan and Statius, has become the normal pattern in Claudian. In his most ambitious poem,

the *Rape of Proserpine* (*Persephone*) (*De Raptu Proserpinae*), the alternate set speeches and descriptions squeeze the narrative into mere bridging passages. But Claudian was a first-rate painter with words, and wrote with a panache that one admires more easily than his subject matter. The poet died, or at least disappeared, in A.D. 404. Six years later Alaric sacked Rome.

The periods of literary history are never as sharply defined as those of political history. Nonnus and Claudian mark the termination of the ancient culture mainly in the sense that what they achieved was never afterward equaled or even attempted. Claudian was a pagan of sorts, and Prudentius, who wrote immediately after him, a Christian and an exponent of the allegorical method that hallmarked serious literature for the next millennium. The break looks clear enough, yet the *Battle of the Soul* (*Psychomachia*) too is a series of tableaux with little real narrative. Even as late as the mid sixth century A.D. the African Corippus could write a historical epic (*Johannes*) in eight books. On the Greek side the ancient culture faded by very slow degrees and any terminus looks arbitrary.

BIBLIOGRAPHY

SOURCES

Homer, *The Iliad,* A. T. Murray, trans., 2 vols. (1924–1925); Pliny the Younger, *Letters and Panegyricus,* Betty Radice, trans., 2 vols. (1969); Suetonius, *The Lives of the Caesars,* J. C. Rolfe, trans., 2 vols. (1914).

STUDIES

Prehistoric Origins

Cecil Maurice (Sir Maurice) Bowra, *Heroic Poetry* (1952); Arthur T. Hatto, ed., *Traditions of Heroic and Epic Poetry* (1980); Felix J. Oinas, ed.,

Heroic Epic and Saga: An Introduction to the World's Great Folk Epics (1978); Peter Walcot, *Hesiod and the Near East* (1966); Thomas B. L. Webster, *From Mycenae to Homer* (1958; repr. 1964).

Greek Primary Epic and its Offshoots

Howard Clarke, *Homer's Readers: A Historical Introduction to the Iliad and the Odyssey* (1981); Jasper Griffin, "The Epic Cycle and the Uniqueness of Homer," in *Journal of Hellenic Studies*, **97** (1977); George L. Huxley, *Greek Epic Poetry from Eumelos to Panyassis* (1969); Geoffrey Stephen Kirk, *The Songs of Homer* (1962), and *Homer and the Oral Tradition* (1976); Joachim Latacz, ed., *Homer: Tradition und Neuerung* (1979); John Linton (Sir John) Myres, *Homer and His Critics*, Dorothea Gray, ed. (1958); Gregory Nagy, *The Best of the Achaeans: Concepts of the Hero in Archaic Greek Poetry* (1980); Adam Parry, ed., *The Making of Homeric Verse: The Collected Papers of Milman Parry* (1971); Kirsti Simonsuuri, *Homer's Original Genius: Eighteenth-century Notions of the Early Greek Epic* (1979); Alan J. B. Wace and Frank H. Stubbings, eds., *A Companion to Homer* (1962); Cedric H. Whitman, *Homer and the Heroic Tradition* (1958).

Hellenistic Literary Epic and Derivative Forms

Gerald F. Else, *Aristotle's Poetics: the Argument* (1957); Hermann Fränkel, *Noten zu den Argonautika des Appollonios* (1968); Peter M. Fraser, *Ptolemaic Alexandria*, vols. 1–3 (1972); Severin Koster, *Antike Epostheorien* (Palingenesia 5, 1970); Thomas B. L. Webster, *Hellenistic Poetry and Art* (1964); Konrat J. F. Ziegler, *Das hellenistische Epos* (1934; 2d ed. 1966).

Early Roman Epic

Erich Burck, ed., *Das römische Epos* (1979); Reinhard Häussler, *Das historische Epos der Griechen und Römer bis Vergil* (1976); Werner Suerbaum, *Untersuchungen zur Selbstdarstellung älterer römischer Dichter* (1968); Konrat J. F. Ziegler, *op. cit.*

Neoteric and Augustan Epic

Cecil Maurice (Sir Maurice) Bowra, *From Virgil to Milton* (1945); Erich Burck, *op. cit.;* Robert Coleman, "Ovid and the Anti-Epic," in *Classical Review*, **17** (1967); Karl Galinsky, *Ovid's Metamorphoses* (1975); Jasper Griffin, "Augustan Poetry and the Life of Luxury," in *Journal of Roman Studies*, **66** (1976); Brooks Otis, *Virgil: A Study in Civilized Poetry* (1964), and *Ovid as an Epic Poet* (1966; 2d ed. 1970); Kenneth Quinn, *Virgil's Aeneid: A Critical Description* (1968); Ronald Syme, *The Roman Revolution* (1939); Eustace Mandeville Tillyard, *The English Epic and its Background* (1954); Gordon Williams, *Technique and Ideas in the Aeneid* (1983).

Roman Rhetorical Epic

Joachim Adamietz, *Zur Komposition der Argonautica des Valerius Flaccus* (Zetemata, Heft **67**, 1976); Henri Bardon, *La littérature latine inconnue*, **1** (1952), **2** (1956); Erich Burck, *op. cit.;* Pierre Miniconi and Georges Devallet, *Silius Italicus: la guerre punique* (Collection Budé, 1979); Mark Percy O. Morford, *The Poet Lucan* (1967); David Vessey, *Statius and the Thebaid* (1973); Gordon Williams, *Change and Decline: Roman Literature in the Early Empire* (1978).

The Epic of the Greek Revival

Alan Cameron, *Claudian: Poetry and Propaganda at the Court of Honorius* (1970); Francis Vian, *Quintus de Smyrne: la suite d'Homère* (Collection Budé, **1**, 1963; **2**, 1966; **3**, 1969), and *Nonnos de Panopolis: les Dionysiaques* (Collection Budé, **1**, **2**, 1976); Sven Albert Wifstrand, *Von Kallimachos zu Nonnos: metrisch-stilistische Untersuchungen zur späteren griechischen Epik und zu verwandten Gedichtgattungen* (1933).

Greek Lyric and Elegiac Poetry

JOSEPH RUSSO

INTRODUCTION

It is convenient, and reasonably accurate, to divide Greek poetry into three major classes: epic, lyric, and dramatic. They reached their respective heights in that order, their greatest recorded achievements coming roughly in the eighth, seventh-to-sixth, and fifth centuries B.C. Lyric may well be the oldest of the three, having its roots in the folk songs, ritual and magical chants, prayers, curses, laments, and other occasion-based singing that is surely as old as any human verbal art can be.

In the early seventh century, not long after Homer and Hesiod, lyric first emerged as the creation of known individuals and attained—perhaps after years in oral circulation—a written form that guaranteed its survival. For the next 200 years the best poetic talents of archaic Greece continued to express themselves in lyric forms (which for our purposes include elegiac, iambic, and related meters) throughout the seventh, sixth, and first half of the fifth centuries. We may therefore speak of a "Lyric Age of Greece," situated between the "Epic Age" and the fifth century, in which Athenian drama was the preeminent poetic form.

Our first step toward understanding Greek lyric and elegiac poetry is to abandon some of the English connotations of the words *lyric* and *elegiac* and to replace them with Greek meanings. Today *lyric* suggests a short poem, spoken as the voice of a sensitive consciousness, expressing in condensed fashion an individual feeling or perception that is meant to convey universal insight to the hearer or reader. The term *elegiac* means simply sad or mournful, referring especially to lamenting the passing of something valued. These meanings, although derived from the Greek, no longer reflect it accurately. The Greek word *lyrikos* designated poetry sung to the lyre, and "lyric" in the ancient sense should refer only to such verse. The nouns *elegos* and *elegeia* designated verses spoken or chanted (but not sung) aloud, often or sometimes (the question is still being debated) to flute accompaniment. Both these ancient forms of poetry are the literary ancestors of most subsequent poetry in the Western tradition, and of all Western poetry that is not narrative or satirical or dramatic (although satire too has some roots in ancient lyric). But these ancient genres differed greatly from their modern descendants in one vital aspect: verbal art in performance played an enormous role in the social, religious, aesthetic, and political life of the ancient world, as indeed it always has in traditional, archaic cultures.

There is an enormous difference between the role of the poet in the ancient and modern worlds, and between the means of production, dissemination, and "consumption" of poetry in each system. Modern poets compose idiosyncratically in a style that they work at making their own, primarily for their own satisfaction, for an audience they will never see and need not strive to please. Our poets are considered outside the cultural mainstream, odd types in a society that is organized to an extreme degree around non-artistic values and activities. Therefore, they have little influence or money. But the situation of the ancient Greek poets was quite the opposite. Their social prestige was enormous, they were favorites at the courts of tyrants and kings, they influenced politics, and they eventually charged large fees. Money was not a problem in any case, since they were usually from aristocratic families. In composing their poetry they were guided not so much by individualistic criteria as by the demands of tradition and the tastes of a public well-steeped in that tradition. Thus, the nature of the occasion and the audience for a given performance strongly influenced the choice of genre, which in turn determined subject matter, poetic diction, meter and dialect, and other formal aspects of the verse. Every poetic text, therefore, is one piece in an interlocking set of variables, the demands of which the individual poetic talent mediates along two axes—that of past precedents and that of present situation.

One of the fundamental determinants of form in Greek lyric is the distinction between solo song, or monody, and choral song. Our oldest testimony for such diverse genres is Homeric epic, which already describes the performance of group song, group song accompanied by dance, and solo song. Although the word *choros* means "dance" or "dancing group," some choral genres—to the best of our knowledge—involved no dancing, including the hymn to Apollo for deliverance from harm (*paian*), the ritual lament for a death (*threnos*), and the wedding song (*hymenaios*). Choral song was accompanied by the lyre or the flute, true lyric only by the lyre, elegiac poetry by the flute (or perhaps at times it had no accompaniment, and was recited rather than sung); iambic poetry was simply recited or chanted.

The great poets of choral lyric are Alcman, Stesichorus, Simonides, Bacchylides, and Pindar, while the great monodists are Archilochus, Sappho, Alcaeus, and Anacreon. Some of them composed in several genres, so that some of the monodists' hymns were probably choral, such as Sappho's wedding songs (*epithalamia*), while Alcman and Simonides have songs that are meant for the solo voice.

Monody was usually brief, and most have not survived in full, so that our texts of solo lyric are quite fragmentary. Even so, they are eloquent testimony to the remarkable talent of these composers, and the more complete poems often astound us with their beauty and intensity. Choral lyric usually runs to some length, and the earliest example from the seventh-century work of Alcman is already quite long and complex in structure. Length and complexity grow even greater in the last great flowering of choral lyric, the fifth-century victory odes (*epinikia*) of Bacchylides and Pindar.

To conclude our general discussion of types, we must further define two kinds of monody not sung to the lyre and therefore not "lyric" by the strict definition: elegiac and iambic verse. The term *elegiac* covers all poetry composed in elegiac couplets, regardless of content or tone. Elegiacs were used for political comment, military exhortation, moral essays in verse, love poetry, sympotic (drinking-party) poetry, epigram, tombstone epigraphs, and various kinds of formal inscription cut into stone for public display. The elegiac couplet is composed of one dactylic hexameter line (the meter of epic) followed by one pentameter, which is a derivative of the hexameter, consisting of what amounts to two hexameter line openings joined together (– ˘ ˘ ˘ – ˘ ˘ –|– ˘ ˘ – ˘ ˘ –). This formal structure itself suffices to show that elegiac was created in the shadow of epic, requiring only a small modification in epic meter to produce a new unit that moves by couplets rather than by single lines. This small change ushered in a radically new kind of poetry, based on short rhetorical units, spoken from a personal rather than an impersonal viewpoint, addressing the here and now rather than narrating traditional stories, and applicable to a vast range of topics in no way connected with epic. Thus the development of the elegiac reveals the Greek creative genius at its most inventive.

Iambic poetry was normally a vehicle for satire and invective, moral suasion and criticism, and general comment and advice about life. Iambic poetry came closest to the rhythm and diction of ordinary speech, being quite devoid of the loftier phrasing and epic echoes that constantly turn up in the dactylic cadences of the elegiac. Once the zenith of monodic poetry had passed, and Athenian drama was developing its form in the late sixth and early fifth centuries, iambic was taken as the standard meter for the spoken dialogue, but not the sung portions, of tragedy and comedy.

All three kinds of solo poetry we have discussed, lyric, elegiac, and iambic, have something in common with our modern notion of lyric: poetry speaking for an individual and expressing judgments and feelings from a personal point of view, the author's "I." In this respect choral lyric differs greatly, because its concern is with group values and attitudes and it makes generous use of communal material in the form of myths and legends. Because it runs to considerable length, choral poetry lacks the intensity that comes with the concision of lyric, and because it speaks for the community, it lacks the urgency generated by the authorial "I."

EARLY MONODIC POETRY

Archilochus

We begin our discussion of outstanding monodists with Archilochus of the island of Paros, who was active in the first half of the seventh century and died about 640, killed in battle according to tradition. His is perhaps the clearest and most self-asserting poetic personality on record from archaic Greece, whether or not his poems are to be read as autobiography. Even if he speaks with more than one poetic persona, his very choice of poetic masks reveals his personality through the choice of roles he likes to play for his audience. As a colonist from Paros to Thasos and something of a soldier of fortune, he led a life filled with violence and the unexpected. The dominant themes of his poetry are the power of the unexpected, the joy and pain of love, and the military life of an island rover. His favorite meters, to judge from the surviving poetry, are elegiac, iambic trimeter, trochaic tetrameter, and epodic meters that combine dactylic and iambic movement and alternate a long line with a short one.

Here are two poems in trochaic tetrameter (– ˘ – ˘|– ˘ – ˘|– ˘ – ˘|– ˘ –), neither likely to be complete, but representative of this poet at his best:

> Glaukos, look, the deepest ocean stands
> with churning waves by now,
> And around the Gyrean peaks a cloud is
> lifted to the heavens,

Sign of storm: a sense of danger rises
   from the unexpected.
                 (Diehl 56; West 105)

Anything the gods should want, they do;
   how often out from troubles
They lift a man back on his feet, who was
   down on the black earth;
And other times they'll take a man who's
   walking well, and flip him
Down on his back, and then his griefs
   begin: without
A livelihood, his mind unhinged, he has
   to wander.
                 (Diehl 58; West 130)

The following is in elegiac form:

Along the benches of the swift ship,
   come on, go with your cup, lift the
   lids off the jars;
Chase all the red wine to the dregs, for
   how could we manage,
Standing guard like this, ever to be
   sober?
                 (Diehl 5a; West 4)

In epode form, we have the fragment:

Such an erotic yearning has slipped its
   way into my heart,
   Pouring a veiling cloud on my eyes
Snatching my delicate wits right out of
   my body.
                 (Diehl 112; West 193)

The following four-line trochaic tetrameter
may be complete:

I don't care for the tall captain, the one
   with the long stride;
For the one who's proud of his curly
   locks, or too carefully shaved.
Let me have a little fellow, let him have
   crooked legs:
A man who's steady in his walk, a man
   who's full of heart.
                 (Diehl 60; West 114)

From these samples it is evident that we are in the presence of a strong poetic personality. Equally powerful is the fifty-three-line fragment discovered and published in 1974, the so-called Cologne Epode (Page, *Supplementum Lyricis Graecis* 478), which is the longest surviving Archilochean poem and the most detailed description we have of sexual seduction in ancient Greece. It uses extended dialogue and leads up to a sexual act whose exact nature is still disputed in scholarly journals (see Van Sickle [1975] for translation and commentary).

In this same archaic period there are some good elegiac poets whom we must pass over briefly. The most enjoyable is Mimnermus of Colophon (670–600), who wrote movingly about the joys of love and the sad necessity that these fade with old age. Callinus of Ephesus (mid seventh century) wrote good hortatory poetry encouraging his townsmen to military struggle. Tyrtaeus of Sparta (middle to third quarter of the seventh century B.C.) similarly encouraged his people to battle in elegiac verses that draw heavily on epic language and sentiments. The great Athenian politician Solon, at the beginning of the sixth century, composed long elegiac poems and also iambic and trochaic pieces. The latter are all political, but in the elegiacs he rises to greater heights by setting issues of political morality in a wider context of human life as a whole and man's relationship to the gods.

Theognis

The greatest output of any elegiac poet is that of Theognis of Megara (550–480?), the only poet of this group whose work survives not in papyrus fragments or quotation by later writers but in direct manuscript form. Unfortunately he is a mediocre poet, and the 1,400 verses attributed to him (some surely spurious, but there is controversy over how many) are difficult to read straight through with enjoyment. They include many repetitions, and attempts have been made to edit them into many small poems. Theognis' favorite themes are political harangue against the new class that has taken over political power in Megara from the landed aristocrats (his own class), love, and drinking parties. Some of this poetry is addressed affectionately to a young man called Cyrnus, about whom we know nothing else.

Semonides

One of the most interesting early archaic poets, Semonides of Amorgos (mid to late seventh century), was one of Greece's first intensely misogynistic poets (the other being Hesiod). His statements are negative, querulous, and small-minded, but expressed with vigor and an awkward bluntness that effectively conveys strong feeling. His famous poem 7 is a 118-line iambic diatribe against women, whom he catalogs according to the nature they were given by the deity at creation. They were all fashioned out of various animals (pig, vixen, dog, ass, weasel, mare, monkey, and bee) or out of the earth or the sea, and consequently bear these natures. Only the bee woman is singled out for praise, because she embodies the beelike virtues of good housekeeper and faithful servant of her husband's wishes. This poem may be read as a catalog of all the qualities that Greek men disliked and feared in their women, which, taken together with some of Hesiod's comments in his *Theogony* and *Works and Days* concerning Pandora, constitute the earliest documentation in the long unfortunate history of Greek misogyny.

THE FLOWERING OF LYRIC POETRY

Of the poets presented thus far, none is strictly lyric in the ancient sense. Among those who did sing to the lyre, the supreme masters of the genre are Sappho and Alcaeus of the island of Lesbos (*ca.* 600 B.C.) and Anacreon of the island of Teos (*ca.* 575–*ca.* 490).

Sappho

The greatest of the monodists and the one whose poetry and social context offer the most interesting and complex connection is Sappho. Both her monodic poems, which are spoken from her personal perspective, and her wedding songs and hymns, meant for choral presentation, are sung within a group setting with a certain inevitable ritual quality to the performance. Therefore, we should not take her intense, personal-sounding lyrics to be the exact equivalent of their modern counterparts. A Sapphic ode is not a solitary cri de coeur, but a public statement on a specific occasion before a familiar audience of a strong sentiment that involves the members of the group. Thus Sappho's intense feelings become a group possession, and the assimilation of and identification with these feelings a group function. When Sappho praises the beauty or laments the absence of a young woman, each member of the audience responds internally through her own emotional attachment to Sappho, to the woman in the song, and to other women in the audience with whom she may have shared some of the same feelings that exist between Sappho and the girl she loves. Thus the public performance creates much more in the live audience than the distant vicarious identification with the poet's feelings that characterizes the modern response to lyric poetry. We, as moderns, must realize that ancient "literature" of this type is to be thought of not as a text but as an event.

Sappho's poetry has survived almost entirely in fragmentary form, although we know that originally her poems were edited in nine books by Alexandrian scholars. Any lover of poetry is advised to find a modern translation and read all that survives of Sappho, which may come to less than fifteen pages but is incredibly fine. She has a great capacity for dramatic externalization of her private feelings and for giving life to the small universe of love ties and losses that formed the emotional center of her group. Consider the following (Lobel and Page, *Poetarum Lesbiorum Fragmenta* [*LP*] 94.1–17; all numbers given hereafter for Sappho and Alcaeus refer to this edition):

> "I really wish I were dead."
> She wept strongly as she left me, and
>   added,
> "What terrible things have come for us!
> Sappho, it's against my will that I leave
>   you."
> And I answered, "Go and be well, and
>   think of me:
> You know how we cared for you.
> If you don't, let me recall to you . . .
>   good for us.
> How many times, at my side, did you put
>   on . . .
> Wreaths of roses, crocus, violets, and
>   how many
> Woven garlands, twisted with flowers,
>   under your delicate neck?"

There follow twelve more verses in increasingly fragmentary form, which apparently continue to list various past delights (myrrh and other ointments are named) that Sappho and the unnamed young woman have shared. It is clear that the activities of Sappho's group were designed to create and intensify tender and romantic feelings through the almost ritualized use of unguents, flowers and wreaths, and overt declarations of physical admiration and attraction. Scholars in the past have often been embarrassed by Sappho's homosexual feelings and have tried to minimize them, but we cannot understand her poetry without appreciating how sexually charged it is. This

poem in fact happens to contain the one clear reference in Sappho's surviving texts to physical sexual activity, as it would seem from lines 21–23 of poem 94:

> and on soft bedding
> (and) delicate . . .
> you satisfied your longing.

Poem 94 vividly presents a pattern of separation and deep sense of loss that seems to be built into the very nature of Sappho's group. Compare poem 96, which describes how a woman, although now in Sardis (in Lydia), is still strongly bound in thought and feelings to the group in Lesbos and particularly to Atthis, who was her favorite, "whose tender heart is consumed because of your fate." The absent woman is said to stand out among the Lydian women as the moon outshines the stars once the sun has set. Such comparisons, using the brightness of heavenly bodies to describe the radiance of female beauty, are common rhetorical features of archaic Greek lyric (see the maiden song of Alcman, discussed below). From poems 94 and 96 we may infer that the ultimate purpose of Sappho's group was to send off its young members, presumably to marriage, once they had attained sufficient cultivation of the arts of Aphrodite through the group's regular activities. Other poems (1, 2) show that Aphrodite's presence was of prime importance, and the arts of this goddess have to do not just with sexuality but also with all the decorative touches (perfumes, flowers, song, clothing) that foster the development of erotic feeling.

The exact nature of Sappho's group is a question that has burdened past scholarship and evoked a variety of responses. It used to be fashionable to imagine that Sappho was head of a sort of finishing school, in which young women of good families received musical education. This comparison is not far off the mark if we substitute the Aphroditic arts for music—although we see that they include music under the form of song (poem 96 mentions how someone, presumably Atthis, used to enjoy the singing of the now absent woman). After learning all these arts, the young women probably left, in most cases to marry. Here poem 31 may give us a further clue, if the man named at the beginning is the prospective husband of the woman he sits with. Sappho begins by calling this man "equal to the gods" because of his fortunate position opposite the woman Sappho loves. She describes herself as overwhelmed with grief because the woman is apparently enjoying this man's company, since she smiles and laughs in reaction to him. The poem concludes (31.9–16):

> My tongue is broken,
> A tender fire runs under my skin, my
>   eyes
> See nothing, my ears roar, a cold sweat
>   takes me,
> And trembling seizes me everywhere. I
>   grow more pale
> Than grass, I think I'm about to die.

It is vital for understanding Sappho to see that her chief raison d'être, as defined in her poetry, is the cultivation of love relationships. What one loves, she says in poem 16, becomes the fairest thing in the world. The poem begins:

> Some say a host of cavalry, some say
>   infantry,
> Some say a host of ships, is the loveliest
>   thing
> Upon this dark earth; but I say
> It's whatever you love.

This poem leads again to the familiar theme of the beautiful beloved who is now gone and sorely missed. Here it is Anactoria whose beautiful walk and shining face, Sappho says in the fifth stanza, she would rather see "than all the chariots of Lydia and its

fully armed infantry." Since these details echo the set of contrasts that opened the poem, it is likely that this poem is complete in the five stanzas that survive, although missing a crucial word in the third stanza and about half of the fourth.

The only completely preserved Sapphic poem is the famous "Ode to Aphrodite," numbered 1 in all editions. It is a perfect self-revealing statement of Sappho's commitment to a life centered on love affairs, of her awareness of the painful price this life sometimes exacts, and of her total dependence on Aphrodite as the goddess who controls our falling into and falling out of love. The poem is too long to quote here, but the reader is urged to use the outstanding translation by Thomas G. Rosenmeyer included in the excellent analysis by Walter Ralph Johnson in *The Idea of Lyric* (1982). Like poems 16 and 31 quoted above, this text is in the meter that Sappho made famous, which was called "Sapphic" for that reason. An English approximation can be found in the 1960 translation of Richmond Lattimore.

When Sappho is not singing about individual loves she often performs as group spokeswoman, in poetry that has less intensity but is no less graceful or beautifully worded. These nonerotic fragments include pieces of wedding songs (*epithalamia*), some teasing banter that seems also to have formed part of the wedding ritual, and poems meant to exalt her own group against a rival group whose leader Sappho criticizes. The one sizable fragment among these wedding songs (44) is a description of the wedding of Hector and Andromache, done in quasi-epic dialect and perhaps performed to serve as an *epithalamium* for the marriage of one of Sappho's young women, if we can imagine that it was customary to enhance the immediate moment with parallels from the legendary past. More clearly part of customary practice in *epithalamia* was the comparison of bride and groom to beautiful plants or flowers in formal similes, as in 105a:

> Just as the sweet apple reddens, up on
>   the highest branch,
> Atop the very top, and the apple-pickers
>   forgot it—
> No, they didn't forget it: they simply
>   could not reach it.

In such comparisons the young bride's virginity is metaphorically presented through images of the delicate, sweet, but so far inaccessible growth. In fragment 105c the image is more troubled, that of a hyacinth whose purple flower the shepherds have (carelessly?) trodden down:

> Just like the hyacinth that shepherds with
>   their feet will walk on
> In the mountains, and the purple flower
>   on the ground.

Since we have only two lines, we cannot tell in what direction Sappho developed this image of delicacy wounded.

We have given considerable space to Sappho's poetry and the world it was created to serve, in the belief that she is the greatest of the lyric monodists and one of the world's greatest poets. Among the Greeks only Archilochus can match her intensity (but not her delicacy), and only Anacreon comes close to her perfect choice and placement of words.

Alcaeus

The poet Alcaeus was, like Sappho, a native of Lesbos active in the late seventh and early sixth centuries. He also sang of love, but gave more poetic energy to songs about political conflict and to drinking songs, if the surviving poems are representative. Many of his poems are, like Sappho's, the direct product of his personal life and read like pieces of autobiography. In place of Sappho's female circle we have Alcaeus' political *hetaireia* or body of political friends. Just as Sappho performed her songs before a group who shared her ideals of female beauty and her susceptibility to love and the pain of separation from a loved one, so Alcaeus performed before friends who shared his political beliefs and animosities, as well as his sensitivity to the pain of exile and separation from power.

The political biography of Alcaeus consists of constant struggle to be at the center of power in Mytilene, the chief city of Lesbos. At first his brothers were allied with a certain Pittakos in overthrowing the tyrant Melanchros, during 612–609 B.C. Pittakos remained the leading political figure in Mytilene during this period, and Alcaeus speaks of alliance with him in opposition to a new tyrant, Myrsilos (poem 129). But at some point Pittakos defected to Myrsilos (poem 70). Then we have a fragment of a poem of intense rejoicing at Myrsilos' death (poem 332)—a poem imitated by Horace in his famous opening "Nunc est bibendum" (Now let there be drinking), of *Odes* 1.37—but Alcaeus' continued vituperation against Pittakos shows that his faction remained excluded from power. We have two poems complaining of exile in some rural area of Lesbos (poems 129 and 130b), and we know that he traveled to the East, to Egypt, perhaps also in exile from Lesbian politics. All other evidence suggests that Pittakos was a good ruler who in fact granted clemency to Alcaeus; so that the personality of Alcaeus that emerges from the poetry is that of a man who is an implacable, unforgiving opponent in politics, capable of deep and abiding animosity. This same strong personality is transformed in the convivial drinking songs into one that intensely enjoys his good times, and the friends he drinks with and speaks to in these poems are no doubt the same men who are his political allies.

In both the political and drinking songs, we must admire Alcaeus' capacity for the sharp, memorable metaphor. The metaphoric relationship is at times sustained to yield an effective allegorical picture. It can be seen in several political poems where weather represents the political climate, and survival or distress at sea stands for the poet's shifting political fortunes. The most famous of these poems is the "Ship of State," poem 326, the earliest known use of what became a stock political metaphor in antiquity (used, for example, in Sophocles' *Antigone* and *Oedipus the King,* and in Horace *Odes* 1.14) and remains a commonplace metaphor today. An ancient critic quotes this much of the poem:

> I don't understand the wind's movement:
> One wave rolls from this side, one from
>   another,
> And we in our black ship
> Are carried between them
>
> Shaken by this great storm.
> Bilge is up to the mast stand, the whole
>   sail
> Torn through with big holes everywhere.
> The anchors [ropes?] won't hold, the
>   rudders . . .

Here the quote breaks off. A possible supplement from a papyrus fragment would add, "Both feet are tangled in the sheets: this alone holds me safe" (Page, *Sappho and Alcaeus* 185–189). A similar metaphoric picture is developed in poem 6, in much more fragmentary form. Both poems are called "allegorical" in a commentary from late antiquity, Heraclitus' *Homeric Allegories* (first century A.D.); but even without this judgment we might have assumed as much from a careful reading of the texts. As early as Homer's *Iliad* (15.381–384) we find the Trojans' attack compared to ocean waves coming over the side of a ship. Archilochus (Diehl 56; West 105, quoted earlier) contin-

ues this tradition, and Alcaeus is simply building on an established poetic convention.

Other poems of Alcaeus are immediately appealing for their simple delight in drink and the fellowship of the symposium, a type of poetry known as sympotic. Fragment 346 begins:

> Let's drink! Why wait for the lamps? A
>   finger of daylight remains.
> Take down the big drinking cups with
>   elaborate handles.

Fragments 38A and 347 begin:

> Drink and get drunk, Melanippus, with
>   me. Why
> Do you think, once you've passed over
>   Acheron's
> Eddying waters, you'll see the sun's pure
>   light again?

and

> Moisten your lungs with wine: the
>   dogstar is back,
> It's a hard [summer] season, the heat
>   makes everything thirst.

Although political and sympotic poems make up the majority of Alcaeus' work, the other two significant genres represented in his limited surviving corpus are hymns and poems on mythological themes. We have hymns to Apollo, Athena, the Dioscuri, Hermes, and the god Eros, and mythological poems dealing with Achilles and Thetis, Perseus and Medusa, and the ever-popular figure of Helen of Troy, who appears in two poems, 42 and 283. In contrast to Sappho's seemingly sympathetic portrait in her poem 16, Alcaeus paints Helen in a strongly negative light. One may sense here the same moral fervor that colors his political poetry, as well as a natural disinclination to sympathize with a woman's position.

Of the ten books of poems collected in late antiquity, relatively little of Alcaeus survives, and none of the poems we have is more than a fragment. Poem 42 seems nearest to a complete text in four stanzas, although lacking the final few words of most lines. His favorite meter seems to have been the Alcaic stanza, named after him, which he may have invented and which became a favorite meter for Horace in his *Odes.* He also composed in Sapphics and in several non-stanzaic meters like the greater and lesser Asclepiadic (also Horatian favorites) and various expanded glyconics.

Anacreon

The third in our trio of pure lyricists, Anacreon (*ca.* 575–*ca.* 490), seems less intense than Sappho and Alcaeus because of the greater distance that separates the speaker of the poems from the sentiments expressed. Anacreon's passions are presented as kept more consciously under the objective, even amused, scrutiny of the poet than are those of the two Lesbians. This distance is created through several devices, one of them being the poet's conscious use of his middle-aged perspective and another being the almost self-conscious deliberateness of his word placement. His age is used to give the appearance of the experienced, blasé gentleman who, as veteran of many love affairs, knows how to enjoy himself without letting himself be totally carried away. This detachment lends a spirit of irony and playful self-awareness to his songs. In addition, he is such a skilled practitioner of the art of word placement and careful construction that his finely wrought little word pictures, so manifestly under control, serve as iconic representations of an emotional drama that is also under total control. The speaker of such language is, we feel, acting his role for us, rather than transcribing literal reality, which is the impression that Alcaeus and Sappho seek to convey. This distinctly Anacreontic quality may be illustrated by two of his best and apparently complete poems, "The Girl from Lesbos" and "Thracian Filly." The first reads (Diehl 5; Page, *Poetae Melici Graeci* [hereafter *PMG*] 358):

> Once again with a bright red ball
> Golden Eros hits me,
> And with a girl with fancy sandals
> He calls me forth to play.
>
> But she, since she comes from famous
> Lesbos, spurns my head because
> It is gray, and toward some other
> Girl goes gaping.

This little drama unfolds with neat, controlled irony, moving from the presentation of Anacreon as the victim because he is too old to a more complex picture: the attractive Lesbian girl has a second reason for rejecting the narrator, which comes as a late surprise when the Greek feminine gender of "some other" appears in the last line of the poem. Now a second meaning for "famous [literally, "well-established"] Lesbos" emerges. The girl is more attracted to women than to men, and we see that the adjective "Lesbian" has moved, in the half-century since Sappho, closer to its modern meaning. In the original Greek this poem is remarkable for its skillful word arrangement. The finite verb forms appear only at the end of lines 4, 7, and 8, suspending completion of the crucial idea and then bringing it home with emphasis. The last verb in the poem, "gapes," the final word of the second quatrain and of the whole poem, carries a sting in its sudden revelation that the haughty woman is herself in thrall to an overpowering passion. There may even be a nasty sexual innuendo in the picture of the girl's open mouth, which would make the closing word *khaskei* still more forceful.

In "Thracian Filly" (Diehl 88; *PMG* 417)

the poet is again considering a sexual liaison with a young woman, this time an encounter apparently within his power to achieve. The entire poem consists of a sustained metaphoric correspondence between the poet breaking in and riding a young, untrained filly and the sexual referent for each detail of this procedure. The word play therefore abounds in clever double entendres, culminating in the word *epembatēn*, normally translated "rider" but literally "one who goes on top" and so here clearly sexual.

> Thracian filly, why do you give me that
>   sideways look,
> Cruelly flee me, and think I have no
>   skills?
>
> Know that I could put the bridle neatly
>   on you,
> Take the reins and turn you around the
>   track.
>
> Now you graze the meadows, and play
>   with a light skip:
> You still have no one skilled in
>   horsemanship to ride you.

The poem is neatly organized into three couplets. The meter is trochaic tetrameter, which approximates the rhythm of speaking voices as the more artificial lyric stanzas of the preceding poem could not. In this monologue, as in "The Girl from Lesbos," Anacreon goes beyond the poetic postures taken by Sappho and Alcaeus by using wit to offset passionate sincerity. As Sir Maurice Bowra puts it, "His head understands his heart, but refuses to make too many concessions to it" (1961, p. 272).

In Anacreon we may well have an important turning point in the history of Greek solo lyric: a major step forward in the use of verbal play and the self-conscious stance to distance the poet from his elemental feelings. Such verbal refinement will grow to characterize the later epigrammatic tradition and the entire style of the Hellenistic age. This kind of poetry is less dependent on an audience of sympathizers or supporters; as a work of perfected verbal art, it has less need of specific social context to be fully appreciated. Unlike Sappho or Alcaeus, Anacreon is not rooted in any one social network. We know that he left his native Teos for extended residence at the courts of the tyrants Polycrates of Samos and Hipparchos of Athens, among other patrons. Anacreon thus represents the emergence of a new kind of lyric poet—the traveling professional whose poetry pleases because of its technical brilliance and the generic appeal of its themes. (We might say that at this stage lyric is playing a role similar to that which was normal for epic in Homer's day.) If there are no major monodists after Anacreon, it may be because this kind of poetry was more suited to the traditions and performance style of choral lyric, with its emphasis on the communal rather than the individual point of view. Indeed it is the choral poets of the two generations after Anacreon (Simonides, Bacchylides, Pindar) who will continue the tradition of the poet as traveling professional, composing what each patron wants (and pays for) rather than what his personal experience urgently drives him to express.

CHORAL LYRIC

Alcman

We know that choral lyric was practiced in Greece long before the period of our first surviving texts, the poems of the Spartan Alcman, dated with some uncertainty to the late seventh century. The very complexity of Alcman's technique implies a long tradition behind him. His nationality has been disputed, following an ancient tradition that he came from Sardis in Lydia. It is, however, more than likely that he was Spartan, since Sparta in this period was one of the centers of Greek poetry and music. (We noted earlier the Spartan Tyrtaeus among the earliest elegists.)

Alcman's surviving texts amount to two fragments of maiden songs (*partheneia*) and many other small fragments, some of them gems of lyric. The one fragment sufficiently long to allow us to admire this poet's complexity, grace, and subtlety is the so-called Louvre Partheneion (its papyrus was first published in Paris and is kept in the Louvre). It consists of 101 lines, not all complete, of an original 140, enough to delight the scholar and the reader of good poetry, but at the same time a source of much puzzlement because of the obscurity of its references. We can see a kind of ritualized rivalry between two groups or semichoruses of young women, in which praise is first given to the radiant Agido, but then even greater praise is bestowed upon an apparent rival, the chorus leader Hagesichora (whose name in fact means "chorus leader," so that we are dealing with a role being played).

The chorus members are carrying a robe (although the word could possibly mean "plow") as an offering to the goddess Aotis, who may be a dawn goddess, a fertility and marriage goddess, or both. There is a mysterious reference to the Pleiades as rivals, which has baffled commentators and led to divergent hypotheses. Some think that this is a rival chorus, others that the present chorus is in rivalry with the constellation in some connection lost to us; but it is also possible that the Pleiades are Agido and Hagesichora, since these two are said to "rise like Sirius through the ambrosial night." It is frustrating to have such a long and rich specimen of archaic Greek choral song and yet to face so many unanswered questions, not just about the details of the poem but about its overall purpose. One intriguing recent theory, put forward by Alan

Griffiths (1972), is that the maiden praised most highly after the leader Hagesichora is being prepared for marriage, and that this kind of *partheneium* is essentially part of the *epithalamium* tradition, a bridal song meant to enhance the prestige of the young woman in a ritual public performance. According to this theory, as each member of the chorus is married off, the remaining group continues to perform with one less member; hence the obscure statement at lines 98–99, "Instead of eleven girls this group of ten is singing." But whatever the full purpose of this choral song was, even in its enigmatic allusiveness it continues to attract readers through its rich imagery and its playful, humorous dramatization.

Among Alcman's shorter fragments there are several lovely poems, perhaps monodic, of which one must suffice to illustrate this poet's capacity to create a mood through significant choice of detail (*PMG* 89):

> Asleep now are the mountain peaks and clefts,
> Headlands and ravines,
> Each animal race that the dark earth feeds,
> The mountain beasts, the tribe of bees,
> And strange creatures down in the deep of the dark blue sea;
> Asleep, too, are the races of birds with their long thin wings.

Stesichorus

After Alcman the next important figure in choral poetry was Stesichorus (632/629–556/553 B.C.), the earliest Greek poet to come from the colonies that flourished in southern Italy and Sicily. Although possibly born in southern Italy, he spent most of his life in Himera, a city on Sicily's northeastern coast founded from Zankle (Messina). His place in the development of choral lyric was known from ancient testimony to be an important one, since his fondness for extended narrative served as a bridge between epic and lyric; but until recently there were no fragments long enough to substantiate this judgment. Papyrus finds over the last fifteen years have now filled in some of the picture, giving us sizable fragments of poems titled "The Sack of Troy," "Geryoneis" (the tale of Geryon, a triple-bodied giant whose cattle Heracles carried off as one of his twelve labors), "Eriphyle," and an interesting one-hundred-line fragment of the Oedipus story in which a speech by Jocasta is preserved almost completely. Such texts, together with the already known fragments on the Oresteia, the Calydonian Boar Hunt, Helen of Troy, the Returns of famous heroes from Troy, and stories of the adventures of Heracles, suggest clearly Stesichorus' preference for typically epic and mythological material. His narrative style, although cast in lyric meters, strongly suggests epic in its leisurely pace, abundant use of detail and repetition, full speeches, and echoes of Homeric phraseology. It is hard to know how much of Stesichorus was chorally performed. For the longer pieces it is hard to imagine a chorus dancing for hours, and many believe that these poems were simply recited to the lyre.

Ibycus

The poet Ibycus deserves brief notice here, appropriately next to Stesichorus, since he is the other important poet of the western colonies. A native of Rhegium (Reggio), he wrote during the second half of the sixth century and spent much of his career at the court of Polycrates of Samos, who also hosted Anacreon. His use of epic and mythic themes shows him to be a follower of Stesichorus; but another favorite theme was love, and a few good examples survive of erotic poetry in praise of handsome boys. Because we know so little of Ibycus, it is not certain whether his poetry was choral or mo-

nodic. Certainly the surviving erotic fragments suggest the solo voice used in intense personal expression, in the spirit of Sappho, Alcaeus, and Anacreon, as in poem *PMG* 287:

> Again Eros looks at me meltingly,
> Glancing from under dark eyelids,
> And drives me with all his many
>   enchantments
> Into Aphrodite's endless net.
> Indeed I tremble at his coming,
> Like an aging racehorse under the yoke
> Drawn to compete, unwilling, against
>   swift chariots.

Simonides of Keos

The development of choral lyric takes us now to Simonides of Keos (556–468 B.C.), an important transitional figure between the archaic poetry of Alcman, Stesichorus, and Ibycus and the final flowering of choral lyric in the victory odes, paeans, and dithyrambs of Bacchylides and Pindar in the first half of the fifth century. Simonides was born on the island of Keos but buried in the Sicilian city of Akragas (Agrigento). These facts reflect his international career, which took him on extended visits to Thessaly, Athens, and Sicily, in each case the honored guest of the local aristocracy (in Thessaly) or tyrant (Hipparchos at Athens during 527–514, Hieron of Syracuse at the end of Simonides' career). He seems to have been the first ancient poet to charge fees of his wealthy patrons. Hence he acquired a reputation for avarice, which engendered amusing anecdotes in later antiquity. His compositions covered a wide range of genres and meters, from elegiac couplets to dithyrambs, dirges, paeans, and many epinician (victory) odes. Most famous from antiquity to the present are his sepulchral epigrams composed for the various Greeks who lost their lives warding off the Persian invasion at the battles of

Marathon, Thermopylae, Artemision, Salamis, and Plataea.

Aside from these sepulchral epigrams, we have no complete poems by which to judge Simonides' poetic craft in making a large, complex statement. But some of the fragments are long enough to give us a taste of what antiquity admired as characteristic Simonidean pathos. The uncertainty of human fortune is a prevalent theme, as seen in the fragment below (*PMG* 521), with its vivid closing image:

> Being human, you can never say what
> will happen tomorrow,
> Nor, seeing a fortunate man, how long it
> will last.
> The turnover is swifter even than the
> quick
> Flit of the dragonfly.

One of his more interesting fragments (*PMG* 543) shows how he can use myth, describing Danae and her infant Perseus afloat in the chest in which Danae's father Acrisius had placed them to drown at sea. It is not gnomic and philosophical like many of his other fragments, but gives instead an example of his narrative style. Most of the surviving piece consists of Danae's speech to her child, a warm and moving characterization through language revealing a master poet at work and suggesting how much we have missed through the loss of so much of this poet's work.

LATER CHORAL WORKS: THE VICTORY ODES

For the final period of choral lyric and the only examples we have of complete choral poems, we turn to Pindar and Bacchylides, the two masters of the victory or epinician ode. Both were active in the generation after Simonides (Bacchylides was Simonides' nephew), roughly the first half of the fifth century. Both composed in the usual choral genres, including dithyrambs, paeans, hymns, dirges, and encomia; and indeed there are some fine pieces of poetry in Pindar's fragments of these genres. But it is Pindar's epinicians (odes in honor of victors in the Greek games) that stand supreme as complex art forms embodying many fundamental values of Greek culture. To some extent these values are conservative and aristocratic, since the patrons who commissioned the poems came from the elite—the only Greeks who had the time and money to train for these games and to enter the racehorses and chariots that some of the contests required. These were often the leaders of the international Hellenic community, and included princes, aristocrats, and tyrants. Thus we find Bacchylides and Pindar to be inheritors of Simonides' role of the poet as international figure, a well-traveled professional who is handsomely paid for his services.

Pindar

Pindar composed *epinicia* for the four great athletic contests of Greece, held at Olympia, Delphi, Nemea, and Isthmia (the Isthmus of Corinth). The games were intended as religious celebrations honoring Zeus at Olympia and Nemea, Apollo at Delphi, and Poseidon at the Isthmus. As in the Athenian dramatic competitions held to honor Dionysus, the religious basis of the event meant that a recurring theme of the poetry would be the place of the divine in human affairs. Pindar shares the general Greek belief that human success is unstable and ultimately beyond our control, and is dependent upon divine favor as well as the requisite human skill and courage. Not only, then, are the athletic victors sharing momentarily in the grace of divine favor, but their victorious deed is the very manifestation among us of divine presence, which lifts them for their fleeting moment of glory above all the human race.

Greek culture was highly competitive generally, and here in the games we have that competitiveness formalized and organized in its purest form. Men competed in the four-horse chariot race, single-horse race, mule-cart race, men's and boys' boxing and wrestling, footraces, racing in armor, boxing and wrestling combined (*pankration*), and the pentathlon, a combination of discus and javelin throw, wrestling, running, and broad jump. The prizes were not monetary but simple wreaths, symbols of the great honor achieved. Such honor was a valued commodity among the Greeks, conferring distinction on both the victor and his city. Pindar's attitude as expressed in these praise poems is one of deep identification with the glory conferred by such achievement, based as it was on innate excellence enhanced by training. A true believer in the old aristocratic virtues, Pindar found in the games and in his role as their encomiast a perfect combination of ideology and professional practice. It is significant that after Pindar there is no more distinguished epinician poetry. The genre seems to come to a sudden halt. Perhaps his supreme achievement discouraged further efforts (as apparently happened with Homer and the epic). But the decline of the genre must also have been due to the shift in mid- and late-fifth-century thinking away from the old aristocratic values in favor of the more exciting new thought emanating from Athens, the intellectual center of Greece. In politics democratic ideology was replacing the more conservative value system so dear to Pindar; and in the realm of speculative thought the old religious pieties so often framed as aphorisms in Pindar's verse were being replaced by new modes of philosophical and scientific thought about man, God, and the universe.

In the poetry of Pindar and his lesser rival Bacchylides we therefore see the last great poetic claim for the old aristocratic vision of life.

In what poetic form was this vision cast? The typical epinician ode was framed in groups of three stanzas, a triad in which the first two stanzas were metrically identical and the third was distinct. All triads in a given poem were metrically repeated, their meters being among the most complex in all Greek poetry. The usual length of an ode was three to five triads, although there are poems as short as one triad and one exceptionally long ode, *Pythian* 4, that reaches fourteen triads. There are also a few "monostrophic" poems, consisting of identical stanzas without triadic structure. Internally, the odes are structured in an *a b a* pattern of thought, but without tight symmetry. They begin with praise of the victor and name him, the nature of his achievement and the place; then proceed to use a myth to comment by analogy on heroic achievement, its sweetness and its pitfalls; then return to a brief concluding mention of the victor with a final word of advice, praise, or some topical comment. This scheme holds true for the typical epinician ode, while the shorter ones usually omit the myth. At transitional points in this three-part structure Pindar likes to insert gnomic comments, succinct general truths that ring with proverbial wisdom. Characteristic examples are "All achievements come from the gods" (*Pythian* 1.41); "What is anyone? What is he not? Man is the shadow of a dream" (*Pythian* 8.95–96); "The wave of Hades breaks over all" (*Nemean* 7.30–31); "Excellence without risk is not honored among men or in hollow ships" (*Olympian* 6.9–11). As such statements make evident, Pindar has a strong gift for metaphor, and much of the pleasure in his poetry (which is not always lucid or easy to follow) comes from his rich application of metaphor, imagery, and mythic paradigm to the inherently unpromising task of praising an athlete in a commissioned poem.

Bacchylides

The surviving poetry of Bacchylides consists of fourteen epinicians and six dithyrambs, some complete and some fragmentary. They were discovered in 1896, before which time only scattered fragments from quotations in ancient authors were available. In form and intent his poems resemble Pindar's, and yet there are distinct differences in style and narrative habit that set Bacchylides apart as the lesser of the two poets. He is clearer and more direct than Pindar, but thereby misses the grandiloquence and intricacy of his rival. He has a good sense for quick narrative movement and the use of dialogue for dramatic effect. Poem 17, apparently a dithyramb on a mythological theme, presents a quarrel between Theseus and King Minos aboard the ship taking the young Athenian victims to Crete, and consists largely of dialogue (at least within the surviving 132 lines). Poem 18, also a dithyramb, consists in its surviving sixty lines entirely of a dialogue sung between a chorus and the legendary King Aegeus of Athens (Theseus' father).

Among the epinicians, we have two examples written for a victory that Pindar was also commissioned to celebrate, and a comparison of the rival poets' technique is instructive. Poem 5 and Pindar's *Olympian* 1 were both written for the victory of Hiero tyrant of Syracuse in the horse race at the Olympian Games of 476; and poem 4 is a short epinician written for the same patron's chariot victory in the Pythian Games of 470, for which Pindar wrote *Pythian* 1. The first pair represents a perfect match, revealing each poet at his best. Bacchylides' work is a fine poem, showing a rich use of myth in its account of Heracles' meeting with Meleager in

the underworld, and skillful in its use of the theme of these great heroes' misfortune to allude to some misfortune that clouds Hiero's life (presumably an illness). But Pindar's poem shows a richness of metaphor, density of thought, and complexity of organization that are beyond Bacchylides' powers. It moves at a higher level of eloquence and power from its opening lines, the famous:

> Water is best, but gold like a shining fire
> Shows bright in the night beyond all
>   lordly wealth.

CONCLUSION

Pindar and Bacchylides represent the end of choral poetry as a major successful independent genre. The tradition continues, however, in the choruses of Athenian drama—a genre that is rising to prominence as the new fifth-century poetic art form, even as Pindar and Bacchylides are concluding their careers as practitioners of the old one. It is democratic Athens that will foster tragedy and comedy and spread them throughout Greece. This new and more ambitious literary genre will be able to revive old legends as did epinician poetry, but will use them to address the political and existential concerns of whole citizen bodies, not just the small aristocratic elites for whom the older poets composed.

As for the subsequent history of monodic lyric, we have a few samples from poets after Anacreon, such as Corinna the Boeotian, of uncertain date but perhaps a contemporary of Pindar; Praxilla of Sicyon, active about 450; Timocreon of Rhodes, active in the 470s; and other minor figures. But outstanding monodic poetry essentially ceases with the death of Anacreon about 490. As with choral lyric, we may view the genre as undergoing a kind of natural exhaustion, as the social conditions that especially favored lyric creation and performance were altered and the energies of its potential poets went elsewhere. But there can be no easy explanation or single cause to explain why certain genres flourish only at certain periods within a given society. We are left with the historical fact that in the period when no new epic poetry of importance was being created in Greece, her poets expressed themselves primarily in lyric song of great beauty and technical finesse for over two centuries, until the ascendancy of Athenian drama in the fifth century marked the close of this "Lyric Age of Greece."

BIBLIOGRAPHY

SOURCES

The following are the basic editions of the lyric and elegiac poets: David A. Campbell, ed., *Lyra Graeca*, vol. 1 (1982); Ernst Diehl, ed., *Anthologia Lyrica Graeca*, 3 vols. (1924–1952); Bruno Gentili, ed., *Anacreon* (1958); Bruno Gentili and Carlo Prato, eds., *Poetarum Elegiacorum Testimonia et Fragmenta*, pt. 1 (1979); Edgar Lobel and Denys L. Page, eds., *Poetarum Lesbiorum Fragmenta* (*LP*) (1955); Denys L. Page, ed., *Poetae Melici Graeci* (*PMG*) (1962), and *Supplementum Lyricis Graecis* (1974); Bruno Snell and Herwig Maehler, eds., *Bacchylides*, 10th ed. (1970), and *Pindari Carmina cum Fragmentis*, 2 vols. (1975, 1980); E. M. Voigt, *Sappho et Alcaeus* (1971); Martin L. West, *Iambi et Elegi Graeci ante Alexandrum Cantati*, 2 vols. (1971–1972).

Among the best available translations of the poets discussed in this essay are: Willis Barnstone, *Greek Lyric Poetry* (1962); Robert Fagles, *Bacchylides: Complete Poems*, with notes by Adam Parry (1961); Richmond Lattimore, *The Odes of Pindar* (1947), and *Greek Lyrics*, 2d ed. (1960); Frank J. Nisetich, *Pindar's Victory Songs* (1980).

The best editions with commentary are: David A. Campbell, *Greek Lyric Poetry: A Selection of Early*

Greek Lyric, Elegiac, and Iambic Poetry (1967); Douglas E. Gerber, *Euterpe: An Anthology of Early Greek Lyric, Elegiac, and Iambic Poetry* (1970); Sir Richard Claverhouse Jebb, *Bacchylides* (1905; repr. 1967); Gordon M. Kirkwood, *Selections from Pindar* (1982); Denys L. Page, *Alcman: The Partheneion* (1951; repr. 1979), and *Sappho and Alcaeus: An Introduction to the Study of Ancient Lesbian Poetry* (1955); Herbert Weir Smyth, *Greek Melic Poets* (1899; repr. 1963).

STUDIES

Arethusa, **9** (1976), a symposium on the Cologne Epode of Archilochus; Sir Cecil Maurice Bowra, *Early Greek Elegists* (1938), *Greek Lyric Poetry: From Alcman to Simonides*, 2d ed. (1961), and *Pindar* (1964); Andrew Robert Burn, *The Lyric Age of Greece* (1960); Anne Pippin Burnett, *Three Archaic Poets: Archilochus, Alcaeus, Sappho* (1983); Claude Calame, *Les choeurs de jeunes filles en Grèce archaïque*, 2 vols. (1977), the most extensive study of Alcman's poetry and its social context; John Armstrong Davison, *From Archilochus to Pindar* (1968); *Fondation Hardt pour l'étude de l'antiquité classique: Entretiens*, vol. *10*, *Archiloque* (1964); Hermann M. Fränkel, *Early Greek Poetry and Philosophy*, Moses Hadas and James Willis, trans. (1975); Bruno Gentili, "La veneranda Saffo," in *Quaderni Urbinati di Cultura Classica*, **2** (1966); Alan Griffiths, "Alcman's *Partheneion*: The Morning After the Night Before," in *Quaderni Urbinati di Cultura Classica*, **14** (1972).

James W. Halporn, Martin Ostwald, and Thomas G. Rosenmeyer, *The Meters of Greek and Latin Poetry*, rev. ed. (1980); A. E. Harvey, "The Classification of Greek Lyric Poetry," in *Classical Quarterly*, **49** (1955); Walter Ralph Johnson, *The Idea of Lyric: Lyric Modes in Ancient and Modern Poetry* (1982); Gordon Kirkwood, *Early Greek Monody: The History of a Poetic Type* (1974); Giuliana Lanata, "Sul linguaggio amoroso di Saffo," in *Quaderni Urbinati di Cultura Classica*, **2** (1966); Hubert Martin, Jr., *Alcaeus* (1972); R. Merkelbach, "Sappho und ihr Kreis," in *Philologus*, **101** (1947); Sir Arthur Pickard-Cambridge, *Dithyramb, Tragedy, and Comedy*, 2d ed., rev. by T. B. L. Webster (1962); David S. Raven, *Greek Metre*, 2d ed. (1978); Bruno Snell, *Poetry and Soci-*

ety: The Role of Poetry in Ancient Greece (1961); Max Treu, *Von Homer zur Lyrik: Wandlungen des griechischen Weltbildes im Spiegel der Sprache,* 2d ed. (1968); John Van Sickle, "Archilochus: A New Fragment of an Epode," in *Classical Journal,* **71** (1975); Martin L. West, *Studies in Greek Elegy and Iambus* (1974); Michael Wigodsky, "Anacreon and the Girl from Lesbos," in *Classical Philology,* **57** (1962).

BIBLIOGRAPHIES

Excellent annotated bibliographies of Greek lyric poetry were published by Douglas E. Gerber in *The Classical World,* vol. 61 (1967–1968), covering the period 1952 to 1967, and vol. 70 (1976), covering 1967 to 1975. For publications after 1975 one can consult *L'Année philologique* for each year.

Roman Lyric and Elegiac Poetry

GORDON WILLIAMS

INTRODUCTION

Elegy and lyric flourished brilliantly in Rome and in forms quite different from those of their Greek counterparts, but for only a brief period, the seventy-five years or so that extend from the activity of Catullus around 60 B.C. to the death of Ovid. Although much poetry from this period has been lost, we possess the work of the five great masters of the two genres: Catullus, Propertius, Tibullus, Ovid, and Horace. So distinctive was the stamp imposed by each on the form that it is impossible to talk generically about elegy and lyric in Rome. Rather, one is compelled to consider the work of each poet separately. However, four general features of the period are important to all of this poetry.

Poetry came late to Rome, in the middle of the third century B.C., and it came from Greece. Roman aristocrats adopted the same attitude to poetry as they had, for instance, toward painting and sculpture: they saw all such arts as decoration, a pleasant adornment of life that should be left to hired artisans to create. All poets in Rome until late in the second century were of inferior social status. Important Romans wrote only prose, to share with a deserving world their own expertise in agriculture or law or some other such technical field (history was included among these since such Romans made it).

This was all changed by the aristocrat Gaius Lucilius who, around 135 B.C., invented the genre of satire. The characteristic of his poetry was that it concerned his own life. Anything that happened to him, however trivial, acquired interest because of his own individuality and was worthy subject matter for poetry. This aristocratic attitude had no parallel in Greece and was deeply Roman. In this period several prominent Romans wrote their autobiographies. Romans, contrary to the Greek tendency to favor generalization, had a great interest in the particular, and especially in the details of individual lives. (The publication of Cicero's private letters is a striking example, but one can also think of the Roman liking for unflattering realistic portraiture.) What Lucilius did, then, was to make the writing of poetry a respectable activity for Romans of the upper classes.

Roman love elegy owed its invention to

this interest in the individual, for it had no Greek predecessor. A distinction is sometimes made between objective and subjective narrative, and it is then argued that there probably existed subjective narrative of myth in the Hellenistic world. But this is to miss the distinctive feature of Roman love elegy. It has nothing to do with its being subjective; it is that the poetry purports to be strictly autobiographical and that the poet composed by a process of self-examination. This is not to deny that these Roman poets could invent and that in such invention they were often inspired by Hellenistic predecessors such as Callimachus; but it is to insist that the form is expressly that of autobiography and that this marks it as Roman and not Greek. All the poetry of this period is far more directly referential to a contemporary reality than any Greek poetry, and this is no less true of the love elegists than it is of Horace's lyric poetry.

The second feature is the changed social reality that lay behind love elegy. Whereas absolute fidelity had been demanded always of Roman married women, their husbands were free to engage discreetly in casual liaisons with courtesans (normally freedwomen) and slaves (not, of course, with free women and certainly not with married women). That situation was changing early in the first century B.C., and we know of many women in the half century before the rise of Augustus (31 B.C.–A.D. 14) who were married to husbands of distinguished families and yet were notorious for having affairs with other men. It was against this licentiousness, which was threatening to marriage, that Augustus directed his moral legislation. Here was the social reality in which Roman love elegy was born. The Lesbia of Catullus' poetry was named Clodia and she was married to Quintus Metellus Celer, consul of 60 B.C. Ovid (*Tristia* 2.437–438) tells of a poetically celebrated Perilla who was well known to be a real woman named Metella. Propertius' Cynthia was named

Hostia and Tibullus' Delia was really Plania (this information comes from Apuleius in *Apology* [*Apologia*] 10).

All of these names suggest women of respectable social class (in fact the only known freedwoman was Gallus' Lycoris—she was Volumnia Cytheris in real life), and the poets sometimes seem to treat them as married women. But here lies a difficulty. For the women tend to change somewhat from poem to poem as the dramatic situation changes, and a married woman behaving promiscuously is sometimes hard to distinguish from a high-class courtesan. These poems are not historical documents. A further fact that enforces the distance between poetry and life is that the love elegists address their women by false names that are the metrical equivalent of their real names. This in itself suggests a step back from close referentiality to a real person and gives room for poetic imagination to invent. But a social reality lies behind the poetry, and it is no accident that the genre died out when Augustus' moral legislation began to bite. The problem is important because the autobiographical form constantly challenges the reader to test the authenticity of the poet's assertions, and these poems were intended to hold much more meaning for contemporary readers. The word for "affairs" regularly used by these poets is *furta* (thefts), and one assumes that the reader is intended in general to appreciate both the dangers and delights of adultery. However, every context needs separate interpretation.

The third important feature is political as well as social. In this period, as never before, and increasingly after 40 B.C., the concrete political problems of the time became recognized subject matter for poetry, and they loom large both in elegy and in lyric. It was a grim time for Roman citizens, with successive waves of devastating civil war breaking out until Octavian (the future Augustus) finally triumphed at the battle of Actium in 31 B.C. The poets devised various ways of dealing with such subjects, but the problem became really urgent after the battle of Philippi in 42 B.C. since Propertius, Tibullus, and Horace all lost their estates in the aftermath of the war. This made them targets for patronage and consequently increased the pressure on them to make political statements in their poetry. In the end this led to Augustus' becoming the patron of literature and thus inevitably to the imposition of constraints and censorship. Tibullus, Propertius, and Horace, however, were dead before this happened, and it affected only Ovid.

The fourth general feature of the period concerns style, but it does not include Ovid, who turned Roman poetry in a new direction. (However, this is a very complex and difficult problem that can be only briefly mentioned here.) Essentially, poets from Catullus to Horace saw it as a prime poetic virtue to say one thing and yet also mean something else that the reader, working in imaginative sympathy with the poet, had to discover for himself. This was meditative poetry that was not immediately intelligible at each stage of a poem, but demanded a suspension of judgment by the reader until the whole poem had been read; such poetry has more to give on each subsequent rereading. The technique was a sophisticated application of figures of thought in a way analogous to figures of speech: what was not said was related to what was said by modes either of metonymy (that is, by being contiguous with it) or of metaphor (that is, by being similar to it). The poet assumed a specially intimate relationship with his reader who possessed, or was capable of acquiring, a privileged access to the poet's private processes of thought.

ELEGY

Elegy is defined as poetry written in elegiac couplets, a sequence of dactylic hexameter and pentameter. In Rome during this period and before Ovid extended the scope of the subject matter, it was virtually confined to love elegy. This type of poetic composition was the invention of Catullus (?84 B.C.–?54 B.C.).

Catullus

What is without parallel in Catullus' poetry about Lesbia is that, following the general lead of Lucilius, he took a particular human experience (his own, he asserts, and a reader feels no inclination to disbelieve) and subjected it to intimate and painful psychological analysis, expressing its contradictions, basically "odi et amo" (I loathe and yet I love—desire linked with dislike), by viewing the relationship in the framework of two Roman institutions that generated mutual obligation: that of friendship (*amicitia*) and that of marriage. This type of clinical analysis is virtually confined to his epigrams, and in poem 76 (the longest of the collection of epigrams and going well beyond the limits of the form) he expresses in tortured terms of self-pity his sense of having discharged fully (and more) his obligations, whereas Lesbia has flouted hers. He treats the sexual desire he feels as a mortal illness of which he hopelessly prays to the gods to be cured. No previous poet (and certainly no Greek) had written to lay bare so painfully and convincingly the misery of his inmost being.

But the poem from which Roman love elegy arose was the long elegy, poem 68. This is so complex a composition that there is disagreement even about its structure. Some scholars regard it as three separate poems, others as two; along with still others, I see it as one poem of which the opening (1–40) and the close (149–160) form an epistolary address to a Manius, enclosing a highly elaborate poem (40–148) addressed to the Muses and ostensibly celebrating the same man (here more formally designated in the third person as Allius). Unity is achieved by nearly word-for-word repetition in the central poem of a passage in the epistolary opening, in which Catullus bitterly laments the death of his brother.

Allius is hymned to the Muses as the poet's benefactor—he provided a house in which Catullus could meet his Lesbia. Their love is the real subject of the central poem, but it is not confronted directly. A sense is allusively created of a love that is hot but torturing, in highly ornate language and a double simile (51–69). Lesbia's arrival is symbolized in the sound of her foot on the doorstep (70–72). The poet then arbitrarily asserts that this was like Laudamia visiting Protesilaus, and that myth takes over (73–130) until return is made to the context with the modified assertion (131), "Well, Lesbia's love is the equal of Laudamia's—or nearly so." The poem ends with the poet desperately trying to come to terms with the fact that Lesbia's love for him is actually far inferior to Laudamia's (135–48). The myth is clearly used here to substitute for a context that the reader has to reconstruct for himself. Further, the myth is broken by an extraordinary connection of thought by which the poet uses the name Troy to shift from the myth to his own brother's death at Troy. In this way, two aspects of love are introduced: sexual passion and the kind of affection that is combined with respect and loyalty. These aspects coincide with the contradiction between desire and dislike within him that Catullus analyzes in the epigrams.

In this extraordinarily original poem Catullus invents a technique of indirection that allows him to suggest, to wrestle with, and desperately to try to come to terms with an exceedingly painful and threatening human situation. The reader overhears, as it were, the poet as he grapples privately with his dilemma, and from that very allusive one-sided conversation must reconstruct a complex relationship. This poem was the in-

spiration for later poets to explore in their own ways the drastic problems that are created when two human beings are afflicted with love. It should be said that Catullus gives a reader the sense of being put in more immediate touch with what purport to be the realities of the poet's own life than do later poets. Propertius and Tibullus both give the impression of being more literary, at a greater remove from concrete reality. This is true and understandable: they both had the poetry of Catullus as a model, and that not only of itself created a distance from actuality, but it also made more accessible to them the work of other predecessors, especially of the great Alexandrians such as Callimachus, Theocritus, and others.

Propertius

So it is that with Propertius (*ca.* 50 B.C.–*ca.* 16 B.C.) a series of conventional frameworks is used to represent the love relationship. (Propertius was born around the time Catullus was writing poem 68.) Catullus had used those of friendship and marriage, and Propertius makes some use of both. In addition, he invented two others that were to have a long life in European poetry: the idea of love as slavery (*servitium amoris*) and the idea of the lover as a soldier whose warfare is love (*militia amoris*). He also established another connection of ideas that was destined to last: the close link between love and death. Propertius constantly and morbidly reflects on his own death and the effect it will have on his love. It should be noted that the two frameworks of love as slavery and love as warfare are not to be dismissed as metaphorical (any more than those of friendship and marriage). They have, of course, a basis of similarity, but all such frameworks show the poets reaching to explain an extraordinary sensation in terms of one more concrete and factual. Slavery and warfare were commonplace and important features of Roman life, the one signifying the ultimate in degradation, the other in hardship. In a real sense the poet represents himself as a slave (without civil rights) and as a soldier (compelled by superior orders to fight for his life).

The more literary approach of Propertius to love elegy can be seen in an innovation: he composed three books of elegies intended to have a coherence and unity that depended on Cynthia as the focus of all his erotic vicissitudes. Elegy 1.1, which treats an early stage of the affair, is thematically echoed in 3.24 and 3.25, where the poet curses Cynthia and resolves to regain his sanity and have nothing further to do with her. There is a similarly loose structural unity in Horace's *Odes* 1–3. In no sense does Propertius present the narrative of an affair, and poems that do not concern Cynthia are scattered among poems that do (to the greatest extent in Book Three). Yet, whereas Catullus' Lesbia poems are distributed over his work, and form only one aspect of it, Cynthia dominates Propertius' books one through three and is normally to be assumed as present in poems that do not actually address her.

Propertius' technique in these books is that of dramatic monologue, and the reader has to construe the actual situation for himself. In Book One the poems are relatively short and the addressee is usually a man who has a relevance to the affair. Book Two is far bolder: it is very long and is made up of sequences of poems, each of which refers to one continuous dramatic series of events in the affair. The poems are much longer and develop Catullus' techniques of indirection and connections of thought to a very high point of sophistication (to such an extent that editors have felt obliged to break up many poems into shorter separate units). Book Three is more literary and self-conscious, appealing to the Alexandrians Callimachus and Philetas as models, and many poems do not concern Cynthia.

The publication of Book One clearly caught the attention of Augustus' friend Maecenas, who brought the poet into his circle of patronage. So Maecenas has poems 2.1 and 3.9 addressed to him, but political topics also make their appearance in books two and three. There is almost no politics in Book One, except that Tullus (to whom the book and—since he is again addressed at 3.22—books one through three are dedicated), nephew of Lucius Volcatius Tullus, the consul of 33 B.C., is accompanying his uncle on proconsular duty, and the poet reflects on the clash between public service and love (1.6 and 14). The book ends with two striking poems (in the form of epigrams) lamenting the loss of a relative at the siege of Perusia in 40 B.C. But Propertius devised an ingenious way of treating political themes so that his integrity as lover was not compromised: he wishes that he could celebrate the great achievements of Augustus (which he mentions), but regrets that his capacities as a love poet do not enable him to do so. Such is his integrity, in fact, that he even writes a poem (2.7) in which he and Cynthia rejoice at the rejection of Augustus' moral reforms in 28 B.C. (which would have separated the lovers).

Book Four shows a dramatic change that reflects Augustus' taking over literary patronage from Maecenas. Only three poems mention Cynthia (in poem 7 her ghost reproaches Propertius for his behavior), and the rest are on great topics of Roman history and contemporary politics. Poem 6 celebrates Augustus' victory at Actium in 31 B.C., and in the superb funeral elegy for Cornelia (poem 11) the injunctions of Augustus' legislation regulating sexual conduct (passed in 18 B.C.) are held up as shining ideals. The style of composition is grander and makes both explicit and implicit claims to Callimachus as its model. But the most striking feature is the constant celebration of Rome under Augustus.

Tibullus

Tibullus (*ca.* 48 B.C.–19 B.C.) was a contemporary of Propertius, but his poetry did not catch Maecenas' eye and his patron was the aristocratic Marcus Valerius Messalla Corvinus. So politics (as distinct from the achievements of his patron) plays little part in his poetry. His poetic output was small: two books, the first of ten poems, the second of six. In the first book, five poems are concerned with his girl Delia, but three address a young male lover called Marathus (4, 8, and 9). Only three poems of Book Two are concerned with a lover, who is now called Nemesis (3, 4, and 6); the other three are directed to his patron. Tibullus devised a technique of composition that is all his own: he addresses people, he seems to go places and do things, but there is no sense of people present in the poem and nothing actually happens in it. Instead everything is happening inside the poet's head; in fact, Tibullus anticipated the "stream of consciousness" technique. This allows extraordinary thematic complexity to exist within a naturally coherent unity. At the very core of Tibullus' imagination lies the same type of contradiction that Catullus found so stimulating: with Tibullus it is the clash between love of the country (he was, like Propertius, an equestrian, and owned a country estate) and the necessity for military service (he was a soldier and was decorated). As with Catullus, the tension was never resolved and was susceptible of variations such as peace versus war, or country versus city, or love versus war.

Ovid

Catullus' love elegy is a painful search for a means of expressing his complex emotions, in an intensely personal tone, and with the drama internal to himself. Propertius creates a dramatic situation and explores its rhetorical possibilities by means of dramatic monologue, with himself alone on the stage. Tibullus' poetry is a continuous act of self-musing, with a stream of images passing through his mind. Such were Ovid's predecessors. Ovid was born in 43 B.C. (*d. ca.* A.D. 18) and so was a generation later. He did not experience the civil wars or suffer any loss in them. He came of a family of wealthy equestrian landowners, and could mix with the elite of Roman society.

Ovid's *Loves* (*Amores*) appeared in a first edition around 15 B.C. in five books; the work was reduced to three books in a second edition (as a witty introductory epigram tells us). The work assumes the existence of love elegy as a generic web of conventions and plays against this. The witty, self-consciously literary nature of this poetry appears from its alleged inception (1.1–3): the poet tries to write epic, but Cupid takes a foot from every second line (making them pentameters and the meter elegiac couplet) and then wounds the poet with an arrow; now he can write only love elegy, but he does not even know a girl. This plays with the tradition of the lover-poet: the poet must become a lover to write in his chosen genre.

With Ovid love becomes play, but as much literary as amorous play. He constantly takes themes and situations from his predecessors, but not for parody (since he does not mock them); rather he plays with the audience's knowledge of predecessors and with its expectations to extract humor from his own performance. For an important change has taken place and Ovid exploits it to the full. The earlier poetry had been directed to the private reader, but public recitations of poetry, after the Greek fashion, were introduced into Rome, and Ovid was the first to take advantage of the custom. So he is always conscious of playing before an audience, with the literary equivalents of winks and nudges and asides and jokes with the audience that target himself, his girl and especially earlier poets. The style of composition, too, is quite different: it is much more explanatory and exhaustive; repetition in the form of theme and variation is constant; the earlier compression, startling leaps of thought, and demands on the reader for rigorous imaginative sympathy and for his understanding of what has not been said—all of this is abandoned by Ovid in favor of a style that is endlessly witty and pointed. So successful was this that not only all later elegists but all later poets aspired to an Ovidian technique.

Ovid's *Loves* has the same type of unity as Propertius' books one through three: they are focused on one girl, named Corinna. There is, however, hardly any politics in the work, apart from a few flattering references to Augustus, so wittily linked to their undignified contexts as to give little pleasure to the emperor. Ovid belonged, like Tibullus, to the circle of Messalla, but Tibullus had died in 19 B.C. and Augustus was now supreme literary patron, so that Ovid was in no position to avoid imperial pressure. There was a further ominous fact: Corinna is represented on some occasions as married, so Ovid's putative relationship with her was adulterous and flouted Augustus' sexual legislation of 18 B.C.

Ovid's next work retreated into the safety of Greek mythology. His *Heroines* (*Heroides*) consists of letters from abandoned women to their forsworn lovers; he later added a series of double letters in which the perjurers reply to their wronged ladies. It was a work perfectly devised for Ovid's wit: there is no sense of tragedy or heartbreak here, only constant wit and point (so that it becomes wearisome after a time).

But his *Art of Love* (*Ars Amatoria*), published about A.D. 1, was disastrous for him. This work cleverly took the tradition of didactic poetry in the high style, such as Lucretius' *On the Nature of Things* or Vergil's *Georgics*, and transformed it from an epic genre to love elegy by altering the meter to elegiacs. Two books give full instructions, right to the point of consummation, to men; a third book is added (the poet alleges) at the urgent insistence of women to do them a similar favor. The work flew full in the face of Augustus' moral ideals. Ovid realized this and tried to avert trouble by two means: first, he insists that the women with whom the work deals are courtesans, not married ladies; second, he incorporated a very extensive panegyric of Augustus. Neither worked. The former was totally unconvincing, and the panegyric was so wittily linked to highly improper contexts that it could only have made things worse. Augustus waited until A.D. 8, when he revealed that the younger Julia, his granddaughter, had been committing adultery (her mother had been caught and exiled in 2 B.C.). He connected Ovid with this in some obscure way, added the offense of the *Art of Love*, and sent Ovid to the cruelest form of exile in the savage region of Tomis (Constanţa) on the Black Sea.

After the *Art of Love* Ovid turned to safe material once again for elegiac poetry and wrote *The Roman Calendar* (*Fasti*); he finished just six books (representing six months) and published them only very late, after A.D. 14. He never came back from exile, but composed from there an entirely new type of work in elegiacs—letters. The first collection of these, called *Tristia*, is in four books, and the letters are seldom addressed to named people (lest contact with a condemned man should harm them). But the second collection, *Letters from the Black Sea* (*Epistulae ex Ponto*), are all addressed to specific individuals. All of this poetry had one main aim: to gain pardon and return to Rome. Even when miserable and despairing, as it often is, it is still witty and clever and pointed.

Love elegy virtually died with Ovid, killed largely by the moral oppression of Augustus and the regime, but also by Ovid's making it impossible for anyone to treat the genre seriously after him. However, the work of two poets in the circle of Messalla has been preserved as books three and four of the collection of Tibullus' poems: a series of love elegies by one called Lygdamus shows much dependence on Ovid, and six very short love elegies (amounting to forty lines in all) are attributed to a Sulpicia (possibly a ward or niece of Messalla). Elegiac poetry thereafter continued to be written from time to time, but it never again in ancient Rome regained the prestige it had during the short period from Catullus to Ovid.

LYRIC

Catullus

When Eric Havelock published in 1939 what is still the finest study of Catullus' poetry, he entitled it *The Lyric Genius of Catullus.* But, strictly speaking, Catullus was a lyric poet in only a few poems, written in specifically lyric meters such as Sapphics (poems 11 and 51). Yet, in a more modern sense, Catullus is the outstanding lyric poet of antiquity, for his directness of emotional intensity combined with extreme formal sophistication and learning. He was the first Roman poet to give full attention to the Alexandrian standards of technical finish in verse. (What is in question here is the series of short poems, 1–60, although one could not exclude the long lyrical marriage hymn, poem 61.) Catullus (and his friends) self-consciously broke with the Roman literary past in this respect and drew from Cicero the disapproving title of "newfangled poets." The poems about Lesbia among 1–60 can be contrasted with those among the larger poems and the epigrams; what is missing is the indirectness of poem 68 as well as the cool analysis of contradictory emotions in the epigrams. Instead there is an extraordinary combination of direct emotional intensity (frequently expressed in plain obscenities) with the height of technical artistry.

In two poems about Lesbia (11 and 51) Catullus anticipates Horace's use of the Sapphic stanza. In poem 51 he translates a poem of Sappho, but adds a final ironic stanza that totally alters the tone; in poem 11 he commissions two friends to say good-bye for him, in most obscene terms, to his girl (clearly Lesbia, although she is not named). In poems 2 and 3 he writes about his girl's (again Lesbia's) sparrow, relating it to his love affair. The enjoyment of Lesbia's kisses is the subject of poems 5 and 7. In poem 8 he engages in a tortured self-debate to try to persuade himself to forget Lesbia. In poem 58 he briefly describes the sexual activities of Lesbia in words of extreme obscenity. These are the Lesbia poems, but the range of subject matter covers every activity in a young Roman's life: from the writing of poetry to delight in the jewel-isle of Sirmio; from obscene attacks on individuals (including prominent political figures like Pompey and Julius Caesar) to a witty account of a meeting with a friend's girl (told against himself); from a joking invitation to dinner to an attack upon a napkin thief. Immediacy, combined with artistry, makes the paradoxical essence of Catullus' lyric. That sense of immediacy is emblematized in poem 1, which begins with the poet wondering to whom to dedicate his poems. It takes him two lines to decide that it shall be the biographer Cornelius Nepos. All of this persuasively offers the authenticity of autobiography.

Horace

That immediacy was no part of Horace's aim in his lyric poetry. Catullus died in the late 50s, and Horace (65 B.C.–8 B.C.) began writing lyric ten years or so later. Catullus was his predecessor in his earliest lyric work, his *Epodes,* but Horace ignores the Roman predecessor and claims the Greek poet Archilochus of Paros as his model (*Epistles* 1.19.23–25). There was good reason for this. Just as a distance divided Propertius from his subject matter in contrast to the immediacy of Catullus, so too with Horace, and he figures this by referring to Archilochus. A reader feels the bitter anger and contempt of Catullus, but the iambic anger of Horace is an element of the artistry. A further difference lies in the autobiographical technique. With Catullus one is easily convinced that this is his real life. The analogue to that lies in Horace's *Satires,* but in his lyric he constructs a persona that varies from poem to poem. It is significant that there is virtually no political statement in the *Satires,* but the *Epodes* are closely engaged with the urgent issues of contemporary politics. For this purpose the poet invented a particular persona that would lend his voice more authority than the mere assertion of the private individual Quintus Horatius Flaccus. He appropriated the word *vates* (in the sense of "prophet," "seer," almost "priest") to express the idea that the poet could examine his own society with a vision that had the greater authority of inspiration.

The *Epodes* were written from soon after the battle of Philippi in 42 B.C. to just after the battle of Actium in 31 B.C., and they fully reflect the political anxieties of that period of the civil war; only the two late poems on the battle of Actium (1 and 9) express optimism. This was the period when the poet was being drawn into the circle of Maecenas and persuaded that Octavian (soon to become Augustus) held the key to peace. An important feature of the *Epodes* becomes canonical in the *Odes:* the blending of Greek and Roman elements into an imaginative unity that establishes a carefully devised dis-

tance from immediate reality. Two of the poems (8 and 12) are vicious attacks on aging women, with the grossest physical details and sexual obscenities. Neither woman is named and, since this type of poem was characteristic of Archilochus, the lack of any claim to immediacy (in contrast to Catullus) gives room to poetic imagination.

Odes 1–3 were designed as a unit, with the last ode (3.30) echoing the meter and themes of the first. The work as a whole is dedicated to Maecenas and many odes throughout are addressed to him. Horace explicitly claims this as a Roman re-creation of the Greek lyric poetry of Sappho and Alcaeus, and once more (3.30) he ignores Catullus as a predecessor, reaching beyond him to the Greek poets. Again, controlled poetic distance is substituted for immediacy. The range of the *Odes* is as wide as that of the two Greeks (claimed explicitly in *Odes* 1.32): there are hymns and prayers, symposium poems, erotic poems, and political poems. Horace displayed a technique of using a form such as hymn or symposium poem as a framework, usually distinguished by Greek elements, within which he could express general ideas with the indirection that is his characteristic. He also made strikingly original use of the figures of thought that enabled poets to say one thing and also mean something else left unsaid. As a result many of his odes were soon misunderstood by those who read them with Ovidian and post-Ovidian expectations. Horace's love poems are totally unelegiac. They are detached, ironic, and humorous, and the persona is that of a practiced philanderer, vulnerable to passion but ready to mock himself and laugh at others, and always (unlike the elegiac poets) conscious that love is fleeting as well as ridiculous.

The political odes cover a wider range of actual contemporary problems than any other poetry of the period—for instance, uncertainty about Augustus' tenure (1.2); the problem of the succession (1.12); the significance of the battle of Actium (1.37); the dangers of civil war (1.35 and 2.1); opposition to Augustus (3.4); Augustus' program of temple restoration and the failure of his moral legislation (3.6). It is notable that in several of these poems (especially 1.12 and 3.4) Horace makes appeal not to poems of Alcaeus but to specific odes of the Greek poet Pindar, giving those poems thereby a grander scale.

There is an important feature of all the political poetry of this period, but especially of Horace's: the issues, social, moral, and political, are unresolved, open to discussion and discussed—however clear the solutions may be. The problems concern public and private morality, social justice and values, military dangers, and above all a society divided against itself by civil war. But 17 B.C. is a turning point. That was the year Horace, at Augustus' request, wrote the *Centenary Hymn* (*Carmen Saeculare*), celebrating the achievements of Augustus.

The business of poets had changed: it was now their task to celebrate the solution of all problems, and the danger of a lapse into panegyric thus became acute. It is the time when Propertius' poetry changes with Book Four, and Horace's too changes with *Odes* 4. There is direct evidence (in the biography that derives from Suetonius where actual letters of Augustus are quoted) that Augustus took over patronage of literature and made direct requests for poems on specific political topics. The poems of *Odes* 4 are far more laureate and Pindaric (although, as with Propertius, there is a central core, 10–13, of the earlier, more personal type), and Horace devised an unparalleled formula, often repeated: a bare factual list, with unpoetic technical language, of the successful solutions found by Augustus for Rome's problems. The dangers of mere panegyric were largely avoided by Horace (and Propertius),

but Ovid and all his successors fell victim to them.

Lyric poetry on the Horatian scale thereafter died out. Seneca the Younger closely imitated Horace's poetry in the choral odes of his tragedies, but the imitation is totally unlike the model, since expansiveness and structures like theme and variation had become fashionable by Seneca's time. Statius wrote a few Horatian-type odes in his *Silvae*, but then there is a gap (broken only by a few fragments and Hadrian's little poem to his soul) until the poetry of Ausonius and the Christian hymns of Prudentius and Ambrose.

BIBLIOGRAPHY

Detailed bibliographies will be found in *The Cambridge History of Classical Literature, Vol. 2: Latin Literature,* E. J. Kenney and W. V. Clausen, eds. (1982). There are translations of all the poets mentioned in the series of Penguin Classics.

TEXTS AND COMMENTARIES

Catullus

C. J. Fordyce, *Catullus: A Commentary* (1961); G. P. Goold, ed. and trans., *Catullus* (1983); Kenneth Quinn, *Catullus: The Poems,* 2d ed. (1973).

Horace

R. G. M. Nisbet and Margaret Hubbard, *A Commentary on Horace: Odes, Book 1* (1970), *Book 2* (1978); Edward Charles Wickham, *The Works of Horace, Volume I: The Odes, Carmen Saeculare, and Epodes,* 3d ed. (1896); Gordon Williams, *The Third Book of Horace's "Odes"* (1969).

Ovid

John A. Barsby, *Ovid Amores I* (1973); Guy Lee, *Ovid's Amores* (1968).

Propertius

W. A. Camps, *Propertius: Elegies,* books 1, 2, 3, and 4 (1961, 1967, 1966, 1965).

Tibullus

Guy Lee, *Tibullus: Elegies* (1982); Michael C. J. Putnam, *Tibullus: A Commentary* (1973); K. F. Smith, *The Elegies of Albius Tibullus* (1913; repr. 1964).

STUDIES

John A. Barsby, *Ovid* (1978); J. W. Binns, ed., *Ovid* (1973); Francis Cairns, *Tibullus: A Hellenistic Poet at Rome* (1979); Steele Commager, *The Odes of Horace* (1962); Eduard Fraenkel, *Horace* (1957); Eric A. Havelock, *The Lyric Genius of Catullus* (1939; repr. 1957); Margaret Hubbard, *Propertius* (1974); Georg Luck, *The Latin Love Elegy,* 2d ed. (1969); Kenneth Quinn, *The Catullan Revolution* (1959; rev. ed. 1969); David O. Ross, *Style and Tradition in Catullus* (1969), and *Backgrounds to Augustan Poetry: Gallus, Elegy, and Rome* (1975).

John Patrick Sullivan, *Propertius: A Critical Introduction* (1976), and ed., *Critical Essays on Roman Literature* (1962); Paul Veyne, *L'Elégie érotique Romaine* (1983); David West, *Reading Horace* (1967); L. P. Wilkinson, *Horace and his Lyric Poetry,* 2d ed. (1951), and *Ovid Recalled* (1955); Gordon Williams, *Tradition and Originality in Roman Poetry* (1968), *Horace* (1972), *Figures of Thought in Roman Poetry* (1980), and *The Nature of Roman Poetry,* 2d ed. (1983); Timothy Peter Wiseman, *Catullan Questions* (1969), and *Cinna the Poet* (1974).

Bucolic Poetry

DAVID M. HALPERIN

BUCOLIC POETRY WAS INVENTED by Theocritus early in the second quarter of the third century B.C. (around 275, let us say, or shortly thereafter). Theocritus was a native of Syracuse, a Greek city on the eastern coast of Sicily, but he seems to have composed his bucolic poems (or Idylls, as the poems comprising the Theocritean corpus came later to be called—though few are in fact idyllic) in Alexandria, the capital of Hellenistic Egypt, where he passed the most productive period of his career. During the two succeeding centuries a number of lesser Greek poets laid claim to the bucolic mantle of Theocritus: we currently possess a slim volume of their work along with two names, Moschus and Bion, to which most of the post-Theocritean bucolic efforts have at one time or another been attached. At least one Roman author, Marcus Valerius Messalla Corvinus, is reported to have composed bucolic poetry in Greek during the latter part of the first century B.C., but despite this and other signs of a limited interest in Theocritus on the part of Roman literati, no

Roman poet attempted to render the form in Latin until Vergil undertook his first major work, the *Bucolics* (sometimes called the *Eclogues*), probably between the years 42 and 35 B.C. A number of surviving Eclogues in Latin from the first five centuries A.D. testify to the enormous popularity and influence of Vergil's *Bucolics* in later antiquity; among these various imitations a virtual monopoly of literary value is held by the poems which are ascribed in manuscript sources to the authorship of Calpurnius Siculus and Nemesianus and are most plausibly dated to the third century A.D. The ancient tradition of bucolic poetry is characterized in general by an unusually high degree of literary self-consciousness on the part of its contributors and by the remarkable stability of its artistic conventions: themes, compositional forms, dramatic situations, tropes, diction, and even the names of bucolic characters are repeated from one poem to another over the centuries in an intricate network of allusion and cross-reference within which individual meaning is achieved by novel combinations of familiar elements and by the distinctive reworking of borrowed material.

THE GREEK BUCOLIC TRADITION

The distinguishing features of ancient bucolic poetry can be described most economically by comparing and contrasting them with the established features of ancient epic poetry. Bucolic poetry invites such a comparison, in fact, because according to Alexandrian schemes of literary classification it belongs on formal grounds to the same poetic category (or genre) as epic. Throughout the Hellenistic period meter constituted the single most important determinant of poetic genre, and bucolic poetry—with the sole exception of Idyll 8.33–60, set in elegiac distichs—was invariably composed in the dactylic hexameter, the same form of versification used by Homer, Hesiod, and all the other Greek and Roman epicists of antiquity. The dactylic hexameter verse form, moreover, provided bucolic poets with a framework for echoes and reversals of conventional epic phrasing, diction, tropes, and themes, thereby enabling the poets to maintain—in the very act of revising the epic tradition—an underlying continuity of artistic purpose within it. In short, bucolic poetry looked to epic as to a benchmark against which to measure the character and extent of its own programmatic deviations from a preexisting literary norm, for it was chiefly by means of such deviations that bucolic poetry acquired its unique and distinctive literary profile. Through a variety of calculated and selective departures from tradition, then, Theocritus was able to prolong and renew the life of the Greek epic, bringing it into conformity with "modern" (that is, Alexandrian) aesthetic ideals of refinement, learning, subtlety, indirection, and freshness of feeling. The bucolic program of poetic revisionism comprises, specifically, a series of radical innovations within at least six departments of traditional epic style, each of which requires brief exploration.

MAGNITUDE. Heroic epic is a lengthy affair; in the words of Callimachus of Cyrene, an Alexandrian contemporary of Theocritus and fellow-traveller in matters of aesthetics, it is "one continuous poem in many thousands of lines." Bucolic poetry is brief: a Theocritean Idyll seldom exceeds 150 lines and a Vergilian Eclogue rarely attains 100. The Greek bucolic corpus even contains a complete hexameter poem (Idyll 19) totaling eight lines—and the little work is entirely unapologetic about its size:

> A cruel bee once stung the thievish Love-god as he was stealing honey from the hives, and pricked all his finger-tips. And he was hurt, and blew upon his hand, and stamped and danced. And to Aphrodite he showed the wound, and made complaint that so small a creature as a bee should deal so cruel a wound. And his mother answered laughing, "Art not thou like the bees, that art so small yet dealest wounds so cruel?" (A. S. F. Gow, trans., vol. 1 [1952], p. 147).

This diminutive epic, which by its very subject calls attention to the piquant aesthetics of tininess, valiantly defends the artistic potency of a diminished thing.

THEMES. War and other forms of conflict, struggle, or competition furnish the themes of heroic poetry; love hovers about the periphery of the action, supplying a motive or a goal for the combatants. Theocritus substitutes the agony of frustrated desire for the agony of mortal strife and transfers the locus of competition from the military to the poetic arena: rival lovers vie with words, cap each other's verses, or compose serenades in an effort to sway the objects of their love and vent their own feelings.

LANGUAGE. Homer and his followers inherited from their preliterate forebears a technique of oral composition which employed, mostly for the sake of metrical convenience, an amalgam of Greek dialects never so combined in the actual speech of any historical culture. Theocritus similarly used an artificial and unexampled mixture of dialects, but he reversed the proportions of the linguistic ingredients in Epic by replacing the dominant strain (Ionic) with an almost wholly excluded one (Doric), which he then proceeded to contaminate with a fluctuating but apparently calculated blend of Aeolic and Ionic forms, just as Homer had seasoned his Ionic with Aeolic and with what Theocritus may have taken to be an occasional Doricism. Theocritus' linguistic inventiveness extends beyond the mere combination of divers linguistic elements to the learned creation of unreal, cross-dialectal coinages that are designed to recall the hybrid morphology of individual words in Homer. This dimension of bucolic artistry was necessarily lost when Vergil took it over, for Latin does not possess a system of dialects associated respectively with different literary genres: Vergil had to content himself instead with a largely symbolic gesture in the direction of subliterate, rustic speech at the start of his Third Eclogue (*cuium pecus* for *cuius pecus*), and he was taxed by his contemporaries for taking such liberties with the language.

TONE. Heroic epic is lofty, noble, and grand; it relates the achievements and sufferings of princely warriors. Because its characters are morally serious and engaged in great enterprises, epic invites the audience's sympathetic identification with their vicissitudes. Bucolic poetry is concerned with the trivial pursuits of "little people" whom it tends to treat with amused detachment; it keeps its audience at a distance from its subject, substituting comic irony for tragic sympathy, and achieves its best effects through a complex combination of suavity, mischievousness, wit, allusiveness, and a controlled emotionality. Here, in Idyll 1.45–54, is a typical bucolic scene:

> And not far away . . . is a vineyard
> Heavily laden with ripening clusters
>   of grapes,
> Where on a dry-stone wall a small boy
>   sits on guard.
> Two foxes flank him: one prowls up and
>   down the vine rows,
> Pilfering the already ripe fruit, while
>   the other
> Directs all her cunning toward the boy's
>   wallet, and vows not to rest
> Until she has left him lean fare for
>   his breakfast.
> But he, plaiting with asphodel stalks a
>   fine cage for locusts,
> Fits in a reed and thinks not at all of
>   his wallet
> Or of the vines, so great is his joy in
>   his weaving.
> (Thelma Sargent, trans. [1982], pp. 2–3)

A sense of unencumbered delight in the trivial but amusing situation, in a miniature scene that can be conveyed with delicacy and wit; a good-natured, almost irresponsible detachment from the material; and a subtle but precise expressivity achieved through a careful balance of the emotional values associated with the images—these are all characteristic features of Theocritus' tone.

COMPOSITIONAL FORM (or mode of representation). In the classification of literature according to speaker, epic traditionally belongs to the mixed genus, because in it both the poet/narrator and his characters speak directly to the audience. Bucolic often assumes a dramatic form in which only the characters speak and the narrative frame is absent; in this as well as in its low-mimetic subject (described in the next section) bucolic resembles another genre popular in the Hellenistic period, the mime (a kind of realistic dialogue, in prose or verse, set among humble folk). Unlike true drama, however, bucolic is not designed to be spoken by actors or performed in a theater but, once again like mime, to be read from the written page.

CAST OF CHARACTERS. The protagonists of heroic poetry are members of a military aristocracy and behave according to an ethical code specific to their class. Herdsmen, artisans, laborers, and other humble folk are introduced into heroic poetry, usually in the course of epic similes, in order to provide an enlarged perspective on the activity of the heroes. Theocritus reverses this procedure: his protagonists are agricultural field hands, housewives, shepherds, goatherds, fishermen, and mercenaries whom the poet surrounds with deliberately incongruous heroic reminiscences; should a genuine hero put in an appearance, Theocritus depicts him in a homely situation and with all the veristic detail appropriate to a low-mimetic subject.

The star of Theocritus' motley crew is the herdsman: it is he who gives bucolic poetry its name ("bucolic" means "of or pertaining to cowherds" in Greek). Of the thirty-odd poems in the preserved Theocritean corpus (Idylls 8, 9, 19, 20, 27, and possibly others are the work of Theocritus' imitators) only about a third involve herdsmen, and of these many closely resemble other poems by Theocritus that altogether lack a pastoral subject; nonetheless, already in the latter half of the third century B.C. Theocritus' readership seems to have singled out for special attention those Idylls which feature a rustic setting and cast of characters and to have come to regard poetic competition among herdsmen as the preeminent bucolic theme. This interpretative tendency was carried to its conclusion by Vergil, who, in his creative reworking of the Idylls, converted pastoral and nonpastoral subjects alike to a rustic design. Vergil's achievement essentially created the rules for the later genre of pastoral, which first attained wide popularity in fifteenth-century Italy, and it is he, rather

than Theocritus, who can claim to be the true founder of the European pastoral tradition. Vergil's "pastoralization" of ancient bucolic poetry has led to the conflation of bucolic with pastoral, and it is therefore necessary to say something about the differences between the two in order to avoid approaching the ancient historical phenomenon with inappropriate expectations. What, since the Renaissance, we have been accustomed to call *pastoral* is a literary form which can now, in retrospect, be seen to have flourished in every period of Western culture; in the hands of modern critics, therefore, pastoral represents a descriptive and transhistorical concept. Pastoral is most usefully distinguished from other kinds of literary discourse by the characteristic set of attitudes to the relation between man and nature that it expresses. It is typical of pastoral to contrast the "great" world of urban culture, centralized power, social hierarchy, and artifice in general with the "little" or "green" world of natural simplicity, rural leisure, freedom, and spontaneity—always to the moral and sensual advantages of the latter. The traditional if inessential vehicle for conveying such a contrast is the representation of the lives, loves, and songs of shepherds, inasmuch as shepherds are considered (for literary purposes) to enjoy the privilege of a special intimacy, sympathy, and harmony with their natural surroundings. The bucolic poems of Theocritus and Vergil afford many quintessential examples of pastoral in this sense and came to provide later pastoralists with a canonical definition of the genre. But because pastoral conventions emerged from rather than shaped the work of Theocritus and Vergil, we must endeavor to account for their artistic choices without reference to later assumptions about the purpose or function of pastoral.

Theocritus lived in a sophisticated, self-conscious age in which it was difficult for writers to express strong emotion directly and still maintain the artistic credibility of their work. Alexandrian poetry could not reproduce the terrifying and pathetic effect of Ajax's prayer in *Iliad* 17, "Destroy us in the light!", which the author of *On the Sublime* would later use to exemplify the most noble poetic subject: human greatness in extremis. Theocritus had to search for new means of achieving freshness and expressivity within the classical poetic forms. He found what he was looking for not only in the shifting dialect and lexical variation of an artificial language but also in a low-mimetic subject, the lives of little people. Such humble folk did not exert the same claim on the ancient reader's sympathy that the Homeric heroes did, and so Theocritus' choice of subject created an ironic distance between his material and his readership; this very distance, further increased by the supremely artful language of Theocritus' low characters and by the humorous incongruities arising from the poet's manipulation of epic diction and tropes, allowed the treatment of love and loss to recover a limited measure of dignity and seriousness within a credible artistic medium. Perhaps the best example of this technique—for which modern analogies can be found in such works of American literature as "Mr. Flood's Party" by Edwin Arlington Robinson or, more recently, the plays of Sam Shepard—occurs not in Theocritus' pastoral efforts but in Idyll 2 (155–161), the passionate if inadvertently comical effusion of a seduced and abandoned suburban teenager:

For once he used to visit me three and four times a day and would often leave in my keeping his Doric flagon of athletic oil; now it is twelve days that I've not set eyes on him. Mustn't he have found some pleasure elsewhere and forgotten me? That's why I'll trammel him up by my spells. And if he should still grieve me, then by the Fates it's the gates of hell he shall pound on (since he won't pound on mine)—such are the evil drugs I claim to store in my casket for him.

This latter-day Medea would have aroused in Theocritus' audience a social response hardly different from that evoked by the countrymen of his pastoral Idylls, and it is no accident that William Empson's description in *Some Versions of Pastoral* of the classical shepherd-poem can apply equally well to Theocritus' entire range of low-mimetic poetry: "The essential trick of the old pastoral, which was felt to imply a beautiful relation between rich and poor, was to make simple people express strong feelings (felt as the most universal subject, something fundamentally true about everybody) in learned and fashionable language (so that you wrote about the best subject in the best way)" (pp. 11–12).

The success of Theocritus' pastoral Idylls can be described in similar terms. Adopting an illusionary technique previously employed by Homer in the *Odyssey*'s rural interludes, by Euripides in some choral odes of the *Hippolytus* and *Ion,* and by Plato in the *Phaedrus,* Theocritus creates a landscape halfway between the sensuous descriptions of the classical poets and the sentimental metaphors of the romantics—a landscape at once realistic and artificial, distant and familiar, in which the sophisticated reader and the passionate shepherd are equally at home. Within such a setting the erotic vicissitudes of herdsmen can take on a certain dignity and emotional grandeur, can achieve what Adam Parry has called a heroism unspoiled by irony:

Daphnis, indeed, lives in a world where it is possible to be a hero. But this world is no longer quite the poet's own—or the audience's. . . . By a subtle device, it is the very magical unreality of the poetic landscape in the first Idyll that prevails upon us to accept Daphnis' words as straightforward heroic speech, and to take pleasure in them as spontaneous dramatic utterance; for this unreality wins us to itself. . . . Pastoral might be described as a cover in an age of irony (1957, pp. 11, 14).

Lastly, and most important, the pastoral economy furnished Theocritus with a figure who could serve as a distant reflection of himself and of his poetic vocation. From the Bronze Age to the present day herdsmen have been observed to while away the hours they spend watching their flocks by singing and playing musical instruments—they have plenty of time and nothing better to do with it. Moreover, they perform solely to entertain themselves, not to instruct their audience or impart wisdom to their community. Theocritus' assumption of a pastoral persona expresses a typically Alexandrian refusal to play the roles of teacher, prophet, and sage which had previously attached themselves to the profession of poet in the heyday of classical Greek culture. It also accords well with the inverse snobbery of Alexandrian poets who tended to disparage the nobility, grandeur, and social significance of their own work in proportion as they prided themselves on its delicacy, sophistication, and refinement: beneath Theocritus' pastoral disguise is plainly visible the face of the learned Alexandrian practitioner who lavishes in an ostensibly playful and leisurely fashion, and for no loftier purpose than his own amusement, an infinite amount of care upon what he pretends to regard as a humble or pedestrian craft.

THE ROMAN BUCOLIC TRADITION

It was precisely this self-reflexive dimension of Theocritus' pastoralism that commended bucolic poetry to Vergil's attention. It is characteristic of Vergil's artistic method to thematize the conventions of whatever genre he is working in until he has forced them to yield a figure for the subject he has chosen to treat: in this way, the pastoral setting of his *Bucolics* becomes a metaphor for the inwardness, aesthetic detachment, and creative liberty of the human imagination. Theocritus had appealed to the herdsman as a poetic self-image and had treated him as an emblem for the free, unencumbered, and self-gratifying pursuit of artistic impulse. Vergil makes such "pastoralism" the true subject of his bucolic poetry: through a cluster of recurring images he dramatizes the inevitable and potentially tragic conflict between the poet's necessary absorption in the private world of his creative imagination and his inescapable involvement in the historical community of which he is a member. Vergil thus exploits the pastoral convention for the purpose of articulating the pleasures, the dangers, and the limits of literary art.

The pastoral world provided Vergil with a peculiarly appropriate metaphor for one particular kind of poetic endeavor—namely, for the very school of Alexandrian poetry whose aesthetic creed Theocritus had so memorably symbolized in the figure of the herdsman. Vergil, along with his teachers and contemporaries, had been immersed in the work of the Alexandrians and had learned, in the course of a long and arduous literary apprenticeship, to write poetry that was—like theirs—learned, allusive, disengaged. But the generation of poets to which Vergil belonged was also somewhat skeptical about the possibility of converting the Alexandrian heritage into the basis of a genuinely national literature: in his *Art of Poetry* (*Ars Poetica*) 351–365, for example, Horace implicitly criticizes the Alexandrian cult of artistic refinement for its tendency to inspire coterie verse, poetry designed to be read only in the privacy of one's cabinet and unfit to be seen in the light of day. Elaborating a similarly contrastive image for the opposition between the tranquil shade of the poet's private sanctum and the glare of public attention, Vergil frames his own *ars poetica* in the *Bucolics* by creating an evocative spiritual landscape marked out by alternating patches of exposed sunlight and cool, protected shade.

The theme is clearly sounded in the opening lines of the First Eclogue: "You, Tityrus, reclining beneath the protection of a spreading beech, rehearse the woodland muse on a slender oat; we are leaving behind us the bourn of our fatherland and our sweet fields: we are banished hence. Tityrus, you, at ease in the shade, teach the woods to echo the name of lovely Amaryllis" (1.1–5). The speaker is Meliboeus who, along with his flock, has been driven from his ancestral farm by the land confiscations of the Triumvirs; his wondering gaze and pathetic eloquence have been elicited by the spectacle of an elderly slave's solitary felicity. Tityrus, as we subsequently learn, had journeyed to Rome in order to purchase his freedom but received instead the apparently unsolicited permission to remain at home, as before, and to enjoy the compensatory pleasure of *poetic* liberty: he has been granted leisure and the freedom to play whatever he wishes on his rustic pipe. The hierarchical power of Rome, which makes one man god to another, also creates artificial, administrative calamities in the countryside that, unlike natural disasters, do not affect all the inhabitants alike but render one man happy in isolated security while hurling his neighbor headlong into exile, sickness, and death. The musical Tityrus, however, is able at the conclusion of the conversation to project a visionary image of life in which such inequities are transcended and reconciled—if only momentarily, solipsistically, and somewhat ominously: "Here, nonetheless, you might repose with me tonight upon green foliage; we have ripe fruit, soft chestnuts, and an abundance of drained curds—and already smoke is rising from the far-off cottage roofs, and deeper from the high mountains fall the shadows" (1.79–83).

The Second Eclogue also begins under the "shady summits" of thickly branching beeches (2.3), where the shepherd Corydon bewails his unsuccessful suit for the love of Alexis, his master's favorite. His passion leads him out of the shade, where at noon every beast and reptile sleeps, into the burning sunlight, where he sees his life from the outward and disdainful perspective of the cultivated boy he adores; at the end of the poem, however, he returns to his neglected rustic occupations, resigning himself to unalterable fate: "See, how the bullocks carry home the plows hung from their yokes and the sun, declining, redoubles the growing shadows; love still scorches me, for what measure is there in love? . . . Since this Alexis spurns me, I shall find myself another" (2.66–73). Roman and erotic realities continue to alternate in the succeeding Eclogues (*ROMA* is *AMOR* spelled backward), testing poetry to discover what, if anything, it can make happen in the face of them. The poetic imagination achieves a momentary triumph in magnificent works of prophecy, elegy, and cosmological mythology (Eclogues 4, 5, 6), but by the Ninth Eclogue we find the rustic poets banished, escaping barely with their lives, and leaving behind them the "now broken summits of ancient beeches" (9.9). In the Tenth Eclogue Gallus, the love-poet, unlike Corydon in Eclogue 2, finds no repose in Arcadia; rather, he abandons it with the words, "Love conquers all, and we too must yield to love" (10.69). Vergil then takes leave of his work, picturing himself in the guise of Theocritus' absorbed and negligent watch-boy in the passage quoted above, "sitting and plaiting a wicker basket with supple marsh mallow"; but he shakes off his frivolous pastime and rouses himself at last: "Let us rise. Shade is wont to be harmful to singers, harmful is the shade of the juniper; crops, too, are marred by shade. Go home, my goats: it is evening, you are full; go home!" (10.70–77). In short, the *Bucolics* can be thought of as an inquiry into the advantages and liabilities of the umbratile life: a preparation for a poetics of engagement.

Unlike the wholly independent and autonomous Idylls of Theocritus, of which some may at one time have formed a single collection, the ten Eclogues comprising Vergil's *Bucolics* are not occasional pieces—whatever may have been their individual origins—but parts of a single and integrated work. They are arranged in such a fashion as to display the spectacle of the pastoral world initially succeeding (though not without considerable cost) and ultimately failing to meet the challenge of the threats to its existence which arise both from within and from without its fragile boundaries: the external, invasive threat of public authority to destroy the poet's livelihood, on the one hand, and the internal, disruptive threat of erotic desire to destroy the poet's creative equilibrium, on the other. The *Bucolics* is an exploration of the imperiled dream-world of language, of a poetic vision which can alternately transcend, redeem, or falsify the harsh world of historical reality but is ultimately powerless either to sweeten it or to save itself. Thus Vergil describes both the outward and the inward constraints upon his art. Until the reflowering of pastoral poetry in the Renaissance, Vergil's imitators could do little more than rearrange the symbolic landscape that he bequeathed to them.

BIBLIOGRAPHY

SOURCES

Texts and commentaries: A. S. F. Gow, ed., *Theocritus*, 2 vols. (1950; 2d ed. 1952); A. S. F. Gow, ed., *Bucolici Graeci*, Oxford Classical Texts (1952; 2d ed. 1958); K. J. Dover, ed., *Theocritus: Select Poems* (1971); R. A. B. Mynors, ed., *P. Vergili Maronis Opera*, Oxford Classical Texts (1969; rev. ed. 1972); M. Geymonat, ed., *P. Vergili Maronis: Opera* (1973); Robert Coleman, ed., *Vergil: Eclogues*, Cambridge Greek and Latin Classics (1977); R. D. Williams, ed., *Virgil: The Eclogues and Georgics* (1979); H. Schenkl, *Calpurnii et Nemesiani Bucolica* (1885); J. Wight Duff and Arnold M. Duff, eds., *Minor Latin Poets*, Loeb Classical Library (1934; rev. ed. 1935).

Translations (in addition to those contained in Gow, *Theocritus*, Duff and Duff, and in Alpers, Berg, and Klingner, below): Anthony Holden, trans., *Greek Pastoral Poetry*, Penguin Classics (1974); Anna Rist, trans., *The Poems of Theocritus* (1978); Thelma Sargent, trans., *The Idylls of Theocritus* (1982); Daryl Hine, *Theocritus: Idylls and Epigrams* (1982); Guy Lee, trans., *The Eclogues (Bucolica)*, rev. ed., Penguin Classics (1984).

STUDIES

Paul Alpers, *The Singer of the Eclogues: A Study of Virgilian Pastoral* (1979); William Berg, *Early Virgil* (1974); Karl Büchner, *P. Vergilius Maro. Der Dichter der Römer* (1955; repr. 1959); Phillip Damon, "Modes of Analogy in Ancient and Medieval Verse," in *University of California Publications in Classical Philology*, **15** (1954–1961); William Empson, *Some Versions of Pastoral* (1935; rev. ed. 1974); Gianfranco Fabiano, "Fluctuation in Theocritus' Style," in *Greek, Roman, and Byzantine Studies*, **12** (1971); David M. Halperin, *Before Pastoral: Theocritus and the Ancient Tradition of Bucolic Poetry* (1983); Friedrich Klingner, *Virgil. Bucolica: Hirtengedichte* (1977); D. Korzeniewski, *Hirtengedichte aus Neronischer Zeit*, Texte zu Forschung (1971), and *Hirtengedichte aus spätrömischer und karolingischer Zeit*, Texte zu Forschung (1976).

Gilbert Lawall, *Theocritus' Coan Pastorals: A Poetry Book* (1967); Eleanor Winsor Leach, "Corydon Revisited: An Interpretation of the Political Eclogues of Calpurnius Siculus," in *Ramus*, **2** (1973), and *Vergil's "Eclogues": Landscapes of Experience* (1974); Philippe-Emmanuel Legrand, *Étude sur Théocrite* (1898; repr. 1968); Brooks Otis, *Virgil: A Study in Civilized Poetry* (1963); Adam Parry, "Landscape in Greek Poetry," in *Yale Classical Studies*, **15** (1957); J. Perret, *Virgile, l'homme et* *l'oeuvre* (1952; 3d ed. 1970); Viktor Pöschl, *Die Hirtendichtung Virgils* (1964); M. C. J. Putnam, *Virgil's Pastoral Art* (1970); Thomas G. Rosenmeyer, *The Green Cabinet: Theocritus and the European Pastoral Lyric* (1969); E. A. Schmidt, *Poetische Reflexion.* *Vergils Bukolik* (1972); Charles Segal, *Poetry and Myth in Ancient Pastoral* (1981); Otto Skutsch, "Symmetry and Sense in the *Eclogues,*" in *Harvard Studies in Classical Philology,* **73** (1969); John Van Sickle, *The Design of Virgil's "Bucolics"* (1978).

Drama

PETER D. ARNOTT

GREECE

The Origins of Greek Drama

The drama of the Western world was born in Greece. It evolved in large part from religious practices, which already contained a strong mimetic element. We know, for instance, of a sacred play at the shrine of Eleusis, not far from Athens, which offered an annual reenactment of the death and resurrection of Persephone. Such priestly ceremonies contained the seeds of drama. A major impulse was provided by the institution of choruses, which, in major cities and smaller communities, celebrated native deities in song and dance, using narratives composed by local poets to relate the adventures of gods or goddesses. The Greeks themselves believed that the transformation from narrative to drama was effected by Thespis, who took it upon himself one day to step out of the chorus and sing a solo role, not about the god but as the god. With this introduction of the first actor, dialogue between principal and chorus became possible, and the members of the chorus could accept characterizations as the god's worshipers or as participants in his adventures.

The Greeks loved to personalize their history, and it is doubtful whether Thespis did, as the legend asserts, single-handedly create a new art. There does seem, however, to have been a historical Thespis, known for his performances in the Attic countryside, who acted in Athens in 537 B.C. But there must have been additional contributing factors. We know of early poets who apparently were experimenting with lyric tragedy; and a strong influence may have come from the Homeric poems. The *Iliad* and the *Odyssey* are intensely dramatic and contain a good deal of first-person narrative. They were recited by professional bards at a quadrennial Athenian festival. The Thespis story, however, is true in its general terms.

The chorus, originally the major element in Greek drama, remained important through its most productive period, and its members acquired several functions. They could be elders, soldiers, people of a city, or whatever else the story required; or they could step out of the action and become narrators, giving additional information to the audience, commenting objectively on the scene that had just been played, and relating the action to other legends or giving it a wider social context. The flexibility of the chorus gives Greek drama some of its most characteristic features. Greek drama was also a musical performance. The chorus sang and danced; the actors, too, probably delivered their lines as recitative, breaking into impassioned song at the emotional high points of the play.

The music of Greek drama has been lost. We have only fragments of a lyric from Euripides' *Orestes,* which is impossible to recreate convincingly in modern notation. Some choral music survived for centuries after the disappearance of the drama, having been adapted for hymns in the Byzantine church. This too was swept away by liturgical reform, although there are tantalizing hints that portions may survive in the Soviet Union. Musical performances of Greek tragedy are now rare. It must be remembered, however, how important music was to the original conception of Greek tragedy and that, in reading a drama, we essentially only get to know the librettos of operas of which the musical scores have been lost. The earliest composers of Italian opera knew this; their intent was to reconstruct the vanished musical art of Greek tragedy.

Although the music is lost, something is known of its instrumentation. The double flute, *diaulos,* was used, probably not only for the choruses but also to give a musical beat to the actors' declamations. Drums and trumpets were also used, with the occasional addition of exotic instruments such as tambourines and maracas. As they sang, the choruses also danced, in formations that (like much modern Greek folk dancing) seem to have been primarily circular. Each form of drama had its appropriate dance, though the names of some dance figures for tragedy suggest wild—even abandoned—movement. Clearly, these performances were anything

but sedate and relied on the power and spectacle of mass movement to interweave and underline the spoken words of the play. It is even possible that the movement of the chorus was continuous, offering a running visual counterpoint to the actors' speeches. In modern productions the chorus is often seen as an intrusion and embarrassment. In the original productions it was both physically and figuratively central, and the Greeks spoke of the chorus as virtually synonymous with the play.

The earliest plays, then, were monodramas, performed to the accompaniment of an omnipresent chorus. Some idea of what they must have been like is given by Aeschylus' tragedy *The Suppliants,* which, though not early in date, retains an early form. Here, the chorus carries the burden of the play, and the acted scenes are mainly monologues. Aeschylus himself is credited with introducing a second actor, and Sophocles a third. In tragedy the number never rose above this, although each actor could play several roles, and nonspeaking characters and supernumeraries could be added if necessary. The introduction of more actors increased the possibilities for complex scenes and dialogue and gradually reduced the central importance of the chorus. Tragedy assumed a regular, but not invariable, pattern. The extant plays usually open with a *prologos* (prologue), either a monologue (as in Euripides' *The Bacchants* [*Bacchae*]) or a complex scene with several characters (as in Sophocles' *Oedipus the King* [*Oedipus Rex*]) establishing the main line of the story. Then comes the formal entrance of the chorus (*parodos*); the action proceeds as an alternation of acted scenes, *epeisodia* (episodes), and choral songs (*stasima*). Sometimes, when one of the characters dies, actors and chorus sing together in a formal lament (*kommos*). The exit of the chorus (*exodos*) marks the ending of the play.

Although every city of importance, and

many smaller places, had their own theaters, only those plays written in Athens have survived. As in so many other areas, therefore, we are compelled to look at an important aspect of Greek life through Athenian eyes. The earliest extant play, Aeschylus' *The Persians* (472 B.C.), deals with a contemporary event, the defeat of an invading power by a largely Athenian navy eight years earlier. This choice of topic is not typical. Subject matter was normally drawn from myth and legend, using a body of stories that, in their general outline, would have been familiar to the audience.

The dramatist's originality lay in his unique adaptation of these well-loved tales and continuous reinterpretation of their meanings. There are, for example, three treatments, by three different dramatists, of Orestes' murder of his mother, Clytemnestra. They are similar only in the outline of the story. Aeschylus' version places the incident in the context of an inherited blood-guilt and uses the family vendetta to explore wider issues of cosmic justice. Sophocles employs the story to examine the social and familial consequences of murder. Euripides adapts the tale to depict the corruption of the human spirit by penury and violence. The fortunes of Orestes and his family provided the inspiration for numerous other plays. Another favorite source was the story of the royal house of Thebes, including Laius and Jocasta, their son Oedipus, and his children, Antigone and her doomed brothers. The Trojan War provided other subjects for the Homeric poems or for other early epics that we now know only by name.

Greek Plays in Performance

The plays were performed in theaters whose characteristic shape affirms the traditional view of the origins of the drama. There is increasing archaeological evidence that the earliest structures were rectangular, having affinities with similar stone-paved areas that have been uncovered in Crete. By the early fifth century B.C., however, when the drama was fully established, the theaters were undoubtedly circular—perhaps more elaborate developments of the circular stone threshing floors found in every Greek village, which could have served as dance floors for the local choruses. This large circular dancing space (*orchestra*) is the central, and most distinctive, feature of fifth-century theater building. Here the choruses performed their complex evolutions, almost completely surrounded by an audience packed into tiers of stone seats rising steeply up the hillside.

Greek theater was performed as theater-in-the-round. That portion of the rim of the orchestra circle not taken up by spectators held the *skene* (hut or tent), a simple building that served as an architectural background for the action, as a sounding board for the actors' voices, and as dressing room and storage space. A single door gave actors the necessary focus for their entrances, and an upper level provided an area that could conventionally stand for heaven, in which the gods appeared. Probably a low platform in front of the *skene* raised the actors a few feet, making them more prominent and distinguishing them from the mass of the chorus—although the actors could descend to orchestra level if the situation demanded, just as the chorus could ascend by ramps or steps to the *skene.* The chorus made its own processional entrances and exits down long aisles (*parodoi*) located at either side of the *skene.*

Simple but spacious and imaginatively flexible, the fifth-century theater provided an appropriate setting for a poetic drama in which most effects were suggested by the spoken word. Although *skene* is the origin of the word "scenery," the Greek theater had no stage settings. The decoration was limited to the architectural embellishment of the *skene;* everything else is conveyed through words. Characters tell us where we are supposed to be: in front of Oedipus' palace in Thebes; outside Medea's house in Corinth; on a mountain peak at the edge of the world, where Prometheus is hung in chains; near Philoctetes' cave on the barren isle of Lemnos. Such mechanical effects as the theater possessed were of similar simplicity. There was a crane or derrick called the *mechane* (machine), which could swing characters through the air in an illusion of flight. Gods sometimes entered in this way, and Euripides exploited the device in one play, now lost, to show Bellerophon riding on his winged horse, Pegasus. The Latin phrase *deus ex machina* (god from a machine) derives from the charge that some playwrights resolved insoluble plots by the arbitrary introduction of an airborne deity to settle human dilemmas by miraculous means. However, the Greek plays that we have do not abuse the *mechane* in this way.

Another device was the *ekkyklema* (something rolled out), a small platform that could be pushed out through the *skene* door, bearing a tableau—often dead bodies, to provide a focus for the lament and discussion on stage. This is probably the way the corpses of Agamemnon and Cassandra appeared in Aeschylus' *Agamemnon,* after Clytemnestra murders them offstage. This was the sum of fifth-century B.C. stage mechanics; they performed a function that, in the modern theater, would normally be accomplished by lighting. Greek theater performances were outdoor events, in full sunlight, and the sudden, emphatic introduction of a character had to be secured by mechanics rather than by a spotlight.

Greek tragedy, however, remained rhetorical rather than spectacular in its effects. It was a medium in which what the audience heard was more important than what it could see. To an extent, this reliance on language was imposed on the dramatists by theatrical conditions. In the principal cities, the theaters were enormous. The Theater of Dionysus at Athens, where the extant plays were first performed, held 15,000 people. To those sitting far back in the theater, the actors were dwarfed by their surroundings. The group movement of the chorus could be seen as continually changing patterns against the orchestra floor, but the smaller, more personal gestures on which a modern actor builds his performance would have been hopelessly lost. To compensate for the lack of visual impact, the acoustics of the Greek theaters were excellent. The theater of Epidaurus, although not built until the early fourth century, remains the best surviving example of the fifth-century plan: a coin dropped in the center of the orchestra can be heard in the farthest tier of seats.

Much, therefore, that in modern drama would be expressed in visual terms is in Greek plays conveyed by words. Characters announce themselves or one another; they describe their movements, feelings, and expressions; their speeches are cast in the patterns of formal rhetoric. For Athenian audiences, rhetoric was a familiar feature of their lives. They spent a good portion of each day in the assembly, listening to carefully prepared and powerfully delivered speeches, or in the lawcourts, hearing advocates argue cases with elaborate and meticulously rehearsed eloquence. Rhetoric was a major element of Greek education, and Athenian audiences were trained to listen as modern audiences are not. The playwrights addressed their public in familiar rhetorical terms. Often, the nucleus of a play is a formal debate; speech is used where modern drama would provide action. Often the whole play is, in effect, a debate, building up a powerful argument first for one side, then for the other, and asking the audience to reach a decision. Modern audiences sometimes find Greek tragedy unnecessarily verbose. Given the original circumstances of presentation, however, and the kind of society for which these plays were composed, language was the most effective medium for conveying the argument.

Plays were given as part of a religious festival and were performed competitively. Dionysus, one of the younger gods of the Olympic pantheon, who had been previously associated with fertility and nature worship, was adopted as the patron deity of the fledgling drama; and the theater in Athens was built in conjunction with his temple, at the foot of the Acropolis. There were three festivals involving plays, all held during the winter and early spring. Of these, the most important was the City Dionysia, which attracted visitors from all over the Greek-speaking world. As the first step in the long process of production, dramatists submitted their scripts to the archons, who chose from among them. Each tragic writer was required to submit three tragedies. Early practice was to write a trilogy of closely related plays: each play, although it could be performed independently, was in fact merely one act of a larger drama, whose performance time would have come close to five hours. Later practice favored the writing of three plays separate in theme and intent.

Each tragedian was also required to submit a satyr play, a short comic afterpiece to the tragedies. Only one example of this popular genre, Euripides' *Cyclops*, has survived complete, but we may judge that the satyr play was a burlesque of mythology—perhaps a parodic version of one of the stories that the audience had just seen as tragedy—with a chorus of satyrs, the half men, half animals who were the buffoons of Greek folklore. For the most part, tragic writers confined themselves to tragedy, and comic writers to comedy; but the satyr play served as a meeting ground for the two genres, demanding that the tragic dramatist also demonstrate his skill with knockabout farce.

The plays of three tragedians were selected for performance in the festival. Each of the dramas was then allotted a chorus, which involved considerable expenditure of public money. The chorus members themselves were amateur volunteers, drawn from the public at large. They contributed their services as a public duty, just as they contributed their time and energy to the army or the lawcourts. Early choruses may have numbered as many as fifty; this was later reduced to twelve or fifteen (traditionally in the mid fifth century B.C.). Even so, a considerable number would have been involved, and over the years a large proportion of the adult male population would have done duty in the theater, creating a highly knowledgeable audience. Choruses had to be trained and costumed. This was expensive. Rehearsals seem to have occupied the better part of a year, and costumes could demand a ruinously large sum. This money came largely from taxation. A particularly wealthy citizen might be asked to pay for outfitting a chorus as a *leitourgia* (liturgy) or special tax, just as he might be asked, in other circumstances, to pay for outfitting a warship.

Athens saw the dramatic festivals as one of the regular and normal operations of the state, and financed them accordingly. Actors were professionals, paid for their festival services; and many undoubtedly found occasional work elsewhere, in smaller local festivals or as guest artists outside Athens. It was almost certainly impossible, however, to earn a living as a full-time actor. The opportunities did not yet exist. Some actors worked part-time as teachers of rhetoric, an art to which their own was closely allied. Some served the state in other capacities, as spokesmen for diplomatic missions or in political offices. Acting was still a prestigious profession. There was as yet no stigma on the theater, and in a society where the art of public speaking was of cardinal importance, an actor could expect to make his mark in places other than on the stage.

We must still refer to actors in the masculine. There were no actresses in the Greek theater; all female parts were played by men. Besides a fine voice, an actor needed considerable physical stamina. Within one play, he would normally be expected to take several roles; the change of character was indicated by a change of mask and costume. In the fifth century, masks were still simple and expressive, not the grotesque distortions they were later to become. Probably made of leather, and worn with a heavy, boldly colored, stylized costume, they helped to give the actor definition in the huge theater and to make the characters instantly identifiable. They also imposed on the actor the necessity of conveying emotion not with the face but with the whole body. Actors consequently trained as rigorously as athletes and accepted the same disciplines.

Fifth-century productions were still largely in the hands of the author, who, in the earliest phase of the theater, was director, composer, choreographer, designer, and chief actor for his own play. Inevitably, some of these functions became more specialized. Professional chorus trainers were sometimes employed. In 449 B.C. the institution of a separate prize for actors, distinct from that for dramatists, signaled the growing breach between the literary and performing arts. But although the dramatist ceased to take major roles in his own plays, he continued to exercise overall control of the production. Greek drama of this period enjoyed a unity of theatrical conception that later ages have only occasionally—and with great difficulty—recaptured.

At the close of the festival, prizes were awarded by a panel of judges. We do not know the basis on which they made their decisions: whether they were influenced by audience response or responsible only to their own judgments. Winners' names were inscribed in the city archives, and the *choregus,* the tax-paying citizen who had financed the production, was allowed to erect a columnar monument to his victory, at his own expense. To the dramatist went a victory wreath and a small cash prize. The surviving plays do not necessarily owe their preservation to success in competitions. Some works now considered among the finest examples of Greek tragedy did not do well in their time. Their more successful competitors exist for us now only as names and their works only as scattered fragments of verses.

Because the plays were part of a state festival, attendance was a civic duty. The theaters were large enough that most of the population could be packed into a single performance, and we know of only one case in the fifth century when a play—Aristophanes' *Frogs*—was repeated at a festival. The exact composition of this audience remains problematical. It is still debated, for example, whether or not women were admitted. But we do know a certain amount about audience behavior and must beware of confusing Greek notions of religious festivals with our own. These were clearly not solemn occasions but, rather, public holidays, eagerly anticipated and keenly relished. The plays were but one part of a whole complex of ceremonial activities that lasted from dawn to dusk for days on end. Nor was the audience slow to express its opinion. We know of several cases when the play was halted by a hostile crowd, who threw stones and fruit and abused the author.

Playwrights respected the temper of this mass of people. Both tragedy and comedy contain obvious crowd-pleasing devices, passages designed to flatter the political susceptibilities of an audience and bring it cheering to its feet. Indeed, although these were religious occasions, the Greek audience did not go to a play as we go to a sermon, nor were the plays necessarily about religion. Although several of the extant works explore the ways of gods with man, others are largely humanistic in their themes; and a number of the later works are openly derisive of traditional religion. Yet, in Greek terms, all of these could be assembled as components of a religious festival. It would be more accurate to see the plays as extensions of the democratic process, serving up to the public, in fictional form, arguments similar to those heard in the assembly. The theater in Greek society was the most public, and the most exciting, way of disseminating opinions.

Writers of Greek Tragedy

Time has robbed us of most of the tragic writers' output. We have complete plays of only three authors, out of a vastly larger number, and even these represent only a small proportion of their writings. Fortunately, the plays that have survived—selected by Alexandrian scholars, primarily for schoolbook use—seem reasonably representative of the development of the art. Aeschylus (525–456 B.C.), seven of whose plays have been preserved, was regarded by the Greeks as the second father of the theater, after Thespis, and as the innovator of several of its traditional practices. He preferred the trilogy structure; and one such trilogy, the *Oresteia,* has survived complete, though without the satyr play that originally accompanied it. He used this structure to deal with enormous themes, in which great figures from the remote, mythic past wrestled with cosmic questions of divinity and justice. His characters are the gods themselves or mail-clad supermen; and because he depicts a universe in which human beings are merely small cogs in the divine machine, his plays show more interest in the overriding argu-

ment than in individual characterization. His language is rich, dense, allusive, and often cryptic; even the Greeks of the next generation sometimes found him hard to follow.

By contrast his successor Sophocles (495–406 B.C.) wrote plays more focused on human issues. His seven extant tragedies are concerned with such things as the true definition of heroism, the rights of the individual as opposed to those of the state, and the extent to which man may control his own destiny. His work shows much more emphasis on the characters and their interrelationships and correspondingly less on the chorus. Euripides (480–406 B.C.), though Sophocles' near contemporary, works from radically different principles. His nineteen surviving tragedies, although deriving from myth and legend, use these well-known stories to question traditional beliefs and values in front of an audience whose own standards were being eroded by the bitter years of the Peloponnesian War (431–404 B.C.). Euripidean tragedy is so contemptuous and parodic that it virtually creates a new genre, verging on black comedy.

Old Comedy

Comedy came late into the festivals and loosely imitated tragedy in its general structure. It too had a chorus, twenty-four in number, and suggests an early influence of nature worship by the fact that many of these choruses were characterized as animals or birds. Like tragedy also, it developed as an alternation of sung choruses and acted scenes. In comedy, however, the pattern was less regular. The chorus may predominate in one half of the play and virtually disappear during the other. The most obvious difference between tragedy and comedy, however, is in the plot material. Tragedy takes its subjects from myth. Comedy, although it may borrow elements from myth, largely invents its situations. Greek comedy is also fiercely immediate and personal. It deals with contemporary issues and events, peopling its stage with broad caricatures of notabilities of the time. Greek comic writers were licensed jesters: Athens had no laws regarding slander or libel to control the stage, and any prominent or notorious citizen might expect to see his masked simulacrum strutting before a gleeful audience.

One of the three Athenian dramatic festivals, the Lenaea, was devoted to comedy. The form also occupied a subordinate place in the other festivals and produced a number of writers celebrated in their time. Unfortunately, surviving evidence for fifth-century comedy is even slimmer than for tragedy, for we have only eleven plays by one writer, Aristophanes (*ca.* 450–*ca.* 385 B.C.). His work shows, however, some consistent patterns that presumably represent the norms of his time. His plays usually begin, like tragedies, with a prologue; this often commences with general, irrelevant patter, to engage the audience's attention and secure their good humor before the subject of the play is introduced. Most of Aristophanes' plays were composed under wartime conditions, when the normal lives of his audience had been disrupted; it is significant that his characteristic hero is a displaced person, frantically attempting to find peace and security in a world that will not let him rest. To extricate himself from his difficulties the hero devises a fantastic plot, in which he is sometimes resisted, sometimes abetted, by the chorus, who, as in tragedy, enter in a lengthy *parodos.* A recurrent feature of the plot is the *agon* (contest), sometimes a physical fight, sometimes a verbal conflict—the rhetorical arts of debate play no less a part in comedy than in tragedy.

About halfway through the play a point of rest occurs. The situation has now been set up, and action ceases while the chorus members address the audience directly in a long harangue known as the *parabasis* (turning around). They may speak in or out of character, often on subjects of topical importance that have no direct connection with the play, such as calendar reform or voter registration. Aristophanes sometimes uses the parabasis for statements of his views about comic art, defending his plays and deriding his critics. The second half of the play, after the parabasis, tends to consist of a string of loosely knit scenes, almost independent sketches illustrating various comic consequences of the situation already established. Finally comes the *komos,* the almost obligatory final revel, a grand burst of song and dance, eating and drinking, packed with sexual innuendo, which sweeps actors and chorus off the stage together and brings the comedy to a lavish conclusion. Like the animal nature of the chorus, this festive finale may possibly derive from the fertility celebrations of earlier ritual.

The loosely knit plots address various aspects of the Athenian condition: the varying fortunes in war, contemporary views of education, politics and politicians, the judicial system, plays and playwrights. The dramatis personae comprise fictional characters, figures out of myth and legend—in several cases, the gods themselves—and caricatures of contemporary citizens. The action shifts from one imagined location to another; jokes and references are often wildly anachronistic; the language fluctuates between exquisite poetry and earthy and vernacular reference. Often, the plot may seem to change direction arbitrarily, as the play proceeds. But there is usually a strong and discernible theme, to which the other elements are subordinate. To modern ears, Aristophanes seems to combine many types of comedy into one play—situation comedy, political and social satire, and broad farce—and to present them with techniques that might now seem more appropriate for an intimate revue than for the legitimate theater.

The bulk of Aristophanes' work, distinguished by the characteristics listed above and generally referred to as Old Comedy, appeared before the end of the fifth century. As the Peloponnesian War drew to its unhappy close, however, various constraints began to appear that were to change this format substantially. With increasing pressure from outside, Athens could no longer tolerate such outspoken criticism from within. Comedy became less abrasive, turning from political and social satire to a milder and more generalized style of humor, with all the pungency and personalities removed. Aristophanes' last play, *Wealth,* is little more than a gentle allegory and is seen by critics as belonging to a different, transitional genre, Middle Comedy.

The loss of the war, and consequently of political power, by Athens, brought many changes to the city and its distinctive arts. These changes were accelerated by the growing professionalism of the theater, which, from the fourth century on, sought audiences beyond those offered by the annual festivals. Although these festivals continued to exist—indeed, they retained much of their prestige through Roman times—the later Greek theater was largely in the hands of touring companies that operated for profit, performed whenever and wherever they could, and developed a star system in which the actor replaced the poet as the focus of the audience's attention. With a dearth of new dramatists, the theater turned increasingly to revivals of fifth-century masterpieces and particularly to Euripides, who, his personal odium forgotten, was now seen as a creator of sensational roles for leading actors. As a tragedian whose plays relied least upon their chorus, Euripides also lent himself happily to the new system. Touring companies preferred a repertory that needed minimal personnel. Thus, in revivals, the chorus shrank to nine. In new plays, the chorus tended to disappear altogether or, at best, to perform perfunctory musical divertissements between episodes. The old sense of civic duty that had brought the chorus into being no longer existed.

New Comedy

Touring possibilities increased rapidly as Greek influence spread eastward through the conquests (336–323 B.C.) of Alexander the Great. Actors could now expect to play not merely in Greece itself, or in the older colonies of Italy and Sicily, but also as far away as the hinterland of India. They chose their material accordingly. The favored tragedy was violent and sensational; Euripides, again, was seen as suitable. But comedy had largely replaced tragedy in the affections of an age that sought diversion rather than involvement. This could no longer be Old Comedy, whose local allusions would not be understood outside Athens. A different genre evolved, New Comedy, virtually without a chorus and concerning itself with themes more generally understood—situation comedies, which explored the common world of family relationships. Romantic love was now established as a prolific source of plots. Mistaken identities—identical twins, long-lost children, broken families reunited after much misunderstanding—proved equally fruitful. The focus of comedy had narrowed from the state to the family. Expanding audiences created a demand for more material, but the same simple formulas, with names and settings changed and different dialogue, could produce a multiplicity of plays.

No less than the plots, the dramatis personae of New Comedy show a different world. Gone are the topical personalities of Aristophanes. Characters are now types, distinguished by easily recognizable masks that label them at first appearance, and offering predictable patterns of speech and behavior. Later writers list these types: cross old man, genial old man, playboy son, cunning slave, and stupid slave. Each has stage business from which he never departs. Costumes were now more realistic, and the acting style had moderated its original formality.

For a long time, plays of this period were known to us by reputation only. The leading playwright of the fourth century B.C., Menander, was a legend in his time and a powerful influence on the Roman dramatists who followed. Ancient criticism is lavish in his praises; the scholar Aristophanes of Byzantium wrote, "O Menander and life, which of you imitated the other?" But, until the twentieth century, no portion of his work substantial enough to construct even the outline of a plot was available. Then fragments began to appear, and finally, in the 1950s, a complete play, *Dyskolos* (*The Grouch,* or *The Man Who Hated People*), was discovered in Cairo. It is at last possible to see what the Greeks of Alexander's time laughed at. Set in the barren Greek countryside, *Dyskolos* is a simple but charming tale of a crotchety old farmer, his lovely daughter, and a rich city boy who falls in love with her. After vainly trying to prove himself in the father's eyes, the boy seizes his chance when the old man tumbles down a well. Grateful for his rescue, the grouch allows his daughter to be married and, at the end of the play, is carried off to join in the wedding party. Modern critics claim to find this comedy disappointing. But its charm lies in the performance rather than in the reading; it illustrates some key characteristics of this period of the theater. Most significant is what has happened to the chorus. Although present in the flesh, it no longer has any spirit. Annotations for chorus entries appear at intervals throughout the work, but there is no special material for them to sing. Presumably they sang folk songs or anything that was popular at the moment; in *Dyskolos* the chorus has become peripheral, marking the end of an era of Greek drama.

Theater structure reflected literary and social changes. With the chorus no longer central, or vanished altogether, there was no longer any need for the orchestra. In the Hellenistic theaters, therefore, it was reduced. The growing size and magnificence of the stage buildings impinged upon it from one side and the auditorium—with seats now placed inside the rim of the orchestra—from the other, and the full circle was cut to half. The *skene* had new doors added to it, and new types of stage machinery appeared, notably the *periaktoi,* revolving scenic panels located on either side of the stage, which indicated changes of scene by showing different faces to the audience.

But more important than any mechanical change was the change in attitude embodied in the new theater. What had been a formal and conventional drama became realistic and specific. In the fifth century, the setting had been created largely in the audience's imagination, prompted by the poet's words. In the fourth, the *skene* with its doors was taken as a realistic representation of a row of houses fronting on a street. The prologue identifies the occupants of the houses for each new play but, once established, the location never changes. Costumes, stage behavior, and a language approximating the vernacular much more closely combine to suggest a slice of life. As the themes of drama become more mundane, its presentation becomes more realistic.

Most of the ancient theaters that we can still see in the Mediterranean countries are of the Hellenistic pattern. Every important city had its own; where there was none, companies played on portable stages that replicated the main features of the permanent structures. This period too saw the organization of the first actors' union, a guild known as the Artists of Dionysus, with headquarters on the island of Delos. It laid down conditions of employment for its members, negotiated contracts, and attempted to establish standards for the profession. Prominent actors traveled the length and breadth of the Mediterranean, going from festival to festival, much as operatic superstars do now, and commanding huge salaries. Compared with the fifth century, however, the status of the actor slumped, and the days of the honorable amateur were over.

ROME

The Roman Theater

The Greek colonies in southern Italy and Sicily, many of them dating from the eighth century B.C., saw a great deal of theatrical activity. Such cities as Taras (modern Taranto) and Syracuse had large theaters of their own, produced both spectacular tragedy and New Comedy, and introduced Greek drama to the emergent power of Rome. Rapidly outgrowing and absorbing its neighbors, Rome had little time or inclination to develop artistic standards of its own. Instead, it borrowed from the earlier powers with which it made contact. North of Rome, occupying roughly the district now known as Tuscany, were the Etruscans, a people of mysterious origins who supplied Rome with her first kings, her earliest architecture, and some of her oldest institutions. Among these was a sacred dance, traditionally brought in to avert a disastrous plague in 364 B.C., which the Romans claimed as the origin of their theater. Onto this were grafted plots taken from the Greek. As Roman influence pushed southward, and the prosperous Greek colonies were taken over one by one, Greek plays became increasingly familiar. The Romans credited one Livius Andronicus with the first performance of Greek plays in the Latin language at Rome. He was believed to be a Greek captured in the wars, to have come to Rome as a slave, and to have distinguished himself so by his learning that he gained his freedom. The year 240 B.C. is cited for his first performances.

As with Thespis in Greece, the story of Livius Andronicus may be a simplification of a much more complex historical process. In general terms, however, it is undoubtedly true. Greek plays in translation became the staple of Roman drama, and in the early years, it seemed that the art might be as prestigious in the new world as it had been in the old. Livius and the dramatists who immediately succeeded him were given high honors. A college of poets was established. Plays were performed regularly at major civic and religious festivals—more frequently, indeed, than in Greece, for in Rome the number of such festivals multiplied, and performances could also be given at special celebrations such as the funeral games of a distinguished citizen or the dedication of a new temple. As in Greece, the financing of productions was a state responsibility. Although the plays were borrowed, the organization of the theater, and its place in society, seemed superficially the same.

In reality, the theater in Rome never achieved the dignity and importance that it had possessed in fifth-century Greece. Soon after its inception, it came to be regarded as mere entertainment, lacking the educative qualities of Greek tragedy or the social involvement of Old Comedy. Roman tragedy, significantly, had a brief life. Writers increasingly preferred comedy, and few fragments of republican tragedy have come down to us. Roman comedy also showed tendencies even more escapist than those of its Hellenistic models, and any hint of political commentary was frowned upon. Although the process of adaptation varied from author to author, the comedies tended to retain their Greek characters, settings, and costumes, while salting the Latin text with Roman allusions. This created the semblance of a fantasy world, a never-never land devoid of contact with Roman actuality. It could be argued, indeed, that the one remaining civic function of the theater in Rome was to act as a vote-catching device; lavish expenditure on festivals by incumbent officials ensured that their names would be remembered at election time.

It is indicative of the low status of the theater at Rome that no building was erected specifically for the performance of plays in the capital until 55 B.C. While the Greek colonies, now Roman dependencies, had had theaters for hundreds of years, the citizens of Rome made do with makeshift structures. A strong puritanical faction in the senate argued that drama was a product of Greek decadence, unsuitable for a virile and aggressive race. Thus, companies performed plays where they could: in temple precincts or on wooden stages erected in the market square or stadium for the duration of a festival. Such evidence as we have suggests that these portable theaters followed the form of their more solid Hellenistic predecessors. A low wooden stage served for the actors, closed in at the rear by curtains or a painted architectural backdrop. Steps led down from the stage, for occasional entrances at ground level, and some plays needed divine appearances at roof height.

These flimsy theaters were tenanted by companies formed and operated as commercial enterprises. Each was headed by a *dominus,* an actor-manager who played the principal parts, served as spokesman for the troupe, negotiated with the authorities, and haggled with playwrights. Rank-and-file actors might be slaves—a well-trained slave fetched good prices and was a valuable asset—or free citizens whose lives could not have been much better than those of slaves. Companies were kept small, for financial reasons, and doubling and tripling of parts was common. The chorus had now almost entirely disappeared. Some element of music remained, both in flute accompaniments performed by players sufficiently accomplished for their names to be recorded separately on the bill, and in *cantica,* solos sung by the principal characters. Actors therefore had to be skilled singers and dancers, and probably acrobats as well, for Roman comedy was physically demanding, and versatile enough to play several characters in an hour's performance. The mask, another carryover from the Greek theater, served to define character, and Roman plays tended to use the same limited range of broadly differentiated types.

Roman Comedy

In a culture where the theater was a trade, plays were regarded as mere merchandise. Authors sold their works outright and retained no further control over them. There were neither copyrights nor royalties. A play might remain in the repertory for years, cut or added to as the whim of the public or of the *dominus* dictated. This explains the shabby state of some of the texts of Roman comedy. The works of only two authors survive from this period. Titus Maccius Plautus (*ca.* 254–*ca.* 184 B.C.), undoubtedly the most popular author of his time, was, by tradition, an actor who recouped his fallen fortunes by writing plays. His prolific output is represented by twenty-one surviving examples, most of which exploit the well-worn domestic situations for broad laughs, though one or two strike a more serious or sentimental note. According to tradition, his successor Publius Terentius Afer (*ca.* 195–159 B.C.), more familiarly known as Terence, a captured slave like Livius Andronicus, was liberated and subsidized by wealthy patrons who recognized his genius. Terence's comparatively meager output of six comedies suggests that he did not need to write for a living. In addition, the more serious tone of his work, bare of slapstick humor or romanizing allusions, indicates that he wrote for a literary elite with greater knowledge of the Greek originals.

Terence had been long dead when Rome's first permanent theater was built in 55 B.C. This break with long tradition was the work of a prominent general and statesman, Cnaeus Pompeius Magnus (Pompey the Great), who used his influence to outweigh the moralists. He constructed a theater modeled on that of the Greek island city of Mytilene as part of a large building complex near Rome's center. It was coupled with a temple dedicated to Venus, and the huge structure was inaugurated with processions, play productions, and wild beast hunts, the last an unhappy omen for the future. A spate of theater building followed, accelerated in the early empire as each new ruler sought to make his mark on the city's architecture; but Pompey's theater was venerated as Rome's first and for centuries was something every tourist to the capital felt bound to see. Although most of its fabric has disappeared, its outline can still be traced in aerial views of the city streets, and one corner of it—perhaps the very spot where Julius Caesar was assassinated in 44 B.C.—has been excavated underneath the modern thoroughfare.

Other Entertainments

Ironically, Pompey's structure came too late, for the drama was already as good as dead. The mass of the population, whose interest in the theater had been perfunctory at best, increasingly sought diversion in cruder forms of entertainment. Gladiatorial combat, whose origins can be traced back to acts of ritual slaughter in Rome's remote past, saw a surge of popularity as a spectator sport. Julius Caesar's foreign conquests in the last years of the republic brought back masses of expendable captives to Rome. The public loved to see them fight to the death with the armor and weapons of their native countries. As this new sport grew more sophisticated, major gladiatorial schools were established in Rome and the provincial cities, using slaves who chose this career for the faint hope of freedom that it offered to a champion. In the later empire freemen, and one emperor, Commodus, were to join the gladiatorial ranks. Their showplaces were called amphitheaters (double theaters), as though two semicircular orchestras had been built face to face, so that the packed, tiered seats surrounded an elliptical arena. The most famous of these structures, and the largest in the Roman world, was the Colosseum, dedicated in A.D. 80 as a political act to celebrate the Flavian dynasty. Occupying the site of an earlier imperial palace, it was originally designed to be flooded, so that the arena could be used for mimic sea battles. Such aquacades were a favorite Roman entertainment, and several theaters were constructed or adapted to hold them. Underneath the Colosseum floor lay an elaborate network of passages, cells, and cages for wild beasts, with elevators to bring the animals to the surface. As brute slaughter began to pall, various dramatic colorations were adopted. The fights were given an elaborate scenario, often drawn from mythology. Complex settings were constructed, changed by the apparatus of lifts and tunnels that the amphitheaters already provided.

Against such competition the poor remnants of the drama languished. Tragedy was still being written in the early empire, but often as a literary diversion merely, with no intention of performance. The only surviving tragic drama from this period is represented by ten works attributed to Seneca (*ca.* 4 B.C.–A.D. 65), philosopher, statesman, and tutor to the young emperor Nero. Based mostly on Greek models—in several cases, on originals that we still possess—the Roman plays show a radical change in treatment and perspective. True to their age, they show a fascination with the morbid, perverted, and bizarre. The language is ornate, rhetorical, and studded with obscure mythological allusions. The plays may never have been intended for the stage at all, but merely for declamation in the fashionable schools of rhetoric. Some of the effects they seem to call for would make staging them extremely difficult.

More popular by-products of tragedy were the performances of the *pantomimi*, solo dance recitals using a succession of masks to present the various characters of myth and legend. These could be performed to music alone or accompanied by the chant of a narrator. At a lower level of taste came the *mimi* (mimes); not, as in our sense, wordless performers but something closer to vaudeville performers, offering a mélange of songs, skits, and dances interspersed with juggling, beast acts, and acrobatic skills. Scenes and characters from early Roman comedy undoubtedly passed into the mime repertoire and were thus kept alive long after formal drama had disappeared. The mime performances also offered virtually the only opportunity for women to appear on the stage; troupes of women, and even female managers, were known, while the rest of the theater was still entirely male.

Weakened by apathy and the shift of popular taste, the classical theater was dealt a fatal blow by the advent of Christianity. The adherents of this new religion, distrusted from the beginning in Rome and suspected of treasonable activities, were apt targets for ridicule on the stage. Christian rites and practices were regularly burlesqued by the mimes. According to tradition, Saint Genesius, the patron saint of actors, was one such mime who converted in midperformance and went to his death in loyalty to the religion that he had once mocked in the court of Emperor Diocletian. As Christian apologists acquired a louder voice in Roman society, the theater came under attack. The most prominent critic was the fiery African Tertullian, who assailed Pompey's theater in Rome as the abode of two of the most pernicious pagan gods, Venus and Bacchus. With the growing respectability of Christian worship, and eventually its official acceptance, the theater was increasingly stigmatized. Some Christians were prepared to distinguish between the obscenity of the mimes and the more civilized utterances of the classical past; but most dismissed all manifestations of theater under one blanket condemnation, leaving a legacy of odium that the art has never entirely shaken off.

As the center of power began shifting from Rome to Constantinople in the sixth century, the writing of drama virtually disappeared. There was still, however, an extraordinary diversity of entertainment. In the Greek-speaking East, plays of Euripides were being revived well into the Christian Era. In the amphitheaters, vast balletic extravaganzas were staged, clearly using a complex theatrical technology now completely lost. Despite the disapproval of the church, the mimes flourished, with some winning great reputations. One, Theodora, rose from humble beginnings to marry Emperor Justinian and become mistress of the Byzantine Empire. In Greece and Italy, however, the major theatrical sites were allowed to fall into decay. By the Middle Ages, the theaters of Rome served only as fortifications in the endless wars among the city's feuding families; and the Colosseum, long desolate, was shunned by the superstitious as an anteroom to hell. In the once prosperous Roman colonies of southern France, the walls of theaters, their original purpose forgotten, were used to shelter whole villages.

REVIVALS AND INFLUENCES

The production history of classical drama since its own time has been sporadic. An Athenian dramatist of the fifth century B.C. could expect only one performance of his work in his lifetime, although plays were occasionally taken to festivals elsewhere. The fourth century, though largely an age of revivals, was still selective, and many plays never saw the stage again after their premieres. Toward the end of the fourth century the Athenian authorities, conscious that they were in danger of losing their dramatic heritage, assembled troupes of actors and, from their memories, prepared official copies of a number of plays. These were first placed in the Athenian archives and then spirited off to the Library at Alexandria, where a further selection took place for use as school texts. Those chosen were, substantially, the ones we know today through medieval copies of the long-vanished originals. With the decline of the classical world, Greek plays disappeared almost entirely from performance, surviving only as dusty relics on library shelves. Even with the rediscovery of classical literature in the Renaissance, Greek plays were slow to come into their own. For centuries they were read rather than performed or, if performed at all, were presented merely as educational exercises designed to illuminate the text.

Greek tragedy returned to the stage only in the nineteenth century. Much impetus was given by the universities, both in Great Britain and the United States, and in the early decades of the twentieth century a series of theatrically viable translations by Gilbert Murray made the works of this genre accessible to a wider audience. In Greece itself the excavation of important theaters made it once again possible to produce Greek plays in the surroundings for which they had been designed. Although the Theater of Dionysus in Athens is in ruins and unusable, the theater of Epidaurus has been restored to the point where it can be used for annual festivals of ancient drama. In Athens the smaller Greco-Roman Odeum of Herodes Atticus houses the Athens Festival. Thus it is now possible to see, both in their own country and in major theaters through-

out the world, revivals of the works of Aeschylus, Sophocles, Euripides, and Aristophanes; once again, Euripides has proved the most popular. Aristophanic comedy was for a long time barely understood. In the nineteenth century its gross indecency made performance, and even complete translation, impossible. But more modern forms of humor have revived the Aristophanic spirit, and the comedies are now frequently staged.

The Romans suffered a less fortunate fate. Plautus, despite his enormous theatrical popularity, largely disappeared from sight. A number of his plays were lost, not to be rediscovered until the fifteenth century. It was, oddly, Terence who survived, despite his lack of success in his lifetime. Held in high regard for their elegant Latinity, his comedies remained in constant use as schoolbooks and were regularly performed during the Middle Ages, exercising a great influence on later forms of comedy. Italy, like Greece, now offers regular festivals of ancient drama in the original settings.

The literary influence of classical drama has been enormous. Senecan tragedy provided a bridge from the ancient world to the Renaissance while Greek was still struggling to reestablish itself in the universities. Thus a new age of dramatists rediscovered Greek tragedy, albeit at second hand. Read in schools and declaimed in Jesuit colleges, the Latin plays were soon translated into French and English and inspired numerous imitations of both their form and subject matter. For English dramatists of the age of Shakespeare, it was the themes that were most appealing. The revenge story of Orestes, returning home to murder his mother, begot a spate of imitations and adaptations, of which *Hamlet* is merely the most famous. Elizabethan playwrights responded to the violence and savagery of Euripides as adapted by Seneca for his half-crazed characters.

In France almost a century later, playwrights shunned Seneca's sensationalism and violence but proved more susceptible to classical form. French seventeenth-century tragedy—the works of Racine, Corneille, and their contemporaries—represents a conscious attempt to reproduce what were considered the key elements of the classical style: economy, simplicity, dignity, and a carefully balanced structure in which scene answers to scene and each motif is woven into a carefully textured whole. Writers of this period were delighted to find what seemed a book of rules for writing Greek tragedy; Aristotle's *Poetics,* written in the fourth century B.C. and lost for centuries to most of the world, was rediscovered in the Renaissance and edited and expanded by French and Italian critics. Obscure in expression and incompletely understood, the *Poetics* imposed, among other things, the famous doctrine of the three unities—time, place, and action—on the stage.

Greek comedy was less influential. Roman comedy, however, which had never entirely disappeared from sight, was all-pervasive. French, English, Spanish, and Italian writers not only stole liberally from Plautine and Terentian plots but also adopted the Roman character stereotypes. The angry fathers, braggart warriors, foolish pedants, and sharp-witted slaves of Plautus have many echoes in Shakespeare, Molière, and Goldoni. Modern situation comedy, in fact, is still faithful to the spirit of the New Comedy, as learned through its Roman imitators.

Although Racine adapted one comedy of Aristophanes (*Les plaideurs* [*The Litigants*] was adapted from *The Wasps*), no serious attempt was made to reproduce his eclectic vitality on the stage until the late nineteenth century, when Gilbert and Sullivan produced their series of popular comic operas. These owe much to Aristophanes, both in the letter and in the spirit. Gilbert, who had enjoyed the normal classical education of his time, uses many Aristophanic subjects and assails the pretensions of society in the same way. There are clear similarities between the comparison of rival schools of poetry in *Patience* (1881) and the comparison of rival schools of tragedy in Aristophanes' *The Frogs;* between the political satires of *Iolanthe* (1882) and Aristophanes' *Acharnians,* both of which ridicule mortal institutions by the introduction of supernatural elements; and between the feminist takeovers in *Princess Ida* (1884) and Aristophanes' *The Congresswomen.* Even the meters are similar; whole passages of Aristophanic Greek can be sung to Sullivan's music. In their mixture of fantasy, satire, and lyrical invention, these works come perhaps closer than anything in the post-Greek world to an Aristophanic revival.

The twentieth century has produced a number of works modeled on the Greek. Many of these come from France, where the classical spirit has always been strong. Modern dramatists have realized, as the Greeks did centuries before them, that familiar myths could serve as persuasive metaphors for contemporary experience. Thus, Gide, Cocteau, Anouilh, and Giraudoux have all sought inspiration from the Greek; some have adapted (although with a single speaker) the characteristic Greek device of the chorus. In English, T. S. Eliot devised elegantly worded, although less theatrically powerful, adaptations of both Greek tragedy and New Comedy. The United States offers one towering achievement, Eugene O'Neill's *Mourning Becomes Electra* (1931), which transfers Aeschylus' *Oresteia* into the agony and frustration of a society torn by the Civil War. In this and other plays, O'Neill's experimentation with choruses and masks shows how far-reaching the effects of Greek drama have been. And, finally, Roman comedy has received the ultimate accolade of the American theater by being turned into a musical. Stephen Sondheim's *A Funny Thing Happened on the Way to the Forum* (1962) takes several plays by Plautus, adapts them, combines them, and tailors them to suit contemporary mores—which is exactly what, almost two millennia ago, Plautus did to the Greek originals.

BIBLIOGRAPHY

SOURCES

The Plays

A number of translations are readily available, notably *The Complete Greek Tragedies,* David Grene and Richmond Lattimore, eds., 9 vols. (1953–1959); Aristophanes, *Three Comedies: The Birds, The Clouds, The Wasps,* and *Four Comedies: Lysistrata, The Congresswomen, The Acharnians, and The Frogs,* William Arrowsmith and Douglass Parker, trans. (1969); Plautus, *The Rope, and Other Plays,* and *The Pot of Gold, and Other Plays,* E. F. Watling, trans. (1964 and 1965).

Ancient Commentaries on the Theater

Cicero, *De Oratore (On Oratory),* Book 3, together with *De Fato (On Fate)* and others, E. W. Sutton and H. Rackham, trans. (1942); Lucian, *On the Dance,* A. M. Harmon, trans. (1913); Alois M. Nagler, ed., *Sources of Theatrical History* (1952), contains translations of key passages from Pollux, Vitruvius, and others; Quintilian, *Institutio Oratoria (Education of an Orator),* H. E. Butler, trans. (1913); Vitruvius, *The Ten Books on Architecture,* Morris Hicky Morgan, trans. (1914; repr. 1960).

STUDIES

Peter Arnott, *An Introduction to the Greek Theatre* (1959), and *Greek Scenic Conventions in the Fifth Century B.C.* (1962); William Beare, *The Roman Stage,* 3d ed. (1965); Margarete Bieber, *The History of the Greek and Roman Theater,* 2d ed. (1961); George Duckworth, *The Nature of Roman Comedy* (1952); Roy Flickinger, *The Greek Theater and Its Drama,* 4th ed. (1936); Anthony E. Haigh, *The Attic Theatre,* Sir Arthur Pickard-Cambridge, ed., 3d ed. (1968); John Hanson, *Roman Theater-Temples* (1959); Lillian Lawler, *The Dance in Ancient Greece* (1965); Sir Arthur Pickard-Cambridge, *The Theatre of Dionysus in Athens* (1946), and *The Dramatic Festivals of Athens* (1953); Gregory M. Sifakis, *Studies in the History of Hellenistic Drama* (1967); J. Michael Walton, *Greek Theatre Practice* (1980); Thomas B. L. Webster, *Greek Theatre Production,* 2d ed. (1970).

Epigrams and Satire

J. P. SULLIVAN

EPIGRAMS

In 480 B.C. the great lyric poet Simonides of Ceos (*ca.* 556–468 B.C.), according to ancient belief, wrote this epitaph for the Spartans who died in the battle of Thermopylae to save Greece from conquest by Persia:

> For a message to the Spartans, stranger,
> pause:
> Tell them we lie here, obedient to their
> laws.

A paradigm of the later genre, this incisable and incisive poem in elegiac verse, which had popular associations with death and mourning, purports to be the inscription on the tomb of the fallen. This represents perhaps the earliest and certainly the most enduring aspect of epigram. Originally "epigram," in Greek *epigramma,* meant any words inscribed on artifacts, votive offerings, graves, monuments, or buildings, representing the owner, the maker, the donor, the dedicatee, or simply the message itself. The classical application of the word to sepulchral, commemorative, or dedica-tory inscriptions in easily memorable verse prompted the extension of its use in the early Alexandrian period to cover a whole literary genre of brief poems. These productions were reminiscent of, or analogous to, such inscriptions, but they now dealt with almost any subject, sentiment, event, or occasion. There were of course models. Short poems of this type had been written by numerous archaic and classical authors, including Sappho, Alcaeus, and Pindar. These were gathered and preserved in later collections of epigrams.

Such apparently unpretentious poems had been given the general title of *paegnia* (playthings). Compared with the elevated genres of epic, lyric, and tragedy, epigrams were light and occasional verses. In Rome they were defensively termed *lusus* (play), *ioci* (jokes), or even *nugae* (trifles). The epigram never quite lost its apologetic stance, despite its frequent brilliance in the hands of a master and its great popularity.

Important influences on the Hellenistic epigram were the convivial, hortatory, and erotic themes associated with elegiac verse in general. There were hexameter verse inscriptions on pottery as early as the eighth century B.C., but the elegiac couplet soon prevailed over almost all other poetic forms, although meters such as hendecasyllables and scazons were popular with Roman epigrammatists. The elegiac couplet was found preeminently suitable for a wide range of topics. Moreover, its self-contained concision was artistically adaptable. An epigram would typically consist of one to five of them, sometimes more, but the unit itself also encouraged certain characteristics such as wit, terseness, and antithetical point, enjambment being rare. Indeed, it was this quality of the verse that led eventually to the use of the word in English to mean not only an epigraph, sepulchral or otherwise, but also, after 1538, a short, witty poem; and then, since 1796, any pointed or antithetical sentiment in prose or verse.

No literary genre in the course of a long development has been put to so many purposes or taken on such protean shapes. But the mildly pejorative connotation the term still has, inherited from the sometimes deprecatory use of it by Martial and his successors, should not hide the fact that we are often dealing with superb poetry just "writ in small."

The development of the epigram as a separate genre by Hellenistic poets of the early third century B.C., such as Leonidas of Tarentum, Asclepiades and Posidippus of Samos, provided a tempting outlet for Greek, Roman, and Byzantine poetic talents, great or small, pagan or Christian, for more than a millennium. Real grave inscriptions and dedications had inspired the fictitious examples, but the Alexandrian poets soon broke away from such limitations in favor of a great variety of personal, artistic, and general themes, introducing experimental refinements on their classical precursors. New notes were to be introduced by Christian and Byzantine poets, but the Alexandrian age more or less defined the different types of epigram and also, for Greek practi-

tioners, its artificial archaic language, incorporating epic, Ionic, and Doric dialectal elements.

The traditional classifications of epigram by subject are roughly, and somewhat confusedly, preserved in the *Greek Anthology,* a modern collection in sixteen books of more than 4,000 epigrams taken from the *Palatine Anthology* (*AP*) of John Constantinus and the overlapping "Anthology" of the monk Planudes. Both of these late-tenth-century compilations derive mainly from the comprehensive anthology of Greek epigrams put together *ca.* A.D. 900 by Constantine Cephalas, although they have incorporated additional, usually Christian, material. Cephalas himself had drawn on earlier highly popular anthologies discussed below.

The usually accepted subdivisions of epigram were: (1) votive inscriptions and dedications, *anathematika* (*AP* 6); (2) epitaphs or tomb inscriptions, *epitumbia* (*AP* 7, 8); (3) amatory and pederastic epigrams, *erotika* and *paedika* (*AP* 5, 12); (4) "epideictic" epigrams, which were clever, rhetorical, or informational poems on curious facts or incidents, famous personages or places, as well as "ecphrastic" descriptions of works of art, *epideiktika* (*AP* 2, 3, 9); (5) versified reflections and advice on life and morality, *protreptika* (*AP* 10); (6) convivial pieces, *sympotika* (*AP* 11); and (7) abusive and satirical epigrams, *skoptika* (*AP* 11).

The *Greek Anthology* also separates from these conventional groups some epigrams on formal subjects in unusual meters (*AP* 13); numerical, historical, and literary puzzles in verse (*AP* 14), and miscellaneous epigrams which include the so-called *technopaegnia,* in which the arrangement of the words and lines imitates the shape of such objects as an egg, an ax, a pipe, or an altar (somewhat reminiscent of *poésie concrète*). From the many historical strata of the *Greek Anthology* we can discern fashions and innovations in the development of the genre.

For Latin epigrams we are not so fortunate as with Greek. The so-called *Anthologia Latina* is not a comprehensive and diachronic collection of epigrams proper, but merely a few hundred poems of differing length, not all epigrams, put together around A.D. 533, the core being a miscellany from a score of roughly contemporary poets living in provincial North Africa under the domination of the Vandals. To the basic collection was added the work of various other earlier writers of epigram such as Petronius and Seneca. The modern *Anthologia Latina,* compiled in 1894 by Riese, Buecheler, and others, simply added to this core verse inscriptions and epigrams found in Renaissance manuscripts. Fortunately the epigrams of most well-known Latin epigrammatists survived independently.

The most famous Hellenistic writer of epigram was perhaps Callimachus of Cyrene (*ca.* 305–240 B.C.). His delicate and allusive work was to have a profound effect in general on Roman literature. Already by the time of Ennius (d. 169 B.C.), the elegiac epigram replaced earlier Latin meters for Roman funeral inscriptions, and some erotic epigrams were based on Greek models by the early Roman admirers of Alexandrian poetry. These were the immediate predecessors of Valerius Catullus (84–54 B.C.), whose genius for short erotic lyric and invective was to make him the main model for the greatest of Latin epigrammatists, Martial.

The Catullan circle popularized epigram, but its practitioners still looked to Greece, where it had made steady progress in the descriptive and sepulchral epigrams of Antipater of Sidon (*ca.* 120 B.C.) and the sensual love poems of Philodemus of Gadara (*ca.* 110–37 B.C.). The most important phenomenon of the period, however, was the anthology, mainly of erotic verses, culled from six centuries of epigram and published as *The Garland of Meleager* sometime around 80 B.C. The Latin epigram, whether erotic or satiric, was flourishing by the Augustan period. Albinovanus Pedo and Domitius Mar-

sus are especially singled out by Martial, but Augustus himself was not above using the form for obscene abuse of his enemies.

Satiric epigrams of a highly political nature in fact flourished in the early empire. Often circulated anonymously, they contained attacks on the imperial court and, in addition to Augustus, various upper-class Romans also made frequent use of them. Of course traditional Greek themes were also borrowed and erotic epigram in particular was popular. Pliny the Younger, in his self-conscious defense of the genre, gives a list (*Letters* 5.3) of more than twenty famous practitioners up to his own day. It includes such names as Cicero and Vergil as well as most of the first-century rulers such as Nero and Nerva. The Romans contributed therefore a political dimension to the genre, as well as a certain earthiness and realism.

By the age of Nero, Philippus of Thessalonica could gather his own *Garland* from about fifty poets who had written in Greek since the time of Meleager. This was a mannered and overingenious collection. Some of the standard divisions are represented: imaginary epigraphs and dedications, and epideictic topics and moral exhortations. Erotic and satiric epigram are underrepresented. Its stars were, apart from the editor himself, Crinagoras, Antipater, and the witty Marcus Argentarius. One surprising feature of the book is the glimpse afforded, through Crinagoras especially, of aspects of contemporary, even upper-class, Roman life. There are also requests for patronage.

But perhaps the most important advance in the writing of epigram came a few decades later under Nero, when with the verses of Lucillius and Nicarchus there is an upsurge in satiric themes and a noticeable sharpening of the "line of wit," often directed at contemporary literary and dramatic enthusiasms.

These writers were, however, obscured by their successor, the master epigrammatist Marcus Valerius Martialis (*ca.* A.D. 40–104), whose range and output (more than 1,500 poems in fifteen books) were enormous. His satiric and obscene wit became the admiration and envy of all future epigrammatists in English and the Romance languages. He defended the obscene aspect of his writings by linking it to fertility festivals and artistic realism in the depiction of life, insisting that this element was a quintessential part of the genre. And it is he who pressed, mock-modestly, the claims of epigram to artistic superiority over outworn literary genres such as mythological epic and tragedy.

Martial wrote on gladiatorial shows in the amphitheater and on the pleasures of country life as well as the more dubious enjoyments of city living. Touching epitaphs on dead boy and girl favorites were juxtaposed with acid descriptions of the countless types his dependent life as a client allowed him to observe: the ostentatious, the pretentious, the depraved, and above all the parsimonious. Wittily turned dedications, memorials, and compliments flowed from his adaptable pen. His variations on the age-old poetic themes of "live for the day" and "the happy life" were to affect profoundly generations of English epigrammatists, who constantly tried to modernize his great poem (10.47) on the life of contentment and ease. He often translated, or borrowed from, his Greek precursors and even added a new subdivision to the form: short couplets suitable for the presentation of gifts to friends (the *Apophoreta* and *Xenia*).

After the *Garland of Philippus,* in the age of Hadrian (A.D. 117–138), pederastic epigrams enjoyed a revival in the *Musa Puerilis* of Straton, and satirical and convivial epigrams were emphasized in the *Epigrammaton Anthologion* by Diogenianus of Heraclea. The next visible revolution, however, in the writing of Greek epigram was the use of the epigram form for Christian subjects, notably by St. Gregory Nazianzen (A.D. 329–389).

The epigrammatic tradition of grave and dedicatory inscriptions flourished in the Byzantine period, and Book One of the *AP* contains numerous examples from Byzantine churches, in which the motifs of Christ, the Virgin, and other religious and biblical topics are used, replacing almost entirely the mythological paraphernalia of the earlier epigrammatists. Only the pagan Palladas of Alexandria in the fourth century managed to revitalize the tradition of erotic, moralizing, and satiric epigrams (the last sometimes directed at Christianity).

For the period of Justinian I and earlier, Agathias Scholasticus of Myrina in his *Cyclus* (A.D. 567–568) preserved the best work of himself, his contemporaries, and a few older poets. These were on all the standard themes, their authors mainly public officials and lawyers with literary pretensions. After Agathias himself, perhaps Paulus Silentiarius is the best. The collection at least proved that the genre in all its diversity still flourished, and much of the mythological apparatus rejected by earlier Christian writers now reappeared, in somewhat uneasy combination, alongside the natural Christian beliefs of the Agathias authors. The satirical epigrams of Book Five, however, were unaffected by this and drew on Lucillian models to attack professions, character types, and physical deformities. The misogynistic streak, a constant feature of all Greco-Roman epigram, makes its appearance here also.

This was the last important collection by practicing poets. The Greek epigram now slowly died out as a creative form, although metrical inscriptions for religious purposes were still in demand.

As for Latin epigram, Martial represented the summit of its achievement, and later Roman epigrammatists could add little to the norms he established. Only Christianity, as with the Greek epigram, could add new topics. The more important classical successors of Martial were Claudian (d. ca. A.D.

404) and the North African poet Luxorius (*ca.* A.D. 525). Decimus Magnus Ausonius (*d. ca.* A.D. 395), although a Christian, kept to classical models in his Greek and Latin epigrams. There was, however, a reaction to Martial in one of the last of the Roman poets, Venantius Fortunatus (*ca.* A.D. 540–600), who revived the moralistic Greek approach to epigram, an approach found also in the *Epigrammata Bobiensia,* which is mainly the work of Naucellius (*ca.* A.D. 400).

Martial, however, was the great influence in the Renaissance, and his work had its greatest impact on English and European poetry between 1550 and 1700, when practically every nondramatic poet aspired to be the Martial of his day, whether in English or, as with John Owen (*ca.* 1560–1622), in neoclassical Latin. Since then an interest in the genre has persisted, but generally as a by-product of writers whose main poetic direction was more ambitious.

SATIRE

Epigram required some time to develop its meaning of a brief, pointed, and often caustic sentiment expressed in either verse or prose. Satire, however, took on its standard meaning fairly quickly.

Satire as a literary genre in its own right was first developed by the Romans, and Quintilian's boast (*Education of an Orator* 10.1.93), "Satura quidem tota nostra est" (satire at least is a wholly Roman achievement), is not without foundation. Whatever its primitive origins and foreign influences, there was early established in Roman literature a broad, multifarious genre called *satura,* one important strain of which usurped the name as its prerogative, even in classical times. It was this historical refinement of the broader poetic form that became the paradigm of "satire" in our sense. Even then it retained some topics and ele-

ments of technique from earlier stages of its development and many poetic compositions called *satura* by the Romans were not satire, except in a purely historical sense. By the time of Horace, however, and even more so for Persius and Juvenal, *satura* meant primarily artistic denigration of a moralizing or aesthetic kind, even if earlier models allowed the introduction of much else, such as autobiographical reflection and literary discussion.

The origins of the word *satura* are disputed. Varro in the first century B.C. suggested several derivations: from *satyr,* because of the ridiculous and obscene content of the genre; from the *lanx satura,* the full plate of mixed fruit offered to the gods; from a stuffing of all kinds of things, which was also called *satura;* or from the so-called *lex satura,* an omnibus law containing unrelated provisions. The Etruscan word *satir* (to speak) has also been invoked to explain the term.

Whatever the etymology, Quintus Ennius (239–169 B.C.) was described by Horace as the "first originator" of the broader, miscellaneous *satura,* which is absent from Greek literature, but it was Gaius Lucilius (*ca.* 168–102 B.C.) who became the most important figure in the history of verse satire, and Horace rightly describes him as its true founder. It was Lucilius, with his biting personal and general attacks on prominent figures and contemporary vices, who gave *satura* its predominantly satiric note and its modern connotations.

Lucilius' other important influence was on its form. Although initially he had used other meters, his exclusive use of the hexameter in his powerful second volume made this meter the obvious one for succeeding satirists. Naturally the particular qualities, aims, and techniques that make Latin satire what it is in modern eyes were not original to Latin literature; they could, after all, be used in other literary genres, including prose, and the satiric spirit can be discerned in retrospect in earlier Greek writing.

The anonymous *Margites* (*ca.* 700 B.C.) had combined parody of Homer with satire of a hen-pecked Simple Simon. Archilochus of Paros (*ca.* 648 B.C.) was the first great Greek satirist, whose sarcastic iambics describe his personal problems in a world of changing values. This tradition of aggrieved sardonic rage continued with Semonides of Samos (*ca.* 600 B.C.), who wrote one of the earliest attacks on that favorite target of the satirist—the monstrous regiment of women. Hipponax of Ephesus (*ca.* 540 B.C.) introduced a brutal realism which later made him attractive to Alexandrian literary circles, whereas Xenophanes of Colophon (*ca.* 500 B.C.) was the first theological satirist, ridiculing the anthropomorphic religious beliefs of Homer and Hesiod and the Pythagorean belief in the transmigration of souls.

For Horace, the spiritual precursors of Roman satire were the playwrights of Attic Old Comedy: Eupolis, Cratinus, Aristophanes (*ca.* 450–385 B.C.), and the surviving Aristophanic comedies may be taken as representative. The fantasy and comic invention do not blunt the weapons of irony, ridicule, parody, and obscenity, which he deployed against contemporary personages such as Socrates and Cleon.

Directly political satire and invective depended upon the liberal and self-confident attitudes of the democratic society of fifth-century Athens, where great freedom was allowed and taken. Once these social and political conditions passed away, after Athens' defeat by Sparta in 404 B.C., personal attacks and political criticism had to be muted into social strictures of a less offensive kind.

Hellenistic literature too was important to the Roman satiric tradition in various ways, notably in its strong philosophical bias. The political structure of the city-state had given way, in the third and second centuries B.C.,

to the supranational allegiances demanded by Alexander and Rome. Patriotism was supplanted by a desire for security and prosperity. Spiritual regeneration and happiness must come through moral philosophy, in the Cynic rejection of fortune and conventional goals, the Stoic pursuit of virtue, or the Epicurean's cultivation of inner tranquillity.

The most important literary vehicle for this was the *diatribe,* a hortatory sermon enlivened by quotations, parody, dialogue, anecdote, and the witty ridicule of human folly, all of which were taken over by the great Roman satirists. The main practitioner of the genre was Bion the Borysthenite (*ca.* 320 B.C.), whose homilies, admired by Horace, were directed against human passions and prejudices. The tone aimed at was a mixture of humor and seriousness, the *spoudogeloion,* more familiar in Horace's phrase "ridentem dicere verum" (speaking the truth with a smile).

This style of writing was further developed by Menippus of Gadara (*ca.* 275 B.C.). The earlier *diatribe* had included verse quotation and parody, but Menippus gave his name to a satiric genre that alternated deliberately between prose and verse. These *Saturae Menippeae* were taken over into Latin literature as a separate art form by Cicero's friend Varro. It developed alongside the classical hexameter satire: two great examples survive from the Neronian age in Seneca the Younger's *Apocolocyntosis,* a vitriolic but amusing attack on the late emperor Claudius, and Petronius' *Satyricon,* an erotic picaresque novel of adventure, incorporating social satire against freedmen and sexually liberated women together with criticism and parody of contemporary poetry and philosophical writing. The literary form, although robbed of its satiric impulse, was continued in the didactic work of Martianus Capella (*ca.* A.D. 425) and in Boethius' *On the Consolation of Philosophy* (A.D. 524).

In Greek, however, Menippus' true descendant was the talented prose satirist Lucian of Samosata (born *ca.* A.D. 120). A skeptic and a rationalist, who anticipates Swift's *Gulliver's Travels* in his *True History,* Lucian mocks such traditional subjects for satire as the unhappiness of riches and power, the follies of women and philosophers, and religious fakery.

With Roman verse satire, it is important to stress that we are dealing with a literary genre, and that whatever light satire throws on contemporary life or whatever its moral lessons, its aim is art. The great satirists may achieve an intimate fusion of morality and literature, but what makes them satirists per se is their mastery of what is often regarded suspiciously as an impure form straddling life and literature.

That we are dealing with a literary genre is clear from Horace's criticisms of Lucilius. Lucilius had created the form and substance of satire. His subject range was wide and many Greek, specifically Hellenistic, influences were imported as grist for the Roman satiric mill. There is evidence in the fragments of his work of literary discussions, autobiographical anecdotes, descriptions of journeys, and dinner parties. But his most striking contribution to literature was his strictly satirical writing on politics and society. From this the other manifestations of satirical realism sprang: offensive sexual description, cynicism about human motives, and graphic portraits of individuals or types best seen in Juvenal. Naturally the form absorbed all manner of literary techniques: mockery of mythology, epic parody, historical anecdote, and popular fable. Lucilius' colloquial manner, his avoidance of elevated diction, was the basis from which the poetic styles of his successors developed. The subject matter and language of satire was in sharp contrast with those of the lofty poetic genres such as epic or lyric.

Quintus Horatius Flaccus (Horace) (65–8 B.C.) modestly claimed second place in the development of satire (*Satires* 1.10.46 ff.). His early choice of satire as a literary form may be explained by the challenge he saw in Lucilius' unpolished products. Horace provided a new standard of artistry for hexametric satire in language, rhythm, and tone, rather than deeper moral philosophy or sharper social criticism. Unlike Lucilius, Horace rarely attacked identifiable or living persons. His *Satires* (34–30 B.C.) and his later *Epistles* cover such topics as the vanity of human wishes and the absurdities of philosophers; the dangers of adultery, envy, discontent, and moral inconsistency. He tightens the structure of his predecessor's apparently artless rambling and in his defense of his own work ("apologia pro opere suo") (*Satires* 1, 4) self-consciously redefines satire. Horace's defense is that his satires do not profess to be poetry and are not motivated by malice; he is simply giving moral advice by pointing to everyday examples of what was to be avoided in personal life. His defensive posture was to be replaced by the later satirists' pretense of helpless indignation.

Aulus Persius Flaccus (Persius) (A.D. 34–62) is regarded as a "serious" satirist, but it was his literary qualities that gave him his contemporary and later popularity, rather than his derivative philosophy. His themes are standard: the debased morality underlying bad writing (*Satire* 1); hypocrisy and the wickedness of men's prayers (3); and the desire for popular acclaim (4). His positive teaching is strongly Stoic, stressing self-knowledge (4); true freedom, that is, freedom from base passions (5); and the proper attitude to money (6). Like Horace and Juvenal, he uses imaginary dialogue, literary and autobiographical reminiscence, parody, and illustrations from everyday life. His first satire announces his place in the satiric tradition of Attic Old Comedy, Lucilius, and Horace. His description of contemporary bombastic writing on mythological subjects points up his own carefully jagged style, which tries to represent the fluctuations, and highly allusive imagery, of an inner monologue.

Between Persius and the most famous writer of satire in Latin we hear of only a few names such as Turnus (mentioned by Martial), but Decimus Junius Juvenalis (*ca.* A.D. 60–140) was the culmination of the tradition and the writer who most affected its prestige and changed its associations in the eyes of later generations.

Juvenal's sixteen hexameter satires, published at intervals between 100 and 140 A.D., differ in one important respect from the work of his predecessors: he adopted as his persona the mask of the indignant and disgusted observer who cannot help attacking, albeit with some caution, the iniquity of the Roman world he lives in.

The first satire offers Juvenal's program. Moral indignation forces him to write satire in the style of Lucilius and Horace, satire in the now established sense of attacking the vices of the age with all the literary weapons available to him, rejecting the unreal and irrelevant mythological themes still dominant in poetic circles. Juvenal's imaginary interlocutor points out its possibly lethal consequences, to which Juvenal replies that he will make examples of characters long dead.

Juvenal nevertheless gives us vivid, though distorted, glimpses of Roman society: his pictures of the sorry plight of poor clients, humble guests at rich tables, and struggling writers have the brushmarks of authenticity, and his xenophobia is Roman enough to be convincing. Similarly, although his attack on women in *Satire* 6 is so rhetorical and prurient that the reader might well doubt his moral sincerity, not all of the moral norms invoked in his work are therefore perfunctory. It merely reinforces the point that his morality and realism are subordinate to his artistic intentions, to sub-stitute for the subtle humor of Horace and the allusive packed wordplay of Persius the forensic verbal wit of the rhetorician and the characteristic pointed style of Silver Age Latin.

Juvenal is an artist, a "supreme manipulator of the Latin language," rather than a radical social reformer or a Christian preacher. Like his friend Martial, he is not discontented with a social order based on the oppression of women and the ownership of slaves. He merely argues that women and ex-slaves should be kept in their place and that respectable Roman males like himself should have their proper due, socially and materially.

To achieve his exaggerated effects, Juvenal uses detailed and compelling touches and rapid cinematic shifts to blow up his vignettes of everyday life. The sonorous hexametric verse manages to display Dickensian powers of observation with a concision and wit worthy of Pope. Even his familiar epigrams such as "sit pro ratione voluntas" (let my wish be the reason) have additional, sometimes ironic, point when not treated as detachable gems but regarded in their proper poetic setting.

Juvenal's satires of indignation marked the climax of the Roman satiric tradition and became its hallmark. The traces of the genre in the next few centuries are disappointing. Christian writers such as Tertullian, Arnobius, Ambrose, and Jerome turned to prose to express their spleen and ridicule their enemies. Within the Latin literary mainstream, Decimus Magnus Ausonius (A.D. 310–395), Rutilius Namatianus (*fl.* A.D. 416), and Sidonius Apollinaris (A.D. 430–480) all show flashes of the satiric spirit in their work and in their epigrams. The satiric epigram of course continued to flourish in both Greek and Latin; more sustained attempts at longer satire are disappointing.

The only pretender to being the last of the

Roman satirists is Claudius Claudianus (*ca.* A.D. 374–404), whose two long hexameter satires, *Against Rufinus* and *Against Eutropius*, directed at ministers of the emperor Arcadius, have something of the generalizing power and literary techniques of Juvenal. And perhaps it is fitting that personal satire, naming names and prompted by individual spleen, should make its reappearance at the end, as it had at the true beginning of Latin satire. It was only in the sixteenth and seventeenth centuries that satire in the Roman mode came back into its own with the work of Boileau in France and, in England, with Donne, Oldham, Dryden, and Pope, just as epigram found its new masters in Ben Jonson, Robert Herrick, and the poets of the Restoration.

BIBLIOGRAPHY

SOURCES

The Greek Anthology, William R. Paton, ed., Loeb Classical Library (1960); *The Greek Anthology: A Selection in Modern Verse Translations,* Peter Jay, ed. (1973); *The Greek Anthology: From Meleager to Planudes,* Alan Cameron, ed. (1987); *Epigrammata Graeca,* Denys L. Page, ed. (1975); *Anthologia Latina,* Franz Buecheler, Alexander Reise, and Ernst Lommatzsch, eds. (1894); *Epigrammata Bobiensia,* Wilhelm Speyer, ed. (1963).

Lucilius, *Lucilius Satiren,* Werner Krenkel, ed. (1970); Catullus, *Catulli Carmina,* Roger Mynors, ed. (1958); Horace, *Horatius,* Friederich Klingner, ed. (1959); Petronius and Seneca the Younger, *Petronius: The Satyricon and Seneca: The Apocolocyntosis,* John P. Sullivan (1977); Martial, *M. Val. Martialis Epigrammata,* Wallace M. Lindsay, ed. (1929); Persius and Juvenal, *A. Persi Flacci et D. Iuni Iuvenalis Saturae,* Wendel V. Clausen, ed. (1959).

STUDIES

Alan Cameron, *Claudian: Poetry and Propaganda at the Court of Honorius* (1970); Michael Coffey, *Roman Satire* (1976); Donald R. Dudley, *A History of Cynicism, from Diogenes to the Sixth Century* A.D. (1937); Victor Ehrenberg, *The People of Aristophanes: A Sociology of Attic Comedy* (1951); Gilbert Highet, *Juvenal, the Satirist* (1954); Rudolph Keydell, "Epigramm," in Th. Klauser, ed., *Reallexicon für Antike und Christentum* (1941–); Harold A. Mason, "Is Juvenal a Classic?" in J. P. Sullivan, ed., *Critical Essays on Roman Literature: Satire* (1963).

Niall Rudd, *The Satires of Horace* (1966), and *Themes in Roman Satire* (1986); John P. Sullivan, *The Satyricon of Petronius: A Literary Study* (1968); Charles A. Van Rooy, *Studies in Classical Satire and Related Literary Theory* (1965); Arthur H. Weston, *Latin Satirical Writing Subsequent to Juvenal* (1915).

Music and Dance

EDWARD KERR BORTHWICK

THE GREEK WORD for music, *mousike*—the art patronized by the Muses—means much more than its English equivalent, for it embraces all forms of artistic cultivation. To be unmusical (*amousos*) was to be without refinement, a boor. When used in its more restricted sense, referring to lyric and melody, the unity of words and music—whether in solo or choral compositions—was so close that the idea of a composer putting to his own music the text of another was quite strange, at least in the classical period. However, in a late, and not necessarily accurate, reference (Plutarch, *Moralia: On Music* 3) the seventh-century Greek Terpander is said to have sung Homeric texts to his own music at festivals. Indeed, even the choreography of a choral ode—and dancing was a regular ingredient of musical compositions—was thought part of the basic craft of an individual poet-musician.

GREEK INSTRUMENTS

Reverence for the divine nature of music made the Greeks create myths in which their very instruments were invented and mastered by their gods. Apollo, the classical Hellenic god par excellence, appears at the end of the first book of the *Iliad* accompanying the Muses in entertaining the other Olympians at banquet. Apollo, however, is not credited with the actual invention of his lyre, for the charming legend of the fourth *Homeric Hymn* tells how he had received it from Hermes. The young Hermes had discovered the musical potential of sheep gut stretched taut and attached to a resonator— the eviscerated carapace of a tortoise.

Sometimes Athena was credited with the invention not only of the martial trumpet (*salpinx*), but also of the principal Greek wind instrument, the aulos. It should be noted, though, that at a period when superiority was accorded to the Apollonian lyre (symbolized in the myth of a musical contest between Apollo and the Phrygian satyr Marsyas, which was won by the god because, unlike his aulos-playing opponent, he could sing to his own accompaniment), Athena was declared to have exhibited her superior intelligence and good taste by throwing away the less cultured aulos, which had come to be associated with unrestrained, and therefore un-Hellenic, music of lamentation or orgiastic excitement. Aristotle (*Politics* 1340a10) refers to the auletic compositions of Olympus, a Phrygian musician of about the seventh century, sometimes said to be a pupil of the satyr Marsyas himself.

The common translation of aulos as "flute" is both incorrect and misleading; it was a double-reed, oboelike instrument, usually played in pairs, and its deep-toned "booming" (*bombos*) is often alluded to. This suggests that, at least in the case of the lower-pitched of the so-called Phrygian pipes of unequal length, a drone may have been sustained. Vase paintings often show the player blowing with great intensity, the inflation of the cheeks controlled by a leather strap called *phorbeia*.

It is of some interest that of the earliest allusions to the music of men (rather than of gods), the greatest Greek hero, Achilles, sings tales of heroic deeds to his own lyre accompaniment (*Iliad* 9.186), while the sounds that come from Troy are of the aulos and the pastoral syrinx, the shepherd or Pan pipes (*Iliad* 10.13). In fact, the musical influence of the East on mainland Greece probably encompassed string and wind instruments alike, and even the worship of Apollo himself (a champion of the Trojans in the *Iliad*) seems to have originated in Asia Minor before he was adopted by the Greeks.

The wide distribution in the ancient world of various types of lyrelike or harplike instruments makes historical and chronological development difficult to determine. Certain generalizations can be made, however. While polychordal instruments, with angled frame and strings of unequal length, are well known in Sumerian, Babylonian, and Assyrian iconography from the third millennium onward, and also from Egyptian examples, these never made great inroads into native Greek music and were often despised as exotic and effeminate. Yet, even the familiar form of Greek lyre and kithara had proto-

types in the eastern Aegean and Near East. The kithara, like the lyre, had strings of equal length and different thickness or tension, but it had a more substantial wooden sound box and set of arms. It was played with the fingers of the left hand and a plectrum in the right (bowed instruments were unknown to Greece), and held in an upright position; the lyre is usually pictured held at an angle leaning away from the body, the base resting against the player's waist.

GREEK MUSICIANS AND COMPOSERS

The *Iliad* contains references to choral singing both in supplication to the gods (at 1.473, the Greeks raise a *paian* to Apollo to invoke the cessation of his wrath) and in lamentation for the dead (at 24.719 ff., the Trojan women join in a mourning refrain over the body of Hector after individual solo voices "lead off"—the verb *exarchein* was to become virtually a technical term in various sorts of music thereafter). It is in the *Odyssey* that we first find the professional musician as part of everyday life, in the persons of the bards Phemius and Demodocus. The descriptions of their recitations of episodes from the Trojan War must reflect the conditions under which the Homeric and other epics were performed at the time of composition, some twenty-seven centuries ago. This inference is supported by evidence from literature and vase paintings that the reciter, the rhapsode, if not literally singing at least used as a sort of accompaniment the phorminx, the precursor of the more elaborate form of kithara used by later professionals. Modern writers who like to see in twentieth-century Balkan epic recitations a resemblance to conditions in Homeric Greece can point to the use of the *gusle*, a single-stringed bowed fiddle, by Slavic exponents of this art.

Between the Homeric period and that

dominated by Athenian culture, the classical period, many of the important poets and musicians of monody or choral lyrics sprang from the Asiatic mainland, the Aegean Islands, Crete, or the Greek colonies to the west. Alcman, composer of maiden songs (*partheneia*), of which one substantial piece and some smaller fragments survive, probably came from Lydia; Thaletas, a shadowy but perhaps important figure, came from Crete. Terpander, a great musical innovator, particularly in the genre of solo song with kithara accompaniment called the *nomos* (literally "law," but musically/poetically a fixed pattern with a traditional melic and rhythmic character), came from Lesbos but, like the two already named, was associated with the flowering of poetry and music in Dorian Sparta. In Lesbos a musical and lyric tradition was later maintained by Sappho and Alcaeus, whose poetry was sung to a longer, more slender form of lyre, often pictured on vases, called *barbitos*. Another notable innovator, Stesichorus, and Ibycus, a poet of erotic themes, hailed from Magna Graecia, although the latter's career took him to the court of Polycrates of Samos, one of many of the so-called tyrants of the city-states in and around Greece who cultivated the arts. The patronage extended to artists in the city-states might be compared in its effect to that offered by the archdukes and princes within the Austro-Hungarian tradition of our own classical period of music. It gave rise to a new and flourishing professionalism and stimulated public interest in poetry and music on an international scale.

The elaborate choral compositions of Pindar, a Theban whose career was greatly enhanced by association with great courts as far afield as Sicily and Cyrene, extended into the various poetic genres: hymns, paeans, encomia, laments (*threnoi*), processionals, and, above all, *epinicia*—triumphal songs celebrating victories in chariot racing or other sporting events in the great festivals at Olympia and elsewhere. Such compositions increased the fame of both patron and composer, whose services for the composition itself and for training the performers would be sought at a price. In the aftermath of the Persian wars, fifth-century poets such as Simonides and Bacchylides (both from the island of Ceos) would be engaged to compose not only the types of song already mentioned, but also commemorative odes for the fallen, or thanksgivings for victory and deliverance. A number of the major festivals included musical competitions for singers to the kithara or aulos, and even solos for these instruments. Pindar's twelfth Pythian ode commemorates such an auletic performance for a Sicilian virtuoso, and a century earlier a famous player, Sacadas of Argos, had written for Delphi a remarkable composition in many "movements" describing the fight between Apollo and the Python—just the type of blatantly "imitative" music deplored later by Plato.

In the generation before Pindar, the Athenian tyrant Pisistratus and his sons were similarly promoting the public performance of poetry and music, an activity that was to make Athens a cultural focal point in the fifth century. In addition to his celebrated organization of recitals of Homer at the panathenaic festival, Pisistratus fostered two poetical genres in which music, dance, and spectacle were to play their part. These, the dithyramb and tragic drama, were to be of the utmost importance in musical history. Whether Aristotle in his *Poetics* was right in his view that the latter actually developed from the former remains controversial, but both were to give great stimulus to composer and performer alike.

The dithyramb was traditionally linked with the worship of Dionysus and grew in sophistication from the spontaneous song of revelers into a formalized cyclic dance with text and music, performed by a choir of fifty. Among the earliest known composers was Lasos from Hermione in the Peloponnese, who settled in Athens to become a prominent innovator in music and an organizer of dithyrambic competitions. In the earliest tragedies (also closely connected with Dionysus worship), the choral and musical part was more prominent than it came to be toward the end of the fifth century and beyond, when separate entr'actes might be used simply to punctuate the various dramatic scenes. Composers such as Phrynichus and Aeschylus drew on and added to the rich tradition of Dorian choral lyric. In his *Persians,* Aeschylus introduced the type of dirge music associated with the Eastern world, and in his masterpiece the *Oresteia* the odes are elaborate symphonic structures of much rhythmical subtlety and complexity. Sophocles, we are informed (*Life of Sophocles* 23), introduced music characteristic of the dithyrambic style and Phrygian melody.

GREEK DANCE

As both dithyramb and tragedy introduced group dancing, it should be said that this was true also of the various choral genres already mentioned. Dancing together by members of the opposite sex occurs in early poetry, notably in the description of a festive scene on the shield of Achilles (*Iliad* 18.590), where the dancing floor is likened to that once made by Daedalus for Ariadne at Cnossus. Plutarch (*Theseus* 21) describes such a dance, called *geranos* (crane), which Theseus and his youths and maidens performed at Delos on their return after escaping from the labyrinth of Minos. But mixed dancing apparently became rare, at least among adults, as the sexes were normally segregated in their rituals and festivals. The performers in tragic choruses were, of course, always male, whatever role they were playing. Only at all-male symposia in Athens and elsewhere would dancing and music be provided by women—the professional courtesans known as *hetairai.*

Athenian youths were expected to attend dancing classes as part of their normal education, and armed dances, like the Pyrrhic, were notable events at festivals such as the Panathenaea and in the predominantly military society of Sparta. Socrates is reported as declaring that those who danced best were also best at war, and in the *Iliad* (16.617), the agility in battle of the Cretan Meriones was ascribed to his dancing experience. The acrobatic dancing of Cretans is familiar from Minoan art. Their skills were sometimes attributed in legend to the time when semidivine youths called Curetes danced, clashing their weapons to drown the cries of the infant Zeus who lay concealed in the Dictaean cave, so as to prevent his discovery by a vengeful father bent on his destruction. Often the Curetes were equated with the Corybantes, ecstatic dancers in the cult of the Asiatic fertility goddess Cybele, male equivalents of the bacchantes, or maenads, of Dionysus worship. The bacchantes are a familiar image in ancient art; they are shown stimulated by wine, nighttime dancing, and aulos music, and are portrayed with bulging throats, disheveled hair, and startled eyes. Corybantism, or maenadism, may prefigure genuine outbursts of the dancing mania attested periodically much later in various parts of Europe.

INSTRUMENTATION, PERFORMANCE, AND TRADITION

Choral singing in Greece seems normally to have been homophonic, although a degree of heterophony may have been introduced in the accompaniment. In tragedy the double aulos was regularly employed, but in plays such as Euripides' *The Bacchants* (*Bacchae*), with its hypnotically rhythmical choruses of ecstatic maenads and abundance of musical references, the percussive addition of *tympana* (hand drums or tambourines) is likely to have been used also. It is interesting that in both the Greek and Roman civilizations, the drum, which we tend to think of as having a masculine sound, was usually associated with women, whether in cult or entertainment music, as were cymbals, castanets, and rattles (Gk. *krotala,* Lat. *sistra;* they figured prominently in exotic cults such as that of Isis). The tonal range and emotional character of the aulos began to influence even the more conventional music of the kithara. In early art instruments of the lyre type have three to seven strings, but seven became the norm, the octave note readily being obtainable by stopping the appropriate string at its midpoint. Whether or not further stopping (easier on the substantial concert kithara than on the simple lyre) was used at an early stage is not susceptible of proof. But certainly toward the end of the fifth century not only were more sophisticated playing techniques introduced, but also a new school of "avant-garde" composers—again many of non-Greek origin—extended the kithara's compass with additional strings. The deviations from tradition were characteristically disapproved of by conservative musicians. A celebrated anecdote tells how the Spartan authorities at a festival of Apollo were so incensed by a performance by the most notorious of this group, Timotheus (not the aulos player of the same name who is said to have so aroused Alexander the Great by his playing two generations later), that they insisted on removing the untraditional strings from his kithara.

The comic poets, always conservative in the arts, enjoyed deriding these composers, who apparently influenced the tragic poets Euripides and Agathon, for their sinuous, chromatic (and therefore effeminate) melodies, to which the cant terms "bends" or "ant-tracks" were applied. In his *Women at the Thesmophoria,* Aristophanes offers a delightful parody scene in which Agathon, in female dress, takes his strophes out into the sun to bend them. And in *Frogs* (1301–1303) Aristophanes makes Aeschylus accuse Euripides of taking his lyrical style from "songs of harlots, drinking songs, Carian pipings, dirges, and dance music." Plutarch's *On Music* quotes the remarkable fragment (no. 145) of the comic poet Pherecrates from his *Cheiron* (an allusion to the musical and moral pedagogue who educated Achilles); the poet has a female figure, Music, complaining in a series of double entendres drawn from musical terminology how she has been sexually assaulted and degraded by Timotheus and his gang. Ironically, of the great tragedians it was the work of Euripides that was to become the most popular and influential in subsequent centuries.

The *Persians* of Timotheus was to become a classic in its own right. However, bereft of its no doubt colorful music, the operatic extravagance of this famous *nomos,* discovered on papyrus in the last century, does not have much apart from its curiosity value to attract the modern reader. The choral fragment ends with self-praise for the author's giving new life to his eleven-stringed kithara and thus joining the company of Orpheus and Terpander.

MUSIC AND PHILOSOPHY

In terms of their dislike for musical innovation, which seemed to go against the severity and serenity of traditional Hellenic musical idioms, the comic poets are strange allies of the philosophers of following centuries, and especially of Plato. Periclean Athens had considerable hostility to foreign influence in civic life, in religion, and in the arts. In Plato's *Republic,* Socrates is made to refer approvingly to the musical doctrines of Damon, a distinguished music teacher and theorist who also advised Pericles in political and social affairs. Damon's strikingly uncompromising views about the potentially corrupting effect of bad music on the individual citizen and the state were to lead Plato to have Socrates recommend censorship of musical compositions in the education of the young (a theme that Plato returns to in his later work, the *Laws*). Censorship, for Socrates, would involve outlawing certain musical styles and even forbidding aulos music entirely. These styles were identified by the basic musical materials out of which they were built, ethnically associated modal scales called *harmoniai*. Thus, in order to preserve the ethical purity of the so-called Dorian *harmonia* (associated with courage) and the Phrygian (known for its therapeutic value), the Ionian and Lydian modes, enervating and lugubrious by reputation, would be outlawed.

It is not possible in this synopsis to enter upon the controversy that surrounds these so-called modes of classical Greek music, the ethnic names of which (Ionian, Lydian, Dorian, Phrygian) were to be retained and adopted in the later systematized scales associated chiefly with Aristotle's pupil Aristoxenus. Suffice it to say that the Greeks seem to have been unusually sensitive to stylistic differences involving intervals in the scale (diatonic, chromatic, or enharmonic), pitch, rhythm, and instrumentation, in close association with the verbal and subject matter of religious or secular texts.

More tolerant of public taste than Plato, Aristotle (chiefly in his *Politics*) nevertheless agrees basically with the view that music both "imitates" and manipulates character, but is readier to admit—at least for adults—some emotional music rejected by Plato, because of its cathartic effect on the listener. The close bond between music and philosophy (in *Phaedo* 61a, Plato describes philosophy as "the greatest *mousike*") has a distinguished history in Greek thought. Among early pre-Socratic thinkers, Heraclitus had envisaged the equable constitution of the whole *kosmos* as being due to a prevailing tension "as in the bow- or lyre-string," and some later medical theorists considered the health of the human body to be dependent on the correct attunement of its constituent parts, as in a musical *harmonia*. Above all, Pythagoras, who in this may have been influenced by philosophic thought already prevailing in the East, saw the world and human soul alike as bearing a relation to the numerical ratios and proportions of a mathematically constituted scale. The doctrine of "the music of the spheres," attributed to Pythagoras and developed with mathematical and astronomical ingenuity by Plato and subsequently by Neoplatonists and Neopythagoreans, exerted a profound influence on both philosophic thought and musical theory. Indeed, it is perhaps unfortunate that much extant Greek musical literature tells us more about the abstract and unworldly music of the mind than about the sounds of real, man-made music.

ROMAN ATTITUDES TOWARD MUSIC

The ethical approach to music maintained its ground into the Roman period of Greek culture, as witnessed in a number of Plutarch's essays in *Moralia* even if the most substantial musical essay, *On Music,* may not be authentic. This approach was opposed, however, by followers of Epicurus, notably Philodemus, a Judean whose adult career at Herculaneum was largely devoted to Greek philosophy. His castigation of Damonian/Platonic/Aristotelian (Peripatetic) doctrines is contained in a tantalizingly mutilated remainder of his substantial work *On Music,* preserved on carbonized papyrus rolls from a library engulfed in the volcanic destruction of Herculaneum in A.D. 79. (Included among other artifacts recovered from the same cataclysm, which also destroyed Pompeii, are contemporary auloi of complex mechanism and a number of brass instruments.)

It is hardly surprising that a well-to-do Greek living in a comfortable Roman milieu should have a hedonistic attitude toward music as a luxurious entertainment. Even if, as some recent writers have claimed, ancient Rome, in comparison with Greece, has been too much disparaged as "a land without music," the Romans appear on the whole not to have assigned to music so exalted a place in their education and daily life as did the inhabitants of classical Athens. Nevertheless, there is evidence of an indigenous music of folk song, work, love, and marriage songs, and the like. And in the theater (our evidence is strongest for comedy, in view of the number of extant plays of Plautus and Terence), music of tibiae (like auloi, reed-blown pipes) was employed particularly for the songs (cantica) and in instrumental interludes.

ROMAN INSTRUMENTS

The Romans were nothing if not receptive of foreign fashions, first from the Etruscans, then from Greece, Egypt, and Syria. If the music of string instruments played a less notable part until the empire, when Greek virtuosos could command public lionization, imperial patronage, and high fees, the tibia was from an early period also a popular instrument in cult. An Etruscan fresco from a tomb in Tarquinia of the fifth century B.C. showing a piper (tibicen) is well known. In the period of Rome's early kingship, guilds (collegia) of pipers were formed. They played, often in large numbers, at sacrifices and funerals, attesting to the primitive superstition that sustained and noisy music might deter evil spirits. From Etruria, too, the Romans inherited a strong tradition of the construction and playing of various sorts of brass, or other

lip-reed, instruments (which are mentioned surprisingly rarely in classical Greek literature, although the "Tyrrhenian," that is, Etruscan, trumpet is sometimes named). The trumpet (the straight tuba and curved lituus) and the horn (cornu, sometimes little differentiated in usage from the buccina) were preeminently martial instruments, with recognizable calls specifying different tactical or organizational functions. They were, however, used also in ensemble, and their practitioners formed guilds as early as the fifth century B.C., in accordance with the liberal reforms attributed to King Servius Tullius. Such groups played at funerals, in the theater, and at gladiatorial spectacles in the amphitheater, where they contributed to the noise and excitement of the occasion. That magnificent vulgarian Trimalchio, in the Satyricon of Petronius, declares that the only things he really enjoys are horn players and acrobats.

A well-known mosaic from Sugolin (Zliten) in North Africa (first century A.D.) shows players of trumpets and horns accompanying gladiators alongside a water organ. This instrument, the hydraulus, used water pressure to compress the air blown into the pipes. It is said to have been invented in the third century B.C. by an Alexandrian Greek, Ctesibius, at a time when there was a public demand for musical performance on a grand scale. Athenaeus, an Egyptian Greek of the second century, in his amiable and discursive The Learned Banquet (Deipnosophistae 201e), a mine of information and anecdote about musical instruments and performances, preserves a detailed description of a lavish procession in Alexandria organized not long before Ctesibius' time by Ptolemy II Philadelphus, which in addition to pipers and trumpeters featured a choir of 600 and 300 players of golden kitharas. The hydraulus appears accompanying a solo hornist on a handsome third-century mosaic from near Trier. That the new instrument became widely disseminated is shown by the discovery of substantial remains of a water organ of the same century at Aquincum in Pannonia (Budapest, Hungary); reconstructions of this instrument have been attempted. There are ancient reports of the "deafening sound" of which the organ was capable, and of unusual interest is the inscription from the same area on a sarcophagus of one Aelia Sabina, young wife of a Roman legionary, who "alone outshone her husband . . . in public concerts on the hydraulic organ." Ironically, the organ immediately aroused distaste among early church fathers because of its association first with the pagan amphitheater, then with the Byzantine hippodrome, before its appropriation by the Christian church led to a new era of both music and civilization itself in Europe.

ROMAN DANCE AND PERFORMANCE

Another novel development in the arts of music and dance in Rome from late republican times must be mentioned, namely the displays of solo dancing, with the accompaniment of wind and percussion, by Greek dancers of both sexes called *pantomimi*. While we have surprisingly little clear information about serious music at the time of Augustus (the claim made that the odes of Horace were intended for musical performance has on the whole not found approval, save in the special case of his *Secular Hymn* [*Carmen Saeculare*], commissioned in 17 B.C.), the theatrical exhibitions of pantomimists such as Bathyllus and Pylades are well attested. They excelled in the highly stylized presentation of mythological themes, serious or comic; finely dressed and masked, they performed with wordless dance and gesture. Later performers in this popular genre, such as two artists called Paris in the

reigns of Nero and Domitian, were to meet with the censure of moralists and the lash of Juvenalian satire—the younger of the two seems to have attracted the sort of adulation, and often riotous audience reaction, which today we associate with the leading lights of popular music—but the artistic quality aroused genuine admiration in as cultivated a Greek as Lucian of Samosata in the second century A.D.

Too well known to need more than passing mention is the passion for music of the emperor Nero, player of several instruments, including the hydraulus and a sort of bagpipe, and indefatigable singer to the kithara at public contests. The musical reputations of a number of his imperial successors have come down to us. Notable are Elagabalus, singer and player of trumpet, tibia, organ, and three-stringed pandura; and Carinus, military ruler of the western empire, who in A.D. 284 pandered to the public taste for gargantuan music with celebratory games involving, we are assured (*Life of Carinus* 19), one hundred each of trumpeters, hornists, and two different types of auloi. From the Neronian period, Greece and her traveling virtuosos remained the dominant influence, and the patronage of the Cretan composer Mesomedes by the second-century emperor Hadrian introduced a perhaps more tasteful cultural dimension to Roman music. For a long time the only coherent surviving examples of actual music of the classical world (apart from a notorious Pindaric forgery by the polymath Athanasius Kircher) were a number of hymns, one or more of which were attributed to this musician.

THE HERITAGE OF ANCIENT MUSIC

In the last hundred years or so a more extensive corpus of musical fragments inscribed on stone or papyrus has been recovered. With the help of texts that record the notation used at least in postclassical times, they have provided a faint resonance from the past. The most tantalizing are scraps of two plays of Euripides (*Orestes, Iphigenia in Aulis*), and the most performable are larger portions of two hymns of the second century B.C. found at Delphi, one at least composed by a certain Limenius, and an agreeable little melody known as the Seikilos song of about the same period found at Tralles (Aydın) in Lydia (western Asia Minor). Worth mentioning too, from the Oxyrhynchus papyri, are scraps, now in Oslo, of tragic texts that may be from the copy actually belonging to its second-century A.D. composer or singer (*tragodos*), and a Christian hymn of orientalizing style from the following century.

But it was the preservation not of the music itself, but of Greek theory, in late writers such as Aristides Quintilianus and Boethius, that was to sustain interest in "the music of the ancients" into Byzantine and Renaissance times. Aristides, with his Greco-Roman name, is an enigmatic writer of the third or fourth century A.D. who deplores the cultural degeneracy (*aphilomousia*) of his own age and attempts to revive the ethical and educational principles of Pythagoras, Damon, Plato, and Aristotle, with much interesting material about the therapeutic value of music for the human soul and body. But while the theorists continued to meditate on Pythagorean ratios, Aristoxenian scales, and the music of the spheres, the future of actual music was being determined by professional performers adapting themselves to social, political, and religious upheavals. Continual Eastern influence, and the unequivocal impact of Turkey, brought Greece more and more into an environment that cut her off from contact with the flowering of the most valued of our own classical Western music. But Rome, having benefited first from Greek culture, was ultimately compensated for being overshadowed so long by her erstwhile teachers as her contacts extended ever farther north and west.

It is a matter of regret for philhellenes that, as the focus of European musical culture gradually but decisively shifted northward to the Rhine and the Danube, and while Italian composers from Palestrina to Verdi—via Monteverdi, Scarlatti, Vivaldi, Cimarosa, Boccherini, Cherubini, and Rossini—at least played a distinguished part, the land of Apollo and the Muses was isolated from participation in the development of the art to which in the beginning it had so significantly contributed.

BIBLIOGRAPHY

SOURCES

Nearly a thousand items are listed in Thomas J. Mathiesen, *A Bibliography of Sources for the Study of Ancient Greek Music,* Music Indexes and Bibliographies, No. 10 (1974). Not all the Greek writers on music are available in English translation, but the following will be found useful: Aristides Quintilianus, *On Music, in Three Books,* Thomas J. Mathiesen, trans. (1983); Aristoxenus, *The Harmonics,* Henry S. Macran, ed. and trans. (1902); Athenaeus, *The Deipnosophists* (*The Learned Banquet*), Charles B. Gulik, ed. and trans., 7 vols. (1927–1941), books 4 and 14 contain much of the musical material; Plutarch, *De Musica (On Music)* in his *Moralia,* XIV, Benedict Einarson and Phillip H. de Lacy, trans. (1967).

STUDIES

Warren D. Anderson, *Ethos and Education in Greek Music* (1966); Andrew Barker, *Greek Musical Writings I—The Musician and His Art,* in *Cambridge Readings in the Literature of Music* (1984); E. Kerr Borthwick, "Dance: II, Western Antiquity," in *The New Grove Dictionary of Music and Musicians,* V (1980); Jacques Chailley, *La musique grecque antique* (1979); Günter Fleischhauer, *Musikgeschichte in Bildern, Etrurien und Rom* (1964), and "Rome:

I, Ancient," in *The New Grove Dictionary of Music and Musicians,* XVI (1980); Mary I. Henderson, "Ancient Greek Music," in *The New Oxford History of Music,* I (1957); Lillian B. Lawler, *The Dance in Ancient Greece* (1964).

Solon Michaelides, *The Music of Ancient Greece: An Encyclopedia* (1978); James F. Mountford and Reginald P. Winnington-Ingram, "Music," in *The Oxford Classical Dictionary,* 2d ed. (1970); Jean Perrot, *The Organ from its Invention in the Hellenistic Period to the End of the Thirteenth Century,* Norma Deane, trans. (1971); Egert Pöhlmann, *Denkmäler altgriechischer Musik* (1970); Curt Sachs, *The History of Musical Instruments* (1940), and *The Rise of Music in the Ancient World* (1943); J. E. Scott, "Roman Music," in *The New Oxford History of Music,* I (1957); Max Wegner, *Musikgeschichte in Bildern, Griechenland* (1963); Günther Wille, *Musica Romana, Die Bedeutung der Musik im Leben der Römer* (1967); Reginald P. Winnington-Ingram, *Mode in Greek Music* (1936, repr. 1968), "Ancient Greek Music 1932–1957," in *Lustrum,* **3** (1958), and "Greece: I, Ancient," in *The New Grove Dictionary of Music and Musicians,* VII (1980).

Literary Criticism

FREDERICK T. GRIFFITHS

HOMER, HESIOD, AND THE CONTEST SYSTEM

Poets were the first critics. The near approaches to formal criticism in Aristophanes and Plato, followed by Aristotle's definitive *Poetics,* distill critical habits that are implicit when Homer summons his Muse and unmistakable as later poets continually conjure Homer as the foil for their new departures. Within a rapidly evolving and ramifying tradition, poets must keep reeducating audiences and patrons about their craft: the esteemed bards in the *Odyssey* do not just sing other "Iliads"; nor does Odysseus, since the *Odyssey* poet himself has quite a different project in mind. That is, this first sequel, like many texts to follow, comes equipped with arguments for its own existence.

This epochally productive habit of honoring received tradition by altering it partakes of the extreme competitiveness of Greek life. The ritualized conflict that pitted warrior against warrior extended to athletes, politicians, and (adds Hesiod) farmers, potters, carpenters, beggars, and bards. In celebrating the contests of these other groups,

poets inevitably sang themselves into the same agonistic system. Homer and Hesiod (eighth or seventh century B.C.) bear witness to a society where the singer of traditional tales is the chief transmitter of received values and information, but one not protected or shackled by a religious establishment. Such tales deal with what is worth knowing about the past (the sieges of Thebes and Troy, voyages of discovery, the births of the gods) and convey the civic and military virtues that the young must absorb. In claiming guidance from the Muses, the singers reveal that they do not, as often in other ancient cultures, speak as priests or prophets. Homer characterizes bards as *demiourgoi* (craftsmen, sometimes itinerant, like physicians, carpenters, and heralds); though a provincial farmer, Hesiod needs only the Muses' help to codify Olympian traditions in the *Theogony.* Especially in the *Odyssey* such songs, lacking scriptural authority, are continually shown as subject to evaluation by audiences as to truth value, delight, and suitability to the occasion. Hesiod himself won a singing contest. The act of judging verse was habitual, sometimes institutionalized, and drawn inevitably into the values of the poets themselves from the first: the major texts all contain some implicit celebration of their own artistry, possibly with a dismissal of what precedes, as for example when the *Odyssey* relates that craft (Odysseus' Trojan horse), not raw Achillean courage, won the war. Even outside of contests, the bard would in effect compete with earlier singers of the same traditional material.

Homer accounts his purveying of heroic fame (*kleos*) as a direct extension of the heroic society that he depicts. When not fighting, Achilles himself sings the glories of men (*klea andron*) in *Iliad* 9.189, just as Helen, in the midst of causing the war, embroiders the battle into a scarlet robe and proposes that such misery has been visited on her so that she may be a theme of song for future generations (*Iliad* 6.358). The heroes who have died to achieve fame necessarily perish in vain without bards to purvey that fame, as bards do quite successfully in the *Odyssey,* where Odysseus finds that his fame accurately goes before him even into fairyland. In books nine through twelve he tells much of his own tale himself. In regaining his kingdom, telling tales proves as crucial as shooting arrows. Homer, in all, inclines more to situate his craft within the agonistic world of action that he memorializes than to claim some aesthetic or hieratic superiority to that world. In these epics, song most often attracts adjectives conveying sweetness and delight, but such simple pleasure exists unalloyed only on Olympus. On earth song infallibly works more importantly to edify, galvanize, or seduce audiences.

Hesiod embodies the educational mission of the singer quite directly in singing of justice and work, as well as of the nature and origins of the gods. He strongly insists on the truth of what he sings and its utility. In letting his name and personal problems figure in his disquisitions, Hesiod deviates from the bardic anonymity of the Homeric tradition, as do the lyric poets.

LYRIC AND DRAMATIC POETS

The texts of the seventh through fifth centuries present a new spirit: lyric poets identify themselves and speak subjectively about their own emotions. Loved ones or enemies begin to supplant the Muses as inspirers of song, and song itself is regarded increasingly as an artifact, finally a *poiema* (making; *poiesis* was used first by Herodotus [2.82] for poetry). The spread of writing presumably shapes the new perceptions of the medium, as well as preserving a broader range of forms. The quirks of preservation, however, play an indeterminate role in this movement: strong, individual voices like those of Archilochus (seventh century B.C.) or Sappho (late seventh to sixth century) would easily have been lost before literacy spread.

The remains allow a tantalizing view of a multiplicity of audiences. The Homeric *Hymn to Demeter* (seventh or sixth century) with its connection to the Eleusinian Mysteries directs itself to the myths and frame of reference of women. Sappho raises the possibility that women had their own highly evolved tradition with its own distinct poetics, which she presents with evocations of Homeric diction, myth, and values as foil. The one specialized audience that we know well are the victors in the Olympic and other athletic games, along with their communities, to which poets like Pindar (518–438) and Bacchylides (*ca.* 518–after 452) wrote victory odes. The continually renegotiated relationship of poet and patron made the roles of each a central theme of the celebration. The attendant self-consciousness illuminates the relationship not only of artist and patron, but also of poet and athlete, of writer and performer, as well as of suprapersonal tradition and the individual talent through which it speaks. Pindar elaborates the Homeric notion that the singer embodies something of the same distinctive capability or virtue (*arete*) that distinguishes his heroes (here, victorious athletes), but also that the poet is a *prophetes* possessed of a special wisdom (*sophia*). Pindar is the richest Greek source of metaphors for poets and poetry.

The poets' influence as teachers provoked criticism on moral and philosophical grounds well before complex aesthetic judgments came to be recorded. Following Hesiod, warnings about the mendacity of bards are heard from Solon (early sixth century; frag. 21 Diels) and Pindar (*Nemean* 7.20 ff.), who sometimes explains that he has had to expurgate the old tales. Xenophanes (end of sixth, beginning of fifth century; frags. 11–16 Diels) complains of the misbehavior of Homer's Olympians and debunks anthropomorphism in general. The rise of scientific speculation in this period also encouraged rationalization of the old Olympians through allegory, so that, for instance, their battles could be seen as the strife of earth, air, and water or of social and political principles. Theagenes of Rhegium (late sixth century) may have been the first allegorizer, and the technique was taken up by some Sophists and later by the Stoics.

In the fifth century Homer and the lyric poets continued as the basis of formal education, and drama attained a central role in Athenian public life. The performance of comedy and tragedy in competition for prizes stimulated critical judgments, while audiences' responses provided concrete demonstrations of literary impact. The playwrights constant reworking of each other's material produced a refined mode of implicit criticism, which Euripides occasionally opens out into parody. His often self-conscious and incongruous restagings of traditional material call into question the interactions of myth, ritual, and song. Old Comedy satirized poetry along with the rest of life, and Aristophanes took Euripides as a special target (*Acharnians, Women at the Thesmophoria*). The breaking of illusion in the *parabasis*, where the chorus speaks for the playwright himself, provides a ritualized occasion for literary commentary. *The Frogs* contains a notable example of comparative criticism in pitting the lofty and old-fashioned Aeschylus against the (to Aristophanes) shoddy, modern, morally subversive Euripides. Their contest not only affirms the social importance of the poet as teacher, but also adumbrates the later contrast between "high" and "low" styles. The play strongly claims a central role for poetry not only in memorializing Athenian civic heroism, but also in engendering it in the first place.

THE SOPHISTS AND PLATO

The Sophists' speculations on literary form apparently broadened the analysis of style, though we have only sparse fragments of them. Gorgias (483–376 B.C.), who may have had a systematic theory of poetry, defends the fiction of tragedy in his paradox that "the deceiver is juster than he who does not deceive, the deceived is wiser than the undeceived" (Plutarch, *On the Glory of the Athenians* [*De Gloria Atheniensium*], 348b–c).

Although the Socratic circle wrote treatises on the poets, Plato (429–347 B.C.) eschews literary criticism and theory as a discrete study. However, in pursuing his lifelong project of dislodging the poets and Sophists from their educational monopoly and immense public influence, Plato opens up questions about literary art more fruitfully than did its many apologists. In prose he has no rival as a parodist (*Symposium, Phaedrus*).

Plato widens the traditional notion of poetic inspiration (*enthousiasmos*) into an exploration of creativity as madness, divine possession, or subrational thinking (*Phaedrus* and *Ion*). He sees danger in the process of emotional participation (*mimesis*) whereby the dramatist must experience the feelings of his characters, as do in turn the actors and audience (*Republic* 2). Under a different application of *mimesis,* Plato dismisses poetry as being a representation of the phenomenal world, which itself imperfectly imitates the world of forms; on that view, poetry stands twice removed from truth (*Republic* 3; 10).

Plato puts particular emphasis on the varieties of verbal media, classifying poetry by whether it consists of narration (tales), impersonation (drama), or a mixture (epic). He gravely suspects written communication as opposed to oral questioning (*Phaedrus, Letter* 7). The mystifying *Cratylus* provides the earliest codification of theories about the nature of language.

In banishing poets from his ideal state, Plato provides the first theoretical consideration of the role of poetry in society and defines the problem to which defenses of poetry still respond. The incompatibility of his own literary practice with his theoretical strictures has made his critique a perpetually rich source of controversy. Are we to believe his denunciations of writing or his brilliant development of it as a medium? Are we to believe his debunking of myths or his own seductive mythmaking?

ARISTOTLE

The *Poetics* of Aristotle (384–322 B.C.) constitutes the only piece of systematic literary theory from antiquity, one restricted to tragedy and to epic as the source of drama. By stimulating the pity and fear of the viewers, tragedy can, in Aristotle's view, provide a purgation or purification (*katharsis*) of these emotions. Possibly in answer to Plato's attack, Aristotle demonstrates an educational

role for poetry that is positive, though one less central than that which Plato assumes and strives to undermine.

Where Plato denounces poetic *mimesis* as a counterfeiting of phenomenal reality, Aristotle shows the playwright extracting from the confused particulars of everyday experience a generalized or idealized representation that has claims to be "more philosophical" than history. Character portrayal, versification, and staging all serve the dramatist's central act of building a structure of action, a plot (*mythos*) that instructively captures an essential truth about men acting in the world. The beauties of such a structure derive from its "unity of action," that is, the coherence of events following one upon another in necessary or probable succession, as well as from the symmetry of the parts and an imposing but not unassimilable length for the whole work. Everywhere Aristotle assumes the text to be an organic entity with inevitable characteristics (such as the complication and denouement of the *mythos*). The changes of fortune that constitute a plot may be from happy to unhappy or the reverse, may progress simply or, in complex plots (the preferred type), by a sudden and unforeseen reversal (*peripeteia*) and/or recognition (*anagnorisis*)—ideally by a reversal hinging on recognition, as in Sophocles' *Oedipus the King.* The hero's fall ideally results from some *hamartia,* a term for "error" that seems to include misguided decisions and passionate acts. The tragic character, fallible rather than wicked, should be credibly realistic and self-consistent. Drama has its impact through the viewers' emotional identification of themselves with the characters' experience. Action, not character, is the essence of drama.

Aristotle's discussion of comedy is largely lost to us, but it apparently disparaged the formlessness and topicality of Aristophanes and Old Comedy, preferring the greater uniformity and more exemplary character portrayal of Menander and the New Comedy. The *Poetics* also evaluates epic by the standards created for tragedy, although Homer retains his traditional supremacy in being designated the fountainhead of drama. The epic poet is permitted to digress and dabble in the supernatural.

The three books of Aristotle's *Rhetoric* set the pattern for later handbooks on the subject. The observations on audience psychology (especially anger, pity, and fear) bear comparison to the *Poetics*. Book Three, with its discussion of diction and compositional arrangement, has the most importance for criticism in general.

It should be noted at once that the term "Aristotelian" in modern criticism often has little to do with the philosopher, who has enjoyed several posthumous careers as a critic. Since the text of the *Poetics* was lost for much of antiquity, he mostly stood as a looming presence behind his pupil Theophrastus (*ca.* 370–288 B.C.) and the distinguished Neoptolemus of Parium (third century B.C., presumed to be a large influence on Horace), but a presence imperfectly known to his own school. The Renaissance rediscovered, canonized, and rewrote Aristotle's texts, so that, for example, the "three unities" (action, time [added by Giraldi Cinzio], place [added by Ludovico Castelvetro]) extend and rigidify his observations about integrated plot and a tendency to compress the time frame. A Christianized notion of "fatal flaw" grew from his notion of *hamartia,* which may come closer to "mistake."

HELLENISTIC SCHOLARS
AND POETS

No critical masterpieces survive from the third to the first centuries B.C., but it was in these years that the role of the critic largely took shape. Literary scholarship found an institutional home, most notably in the Library and Museum of Alexandria, and canonized the poetry from Homer to Euripides as "classics," the models of all possible literary attainment. The term "criticism" derives from the judgment of poems (*krisis poiematon*), and the rebirth of poetry after a century dominated by prose saw the emergence of the scholar-poet, a figure whose literarily self-conscious verse was to remain a major vehicle of criticism throughout antiquity. Verse was now reborn silent, a written artifact more than song or performance, so that something like the modern notion of the text began to gain currency.

With the systematic study of literature (grammar, philology, editing and cataloging texts, literary history) and the retrospective view of texts as classics came a new reliance on genre. Each literary type, defined usually by meter, was thought to have its own laws of subject, composition, dialect, and style, as well as its own master (Homer for epic, for example, Archilochus for "iambic" poetry, and so on). With system came lists (the Nine Lyric Poets, the Three Tragedians).

The professionalization of literary study, as well as the involvements of scholar-poets, Peripatetics, Stoics, and Epicureans, led to a proliferation of controversies. Where the Stoics asserted that poetry should provide ethical instruction, poets like Callimachus and Theocritus (early third century) espoused art for art's sake or, as Eratosthenes theorized, for delight. The competing claims of pleasure and edification (*dulce et utile*) continued to preoccupy critics into the Renaissance. Similarly, the traditional rivalry of talent (*physis, ingenium*) and art (*techne, ars*) found new elaborations, as did the discrimination of subject matter from expression. The Aristotelian view that the objects of poetry are universals gave way to an acceptance of history and science, saga, and pure fiction as fit subject matter. With the full flowering of classicism came the first skirmishes between the ancients and the moderns.

Had this first age of professional critics not existed, we should have had to invent it, and to some large degree perhaps we have. Critical treatises have not survived intact; controversies must be reconstructed from later references and from Roman imitation; and the new literary values must largely be divined from the notorious obscurity of Alexandrian verse. The extant bits of literary scholarship preponderantly concern individual words ("Could Homer have used this word?"), as does the erudite play in the poets. The new theoretical issues that loom large in our history may have played only a peripheral role in an age more concerned with rare words.

GREEK AND ROMAN RHETORICIANS

Already in the fourth century Isocrates and other rhetoricians were competing with the philosophers in providing higher education. In Rome from the first century B.C. onward the rhetoricians dominated education, influenced poetic style, and monopolized formal criticism other than that of Horace. In the practice of the schools, the imitation of literary models (*imitatio*) replaced the Greek concern with embodying phenomenal reality (*mimesis*). The emulation of classical authors included poetry along with prose. The analyses of the philosophical schools were reduced to formulas: the three "styles" (high, plain, intermediate) and the four "virtues of diction" (latinity, clarity, appropriateness, and elaboration, with brevity later added as a fifth).

The rhetorical schools thrived on handbooks, of which we have *On Style*, ascribed to one "Demetrius" (probably first century B.C.), and *On Literary Composition* by Dionysius of Halicarnassus (late first century B.C.),

who discusses the placing of words. Literary practitioners produced work of a different order: Cicero's judgments about oratory are unsurpassed in antiquity, while his observations about poetry show wide reading and respectable talent as a poet. Throughout his career he emphasized the importance of a literary education for the orator. Noting the lack of great topics for the rhetorician to address, the historian Tacitus' *Dialogue on Orators* (*ca.* A.D. 100) ties the decline of letters to social decay and thereby provides a rare bit of literary sociology. Quintilian (*ca.* A.D. 30–100) wrote literary history, also rare, in Book Ten of *Education of an Orator* (*Institutio Oratoria*).

ROMAN POETS

More Greek controversies were resolved by the way the Romans wrote poetry than by any theoretical discussions. The allegorical uses of myth, long imputed to Homer, became a medieval habit in the wake of Vergil's *Aeneid.* The sophistication and self-consciousness of the Romans as they created their own literature in imitation of the Greeks tipped the scales from *ingenium* to *ars* as the poet's chief virtue. With serious drama occupying a peripheral position after the second century B.C., questions of how literature imitates life lost urgency. Since poetry now more exclusively addressed an elite, educated audience than it had among the Greeks, it could more credibly reconcile the claims of the *dulce* and the *utile* in claiming its refined delights as edifying and its instruction as a pleasurable exercise. The ancient feud between poetry and philosophy lapsed as the Romans failed to develop much of a taste for the latter and poetry became too socially peripheral to excite much resistance. It was through the practice of Roman poets that various more or less fluid traditions, sometimes distinguished in

Greek practice only by differences of meter and dialect, became fixed as independent forms, such as pastoral, georgic, love elegy, and the "short" epic, thereby solidifying the very concept of genre. The form that Romans claimed entirely as their own, satire, normally includes literature and the literary life among its targets; and self-expressive modes (pastoral, lyric, elegy, literary epistle) regularly include the poet's professions about his calling and attainment. Poets like Catullus, Horace, and Ovid present a highly articulated persona in their verse. In all, poetry about poetry captured the Roman imagination far more than it ever did the Greek.

Horace

Of the poets it is Horace (Quintus Horatius Flaccus, 65–8 B.C.) who speaks about literature most pungently, influentially, and often. His chief contributions center on style, especially on the need to polish more and publish less, and on the prospects of creating a literature to rival that of the Greeks without in the process ceasing to be Roman. The Roman resolution to the conflicts of tradition and originality, articulated most famously by Horace, was to guide emerging vernacular literatures up through the Renaissance.

Horace occupies a primary position both as a commentator on poetry in his *Satires* and *Odes* and as a prophet of a progressive, proudly Roman classicism, chiefly in his versified *Epistles*. His *Epistle to Augustus* (2.1), in affirming the prospect of a first-rate Roman literature, disparages the influence of popular taste, as well as blind veneration of the indigenous literary tradition, and urges instead judicious emulation of the Greeks. The *Epistle to Florus* (2.2) further discourages haste and tawdriness, urging instead the endless polishing of texts, a doctrine further developed in the *Epistle to the Pisones* (2.3), the so-called *Art of Poetry*. This handbook of poetry exercised supreme influence on Roman and Renaissance theorists, although it has become less fashionable in this century. Apparently following on Neoptolemus of Parium, a Peripatetic of the third century, Horace organized his observations around the distinction between the process of selecting and arranging subject matter (*poiesis*), the text itself and its style (*poiema*), and the poet as creator (*poietes*). This witty and discursive epistle mixes the poet's own favorite observations, mostly stylistic, with an emphasis on drama entirely foreign to the contemporary literary scene. The text has provided a rich supply of literary bon mots ("purple patch," "in medias res," "even Homer nods") and judicious resolutions of old controversies: the poet may either please or profit, preferably both, and needs both ability and long practice. Questions of representation or *mimesis* now play a minor role.

"Longinus"

The major ancient rival to the poetic handbooks of Aristotle and Horace is the *Peri Hypsous* (*On Great Writing*, or more commonly, but misleadingly, called *On the Sublime*), once attributed to Cassius Longinus (*ca.* A.D. 213–273) but now believed to be by an anonymous rhetorician of the first century A.D. This lively and unusually nontechnical description of *hypsos* (height, elevation) in poetry and prose stands apart from the main currents of ancient criticism, but speaks to modern readers with unique directness.

Skirting the technicalities of style, the treatise explores the spiritual sources and workings of literary greatness. *Hypsos* is a spark that leaps from the soul of the author to the soul of the reader, "the echo of greatness of spirit." Technique is needed to prevent misdirected or excessive feeling, but the process can start only with the initial thrust of genius. Such greatness results from a natural endowment of great thoughts and noble sentiments, and only secondarily from the techniques of heightening through figures, diction, and arrangement. The spirit of a great and greatly flawed Homer outweighs the perfections of an Apollonius Rhodius, just as Sophocles, Plato, and Demosthenes outshine their more careful but mediocre rivals. In analyzing notable passages to support this judgment the author strikingly anticipates modern comparative criticism.

Late Roman Writers

The second century saw a turn to archaism. Writers like Aulus Gellius and Fronto advocate a return from the standards of Cicero and the Augustan poets to the earlier stages of the national literature. In the late empire scholars, such as Servius on Vergil and Donatus on Terence, preserve many valuable fragments of literary scholarship in scholia and commentaries on the classical texts.

SURVIVAL AND INFLUENCE

Of the Greek critics, only Aristophanes, Plato, and Aristotle directly survived antiquity. Plato was imperfectly known in the West until the Renaissance and even then remained hostage to the Neoplatonists, who had developed their own sophisticated, although often quite non-Platonic, theories concerning *mimesis,* compositional unity, the organic nature of the text, and the poet's claim to superior knowledge. As mentioned above, Aristotle's *Poetics* was mostly lost. Horace and the Roman rhetoricians continued to be known and studied, though much of Cicero and Quintilian was lost until the Renaissance. Poetics played a minor role in the medieval trivium as a part of grammar.

The Renaissance revived ancient criticism, working from the latest to the earliest. Among Petrarch and the humanists of the early Renaissance, the ideal of the *Poeta Orator* derived largely from Horace and the rhetoricians. The recovered texts of Cicero and Quintilian became of primary concern in the revived interest in Latin style. The conflict between the taste for pagan literature and the Christian resistance thereto created the need for systematic defenses of poetry, which brought Plato into the picture, sometimes on both sides of the same debate.

The rediscovery of Aristotle's *Poetics* in the sixteenth century (Aldine, *editio princeps* 1506) inspired the fashion for systematic theorizing about poetry, its composition, forms, and impact. Valla's Latin translation (1498) and Segni's Italian (1549) supported Aristotle's ascendancy, a movement consolidated by Castelvetro's commentary (1570), Minturno's *De Poeta* (1559), and Scaliger's *Poetices Libri Septem* (1561), though Renaissance literary Aristotelianism tended to have a Horatian tinge.

"Longinus" enjoyed a fashion among the romantics, but otherwise the influence of classical poetics has steadily declined, with the Greeks surviving better than the Romans. The many currents of twentieth-century criticism have recurrently brought Aristotle back into favor, as, for example, among the so-called Chicago critics. Poststructuralist critics have paid particular attention to Plato (for example, Jacques Derrida on the *Phaedrus*) as the critic with the most to say about the nature of language and of the creative experience, the differences between oral and written literature, and the relation of fiction to truth. Criticism in the second half of the twentieth century, with its proliferation of perspectives, seems to be finding neither scripture to replace the *Poetics* nor a more persuasive prototype for criticism as an orderly and scientific study. By contrast, radicals and puritans, iconoclasts and ideologues all find support one place or another in the protean perspectives of Plato.

BIBLIOGRAPHY

SOURCES

Early Greek texts are collected in Giuliana Lanata, *Poetica Pre-Platonica* (1963). Anthologies of texts in translation are available in John D. Denniston, ed., *Greek Literary Criticism* (1924); Donald A. Russell and M. Winterbottom, eds., *Ancient Literary Criticism* (1972); and Alexander Preminger, Osborne B. Hardison, Jr., and Kevin Kerrane, eds., *Classical and Medieval Literary Criticism* (1974). Of the many available translations of Aristotle's *Poetics*, the edition by Samuel H. Butcher, *Aristotle's Theory of Poetry and Fine Art* (4th ed. 1911; repr. 1951) with facing pages of Greek and interpretative essays is particularly useful, and there are also commentaries by Ingram Bywater (1909) and Donald W. Lucas (1968).

For Horace, see Charles O. Brink, *Horace on Poetry* (1963 and 1971) the second volume of which has text of and commentary on *Ars Poetica;* for "Longinus," see *On the Sublime,* Donald A. Russell, ed. (1964). The following authors are available in the Loeb Classical Library with the Greek and English translations on facing pages: Aristotle, *The Poetics* and "Longinus," *On the Sublime,* W. H. Fyfe, trans., and Demetrius, *On Style,* W. Rhys Roberts, trans. (1927); Horace, *Ars Poetica* (*Art of Poetry*), Henry Fairclough, trans. (1926); Quintilian, Harold E. Butler, trans., 4 vols. (1920–1922); Tacitus, *Dialogus* (*Dialogue on Orators*), William Peterson, trans. (1925).

STUDIES

John Atkins, *Literary Criticism in Antiquity,* 2 vols. (1934); Fran Cairns, *Generic Composition in Greek and Roman Poetry* (1972); James A. Coulter, *The Literary Microcosm: Theories of Interpretation of the Later Neoplatonists* (1976); John F. D'Alton, *Roman Literary Theory and Criticism* (1931); Gerald F. Else, *Aristotle's Poetics: The Argument* (1957); George C. Fiske and Mary A. Grant, *Cicero's De Oratore and Horace's Ars Poetica* (1929); Arnold W. Gomme, *The Greek Attitude to Poetry and History* (1954); George Grube, *The Greek and Roman Critics* (1965); Rosemary Harriott, *Poetry and Criticism before Plato* (1969); J. Jones, *On Aristotle and Greek Tragedy* (1962); Donald A. Russell, *Criticism in Antiquity* (1981); George Saintsbury, *History of Criticism,* I (1900); Edward Sikes, *The Greek View of Poetry* (1931); Paul Vicaire, *Platon: critique littéraire* (1960).

Greek Historiography and Biography

STEPHEN USHER

HISTORY

Historiography began as a close companion of geography, both emerging as areas of knowledge explored in the general movement of scientific inquiry initiated in Ionia in the sixth century B.C. Attempts by the Milesians Thales and Anaximander to explain the structure of the physical world were paralleled by researches into the origins of human societies. Less speculative and esoteric, fueled by rich source material, and attractive on a practical level because of its dependence upon popular tradition, this new form of inquiry (Gk. *historia*) attracted many variously gifted writers. They wrote in prose rather than verse, the earlier medium, for two main reasons: first, because their source material, temple and civic records and oral informants, were purely factual, and in the former cases documentary; second, because the authors wrote in the same spirit of scientific inquiry as Anaximander and Anaximenes, the great Milesian philosophers, whose writings on nature were the first known Greek works in prose. But much of this material was as mythical in character

as the stories in Homer and Hesiod, and was often related to them. Later critics declined to dignify most of these early writers with the name historian, preferring to call them merely logographers (prose writers) because of their modest aim of making the records they had seen and the stories they had been told more generally known, without adding to or subtracting from them.

Although much of the writing of these early logographers survived into Roman times, only scanty fragments now remain. Cicero was thus in a much better position than we are to pronounce his famous judgment that the father of history was Herodotus of Halicarnassus; yet some qualification is required. His most important predecessor, Hecataeus of Miletus, had certain claims to the title. The two main works that he wrote, the *Genealogiai* and the *Journey Around the World* (*Periegesis*), were mainly factual and written in an unpretentious style, but he claimed to have applied critical judgment in the selection of his material, telling only stories which seemed credible to him, "for the stories of the Greeks are many and ridiculous, as it seems to me." Hecataeus was also probably the most widely traveled of the logographers, and also found time to play a part in Milesian politics. He tried to discourage his fellow citizens from undertaking a war of liberation against their Persian overlords, and when this advice was rejected he urged them to gain supremacy at sea, but was unheeded once more. His travels included Egypt, and his findings there were used by Herodotus to supplement his own. But he was a geographer rather than a historian.

In the writings of Charon of Lampsacus and Xanthus of Lydia, which like those of Hecataeus have survived only in fragments, storytelling rather than serious history probably predominated. Herodotus' aims were altogether more ambitious, as he reveals in the first sentence of his *Histories:*

> The following is an exposé of the researches of Herodotus the Halicarnassian, in order that the memory of men's actions may not be erased by the passage of time, nor the mighty and wonderful deeds of both Greeks and barbarians be without glory; and in particular it is my purpose to establish the cause of their conflict.

The tension between literary and scientific aims, which became a permanent feature of ancient historiography, is already present. The desire to commemorate the great deeds of men is shared by epic and lyric poets, and with the latter Herodotus also shared the experience of reciting his own work to audiences in the cities he visited on his travels. An understanding of the public for which he wrote was essential, and he sought to satisfy a wide range of taste and intelligence. He set out both to instruct and to entertain, leaving individual members of his audience to decide how much of each they wanted. This purpose explains his catholic inclusiveness, which he states thus (*Histories* 2.123.1):

> Any person who finds such stories credible may adopt the account given by the Egyptians: for my part, it is my principle throughout the whole history to record what I have heard said by each of my informants.

This statement makes Herodotus appear less scientific than Hecataeus. But in practice he often tells more than one version of a story and states which he believes, weighing probabilities where factual evidence has been wanting.

Herodotus and Thucydides

Herodotus was born a few years before Xerxes' invasion of Greece in 481–479 B.C., and the last three books of his *Histories,* which was divided into nine books by later librarians, describe that invasion. Thucydides the Athenian, son of Olorus, was born perhaps a generation later, but took an entirely different view of the historian's task, and indeed of the limits of his competence. He chose as his subject the Peloponnesian War (431–404 B.C.) and took his narrative down to the year 411 B.C. He served his city as a commander until defeat and exile in 424 B.C. imposed retirement, but he had decided on his vocation earlier when he realized the magnitude of the conflict. In explaining his decision he stresses the difficulty of obtaining accurate information, and concludes that the only serious history is contemporary history. The product of this process of rigorous inquiry and examination is not intended for mere entertainment (*History of the Peloponnesian War* 1.22.4):

> It is a work which will give but little pleasure to those who seek only romance and sensationalism; but if it is of some use to those who wish to have a clear view of the past, and through it a guide to the future, since human nature is a constant factor, I shall be satisfied.

It is composed as a possession for ever, not as an occasional piece for a single hearing.

With a superb disdain of all that makes no intellectual demands, Thucydides appeals to the genuine student by claiming specific practical powers for his kind of history, but also, in this passage and elsewhere, by taxing to the full his interpretive ability. His style is difficult, especially in reflective passages, where the thought is sometimes condensed to the point of gnomic obscurity, and at other times forced into a rigid antithetical framework. The intellectual demands that he made upon himself in the collection and presentation of his material were no less exacting, but are largely concealed from his readers. Apart from telling them once that as many as possible of his informants were eyewitnesses, he makes no comparisons between conflicting accounts, but presents them, except in those parts of books five and eight (the last book), which he did not revise, with the results of his own adjudications in an editorialized and self-consistent narrative.

The reporting of live speech presented a special challenge to the two historians. The important part that it played in earlier literature, especially in Homer, afforded precedents and models. Both historians, moreover, regarded the inclusion of what was said as necessary in order to explain what was done. Herodotus reproduces many conversations and a much smaller number of longer speeches. He devotes a substantial part of Book Seven to the deliberations that led Xerxes and his advisers to the fatal decision to invade Greece. Elsewhere, live speech frequently arises naturally in the course of the narrative, providing relief, color, variety, and motivation. In Thucydides, speech, or rather speeches, play a more positive and pervasive role. Most of them occur in pairs, presenting opposing arguments, a technique used by the sophistic writers of the period, whose influence is also seen in the moral and philosophical issues discussed—might and right, justice and expediency, reason and emotion. Another contemporary influence was the new art of rhetoric, which originated in Sicily. The three types of oration established by its proponents—deliberative, epideictic, and forensic—are represented. Deliberative oratory predominates, since most speeches are concerned with political decisions. These, by showing on what rational grounds important decisions were reached, and by including information supplementary to that given in the narrative, contribute very significantly to an understanding of the course of events. The most famous epideictic speech is Pericles' Funeral Oration. It serves several purposes, the most important of which is to display the persuasive powers of the greatest Athenian. His idealization of Athenian imperialism and praise of her culture and democratic institutions are intended for a wider audience, in addition to showing how Athenian morale was raised when it was wavering at the sight of the first casualties of the war. Thucydides also puts speeches into the mouths of field and naval commanders before battles. These are hortatory rather than deliberative, but always contain a strong rational element.

In his first sentence Herodotus specifies inquiry into causes as one of his objectives. The inquiry is wide-ranging, but a comprehensive view of the nine books reveals their thematic unity. Herodotus saw the Greeks and barbarians as inhabiting two irreconcilable worlds. In the barbarian world absolute rulers reigned over enslaved subjects, and their decisions, like that of Croesus to invade Persia, changed the course of history, yet were often reached irrationally because fear prevented their advisers from giving good counsel. The Greeks, by contrast, with their individual freedom of speech and action, were factious and indecisive, but fought more purposefully when battle had been joined. This antithesis is genuine enough, but Herodotus' preoccupation with the whims of potentates led him to ascribe personal motivation to events when other explanations should have been considered. For example, in describing the antecedents of the Ionian Revolt (500–494 B.C.) he concentrates on the intrigues of the despots Histiaeus and Aristagoras and does not consider why there was widespread discontent in Ionia at that time. Yet his practice of recording all he had been told by his various informants in the many places he visited has produced a treasure house of source material concerning periods and countries remote from the subject matter of his main narrative. But these oral sources were often partisan, being personally involved in the stories they told, so that motives of greed, revenge, and fear figure largely in them. Thucydides edited and impersonalized his sources. Even the speeches, which afforded an opportunity to represent character, were composed primarily as vehicles of reasoned argument and, to a lesser extent, of emotional appeal. They were fitted to the situation rather than to the individual. His study of events and causes led him to conceive two kinds: long-term causes, which gradually produce a certain state of mind that leads to action, and immediate causes, which precipitate action. Corresponding with these are the two mainsprings of human motivation: the desire for power, which is a constant source of action, and irrational optimism in pursuit of it, which leads men to go to war because of some imagined temporary advantage. These ideas led Thucydides to the belief that parity of strength between powerful states afforded no guarantee of peace, while frequent engagement in minor military operations in times of general peace made states more prepared to enter a major conflict.

The central position occupied by human agency and calculation in Thucydides' scheme of things accords with the Sophistic view that "man is the measure of all things." But it contrasts sharply with the traditional religious view, which Herodotus represents unequivocally, of man's subjection to divine will and to the vaguer but no less strong power of fate. This view profoundly affected Herodotus' interpretation of events, their causes and their consequences. If an enterprise resulted in failure, he tended to regard it as doomed from the outset, and he often foreshadowed its outcome by highlighting actions which display the *hybris* (arrogance, excess) that inevitably leads to *nemesis* (divine retribution). Far from emphasizing man's control over his destiny, he tells many stories that dwell upon the instability of human fortune, especially in cases where success has been so great as to incur divine jealousy. He also professes belief in the prophetic powers of oracles and tells stories of divine intervention. But he does not absolve men from responsibility for their decisions, and says that they should not blame the gods when their unreasonable hopes are not realized. Similarly, Thucydides' anthropocentric rationalism is tempered by a recognition of the importance of religion as a state institution. He also describes the plague and the occurrence of natural disasters in language which some commentators have found sufficiently powerful to suggest that the historian may have thought that some demonic agency produced them. Again, rationalism does not banish human feeling. This expresses itself explicitly in his comments on acts of barbarous cruelty, but more generally and pervasively in his narrative of momentous events. In his account of the battle in Syracuse harbor, which decided the fate of the Athenian expedition to Sicily (415–413 B.C.), more description is devoted to the emotions of the spectators and the combatants than to the actual fighting. His description of the plague at Athens, while full of medical detail, also portrays the victims' own reactions to their sufferings. These and many other narratives display more emotional involvement on the historian's part than the tales (*logoi*) of Herodotus, in which the storyteller's catholic interest is spread widely and thinly over time and space, and curiosity and wonderment are stronger than sympathy.

Comparison of the two greatest Greek historians is thus a matter of considerable complexity. The approach of each was idiosyncratic, yet not simply complementary to the other in spite of Thucydides' conscious desire to correct what he saw as the faults of earlier writers. The greatest contrast is between Herodotus' epic or Homeric conception of a wide-ranging inquiry, in which almost the whole of the known world and the accounts of all his informants are included, and the strict limit of subject, the careful chronological framework, and the editorial censorship that Thucydides imposed upon his material. As a source of multifarious information, Herodotus is the most valuable of the ancient historians to modern scholars, and his popularity in his own time shows that he was attuned to contemporary views and literary taste. Thucydides made uncompromising demands upon his readers, and his generally unidealized, even pessimistic view of his man-dominated world appealed more to practical politicians like Demosthenes than to ordinary readers. To later students of history, therefore, his preoccupation with human psychology seemed to set the subject on a fittingly higher intellectual plane and ensured his lasting influence on the genre.

Xenophon

The next generation produced no historians to match the genius of either Herodotus or Thucydides. The only one whose work survived in quantity was Xenophon the Athenian, a prolific writer whose wide interests included philosophy, politics, military matters, and horsemanship. In all his writings he displays a gift for communicating with the reader of average intelligence, but his historical writing reflects his own interests rather than the relative importance of events, and generally lacks analytical penetration. His *History of Greece* (*Hellenica*), in seven books, which occupied him intermittently during the last two-thirds of his life, purported to be a history of Greece down to the battle of Mantinea (362 B.C.). It starts where Thucydides ends (410 B.C.) with the words "After these events . . . ," and in the first two books Xenophon attempted to follow Thucydides' chronological division of events down to the end of the Peloponnesian War (404 B.C.). But he was never at ease when recounting events in which he had played no part unless they were enacted by personalities whose qualities he could admire. The unbalancing effect of this preoccupation is already evident in the first two books, in which important events are omitted while prominence is given to characterization. In spite of this, however, these two books contain a mainly satisfactory account of the years 410–403 B.C., including some exciting narrative and effective scene painting, some of which carries the eyewitness' stamp of authenticity. The accounts of the Trial of the Ten Generals after the battle of Arginusae (406 B.C.), the destruction of the Long Walls after the surrender of Athens (404 B.C.), the trial and death of Theramenes (404 B.C.), and the return of the democrats under Thrasybulus (403 B.C.) are all vivid with drama and emotion, and Xenophon's narrative is by far the best account of these events.

Xenophon left Athens in 401 B.C. The last five books of the *History of Greece* cover some forty years of Greek history, ranging widely but not containing all the main areas of activity. The historian himself came within the Spartan sphere of influence through his friendship with King Agesilaus and his residence at Scillus, near Olympia in the Peloponnese. The last vestiges of Thucydidean influence disappear in these books, and personal caprice increasingly dictates the choice of material. There are some glaring omissions and misrepresentations: for example, the foundation of the Second Delian League (378 B.C.) is not mentioned. The great Theban leaders Pelopidas and Epaminondas are given far less prominence than they deserve, while the exploits of Agesilaus and other Spartan leaders are recounted in minute detail. Restricted both as to his sources of information and by his own criteria of what was worth recording, Xenophon tended to concentrate upon events that illustrated his views on leadership, loyalty, and piety—on the last of which he held strong but conventional views—or that simply made good stories and exercised his narrative talents. The speeches he wrote are lively and combative, and probably reflect quite faithfully the temper of fourth-century politics. But he makes no attempt to establish causal connections between events, and the state of confusion (*tarache*) in which he leaves the Greek world in his concluding sentence is shared by his readers at many points in the course of his narrative. His talents, which may be compared to those of a high-class journalist, are deployed to the greatest advantage in the *The March Up Country (Anabasis)*, his justly famous account of the March of the Ten Thousand into the heart of the Persian Empire and out again (401–399 B.C.). As a constant eyewitness who emerged in the crisis after Cyrus' death to play a leading part in securing the safe return of the expedition, he was stimulated by the constant dangers, frequent emergencies and clashes of personality, and also by the strange places and tribes encountered.

Autobiography and biography were more to his taste than historiography.

Other Fourth-century Historians

For the assessment of the other fourth-century historians fragments and the judgments of later critics must serve. It was a transitional period in historiography. The brilliance and originality of the two men who established an identity for the genre in the fifth century could not be reproduced, but the Thucydidean idea of its permanent educative value persisted, and it was complemented by the formation of a link between historiography and rhetoric that was to prove no less durable. The two most important historians of the fourth century, Theopompus of Chios and Ephorus of Cyme, were pupils of Isocrates, whose school of rhetoric at Athens also trained famous politicians and generals in the art of persuasive discourse. The contemporary political scene supplied some of the topics chosen, and Isocrates' own views found expression in the discourses he wrote as models for his pupils, who were naturally influenced by them. Ephorus' *Histories* covered a period of more than 700 years. He had finished twenty-seven of its intended thirty books when he died in about 330 B.C. The work incorporated the Isocratean idea of the superiority of Greeks over barbarians. Ephorus was also pro-Athenian and anti-Spartan, and apparently followed the plan proposed by Isocrates in his *Panegyricus* for the leading role of Athens. But the incorporation of these themes did not give Ephorus' history a strongly rhetorical character. Isocrates himself is reported to have contrasted the temperaments of his two pupils by saying that Theopompus needed the rein, Ephorus the spur. Apart from having a mildly moral flavor, Ephorus' narrative appears, from later historians who used it as a major source, to have lacked any individual imprint. But it may have been this very characteristic that inspired confidence and ensured for Ephorus, in spite of his ignorance of military matters, a wider reading public than that of any historian since Herodotus.

Theopompus' powerful style and the prominent vein of censure in his moralism made him a more controversial figure, but his reassertion of the Thucydidean principle and practice of writing contemporary history suggests a serious purpose. The first of his two main works, the *Hellenica,* was a history of Greece from 411 to 394 B.C. in twelve books, a continuation of Thucydides but apparently even more concentrated and detailed; and his magnum opus, the *Philippica,* perhaps inspired by the latest of Isocrates' ideas for the unification of Greece under one leader, was in fifty-eight books, making its scale the most ambitious so far conceived. Like Ephorus, he lacked military knowledge and experience of public life, but the surviving fragments reveal a wide interest in geography, ethnology, and mythology. Some of his critics interpreted his taste for censure as bias, but as Philip II of Macedon was the most celebrated object of it, their opinion, in view of the title of the work, hardly carries conviction. Theopompus simply reveled in the color and vitality that censure conferred upon his narrative, and set a fashion for it which several Hellenistic historians followed.

The remaining fourth-century historians are little more than names to us. The most respected in his own time was probably Cratippus, a continuator of Thucydides who reputedly excluded speeches from his history in the interests of strict veracity. Philochorus was a chronicler of Athenian local history rather than a historian, but he provided valuable source material for later historians and biographers. The unknown author of a famous fragment covering the years 396–395 B.C. in detail, the *Hellenica Oxyrhynchia,* may have been a considerable historian. Because of the Boeotian interest in the account, the name of Daimachus of Plataea as author has been suggested, but the question must remain undecided.

The death throes of the free city-state and the turmoil that attended its demise suggested a change of direction in the development of historiography. The relation between history and tragedy had not been lost on Herodotus, who was acquainted with the dramatist Sophocles. But Duris of Samos, who wrote a history of Greece from 370 to 281 B.C. and other historical and literary works, aimed overtly in his narratives at the excitation of emotion, believing that historians should try to affect their audiences in the same way as dramatists. His lead was followed by a historian of the succeeding generation, Phylarchus of Athens, who was one of the most important Greek historians of the third century. Both Duris and Phylarchus attempted through their style to draw the maximum of emotional response from their readers by dwelling on scenes of horror and pathos. They attempted to entertain their readers with picturesque anecdotes. In their hands history was separated by only a thin line from imaginative literary art.

But even in this period the tradition of sober historiography was upheld by Hieronymus of Cardia, who wrote a history of the period 323–263 B.C., which was a major source for Diodorus, Arrian, and Plutarch.

Next may be considered two contrasting historians from Sicily. Philistus of Syracuse witnessed the Sicilian expedition (415–413 B.C.) in his youth. He was said to have imitated Thucydides when he wrote his *History of Sicily* in at least twelve books while in exile, like his model. Before his exile and after his return he was active in the courts of Dionysius I and II, and there is some reason for supposing that his political acumen, born of experience, served him well in his writing, as did a disciplined and succinct style.

The long lifetime of Timaeus of Tauromenium extended from the mid fourth almost to the mid third century B.C. His father, Andromachus, was tyrant of his native city until it was captured by Agathocles of Syracuse (312 B.C.). Thereafter Timaeus lived in Athens from about 329 to 289 B.C., but his *History* in thirty-eight books dealt primarily with Sicily. Events in Italy and Africa also came within his scope, making him the first Greek historian to write about Roman affairs. Indeed, his range was remarkable, in time, space, and subject matter. He made the Olympiad his unit of chronology, an innovation adopted by many later historians, beginning with the First Olympiad (776 B.C.), and including, in the manner of Herodotus, a variety of material of an antiquarian rather than strictly historical nature. Also, writing about Sicily past and present while residing at Athens, he obtained his material from increasingly available literary sources, but at the inevitable expense of fieldwork and research at first hand. However, this fault did not prevent him from becoming one of the most popular historians. His popularity was still high a century later, when his work came under the hypercritical scrutiny of the greatest Greek historian after Thucydides, Polybius of Megalopolis.

Polybius

Born shortly before 200 B.C. into the complex and factious political environment of the Achaean League, Polybius was the son of Lycortas, a leading statesman. In 170–169 B.C. he held one of the league's senior offices, that of cavalry commander (hipparch), but after the Battle of Pydna (168 B.C.) he was one of the thousand Achaeans deported to Rome. Internment opened up a new career to Polybius through a chance meeting and subsequent friendship with Scipio Aemilianus, whose patronage enabled him to reside in Rome and to travel and see the Roman military machine at work. His study of Rome's military, and to a lesser extent her political institutions, in both theory and practice, led him to conclude that no rival power could withstand her. Earlier plans to write a history of Achaea were revised, and Rome was made the central subject of a newly projected work. He states his purpose in these words (3.1): "The one aim and object, then, of all I have undertaken is to show how, when, and why all the known parts of the world fell under the dominion of Rome."

Confidence in his ability to achieve this aim permeates Polybius' many personal statements. He described his work as "pragmatic" history because it predominantly incorporated material obtained through his own direct contact with men, places, and reliable documents and by analysis based on his own experience as a man of action and as a confidant of such men. His somewhat priggish dismissal of historians who lacked his special qualifications becomes understandable when the extent to which historiography had become amateurish is realized. Polybius is also critical of sensationalism, and repeatedly states that history should be useful and truthful rather than merely enjoyable to its readers.

Of the forty books of the *Histories* the first five have survived almost complete. The fragments of the remainder amount to about one-fifth of the whole work, and are sufficiently well distributed to indicate its scope and plan. It narrates in detail the events in the Greek and Roman worlds between 220 and 146 B.C., but the first two books contain selective accounts of events before 220 B.C., including the First Punic War and the interwar years. Book Six is a discussion of the Roman constitution and military system; Book Twelve is an extended polemic against other historians, especially Timaeus; and Book Thirty-four is geographical. Polybius' interests lay mainly in practical matters, especially military matters. He wished to discover and explain how and why things worked. This was easier to do with regard to the mechanical aspects of both the Roman constitution and the army than it was with more abstract and intangible factors such as the ideals of the Roman aristocracy and the operation of clientship and patronage, *gratia* and *amicitia,* of which he shows no deep understanding. However, wars and diplomatic exchanges form a large part of his story, and his treatment of such matter is more than merely competent and almost invariably the best available. In his mission to convince his compatriots of the inevitability and permanence of Rome's dominion he discusses many issues digressively, but most of these discussions can be traced to earlier writers. In particular his discussions of the origins of society and of different types of constitution can be traced back to Aristotle and beyond; while his discussion of the causes of the Second Punic War in Book Three, although more stratified and focused on personal motivation, is obviously indebted to Thucydides. But he is the first historian to relate these and other matters to the success of a nation. Thus in his scheme of things history furnishes clearer lessons than his predecessors felt able to assign to it. But it is characteristic of his cautious and balanced approach to impose one limit that effectively adds a further lesson. It was the part played by Chance (*Tyche*) in human affairs, and the realization that it could upset all human calculations: this capacity made it an integral part in the historical process.

Roman history continued to preoccupy Greek historians. Poseidonius of Apamea combined the role of Polybius' continuator with a wide range of other interests that included geography, astronomy, and natural science. He was also a pupil of the Stoic philosopher Panaetius. His *Histories* narrate events to 82 B.C., but for an estimate of their importance we must depend on references and opinions of contemporaries, since the work is lost. He was oligarchic and also supported Pompey. The unification of the world under a Roman Empire with strong leadership satisfied his Stoic ideal of a human commonwealth; his death in 51 B.C. may have been timely in saving him from disappointment. The ideas of Polybius influenced Cicero, Sallust, Caesar, Tacitus, and Plutarch, although to what degree has been the subject of heated debate in this century.

Dionysius

No successor of Polybius could be unaware of the dangerous influences awaiting him, but rhetoric and dramatic sensationalism were not to be banished by the virtuous example of a single historian. In the event, the affinity of history with rhetoric was consolidated in the first century B.C. as more historians, mostly Roman, turned to the writing of laudatory monographs. The use of rhetorical techniques was also the way to reach a wider public in an age when declamation was becoming an increasingly popular form of entertainment; the subjects were often historical in character. On a more esoteric level, literary critics, reflecting popular taste, demanded that historians should pay as much attention to style (which included rhetorical effects) as to content. Dionysius of Halicarnassus was both a literary critic and a historian. His *Roman Antiquities (Antiquitates Romanae)* attains the high point of rhetorical history, and exhibits both its virtues and its vices. It contains a very high proportion of live speech, mostly long formal orations, the content of which is inevitably purely imaginative; the historical episodes with the greatest potential for rhetorical exploitation also are accorded disproportionate prominence. Yet Dionysius shows himself acutely aware of the Thucydidean and Polybian tradition of scientific historiography. He spent almost the whole of his period of residence in Rome, from about 30 B.C. until his death, working on this magnum opus. He learned the Latin language in preparation for his researches, the sources for which were both oral and documentary. He compares these sources conscientiously in his efforts to arrive at truth and justice. But his rhetorical preconceptions undermined his best intentions and prevented him from giving adequate narrative coverage of events. Nevertheless, because his choice of rhetorically attractive material was not always the same as Livy's, he often fills gaps in that historian's account.

Diodorus

Diodorus Siculus was a writer of more modest pretensions. The title he gave to his work, *Library of History,* composed in forty books, mostly between 60 and 30 B.C., suggests that he claimed to be no more than a compilator, and in his introduction he explicitly disclaims deep intelligence or insight. Occasionally the motivation behind his vast project, the Stoic doctrine of the brotherhood of man, comes to the surface, as when he describes with feeling actions and conditions of extreme cruelty, especially those involving slavery. For the most part, however, Diodorus is dependent on his sources, the most important of whom was Ephorus, for most of the opinions expressed and for the degree of rhetorical treatment and moral tone. But his account of Greek history provides invaluable secondary information for some periods and is the only continuous full narrative for others, including the all-important *Fifty Years (Pentekontaetia)*, the fifty-year period (479–431 B.C.) between the Persian and Peloponnesian wars. His account of the part played by Thebes and her leaders Epaminondas and Pelopidas restores some

balance to the historical tradition of the earlier part of the fourth century, tendentiously treated by the pro-Spartan Xenophon. Reliance on a plurality of sources, which he did not always find the time to compare and reconcile, produced some confusion of chronology. Judged by the strictest standards set by the best historians, Diodorus' *Library* is third-rate history; but its clear narrative, agreeably free of superfluous rhetoric and digressive clutter, makes it at worst a useful and at best an indispensable part of the historical tradition.

Subsequent Historians

No Greek historian after the reign of Augustus added significantly to the development of the genre. The best was probably Flavius Arrianus. The military experience he acquired as governor of Cappadocia from A.D. 131 to 137 qualified him well for the literary task on which he embarked after an early retirement. He entitled his account of Alexander the Great's expedition *The March Up Country (Anabasis)*, and on several occasions expresses his admiration of Xenophon. But he also inherited the critical spirit of the Hellenistic age and manifested it in his many discussions of sources and their merits. Remoteness from events brought advantages not enjoyed by the historians in Alexander's entourage: Arrian was no hero-worshiper, noting occasions when Alexander failed to act with self-control, an essential quality in the Stoic ideal of a king, to which Arrian, following his teacher Epictetus, subscribed. Again, Arrian's technical knowledge of the arts of war could be applied effectively to Alexander's campaigns, since these had changed little in the intervening years. The *Anabasis* is easily the best account of Alexander's exploits.

A close contemporary of Arrian, Appian of Alexandria, wrote a *History of Rome* from earliest times. The eleven books that survive from twenty-four include five covering the years 133–130 B.C., providing an important source. His impartiality guides his readers through a minefield of controversial events that most Roman commentators were quite unable to interpret without reference to their own political prejudices. Indeed, in its extreme form his sobriety is perhaps his worst fault. Apart from an occasional nicely turned phrase, his almost continuous bare narrative leaves an impression of a writer uninterested in style. In a work otherwise lacking in originality, indifference to literary form is a fatal flaw. Cassius Dio Cocceianus of Nicaea was more ambitious in both his political and his literary career. He attained the consulship during the reign of Septimius Severus, and his *History of Rome* brought events down to A.D. 229 in eighty books. In it much is sacrificed to the maintenance of narrative momentum. The thread is too narrow, and details are passed over. His interest in constitutional matters is restricted to general questions about the strengths and weaknesses of the different forms of government, on which he has nothing original to say. He is also no military historian, although this weakness did little harm to his reputation because it was shared by more illustrious predecessors like Livy, with whom he shared the distinction of having his *History* epitomized by later scholars. As a vital, developing genre, Greek historiography was now dead.

BIOGRAPHY

The predominance of poetry in early literature, its association with divine inspiration, and its mainly mythical, divine, and heroic subject matter, had the effect of delaying the assertion of individualism. This influence affected prose writers, especially those who sought to appropriate certain qualities of the poet's art. A writer who chose a contemporary mortal's career as the theme of a work of literature would have risked as transient a period of fame as his subject. On the other hand, reliable material about famous men of the past, containing the kind of detail needed for effective biography, was difficult to find. Certain episodes in Herodotus, by concentrating for a time on the actions of one man, acquire the temporary flavor of biography. Thucydides gives swift sketches of the salient characteristics of leading men, and allows these and others to emerge in their speeches and in the course of the narrative. But neither historian explored the whole life, and through it the psyche of any individual, in a systematic and complete way.

Nevertheless, the beginnings of biography are to be sought among their contemporaries, some of the many fifth-century writers whose works are lost or fragmentary. The most important of these was Stesimbrotus of Thasos, whose interest in statesmen led him to write pamphlets about Themistocles, Thucydides, son of Melesias (not the historian), and Pericles, fragments of which survive. Another subject of biography was the philosopher Empedocles, and Xanthus (probably the Lydian) was his biographer. The Ionian Scylax of Caryanda, who influenced Herodotus, wrote a life of the tyrant Heraclides of Mylasa. The personal daily recollections (*Epidemiai*) of Ion of Chios are almost as much autobiographical as biographical, and his extensive travels add color to them. Exposure of these Ionian writers to oriental tales may have fueled their interest in biography, while both in the East and nearer home kings, tyrants, and sages were a natural focus of interest. The stories of the Seven Wise Men, who belonged to all three of these classes, seem to originate in the fifth century or even earlier.

Xenophon, Isocrates, and Others Before Plutarch

The first extant biographical studies appear not in works written purely in this form but in the autobiographical *The March Up Country* (*Anabasis*) of Xenophon. They are the obituary pen portraits that he gives of the Greek mercenary leaders and the Persian prince Cyrus (at the end of Book Two) after describing their treacherous murder by Tissaphernes. In them he attempts to relate character to environment, and carefully marks its development, even if only over a short span of time. They also contain elements of praise and blame that link them with epideictic literature, but their precise relationship to this is uncertain. As a companion of these men, Xenophon was especially interested in those qualities that affected their performance as leaders, and his portraits of them focus firmly on this question, thereby narrowing their scope. But their importance in the history of biography is considerable. The first monograph devoted to a historical figure is the *Euagoras* of Isocrates (*ca.* 365 B.C.). It is a commemorative discourse addressed to the Cypriot king's son and successor, Nicocles. In it is seen the full effect of the fourth-century interest, projected through the rhetorical and philosophical schools, in the education and cultivation of self-discipline and responsibility of men in positions of power, and in the nature of leadership in a world in which monarchy was increasingly seen as the salvation of the Greek world. In an otherwise chronological arrangement of events, the *Euagoras* contains a description of the king's character when he was at the height of his power. But Isocrates disliked narrative, and the work's main strength lies in its rhetorical resource, which is used effectively in describing the impact that the king's actions had on the ambitions of other leaders.

Xenophon's *Agesilaus*, written a few years after the *Euagoras* and indebted to it at least in conception, draws more fully on personal acquaintance. Far from eschewing narrative, Xenophon makes it an integral part of the monograph's structure, adapting passages from his *History of Greece* and thereby basing his encomium, which he calls *epainos* (praise), on specific actions. This, together with his own experience, places the *Agesilaus* in closer conjunction with historical reality than the *Euagoras*. Finally, by dividing the work into two parts—a chronological account followed by a systematic examination of the king's virtues, with examples—Xenophon set a pattern for later biographers to adapt to their own subjects. He affirmed his interest in the genre by devoting his longest work, the *Education of Cyrus* (*Cyropaedeia*), to the life of the founder of the Persian Empire. But this is largely imaginative in content and dismisses most of Cyrus' reign in a few sentences. As the earliest historical romance, however, it provides another example of Xenophon's talent for literary innovation. His *Memorabilia of Socrates* contains biographical material, though to a limited degree, concentrating as it does primarily on his master's teaching.

For some time biography merged with fiction while undergoing the influence of rhetoric. History too, at least in some hands, acquired a stronger biographical content. Theopompus wrote excursuses on men's lives and characters in his *Philippica;* and the histories of Alexander had obvious biographical tendencies. Indeed, with the works of these historians history and biography seem to merge, and the latter needed a new stimulus to enable it to reestablish a separate identity. The stimulus came from scholastic quarters.

Aristotle and certain of his pupils were interested in individual writers. This interest arose from their study of literature, especially drama and rhetoric, so that purely biographical information about authors was probably sought only insofar as it contributed to an understanding of their writings. One author, Chamaeleon, deduced details of the lives of Sappho, Anacreon, and Aeschylus from their writings, a hazardous and unscientific procedure that nevertheless demonstrates the priority of his interests. Even works like Didymus' *On Demosthenes,* though containing biographical material, were not biography in the most complete sense. Most of these literary and philosophical biographers produced specialized accounts of their subjects emphasizing their peculiar contribution to their discipline.

The first fourth-century author to write rounded, balanced, and comprehensive biography was probably Aristoxenus of Tarentum. His subjects were chiefly philosophers, and comparison played a part in his treatment of them. He was, or became, a disciple of Pythagoras, and contrasted that philosopher's life and teachings with those of Socrates and Plato, not without malice toward the latter two. Their side was upheld by Clearchus, who wrote an encomium of Plato, but this was a reversion to the Isocratean model. Phaenias of Eresus completes the list of biographers from the first generation of Peripatetics, and his works on political men, especially tyrants, were used by Plutarch.

The organization of the great royal libraries at Pergamum and Alexandria in the third century involved the identification and classification of authors, in the process of which it was necessary to establish the scope, nature, and quality of their work. Perhaps influenced by Peripatetic teaching, librarians looked to the lives of their authors to supply the answers to their questions, and to this end assembled much of the biographical material that became available to men like Hermippus of Smyrna, who lived in Alexandria around 200 B.C. In a parallel manner to some of the historians of his time, Hermippus included melodramatic scenes in his bi-

ographies of the Seven Wise Men, Pythagoras, Gorgias, Isocrates, Aristotle, and their several followers, but not at the expense of really valuable factual detail, which placed later historians and biographers greatly in his debt. Two contemporaries of Hermippus, Antigonus of Carystus and Aristo of Ceos, were also interested mainly in philosophers, but little is known about these biographers. Living perhaps a generation later than these in Alexandria, Satyrus may have attempted to refine the genre by writing in dialogue form. His known works include lives of the tragedians Aeschylus, Sophocles, and Euripides.

In late republican Rome biography could afford publicity to ambitious politicians, some of whom even commissioned writers for this purpose. Such a writer was the historian Theophanes of Mytilene, who accompanied Pompey in his third campaign against Mithradates. His account of that war was published around the time of Pompey's return to Rome (62 B.C.) and was intended to influence opinion in his favor. This was hardly biography in the fullest sense, any more than were Sallust's monographs on Jugurtha and Catiline. But its laudatory character, indicated by the fact that Theophanes compared Pompey's exploits with those of Alexander the Great, set it in line with the earlier tradition of encomiastic biography, although it must have been less comprehensive than Xenophon's *Agesilaus* and was probably less rhetorical than Isocrates' *Euagoras.*

The most talented Greek writers of this period turned to history. One of these, Nicolaus of Damascus, was also very versatile, producing tragedies, comedies, and philosophical and scientific works in addition to a universal history in 144 books, now lost apart from a few excerpts. He found time as well for autobiography, and for a panegyrical life of Augustus, who was an almost exact contemporary. This work projects Hellenistic ideas of kingship into the Roman milieu and emphasizes dynastic continuity by relating Octavian's aims and actions to those of Julius Caesar, his adoptive father.

Plutarch

The next Greek biographer of note was indeed the greatest of them all, Plutarch of Chaeronea, who lived from about A.D. 45 to 120. The corpus of his surviving work is voluminous: forty-eight lives, of which forty-six are arranged in parallel pairs, and over two hundred other works on a wide range of subjects, but collectively called *Moralia*. The subjects of his *Parallel Lives* were remote from him in time, and his purpose was not to influence their reputations or even to honor their memory but to draw moral and philosophical lessons from their actions and words. He wrote for an intelligent readership, some of whom might be expected to entertain ambitions for high office, and it is against this background that the conception of parallel lives (which was not new) is to be understood. During Plutarch's lifetime many Greeks held important positions in the imperial administration. Earlier Greek writers had regularly reminded their fellow countrymen of past glories, and some had, in various ways, anticipated a Mediterranean empire that combined the best in Greek and Roman civilization. Nothing therefore seemed more natural and practical than to portray side by side the best men of both nations. Plutarch shows no partiality, nor is his characterization uncritical, passing over flaws and mistakes. The total picture of the subject's achievement is constructed from the main events of his life. A broadly chronological treatment serves Plutarch's moral purpose well in most cases, drawing the reader through a sequence of early promise and crowning success, often followed by decline brought about externally by the envy of others, or internally by moral corruption. When a particularly important characteristic emerges, chronology is temporarily suspended while it is illustrated further from other events in the subject's life. Choice of material is determined by its relevance to the central purpose of characterizing and exemplifying the *arete* (an untranslatable word that combines moral excellence with practical efficiency) of his subject. To this selective narrative is applied a critical morality that derives its principles ultimately from Aristotle's *Ethics*, according to which a virtue is a mean between two extremes. Prominent also are the ideas that the best of men's actions spring from reason rather than passion, and that consistency of policy is praiseworthy even if it results in failure (as in the case of Demosthenes), provided that the moral principles on which it has been based are sound. A philosophical rather than populist attitude is also to be noted in his views on the role of ambition. He concedes that a public figure must aim at honor and a good reputation, but solely for the practical reasons that without these he cannot perform great deeds, and that praise will actually encourage him to do good ("Agis" 2.1–2). Plutarch appears not to have believed that a man's character could change, but, like Tacitus in his portrayal of Tiberius' character, preferred to attribute apparent changes to the emergence of a man's true nature from deliberate concealment.

The number and variety of Plutarch's sources, and his own wide and easily diverted interests, make it hazardous to seek a rigid pattern in the composition of the *Parallel Lives*. Plutarch was at the mercy of his sources, but he was also himself much given, in the donnish Hellenistic writer's manner, to personalized digression on any matter that attracted him. Remembered or imagined conversations often figure in these digressions, and these serve only to relax further an already loose structure. But he is tireless in pursuit of his central aim, which is to exemplify the character of his subject and show how it affected his career. A man's public and private behavior from day to day might be more illustrative of his character, and might account more directly for his success or failure, than his policies or his diplomatic skills. Again, Plutarch is often our only historical source for popular opinions, which were very important, especially in democracies like Athens. Full of explanations of personal motives and of epithets describing those who held them, and freely interlarded with conjecture, illustrative stories, conversational tableaux, and personal judgments, the *Parallel Lives* are not history, as Plutarch himself well knew. However, a continuous narrative that merely traces the course of a man's military or political career does not provide its readers with insight into his soul. The biographer is the best portrayer of the whole man, whose weaknesses and failures are as instructive as his virtues and his successes.

Plutarch's *Parallel Lives* marks the summit and the end of innovation in ancient Greek biography. After Plutarch, Flavius Philostratus wrote *Lives of the Sophists,* probably early in the third century A.D. A little later Diogenes Laertius wrote biographical sketches of both earlier and later philosophers, which provide valuable source material in the absence of anything more thorough and professional. Porphyry of Tyre (A.D. 232/233–305) wrote copiously on philosophical subjects, and his works include lives of Pythagoras and Plotinus, the former as part of a longer history of philosophy. The list of biographers of the Second Sophistic is completed by Marinus and Damascius. The former wrote a laudatory biography of Proclus, the Neoplatonist philosopher of the fifth century A.D.; the latter wrote a life of Isidorus the historian and polymath of the sixth century A.D.

BIBLIOGRAPHY

SOURCES

Texts and Translations

There are Oxford Classical texts of Herodotus, Thucydides, and Xenophon, and texts in the Bibliotheca Teubneriana of Thucydides, Xenophon, Polybius, Diodorus, Dionysius, Arrian, and Plutarch. Other minor and fragmentary historical writings are collected in F. Jacoby, *Fragmente der griechischen Historiker* (1926–). Texts and English translations of all these authors, together with Appian and Dio Cassius, are published in the Loeb Classical Library. The Budé series has texts and French translations of all except Appian and Dionysius. The Penguin Classics translations of Herodotus, Thucydides, Xenophon, Arrian, and Plutarch contain valuable introductions, as does the reprint (1974) of E. S. Shuckburgh's translation of Polybius.

Commentaries

Arnold W. Gomme, Anthony Andrewes, and Kenneth J. Dover, *A Historical Commentary on Thucydides* (1944–1981); Walter W. How and Joseph Wells, *A Commentary on Herodotus* (1912); George E. Underhill, *A Commentary on the Hellenica of Xenophon* (1900); Frank W. Walbank, *A Historical Commentary on Polybius* (1957–1979).

STUDIES

Historiography

Norman Austin, *The Greek Historians* (1969); John B. Bury, *The Ancient Greek Historians* (1909;

repr. 1958); Moses I. Finley, *The Greek Historians* (1959); Michael Grant, *The Ancient Historians* (1970); Guy T. Griffith, "The Greek Historians," in Maurice Platnauer, ed., *Fifty Years (and Twelve) of Classical Scholarship* (1968); Albin Lesky, *A History of Greek Literature* (1966); Arnaldo D. Momigliano, *Studies in Historiography* (1966); Lionel Pearson, *Early Ionian Historians* (1939); Stephen Usher, *The Historians of Greece and Rome* (1969); Frank W. Walbank, *Speeches in Greek Historians* (1965).

Biography

Ivo Bruns, *Das literarische Porträt der Griechen* (1896; repr. 1961); Friedrich Leo, *Die griechisch-römische Biographie* (1901; repr. 1965); Georg Misch, *History of Autobiography* (1931), translation of the original (1907) German edition; Arnaldo D. Momigliano, *The Development of Greek Biography* (1971); Duane R. Stuart, *Epochs of Greek and Roman Biography* (1928).

Individual Historians

Charles W. Fornara, *Herodotus: An Interpretative Essay* (1971); Terrot R. Glover, *Herodotus,* (1924); Henry R. Immerwahr, *Form and Thought in Herodotus* (1966); John L. Myres, *Herodotus, Father of History* (1953).

Frank E. Adcock, *Thucydides and His History* (1963); Charles N. Cochrane, *Thucydides and the Science of History* (1929); Francis M. Cornford,

Thucydides Mythistoricus (1907); Kenneth J. Dover, *Thucydides* (1973); John H. Finley, *Thucydides* (1963), and *Three Essays on Thucydides* (1967); Virginia J. Hunter, *Thucydides, the Artful Reporter* (1973); Henry D. Westlake, *Individuals in Thucydides* (1968); Arthur G. Woodhead, *Thucydides on the Nature of Power* (1970).

John K. Anderson, *Xenophon* (1974); Edouard Delebecque, *Essai sur la vie de Xénophon* (1957); William E. Higgins, *Xenophon the Athenian* (1977).

Godfrey L. Barber, *The Historian Ephorus* (1935); Truesdell S. Brown, *Onesicritus* (1949), and *Timaeus of Tauromenium* (1958); Lionel Pearson, *The Lost Histories of Alexander the Great* (1960); Paul Pédech, *La méthode historique de Polybe* (1964); Frank W. Walbank, *Polybius* (1972).

Benjamin Farrington, *Diodorus Siculus: Universal Historian* (1937); Emilio Gabba, "La 'Storia di Roma arcaica' di Dionigi d'Alicarnasso," in *Aufstieg und Niedergang der römischen Welt* II.30.1 (1982), and *Appiano e la storia delle guerre civili* (1956); Fergus Millar, *A Study of Cassius Dio* (1964).

Individual Biographers

Reginald Barrow, *Plutarch and his Times* (1967); A. John Gossage, "Plutarch," in Thomas A. Dorey, ed., *Latin Biography* (1967); Christopher P. Jones, *Plutarch and Rome* (1971); Donald A. Russell, *Plutarch* (1973); Alan E. Wardman, *Plutarch's Lives* (1974).

Roman Historiography and Biography

RONALD MELLOR

To be ignorant of what has happened before your birth is to remain always a child. For what is the meaning of a man's life unless it is intertwined with that of our ancestors by history?
(Cicero, *Orator* 120)

THE ROMANS' DEVOTION to their ancestral and national past is manifest in their literature and art, their political and legal institutions, their religion and legends, their festivals and their funeral celebrations. They were proud of their traditions, and what had begun as family memories became over the centuries a collective national mystique—to be tended as assiduously as the Vestal Virgins tended the communal hearth. Cicero's comments are an important reminder that for the Romans the past was a validation of their present greatness: it had to be preserved to give meaning to the present.

Heroic legends of Rome's past were transmitted from oral traditions into written epic poems, and the same stories appeared later as prose history and biography. But for the Romans, history, biography, and autobiography were quite distinct literary genres that were written to serve different purposes. We should examine separately how each form was used by the Romans to preserve the memory of the past.

HISTORIOGRAPHY AT ROME

Cicero said that history must be both useful and moral: useful in keeping the public man aware of precedents in legislation, foreign policy, and military affairs; moral in providing models of conduct from Rome's past to help its leaders act virtuously in the public interest. History, by linking the present with the past, should illuminate the contemporary state of society and provide both moral and practical guidance. A Roman was encouraged to emulate the personal and civic virtues of his ancestors at the family hearth, in the Forum, or on the battlefield. This closely intertwined code of public and private conduct (*mos maiorum*) formed the core of moral and political education at Rome.

Thus Roman historical writing must do more than tell pleasant stories; it must make moral judgments. The Romans used history to discuss the moral dimension of political questions while the Greeks used philosophy. Thus the problem of Rome's decline was regarded as a moral question by Sallust, by Tacitus, and even by Edward Gibbon in the eighteenth century. Such historians do not merely ask what occurred and how, but most importantly why certain events came about.

History at Rome was written mostly by senators for senators: this explains its narrow focus on political conduct. As a result, it was less interesting to the general public, and schoolteachers preferred to find moral exempla in poetry, biographies, or collections of anecdotes. But if the general public was indifferent to historiography, senatorial historians cared little, since their work was an extension of political life and was aimed at those with political power in the Roman state.

HISTORIOGRAPHY IN THE ROMAN REPUBLIC

In historical writing as in so much else, the Romans looked to the Greeks for models. But equally important were indigenous traditions which shaped the form and subject matter of Roman historiography for centuries. Though no Roman wrote historical prose before the end of the third century B.C., the Romans had long preserved the real or imagined achievements of their ancestors. To keep the memory of famous forebears before the young, encomia were said to have been pronounced at dinners and wax masks (*imagines*) of ancestors were kept for display in funeral processions. Funeral addresses, which linked the achievements of the recently deceased with the exploits of his ancestors across the centuries, were passed orally from generation to generation with embellishments and distortions. However untrustworthy, these encomia are an early expression of the Roman desire to illuminate and guide the present through the past.

Other family records were kept in written form. Roman magistrates kept the accounts of their tenure in office among private documents in their homes. Epitaphs on placards might also be carried beside the masks at family funerals. These epitaphs, best known from the group found in the tomb of the Scipios, contained details of careers in public life.

Besides these family records, the Romans preserved a variety of public documents. The Twelve Tables were set up in the Forum, and the Romans had long displayed treaties. Thus there is no reason to doubt Polybius' report that he saw on a bronze tablet the treaty with Carthage from *ca.* 500 B.C. Decrees of the senate were kept in the treasury (*aerarium*) in the temple of Saturn, and resolutions of the Plebeian Assembly were preserved in the temple of Ceres. The most important of the early records were the *annales maximi*. These annual lists, kept by the *pontifex maximus* (chief priest), who gave them his title, were initially inscribed on white notice boards. They recorded the consuls, military triumphs, religious prodigies, and other important events of the year. Cato the Elder derided the *annales* as merely recording eclipses, the price of grain, and other trivia; but consular names alone, if accurate, could be of enormous use in establishing a chronological framework. Although the accuracy of the version published in the 120s is difficult to ascertain, the names were probably reasonably reliable for the third and second centuries, questionable for the fourth century, and fanciful for any earlier period, since all such records would have been destroyed by the Gallic sack of Rome about 390 B.C.

By 265 B.C., Rome had control of the entire Italian peninsula and cultural life came increasingly under the influence of the Greek cities of southern Italy. The earliest surviving fragments of Latin poetry are from a translation of Homer's *Odyssey* into Latin by Livius Andronicus, a Greek slave captured at Tarentum. The Romans used Greek models for history as well, but drew less on Herodotus and Thucydides than on writers of the Hellenistic age. Some Hellenistic historians emphasized the dramatic and rhetorical aspects of historical writing that elicited an emotional response from their readers, but Polybius, much of whose history of Rome's conquest of the Mediterranean does survive, harshly criticizes this "pathetic history" and prefers an analytical, pragmatic history written for political leaders.

But even with Greek models available, the Roman historiographical tradition developed differently. Greek historical writing had begun with studies of the lands and customs of different peoples, and these concerns remained central. Both travel and research were important elements in the Greek historian's preparation for writing his book. There was a lack of parochialism that allowed Greek historians to exhibit a Homeric sympathy for both sides in a conflict, which can be seen in the accounts of the Persian and Peloponnesian wars by Herodotus and Thucydides, respectively.

From its very beginnings Roman historical writing was narrower in scope and less tolerant in its attitudes. Roman historians began with an interest in the Roman state and the political life of the community. In Rome's desire to rival the ancestry of the Greeks, there developed a chauvinistic historiography whose ethnocentrism left little sympathy for Rome's opponents. And this polemical, partisan, moralizing strain, first used by historians against Rome's enemies, was increasingly deployed against one faction or another in the struggles in Roman political life.

As in Greece, the earliest Romans to write about Rome's past were epic poets, though only fragments of their works survive. Gnaeus Naevius (270–201 B.C.) did reproduce certain Homeric elements: even though he had served in the First Punic War he portrays gods on its battlefields. But his polemical politics are far from Homeric and his fierce attacks on the aristocratic Caecilii Metelli family caused Naevius to end his life in prison. His successor Quintus Ennius (239–169 B.C.) was far more laudatory of Rome's preeminent families in his account of the Second Punic War in his *Annales,* and he became closely linked with the circle of hellenizing writers associated with the Scipios. Though a poet and a dramatist, Ennius emphasized national pride and the moral power of Rome and thus greatly influenced later prose historiography and historical epics. Vergil's *Aeneid* may hardly seem historical to us, but Augustus was praised for demonstrating his concern with Rome's "history" by saving the manuscript from the flames. From Ennius, Vergil, and Lucan's *Civil War* (*Pharsalia*) many Romans learned their national history.

The first Roman to write prose history was the senator Quintus Fabius Pictor (late third century B.C.) who wrote in Greek an account of Rome's early history. There was as yet little literary prose in Latin, and the use of Greek was quite normal in the wider context of Hellenistic civilization: Syrians, Egyptians, Babylonians, Jews, and Carthaginians had begun to use Greek for literary works and philosophical discourse. Writing soon after the Hannibalic War, Fabius wished to explain Roman policy and values to the Greek world in the form of a history from Rome's foundation to the First Punic War (264–241 B.C.). With few native records to draw upon, Fabius stitches together Greek accounts of Rome's early history and parades Roman greatness with an emphasis on moral superiority. Few fragments survive, but Polybius' use of Fabius allows us to discern his moralizing, nationalistic attitudes: praise for the wisdom of the senate and, of course, the Fabian family, together with criticism of the stupidity of the popular assembly.

For two generations Fabius' successors continued to write what Cicero called *Graeci annales.* It was the censor Marcus Porcius Cato (234–149 B.C.) who first wrote history in Latin. The work survives only in fragments, quoted verbatim by later authors interested in Cato's archaic Latin. The *Origins* (*Origines*) traced in seven books Rome's history from the beginning down to 149, with particular attention to the growing unification of Italy. Although Cato carefully fostered his reputation as a conservative who despised corrupting foreign influences, his history displays many characteristics of Greek historiography: interest in the geography and customs of Italy, which had already been recorded by the Sicilian Greek Timaeus, and the inclusion of speeches. He relied on Greek sources for the early books and, after a skimpy account of the early and middle republic, for which the sources were sparse, his treatment greatly expands in his own lifetime. A notable characteristic is Cato's partisan position in support of the plebeians. He not only rejects the ideology of the Scipios but also avoids mentioning the names of consuls. He views the Roman people as sovereign, and resents the glory that Fabius, Ennius, and even the *annales maximi* attached to individual Roman families. His disdain for personal aggrandizement did not, however, restrain him from including his own speeches in the later books. Cato's purpose in writing his history was to instruct Rome's future leaders both in pragmatic politics and, especially, in the moral standards of their ancestors, which needed to be retained to combat the corruption of increasing hellenization. The last three books dealing with Cato's own political career begin the tradition of political autobiography at Rome and set a clear precedent for the partisan nature of later Roman political history.

Between Cato and Sallust a century later there survive only fragments of those annalistic historians derided both now and in antiquity. With the pontifical annals as a model, these historians provided a year-by-year account of the major officials and important events, but such a structure obviously precluded treatment of longer-term political, social, or economic tendencies. They invented episodes to embellish bare names and dates, and Gnaeus Gellius wrote a history of Rome down to at least 146 B.C., including fifteen books on the period before 389 B.C., of which almost nothing could have been known. The sparse record of the distant past was also expanded by the anachronistic treatment of legal and constitutional questions. Once again, the political and ideological controversies of contemporary Rome were imposed upon the shadowy past to create a nationalistic pseudohistory. There were occasional exceptions: Lucius Coelius Antipater actually checked documentary sources for his history of the Hannibalic Wars, and Sempronius Asellio, who ambitiously wished to imitate Polybius, scorned *annales* as mere records and attempted in his own *historiae* to explain why events took place. Little remains of their work, though there is ample evidence that the annalists did more than recount bare facts. During the political struggles of the first century B.C. they turned with equal invention to contemporary history and devised fictions to attack or defend the Gracchi, to praise or damn Sulla. Valerius Antias, who was used by later historians, went so far as to invent documents. This corpus of untrustworthy material was all that historiography had achieved by the end of the republic. Atticus' *Liber Annalis* and Cornelius Nepos' *Chronicles* (*Chronica*) provided chronologies to facilitate the work of historians and orators, and Caesar had written his autobiographical *Commentaries* (*Commentarii*), but history did not yet exist as a literary genre.

The major intellectual and literary figure of the late republic, Marcus Tullius Cicero (106–43 B.C.), speculated on the theory of history in his literary and philosophical essays. He distinguished history from poetry by its devotion to truth, yet he believed literary ability to be absolutely essential and had only contempt for the inept products of the annalists. Rhetorical training was fundamental if the historian was to make his work persuasive and affect future political life, which Cicero believed should be his goal. Here, as so often in his work, Cicero explores the link between oratory and political action, since in republican Rome the most effective orators were in fact at the center of the political stage. Although Cicero defined the genre of moral historiography at Rome and was Rome's greatest historical theorist, his political interests and perhaps a fear of increasing his already large number of enemies kept him (as Cornelius Nepos lamented) from doing for history what he had done for oratory and philosophy: creating a Latin genre based on Greek achievements, but with a uniquely Roman style and form.

SALLUST

Gaius Sallustius Crispus (86–35 B.C.) was born into a municipal Sabine family that provided him with a good Greek and Latin education. He rose to the tribunate before being expelled from the senate for immorality in 50 B.C. In the following year he was one of Caesar's commanders in the civil war and later served as praetor. In 46 he was appointed the first governor of Africa Nova (Numidia). Charged with financial corruption, he escaped conviction only by bribing Caesar himself. In bitterness, he withdrew from public life to his Roman villa with its famous lavish gardens, there to chronicle the decline of Roman morality.

His first monograph, *The Conspiracy of Catiline,* places the rebellion of 63 B.C. in the context of the economic and social dislocations that resulted from the settlement of Sulla's veterans throughout Italy. In *The*

Jugurthine War Sallust emphasizes the avarice and corruption of the Roman nobility as the backdrop to the war. The work is a moral critique embellished with speeches and exotic descriptions of North Africa. Although his chronology is sometimes weak, Sallust employed a novelist's skill in dramatizing scenes and presenting vivid portraits of historical personalities. He presents the collapse of old Roman virtue in a state where political faction was merely a mask for personal ambition and greed. The crisis of the Roman Republic was for Sallust a moral crisis in which the political instability resulted from the abandonment of traditional values.

Sallust created literary historiography at Rome, but it was far from a Ciceronian ideal. Just as he opposed Cicero's politics, so Sallust also wrote in a style that Cicero would have abhorred. "Hard and dry," the Ciceronian Livy called him, and Quintilian, who regarded Sallust as the "Roman Thucydides," counseled young rhetoricians not to imitate his style. Sallust favored Cato's archaic style and brought to it an abhorrence of balance and harmony. Ciceronian periods were thought to disguise political reality; Sallust's epigrammatic and dense prose followed his model Thucydides in trying to unmask it.

Sallust died *ca.* 35 B.C., and his incomplete *Histories* cover the period from 78 to 67. Only fragments survive, usually speeches or letters quoted in later authors. Sallust soon became a great favorite whose reputation was surpassed only by that of Vergil and Cicero. Martial called him the greatest Roman historian, but it was Tacitus who paid him the highest compliment of imitating both his biting style and his bleak moral vision. Augustine and other Christian writers found his views congenial, and he was much quoted and copied in medieval monasteries.

The blatant hypocrisy and overt bias of Sallust pushed him out of favor with nineteenth-century scholars. But his reputation has risen again as more scholars have come to approve of his general conception of the late republic. Despite factual inaccuracy, chronological confusions, and partisan invective, Sallust's picture of social and economic changes affecting the moral fabric of the Roman ruling class is a cogent historical reconstruction that demands serious attention and respect.

LIVY

Roman historians were typically men of wide military and political experience who held high public office and served in the senate. Titus Livius (ca. 59 B.C.–A.D. 17) is the outstanding exception. Born in Patavium (Padua) in Cisalpine Gaul (north Italy), he received excellent rhetorical training, although he never attained that fluency in Greek which characterized nearly all members of the Roman intellectual elite. Since Livy held no public posts, fought no wars, and seemingly had traveled little, his history depends almost totally on what he learned from books.

Livy is a natural conservative whose work so exudes a nostalgic, antiquarian republicanism that his friend and patron Augustus rightly chided him as a "Pompeian." Like Sallust, Livy saw Rome's decline as a moral problem, though his political attitudes were quite the reverse of his predecessor: anti-Gracchan, pro-Sullan, and unsympathetic to Julius Caesar. Livy was a Ciceronian in his approach to politics as well as in style. Thus he prudently refrained from publishing his last twenty-two books, covering the period 43 through 9 B.C., until after the death of Augustus. He traces Rome's predestined rise to world domination before turning to the bitter story of the destruction of the republican political system. If not as pessimistic as Sallust or Tacitus, Livy nonetheless waxes melancholic at the cost that imperial success had exacted of the Roman people: civil war, social disorder, and finally monarchy.

Livy wrote his *History of Rome* (*Ab Urbe Condita*) on an enormous scale: 142 books covered the foundation of the city to 9 B.C. The 35 books that survive are from the first third of the work, so that the last surviving book (45) only comes down to 167 B.C. What survives necessarily glorifies Rome: the expulsion of the Etruscan kings; the conquest of the Italian peoples; Hannibal's invasion of Italy in the Second Punic War (218–201 B.C.) and his eventual defeat by Scipio Africanus Major; and Rome's conquest of Greece, Macedonia, and Asia Minor. But the ancient book-by-book summaries (*Periochae*) provide a general idea of Livy's interests and attitudes toward the late republic. There he expresses his pessimism at the breakdown of traditional Roman institutions and values during the last century of the republic, a pessimism that perhaps grew deeper after the civil wars resulted in the permanent establishment of a monarchy.

Ancient critics praised Livy's clarity of style and compared the richness and color of his language to poetry. He excels in writing exciting narratives and in depicting the broad sweep of events with drama and psychological insight. Although many of his portraits resort to rhetorical stereotypes, leading figures such as Scipio, Cato the Elder, and Hannibal are better developed, with speeches well adapted to their characters. But Livy had greater difficulty imposing an overall structure on the dramatic episodes, explaining cause and effect, and breaking out of the straitjacket of annalistic structure.

Even in antiquity Livy's accuracy was impugned. Though we may smile at the emperor Caligula's desire to burn the history as "verbose and careless," Quintilian's comment that Livy's work was more beautiful than truthful is harsh coming from a critic who so much prized style over content. Livy disdained to go even to the Capitol to consult a document, much less travel in Italy or beyond to examine inscriptions or visit battle sites. He makes statements that were confuted by buildings visible in Rome in his own day, and he did not use the work of antiquarian researchers such as Varro who would have kept him from numerous anachronisms. He did not regard inscriptions or monuments as more reliable than the historical accounts he preferred. Livy did read widely among the historians but he lacked the critical ability to correct conflicts in his sources. His version, including pieces of information taken from contradictory sources, is sometimes utterly confused, and tends to retain patriotic annalistic inventions while concealing Roman brutality. He is honest but uncritical, warning his readers of the unreliability of the legends of earliest Rome while accepting incredible inventions from much later periods. Yet he personally did not invent fictions and he used some excellent sources, such as Polybius. If Livy does not satisfy our own standards of historiography, it must be said that he took the flawed tradition of annalistic historiography and improved it enormously.

Livy was severely criticized by the pragmatic historians of nineteenth-century Germany, but his reputation stands far higher now. If he was unable to impose a vision on his sprawling subject, his comprehensive treatment has preserved much material that would otherwise have perished: not only the names of officials, but details of Roman religion and Roman law. And if the early books are filled with legend, archaeology has confirmed certain aspects of his story, such as the Etruscan urbanization of the Forum. If some such details had survived until the Augustan Age, through Greek writers, oral tradition, or folk memory, Livy did a great service in preserving them. But Livy's importance has been based on his telling stories as exempla of republican values. From the Renaissance to the French Revolution, Livy's tales of Lucretia's virtue in the face of tyranny, of Brutus killing Tarquin and establishing the Roman Republic, and of the Horatii fighting to defend their fatherland have done much to stimulate poets and painters, and to nourish dreams of liberty.

MINOR IMPERIAL HISTORIANS

No Augustan historian except Livy has survived, and the loss of Gaius Asinius Pollio (76 B.C.–A.D. 5) is to be particularly regretted. This general of both Caesar and Antony wrote an eyewitness history of the civil war beginning with the First Triumvirate in 60 B.C. and culminating at Philippi (42 B.C.). His work was used by Livy, Suetonius, and Plutarch, as well as quoted by the elder Seneca. We see the dyspeptic old soldier in his criticism of his commander Caesar's inaccuracy, his sneers at Livy's provincialism (*Patavinitas*) and Sallust's archaisms, and his continuing hostility to Cicero so many years after his death.

The Gaul Pompeius Trogus wrote one of the few Latin attempts at universal history. His *Historiae Philippicae*, named after their central feature, the Macedonian empire established by Philip II, survives only in Justin's third-century abridgement. This work, in which Trogus avoided the traditional practice of including speeches, remains a useful source for certain badly documented periods in Hellenistic history. Under Augustus the highly rhetorical Aulus Cremutius Cordus read publicly from his history of the civil war, but he later came to grief when the creatures of Tiberius' minister, Sejanus, accused him of praising Caesar's assassins, Brutus and Cassius.

The summary history of Velleius Paterculus does survive: two books from the fall of Troy down to A.D. 31. Velleius was a child of the camps and his blind loyalty to Tiberius (and Sejanus) has caused his history to be dismissed as mere propaganda. Expanding its scope as it reaches his own time with adulatory accounts of Caesar, Augustus, and Tiberius, he unashamedly presents Tiberius' self-imposed exile in Rhodes (6 B.C.–2 A.D.) as a proconsulship. But the slavish devotion seems sincere, and reflects the popularity Tiberius enjoyed in Italy and the provinces more accurately than such senatorial sources as Tacitus. This modest work, though ill-served by its inept rhetorical approach, treats such interesting topics as provincialization, colonization, and cultural history (Greek poetry and drama), which are ignored in the relentlessly political senatorial histories.

Valerius Maximus' *Memorable Deeds and Sayings* (*Facta et Dicta Memorabilia*) is not a history but a compilation of almost a thousand anecdotes classified under such topics as "religion" and "Roman virtues." Writing under Tiberius, Valerius particularly relied on Cicero, Livy, and Nepos for these exempla. He made clear that his work was intended as a shortcut to avoid the onerous task of reading entire historical works. Used by orators as Bartlett's *Quotations* has been used in more recent times, this compendium attained great popularity in the Middle Ages and survives in more Renaissance manuscripts than does any other ancient work. This pragmatic, and sanitized, view of historical writings gave rise to the epitomizers and excerpters of the later empire and the Byzantine era, through whom long selections or summaries of lost ancient historians have been preserved. No other Julio-Claudian or Flavian histories survive. Claudius wrote eight books on the Carthaginians and twenty on the Etruscans in addition to his Roman history. Servilius Nonianus and Aufidius Bassus are favorably cited by Quintilian, while Fabius Rusticus and Cluvius Rufus were sources for Tacitus. But the works are completely lost and were not perhaps of high quality. Romans believed that political conditions were unfavorable to history, while the younger Pliny pointed out that in a vicious age there is more to blame than praise. This did not deter his friend Tacitus, but the latter wrote his history only after the fall of Domitian and the establishment of a new, more liberal regime.

TACITUS

Born in southern Gaul, Cornelius Tacitus (A.D. 55–*ca.* 120) made an excellent marriage to the daughter of the Gallic senator Julius Agricola. Tacitus' political career advanced rapidly until he held the praetorship in A.D. 88. He then withdrew from Rome for five years and on his return preferred his researches to public life until the assassination of Domitian in 96. He was consul in 97 and was on good terms with the emperors Nerva and Trajan.

Tacitus' strong political views were formed in the terrible years of Domitian, and it is Domitian that we find projected back into the monstrous portrait of Tiberius. Some senators groveled before the tyrant while others publicly opposed the regime and were executed. Tacitus chose to withdraw into voluntary exile and study and to yearn nostalgically for the *libertas* of the republic. Thus his writings display bitter resentment mixed with a certain defensiveness toward the senatorial martyrs. His ambivalence toward the principate is clear and mingled with self-justification. Thus he attacks the tyrants but finds the Stoic opposition too inflexible: he prefers passivity to the danger of civil war. Tacitus' work shows political ideals and a sensitive conscience that he cannot easily reconcile with political reality.

In his early *Dialogue on Orators* Tacitus explores the role of oratory in the empire and the need to connect literature with political reality. To do this, Tacitus said, one must write history. In 98 he published two monographs: the biography of Agricola and an essay on Germany. In the *Germania,* Tacitus expands the geographical and ethnographic digression, used by Cato and Sallust, into a monograph. He discusses the religious, social, and political life of the Germans and shows a certain admiration for their high moral standards. The *Agricola* is a far more personal work containing elements of family eulogy and ethnography, all shot through with Tacitus' defensive justification of Agricola's passive behavior under Domitian.

But Tacitus' masterpiece and the greatest achievement of Roman historiography is his history of the empire from the death of Augustus to the death of Domitian. He first wrote twelve books covering the period from the civil wars of 69 to 96. Of these, which we call the *Histories,* only four books and a fragment of the fifth survive. They cover only the period from Nero's death in 68 to the suppression of the Jews in 70—the most detailed extant treatment of a period in ancient historiography. Tacitus then wrote eighteen books (*Annals*) on the Julio-Claudians. The first six books covering the reign of Tiberius survive, though there is only a brief fragment of Book Five, together with books eleven through sixteen, which cover the latter part of Claudius' reign and much of the reign of Nero. Although these books ostensibly retain the annalistic structure and begin each year with the names of the consuls, Tacitus has transformed the genre and skillfully combined biography, ethnography, and rhetorical elements in the service of history.

Tacitus was not a mere storyteller; he wrote history to pass moral and political judgments on the past and thereby affect the future. Since no autocrat can control the future, his fear of future condemnation should restrain his present cruelties. Therefore Tacitus creates one of the most compelling psychological portraits of tyranny in historical literature. Amidst all the carnage and intrigue, the historian holds before us models of dignity, liberty, and personal courage. Economic and sociological explanations hold no interest for Tacitus, nor do the far-off provinces. He is not writing a history of the empire, but of political life and the loss of liberty. In that he has no peer.

Although Tacitus professes to write "without anger or favor," he openly passes personal judgments. Yet even where his prejudice is clear, as when he writes on the Jews, he does try to ascertain the truth. He is skeptical of his sources, so his facts are usually quite accurate. But he will often weave facts into a misleading picture. He refers to a "continuous slaughter" as a result of treason trials at the court of Tiberius and describes several executions and enforced suicides. But there were only a few dozen such executions—hardly as shocking (in a reign of twenty-three years) as Tacitus would have us believe and mild by comparison with modern despots. Yet here and elsewhere Tacitus can distort without once falsifying the facts.

Tacitus took the intense, asymmetrical style of Sallust and honed it to a knife-edge. His words analyze and reveal, they do not conceal. Though he draws on such poets as Vergil and Lucan, the biting wit and devastating epigram are uniquely Tacitean. The style becomes elaborate where the argument is questionable, but the spare aphorisms that often end chapters—perhaps, as with Jane Austen, the result of writing for being read aloud—demonstrate a confidence in his literary art.

His rhetorical training is obvious throughout the historical works. Characterizations of tyrants, victims, and martyrs often rely on descriptions of type-characters known from school exercises. But Tacitus goes far beyond this in his great, subtle portraits of Nero and Tiberius as well as the wonderful vignettes scattered through the books: Petronius, Galba, Messalina, and Agrippina. That his speeches are persuasive is clear when we compare his version of Claudius' speech on the Gallic senators to the original preserved on a bronze tablet: Tacitus' version is far more effective.

Tacitus is weak on geography, the provinces, and military and legal history. His focus is narrow: the imperial court. Yet his subject is broad. He is interested not only in what has been done and said (*facta et dicta*) but also in the effects of words and deeds on the minds and characters of the rulers and the ruled. Gibbon regarded Tacitus as the supreme "philosophical historian" and his histories examine psychological and political issues that are still very much with us.

LATER IMPERIAL HISTORY

Tacitus marked the end of serious historical writing at Rome for 250 years. As the Roman creative spirit dried up in other intellectual and literary fields, so it did in history. Serious history was regarded as too long and too complex, so the age turned to abridgments and summaries. In the second century P. Annius Florus wrote an admiring panegyric of Roman history that depended heavily on Livy. Florus urged his readers to employ his brief summary the way travelers use a pocket map. A century later Justin alternately abridged and summarized Pompeius Trogus. He calls this work a collection of choice "flowers" and candidly tells his readers that he has omitted all that is unpleasant to know or unnecessary to imitate.

Important work was being done in Roman history during the second and third centuries, but it was written in Greek. Appian of Alexandria, Cassius Dio of Bithynia who was twice consul, and the Syrian Herodian all wrote books on Roman history far more significant than anything being written in Latin. In the fourth century Eutropius and Festus wrote abbreviated histories of Rome. In fifteen printed pages Festus covers the period from Rome's foundation to his own time so superficially that the Punic Wars are described with the simplistic phrase "three times Africa revolted."

Ammianus

A Greek from Syrian Antioch, Ammianus Marcellinus (A.D. 330–ca. 395) had excellent literary and rhetorical training in Greek and Latin before joining the Roman army. He served in Julian's army in Gaul and Germany before being transferred to the Persian front where he served in Julian's final ill-fated expedition in 363. After some years of travel, Ammianus settled in Rome about 378 and began to write history. His work is a continuation of Tacitus, beginning in A.D. 96 and concluding with the battle of Adrianople in 378. Of the thirty-one books, the final eighteen survive (14–31); they cover the years 353 to 378—a quarter century of very detailed contemporary history.

The history is a masterpiece. Gibbon called Ammianus his "accurate and faithful guide." And so he is. His breadth of interest is extraordinary: he surveys not only the political and diplomatic history of his time but, rare in any ancient historian, also the administration and the bureaucracy. His eastern origin gave him an interest in peoples throughout the empire, and his learned digressions on Thrace or Persia were both sensible and sympathetic. His attention to detail is impressive: wherever the work can be checked against independent Greek, Latin, or Syriac sources, Ammianus is confirmed.

Ammianus was personally devoted to Julian and the apostate became the hero of his history. Though a pagan, Ammianus supported religious toleration and believed the senate and the emperors could work together if the emperors respected traditional institutions. In this, as in much else, Ammianus harks back to the early empire, and echoes of Tacitus abound in his work.

His rhetorical training is much in evidence, but we find little of the rhetorical distortion of earlier historians. There are in fact very few speeches; Ammianus prefers to characterize by anecdote. The breadth of Ammianus' reading was vast, and his history is filled with allusions to Greek and Latin literature. And this is not schoolbook learning. Ammianus was deeply imbued with the culture and values of an earlier time, and his scathing judgments on many of his contemporaries show his profound dissatisfaction with the philistine attitudes of the nobility of his own day. After two centuries of barrenness in Latin literature, the work of this Syrian Greek formed part of a final florescence of pagan Latin letters. He was the last of the great Roman historians and, one might well add, the last outstanding pagan writer of classical antiquity.

HISTORICAL METHOD

Research and Accuracy

Little evidence for the earliest period of Roman history was available for the later historian. But during the course of the republic an increasing documentary record was preserved in addition to oral and family traditions. Even without a state record office, treaties, laws, and decrees of the senate were often preserved in addition to the pontifical annals that were open to senators. Magisterial state records, including the results of the census, were sometimes retained in family archives. Sulla constructed the enormous public record office (*tabularium*),

which still stands above the Forum at the foot of the Capitoline. Julius Caesar had the minutes of the senate recorded, and these *Acta Senatus,* together with the reports of returning governors and generals, ensured that the history of the entire Roman world was documented in archives at Rome. Yet most Roman historians had limited interest in documentary material and preferred to gather material from the works of other historians.

The practice of history was not thought to be research; it was, rather, an act of literary composition. Quintilian regarded research as mere pedantry. Unlike the Greeks, Roman historians never discussed research in their prefaces: they expected to rearrange data already available. Most Roman historians used only a single source for a specific section of their work, though other historians who disagreed with the principal source are sometimes patched in (not unlike the work of the contemporary student who paraphrases an encyclopedia article while adding a few quotations or facts from other books). The author then recasts the material (including speeches and even documents) into his own prose. Of course the greatest historians may impress their conception and style on the material so effectively as to change it radically, but the fact remains that there was little genuine research. History was, in most cases, written from other books.

Since Roman historians did so little research with primary evidence, how accurate are they? In his essays Cicero criticizes deceptive family records and says the first law of history is "that an author must not dare to tell anything but the truth. And the second that he must make bold to tell the whole truth" (*On Oratory* [*De Oratore*] 2.15.62). This is familiar ground until that same Cicero, in a private letter to his historian friend Lucius Lucceius, asks him to "celebrate my exploits with even more enthusiasm than you perhaps feel, and in this case disregard the principles of history. . . . Indulge your affection for me a trifle more even than strict truth would allow" (*Letters to Friends* 5.12). The gap between high-minded theory and actual practice was considerable.

Of all ancient historians, only Thucydides and Polybius had a passion for accuracy in a modern sense. Other Greek and Roman historians also wished to avoid untruths, but they lacked the critical skills to evaluate their evidence properly and they made no serious distinction between primary and secondary sources. They were certainly eager to reject divine explanations in favor of human ones, but there as elsewhere their fundamental criterion was verisimilitude. As teachers of rhetoric emphasized the importance of probability in constructing a persuasive argument, so this became the basis of historical argument as well. As long as there was no blatant improbability and no obvious bias, a Roman historian would accept his source at face value. That the source contained information that could not possibly be based on knowledge or verified is irrelevant: Livy recounts with aplomb events that had occurred seven centuries earlier. For the Romans the important issues were moral questions and not matters of names and dates. Quintilian says that Greek historians were permitted quasi-poetic license. This surely applies equally at Rome where historians attempted to conceal that the Gauls actually captured the city around 390 B.C. Cicero arbitrarily chose one of several versions of the death of Coriolanus. Even Tacitus, through his language, dramatic construction, and use of innuendo, created a powerful picture quite at variance with the facts that he accurately reported. To the Roman, Tacitus was writing moral history to address the larger truths of tyranny and political freedom. Concern with minor details was for a pedantic antiquarian, not a historian.

Literary Artistry

The Roman historian was primarily a literary artist. He exercised great care over Latin prose, for the style itself revealed the author's attitudes. Livy's richness is well suited to a master storyteller, but Sallust and Tacitus use a leaner, harsher, and more intense Latin to uncover political realities. By the early second century, Pliny the Younger saw history as harsh and dry while oratory was bland and pleasant. As the panegyrist of the emperor Trajan, he was well placed to know. Livy presented a genial face in recounting the heroic exploits of Rome's past, but contemporary political history required epigrams and biting wit more in keeping with our modern conception of a political essayist.

Hellenistic historians wished above all to entertain. This often took the form, as in the tabloid press or the Gothic novel, of shock and horror which induced a most pleasurable pity. They brought poetic devices into their histories, which Lucian condemned as artificial beauty, like dressing an athlete to look like a harlot. Surviving Roman historians can hardly be so described, but there is ample evidence that these values lay not far below the surface, as when three historians cast lots whether to write an account of the Social War in Greek or Latin, prose or poetry (Plutarch, *Parallel Lives,* "Lucullus" 1). Quintilian described history as "a poem in prose" and Cicero called the historian an "embellisher of events" (*exornator rerum*) who would bring pleasure by depicting changes of fortune. But these are rhetoricians with an outsider's view of history, and Cicero never found a historian willing to write his authorized version of the Catilinarian conspiracy. The goal of a Tacitus or an Ammianus is not to forgo literary techniques in the interest of accuracy, but to deploy his considerable stylistic and rhetorical skills to present historical truth more convincingly.

By the first century B.C. Roman education had become rhetorical education, and all the great Roman historians display this rhetorical training. The use of rhetoric in their histories goes far beyond the construction of speeches to the use of language, the structure of argument, and the organization of episodes. The universally known rhetorical character types provided historians with a shorthand method of characterization. Likewise, historians could characterize by juxtaposition so that Tacitus makes Nero and his mother Agrippina resemble Tiberius and Livia, and Sallust's Catiline lies behind Tacitus' portrait of Sejanus. These portraits, together with certain formulaic scenes (death scenes, battles, trials) appealed to the reader's own rhetorical training and thus enriched the texture of the historical narrative.

Cicero says that history consists of events and speeches, and speeches were indeed used by virtually every Roman historian as they had been by their Greek predecessors. For the early republic there could have been no evidence; thus the reported speeches are wholly fictitious, although certain themes may have been transmitted through Rome's very tenacious oral tradition. Even such conventionalized speeches as those delivered by generals before battle have a certain psychological truth, since speeches actually delivered on such occasions consisted of traditional formulas. In Livy's account of Rome's conquest of the East, his speeches can be checked against the Greek versions in Polybius, who was a contemporary of those events. At times Livy reliably retained the substance of the speech, but sometimes he created both the occasion and the speech out of whole cloth, preferring to follow an untrustworthy annalistic account. It is Tacitus who provides the only opportunity to check a literary speech against the text as

delivered. A bronze tablet has fortunately preserved Claudius' speech in A.D. 48 on the admission of Gauls to the senate. It is clear that Tacitus' version (*Annals* 11.24) preserved the substance while immeasurably improving its rhetorical force.

Historians regarded speeches as a method of analysis by which the motives of a character could be made explicit. A modern historian delivers analytical judgments in his own voice, but ancient historians preferred the dramatic and rhetorical mask of a speech. In Athens or republican Rome, a speech was a political act and Sallust so records Caesar's and Cato's proposals for the Catilinarian conspirators. But the imperial historians realized that imperial autocracy had reduced speeches to occasions for display rather than for genuine persuasion. In an autocracy, speeches, indeed words in general, are used to disguise and conceal rather than to reveal the truth. Thus Tacitus and Ammianus used speeches far less frequently and then only where a speech was actually delivered.

The use of dramatic elements goes back to the origins of ancient historiography when Herodotus divided his work into dramatic episodes, but it was the Hellenistic historians who vastly expanded the use of drama and passed these traditions on to Rome. Since history, like tragedy, intended to recount the deeds of great men (real or mythic), there is a similar preference for personalities and the human element. Livy's account of the sack of Alba Longa paints an almost cinematic picture of personal and communal destruction. But it is Tacitus who employs the full array of dramatic devices: the dramatic prologue to an episode; foreboding built up by omens as well as mood; reversals of fate and dramatic irony. His story of Germanicus' death in *Annals* 2 is a more effective tragedy than any written for theatrical performance in the early empire. It is no surprise that the French classical dramatists Corneille and Racine found much tragic material in the Roman historians.

SENATORS AS HISTORIANS

Cato the Elder's immodest comment that history, unlike poetry, was written by great men simply means that Roman historians in his day were members of the senatorial elite who had held high public office. Only senators would have access to state and family records and only they had sufficient prestige (*auctoritas*) to write convincingly on political matters. Thus in the second century B.C. nearly all historians were senators or members of senatorial families. Since they wrote for other members of the same class, their histories show a continuing interest in the political battles of the Forum and senate house.

By the first century B.C. literacy had increased and some writers appealed to this wider readership. In the highly partisan atmosphere it is not surprising that historians were supported by various political factions: Antias by the Valerii; Sisenna by Sulla; and several (in Greek and Latin) by Pompey. But this era of patronage was brief and uncharacteristic of Roman historiography. In Hellenistic Greece literary patronage was widespread and even Roman poets sought out and flattered patrons, but only Livy relied on Augustus in this way and he was, perhaps for this reason, the least political of the major Roman historians. Otherwise the greatest Roman historians—Cato, Caesar, Sallust, Asinius Pollio, Tacitus, and Ammianus—were all men who had carved out niches through their own political or military achievements.

Although histories were still primarily intended for the political elite, the move to a wider audience in the first century B.C. led to public readings by historians. Though originally intended for small private parties, these recitations later moved to the theaters and the baths with enormous audiences sometimes in attendance. Livy's fame even reached Gades (Cadiz), whence an admirer came to Rome merely to see the historian. Oral recitations afforded publicity to the historian and entertainment to his audience and were particularly appropriate in a society in which even private reading was done aloud.

BIOGRAPHY AT ROME

Biography was one of the most popular forms of historical writing in the ancient world, though it was regarded as a genre inferior to history. Ancient biography originated in the ethical concern with the formation of moral character. The tradition began in fourth-century Greece with Xenophon's *Agesilaus* and Isocrates' *Evagoras* as well as Plato's depiction of Socrates in his *Dialogues*. Aristotle and his successors in the Peripatetic school also taught that an individual's character was fixed, although it might be only gradually revealed during one's life. Thus we find an emphasis on character types, and the Peripatetic biographer did not seek to chronicle an entire life or show the importance of his subject in history, but to illuminate his character and thereby teach moral lessons. As Plutarch says, "I must be allowed to give my more particular attention to the marks and indications of the souls of men, and while I endeavor by these to portray their lives, may be free to leave more weighty matters and great battles to be treated of by others" (*Parallel Lives*, "Alexander" 1).

The scholars at the Museum in Alexandria developed another form of biography for the lives they appended to editions of poets.

Written without any moral purpose, these lives were simply compilations of anecdotes organized by categories.

Rome did not wholly depend on Greek models of biography since there was the independent tradition of funeral orations. Though no proper biographies survive from the Roman Republic, long passages in Cicero's orations that describe his client's background approach biography. After Varro first brought biography to Rome, Brutus wrote a famous eulogistic life of the younger Cato, which provoked a sharp pamphlet in reply by Caesar himself. This began a tradition of Stoic political hagiography that continued into the Roman Empire.

NEPOS

Cornelius Nepos (*ca.* 99–24 B.C.), born into a wealthy family in Cisalpine Gaul, wrote the first surviving Latin biographies. A close friend of the poet Catullus, Nepos took an active part in the cultural life of the capital while studiously avoiding political involvements. Nepos' *Lives of the Famous Men,* dedicated to Cicero's friend Titus Pomponius Atticus, presented in sixteen books the lives of Roman and barbarian kings, generals, lawgivers, orators, philosophers, poets, historians, and grammarians. We have only the book on foreign generals (including Alcibiades and Hannibal) and the lives of the elder Cato and Atticus from the Roman historians.

Nepos had no intention of writing history and his modest goal was to draw moral lessons from Peripatetic biographies. But his limited ability produces confusions, contradictions, and exaggerations, and Nepos displays little critical ability in dealing with his sources. The life of Atticus is by far the most successful since there Nepos could rely upon personal knowledge and he had an obvious sympathy for his subject. At his best, Nepos can tell anecdotes well, and his clear, pleasant Latin was long popular with schoolboys. But he is hardworking rather than gifted and only useful as a historical source for the light he sheds on his own time in the life of Atticus. Since Roman historians wrote with moral aims and made considerable use of character types from their rhetorical training, history moved closer to biography in the imperial era. The history of Alexander by the first-century rhetorician Quintus Curtius Rufus seems to straddle the line between the two genres. Rufus skillfully presents in great biographical detail the standard Roman portrait of the heroic Alexander who is gradually corrupted. He also includes geographical and ethnographic digressions that seem quite extraneous to a biography. The result is that of a well-written and even exciting, though none too accurate, biography, with exotic digressions added for entertainment.

A mixture of biography and history informs Tacitus' *Agricola,* which was written as a tribute to his father-in-law and as a self-justifying account of the tyranny of Domitian. Biographical elements also occur in Tacitus' more conventional *Annals* and *Histories*—so much so that three centuries later St. Jerome referred to these books as Tacitus' *Lives of the Twelve Caesars.* The early Christians patterned their lives of martyrs on the adulatory biographies of such Stoic heroes as Thrasea Paetus and Helvidius Priscus, and with the same end: to provide models of moral behavior.

SUETONIUS

Born in North Africa of an equestrian family, Gaius Suetonius Tranquillus (*ca.* A.D. 70–140) eschewed politics for a career in the imperial archives and secretariat. He moved in senatorial circles and was a friend of Pliny the Younger, who called him "most learned" (*eruditissimus*). Suetonius embarked on a series of biographies of illustrious men: poets, orators, historians, grammarians, philosophers, and, of course, the emperors. But aside from the twelve biographies in the *Lives of the Twelve Caesars,* only lives of the grammarians and of several poets survive. His lives of the Caesars made a lasting impression and became the model for biographers of later antiquity.

The ethical concerns of Peripatetic biography held no attractions for Suetonius, who much preferred the antiquarian scholarship of Alexandria. He rejected Plutarch's chronological organization and instead prefaced each life with a very brief narrative. He then organized the bulk of his material by topics before appending a few chapters on the emperor's death.

The popular image of Suetonius as a crude scandalmonger obscures his formidable skills. He stands outside the mainstream of Greco-Roman historical writing because he is not primarily a literary artist, but an ancestor of the modern scholar. As we read Suetonius we can see his card index (or its Roman equivalent) at work, sorting anecdotes according to theme. He includes everyday, even vulgar, stories that lack the grandeur necessary for history. He sometimes gives the verbatim text of letters—intolerable for a Roman historian who was expected to recast documents in his own style, but much appreciated by present-day historians. He presents his tales with little moralizing, although his dry impartiality at times approaches irony. Despite Suetonius' lack of stylistic artistry, he can be an excellent storyteller. His accounts of the assassination of Julius Caesar and the accession of Claudius are masterful dramatic narratives. Suetonius brings a novelist's skill to individual episodes, as in his melodramatic account of Nero's death, which describes the emperor's dreams and feelings.

Suetonius once served Trajan as chief librarian and had open access to the archives. Though he rarely cites sources by name, his long quotations from imperial correspondence were surely taken directly from the originals. But in 122 Hadrian dismissed Suetonius from his post as director of imperial correspondence for disrespect toward his empress Sabina. We know nothing more of his life, though it has been suggested that the lack of detail in the later lives was due to the inaccessibility of the archives.

By ancient definition Suetonius was not a historian, but he remains an invaluable historical source. His lives are particularly useful for the reigns of Gaius (Caligula) and the early years of Claudius, where Tacitus is lost. And his prodigious learning provides much that cannot be found elsewhere, especially information about literary, cultural, and scientific developments. These scattered data are especially valued by the modern historian because, unlike other biographers and historians, Suetonius did not select material to support a political or moral argument. And if he is a lesser intellectual figure than his Greek contemporary Plutarch, he is often a more useful historical source.

HISTORIA AUGUSTA

This name was given in the seventeenth century to a collection of thirty biographies attributed to six writers of the ages of Diocletian and Constantine the Great and gathered together in the manuscript tradition. These biographies (which often contain several lives, such as the three Gordians) extend from A.D. 117 (Hadrian) to 284 (Numerian) and include heirs and pretenders as well as emperors. They are modeled on Suetonius, with a short chronological account followed by numerous anecdotes arranged topically. Like Suetonian lives, these biographies contain the texts of letters, documents, official decrees, and senatorial acclamations.

These lives, which have puzzled and infuriated scholars ever since they were first discovered, are now regarded as a forgery. They probably were written late in the fourth century by a single hand, and the six putative authors are invented. Likewise, the letters and documents quoted are virtually all fraudulent. The work abounds with personal names, many of them bogus, as well as detailed references to imaginary sources. In fact, these biographies are largely fictions built on a skimpy foundation of fact. The composition is so careless that we can discover contradictions and lies from internal evidence alone, as when an emperor refers to events that occurred only after his death. Literary forgery was common enough in the ancient world, but rarely was the work attributed to completely imaginary authors. The motivation for this colossal fraud remains obscure, although the pagan and senatorial bias of the work has led scholars to hypothesize an author in the circle of Symmachus or Ammianus Marcellinus writing in the last decade of the fourth century.

AUTOBIOGRAPHY AT ROME

The earliest autobiographies written in republican Rome were political and military memoirs based on Greek literary models such as Xenophon's *The March Up Country* (*Anabasis*). The Romans even used the Greek name *hypomnemata*—there was no Latin title. As early as 190 B.C. the elder Scipio published in Greek a pamphlet in letter form describing his battles in Spain, and a generation later Cato included autobiographical material in the last books of his *Origins*. Other prominent Romans followed these precedents in writing memoirs to justify their careers: Tiberius Sempronius Gracchus (consul of 177 and 163); Marcus Aemilius Scaurus (consul of 115); Quintus Lutatius Catulus (consul of 102); and Publius Rutilius Rufus (consul of 105), who, exiled to Asia for his obstinate integrity in opposing equestrian corruption, wrote a heavily Stoic autobiography. Unhappily none of these survives.

The other type of memoir (*commentarius*) grew from the private diary and pretended to be a personal memorandum of the bare facts, which might later be turned into literary form by a historian or biographer. Thus a *commentarius* was not a literary genre in itself. Sulla called his own nothing more than the "raw material of history." The surviving fragments show that it was written in an unadorned style, yet this composition in twenty-three books effectively presented Sulla's case and was much used by later historians and biographers. Sulla's success was not lost on Cicero and Caesar, who followed his example. When Cicero sent a *commentarius* on his defeat of Catiline to a distinguished Greek historian to entice him to write a formal history, Posidonius shrewdly replied that the memo was such a masterpiece that it could not be bettered.

Julius Caesar

The political career of Julius Caesar (100–44 B.C.) is well known: consul in 59, he served as governor of Gaul for a decade and subdued that province before marching into Italy in 49 to confront Pompey and the senatorial forces in the civil war. After their defeat he ruled Rome as dictator until his assassination in 44 B.C. What is less well known is his extraordinary literary achievement. The *Gallic War* is far from the schoolboy's perception of a general's dull reminiscences; it is a skillful work by a literary master who was also a poet and Cicero's rival in oratory.

Caesar's *Gallic War* and *Civil War* are the only extant Roman *commentarii*. To the Roman mind they were not histories. There are no reflective prefaces or background information to set the work in its historical context, nor is there any clear moral purpose. The *Gallic War* was written in a bare, precise style that brings clarity and swiftness to the narrative. Even Cicero, who was hardly sympathetic to this so-called Attic spareness, complimented his political rival on the style but still regarded it as a skeleton of history. Referring to himself in the third person, Caesar endows the book with an aura of plain-spoken objectivity that can deceive the unguarded reader. Here, as the Latin epigram says, "art lies in concealing artifice."

Caesar subtly developed the form of the *commentarius*. Each of the first seven books describes an annual campaign (the eighth was written by his deputy Hirtius). They were forwarded to Rome to keep Caesar's image before the senate and the people. That image of decisive swiftness together with clemency toward former opponents would play an important part in Caesarian propaganda during the civil war. The latter books of the *Gallic War* include his speeches, and these speeches become still longer in the surviving books of the *Civil War*. The *Civil War* is more explicitly partisan, but even here Caesar shrewdly includes speeches by his opponents. This work is far more restrained than the slanderous anti-Caesarian pamphlets, and thus more persuasive.

Caesar's *Gallic War* is the only detailed account of ancient battles by a field commander and, not surprisingly, his descriptions are infinitely superior to any other ancient historical accounts. Despite the attempts of some modern scholars to see gross distortion, military historians attest to Caesar's general accuracy even though he naturally emphasizes his successes and distances himself from any reverses. Caesar's *Commentaries* are hardly bare memoranda to be embellished by a literary historian. That is the pretense, but in fact Caesar creates through these masterpieces a new literary genre that has been a far more effective tool of propaganda than overblown rhetorical bluster.

Imperial Autobiography

Since triumphs were celebrated only by the emperor or his family, private military memoirs were rarely permitted under the empire. The eminent general Gnaeus Domitius Corbulo wrote his memoirs during the reign of Nero, but this was numbered among the faults that drove him to suicide. It was for emperors alone to write autobiography, from Augustus' account of his early life through Tiberius' grim notebooks that so inspired Domitian's cruelties to the books of the warmhearted Claudius and the troubled Hadrian, which survive only through the fictional re-creations of Robert Graves and Marguerite Yourcenar. All these, and many others, have been lost, but there survives a single magisterial imperial autobiography engraved in Greek and Latin on the walls of a temple in Ankara. The *Res Gestae* of Augustus was displayed in Rome on bronze tablets before his tomb and throughout the empire. But the Ankara text aptly recalls its similarity to those monumental autobiographical texts carved on mountainsides by the Achaemenid Persian monarch Darius I and by Antiochus I of Commagene, in northern Syria. There is deception in his discussion of Sextus Pompey and Antony in the civil wars, but Augustus wrote almost half a century after those events and his majestic disregard for the squabbles and constitutional niceties of the dying republic was surely (in his own mind) vindicated by the establishment of peace and prosperity. The *Res Gestae* is fundamentally honest in representing the retrospective view of the emperor in his seventy-seventh year.

Other Romans wrote more specialized autobiographical essays, such as Cicero's account of his education in the *Brutus* and Marcus Aurelius' philosophical *Meditations,* written in Greek. These survive, as does Apuleius' autobiographical *Apology.* But perhaps the most self-revealing work by any ancient pagan is not a formal autobiography but Cicero's letters to his close friend Atticus. These letters range from Cicero's involvement in the highest affairs of state to the most intimate family troubles. His conflicts and confusions become clear, and his weaknesses are revealed. We come closer to knowing his soul than that of any other Roman before Augustine of Hippo. His display of weakness and vacillation, of pride and shame, of deception and self-deception, finally make Cicero a more interesting and even more noble character than his self-serving and pompous orations would ever have allowed us to appreciate. Only at the end of antiquity does Augustine take autobiography one step further to spiritual self-scrutiny—but that falls outside the scope of this essay.

CENSORSHIP

Though the word "censorship" derives from the Roman censor, who exercised a certain moral scrutiny over the membership roll of the senate, the modern conception of state censorship did not exist in the Roman Republic. There was a prohibition on defamatory songs in the laws of the Twelve Tables, but this was a matter for civil litigation by the aggrieved party. And the poet-historian Naevius was imprisoned by aristocrats whom he had lampooned, not by the state. Aside from the self-censorship that kept Cicero and others from writing history, there was no suppression of historical works during the Roman Republic. With some justice Tacitus regarded historical candor as a privilege of republican authors.

The empire was quite another matter. While Julius Caesar responded to scurrilous republican pamphlets with words, his successors banned and burned critical writings. When Timagenes of Alexandria was banned from the imperial palace by Augustus, he went to live with Asinius Pollio and burned his account of Augustus' own accession. But when the Pompeian Titus Labienus' books were burned in 12 B.C., he preferred to die with them. Seneca the Younger remarks on the good fortune that the Triumvirs were content to kill Cicero, and allowed his books to survive. Augustus ordered the imperial librarian to suppress some early works of Julius Caesar, but that must have been an aesthetic rather than a political judgment.

Under Tiberius writers were prosecuted under the newly revived *lex maiestatis,* which functioned like a treason law. Although others were killed or exiled for plays or verses, Tacitus' long report on the trial of Aulus Cremutius Cordus provides the earliest account of a historian's trial for treason on the basis of his published work. In A.D. 25, sixty-eight years after the Ides of March, Cremutius was charged before the senate for praising Brutus and Cassius in his history. In his defense, Cremutius pointed out that Livy had praised Pompey and remained a friend of Augustus, while Asinius Pollio praised the tyrannicides and lived peaceably afterward. He goes on to say that among the Romans

> there has always been complete, uncensored freedom to speak about those whom death has placed beyond hate or favor. . . . They have their place in the historian's pages. Posterity gives everyone his due honor. If I am condemned, people will remember me as well as Cassius and Brutus (Tacitus, *Annals* 4.35).

He starved himself to death and state officials burned his books. Cremutius was right;

it is for this that he has been remembered. Labienus, Cremutius, and other banned authors were republished under Caligula, who claimed that he wished future generations to have access to all the historical facts, but that bizarre figure also contemplated suppressing Homer, Vergil, and Livy.

Claudius was the only emperor who actually wrote history, so it is not surprising that there is no evidence of censorship in his reign. As a youth he himself had planned a book on the civil war, but his mother and grandmother (Livia) persuaded him that he would not be allowed to publish a true account of that sensitive period, so he simply left a long lacuna. Perhaps the memory of his lacuna and Augustus' tolerance for his old teacher Livy made him more indulgent.

The Flavian era saw expulsions of philosophers and astrologers from Rome, and laudatory biographies of the Stoic dissidents Thrasea Paetus and Helvidius Priscus were burned. But an even more gruesome story is told of Hermogenes of Tarsus, who died under Domitian for some incautious allusions in his history. The emperor ordered that the slaves who had merely copied his book be crucified.

The Antonine emperors ushered in a new era of toleration. Historical accounts of the horrors of the preceding century only glorified the new Golden Age, so Tacitus and the many Greek historians writing in the second century had few restraints or fears. Tacitus spoke for this more enlightened time when he commented on the trial of Cremutius:

> This makes one deride the stupidity of people who believe that today's authority can destroy tomorrow's memories. On the contrary, repressions of genius increase its prestige. All that tyrants, and imitators of their brutalities, achieve is their own disrepute and their victims' renown (*Annals* 4.35).

It is precisely that disrepute and the victims' renown that Tacitus achieves so brilliantly in his history.

CONCLUSIONS

Roman historiography grew out of the political life of the city. Save for an occasional entertaining ethnographic digression, Roman history centered its interest resolutely on the public life of the Roman people, whether in the Forum, in the senate house, on the Palatine, or on military campaigns. Since their concern was Rome, the historians rarely found it necessary to leave the city in quest of evidence. Chauvinism and a resulting xenophobia were endemic, and there was little interest in the universal history that had so inspired their Greek forerunners.

There are of course differences between the narrow vision and rigid structure of the early annalists, Tacitus' flexible use of annalistic form, and Ammianus' broad range of interests and sympathies. This is hardly surprising; from Cato the Elder to Ammianus is a longer period than from Columbus to the present day. But the continuities over five centuries are far more extraordinary: though rhetorical in expression and parochial in its scope, Roman historiography never lost its lasting concern with the moral dimensions of political issues.

This concern led Roman historians to themes of universal importance. They looked nostalgically to a lost Golden Age and repeatedly explored the decline of republican Rome. Rome had not been conquered and her empire was larger than ever, but her moral values and political institutions had been eroded from within. Conquest, wealth, and perhaps civilization itself had corrupted the free Roman people and left them the subjects of a new monarchy.

Moral historiography became the conscience of the Roman people, and it is in Sallust, Livy, Tacitus, and Ammianus that we find the most cogent Roman discussions of freedom versus tyranny, the corrupting effect of individual or civic power, and the decline of political and social institutions. And these remain central issues for the historian of any age.

The genre of history occupies an important place in Latin literature, but Roman historiography is more than a literary record of the past; it is an extension of political life. Speeches were political acts in republican Rome and Tacitus did not turn to history to escape into the past but to take a political stance in his own time. The language of history functioned as a principal mechanism of political discourse and social analysis.

From antiquity to the present day Roman history has been read for its exempla of heroic conduct. Succeeding peoples have commemorated the Romans in poetry, drama, and painting. This goes beyond nostalgia. These texts kept the dream of liberty alive to be reborn in Cola di Rienzo's medieval Roman republic (1347–1354), the Italian communes of the Renaissance, and the American and French revolutions. Tacitus believed that the function of history is to affect the future and, by that standard, Roman historiography succeeded and continues to succeed. It remains, as Cicero hoped it would be, "the witness of the past, the light of truth, the survival of memory, the teacher of life, the message of antiquity" (*On Oratory* 2.9.36).

BIBLIOGRAPHY

SOURCES

Caesar, the *Historia Augusta,* Livy, Ammianus Marcellinus, Cornelius Nepos, Sallust, Suetonius, and Tacitus are all available in the Loeb Classical Library and Penguin editions.

STUDIES

Roman Historiography

T. A. Dorey, ed., *Latin Historians* (1966), and *Empire and Aftermath* (1975); Charles W. Fornara, *The Nature of History in Ancient Greece and Rome* (1983); Michael Grant, *The Ancient Historians* (1970); M. L. W. Laistner, *The Greater Roman Historians* (1947); A. H. McDonald, "The Roman Historians," in M. Platnauer, ed., *Fifty Years (and Twelve) of Classical Scholarship* (1968); Arnaldo Momigliano, *Studies in Historiography* (1966), and *Essays in Ancient and Modern Historiography* (1977); Timothy Peter Wiseman, *Clio's Cosmetics: Three Studies in Greco-Roman Literature* (1979).

Early Roman Historians

E. Badian, "The Early Historians," in Dorey, *Latin Historians* (1966); Bruce W. Frier, *Libri Annales Pontificum Maximorum: The Origins of the Annalistic Tradition* (1979); A. D. Leeman, *Orationis Ratio* (1963); R. M. Ogilvie, *A Commentary on Livy Books I-V* (1965).

Cicero on Historiography

P. A. Brunt, "Cicero and Historiography," in *Miscellanea di studi classici in onore di E. Manni,* I (1979); M. Rambaud, *Cicéron et l'histoire romaine* (1953).

Sallust

D. C. Earl, *The Political Thought of Sallust* (1961), and "Sallust," in Torrey James Luce, ed., *The Ancient Writers,* II (1982); A. D. Leeman, "A Systematical Bibliography of Sallust (1879–1964)," in *Mnemosyne,* Supplement 4 (1965); Ronald Syme, *Sallust* (1964).

Livy

T. A. Dorey, ed., *Livy* (1971); I. Kajanto, *God and Fate in Livy* (1957); J. Lipovsky, "Livy," in

Torrey James Luce, ed., *The Ancient Writers*, II (1982); Torrey James Luce, *Livy: The Composition of His History* (1977); Ronald Syme, "Livy and Augustus," in *Harvard Studies in Classical Philology*, **64** (1959); P. G. Walsh, *Livy, His Historical Aims and Methods* (1961), "Livy," in Dorey, *Latin Historians* (1966), and *Livy: Greece and Rome*, in *New Surveys in the Classics*, no. 8 (1974).

Tacitus

T. A. Dorey, ed., *Tacitus* (1968); Francis Richard David Goodyear, *Tacitus: Greece and Rome*, in *New Surveys in the Classics*, no. 4 (1970); Torrey James Luce, "Tacitus," in Luce, *The Ancient Writers*, II; Ronald Martin, *Tacitus* (1981); Ronald Syme, *Tacitus*, 2 vols. (1958), and *Ten Studies in Tacitus* (1970); B. Walker, *The Annals of Tacitus* (1952).

Ammianus Marcellinus

R. C. Blockley, "Ammianus Marcellinus: A Study of His Historiography and Political Thought," in *Latomus*, **141** (1975); G. A. Crump, "Ammianus Marcellinus as a Military Historian," in *Historia Einzelschriften*, **27** (1975); J. F. Matthews, "Ammianus Marcellinus," in Luce, *The Ancient Writers*, II (1982); E. A. Thompson, *The Historical Work of Ammianus Marcellinus* (1947).

Biography and Autobiography

T. A. Dorey, ed., *Latin Biography* (1967); G. Misch, *A History of Autobiography in Antiquity* (1950); Arnaldo Momigliano, *The Development of Greek Biography* (1971); D. R. Stuart, *Epochs of Greek and Roman Biography* (1928); Alan Wardman, *Plutarch's Lives* (1974).

Julius Caesar

F. E. Adcock, *Caesar as a Man of Letters* (1956); J. H. Collins, "Caesar as Political Propagandist," in *Aufstieg und Niedergang der römischen Welt*, I, 1 (1972); B. N. Quinn, "Caesar," in Luce, *Ancient Writers*, I (1982); L. Raditsa, "Julius Caesar and his Writings," in *Aufstieg und Niedergang der römischen Welt*, I, 3 (1973); C. E. Stevens, "The *Bellum Gallicum* as a Work of Propaganda," in *Latomus*, **11** (1952).

Cornelius Nepos

Edna Jenkinson, "Nepos—An Introduction to Latin Biography," in Dorey, *Latin Biography* (1967).

Suetonius

G. B. Townend, "Suetonius," in Luce, *Ancient Writers*, II (1982); Andrew F. Wallace-Hadrill, *Suetonius: The Scholar and His Caesars* (1983).

Historia Augusta

T. Barnes, "The Sources of the Historia Augusta," in *Latomus*, **155** (1978); N. H. Baynes, *The Historia Augusta: Its Date and Purpose* (1926); A. R. Birley, "The Augustan History," in Dorey, *Latin Biography* (1967); Arnaldo Momigliano, "An Unsolved Problem of Historical Forgery: The *Scriptores Historiae Augustae*," in *Journal of the Warburg and Courtauld Institutes*, **17** (1966); Ronald Syme, *Ammianus and the Historia Augusta* (1968), *Emperors and Biography: Studies in the Historia Augusta* (1971), and *Historia Augusta Papers* (1983).

The Novel

JOHN J. WINKLER

CONVENTIONAL WISDOM, as stated in the justly famous *The Rise of the Novel* by Ian Watt, has it that the eighteenth-century English writers Defoe, Richardson, and Fielding created a new form of literature (the novel) and that long fictional works in prose before them were something else—call them "romances." It is certainly true that those writers' fictions, produced for an expanding and newly dominant middle class, set up a different set of conventions, often called "realism," for long storytelling than had hitherto been accepted. But the restriction of the term *novel* to that subclass of lengthy fictions depends on erecting what Watt calls "a definition sufficiently narrow to exclude previous types of narrative and yet broad enough to apply to whatever is usually put in the novel category." Since the novel nowadays includes works that reject those fairly narrow bourgeois conventions in many different ways—such as the work of Proust, Joyce, Pynchon, Marquez, Genet, and Lessing—a more up-to-date map of the field must print NOVEL in large letters covering everything fictional and in prose from Chariton and Petronius to the present, using another name for the limited territory of middle-class "realism," whose residents once thought of themselves as the central Manhattan of the known fictional world.

The need for a new survey and remapping of the field of Greek and Roman novels is particularly pressing for three reasons. First, new discoveries of novel fragments on papyrus in the last decade have dramatically increased our library catalog of ancient novels and radically altered our sense of its contents and proportions. Second, the old stereotype of classical novels, especially those in Greek, as unoriginal, repetitive, schmaltzy, and trite, has been revealed by more informed readings to be no more than a slander by unfriendly proponents of a different set of conventions. Third, as our knowledge of Greco-Roman drama, folktales, and historiography increases, the boundary separating the novels from other kinds of writing and performance-text diminishes. The result of these changes is that the ancient novels are proving to be not a late and insignificant sport but a cultural form as central to and revealing of the Greco-Roman world after Alexander as tragedy and comedy were to the city-state of Athens in the fifth century. Further, they invite appreciation as sustained and profound as that accorded any tragedy or lyric poem.

THE ORIGINS OF NARRATIVE

The story elements used by Greek and Latin novelists had been circulating in the form of oral tales, legends about local heroes, or the adventures and passions of ordinary people as far back as we can trace Mediterranean culture; the important exception to this is the Hellenistic development of romantic fantasy, which will be discussed in the last section of the essay. Folktales, in their very nature as performance pieces outside the institutions of writing, are preserved only when a collector undertakes to gather them. Two important collectors were Herodotus and Pausanias, whose works are treasure troves of local tales. But many other writers too had sufficiently large networks of interests to catch living specimens of popular narrative, for instance Strabo, who records a version of the tale we now know as Cinderella—in a Greco-Egyptian setting (*Geography* 17.1.33). The narrative lines of Homeric epic seem to be of this type. The development of the novel proper in the Hellenistic and imperial eras is a story, therefore, not of the invention of a wholly new genre but rather of the gradual entry of popular narrative into the accepted formats of established writing.

In the fifth century many contemporaries and predecessors of Herodotus assembled oral traditions. They are sometimes referred to as logographers (recorders of narrated accounts) rather than historians, but this is a partisan description by a different kind of historian. The native perception of such local tales is rather a skeptical traditionalism, which acknowledges that they do indeed contain much that is fabulous but which insists nevertheless on preserving them. Most of these collections are lost, but one reader, Dionysios of Halikarnassos, gave a general characterization of them as containing "tales [*mythoi*] that have been believed for a very long time, and some theatrical peripeties that make them seem rather silly to the present generation" (*On Thucydides* 5). The sort of thing Dionysios was reading in those early historians can be illustrated from Greek folklore by the Kalydonian tale of Koresos, a priest who was about to perform a public human sacrifice on Kallirhoë—a maiden who had rejected his love—but who at the last moment turned the knife on himself (Pausanias, 7.21). It is instantly obvious that the entertainment value of such a story will guarantee it a long life and frequent elaborations by the skilled tale-tellers who are found in every preindustrial village, and also that "serious" writers will dismiss it as too good (a story) to be true.

The peripeties (sudden reversals) that Dionysios mentions were an essential element of a good dramatic plot (*mythos*). Aristotle's analysis of what made tragedies so impressive shows that he was thinking of them primarily as stories ("the plot should be so framed that even a person who does not see the events performed but simply hears an account of them will have the same strong emotional reaction" [*Poetics* 6]), and in a certain real sense as novels before the fact, on the condition that they be tightly plotted ("in the nature of things a longer story is always better than a shorter one, with the strict proviso that the audience can remember and see as a whole the beginning, middle, and end of the entire plot" [*Poetics* 7]). Modern criticism tends to emphasize the psychology and metaphysics of Greek tragedies. But their basic plots were traditional legends and thus it is that we find in tragedy, alongside historiography, a second major repository of novel-like narratives.

On the spectrum of greater or less closeness to popular narrative, Euripides is easily the closest of the surviving playwrights: his *Ion, Helen,* and *Iphigenia in Tauris* (Aristotle's favorite example, along with the equally well-plotted *Oidipous Tyrannos*) have almost all the elements so often exploited by the later novels—travel to distant lands, truly wicked villains, separation and reunion, disguise and recognition, tender family feelings, a happy ending. (For the missing element of teen sex, see the discussion of romance below.)

For an example of the sort of play Aristotle probably saw, consider the following drama of unknown authorship recovered from Hyginus, a Greek librarian under Augustus. A maiden named Theonoë is captured by pirates and taken to Karia where she becomes the king's mistress; her father Thestor goes searching for her but is shipwrecked off Karia and sold into slavery. The remaining sister, Leukippe, is told by the oracle at Delphi that she will find her family if she searches for them in the guise of a priest of Apollo, so she cuts her hair and travels as a young man. Arriving in Karia, she has an interview with the king's mistress, who falls instantly in love with the handsome stranger and propositions him/her. Leukippe rejects the offer. Theonoë has her/him locked in a room and commands that a slave be sent from the mines to do a job. Thestor is sent to her; Theonoë hands him a sword and orders him to kill the visiting priest of Apollo. As he stands with sword drawn above the helpless victim he laments his fate, mentions the names of everyone in his immediate family and is about to kill himself, when Leukippe exclaims, "Father!" and wrenches the sword from his hands. Together they then plot to kill the wicked concubine, but that horror too is averted by a timely recognition, and the happy threesome are sent home with gifts by the king (Hyginus, *Tales* [*Fabulae*] 190).

If we leave Thucydides and the more static tragedies to one side (and both are arguably unrepresentative of their genres in the late fifth and early fourth centuries), it is an open question whether tragedians or historiographers have the better claim to be protonovelists. A too-incisive slicing up of narrative into tragedy and history and folktale, like the partitions of nations in European history, does violence to the cultural unity and ease of passage from one to the other. Our records and fragments of Greek historians show that most of them had a keen eye for the melodrama of complex tales and a sure touch in satisfying their audience's love of pathos and rhetoric—hence the designation "tragic (or romantic) historiography" for the works of Ktesias, Xanthos, and numerous others. Xanthos' *Lydiaka,* for example, contains in one episode kings, innkeepers, assassins, a trapdoor, a fake head in a box, and a marriageable princess (Jacoby, 90 frag. 44). Tragedy and historiography, then, are the two forms of classical writing that provide us with the best access to the oral art of fictional narrative, and they were the main points of entry for novel-like tales into the canon of literature.

There are two subsidiary genres that also display the development and exploitation of storytelling skills; the first of these is philosophy, conceived in the broad manner that was usual in the ancient world. Works such as Xenophon's *Education of Cyrus* (*Kyropaidia*) and Plutarch's *On the Daimon of Socrates* are brilliant re-creations of a historical career or event, which only fall short of being novels insofar as the guiding purpose of the composition is the discussion of issues in practical or theoretical philosophy. The same restriction applies to the fabulous travel narratives of Iamboulos (a Hellenistic writer preserved in Diodoros, 2.55–60), who describes a Utopian culture on Ceylon, and of Euhemeros, whose *The Sacred Record* describes another island in the Indian Ocean where a golden stela tells the history of famous rulers named Zeus, Artemis, and Apollo, who were later regarded as gods (Diodoros, 5.41–46; 6.1). Since the fictionalized background is strictly secondary to the purpose of such compositions—which is explicitly to present the author's serious views on politics, theology, or other philosophical topics rather than to tell a story—we must say that they employ novel-like materials but that they are not novels.

The other tangential genre is New Comedy, which is closer in form and style to Euripides than to Old Comedy. The "Upstairs-Downstairs" intrigues of wealthy families and their slaves, which are the central concern of New Comedy, can be seen to some extent in the novels of Chariton and Achilles Tatius. But since the later novelists lavished most of their efforts either on legendary nobility or on contemporary lowlife—a step up and down respectively from the domestic arena of New Comedy—those plays remain tangential to the great tradition of fiction.

The livelier, less arty and precious plays performed by traveling troupes in the Hellenistic period may already have developed the novel-like plots of *Charition* and *The Jealous Mistress*, two actors' scripts (with working revisions right on the page) that have survived from the second century A.D. (*Oxyrhynchus Papyri* 413). *Charition* is a campy remake of *Iphigenia in Tauris*, with some of the *Cyclops* thrown in; *The Jealous Mistress* is a splendidly wicked Joan Crawford-like part, a woman who rages, seethes, and murders right and left—descendant of Euripides' Medea, ancestress of Queen Persinna in Heliodoros' *Aithiopika*. Popular drama suffered of course from the same contempt that was directed by

establishment writers against folktales. This contempt is at the same time a cause for the loss of most popular drama (which might have been recorded if writers were interested in doing so) and a sign that it was an important location for that narrative make-believe that achieved sustained and carefully written form only with the first novelists—Dionysios, nicknamed Skytobrachion ("Leather Arm"), a native of Miletos who lived and worked in Alexandria, and Chariton of Aphrodisias.

THE EARLY NOVELS

Dionysios is a problematic case, since we have only Diodoros' paraphrase of his Argonautic saga (4.40–56), but even in summary it reads with a dramatic excitement and an originality of invention, motivation, and physical detail that mark it as a fine work of fiction. Medea's singularity of conscience, the jailbreak at Troy with Priam's help, the heroic suicide of Jason's mother, and the drug-filled icon of Artemis are some of the high points in this vivid portrayal. There may have been a point to Dionysios' Argonautic novel, as there certainly was to his accounts of the Amazons and Dionysos, namely to demythologize and naturalize the old fables of gods and godlike beings walking the earth. But in doing so with full attention to the narrative itself rather than to the argument, Dionysios' *The Argonauts* has a good claim to being the first novel on record.

Another Alexandrian, Hegesianax, wrote a novel (now lost) about the Trojan War from the perspective of a local Troadic villager named Kephalon. Hegesianax seems to have spoken in his own person in the preface about the current state of Troy's dilapidation (Strabo, 13.1.27) and then to have presented the narrative as an ancient document that he had discovered. At least, later writers who cite or retell episodes from this account attribute them to Kephalon himself (for example Parthenius, *Love Stories* 4.34). Dionysios also used this device in his *Phrygian Composition,* purportedly written first in ancient Pelasgian script and dialect by a contemporary of Orpheus named Thymoites, who traveled to Libya and learned there the true history of the wise king (later regarded as a god) Dionysos (Diodoros, 3.67). The "discovery" of ancient writings was a popular way to frame a novel whose action was set in archaic times: we know of at least four other novels supposedly written by Greeks or Trojans about their war experiences (Korinnos of Nauplia, Sisyphos of Kos, Diktys of Krete, and Dares of Phrygia). The latter two survive in Latin translation and were much admired and imitated in the Middle Ages; Greek fragments of Diktys were found in this century at Tebtunis.

Undoubtedly the masterpiece of novels in the format of a "discovered" ancient document is Antonius Diogenes' *Marvels Beyond Thule*—purportedly written on cedar tablets by an Athenian scribe in Tyre taking dictation from an Arcadian exile who had wandered the world and had had many adventures with magic. The tablets were "discovered" by one of Alexander's generals in a tomb near Tyre. For complexity of structure and sheer imaginative fantasy, *Marvels Beyond Thule* is the closest Greek fiction came to *The 1001 Nights.* The main narrative is spoken by the Tyrian heroine Derkyllis, who has been cursed by the wicked Egyptian magician Paapis to live by night and lie dead by day. We may guess that the breaking off of her story as she apparently died each dawn served neatly for a Scheherazade-like suspense.

A minor masterpiece of historical impersonation is the *Letters of Chion of Heraklea,* a collection of seventeen letters from a young man who went to Athens in the mid fourth century to study with Plato. Though seriously attracted to mysticism, he decides he must leave the Academy and return to the political turmoil of his own city, which is now controlled by a dictator. He becomes a martyr of the revolution, or so we are left to infer from the last letter, which speaks of his part in a plot to kill the tyrant on the following day. Chion himself is a real historical figure; his *Letters* are an epistolary novella of the first century A.D.

Another device for inveigling fiction onto the library shelves of history was to impersonate an older historian. The *Life of Alexander* was one of the most popular of all novels; the fact that it was circulated under the name of Kallisthenes, a great-nephew of Aristotle who accompanied Alexander on his campaigns and wrote of his deeds, gave an unknown author's brainchild a chance to survive.

In the case of "discovered" documents and consistent impersonations it is hard for us to judge how many of their readers understood them to be operating under the convention of a discourse that is neither a lie nor the truth. By long acculturation we have become comfortable with this category of writing and have labeled it fiction, but it made ancient readers and writers feel quite nervous. There were very real pressures that made an expenditure of time or papyrus on producing written records of historical lies seem a foolish waste. (Those pressures did not really disappear until the production of cheap paper in 1820.) The essential fact about ancient novels is that they were a luxury product.

Therefore it is all the more surprising that Chariton (*ca.* 50 B.C.–A.D. 50?), in his eight-book *Chaireas and Kallirhoë,* clearly defines his subject as one of historical verisimilitude and himself as a storyteller, not a historian. His opening verb is *diegesomai* (I shall narrate), with never a reference to researches or documents, though his heroine is the daughter of the famous Syracusan general

Hermokrates who defeated the Athenian armada in 412. The author's role in narrating is quite like that of a person describing a theatrical drama he has seen—the settings, the timing, the turns of event are all recognizably stagey—but Chariton's access to intimate thoughts, such as Kallirhoë's confused and half-conscious feelings when she wakes up in a tomb, far surpasses anything that conventional drama or historiography could encompass. With Chariton's ambitious project, mastering a complex set of intrigues in different parts of the world and a synoptic clarity of plot, Aristotle's prophetic reference to just such a work has come true.

Though with Chariton the novel has decisively arrived, there is at this time still no name for the genre (ten centuries later Photios was still calling them "dramas") and little official respect. Yet they proliferated nonetheless. Bound with Chariton in a handsome seventh-century codex was a copy of *Chione:* a few surviving columns describe the maneuvering of several parties before an approaching dynastic marriage. Herwig Maehler has brilliantly demonstrated that the fragmentary *Metiochos and Parthenope* was also a historical novel, set in the time of Polykrates of Samos (sixth century B.C.). The main characters discuss the nature of desire (eros) at a symposium with the philosopher Anaximenes. Seven columns survive from a historical novel about Ninos and Semiramis, portrayed as young lovers who must overcome parental opposition to their early marriage. Because the lucidity of Xenophon was much admired in the early empire as a stylistic model, several novels were written by "Xenophons"—a *Babyloniaka* (conceivably our Ninos fragment) by Xenophon of Antioch, a *Kypriaka* concerning characters named Kinyras, Myrrha, and Adonis (not necessarily mythological) by Xenophon of Cyprus, and an *Ephesiaka* by Xenophon of Ephesos. This last survives in a five-book abridgement of its original ten. The passages of this novel

that have been summarized rather than reproduced intact are betrayed by their blissful obliviousness to hiatus. For however low the prestige of novels, it was not due to their authors' faulty writing. Most of them show perfect mastery of the techniques of clausular rhythm, hiatus avoidance, and similar tokens of elegant writing.

The important exceptions to this rule are two novels that have some claim to being genuine folk books—*Apollonios of Tyre* and the *Life of Aesop. Apollonios,* which Shakespeare adapted as *Pericles, Prince of Tyre,* tells of a wandering prince whose kindnesses are rewarded only after a long series of betrayals and misadventures. The many Latin versions show its medieval popularity; two Greek fragments concerning an Apollonios have been found, but it is not clear whether they are the same tale or another. Aesop's life was a favorite oral tale as early as the fifth century B.C. Over the centuries stories about the ugly, wily slave accumulated, including an adaptation of a popular oriental tale (known in Aramaic and demotic versions) about the wise vizier Akiqar. The episodes are wonderfully irreverent, frequently obscene, and filled with a kind of Socratic wisdom about pretenders to knowledge.

The bold, Charitonian stance of authority over the minds and hearts of characters whose lives are both storied and verisimilar is found in the two novels that later ages most admired—Longus' *Daphnis and Chloe* and Heliodoros' *Aithiopika.* Both authors make it quite clear from the beginning that what they narrate did not actually take place: Longus by stating that his work is a verbal correlative to a painting he once saw; Heliodoros by describing a variety of perspectives and private events to which no single person could have had access. In many ways these two works are polar opposites to each other.

Daphnis and Chloe tells the story of how two country teenagers begin to notice their adolescent hormones working and how they cope with the painful comedy of learning about adult sexuality. The process is particularly painful to Chloe, who finds that nature and culture have conspired to put her needs in subordination to those of Daphnis, who must become her responsible male (*kyrios*) instead of her playmate. The delicious play of changing seasons, of brief country scenes and erotic vignettes, the impingement of animal worlds and dream worlds onto the sometimes harsh realities of rural work, all couched in a style that seems to capture the aroma of an overripe peach, make Longus' novel a miniature masterpiece of sensuousness, though hardly a challenge to serious thought.

Heliodoros, by contrast, is a novelist not only of Technicolor, wide-screen panoramas but, like Proust, Mann, and Tolstoy, of very high I.Q. His *Aithiopika* is a slowly unraveled mystery involving Kalasiris, an Egyptian priest in voluntary exile; his son Thyamis, the leader of the marsh bandits; Theagenes, a descendant of Achilles who leads a pageant at Delphi; Charikles, the priest there of Apollo; Charikleia, his beautiful and smart foster daughter; Persinna, the sultry wife of the Persian satrap in Egypt; and many more. The power of its tightly wound plot, which begins with a stillness like the eye of a hurricane and expands to take in three cultures on two continents, makes it the supreme development of that narrative craft and craftiness whose distant point of origin was the Greek folktale.

All of these novels deal in the main with the noblest level of a hierarchical, class-conscious society. (*Daphnis and Chloe* seems at first to be an exception, but they turn out to be rich city kids after all.) Most are also projected several centuries into the historical past. There was also a type of novel altogether different from these, which suffered from a double oppression not only for being fiction but also for dealing with criminal and quite indecorous behavior, usually set in the present time and among the lower orders.

Until 1971 this type seemed to exist only in Latin—Petronius' *Satyrika* (*Satyricon*) and Apuleius' *The Golden Ass* (though the latter was clearly based on a Greek novelette called *Lucius, or the Ass*)—but since then fragments of three hitherto unknown Greek novels have been published that indicate that outrageous indecency and Grand Guignol flourished as much in Greek as in Latin. The first is *Oxyrhynchus Papyri* 3010, tentatively described by Peter Parsons as "a Greek Satyricon." It features one Iolaos, whose friend has just been initiated as a castrated priest of Cybele (*gallos*), and the narrator switches without warning into verse, as does Petronius in the *Satyrika*. The second (P. Turner 8) involves a magus named Tinouphis, an imminent execution, an adulterous woman, and a movable brick. The relation of these is not entirely clear, but the fact that part of the text is in verse is an additional guarantee that it too falls in this category. The third and most extensive is Lollianos' *Phoinikika* (P. Colon. inv. 3328), of which we have three substantial fragments, one of which had been published earlier without its source being known (*Oxyrhynchus Papyri* 1368). In this last a certain Glauketes meets a ghost. In one of the Cologne pieces, the male narrator, after a wild party where something or someone is being thrown off the roof, loses his virginity to a woman named Persis. She tries to give him a gold necklace but when he refuses she tells Glauketes to take it elsewhere, and at that moment her mother bursts into the room and scolds her. A second fragment recounts a scene of (pretended?) human sacrifice, accompanied by a terrible bandit oath of resistance to authority, and then general flatulence and nausea. Later that night some of the desperadoes dress up as ghosts, all in white or all in black, just as their counterparts do in Apuleius.

The problems we have in reading Petronius and Apuleius are considerably eased by knowing that they are not simply individual sports in the genre of ancient fiction but rather examples of a type that purposely expended the precious resources of good writing on illicit subjects. Our cultural emblem for this mischievous desecration might well be Nero, who prowled the alleys at night in a hooded cloak, committing crimes against property and persons (Suetonius, *Lives of the Twelve Caesars,* "Nero" 26), forced the noble orders to perform as gladiators in public shows (12), and urinated on the statue of the Syrian Goddess (56).

Of Petronius we have too little; of Apuleius, in a sense, too much. The *Satyrika*'s substantial but mutilated remains seem to come from a mock *Odyssey* in which the Greek-named but Latin-speaking scamp Encolpius (Crotch) is pursued by the wrath not of Poseidon but of Priapus. The eroticism is polymorphous, the literary style a brilliant pastiche of incompatible genres. The same may be said of *The Golden Ass,* but where the *Satyrika* is tantalizingly incomplete, Apuleius' novel of witches, bandits, and other nonexemplary types concludes with a final book of apparently straight-faced religious indoctrination. The key to this extrageneric addendum may be the continuous attention throughout the novel to facetious issues of truth and fiction, clustering around the numerous subnarrators who tell incredible tales to the hero-narrator Lucius. At the end of *The Golden Ass,* when the narrator himself is unexpectedly converted to the worship of Egyptian Isis, the reader is left to ask seriously the same questions about this frame-tale that were put humorously to the inset tales: "Could this possibly be true?" and "What is the real identity of the narrator?"

One of the bonuses from the recent discoveries of such criminal fiction is that it clarifies Achilles Tatius' novel *Leukippe and Kleitophon* as an experiment combining nobly placed characters with situations and motives of the criminal type. Thus the hero and heroine are rich and beautiful members of polite society but can't wait to get to bed together. Only a series of incredible accidents keeps them technically chaste, as they are put through cartoon catastrophes of the most grisly sort. The episodes of cross-dressing and of human sacrifice and the frequent allusions to mystery rituals are also characteristic of *Iolaos,* the *Phoinikika,* the *Satyrika,* and *The Golden Ass.*

This may also be the right context for Iamblichos' *Babyloniaka,* one of the strangest and most interesting of the lost novels. Iamblichos claimed that the plot of his novel was an old Babylonian tale that he had learned from one of the royal scribes who was taken as a prisoner of war when Trajan conquered Babylon. Be that as it may, his very long novel (known from excerpts and a summary by Photios) is a rich mixture of exotic persons and events: bees who make poisoned honey, a cannibal bandit, a priestess of Aphrodite whose children Tigris and Mesopotamia are look-alikes for the hero and heroine, a Lesbian queen of Egypt, a farmer's daughter, and an escape from prison by cross-dressing. The excerpts are very stylish indeed. If the sands and mummy cartonnage of Egypt continue to be kind, they may yet provide us with the sixteen (Photios) or thirty-nine (*Suda*) books of the *Babyloniaka.*

ROMANCE

A problem strictly separate from the development of the novel but often confused with it is the change in social and cultural forms concerning love and marriage. In all circum-Mediterranean societies marriage was not a private "dream of passion" but a carefully negotiated business arrangement between clans and families. In such a context adolescent passions are likely to be a threat to social stability; hence while most early Greek stories and poems about sexual desire (eros) may celebrate its pleasures both in and more often out of marriage, they never present eros as a motive for marriage. The notion that two young people who felt mutual love and desire should try to ratify those feelings by marriage was subversive, to say the least.

When political power in the post-Alexandrian period was somewhat less in the hands of the adult male citizens in each polis, there may have been a certain relaxing of patriarchal rigor, at least enough to tolerate the existence of idle fantasies in which lovely youths found a permanent erotic happiness that had nothing to do with property or parental arrangement. If "romance" is defined as the plot in which two young people in love get married, we may say that romance was invented in Hellenistic Greek lands as a cultural form but not as a social norm, as a plot of literature but not a plot of life.

Because the novels had no place in the serious curriculum of cultural honors but were rather a luxury product for the wealthy and a diverting entertainment for the less privileged, they were an available location for the outcropping of such impractical figments of the imagination. If anything, those novels that are also love stories show that romance was not a much-sought-after ideal but a fantasy of the significantly impossible. The typical young persons who fall in love in a novel take to their beds, sick with anxiety and certain that if they reveal their feelings to their parents they will be clobbered from here to doomsday. The young men, like Chaireas and Kleitophon, are of an age where the normal form of erotic socialization is still with other young men in the gymnasium. That Kallirhoë's parents, who at no time consult her wishes in the matter, are persuaded by popular demand to give her in marriage to Chaireas, the man of her dreams, is only the first of many unexpected turns in a narrative that excels in contriving them for our pleasure.

Some of the ancient novels, then, may be used to illustrate the invention of romance, but the notion that love leads to marriage is a particular Hellenistic novelty, whereas the plotting and performance of long fictions is not. The coincidence that most of the surviving evidence about this romantic fantasy is contained in novels has long been a source of confusion, obscuring both the nature and the variety of erotic ideologies in the novels and overshadowing the breadth of their other subject matter.

BIBLIOGRAPHY

SOURCES

Translations of the major Greek novels and fragments will soon be available in two volumes: *The Ancient Greek Novels*, translated by various hands under the editorship of B. P. Reardon (forthcoming), and *Fragments of Ancient Greek Novels*, edited and translated by John J. Winkler and S. E. Stephens (forthcoming). The latter will also contain a selection of texts illustrating the extent and development of ancient fiction outside the usual major works. The authors mentioned in this article are at present available as follows:

Apuleius, *The Golden Ass*, J. P. Sullivan, trans. (1965); Chariton, *Chaereas and Callirhoe*, Warren E. Blake, trans. (1939); Lloyd W. Daly, trans., "Life of Aesop," in *Aesop Without Morals* (1968); Ingemar Düring, trans., *Chion of Heraclea: A Novel in Letters* (1951); Heliodorus, *Ethiopian Story*, Walter Lamb, trans. (1961); Felix Jacoby, *Die Fragmente der griechischen Historiker*, IA (1926); Longus, *Daphnis and Chloe*, Paul Turner, trans. (1968); Lucian, "Lucius, the Ass," in *Selected Satires of Lucian*, Lionel Casson, trans. (1968); Petronius, *The Satyricon*, J. P. Sullivan, trans. (1965); *The Story of Apollonius, King of Tyre*, Zoja Pavlovskis, trans. (1978); Achilles Tatius, *Leucippe and Clitophon*, S. Gaselee, trans., rev. by E. H. Warmington (1969); A. M. Wolohojian, trans. from the Armenian, *The Romance of Alexander the Great by Pseudo-Callisthenes* (1969); Xenophon of Ephesus, "An Ephesian Tale," in *Three Greek Romances,* Moses Hadas, trans. (1953).

Diodoros, Pausanias, Plutarch, Strabo, and Xenophon are all available in the Loeb Classical Library editions.

GENERAL STUDIES

Graham Anderson, *Eros Sophistes: Ancient Novelists at Play* (1982); Martin Braun, *History and Romance in Graeco-Oriental Literature* (1938); Linda Dégh, *Folktales and Society* (1969); Northrop Frye, *The Secular Scripture: A Study of the Structure of Romance* (1976); Thomas Hägg, *The Novel in Antiquity* (1983); Arthur Heiserman, *The Novel Before the Novel* (1977); Peter Parsons, "Ancient Greek Romance," in *London Review of Books* (10 August 1981); Ben E. Perry, *The Ancient Romances* (1967); Erwin Rohde, *Der griechische Roman und seine Vorläufer* (1876; 5th ed. 1974); Sophie Trenkner, *The Greek Novella in the Classical Period* (1958); Ian Watt, *The Rise of the Novel* (1957); John J. Winkler, "The Invention of Romance," in *Laetaberis* (Journal of the California Classical Association), n.s. 1 (1982).

STUDIES OF INDIVIDUAL AUTHORS

William Arrowsmith, "Luxury and Death in the Satyricon," in *Arion,* **5** (1966); Anne P. Burnett, *Catastrophe Survived: Euripides' Plays of Mixed Reversal* (1971); Rhys Carpenter, *Folk Tale, Fiction and Saga in the Homeric Epics* (1946); Gerald K. Gresseth, "The *Odyssey* and the *Nalopākhyāna,*" in *Transactions of the American Philological Association,* **109** (1979); Richmond Lattimore, *Story Patterns in Greek Tragedy* (1964); Herwig Maehler, "Der Metioches–Parthenope–Roman," in *Zeitschrift für Papyrologie und Epigraphik,* **23** (1976); William McCulloh, *Longus* (1970); Denys Page, *Folktales in Homer's Odyssey* (1973); Peter Parsons, "A Greek Satyricon?" in *Bulletin of the Institute of Classical Studies,* **18** (1971); B. P. Reardon, "Theme, Structure and Narrative in Chariton," in *Yale Classical Studies,* **27** (1982).

James Tatum, *Apuleius and "The Golden Ass"* (1979); John J. Winkler, *Auctor and Actor: A Narratological Reading of Apuleius's "The Golden Ass"* (1985), and "The Mendacity of Kalasiris and the Narrative Strategy of Heliodoros' *Aithiopika*," in *Yale Classical Studies,* **27** (1982).

Letter Writing

ROBERT GLENN USSHER

THEORY

The ancient theorists asked: What is a letter? What style and contents are appropriate in a letter? How may letters be distinguished according to their purpose? To the first question, one Artemon (of unknown date, but editor of Aristotle's letters) replied "the one side of a literary dialogue" (Demetrios, *On Style* 223). Demetrios himself (early first century A.D.?) accepts the analogy insofar as both dialogue and letter—an especially self-revelatory form—reveal the character (*ethos*) of the writer: the letter, one might say, is an "image" (*eikon*) of the writer's soul (*psyche*) (227). To the second question he answers, "Plain style, clarity, and brevity" (though circumstances may slightly alter cases [234]) "with some degree of freedom in the structure" (223, 226, 228, 229). A letter admits no academic subtleties: its sole philosophy is conveyed in homely maxims expressive of goodwill and friendship (*philophronesis*) (231, 232). It is still, however, a literary art form: its plain style should also be graceful (*kharieis*), and more elaborate than de-manded by the dialogue (235, 224). Such elaboration—in length or expression—should not, at the same time, produce a thesis (*syngramma*) (228, 234).

Demetrios' comments—in their context, an aside—are echoed and amplified in other writers. Two technical manuals, out of many, have survived, the work of Demetrios (called, in the best manuscript, "of Phalerum") and Proklos. Demetrios (at an unknown date, in Egypt) wrote *Forms of the Letter* (*Typoi Epistolikoi*) and Proklos (pseudo-Libanios, fourth century A.D.?) wrote *Styles for Letters* (*Epistolimaioi Kharakteres*). Both answer the third question above by classifying letters—Demetrios in twenty-one, Proklos in forty-one divisions—as conveying, for example, information, consolation, recommendation (including introduction), thanks, congratulation, censure. Brief models (very brief, in Proklos) are added to illustrate each type. Three of these illustrative models, presented in free translation, will suffice.

Consolatory (*paramythetikos*, sc. *typos*):

When I heard of the terrible misfortune you had met with, I was deeply grieved and consid-

1573

ered it had happened not any more to you than to myself . . . I reflected, however, that such is the natural lot of all men . . . since I could not comfort you in person I decided to do so in a letter. So take what has happened as lightly as you can, and offer yourself your own advice to others (Demetrios, 4.20).

Recommendatory (*systatikos*):

So-and-so who is bringing you the letter has been proved by me. I esteem his loyal nature very highly. I shall appreciate it if you see fit to receive him, for my sake, for his, and for your own (Demetrios, 3.16).

Conveying thanks ([*ap*]*eukharistike*, sc. *epistole*):

I owe your goodness thanks for many other benefits, but especially for this one (Proklos, 23.5).

Both these writers recall Demetrios (*On Style*), his namesake by stress (1.5) on literary form, Proklos by a similar emphasis (13.4) and by repetition (19.18) of the primary need for brevity (*syntomia*) and clarity (*sapheneia*). Proklos is following (and quoting from) Philostratos (late second, early third century A.D.), one of two practitioners of literary letters who offer epistolary guidelines. Philostratus saw clarity—a "good guide" in any kind of literary discourse—as lending the persuasiveness often needed in a letter (Kayser, 1871); Gregory of Nazianzos (fourth century A.D.) sees "the best and finest letter" as that which, by its clarity, convinces both the ignorant and the learned (*Letters* 51.4). Brevity, it follows, is subordinate to clarity, whose primacy is axiomatic in Demetrios (*On Style* 226)—and may, within limits, be abandoned in its interest (Gregory, 51.2; Proklos, 20.14). Finally, the letter as an "image of the soul" is echoed in St. Basil: "Words are truly the images of souls," "I saw your soul in your letter" (*Letters* 9,

163). Demetrios, or his Aristotelian sources, could still, it seems, influence epistolary theory in the third and fourth centuries A.D. The influence, however, may not be a direct one, for schools of rhetoric had long, in their curricula, included letter-writing theory and practice (a second-century B.C. "practice-piece" survives from Egypt) and Basil's figure, in fact, has common ancestry in Demetrios and in the noted rhetorician (late first century B.C.) Dionysios of Halikarnassos (*Roman Antiquities* 1.1). Such ideas, whoever first expressed them, were soon the commonplaces of the schools.

The concept of the letter as "the one side of a dialogue," along with its basic requirement of friendship, assisted the view of it as "written conversation" (*homilia engrammatos*) (Proklos, 14.1) between two physically separated persons—particularly between separated friends (Proklos, 23.11): it creates the appearance (*phantasia*), in the mind of the recipient, of the presence (*parousia*) of the writer (Synesios, late fourth century A.D., *Letters* 138.1). It is conversation (*homilia*) or the illusion of it (*skia*), and evokes a physical presence as a work in *skiagraphia* produces its illusion at a distance (Gregory, 87.2; 93.2; 51.3). These ideas are once more commonplaces in St. Basil: "Take any excuse that from time to time arises for writing to me and granting me the solace of this long-interrupted conversation" (163). He even speaks of "visiting by letter" (62, 101). A feeling of spiritual communion is implicit ("even though I am separated from you by great distance, I suffer this only in the body"; Demetrios, 3.6): as St. Paul writes, "For though I be absent in the flesh, yet am I with you in the spirit" (Letter to the Colossians 2:5).

These tenets of fourth-century A.D. Greek epistolographers are echoed in contemporary Latin: they recur in Jerome, Augustine, and Paulinus. Julius Victor, whose work enshrines the traditional Greek epistolary teachings, recommends the occasional use of direct, colloquial language in a "face-to-face conversation, so to speak" (*quasi praesentem alloqui; Art of Rhetoric* 27, Halm 1863). His words recall, and are meant to, those of Cicero (*tecum ut quasi loquerer; Letters to Atticus* 9.10.1; *cum de me apud te loquor,* "when I am speaking"—through a letter—"in your presence"; 1.16.8), who often writes in this way to his friends. Letters, indeed, are the "personal conversations" (*colloquia*) of separated friends (*Philippics* 2.4.7) whose exchange can lighten care in sender or receiver (*Letters to Atticus* 12.39.2; St. Basil, 163, above). The figure is natural in letters from an exile (Ovid, *Letters from Pontus* 2.10.49; 3.5.50; St. Jerome, *Letters* 7.2), and a lover aims, in writing to his mistress, "to seem to be speaking face-to-face" (Ovid, *Art of Love* 1.468). This view implies the appropriateness of conversational style (*familiaris sermo;* Cicero, *Letters to Atticus* 1.9.1), and Seneca, who shares it (*Moral Letters* 40.1; 67.2) is explicit: "I want my letters to be spontaneous and easy, just like my talk were we together" (75.1). Epistolary style, that is, should not be labored (Demetrios, *On Style* 229) and should incline toward spoken language (Gregory 51.4; Julius Victor); the love letter, for example, will persuade by "believable language and ordinary words" (Ovid, *Art of Love* 1.467). Quintilian, who like Artemon groups letters with the dialogue, believes them (like Demetrios, 231) an inappropriate medium for discussion of academic subjects: when not required to perform "above their nature" their style is loose, *soluta* (*Education of an Orator* 9.4.19). The slight stylistic heightening Greek theory desiderates (Demetrios, 224, 234; Proklos, 19.9; Philostratos, Kayser, p. 258, 11. 8ff; Gregory, 51.5) is nowhere explicit in the Roman; but the Greeks had foreseen the risk, in seeking style, of falling into affectation (*kompsologia,* Proklos, 19.11; Philostratos, Kayser, p. 258, 1.11 Gregory, 51.7) and Seneca, censured by Lucilius for

"careless" (in the sense of informal, "unliterary") writing, defends himself by asserting that his letters are, for that very reason, free from affectation (75.1). Philostratos had prescribed the happy medium—clarity is best served by common thoughts expressed in new and new thoughts expressed in common, language (*koina kainos; kaina koinos*).

HISTORY AND PRACTICE

A letter, whatever it might be in theory, was in practice an *epistole:* it was "sent to" (*epistellein*) an addressee. What was its portable form and who conveyed it? Both Greeks (from early times; Homer, *Iliad* 6.168–170) and Romans (though perhaps in later times for short notes only; Cicero, *Letters to Atticus* 12.7.1; Pliny, *Letters* 6.16.8) used tablets: of lead (the Berezan letter, sixth/fifth century B.C., the letter of Mnesiergos, fourth century B.C.), of ivory (St. Augustine, *Letters* 15.1), or (commonly) of wood (the finds at Vindolanda; Aristophanes, *Women at the Thesmophoria* 775, Propertius, 3.23.8) with a waxed surface (Herodotus, 7.239.3; Plautus, *Weevil* [*Curculio*] 410) on which the characters were chiseled (Quintilian, *Education of an Orator* 1.1.27). The sharp-pointed pen (Greek *graphis;* Latin *stilus*) when inverted could act as an eraser (Cicero, *Verrine Orations* 2.2.41), allowing repeated use of the same tablet (Propertius, 3.23.3). The tablets (Greek *deltoi, pinakes;* Latin *tabellae, codicilli, pugillares*), in which two or more "leaves" could be folded (Herodotos, 7.239.3; Symmachus, late fourth century A.D., *Letters* 2.81.2; Euripides, *Iphigenia in Tauris* 727) were secured with thread or tape, and sealed with wax and the impress of a signet ring (Euripides, *Hippolytos* 862–865; Plautus, *The Two Bacchises* 748). The common medium, however, was papyrus (Latin *charta*), inscribed with a reed pen (*kalamos, calamus*) in black ink (*melan, atramentum*): "I shall write this letter with a good pen, in well-mixed ink, on ivory-polished paper" (Cicero, *Letters to Quintus* 2.15.1). Sheets were pasted together, folded or rolled up, and tied and sealed (Cicero, *Letters to Atticus* 12.1.2; Ovid, *Tristia* 4.7.7; Basil, 3.1). Papyrus, of whatever grade (Pliny the Elder, *Natural History* 13.74–76) was flexible and durable, and offered a smooth surface to the writer (Lewis, 1974); when neither it nor tablets were available St. Augustine used parchment (*membrana; Letters* 15.1).

Private letters required private messengers, for neither in Greece nor in Rome were there facilities for other than official public mails. A writer without available slaves or freedmen of his own—a bishop could employ a priest or acolyte (St. Augustine, 191.1)—depended, at all periods, on finding someone "going there," and travelers on some routes were infrequent (Cicero, *Letters to Atticus* 8.14.1; 1.9.1). Iphigenia had nobody to take a letter back to Argos (Euripides, *Iphigenia in Tauris* 588–589) and St. Basil sent a letter with Sophronios when he found him "setting out in your direction" (105; St. Augustine, 80.1). In Rome, however, leading citizens had access to private couriers (*tabellarii*) employed on state or other business—in particular, those of the tax collectors (*publicani*), who moved regularly between the provinces and Rome (Cicero, *Letters to Atticus* 5.16.1); Cicero (at Antium) writes hastily on learning that the quaestor's boy is leaving for the city (*Letters to Atticus* 2.9.1). Delays were frequent, if only from bad weather (Basil, 121), and Ovid, in exile at Tomis, estimates that for a letter to reach Rome from the Black Sea and be answered takes a year (*Letters from Pontus* 4.11.15–16). Messengers, moreover, could meet with mishaps or be unfaithful: Iphigenia gives Pylades her letter under oath—in case, his life once assured, he should forget it—and after he has mastered the contents, which she reads to him, in case he should lose it by the way (Euripides, *Iphi-*

genia in Tauris 727–787; Cicero, *Letters to Atticus* 2.8.1; 7.9.1). They were sometimes tempted to inspect a letter's contents (Cicero, *Letters to Atticus* 1.13.1), and this fact, with the uncertainty "in the disturbed state of the world" of a letter's reaching its addressee, makes St. Basil (173) hesitant in writing.

Letters, despite difficulties, were delivered, and hundreds of them (written on papyrus, the earliest from the third century B.C.) survive from the rubbish heaps and cemeteries of settlements (Oxyrhynkos, Tebtunis) in Greco-Roman Egypt. They preserve, with their fold marks, an address upon the back, and the letter itself begins (Demetrios, *On Style* 228; Proklos, 21.11) and ends with formulas that, after the earlier Herodotean prescript ("Amasis to Polykrates says thus"; *Histories* 3.40.1), vary little over centuries (Xenophon, *Education of Cyrus* 4.5.27 and 33):

> Isias to her brother Hephaistion, greetings [*khairein*, literally "joy"; Mnesiergos' letter combines this with the Herodotean formula (Witkowski, 1911, p. 135); Christian letters add "in God" or "in the Lord"]. If you are well . . . it would accord with the prayers [or elsewhere, "obeisance," *proskynema*] I continually make to the gods [in Christian letters "to God" or "to the Lord"]. I myself . . . enjoy good health. . . . I shall be pleased if you look after your body to stay healthy. Good-bye [*erroso*, literally, "be well"] (Hunt and Edgar, 1932, p. 283).

Addresses are, naturally, in hand-delivered letters brief: "to Hephaistion," "to Flavianos from Demetrios," "deliver at Pathyris to my father" (Hunt and Edgar, pp. 283, 387, 291); but sometimes the letter requires being forwarded ("deliver this letter from Apion to Ioulianos at the camp . . . to reach his father Epimakhos" [p. 307]), or itself includes such instructions for replying ("if you write . . . send it to . . . Hermes at Artemas' house, so that he can deliver it to me"; (Youtie, 1976). The month and year are often added.

The letters deal with administrative details (in correspondence with agents such as Zenon), the management of agricultural estates (in letters to the steward Heroneinos), with social, and, predominantly, family concerns. Family marriages, births, sicknesses and deaths, quarrels and offers of reconciliation, the trivia or temporary crises of the day, are matters for relatives to write of: a naval recruit, en route to Misenum, sends a note from Rome to reassure his mother; a boy, away at school, asks his father for a visit, endearingly adding, "Don't forget our pigeons"; Theon writes to an official recommending the carrier, his brother: "Herakleides, the bearer of this letter, is my brother. . . . I shall very much appreciate it if he happens to gain your favorable notice" (Hunt and Edgar, pp. 303, 339, 297). The form of the last and similar letters recalls Demetrios. Papyrus letters, if sometimes written by (through professional scribes) and to illiterates, or at least to recipients ignorant of Greek, sometimes also—apart from their brevity, which could be eked out by verbal information from the messenger— show knowledge of the teaching of the schools. "Look at this letter, my lord, and imagine I am talking with you" (in a Latin letter to a military tribune); "I received your letter, through which I seemed to see you" (to a brother). Both letters date from the second century A.D. (Hunt and Edgar, p. 323; Youtie, 1976).

The Christian Epistolary Tradition

Pagan and Christian papyrus letters closely parallel the style of the New Testament Epistles. A striking resemblance is in the lists of relatives, friends, and fellow Christians from whom and to whom the writer sends a greeting. Thus (for example) a student writes, in a letter to his father: "I greet my mother [named, like all these rela-tives] and my sister . . . and my brother . . . I greet Melanos and Timpesouris and her son. Gaia greets you all . . . Horeion and Thermouthis greet you all" (Hunt and Edgar, p. 345), and St. Paul (who sometimes, like Cicero, wrote in his own hand; Letter to the Galatians 6:11) ends a long list of similar greetings ("Greet Prisca and Aquila") with "The churches of Christ salute you" (Letter to the Romans 16:3–16). Differences are the distinctive Christian prescript and valedictory benediction and the generally greater length of the Epistles. This is required (Gregory, 51.2; Proklos, 20.14) for the letter to fulfill its primary task of expounding and disseminating doctrine; for though letters were early exchanged in Christian circles (Acts of the Apostles 18:27), the New Testament writers stand in the tradition of those (philosophers, political and literary theorists) who used letters to propagate ideas. Plato, for example, treats the problems of philosophy, writing to the Syracusan Dion and his friends, in Letters 7.340c–345c (a letter regarded as a treatise by Demetrios, On Style 234); Isokrates airs his theories in letters to the Macedonian princes, as did Aristotle, whose letters are both praised and criticized by Demetrios (230, 234); Dionysios of Halikarnassos, like Horace, uses the letter form as a medium for literary criticism. Yet even here the didactic note does not exclude the personal: Plato's letter is largely autobiographical, and Isokrates finds a personal, informal tone in recommending Diodotos to Antipater (Letters 4). The combination, marked in the apostolic letters, recurs in the group of Greek epistolographers who span the fourth century A.D. Among them are Libanius, a pagan rhetorician, and these—a few out of many— leading churchmen (the three last-named probably his pupils): Synesios, bishop of Ptolemais, for whom letters are "not a gift from any man" (in reference to Demetrios, On Style 234?), but rather a gift from God to men (138.1); John Chrysostom, bishop of

Constantinople; Gregory, who supplied model letters for his pupil (52.2); and Basil, bishop of Caesarea.

Of these, and their Latin counterparts (Jerome, Augustine, Paulinus, and the militant pagan Symmachus) the scope of this essay allows only passing mention. For general readers, Basil and Jerome excel in interest: theological controversy, advice on Christian living (particularly on the duties of the monk, as in Basil, 22 and Jerome, 125), reproof of a wayward monk or boastful emperor (Basil, 44; Jerome, 14; Basil, 41 to Julian, himself a letter writer), and exposition of the values of virginity and widowhood (Jerome, 22, 54) mingle with consolation to individuals and churches ("Since . . . I could not join you in person, it remained for me to share your present griefs by letter" [Basil, 28; Demetrios, 4.20]), praises, embodied in consolatory letters, of good women (Jerome, 39, 77), and occasional family and personal details such as recurrent illness (Basil, 139, 163; Jerome, 7). Both writers stand in the espistolary tradition of St. Paul ("Greet Paula and Eustochium . . . greet your mother and sisters . . . along with Marcellina and Felicitas" [Jerome, 45.7]), as well as in the classical tradition. St. Basil advised on how to profit from Greek literature (*Address to Young Men*). Jerome was torn between his two conflicting loyalties ("What has Cicero to do with the apostle?") and agonized over heaven's accusations of his being "a Ciceronian, not a Christian" (22.30). He stands at the end of a group of Latin writers who, following Cicero, ensured epistolography a high rank in the literature of Rome.

The Roman Classical Tradition

CICERO. Cicero's letters to his brother Quintus, Atticus, and his friends span the years 68 to 43 B.C. They cover the turbulent history of the late Roman Republic, including the writer's own consulship and exile, and offer (especially those to Atticus in Greece) a privileged insight into Cicero's ambitions, his shifting political allegiances (as a Pompeian attracted by Caesar's personality; *Letters to Quintus* 2.14), his public hurt, and his private grief. The letters, depending on the addressee and occasion (Demetrios, *On Style* 234), are sometimes of studied formality and stiffness (*Letters to Friends* 5.7, to Pompey), at other times they are dashed off informally (between the courses of a meal, or by the roadside [*Letters to Atticus* 14.21.4; 5.16.1]). Cicero himself defined three categories (*genera*) of letters. The first is the "familiar and jocular" (*familiare et iocosum*); the jocular is best seen not in Cicero but in Caelius, the colorful young friend whom he appointed his informant while he himself was absent in Cilicia (*Letters to Friends* 8.1.1), the familiar in the letters (written in his own hand when possible and not, as usual, dictated to his freedman) to Atticus and Quintus (*Letters to Quintus* 2.2.1; 2.16.1; *Letters to Atticus* 2.23.1; 13.9.1). The second is the "serious and grave" (*severum et grave*), as seen in the letters to Pompey (above) and Spinther (*Letters to Friends* 1.1). The third is the "most authentic" (*unum illud certissimum*), which (in accordance with the letters' raison d'être) "inform the absent of what it is desirable, in their interests or ours, for them to know" (*Letters to Friends* 2.4.1). Such newsletters (*apangeltikai*) (Proklos, 29.1), in familiar style and language ("those somewhat loose and Cicero-like letters of yours" [Fronto, *Letters to Marcus Aurelius* 1.9.4]) kept Atticus abreast of affairs of public interest and matters of personal or family concern—the difficulties between Quintus and his wife (the shrewish Pomponia, Atticus' sister), the birth of "a little son, with Terentia well" (*Letters to Atticus* 5.1.3–4; 1.2.1). Clarity here may be sacrificed to secrecy: agents in private transactions have pseudonymous Greek names (*Letters to Atticus* 1.14.7). The use throughout of Greek words and quotations, partly playful, is also the earnest of a culture shared with Atticus ("the parts of my speeches that have met with your approval now seem to me much *attikotera* [more Attic]") (*Letters to Atticus* 1.13.5). Specific echoes of Greek theorists are heard in the consolatory letter from Sulpicius:

> When the news of the death of Tullia, your daughter, was conveyed to me, I was deeply upset . . . and considered the great loss one we shared. . . . Had she not met her appointed day at this time, she must yet have died a few years later, since she had been born a human being . . . bring to your own attention and set before your mind the advice which you usually give others (*Letters to Friends* 4.5.1, 4, and 5; cf. Demetrios, 4.20).

The letters of recommendation (*epistulae commendaticiae*) (*Letters to Friends* 5.5.1), which occupy completely Book Thirteen in that collection, similarly follow the theorists' prescription of praise for the person recommended in the letter and gratification in the person recommending should the addressee accede to his request (*Letters to Friends* 7.5.3; 13.11.3; Demetrios, 3.16). The formulas of Greek letters are recalled in prescripts, "Cicero to Atticus [gives] greetings"; in conventional expressions of goodwill, "if you are well I am," or "it is, well"; and in endings, which transmit greetings to and from third parties ("Please greet Attica," "Terentia sends you hearty greetings" [*Letters to Atticus* 14.19.6; 2.12.4]), before the formal valediction, "Be well" (*vale*), "See that you keep well" (*cura ut valeas*) (*Letters to Friends* 7.6.2). The formal ending, however, is exceptional: Cicero, and his correspondents, tend to finish curtly (*Letters to Friends* 10.28; 8.1), and he only very rarely adds a date.

SENECA. Publication of the letters, though considered and discussed, did not occur in Cicero's own lifetime. They are first referred to by the Senecas, who quote from them, and may have suggested to Seneca the Younger (*d.* A.D. 65) the use of the epistolary form. Seneca's *Moral Letters* are an excellent example of Demetrios' treatise with a prescript (Demetrios, *On Style* 228): they are philosophical musings, often in reply to queries from Lucilius, his addressee, which stand in the tradition of letters used to disseminate ideas (three letters of Epicurus, for example, are preserved in Diogenes Laertios, *On the Lives of the Famous Philosophers* 10.35). They tell us much of Seneca, and something, incidentally, of Lucilius, himself of philosophical interests and a writer (40.2; 46.1), and their interest is literary more than philosophical: the description, for example, of "the happy man" (45.9) belongs in the tradition of the *character*. The Senecan letter—essentially an essay—and its style—more careful than Seneca's words suggest—point forward to the novel work of Pliny.

PLINY THE YOUNGER. Pliny the Younger (*ca.* A.D. 61–112) collected and edited letters "written with some care" (*epistulae curatius scriptae*) (*Letters* 1.1). The care for style (contrast Cicero) is Senecan, the pictures of social life and the range of correspondents (contrast Seneca) are Ciceronian. The correspondence is in origin practical (Pliny was a property owner, lawyer, and governor of Bithynia under Trajan) and was also the exchange of belletristic compositions between himself and other men of culture (9.28.5). It emerges, in its published form, as a new literary genre that rivals Cicero's variety of topics (despite a disclaimer; 9.2.2) and offers an anthology, in epistolary form, of short and elegant literary essays. Many concern his own life, in Rome or in the country (1.9; 9.36), his aspirations to literary fame (based, however, on his speeches, not his letters; 1.2), and his pride in success, both as advocate and writer (9.23). Some describe a contemporary banquet (1.15; 2.6), others give the darker sides of Roman life (a slave-owner's cruelty resulting in his own death; 3.14). We learn of his own humane attitude toward slaves (5.19; 8.16, though this is, perhaps, a literary topic; compare Seneca,

47), his practical interest in children's education (he founded a school in his native Comum [Como]; 4.13), and his views on the futility of public games (9.6; compare again Seneca, 70.26). This last letter (like 5.8, on writing history) echoes Cicero (*Letters to Friends* 7.1, a uniquely literary letter; 5.12, to the historian Lucceius): it also illustrates Pliny's practice of devoting each letter/essay to one theme. Many are characters (as in Seneca) or portraits (especially of women): Calpurnia is objectively portrayed as "the good wife" (4.19).

Some of the letters are merely anecdotal (a trio of ghost stories, 7.27; the dolphin of Hippo Regius, 9.33), but two are of surpassing historical importance—the description (to Tacitus) of the Vesuvius eruption (A.D. 79) and that (to Trajan) of Christians in Bithynia (6.16, 20; 10.96; the collection, in a tenth book, of official correspondence, is copied in Symmachus' letters). Epistolary teaching dictates the formal language of recommendation and of thanks: "You will have me, you will have himself, your very grateful debtor"; "I have to thank you for many acts of kindness, but you have really helped me in—" 3.2.6; 5.3.1). Short letters often end (as Philostratos advised) with a reference back to their beginning (3.16; 8.24): brevity is stressed (2.5.13), as frequently in Fronto (*Letters to Marcus Aurelius* 4.3.8).

FRONTO. The correspondence of Fronto with his pupil the future emperor Marcus Aurelius and his friends—discovered only in the early nineteenth century—has interest for students of rhetoric and language. Fronto aimed at a "modern style" of Latin (*elocutio novella*) (*On Eloquence* 5[4].1), but offers less to attract the common reader than Pliny or Cicero, whose familiar style it mentions (1.9.4). Yet despite their content—the academic mixed with the trivial—the letters of both Fronto and Marcus Aurelius (praised as a letter writer by Philostratos) have a freshness that eludes the prose of those for whom (like Seneca) the letter form is merely a convention.

EPISTOLOGRAPHY IN VERSE

Not all epistolography, however, is in prose: "The elasticity of the epistle form, especially as a receptacle for literary creation, had been long recognized by the Romans" (Jacobson, 1974). Horace in his *Epistles* (following Lucilius, second century B.C.) employed it to effect (in poems addressed to a wide range of correspondents, including the emperor Augustus), for example, to express his views on literature and ethics (1.19; 2.1; the "good man" is depicted in 1.16) or to issue an invitation to or recommend a friend (1.5.9). There are personal details (his appearance, age, and character; 1.20.19–28, and his route to poetry; 2.2. 41–52): he can laugh at himself as "a porker from the herd of Epicurus" (1.4.16). His *Art of Poetry,* or *Epistle to the Pisones,* stands apart: it deals, in particular, with dramatic composition (86–294). The style of the *Epistles* blends the poetic with the familiar (they seem to be included in "conversations" [*sermones*]; 2.1.250–251), and lends itself to proverbial quotation (*Epistles* 1.11.27; *Art of Poetry* 78; 139).

Epistolary form is again employed by Ovid. *Heroines* (*Heroides*) are imaginary letters (the word is Ovid's, *Art of Love* 3.345)—rhetorical, epigrammatic, and ingenious, if monotonous—from heroines of mythology to husbands or lovers who have left them (Medea to Jason, Dido to Aeneas). They offer, at times, a metrical attempt at formal prescript or valediction (4, 16, 18; 9, 13, 21) but, like *Letters from Pontus* (to Ovid's wife and certain friends) with their quasi prescripts (1.7; 3.4), have little other claim to rank as letters. No Greek model is known for the love letter in verse, and Ovid's claim to have created it (prompted, perhaps, by the letter in Propertius, 4.3) may be justifiably accepted (*Art of Love* 3. 346).

Real love letters, of course, were commonly exchanged (Ovid, *Art of Love* 1.455; Plautus, *Pseudolus* 41), but the prose love letter (Proklos, 33.5) may date, as a literary form, only from Lesbonax (of Mytilene, second century A.D.): it is sometimes traced, improbably, to Lysias' discourse (Plato, *Phaidros* 230e–234c). Philostratos' brief *Love Letters* (to both sexes) are of interest because of their influence on Ben Jonson, "To Celia" (2, 32, 33, 46) and Robert Herrick, "To the Virgins" (55). "Aristainetos'" erotic letters (date unknown) include one (2.1) partly modeled on Aelian, *Farmers' Letters* 7 (late second, early third century A.D.): but the best love letters are found in (Aelian's slightly older contemporary?) Alkiphron, who himself appears in "Aristainetos" (1.5) and whose *Letters from Courtesans,* like those from *Farmers, Fishermen,* and *Parasites,* purport to be written, in the language of the day, by contemporaries of Menander. The letters between Menander himself and Glykera are famous (4.18, 19). Menander's influence on these writers is paramount (notably in "Aristainetos" and Aelian 13–16), and Alkiphron especially, despite his patent bookishness and an insecure grasp of the language of his period, has much that is fresh and interesting to offer.

The imaginary letters of an Ovid or an Alkiphron pay scant respect to epistolary theory or, apart from brief prescripts, current practice. It is fitting to end, then, with those of "Khion of Herakleia" (ostensibly of the fourth century B.C., but written, perhaps, in the early first century A.D.). His letters, which constitute an epistolary novel, are the finest exemples of the precepts of the Demetrii, Philostratos, and Proklos.

It is idle to search for the creator of letters as a literary genre. This essay offers not a literary history, but merely a succinct examination of epistolary theory and practice, and the sole distinction recognized is between real and imaginary, not literary and nonliterary, letters.

BIBLIOGRAPHY

SOURCES

Alciphron, Aelian, Philostratus, *The Letters,* L. A. Post and E. H. Warmington, eds., Allen Rogers Benner and Francis H. Fobes, trans. (1949); Aristaenetus, *Epistularum libri duo,* O. Mazal, ed. (1971); St. Augustine, *Select Letters,* L. A. Post and E. H. Warmington, eds., James Houston Baxter, trans. (1930); St. Basil, *The Letters,* L. A. Post and E. H. Warmington, eds., Roy J. Deferrari and Martin R. P. McGuire, trans., 4 vols. (1926–1934); *Chion of Heraclea: A Novel in Letters,* Ingemar Düring, trans. (1951); Cicero, *Letters to Atticus,* D. R. Shackleton Bailey, ed. and trans., 6 vols. (1965–1967), *Epistulae ad Familiares* (*Letters to Friends*), D. R. Shackleton Bailey, ed., 2 vols. (1977), *Epistulae ad Quintum fratrem et M. Brutum* (*Letters to my Brother Quintus and to Marcus Brutus*), D. R. Shackleton Bailey, ed. (1980), and *Letters to his Friends,* D. R. Shackleton Bailey, trans., 2 vols. (1978).

Demetrius, *On Style,* W. Rhys Roberts, ed. and trans. (1902); Marcus Cornelius Fronto, *Epistulae,* I, M. P. J. van den Hout, ed. (1954), and *The Correspondence,* L. A. Post and E. H. Warmington, eds., C. R. Haines, trans., 2 vols. (1919, 1920; rev. ed. 1928, 1929); St. Gregory of Nazianzos, *Lettres,* Paul Galley, ed. and trans., 2 vols. (1964, 1967); Carolus Halm, ed., *Rhetores Latini Minores* (1863); Horace, *Satires, Epistles and Ars Poetica* (*Art of Poetry*), E. H. Warmington, ed., H. Rushton Fairclough, trans. (1926; rev. ed. 1929); *Isocrates,* III, E. H. Warmington, ed., Larue van Hook, trans. (1945); St. Jerome, *Select Letters,* L. A. Post and E. H. Warmington, eds., F. A. Wright, trans. (1933); Julius Victor, *Ars Rhetorica* (*Art of Rhetoric*), 26, 27 (see Halm, *Rhetores Latini Minores*).

Ovid, *Heroides, Amores* (*Heroines, Loves*), T. E. Page and W. H. D. Rouse, eds., Grant Showerman, trans. (1914), and *Tristia, Ex Ponto* (*Letters from Pontus*), G. P. Goold, ed., Arthur Leslie Wheeler, trans. (1924; repr. 1975); Philostratus, *Opera,* II, C. L. Kayser, ed. (1871); *Plato,* VII,

L. A. Post and E. H. Warmington, eds., R. G. Bury, trans. (1929); Pliny the Younger, *Letters and Panegyricus,* E. H. Warmington and G. P. Goold, eds., Betty Radice, trans., 2 vols. (1969); L. A. Post and E. H. Warmington, eds., A. S. Hunt and C. C. Edgar, trans., *Select Papyri* I (1932); Symmachus, *Lettres,* Jean Pierre Callu, ed. and trans. (1972); Synesios, *Epistolae,* A. Garzya, ed. (1979), and *The Letters,* Augustine Fitzgerald, trans. (1926); V. Weichert, ed., *Demetrii et Libanii qui feruntur* Τύποι ἐπιστολικοί *et* Ἐπιστολιμαίοι χαρακτῆρες (1910); Stanislaus Witkowski, ed., *Epistulae Privatae Graecae* (1911).

STUDIES

W. Geoffrey Arnott, "Pastiche, Pleasantry, Prudish Eroticism: The Letters of 'Aristaenetus,'" in *Yale Classical Studies,* **27** (1982); Alan K. Bowman, *The Roman Writing Tablets from Vindolanda* (1983); A. Buelow-Jacobsen, "Family Letter," in *Zeitschrift für Papyrologie und Epigraphik,* **29** (1978); O. A. W. Dilke, "Horace and the Verse Letter," in C. D. N. Costa, ed., *Horace* (1973); Reginald Hackforth and Brinley Roderick Rees, "Letters, Greek," in *The Oxford Classical Dictionary* (1949; 2d ed. 1970); Howard Jacobson, *Ovid's Heroides* (1974); Robert Graham Cochrane Levens, "Letters, Latin," in *The Oxford Classical Dictionary;* Naphtali Lewis, *Papyrus in Classical Antiquity* (1974).

D. A. Russell, "Letters to Lucilius," in C. D. N. Costa, ed., *Seneca* (1974); Eric Gardiner Turner, *Greek Papyri* (1968); J. G. Vinogradov, "A Greek Letter from Berezan," in *Vestnik Drevnej Istorii,* **118** (1971); J. G. Winter, *Life and Letters in the Papyri* (1933); H. C. Youtie, "*P. Mich. Inv. 241:* ἐδοξά σε Θεωρεῖν," in *Zeitschrift für Papyrologie und Epigraphik,* **22** (1976).

PHILOSOPHY

Greek Philosophy

G. E. R. LLOYD

ORIGINS AND SOURCES

The idea that Thales of Miletus is the father of philosophy has its ultimate origin in a judgment of Aristotle's in his discussion of his predecessors in the first book of the *Metaphysics.* Yet it can be accepted, if at all, only in a very restricted sense. Aristotle himself does not suggest that Thales originated the whole of what he includes under the rubric of philosophy. Nor—it should be stressed—was Aristotle attempting to write a purely historical account. Rather his interest, as always, is in substantive philosophical or scientific questions. The particular issue he is dealing with, in the text in question, is the types of account (or "causes") that earlier thinkers had tried to give. According to Aristotle, one kind of question that can be asked concerning any physical object is directed to discovering what it is made of, or what is its matter. That will elicit a simple answer, at any rate as a first approximation, where most artifacts are concerned: the reply will take the form that a sculpture, for instance, is made of bronze or marble or wood or wire. But obviously to say what the

material constituents of some natural objects are is often much more difficult: What are marble or limestone or wood or blood or hair made of? In some cases the inquiry will correspond to what we should call chemistry or to biochemistry. But the questions can be pressed further back and generalized. If we decide to call limestone a kind of "earth" and blood a kind of "water," it would still be open to us to ask what earth and water themselves consist in. At the limit, the question is one concerning the fundamental elements, their differentiation and their methods of combining, and so one that corresponds to physics as much as to chemistry in modern terms.

Aristotle's contention (*Metaphysics* 983b18 ff.) is that Thales was the first to investigate the material causes of things, that is, the physical elements, and he reports that Thales held that the "principle" of all things is water. Our other early information about Thales allows us to infer that even before Aristotle he had a reputation as some kind of genius. "The man's a Thales," remarks a character in Aristophanes' *Birds* (1009). Plato includes him in the list he gives of the

Seven Wise Men (*Protagoras* 343a). Evidence in Herodotus (for example, 1.170) indicates that Thales was involved in the political affairs of his hometown of Miletus and offered his advice about how the Ionian cities of the western seaboard of Asia Minor should respond to the threat posed by the Persian Empire. Herodotus also reports (1.74) that Thales predicted an eclipse of the sun "to within a year." The eclipse in question—which coincided with a battle between the Lydians and the Medes—enables us to give a precise date to the event, 585 B.C., even if the form of Thales' prediction, and its basis, are otherwise matters of mere conjecture. Later sources leave out Herodotus' qualification "to within a year," and fanciful suggestions have often been made that Thales had access to Babylonian astronomical lore and used this to make his prediction. But caution is necessary. At no stage in the ancient world could anyone, Greek or non-Greek, accurately predict that a solar eclipse would be visible at a given location on the surface of the earth: the most they could do was to say when an eclipse of the sun might occur or when one was ruled out. It is not impossible that Thales may have heard something about Babylonian eclipse observations. However, it is as well to insist that there is no reliable direct evidence whatsoever that he had access to Babylonian astronomical records or, more important, to someone who could have interpreted such records to him or reported their contents in an intelligible fashion. Thales himself, we may be sure, would not have been in any position to understand, unaided, the technical astronomical cuneiform tablets that modern archaeology has unearthed from Mesopotamia.

Aristotle himself shows great diffidence in interpreting Thales' opinion about water as the principle. The contrast with later commentators is again striking. Aristotle's own frequent discussions of earlier thinkers stimulated an important tradition not so much of complete histories of early Greek philosophy and science as of collections of the opinions of notable theorists. Aristotle's successor as head of the Lyceum, Theophrastus, composed a work entitled *The Opinions of the Natural Philosophers,* now extant only in fragments, and it probably served as the basis and model for many later so-called doxographical accounts (records of the opinions of earlier philosophers). There is, moreover, a marked tendency in this tradition for the confidence with which attributions are made to increase the greater the distance in time between the commentator and the person he is commenting upon, and wherever (as quite often) we have to rely solely or even principally on such sources, the conjectural nature of any reconstruction must be emphasized. As regards Thales himself, if, as seems likely, the tradition that has it that he left nothing in writing is correct, Aristotle's diffidence is readily understandable. He does not claim to know precisely why Thales made the suggestion about water that he did. As Aristotle puts it in *Metaphysics* 983b22 ff.:

> He may have derived his supposition from seeing that the nourishment of all creatures is moist, and that warmth itself is generated from moisture and lives by it, and that from which all things come to be is their first principle. Besides this, another reason for his supposition would be that the seeds of all things have a moist nature, and for moist things water is the principle of their nature.

The limitations of what we can confidently ascribe to Thales thus emerge very clearly. There is, for example, no suggestion in our extant evidence that he was interested in political and moral philosophy—as opposed to practical politics. Nor, so far as we know, was he concerned with logic or with the theory of knowledge. His chief interests were in a small area in the study of nature, rather than in what we call philosophy nowadays. Doubts too must be expressed about precisely what questions he addressed in that area. Aristotle's view was that Thales held that water is the material element of all things, that is, that all things are made of water. At the same time it is as certain as anything can be about Thales that he did not speak of "matter" as such, the Greek term for which, *hyle,* is a coinage of Aristotle's own. He may not even have spoken of water as the *arche* or principle, for *arche* was a term that his immediate successor Anaximander is reported to have been the first to use in relation to *his* principle, the Boundless. Moreover, even if that had been Thales' word, an important ambiguity in it, and in cognate expressions referring to that "from which" things arise, enables us to distinguish more clearly than Aristotle does in the text quoted between two possible questions that Thales may have been addressing: first, that of the elementary constituents of physical objects, and second, that of their chronological origin. If we accept the account in Aristotle at all, we may be confident that Thales was interested in the second of these two questions. Whether he was also interested in the first—that is, whether he thought of water as what things are made of now, as well as that "from which" things originated—is more doubtful.

Obviously the question of Thales' relationship to earlier thought depends on the position we take on that issue. His ideas about water, which include also the notion that the earth floats on water, have often been compared, in ancient and in modern times, with earlier myths, both Greek and non-Greek. Aristotle himself refers to the idea that Ocean and Tethys are the parents of the gods in this very connection—not that he endorses the view that such an idea was in any real sense an anticipation of Thales. Babylonian and more especially Egyptian

myths about primeval water deities have also been adduced by ancient and by modern commentators. Yet stories that Thales visited Egypt, for instance, may be rather fragile grounds for the supposition that he studied Egyptian mythology, even though, equally obviously, the possibility that he was aware of some of its themes and motifs cannot be discounted completely. It would, however, undoubtedly be simplistic to think of Thales as straightforwardly "demythologizing" earlier myths, whether Greek or non-Greek. What would it mean, we must ask, at this stage to set out to demythologize myth—for the explicit category of myth as such, in the sense of fictional narrative account, is once again a later invention. Nor was Thales ridding the world, or the world picture, of gods. Quite to the contrary: another report in Aristotle (*On the Soul* 411a8) says that he held that "all things are full of gods." This may in turn be connected with a further testimony (*On the Soul* 405a19 ff.) to the effect that the magnet possesses soul, in which case Thales may have been impressed by the evident capacity for motion, and for causing movement, in some apparently inert objects, though clearly we are in no position to say for sure that that was his idea.

If we restrict ourselves to the Greek writers Thales definitely did know about, perhaps the most likely suggestion is that his ideas about water should be seen against the background of the story of the origins of gods and men in Hesiod's *Theogony.* Hesiod had put it (*Theogony* 116 ff.) that "first of all chaos came to be," where "chaos" is probably to be interpreted not as disorder so much as a yawning gap, perhaps the gap between heaven and earth, assumed originally to have been a single undivided form. Certainly Hesiod then goes on to talk of the genealogies of divine beings, some generated, as he puts it, "without love," but most by sexual union. What Thales' suggestion about water has in common with such an account is that it offers an answer to the question of the origins of things. If that was Thales' chief concern, there would be no need to ascribe to him any further, more sophisticated conception of the underlying material substratum of all physical objects, in addition, that is, to that interest in beginnings. But where Thales' account differs from Hesiod's is that it refers not to some imagined primeval yawning gap but to a familiar substance, water: whatever Hesiod meant by "chaos," it is not an object we can see around us in the world we know. Thales' suggestion, on the other hand, was that the multiplicity of physical objects in everyday experience originates—in some way he may have left quite unclear—from water. The guess in Aristotle, as we saw, was that water is essential for life, for nutrition, and for generation: on that view Thales' primary concern would be to account for the origin of living things.

This line of interpretation, it must be repeated, remains, like all others, a conjecture. While many scholars have been less reluctant to accept the implication, from Aristotle, that Thales' water answers the question of what things are made of as well as what they come from, the view presented here has not only the advantage of caution—it is indeed a minimalist interpretation—but links Thales more closely with, even while it allows that he reacted differently to, earlier preoccupations, in mythology, with origins. It receives some support, too, from a consideration of Thales' immediate successors, the next two Milesian philosophers, Anaximander and Anaximenes, generally assumed to have been active in the middle and at the end of the sixth century, respectively. Here too our evidence is lacunose, but it appears that they did not just offer alternatives to Thales' principle, but show a greater awareness of precisely the questions that, on the view offered here,

Thales himself had not confronted. The development of early Greek natural philosophy is as much a development of such an awareness of the questions to be asked as one of the answers given.

The names that Anaximander and Anaximenes gave their first principles are well attested, namely the Boundless and Air. Our sources also provide hints concerning the possible motivations underlying these proposals, though as usual reservations must be expressed about just how trustworthy those sources are. Aristotle in the *Physics* (204b24 ff.) reports an argument that he says was used by some of those who advocated the Boundless, and although he does not here mention Anaximander by name, we have it on the authority of Simplicius, in the commentary he wrote on Aristotle's *Physics* in the sixth century A.D., that Anaximander argued along these lines. The starting point of the argument may be the realization that there is an obvious objection that theories such as Thales' encounter, namely this: If the primary substance is water, how can its opposite, fire, ever have come to be, for each destroys the other? If that point is generalized, the conclusion would be that the original substance is not any definite identifiable entity, such as water, fire, or air, but rather an indeterminate conglomerate from which such entities emerged. This conglomerate was called Boundless not in the sense that it was infinite in extent, but rather because of its indeterminate nature.

If we can accept that this was indeed Anaximander's reasoning, two fundamental features stand out. First, his chief concern is still with origins: the Boundless is not something that the determinate objects of the world around us are made of, but what they came from. However, other doxographic evidence suggests that Anaximander may also have given some account of the processes by which a differentiated world arises from the indeterminate primeval state. This process begins when some opposed substances emerge from the Boundless and thereby start a sequence of interactions that leads eventually to the formation of the world as we know it. The details in our late sources may well be unreliable, and we can be certain that whatever Anaximander's story was it was subjected to heavy reinterpretation. The point that may remain, however, is that he may have felt the need to offer some account of the cosmogonical process—though that account may not have been much less fantastic than many myths that treat of similar themes.

But the second and even more important feature is that Anaximander's idea stems from rational criticism of Thales'. A second example where this may also be the case relates to the suggestion he appears to have made concerning the position of the earth and why it apparently remains at rest. Where Thales had conjectured that it floats on water, Anaximander is said to have held that the cause of its being at rest is its "indifference." As Aristotle reports the argument (*On the Heavens* 295b10 ff.), it was that what is in the center and equably related to the extremes has no impulse to move in one direction rather than in any other. If this was indeed Anaximander's thought, it provides a notable example of the use of what we may call the principle of sufficient reason; and again the stimulus may well have come from reflection on the difficulties presented by Thales' view (and by all like it), namely, if water holds the earth up, what holds the water up? Such critical reflections on earlier views or common assumptions provide the chief foundation for the claim that the principal originality of the Milesians lay in their attempts to give cosmological accounts a rational basis.

By the time we come to the third Milesian thinker, Anaximenes, the evidence of a concern with the question of what physical objects consist in now is far more definite. Unlike Anaximander's Boundless, Anaximenes' Air is as familiar an entity as Thales' Water. But Anaximenes now appears to have asked, and answered, the question of the transformations that air undergoes to appear as other things. His answer referred to the twin processes of condensation and rarefaction. Water, ice, even earth and stones are, in his view, just condensed air, and fire is air that has been rarefied. Here at least, or we may even say at last, the notion of an underlying physical element appears fairly clearly, accompanied now by its essential concomitant, a theory concerning the changes it undergoes such that other objects can be interpreted as varieties or modifications of a single substance.

THEORIES OF CHANGE AND OF KNOWLEDGE

What we should consider to be more strictly philosophical concerns begin to figure more prominently in the work of Heraclitus of Ephesus and Parmenides of Elea, both thought to have been active around 500 B.C., both of whom raise, if still somewhat indirectly, problems relating to the foundations of knowledge, for instance, and to the relationship between language and reality. In both cases the evidence we have to go on is far more substantial than that available for any of the three Milesian thinkers we have just discussed. Yet although for Heraclitus, for example, we have more than a hundred sayings quoted as what are known as "fragments" by later writers, in every case it is not just legitimate but necessary to consider why the later writers in question gave us the quotations they did and how they interpreted them and Heraclitus' philosophy in general. Already in antiquity Heraclitus was famous for his obscurity. Such statements as "The way up and down is one and the same" (frag. 60), "The connections between things are wholes and not wholes" (frag. 10), and "The only wise thing is and is not willing to be given the name of Zeus" (frag. 32) are evident paradoxes, and although the tendency of a good part of a long tradition of commentators has been to try to fix their sense, their polyvalence of meaning is far more likely to have been deliberate and indeed an important part of Heraclitus' message. In such cases to seek a single determinate sense is to miss the point, or one of them.

Many sayings make great play with pairs of opposites. "Justice is strife" (frag. 80). "God is day, night, winter, summer, war, peace, satiety, hunger" (frag. 67). "Sea is the purest and the foulest water," and our source continues, "for fish it is drinkable and healthy, but for men it is undrinkable and deadly" (frag. 61). "Immortals mortals, mortals immortals, living the others' death, and dying the others' life" (frag. 62). "To God all things are fair and good and just, but men have distinguished just and unjust" (frag. 102). Faced with this bewildering array of tantalizing apothegms, commentators ancient and modern have often reacted with attempts to distill a single coherent doctrine, in this case concerning the "unity of opposites." In some instances what appears in our modern editions of Heraclitus as part of the fragment—that is, what is claimed as part of Heraclitus' original saying—appears to give us a lead. If the gloss on the remark about seawater in fragment 61, for instance, was indeed part of what Heraclitus himself said (and the question cannot be ignored, although in this case we have no particular reason to reject the addition), this seems to go some way toward alleviating the paradox. Sea is not both purest and foulest to the same creatures, but purest to one kind, foulest to another. Yet it would be a mistake to suppose that Heraclitus' sole

or chief purpose was to offer some fairly easily solvable puzzles. Thus it is undeniably true of an actual road (as it might be from Ephesus inland to Smyrna) that, traveled in one direction it may be "up," in the other "down": yet this fact does not exhaust the sense of fragment 60; it does not even begin to do so. For the statement may have application to any number of metaphorical roads or transitions: one favorite ancient way of taking it is to apply it to the physical changes that take place between major cosmic entities, fire, water, earth. But reflection should suggest that none of these possibilities should be privileged to the exclusion of the others. Any such restriction seems quite foreign to Heraclitus' vision, which is, rather, one of the connections between at first sight quite diverse facts, events, and contexts.

While in one respect the cacophony of divergent interpretations of Heraclitus may lead the student into some despair, in another those very divergences may well have an important moral for us (and one that Heraclitus would have approved). At one level the remarks that justice is strife, or that war and peace are one, indicate the interdependence of these concepts. There would be no peace if there had been no such thing as war. But the more important generalizable implication from such statements is that judgments of this kind are relative to the, or a, human categorical or conceptual framework. Men were responsible for distinguishing just and unjust. Not that Heraclitus means that there is no such thing as justice at all. Otherwise he would not have said that to God all things are just—despite the fact that there is no way, no ordinary mortal way, to have "just" on its own. It is our way of dividing up the world that has introduced such oppositions. Yet Heraclitus' own statements are themselves inevitably made in human language, the total inadequacy of which as a vehicle for making discriminations is one of the chief points he is trying to drive home. He has, of course, no way of conveying that lesson otherwise than by the very means that that lesson undermines or teaches us to treat with radical skepticism.

It goes without saying that that view is no more than just one other reading of Heraclitus, or rather of a part of his sayings. That he offers a radical challenge to accepted human judgments is, however, agreed on all sides. Many sayings express his contempt not just for those who had a special reputation for being wise—Homer, Hesiod, Pythagoras, Xenophanes, and many others—but for the vast majority of mankind in general. "This word which is, always men prove incapable of understanding once they have heard it, as before they have heard it at all. . . . The rest of men are not aware of what they do when awake, just as they forget what they do when asleep" (frag. 1). "Eyes and ears are bad witnesses for men if they have souls that cannot understand their language" (frag. 107)—though Heraclitus also says, "Things which can be seen, heard, learned, these are what I prefer" (frag. 55). Men are mistaken, it seems, not just—to use our terms—because they have an unjustified confidence in the coherence of their conceptual framework, but also because they assume that the world itself is a stable entity, a stable object of reference for language, thought, and meaning.

When Heraclitus speaks of the invisible attunement being stronger than a visible one (frag. 54) or remarks that "nature loves to hide" (frag. 123), he warns us, at the very least, that appearances may be deceptive. Whether or not he ever made the statement that "everything flows" (*panta rhei*), which is often ascribed to him or represented as an encapsulation of one of his most important thoughts, a series of fragments suggests that he held that physical objects are always changing. Now whether that "always" is to be understood strictly, as implying constant change at every instant of time, is, like so much else, problematic and controversial. Some have argued that those ancient critics, beginning with Plato, who took Heraclitus in that sense are mistaken, and that all that we should ascribe to Heraclitus himself is the much weaker thesis that every physical object undergoes change sooner or later. Modern scholarship now tends to favor the Platonic view, at least on that point, although the issue is not one that can be settled decisively. It is, however, more generally agreed, at least, that when we are told, for example, that "this world order is an ever-living fire, kindling in measures and going out in measures" (frag. 30), we are to understand "fire," if not as pure process, at any rate as symbolic of process, and itself essentially subject to change.

This allows us to link but also to contrast Heraclitus with the Milesians. Although Aristotle and others attributed a more or less conventional element theory to Heraclitus, treating his fire as a substratum like Anaximenes' Air, it is far more likely that he was less intent on describing the various processes of change that apparently different physical objects undergo to become the objects they appear to be (the problem mentioned above in connection with Anaximenes) than he was on emphasizing the universality of the process of change itself.

It is not clear whether either Heraclitus or Parmenides knew of the other. The contrasts between the two, in style and in the content of their thought, are extreme, though the one thing they both assert firmly is that conventional human views of the world are radically mistaken, even if what Parmenides saw as the truth is very different from Heraclitus' teaching. Whereas Heraclitus produced a series of highly puzzling oracular pronouncements, Parmenides chose hexameter verse as his medium, thereby aligning himself with earlier epic. Indeed, after an introductory proem describing how he travels to the Gates of Day and Night and is there greeted by a goddess, the whole of the rest of the poem is represented as the revelations of this goddess. Yet the content of his verse is anything but traditional. Its originality consists not least in the tight-knit philosophical argumentation it contains. The major section of the argument has been preserved as a whole and it represents the first sustained piece of philosophical reasoning in western European thought. The problems of interpretation here do not stem so much from the selectivity—if not the actual prejudices—of our sources, as rather just from the difficulty of the original thought.

While Heraclitus had cast doubt on the reliability of the senses in certain contexts, or rather on the way ordinary humans use them, Parmenides states categorically that reasoned argument (*logos*) alone is to be trusted. The strategy of the first part of the poem, called the Way of Truth, is to explore what follows from what is claimed to be its incontrovertible starting point. Once those consequences have been spelled out, Parmenides returns in the second, far more fragmentary part of the poem, the Way of Seeming, to sketch out an account of the generation of the world of appearances corresponding to the opinions of ordinary mortals. In that section of the work Parmenides uses the twin concepts of Light and Night as the basis of a cosmological story that joins, though it undercuts, the tradition of such accounts that goes back to the Milesians. Nevertheless it is now generally agreed that although this cosmology is asserted to be superior to any other, it has no claim to be true. Its superiority must then be justified either because it is more economical than other accounts, or because it is represented as more coherent, and more self-conscious, than they: given certain premises the consequences are as Parmenides states them, but the whole account is explicitly said to be deceitful. Only the Way of Truth is true.

The more important part of the poem begins by considering what possible ways of inquiry there can be. Two ways are identified, one that "it is" (*esti*), the other that "it is not" (*ouk esti*). This immediately poses two major problems, the subject we are to understand (for none is specified) and the sense of the verb *to be.* Both remain highly disputed issues, but on the second question it emerges fairly clearly that what we may call existence claims are involved; and on the first, a first remark would be this: Given that we are about to engage on an inquiry, it may be that initially we should think of the subject of the verb *to be* as being whatever it is we are going to inquire into. Parmenides certainly identifies "it" with the object of thought, and in practice the subject becomes specified and characterized as the argument proceeds.

But having specified two possible ways of inquiry Parmenides immediately rules one out. It is and it cannot not be: "that is the path of persuasion for it accompanies truth." The second way, that it is not and that it needs must not be, is a path from which nothing can be learned. "For you could not know what is not [or, in an alternative interpretation, you could not know it if it were not] nor could you assert it" (frag. 2). "For it is the same thing that can be thought and that can be" (frag. 3). Indeed, "What can be spoken and thought of must be: for it is possible for it to be, but impossible for nothing to be" (frag. 6). In this last remark, especially, Parmenides seems to go from its possibility that it is to its necessity by a fallacious, if plausible, move. The idea may be that the possibility that what can be thought of is would be agreed on all sides. But then of nothing it is not true even that it could be. So a thing that can be thought of cannot be nothing, but is something, indeed it must actually be.

Fragment 8 then proceeds to draw certain conclusions about the character of what is, where Parmenides shows that it cannot come to be nor be destroyed, nor be subject to change, nor even be differentiated in any respect. Each of these later conclusions is established by means of a tightly structured argument that builds on the results obtained earlier. Thus in the first particularly important stretch of argument Parmenides puts it that what is cannot be subject to coming-to-be or to destruction, since the only thing it could come to be from or be destroyed into is what is not, and that has been ruled out, since what is not cannot be thought of. The point is enforced by an appeal to what we may again call the principle of sufficient reason: "What need would have raised it to grow later or earlier, starting from nothing?" As later commentators put it, there was a dilemma. What is either comes to be from what is (but then it does not come to be, but is already) or from what is not: but that is totally nonexistent and nothing can come to be from nothing. The conclusion, that what is cannot come to be from what is not in the sense of the totally nonexistent, is accepted not just by Parmenides' own followers but by later natural philosophers who otherwise opposed him and, indeed, by Plato and Aristotle themselves. Only with Christian theology did the notion of creation from nothing—ex nihilo—gain credence, and then for theological reasons—the notion of the omnipotence of the divine Creator—not for purely cosmological ones. Nor does the challenge initiated by Parmenides lack relevance to cosmological discussions in the twentieth century. If current astronomical arguments favor the "big bang" over the "steady state" hypothesis, we must still acknowledge the paradoxicality of the concept of the universe having a beginning in time. How, Parmenides will still ask, could it come to be from what is not? And why at any particular time, time *t,* rather than any other?

The rejection of coming-to-be and de-

struction is in turn the basis for the denial of change and movement of any kind, for they are construed as implying a coming-to-be (of a kind) from what is not and so are ruled out. Similarly what is is continuous, indivisible, complete, undifferentiated and unitary not just in the sense that it is whole, but also in the sense that there is only one thing. Parmenides thus states conclusions that completely overthrow all normal human assumptions: and even more important than these conclusions is the method he uses to arrive at them, starting from what is represented as a self-evident premise and then proceeding through a carefully linked sequence of deductive arguments.

We have discussed early cosmological speculations at some length since they contain not just some of the most puzzling but also some of the most penetrating and challenging Greek thinking on the subject. The late pre-Socratic period contains a great variety of systems, treatment of which here has to be drastically selective. In the broadest possible terms, those whom we conventionally classify chiefly as philosophers were divided into two main camps, the followers of Parmenides and the natural philosophers who tried to resolve the problems he posed.

First there were those who agreed with the conclusions of Parmenides, notably in denying plurality and change. Zeno of Elea especially undertook a devastating attack on all types of plurality. In particular he assailed commonsense notions about motion in a series of paradoxes that have continued to provoke discussion ever since. His strategy, in these, was to show that impossible or absurd consequences follow whether it is assumed that space and time are continual (that is to say infinitely divisible) or whether they are not. Thus a runner cannot traverse a stadium because he has to traverse half of it first, and to do that he has first to traverse a quarter. Given that this division can be continued indefinitely, a point can always be found between the point to be reached and the starting point, and so movement cannot begin. Again, and conversely, an arrow at each moment in its flight occupies a space equal to itself; but what occupies a space equal to itself is (for that time) at rest; so the arrow is at rest at each moment of its flight and therefore, it is claimed, throughout the flight, and so it does not move.

Melissus of Samos, in turn, developed and modified Parmenides' monism. Where Parmenides had argued that what is must be complete and finite, Melissus concluded that it must be infinite in magnitude, although in both cases the argument appealed to the same factor, namely the impossibility of what is not. Melissus took this to indicate that what is is never bounded (a limit would bring it up against the void or what is not), while Parmenides had insisted rather that what is is spatially invariant, because the only conceivable way of producing differentiations within the bounded whole would have to invoke what is not.

But while some late-fifth-century philosophers thus elaborated aspects of Parmenides' thought, others attempted to reinstate coming-to-be, change, and plurality, even while (as noted) they agreed that it is impossible for what is to come to be from what is totally nonexistent. The first two such natural philosophers postulated an original plurality of existing things and interpreted coming-to-be as the mixture and separation of these elements. These were Empedocles of Acragas and Anaxagoras of Clazomenae (Klazümen), both at work in the mid to late fifth century. But although their systems have that much in common, they were otherwise markedly different in their interests, aims, and motivations.

Empedocles owed much to Pythagorean thought and is indeed one of our most important sources for early Pythagoreanism. Pythagoras himself lived in the late sixth century, and although much of the evidence for his ideas is unreliable, since it comes from later neo-Pythagorean writers eager to represent him as the propounder of many of their own ideas and theories, two points that are reasonably well attested are, first, that he taught a way of life (a matter of rules of behavior, probably, rather than a formal moral philosophical system) and, second, that he held various views we should class as religious as much as philosophical, the most important of which was the doctrine of the immortality of the soul. On death, the souls not just of human beings but also of animals survive, not in a disembodied state (let alone as wraiths in Hades) but as the souls of other living creatures. All living things are akin and according to how one had lived his life his soul was reborn in a higher or in a lower kind of creature. The welfare of one's soul was of paramount concern, and the ultimate hope was to escape from the cycle of rebirth altogether. The origins of this belief are obscure; but certainly some early Pythagoreans seemed to some early commentators, notably to Herodotus, to have certain beliefs in common with, and even to have obtained them from, Egyptian religion. As for the future of this and other versions of the doctrine of the immortality of the soul, they were to be enormously influential, and we shall return to this topic in discussing Plato especially.

Aspects of Empedocles' teaching deal with themes directly inherited from Parmenides. He is concerned, for instance, to reinstate the validity of the senses, at least if used critically, as the, or a, source of knowledge. Change is interpreted as the mixing or separating of four elements, or "roots": earth, water, air, and fire. Briefly, their mixture is the work of a principle Empedocles called Philia or Love, their separation that of an opposing principle of Strife. Some specific suggestions about the proportions of the roots that go to make up such natural substances as blood and flesh are recorded, as well as some quite detailed discussions of the physical processes involved in respiration and in vision. At the same time many statements in his poems relate to the welfare of the soul. There is an impassioned prohibition of bloodshed, including animal sacrifice (one of the central Greek religious rituals), and other statements stress the kinship of living things, including plants. Empedocles even tells us that he himself has been a boy and a girl, a bush, a bird, and a fish (frag. 117). He even claims to go about among the people of Acragas now as an "immortal god," sought after for the advice he can give as a healer and wonder-worker. He promises too to teach not just remedies for diseases and old age but also how to control the winds and rain and drought, and even how to bring the dead back to life.

This apparent mixture, as it is often represented, of scientist and wonder-worker has often puzzled commentators, who have sometimes suggested that there may have been a radical shift or development within Empedocles' career, one that separates the work *On Nature* from that known as the *Purifications.* Yet it would be quite mistaken to think of the discussion of physical problems in *On Nature* as devoid of religion, let alone as opposed to the religious beliefs of the *Purifications.* This is not just a matter of style—of his referring sometimes to the four physical elements, for instance, by the names of gods: Zeus, Hera, Aidoneus, and Nestis (though which name stands for which element was disputed already in antiquity). The more important point is that the role of the two principles, Love and Strife, is the guiding theme of both works, of both the scientific and the religious doctrines. It may be helpful for us to think of Love as some principle of attraction, Strife as one of repulsion: but their work and functions are loaded with significance—ambivalent significance at that—of a moral and religious kind in what we should call physical contexts

as well as when Empedocles offers advice and warnings on the subject of the purities and impurities of the soul.

Anaxagoras represents a quite different type of investigator, in the tradition of Ionian *historie,* the word that we can translate "research" but that covers such diverse interests as the geographical studies of Hecataeus and the histories (in our sense) of Herodotus and Thucydides, as well as the natural philosophical inquiries of the Milesian thinkers. Anaxagoras' answer to Parmenides was, again, to postulate an original plurality. Again he was careful to reinstate the senses as sources of knowledge and indeed to enunciate the principle that "appearances" are the "vision" of the obscure, that is, that visible evidence can be used as the basis of inferences concerning what is not directly perceptible. But in marked contrast with Empedocles, Anaxagoras' physical speculations are not permeated by religious and moral interests. Indeed, his assertion that the sun is a fiery stone was one factor that led to his being charged with impiety and exiled from Athens (though a further consideration was his association there with Pericles).

One application, in Anaxagoras, of the principle that nothing comes to be from nothing was to such natural substances as blood and flesh. As a late source puts it, how could hair come to be from not-hair? Generalizing this point, Anaxagoras held that "in everything there is a share of everything," taking "everything" to range without restriction across natural substances. Wheat and water, for instance, contain blood and flesh and hair, and blood and flesh and hair in turn contain wheat and water and indeed everything else, for with the exception of "mind" no substance ever exists in separation from every other. "Mind" not only accounts for rational activity on the part of living creatures but is also given a cosmic role, as that which sets the cosmogonical process in motion. This physical theory is certainly extravagant in the number of kinds of things postulated; at the same time it is highly economical in the number of assumptions it appeals to: indeed the single assumption that "everything has a share in everything" is used to explain every type of change in terms of modifications in the proportions of different things that the objects we see possess.

There was no shortage of other "solutions" to the question of the elements in the late fifth and early fourth centuries, but we have space merely to note one more, and the most famous, namely the atomic theory originally propounded by an otherwise shadowy figure, Leucippus, perhaps around 430 B.C., and then elaborated by Democritus in the final decades of that century. This too was a theory that had its origin in the philosophical challenge posed by Parmenides. There is no question of the original atomic theory being the product of what we should call empirical research. Indeed of the various fifth-century responses to Parmenides that we have considered, atomism stays closer to the tenets of Parmenides himself than either Empedocles or Anaxagoras had done. It does so because it does without the assumption of a plurality of different kinds of substances. In its fifth-century version, the original postulates of atomism were that atoms and the void alone exist. The atoms themselves, however, do not differ in substance, only in shape, size, and arrangement (it is disputed whether Democritus also held weight to be a primary property of the atoms, but this is possible). The void is simply the space that separates the atoms, and the closeness of the connection with Parmenides may be further suggested by the apparent riposte directed at him in the dictum (ascribed to the atomists by Aristotle, *Metaphysics* 985b4 ff.) that not only what is exists, but also what is not, namely, the void.

The void is used to secure movement and change as well as plurality. Aristotle complained, among other things, that the atomists gave no explanation of movement, no explanation, that is, of the kind that he himself offered when he distinguished between natural and forced motion and saw natural motion as the property of the four elements. Yet it appears that Leucippus and Democritus took as their starting point not the idea of inert atomic particles but that of particles in motion. Their postulate was not just atoms, but atoms in motion through a void. In their random collisions suitably shaped atoms combine, giving rise in turn to larger agglomerations, eventually to the formation of worlds as we know them. The process that produced our cosmos is not unique but is repeated at different times and places to generate an infinite number of worlds. As for the variety of things we encounter in our world, these all depend ultimately on differences in fundamental atomic structure. What appears to us as sweet or hot or red is merely a matter of convention. But while the senses are described as yielding only "bastard" knowledge, as opposed to the "legitimate" knowledge that is separate from this, directed to atoms and the void themselves, Democritus appreciated that mind, itself conceived as corporeal, derives its data from the senses, and in a further fragment (125) represents the senses objecting to the criticisms of mind: "Wretched mind, taking your proofs from us, do you overthrow us? Our overthrow is your fall."

SOPHISTS, MATHEMATICIANS, DOCTORS, AND SCIENTISTS IN THE LATE FIFTH AND EARLY FOURTH CENTURIES

Our discussion of Empedocles, Anaxagoras, and Democritus has already suggested something of the variety of late-fifth-century natural philosophy. But in the last decades of the fifth and the first half of the fourth century there was an extraordinary expansion of intellectual interests of every kind. Much of this is commonly discussed under the general rubric of the "sophistic movement." Yet that movement itself is often interpreted rather narrowly. The chief reasons for this are clear: almost all of the Sophists' own works are now lost, with the exception of some speeches and a philosophical treatise of Gorgias, together with some fragments from Antiphon and others. Our earliest main source is, then, Plato, but he exercised his very considerable arts of persuasion first to insist on the contrast between the main Sophists and Socrates—for him Socrates was no Sophist—and secondly to attack many of the positions he associates with their teaching, especially the moral relativism of Protagoras and the amoralism for which Plato makes Callicles and Thrasymachus the passionate spokesmen in the *Gorgias* and *Republic.* Furthermore, in the *Laws* (Book 10) unnamed "atheists" are attacked for attempting nonmoral—or as Plato thinks, positively immoral—mechanical or physical explanations of the cosmos.

Plato remains an important witness, yet to gain a more accurate perspective on the intellectual movements of the late fifth and early fourth centuries the range of our discussion must be broadened beyond the work of the main figures Plato attacks by name (Protagoras, Gorgias, and so on) and even of the generality he abuses. The term Sophist (*sophistes*) itself is one that before Plato and even sometimes in his works carried no automatic pejorative undertones. For Herodotus (4.95), for example, Pythagoras is "not the weakest of the Sophists." Elsewhere the Seven Sages are sometimes called such, and the distinction between *sophistes* and *sophos,* wise man, is sometimes a fine one. Nor should we suppose straightforwardly that the defining characteristic is teaching for money. It is true that Plato contrasts

Protagoras and later figures with some earlier teachers in this respect especially. But plenty of ordinary artists and craftsmen regularly taught their trades and were paid for it, and doctors also did. At the beginning of Plato's *Protagoras* the idea that a young man might pay to be taught medicine is considered quite unexceptionable. Rather Plato's attack was directed more specifically at teaching excellence or virtue (*arete*) for money, and of course the stridency of his objections stems in part from his disagreement with the Sophists on what moral excellence consists in.

When we distance ourselves from Plato's polemic it is possible to see one important development in the late fifth century as an extension in the education that became available. The ordinary education of the (male) children of citizens consisted chiefly of instruction in *grammatike* (including reading and writing) and in arithmetic, as well as in athletics and music. Pride of place among the subjects that several who passed as Sophists claimed to teach was rhetoric, the art of public speaking. In the context of the institutions of the Greek city-state this is readily understandable, since involvement in both political debates and in lawsuits was far greater than anything we are used to in modern large-scale representative democracies. In their democracies the assembly was the sovereign body that took major decisions, about peace or war for example, and any citizen could and many did attend their debates. No doubt those who were regular speakers were only a small minority. But it has been calculated that some 30 or 40 percent of Athenian citizens served at one time or another on the council, the main executive body. The Athenian passion for litigation was proverbial, but again this is just the most marked example of a common characteristic in Greek city-states, including some that were not democracies.

Moreover in the lawcourts the prosecutors and defendants represented themselves: the possibility of hiring a professional speech writer (such as Lysias) to compose a speech is one of the developments connected with the changes we are concerned with. Of course those who disapproved of those developments—such as Aristophanes and Plato—represented what the Sophists were doing as teaching how to make the "worse" cause appear the "better." Arguing on either side of a case—familiar enough to us in debating societies and in the professional conduct of barristers—was no doubt part of the normal training of the skilled orator: the paired speeches of the orator Antiphon, setting out what might be said for the defense and for the prosecution in imaginary trials, provide models that might well be used in such training. But we should hesitate before accusing of immoralism all who provided such instruction.

Those who began to offer to teach rhetoric were, then, answering a reasonably widespread practical need, and certainly served a practical function. The general intellectual importance of this aspect of the sophistic movement is twofold. First, an interest in the analysis of argument develops in this area, a factor that contributed to the eventual development, with Aristotle, of the explicit study of formal logic as well as of the techniques of persuasion. Second (and this provided the chief grounds for Plato's attack), when skill in advocacy was divorced from questions of the moral content of what was advocated, this helped indirectly to increase awareness of the conventionality of customs and of certain beliefs about right and wrong. It should however be stressed that a realization that human laws and customs are not universal was widespread both before and outside the sophistic movement.

If rhetoric was a chief interest, it was far from being the only subject that could be and was taught for a fee. If we piece together the evidence in Plato and elsewhere, it ap-

pears that the Sophist Hippias, for instance, was prepared to offer instruction in a wide range of subjects that included astronomy, mathematics, "music," and "philology." One way the Sophists publicized the teaching they offered was through the demonstration lecture, or *epideixis:* we know, for example, that these were sometimes given at large gatherings such as the Olympic or the Pythian games. We have examples of this loosely defined genre not just from Gorgias, but also in the considerable body of extant medical literature from the late fifth and early fourth centuries, for some of the Hippocratic treatises appear to be, or to have originated in, just such lectures.

Plato's criticism here was that what the Sophists did was simply to teach their pupils how to win arguments, not how to be a good astronomer or mathematician, let alone a good doctor. But again we must beware. There is no reason to doubt that some of those who engaged in public debate in such domains did so on the basis of little or no practical experience—and with no ambition to acquire it. At the same time we need not and should not deny that a serious interest in mathematical problems was shown by several Sophists. The distinction between a professional and a merely general interest in many such subjects was far from hardedged. The point can most easily be illustrated in connection with medicine, where our extant Hippocratic treatises contain not just practical notebooks composed by practitioners for fellow practitioners but, at the opposite end of the spectrum, general lectures for a lay audience, written in some cases by individuals who themselves appear to have no clinical experience at all. We do not have anything like such good direct evidence for such fields as mathematics or astronomy at this period, but similar points may well apply. Our reports suggest that both Hippias and the Sophist Antiphon did original work in mathematics, for example in connection with such problems as that of squaring the circle, and Protagoras raised an important issue in what we may call the philosophy of mathematics when he denied that a circle touches a tangent at a point.

It would once again be mistaken to divorce the kind of instruction offered by Sophists too rigidly from the interests in philosophy, including natural philosophy, that we discussed in the last section. This point can be exemplified in connection with Gorgias particularly. In one of his works, entitled *On What Is Not,* he undertook to prove that nothing exists, that even if it did exist it could not be understood, and that even if it could be understood, it could not be communicated to anyone else. The reaction to this work has often been one of dismissal. It is argued that it cannot itself have been a serious philosophical piece, and moreover that the fact that Gorgias wrote it casts a general doubt on any claim that he might have to have been more than an intellectual playboy. Such a reaction is exaggerated, if not badly mistaken. A first grounds for hesitation might be that according to ancient tradition Gorgias belonged to a line of philosophers that began with Parmenides and continued through Empedocles, who is reported to have been Gorgias' teacher.

But there are two main reasons for not dismissing Gorgias as a philosophical thinker too quickly. First, we should distinguish between, on the one hand, the serious exploration of fundamental ontological difficulties (that is, problems about being) and, on the other, the endorsement of the conclusions to which such an exploration might lead. Second, we should further distinguish between the possible motivations for raising a puzzle and the importance of the puzzle itself. No one doubts the seriousness with which Parmenides carried out the analysis of the issues presented in the Way of Truth. Yet if Parmenides accepted the force of his own demonstration, he would have to admit that along with change and plurality, he was himself a mere illusion, a mere participant in the Way of Seeming. That his Way of Truth had, at the limit, not just paradoxical but self-refuting consequences in no way detracts from its importance in presenting a challenge to common beliefs, a challenge that takes the form: If we choose to continue to maintain those beliefs, and to hold that change occurs, how can this be validated? If we do not accept Parmenides' conclusions, how can we evade them or show where his argument goes wrong?

A similar point seems relevant also to Gorgias, though no one would claim for his thought the originality that characterizes that of Parmenides. At the very least Gorgias appreciated that arguments like those of Parmenides and the Eleatics could be used not just to defeat conventional ideas about change and plurality, but also the Eleatics' own conception of what is. For what is must either (1) come to be or (2) be eternal or (3) be both. But against (1) Parmenidean arguments can be deployed: How can anything come to be from what is not? Or again from what is, for then it will not come to be, but be already. Moreover, against (2) Gorgias argued that the notion of something being without ever having come to be is incoherent. Finally, against (3) the chief consideration was that the conjunction, taken as a conjunction, is itself a contradiction (what is cannot be both eternal and generated); and we may add that if we take each of the conjuncts separately, we are back to the difficulties already identified under (1) and (2). Nor should we dismiss too quickly the arguments later in the work that purport to establish that even if what is could be said to be, it could not be understood, nor communicated. Their interest consists in, among other things, their exploring the status of purely imaginary objects and the question of how they are to be differentiated from those that are real. To be sure, in the last section especially the problem of self-refutation looms large. Yet at the very least—to repeat—Gorgias produced a notable demonstration that Parmenidean arguments could be applied to Parmenides' own position as much as to the conventional beliefs that the Eleatics themselves attacked. Even if his intention was merely to suggest how such arguments could be reduced to absurdity, the question of specifying how and where they are mistaken still remains. As so often in philosophy, that may be a far harder task than those who are confident that such arguments are mistaken expect or assume, and in Gorgias' case the ingenuity, power, and scope of the challenge that some of his arguments present remain considerable.

PLATO (427–347 B.C.)

Plato is one of the most elusive as well as one of the most influential of European thinkers, and the history of Platonism is a history not of one movement or dominant idea but of a multiplicity of different interpretations of Plato. If there is some truth in Alfred North Whitehead's celebrated dictum in *Process and Reality* (1929) that the safest general characterization of the European philosophical tradition is that it consists of a series of footnotes to Plato, this is in large part because of the complexity and obliqueness of the text to which those footnotes are appended. That text, the extant dialogues, shows Plato to be an unsurpassed master of a literary form that not only enables him to preserve much of the vividness of ordinary conversation but also captures and reproduces essential features of live dialogue, notably in the importance attached to the contexts in which remarks are made, in the interplay between characters, and in the way in which later exchanges can modify, gloss, and even

undermine earlier ones. Even when agreements are reached between Socrates and his interlocutors and they express confidence in their soundness, this is always within the frame of the situation as given. Those who extract systematic doctrines from those texts ignore this frame at their peril. Such a danger is particularly prominent in any brief account of Plato's thought, and what follows must be understood as subject to express reservations, not only (most obviously) on the score of a lack of comprehensiveness, but also in relation to illusions of systematicity inevitably generated by a highly selective discussion.

For Aristotle, writing his account of earlier thinking about causes, which we have cited before, Plato owed most to Heraclitus and the Pythagoreans, and Aristotle's testimony carries particular weight here since he was a pupil of Plato for twenty years in the Academy, the school Plato founded. According to Aristotle, Plato was impressed by problems that Heraclitus and his followers had raised about the world of perceptible phenomena. Yet whatever may be true about Heraclitus' own view, Plato certainly distanced himself from an extreme position according to which perceptible phenomena are in some sense incoherent. What he did agree with was both that physical objects are subject to change and that sense perception is not the best guide to truth. But the changes that perceptible phenomena undergo are certainly not such as to make it impossible to characterize them in any way at all, even if those characterizations are—as we shall see—subject to certain qualifications. That sense perception is inferior to reason as the way to the truth is, moreover, a point that owes as much, or more, to Parmenides as to Heraclitus.

The second influence mentioned by Aristotle, Pythagoreanism, is to be seen first in the importance of mathematics as a model for knowledge and perhaps also in a particular view about mathematical objects. Some Pythagoreans, but maybe not before the mid fifth century, held that all things are numbers, an obscure doctrine open to widely divergent interpretations, ranging from a literalist view that has it that physical objects are made up of units that correspond to numbers, to various ideas according to which, for instance, the essential relations between things are expressible in numbers, as in the famous example of the musical harmonies of the octave, fifth, and fourth, expressible by the ratios 2:1, 3:2, and 4:3. Toward the end of his life Plato may have held a version of the doctrine that numbers are some kind of intermediate entities (between Forms and particulars) and that other things arise from combinations of principles called the One and the Many or the Indefinite Dyad. However, not only are such doctrines highly obscure and their interpretation disputed, but also they are not recorded in any of the texts of Plato that we have. For our purposes the chief point Plato's epistemology shares with Pythagoreanism is the idea that the true objects of knowledge are not perceptible but intelligible, not the circle drawn in the sand but the abstract circle we reason about. Second, Plato was evidently impressed by Pythagoras himself as a founder of a way of life, and third, as already noted, the Pythagoreans were the chief pre-Socratic proponents of the doctrine of the immortality of the soul.

Those last two points take us to moral questions, and to the man who was by far the most important single influence on Plato, namely Socrates. The exact order in which Plato composed the dialogues that are extant is subject to considerable dispute, although broad agreement exists about the three main periods in the development of his thought. The dialogues that come from the earliest, so-called Socratic, period do not contain the set of ideas referred to under the rubric of the "theory of Forms." This is

clearly expressed and elaborated only in the so-called middle period, in such works as the *Phaedo* and the *Republic*—before being submitted to some devastating criticisms and probably also modifications and revisions in works of the latest period represented by our texts.

The chief concerns of the Socratic dialogues are clear: they deal with moral issues. Socrates was famous for the persistence of his dialectical attack on these questions—one factor that led to his unpopularity at Athens and eventually to his condemnation and death. But there is no reason to doubt that his concern was not just to arrive at correct solutions to moral problems, but the practice of the good life. The circumstances that led up to Socrates' trial, the motivations of his accusers, the impression that his own defense made on the mass of the jury responsible for judging him (and that defense, as we have it from Plato, was not short on arrogance) are all problematic. But once the death sentence was passed, his refusal to accept offers to help him escape stemmed from his conviction that his being able to practice the kind of philosophical inquiry he believed in in Athens meant more to him than saving his skin. If the Athenians chose to condemn him to death, that was a decision he would stick by, though Plato has him insist openly that in getting rid of their gadfly the Athenians are the losers.

In part, no doubt, to vindicate his friend and teacher, Plato composed not just the *Apology*—the account of his trial—but also a series of dialogues in which Socrates is represented as exposing the ignorance of those who explicitly pretended to, or simply assumed they had, knowledge. Socrates is pictured, for example, as meeting a self-styled religious expert, Euthyphro, who is just about to prosecute his own father, deemed to be responsible for the death of a slave, but by the end of the dialogue Euthyphro has been unable to satisfy Socrates with his answers to the question of what holiness is. Socrates is supposed to have said that he knew nothing except that he knew nothing, an exception that was represented as justifying the verdict of the Delphic oracle that no one was wiser than he: it may have been Socrates' puzzlement at that verdict that stimulated his inquiries.

The overt conclusions of the Socratic dialogues are all negative: the interlocutors agree that they have reached no satisfactory answer to the question in hand, which usually takes the form of a demand for the definition of some moral excellence, holiness, courage, friendship, and so on. Socrates is, however, implicitly committed to certain positive convictions, especially those expressed in the paradoxes that no one does wrong willingly and that "virtue" (or, better, excellence) is knowledge, although, being the paradoxes they are, quite what positions they represent is not transparent. In several passages, however, arguments are developed that suggest that when it appears that someone does wrong while knowing what is right, the truth of the matter is that he or she acts in ignorance of some kind. If one really knew what is right, and that it is deemed to coincide with what is in his own best ultimate interests, he would not act in a way contrary to that knowledge. It goes without saying that a person pursues his own *eudaimonia*—less a matter of being happy, as we in English speak of that as a state or feeling that comes and goes, as a matter of being blessed or fortunate. But if a person really knows what would make him blessed, he would never be distracted by short-term pleasure or gain. Virtue or excellence consists, then—in the second paradox—in just such knowledge. Certainly such knowledge is a necessary condition for excellence—no one can practice excellence without it. And in certain texts in the dialogues it is suggested that such knowledge is also a sufficient condition of excellence, or that excellence is constituted of that knowledge.

These positions are often in view when Plato's moral philosophy—often also Greek moral philosophy in general—is accused of being excessively intellectualist. Yet the knowledge in question is not just a matter of intellectual apprehension. Our distinction between intellectual and emotional—largely a legacy of the romantic movement—cuts across Greek distinctions, not that "knowing" in English is confined to matters of intellectual knowledge (think of knowing how to ride a bicycle, or of knowing in the sense of being acquainted with the President of the United States). Greek words for cognition, *epistasthai, eidenai, phronein,* often have an important dispositional element—that is, they convey an idea not just of what a person knows but of character, attitude, or disposition. One way to express the idea of being friendly or hostile to someone is to use the verb *phronein,* often literally translated "think," in a combination with an adjectival or adverbial phrase, in expressions whose literal rendering would be something like "think in a friendly/hostile way toward." Again one way to express the idea of a tendency or ambition toward tyranny is to use a phrase that literally suggests "thinking" tyrannical things (*phronein ta turannika*). In any event, when in Plato's early dialogues Socrates asks for definitions of certain moral qualities, it is clear that his concern is not just with knowing the answers to certain theoretical questions, but with being good; not just with knowing what to say, the formula to give, in answer to the question of what courage is, but with being courageous, though that excellence, as noted, will consist in what can still be called knowledge of a kind.

As noted, these early dialogues do not contain anything that can be called a theory of Forms. That is the expression used of certain positive philosophical positions that Plato maintained in the middle period, especially in such works as the *Symposium, Phaedo, Republic,* and *Phaedrus.* Yet Plato nowhere presents in the mouth of Socrates or of anyone else a systematic exposition of what that theory is taken to stand for. This being so there is plenty of room for disagreement on what that "theory" consists in, especially as it is brought to bear in different contexts on very different types of problems, in the theory of knowledge and meaning, in moral and political philosophy, eventually in cosmology. As for how much of that theory survived Plato's own criticisms of it in such late dialogues as the *Parmenides* and the *Sophist,* that is more difficult still.

It is already implicit in the search for definitions in the Socratic dialogues that the objects they are trying to define, the definienda, are not to be identified with any of their instances. To mention an act of courage, or even a type of courage, will not do by way of answer to the question of what courage itself is, that in virtue of which all courageous acts are courageous. But it appears unlikely that either the historical Socrates or Plato when he wrote the earlier dialogues had a clear idea about just what kind of entity "courage," "holiness," "friendship," and the like themselves were. Rather, as noted, the interest is in exploring moral questions with the hope of thereby becoming better, not in the "second-order" questions concerning the nature of the difference between (for instance) a particular instance of a quality and the quality itself. An interest in those second-order questions does undoubtedly come to the fore in the *Symposium,* in connection with the nature of beauty, and in the *Phaedo,* in relation to a wide range of moral qualities and mathematical objects. In both works the view is put forward that knowledge has as its objects not the perceptible particulars, but intelligible, abstract, and unchanging Forms.

Thus in the *Symposium* a series of contrasts is suggested. Any given particular beautiful object comes to be and passes away: it appears beautiful in some respects but ugly in others, beautiful at one time but not at another, in comparison with some things but not with others, in one place but not in another, or to some people but not to others. But the beautiful itself, it is claimed, is not similarly subject to any such reservations or qualifications: it is what beauty is, and the true object of our love and aspiration. Again in the *Phaedo* an argument is developed that equality itself differs from any of its exemplifications. Pairs of equal sticks or stones are also unequal (to other things, for instance) whereas that cannot be true of equality itself. Moreover if we are concerned to study equality, it is equality itself that we should try to focus on in our thought, rather than its examples, for they are bound to be unreliable guides since they can be said to be unequal as well as equal.

The Forms—to use the conventional term used to correspond to a variety of Greek words that Plato uses and that he never turned into a technical vocabulary—are intelligible and eternal unchanging objects of knowledge. While the particulars have the qualities or properties they have in a way that is always subject to qualifications and reservations, that is not true of the Forms themselves. However, the particulars have such a claim to exemplify qualities or properties in virtue of their relationship to the Forms, expressed—admittedly, rather unsatisfactorily—in the metaphors of "participating" in the Forms or of "imitating" them.

The fundamental importance of this set of ideas can hardly be exaggerated. Although the arguments supporting the distinction on which the theory rests relate to mathematical and logical examples as much as to moral ones, the implications for moral philosophy are especially important. Plato's preoccupations with what he saw as the damaging effects of sophistic relativism and immoralism have been noted before. Protagoras, for instance, had maintained that "man is the measure of all things," including right and wrong: what appears to different people to be right may differ, but there is no objective standard by which to settle which of them may be mistaken—indeed, for Protagoras neither can be. One function the Platonic theory of Forms serves is to provide an answer to the question of the nature of moral entities and to secure their objectivity. Yet of course Plato did not simply invent the Forms just because he wanted to defeat Protagorean relativism or Calliclean immoralism. That would have amounted to no more than wishful thinking. Rather he believes he has good independent grounds for insisting that intelligible Forms exist. Only if they do can we understand not just moral questions, but also mathematics and indeed our ability to make some sense of the world of ordinary experience. For us to have the concepts not just of equality and justice, but also of largeness, there must be intelligible objects that correspond to these, not just examples to which unequal as well as equal, unjust as well as just, small as well as large, are equally applicable.

Moreover, in the domain of politics an elaborate superstructure is based on this philosophy. Human happiness cannot be secured unless states are well governed, but for states to be well governed they must be ruled according to these objective, indeed absolute, moral values. The rulers must be statesmen who have been trained to apprehend the Forms. States will not be well governed, as Plato writes in the *Republic,* until either philosophers become kings or kings become philosophers. That is an ideal to be aimed at, nor does Plato shirk the task of spelling out the consequences in detail. Education is of crucial importance, first and foremost the education of the philosopher-kings themselves. These have a demanding course of study, first in mathematics and the mathematical sciences and then in dialectic itself: the latter is not just a matter of the apprehension of the Forms and of the supreme Form, the Good, on which the other Forms themselves depend, but one of being able to give an account to themselves and to others of what is true. Dialectic, thus conceived, is no mere matter of the contemplation of eternal entities—though it depends on them—but one of the development of an ability in question and answer.

But education of an admittedly different kind is also necessary for the other members of the ideal state. Each individual soul has not just a reasoning faculty, but also faculties that correspond to spirit (in the sense of the high-spirited) and to appetite. So too the state is organized into three classes, the philosopher-kings, the auxiliaries, and the rest, though Plato would claim that the two arms of this analogy are established independently. Nevertheless so far as the other classes of the ideal state are concerned, their acquiescence in the disposition of things is essential and for this they too must be persuaded, if necessary with what are called "noble lies," fictions that are justifiable in the interests of the good of the whole. The state thus described in the *Republic,* self-confessedly an ideal, though not one that deals in impossibilities, is a highly elaborate and ultra-authoritarian structure, and the challenge it presents to us today is a powerful one despite, or rather because of, our rejection of authoritarianism. It is a challenge that relates to such questions as the nature of political knowledge, the qualifications we should expect or require of statesmen (or of voters), the accountability of politicians, the nature and scope of education, and the relationship between the content of the educational program and governmental control. In each case Plato raises the issue in the sharpest possible terms, and if his authoritarian and absolutist solutions are unacceptable, what alternatives to propose, and how alternative proposals can be rationally justified, are questions that have lost none of their importance, even though we must be less sanguine than Plato appears to be on occasion (in the context of the Greek city-state) about the prospects of practical reform of existing political institutions.

Corresponding to the tripartite state, the individual soul, too, as we noted, is imagined as possessing three distinct faculties. That the soul is immortal is a firm and constant belief of Plato's—and one that he believes to have important ethical implications, reinforcing his notion that the primary concern of a human being should be the care of his soul. Nevertheless he maintains that the main ethical and political theses of the *Republic* can be established independently of the belief in immortality. That justice pays, and even that it is better to suffer wrong than to do wrong, are doctrines shown partly on the basis of the analogy with health; for justice is seen as the correct, balanced relationship between the parts of the soul in the individual just as it is a matter of the correct relationship between the classes in the state. Again the influence on the later philosophy of mind was immense, for this is the first clear statement of a dualist view according to which the soul or the mind is different in kind from the body, the former incorporeal, the latter corporeal. The texts that introduce the tripartite soul initiate the exploration of problems concerned with the classification of the various vital faculties and with the tensions between them. Moreover, at the end of the *Republic* (611a ff.) Plato explicitly recognizes that there are difficulties in saying precisely how the soul, if tripartite, can be immortal, not that Plato is in any doubt that both doctrines are true.

The Forms are thus brought into play in a number of fundamental contexts—many more than can be indicated here—in the middle-period dialogues. Yet several important questions about them remain unanswered. Some of these questions become the focus of explicit attention in works of the latest period of Plato's literary activity—not that attention paid to these issues ever ousted Plato's ongoing concern with moral

and political problems. Two types of question are explicitly confronted in the *Parmenides.* The first concerns the scope of what we have been calling the theory. Although if there are Forms at all, we can be sure that there are Forms of moral excellences (justice, the good itself, and so on), of mathematical properties (equality), and of logical ones (sameness, difference), whether there are also Forms that correspond to natural kinds (man or ox) or to physical elements (fire, water) let alone to objects of minimal value or significance (such as hair, mud, and dirt) is problematic. The question is a telling one, and what Plato's answer would be is highly debatable. The main arguments used to establish that there are Forms (for example that sketched out above from the *Phaedo* in relation to equality) are never in fact deployed in connection with such entities as man, let alone hair. There is, too, much less plausibility in claiming that particular men are also in some way not men, than there is in making the corresponding claim about beautiful things or pairs of equal objects. On the other hand there is nothing puzzling about requiring a clear definition of man or fire or even dirt. Thus one consideration would tell for restricting Forms to moral, mathematical, and logical entities. But the need for definitions would point rather to a theory ranging unrestrictedly over what we think of as universals.

The second main problem raised in the *Parmenides* strikes at the very heart of the nature of Forms themselves. It concerns the relationship between particulars and Forms and the question of whether the Forms themselves merely are, or have, the qualities of which they are the Forms. The implicit assumption in the middle period is that "beautiful" is true of the Form beauty itself (and even that "equal" is true of equality itself), although in an importantly different way from the merely relative way in which the predicate is true when applied to any particular. It follows that the Forms are in some sense paradigms or ideals or exemplars. On one view this means that they are not merely themselves the qualities: rather, they manifest those qualities, indeed to a supreme or absolute degree. But in the case of largeness, it seems absurd (as the *Parmenides* now suggests) that the Form itself is in some way superlatively large. If it is, there will be a vicious regress, since if we need one Form to explain what it is that all large things have in common, we will need a second to explain what all of them and the large itself do—a process that can be continued indefinitely.

No definite answers are provided by Plato in the exchanges between Socrates and Parmenides in the dialogue in which these difficulties are explored, and the question of Plato's own reaction to the problems remains the most disputed issue in Platonic scholarship today. Some scholars maintain that the difficulties depend merely on misunderstandings of the theory of Forms, and that that theory itself, properly understood, is quite immune to them. Others, at the opposite end of the spectrum, hold that Plato must have abandoned the central assumption of paradigmatism, while still others maintain that Plato may well not have seen his way clear to solutions to the problems. But some points at least are clear. In the *Parmenides* and elsewhere in the late dialogues Plato is as emphatic as ever that for communication to take place definition must be possible and that there must be objective entities to which such definitions correspond. Whatever else Plato may have abandoned, a belief in the objective realities that underpin thought remains.

Second, it is clear from the more elaborate explorations of the problems of knowledge, meaning, and dialectic, in the *Theaetetus, Sophist,* and *Philebus* especially, that the Forms by themselves cannot be said to provide the entire answers. It is important to recognize that there is a marked shift in emphasis in these works, from construing the problems as to do with individual entities taken in isolation to considering them as concerned with networks of relations between such entities. Meaning is not now discussed on the model of a target that is hit or missed, but rather in terms of relationships between complexes. It would be too simple to claim that Plato was no longer concerned with the relationship between perceptible particulars and the intelligible Forms, but that concern certainly takes second place to the interrelations of the Forms themselves.

The one dialogue after the *Republic* where paradigm Forms are indubitably deployed in significant roles is the cosmological work, the *Timaeus,* but whether this was composed before or after the *Parmenides* is disputed. Moreover paradigms are there part of a complex metaphor: they are the patterns the divine Craftsman or Demiurge refers to in bringing the world from disorder into order—and it would be rash indeed to press the literal interpretation of this imagery. The chief importance of the *Timaeus,* however, is that it provides the most powerful and detailed statement of a theme that appears in many other indubitably late works (the *Sophist, Politicus, Philebus,* and *Laws*), namely, that the universe is the product of intelligent design. One of the paradoxes of Plato's reputation is that he is often represented as turning his back on the physical world. Certainly in prominent texts of different periods, but most notably in the account of Socrates' last hours in the *Phaedo,* the themes of the distractions of ordinary appetite, the need to cultivate reason, and the image of the body as a prison from which the soul longs to escape are strongly developed. Certainly in the *Timaeus* itself only what is called a likely account is possible of the physical world. Yet Plato always held, and unequivocally proclaims, the goodness and the order of the universe, seen as the work of a benevolent craftsmanlike deity. True, that deity has to bring it from disorder into order, and many signs of residual disorder are detectable: he has to work with resistant material. More important, in the *Laws* it is recognized that the soul is responsible for evil as well as good. Yet while Plato provides some of the most striking descriptions of the potential corruption, degradation, and destructiveness of human beings, he also offers clear and ringing statements of the goodness of the universe as a whole. As the *Timaeus* puts it (92c), it is a perceptible God, greatest, most good, most beautiful, and most complete.

ARISTOTLE (384–322 B.C.)

The range of Aristotle's interests surpassed that of any other ancient philosopher. He can be called the inventor of formal logic, and he produced not just the first analysis of the validity of schemata—that is, forms or patterns—of argument in the theory of the syllogism in the *Prior Analytics,* but also a comprehensive study of informal argument and methods of persuasion in the *Rhetoric* (though here he was clearly drawing on a tradition that is mostly lost to us). In his metaphysics, his doctrines of the categories and of substance, as well as his often acute discussions of problems connected with time, place, continuity, and the infinite (for him part of "physics" or the study of nature) all build on earlier thought but go beyond it and break new ground; so too do his development of the four element theory and his study of the varieties of mixture and combination, and, in his psychology, his views of the relationship between soul and body and his analyses of perception, imagination, and reasoning. He undertook the first systematic studies in the area we should call zoology. In ethics, in political theory, and in aesthetics,

especially, his ideas remain, today, both influential and challenging. He himself is concerned to differentiate between different disciplines, and he repeatedly underlines, for example, the contrasts between the study of nature (physics) and mathematics, or between exact studies and inexact ones (the latter include ethics). There is certainly nothing predictable about his contributions to different areas of thought. There are, however, recurrent ideas that run through his discussion of many different topics, and these provide important links between them. He has often been represented as not just a systematic but a dogmatic thinker. That tends to discount the clear signs of development in his thought (about which a little will be said below) and to underestimate the tensions within it. On some of the most problematic issues in his metaphysics he appears never to have settled on a definitive view. In an important sense he is a problem raiser as much as a problem solver, tentative on many occasions, even though on others he expresses his confidence in the solutions he proposes for the difficulties he identifies. Yet the element of truth in the representation of his thought as systematic lies in those recurrent themes, methods, and motives. This, rather than any attempt to discuss his individual contributions across the wide range of subjects he tackled, will be the focus of our attention here.

He was, for twenty years, a member of Plato's Academy. There can be little doubt, on general grounds, that he was, to begin with, an adherent of some version of Plato's theory of Forms. We know that he composed a number of literary works, many of them dialogues modeled on those of Plato, though only fragments from some of these are extant in the quotations, paraphrases, or imitations of later writers. It is commonly held that in some of these lost works that stem from the earliest period of his literary activity (not all do), he maintained Platonic positions not just on the Forms, but also, for example, on the soul and its relationship with the body. It is moreover from these literary works that Aristotle was chiefly known to the generations that followed him, rather, that is, than from the treatises that make up the Aristotelian corpus that we have (treatises that represent for the most part notes, in many cases incomplete and unedited notes, for the lecture courses he gave in the school he eventually set up in the Lyceum at Athens toward the end of his life). The hypothesis of an earliest period during which Aristotle adopted more or less orthodox Platonic positions on a number of topics has a good deal of prima facie plausibility. Nevertheless this remains a hypothesis: in not one of the extant treatises does he defend Plato's views on Forms, for instance. Although the severity and the manner of his criticisms vary from context to context (and may also have varied from period to period), he was always critical of the assumption of Forms that exist independently of the particulars that exemplify them.

While Aristotle's own doctrines of form, particular, substance, and causation all diverge in various fundamental ways from Plato, he remained, in important respects, a Platonist, or at least took Plato's side on many debates on basic issues. Though he criticized Plato for "separating" the Forms and held that form is an aspect of the particular concrete thing which is itself construed as a composite of form and matter, he agreed with Plato nevertheless in emphasizing the importance of the investigation of that aspect and in stressing that forms are the primary objects that we can be said to know or understand. He shared, too, Plato's view that the cosmos is a well-ordered whole, though he preferred the idea of the craftsmanlike activity at work in natural objects themselves to the image of a divine creator-god. In our attempts to understand events or objects it is essential to ask what

their end is, what good they serve, what they are for. He is, in fact, an out-and-out teleologist, like Plato, even though he recognizes (as Plato too had done) that there is not always going to be an answer to the question that seeks a final cause. Some things are as they are because they have to be so or because they just happen to be so (the color of one's eyes, for example). Again he takes Plato's side on the issue of the objectivity of moral values and in rejecting moral relativism, though he again diverges from Plato in denying the absoluteness of moral values and in insisting that ethics and politics are not exact studies. Finally, although his view of the soul is in some ways antithetical to Plato's (for while Plato represented soul as an independent substance, Aristotle thinks of the vital faculties, for the most part, as the activities of the corresponding parts of the body and as inseparable from them) he again remained in agreement with Plato in holding a (but not the same) doctrine of the immortality of the soul. For Aristotle this was a matter of the immortality of what he called the active reason, a difficult and obscure doctrine we shall return to later.

These links with Platonic positions remained strong even when Aristotle severely criticized many of his master's central beliefs. While the eventual scope of Aristotle's intellectual activities far outstripped Plato's, it is mistaken to see his development as the transformation of a (rather naive) Platonist into some kind of inductivist devoted to disinterested empirical research. That underestimates, first, the complexity of his relation with Plato. But it also misrepresents the nature and aims of his empirical studies. As noted, he carried out extensive research in zoology and encouraged his colleagues and pupils in the Lyceum to pursue similar work in other areas of the study of nature; Theophrastus' extant botanical treatises are the most obvious example of studies carried out on the model set by Aristotle himself. Again

Aristotle undertook or initiated equally comprehensive studies in political history (in the analysis of the constitutions of Greek city-states; 158 of these are said to have been produced, not all by Aristotle himself, no doubt, though the only example that has survived is the *Constitution of Athens*), and in the history of earlier thought. Thus the histories of physical speculation and of psychology undertaken by Theophrastus, those of mathematics and astronomy by Eudemus, and that of medicine by Meno all follow Aristotle's lead and the pattern that is already discernible in several of his own treatises where he engages in surveys of previous thought before embarking on his own attempted resolution of the problems. But in every case he had clearly defined theoretical interests, though that does not mean to say, of course, that he undertook these studies simply to prove a particular thesis.

Thus the wide-ranging zoological studies (which together amount to more than a quarter of the extant corpus) were clearly in no sense merely descriptive works. The zoologist is out to provide the explanations of the data he collects. In the first book of *On the Parts of Animals* Aristotle writes a passionate protreptic, or exhortation, to the study of animals. Countering those who might maintain, or who had maintained, that such subject matter is trivial or plain nasty, he insists on the value and importance of the study of animals, including the study of their material constituents. But the justification he offers is in terms of the beauty and the goodness of nature that is thereby revealed, and he is careful to underline that the chief objects of the zoologist's attention are the form and finality present in animals and their parts. Similarly the study of political constitutions is one eventually directed to the question of their forms and to the analysis of the changes they undergo, even though in the extant *Constitution of Athens* this concern does not obtrude, and the frame-work of the account is provided first by the chronological narrative and then by the description of the existing constitution.

The analysis of earlier thought on particular subjects takes us to a central topic in Aristotle's methodology. Although he is often critical of what ordinary people, or particular so-called experts, hold on particular issues, he has a profound respect for their views. It is mainly by considering what had been assumed or asserted on any given subject that the problems it poses can be identified. He sometimes expresses his own aim as being simply to disentangle those problems. As he says in the *Nicomachean Ethics* (1145b2 ff.), if that has been achieved, and what is sound in common assumptions has been preserved, then the subject has been demonstrated sufficiently. In moral philosophy, especially, common beliefs are an important, indeed the chief, guide to what is the case, though in ethics as in other areas common beliefs, when analyzed, often turn out to contain incoherences, or to be partial or oversimplified. This principle—of the respect for ordinary opinions and for the views of those who had studied the questions before him—does not prevent him from sometimes diverging very radically from common beliefs by the time he reaches the end of his discussion. Yet those opinions provide the most usual starting point for his study, even though in such areas as zoology what was commonly believed will need to be supplemented extensively by original research.

Just as Aristotle sets out clear methodological principles for his inquiries, so too he is explicit on the topic of the kinds of question to be investigated. As we noted before, the so-called theory of causes is a theory of the types of explanation to be sought. Of any object we can ask what it is made of, what sort of thing it is, who made it (or what initiated the process that produced it), and what it is for (what good it serves), and of events similar questions also can be asked.

The example of a physical object is the easier to illustrate but should not be thought to dominate Aristotle's schema. With an artifact such as a chair, for instance, the four kinds of question yield answers in terms of the matter it is made of (as it might be, wood) the form (what makes the wooden object a chair, not any other kind of object), the craftsman who made it (the carpenter) and the purpose it serves (providing somewhere to sit). But we can ask similar questions about an event, such as an incursion into foreign territory, a raid, or an invasion. Its efficient cause will be what provoked it (it was in response to an act of aggression, maybe) and its final cause will be given by the end the agents had in view (to win an empire). The question about form will be relevant too, since there are relevant distinctions between, for example, declared and undeclared hostilities that must be taken into account in characterizing the event in question. Aristotle does not expect all four questions to be answerable in every case. On the contrary, as already remarked, there will be plenty of instances where we cannot say what good an object or event serves, and these include many instances in the study of animals, an area where Aristotle's teleological bent is particularly prominent, not to say notorious.

The interdependence of the items picked out in the answers to different questions relating to the "causes" emerges from such a case as that of a living creature, where the kind of animal it is—its form or species— answers not only to the formal cause, but also, under different aspects, to the efficient and final causes. The efficient cause of a man, in Aristotle's view, is the male parent, and while the end, or the good, that human life can serve can be answered fully by reference to the various vital functions and moral and intellectual capacities we possess, to say what a human being is is a shorthand way of referring to this end or good. We should

also remark that form and matter are correlatives. The matter of a chair may be wood: but of wood itself we can ask questions about its form and matter, about what makes it wood. Here Aristotle will answer in terms of his theory of the four simple bodies—earth, water, air, and fire—each of which is characterized by a pair of the fundamental qualities—hot and cold, wet and dry.

What primarily exists, in Aristotle's view, are the individual substances, such as Socrates or Callias or this dog or that horse, but each individual substance is analyzable in terms of its matter and its form. In two respects especially Aristotle makes a radical break from Plato: first, in distinguishing between substances and the other categories of things, and second, in his doctrine of substance itself. The doctrine of categories classifies the most general answers to the kinds of things there are: these kinds correspond in some cases to linguistic distinctions, but they are not themselves merely linguistic categories, but rather the categories of what there is. Thus red is a kind of color: if we ask what color, in turn, is, the answer is a kind of quality. But when we reach that reply, we can go no further: that answer picks out a basic category. Whereas Plato's theory of Forms had been applied not just to what Aristotle would call qualities (beautiful, just) and to relations (equal) but also to substances (man, ox), Aristotle insists on fundamental distinctions between these different categories. He insists too that qualities are always dependent on substances, that there can be no disembodied qualities. Substances are the primary category in that if there were no substances, there could be no qualities, no quantities, places, or times. Yet Aristotle has been criticized, and is to some extent open to criticism, in that he occasionally represents substances as themselves capable of independent existence. While, to be sure, any given substance can exist independently of a given determinate quality, it can hardly do so independently of any determinable quality whatsoever.

The same doctrine provides an essential part of his answer, also, to problems that went back to Parmenides, concerning the possibility of coming-to-be and change. Locomotion, for instance, is to be defined as change in the category of place. Growth is change in the category of quantity, and both of these must be distinguished from, and are independent of, qualitative change (alteration) and the coming-to-be of a new substance—though that does not happen ex nihilo. Aristotle agrees with Parmenides that nothing comes to be from nothing, but admits coming-to-be of new substances nevertheless, analyzing this in terms of the acquisition, by matter of a particular type, of form of a particular type. Neither the form nor the matter itself comes to be: it is rather their combination that does so. But, more important, Aristotle can now use his distinctions between types of change and coming-to-be to rebut Parmenides when he ruled out change of any kind on the grounds that it involved a coming-to-be (of some type) from not-being.

The doctrine of substance puts the emphasis on the individual members of a species, the particular human beings, dogs, or horses. Where Plato had privileged the universal and downgraded the particular, Aristotle from some points of view reverses the order of priorities and insists that for the universal to exist, there must be at least one particular instance of it (though he does not deny, indeed he asserts, that for animals to exist there need not be human beings, or any particular human being, though the converse holds). This is however an example where important developments can be detected in his thought. Initially, in the *Categories*, he was content with a broad distinction between primary and secondary substances, the former the individual such as Socrates, the latter the species and genera (such as man, animal) that the individual exemplifies. Within that distinction the claim was that secondary substances depend on primary in the sense explained. Yet when he wrote the central books of the *Metaphysics* he came to press certain questions that were not raised in the *Categories*. The point is a complex one but may be expressed like this. It is all very well to claim that the individual primary substance is what exists fundamentally, but we must ask what makes a substance a substance—as opposed to just a random conglomeration of things or, as Aristotle puts it, a heap. If that question is pressed, it must be answered in terms of the form of the thing in question, that is, in terms of what it is to be that particular thing, or its essence. It turns out, in fact, that from some points of view what is primary is form, for it is this that makes the substance what it is. Yet Aristotle remains emphatic that form cannot be said to exist separately, and his disagreement with the transcendent Forms of Plato's middle period remains as fundamental as ever.

There is no space here to pursue the ramifications of the applications of these methodological and metaphysical principles to the various multifarious areas of Aristotle's intellectual activity. We must limit ourselves to some brief comments on some of the most important ideas in his ethics and philosophy of mind, focusing as before on the connections between various aspects of his thought and on the role of certain major articulating conceptions.

In ethics, Aristotle rejects both Platonic absolutism and moral relativism and subjectivism. Moral excellence is defined as a disposition involving choice and lying in the mean relative to us as defined by reason and as the man of practical intelligence would define it (*Nicomachean Ethics* 1106b36 ff.). But "relative to us" does not mean that it is simply a matter of our personal judgment. It allows merely that there are differences between one individual and another that are relevant to what we should say about how they should behave. But in every case there is, for each individual, an objectively determinable disposition that will correspond to moral excellence. But against the Platonist, in turn, Aristotle insists that ethics is no exact science, and argues that even if there were such things as transcendent Forms they would be of no practical use in deciding moral questions. Such an excellence as courage is not a matter of precise measurement, but will be a disposition falling within a certain range. The point may perhaps most easily be illustrated in relation to generosity. A generous donation is not to be defined in terms of an exact sum of money, but will fall within certain limits (which will differ according to the means of the individual concerned). But generosity itself is not just a matter of acts, but one of a settled disposition: the acts create the disposition—they give us the character we acquire—though some dispositions, once acquired, may be hard or impossible to reverse. Furthermore, acts must be the result not just of knowledge of the circumstances of the case (one cannot be said to have done something courageous if he was quite unaware of the dangers of the situation), but also of deliberate choice, *proairesis,* which will reflect a certain view concerning ends as well as means.

Courage, for example, consists not merely in having the right feelings of confidence, but in having them in relation to the right objects, from the right motives, in the right way, and at the right time—all factors that are the province of practical intelligence, *phronesis.* This is itself one of the so-called intellectual excellences, that is, an excellence of reasoning (like art) and one way in which these differ from the moral excellences is that they can be taught, while moral excellence comes from habituation. But practical intelligence has a special role in that it and moral excellence are interdependent and inseparable. Conceptually

they can of course be distinguished, the one to do with reasoning about moral decisions, the other to do with desire for the ends, but Aristotle holds that a person cannot have moral excellence without practical intelligence and vice versa. If reasoning in moral matters is not illuminated by a correct conception of the ends (correct, but not exact), it amounts to no more than mere cleverness. Conversely, moral excellence without practical intelligence would be at best what he calls "natural excellence," a natural disposition that children and animals may share, but which needs both training and reason to develop into true moral excellence. This conception of the interdependence of character and judgment offers an important insight into the nature of morality and one that is in sharp contrast both with earlier Platonic and with most later, including modern, ethical theory.

Aristotle's view of the highest excellence of man is that it consists of what he calls *theoria,* conventionally translated "contemplation." This is the exercise of reason in theoretical domains—in philosophy itself—and ranks as the supreme excellence (and the most important constituent of human happiness), as it is the exercise of the highest faculty of soul. In the *Nicomachean Ethics* (1177b30 ff.) he says:

> If reason is divine in comparison with man, then life according to reason is divine in comparison with human life. But we must not follow those who advise us as we are men to have human aspirations, as we are mortal to have mortal aspirations, but we must, so far as we are able, make ourselves immortal and do everything we can to live in accordance with the best thing in us.

Nevertheless, Aristotle also emphasizes that man is essentially a creature who lives in a social community (*politikon zoon*). While reason is the divine part in us, we cannot just engage in a life devoted to nothing but theoretical study. As human beings, we should also exhibit the social and political excellences, doing just and brave acts, performing our duties with regard to contracts and the like: indeed it is just such activities and their corresponding excellences that are, in his eyes, typically human.

In his philosophy of mind, once again, Aristotle offers a solution to the problems that differs radically from Plato's. As form and matter are interdependent, so too are soul and body. Indeed the soul is the form, the body the matter of the individual human being. In general, Aristotle asserts (*On the Soul* 412b6 ff.) that it is as unnecessary to investigate whether the soul and body are one as it is to ask whether the ax and its function, chopping, are one. With the single, qualified exception of the faculty of reasoning, all the vital functions are functions of parts of the body. They include reproduction, nutrition, perception, imagination, and locomotion. Aristotle shows considerable interest in the detailed answers to such questions as which animals can smell, which can hear, how different animals move, and how they reproduce. The zoological treatises are in an important sense a continuation of the treatises dealing with the faculties of soul, themselves clearly stated to belong to the study of nature.

The analysis of perception in particular is complex and subtle. The primary objects of sight, for instance, are colors, though we also say that we see Socrates, and Socrates would be an example of what Aristotle calls an incidental object of perception. In the act of perception, the perceptible form of the object seen (the color) is received by the sense organ, the eye, but strictly it is not the eye that sees. The impression it receives must itself be interpreted by a central faculty of perception, which is also responsible for coordinating perceptions and for the apprehension of what Aristotle calls the "common

sensibles," such as movement and shape. There is, for sure, what may be called a physiological component to perception; but there is also a psychological one. For whatever happens in the eye treated as a mere receptor of an impression is not what seeing is, though it is a necessary condition for it. Similarly with the feelings: anger is not the seething of the blood around the heart, though it is accompanied by it. Aristotle thereby avoids both a materialist psychology and a dualist one, according to which soul and body are two entities. In his theory of the reasoning faculty, however, he finds a place for immortality. Reason too has intelligible objects, analogous to the perceptible objects we see or hear, and these must, in a way, be received by a part of the reasoning faculty he calls the passive reason. But what ensures that reasoning can take place—what is said to fulfill the role of light in vision— is what he calls the active reason, and it alone can be and is immortal. This is, however, clearly no personal immortality: the active reason, if not to be identified with God himself, corresponds to a divine principle whose role is to render potentially intelligible forms actually intelligible.

This obscure, even opaque, doctrine is adumbrated in a single elliptical chapter of *On the Soul,* which exemplifies not just the speculative but also the tentative character of Aristotle's thought. The divine is what is supreme in the hierarchy of nature. Aspects of that hierarchy can be understood readily enough. Plants, animals, and human beings are stratified according to the vital faculties they possess: plants have the power of reproduction and nutrition alone, man alone has the power of reason. But God is not just described as pure reason, but also as the ultimate source of movement and change in the universe, conceived as an "unmoved mover." Such a mover could not himself be subject to change, for any change would be away from the perfection he perpetually enjoys. But he must also be totally unmoved, for movement implies lack of fulfillment. At the same time his perfection is not one of inactivity, but rather one of the actuality of reasoning, the one activity, in Aristotle's view, that can be carried on without remission, let alone without fatigue. The way in which such a principle secures movement and change in the universe as a whole cannot be as an efficient cause (for there action is always accompanied by reaction). Rather it acts as a final cause: it is the good to which, directly or ultimately, everything else aspires. Here in the notion of a supreme being—of God as reason, as the good, as the source of motion, and as final cause—Aristotle's philosophy of mind, his ethics, his cosmology and his theory of causation come together in a synthesis that has, for sure, Platonic traits and in places exhibits Platonic influence, but which is nevertheless distinctly Aristotelian and a reminder of the speculative ambitions of his thought.

HELLENISTIC PHILOSOPHY

The conquests of Alexander brought about far-reaching changes in the Greek world, which had their reflection in speculative thought. Although many city-states retained their independence, in some cases that was a merely nominal matter. Alexander's conquests and their aftermath contributed to improving communications between parts of the eastern Mediterranean and Near East, and although the Greeks always remained Hellenocentric, some thinkers adopted a rather more internationalist perspective. Major contributions to both philosophy and science were made in the Hellenistic period by individuals who, though they wrote in Greek, were not of the Greek race, and some centers of learning—especially Alexandria itself—were cities whose populations were multiracial, though we should beware of overestimating the closeness of the contacts

there and elsewhere between ruling Greeks and the populations they ruled. Athens, meanwhile, remained the chief center of philosophical activity, not just for those such as Epicurus, who was an Athenian citizen (though born in Samos), but also for the main leaders of other schools, including some, like Zeno of Citium, the founder of Stoicism, who came from cities with strong non-Greek elements in their populations (in Zeno's case some admittedly disputed reports have it that he was himself of Phoenician origin).

The Hellenistic period also sees modifications in the way in which both philosophy and science were construed, in their aims and motivations. In both a growing practical orientation is detectable, and as we shall see, especially in the next and final section on science, there are trends toward greater specialization. In philosophy, the practical slant is marked: it took the form of an emphasis on the need for philosophy to be applicable—and to be applied—to the problems of life. Merely theoretical studies were of little or no interest to most Hellenistic philosophers. Everything they studied was directed immediately or ultimately to the end of happiness, and the focus of attention was often not so much on the positive characteristics of the good life as on the negative ones, the need to secure freedom from fear and anxiety. The good life and happiness themselves were now often, indeed usually, seen in terms of *ataraxia*, freedom from such anxiety. This did not, however, prevent philosophers from continuing to engage in such studies as the theory of knowledge and logic, physics, and cosmology. But these inquiries were undertaken not for their own sakes, but for their relevance to moral philosophy. Thus epistemology was necessary because the philosopher must be confident of the answers to give to questions about the foundations of knowledge. Physics too is important because if we do not understand natural phenomena, we will not be free from anxiety about them, from superstitious fears, for instance, about divine intervention in human affairs, about the gods causing earthquakes, thunder, or eclipses. But once that specific end has been achieved, further research is pointless. As Epicurus put it, in the *Principal Doctrines* (11): "If we were not troubled at all by apprehensions about things in the sky and concerning death, lest it somehow concern us, and again by our failure to apprehend the limits of pain and desires, we should have no further need of the study of nature." Even so, quite detailed studies, especially of the problem of the fundamental elements and their interactions, were undertaken by people whose chief concerns were philosophical.

While there are some marked continuities between classical and Hellenistic philosophy, the two periods can be broadly differentiated along the above lines. Some Hellenistic doctrines were undoubtedly elaborated as responses to or in reaction to the ideas of Plato and Aristotle (though the extent to which the latter's treatises were known is not clear). But there is a new urgency in asking, and answering, questions about the very possibility of knowledge, and in making philosophy relevant to life. In what was an open and complex situation, three main schools or traditions stand out— Epicureanism, Stoicism, and the various types of skepticism—and we may deal with each of these in turn very briefly, although no claim can be made that this offers any more than a very selective sketch of the variety of philosophical positions advanced, some of which were personal and idiosyncratic and fall outside the three main schools we shall be discussing.

Epicureanism

We have two main sources for the philosophy of Epicurus: three letters, preserved by Diogenes Laertius, in which Epicurus pro-

vides instruction in physics and ethics at a fairly elementary level, and the account of his ideas in the Roman poet Lucretius. But Epicurus' own more technical treatises are either completely lost or, as in the case of the important work *On Nature,* preserved only in very fragmentary form.

Epicurus rejected formal logic as of no relevance to philosophy, but he recognized the importance of considering the question of the criteria on which claims to knowledge could be based. He identified three such criteria: perception, preconception (*prolepsis*), and pleasure and pain. Pleasure and pain provide the basis of judgments about good and evil in Epicurus' ethics and we shall come back to them shortly. By preconception he has in mind the clear and distinct ideas we have about, for example, what a man is (though the Epicureans are in some difficulty differentiating such acceptable preconceptions from false assumptions or beliefs, especially when, as in the case of God, which will be considered below, they wish to accept some parts of what is commonly assumed but reject others). But the ultimate basis of knowledge is perception. Thought itself, the activity of mind or soul, is construed in material terms, for mind or soul themselves are atoms of a particular kind.

The physical system is a modified version of the atomic theory of Leucippus and Democritus (not that Epicurus himself usually acknowledges his debts to earlier thinkers). Atoms and the void alone exist. But whereas the earlier atomists had probably not distinguished clearly between physical and conceptual indivisibility, Epicurus differentiated these two—perhaps in part in response to criticisms that Aristotle had leveled at the earlier theory. The atoms are physically indivisible: they cannot be split. But they are conceptually divisible. But at the conceptual level there is an analogue to the atom, what Epicurus called the minimum in the atom, and this minimum is construed as itself conceptually indivisible. Matter, space, and time are all made up of indivisibles. Epicurus recognized that this conflicted with conventional Greek geometrical notions—which presupposed the infinite divisibility of spatial magnitudes—but he argued that such conventional notions were mistaken.

The primary properties of the atoms include weight as well as shape, size, and arrangement, and in the precosmic state the atoms are imagined as all moving at the same speed downward through the void. To account for the first interactions of the atoms he postulated a minimal swerve: this swerve has itself no cause; it is rather assumed to be an interruption in the otherwise unbroken chain of physical causes and effects. The swerve plays a vital role in his system in two ways. First, it is necessary to account for the formation of worlds (plural, for like the earlier atomists he held that this is not the only possible cosmos). Given that there is the differentiated variety of objects with which we are familiar, something must have happened to bring about an initial interaction between atoms, though once one such interaction had occurred its effect could be cumulative. As in the earlier atomic theory, compounds are formed by appropriately shaped atoms colliding and cohering. He gave, in fact, quite elaborate accounts of a variety of natural processes and phenomena, in part in order to release men from anxiety about possible supernatural or divine intervention. But he was emphatic that one should not dogmatize when giving such explanations: if several different accounts of the same phenomenon seem possible, none should be ruled out. The object of the inquiry was, always, to secure that some physical account could be given.

The second important function of the doctrine of the swerve was to secure free will. Quite how he saw choice as related to the atomic swerve is controversial, for an arbitrary and uncaused swerve of atoms in the soul at the moment of decision seems a bizarre way to account for free will and responsibility. It is however clear that his view was that, negatively, such a swerve is the necessary condition of free will. There must be some break, at some point, in the otherwise inexorable chain of cause and effect, if not at the moment of choice, at least at some stage in the past history or development of the living creature.

In ethics good is identified with pleasure, though this is largely construed negatively as freedom from pain, both bodily pain and mental anxiety. Epicurus appeals for example to the evidence of animals and children to support the claim that it is basic to all living creatures that they pursue pleasure and avoid pain. Human beings, too, he held, would do so, but for the fact that many of them have become contaminated by false opinions and myths in the process of being brought up and socialized. It was the chief aim of the Epicurean philosophy to free us from such mistaken beliefs and to return once again to the realization that pleasure is the good.

In some occasionally deliberately provocative remarks he claims, for instance, "I at any rate do not know how to conceive the good apart from the pleasures from tastes, or apart from the pleasures from sex, from sounds, and from shape" (Diogenes Laertius, 10.6). But more often the lesson he teaches is a prudential one. The emphasis is not on any attempt to maximize sensual pleasures, for that leads to discontent, frustration, and anxiety; besides, it was an important part of his teaching that there are natural limits to physical pleasures, or, as he puts it in *Principal Doctrines* 3, "The removal of all pain is the limit of the magnitude of pleasures." Rather, the focus is on avoiding pain and anxiety. If ill, or faced with unavoidable physical discomfort, the Epicurean remains happy, for he will reflect on the joys of past philosophical discussion. A letter purportedly written by Epicurus when close to death runs: "As I live this blessed day, the last of my life, I write this to you. Strangury is with me continually, and so too dysentery, so great that nothing could increase them. But over against all of these things there is the joy in my soul at the memory of our past conversations" (Diogenes Laertius, 10.22).

Clearly the follower of Epicurus is no Epicurean in the colloquial English sense, since he will be far too alert to the possible disadvantages in indulgence in pleasures of the table to pursue them. Rather the simple life is the surest way. "Send me a little pot of cheese," Epicurus is reported to have said (Diogenes Laertius, 10.11), "that I may when I like have a feast." Again the *Letter to Menoeceus* (130 f.) puts it that "plain savors give as much pleasure as a luxurious diet, when once the pain of want has been removed; and bread and water offer the most extreme pleasure when someone who needs them takes them." Once this moral message is grasped, Epicurus believes, the good is within reach. But it follows that the Epicurean will not, from choice, engage in such activities as politics or raising a family, for the calculation of the balance of likely pleasures and pains is unfavorable. Yet he will follow the customs of the society in which he lives and will act justly in relation to his fellows. As two of the *Principal Doctrines* put it: "The just man enjoys the greatest freedom from trouble, while the unjust is full of the greatest disturbance" (17); and, "It is impossible for a man who secretly violates a mutual contract with others . . . to feel confident that he will remain undiscovered, even if he has already got away with it innumerable times up till the present" (35). As for the Epicurean attitude toward the gods, he does not deny their existence (the common conception among mankind that there are such beings is to be accepted thus far);

but the gods have nothing to do with this world, and are imagined as living a blessed, trouble-free life in the infinite spaces between the worlds. So the notion of the divine that Epicurus ends up by advocating turns out to be one far removed from ordinary beliefs, which are, indeed, in his view, full of superstition.

While the prudential and negative characteristics of Epicurean morality are marked, it is fair to add that the positive value set on friendship and on partnership in the enjoyment of pleasures is an important tenet in the school. It is even said that on occasion the Epicurean may even die for a friend. Clearly too the circle of pupils and associates that collected around Epicurus attempted to practice what he preached, and he himself was positively revered as one who had released them, and who could release men in general if only they would listen to him, from an oppressive burden of fear generated by error.

Stoicism

The main rival positive or dogmatic philosophical school, Stoicism, was founded by Zeno of Citium in the early third century and developed especially by the third head of the school, Chrysippus, in the latter part of that century. The Stoics agreed with the Epicureans in stressing the importance of freedom from anxiety and in representing the good as within our grasp. For the Stoics, too, the wise man is happy even on the rack. But where Epicurus had defined the good as the pleasant, the Stoics identified it with excellence, virtue, *arete*. This position too was supported by an appeal to what is represented as natural, but it was argued that what all animals and children pursue is not pleasure, but rather their own self-preservation. This doctrine of *oikeiosis* has it first that in making the animal, nature made it "dear to itself," and second that human society is similarly built up because the ties of family, kin, community, and state are also naturally "dear" to us. Thus when the aim of life was said to be to live "in accordance with nature," "nature" was broadly conceived, both as human nature and as the nature of the universe: in the final analysis there is or should be no conflict between these. Pleasure, however, like other emotions and affections, arises from false opinions and is a kind of sickness of the soul, to be cured, as far as possible, by philosophy. The wise man does not just minimize his passions, he extirpates them.

Excellence is the only good. Most of what are commonly judged goods, such as health, beauty, wealth, and good birth, are indifferent, neither good nor bad; the wise man can be happy without them. They are, however, to be preferred, even though we can do without them. The wise man is secure in the knowledge that the only good, excellence, is within his power. There were, however, duties (*kathekonta*), actions that are befitting in that a reasonable defense can be adduced for them, some conditional (dependent on the circumstances one finds himself in), others unconditional, such as caring for one's parents. Accordingly, unlike the Epicureans, the Stoics were prepared to allow considerable involvement—even if an ultimately uncommitted involvement—in social and political activities, with the aim of promoting excellence and removing its opposite, vice (*kakia*).

This moral doctrine was supported by an elaborate theory of knowledge and a sophisticated physics and cosmology. In the former, perception is again seen as the ultimate basis of claims to knowledge: but from perceptions come presentations or impressions (*phantasiai*). Some presentations do not correspond to real objects (those we have in dreams, for instance). But those that do, the so-called "apprehensible presentations" (*phantasiai kataleptikai*), are defined as proceeding from an existing object, as impressed and stamped according to the object, and such that they could not come from a nonexisting object. When the presentation is clear, we are in no doubt, and it is these presentations that act as the chief criterion of the truth. The full definition of this key notion in their epistemology is probably the work of Chrysippus, who was certainly responsible for other developments in Stoic logic, the doctrine of signs, work in linguistics, and especially the analysis of arguments. While, as noted above, Aristotle produced the first formal logic in his theory of the syllogism, this was essentially a logic of terms: to the Stoics, and especially to Chrysippus, goes the credit of the first propositional logic.

Physics and cosmology are, as in Epicureanism, strictly relevant to morality, studies undertaken to achieve peace of mind. But against Epicurean atomism, the Stoics maintained a thoroughgoing continuum theory. They denied there is void within the world (although outside it there is infinite void). They rejected the argument that the void is necessary to account for movement. The world is a plenum, but that does not prevent movement taking place within it. As fish move through water, so any object can move through the plenum, conceived as an elastic medium. Matter, space, and time are all infinitely divisible continua.

In contrast to the quantitative theory of atomism, Stoic physics was essentially qualitative. The starting point of their cosmology is the distinction between two fundamental principles, the active and the passive. The passive is qualityless matter, the active variously identified as the cause, God, reason, breath or vital spirit (*pneuma*), and fate. Both these principles are corporeal, and to describe the relation between them the Stoics used the term "total mixture" (*krasis di' holon*). Mixture (*krasis*) is defined as the total interpenetration of two or more substances, as exemplified in the mixture of two liquids such as wine and water. It is distinct both from the mere juxtaposition of parts (*parathesis*), as in a mixture of two kinds of seeds, and from *synchusis,* where, as in our chemical combination, the component substances are destroyed and a new substance results.

The active principle is, then, thought of as inherent in the world and permeating every part of it. The universe is indeed not simply like a living creature, it is one. Like a human being, it is pervaded with vital spirit (*pneuma*), life (*psyche*), and reason (*nous*). The active principle is not only a principle of cohesiveness, but also a generating force. In accounts of the cosmogonical process, God is described as the seminal formula of the universe. The reason that pervades the cosmos is, moreover, not merely an intelligent but also a providential cause. But divine providence implies no break in the chain of physical causes and effects. On the contrary, it is the name for that chain. The sequence of cause and effect is both fate and the will of God. Chance is eliminated or interpreted purely subjectively, as what is obscure to human cognition. But this physical determinism was not held to conflict with human moral responsibility. This they justified with the help of a distinction between different kinds of cause: some part of our action is "in our power" in the sense of depending on our character. Yet the Stoics consistently maintained that there were no exceptions to the nexus of physical causes and effects, and if pressed on how character itself is formed they had to trace its formation back through acts and processes that all themselves belonged to that nexus.

Skepticism

Both Epicureanism and Stoicism offered positive and essentially dogmatic philosophical systems, though Stoicism was flexible enough to allow some modifications, fairly considerable ones in the case of some later adherents of the school, such as Posidonius in the first century B.C. Skepticism took different forms at different periods, and the reconstruction of the ideas of the first Hellenistic skeptic, Pyrrho of Elis, active in Athens in the early third century B.C., is problematic since he wrote nothing and, as usual, many of the reports of his teaching are tendentious. It seems clear, however, that his basic strategy was to undermine dogmatism in any form, to throw doubt on claims to knowledge, on the criteria used to justify such claims, and on the systems built upon them. Then later in the third century a form of skepticism appears to have been adopted by Arcesilaus, the then head of Plato's Academy, and a further shift in the traditions of Plato's school took place with Carneades in the second century, though how far he adopted a radical or just a qualified version of skepticism is a matter of dispute. What is clear is that he gained a formidable reputation as a dialectician, notably in undermining the positions of Chrysippus.

By far the most important of extant sources for skepticism is Sextus Empiricus, writing in the second century A.D. From him it appears that a distinction may be drawn between the Pyrrhonist position (which Sextus himself supported) and that of the Academic skeptics, or at least Arcesilaus. Where the latter asserted that nothing can be known, the Pyrrhonist suspended judgment on the question. He saw, in fact, that the insistence that nothing can be known can be used in relation to that position itself. What he advocated was, rather, the practice of suspension of judgment (*epoche*), on this as on every other issue that relates to the reality of things.

The skeptics' strategy was to point out that on the central questions disputed between the opposing dogmatic schools, no certainty was to be obtained. It was impossible to justify reason, or the senses, as the criterion of truth, for instance. On all such issues the skeptic used destructive arguments to undermine both positive positions. The Pyrrhonist follows appearances and makes no assertions about underlying realities. He will say that the honey appears sweet to him, but he will suspend judgment on whether it really is sweet. In everyday life he will go along with the customs and conventions of the society he lives in, and he will occupy himself by practicing an art or craft (Sextus himself was a doctor). But he makes no claims to knowledge and holds such beliefs as he does undogmatically.

Ancient skepticism thus offered a radical, at points subtle and sophisticated, challenge to dogmatic philosophy, and in time skeptical themes were to prove immensely influential in later European philosophy—and not just on Montaigne, Descartes, Hume, and others who explicitly took up skeptical arguments. This influence has only recently come to be fully appreciated. In its ancient form, moreover, skepticism was a point of view with moral implications. The skeptic was an inquirer—that was indeed the root meaning of the term *skeptic* in Greek—and he sets out initially with the aim of arriving at resolutions to the fundamental issues debated in philosophy. But when he finds that there is just as much to be said on both opposing sides on the chief questions concerning truth and reality, this discovery brings peace of mind (*ataraxia*). He does not search for this, but it supervenes on suspension of judgment. The skeptics compared the situation with a story told about the painter Apelles who, trying but failing to represent a horse's foam, flung his sponge in desperation at the painting—only to find that the mark left by the sponge produced exactly the effect he had been aiming at. The skeptic, too, like his dogmatist counterparts, achieves freedom from anxiety and independence from the vagaries of fortune, but he does this not by adopting pleasure or excellence as the good but by suspending judgment.

HELLENISTIC MATHEMATICS AND SCIENCE

Discussion of the chief achievements of Greek science has been postponed until the end of our summary account of philosophy in part simply for convenience of exposition, but in part because in fact much of the most important work in Greek science was done during the Hellenistic period. A brief analysis has already been given of early Greek natural philosophy and some mention made of the intellectual developments associated with the sophistic movement in the fifth century. But with the exception of Aristotle's zoology and Theophrastus' botany, earlier work was generally superseded by that done in the Hellenistic period. This is true, for instance, of other areas in what we call the life sciences, such as anatomy and physiology, where investigations were usually carried out by doctors and often had practical ends in view, namely, their applications to medicine. Medicine itself, to be sure, expanded considerably in the fifth and fourth centuries, during which time there were important interactions between it and natural philosophy. Several of the Hippocratic treatises contain theories about the fundamental constituents of physical objects as a whole or of human beings, for instance, and some enter the debate on the nature of knowledge and causation. Several, for example, insist that medicine is a rational discipline (*techne*), even though it is not exact. The treatise *On Ancient Medicine* contrasts medicine and natural philosophy, claiming that the former, unlike the latter, needs no arbitrary hypotheses, and this work also distinguishes clearly between causal and merely concomitant factors.

Yet most of the writers who are represented in the Hippocratic corpus had only comparatively limited knowledge of human anatomy, obtained usually from surgical practice or from the observation of lesions. It was Aristotle who first made extensive use of dissection (on animal subjects), and even his anatomical knowledge was primitive in comparison with that of the great Hellenistic biologists, Herophilus and Erasistratus, who were active at the end of the fourth and the beginning of the third century. It was they who first dissected human subjects (they are even reported also to have carried out vivisections on "criminals received out of prison from the kings," as Celsus tells us [*On Medicine,* Proem paragraphs 23 f.]), and they were responsible for a series of brilliant advances in anatomy and in physiology, the most important of which were the discovery of the nervous system and that of the valves of the heart. Of greater importance for our discussion, however, are developments in mathematics and the exact sciences, especially astronomy.

Mathematics

The Greeks were, of course, far from being the first in the field in the development of mathematics. Both Babylonian and Egyptian mathematics had already reached a state of considerable sophistication in the second millennium B.C. In such areas as the solving of quadratic equations, Babylonian mathematics always remained superior to Greek. Where Greek mathematics eventually diverged from the mathematics we know about from the great ancient Near Eastern civilizations is primarily in the concentration of interest on the question of mathematical proof—in the strict sense of the demonstration by deductive argument from clearly identified premises. For the early stages of this development we have to rely on the meager remains of pre-Euclidean mathe-matics—the very success of Euclid himself led to the almost total eclipse of earlier mathematics. But we are told by ancient historians of mathematics that the first person to compose a book of *Elements* was Hippocrates of Chios (not to be confused with the doctor of the same name, who came from Cos), and this may have been around the middle of the fifth century B.C. Those historians also indicate that there was a whole series of mathematicians who continued this work between Hippocrates and Euclid himself, but Euclid's *Elements,* generally dated to around 300 B.C., was both more systematic and more comprehensive than any earlier work.

The object of such books of "Elements" was to systematize geometrical knowledge and exhibit the relations between elementary propositions and those derivable from them—the term "elements" itself was used of such elementary propositions. In Euclid, Book One, for instance, begins by setting out the definitions, those "common opinions" (axioms) and postulates on which the geometry in that book is based. Ideally these are all and the only assumptions to be made for the deductions that follow, and Euclid approximates tolerably closely to that ideal. These starting points are themselves not proved, but merely asserted. In a passage in the *Republic* (510c) Plato complains that mathematicians give no account of their hypotheses (illustrated here by such examples as the odd and even and the three kinds of angles). Rather they take them as evident to everyone. In Aristotle's analysis of demonstration, in the *Posterior Analytics,* he insists that the starting points (which he specifies as definitions, axioms, and hypotheses) must themselves be indemonstrable (on pain of an infinite regress) but they must be known to be true.

Quite what Euclid himself thought about the status of his starting points is a matter of guesswork. He makes no direct comment on that question, and we should not assume that he took them all to be self-evident. Their role is certainly to identify the assumptions on which the geometry that follows will be based. But he must have known that not all of them are uncontroversial. Alternative definitions of number, for example, are given in different Greek mathematical texts. In such a case Euclid has at least had to be selective. In the more interesting instance of the parallel postulate, which states that nonparallel straight lines meet at a point, it is possible that he was not just responsible for but also appreciated the significance of including it *as* a postulate. A passage in Aristotle (*Prior Analytics* 65a4 ff.) shows that fourth-century mathematical theory on the topic of parallels was open to the charge of circularity, for he remarks that mathematicians who "think they can construct parallels unconsciously assume such things as cannot be demonstrated if parallels do not exist." It seems likely, then, that Euclid's introduction of a postulate to cover this was a deliberate move. Certainly the geometry developed on its basis depends crucially on this assumption. Later Greek mathematicians, including Ptolemy (second century A.D.) and Proclus (fifth century A.D.), standardly objected that the parallel postulate should have been proved, not assumed, and they offer varieties of attempted demonstration, none of which avoids the circularity that had been mentioned by Aristotle. It was, too, an attack on this problem that eventually led to the development of non-Euclidean geometries such as those of Lobachevsky and Riemann in the nineteenth century. Although there is no evidence that Euclid or any other Greek geometer envisaged the possibility of such geometries, it may be noted that his *Elements* are not merely an axiomatic but also a hypothetical system, in the sense, at least, that it was based on a set of assumptions that include propositions that he must surely have known

to have been questioned or denied by other Greek thinkers. Those later developments in geometry also enable one to see the wisdom of Euclid's desisting from any attempt to provide the parallel postulate.

Once the starting points are set out, a body of theorems is demonstrated in systematic order. We have noted above that rigorous deductive argument was used in philosophy as early as Parmenides, and that first Aristotle and then the Stoics provided formal analyses of valid and invalid arguments. Yet it was mathematics that provided the star example of orderly sequences of conclusions established by deduction from clearly identified premises. Thus while ancient Near Eastern mathematics used various approximations to what we should call the square root of 2, there is no evidence that the Babylonians or Egyptians knew that the ratio between 1 and the square root of 2 cannot be expressed as an integer, or that they appreciated the significance of that fact. The distinctive Greek contribution was to demonstrate that the side and the diagonal of the square are incommensurable by showing that if the reverse is assumed, absurd consequences follow.

This argument schema, reductio ad absurdum, which assumes the contradictory of what is to be proved and shows that this assumption leads to absurdity, is the most common method of argument in the *Elements*. But Euclid also employs the particular form of it known as the method of exhaustion, which is generally thought to go back to the mathematician and astronomer Eudoxus of Cnidos, a younger contemporary and associate of Plato. The principle that underlies the method is set out in Euclid, 10.1. If there are two unequal magnitudes, *A* and *B*, and from the greater, *A*, there be subtracted more than its half, and from the remainder more than its half, and this process is repeated indefinitely, there will be left some magnitude that is less than the lesser of the two given magnitudes (*B*). By repeating the process of subtraction as often as one likes, one will eventually arrive at a remainder that is smaller than any given magnitude at all. One obvious application in geometry is to determine a curvilinear area such as a circle. This can be done by inscribing in it regular polygons that approximate successively more closely to the area of the circle itself. By repeating the process one can increase the area of the inscribed figure until the difference between it and the area of the circle is less than any given magnitude, although the Greeks standardly denied that the inscribed polygon can be identified with the circle (exhaustion is in this sense a misnomer, in that the area is never in fact deemed to be exhausted).

Euclid's textbook contains most elementary geometry and number theory. Thereafter, in the third century, Greek mathematics produced a series of masterpieces, the work first of Archimedes (notably such treatises as *On Spirals* and *On the Quadrature of the Parabola*) and then of Apollonius of Perga, whose study of conic sections is extant. With the exception of Archimedes' *Method,* these, like other Greek mathematical works, all present results and give no indication of how either the theorems or their proofs were discovered. The *Method* is exceptional and exceptionally important both in that it refers to discovery as well as giving demonstrations and in the actual method that Archimedes there recommends. This involves the application of mechanical notions, the law of the lever, to geometrical problems; and it also assumes that a plane figure may be thought of as consisting of the set of parallel lines it contains. Thus by thinking of a plane figure as composed of a set of such lines indefinitely close together, and then thinking of these lines as balanced by corresponding lines of the same magnitude in a figure of known or determinable area, he finds the desired area in terms of the known

one. Yet with a typical Greek insistence on rigor, Archimedes remarks that this method is not a proof, it is only a method of discovery (whether because of the mechanical assumptions it uses, or in some views more probably because it depends on infinitesimals). He accordingly gives a strict geometrical demonstration, using reductio and the method of exhaustion, of the theorems concerning the area of a segment of a parabola that he tells us he had discovered by the mechanical method. Although he found the theorem for the area by such a method, he proved it by showing that the area is neither greater nor less than four-thirds of the triangle with the same base and height.

In two respects Archimedes' procedures have been hailed as anticipating the integral calculus: first in his use of infinitesimals in the *Method* (where areas and volumes are treated as composed of their line and plane elements, respectively) and second in certain applications of exhaustion in determining areas or volumes. Thus in *On the Quadrature of the Parabola* the theorem for the area of a parabolic segment is obtained by taking the sum of an infinite series, that is, of a series of *n* terms plus a remainder that can be made as small as desired. Strictly speaking, no Greek mathematician used the integral calculus, since this depends on the rigorous definition of the concept of a limit of an infinite series, an idea generally alien to Greek mathematics. Indeed the method of exhaustion, in which the difference between two magnitudes is made as small as desired, is, in general, a way of avoiding integration. Yet Archimedes' procedures, while not based on a general theory of integrability, are practically equivalent to integration, in that they yield, case by case, results that would now be obtained by that method.

Mathematics provided the chief model of demonstration not just for certain areas of natural philosophy but also for the exact sciences. The Hellenistic period sees remarkable advances not only in astronomy—which we shall come to in due time—but also in theoretical geography and geophysics, in acoustics, in optics, and in statics and hydrostatics, although in several of these disciplines, acoustics especially, there was earlier work on which to build. There was, to be sure, no consensus among those who engaged in these studies about their aims or methods. Nor was the effort of Greek scientists wholly devoted to the applications of mathematics to these fields and to the bid to turn them into exact sciences. In most cases notable empirical work was also done in these inquiries, which we must also take into account. We may illustrate the diversity of work with some brief examples from some of these studies, referring where necessary to the pre-Hellenistic background.

Descriptive geography goes back to Hecataeus in the late sixth century, and Herodotus would certainly have seen his *historie* as including this as well as what we should call history in the stricter sense. Theoretical geophysics is represented in the pre-Aristotelian period by such debates as that on the shape of the earth. By Plato's time, at least, its sphericity was accepted by others besides Plato himself, though it is notable that the atomist Democritus still held that the earth was flat. Aristotle's treatise *On the Heavens* provides a battery of arguments for the earth's sphericity. Some of these are based on the Aristotelian theory of natural movements. Heavy objects are held to fall toward the center of the universe, deemed to coincide with the center of the earth; but the shape of the earth formed by the collection of the heavy objects at the center is (roughly) spherical. But he also uses impressive empirical arguments for the same conclusion, referring first to the shape of the earth's shadow in lunar eclipses, and second to the changes in the configurations of the constellations when observed from different latitudes.

Aristotle also records the first known attempt to determine the size of the earth. In *On the Heavens* (298a15 ff.) he says that "those mathematicians who try to calculate the circumference say it is 400,000 stades." Since it is not certain which of the several kinds of stade, each with a different absolute value, is in question, this result cannot be interpreted exactly, but on any view it is a considerable overestimate.

Aristotle does not mention the method these mathematicians used, but we know from other sources, notably Cleomedes, how two Hellenistic investigators proceeded. In the third century Eratosthenes based his calculation on observations of the shadow cast by a gnomon (the upright rod or pointer on a sundial at right angles to the surface) at noon on the day of the summer solstice at two points on the earth's surface (Alexandria and Syene) assumed to be on the same meridian. At Syene there was no shadow; at Alexandria one of 7.2 degrees. Taking the distance between the two places to be 5,000 stades, he arrived at a figure of 250,000 stades for the circumference of the earth by simple geometry. Then in the first century B.C. the eclectic Stoic philosopher Posidonius obtained a figure of 240,000 stades by comparing observations of the altitude of the star Canopus above the horizon at Rhodes and at Alexandria (again taken to be 5,000 stades apart on the same meridian). It has commonly been assumed that the stade Eratosthenes used corresponds to 517 feet (157.5 m), which gives a polar circumference of 24,608 miles (39,690 km), compared with the modern figure of 24,806 miles (40,009 km). But first there are at least two other distinct possibilities, stades of one-eighth and one-tenth of a Roman mile, that is, roughly 610 feet (186 m) and 488 feet (148.8 m), which give results a good deal less close to the true figure, about 17 percent too high or 6 percent too low. Second, it is clear that both in assessing the angles and calculating the distance between the base points both Eratosthenes' and Posidonius' procedures involved a fair amount of approximation and rank guesswork.

The specific issues of the shape and size of the earth are of particular interest, but mathematical geography eventually included sophisticated discussions of, among other things, such problems as those of cartographic projection. In the second century A.D. Ptolemy's *Geography* begins with a theoretical section in which he deals with these issues before establishing the various zones or climata of the earth (determined by the maximum hours of sunlight in each) and entering on the more descriptive parts of the work.

In acoustics, too, considerable work had already been done in the period before Plato, and some of the important methodological debates go back as far. One of the chief sources is Aristoxenus, writing in the late fourth century B.C. It is clear that he knew already of a spectrum of positions adopted on the nature and criteria of music theory. At one extreme there were those who sought to reduce the subject to number theory (as was indeed recommended by Plato in the discussion of the part acoustics might play in the education of the Guardians in the *Republic* 530d ff.). Thus because the ratio that corresponds to the interval of an octave and a fourth (8:3) is neither a multiplicate one (like 1:2 and 1:4, corresponding to the octave and the double octave), nor again superparticular (as are 2:3 and 3:4, corresponding to the fifth and fourth), that interval cannot be a concord, even if it may sound like one. Yet to that Theophrastus is said to have objected, pertinently, that what is heard is not a number, even if it can be expressed numerically.

At the opposite end of the spectrum there were those who were interested purely in musical practice to the exclusion of any theoretical studies. Aristoxenus himself represents his own position as a via media. He has criticisms to make both of the ultraempiricists and of those who dismissed the evidence of the senses entirely. It is quite wrong to assimilate music theory to geometry completely. The geometrician makes no use of his faculty of sense perception, while "for the student of musical art accuracy of sense perception is a fundamental requirement" (*Elements of Harmony* 2.32–33). Yet Aristoxenus is unable to carry through his program of basing music theory on the use of intervals that can be discriminated by sense, and he is in turn criticized by later theorists, such as Ptolemy, for an excessive empirical bias.

Optics, statics, and hydrostatics all show the influence of the model provided by Euclid's *Elements*. Euclid's own optical treatise begins with the postulates necessary and then proceeds to a geometrical study of the problems connected with reflection especially. Yet here too later Greek studies contained important empirical work, especially the detailed investigations of refraction carried out by Ptolemy. His *Optics* (which exists only in a Latin version of an Arabic translation) not only engages in a theoretical analysis of the phenomena of refraction but sets out the results of the study of the actual amounts of refraction between three pairs of media, air to water, air to glass, and water to glass, for angles of incidence at 10-degree intervals from 10 degrees to 80 degrees.

Finally Archimedes' work in statics and hydrostatics again proceeds deductively, *more geometrico*, on the basis of assumptions set out at the start of his treatises. Thus the work *On Floating Bodies* begins by specifying a postulate that corresponds to the assumption of the absolute inelasticity of fluids. Book One demonstrates, for example, that "any solid lighter than a fluid will, if placed in the fluid, be so far immersed that the weight of the solid will be equal to the weight of the fluid displaced" and the so-called principle of Archimedes itself that "solids heavier than the fluid will, if placed in the fluid, be carried down to the bottom of the fluid, and they will be lighter in the fluid by the weight of the amount of fluid that has the same volume as the solid." The proofs of subsequent propositions and the geometry they use become increasingly complex. In Book Two, for instance, he turns to problems concerning paraboloids of revolution (the figure generated by rotating a parabola on its axis) and investigates the conditions of stability of paraboloids of varying shapes, and of varying specific gravities, in a fluid.

The treatise on statics, *On the Equilibrium of Planes,* takes a similar form. The use of the balance and levers had long been familiar in many practical contexts, and the treatise *On Mechanics* that appears in the Aristotelian corpus (though it is probably not by him) had discussed various problems in this connection. What is new in Archimedes is the rigorous deductive proof of the basic propositions in statics. Seven postulates are first set out, and a series of propositions then demonstrated on their basis, including the law of the lever in propositions 6 and 7, first for commensurable, and then for incommensurable magnitudes. The rest of books one and two deals with the problems of determining the centers of gravity of various plane figures, such as a parallelogram, a triangle, and a parabolic segment. In complete contrast to the repeated references to empirical data in *On Mechanics,* Archimedes deals with statical problems formulated in ideal, mathematical terms. Friction, the weight of the balance itself, indeed every extraneous factor, is discounted. The treatment is geometrical throughout and the whole is an exercise in deductive proof on the lines of Euclid's *Elements* and itself a model, in turn, of the application of mathematics to physical problems.

Astronomy

As with mathematics, so too with astronomy; there are interesting continuities and discontinuities between Greek studies and work done much earlier in the ancient Near East. Babylonian observational astronomy goes back to the second millennium B.C. The focus was on particular phenomena that were believed to be significant for events on earth—for the fortunes of the king and the kingdom, especially—and Babylonian astronomers constructed tables determining certain astronomical periodicities. Eventually the Greeks had access to, and used, Babylonian data extensively: in the second century A.D. Ptolemy took the first year of the reign of King Nabonassar (747 B.C.) as epoch, that is, as the base line for his calculations, and he also cites several precisely observed lunar eclipses from the eighth, seventh, and sixth centuries B.C. But this important cross-fertilization between the two main ancient astronomical traditions became a significant factor only in the period after the conquests of Alexander. Before the end of the fourth century B.C. Greek knowledge of Babylonian in this field was, at best, patchy, and probably confined largely to the use of Babylonian figures for the periodicities of the planets.

The distinctive Greek contribution was the construction of geometrical models to represent the movements of the moon, sun, and planets. Interest in this question goes back to the pre-Socratic period. When Anaximander, for instance, is reported to have located the sun, moon, and stars on separate circles around the earth, this was no more than the most schematic representation—as is shown by the fact that he took the stars to be less distant than the sun and moon. The Pythagoreans in the fifth century had advanced to the point of assigning each of the planets as well as the sun and moon to separate circles, but how far they had worked out a detailed theory of planetary motion is not clear. Aristotle reports and criticizes speculative ideas such as that of the counterearth, held to be responsible for some lunar eclipses, and he also tells us (*On the Heavens* 293a21 ff.) that some Pythagoreans held that the earth itself moves, circling a postulated central fire like one of the planets. (This was, then, the first non-geocentric system, though it was not a heliocentric one.) Tantalizing as the evidence is, the attempt to reconstruct a coherent astronomical system, even for Philolaus in the late fifth century, the most sophisticated Pythagorean astronomer of whom we hear, fails—and probably not just through the lack of reliable evidence.

Plato's *Timaeus,* which draws, no doubt, on earlier work, certainly introduces a key astronomical distinction, namely that between what he called the "Circle of the Same" and the "Circle of the Other." The former accounts for the phenomena we should explain in terms of the daily rotation of the earth about its axis; for most Greek astronomers, the outermost sphere of the "fixed" stars rotates once in every twenty-four hours. The Circle of the Other corresponds to and accounts for the independent movements of the sun, moon, and planets along the ecliptic. This simple hypothesis enables a considerable body of data to be accounted for at least in qualitative terms: but even Plato draws back from a detailed description of the individual planets, mainly contenting himself with references of a general kind to their varying speeds and to the firm assertion in the *Laws* (822a) that, contrary to what their Greek name (wanderers) suggests, the movements of the planets are regular and indeed simple.

The first reasonably detailed and coherent solution to the main problems posed by the apparent irregularities of the movements of the planets was the work of Plato's younger contemporary Eudoxus of Cnidos (whose mathematics has been mentioned

above): and some have assumed that it is Plato's knowledge of Eudoxus' system by the time he came to compose the *Laws* that accounts for the firmness of the statement just mentioned. In this system each planet is imagined as located on the innermost of a series of concentric spheres. The combined motion of these spheres produces the resultant complex apparent motion of the planets, including the phenomena known as their stations and retrogradations. A similar but simpler model is proposed also for the sun and moon, where there are no stations and retrogradations to explain. Eudoxus is said to have proposed four spheres for each of the planets, but needed only three each for the sun and moon.

Our two main sources for Eudoxus' system are a passage in Aristotle's *Metaphysics* and the commentary on this by Simplicius. These tell us the number of spheres Eudoxus used for each heavenly body and give certain information about their speeds (the periods within which they rotate) and their angles of inclination to one another. It is the inclinations of the two innermost spheres that produce the geometrical figure known as the hippopede—roughly a figure of eight—and that yield the stations and retrogradations of the planets. There are, however, gaps in these reports at certain points that prevent definitive answers to two key questions.

First, it is not clear just how far Eudoxus had worked out a fully quantitative and exact solution for each of the planets, sun, and moon. Although the two main periods for each are recorded, we lack definite information on his estimate of the maximum length of the retrograde arc of each planet. Our sources do not report the angle of inclination of the fourth sphere to the third, and although modern reconstructions usually take the true modern determinations of the retrograde arcs as their starting point, to suppose that Eudoxus had accurate information on this point is wildly unlikely and methodologically quite unsound. Moreover, even taking the most optimistic figures possible the system breaks down for two of the planets, Mars and Venus, where the evidence given by Simplicius fails to provide for retrogradation at all. That Eudoxus gave some definite parameters is clear. But the shortcomings of the theory suggest that it may well not have been fully determined, and that once Eudoxus had solved the problem of the main motions of the planets, sun, and moon qualitatively, and given some interpretations in quantitative terms, that was as far as he proceeded.

The second point at which the information is inadequate concerns the nature of the spheres themselves. So far as the reports in Aristotle and Simplicius go, nothing is said about the physical substance and character of these. The modification that Aristotle himself introduced, when he postulated further retroactive spheres whose function it was to counteract the movements of the higher spheres, makes it clear that he interpreted his version of the system in physical and dynamic terms: the spheres consist of the fifth element, ether (*aither*), which has the property of naturally moving in a circle, and movement is clearly transmitted from one sphere to the next. It has often been assumed that in contrast to Aristotle's dynamical and physical view, Eudoxus' original theory was purely kinematic and mathematical, dealing with the motions of the heavenly bodies independently of any consideration of the forces that cause their movement. That assumption may be correct, but it must be stressed that it goes beyond the evidence we have. It is perfectly true that the reports deal purely with the mathematics, that is, the geometry of the problems. So far as our evidence goes, Eudoxus *may* have ignored all physical questions. Equally clear, however, is that the absence of any discussion of those questions in

the sources may simply reflect the particular interests of those who compiled them. It has been argued, for example, that if Eudoxus were concerned purely to give a geometrical account, he could have done so far more simply than he actually does, and that each of the four spheres in each case is thought to have a physical interpretation. That remains a controversial view, but it is only prudent to repeat that the question of what assumptions, if any, Eudoxus made about the physics of the heavenly spheres remains an entirely open one.

This takes us to what is one of the thorniest general questions in the understanding of Greek astronomical model building, namely, the interpretation of the aim often encapsulated in the slogan "to save the phenomena." It is agreed on all sides that the chief effort of Greek theoretical astronomy was to reduce the apparent complexity of heavenly movements to simple, by which is understood circular, motions. A passage in Simplicius suggests that such a program was already recommended by Plato to contemporary astronomers. As our discussion of Eudoxus has already indicated, however, the question of whether Greek astronomical theories were purely mathematical is a separate issue. In many cases the available evidence does not allow us to resolve the problem, although there are certainly texts where astronomical questions are discussed—at least for the time—in purely geometrical terms. Autolycus' work *On the Moving Sphere*, in the fourth century B.C., is the first extant example of such a treatise, and another is Aristarchus' sole surviving work, *On the Sizes and Distances of the Sun and Moon* (written sometime in the early third century).

In that work Aristarchus analyzes the geometry of the problems of determining the distances of the sun and moon, and of estimating their sizes. For the sake of his analysis he adopts a series of postulates that includes some that are quite arbitrary (as when he takes it that the moon subtends an angle of 87 degrees to the sun when it appears to be halved, a precise figure he could not have obtained by observation) and others that he must have known to be well wide of the mark (as in the notorious case of the figure of 2 degrees assumed for the angular diameter of the moon, when the usual Greek approximation was one-half degree, a figure that is indeed attested for Aristarchus by Archimedes). But for the sake of the analysis of the geometry of the problems, it does not matter that the assumptions include some that are moderately and others extravagantly inaccurate. The value of the geometrical study remains, since its aim is to identify how one can get to determinate solutions to the problems from given assumptions. No actual solutions, in absolute figures, are presented by Aristarchus himself in the work, but the fact that the ones implied by his figures are well off target does not detract from the value of the geometrical discussion.

In such a case, then, we find a concentration on the mathematics of the problem and at least a temporary indifference not merely to the physics of the heavenly spheres but also to some of the known empirical data, astronomical parameters obtained or obtainable from observation. On the other hand, elsewhere we find an equally obvious interest not merely in providing definite solutions to astronomical parameters but also in giving an account of the substance, nature, and motive forces of the celestial bodies.

The question of whether to take the earth or the sun as the center of the system will enable us to illustrate both the variety of possible positions on the matter of the relevance of physical issues and the strongly realist assumptions at work in at least some parts of Greek astronomy. It appears from a report in Archimedes (*Sand-reckoner* 1.4 ff.) that Aristarchus suggested as a hypothesis that the phenomena could be explained on the assumption that the sun is at rest in the cen-

ter of the system and that the earth moves around the sun like the other planets. (Although Archimedes does not specify that Aristarchus also assumed the daily rotation of the earth around its axis, that was clearly part of the set of hypotheses he adopted.) Plutarch in turn reports (*Platonic Questions* 8.1.1006c) that Aristarchus only suggested this as a hypothesis, that is, merely for the sake of argument, and he contrasts Aristarchus' position in this respect with that of the only other ancient astronomer whom we know definitely to have adopted heliocentricity, namely Seleucus of Seleucia (who lived around the mid second century B.C.). That certainly confirms that for at least one ancient astronomer heliocentricity was no mere hypothesis; but whether Plutarch was right about Aristarchus' position is disputed.

It is, however, beyond doubt that heliocentricity was rejected by others in part for straightforward physical reasons. The chief evidence for the considerations that weighed with the astronomers comes from Ptolemy, who discusses the question of whether any movement can be attributed to the earth in the first book of his astronomical treatise, the *Syntaxis* (also known from its Arabic name as the *Almagest*). This discussion makes it absolutely clear that Ptolemy, at least, rejected any such notion partly on astronomical grounds, but partly, indeed largely, also on physical ones. If the earth rotated, for instance, we would expect visible effects on the objects around us. Clouds and missiles in the air would never move eastward, for example, for the movement of the earth would always anticipate them. There is no question here, then, of allowing a hypothesis that might have nothing to be said against it mathematically when it conflicts with basic physical assumptions.

It is true that in the almost totally unanimous rejection of heliocentricity in antiquity, other factors weighed besides physical arguments (which included not just the absence of visible effects on the earth's surface but also an appeal to the "commonsense" Aristotelian doctrine that all heavy objects must be subject to the same laws and move in the same direction, namely, to the center of the earth). Thus we know that outside the circles of specialist astronomers some were scandalized by the suggestion that the earth moves. In the early third century B.C. the Stoic philosopher Cleanthes is said to have "thought that the Greeks ought to indict Aristarchus of Samos on a charge of impiety for putting in motion the Hearth of the Universe, that is, the earth" (Plutarch, *On the Face of the Moon* 923a). We must, however, be cautious.

First, there is no evidence that any Greeks actually took Cleanthes' advice and attempted to prosecute Aristarchus. Second, we must recall that the situation in the ancient world was appreciably different from that of the seventeenth century, when geocentricity was represented as being implied by passages in the Bible and was the orthodox teaching of the church. In pagan antiquity there was no such established religion as Christianity became, and no institutions such as the church with legal sanctions that could be applied to discipline deviants. Third, we should not assume that such quasi-religious considerations as might be deemed to be relevant to this issue all told for the common belief that the earth is at the center. In *On the Heavens* (293a30 ff.) Aristotle suggests that among the reasons that some fifth-century Pythagoreans held that the earth is not at the center was that it was not considered noble enough for that place, the most important in the universe, which must, rather, be held by fire. Clearly symbolic factors could tell against as well as for geocentricity.

Finally, from the immediate point of view we are concerned with here it may be noted that there would have been no need for Cleanthes or anyone else to be scandalized by Aristarchus' view if it had been merely hypothetical. This evidence tells, then, if anything, in favor of the idea that that view was not just a mathematical hypothesis but intended as the physical truth.

Among the chief astronomical considerations that told against heliocentricity two are most important. First, there was the absence of visible stellar parallax, that is, differences in the configurations of the constellations observed at different points on the earth's orbit around the sun (stellar parallax was only confirmed by the work of Bessel and others around 1835). But here a possible counter may well have occurred already to Aristarchus. Archimedes reports that he assumed that the sphere of the fixed stars may be treated as infinitely far away (that the orbit of the earth around the sun is as a point in relation to the sphere of the fixed stars). Archimedes comments that all that Aristarchus needed is that the sphere of the fixed stars should be indefinitely far away; but in either case one would expect no visible stellar parallax. It would seem that Aristarchus realized that this had to be included in the assumptions to block an otherwise damaging apparent objection, and the fact that the assumption could not be confirmed did not, of course, mean that it was not true.

Second, what may well have counted with some Greek astronomers is the success of the preferred astronomical model that superseded Eudoxus' system of concentric spheres. This was the epicycle-eccentric theory proposed first by Apollonius at the end of the third century and then used by both major theoretical astronomers after him, first by Hipparchus in the mid second century B.C., and then by Ptolemy in the second century A.D. The key point is that some such model was necessary in two cases where the issue between heliocentricity and geocentricity was not relevant. For both the sun and the moon a simple circular orbit did not account for the observed irregularities—for example, the inequality of the four seasons as measured by the equinoctial and solstitial points. If in such simpler cases, either epicycles or eccentrics, or in the case of the moon a combination of both, proved necessary, and to a very large extent adequate, then the application of a similar model also to the planets must have seemed reasonable enough. We do not in fact know how far Aristarchus himself had worked out detailed planetary models on the basis of the heliocentric assumption (his work antedates the development of the epicycle-eccentric theory) and the extent to which he or others realized the simplifications that could be made on that basis cannot, therefore, be confirmed in detail.

From Hipparchus onward, if not already from Apollonius, the chief effort of Greek theoretical astronomy was to develop the epicycle-eccentric theory to account for the main data concerning the movements of the sun, moon, and planets. The data themselves were now increasingly accurate and, as already noted, both Hipparchus and Ptolemy were able to draw on some relevant observations made much earlier by the Babylonians. In the eccentric theory, the heavenly body is imagined as moving on a circle whose center does not coincide with the earth. Such a model could be used, for instance, to account for a problem that had proved difficult for the earlier Eudoxan model of concentric spheres, namely, the inequality of the seasons: the sun moves at uniform speed on its circle, and the unequal lengths of arc it traverses from one equinoctial or solstitial point to the next merely reflect the fact that the earth is not at the center of that circle.

A similar result could also be obtained by the epicycle hypothesis, according to which the earth is at the center, but the heavenly body—in this case the sun—is imagined as moving on a circle whose center itself moves around the circumference of the circle (the deferent) that has the earth as center. For both the sun and moon, Hipparchus' results already reached what was, for the time, an impressive degree of accuracy. How far he had also arrived at detailed solutions for the models of the planets is not clear. Ptolemy says that he contented himself with trying to improve and organize the observational data available for the study of the planets. If that is so, Ptolemy's own solutions to planetary motion represent important original theoretical work (as also, certainly, does his modification of Hipparchus' lunar theory to account for what is called the second anomaly). For the planets and the moon Ptolemy has to combine both epicycles and eccentrics, and sometimes (for the moon and Mercury) has the center of the deferent itself move around a circle revolving around the center of the system. He also introduced the notion of the equant, or center of uniform motion, in each of these models. The epicycle's center is carried around on an eccentric circle, but its motion is uniform neither with respect to the center of the eccentric nor with respect to the earth, but with respect to a point on a line joining these two centers and produced. He undertakes to determine the position of this equant point in each case and it turns out to be, for most of the planets, at a location such that the center of the ecliptic is midway between equant and earth.

The notion of the equant was to be bitterly attacked by Copernicus, who argued that it breached the cardinal principle on which theoretical astronomy was based, namely, that of uniform circular motion. Yet the use of eccentric circles, or even of epicycles, might already be thought to deviate from that principle if taken in its purest form. Certainly in its original Platonic, Academic, or Eudoxan guise the program was limited to finding concentric circles whose center is the earth. The notion of the equant, like the introduction of a further circle around which the center of the deferent revolves in the case of the moon and Mercury, might have been represented by Ptolemy as developments of the model in line with the way in which it already dealt with other irregularities. And Ptolemy would no doubt have justified its use primarily on the grounds that it gave more accurate results.

The epicycle-eccentric theory is, in fact, a marvelously flexible model—and, despite frequent criticisms to the contrary, an extraordinarily simple one, in relation to the complexity of the data that it can be adapted to explain. Moreover, although the whole system in both Hipparchus and Ptolemy is geocentric, the movements of the planets contain one element that directly and explicitly depends on the position of the sun. Finally, we should repeat that Ptolemy's ambition was not merely to provide a geometrical model from which the positions of the heavenly bodies could be determined and predicted. We have already noted that in the rejection of the ascription of any movement to the earth, the whole system of the *Syntaxis* is firmly based on certain physical assumptions. Moreover, in a later treatise, the *Planetary Hypotheses*, he attempts a fully fledged physical account. Here he tackles not just the kinematics of heavenly motion (how the heavenly bodies move) but their dynamics (why they move, their motive forces). Each of the heavenly bodies is imagined as moving on a strip of a sphere (this is now the physical counterpart of the epicycles, eccentrics, and deferents of the *Syntaxis*) and the source of its motion is its own vital force— the heavenly bodies move because they are alive.

The intriguing details of Greek astronomical theory cannot be pursued further here. But it is important to note that Greek astronomers excelled not just as theorists. Hipparchus in particular was an outstanding observational astronomer. He was responsible for the first comprehensive star catalog (it has been estimated to have contained some 850 stars), the basis for Ptolemy's own work in this area: the catalog in *Syntaxis* 7 and 8 gives the celestial coordinates of about 1,020 stars with an average error of less than one degree in longitude and of half that in latitude.

A comparison of his own observations with those of some earlier positions caused Hipparchus to remark the displacement of the equinoctial point in relation to the bright star Spica. He was thus led to the brilliant discovery of the phenomenon known as the precession of the equinoxes. The positions of the equinoctial points (where the ecliptic intersects the celestial equator) do not remain constant in relation to the fixed stars, but are displaced from east to west at a rate of about 50 seconds of arc a year. (The phenomenon is now explained as largely due to the fact that the earth is not a perfect sphere, but bulges slightly at the equator: the attraction of the sun and moon tend to pull the equatorial bulge into the plane of the ecliptic. The earth's axis is thus caused to oscillate slightly and it turns very slowly about an axis perpendicular to the earth's orbit, completing a single revolution in a period of about 26,000 years.) Furthermore, Hipparchus fixed as a lower limit to precession a movement of one degree in one hundred years. Unfortunately Ptolemy was to adopt this not as a lower limit but as the correct figure (partly perhaps because of its convenience), and this was in time to generate a considerable mismatch between his theory and the observational data. Yet later Greek commentators found it hard enough to accept the notion of precession at all, and usually flatly denied what Hipparchus had discovered.

This last example illustrates, no doubt, a point about the decline of Greek science after the second century A.D. But it also suggests the gap that had opened up between advanced theoretical work and what the reasonably well educated, even learned, layman understood. There were certain aspects of astronomy that impinged on everyone's life. One of the chief motives for early Greek astronomical observation was the attempt to regulate the calendar. As early as Hesiod astronomical data were one way of organizing seasonal work in agriculture. Yet otherwise the main context in which an interest in the heavenly bodies was developed, outside and within the circles of specialist astronomers, was the assumption that these bodies influence events on earth. Astrology took many forms, and in some, such as the casting of horoscopes (which begins to be frequent in the sources only in the Hellenistic period), not only fairly precise observations were necessary but also a fair amount of mathematical theory. Both Hipparchus and Ptolemy, like many Renaissance astronomers, also practiced as astrologers, and Ptolemy composed a four-book treatise on the subject, the *Tetrabiblos,* expressing a tolerably cautious view of the limitations of the subject. The more important point is, however, that astrology probably helped to keep at least a part of astronomical theory alive, for the same basic framework of theory underpinned both studies. Yet beyond that basic framework the kind of advanced work represented in the *Syntaxis* was always the preoccupation of a tiny minority.

Astrology is one point at which the work of those who were primarily scientists (in our terms) overlaps with that of the philosophers. The concomitant of the Stoic belief in determinism was one in the possibility of predicting the future. We may conclude our brief survey by noting some other contexts in which a similar overlap occurs. We are, as usual, in the dark about the primary motivations of many of those responsible for the major achievements of Greek science. But in late antiquity, especially, some articulate individuals lay great stress on the contribution that the study of nature can make both to happiness and to morality. Ptolemy himself

takes up a theme that goes back to Plato when he underlines how the study of astronomy improves men's characters—the study of celestial order encourages us to be more orderly in our everyday lives. The medical writer and biologist Galen, too, emphasizes how the study of living creatures, their anatomy and their physiology, can contribute to an appreciation of the beauty and goodness of nature. Just as Aristotle had justified the study of zoology on similar grounds, so Galen thinks of his biological investigations as supporting a teleological viewpoint that has important moral implications. The principle that "nature does nothing in vain" is the leitmotif of Galen's treatise *On the Use of Parts,* which is indeed explicitly devoted to establishing that thesis through a comprehensive study of comparative anatomy. Galen describes his work as a "sacred book which I compose as a true hymn to him who created us; for I believe that true piety consists not in sacrificing many hecatombs of oxen to him or burning cassia and every kind of unguent, but in discovering first myself, and then showing to the rest of mankind, his wisdom, his power, and his goodness."

But if teleology is thus one of the main links between the work of some "scientists" and that of some "philosophers," there is an important difference between the nature and aims of the investigations carried out by such as Ptolemy and Galen on the one hand and by the Stoics (let alone the antiteleological Epicureans) on the other. The philosophers, we said, studied nature to secure peace of mind; once anxiety was removed, further research was superfluous. Galen and Ptolemy agree in seeing the study of nature as anything but a morally neutral activity, but for them continued research is of the essence. At no point can the scientist simply relax. In his *On Habits* (1) Galen quotes with approval a statement of the biologist Erasistratus on the difficulties of research and the persistence and determination needed to pursue it—a fitting final testimony, perhaps, to the energy that Greek scientists brought to the study of nature:

Those who are completely unused to inquiry are in the first exercise of their mind, blinded and dazed and straightway leave off from mental fatigue and an incapacity that is no less than that of those who enter races without being used to them. But the man who is used to inquiry tries every possible loophole as he conducts his search and turns in every direction, and so far from giving up the inquiry in the space of a day, does not cease his search throughout his life. Directing his attention to one idea after another that is germane to what is being investigated, he presses on until he arrives at his goal.

BIBLIOGRAPHY

SOURCES

The extant fragments of the teaching of the pre-Socratic philosophers and the Sophists are collected in Hermann Diels and Walther Kranz, eds., *Die Fragmente der Vorsokratiker*, 3 vols. (1903; 9th ed. 1959–1960). An English translation of the main fragments appears in Kathleen Freeman, *Ancilla to the Presocratic Philosophers* (1948; 2d ed. 1949).

The standard edition of the works of Plato is that of John Burnet, 5 vols. (1900–1913) and many excellent English translations and commentaries exist, for example those in the Loeb Classical Library series and the translations and commentaries in the Oxford Clarendon series.

Aristotle is standardly cited according to the Berlin Academy edition, Immanuel Bekker, ed., 5 vols. (1831–1870) but many treatises have also been edited in the Oxford Classical Texts series and translated in *The Works of Aristotle Translated into English,* William David Ross, ed., 12 vols. (1908–1952), in the Loeb Classical Library series, and in the Oxford Clarendon series.

The editions and commentaries by William David Ross of the *Physics* (1936; 2d ed. 1955), the *Metaphysics,* 2 vols. (1924), the *De Anima* (1961),

and the *Parva Naturalia* (1955) are especially important.

The most important editions and translations of the extant remains of the main Hellenistic philosophical schools are as follows: Hermann K. Usener, ed., *Epicurea* (1887); Cyril Bailey, *Epicurus: The Extant Remains* (1926); Graziano Arrighetti, *Epicuro: Opere* (1960; 2d ed. 1973); Lucretius, *De Rerum Natura,* Cyril Bailey ed., 3 vols. (1947); Hans Friedrich August von Arnim, *Stoicorum Veterum Fragmenta,* 4 vols. (1903–1924); Fernanda Decleva Caizzi, *Pirrone: Testimonianze* (1981); Sextus Empiricus, *Opera,* Hermann Mutschmann and J. Mau, eds., 4 vols. (1912–1962; vol. 4, K. Janáček, ed.); Robert G. Bury, ed. and trans., 4 vols. (1933–1949). An important general source for Hellenistic philosophy is Diogenes Laertius, *Vitae Philosophorum,* Herbert S. Long, ed. (1964); R. D. Hicks, ed. and trans., 2 vols. (1925).

For pre-Hellenistic Greek science, the most important sources, in addition to the works of the philosophers mentioned above, are the following: Émile Littré, ed., *Oeuvres complètes d'Hippocrate,* 10 vols. (1839–1961), which can be supplemented with the Hippocratic treatises edited by Johan Ludvig Heiberg, *Corpus Medicorum Graecorum,* I, 1 (1927) and by other editions of individual treatises, notably André J. Festugière, *L'Ancienne médecine* (1948) and Iain M. Lonie, *The Hippocratic Treatises "On Generation" "On the Nature of the Child" "Diseases IV"* (1981). For pre-Euclidean mathematics no complete collection exists, but some of the extant material is collected and translated in Ivor Thomas, ed., *Greek Mathematical Works,* 2 vols. (1939–1941).

The major works of Greek mathematics and astronomy have been edited and translated as follows: Euclid, *Opera Omnia,* Johan Ludvig Heiberg and Heinrich Menge, eds., 9 vols. (1883–1916; the first five volumes appear in a second edition, Evangelos S. Stamatis, ed., 6 vols.; 1969–1977); Thomas L. Heath, *The Thirteen Books of Euclid's Elements,* 3 vols. (1908; 2d ed. 1926), and *Aristarchus of Samos* (1913); Johan L. Heiberg, ed., *Archimedis Opera Omnia,* 3 vols. (1910–1915); Thomas L. Heath, *The Works of Archimedes* (1897; with supplement 1912); Apollonius Pergaeus, Johan Ludvig Heiberg, ed., 2 vols. (1891–1893);

Thomas L. Heath, *Apollonius Pergaeus' Treatise On Conic Sections* (1896); Hipparchus, *In Arati et Eudoxi Phaenomena,* Carolus Manitius, ed. (1894); Ptolemy, *Opera,* Johan Ludvig Heiberg, ed., 3 vols. (1898–1952); G. J. Toomer, *Ptolemy's Almagest* (1984). In addition, Thomas L. Heath, *Greek Astronomy* (1932) contains selections of Greek astronomical writings in translation.

Among later Greek medical writings of importance should be noted the medical encyclopedia of Celsus, Friedrich Marx, ed. (1915); Walter G. Spencer, trans., 3 vols. (1935–1938); the gynecological treatise of Soranus, Ioannes Ilberg, ed. (1927); O. Temkin, trans. (1956); and especially the works of Galen. The most complete edition of these is that of Carl G. Kühn, 20 vols. in 22 (1821–1833), but among recent important editions and translations are Vivian Nutton, *Galen On Prognosis* (*Corpus Medicorum Graecorum,* V 8 1, (1979) and Phillip de Lacy, *Galen On the Doctrines of Hippocrates and Plato,* 2 vols. (*Corpus Medicorum Graecorum,* V 4,1,2; 1978–1980). Finally, Morris R. Cohen and Israel E. Drabkin, *A Source Book in Greek Science* (1948; 2d ed. 1958) contains English translations of a wide range of passages of Greek scientific works dealing with the exact and life sciences and with technology.

STUDIES

The most reliable general study of the history of Greek philosophy down to Aristotle is the six-volume work of William Keith Chambers Guthrie, *A History of Greek Philosophy* (1962–1981). On the pre-Socratic philosophers consult also Edward Hussey, *The Presocratics* (1972); Jonathan Barnes, *The Presocratic Philosophers,* 2 vols. (1979); Geoffrey S. Kirk, John E. Raven, and Malcolm Schofield, *The Presocratic Philosophers* (1957; 2d ed. 1983); and for the evidence for early Pythagoreanism in particular, Walter Burkert, *Lore and Science in Ancient Pythagoreanism* (1972). In addition there are important articles in David J. Furley and Reginald E. Allen, eds., *Studies in Presocratic Philosophy,* 2 vols. (1970–1975); Alexander P. D. Mourelatos, ed., *The Presocratics* (1974); and (not confined to the pre-Socratic period) John P. Anton and George L. Kustas, eds., *Essays in Ancient Greek Philosophy* (1971). For the

Sophists consult G. B. Kerferd, *The Sophistic Movement* (1981); Carl L. Classen, *Die Sophistik* (1976).

On Plato consult William D. Ross, *Plato's Theory of Ideas* (1951); Richard Robinson, *Plato's Earlier Dialectic* (1941; 2d ed. 1953); I. M. Crombie, *An Examination of Plato's Doctrines,* 2 vols. (1962–1963); Gregory Vlastos, *Platonic Studies* (1973; 2d ed. 1981), and *Plato's Universe* (1975); the collections of articles in Reginald E. Allen, ed., *Studies in Plato's Metaphysics* (1965); Renford Bambrough, ed., *New Essays on Plato and Aristotle* (1965); Gregory Vlastos, ed., *Plato,* 2 vols. (1971).

On Aristotle consult Werner Jaeger, *Aristotle: Fundamentals of the History of His Development* (a translation by Richard Robinson of the 2d ed. of *Aristoteles: Grundlegung einer Geschichte seiner Entwicklung,* 1934; 2d ed. 1948); William D. Ross, *Aristotle* (1923; 5th ed. 1956); Friedrich Solmsen, *Aristotle's System of the Physical World* (1960); Geoffrey Ernst Richard Lloyd, *Aristotle: The Growth and Structure of His Thought* (1968); Donald J. Allan, *The Philosophy of Aristotle* (1952; 2d ed. 1970); J. L. Ackrill, *Aristotle the Philosopher* (1981). Many of the most important articles are collected in Jonathan Barnes, Malcolm Schofield, and Richard Sorabji, eds., *Articles on Aristotle,* 4 vols. (1975–1979), and there is a recent bibliography: Jonathan Barnes, ed., *Aristotle: A Selective Bibliography* (1977).

For Hellenistic philosophy in general consult A. A. Long, *Hellenistic Philosophy* (1974), and for late ancient and early medieval philosophy, Arthur H. Armstrong, *The Cambridge History of Later Greek and Early Medieval Philosophy* (1967). There are important articles on Hellenistic philosophy and science in two recent collections: Malcolm Schofield, Myles Burnyeat, and Jonathan Barnes, eds., *Doubt and Dogmatism* (1980), and Jonathan Barnes, J. Brunschwig, Myles Burnyeat, and Malcolm Schofield, eds., *Science and Speculation* (1982). On particular schools, consult also David J. Furley, *Two Studies in the Greek Atomists* (1967); Samuel Sambursky, *Physics of the Stoics* (1959); A. A. Long, ed., *Problems in Stoicism* (1971); Francis Sandbach, *The Stoics* (1975); John Rist, ed., *The Stoics* (1978); J. Brunschwig, ed., *Les Stoiciens et leur logique* (1978); Mario dal Pra, *Lo scetticismo greco* (1950; 2d ed. 1975); Gabriele Giannantoni, ed., *Lo scetticismo antico* (1981); Myles Burnyeat, ed., *The Skeptical Tradition* (1983).

On Greek science in general consult Bartel L. van der Waerden, *Science Awakening,* Arnold Dresden, trans., 2 vols. (1954; 4th ed. 1974); Otto Neugebauer, *The Exact Sciences in Antiquity* (1951; 2d ed. 1957); Samuel Sambursky, *The Physical World of the Greeks,* Merton Dagut, trans. (1956); Benjamin Farrington, *Greek Science* (1940–1944; 2d ed. 1961); Geoffrey Ernst Richard Lloyd, *Early Greek Science: Thales to Aristotle* (1970), *Greek Science after Aristotle* (1973), and *Magic, Reason and Experience* (1979).

On early Greek mathematics the classic work remains Thomas L. Heath, *A History of Greek Mathematics,* 2 vols. (1921). On the background to Euclid consult Wilbur R. Knorr, *The Evolution of the Euclidean Elements* (1975); Ian Mueller, *Philosophy of Mathematics and Deductive Structure in Euclid's Elements* (1981); Arpad Szabo, *The Beginnings of Greek Mathematics,* A. M. Ungar, trans. (1978). Apart from Heath's editions of Greek mathematical texts, cited above, there is an extended commentary on Archimedes in Eduard J. Dijksterhuis, *Archimedes* (1956).

On Greek astronomy the most important general study is that of Otto Neugebauer, *A History of Ancient Mathematical Astronomy,* 3 vols. (1975). Among other useful discussions are: Thomas L. Heath, *Aristarchus of Samos* (1913); D. R. Dicks, *Early Greek Astronomy to Aristotle* (1970); Olaf Pedersen and Mogens Pihl, *Early Physics and Astronomy* (1974); Olaf Pedersen, *A Survey of the Almagest* (1974).

On the exact sciences the following is a brief selection of important work: D. R. Dicks, *The Geographical Fragments of Hipparchus* (1960); Albert Lejeune, *L'Optique de Claude Ptolémée* (1956); G. J. Toomer, *Diocles on Burning Mirrors* (1976); Ingemar Düring, *Ptolemaeus Harmonica* (1930), and *Porphyrios Kommentar zur Harmonielehre des Ptolemaios* (1932).

On the life sciences the following works will provide an introduction: William A. Heidel, *Hippocratic Medicine: Its Spirit and Method* (1941); Louis Bourgey, *Observation et expérience chez les médecins de la Collection Hippocratique* (1953); Ludwig Edelstein, *Ancient Medicine,* Owsei and C. Lilian Temkin, eds. (1967); Owsei Temkin, *Galenism: Rise and Decline of a Medical Philosophy* (1973); Wesley Smith, *The Hippocratic Tradition* (1979); Vivian Nutton, ed., *Galen: Problems and Prospects* (1981).

Roman Philosophical Movements

ELIZABETH ASMIS

THE ROMANS LEARNED PHILOSOPHY from the Greeks. From the second century B.C. Greek philosophers increasingly visited Rome. Many Romans received them with enthusiasm, although others were mistrustful and hostile. When the three most prominent Greek philosophers, Diogenes (head of the Stoic school), Critolaus (head of the Peripatetic school), and Carneades (head of the Academy), came to Rome on an embassy in 155 B.C., they lectured widely with great success, but were denounced by Cato the Elder. By the latter part of the century, Greek philosophy was well established among the ruling Romans. The Stoic Panaetius was a friend of Scipio Aemilianus. This friendship marks the beginning of more than three centuries of Stoic influence on Roman thought.

In the first century B.C. it became common for Romans to visit Greece to study philosophy. The Romans now undertook to translate Greek philosophy into Latin and to create their own philosophical literature. The two founders of Roman philosophy were Titus Lucretius Carus (*ca.* 98–55 B.C.) and Marcus Tullius Cicero (106–43 B.C.).

LUCRETIUS

Lucretius was an Epicurean and a poet who made it his mission to impart the teachings of Epicurus (341–270 B.C.) to the Romans. With evangelical zeal, he composed a poem, *On the Nature of Things,* to explain Epicurus' atomist physics. We know nothing about his life except the little that can be gathered from his poem. There is an untrustworthy rumor, reported by the Christian Jerome in the fourth century, that he became mad after drinking a love potion and eventually committed suicide. Cicero admired Lucretius' poetry. He wrote in a letter to his brother (2.11.5) in 54 B.C. that "Lucretius' poetic compositions have, as you write, many flashes of genius, but also much skill."

Lucretius' poem was the first, and indeed only, attempt to present Epicurean physics in Latin verse. Lucretius' aim was to sweeten the bitter medicine of Epicurus' scientific doctrine by giving it poetic form. Through scientific knowledge, Lucretius hoped to free the Romans from the two great fears that marred human existence, fear of the gods and fear of death. The entire poem is devoted to an exposition of physical doctrine; but Lucretius draws from the physics a message that is ethical.

Lucretius conceived his poem on an epic scale. The enemy is traditional religion, as exemplified by the sacrificial slaughter of the innocent Iphigenia by her father, Agamemnon; and the hero is Epicurus, who is portrayed as passing beyond the fiery walls of the world to slay the monster of superstition that raised its horrible head in the sky. Throughout the poem, Lucretius proclaims a new religion. The gods, he teaches, have nothing to do with anything that goes on in this world. Rather, they live beyond the edges of the world, in the interspaces that separate the infinite number of worlds, enjoying a life of utter bliss and total disregard for human beings. In the prologue to the third book, Lucretius sketches a new Olympus. Addressing Epicurus as the "father" whose divine truths dispel the terrors of the mind, he has a vision of the walls of the world parting: the gods appear to him in a blaze of light, enjoying undisturbed happiness; and there is no Hades. True piety consists in worshiping the remote gods as models of happiness.

All responsibility for human happiness thus belongs to humans alone. Freed of the shackles of traditional religion, they can live a life that approaches that of the gods in happiness. There is nothing more pleasant, Lucretius asserts in the prologue to his second book, than to look down from the "serene temples" of scientific knowledge upon the vain struggles of others. Fortified by truth, humans can be happy because they know that happiness consists of the absence of pain, and that this goal requires very little. The happy person does not pursue power or wealth or sensual gratification and knows how to be content with little. As an ideal picture of human bliss, Lucretius pictures a person stretching out among friends along the grassy bank of a river in summer under the shade of a tall tree.

Lucretius' poem consists of six books. The first two books set out the fundamentals of Epicurus' atomic theory; the third and fourth deal with the soul; the fifth explains the growth and decline of worlds and of human society; and the sixth explains various natural happenings, including thunder and lightning. The poem ends with a vivid description of the horrors of the plague at Athens. This picture balances the portrayal of joyful procreation at the beginning of the poem. This contrast between birth and death, or optimism and despair, may be seen as a theme that extends throughout the poem.

In the prologue to the first book, which serves as a prologue to the entire poem, Lucretius appeals to Venus (Aphrodite), as ancestress of the Romans, goddess of pleasure, and sole ruler of nature, to help him compose his poem. This invocation is surprising, since, as an Epicurean, Lucretius believes that the gods have nothing to do with this world. The appeal can be explained, however, if one understands Venus as a personification of the forces of nature. Lucretius begins his poem by viewing nature as a divine force, then goes on to explain that this divine power is nothing but atoms moving about in empty space. Lucretius presents Epicurus' philosophy not only poetically, but also by applying the rhetorical precepts that were so much a part of Roman culture. The prologues to his books are rhetorical prefaces that aim to involve the listener and remove prejudice. In the first prologue, Lucretius aims to show that, contrary to common belief, Epicurean philosophy is not impious. He appeals, therefore, to a traditional divinity, Venus, with the intention of revealing later what this divinity really is.

In his first prologue, Lucretius also mentions the difficulty of translating Greek terminology into Latin. He notes that his subject matter is new and that Latin has few words for it. As it turns out, Lucretius succeeds admirably in turning Greek philosophical vocabulary into Latin. Cicero and Seneca the Younger later made numerous additions to this fund of philosophical language, demonstrating that Latin can be a suitable vehicle for philosophical expression.

Lucretius claims that he follows in Epicurus' footsteps and that, just as a bee culls nectar from flowers, he culls Epicurus' own teachings. There has been much debate about how closely Lucretius follows Epicurus. It is impossible to answer this question with precision, because a very large part of Epicurus' writings is no longer extant. However, Epicurus' extant summary of his physical doctrines, the *Letter to Herodotus,* provides a check against Lucretius' presentation, especially for the first two books of the poem. A comparison shows that Lucretius refashions Epicurus' arrangement and construction of arguments in conformity with rhetorical theory. In contrast with Epicurus' impersonal summary of doctrines, Lucretius always keeps in mind the student, as he attempts (to use his own metaphor) to disperse the darkness and terror of ignorance with the light of scientific truth. Lucretius attempts to persuade the student by reprobation, sympathy, encouragement, clarity and detail of proof, vivid imagery, frequent anticipations of what is to come and reminders of what has been established, and vigorous refutations of rival views.

In his first book, Lucretius attempts to prove that: (1) nothing comes to be from nothing, and nothing is destroyed into nothing; (2) there is void in addition to bodies; (3) there are ultimate, indivisible bodies (that is, atoms); and (4) the universe is infinite. The argument continues in the second book with proofs that: (5) the atoms move continuously through void, either in a straight downward direction randomly interrupted by swerves, or sideways as a result of blows; (6) the atoms have different shapes; (7) the atoms have no properties except shape, size, and weight; and (8) the number of worlds is infinite. Each book thus consists of several main topics, which are closely connected with one another.

This arrangement is rhetorically effective. It is clear and easy to follow, but not always strictly logically correct. As a result, Lucretius has been accused of disregarding logical sequence and, in general, of masking the weakness of his arguments with the splendor of his poetic imagination. This is an unfair charge. Lucretius is well aware of the demands of logic. But he sometimes rejects logical sequence in favor of a clearer, more persuasive arrangement. Contrary to the rules of logic, he sometimes takes as a premise a proposition that is yet to be proved. In these cases, however, either the particular argument could be omitted or the arrangement could be altered without any detriment to the overall conclusion. Lucretius anticipates what is yet to be proved, confident that his doctrines hang together as a coherent system of which any part supports any other.

Like Epicurus, Lucretius considers that scientific knowledge is knowledge of what cannot be observed, and that it consists of inferences from what is observed. In contrast with other philosophers, therefore, Epicurus and Lucretius view the two basic propositions that nothing comes to be from nonbeing and that nothing is destroyed into nonbeing as deductions from the phenomena, not as self-evident truths.

Lucretius proves the first proposition, that nothing comes to be from nothing, by arguing that otherwise any kind of thing would be observed to come from any other kind of thing, at any time, and in any place. The new student, who may be encountering philosophical argument for the first time, might well be deterred by such an argument.

But Lucretius enlivens it right away with absurdities that are familiar literary commonplaces: humans, he says, would be born from the sea, fishes would arise from the earth, birds would break out from the sky. Here, as throughout the poem, argument is inseparable from poetic visualization, and the latter is subservient to the former. When Lucretius comes to the complementary proposition, that nothing is destroyed into nothing, he paints an idyllic picture of newborn animals frolicking in the pastures, drunk with milk from their mothers. The delightful scene provides evidence of a cycle of birth and death that rests on the existence of unchanging, unobservable particles.

After these first two doctrines, not only the method of proof but also the doctrines are far different from those of any other philosophical system. Lucretius does his utmost to win the student's assent. He vows that he has in reserve a plethora of arguments that he could cite, in case the student won't believe that there is empty space in the world. He does cite numerous arguments for the atomicity of bodies; and he prefaces his proof of the infinity of the universe with a new prologue, in which he tells of his great joy in being the first to use poetry to reveal truths that free humans from the bonds of religion. When he returns to the topic of infinity at the end of the second book, he marvels at how novel and wonderful is the discovery that he is about to reveal.

The second book ends with a picture of a farmer who is distressed at the barrenness of the fields in the present age. After taking the student on an exploration of infinite time and space, Lucretius now returns to the reality of this world. In his journey, he has aimed to show, following Epicurus, that the gods do not control anything in this or in any other world.

The third book is a closely unified composition the purpose of which is to free humans from the fear of death. Lucretius proceeds by arguing, first, that the soul is corporeal, and, second, that as a corporeal entity, the soul is destroyed upon death. After heaping proof upon proof, he uses rhetorical devices, including the personification of Nature, to console and chide anyone who still has lingering doubts about the finality of death.

In the fourth book, Lucretius discusses the functions of the soul. He ends with a discussion of procreation, which includes a strong denunciation of the passion of sex. This attack may seem surprising in view of Epicurus' claim that pleasure is the supreme good. But Epicurus also held that the supreme pleasure is the absence of pain; and he warned that this goal is incompatible with sexual profligacy. Lucretius reinforces Epicurus' warning by supplying vivid details.

The fifth and sixth books are designed to add further proof that the gods have nothing to do with human existence. Lucretius attempts to show that worlds are created and destroyed merely as a result of atomic motion, without any divine plan. He outlines how humans progressed from an animal-like condition to the present state of technological and cultural refinement. In the sixth book, he explains phenomena that were often attributed to divine action by claiming that atomic motion is sufficient to account for them. In the prologue to the fifth book, he promises to explain how the gods live; but he never fulfills this promise. Perhaps he left the poem unfinished. In any case, he fulfills his aim, which is to explain that the gods are external to the world and so leave humans entirely free to forge their own happiness.

CICERO

Cicero studied Greek philosophy as a youth. On a visit to Greece from 79 to 77 B.C., he became a friend of Antiochus, head of the Academy, and attended lectures by the Epicurean Zeno; he also came to know the Stoic Posidonius. Cicero remained interested in philosophy throughout his political career, although he did not start writing philosophy until quite late in his life.

His first philosophical work was *On the Republic*, written between 54 and 51 B.C. This work was preceded by a rhetorical work, *On the Orator*, published in 55 B.C., in which the main spokesman, Crassus, calls for an alliance of oratory and philosophy; the truly accomplished orator, he maintains, must be a philosopher, and the accomplished philosopher must be an orator. After finishing *On the Republic* Cicero began composing a sequel, *On Laws*, which he did not complete until about 45 B.C. In 46 B.C. Cicero wrote *The Paradoxes of the Stoics* and a number of rhetorical works.

The bulk of Cicero's philosophical writings belongs to a short period of some twenty months, following the death of his daughter, Tullia, early in 45 B.C. In a feverish attempt to forget his deep, private sorrow, he wrote in quick succession *Consolation* (not extant), *Hortensius* (surviving only in a few fragments), *Academica*, *On the Chief Good and Evil*, *Tusculan Disputations*, a translation of Plato's *Timaeus* (of which only a few fragments remain), *On the Nature of the Gods*, *On Divination*, *On Fate*, and finally *On Duty* (completed late in 44 B.C.). About the time of the murder of Caesar, Cicero also wrote two short essays, *Cato on Old Age* and *Laelius on Friendship*.

In a letter to his friend Atticus (12.52.3), written in May 45 B.C., Cicero says of his philosophical writings: "They are mere transcripts; they are not much labor; all I provide is words, of which I have plenty." These self-deprecating remarks are misleading. Although Cicero disclaims originality, he also denies that he is merely a translator. In response to the objection that it is preferable

to read the Greek works in the original language rather than in Latin translation, he claims that he does not merely translate, but adds his own judgment and arrangement (*On the Chief Good and Evil* 1.6). Cicero admits that he lags behind others in philosophical knowledge, but he takes pride in his ability to suffuse philosophy with rhetorical adornment (*On Duty* 1.2). In *Tusculan Disputations* (1.5–6; 2.5–7) he notes that up to his time philosophy was neglected by the Romans; the only Latin works, he claims, were crude Epicurean writings. (He does not here take into consideration Lucretius' poetry.) By contrast, he aims to make philosophy attractive by combining it with rhetoric, a goal that he enunciated earlier in *On the Orator*. The "perfect philosophy," he writes in the preface to the *Tusculan Disputations* (1.7), "is that which can treat the greatest issues with abundance and adornment." In his last philosophical work, *On Duty* (1.3), Cicero claims that he has achieved a special distinction in practicing not only forensic rhetoric but also philosophical rhetoric.

Cicero's philosophical writings have sometimes been described as an encyclopedia of philosophy. This is inaccurate on two counts. First, Cicero imparts style to philosophy; his compositions are rhetorically fashioned debates or exhortations. Second, although it was Cicero's ambition to cover the whole range of philosophy, he is selective with respect to the topics and positions that he treats. Of the three generally recognized parts of philosophy—logic, physics, and ethics—he omits logic except for epistemology, and he gives little attention to physics except for theology and related problems. His main interest is ethics. Nor does he give equal treatment to the various philosophical positions. Cicero considered himself a skeptical Academic, but his skepticism is mixed with a strong inclination toward Peripatetic and Stoic ethics. Cicero himself is aware of this bias and defends it by saying that his Academic skepticism leaves him free to adopt the most probable position.

In his *On the Republic,* which is only partially preserved, Cicero imagines a conversation, set in 129 B.C., among Scipio Aemilianus and his friends. The use of the dialogue form is Platonic, as is the general topic. The topic is the ideal state; and Scipio argues that the ideal state is a mixed constitution, formed by a combination of monarchy, aristocracy, and democracy. This ideal state, Scipio maintains, is represented by Rome. Scipio is said to have discussed the topic with the Stoic Panaetius and the Greek historian Polybius; and clearly Cicero is drawing on these two sources in much of his work. Another influence seems to be neo-Pythagoreanism, as reflected in the dream of Scipio in the sixth book. Here Scipio tells of seeing the whole world, with its nine heavenly spheres moving in harmony with one another. Although many of the ideas presented in *On the Republic* are derivative, the treatise as a whole is a personal statement, having relevance to the present political situation. By recalling the past, Cicero sketches out a vision of Rome's political future; he depicts an ideal that, he hopes, may yet be revived.

Cicero's next work, *On Laws,* which is also preserved only in part, continues the theme of *On the Republic.* Similarly to Plato, Cicero follows up his account of the ideal state with a discussion of the laws of the best state. The scene has now shifted to contemporary Rome, where Cicero is having a conversation with his brother Quintus and his friend Atticus. This change of setting reflects an increasing concern on the part of Cicero to apply political theory in practice. In the first book, Cicero sets out the universal foundation of all actual laws. Following Stoic doctrine, he maintains that the laws of any society must be based on the universal law of nature. This universal law is the rationality (that is, reason or *logos*) that inheres in na-

ture; and this rationality is an aspect of God. In the other two extant books, Cicero sketches the laws of religion and the laws concerning magistrates. Cicero notes that there is little that is original in these laws; they are dependent, he says, on ancestral custom and on his philosophical predecessors. Still, the work is the fruit of Cicero's own political thinking; he has selected the laws that he thinks are best for Rome.

The *Paradoxes of the Stoics* is a rhetorical exercise, in which Cicero tries his hand at presenting in a popular, rhetorical manner the subtle and paradoxical ethical teachings of the Stoics. The work is addressed to Brutus (Caesar's assassin), who also composed philosophical works in Latin (none of which has survived).

In *Academica,* an epistemological work, Cicero defends the skepticism of the new Academy, as developed by Arcesilaus and Carneades, against the dogmatism of the later head of the Academy, Antiochus. Cicero presents with admirable clarity the debate between the Stoics (followed by Antiochus), who maintained that it is possible to have knowledge, and their Academic opponents, who argued that one cannot be sure of knowing anything. The work is invaluable as a source for the history of skepticism; and Cicero performs an important service in creating a Latin epistemological vocabulary.

In *On the Chief Good and Evil,* Cicero responds to an even greater challenge, that of translating Greek ethical vocabulary, in particular that of the Stoics. This treatise consists of five books: the first two are a defense, followed by a refutation, of Epicurean ethics; the next two are a defense and refutation of Stoic ethics; and the last is a defense of Antiochus' ethics, which may be categorized as Peripatetic, together with some brief criticism. Cicero takes the part of critic throughout the treatise. He shows strong disdain for Epicurean ethics, which he thinks is immoral because it subordinates virtue to the goal of pleasure. He accuses the Stoics of neglecting the whole person; for they identify the supreme good with virtue, which consists entirely in the exercise of reason. In this work, Cicero inclines toward Peripatetic ethics, in which the supreme good is defined as virtue combined with a moderate amount of external advantages.

The major influence on *Tusculan Disputations* is Stoic ethics. Cicero sets up five theses and refutes them in turn. They are: (1) death is an evil; (2) pain is the greatest of evils; (3) the wise man is not free from distress; (4) the wise man is not exempt from all disorders of the soul; (5) virtue is not sufficient for a happy life. The Stoics opposed each of these theses; and in developing his argument, Cicero draws heavily on them, although he mixes in Platonic views, notably the view that the soul is immortal.

Cicero describes his method of argument in *Tusculan Disputations* as the Socratic method of refuting an opponent by dialectical discussion. But his method is more rhetorical than dialectical. He invites anyone to state any belief at all, so that he may refute it; and after a few preliminary questions and answers, he quickly lapses into continuous speech. Cicero compares his speeches with those he previously pleaded as a lawyer in court; they are the "declamations of my old age" (1.4.7). There is much rhetorical spontaneity and liveliness in these speeches, which are full of interesting historical examples. Along with *Cato on Old Age* and *Laelius on Friendship*, the *Disputations* are the most accessible, least technical of Cicero's philosophical works.

On the Nature of the Gods is a dialogue set in Rome in 77 or 76 B.C. The young Cicero is shown visiting with three leading representatives of Roman philosophy, the Academic Gaius Aurelius Cotta, the Epicurean Gaius Velleius, and the Stoic Quintus Lucilius Balbus. In the first book, Velleius briefly sets out Epicurean theology, then Cotta refutes it at length. In the second book, Balbus sets out Stoic theology, which is then refuted by Cotta in the third book. We might expect Cicero to side with the Academic Cotta throughout. But he says at the end that Balbus' account of Stoic theology seems to him more probable than Cotta's refutation. The Stoics believed that there is an immanent God who controls everything in the world. This belief seems to Cicero more worthy than the skepticism that casts doubt on the very existence of God. The Epicureans again come off very badly. The dialogue provides a wealth of interesting information not only about Stoic theology, but also about Stoic physics in general.

Cicero's endorsement of Stoic theology does not extend to the Stoic belief in fate and divination. In his two works on these topics, Cicero argues strongly (following the Academics) that there are chance events and that divination is quackery.

His last philosophical work, *On Duty,* is an exhortation to his son, who has been studying Peripatetic philosophy in Athens. It is a kind of testament, in which Cicero encourages his son to abide by Peripatetic and Stoic ethical precepts. The work is in three books: the first deals with what is morally good; the second deals with what is expedient; and the third aims to show that there is no conflict between these two notions. The first two books are based on a work by the Stoic Panaetius. But Cicero assures his son that what he has written does not differ much from Peripatetic doctrine. Cicero's aim is to train his son to be a leader among the Romans; accordingly, he cites numerous examples from Roman history and treats the reader to his own personal interpretation of these events.

Cicero's contribution to philosophy is not originality of thought, but a judicious eclecticism, presented in an attractive style. Cicero is the first Western philosophical essayist whose works have come down to us. He selects views that have relevance to contemporary life and gathers them into coherent, often stimulating debates.

Both Epicureanism and Stoicism had an important influence on Roman life and literature in the first century B.C. The influence of Epicureanism, however, soon waned, and in the first and second centuries A.D. the dominant philosophy at Rome was Stoicism. The two most prominent Roman representatives of Stoicism in this period were Lucius Annaeus Seneca (*ca.* 4 B.C.–A.D. 65) and the emperor Marcus Aurelius (A.D. 121–180).

SENECA

Seneca wrote three types of philosophical compositions: a group of essays (consisting of *On Benefits, On Clemency,* and ten other pieces traditionally entitled *Dialogues*) that may be called *Moral Essays; Letters to Lucilius;* and *Natural Questions.* In all of these writings, Seneca develops further the art of the philosophical essay. The *Moral Essays* deal with various ethical topics and include a number of *Consolations.* The *Letters* focus on ethical concerns of everyday life; the *Natural Questions* deal with physics. The latter two works were composed in the last years of Seneca's life, after his retirement from Nero's court in 62.

Like Cicero, Seneca was a prominent politician. He incurred the anger of the emperor Claudius in 41 and was exiled by him to the island of Corsica. Claudius recalled him eight years later to be the tutor of the young Nero. When Nero became emperor in 54, Seneca was one of his most important advisers. By 62 Seneca had fallen out of favor sufficiently to ask Nero to let him retire. Although Nero turned down the request, Seneca withdrew from the activities of the court. He was charged in 65 with conspiracy against Nero and was forced by the emperor to commit suicide.

Seneca was a committed Stoic, who also accepted some Platonic psychological theories and who in the last years of his life welcomed Epicurean ethics as partly compatible with Stoic ethics. Like Lucretius and Cicero before him, Seneca refashioned Greek philosophy by exercising his own choice and applying rhetorical art. In his use of Greek sources, he seems more independent than Cicero. He read widely, and he often seems to write from memory rather than to translate from a text that is directly before him. Seneca continued the task of coining Latin philosophical vocabulary.

Like Lucretius, Seneca does not merely present a philosophical view, but aims to convert and "heal" the listener. In applying Stoic teachings to everyday life, Seneca mellows the sternness of the doctrine. He claims that it is a misconception that Stoicism is excessively harsh. "There is no school," he writes, "that is kinder and milder, none more loving of humans and more attentive to the common good" (*On Clemency* 2.5.3). Throughout his writings, Seneca emphasizes the kinship among all human beings and calls for mutual love and forgiveness. The key concept of his ethics is "humanity" (*humanitas*); and his chief message is "let us cultivate humanity" (*colamus humanitatem; On Anger* 3.43.5). More than any other ancient philosophical writer, Seneca insists that slaves are fellow human beings, who should be treated with the same respect as any other human being. Insofar as we are subject to passion, Seneca argues, we are the real slaves, not the persons who have been bought.

Although Seneca has enjoyed great popularity over the centuries, his reputation has been clouded by the charge of hypocrisy. He claims in his writings that virtue is the supreme and indeed only good, and that wealth and power make no difference to happiness; and he extols poverty and the simple life. Yet Seneca seems to have been strangely tolerant of Nero's murders and other abuses, and he himself secured great power and amassed great wealth. In defense of Seneca, it may be said that he used his influence at court to curb Nero's excesses and left the court when he could no longer do so. Seneca's praise of the simple life, moreover, seems sincere. Seneca suffered a long period of deprivation when he was in exile, and he knew that he might at any time be deprived of all his influence and possessions. He prepares and consoles himself for this eventuality by contending that adversity is not an evil.

Seneca's *Moral Essays* are like sermons. They are intended to elevate the morals of the listener, and they are often highly dramatic in style. He enlivens his arguments with dramatic scenes and satirical vignettes that are reminiscent of the satirist Juvenal. Although Seneca sometimes develops an argument at unnecessary length (out of a desire to omit nothing that can be said for or against a position), he also has a marvelous gift for summing up his thought in short, memorable phrases.

The essay *On Clemency* sheds considerable light on political affairs at Rome. Seneca addressed this work to Nero in 55 or 56, about a year or less after the murder of Britannicus, Nero's stepbrother and rival. Praising clemency as the most humane of all virtues, Seneca appeals to Nero to show this quality to his subjects. He views Nero as a ruler who has absolute power, and he urges him to be mild in the exercise of this power. Seneca is lavish in his praise of Nero for the clemency he has already shown; but throughout he is implicitly admonishing Nero not to misuse his power. It is not implausible that Seneca was troubled by the murder of Britannicus and wished to steer the emperor toward a better course.

On the Happy Life is a carefully pruned essay, in which Seneca announces at the outset that he will not bore the reader with a survey of other philosophers' opinions. He says that he will give his own view, which may go beyond any particular Stoic position. Seneca defines the happy life in various ways, some of which appear to be his own adaptations of Stoic ideas. Perhaps the definition that captures his own feelings best is the notion that the happy life is "an invincible power of mind, trained through experience, serene in action, with much humanity and concern for the persons one deals with" (4.2). The essay is reflective and contains much self-revelation. Seneca seems to apologize for his own wealth and power: he says that, although the wise man will not reject them, he will not worry about them and will not care if they depart.

On Leisure is overtly personal. Seneca here defends his decision to retire from public life. He admits that Stoic teaching demands that one should never cease serving the public. But, he points out, earlier Stoics did not follow this precept; and he will follow their example.

Among the best of the *Moral Essays* is *On Anger,* in which Seneca shows with numerous, deftly sketched examples what havoc anger can bring. As an accomplished rhetorician pleading the case against anger, Seneca refutes one objection after another; and in the manner of a physician who is trying to heal the sick, he gives advice on how to cure oneself of anger.

Of Seneca's remaining *Moral Essays, On the Shortness of Life* deserves special mention. Here Seneca offers the interesting consolation that one can extend life by making the past one's own. By acquainting ourselves with people such as Socrates and Aristotle, it is possible to enrich and lengthen our own brief existence.

The *Letters to Lucilius* are judged by many to be the best of Seneca's philosophical writings. They are scintillating, succinct, beautifully crafted, and remarkably candid. The letters reveal, as no other work, Seneca's personal anxieties and hopes. Although the *Letters* are addressed to a friend, they often seem to be a dialogue of Seneca with himself. Seneca is now living in retirement, and he is taking stock of his present and past life. He is still a Stoic, but he welcomes Epicurus as a philosophical friend. He does not give up the Stoic idea that virtue is the supreme and only good. But he interprets Epicurus' hedonism in such a way that it is compatible with Stoicism; and he quotes Epicurus more frequently than any other philosopher. In one letter (21), he quotes the inscription in Epicurus' garden: "Friend, here you will have a good stay; here the supreme good is pleasure." Seneca describes the guardian of the garden as a "hospitable and humane" host, who will treat his guest to the simple pleasure of barley-meal and water.

One reason that Seneca was so attracted to Epicureanism at this time is that he was now practicing the Epicurean precept that one should live a life detached from politics. Seneca excuses his retirement from politics by saying that it allows him to serve future generations. But more than anything he now devotes himself to the goal of withdrawing into himself and ridding himself of his private fears; this is an aim he shared with the Epicureans. Commenting on a lawsuit of Lucilius, Seneca urges his friend not to fear imprisonment or exile or death; it seems that Seneca is here exhorting himself as well as his friend (*Letters* 24).

Seneca emphasizes in his *Letters* that philosophy is without value unless it has a practical application. A study of philosophical theory has value only if it is accompanied by a recognition of the practical consequences. Seneca says repeatedly that the philosopher should avoid theoretical hair-splitting. With satirical mock seriousness, he demonstrates this defect in laborious detail in a letter (113) in which he debates whether the virtues are animate beings. Seneca is well acquainted with philosophical theory in all three departments—logic, physics, and eth-ics—but the ethical application is of primary importance to him, as it is in Roman philosophy in general.

Seneca agrees with Lucretius that physics is the theoretical underpinning of ethics (*Letters* 95). That is why, at the same time as the *Letters,* he composed a physical text, *Natural Questions.* This work deals primarily with sublunar events and draws on numerous sources, among them pre-Socratics, Aristotle, and, of course, the Stoics. Seneca's endeavor as a whole is inspired by Lucretius. Like Lucretius, he draws ethical lessons from the physical theory; and he tries to remove the fear of natural phenomena by providing scientific explanations. The underlying difference is that Seneca believes that God is immanent in the world and determines everything that occurs in it.

Seneca was the last major Roman writer of the pagan era to write philosophy in Latin. The period of pagan Latin philosophical writing was short, but fruitful. Lucretius gave the impetus with his poetry, and Cicero and Seneca responded by developing a philosophical rhetoric in prose. Each of the three writers succeeded in creating a distinctively Roman philosophy, having relevance to Roman society.

MUSONIUS, EPICTETUS, AND MARCUS AURELIUS

After Seneca, Greek became reestablished as the proper language of philosophical inquiry, but Rome remained a center of philosophical activity. The Stoic Gaius Musonius Rufus (ca. A.D. 25–100) usually receives little, if any, notice in histories of ancient philosophy. He lectured in Rome, but was exiled for a time by Nero and again by Vespasian. His lectures are preserved in Greek. They are remarkable because they contain the clearest statement of the equality of women of any ancient philosophical document (with the possible exception of

Plato, on whom Musonius seems dependent). Musonius maintains that women must study philosophy, just like men, because they have the same abilities; and he urges parents to give daughters and sons the same education, since the virtues are the same for the two sexes. Musonius also claims that the aim of marriage is not only procreation, but also "a communion and concern of the husband and wife for each other, in health and in sickness and at all times" (13a).

Epictetus (*ca.* 50–120 A.D.) heard Musonius at Rome. He was a Phrygian who had come to Rome as a slave and was freed subsequently. He taught Stoic philosophy, with a focus on ethics. After the emperor Domitian exiled philosophers from Rome in 89 or 92, Epictetus went to Nicopolis in Epirus to teach at his own school. Epictetus' teachings are preserved in two works, written in Greek by a student, Arrian. They are a collection of discussions held by Epictetus, called *Discourses,* and a brief *Manual.*

The *Discourses* reveal Epictetus above all as a dedicated teacher, whose goal is to change the thought and behavior of his students. The main theme of his discussions is freedom. Epictetus maintains that we are all free in that we have a mind, which is ours; it is a gift of God, and a part of God (thus making each one of us a part of God), and nothing else matters. "Only the educated," he said, "are free"; for only those who keep their minds pure in the contemplation of God are fully in control of their destiny.

Marcus Aurelius, emperor of Rome from 161 to 180, read and admired the *Discourses* of Epictetus. He wrote twelve books of personal reflections in Greek, entitled *To Himself* (commonly known as *Meditations*). The work may be called a diary, the first in Western literature; it is the most introspective of any ancient philosophical writing. There is in it a remarkable tension between Marcus Aurelius' position as ruler of the Roman world and his deep sense of the nothingness of human, and in particular his own, existence. The emperor has written a consolation to himself for the intrigues and enmities that surround him, and for his own sense of inadequacy.

Marcus Aurelius endorses the common Stoic view that the world is governed providentially by God and that humans should accept whatever lot is assigned to them. But his attitude toward this cosmic order is unique. He is deeply resigned to whatever happens, and he takes comfort in the thought that life is short and that death means the reabsorption of one's existence in the totality of the universe. The human being lives, according to Marcus Aurelius, only at an instant, the present. Hence a human lifetime is virtually nothing, especially when considered in the context of infinite time. Marcus Aurelius compares infinity to an abyss in which all things vanish. The only thing valuable about a human being is the spirit (or mind) within, which is a divinity and must be served by just actions. The body is nothing but clay and corruption.

Marcus Aurelius spent a large part of his career fighting wars. In his writings, he yearns for peace and tranquillity. He is willing to forgive his enemies on the ground that they do not know what they are doing. Everyone, he agrees with Socrates, errs unwittingly. The court, he says, is a stepmother, from which he takes refuge in his real mother, philosophy (6.12). He wishes for death when he contemplates his associates (9.3). But he reminds himself that since he is joined to all others by a bond of kinship, he will serve them and do nothing to injure them (10.6). In an especially revealing entry, Marcus Aurelius describes how he does not want to get out of bed in the morning (5.1). He exhorts himself with the thought that every creature—ant, spider, bee—has been made by the creator to do some work; thus, he should rise and do the work of a human being.

Throughout his writings, Marcus Aurelius

uses images abundantly, putting them together in simple, harmonious clauses that read like verse. He compares life to an empty pageant, a stage play, the toil of ants carrying their burden, the scurrying of mice, the jerking of puppets on their strings (7.3). Elsewhere he writes, "Everything of the body is a river, everything of the soul is dream and delusion; life is war and an alien sojourn" (2.17). The images underscore the vanity of human existence. The only thing that can help is philosophy, for it teaches us to wait for death as the dissolution of our being.

By the time of Marcus Aurelius, Roman philosophy has become merged with Greek philosophy. It no longer draws special inspiration from Roman history or society; it has now become personal and cosmopolitan at once. Although Marcus Aurelius was a Roman whose family had strong roots in Roman history, he does not cite examples from Roman history or recognize a distinctively Roman use for philosophy at all. He regards himself as a citizen of the world, and he uses philosophy as something that transcends national boundaries.

***

In the third and fourth centuries, the most important development in Greek or Roman philosophical thought was Neoplatonism. In the same period, Christianity spread and became the dominant religion in the Roman Empire. Pagan philosophy, of course, cannot be separated from religion at any stage of its development. All the philosophical schools taught physics and ethics within the framework of a religious doctrine; and when the Romans applied Greek philosophy to their lives, they adopted religious ideas along with the rest. Stoicism influenced Roman religion greatly from the first century B.C. through the second century of the Christian era. Then it yielded to Neoplatonic philosophy or Christian thought, though not without leaving an imprint on both.

Plotinus (A.D. 204/205–270), the founder of Neoplatonism, came to Rome from Alexandria in 244. He began writing late in his life. His writings, which are in Greek, were published as six *Enneads* (six collections of nine treatises each) by his student Porphyry. Plotinus was an original and powerful thinker, who made considerable changes in Plato's metaphysics and ethics. He posited three entities, called "hypostases": the One (or Good), Intellect, and Soul. Intellect and Soul are successive emanations from the One; Intellect is directly dependent on the One, and Soul is directly dependent on intellect. Plotinus compared these emanations to light flowing from the sun, and to heat coming from fire; they occur spontaneously, as a kind of overflow from their source. The Intellect is intuitive thought, having as objects unchanging Forms. Soul creates the physical world by acting on matter, which has no existence in itself. Soul is responsible for discursive thought as well as sense perception. The goal of each human being is to ascend from sensory experience to Intellect and, ultimately, to an occasional, momentary union with the One. Neoplatonism is not only a rigorously reasoned philosophical system, but also a mystical movement that had a strong influence on Christian thought.

After Plotinus, the center of philosophical activity shifted to the East, and Roman pagan philosophy came to an end.

BIBLIOGRAPHY

SOURCES

Cyril Bailey has edited Lucretius' *On the Nature of Things* (*De Rerum Natura*) in the collection of Oxford Classical Texts (1900; 2d ed. 1922); Bailey has also published an edition of Lucretius with introduction, translation, and commentary in three volumes (1947). Also recommended is a verse translation, entitled *Lucretius: The Nature of Things*, by Frank O. Copley (1977).

Cicero's philosophical works are available in Loeb editions (containing the Latin text with English translation): *De Finibus Bonorum et Malorum* (*On the Chief Good and Evil*), H. Rackham, trans. (1914; 2d ed. 1931); *De Natura Deorum* (*On the Nature of the Gods*), H. Rackham, trans. (1933); *Tusculan Disputations*, J. E. King, trans. (1927; rev. ed. 1945); *De Senectute, De Amicitia, De Divinatione* (*On Old Age, On Friendship, On Divination*), William Armistead Falconer, trans. (1923); *De Republica, De Legibus* (*On the Republic, On Laws*), C. W. Keyes, trans. (1928); *De Officiis* (*On Duty*), Walter Miller, trans. (1913); *De Fato, Paradoxa Stoicorum* (*On Fate, The Paradoxes of the Stoics*), H. Rackham, trans. (1942).

Seneca's works are available in the following editions: *Moral Essays*, John W. Basore, trans., 3 vols. (1928, 1932, 1935); *Epistulae Morales*, Richard M. Gummere, trans., 3 vols. (1917, 1920, 1925); *Diologorum Libri Duodecim*, L. D. Reynolds, ed. (1977); *Ad Lucilium Epistulae Morales* (*Letters to Lucilius*), L. D. Reynolds, ed., 2 vols. (1965); *Sénèque, Questions Naturelles* (*Natural Questions*), Paul Oltramare, ed. and trans., 2 vols. (1929). The *Letters* are also available in a translation by Robin Campbell entitled *Seneca: Letters from a Stoic* (1969).

For the remaining authors, the following Loeb editions are available: Epictetus, *Discourses*, W. A. Oldfather, trans., 2 vols. (1925, 1928); *The Communings with Himself of Marcus Aurelius Antoninus*, C. R. Haines, trans. (1916; rev. ed. 1930); and five of the projected six volumes of Plotinus, *Enneads*, A. H. Armstrong, trans. (1966-). Another translation of Marcus Aurelius is *Meditations*, by Maxwell Staniforth (1964). All of Plotinus is available in the collection of Oxford Classical Texts: *Plotini Opera*, Paul Henry and Hans-Rudolf Schwyzer, eds., 3 vols. (1964, 1977, 1982).

STUDIES

A general book dealing with Roman philosophy is M. L. Clarke, *The Roman Mind* (1968); a detailed history of Roman philosophy is included in Eduard Zeller's *Die Philosophie der Griechen*, III, pt. 1, 5th ed. revised by E. Wellmann (1923) and pt. 2, 3d ed. (1881).

A. Dalzell, "A Bibliography of Work on Lucretius, 1945–1972," in *The Classical World*, **66** and **67** (1973), is the single most comprehensive bibliography on Lucretius. More recent studies are: Elizabeth Asmis, "Rhetoric and Reason in Lucretius," in *American Journal of Philology*, **104** (1983), and "Lucretius' Venus and Stoic Zeus," in *Hermes*, **110** (1982); Diskin Clay, *Lucretius and Epicurus* (1983); P. H. Schrijvers, *Horror ac Divina Voluptas* (1970).

Elizabeth Rawson includes a discussion of Cicero's philosophical works in *Cicero: A Portrait* (1975; rev. ed. 1983). H. A. K. Hunt, in *The Humanism of Cicero* (1954), argues that Cicero's major philosophical works are united by a common theme. Pierre Boyancé summarizes Cicero's philosophical contribution in "Cicéron et son oeuvre philosophique," in *Revue des Études Latines*, **14** (1936). A detailed study is: Alain Michel, *Rhétorique et philosophie chez Cicéron* (1960).

Miriam T. Griffin analyzes Seneca's theory and practice in *Seneca: A Philosopher in Politics* (1976); Anna Lydia Motto provides a brief overview in *Seneca* (1973). Musonius' writings are discussed by A. C. van Geytenbeek in *Musonius Rufus and Greek Diatribe*, B. J. Hijmans, trans., rev. ed. (1963). For Epictetus and Marcus Aurelius, see Eduard Zeller, *op. cit.*

Works on Plotinus are: Emile Bréhier, *The Philosophy of Plotinus*, J. Thomas, trans. (1958); John M. Rist, *Plotinus: The Road to Reality* (1967). *The Cambridge History of Later Greek and Early Medieval Philosophy*, A. H. Armstrong, ed. (1967) includes a discussion of Neoplatonism and early Christian thought.

THE VISUAL ARTS

Greek Architecture

J. J. COULTON

SIMPLE HOUSES WERE BEING BUILT by the Neolithic communities of southern Greece by at least 5000 B.C., and there were impressive palaces and tombs in the second millennium. However, the subject of this essay is not building in general within the area of Greece. Rather, it is the specific kind of architecture that flourished especially in the classical period and that has influenced Western architecture more or less deeply ever since. It may be helpful therefore to begin by describing in general terms its most characteristic and prestigious building type, the temple (fig. 1), and the system of decoration that was devised for it.

TEMPLE ARCHITECTURE

The heart of a temple was the *cella,* the large inner room that held the cult statue of the divinity concerned (see fig. 2 in GREEK BUILDING TECHNIQUES). Although access to this room was allowed at least in some circumstances, the chief rites took place at the altar outside, normally before the east front. The interior of a Greek temple was thus comparatively little elaborated, but detailed attention was lavished on the outside. The *cella* (fig. 1b) was approached by a porch (*pronaos*) (fig. 1a), which was usually at the east end and consisted of a pair of columns between the extended side walls of the *cella.* In many temples this functional porch was matched by a false porch (*opisthodomos*) (fig. 1c) at the opposite end. Both porches were usually closed off by a grille between the columns; they were used to store valuable offerings, as was the *cella* itself. The exterior of a major temple consisted of a rectangle of massive stone columns rising from a continuous stepped platform. The columns carried stone beams, the entablature, consisting normally of the architrave, frieze, and strongly projecting cornice, above which rose a low-pitched roof whose gables formed triangular pediments. The columns and entablature almost always had the highly refined forms of the Doric or Ionic orders, whose elements are described more fully below. The Corinthian capital (see fig. 5 in ROMAN BUILDING TECHNIQUES), which consists normally of two rows of acanthus leaves from which two pairs of spiral tendrils

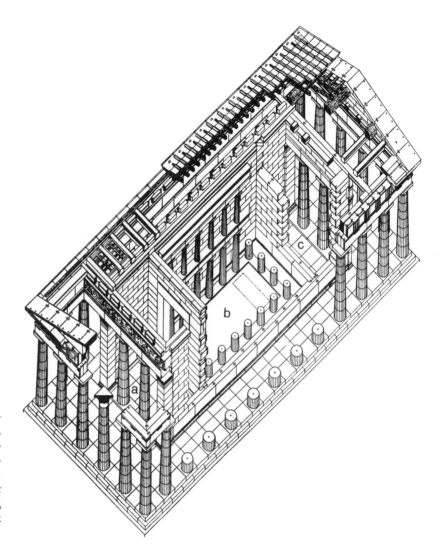

Figure 1. The temple of Hephaestus (the Hephaisteion), *ca.* 450–445 B.C., cutaway drawing by W. H. Plommer: *(a) pronaos; (b) cella; (c) opisthodomos. Reproduced from* ANNUAL OF THE BRITISH SCHOOL AT ATHENS 45 (1950). BY PERMISSION OF THE BRITISH SCHOOL AT ATHENS

spring upward on each face, appeared only in the fifth century. It was never treated as a separate order in Greek architecture, but as a variant capital, usually in an otherwise Ionic order. The chief characteristics of the Doric order (fig. 2a) are its baseless columns, simple capitals, and strongly articulated frieze of grooved, vertical triglyphs, between which are smooth or sculptured metopes, square slabs set back from the face of the triglyphs. The Ionic column (fig. 2b), on the other hand, had a molded base and a more elaborate capital with spiral, scroll-like volutes. Initially it had either a continuous frieze or a low course of pro-

jecting rectangular "teeth" known as dentils; but from the fourth century onward these two forms were increasingly used together.

The origins and development of these orders are treated below; here it may be worth noting their visual effectiveness. The stepped platform of a temple visually as well as actually provides a firm horizontal base for the building; the effect of the concave fluting is to bring out the roundness of the columns and to emphasize their character as vertical supports. The column bases, in Ionic, make a formal transition from the broad platform to the narrow column shafts,

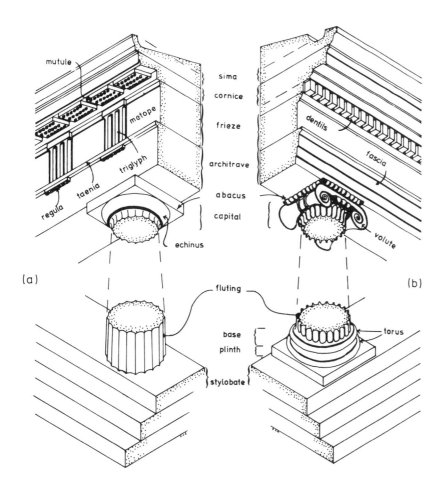

mutule
sima
cornice
metope
frieze
triglyph
architrave
taenia
abacus
regula
capital
echinus
dentils
fascia
volute
(a)
fluting
(b)
base
plinth
torus
stylobate

Figure 2. The Greek orders: (a) Doric; (b) Ionic. *Reproduced from J. J. Coulton, ANCIENT GREEK ARCHITECTS AT WORK* (1977)

while the capitals in both Doric and Ionic make a similar transition—yielding yet resistant—from support to load. Above the columns, the horizontal bands of Doric and Ionic architraves enhance their role as the main horizontal beams of the system. The Doric triglyphs and Ionic dentils reflect in their different ways (and not literally) the beams of the roof structure, while the cornice not only serves to throw clear the rain but also provides a strong visual termination to the whole facade. Thus although the forms of the orders are not merely functional, they constitute an abstract sculpture of the structure of the colonnade, and their visual expressiveness, combined with the cultural prestige of the classical in general and of the Greek in particular, must largely explain the prolonged popularity of such closely defined schemes.

Another notable characteristic of Greek architecture is its use of moldings (fig. 3) to articulate the elements of a building. A number of different profiles were developed—convex, concave, and S-shaped—and with them conventional decorative patterns corresponding to the profile; thus egg-and-dart comes on the convex ovolo molding (fig. 3b), and S-shaped leaf-and-dart is found on the double-curved cyma reversa (fig. 3e). In Doric architecture these patterns were painted, but in Ionic they were both carved and painted. In fact the monochrome appearance of existing Greek ruins is misleading; color was extensively used to reinforce the three-dimensional forms of the orders and of the relief sculpture. The main structural elements, the columns and architrave, were left comparatively plain, while the frieze, cornice, moldings, and ceilings might be richly painted. The main colors were blue and red—as for the Doric triglyphs and metopes—but black, green, and gold were also used.

There was impressive architecture in the second millennium B.C.—the palaces

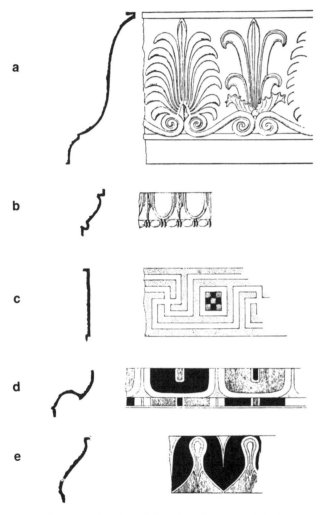

Figure 3. Profiles of Greek moldings and their decorations: (a) cyma recta and cavetto; (b) ovolo and astragal; (c) plain taenia; (d) hawksbeak; (e) cyma reversa. *Reproduced from Hugh Plommer, ANCIENT AND CLASSICAL ARCHITECTURE, SIMPSON'S HISTORY OF ARCHITECTURAL DEVELOPMENT 1 (1956). BY PERMISSION OF LONGMANS, GREEN AND CO., LONDON*

and tombs of Minoan Crete and Mycenaean Greece—and although there seems to have been a complete break in monumental building after the end of the Bronze Age (ca. 1050), memories of this lost glory, and perhaps also some visible remains of it, may have assisted Greek architects in a fresh start. Although its influence remained strong in Crete, Minoan architecture had little direct impact on classical architecture. However, the massive dressed masonry of Mycenaean fortifications and tombs, built mainly in the thirteenth century B.C., may have been more influential, since impressive remains were visible in the northeast Peloponnese, one of the formative areas of later Greek architecture, and tomb and gate facades displayed such features as fluted columns and a capital quite comparable to a Doric one. There are similarities too between the Greek temple and the Mycenaean palace, for the central element of both is a large hall approached by a porch of two columns. Significant differences, such as the shallow anteroom that separates the porch from the main room of the palace, suggest that the similarities may be due not to the direct derivation of the temple from the palace hall but to the common origin of both in a simpler and longer-lasting house type.

From about 1100 to 800 B.C., little was built in Greece besides houses, and most of those were small and simply made. Minoan and Mycenaean houses had been rectangular, often in dense settlements; with the end of the Bronze Age, long, freestanding houses, often with apsed ends and thatched roofs (see fig. 1 in GREEK BUILDING TECHNIQUES), became more normal, in part perhaps a response to a lower population density and to the less permanent materials that unsettled conditions encouraged. Most houses consisted of a single main room with a porch at one end (as in later temples) and sometimes another small room, apparently for storage, at the back. Sanctuaries also existed, although it is rarely possible to demonstrate a continuity of cult from the Bronze Age, and it was only in the eighth century that the practice of temple building developed. Cult statues also began to appear about the same time, and it seems reasonable to suppose that the embodiment of the divinity in a specific form and the provision of a divine residence in a specific place are two aspects of the same attitude to the gods. Ritual dining around a central hearth, a feature of several early temples, may also have encouraged temple construction, at least in Crete; in later sanctuaries such dining, while still important, took place in quite different types of building.

Since a temple was regarded in a sense as a god's dwelling, it naturally followed the form of a mortal's house with main room and porch; but not surprisingly the divine house might be much longer than a human one, a length of about 100 feet (30–35 m) often being considered appropriate. A more enigmatic elaboration of the human dwelling was the ring of posts around the outside of some temples, a feature that became the characteristic outer colonnade of major classical temples. It has no obvious source in the earlier architecture of Greece, Egypt, or the Near East, but new light on its origin is thrown by a recent discovery at Lefkandi (Euboea). In the mid tenth century an apsidal building about 157 feet (48 m) long, built over the site of a contemporary but unusually rich burial, was given a veranda of wooden posts down each side and around the apse. This discovery pushes back the origin of the surrounding portico by at least a century. Furthermore, the building can hardly have been conceived at this early date as an imitation temple to honor a dead hero; pits for storage jars in the rear room indicate rather that it was envisaged as a "glorified house," so suggesting that the veranda arose in a secular, not a sacred context.

Although large and substantially built, the Lefkandi building still has the long apsidal plan of more modest houses. However, the renewed development from the ninth century onward of more compact settlements, sometimes surrounded by fortification walls, generally led to a readoption of a rectangular plan for houses, with temples following. At least by the eighth century houses in more prosperous communities, such as Zagora on Andros Island, began to develop more complex plans, with separate rooms for different functions, sometimes grouped around a court. This development became more widespread in the seventh century, and so houses became quite distinct in form from temples, which continued to be built as long, freestanding buildings.

The seventh century saw two important changes in temple architecture that eventually affected other classes of building as well. These are the mastery of building in large, carefully shaped blocks of stone, and the evolution of sophisticated decorative forms for columns and entablature. As a result major temples of the early sixth century in mainland Greece looked much as they would for the next half millennium. In Crete seventh-century temples at Prinias and Gortyn were decorated with large stone reliefs that probably ran along their lower walls, a Near Eastern practice that parallels other evidence for Near Eastern craftsmen working on the island at about this time. However, Cretan developments show little connection with later Greek architecture, and the Doric and Ionic orders present more complex problems.

The Roman architect Vitruvius thought that both orders were stone versions of preexisting wooden structures, with triglyphs, for example, representing the original roof beams. Although some features of these orders suggest the inspiration of woodwork, the idea of traditional wooden forms translated wholesale into stone is not borne out by present archaeological evidence. Building models of the eighth and seventh centuries show neither specific forms of the orders nor a lavish and elaborate use of wood that wooden versions of the orders would require, and the porticoes in tenth-century Lefkandi and seventh-century Samos all had slender rectangular posts, not sturdy circular ones.

Since the Doric order was fully established by the early sixth century B.C., its evolution must have been comparatively rapid, taking place within a century or less. The adoption of tiled roofs in place of lighter thatched ones must have encouraged a heavier supporting structure, but modern parallels show that this is not a sufficient explanation. And although it seems likely that the first Doric order was built in wood (or wood and terra-cotta), the particular combination of forms was probably chosen because of its satisfying and impressive appearance rather than because each element had a logical place in a traditional wooden structure. Some elements were surely derived from traditional woodwork; however, Mycenaean and Egyptian architecture were probably among other sources drawn on.

The scanty written evidence suggests that this development took place in the area of Argos and Corinth. Seventh-century temples at Corinth, Isthmia, and the Heraeum near Argos all show a move toward a more substantial and elaborate form. The earliest specifically Doric elements are painted terra-cotta metopes from the temple of Apollo at Thermum (Aetolia, *ca.* 630 B.C.), and a broken Corinthian pot from Perachora of about the same date apparently shows a Doric column. But the Doric order can only be fully attested when dressed stonework was used throughout a building, as in the temple of Artemis at Corcyra (Corfu; *ca.* 580 B.C.).

At about the same time that the Doric order was emerging in mainland Greece, monumental architecture was also beginning in the Greek cities east of the Aegean.

Smyrna (İzmir) in Asia Minor had had substantial fortification walls already in the ninth century, but shortly before its destruction in the early sixth century the sanctuary of Athena was given beautifully fitted stone retaining walls and a temple of some importance. Much of its form is uncertain. There were stone columns carrying capitals of the type usually known as Aeolic, with volutes springing vertically, as if from a stem, rather than horizontally, as in the Ionic capital. No consistent forms of base or entablature have been found with these capitals there or elsewhere, so it is perhaps wrong to speak of an Aeolic order, but their distribution mainly in northwest Asia Minor and the adjacent islands testifies to a lively school of architecture in that area during the first three-quarters of the sixth century.

There are earlier parallels for Aeolic capitals in the architecture of the kingdoms of Israel and Judah (Palestine), inspired probably from Phoenicia; but although there are parallels for the Ionic capital in the minor arts of the Levant, as an architectural element it seems a Greek conception. The order as a whole was probably inspired partly by traditional timberwork and partly by various motifs from Levantine art and architecture. It apparently emerged rather later than Doric, but the distinction was primarily geographic: Ionic in the Aegean islands and Asia Minor, Doric in mainland Greece and the western colonies.

Some of the earliest Ionic columns served simply to support statues of sphinxes, but probably at about the same time (*ca.* 570–560 B.C.) a major Ionic temple to Hera was built on Samos. Its scale was colossal (over 160 × 320 ft. or 50 × 100 m), covering about four times the area of the temple of Artemis at Corcyra. Soon afterward the Ephesians, presumably in rivalry, built a slightly larger temple of Artemis; in the second half of the sixth century the Samians rebuilt their temple to Hera larger still. All three temples had a double row of columns around the *cella* to help cope with the exceptional size, and the spacing of the columns was varied, both to align with the walls of the *cella* and to provide a wider opening in front of the temple doorway. In spite of the large spans, the temple of Artemis apparently had a stone entablature; in the two Samian temples the entablature was probably made of wood. The columns all had molded bases, although of varying profiles, and at Ephesus some columns also had sculptured drums, probably just above their bases. The varying treatment of individual bases and capitals shows the fluid character of archaic Ionic, and the finely carved moldings bring out its elaboratively decorative character.

Although the Cycladic islanders were Ionians by dialect, they were also open to influences from the Greek mainland. It is therefore not surprising to find not only some Doric temples on the islands but also a distinctive version of the Ionic order. The most important difference is the inclusion of a continuous frieze in place of the blocklike dentils of Asiatic Ionic. This may in part be due to the islanders' familiarity with the heavier Doric entablature, but it may also be explained by the elaborate marble ceilings that Cycladic builders favored, which demanded more height than the wooden ceilings used elsewhere at this stage. Cycladic marble architecture is attested from the first half of the sixth century; the major Ionic temples on Naxos and Paros belong to the second half.

During the first half of the sixth century the Doric order had become firmly established in mainland Greece and the western colonies. Although it was already a clearly defined system, there was considerable variation in minor elements from one building to another; for instance, spiral fluting is found on the neck of a capital from Kalapodi in Locris. In mainland Greece this artistic freedom was drastically reduced soon after

the middle of the century. The decorative features of some earlier temples were omitted, and the alternating rhythms of the order were clarified by making the slablike mutules (fig. 2a), projecting drip caps atop the columns, all of uniform width. Thus the rhythm of the colonnade was repeated at double frequency in the triglyph frieze and then redoubled in the cornice. The fairly small but well-preserved temple of Aphaea on Aegina (late sixth century) gives a good impression of the style, which continued with little change until the mid fifth century. Variation was generally restricted to a sporadic tightening of the capital profile and to changes in proportion and in the use of some subsidiary moldings.

The second half of the sixth century was a time of considerable prosperity in Sicily and southern Italy, and several large and quite well preserved temples survive at cities such as Syracuse, Selinus (Selinunte), and Poseidonia (Paestum). In these, however, the disciplined mainland style was not immediately adopted. Some early features, such as a fondness for rich terra-cotta roof decoration, were simply retained longer, while specifically local features were also developed. More emphasis was given to the front of the temple than the rear (where the *opisthodomos* was usually replaced by a closed room [*adyton*] behind the *cella*), and the side porticoes were generally deeper than on the mainland. An Ionian component in the population of several western colonies helps to explain the Ionic features in some of these Doric temples (for example, carved moldings), and a few Ionic temples were built. Another aspect of this Ionian influence was the inception of a colossal (though Doric) temple dedicated to Apollo at Selinus (*ca.* 530 B.C.), and its curious rival at Akragas (Agrigento) some fifty years later, where half-columns in a screen wall replaced the usual colonnade.

Temples were architecturally the most important buildings in an archaic Greek sanctuary; however, in terms of function the altar was more important. In form it might simply be a mound of ashes, as at Olympia; more formal altars on the Greek mainland were often long stone platforms decorated with a triglyph frieze, while elaborate altars in Ionia might consist of a substantial raised platform approached by a broad stair and surrounded by a decorated enclosure wall. In the major Panhellenic sanctuaries such as Delphi and Olympia, some individual cities built treasuries to house their dedications to the divinity. Like temples, these usually had a porch in front of a closed main room, but they were smaller, squarer, and lacked a surrounding portico. Since they were themselves prestigious dedications, they were sometimes extremely elaborate: the Athenians had a marble treasury at Delphi with all its metopes sculptured long before there was any such temple at Athens (or Delphi).

Somewhat lower down the scale of importance came stoas, long freestanding porticoes that might be used to house less valuable dedications and to provide shelter for pilgrims, for many might travel some distance to attend an important festival. Although some archaic stoas had columns and entablature of stone, such secondary buildings often continued to have wooden posts and beams. The ritual consumption of sacrificial meat was an important part of Greek religious ritual, and buildings for this purpose appeared early. In later sanctuaries formal dining rooms can often be recognized by their off-center doors, which allowed the most economical arrangement of dining couches.

The arrangement of buildings in an archaic sanctuary was fairly informal. The temple and its altar were sometimes strictly related on a common axis of symmetry, even if (as in the late-sixth-century temple of Aphaea on Aegina) this involved some change in their previous positions. Otherwise buildings were generally placed with more regard for function than aesthetics, with temples dominating the center of the sanctuary, secondary buildings in less important areas, and stoas set along the edges. The sanctuary entrance, often marked by a propylon (monumental gateway) consisting of a small porch inside and outside the door itself, was usually placed to give direct access to the area between the temple and its altar. Thus it gave the pilgrim an oblique first view of the temple, rather than an axial one.

CITY PLANS AND CIVIC BUILDINGS

Most mainland Greek cities grew up gradually and irregularly, and although specific areas might be set aside for public use—such as the Athenian Agora (fig. 4) in the early sixth century—no effort was made to give such areas a formal shape. Where a whole new settlement was laid out at one time, some degree of order was helpful. The foundation of colonies in Sicily, southern Italy, North Africa, and the Black Sea area provided just such a situation, since each colonist was entitled to an equal share of land. At Megara Hyblaea (Sicily; founded *ca.* 725 B.C.) the original street plan consisted of sets of parallel streets with house blocks that were not all rectangular. By the late sixth century some new cities were based on a regular grid of straight streets and rectangular house plots, a system that was for a long time connected with the fifth-century town planner Hippodamus of Miletus.

Civic building received less attention in the archaic period. Some cities had stoas on their agoras (for example, Megara Hyblaea), and Athens is known to have had a prytaneum (*prytaneion*), where the city's hearth burned perpetually and state guests were entertained, and a number of civic

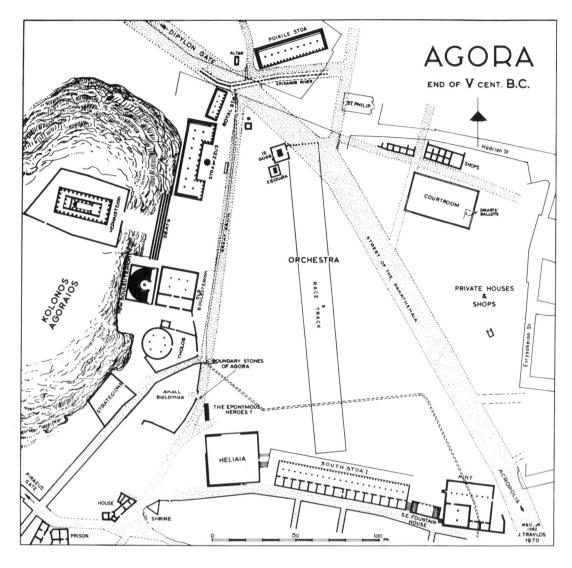

Figure 4. The Agora at Athens, *ca.* 400 B.C., restored plan by J. Travlos and W. B. Dinsmoor, Jr. *Reproduced from* HESPERIA **53**.1 (1984). COURTESY OF THE AMERICAN SCHOOL OF CLASSICAL STUDIES AT ATHENS, AGORA EXCAVATIONS

offices, although none from this period has been rediscovered; the main evolution of Greek civic building comes later. The archaic houses known are also fairly modest buildings, consisting of three or four rooms, sometimes entered from a corridor in front, and with no pretense of architectural elaboration.

While the period between 500 and 480 B.C. saw profound changes in Greek sculpture and painting, there was no comparable change in the architecture of the Greek

mainland. The temple of Zeus at Olympia (*ca.* 470–457 B.C.), for instance, was closely comparable in most ways to the temple of Aphaea on Aegina a generation earlier, except that being twice as large (about 91 × 210 ft. or 27.7 × 64 m) it had noticeably sturdier columns. Such variation of proportion with scale is characteristic of Greek architecture. The temple of Zeus at Olympia, with its fully symmetrical plan, pure Doric forms, and appropriately severe architectural sculpture, constitutes virtually a sum-mation of two centuries of development in mainland Greek architecture.

In the western Greek colonies, however, there was a change, for the variation and experimentation that had still continued there were abandoned in favor of the more architectonic severity of the mainland. The temples of Athena at Syracuse and Nike at Himera (in Sicily), both celebrating the defeat of the Carthaginians in 480 B.C., have capital profiles similar to those of Zeus at Olympia and an *opisthodomos* rather than a closed *adyton*. Temples of similar style were built at Akragas, Selinus, and Poseidonia in the following quarter century, and with minor modifications the style continued in Sicily until the Carthaginian victories of the late fifth century.

A more productive change is embodied in the architecture of Athens in the third quar-

ter of the fifth century. In the thirty years after the Persian sack of Athens (480–479 B.C.) few temples had been built or rebuilt, perhaps because they were intentionally left as a memorial to barbarian impiety. But from about 450 B.C. onward a major program of sanctuary building was undertaken throughout Attica (fig. 5). Much of this falls within the period of Pericles' dominance, and he was personally involved in initiating some of it. But sanctuary building was a civic activity, and in Athens proposals had to be passed by the assembly, which would also allot the sources of revenue and appoint an architect and a board of supervisors. The Athenians at this stage seem to have hired laborers (citizens, foreigners, and slaves) individually or in very small groups, but in other places quite large contracts were let, necessarily involving the contractor in hir-

Figure 5. The Athenian Acropolis, view from northwest: *(a)* the Parthenon, 447–438 B.C.; *(b)* the Erechtheum, 421–405 B.C.; *(c)* the Propylaia, 437–432 B.C.; *(d)* the temple of Athena Nike, 427–424 B.C. Plaster model, restoration by G. P. Stevens and J. Travlos. QUEBEC, LE CENTRE MUSÉOGRAPHIQUE DE L'UNIVERSITÉ LAVAL

ing a labor force; in the archaic period whole buildings may have been contracted for by a single person.

The new temples of Periclean Athens were built of marble, not limestone like most earlier mainland temples. The Pentelic quarries provided a convenient source of the material; many of the skilled masons who carved it probably came from the Cyclades. Marble not only allowed sharper carving; it also allowed the adoption, from Cycladic practice, of marble ceilings over the porticoes and porches of these temples. Cycladic influence may also have suggested the inclusion of Ionic features in what were generally Doric temples, a combination that was particularly appropriate at Athens—which by location and habit belonged to the Doric architectural tradition of the mainland, but which was Ionian by dialect and now dominated a largely Ionian league. Although similar combinations of Ionic with Doric had occurred earlier in the western colonies, the Athenian example seems in practice to have been more influential.

The Parthenon

The Parthenon (fig. 5a), the most important of the Periclean buildings (built between 447 and 438 B.C.), stood on a site previously occupied by an unfinished temple (probably built *ca.* 490–480 B.C.), whose internal arrangements it seems to have followed. Each had a separate room entered from the west as well as the main *cella*. The *cella* of the Parthenon (fig. 6) was unusually wide in comparison to the temple platform, and the inner colonnades supporting the roof were not the usual two rows but continued around behind the cult statue; this provided a particularly effective setting for Phidias' great gold and ivory statue of Athena Parthenos. The *cella* colonnades were Doric and in two stories as usual, but those in the west room were apparently Ionic. Although somewhat larger than

the temple of Zeus at Olympia, the Parthenon (101.4 × 228 ft. or 30.9 × 69.5 m) has smaller columns, so that there are eight rather than the usual six at each end. To prevent the facades appearing squat, the columns were made more slender and close-set.

The Parthenon was unusually rich in sculpture, which filled both pediments, all the outer metopes, and the famous panathenaic frieze (see fig. 8 in GREEK SCULPTURE AND GEMS). This continuous frieze, an Ionic feature, replaced the usual Doric frieze over the two porches and continued along both sides of the *cella* building. But the most remarkable elaboration was the use of "refinements," such as the slight upward curve of the temple platform, the slightly curved taper of the column shafts, and the inward tilt of all the columns. Such refinements were

Figure 6. Interior of the Parthenon *cella* with the cult statue of Athena Parthenos by Phidias, which stood forty feet tall, reconstruction model by N. Leipen. TORONTO, ROYAL ONTARIO MUSEUM

already used in some archaic Doric temples, and from the fourth century at least they occur in Ionia too; nevertheless they are particularly well illustrated in the Parthenon. Ancient writers suggest that these subtleties were intended to correct undesirable optical illusions, and some refinements, such as the slight thickening of the four corner columns, clearly do so; they may also have been intended to give the spring of life to otherwise inert forms. At any rate they effectively illustrate the immense pains taken by the Greeks to refine and perfect temple design within the strict limits of the type.

Many of the features of the Parthenon—the rather slender columns, the inclusion of Ionic features, and especially the Ionic frieze—occur in other Periclean buildings, and there seems to have been a growing interest in interior space as well as the outer form of a building. For instance the temple of Hephaestus (the Hephaisteion, often known, probably erroneously, as the Theseion) shown in figure 1 and three other Attic temples outside Athens apparently designed by the same architect have the *pronaos* entablature continuing across the side porticoes of the temple to create a visual separation of the space in front of the *pronaos*. And in the Hephaisteion there is also a horseshoe inner colonnade like that of the Parthenon, yet it is set so close to the *cella* walls that its intention must be aesthetic, not structural. The Propylaia (fig. 5c), which formed a grand entrance to the Acropolis, shows a similar interest in space: two side wings project forward from the main gate building to frame a formal forecourt, and the resulting combination of separate elements into a single complex building is a unique achievement in fifth-century architecture.

Other Athenian Architecture

Civic building also flourished at Athens to meet the needs of the developing democracy; it belongs mainly to the second and fourth quarters of the century. Two successive council chambers contained a theater-like arrangement of seats with a minimum of interference from columns; and a substantial circular chamber, the tholos, accommodated the councillors on duty (*prytaneis*). To the east of the theater of Dionysus, where little remains of the fifth-century structures, a large concert hall (*odeion*) was built by Pericles, its roof carried by an array of ninety columns set in ten rows. Three or four stoas on the agora included new varieties of plan and new features that were to become conventions for such buildings: for instance, the inclusion of three metopes instead of two above each intercolumniation provided more space with small columns.

Not all Athenian architecture was primarily Doric; the Erechtheum (fig. 5b), which housed the much-revered statue of Athena Polias, was Ionic, and there had been two or three less important Ionic temples earlier. The unusual irregularity of the Erechtheum plan, due to the sacred landmarks on the site, was counterbalanced by elaborate moldings and other carved details typical of Ionic (see fig. 5 in GREEK BUILDING TECHNIQUES), so that it forms a fascinating contrast with the Doric Parthenon just to the south. Ionic in Athens was mainly of the Cycladic type, possessing friezes, but there were important local developments too. For instance, a new base profile was evolved, consisting of convex, concave, and convex elements, and this eventually displaced earlier types.

The influence of Periclean architecture soon spread to other parts of Greece, albeit more slowly to Ionia and very little to Sicily and southern Italy. This could have been through books, like that written by the architect Ictinus on the Parthenon, or by the movement of workmen and architects. Ictinus himself, for instance, is said to have designed the temple of Apollo at Bassai (in Arcadia; *ca.* 430–400 B.C.), and although it is not closely similar to the Parthenon, it shares with it a horseshoe inner colonnade (Ionic and Corinthian, not Doric) and shows a number of other Athenian features. The Corinthian capital, which first appears in a somewhat immature form in the *cella* colonnade at Bassai, was initially used mainly for interiors; in the Roman period it exceeded all other types in popularity. Although its antecedents were mainly Attic, the temple at Bassai seems to stand at the head of a distinctive Peloponnesian school of the fourth and third centuries. The Corinthian capital was developed to something close to its definitive form and was much used for inner colonnades; these were often purely decorative and consisted only of half or three-quarter columns set against a wall. This style, which can be seen in the circular tholos at Delphi, in the fourth- and third-century development of the sanctuary of Asclepius at Epidaurus, and in major temples at Tegea (Piali, in Arcadia) and Nemea (in Argolis), had considerable influence in other areas of Greece, including Macedonia.

Athens in the fourth century lost its former prosperity, and although there are some interesting buildings, like the Corinthian monument of Lysicrates (334 B.C.), a highly decorative little building set up to carry a prize tripod, the Athenians tended to continue fifth-century traditions, sometimes in a frankly retrospective way. A similar backward-looking character can be seen in the architecture of fourth-century Ionia (in western Asia Minor), but here it is revival of archaic ideas since there had been little fifth-century building. The temple of Artemis at Ephesus, destroyed in 356 B.C., was rebuilt virtually to the archaic plan, with the traditional Ephesian type of base and even sculptured column drums. Other Ionian monuments of the period also adopted the specifically Asiatic version of Ionic (with dentils, not frieze). In some respects, however, mainland influence was admitted and can be seen in the fairly general inclusion of an *opisthodomos*. Another feature of the

fourth-century revival in Ionia that broke with archaic practice was a marked rationalism in the plan of formal buildings. This is clearly visible in the small but influential temple of Athena Polius at Priene (Turunçlar, in western Asia Minor; *ca.* 340 B.C.), where all the columns are uniformly spaced, with the square plinths below each column base equaling exactly half the column spacing, and where the wall and column axes all conform to a regular square grid. A similar system governs the huge temple of Apollo at "Didyma" (or Branchidae [Didim] in eastern Asia Minor; late fourth century onward) and this also takes many features from its archaic predecessor; but in the Hellenistic period the grid was often modified by widening the central intercolumniation to emphasize the entrance.

Ionian Developments

There is also a significant difference between the principles of planning on the Greek mainland and in Ionia. In both areas the fourth century saw a growing interest in the formal definition of open spaces, often by means of long stoas. On the mainland each building was treated as a separate entity, as seen in the modifications to the sanctuary of Zeus at Olympia or the Agora at Megalopolis in Arcadia (both mid fourth century), while in Ionia, as in the agora areas of Miletus and Priene (fig. 7) (both later fourth to second century B.C.), the buildings flow into each other without clear boundaries, and porticoes often continue around corners to provide a clearer definition of the space.

Stoas of considerable size and of various sorts—one- and two-aisled, straight and L-shaped, with and without rooms—were common in the fourth century both in sanctuaries and on agoras; the rooms behind the portico might serve as shops or civic offices. Other secular buildings, such as the gymnasium (often with rooms set around a colon-

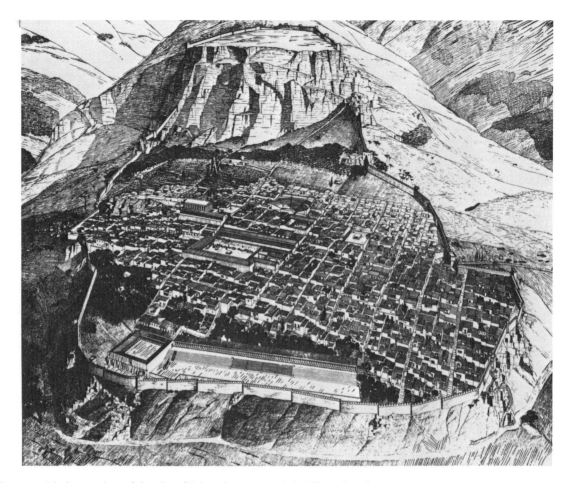

Figure 7. Birds-eye view of the city of Priene in western Asia Minor, late fourth to second century B.C., reconstruction drawing by A. Zippelius. *Reproduced from Martin Schede,* DIE RUINEN VON PRIENE © 1964 BY WALTER DE GRUYTER & CO., BERLIN

naded court), began to attain an established form. One of the most important was the theater. What is known of theaters in the fifth century suggests that although the three elements of orchestra (the area for choral dancing), cavea (audience area), and scene building were present, their form and relation varied from site to site. Only in the mid fourth century (for example, in theaters in Athens, Eretria in Euboea, and Megalopolis) does a clearly defined and popular type emerge, with a circular orchestra, a stone scene building, and more than a semicircle of stone seats rising up the slope of a hillside. At the end of the century the splendidly preserved theater at Epidaurus (fig. 8) already

shows the Hellenistic innovation of a high stage. The stadium, which was a racetrack 600 Greek feet long (about 620 ft. or 186 m) with banks for spectators, also became more formal and might have a vaulted entrance tunnel for the athletes.

Houses became increasingly elaborate in the later fifth and fourth century. Main rooms usually faced south onto a court and included a dining room (*andron*) designed for couches (see fig. 1 in HOUSES). At Olynthus in the Chalcidice (Macedonia) the main rooms formed a row connected by a corridor (*pastas* type, see fig. 2 in HOUSES); at Priene they were set two deep (*prostas* type, see fig. 3 in HOUSES); and at Athens and Eretria

Figure 8. The theater at Epidaurus designed by Polykleitos the Younger, *ca.* 350 B.C., aerial view: *(a)* upper cavea (audience area); *(b)* diazoma (gangway); *(c)* lower cavea; *(d)* orchestra; *(e)* stage buildings. *PHOTO: FATHER RAYMOND V. SCHODER, S.J.* COURTESY OF THE JESUIT COMMUNITY AT LOYOLA UNIVERSITY, CHICAGO

houses based on a colonnaded court (peristyle type) begin to appear.

THE HELLENISTIC PERIOD

After the death of Alexander the Great, the Hellenistic period saw major changes in the geography of Greek architecture. The heartlands of classical Greece generally became unimportant, except as recipients of architectural donations from prestige-hungry monarchs. The cities of Ionia and Rhodes continued to be prosperous and architecturally active, but most of the wealth of the Greek world was controlled by the great Hellenistic kingdoms, with capitals at Pella in Macedonia, Antioch in Syria (modern Antakya, Turkey), and Alexandria in Egypt. The eastward spread of Greek culture exposed Greek architects once more to the influence of Egypt, Mesopotamia,

and Persia. A few motifs, such as the bull's foreparts and some leaf capitals, were borrowed and used sporadically; more important, the preference for an axial arrangement of building complexes that developed in the second century (as in the sanctuaries of Athena at Lindos [Rhodes] and Asclepius at Kos) may have been encouraged by the axiality of Egyptian sanctuaries. In general, however, Hellenistic architecture remained firmly Greek.

Temple building continued to carry high prestige, and colossal temples were begun or continued at Didyma, Sardis (Asia Minor), and Athens, besides many of more normal size. In Ionia, Ionic continued to be popular and had a vocal propagandist in Hermogenes (*ca.* 200 B.C.), who built temples at Teos (Sığacık) and Magnesia ad Maeandrum (near Ortaklar) in western Asia Minor, and whose theories of proportion and temple design were quoted by Vitruvius. Corinthian became increasingly popular, especially in the eastern Mediterranean, and the first Corinthian temples appear. Doric also continued to thrive and became almost universal for secular porticoes.

Secular architecture played an increasing role in this period. Large numbers of new cities were built, and citizens came to expect more elaborate civic amenities—gymnasia, stadia, theaters, council chambers, markets, agoras, and sanctuaries, as well as the massive, towered fortification walls that already in the fourth century were developed to counter increasingly sophisticated siege warfare. Houses also became more monumental, the peristyle type being especially popular (as at Pella in Macedonia, Pergamum, and Delos, which is shown in fig. 4 of HOUSES). To the Greeks, colonnades (fig. 9) in dressed stone were virtually synonymous with formal architecture, and almost all these building types used the traditional orders. The adaptation of forms devised for simple temples to these new needs involved major features such as two-storied facades and smaller ones like half columns and pilasters, and although these had occurred occasionally earlier, they now entered the general repertoire of architecture.

The public budget of a Hellenistic city could rarely cover the quantity of building expected, and in most cases it depended on contributions from wealthy citizens. A whole building might be financed by a single individual and take his name, but the most important architectural patrons were kings who used architecture to promote political

Figure 9. Lower colonnade of the Stoa of Attalos in the Athenian Agora, *ca.* 150 B.C., interior view showing the combination of partially fluted Doric columns on the outside with smooth Ionic support columns inside. Reconstructed in 1953–1956. COURTESY OF THE AMERICAN SCHOOL OF CLASSICAL STUDIES AT ATHENS, AGORA EXCAVATIONS. *PHOTO: ALISON FRANTZ*

ends and project an image of power. Pella has revealed some large and well-decorated houses; Antioch and Alexandria unfortunately lie below modern cities. Scattered architectural elements and some reflections (for example, tomb facades at Petra, Jordan) give tantalizing glimpses of Alexandrian architecture that contrast with the sobriety of the Macedonian architecture so far known. But the only royal capital extensively excavated is Pergamum, the center of a small but proverbially wealthy kingdom in northwest Asia Minor in the later third and second centuries B.C.

Most Hellenistic new cities continued to be based on a rectangular grid plan like those of the archaic and classical periods; but the main streets were now sometimes broadened for effect, as at Alexandria, where they were about 100 feet (30–35 m) wide. However, the hill at Pergamum, rising some 900 feet (275 m) above the surrounding plain, is too steep, and the plan is less rigid, with the main street winding up the southern slopes. The dominating Acropolis (fig. 10) consists of a series of terraces set fanwise around the steeply sloping theater in a way that exploits, but is not just controlled by, the terrain. Although not completely regular, each terrace is a clearly planned entity, and like the theater each is open to the west, making a strong impact on the direction from which travelers would approach the city. But behind this dominating array of public buildings, the modest residences of the "citizen kings" of Pergamum were peristyle houses of the same size and type as those on the slopes below.

The detail too is thoughtfully conceived but, in contrast to the grand general layout, intentionally sober, with Doric the favored order. Corinthian is almost wholly absent, and its place is partly taken by a type of leaf capital that consciously revives a local ar-

Figure 10. The Acropolis of Pergamum in Asia Minor, view from southwest showing the ascending plan of the upper city, *ca.* 200-150 B.C., reconstruction model by H. Schleif. EAST BERLIN, STAATLICHE MUSEEN, ANTIKENSAMMLUNG

chaic form. The main Ionic monument, the great Altar of Zeus, with its writhing frieze of gods and giants (see fig. 15 in GREEK SCULPTURE AND GEMS), follows the Asiatic version of the order; it was probably built to celebrate the Pergamene victory over the Galatians in 166 B.C., which brought Pergamum especially close to the Ionian cities. Thus both in large matters and in small, Pergamum exemplifies the political significance of architecture in the Hellenistic period, an aspect that brings it close to Roman architecture. (Augustus, who wished to present himself as merely first among equals, made much the same point as the Pergamene kings by living in a modest house in Rome.)

Hellenistic architecture may have lacked the perfection of craftsmanship and refined sense of form for which classical Greek architecture is renowned; the enormous output of building almost inevitably meant that the standard of finish declined. But the much greater range and flexibility it developed made Hellenistic architecture the necessary bridge from the Greek to the Roman world and beyond. Although the pedimented colonnade of the Greek temple front was lifted far out of context, it remains to this day a powerful architectural symbol.

BIBLIOGRAPHY

SOURCES

Jerome J. Pollitt, ed., *The Art of Greece, 1400–31 B.C.: Sources and Documents* (1965); Vitruvius Pollio, *The Ten Books on Architecture*, Morris H. Morgan, trans. (1914, repr. 1960).

STUDIES

Birgitta Bergquist, *The Archaic Greek Temenos* (1967); Helmut Berve, Gottfried Gruben, and Max Hirmer, *Greek Temples, Theatres, and Shrines* (1963); Philip P. Betancourt, *The Aeolic Style in Architecture* (1977); Margarete Bieber, *The History of the Greek and Roman Theater*, 2d ed. (rev. ed. 1961); Johannes Boersma, *Athenian Building Policy from 561/0 to 405/4 B.C.* (1970); Philippe Bruneau and Jean Ducat, *Guide de Délos*, 3d ed. (1981); Jens A. Bundgaard, *Mnesicles, A Greek Architect at Work* (1957); Alison Burford, *Greek Temple Builders at Epidauros* (1969); R. M. Cook, "The Archetypal Doric Temple," in *Annual of the British School at Athens*, **65** (1970); J. J. Coulton, *The Architectural Development of the Greek Stoa* (1976), and *Greek Architects at Work*, 2d ed. (1982).

William B. Dinsmoor, "The Gables of the Propylaea," in *American Journal of Archaeology*, **14** (1910), and *The Architecture of Ancient Greece*, 3d ed. (1973); Robert Koldewey and Otto Purchstein, *Die griechische Tempel in Unteritalien und Sicilien* (1899); Arnold W. Lawrence, *Greek Architecture*, 4th ed. rev. by Richard A. Tomlinson (1983); Alfred Mallwitz, *Olympia und seine Bauten* (1972); Roland Martin, *L'Urbanisme dans la Grèce antique*, 2d ed. (1974); James M. Paton, ed., *The Erechtheum* (1927); Francis Penrose, *An Investigation of the Principles of Athenian Architecture*, 2d ed. (1888); William H. Plommer, *Ancient and Classical Architecture* (1956), and "Three Attic Temples," in *Annual of the British School at Athens*, **45** (1950); Mervyn Popham *et al.*, "The Hero of Lefkandi," in *Antiquity*, **56** (1982).

David M. Robinson and J. Walter Graham, *Excavations at Olynthus*, pt. 8: *The Hellenistic House* (1938); Georges Roux, *L'Architecture de l'Argolide aux IVe et IIIe siècles avant J.-C.* (1961); Ione M. Shear, "Kallikrates," in *Hesperia*, **32** (1963); Lucy T. Shoe, *Profiles of Greek Mouldings* (1936); Richard A. Tomlinson, *Greek Sanctuaries* (1976); John Travlos, *Pictorial Dictionary of Ancient Athens* (1971); Theodor Wiegand and Hans Schrader, *Priene: Ergebnisse der Ausgrabungen und Untersuchungen in den Jahren 1895–1898* (1904); Frederick E. Winter, *Greek Fortifications* (1971), and "Tradition and Innovation in Doric Design," in *American Journal of Archaeology*, **80** (1976), **82** (1978), **84** (1980), **86** (1982); Richard E. Wycherley, *How the Greeks Built Cities*, 2d ed. (1962).

Roman Architecture

ROGER LING

THE ROMAN REPUBLIC

Like all aspects of Roman culture, Roman architecture is a diverse field, comprehending many different formal and stylistic currents; the term *Roman* is a convenient peg on which to hang all buildings of any architectural pretension erected in the lands under Roman rule from about the fourth century B.C. to the fourth century A.D. Within this vast area, given the slowness of ancient communications, pronounced regional variations were inevitable; so what is surprising is not the degree of diversity within Roman architecture, but the extent to which common elements united the different regions—for example, building types such as the Roman theater, building techniques such as ashlar masonry and concrete vaulting, and above all the decorative repertoire of the classical columnar orders. Diversity, however, remained an important factor, and one of the recurrent themes of this essay is the interaction of regional strands within the overall framework.

When Rome first came to prominence, the only truly monumental architecture which existed in the Mediterranean basin was that of the Greeks, disseminated by colonization and conquest all along its eastern shores and in scattered pockets along the coasts of southern France and Spain. Rome grew up on the fringes of this civilization and inherited many elements from it, including the columnar orders and ashlar construction. Even after she had become the undisputed mistress of the Mediterranean world, the whole of the eastern part of the empire beyond a line extending roughly from Dalmatia in the north to Cyrenaica in the south remained essentially Greek in culture and thus held comparatively fast to the mainstream tradition of Greek architecture. In the West, however, there developed a new tradition that had its roots in central Italy. This began as a provincial version of Hellenistic architecture, but with an admixture of indigenous elements and, above all, with a new functional and technological flair that made it a perfect tool in the hands of the aspiring world power. From Italy it was carried in the wake of the Roman armies to the northern and western parts of the empire, and it even returned eastward to exert a reciprocal influence in the Greek-speaking lands.

In Italy, where the formative phases of Roman architecture can be traced, the organizational genius and military proclivities of the Roman state were already able by the fourth and third centuries B.C. to express themselves in massive programs of functional and defensive architecture. The so-called Servian Wall of Rome (378 B.C.), constructed in ashlar blocks laid in alternate courses of headers and stretchers, was nearly 6.8 miles (11 km) long and enclosed an area of 1,052 acres (426 hectares); and the military colonies with which the Romans secured their power in central Italy were each provided with impressive fortifications in carefully fitted ashlar or polygonal masonry. Roads, among which the most notable was the Via Appia (begun in 312 B.C.), were constructed to facilitate cross-country communications, often carried on viaducts and arched bridges. The city's water supply was secured by aqueducts such as the Aqua Appia, initiated by the same official as the Via Appia and carefully engineered to achieve a steady gravitational flow. Nor, alongside Rome's functional architecture, were the city's gods neglected. The first major temple of the Capitoline triad (Jupiter, Juno, and Minerva as shown in figure 1) was evidently constructed in the late fifth or early fourth century B.C. and owed much to the Etruscan tradition (which was itself imbued with Greek influence). It consisted of three narrow chambers set flank to flank on a high platform, with a row of columns along each side and a triple colonnade across the front. Here we already have the strong frontal emphasis, reinforced by an approach stairway at the central point, that distinguishes the typical Roman temple from its Greek predecessor; only the low-spreading proportions of the building and its use of a timber and terra-cotta superstructure would have made it appear primitive to later generations.

But the emergence of a distinctive Ro-

Figure 1. The first Capitoline temple in Rome, late fifth or early fourth century B.C., reconstruction model. *GABINETTO FOTOGRAFICO NAZIONALE*

man-Italian style of building belongs to the second century B.C. and is intimately associated with the development of concrete construction. Roman concrete (more strictly mortared rubble) had first appeared in the third century, possibly as an almost accidental by-product of experiments in the pisé technique that was well-established in North Africa (Carthage is said to have had multistoried blocks in this constructional mode). Pisé is a rammed-earth technique in which stiff clay or other cohesive soil is pounded between wooden forms. It received a big impetus when the discovery was made that a mortar mixed with a volcanic earth known as pozzolana possessed extraordinary cohesive powers and the ability to set under water. Although the traditional masonry techniques were retained for buildings of traditional form, concrete found an ideal testing ground in utilitarian architecture. It lent itself above all to vaulted construction, thus avoiding flammable and often costly ceiling timbers, and enabled builders to achieve much greater interior spans than had hitherto been possible. An early beneficiary was a vast warehouse, the Porticus Aemilia, constructed in Rome's dockland in 193 B.C. to house the city's grain supplies; here fifty sets of vaults, each 9 yards (8.3 m) wide, were arranged shoulder to shoulder with interconnecting archways to form a building 533 yards (487 m) long and 66 yards (60 m) deep. A little later the market hall at Ferentinum, southeast of Rome, was constructed with a lofty barrel vault flanked by five lower ones set at right angles to it. These structures were characteristically faced with a network of small irregular fragments of rubble, the so-called *opus incertum.*

By the second half of the century, with ever-increasing intercourse between Italy and the East, the new Italian structural methods began to be combined with the Greek decorative modes to produce a vigorous, independent style of architecture. The evidence from Rome itself is sparse because of later rebuilding, but works of astonishing ambition and maturity were erected in the new style by the wealthy municipalities of central and southern Latium. First in importance was the sanctuary of Fortuna Primigenia at Praeneste (Palestrina) (fig. 2), now dated convincingly to the last decades of the

second century. Here a great axial complex of porticoed terraces was stacked up a hillside, overlooking a plain 1,000 feet (some 300 m) below, and culminating in a semicircular auditorium that formed a kind of prelude to the little cylindrical inner sanctum. Similar schemes with central stairways and ascending terraces had appeared in Greek sanctuaries, but none matched the scale, symmetry, and imperious modeling of the sanctuary at Praeneste. That such grandeur of concept and execution could be attained in Italy was due to the systematic use of concrete, which could be manipulated much more freely than the traditional ashlar (and was thus ideal for shaping platforms on uneven terrain), and which furthermore encouraged an almost industrial style of building in place of the fine craftwork of stonemasons.

The zest of the architect of the Praeneste sanctuary for his medium is shown by bold experiments such as sloping and curving vaults, vaults with recessed coffers (imitating the standard decorative treatment of wooden ceilings), and vaults supported by

Figure 2. The sanctuary of Fortuna Primigenia at Praeneste (Palestrina), late second century B.C., reconstruction model. *FOTOTECA UNIONE, ROME*

colonnades. The combination of vaulting and the Greek columnar orders was a particularly audacious idea and was exploited also in those terraced walls where a series of arched openings was framed by half-columns supporting an entablature in relief. This was to become a favorite motif of Roman architecture. At Praeneste the half-columns were still formed of carefully cut stone drums; but in the sanctuary of Hercules Victor at Tibur (Tivoli), constructed a generation or so later, even this concession to tradition was abandoned and half-columns were fashioned, like the rest of the wall, in concrete with an *opus incertum* facing. The Greek elements here lost all structural significance and became an unashamedly decorative formula designed to articulate a facade.

In Rome the first important surviving structure in the new style is the Tabularium, built in 78 B.C. to house the state archives. In addition to a series of arched openings framed by Doric half-columns and entabulatures, the remains of this building incorporate the earliest known examples of cloister vaults (vaults with four faces that converge) and flat arches (lintels formed of two or more wedge-shaped blocks held in place by a central keystone).

Amid this ferment of structural and stylistic experimentation, various new types of building entered the Roman architectural repertoire. One of the most important was the basilica, a rectangular hall divided into naves and aisles by internal colonnades. Its pedigree is uncertain, but the word *basilica* is Greek, meaning "royal," and the type may have been inspired by some famous hall or portico in a Hellenistic capital. In Italy it generally adjoined the central piazza (forum) of a city and served as an exchange or lawcourt (or both). Little is known about the early examples in Rome—the Porcia, the Aemilia, and the Sempronia—but it is possible to reconstruct the appearance of late-second-century basilicas at Pompeii and Praeneste, where it seems that the clerestory system of lighting familiar in Christian basilicas was not yet employed; the nave and aisles alike were double-storied and light was admitted from windows in the outer wall. A century later, however, the architectural writer Vitruvius accepted the principle of top lighting for the nave as normal. The idea of an apsidal terminus—a semicircular or polygonal projection of the wall—at the narrow end of the basilica did not appear until imperial times, but both Praeneste and Pompeii have yielded, apart from their basilicas, small apsidal halls that served perhaps as council chambers and date from the late second century B.C.; these can be regarded as the forerunners not only of the later apsed basilicas but also of imperial throne rooms.

Another building type to emerge during the late republic was the Roman-style theater. Senatorial prejudice, mistrustful of the political and cultural connotations of the Greek theater, for a long time prevented the construction of a permanent stone building in Rome itself, but such buildings always existed in the Greek cities under Roman sway, and many new ones were put up in areas of Italy during the second and first centuries B.C. They were frequently associated with temples, and when Pompey the Great built the first stone theater in Rome in 55 B.C., one of the means by which he disarmed opposition was to install a small temple, dedicated to Venus Victrix, at the top of the auditorium so that in the Italian manner the entertainments might seem to be presided over by the goddess. Pompey's theater and others after it combined the auditorium and stage building in a single architectural unit, semicircular in plan, which was acoustically superior to the Greek formula (a horseshoe-shaped auditorium and separate, low stage building). More important, taking advantage of Roman concrete,

Pompey's architect was able to build up the auditorium on a network of vaulted substructures instead of cutting it into a hillside. The necessity of Italian builders, who could not always find a convenient slope, was to be turned into a virtue in imperial times when theaters were regularly built on flat land and could therefore be fitted into an urban layout at will, while the substructures were converted into stairways and corridors that enabled spectators to circulate and reach their seats. The supreme example of such mass spectator architecture was the Roman amphitheater, the home of beast hunts and gladiatorial games, evolved by the enlargement of the theater's semicircular auditorium into a circular or elliptical one surrounding a central arena. Although examples had been built in Campania as early as the end of the second century B.C., Rome was again slow to acquire a permanent building. The first recorded, that of Titus Statilius Taurus, dates to 30 B.C.

To this period, finally, belongs the emergence of the Roman-style thermal baths, with rooms of graded heat in the fashion of modern Turkish baths, which are associated with an open exercise area. Although the principle of bath suites with underfloor heating had been introduced in the Hellenistic world, it remained for the Romans to make the heating system more efficient and, with the aid of concrete vaulting, to evolve a formal architectural framework for the type.

AUGUSTUS AND THE JULIO-CLAUDIAN EMPERORS

Roman architecture in a sense came of age with the establishment of the imperial monarchy by Augustus. From then on Rome controlled all the lands around the Mediterranean and many of the empire's principal resources, both material and intellectual, were subservient to the aims and ideals of the state. At the same time, with the free movement of architects and masons in the service of imperial building programs, a still fuller and more fertile exchange of ideas between the East and Italy occurred. The impetus given by Augustus to urbanization in the western provinces led to the adoption of Roman-Italian building types—basilicas and forums, baths, theaters, amphitheaters, aqueducts, columnar temples—in areas previously unaffected by classical architecture.

In Rome itself the beginnings of imperial architecture should be credited to Julius Caesar, whose projects Augustus brought to fruition. Foremost among these was the Forum Julium, first of the imperial fora, a colonnaded piazza decorated with Greek works of art in the tradition of the public porticoes erected *ex manubiis* (from the spoils of war) by triumphant generals. At the rear, placed axially so as to form a dominant focus, was the temple of Venus Genetrix, the mythical ancestress of the Julian family. Little of the original temple survives, but it was possibly the first temple to be executed in the orthodox Roman Corinthian order (see fig. 5 in ROMAN BUILDING TECHNIQUES), with the cornice supported by projecting brackets or modillions.

The subsequent history of Augustan building in the capital was characterized by two leitmotifs: an emphasis on fine marble masonry with exuberant decorative carving, and a periodic flirtation with the forms and motifs of classical Greece. The first theme is illustrated by Augustus' own boast that he found Rome a city of brick (that is, mudbrick) and left it a city of marble. Something of the scale of his achievement can be gauged from the astonishing list of temples which he claims to have built (thirteen in number) or restored (eighty-two), most of which would have involved construction in ashlar. For the style of their ornament we can refer to the remains of monuments such as the emperor's Parthian Arch (*ca.* 20 B.C.) and the temples of Castor and Concord (first decade A.D.), which show an increasing preoccupation with richness and variety of ornament and a bold disregard for the conventions of the classical orders. In contrast, the second theme of Augustan architecture is a classicizing current, demonstrated by borrowings from the monuments of fifth-century Athens. For example the upper story of the porticoes enclosing the Forum Augustum was supported by female statues copied from the caryatids of the Erechtheum in Athens, while Ionic capitals found in the temple of Mars Ultor (dedicated in 2 B.C. and the dominating focus of the new forum) were also inspired by prototypes in the Erechtheum. During Augustus' reign the Erechtheum itself was the subject of restoration work, and its order was reproduced in the small circular temple of Rome and Augustus constructed only a few yards away on the Athenian Acropolis; so it is tempting to argue that the very masons who had worked on these projects were brought to Rome to take part in the forum program.

Another metropolitan structure that reflects strong Athenian influence is the Ara Pacis Augustae, a monumental altar probably modeled on the Altar of Pity in the Athenian Agora and decorated with relief sculptures in the style of contemporary Attic workshops. It would be wrong, however, to think of such works as slavishly imitating their Greek models. The reliefs of the Ara Pacis (see fig. 8 in CLOTHING AND ORNAMENT), for example, are used as the vehicle of a totally new imperial imagery, and the caryatids of the Forum Augustum perform a new function as a kind of decorative screen in front of a continuous wall, in much the same way that Roman architects used the Greek orders to articulate arched facades. A more striking instance of the adaptation of Greek forms is provided by the masonry of the walls of the temple of Mars Ultor, which reproduces precisely a structural syntax familiar in Hellenistic and Roman Asia Minor, but does so partly by means of a superficial veneer of marble imposed upon a basic fabric of inferior stone. This use of veneers and with it an increasing exploitation of colored marbles were to become basic aspects of imperial architectural practice.

Alongside fine masonry construction Augustus' builders did not neglect the concrete medium. The aqueducts built by the emperor's lieutenant Marcus Vipsanius Agrippa to service the capital were made of concrete faced with reticulate masonry— small blocks set so that their exposed square faces formed a network of diamond shapes. Agrippa also certainly employed concrete for the first great public bath building in Rome, the Thermae Agrippae, which possibly incorporated a large domed hall of the type that became important later. The present remains of this structure belong to a later rebuilding, but a more or less contemporary bathing hall at the thermal resort of Baiae (Baia), near Neapolis (Naples), retains its original hemispherical dome, 70.7 feet (21.6 m) in diameter. Among other building types the most interesting monument to exploit concrete vaulting was the Basilica Julia in the Forum Romanum, another project begun by Caesar and completed by Augustus. For the traditional columns and flat ceilings of Republican basilicas this substituted cruciform piers, cloister vaults, and an arcaded facade with framing half-columns.

Outside Italy the impact of Roman architecture was now felt especially in the Alps, Gaul, and North Africa. Gridiron street plans were laid out in Augustan colonies such as Augusta Praetoria (Aosta, northern Italy), Augusta Raurica (Augst, near Basel), and Augustodunum (Autun, east central France); Roman-style temples were erected in cities old and new (for example, the so-called Maison Carrée at Nemausus [Nimes] and the temple of Augustus and Livia at Vienna [Vienne]); commemorative arches were set up at Susa (northern Italy), Glanum (St. Rémy de Provence), and elsewhere; a fine theater, with apsidal recesses and a columnar screen adorning the front of the stage building, was constructed at Lepcis (Leptis) Magna in Tripolitana (Libya). One of the most famous of all Roman utilitarian structures, the Pont du Gard, part of a 31-mile-long (50 km) aqueduct serving the city of Nemausus, also belongs to this phase of urban development. Generally speaking the architecture of Gaul and the Danube and Balkan provinces seems to have been influenced mainly by types current in northern Italy, such as the forum layout with a basilica set transversely across one end and a focal temple placed at the other, or the city gate with an arcaded gallery over the gateways and semicircular or polygonal towers at the sides. In North Africa, on the other hand, influences came chiefly from central and southern Italy; a good example is offered by the African type of bazaar (*macellum*) in which a circular pavilion was set at the center of a court ringed by shops.

After Augustus' intensive and somewhat self-promoting program of public building, the activities of his successors, the Julio-Claudian emperors, might seem by comparison restrained. But in fact they made notable achievements in various fields, especially in the further development of concrete construction, in utilitarian works, and in the evolution of a new semipublic, semiprivate structure, the imperial palace. To their reigns belongs the emergence of concrete faced with brickwork (now of fired bricks, not sun-dried mud-bricks) as a primary building material. The medium of brickwork, more stable, more fire-resistant, and technically easier to handle than previous types of facing, was ideally suited to large-scale and functional buildings; the first major projects to exploit it were the

barracks of the imperial bodyguard (the Castra Praetoria) and Tiberius' palace on the Palatine Hill in Rome. Utilitarian works are chiefly associated with the reign of Claudius, who built new aqueducts for Rome and constructed a new imperial port at Ostia. This emperor's antiquarian spirit is perhaps reflected in the prominence given to ashlar masonry, often deliberately left unsmoothed to produce a curious uncouth rustication.

His successor, Nero, carried on the rusticated style, for instance in the substructures of the temple of Claudius; but he is chiefly renowned for his fabulous pleasure palace, the Golden House (fig. 3). In contrast to the first imperial palaces, built by Tiberius on the Palatine and on the island of Capreae (Capri), both probably enclosed, broadly rectangular blocks rising two or more stories in height, Nero's took the form of a deluxe country villa transported to the city. The main residence, which is partially preserved on the Esquiline Hill under the later Baths of Trajan, spread out expansively with a south-facing colonnaded front (fig. 3a) overlooking an artificial lake, while the whole of the visible landscape was converted, with a blithe disregard of the interests of previous landowners, into the emperor's private park. The wonders of the house—including ceilings that sprinkled perfumes and flowers on diners below, a dome that revolved continually in imitation of the heavens, and decorations "all smeared with gold and picked out with jewels"—were what impressed the ancient writers; but more significant is the evidence that it offers of contemporary structural experimentation and of the new flexibility of planning made possible by a greater familiarity with the concrete medium. At the focal point of the east wing was an octagonal room (fig. 3e) whose walls were pierced by wide openings so that the crowning dome was effectively supported on the eight angle piers (reinforced by buttressing walls behind); light was admitted both directly through a central circular skylight and indirectly via the adjoining rooms. Less daring but equally unconventional (at least in monumental public architecture in the capital) was the five-sided court (fig. 3d) scalloped back between the east and west wings. These new shapes and volumes were not as yet properly reconciled with the rectangular framework of the palace, as can be seen from the awkward, nonfunctional triangular spaces left over; but they represent an important pointer to the future. Later builders were able to solve the problems that had been raised and to create a fully integrated architecture of rectangular, curvilinear, and polygonal forms.

THE MIDDLE EMPIRE: THE FLAVIAN AND ANTONINE EMPERORS

If the Augustan period saw the coming of age of Roman architecture, the period from the accession in A.D. 69 of Vespasian, first of

the Flavian line, to the assassination of Commodus in 192 brought it to full maturity. During these four generations builders in Roman Italy achieved a more or less complete mastery of concrete construction, now generally brick-faced, apart from a brief revival of reticulate masonry under Trajan and Hadrian. In buildings such as the Colosseum they brought about a perfect marriage of the two traditions, ashlar and concrete, the former being used in the main supporting roles and for outward show, the latter reserved for internal divisions and vaulting. Construction entirely in ashlar tended to lose ground, even in temple architecture, to concrete with a stone facing or marble veneer (for example, in the Hadrianic Capitolium at Ostia): only in parts of the empire where fine stone was plentiful and easily accessible, as at Athens and in Asia Minor, or where the available mortar was of poor quality, as in North Africa and southern Gaul (and Asia Minor again), did the traditional cut-stone techniques prevail.

But fine stone was universally in demand for columns and where an impressive finish was desired—even if that finish was to be merely skin-deep. It is in this context that we

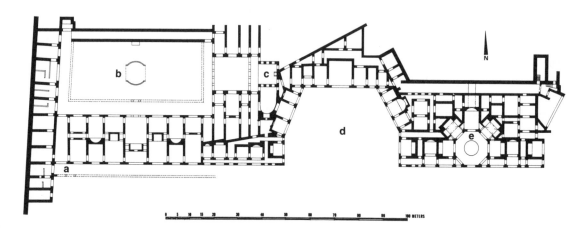

Figure 3. The Domus Aurea (Nero's Golden House) in Rome, A.D. 64–68, plan: *(a)* colonnaded south front; *(b)* peristyle courtyard with central fountain basin; *(c)* artificial grotto or nymphaeum; *(d)* five-sided court; *(e)* octagonal room with oculus (circular skylight). *Reproduced from William L. MacDonald,* THE ARCHITECTURE OF THE ROMAN EMPIRE © 1965 BY YALE UNIVERSITY

must see the vast increase in marble production that took place during the first and early second centuries A.D. and the accompanying internationalization, probably under direct imperial patronage, of the trade in fine building stone of all sorts. Colored materials—the gray and pink granites and porphyry (red basalt) of Egypt, the rich yellow marble (giallo antico) of Simitthus (Chemtou, Tunisia), the serpentine of southern Greece, the green and white marble (cipollino) of Euboea—now became readily available in Rome and other major centers, while the white marbles of Attica and Proconnesus Island in the Propontis (Sea of Marmara) were quarried and marketed on a scale that answered the needs of much of the empire. This new situation had two important corollary effects. First, architectural elements, especially columns, tended to be prefabricated to set sizes and stockpiled in yards until such time as they were needed, a practice that inevitably restricted the freedom of the architect and thus sounded the death knell of the Greek type of columnar architecture, based as it was on a tradition of improvization and fine attunement of proportions. Henceforth the emphasis was placed on grandeur of scale, on contrasts of color, and on elaboration of surface effects. Second, since in ancient as in modern times masons preferred to work the stones to which they were accustomed, unworked or half-worked blocks of marble were accompanied from the quarries to their ultimate destinations by specialist craftsmen who took their styles of carving with them. This more than any other factor contributed to the breakdown of regional differences in architectural decoration and to the emergence of something approaching an imperial style. A vivid example of the movement of craftsmen is provided by the decorative detail of Hadrian's temple of Venus and Rome in Rome, which reveals the direct involvement of eastern stonecarvers, possibly the same men who had worked on

the decoration of the temple of Trajan at Pergamum (Bergama) in Asia Minor.

Among the great monuments of the capital during this period pride of place must go to the Flavian amphitheater, or Colosseum (fig. 4), the masterpiece of its genre, with an auditorium that held about 50,000 spectators and a superbly effective distribution system of corridors and stairways. It inspired a number of amphitheaters elsewhere in Italy and the western provinces, such as those in Verona, Arelate (Arles), and Nemausus. Another important metropolitan building was the last and greatest of the imperial palaces in Rome, that built by Domitian (A.D. 81–96). Terraced into the southern part of the Palatine Hill, this roughly 650-foot (60 m²) square complex was divided into clearly differentiated official and private quarters, and it already announces some of the architectural features that were to characterize late imperial palaces, such as the basilica and audience chamber, each with an apse for the emperor's throne, and a private box overlooking the Circus Maximus. A third major project, apparently begun by Domitian and bequeathed to Trajan to complete, was a new forum complex that set the seal on the development of Roman imperial forums (see fig. 4 in ROMAN BUILDING TECHNIQUES), in much the same way as Domitian's palace had done for the emperor's official residence. Laid out in strict symmetry along one main axis, the complex consisted of four elements: the forum proper with a statue of the emperor at its center, set crosswise behind it the great Basilica Ulpia, the Column of Trajan with its famous spiraling band of reliefs overlooked to left and right by two-storied libraries, and finally, not completed until the time of Hadrian, a horseshoe-shaped court enclosing the temple of the Deified Trajan. Particularly significant is the combination of the forum with a transverse basilica at the rear, a formula that seems to have come to Rome from northern Italy and the western

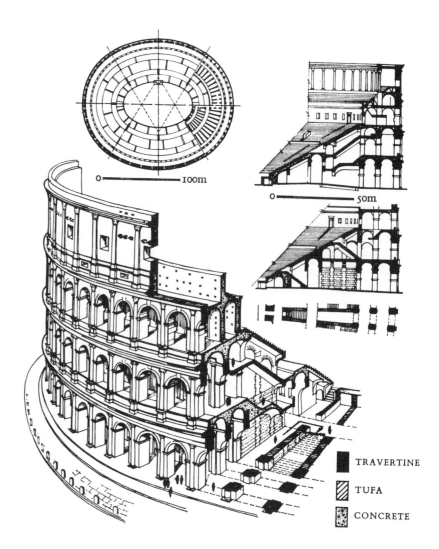

Figure 4. The Amphitheatrum Flavium (Colosseum) in Rome, inaugurated in A.D. 80, plan and sectional view. *Reproduced from Axel Boëthius and J. B. Ward-Perkins,* ETRUSCAN AND ROMAN ARCHITECTURE © 1970 BY THE ESTATE OF AXEL BOËTHIUS AND J. B. WARD-PERKINS

TRAVERTINE

TUFA

CONCRETE

provinces; from now on provincial influences were to become increasingly important in the architecture of the capital.

On a more mundane level, but hardly less significant in the history of Roman architecture, the mid-imperial period saw the technique of brick-faced concrete acquiring its own aesthetic. This can be seen, for example, in Trajan's so-called markets (see fig. 12 in ROMAN BUILDING TECHNIQUES), an aggregation of shops and offices that climbed the hill to the northeast of the new forum. On the one hand this complex, in which the basic unit was the simple wide-doored and barrel-vaulted shop (*taberna*), showed an as-

tonishing flexibility of planning, molding itself to the various levels and angles of a site of unpromising shape and configuration. On the other hand it received a new kind of surface decoration, a delicate play of shallow pilasters and pediments (segmental, triangular, and broken) that framed the openings in much the same way as the applied orders of monumental ashlar facades. Here the brickwork was probably stuccoed over, but elsewhere builders exploited color contrasts between bricks of different type. A good example appears in the little chamber tomb outside Rome popularly known as the Tempio del Dio Redicolo, in which a scheme

1680

Figure 5. Interior of the Pantheon erected by Hadrian *ca.* A.D. 118–128 in Rome, painted by Giovanni Paolo Pannini before 1747. WASHINGTON, D.C., NATIONAL GALLERY OF ART, SAMUEL H. KRESS COLLECTION

of pilasters, half-octagonal columns, niches, and decorative friezes and cornices of molded terra-cotta is carried out in red and buff on a yellow background.

The most important achievements of the age, however, were in the field of curvilinear and domed architecture. Already the palace of Domitian shows a new facility in the integration of curvilinear and rectilinear shapes; particularly successful was a domed octagonal room in which broad rectangular bays alternated with apsidal niches, the latter neatly fitted in the angles of an overall rectangular framework. But something of a climax was reached in the reign of Hadrian (A.D. 117–138) with the concrete domed construction of his buildings in Rome, Baiae, and Tibur. In Rome the hemispherical dome of the Pantheon (fig. 5) had a 142-foot (43.2-m) span that remained unsurpassed until modern times; it was supported by a massive drum of concrete whose upper part acted as a buttress to the outward thrust, while the weight of the dome itself was reduced by diminishing its thickness toward the central point and by carefully grading the aggregate used in the concrete (the topmost parts contain pumice). The result was a vast unencumbered interior which now received much of the decorative emphasis previously reserved for exteriors— the walls dissolved in a play of alternate columnar recesses and projecting tabernacles (aediculae), all enhanced by colored marble veneers; the floor paved with a great checkerboard pattern, again of colored marbles; and the dome punctuated by concentric rows of sunken coffers, presumably once stuccoed, gilded, and adorned with bronze rosettes. By contrast the exterior was plain, a stuccoed cylinder broken only by a couple of projecting cornices; the sole concession to traditional appearances was the pedimented porch, which seems almost irrelevant to the rotunda behind it.

At Baiae and Tibur the domed structures were smaller but in some respects more daring. The so-called temple of Venus at Baiae, actually an octagonal bathing hall that perhaps formed part of an imperial villa, was covered by a dome with sixteen alternate flat and concave segments; the walls were taller than those of the Pantheon and were pierced by windows immediately below the impost. In the emperor's villa at Tibur, a vast landscaped complex barely 12 miles (20 km) from Rome, the same alternation of flat and concave segments found at Baiae is echoed in the semidome of the Serapeum, while simpler forms of "melon" or "pumpkin" vault occur in various smaller rooms. The Tibur villa is in fact a veritable compendium of all that was avant-garde in contemporary architecture: the interlocking of rectilinear and curvilinear forms, the play of curve and countercurve, the thoroughgoing integration of buildings and pools of water. Most important, the builders' total mastery of the concrete medium was accompanied by a willingness for it to dictate its own aesthetic. In the vestibule of the Piazza d'Oro, for example, an octagonal chamber whose walls were opened, like those of the similar room in Domitian's palace on the Palatine in Rome, in an alternation of rectangular and apsidal recesses was no longer set within a square shell or surrounded by rectangular rooms, but frankly avowed its structural "modernity": the exterior was formed simply by the backs of the internal recesses. Under Hadrian the new interiors were beginning to mold the outward appearances of Roman buildings.

Another important trend, this time centered on the eastern provinces, was the adaptation or reinterpretation of the traditional vocabulary of the classical orders to create new, almost "baroque" forms. One is the so-called Syrian arch, a device whereby the central intercolumniation beneath a pediment is spanned by an arch in lieu of a straight lintel. In the true form, illustrated by the monumental entrance to the sanctuary of Jupiter at Heliopolis (Baalbek, Lebanon) and by the facade of the tiny temple of Hadrian at Ephesus, the whole of the architrave arches up into the pediment; but a variant represented by a small temple at Termessos in Pamphylia (southern Asia Minor), as shown in figure 6, has the architrave broken with a separate, smaller arch springing above the gap. It was not a far step to the arcaded colonnade, that is, a colonnade supporting a continuous series of arches. Isolated examples had appeared in domestic architecture in Roman Italy, the arches carried out in mortared rubblework, before the destruction of Pompeii in A.D. 79; but the first attested use of the motif in stone and in monumental architecture belongs to the last years of Hadrian, when it was incorporated in the gigantic temple dedicated to the em-

Figure 7. The Library of Celsus at Ephesus, facade, *ca.* A.D. 117–120. *PHOTO: V. M. STROCKA*

Figure 6. The temple at Termessos in Pamphylia (Asia Minor), second century A.D., drawing by G. Niemann. *Reproduced from Karl Lanckoronski, George Niemann, and Eugen Petersen,* STÄDTE PAMPHYLIENS UND PISIDIENS (1890–1892)

peror at Cyzicus (Balkız) on the Propontis.

Another favorite formula of the new "baroque" architecture, used both internally and externally, was a wall decorated with a columnar screen, often in two or more stories, in which the entablatures advanced and receded over the columns so as to create an ambivalent relationship between the two planes. This effect could be combined with *aediculae,* in which the pediments were triangular, segmental, or balanced in two broken halves. In the most exuberant examples, including the fountain building (nymphaeum) at Miletus and the facade of the Library of Celsus at Ephesus (fig. 7), the ambivalence of planes was compounded with an ambivalence in the vertical dimension, the *aediculae* of the upper story being staggered so as to straddle the spaces between those below. Some of these features, such as the arched intercolumniation, the broken pediment, and the jutting entablature, had been shown in Pompeian wall paintings of the mid first century B.C. and may ultimately have derived from the architecture of Ptolemaic Egypt; but it was only in the second century A.D. that they seem to have won more widespread acceptance in Roman monumental architecture.

FROM SEVERUS TO CONSTANTINE

The period from the accession of Septimius Severus in A.D. 193 to the death of Constantine I in 337 represents the transition to late antiquity: the emperor now became increasingly an absolute monarch, his military power base more overtly stated, and his authority reinforced by religious sanction. The dominant role of Rome was attenuated with the growth of provincial capitals, first for Diocletian's system of collegiate emperors (the tetrarchy) at the end of the third century, then with Constantine's creation of a rival capital (Nova Roma) at Constantinople, formerly Byzantium. The historical situation was naturally reflected in contemporary architecture, which became more clearly propagandist, for example, in its scale and its use of sculpture to glorify the emperor. Further, major imperial building programs were launched in new centers such as Leptis Magna under Septimius Severus; Mediolanum (Milan), Treviri (formerly Augusta Treverorum, now Trier), Sirmium (Sremska, in northern Yugoslavia), and Thessalonica (Thessaloniki, Salonica) under the tetrarchs; and of course Constantinople under Constantine. At the same time there was a new emphasis on fortified architecture, occasioned by the emperor's personal insecurity in a period of repeated internal wars and by the weakness of the northern and eastern frontiers in the face of constant pressures from outside peoples (Rome itself received a new circuit of walls in the 270s, the first since the Servian Wall more than

600 years earlier). Finally, Constantine's adoption of Christianity inaugurated the age of official Christian buildings, first among which were the great basilica churches of Rome itself.

Much of the architectural language of the third century had been heralded in the Antonine age (A.D. 138–192). The idea of arcaded colonnades, for instance, was taken up in the Severan forum at Leptis Magna and later in Diocletian's palace near Salonae (Split, Yugoslavia). Architectural ornament, developing from the coloristic carving of Antonine temples, acquired a striking black and white effect, due to increasing reliance on the drill without the modulations of chiselwork; by the time of Constantine this had declined into a lifeless, almost abstract play of inorganic forms. A similar development characterizes the sculptural decoration that adorned the monuments of the period, but here the declining skill of craftsmen was acknowledged by the designers of Constantine's triumphal arch in Rome, for which the most prominent reliefs (see fig. 11 in ROMAN SCULPTURE AND GEMS) were plundered from second-century buildings. The heyday of sculptural decoration was the Severan period (A.D. 193–235), during which the marble monuments not only of the capital (the Arch of Septimius Severus in the Forum Romanum and the Gate of the Silversmiths) but also of Leptis Magna (the forum, basilica, arch, and fountain building) were richly bedizened with figure reliefs and foliage.

The Severan program of building at Leptis Magna also provides the most vivid testimony of the movement of stonemasons in imperial times, since it incorporates not only lotus and acanthus capitals of Attic style carved in Pentelic marble but also fluting and acanthus capitals of Asiatic type carved in Proconnesian marble, not to mention many other elements typical of western Asia Minor. The Greek origins of the craftsmen are confirmed by inscribed signatures.

Nonetheless, while the layout of the forum and basilica complex and the form of the temple dedicated to the Severan family were indebted to the architecture of Roman Italy, the materials employed came not only from the quarries of Attica and Proconnesus, but also from those of Euboea (cipollino), Egypt (granite), and Tripolitana itself (the yellowish local limestone). Thus the Leptis program can be regarded as truly international, the most eloquent statement of the pooling of resources that was one of the major consequences of imperial patronage.

Monumental architecture in brick-faced concrete during this period is best represented by the great thermal complexes (fig. 8) built for the urban masses in Rome by two soldier-emperors of the beginning and end of the third century, Caracalla and Diocletian. These were the culmination of a tradition stretching back to the public baths of the early emperors, notably Nero, Titus, and Trajan, but in scope and scale they far exceeded their predecessors. In each case the actual bath block was merely part of a huge amenity center including gardens, libraries, lecture halls, exercise areas, and the like, all enclosed by a boundary wall. But it was the bath building that formed the architectural showpiece, now laid out de rigueur in a rigidly symmetrical plan about the minor axis and orientated to face southwest so that the hot rooms were flooded with the light and heat of the afternoon sun. The shorter axis was occupied by a large swimming pool (fig. 8a), its walls enlivened with statue niches

Figure 8. The Baths of Caracalla in Rome, *ca.* A.D. 212–216, reconstruction drawing by C. V. Rauscher: *(a)* swimming pool *(natatio); (b)* the cold room *(frigidarium); (c)* the principal hot room *(caldarium); (d)* colonnaded games courts *(palaestrae). Reproduced from Josef Durm, DIE BAUKUNST DER ETRUSKER, DIE BAUKUNST DER RÖMER, HANDBUCH DER ARCHITEKTUR II.2 (1905)*

and large apsidal recesses, and by the normal Roman sequence of three rooms of ascending heat, culminating in the principal hot room (*caldarium*) (fig. 8c), which here jutted from the main block to secure maximum lighting. The other major element in the plan was a pair of identical colonnaded games courts (*palaestrae*) (fig. 8d), one in either half of the block; the remaining spaces were filled by various service rooms, changing rooms, lavatories, and offices. In all this there was a careful interlocking of elements to make full use of the available space, and everything focused upon a central hall (the cold room, or *frigidarium*) (fig. 8b) with a series of three soaring cross-vaults springing from monolithic columns. Something of the original effect of these great halls can be gauged from the *frigidarium* of Diocletian's Baths, later remodeled by Michelangelo as the Church of Santa Maria degli Angeli; but much is still missing—the gleaming mosaics

of the vaults, the vistas of further rooms along each axis (now closed off), and the decorative statuary, which, like the so-called Farnese Hercules and Farnese Bull in the Baths of Caracalla, would have been appropriately scaled to the context. The importance of statues and statue niches in Roman interiors is often forgotten.

The constructional principle of the triple-vaulted *frigidarium,* in which light was admitted through clerestory windows in the lunettes and buttressing was provided by lower vaults set at right angles to the main hall, reappears in the last major pagan building of Rome, the Basilica Nova (fig. 9), begun by Maxentius and completed by Constantine. Here the central hall was the nave, and the side vaults took the place of aisles (in effect they were separate bays, but large arched openings offered direct passage between them). Again the medium of brick-faced concrete enabled the architect to cre-

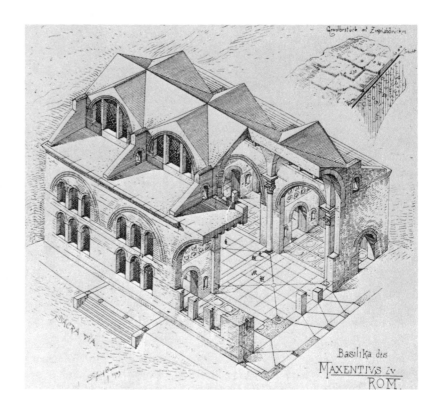

Figure 9. The Basilica of Maxentius (originally called the Basilica Nova) in Rome, begun A.D. 307–312, completed by Constantine after 312, reconstruction drawing. *Reproduced from Josef Durm,* DIE BAUKUNST DER ETRUSKER, DIE BAUKUNST DER RÖMER, HANDBUCH DER ARCHITEKTUR *II.2 (1905)*

ate a vast unobstructed interior, within which we have to imagine the effect of colored wall veneers and marble paving. The vaults were decorated, in a tradition going back via the Pantheon and Domitian's palace to the republican sanctuary at Praeneste, with recessed coffers, here octagonal in shape. Originally the basilica was planned with an entrance and anteroom (narthex) at the east and with the emphasis upon the longitudinal axis; but Constantine turned the building through ninety degrees by putting the main entrance in front of the central bay of the south aisle and opening an apse in the central bay of the north aisle to serve as the setting for a gigantic seated statue of the emperor. This statue, godlike and impersonal, is a fitting comment upon the transformation that had taken place in the emperor's role since the time of Augustus (the "first citizen") and upon the way in which an architectural setting could be employed to display and enhance that role.

Outside Rome two important residential buildings may be selected to illustrate changing styles of architecture in the fourth century. In the relative security of Sicily a Roman aristocrat laid out a luxury villa at Piazza Armerina (near ancient Philosophiana, as shown in fig. 7 of HOUSES) with all the freedom of planning shown by Hadrian's villa at Tibur two centuries earlier; if anything, the shifting of axes is more deliberate, since it occurs within a comparatively restricted area and is not dependent on the shape of the terrain. Curvilinear, including elliptical, forms are more dominant than at Tibur and an important newcomer is the trefoil dining hall (triconch), a feature found also in other fourth-century villas of the western empire, for example at Decentianum (Desenzano del Garda in northern Italy) and at Littlecote in Britain. In sharp contrast to the untrammeled spirit of Piazza Armerina, the palace built for Diocletian's retirement at Salonae (fig. 10) was almost

literally a fortress. It had a fortress' rectangular plan and was enclosed by lofty defensive walls equipped, in third- and fourth-century manner, with bastions for artillery engines. Its internal layout was formulated along military lines with axial roads forming a central T-junction behind which lay (in the place normally allocated to a fort's headquarters building) the main palace block. The fortress form, dictated chiefly by the insecurity of the northern provinces, was however combined with an elaboration of architectural detail that no fortress would have admitted. Arched entablatures were used at several points and in various ways: a Syrian arch above the palace entrance, an arcaded colonnade along either side of its

Figure 10. The Palace of Diocletian near Salonae (Split, Yugoslavia), *ca.* A.D. 300–306, restored view of the Porta Aurea (north gate). *PHOTO: ZVONIMIR BULJEVIĆ*, COURTESY OF THE INSTITUTE FOR THE PROTECTION OF MONUMENTS OF CULTURE, SPLIT

forecourt, and (a particularly baroque detail) an arcade in relief carried on columns bracketed out from the wall above the north gate.

To these eastern devices can be added another: the brick vaulting of Diocletian's mausoleum, which stood in the southeast quadrant of the fortified enclosure. Brick vaults, originally invented in the mud-brick architecture of ancient Egypt and Mesopotamia, were occasionally used in Asia Minor in the mid imperial period, for example, in the dome of the second-century temple of Asclepius at Pergamum; and by the time of the tetrarchs they had reached Galerius' capital, Thessalonica, as well as Salonae. The specimen in Diocletian's mausoleum was remarkably sophisticated, because of the way in which the bricks were set—in a series of fans arranged fishscale-fashion and converging toward the crown. Alongside such eastern features were others whose origins are likely to have lain in the West. The internal plan of the mausoleum, like those of Galerius' mausoleum and of an octagonal hall in his palace at Thessalonica, adopted the familiar Roman-Italian arrangement of eight radial niches: a room within the main palace block took the form of an audience hall of western type with an apse at one end; and along the whole of the south front, overlooking the sea, ran a series of arched windows framed by an engaged order—the Italian motif that we saw first at Praeneste. It is, however, symbolic of the new cosmopolitan architecture that the architrave of the engaged order swung upward at certain strategic points, Syrian style, to form an arch: eastern and western details were now blended in a common architectural repertoire.

EPILOGUE

Within sixty years of Constantine's death the empire was split irrevocably into two halves, and during the following century the western half finally disintegrated. But countless Roman buildings remained standing as an example to future generations, and the living tradition of architecture, especially early Christian architecture, frequently turned back to Roman models for inspiration. In the East the Roman gave way to the Byzantine Empire, and the eastern imperial tradition of architecture was developed in the service of a new theocratic world. What main contributions, we may ask, did Rome make to early Christian and Byzantine architecture, and ultimately to that of more recent times?

One contribution was obviously in building types. The triconch of late pagan villas was taken up by architects at Ravenna and Constantinople in secular contexts, and it was also used for a number of early Christian churches in Egypt and Asia Minor. The semicircular porticoed forecourt, a feature found in the villa at Piazza Armerina and in metropolitan buildings such as the early fourth-century "temple of Romulus" in Rome reappeared at Constantinople in the palaces of the Byzantine emperors. The apsed audience hall also continued into the architecture of early Christian times, appearing, for example, again at Ravenna. The most important survivor of all, however, was the basilica, whose architectural form, together with an apsidal terminus, was copied for Constantine's great churches in Rome and subsequently for many other western and eastern churches. But this was not the only form of church indebted to pagan prototypes. Others developed from the domed rotunda or octagon, a type that had become especially favored for late pagan mausolea, some of which were themselves converted into churches. The mausoleum of Constantine's daughter Constantina, later the Church of Santa Costanza in Rome, initiated an important series by adding an arcaded ambulatory to the rotunda: churches such as those of Santo Stefano Rotondo in Rome and San Vitale at Ravenna were merely elaborations upon this basic theme.

Materials and techniques, notably fired bricks and brick-faced concrete, are an equally obvious and important contribution of Rome to her successors. The outstanding role of concrete was in the creation of vaults and domes, with all their attendant potentiality for the enlargement and modeling of interior space. Here lay Rome's great legacy to posterity. Although later architects used different structural methods, buildings as far afield as the Taj Mahal and St. Paul's in London are the ultimate heirs of the Roman tradition. In Byzantine times the locus classicus for this type of construction is Justinian I's Church of the Holy Wisdom (Santa Sophia, Hagia Sophia) in Constantinople, in which a huge central dome, constructed in mortared brickwork in the Asian manner, rises above a 100-foot-wide (30.5 m) nave; the transition between the angles of the supporting piers and the circle of the dome is effected by pendentives—spherical triangles formed by the intersection of the dome with two adjacent arches—a device never successfully accomplished by the Romans. Domed and vaulted interiors, now regularly provided with clerestory windows and thus attaining greater height than many of their Roman predecessors, created an appropriately majestic and awe-inspiring setting for the new religion. While the Byzantine world passed the dome on to the mosques and tombs of Turkey and other Islamic lands, in the West the architects of Renaissance Italy created it anew under the influence of their humanistic studies and of the surviving Roman examples, especially the Pantheon. They set it over the crossings of their churches and in the boldest examples, such as Michelangelo's dome for St. Peter's in Rome, crowned it with a stone-built lantern.

In terms of architectural decoration, Rome gave Byzantine and early Christian architecture the arcaded colonnade, but the details of the classical orders and of their carved ornament were soon stylized or transformed into new patterns. It was only with the various classical revivals, or "renaissances," that more literal transcriptions of these details occurred. The influence of Rome, as exemplified above all by the Corinthian and "Tuscanic" orders (the latter a native Italian version of Doric established in the peninsula before the direct copying of classical Doric in Roman times), was paramount in the Italian Renaissance of the late fifteenth and sixteenth centuries. Later, in the neoclassical period, the influence of classical Greece and of the Doric and Ionic orders gained ascendancy for a time. But the most specifically Roman contribution to the history of decoration lay in the treatment of surfaces, and especially interior surfaces. The marble veneers and mosaics, the applied half-columns and small ornamental tabernacles, the general play of light and color that characterize the interiors of churches from the Byzantine to the Baroque eras are indebted in greater or lesser degree to the architects of ancient Rome. This type of decoration was an almost inevitable concomitant of the structural liberation obtained by the use of concrete vaults, and once again we return to the basic revolution achieved by the Romans. By breaking free from the tyranny of flat ceilings and internal supports, they created an architecture in which external form became less important than the manipulation and embellishment of the interior.

BIBLIOGRAPHY

SOURCES

Vitruvius Pollio, *The Ten Books on Architecture*, Morris H. Morgan, trans. (1914; repr. 1960), and *De Architectura*, Frank Granger, ed. and trans., 2 vols. (1931–1934).

GENERAL STUDIES

Axel Boëthius, *Etruscan and Early Roman Architecture,* 2d ed. rev. by Roger Ling and Tom Rasmussen (1978); Frank E. Brown, *Roman Architecture* (1961); Ferdinando Castagnoli, *Orthogonal Town Planning in Antiquity,* Victor Caliandro, trans. (1971); Luigi Crema, *L'architettura romana, Enciclopedia classica* III, **12** (1959); *Enciclopedia dell' arte antica: classica e orientale,* 7 vols. (1958–1973), excellent articles on building types and sites; Margaret Lyttelton, *Baroque Architecture in Classical Antiquity* (1974); William L. Macdonald, *The Architecture of the Roman Empire,* I (1965; 2d ed. 1982); Friedrich Rakob, "Römische Architektur," in Theodor Kraus, ed., *Das römische Weltreich* (1967); Giovanni T. Rivoira, *Roman Architecture and its Principles of Construction under the Empire,* G. M. Rushforth, trans. (1925); Donald S. Robertson, *A Handbook of Greek and Roman Architecture* (1929; 2d rev. ed. 1943); Frank B. Sear, *Roman Architecture* (1982); John B. Ward-Perkins, "From Republic to Empire: Reflections on the Early Provincial Architecture of the Roman West," in *Journal of Roman Studies,* **60** (1970), *Cities of Ancient Greece and Italy: Planning in Classical Antiquity* (1974), *Roman Architecture* (1977), and *Roman Imperial Architecture* (1981).

STUDIES OF SELECTED SITES

Ranucchio Bianchi Bandinelli, ed., *The Buried City: Excavations at Leptis Magna* (1966); Ernest Nash, *A Pictorial Dictionary of Ancient Rome,* 2d ed., 2 vols. (1968), with full bibliography of the monuments; Friedrich Ragette, *Baalbek* (1980); John Travlos, *Pictorial Dictionary of Ancient Athens* (1971), includes full bibliography of the Roman monuments in Athens.

Urban Planning

THOMAS D. BOYD

GREEK CITIES

Urbanism in antiquity had its roots in Mesopotamia, preceding the world of the Greeks and the Romans by several millennia. Only in the eighth century B.C., as the Greeks emerged from the post-Bronze Age collapse, did the characteristic patterns of Greek urban life take shape. Towns and cities grew up where water and arable land were available in sufficient quantity and where economic and strategic factors favored their growth. A city regularly included an acropolis, fortified and generally housing shrines; if not in the center of the city as in Athens, it would be nearby and readily accessible as in Corinth. Rarely, however, did an acropolis house the chief temples of a city, and only by accident of topography did this come to be the case in Athens. The basis of Greek urban life was the polis, a term we translate as city, but which in fact had a broader meaning than the physical entity the English term is generally taken to mean. To the Greeks a polis was also the functioning body of participating citizens with their vital institutions. At the heart of a polis was the agora, a term originally meaning a gathering place. It took the form of a large open space, usually in a central location, and was the setting for the market, for administrative facilities, and for the lively political activity of the citizenry. So fundamental was an agora to a polis that when he traveled to Panopeus in central Greece, Pausanias (10.4.1) questioned whether it should be considered a true polis, for it lacked, among other urban amenities, an agora.

It was by the eighth century B.C. also that the Greeks had significantly expanded their maritime trading horizons, becoming increasingly aware of the older civilizations of the Near East. The knowledge of these cultures was opened up to them and the early Greeks eagerly absorbed it in the arts, the sciences, and in the practice of writing. At this time, furthermore, the remarkable phenomenon of Greek colonization began, and colonists were sent out to the west, to North Africa, and to the Black Sea region. It would be difficult to imagine that the Near East had nothing to contribute to the Greeks in these early urban enterprises. Planning played a role in ancient Near Eastern cities, at least to the extent of the principle of the orthogonal (right-angled gridlike) layout that was destined to become the underlying principle in the planning of Greek cities. The Assyrians, dominant in Mesopotamia and the Levant at the time of the colonial expansion of the Greeks, imposed their sense of order; at Nimrud, for example, as later at Babylon and Megiddo, we see elements of orthogonal layouts. The advantages of this simple and practical approach were employed, perhaps not coincidentally, in some of the earliest Greek colonial cities.

The founding of a colony afforded the opportunity to build or at least to plan for the future growth of an entirely new city. The conditions in a new colony would have been pressing, particularly at a previously unoccupied site, for the entire population would have to be accommodated rapidly and efficiently. We must assume that the *oikist* (the leader of a colonial expedition) was responsible for organizing and supervising the land distribution. Among Greeks there was a keen sense of equality among members of the citizen class, and this would have been particularly acute among members of a new colony. The *oikist* must then have seen to the appropriate division of both urban and rural land, although this was not his sole responsibility. If we turn to the Greek literature contemporary with the earliest colonies we see a personification of the *oikist* in a passage from Homer: "God-like Nausithous urged them to get up and move to Scheria, far from men who profit by their toil. Around their city he built a wall, built houses, and set up temples to the gods; and the land he divided into lots" (*Odyssey* 6.7–11). This part of the description of the mythical land of the Phaeacians delineates, in the person of Nausithous, the range of the powers and responsibilities of the chief executive of a colonial enterprise, and the parceling of the land is clearly set out as one of these. It is unfortunate that

this and other references in the ancient texts to those officials responsible for land division offer few details. In the case of the *oikist* we should assume that his role was supervisory and that he had at his disposal a staff whose job it was to conduct land surveys for the purposes of allotment. They cannot be called city planners as such, but it may be nonetheless true to suppose that the *oikist,* land surveyors, and other city officials worked together to coordinate the various needs of the new city and the expectations of the colonists. It is only later, in the classical period, that we have direct evidence of urban planners.

Land surveyors (*geometrai* or *geodaitai*) must have abounded in the Greek world. Land transactions and settlements, boundary maintenance and disputes, and associated taxes would have required their services, and frequently. Their day-to-day activities would have provided the basis for practical approaches and methods of laying out cities. These procedures may be deduced from surviving records and archaeological remains from Egyptian and Roman times. From Egypt come instances of early practical geometry and examples of surveyor's tools: simple sighting devices, plumb bobs, and long cords knotted at regular intervals. These correspond directly to the modern surveyor's transit or theodolite (to measure vertical and horizontal angles), plumb bob, and measuring tape.

But what of the actual process of laying out a rectangular grid for a town? The large number of Greek-planned cities now known supplies important clues. If we examine their typically straightforward plans we find in them the basic determinant the surveyor began with. In many cases city blocks consisted of two rows of houses set back to back. Usually the houses themselves were originally square in plan and measured 50 or 60 ancient Greek feet on a side, and since rows of houses normally abutted city blocks would be twice that in width. (The ancient Greek foot ranged from 0.270 to 0.334 meters in length, varying from place to place and from one historical period to another.) Surveyors found a number of ways to approach the task of dividing up a site in order to achieve the desired results, and the simplest was to balance conditions of local terrain with a consideration of how many of these pairs of back-to-back houses should make up the length of a city block. But in other cases grander schemes seem to have been devised, where a site was first laid out in large squares and subsequently divided into city blocks, a practice linked to patterns of rural land division schemes.

Concerning the physical character of planned cities the ancient sources speak of *plateiai* (avenues) and *stenopoi* (streets), the former distinguished by greater width and the latter by greater number. Typically, early orthogonal layouts featured three or four *plateiai* spaced 300 to 1,000 ancient Greek feet (90 to 300 m) apart, connected by rows of *stenopoi* spaced 100 to 120 ancient Greek feet (30 to 40 m) apart. As time passed the distance between *plateiai* was gradually reduced so that by the Hellenistic period the long blocks of cities like Posidonia (Paestum) were no longer built. As a surveyor proceeded with his task, he set out his *plateiai* first, and clear testimony to this comes from Diodorus Siculus (12.10.7), who describes the layout of the Athenian colony of Thourioi in south Italy in 444/443 B.C.: "They divided the city along its length by four avenues called Herakleia, Aphrodisia, Olympias, and Dionysias, and along its breadth by three which they called Heroa, Thouria, and Thourina. Having filled these with streets for houses, the city appeared well constructed." No doubt a module was employed in the layout of Thourioi, perhaps a large square, though modern investigations have not yet clarified this.

Apart from houses, the simplest modular component of an orthogonal plan was the city block. Attempts have been made to recover their ancient dimensions, for in some cases clues to the surveyor's methods are revealed. It is clear that among the various foot units employed in Greek antiquity two are persistently recurrent and are often referred to as the Ionic foot, about 0.294 to 0.297 meters, and the Doric foot, about 0.325 to 0.328 meters. The city blocks at Olynthos, for example, average 35.50 meters in width and those at Priene 35.40 meters in width. Expressed in terms of the smaller Ionic foot we find that the blocks thus measured 120 feet in width. This figure is significant, for 120 feet is attested elsewhere in antiquity as a linear unit of land measure. Examination of other cities indicates that blocks 100 ancient Greek feet wide were also common. The methods used by land surveyors were flexible, and it is worth pointing out that in other cases the module in all likelihood was the width of a city block plus that of one adjoining street. This seems to be the case at Stymphalos (in the northern Peloponnesos) (fig. 1) where a city block plus one street measures 36 meters, precisely 110 Doric feet.

The residential quarters of Greek cities, planned or not, were utilitarian and lacking refinement. Individual homes in some cases were pleasant, even luxurious, but this would not have been evident from the exterior. In planned cities the urban landscape must have been bleak—row upon row of mud-brick dwellings without so much as whitewash to distinguish the exteriors. Narrow, monotonous streets would have made these quarters resemble modern-day barracks towns. Green, open space, not unheard of in Egypt or in the Near East, was almost entirely lacking in Greek cities. Greeks concentrated their urban refinements in the agora and in major shrines, although the agora remained a simple open space in many cases until the fifth century B.C. By that time the agora in-

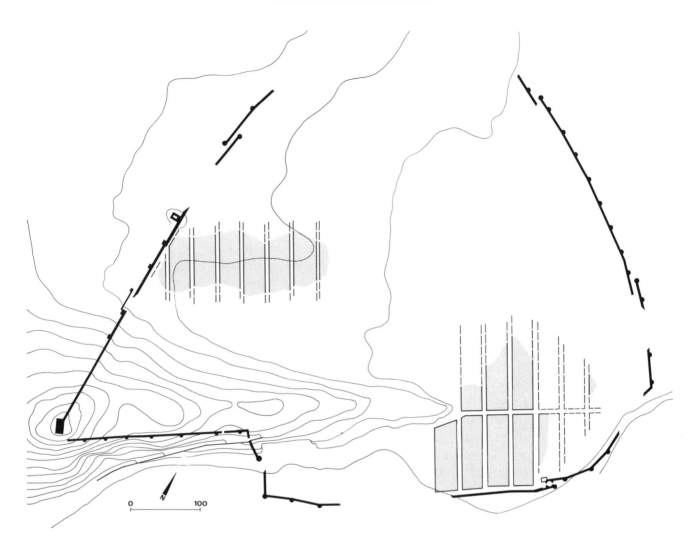

Figure 1. Stymphalos, Greece. Probably laid out in the fourth century B.C. ALL DRAWINGS BY THE AUTHOR

creasingly came to be embellished with care-fully designed buildings of permanent materials and fine workmanship, the most characteristic of which was the stoa or colon-naded hall. These were generally located about the perimeter of an agora, both defin-ing and dignifying the public space. Inter-spersed with stoas, or even incorporated into them, would be fountain houses, council houses, monuments to important citizens, and religious sanctuaries. In orthogonally planned cities the agora would conform to the layout, with the stoas backing onto the surrounding streets. The clearest examples of this are Hellenistic, in cities such as Mag-nesia on the Maeander (Ortaklar) and Mile-tos. In several cases the agora has not yet been detected by archaeologists, and in the case of planned cities we should expect it to have occupied one or more city blocks some-where near the heart of the city.

In the Aegean center of the Greek world from which most colonies were sent out, we have traditionally assumed that towns and cities were not planned, having grown up from very early times, and follow the pattern we are most familiar with, that of Athens. There, centuries of unregulated growth resulted in a tangled maze of streets in most parts of the city. The view

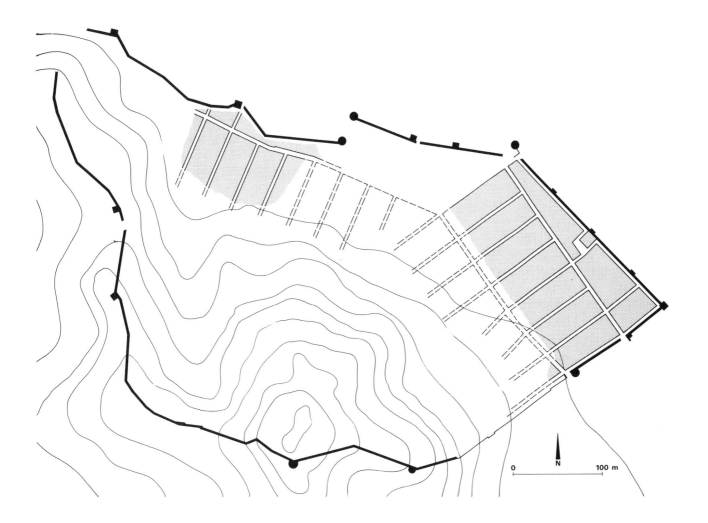

Figure 2. Halieis, Greece. Plan of the city in the fourth century B.C.

that most older cities were like Athens is lent support by Aristotle (*Politics* 7.10.4), who contrasts new, "well divided" cities with "old-fashioned" types. Yet evidence supporting this view exists for only a small number of cities such as Corinth, Eretria, and Thasos. Recent research has revealed that the number of planned cities in the Greek heartland was greater than heretofore assumed, and that the planned city can no longer be viewed primarily as a colonial phenomenon. The layouts of Halieis (modern Porto Kheli, in Argolis) (fig. 2), Halos, and Stymphalos (on Lake Stymphalos, in Arcadia) have recently been documented in

some detail while sketchier elements of the other planned cities in Greece itself have been observed and only await fuller documentation.

The Hellenistic period saw the development of another idea in urban planning, more subtle than the very utilitarian orthogonal city layouts: this was a special appreciation of the landscape that was integrated into overall urban plans. The best known and probably the finest example is Pergamon (Bergama, in Asia Minor), established early in the Hellenistic age. Occupying a steep hill site with an integrated acropolis (see fig. 10 in GREEK ARCHITECTURE), it developed largely unhindered by the earlier settlement. The south approach to the acropolis is relatively gentle, and under the Attalid kings this area was terraced to accommodate a rich array of buildings and shrines, while the royal residences, military installations, and chief shrines of the city occupied the summit. Connected to this remarkably successful architectural grouping was the theater complex on the steep west slope. In the past, Greek architects had demonstrated their ability to exploit a site to great advantage in the placing of individual buildings, but the unity achieved at Pergamon is all the more remarkable because it was the work of several generations of urban planners. Pergamon is not unique, for other Hellenistic cities like Aigai (Nemrud Kalesi) and Alinda (Karpuzlu), both in western Asia Minor, which occupy terraced hills demonstrate the same sort of ability to enhance the relationship between landscape and architecture.

The names of only two urban planners of Greek antiquity have come down to us: Hippodamos of Miletos (born *ca.* 500 B.C.) and Alexander the Great's architect, Deinokrates of Rhodes. Of Deinokrates we know little except that he proposed to shape Mount Athos in the likeness of Alexander and that he built the city of Alexandria in Egypt. Its plan incorporated an orthogonal street system but details of it are obscured by the presence of the modern city. Of Hippodamos we know more, and the ancient sources give us certain information. According to Aristotle (*Politics* 2.5.1) he was a Milesian and planned Peiraeus, the port of Athens; according to Strabo (14.2.9) he planned the new city of Rhodes; and according to late lexicographers (Photios, Hesychios) he took part in the Athenian colony of Thourioi. Diodorus Siculus' comments, quoted earlier, paint a picture of an orthogonal layout at Thourioi, and it is generally assumed that Hippodamos was responsible for it. Scattered excavations in the city of Rhodes re-

veal that it had an orthogonal plan, and if Hippodamos was responsible for it his career would have been lengthy, since Thourioi was founded in 444/443 B.C. and Rhodes in 408/407 B.C. Fragmentary evidence from Peiraeus shows that it had an orthogonal plan, though not a simple one. Aristotle (*Politics* 2.5.1) also tells us that Hippodamos invented the "cutting up" of cities. It was once thought that by this Aristotle meant that Hippodamos invented orthogonal layouts and consequently the phrase Hippodamean planning was applied to any Greek city with a gridlike layout. Aristotle, however, goes on to say that Hippodamos had a theory of an ideal state where the land, the judicial system, and the population were each to be divided into three categories. Recent scholarship has shown that while Hippodamean planning certainly incorporated orthogonal elements, the "cutting up" of cities should be understood in a broader sense, and refers to zones of a city. Peiraeus offers the best evidence of this, where ancient boundary stones have been discovered, referring to specific sectors of the city: agora, port, public land, and others. Here, at least, and perhaps also at Rhodes and at Thourioi, Hippodamean planning signifies a larger, master plan for urban life.

ROMAN CITY PLANNING

The link between the traditions of rural land division by surveyors and urban planning in the Greek world can also be found in the Roman world. Early Rome was the beneficiary of Greek knowledge and experience, particularly since numerous Greek colonies, most of them planned, dotted the coastal regions of south Italy and Sicily. As Rome expanded, first throughout Italy and later the Mediterranean world, colonies once again became an important phenomenon. Unlike the Greek colonies, which became independent city-states, the purpose of the Roman colonies was to establish roots for the expanding presence of Roman power with its centralized rule. Vital to this expansion was the large body of *agrimensores* (land surveyors) and *finitores* (land commissioners), about whose work considerably more is known than about that of their Greek counterparts. According to tradition their profession was of great antiquity. Describing the previous ages of the human race, Ovid (*Metamorphoses* 1.135–136) says of his Age of Iron: "The ground, which had hitherto been a common possession like the sunlight and the air, the careful surveyor now marked with long-drawn boundary line" (Frank J. Miller, trans., 2 vols. [1916]). The duties of the *agrimensores* lay mostly in the countryside, but their skills and services were drawn upon for laying out and building new towns.

The earliest visible evidence of Roman urban planning comes from central Italian towns of the fourth and third centuries B.C. such as Alba Fucens (Albe), Cosa (Ansedonia), and Norba (Norma), whose plans are orthogonal, thus demonstrating influence of Greek practice. The founding of a new Roman town was a matter of great importance attended by solemn rites that included the plowing of a furrow around the intended perimeter, and lifting the plow where gates in the city wall were to be built. The religious observances, however, are not likely to have interfered with the important practical considerations of siting, water supply, and defenses, and the ritual plowing may have been more symbolic than complete. The tradition itself went back to the legendary founding of Rome. Vergil, in a passage recalling Homer's description of Nausithous' acts at Scheria, says of his hero: "Meanwhile Aeneas marks the city out with a plow, and assigns the homes by lot" (*Aeneid* 5.755–756, H. Rushton Fairclough, trans., 2 vols. [1927]). This and other rites represent the religious sanctioning of a primarily political act, and

were held to be of great importance for the well-being of the new community.

The tools of the *agrimensores* differed little from those of the Greeks and the Egyptians. The basic instrument was the *groma*, a simple sighting device consisting of two arms crossing at right angles, balanced on a pivot post. Once a basic orientation had been established, sighting along one arm allowed a line to be extended from the base point where the *groma* was set up. Sighting along the other arm permitted another line to be extended from the base point, but at right angles to the first, and thus the instrument was suited to laying out squares and rectangles.

Today a variety of units exist for both linear and areal measure, for example, inch, foot, mile, square foot, acre, and section. The *agrimensores* also had their measures. In addition to the normal Roman foot of 0.296 meters the basic linear unit was the *actus* of 120 Roman feet. There was a preference for squares in Roman rural land division schemes, and the squares laid out in the countryside almost always had sides whose lengths were multiples of the *actus*. Common areal units included the *iugerum* of two square *actus*, the *heredium* (heritable plot) of two *iugera*, and the *centuria* of 100 *heredia*. With these units and simple equipment vast areas of Italy and other parts of the Roman world, chiefly western Europe and North Africa, were "centuriated." The clear traces of Roman centuriation are still visible in many places today in aerial photographs.

The main survey lines set out for centuriation were often oriented north-south and east-west; they also provided a basis for road systems. A main east-west boundary was known as a *decumanus* and a main north-south boundary a *cardo*. These terms are commonly used to describe the main intersecting streets in a Roman town, *decumanus maximus* and *cardo maximus*. Strictly speaking, these terms are correct only if the point of intersection of the main streets also marks the base point for the survey of the surrounding territory. The close relationship between centuriation and the layout of towns was a distinctly Roman contribution to the character of Mediterranean planned cities.

Colony towns, in numerous instances originally built as garrison towns or settlements for veterans, also owe something of their patterns of layout to the organization of Roman military encampments. The rapid growth of urbanism in other respects was sufficiently great, on the other hand, that we should not overemphasize the contribution of camps to Roman city planning. The relationships are multilayered; in some cases practices in the civilian sector influenced the layout of a garrison town, but in others the reverse was true, particularly on the frontiers where military encampments often crystallized into permanent towns. The military colony of Thamugadi (Timgad) in Algeria established in A.D. 100 is perhaps the most startling example of a town based on a military model (fig. 3). The town quickly outgrew its original limits, and the contrast between the neat but colorless rows of square city blocks of the original layout and the irregular adjacent quarters of succeeding generations is striking.

Nothing is more characteristic of Roman towns and cities than the forum. Like its Greek counterpart, the agora, it consisted of a large open space and was the focal point for shrines, administrative facilities, and markets. Architecturally, a forum was markedly different from a typical agora. Forums tended to be somewhat elongated rectangular spaces formally defined by a surrounding colonnade. This idea was rooted in Greek colonnaded porticoes (stoas), most frequently found around the perimeter of an agora. By Hellenistic times the stoa had lost much of its independent status in many in-

stances, becoming subordinated to the larger entity of the agora. Roman builders dispensed with the stoa altogether and unified a variety of buildings behind a continuous colonnade. A forum typically also had a clear focus to it provided by a large temple centered on the axis at one end. Raised up on a podium the temple contributed to a sense of controlled monumentality of a sort generally lacking in an agora. The finest examples of Roman forums were unquestionably the imperial series in Rome (see fig. 4 in ROMAN BUILDING TECHNIQUES) built to supplement the old Forum Romanum, which had become quite inadequate for a city that had become the seat of an empire. The first of these was a gift of Julius Caesar, completed in the late first century B.C. by his adopted son, Augustus. He, in turn, gave to the city the Forum Augustum. In the first century A.D. the Forum Transitorium was added, and the series came to a close with the Forum Traianum early in the second century. With their axial design and dominating temples, all owed something to the Italic idea of a forum, but the Forum Traianum went a step beyond with a truly innovative design. The architect of this complex, Apollodorus of Damascus, combined the idea of a traditional forum with a basilica, a library, and a new concept in commemorative monuments, a colossal column glorifying the emperor Trajan, who gave the forum.

The formally designed forum was primarily a phenomenon of Italy and the West, while in the East Greek traditions continued to thrive. The agora remained a major component of eastern cities under Roman rule and, as in the Hellenistic era, those of the Roman period were generally designed as a unified whole. It was in the East also that a distinctive new element, the colonnaded street, came to dominate the urban landscape. The earliest recorded ex-

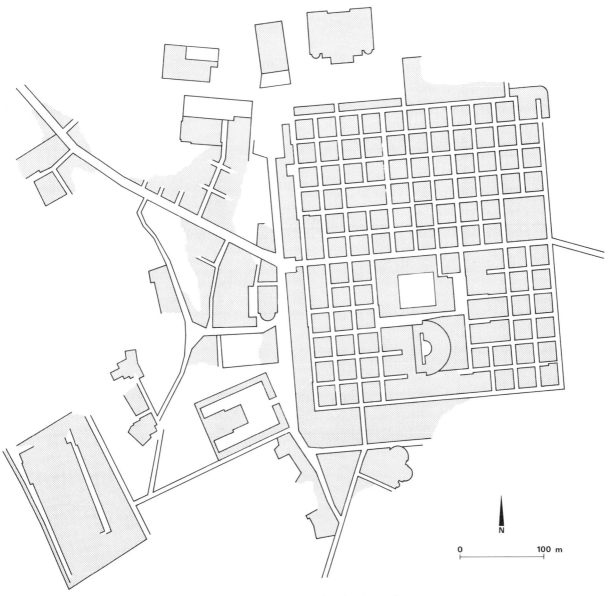

Figure 3. Thamugadi (Timgad), Algeria. Second century B.C.

ample was built at Syrian Antioch (Antakya, in Turkey) in the late first century B.C. at the expense of Rome's client king of Judaea, Herod the Great. Evidently a spectacularly successful innovation, the idea spread so that by the second century A.D. any eastern city of significance boasted at least one such street as a mark of civic pride. In many instances a colonnaded street culminated in an important monu-ment so that the effect was to unify the architectural landscape. Among the finest applications of this important feature are the colonnaded streets of Gerasa (Jerash, in Jordan) where they not only linked the principal monuments of the city, but did so in such a way that, with a sophisticated mathematical precision, a hierarchy of controlled vistas was created.

In contrast to the Greek world, Roman

1699

urban planning was considerably more comprehensive. As a matter of course any new Roman town would be built with a covered water supply and a well-engineered sewage system, a vast improvement over conditions in Greek cities. Moreover, no Roman institution was more ubiquitous than the bath. Whether built by private citizens or by the state, modest or lavish and grand, several baths served most cities, and Rome itself had 856 by official count in the fourth century A.D. The peculiarly Roman taste for public entertainment meant that stadiums and amphitheaters were also common, at least in larger cities, while theaters were found in almost all communities. Basilicas to house judicial functions, public fountains, public lavatories, warehouses, as well as religious sanctuaries completed the range of major facilities provided in a Roman city. The complexity of urban life called for carefully formulated municipal laws to regulate it, particularly in large cities where multistoried apartment dwellings led to crowded conditions. This regulation of urban life for the common good, and the amenities and services provided, created a standard of living not previously realized in the ancient Mediterranean, and not seen again until modern times.

BIBLIOGRAPHY

SOURCES

Ovid, *Metamorphoses,* Frank J. Miller, trans., 2 vols. (1916); Vergil, *Aeneid,* H. Rushton Fairclough, trans., 2 vols. (1927).

STUDIES

Thomas D. Boyd and Michael H. Jameson, "Urban and Rural Land Division in Ancient Greece," in *Hesperia,* **50** (1981); Alfred Burns, "Hippodamus and the Planned City," in *Historia,* **25** (1976); Ferdinando Castagnoli, *Orthogonal Town Planning in Antiquity,* Victor Caliandro, trans. (1971); Mario Coppa, *Storia dell' urbanistica dalle origine all' ellenismo,* 2 vols. (1969), and *Storia dell' urbanistica: Le età ellenistiche,* 2 vols. (1981); Oswald A. W. Dilke, *The Roman Land Surveyors* (1971), the bibliography for chap. 10 is especially good for the vast literature on Roman centuriation; Alexander J. Graham, *Colony and Mother City in Ancient Greece* (1964); Roland Martin, *L'Urbanisme dans la Grèce antique* (1956; 2d ed. 1974); James R. McCredie, "Hippodamos of Miletos," in *Studies Presented to George M. A. Hanfmann,* David M. Mitten, John G. Pedley, and Jane A. Scott, eds. (1971); John B. Ward-Perkins, *Cities of Ancient Greece and Italy: Planning in Classical Antiquity* (1974); Richard E. Wycherley, *How the Greeks Built Cities* (2d ed. 1962).

Greek Sculpture and Gems

JEROME J. POLLITT

TECHNIQUES AND MATERIALS

Because Greek sculpture in stone, especially marble, so dominates the collections of many museums, it is easy to forget that, at least after the beginning of the fifth century B.C., most major works of Greek sculpture were done in bronze. This is clear not only from literary sources, such as Book Thirty-Four of the elder Pliny's *Natural History,* but also from dedicatory inscriptions and surviving statue bases. Stone was used for architectural sculpture and for modest, privately commissioned relief sculptures like votive and grave reliefs, but after the archaic period stone was rarely used for important works of freestanding sculpture. Of the famous sculptors of the classical period, only Praxiteles seems to have had a consistent preference for marble over bronze.

In the development of monumental sculpture, however, perfection in the technique of working stone seems to have preceded the full development of the bronze-caster's technique. The earliest surviving large-scale cast bronze statue, the Peiraeus *kouros,* dates from about 530 to 520 B.C., and it was prob-ably not until this time that the technical problems involved in casting and assembling large bronzes were solved. (Owing to the fact that relatively little bronze sculpture, in contrast to stone, survives, the chronology of the stages in the development of bronze casting remains problematical.) The beginning of sculpturing large blocks of stone and the rapid attainment of a high degree of skill in stone sculpture, on the other hand, can be fixed with reasonable certainty to the middle and second half of the seventh century B.C. The source of inspiration for this great development was Egypt, a land that always fascinated the Greeks and which had had a tradition of large-scale stone sculpture for thousands of years. Under the pharaoh whom the Greeks called Psammetichos I (664–610 B.C.), the Greeks began to develop a firsthand familiarity with Egypt, first by serving as mercenary soldiers and later by establishing trading stations. In this way they not only had a chance to develop a taste for the grandiose stone sculpture of Egypt but were also able to study the methods by which Egyptian sculptors plied their trade. This knowledge was brought back to

Greece and apparently first adopted for local use in the Cycladic Islands, where hard stone, that is, marble, was plentiful and of easy access.

In one of the first great genres of Greek monumental stone sculpture, the figures of striding male youths known as *kouroi* (sing. *kouros*), a connection with Egyptian sculpture both in overall composition and in the rendering of certain details is unmistakable; furthermore, a literary source (Diodorus Siculus, 1.98), attests that early Greek sculptors were familiar with the canons of proportion used by Egyptian sculptors. But it is also clear that from the very beginning the Greeks adapted the Egyptian prototypes to their own needs, uses, and taste, and developed their own tools and techniques for working stone. The Egyptians had used very hard stone that was worked mainly by patient abrasion. Greek marble was softer, and to work it more quickly a variety of iron and bronze tools were developed—punches, several types of chisels, and a drill operated by a bow. In the archaic period, the design of a sculpture was apparently drawn on four sides of a block and then "freed" from the stone, first with a punch and drill, to give rough shape to the figure, and then with a series of increasingly fine chisels (clawed, round-edged, and flat) to attain a smoother surface. Finally, this surface was rubbed with a fine abrasive like emery to remove all or most of the traces of tool marks. The only major change in this technique over the centuries was the addition of a running drill that could be worked nearly parallel to the surface of the stone to create long channels and furrows. It has often been maintained that the development of a running drill facilitated the creation of the "flying drapery" style of the later fifth century B.C., and this contention seems to have the support of Pausanias (1.26.7), who ascribes innovative drill work to an influential Athenian sculptor of that time, Kallimachos. No indisputable archaeological evidence for the use of the running drill exists, however, on any monument dating from before 370 B.C.

It sometimes comes as a shock to modern viewers to discover that the surface of a well-preserved Greek statue in marble, with its sparkling crystalline appearance, was not the final one. All stone statues were brightly painted, and the glistening textures so admired today would have been scarcely detectable in antiquity. Not only were hair, eyes, lips, and drapery painted in strong colors, but in most cases so too was the flesh (in the archaic period, milk-white for women and reddish tan for men; later an "average" skin color). Surviving painted terra-cotta sculptures from the Greek colonies of Italy and Sicily, as well as some architectural sculptures from Greece, give an idea of what polychrome in early Greek sculpture was like. In later times, the Alexander sarcophagus (last quarter of the fourth century B.C.; now in the Archaeological Museum in İstanbul) is the best-preserved example of polychrome work. Even paint, however, was not the final surface of a Greek stone statue. In order to preserve the paint and give the sculpture a lustrous shine, a final coat of wax mixed with oil was applied. This process, mentioned by several literary sources, was known as *ganosis*.

The Greeks began casting solid bronze statuettes at least as early as the eighth century B.C., but it was not until they learned the "lost-wax" technique, apparently from the Near East, that the way was open for casting large works in bronze. The lost-wax technique involves, first, modeling a form in clay; then coating the clay form with wax and modeling or carving final details in the wax; next, covering the wax-covered core with a mantle and doweling the two together; and finally, melting out the wax and using the resulting cavity as a mold into which molten bronze can be poured. The result is a hollow (if the core is removed), relatively light sculptural form. Hollow casting was already in use in the seventh century B.C., and two Greek sculptors of the middle of the sixth century B.C., Theodoros and Rhoikos of Samos, are credited by Pausanias with having "invented" its use for larger statues. It was apparently not until the fifth century B.C., however, that large-scale bronze statuary became common. Classical bronze sculptures were usually cast in pieces, which were then fastened together with rivets. Small details, such as locks of hair, were often made separately and attached. Eyes were made by setting colored, and sometimes semiprecious, stones into a vitreous paste and inserting them into the eye cavity in a cliplike bronze holder. Precious metals were sometimes added to enhance details. (The teeth of one of the classical bronze statues discovered in the sea off Riace, in Italy, and now in the Archaeological Museum in Reggio di Calabria, for example, are coated with silver.) Entire statues, in fact, were sometimes covered with gilding. (Ancient writers and inscriptions speak of gold statues, but these are more likely to have been gilded bronzes, or statues with enough zinc or lead added to the bronze to achieve a yellow, brasslike effect.)

The technique of piecing together bronze statues from separately made parts was also sometimes used, as an economy measure, in stone sculpture. Heads and extended arms, for example, were sometimes carved from small blocks of stone and attached with cement or dowels. Piecing together was also a fundamental part of the technique of making sculpture from mixed materials, such as acrolithic sculpture, in which extremities of stone were added to a torso made of wood; and chryselephantine (gold and ivory) sculpture, like the great cult images by Pheidias, in which hammered gold sheets (for drapery) and carved ivory (for skin) were arranged on an armature made probably of wood, metal, and terra-cotta.

Separate accoutrements, such as jewelry, armor, and weapons, were added to many sculptures and were often made of materials different from that of the sculpture itself, as can be seen in bronze helmets on marble statues.

The use of clay for statuettes was common, but it was rare for large-scale sculptures, except in the Greek colonial cities of Italy and Sicily, where good stone was scarce and often had to be imported.

To what extent Greek sculptors used maquettes made of clay or wax as models for their sculptures is uncertain. In archaic stone sculpture, designs may have simply been drawn on the side of a block to be carved. That models in clay were designed for postarchaic stone sculptures seems likely, even though there is no indisputable evidence for them prior to the Hellenistic period. It has been suggested that a rudimentary pointing device, for transferring the proportions of a clay, wax, or plaster model to stone, may have been in use as early as the second quarter of the fifth century B.C.

In the later second and first centuries B.C., when the Romans had come to dominate Greece and had developed a taste for Greek sculpture, copies of Greek masterpieces were turned out in large numbers to satisfy the needs of avid collectors. These replicas seem to have been produced mainly by taking plaster casts of the original and then making stone versions of the cast by means of a pointing machine. Obviously the finished products of this process seldom did justice to the original. Nevertheless it is to these "Roman copies" (that is, copies made by Greek sculptors for the Roman art market) that we owe much of our knowledge of the personal styles of renowned Greek masters like Polykleitos and Praxiteles.

CHRONOLOGY

The dating of individual works of Greek sculpture is often problematical. Four criteria are frequently used for establishing dates. First, there are literary sources and inscriptions that give historical dates or at least datable historical contexts for particular works. The "fixed points" that can be derived from this kind of information are fairly common in the classical period (for example, the Charioteer of Delphi, 478–474 B.C.; the Parthenon, 447–432 B.C.; and the Mausoleum of Halicarnassus, *ca.* 353 B.C.), sporadic in the Hellenistic period (for example, the Demosthenes of Polyeuktos, 280 B.C.), and rare in the archaic period. Most scholars accept the treasury of the Siphnians at Delphi (*ca.* 530–525 B.C.), and the pediments of the fifth temple of Apollo at Delphi (*ca.* 513–510 B.C.), as fixed points in the archaic period, but otherwise the dates of most archaic sculptures are estimated on the basis of relatively subjective standards.

A second criterion for establishing dates is the letter forms of inscriptions on statue bases, which, while not datable in themselves, resemble the forms of letters on other inscriptions that are datable. Third, a comparison may be made with stylistic features in other media, especially vase painting. The profiles of the heads of early archaic *kouroi,* for example, are compared with figures on Attic black-figure pottery datable to around 600 B.C. The principal problem with this criterion is that the chronology of vase painting is also fraught with many uncertainties.

Fourth, an apparent stylistic evolution may suggest a relative chronology between fixed points, such as the widely adopted use of increasing naturalism in the rendering of anatomy to date archaic sculptures, especially nude male figures. The greatest problems with this approach are that the speed with which such changes took place and the extent to which they were adopted in different areas often remain very uncertain, and there is always the possibility, even the probability, of conservative or *retardataire* works. Nevertheless, in spite of some uncertainties about the dates of individual pieces, the

broad chronological development outlined in the following section is reasonably secure.

STYLISTIC AND ICONOLOGICAL HISTORY

Beginning in the tenth century B.C., Greek sculpture, like Greek civilization as a whole, began to emerge slowly out of the "Dark Age" that separates classical Greek culture from the Mycenaean and Minoan cultures of the Bronze Age. The earliest surviving works dating from the beginning of the first millennium B.C. are unpretentious terra-cotta statuettes. A few of these, particularly those found in Crete, seem to echo ancient Minoan forms; a few others, like the surprisingly early figure of a centaur, painted in the style of Geometric pottery, from Lefkandi in Euboea, anticipate popular forms of succeeding centuries; but most fall into the category of unarticulated and uncategorizable folk art. Not until the middle and late eighth century B.C., toward the end of the Geometric period (*ca.* 900–700 B.C.), did works appear that betray unmistakably Greek aesthetic predilections and that initiate a continuous tradition of formal development that persisted until at least the second century B.C. Although figures in gold and ivory survive, and terra-cottas continue to be plentiful, the most typical works of this period are solid-cast bronze statuettes representing a variety of animal forms (fig. 1), particularly horses, cattle, deer, birds, and beetles. Human figures also exist, but they are usually less sophisticated and less artistically successful than the animals. Some of the statuettes seem to have been designed as votive offerings in religious sanctuaries, while others were probably intended to decorate caldrons, mirrors, wagon poles, and other objects of practical use.

Although its products seem disarmingly simple at first sight, the Geometric style was

Figure 1. Bronze horse, Geometric style, *ca.* 750 B.C. Height 16 cm. WEST BERLIN, STAATLICHE MUSEEN, PREUSSISCHER KULTURBESITZ, ANTIKENMUSEUM INV. NR. 31317

in fact highly sophisticated. In designing figures, the sculptors' method seems to have been to analyze first what were the fundamental component parts of a natural form, then to simplify those parts into their essential underlying geometric shapes (cylinders, triangles, and so on), and finally to recompose those parts into an assemblage that was not so much a representation of a natural form as an analogue to it. This principal of defining the basic components of a form and studying their proportional relationships was perhaps the single most enduring and characteristic feature of Greek sculpture. Among artists and critics of later centuries it was called *symmetria* (commensurability of parts). In the Geometric period the urge for clarity and definition that is behind the *symmetria* principle was undoubtedly more instinctive than self-conscious, but later, in the hands of sculptors like Polykleitos of Argos, a complex philosophical significance, con-

nected with doctrines of ideal beauty, came to be attributed to it.

In the seventh century B.C., as trade and overseas colonization began to bring the Greeks into ever more frequent contact with other cultures of the Mediterranean, a wave of new forms, and with them new sculptural techniques, emanating for the most part from the ancient Near East, swept away the orderly and controlled Geometric style. As was the case in Greek vase painting, the early part of this Orientalizing period was one of experiment and change, while the later part saw the establishment of techniques, forms, and stylistic standards that would dominate Greek art throughout the succeeding archaic period (late seventh century to 480 B.C.).

The most polished and technically proficient sculptures of the early and middle seventh century B.C. were bronze caldron attachments, called *protomai* (things cut off in front), representing the heads and necks of griffins, lions, and other "Eastern" creatures. Some of these were made by hammering metal sheets over a core, but others, as already noted, were hollow-cast by the lost-wax method. The finest of these *protomai* come from Panhellenic sanctuaries like Olympia, where they were part of votive caldrons, offered to the gods in celebration, perhaps, of athletic and military victories. At their best they embody the Greek predilection for definition and order superimposed on new, exotic motifs.

For the representation of the human figure in the seventh century B.C., a new style was developed, which is conventionally called "Daedalic" (after the legendary sculptor Daedalus). Typical features of the style are a head with a flat top, a triangular face with large eyes and a prominent nose, and the hair flanking the face arranged in pendant triangular wedges decorated with horizontal "waves." Standing figures are usually arranged in a rigidly frontal position, with the arms and hands pressed stiffly against the sides. The Daedalic style appears to have originated about 675 B.C. and to have lasted until the end of the seventh century. While the ultimate sources of many of its features seem to lie in the Near East, particularly in Syria, its development in Greece appears to have been centered in Crete. Statuettes in terra-cotta and ivory provide the most plentiful examples of it, but there are also sculptures in stone on a larger scale. Most, if not all, of the works in stone come from Crete (such as the limestone sculptures from the temple of Apollo at Gortyn and from a temple at Prinias, both dating *ca.* 630–600 B.C.) or have Cretan associations. The best known is the Goddess of Auxerre (fig. 2), a limestone figure about 25.6 inches (65 cm) high, now in the Louvre.

Although the Daedalic style is the standard system for representing the human figure in the seventh century, there are traces of experiments in many alternative styles, some of which explore anatomical structure and details in a more elaborate and appealing manner. This probing of new forms finally culminated in the most important of all the innovations of the seventh century—monumental stone sculpture. Some elements of the Daedalic style were initially translated into the new material, especially the Daedalic formula for the head, which appears on some *kouroi* but most obviously on the earliest large-scale female figures, known as *korai* (sing. *kore*), such as the statue dedicated by Nikandre on Delos about 625 B.C. (now in the National Archaeological Museum in Athens). Eventually, however, as archaic stone sculpture became increasingly sophisticated, Daedalic forms were abandoned.

The most typical sculptural form of the archaic period is the *kouros,* and it is in the *kouroi* that the essence and meaning of the archaic style is best studied. *Kouroi* were produced from the late seventh century B.C. to

Figure 2. The Goddess of Auxerre, limestone statuette, *ca.* 630–600 B.C. Height 65 cm. PARIS, MUSÉE DU LOUVRE INV. NR. 3098. *PHOTO: ALISON FRANTZ*

the early fifth century. Some of them were votive offerings, particularly to Apollo, while others were grave monuments. The *kouros* form—a torsionless torso with arms pressed against the sides and one foot, usually the left, stepping forward—has often been seen as a kind of laboratory in which Greek sculptors strove to perfect the realistic rendering of anatomy. From the "Sounion group" of *kouroi* (fig. 3a) early in the sixth century, with their emphasis on block-like, heavy forms (often colossal in scale), through the slender, seemingly aristocratic figures of the middle of the century, like the *kouroi* from Tenea, south of Corinth (now in the Glyptothek in Munich) or Melos (now in the National Archaeological Museum in Athens), to the heavily muscled figures of the last third of the century, such as the figure of a soldier named Kroisos from Anavyssos (fig. 3b) (now in the National Archaeological Museum in Athens), to the spare, modestly scaled figures of the early fifth century, such as the Strangford *kouros* in the British Museum, there is an undeniable growth in anatomical realism. There can be no doubt that Greek sculptors of the archaic period worked diligently to incorporate an increasing number of observations of nature into the canons of proportions that they had inherited or developed at the beginning of the *kouros* series. To conclude from this that realistic depiction was the essential purpose and meaning of the *kouroi*, however, is probably a mistake. The key to what the individual figures, in the context of their culture and time, meant is provided by Herodotus' story (1.31) of the Argive twins Kleobis and Biton, whose statues, powerful versions of the *kouros* type, were set up at Delphi in the early sixth century. The story makes it clear that the *kouroi* were designed to embody and perpetuate a state of human perfection, physical and spiritual, that transcended time, change, and the mutability of fortune. Hence the jewel-like quality that pervades their surface—ears like violin scrolls, beads, and flame-shaped designs for hair—that seems at odds with anatomical realism because it is so obviously and sophistically decorative in intent; and hence the emotional impassivity of the *kouroi*, which are either expressionless or endowed with the blissful "archaic smile." As images of a transcendent permanence, of a more perfect state of being, they were not images of the natural world but rather ideas, in the Platonic sense, that went beyond nature.

This emotionally neutral, jewel-like quality is the essence of the archaic style and characterizes all categories of archaic sculpture. In the *korai* it reaches its peak in the figures found on the Athenian Acropolis (see fig. 13 in CRAFTS AND CRAFTSMEN) dating from the last quarter of the sixth century, with their elaborate coiffures and rich contrasts in drapery textures; but it is also present in earlier figures like the Hera dedicated by Cheramyes on Samos around 560 B.C. (now in the Louvre). Particularly

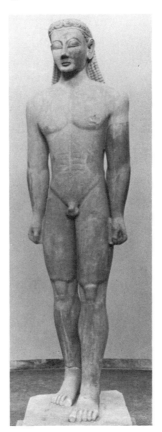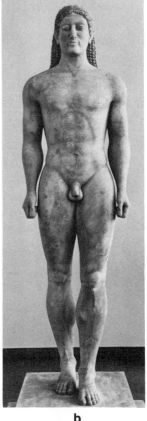

a   b

Figure 3. *(a)* Kouros from Sounion, *ca.* 590–580 B.C. Height 305 cm; *(b)* the Kroisos kouros from Anavyssos (Attica), Parian marble, *ca.* 530 B.C. Height 194 cm. ATHENS, NATIONAL ARCHAEOLOGICAL MUSEUM INV. NRS. 2720 AND 3851. *PHOTOS BY ALISON FRANTZ*

fine examples of the archaic style in other forms of freestanding sculpture are the Rampin Rider of about 550 B.C. (partly in the Acropolis Museum in Athens, partly in the Louvre) and the Sphinx of the Naxians at Delphi.

Much of the finest archaic sculpture is architectural sculpture. The use of stone sculpture to decorate the pediments of temples began early in the sixth century, and was probably preceded by decoration in terracotta. The triangular frame of the pediment with its large center and narrow corners posed problems of composition that sculptors solved in different ways. In the earliest compositions, a large symbolic figure (either apotropaic or embodying the power of the god in the temple, or both) was placed in the center and flanked by smaller, unrelated mythological scenes. The most renowned examples are the temple of Artemis at Corcyra (Corfu), dated about 580 B.C., with its great central Gorgon, and the Hekatompedon pediments from the Athenian Acropolis, with powerful groups of lions attacking bulls flanked by such figures as Herakles wrestling with the sea beast Triton and an enigmatic three-headed monster. This pattern continued to be used for some time, but by the late sixth and early fifth centuries more unified designs were finally developed in which all the figures were on essentially the same scale, and the central figure, while still retaining a certain symbolic and magical role, was integrated into the subject. The sculptures (now in Munich) from the west pediment of the temple of Aphaia at Aegina, with Athena set in the center of a battle scene from the Trojan War, best illustrate the refinement that had been achieved in pedimental sculpture by the end of the archaic period.

The sculptured metopes of the Doric order show a similar evolution in subtlety of composition. The earliest examples, like those from Temple C at Selinus and the Sikyonian Treasury at Delphi (both mid sixth century) have paratactic compositions, that is, vertically arranged figures placed side by side, that follow the basic structural lines of the temple. Later, as, for example, in the metopes of the Treasury of the Athenians at Delphi (ca. 500 B.C.), which depict labors of Herakles and Theseus, figures are often arranged in circular or chiastic designs that bring a unity within the metope frame.

The continuous running frieze, most commonly used in the entablature of Ionic buildings but applicable to a variety of structures, appeared in Crete as early as the late seventh century (at Prinias). One of the most impressive examples of it is the frieze from the treasury constructed at Delphi by people of the Cycladic island of Siphnos shown in figure 4 (dated ca. 530–525 B.C. on the basis of literary evidence). The jewel-like detail of the frieze combined with its vigorous, in some ways childlike enthusiasm, particularly on its north and east sides, which represent a Trojan combat and the battle of the gods and giants, make it one of the most typical and successful works of archaic sculpture.

Besides being used in architecture, sculptured relief was also applied to such monuments as grave stelae (see fig. 15 in CRAFTS AND CRAFTSMEN), statue bases, and votive offerings. Many of these, like the stela of Aristion and the base depicting athletes recovered from the Themistoclean wall (both dating from ca. 510 B.C. and both in the National Museum in Athens) are of particular interest because of their similarity to patterns of composition in contemporary painting.

The naturalism of late archaic art and the need of the artists of the time to extend the range of experience that could be expressed in the visual arts are more apparent in vase painting than in the more conservative medium of monumental sculpture. The seeming conflict between naturalistic detail and stiff, formulaic composition that charac-

Figure 4. The Battle of the Gods and Giants, detail depicting Apollo and Artemis striding forward, overlapping the fleeing giant Kantharos, who looks back at a companion being mauled by lions, portion of the north frieze from the Siphnian Treasury at Delphi, *ca.* 530–525 B.C. DELPHI, ARCHAEOLOGICAL MUSEUM. *ALINARI/ART RESOURCE*

terizes the late *kouroi* needed some great upheaval to resolve it, break down old patterns, and set free a new expressive power among sculptors. That upheaval came in the form of the Persian Wars of 481–479 B.C., in the wake of which a new atmosphere emerged that made the creation of new forms imperative. The Greek victory in that conflict against a force that, on the surface at least, seemed immensely more powerful was seen, as Aeschylus' *Persians* makes clear, as the fruit of moderation, or self-restraint (*sophrosyne*). To express the sobriety and the awareness of moral alternatives that went with this virtue, Greek sculptors of the early classical period (480–450 B.C.) quickly developed what is sometimes called the Severe style. In it archaic ornateness, which had some of its roots in the art of the part of the world from which the Persians had come, was swept away in favor of stark, spare anatomical forms and brooding, heavy facial

features. Drapery, particularly on female figures, became almost like armor or architecture, with shieldlike surfaces over the chest and tubular folds falling to the feet like the flutes of a column.

The most powerful and typical of all the works in the new style of the early classical period are the pedimental and metope sculptures from the temple of Zeus at Olympia, constructed between 470 and 458 B.C. What is most remarkable about these sculptures is their expression of changing states of consciousness. The emotional neutrality of archaic sculpture yielded to a vivid sense of inner awareness. In the figures of Herakles (fig. 5), whose labors were depicted on twelve metopes over the front and rear porches of the temple, one detects fatigue, anxiety, and determination as the hero passes from youth to maturity. In the pedimental sculptures (fig. 6), particularly those of the east pediment, which depicted

Figure 5. Herakles supports the heavens as Atlas brings him the apples of the Hesperides, metope from the temple of Zeus at Olympia, 462–458 B.C. Height 160 cm. OLYMPIA, ARCHAEOLOGICAL MUSEUM. *PHOTO: ALISON FRANTZ*

the moment before the chariot race of Pelops and Oinomaos, aspects of character and emotional reaction, which ancient writers on art referred to as *ethos* and *pathos,* were explored in the context of dramatic scenes that seem to have been influenced by contemporary theatrical productions.

The Olympia sculptures also illustrate new patterns of composition that were developed by early classical sculptors to replace the formulas of the archaic period. For quiet standing figures, whose character and state of mind needed to be emphasized, the biaxial symmetry of the *kouroi* was broken up by making the weight appear to shift to one leg, with a consequent shift in the position of the hips, and by making the head turn slightly to one side. One of the earliest examples of this new design is the Kritios boy, in the Acropolis Museum in Athens, made around the time of the Persian Wars. Mature examples of it are the remarkable bronze warriors (now in Reggio di Calabria) from Riace of *ca.* 450 B.C. For figures in motion the sculptors of the period created a repertoire of "stop-action" patterns that preserved something of the clarity of archaic forms but permitted a more natural and integrated rendering of the body. The term used by ancient art critics for compositions of this sort was apparently *rhythmoi* (sing. *rhythmos*). An early example of it is the Tyrant Slayers group by the sculptors Kritios and Nesiotes, set up in the Athenian Agora

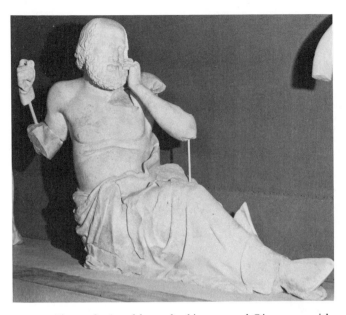

Figure 6. An old seer looking toward Oinomaos with a gesture of dismay, marble sculpture from the east pediment of the temple of Zeus at Olympia, 462–458 B.C. OLYMPIA, ARCHAEOLOGICAL MUSEUM. *SCALA/ART RESOURCE*

in 477 B.C. and now known through copies made in the Roman period; developed examples of it are the Discus Thrower of the sculptor Myron, also known through Roman copies, and the bronze Striding God from Artemision (fig. 7), usually identified with Poseidon or Zeus, now in the National Museum in Athens.

All of the features that are found in a fully developed form in the Olympia sculptures and constitute the essence of the early classical style—severity of form, the exploration of consciousness and change, new patterns of composition—can also be detected in an incipient stage in the sculptures from the east pediment (now in Munich) of the temple of Aphaia at Aegina, generally agreed to be later than the west pediment of the temple and probably created just after the Persian Wars.

Ancient writers record the prestige of, and cite well-known works by, a number of sculptors of the early classical period. Scholars have tried valiantly, if inconclusively, to

recreate a portion of the oeuvre of these artists from among surviving originals and, more often, Roman copies. The style of Kalamis has been seen, for example, in the female type known as the Aspasia or Amelung's Goddess (best copies in Baiae [Campania, southwestern Italy] and Berlin) and in the Omphalos Apollo type (copies in the National Archaeological Museum in Athens and in the British Museum), but few attributions of this sort have won general approval. (The Discus Thrower of Myron is a rare exception.)

After the middle of the fifth century B.C., when the threat from the Persians had receded and the rivalry between the Athenian and Spartan alliances had come to dominate Greek politics, the preoccupation of the early classical period with character, emotion, and morality tended to fade out of Greek sculpture. The style of the high classical period (*ca.* 450–400 B.C.) was shaped by the Athenian sculptor Pheidias (*ca.* 490–430 B.C.), who, as the artistic overseer for the great building program of Pericles, had an opportunity to give visual form to the vision of an ideal culture that Thucydides ascribes to Pericles in the Funeral Oration (2.34–46). The works of Pheidias' own hand, such as the colossal gold and ivory cult statues of Athena in the Parthenon (see fig. 6 in GREEK ARCHITECTURE) and of Zeus in the temple at Olympia, have not survived, and only a hint of their quality can be derived from Roman copies. The power of the Pheidian style can be fully appreciated, however, in the architectural sculptures of the Parthenon. Pheidias seems to have wanted to fuse a sense of a timeless, perfect, absolute state of being with a sense of the transience of the world of everyday experience; to harmonize, in philosophical terms, the immutable truth that Greek philosophers of the archaic period, such as the Pythagoreans, had searched for with the subjectivism of contemporary Sophists, like Protagoras. To do

Figure 7. The Striding God from Artemision, bronze, *ca.* 460 B.C. Height 209 cm. ATHENS, NATIONAL ARCHAEOLOGICAL MUSEUM INV. NR. 15161. *HIRMER FOTOARCHIV, MUNICH*

this he created aloof, serene figures that seem endowed with an eternal youthfulness and are beyond emotion in the ordinary sense. The surface details of these sculptures, however, were designed in a way that required the viewer to react to fleeting, optical impressions produced by subtle undulations and the play of light and shade over them. Drapery, instead of being rendered in schematic patterns, as in archaic sculpture, or in the severe, solid forms of the early classical style, now came to be conveyed through shallow eddies and deep furrows that seemed to flow over the surface of the sculpture. This blend of idealized subject matter with shimmering agitated surface movement is already detectable in the most developed of the surviving metopes of the Parthenon, completed between 447 and 442 B.C., and in the long procession of Athenian citizens on the frieze of the temple (fig. 8)—citizens seemingly raised to the level of the gods yet retaining their natural, casual human mien—it reaches perfection.

Literary sources and archaeological evidence suggest that many, perhaps hundreds, of sculptors, some of whom were not Athenians, were trained in the Pheidian style while working on the Periclean building program, and it was undoubtedly through them that

Figure 8. Procession of maidens being met by marshals of the panathenaic festival, marble slab from the east frieze of the Parthenon on the Athenian Acropolis, *ca.* 442–438 B.C. Height approx. 106 cm. PARIS, MUSÉE DU LOUVRE. *PHOTO: ALISON FRANTZ*

the style came to be broadcast throughout Greece and to dominate Greek art. One of Pheidias' associates, Kresilas, and two Pheidian pupils, Agorakritos and Alkamenes, earned particularly distinguished reputations, and traces of their work survive. Kresilas did a portrait of Pericles, of which a number of copies are known (the best are in the Vatican and the British Museum). Fragments of Agorakritos' cult statue of the goddess Nemesis, placed in her temple at Rhamnous in Attica, are preserved. Alkamenes seems to have inherited the job of artistic overseer of the Periclean building program after Pheidias was driven into exile around 438 B.C. by Pericles' political enemies. A number of his works have been tentatively identified in Roman copies, but his general style is probably best appreciated in the architectural sculptures from the Hephaisteion and the temple of Ares in the Athenian Agora.

Outside of Athens the one sculptor of the high classical period who earned a lasting reputation in antiquity was Polykleitos the Elder, of Argos, whose career extended from around 450 to 420 B.C. Polykleitos was famed above all for a technical book, the *Canon,* in which he delineated a system of perfect *symmetria* for the human body. In essence this treatise seems to have combined Pythagorean ideas about the relationship of numbers to perfect beauty with solutions to practical problems of design that had preoccupied Greek sculptors for centuries. One of his most famous statues, the *Doryphoros* (Spear Bearer) shown in figure 9, seems to have been designed as an illustration of the *Canon.* Roman copies of it are known, and while there is dispute about exactly how the details of the Polykleitan system of proportion can be detected in these copies, their general effect of balance and harmony is striking. Because the style of Polykleitos is so distinctive, a number of other works by him have been identified with reasonable confidence in Roman copies.

In the final stage of the development of the sculptures of the Parthenon, that is, in its

Figure 9. The *Doryphoros* (Spear Bearer) of Polykleitos, Roman copy in marble of a bronze original of about 450–440 B.C. Height 212 cm. NAPLES, MUSEO ARCHEOLOGICO NAZIONALE. *ALINARI/ART RESOURCE*

pediments, executed between 438 and 432 B.C., the balance between idealistic substance and fleeting surface impression in the Pheidian style seems to have tipped in the direction of the latter quality. Out of this change there developed a new ornate style, sometimes called the "elegant" or "flying drapery" style, in which swirling patterns of drapery became an end in themselves, a form of almost abstract expressionism that could convey meaning and states of mind not contained in the immediate subject matter of the sculptures. This was perhaps an appropriate style for Athenian art in the last third of the fifth century B.C., when the trials of the Peloponnesian War began to corrode the idealism of the mid fifth century. Decorative, calligraphic flourishes seem to "paper over" an underlying spirit of tension and wishful thinking. The flying drapery style is best represented by the elegant dancing figures of Nike on the parapet of the temple of Athena Nike (fig. 10) on the Athenian Acropolis (*ca.* 425–420 B.C.). In extant freestanding sculpture the most impressive example of it is the remarkable figure of Nike by the sculptor Paionios (*ca.* 420 B.C.), set on a tall pillar in front of the temple of Zeus at Olympia (now in the Olympia Museum). Literary sources suggest that the Athenian sculptor Kallimachos, whose reputation for drill work has already been mentioned and who was nicknamed "the one who over-refines his art" (*katatexitechnos*), played an influential role in the development of the new style.

The most distinctive characteristic of the sculpture of the last phase of the classical period, from the end of the Peloponnesian War to the death of Alexander the Great in 323 B.C. (a period usually referred to simply as "the fourth century"), is its emphasis on the expression of personal human emotion. In place of the community-oriented themes of the great works of the fifth century, like the Parthenon frieze, sculptors began to ex-

Figure 10. Winged Nike, detail of marble relief from the north side of the parapet of the temple of Athena Nike on the Athenian Acropolis, *ca.* 425–420 B.C. Height approx. 105 cm. ATHENS, ACROPOLIS MUSEUM INV. NR. 11. *HIRMER FOTOARCHIV, MUNICH*

plore basic and universal feelings—pain, fear, tenderness, humor—that were not dependent on the experience of a particular city or group. The most expressive major monument of the first part of this period is the temple of Asklepios at Epidauros (*ca.* 380 B.C.). Its acroteria carry on a modified version of the flying drapery style, as do a number of other monuments of this time, notably the Nereid Monument from Xan-

thos in Lycia (now in the British Museum). In doing so, they represent the first manifestation of a tendency toward classicism, a looking back to the art of the fifth century for inspiration, that was to be a recurring factor in Greek sculpture for centuries to come. The pedimental sculptures of the temple of Asklepios, on the other hand, particularly the head of Priam and the fallen warriors from the sack of Troy represented in the east pediment, show figures contorted by pain in a way that has been called "anti-classical." The anguished quality of the Epidaurian pediments was perpetuated and intensified in the pedimental sculptures from the temple of Athena Alea (fig. 11) at Tegea in Arcadia, constructed somewhere between 360 and 340 B.C. (now partly in Athens and partly at Tegea). Skopas of Paros was the designer of this temple, and the deeply carved eyes with heavy overhanging brows of the heads from the pediments are usually taken as an index of his personal style. On the basis of this index, many works surviving in Roman copies have been ascribed to Skopas, most convincingly the figure of an ecstatic maenad, now in Dresden.

In the exploration of personal emotion by another well-known artist of the mid fourth century, the Athenian Praxiteles, *pathos* seems to have been scrupulously rejected in favor of a lighter, playful mood. An atmosphere of sophisticated, even jaded, urbanity pervades those works of his that can be identified in copies. In the Hermes at Olympia, for example, the amused adult god smiles as he dangles a bunch of grapes before the infant Dionysos and watches the child reach out eagerly for the source of wine. In the Apollo Sauroktonos the soft-looking god lazily swats the Delphian dragon, now reduced to an ordinary Greek lizard. And in the Aphrodite of Knidos (fig. 12), the first really influential rendering of the completely nude female figure in Greek

Figure 11. Head (perhaps representing Telephos), marble sculpture in the style of Skopas, from the west pediment of the temple of Athena Alea at Tegea in Arcadia, *ca.* 340 B.C. Height of face approx. 20 cm. ATHENS, NATIONAL ARCHAEOLOGICAL MUSEUM. *PHOTO: J. J. POLLITT*

Figure 12. The Aphrodite of Knidos by Praxiteles, Parian marble, Roman copy of a Greek original of about 340 B.C. Height with plinth 204 cm. ROME, VATICAN MUSEUM INV. NR. 812. *HIRMER FOTOARCHIV, MUNICH*

sculpture, the goddess smiles enticingly as she prepares for her bath. Along with their languid mood, the soft contours and sinuous, hip-shot poses of these and other Praxitelean sculptures brought a new sensuousness to Greek sculpture that was widely imitated in later centuries.

Still another type of personal emotion—the mood of personal religious devotion—makes its first appearance in the sculpture of the fourth century. It is most obvious in votive reliefs and cult images of Asklepios, a god whose power to intervene miraculously in individual lives in order to alleviate human suffering made him the object of intense reverence during this period. The most impressive image of Asklepios, and one of the finest sculptures of the fourth

century, is the Blacas head, from Melos, now in the British Museum.

The differing emphases in the work of Skopas and Praxiteles point up the fact that there was a wide variety of personal styles in the fourth century. Literary sources mention many masters whose work had a distinct character—Timotheos, Leochares, Euphranor, and the Argive successors of Polykleitos—but attributions of surviving works to them (the original bronze Athena from Peiraeus to Euphranor, or the type of the Apollo Belvedere in the Vatican to Leochares) are controversial. The difficulty in attributing known works to ancient masters is seen most clearly in the sculptures of the Mausoleum of Halicarnassus, which Pliny tells us were done by the workshops of four artists—Skopas, Timotheos, Leochares, and Bryaxis. After years of study, scholars still disagree about which of the surviving reliefs from the tomb (mostly in the British Museum) should be attributed to which sculptor.

A less problematical expression of the stylistic diversity of the later classical period can be found in Athenian sculptured grave stelae. An unbroken series of these runs from the Periclean period down to about 318 B.C., when they are thought to have been outlawed as part of a series of sumptuary laws. The most common form of them consists of seated and standing figures, one of whom is the deceased and the others relatives or servants, set in a frame resembling the front of a small shrine. In the fourth-century examples one encounters revivals of the style of the Parthenon, the flying drapery style, the passionate style of Skopas, Praxitelean grace, and eventually the new proportions of the style of Lysippos.

Lysippos of Sikyon, whose long career extended from about 360 to 320 B.C. or later, can be viewed as the last great classical sculptor and the first great sculptor of the Hellenistic period. In the early part of his career he seems to have been a formalist in the tradition of Polykleitos, and he won acclaim for working out a new canon of *symmetria* that seems to have been designed both to emulate and improve upon its Polykleitan predecessor. In it he prescribed, among other things, that a taller and leaner effect be achieved in sculptured forms by making the head smaller in relation to the body. He also concentrated on designing his sculptures in such a way that the viewer had

to move around them and see them from many angles in order to appreciate them fully. These aspects of his work are best represented by his *Apoxyomenos* (Youth Scraping Himself with a Strigil) (fig. 13), of which there is a Roman copy in the Vatican.

Later in his career Lysippos became the court sculptor of Alexander the Great, who

Figure 13. The *Apoxyomenos* (Youth Scraping Himself with a Strigil) by Lysippos, Roman copy in marble of a bronze original of about 340–330 B.C. Height 205 cm. ROME, VATICAN MUSEUM INV. NR. 1185. *ALINARI/ART RESOURCE*

valued highly the passionate, expressive portraits that the sculptor did of him. These images of Alexander, with emphases on a dramatic turn of the neck, slightly open mouth, and longing expression, are described in literary sources and are preserved in a variety of copies and variants. Almost equally influential was a great monument, consisting of twenty-five or more bronze equestrian figures, commemorating the companions of Alexander who had fallen in the battle on the Granikos against the Persians (334 B.C.). Its immediate historicity as well as a certain theatrical quality made this Granikos Monument so impressive that it established a genre within Hellenistic royal iconography, the king's (and in the Roman period, the emperor's) battles, that persisted for centuries. (The Lysippan monument itself was carried off from Macedonia to Rome in the second century B.C., thus extending the range of its influence.)

In addition to virtually creating Hellenistic royal iconography, Lysippos' later work, also known through Roman copies and literary references, seems to have anticipated other major developments of the Hellenistic period. His allegorical figure of Opportunity (*Kairos*), for example, foreshadowed the Hellenistic taste for learned, didactic subject matter, and his figures of Herakles, such as the original of the famous Farnese type and a bronze colossus at Tarentum, seem to have looked forward to the Hellenistic baroque style.

The sculpture of the first half of the third century B.C. was dominated by Lysippos' pupils, among whom were his sons. Literary sources attest that they received the most important commissions of the period, such as the assignment to make a figure of Tyche for the new city of Antioch, which went to the sculptor Eutychides. (The appearance of the statue, Lysippan in its proportions and design, is known from a variety of copies.)

The most important new artistic development of the early third century, however, the creation of realistic portraits that probed the inner psyche of their subjects, may have owed something to the art of Lysippos but seems to have taken place primarily in Athens, where the Lysippan school did not have its greatest influence. The Greeks had been making portraits since the early fifth century B.C., but their early portraits had by and large emphasized the public image rather than the private personality of the person represented. With the haggard, tense portrait of Demosthenes (fig. 14), set up in the Athenian Agora in 280 B.C. and executed by an otherwise unknown Athenian sculptor named Polyeuktos, a new genre of portraits was born. (The portrait is known in excellent Roman copies, the best of which is in Copenhagen.) This kind of realistic "personality portrait" was one of the major contributions of the Hellenistic period to the Greek sculptural tradition, and its influence has lasted to the present day.

In the period between about 250 and 150 B.C., the major movement in Hellenistic sculpture was the development of the "Hellenistic baroque" style. The roots of this style may have been in the school of Lysippos and are detectable on a humble level earlier in the third century in funerary sculptures from Tarentum. It first really blossomed, however, in the art of Pergamon. King Attalos I of Pergamon saw his defeat of the Gauls in Asia Minor in the 220s B.C. as an act of cultural salvation for the Greeks equivalent to the defeat of the Persians centuries earlier. In celebration of it he set up a series of victory monuments on the citadel of Pergamon, and later on the Acropolis of Athens, that in their pathos, their sense of dramatic crisis, and their deep, exaggerated carving of undulating muscular forms went beyond anything that had been seen before in Greek sculpture. The Dying Gaul and his Wife and the Dying Trumpeter, both in Rome, are the best known of the Roman copies thought to be based on these Attalid dedications. The culmination of the Helle-

Figure 14. Portrait of Demosthenes by Polyeuktos, Roman copy in marble of a bronze original of about 280 B.C. Height with plinth 202 cm. COPENHAGEN, NY CARLSBERG GLYPTOTEK

nistic baroque came in the great reliefs depicting the battle of the gods and giants on the Altar of Zeus at Pergamon shown in figure 15 (now in Berlin), begun around 180–170 B.C. under the patronage of King Eumenes II. In freestanding sculpture one of the most impressive examples of the style is the Nike of Samothrace of about 190 B.C., now in the Louvre.

Along with and in the wake of the Hellenistic baroque there arose a diverse series of stylistic currents that give a very mixed character to the late Hellenistic period. A movement, sometimes labeled "rococo," that specialized in playful children, frolicking nymphs and satyrs, and the like came about, perhaps, as a reaction to the heaviness and drama of the baroque style. Another movement, responding to Roman taste and reflecting a general retrospective atmosphere of the period, revived the styles of archaic and classical Greece, primarily for use on decorative reliefs. Still another rejected the age-old Greek tendency toward idealism in favor of a startling social realism, best represented by the bronze figure of a battered boxer in Rome but also expressed in a variety of figures of old men and women, dwarfs, and grotesques.

Late in the Hellenistic period a good many Greek sculptors migrated to Rome, set up prestigious workshops, and had a major influence on the development of Roman monumental sculpture and portraiture. Roman sculpture throughout its history, in fact, was usually made by Greeks and is only Roman in the sense that it served the needs of Roman culture and, increasingly, expressed Roman ideas and concepts.

THE STATUS AND ROLE OF SCULPTORS

Plutarch (*Parallel Lives*, "Pericles" 2) and Lucian (*The Dream* [*Somnium*] 6–9) both express

Figure 15. The Battle of the Gods and Giants, detail depicting a winged Nike bestowing victory upon Athena as she seizes the giant Alkyoneus away from his mother Ge (Earth), portion of the east frieze from the Altar of Zeus at Pergamum, begun *ca.* 180–170 B.C. Height 230 cm. EAST BERLIN, STAATLICHE MUSEEN, ANTIKENSAMMLUNG.

the view that, while a man of refinement ought to appreciate the art of sculpture, he should not aspire to be a sculptor, because the profession, involving as it does the need to work with one's hands, is a menial and degrading one. These passages were written, however, during the Roman period, reflecting the social prejudices of that time, and seem not to represent the outlook of the classical Greeks. The Greek view of the importance of the artist seems to have fallen somewhere between the disdainful view of the Roman aristocracy and the romantic view, common in post-Renaissance Europe, of the great artist as an inspired, heaven-storming genius. To be a sculptor was a respectable profession in a classical city-state, and a very successful sculptor, like Pheidias,

could become a figure of considerable influence. Moreover, even as early as the fourth century B.C., there is evidence that the workmanship of great artists of the past was remembered with particular reverence (Isocrates, *Exchange of Property* [*Antidosis*] 2, on Pheidias). The average Greek sculptor, however, was viewed as a craftsman with a particular skill that was neither more nor less important than, say, shipbuilding and other crafts.

The major employers of sculptors in the Greek world seem to have been governments and the administrative authorities of large religious sanctuaries, both of which oversaw the erection of public commemorative monuments and the sculptural adornment of temples and public buildings. Private individuals were also patrons for certain types of monuments, such as votive statues or relief sculptures celebrating military victories or victories in some form of public competition, votive sculptures offered to a deity in a spirit of prayer or thanksgiving, and funerary monuments. Even these were quasi-public. There is very little evidence for privately owned "art for art's sake" sculpture prior to the late Hellenistic period.

Most Greek sculptors made a modest living. What little evidence is available about the level of an average sculptor's wages (for example, the building accounts from the Erechtheion and the temple of Asklepios at Epidauros) suggests that a basic subsistence wage, or slightly better, was the norm. Prestigious artists like Lysippos, when he was the court sculptor for Alexander the Great, undoubtedly made more, but the exact amount is not known. In the Greco-Roman art market of the first century B.C., we hear of fabulous prices being paid for works of the popular sculptor Arkesilaos (Pliny the Elder, *Natural History* 35.155–156), but these were late and temporary aberrations from normal practice.

Literary evidence suggests that most Greek sculptors were itinerant and moved, either by invitation or on their own initiative, from city to city as opportunities for employment arose. Pliny (*Natural History* 36.20) and Pausanias (1.20.1) imply that Praxiteles may have had a studio in Athens in which models or replicas of his works were on display, but if such was really the case (both writers lived centuries after the sculptor's time), it was very unusual.

GEMS

The Greeks made engraved gems from stone, ivory, metal, and, occasionally, glass. Gems seem to have had three functions: as seals for documents, treasure boxes, or simply for identification; as magical amulets; and as ornaments or implements for making ornamental designs through impressions. Many were mounted on, or made in the form of, rings; others were strung and worn as necklaces or pendants; still others were simply attached to handles.

Ancient gems are difficult to date in a scientific way. Relatively few surviving examples come from excavations, and even when a datable context is known, it provides only a terminus ante quem for the gem. Stone gems, in particular, are virtually indestructible and can have a very long life "above ground" before being buried. Some Mycenaean gems, for example, were still in use in the Roman period.

The art of engraving hard stones with a drill had reached a high state of development in the Greek Bronze Age, as had techniques for making gems in ivory and gold. These skills were lost during the Dark Age and only slowly recovered in the course of the first millennium B.C. The earliest known Greek gems after the Mycenaean period are pyramid-shaped seals made of ivory, found on the slopes of the Areopagus in Athens and dating from the mid ninth century B.C. They have square faces incised with simple geometric designs similar to those on Geometric-style pottery. Seals made of stone, usually soft stone like serpentine, with their surfaces worked by hand (rather than by drilling) appeared in the mid eighth century B.C. The most common form is a square plaque, equipped with a hole for the attachment of a handle, incised with geometric designs or figures of animals. A few have what may be mythological scenes, such as the example in the Bibliothèque Nationale in Paris with a man shooting arrows at a centaur (Herakles and Nessos?). Seal types similar to these are known from northern Syria, and it is probable that this area of the Near East played an influential role, through trade or by being the source of traveling craftsmen, in the development of early Greek gems. A number of stone, glass, and faience scarabs and scaraboids (stones shaped like a scarab but not actually carved in the form of a beetle) discovered in Greece and datable to this period seem to be Phoenician in origin.

In the Orientalizing phase of the seventh century B.C., the production of gems was subject to the same sort of innovation and experimentation that one finds in pottery and sculpture. Two groups of gems, representing two distinct centers of production, are of particular importance: first, ivory gems that reflect strong stylistic influences from the Near East and are found in the Peloponnesos; second, a category of stone gems from the Cyclades known as "island gems." The ivories, the best-known examples of which come from the sanctuary of Artemis Orthia at Sparta, consist of discs and squares with recumbent animals carved on their backs and their faces incised with animals, Gorgons, the chimera (a monster with lion's head, goat's body, and serpent's tail), and other orientalizing designs. The most remarkable fact about the island gems is that they seem to be deliberate revivals of the shapes and designs of Mycenaean gems. Presumably many of the early gems survived in use, or were rediscovered, particularly on Melos, which had been an important Mycenaean site and later became a center for the production of island gems, and the gem cutters of the seventh century had an opportunity to study them closely. The island gems imitate the lentoid (lens) and amygdaloid (almond) shapes of the Bronze Age seals, but unlike their Mycenaean prototypes they are made of soft stone, the technique for working hard stone having not yet been rediscovered. Most of them are incised with single figures of animals, humans, and orientalizing composite creatures, but a few have mythological scenes, the most notable being a green steatite seal in the Metropolitan Museum of Art in New York City depicting the suicide of Ajax. Enough island gems

survive to make possible a division of them into stylistic phases (ranging from *ca.* 650 to 575 B.C. and evolving from angular to more modeled, rounded forms), and a number of individual examples can be attributed to particular artists (for example, the "Serpent Master," named after another gem in the Metropolitan Museum in New York showing a sea serpent swimming beneath a ship) (fig. 16a).

With the flowering of the archaic period of Greek art at the beginning of the sixth century B.C., major changes took place in the art of cutting and designing stone gems. The technique of engraving hard gemstones with small bronze drills, powered by a bow or a wheel, and abrasive powder was relearned (probably again from the Near East). The scarab and the scaraboid now became the most popular shape. This form was, of course, ultimately Egyptian in origin, but probably reached Greece via trade with Phoenicia and Syria. Unlike the Egyptian version, the scarabs seem to have had no religious significance, and in place of the pharaonic cartouche (a figure with the sovereign's name) that decorated the flat faces of the prototype, the Greeks incised a wide variety of designs. The stone most favored for the new form was quartz of the chalcedony family, especially carnelian.

Because there is such variety in the designs of archaic gems and their designs are so distinctive, it is usually assumed that the majority of them were made as personal seals, which literary sources attest became important at this time, and the increasing prevalence of inscribed names would seem to confirm this. (The lack of variety and distinctiveness in earlier gems suggests that most of them were perhaps made to be jewelry or decorative stamps.) Most of the inscribed names seem to be those of the owners of the seals, but a limited number are indisputably artists' signatures. These signatures suggest that certain gem cutters enjoyed considerable prestige and that their work was sought out. It is not unlikely that many of them also worked as sculptors. This is clearly attested in at least one case, that of Theodoros of Samos, the prestigious archaic sculptor who was commissioned to make a signet ring for the tyrant Polycrates of Samos (Herodotus, 3.41).

Whether most gem makers practiced other crafts or not, archaic gems clearly have all the brilliance of design of archaic vase painting and all the finesse in workmanship of archaic sculpture. Gems of the sixth century have been divided into three stylistic phases: an early "orientalizing" style that draws upon motifs used in the previous century; a "robust" style characteristic of the middle of the century that emphasizes deep carving and rounded forms; and a "dry" style in the second half of the century that has more shallow, angular engraved forms. A particularly fine work of the robust style is an agate scarab in the British Museum showing a reclining satyr, attributed to the "Master of the London Satyr" (fig. 16b). Some of the figures in the dry style, such as the athlete with a discus on a carnelian scarab in the British Museum, resemble the studies of athletes in early Attic red-figure vase painting.

The finest of the sixth-century gem carvers worked in the late archaic period. Epimenes, whose signature occurs on a masterful chalcedony scaraboid (in Boston) depicting a youth restraining an excited horse (fig. 16c), was one of the greatest. Another was the "Semon Master," who made a specialty of two-part combat scenes, such as Herakles and the Nemean lion and a man struggling with a griffin, both in Boston. (The name Semon appears on a gem in Berlin, but it is not certain whether it is the owner's name or the artist's.) On the Cycladic Islands there was a special subgroup of gems, known as "island scarabs," that continued to be made in the soft stones prevalent in the seventh century. Two of the artists who produced these gems, Syries and Onesimos (the latter best known for a steatite scarab in Boston showing a satyr tuning his lyre), are also among the finest of the period.

Rings in gold, silver, and bronze with designs similar to those on gemstones were produced from the seventh century B.C. onward. They are classified according to the varying shapes—for example, cartouche, diamond, and shield—of their faces (bezels).

Like archaic gems, gems of the classical period follow the stylistic currents of their time as known from sculpture and vase painting. The principal technical change of the time is that scaraboids came to outnumber scarabs, and new forms, such as "sliced cylinders" and "barrels," were introduced. The work of the fifth century B.C. was dominated by one very great artist, Dexamenos of Chios, who was active around the time of the Parthenon and deserves to be called the Pheidias of gem carvers. His signed works are scaraboids: two marvelous studies of water birds, now in Leningrad; a penetrating portrait head of a man (fig. 16d), in Boston; and a seated woman facing a maid who holds a mirror and wreath, in Cambridge. Later in the fifth century the classical style as perfected by Dexamenos was taken up with enthusiasm by gem makers in the Greek cities of southern Italy and Sicily, where several workshops produced works of high quality. Gems of the fourth century have been divided into the "common" and "fine" styles, the former relatively simple works that look back to the fifth century for their models, the latter more elaborate pieces that draw upon the taste for elegance of their time (like the Kerch style in vase painting).

In the Hellenistic period, after the conquests of Alexander had opened up the Near East and made available exotic new sources of stone, the character of Greek gems once again changed markedly. Scarabs and scaraboids were given up in favor of convex ringstones. Precious and semi-

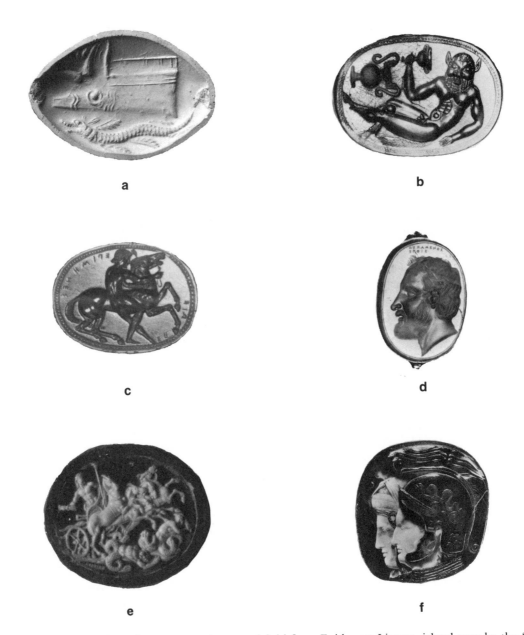

Figure 16. *(a)* Impression of a green steatite amygdaloid from Epidaurus Limera, island gem by the "Serpent Master," second half of seventh century B.C. Length 27 mm NEW YORK, METROPOLITAN MUSEUM OF ART, PULITZER FUND INV. NR. 42.11.11; *(b)* agate scarab carved in the robust style by the "Master of the London Satyr," second half of sixth century B.C. (16 × 22 mm) BY COURTESY OF THE TRUSTEES OF THE BRITISH MUSEUM, INV. NR. 65.7–12.106; *(c)* sapphirine chalcedony scaraboid from the Nile Delta signed by Epimenes, *ca.* 500 B.C. (12 × 17 mm) BOSTON, MUSEUM OF FINE ARTS, FRANCIS BARTLETT FUND INV. NR. 27.677; *(d)* yellow and red jasper scaraboid signed by Dexamenos of Chios, *ca.* 440 B.C. (20 × 16 mm) BOSTON, MUSEUM OF FINE ARTS, FRANCIS BARTLETT FUND INV. NR. 23.580; *(e)* sardonyx cameo signed by Athenion, *ca.* 330–100 B.C. (30 × 35 mm) NAPLES, MUSEO ARCHEOLOGICO NAZIONALE INV. NR. 25848; *(f)* the "Vienna Cameo," sardonyx chalcedony of nine layers, probably early third century B.C. (115 × 113 mm) VIENNA, KUNSTHISTORISCHES MUSEUM INV. NR. IX A81

precious stones, such as garnet, amethyst, and topaz, now appeared. In addition to drilling, some gems now show sharp, incised lines that may have been made with diamonds. Gems made of glass also became common at this time. Perhaps the most striking innovation of the period is the development of cameos, gems made of Indian sardonyx carved in relief and revealing in their designs the multicolored layers of the stone.

Hellenistic gems reflect the same wide variety of styles that characterizes Hellenistic sculpture. A splendid example of the Hellenistic baroque style, for example, is the cameo (now in Naples) depicting Zeus in combat with the giants (fig. 16e), signed by the artist Athenion. Perhaps the most striking development in the subject matter of Hellenistic gems, as in that of sculpture, is the omnipresence of portraits. Most of these represent Hellenistic kings and queens. A particularly fine example is a large cameo in Vienna (known simply as the "Vienna Cameo," as shown in figure 16f) with superimposed portraits of two rulers, probably Ptolemy II of Egypt and his queen, Arsinoë.

The signatures of a fair number of Hellenistic gem carvers survive, but the name and work of the most famous and influential of them, Pyrgoteles, who was appointed official gem maker for Alexander the Great, are known only through literary sources.

BIBLIOGRAPHY

GENERAL

Charles Picard, *Manuel d'archéologie grecque: la sculpture* (1935–1966); Gisela M. A. Richter, *The Sculpture and Sculptors of the Greeks,* 4th ed. (1970); Martin Robertson, *A History of Greek Art* (1975).

PARTICULAR PERIODS

Margarete Bieber, *The Sculpture of the Hellenistic Age* (rev. ed. 1961); John Boardman, *Greek Sculpture: The Archaic Period* (1978); Jerome J. Pollitt, *Art and Experience in Classical Greece* (1972), and *Art in the Hellenistic Age* (1966); Brunilde S. Ridgway, *The Severe Style in Greek Sculpture* (1970), *The Archaic Style in Greek Sculpture* (1977), and *Fifth Century Styles in Greek Sculpture* (1981).

PARTICULAR GROUPS

Bernard Ashmole and Nicholas Yalouris, *Olympia: The Sculptures of the Temple of Zeus* (1967); Frank Brommer, *The Sculptures of the Parthenon* (1979); Rhys Carpenter, *The Sculpture of the Nike Temple Parapet* (1929); Gisela M. A. Richter, *Kouroi* (1960), *The Portraits of the Greeks* (1965), and *Korai* (1968).

TECHNIQUE

Sheila Adam, *The Technique of Greek Sculpture in the Archaic and Classical Periods* (1966); Carl Bluemel, *Greek Sculptors at Work,* 2d ed. (1969); Carl Roebuck, ed., *The Muses at Work* (1969).

LITERARY SOURCES

Texts without translations: Johannes Overbeck, *Die antiken Schriftquellen zur Geschichte der bildenden Künste bei den Griechen* (1868; repr. 1959);

Translations: Jerome J. Pollitt, *The Art of Greece, 1400–31 B.C., Sources and Documents* (1965); Henry Stuart Jones, *Ancient Writers on Greek Sculpture* (1895; repr. 1966).

GEMS

John Boardman, *Greek Gems and Finger Rings, Early Bronze Age to Late Classical* (1970); Adolf Furtwängler, *Die antiken Gemmen* (1900); Gisela M. A. Richter, *Engraved Gems of the Greeks, Etruscans, and Romans* I (1968).

Roman Sculpture and Gems

RICHARD BRILLIANT

THE GREEK HERITAGE

Roman sculpture was not always appreciated by the ancient Romans themselves or by more recent connoisseurs of art. Although deeply influenced by Greek formal and iconographic models, Roman sculpture is not Greek; however, its otherness has not been easy to define. In antiquity Roman collectors often looked to works of Greek sculpture as more worthy of acquisition, and wealthy Roman patrons seem to have preferred artists with Greek names, as if their art had greater legitimacy and prestige, even if the status of the artist, a person who worked with his hands, was not very high. The search for "great name" artists and for the works of art associated with them gave rise to keen competition for famous pieces. When they were not available, then collectors turned to good, recognizable copies of the works of the masters. Still, museums are filled with works of sculpture that bear the label "Roman," indicating something more or less different from Greek, depending on the historical or aesthetic basis of the display.

Works of Roman sculpture, largely the result of excavations over the past 500 years, were highly prized in the Renaissance as survivals of classical antiquity, which comprehended both Greek and Roman civilization and their arts. Several of these prized masterpieces, discovered in the fifteenth and sixteenth centuries, are now in the Vatican Museums, and the vicissitudes of their reputations exemplify the critical problems of reception, evaluation, and interpretation that mark the history of Roman sculpture. Among these works the Belvedere Torso, so admired by Michelangelo, bears an inscription in Greek: "Apollonios, son of Nestor, from Athens, made it." This headless and limbless work was probably made in the first century B.C. by a Greek sculptor for a Roman patron. Is it to be regarded as Greek or Roman? The second of these works, the famous statue of the Apollo Belvedere, a Hadrianic version in marble of a bronze original, attributed to Leochares, a Greek master of the fourth century B.C., brought forth in the eighteenth century the highest praise from Winckelmann and Goethe, who considered it the greatest work of classical antiquity. Again, is it Greek or Roman?

And last, the statue of Laocoön and his sons, discovered in Rome in 1506 and the first work of ancient art appearing in Pliny the Elder's *Natural History* to come down from antiquity, made Renaissance artists wild with excitement. They extolled the expressive quality of the sculpture, satisfied at last that they could verify the judgment of the ancients with their own eyes. Pliny attributed the work to three Rhodian sculptors, Hagesandros, Athanadoros, and Polydoros (*Natural History* 36.37–38), and until fairly recently the Laocoön was thought to be a masterwork of Hellenistic sculpture of the second or first century B.C. However, after World War II a large cache of marble sculptures was discovered in the seaside grotto of the villa of the emperor Tiberius at Spelunca (Sperlonga) in southern Latium. Many of the surviving fragments were recomposed to form two large sculptural groups representing the exploits of Odysseus (Ulysses). Their dramatic style and virtuoso carving closely resemble those of the Laocoön and the work of the Rhodian school of Hellenistic sculptors. In the grotto an inscription was found bearing the names of the same three Rhodian sculptors listed by Pliny in the first century A.D., but now apparently the masters of these dramatic Sperlonga sculptures. It soon became clear to scholars that these unique works of art, carved by Rhodian artists trained in a late Hellenistic tradition, had been created for an imperial Roman patron, in Italy, and in the first century A.D. Are they Greek or Roman?

The question of classification as Greek or Roman is not artificial because it responds to historical realities. Rome was the direct heir of Greece, especially after its expansion into the eastern Mediterranean in the second century B.C. Greek works of art flooded into Rome, acquired as spoils and by purchase, and the possession of such works became the mark of the cultivated person by the late republic. To a degree, works of Greek art either in the original or in copies formed the basis of public and private collections, decorated the houses and estates of the great magnates, and were incorporated in many public monuments. Thus, there was an active presence of Greek art, and Greek artists were employed by Roman patrons to execute original commissions in traditional ways for a very long time. Here one may say that Greek art was in Roman service; in this context the term "Greco-Roman" refers to such works as well as to similar gems or small-scale bronze sculptures, made for a wealthy clientele, sharing similar values and scattered in cities and towns around the Mediterranean.

That clientele, however greedy for original works of Greek art or reasonable facsimiles, was often unsophisticated and was drawn to what looked "Greek." Enterprising Greek artists, or artists with Greek names, came to fill this hunger for Greek culture and invented "Greek" works of art that were eclectic, combining various elements, motifs, compositions, and styles drawn from the history of Greek art. Pasiteles, a Greek sculptor from southern Italy in the first century B.C., excelled in meeting these requirements, as did his followers, Stephanos and Menelaos; and another of these clever artists, Arkesilaos, was commissioned to execute the cult statue of Venus Genetrix for her temple in the Forum of Caesar in Rome in a Greek archaizing style. Pasiteles himself wrote a guidebook to Greek art in five volumes to educate this clientele and to cultivate their taste, probably for such eclectic works as the *Electra and Orestes* in Naples and Rome.

These eclectic works of art, generically rather than specifically, even correctly, Greek, were new creations. They and the artists who made them did more than seduce the unwary Roman collector. A climate open to selective but far-ranging borrowing was created; when reinforced by the ongoing presence of Greek masterworks, the works produced educated upper-class Romans to accept the whole of Greek art as the normative basis for the new art they were prepared to patronize.

Greek art became a common denominator that ran through Roman art until the late empire, even when its power was resisted. By this means Romans brought Greek art to northern and western Europe, thereby creating the first European art. Because it was partly formed out of this eclectic amalgamation of diverse, although categorically Greek, styles, Roman art was subjected to repeated revivals of more purified Greek models, especially under Augustus, Hadrian, the Antonine emperors, and Gallienus. Such revivals probably owed their existence to the fact that the artists and patrons responsible were also making positive statements about the value of the past, of the Greek tradition and its continuation and absorption by the Romans. Here, too, the great number of figural motifs, iconographical models, and compositional types that formed the repertory of Greek art was always available to Roman artists whenever they wanted to portray their gods, themselves, or their exploits.

SCULPTURE MATERIALS

Marble, the favored material for fine Greek sculpture, first came into Roman art as an import from quarries in the Greek east, sometimes with the blocks rough-cut or accompanied by local masons and sculptors. The quarries at Luna (Luni) in Liguria, however, with their fine-grained, opaque marbles, were opened only under Augustus. Terra-cotta, various soft volcanic rocks such as tufa, and a fairly coarse limestone, together with bronze, were the common materials of indigenous sculpture in Italy. The use of these materials for sculpture

had been developed by Etruscan and Italian artists whose work was available to the Romans of the kingdom and early republic. These sculptors worked their craft in the making of architectural sculpture and honorific public commissions and relied especially on terra-cotta and to a lesser degree on costly bronze (for example, the Etruscan late-sixth-century statue of the Roman she-wolf, the *Lupa Romana,* and the third- or second-century mid-Italian portrait known as the Capitoline Brutus) for costly projects, and on tufa for common tasks. But tufa, which cuts very easily, is an unsubtle stone, while bronze and terra-cotta are ductile materials, heavily dependent on modeling and on the incisive detailing of the surface. The making of sculpture in these materials is the very antithesis of the carving techniques required for working marble. Some scholars, especially Kaschnitz von Weinberg (1965), have suggested that these different techniques of making sculpture responded to and reinforced different artistic sensibilities. Accordingly, the indigenous Italian works of art tended to be more descriptive and more schematic than Greek sculptures with their emphasis on fully carved, solid forms. Although this attempt to correlate material differences, structural properties, and expressive possibilities may be difficult to demonstrate in particular objects, there is no question that the native sculptural tradition can be distinguished from the Greek, not just by the eye or hand but most strongly by its diminished interest in that organic coherency of the human form so fundamental to Greek art.

STYLISTIC DEVELOPMENT IN THE REPUBLIC

Roman art, or at least the art of the city of Rome during the republic, seems to have come into being around the time of the Punic Wars when native and Greek artistic traditions began to interact. Far from the many famous works of art in the Conservatori Museum in Rome the assiduous visitor will find four fragmentary reliefs, one placed above another in front of a wall. On the bottom, sterile, regular, and correct, is a section of a marble architrave (fig. 1a) from a building of the late republic, all its elements derived from the decorative repertory of Hellenistic architecture, and rather academically at that; the mason has done his work well, and perhaps that is enough for the purpose, the sober ornamentation of a building. Above it lies a rich, deeply carved acanthus rinceau (fig. 1b), a leaf-motif scroll, in which the irregularities express both the vitality of the plant forms and the mason's skill, nicely kept under the control of the symmetrical composition. This architectural frieze can be dated late in the first century B.C. and reveals the sophistication of Augustan architectural ornament, when the masons had mastered the art of fine stonecutting and had freed themselves from the restrictions of mechanical patterns.

A long limestone frieze (fig. 1c) stretches out at the third level, filled by the frontal busts of six men and women, some old, some young, set bleakly against a clear relief ground, their heads pushing hard against the projecting upper edge of the slab. This late republican relief once decorated the front of a family tomb and served as the bald announcement of the presence of those family members whose ashes lie within and of the pride and (modest) wealth of the group for all to see. This is traditional "old style" Roman portraiture, used here by a successful but hardly prominent group, emulating the worthy images developed for the dignitaries of the Roman state at the end of the second century B.C. These portraits are direct, unlovely, harshly descriptive, and seemingly honest in revealing the physiognomies of these individuals. But more than the grim imagery is harsh and incisive; the style of carving is harsh too, with sharp ridges, linear accents, skull-hard heads, and complicated surface detail. In this sepulchral relief the head is all-important, its primary function to signify the person represented; the draped bust below serves more as a prop than as a body form, the prominently displayed hands an effective attention-getting device, often uncertainly connected to the body of their owner.

Above this tomb relief is an earlier, even starker work (fig. 1d), roughly cut in coarse stone in which the close attention to detail in the human head and in the stalks of grain exposes the primarily symbolic function of the composition. There is nothing Greek about it, but then perhaps the Greek forms and images are anomalous in the context of Italian and Roman art and the difficulty of their absorption by the less hellenized population is to be understood as an aspect of the resistance of the indigenous culture to foreign importations. Thus, the topmost relief and even the family relief below indicate the quality of the indigenous tradition as an established repertory of forms and images, quite distinct from the Greek. A residuum of this native tradition will endure for generations, and it too will provide a basis for change.

The assimilation of these divergent traditions occurred in the late republic, as Rome consolidated its political hold on the Mediterranean world and as the leaders of Roman society absorbed the cultural heritage of ancient and contemporary Greece. Two large reliefs, probably carved in the first quarter of the first century B.C. and conventionally associated with the so-called Altar of Domitius Ahenobarbus, a member of a powerful late republican family, reveal the hesitant, even hybridized, nature of this process. One relief in Munich represents the triumph of the sea deities Neptune and Amphitrite,

Figure 1. Republican and early imperial friezes and reliefs: *(a)* marble architrave; *(b)* architectural frieze with acanthus rinceau carving; *(c)* limestone portrait frieze from a family tomb; *(d)* coarse stone relief. ROME, MUSEI CAPITOLINO, PALAZZO DEI CONSERVATORI. *PHOTO: DEUTSCHES ARCHÄOLOGISCHES INSTITUT, ROME*

accompanied by a cohort of fantastic creatures of the sea, all drawn from the imaginative repertory of Hellenistic art and beautifully carved in marble. The other relief, apparently from the same monument and also in marble, represents the Roman Ceremony of the Census (fig. 2) with its attendant sacrifice, dominated by the taller figures of Mars and of the censor on either side of the central altar. The figures are carefully, if simply, carved, some attention having been given to the anatomical coherence of the poses and to the relation of drapery to the body beneath; the sculptor also endeavored to indicate a real, if shallow, space in which the action quietly unfolds. Yet something of the indigenous tradition survives in the schematic nature of the overall composition, in the careful, even insistent emphasis on detail (of costume, of attribute, of face), and

in the use of hieratic scale: making their figures taller isolates Mars and the censor and focuses the viewer's attention. In this relief, clearly influenced by Greek art, a detailed, descriptive symbolism governs the design, as a traditional Roman office is given a historical reality in the person of the censor, whose identity is at present in dispute.

Thus fact, or the representation of fact, determines the iconography of the Census Relief, a reflection of the annalistic mentality of upper-class Romans at this time. A similar intention informs the frieze on the so-called Baker's Monument beside the Porta Maggiore in Rome; the baker, Eurysaces, who made his fortune baking bread for Caesar's armies, showed just how bread was made in a detailed narrative frieze, precisely because from such matter-of-fact activities his fortune, and hence his prestige,

Figure 2. The Ceremony *(lustrum)* of the Census, portion of marble relief from the so-called Altar of Domitius Ahenobarbus in Rome, late second or early first century B.C. Height 82 cm. PARIS, MUSÉE DU LOUVRE INV. NR. 975. *CLICHÉ DES MUSÉES NATIONAUX, PARIS*

was derived. The monument also bore full-figure portraits of himself and his wife in high relief, prominently displayed on the side of the tomb, which took the unusual form of a large, industrial bread oven. This fascination with fact, with the substantial, even material, realities of life remains with the Romans and shapes some of the most important imperial commissions, including the reliefs of the Column of Trajan.

In the Census relief the iconography of Mars is a romanized version of his Greek counterpart, Ares, consistent with the transference of the Greek pantheon to Rome, at least in the forms of its conventional imagery. Mars's presence brings an allegorical touch to the political theme, qualifying the immediate historical situation and revealing the god's favor in this enterprise. Thematically, if not formally, it is consistent with the extended allegory of the rest of the monument: the portrayal of the marine triumph in the Munich relief relies on a Greek idiom—the victory of Neptune and his triumphant posture—to symbolize a Roman victory at sea. The iconography of military victory, a central theme in Roman art, was developed from Greek sources, and could be used to symbolize the hoped-for triumph over death, appropriated for sepulchral art.

On the side of the monumental Tomb of the Julii, outside of ancient Glanum in Gallia Narbonensis (modern St. Rémy-de-Provence, in southern France), is a large re-lief, depicting a Roman victory over Gallic barbarians. Victory herself appears in confirmation of the victory being won, a symbolic restatement of the action presented in the relief. By virtue of its position on the exterior of the tomb, the motif of battle has been converted into a metaphor of victory over death. Such a victory carries with it the promise of a future life because the upper edge is framed by a garland, borne by *putti* (cupids) and decorated with theatrical masks, evocative of Dionysus (Bacchus) and the promise of his cult. The quality of this late republican monument is remarkable, and so too is the strong pictorial character of the composition, with its apparent faithfulness to Hellenistic, probably Pergamene models, all in a work of art executed in the provinces. Of course, this part of Gaul had been under Roman control for decades, and even before that the Rhône Valley had been penetrated by the Greeks from Massalia (Roman Massilia, now Marseilles), bringing their ideas and their art with them. It is evident that even in this early stage of development, the nature of Roman art in the provinces and the degree of interaction between local and Greco-Roman artistic traditions depended very much on the prior degree of exposure to Greek art and the social level of the patrons.

An analogous process influenced the creation of a handsome bronze statuette of Isis-Fortuna (fig. 3), found in Herculaneum and now in Mainz. The elegant late-first-century B.C. statue with its graceful pose and flowing drapery follows late Hellenistic models very closely, while the iconography combines the attributes of the Egyptian goddess Isis (the feathered crown on her head, the "Isis-knot" on her breast) with those of the Roman goddess Fortuna (the rudder held in the right hand, the cornucopia in the left). This syncretized image assimilated elements drawn from a variety of sources, and it was probably made in Italy. In such a superb work the hybrid art of Rome in the late republic and early empire achieved complete integration of the constituent traditions, bringing forth a masterpiece of small-scale bronze sculpture, a freestanding self-sufficient object on its own base.

Thousands of similar bronze statuettes, some like the Isis-Fortuna about 20 inches (0.5 m) or more in height, others much reduced, have been found throughout the ancient world, many of them imported into the provinces from the major artistic centers. Often such bronzes functioned as models in miniature of large-scale works of art that otherwise were not directly accessible. Small bronzes frequently served the public and private needs of cult observance, where their image value was preeminent. It is likely, given the evidence of bronzes found in the Mahdia shipwreck off the Tunisian coast, as well as the ancient reputation of "Corinthian" bronzes, supposedly made in Corinth and other Greek workshops, that many were of such high quality that they must have been prized as artworks by collectors.

THE AUGUSTAN AGE

Just as the Roman world was never the same after the long reign of Augustus, so Roman art was never the same, becoming much more than it had ever been before, a classic art worthy of a world empire. The hybridiz-

Figure 3. Isis-Fortuna from Herculaneum, bronze statuette, late first century B.C. Height 5 cm. NAPLES, MUSEO ARCHEOLOGICO NAZIONALE

ing tendencies of late republican art reached their culmination under Augustus, a magnificent, ambitious, and manipulative patron who made Rome into a city of marble buildings. He found the fitting expression of Roman dignity and accomplishment in the combination of Roman subjects and attitudes with Greek models, drawn especially from ancient Athens and royal Pergamum.

In this first classic and classicizing period of Roman art, these models provided a suitable inspiration for artists who, like Vergil and Horace, were asked to assert Rome's legitimacy as the rightful, effective continuator of Hellenic civilization.

Ambitious programs of building were undertaken in Rome, in Italy, and throughout the empire to exhibit the quality of Roman civilization and imperial power, of state and emperor. Exquisite workmanship characterized many of these buildings (for example, the Maison Carrée in Nemausus [Nîmes]) the design of which seemed often to depend on a few metropolitan models, adapted to local building conditions and techniques of construction. In Rome itself, the Pantheon of Agrippa (later rebuilt by Hadrian), the Forum of Augustus, the restoration of the Roman Forum as an Augustan complex, and the Altar of Augustan Peace (Ara Pacis Augustae, dedicated 13 B.C., completed 9 B.C.) (see fig. 8 in CLOTHING AND ORNAMENT) relied heavily on architectural sculpture in the round and in relief to display the messages of the Augustan propaganda: peace with victory, prosperity in security, and the rule of law. For these purposes the sculptures of the Athenian Acropolis and the works of the Greek master sculptors of the fifth century B.C. were ideal.

The marble sculpture of the Prima Porta Augustus (fig. 4), now in the Vatican Museum, embodies many of these ideals, clothed in a self-conscious mantle of imperial iconography. The statue was found in the villa of Augustus' wife, Livia, at Prima Porta on the Via Flaminia a few miles north of Rome. When the statue was excavated in the late nineteenth century, traces of paint survived on the cuirass, suggesting that it was meant to look like metal; this fact, as well as the very sharp carving of the motifs on the cuirass, the figured support by the right leg, and the bare feet have convinced many scholars that the Prima Porta statue is a replica of an original bronze, now lost, probably made for Livia herself as a special memento of her husband sometime early in the reign of Tiberius. The original work has been dated to the early second decade of the first century B.C. The relatively flat back of the statue with its simpler workmanship indicates that the figure must have been placed against a wall or in a niche on a fairly high base so that the statue, more than 6 feet (2 m) tall and somewhat remote, would have made a very strong impression on the observer. Standing below and looking up at Augustus, gesturing authoritatively above, the viewer would immediately have understood the power of this being. In its own way the Prima Porta Augustus is a perfect example of the Augustan classic style with its idealizing incorporation of Roman iconographic patterns and familiar Greek imagery.

Pure Augustan art is very much a court style appealing to a highly educated, hellenized elite, and this statue refers explicitly to a famous masterpiece of high classical Greek sculpture, the Doryphorus of Polykleitos (see fig. 9 in GREEK SCULPTURE AND GEMS). This prestigious work was often replicated in the early empire, as in the very correct, slightly academic marble copy in Naples, probably also of Tiberian date. Polykleitos' statue had come to symbolize the classical ideal of the heroic male nude, the most signal image of Greek culture. Its use here by the unknown sculptor of the Prima Porta Augustus marks a deliberate attempt to conflate that image within the idealized, redundant system of references that together present the emperor as the ideal hero of the newly reconstituted Roman state.

Cuirass and uniform reveal Augustus as a general officer, an *imperator* endowed with *imperium*; it follows a well-established Greek convention of the cuirassed statue type, previously employed for some of the great generals of the republic and to be used over and over again throughout the em-

Figure 4. Cuirass statue of Augustus from Prima Porta, Tiberian copy in marble of a bronze original of about 19–15 B.C. Height 204 cm. ROME, VATICAN MUSEUM INV. NR. 2290. *ALINARI/ART RESOURCE*

pire. The spear (a modern restoration) serves as a piece of military equipment at one level of significance, but more profoundly it is here borne as a symbol of supreme power, the power granted to Augustus by the Roman Senate in 27 B.C. The gesture of the upraised right arm, which perhaps once held a baton in the hand, suggests the formal address made by a commander to his troops in the field (*adlocutio*). Here its capacity is more rhetorical, pressing upon the observer, the Roman public by extension, the very exercise of authority itself. This rhetorical ingredient forms an integral part of much of Roman imperial sculpture, because such sculptures were not meant merely to be seen; they were created to impress, to engage the viewer psychologically, and to condition his response. In this case the response would have been most respectful given the lofty stature of the subject, but also because the putto and dolphin support beside the right leg refers directly to the goddess Venus, the divine progenetrix of the Julian line. Augustus was an adopted son of that line through Julius Caesar, who had been carefully, devotedly deified by him. Thus, Augustus can be seen as perfect in body, the scion of a divine house, the son of a god, imperator and princeps, and even *pius*; but that is not all.

His large, noble head with its simplified features, calm expression, and rounded cranium represents an ideal type, an ever-youthful portrait dependent on the Polykleitan model. Only Augustus' long nose and slightly narrow chin sufficed to assure the necessary recognition of the human subject in this work. However, Augustan artists were not always so reticent, as may be seen in the veiled portrait of Augustus as *pontifex maximus* in the marble statue from the Via Labicana in the Terme Museum and in the many portraits of Livia in her long lifetime; but even in these works blemishes and the marks of age simply did not appear. The master of the Prima Porta statue did create a successful type of ideal portrait, which circulated in many replicas, including busts, throughout the empire for many years until the emperor's death. The image of calm grandeur and heroic youth proclaimed the Augustan era and its messianic prospects; it fixed the public concept of Augustus despite the increasing age and infirmities of the man himself and served as well the requirements of the other male members of his house as a fitting model for their portraits. This superb example of image making indicates a keen awareness on the part of artist and patron of the political value of such images as instruments of policy, acting as surrogate appearances of the emperor in the chief places of the empire. Imperial successors of Augustus would fill the world with their images to the same effect.

Augustus wears a cuirass replete with cosmic images: at the top there is the coming of the new era as Dawn streaks across his chest under the protective mantle of the Sky; below, on either side, are the supporting figures of Apollo and Diana, recalling their presence at the naval victory over Antony and Cleopatra at Actium (31 B.C.) and framing a scene in which a pantalooned barbarian hands over a military standard to a martial figure in Roman costume, perhaps Romulus, the proto–alter ego of Augustus. This central motif on the cuirass may refer to the return of the standards lost by Crassus to the Parthians in 53 B.C. and recovered peacefully, through diplomacy. At the bottom edge of the cuirass the personified Earth holds a cornucopia, giving forth her bounty in this time of golden peace, assured for all Romans by the numinous power of Augustus. Except for the historical reference at the center, all these elements have been taken from the allusive repertory of Hellenistic art, especially developed by the Ptolemies. They have been fully absorbed into the imperial repertory, their very Greekness a contribution to their symbolic weight in this romanized setting.

JULIO-CLAUDIAN ART

Many of these same themes, expressed with similar clarity and elegance, permeate the Augustan coinage, the program of the Altar of Augustan Peace with its further allusions to the Parthenon frieze, and the great gems and cameos issuing from the imperial court and its environment. Such luxurious presentation pieces as the Blacas Cameo in London, the famous Gemma Augustea in Vienna, and the Tiberian Grand Camée de France in Paris sumptuously display the special importance of these subjects for Augustus and the successive members of the Julio-Claudian dynasty.

Claudius adopted a similar, if more limited symbolic vocabulary, with a mixture of Greek forms and Roman references, in a splendid cameo in The Hague (fig. 5), representing his Britannic triumph. Accompanied by his wife, Messalina, and his children, Octavia (the future wife of Nero) and Britannicus (Nero's victim), Claudius rides easily, dressed in the civilian costume of the Roman toga, wreathed and brandishing Jupiter's thunderbolt. Victory flies toward him, extending the crown of the triumphator while a trophy rises beneath her, symbolizing the defeat of the Britons. Centaurs, fantastic creatures of Greek myth, draw the imperial biga (chariot) without effort (and without reins), holding out a shield both trophaic and honorific, a shield on which Victory could inscribe Claudius' great deeds. These centaurs also symbolize the wildness of the uncivilized, now quieted by the emperor; they may also stand for the teachers of the martial arts to Achilles, a not-so-veiled reference to the child Britannicus,

armed and holding the hilt of his sword in one hand, a quiver of arrows on his back in the other.

The Hague cameo defines the atmosphere of triumph in which the imperial dynasty flourishes rather than any specific event. The artist has done so with a broader, looser style than the Prima Porta cuirass, in a still elegant manner but less detailed and with larger, more robust shapes. These formal characteristics are to be found in the art of the late Julio-Claudian period, which moves steadily away from the cold classicism of Augustan art to a more plastic, modeled style, influenced by Hellenistic works of art whose active patronage continued under Tiberius (Spelunca, Sperlonga), Nero (the Domus Aurea, Rome), and Domitian of the Flavian dynasty at Rome.

This more energetic Julio-Claudian style penetrated into the northern provinces, as can be seen in the well-preserved toga-clad statue of Lucius Poblicius (fig. 6) from his large tomb in Colonia Agrippinensis (Cologne), dated to the mid first century A.D. The coarse local stone did not permit much subtlety in carving, but the sculptor has made an effort to evoke the plastic treatment of the Claudian toga with its deep folds, and

Figure 5. The Britannic Triumph of Claudius, sardonyx cameo, A.D. 312–315 (21.1 × 29.7 cm). THE HAGUE, ROYAL COIN CABINET

1737

even something of the body beneath the heavy drapery. Typical too of his provincial character as an artist (or of the wishes of his patron) are the frontality of the pose, the simple and inorganic carving of the right forearm, and the globular head with its ruler-straight chiseled nose and large, staring eyes, the pupils deeply hollowed and darkly disturbing. The Poblicius statue is especially interesting because it shows how rapidly changes in Roman art passed from the capital to the provinces and how wealthy provincials were motivated to emulate the style of Rome and of the imperial court as much as possible. The style of the work demonstrates how local attitudes (perhaps one may call them the expression of a "provincial sensibility") at least superficially resemble the reluctance of Romans in the republican period to adopt the forms of Greek art without reservations.

THE FLAVIAN PERIOD

Flavian art at Rome went beyond reservation to the full exploitation of Hellenistic art and of the previous traditions of Roman art itself. Artists developed a richly plastic sculptural style, vividly presented in the broad-faced portraits of Vespasian, Titus, and Domitian, which are filled with physical vitality, and in the handsome portraits of imperial ladies and court beauties. Virtuoso carvers executed these latter works, bent on capturing the tactile quality of female flesh, the sponginess of frizzled hair, the gleam of an eye, as if to bring their subjects alive.

Franz Wickhoff (1900) thought that Flavian art used light and the implication of its movement in a manner comparable to French Impressionist painting, especially when he considered the visual quality of the passage reliefs from the Arch of Titus in Rome. Vivid indeed is this relief, with its sensation of the momentariness of life and

Figure 6. Limestone funerary statue of Lucius Poblicius from Cologne, mid first century A.D. COLOGNE, RÖMISCH-GERMANISCHES MUSEUM. *PHOTO: RHEINISCHES BILDARCHIV, COLOGNE*

its immediacy. The rapid movement of light plays an important role in energizing the sculpted forms, but Flavian sculpture is too substantial to support Wickhoff's comparison, too tied to the materiality of the stone and of the figures carved from it. The Arch of Titus is a Domitianic project of the 90s, honoring the triumphant suppression of the

First Jewish Revolt (A.D. 71). It established the legitimacy of the Flavian dynasty and exalted the memory of his brother, and is a fine example of the emperor's ambitious and sophisticated exercise of artistic patronage in Rome.

The passage relief, shown in figure 7, represents the triumph of Titus, accompanied by Victory, his chariot led by the personified Roma and by lictors. Since the arch is located on the Sacra Via where it is about to descend into the Roman Forum, the apparent movement of the triumphal cortege may be seen to complement the act of entrance itself. The fanning movement of the four prancing horses intensifies this effect, as they pass above the spectator's head. And yet, despite the illusion of figures moving in space, a space enhanced by the deep cutting and the play of dark, broken shadows, the composition is fully contained within the rectangular panel and there is little apparent room for the bodies of the inward horses, contradicting the illusion of spatial sufficiency. Perhaps this effect was induced by the artist to conceptualize the ideal nature of the scene—the triumphator did not, in fact, enter the Forum in a chariot—because the arch is a posthumous dedication, a form of cenotaph. This somber note has been struck by the small relief at the center of the barrel-vaulted passageway in which Titus is borne up to heaven on the back of an eagle, a sign of apotheosis.

At the same time other Domitianic monuments, such as the Cancelleria Reliefs in the Vatican, indicate a return to a more classical, abstract mode of composition, dependent on the processional reliefs from the Altar of Augustan Peace and on the cool forms of Greek art on which they were based. Domitian was strongly philhellenic, and his turn to a more sober classicism may have been an expression of his developing taste. However, an old-fashioned sobriety reappeared in Roman art at the end of the first century,

a phenomenon larger than this instance of a Greek revival, and it triumphed under Trajan. After the so-called excesses of Domitian with his haughty, imperial manner, the end of the Flavian dynasty brought with it a positive reappraisal of republican values, at least in the world of appearances.

TRAJAN: IMPERIAL ART AND THE REPUBLICAN REVIVAL

Shortly after World War II, workmen digging in an Ankara street uncovered a gilded bronze tondo, a sculptured circular medallion-portrait of Trajan, probably once hung on a wall with similar tondo portraits of Roman dignitaries. This resolute portrait reveals a mature, slightly aged man, carefully depicted with his well-defined and familiar physiognomy. The work joins together in harmony the matter-of-factness of the republic with its linear accents and the solid, present forms of later Roman sculpture. Made late in Trajan's life, this honorific work may have been cast by a local master fully capable of work of the highest quality, consistent with the official imperial imagery. The explicit representation of age had been carefully avoided by Roman emperors since Augustus with the exception of Vespasian, a man similarly, or at least publicly, without vain illusions.

However, even the Ankara portrait has fictional, value-laden features. Artists in the early second century had taken a republican revival as an expression of the rebirth of traditional Roman values, conveyed by the worthy imagery of the senior leaders of the state. So Trajan, his wife, Plotina, members of his family and of the imperial court, and many private persons were represented to the Roman public through sober, dignified, mature, and physiognomically descriptive images, giving off an aura of traditional virtue. Nevertheless, during his lifetime Trajan

Figure 7. The Entrance of Titus in his Triumphal Chariot, marble relief panel on the north side of the passage through the Arch of Titus in Rome, *ca.* A.D. 90 (204 × 385 cm). *ALINARI/ART RESOURCE*

did not hesitate to show himself with all the grandiose trappings of the imperial repertory, from heroic nudes to colossal equestrian statues. The appearances of majesty remained the prerogative of emperors, and were even a necessity to them, as Trajan's colossal waxed head in Ostia makes all too evident, and this tendency would become ever stronger in the course of late Roman art.

The republican revival under Trajan did not reject all the lessons of the previous century. Because it elevated the earlier traditions to the highest level of patronage, this movement produced a great number of splendid artworks, including the late Trajanic arch at Beneventum (Benevento) and the spectacular Column of Trajan in Rome. These monuments constitute the classic, mature realization of Roman imperial art itself.

The arch at Benevento, probably executed by the same sculptors' workshop responsible for the Arch of Titus twenty years earlier, represents Trajan's foreign and domestic program in a series of balanced relief panels on both facades and along the central passageway. Here, classical imagery, Roman content and *gravitas,* and an allegorical formality have been fused in an extraordinary composition that achieves the great realization of official Roman art. As P. G. Hamberg (1945) understood so well, the Beneventan Arch stands at the peak of the grand tradition of imperial representation, beginning with the Altar of Augustan Peace, wherein history, politics, and the realities of life, Roman preoccupations, have been encompassed fully within an allegorical mode.

The reliefs of the Column of Trajan (fig. 8) define the alternative mode of narrative representation and are its most complete achievement. Narrative representations have a long history in Roman art, going back to the republic, but the helical reliefs of the column are unprecedented and may have been the idea of Apollodorus of Damascus, the architect supposedly responsible for the design of the Forum of Trajan in which the column is the centerpiece.

Wrapped around the column shaft for hundreds of meters, the relief purports to tell the story of Trajan's campaigns in Dacia (modern Rumania) in about one hundred distinct scenes. The artists have filled these scenes with representations of marching, building, fighting, and resting Roman soldiers, with battling and submissive barbarians, and with the nearly omnipresent and always powerful figure of Trajan; all of this is contained in landscape or urban settings characteristic of the locus of action. This tour de force of narrative representation,

closely related to the Roman annalistic reportorial tradition, enlivened by the artistry of the sculptors, served as the model for the more schematic design of the Column of Marcus Aurelius in Rome in the 180s. The later monument tended to abandon narrative for demonstration in an obvious way through an emphasis on symbolic scenes, dominated by the emperor Marcus Aurelius in his war with the Germans. The Column of Trajan is much more subtle. It offers visual proof of Trajan's conquest of Dacia and the success of Roman arms, but it is very difficult to follow the helical course of the relief, the path of the story line around and up the hundred-foot-tall column shaft. To help the viewer comprehend the true subject of the relief, the glory of Trajan, the designer grouped scenes that would make visual sense, even if they were narratively disconnected. And he showed Trajan, whenever possible, as the veritable focus of events, as if he were the prime cause and master of them. The result is a masterpiece of presentation in which, ultimately, the imperial presence triumphs over detail, and the demands of imperial propaganda over the historical record.

MAGIC REALISM AND SYMBOLIC MODES

The interest in detail, in the magical power of detail, was not restricted to imperial commissions. It forms an essential part of a long tradition in Roman art and was particularly attractive to patrons at a middle level of society. Their portraits, their monuments, and their commissions showed a preference for descriptive detail, often without the high gloss of Hellenic art, and in the middle and late empire this taste became more prominent as these social groups—some would call this class "plebeian"—became more powerful.

Figure 8. The Column of Trajan in Rome, detail showing lower portion of the helical frieze, Parian marble relief, *ca.* A.D. 110–113. Height of frieze approx. 125 cm. *FOTOTECA UNIONE, ROME*

Figure 9. Marble relief slab from the Tomb of the Haterii, A.D. 100–110 (131 × 104 cm). VATICAN, MUSEO GREGORIANO PROFANO INV. NR. 9998. *ALINARI/ ART RESOURCE*

Reliefs from the sepulchral monument of the Haterii (fig. 9) show much of this fascination with descriptive detail in a bizarre combination of sculptural and architectural representations. A work of the Trajanic period now in the Vatican, the Haterii relief exhibits incoherencies of scale, space, and location within the panel, and mixes many types of imagery incongruously together: the bier with the half-recumbent body of the deceased, shown at the final meal as it were, perches on the roof of the elaborate tetrastyle tomb in which, one can guess, she was buried with other members of the family. These discrepant elements, the bewildering profusion of sculptural ornament, perspectival irregularities, and the intrusive crane with its construction crew at the left come together to create an overloaded image of visual abundance beyond ready comprehension. It seems as if everything possible were being crammed into the relief without regard to the spatial and formal implications of the composition. But the whole is different from the sum of its parts; the image itself transcends the limits of legibility in the pursuit of an overall effect of wealth, and the coherencies of space and three-dimensional form, the essential ingredients of Greek art, are ignored. The reliefs of the Column of Trajan and of the Haterii family may stand for different stages in this mode of descriptive representation, but both works adhere to a peculiarly Roman figurative tradition with great consequence for the future course of Roman art.

In the second and third centuries well-to-do persons all over the empire began to purchase carved marble sarcophagi to house the bodies of their deceased inside the tomb. Ateliers specializing in this work were to be found in many of the larger cities of the empire, especially in Asia Minor near the marble quarries from which semifinished sarcophagi were shipped. Roman sarcophagi provide a treasure of motifs, rendered in various regional styles for more than two centuries.

Many of them were decorated with subjects drawn from Greek mythology, converted through metaphorical extension into appropriate sepulchral themes, often featuring some form of salvation from the oblivion of death and conflating a Greek hero—Achilles, Meleager—with the deceased. Such sarcophagi maintained a strong connection to the Greek artistic tradition, however tenuous that association eventually became.

Other sarcophagi displayed subjects drawn from daily life, from the career of high-ranking officers, from scenes of battle, and from private, especially Dionysiac, cults. One sarcophagus, combining mythological and religious themes, was found in Velitrae (Velletri), not far from Rome, and can be dated to about 140 A.D. Carved on all four sides in two major friezes, the sarcophagus (fig. 10) takes the form of a gabled structure, possibly a tomb, and offers to the eye a panoply

Figure 10. The Velletri Sarcophagus, marble relief, A.D. 140–150 (145 × 257 × 126 cm). VELLETRI, MUSEO CIVICO.
PHOTO: DEUTSCHES ARCHÄOLOGISCHES INSTITUT, ROME

Figure 11. The Arch of Constantine in Rome, detail of marble relief on the north facade: *(top)* the Boar Hunt and Sacrifice to Apollo, Hadrianic tondi, *ca.* A.D. 130. Diameter 236 cm; *(bottom)* Adlocutio scene depicting the emperor addressing senators in the Forum, Constantinian frieze, A.D. 312–315 (102 × 538 cm). *ALINARI/ART RESOURCE*

of divine and mythological themes for the benefit of the deceased in the hereafter. The syncretistic program features Mercury (Hermes) and Hercules, who visited Hades and returned to the world of men, presided over in the center of the major frieze by the enthroned figures of Pluto and Proserpine (Persephone), lords of the underworld. Despite the Greek subject matter, the stumpy figural style anticipates the later reduction of the human body, and in frontality the hieratic organization of Constantinian art. Indeed, the projecting lineup of deities and heroes partakes of that same numinous power that gives strength to the awesome image of Commodus-Hercules in Rome and to the numerous votive monuments and religious images of the third century, especially in the service of the cult of Mithras.

Resistance to these stylistic trends was of-fered by Hadrian, who personally intervened as a great patron, strongly philhellenic in his taste. He filled his great villa at Tibur (Tivoli) with many works of art, some originals and many copies of famous Greek statues, a museum of masterpieces of ancient art. Portraits of himself and of Sabina, his wife, relied heavily on the classical forms of the imperial repertory; he wore a beard, probably in emulation of the Greek philosophers he admired, delighted in Greek literature and mythological subjects, and portrayed his lover, the Bithynian youth Antinous, in the manner of a youthful Greek god, if slightly plump. Yet even Hadrian could not resist the changes occurring in Roman art of the second century.

Eight Hadrianic tondi occupy the middle zone of the facades of the Arch of Constantine in Rome (fig. 11), coming from an unknown monument dedicated to the glorification of the hunt and the virtues of the imperial hunter. Two tondi show Hadrian at the left about to spear the boar beneath his flying horse, and on the right with his entourage, offering sacrifice to Apollo; in both reliefs the head of Hadrian was removed at the time of Constantine when the tondi were adapted to their new location. Despite the deep carving of the reliefs and the clarity of their design, the spatial ambiguity of the hunt scene and the paratactic composition, which isolates the individual figures of the sacrifice, have a peculiarly static, even airless character, as if the participants, or images of them, were frozen in time. Stone sculpture does not move, but Greek art emphasized the possibility of movement; the figures in these Hadrianic tondi seem incapable of it.

FROM TACTILE TO OPTICAL SYNTAX IN LATE ROMAN ART

Roman art under the Antonine emperors responds to the continuing tension between these conflicting traditions. Sometimes, as in the surviving base of the memorial column dedicated by Marcus Aurelius and Lucius Verus to Antoninus Pius and Faustina I in Rome, the two artistic languages appeared side by side: the Roman *Decursio* with its abstract circle of horsemen, seeming to ride on the clouds, and the allegorical, flabbily classical *Apotheosis* relief, wherein the busts of emperor and empress are borne up to heaven on the back of a pneumatic, winged male. The dichotomy between these two compositions appears to undo two centuries of Roman art.

German art historians after World War I began to appreciate great change in Roman art in the Antonine and Severan periods. Perhaps because of their own experiences, they found in Antonine portraits, sarcoph-

agi, monumental reliefs (especially on the Column of Marcus Aurelius in Rome), and private commissions an expression of anxious distress which they thought reflected a contemporary awareness of the growing fragility of Greco-Roman civilization under the stress of barbarian invasion and progressive economic exhaustion. Expressionist tendencies do emerge in late-second-century artworks. This is in part a rejection of the imperial facade with its calm, secure imagery, but the effect can also be attributed to a radical change in the techniques of carving. Roman sculptors began to replace the tactile values, produced by carving marble in the round, with optical values, developed by the sharp contrasts between light and dark, solid and void. Thus, what had been taken away came to seem just as important as the solid stone that remained.

The spectacular bust of Commodus-Hercules in Rome (fig. 12), hovering magically on its insubstantial but symbolically loaded base, is sharply, even starkly, carved in hard-edged shapes. Commodus' hairy head is framed within a gaping lion's mouth, an attribute of Hercules, but the deeply drilled folds and the dark shadows around the head seem to cut the figure so that the eye has difficulty in following the continuity of the human form. Indeed, the head floats in a cave of shadow, intensifying its superhuman aspect. Roman sculptors had begun to master these new techniques of cutting in the Aurelian reliefs on the Arch of Constantine in Rome, and in the Aurelian panels (now in the Conservatori Museum in Rome) a few years before.

The next stage appears in the reliefs decorating the pilasters of the Severan Basilica in Lepcis (Leptis) Magna in Tripolitana (Libya). Now the light rebounds from the forward surfaces but disappears into the dark shadows created by the deep, almost straight-back cutting. The effect, resembling textile design, is particularly visible in the

Figure 12. Commodus as Hercules, marble bust, *ca.* A.D. 192. Height 118 cm. ROME, MUSEI CAPITOLINO, PALAZZO DEI CONSERVATORI INV. NR. 1120. *ALINARI/ART RESOURCE*

Figure 13. The Ludovisi Battle Sarcophagus, marble relief, *ca.* A.D. 250 (153 × 273 × 137 cm). ROME, MUSEO NAZIONALE DELLE TERME INV. NR. 8574. *ALINARI/ART RESOURCE*

architectural moldings that appear to function on two levels only. For the most part the decorative elements are cut out only on the surface of the stone and are not rendered in three dimensions. In addition, the bony character of Hercules' body, whose exploits are represented in the central portion of one of the pilasters, marks another retreat from Greek naturalism, also to be found in the reliefs of the Severan Arch in Lepcis.

Among the finest of surviving Roman sarcophagi is the Ludovisi Battle sarcophagus (fig. 13), a masterpiece of the mid third century, now in the Museo Nazionale delle Terme at Rome. The composition epitomizes the traditional battle motif, as the triumphant equestrian leader rises above the fray, his body almost frontal, right arm outstretched in an appealing gesture. His portrait has been identified as that of Hostilianus (249–251), one of the short-lived princes of this troubled time; its hard, dense style has its roots in Severan art and leads on to the Tetrarchy, and seems to deny not the material of which it is made, but rather the human flesh that it no longer fully represents. The relief itself seems bursting with the struggling figures of Romans and barbarians, caught in battle, but no less caught in a compressed space where their bodies have no room to move. The virtuoso carving proves that this does not come about because of a lack of skill in working the stone; instead, it is deliberate, suggesting the idea of violent conflict and ultimate victory without describing how that comes about. Here, too, the pattern of curly-headed men and horses' manes lies on the surface, carrying the eye from place to place as if it were a two-dimensional design.

ART OF THE TETRARCHS AND CONSTANTINE

The stage had been set for the appearance of late Roman art with its optical tenden-

Figure 14. The Tetrarchs ("I Mori"): Diocletian, Maximianus Herculius, Constantius Chlorus, and Galerius, porphyry sculpture at the southwest corner of the Basilica of San Marco in Venice, A.D. 300–305. Height 130 cm. *ALINARI/ART RESOURCE*

cies, schematic compositions, dehumanized forms, and highly symbolic repertory of images. The paired groups of four tetrarchs, the so-called Mori (fig. 14) at the edge of San Marco in Venice, represents the ultimate achievement of the stony, anonymous style in Roman art. Some have seen in such works an artistic metaphor for the ruthless rule of the tetrarchs, hard men in a hard time, as if the resources of the empire were being husbanded in one place. Symbolic language imbued images with a new projective vitality, charged especially by frontal compositions and by centralized schemes of representation, whose insistent focus channeled the

Figure 15. The Triumph of Licinius, sardonyx cameo, A.D. 458–461 (6.8 × 8.4 cm). PARIS, BIBLIOTHÈQUE NATIONALE, CABINET DES MÉDAILLES

possibilities of interpretation. Such is the construction of the early-fourth-century sardonyx in Paris, representing the awesome victory of Licinius (fig. 15), far removed in spirit from the earlier, less forced exploration of this theme in the gem of Claudius, celebrating his generals' victory in Britain.

Now is the time of the repressive state, dominated by autocrats who insist that the abstraction of majesty governs their appearance in public. The Constantinian reliefs from his arch (see fig. 11) embody this principle, as the (headless) figure of the emperor addresses the Roman people directly in the Roman Forum, his central, numinous figure set at the very core of a world that is *his*

stage. The short stumpy figures of Constantine and the Roman citizens have at last thrown off the yoke of Greece, but at a price. And yet, Constantine and his designer still appreciated tradition: his arch is composed of carefully selected fragments from monuments of Trajan, Hadrian, and Marcus Aurelius, remnants of a glorious Roman past to which Constantine and his art were still attached.

BIBLIOGRAPHY

Bernard Andreae, *The Art of Rome* (1977); Ranuccio Bianchi Bandinelli, *Rome: The Center of Power* (1970), and *Rome: The Late Empire* (1971); Margarete Bieber, "A Monument for Guido Kaschnitz von Weinberg," in *American Journal of Archaeology*, **71** (1967); Otto Brendel, *Prolegomena to the Study of Roman Art* (1979); Richard Brilliant, *Roman Art from the Republic to Constantine* (1974); Per Gustaf Hamberg, *Studies in Roman Imperial Art* (1945); Guido Kaschnitz von Weinberg, *Ausgewählte Schriften: Zur Structur* I, *Römische Bildnisse* II (1965); Hans Peter L'Orange, *Art Forms and Civic Life in the Late Roman Empire* (1965); Gisela M. A. Richter, *Engraved Gems of the Romans* (1971); Donald Strong, *Roman Art* (1976); Jocelyn M. C. Toynbee, *The Hadrianic School* (1934); Cornelius C. Vermeule, *Greek Sculpture and Roman Taste* (1977); Franz Wickhoff, *Roman Art; Some of Its Principles and Their Application to Early Christian Painting*, Eugenie Strong, ed. and trans. (1900).

Greek Painting and Mosaic

JEROME J. POLLITT

ANCIENT WRITERS ON GREEK ART make it clear that the most famous painters of antiquity were mural and panel painters who executed their designs, usually on a large scale, on stucco-lined walls, or on wood, or on stone. Unfortunately, prior to the beginning of the Hellenistic period, there is only the scantiest monumental evidence to indicate what such painting was like, and hence, to form a coherent idea of how Greek painting evolved in the archaic and classical periods, one must turn to vase painting.

The finest products of Greek vase painting, particularly the later black-figure and early red-figure work of the archaic period in Athens, have a precision and beauty of draftsmanship unsurpassed in any other artistic tradition. "You cannot draw better," as Sir John Beazley said (in his book on red-figure painting [1964]) of the great cup painter Epiktetos, "you can only draw differently." It must be remembered, however, that the medium of painted pottery imposed certain formal requirements and technical limitations on vase painters that would not have been found in other media. The vase painter had to adjust his designs to the curving surface and shape of the vessel that he decorated, and the range of colors that he could employ was limited to those that could withstand firing in a kiln. In the archaic period these requirements seem to have resulted in only a minimal difference between vase painters on the one hand and mural and panel painters on the other. A painted wooden plaque of the second half of the sixth century B.C. from Pitsa near Corinth, for example, exhibits a wider range of colors than is found on painted pottery (such as blues), but its technique of drawing and principles of composition are very similar. In the classical period, however, when shading, perspective, and more elaborate spatial settings were introduced into Greek painting, the technical limitations of vase painting made it impossible to reproduce many of the effects of large-scale painting. Later classical vase painting continues to be of interest as a genre of the decorative arts in Greece, but it tells us less about what the work of such artists as Zeuxis, Euphranor, and Apelles must have been like.

VASE PAINTING TO THE END OF THE ARCHAIC PERIOD

At the very beginning of the post-Bronze Age tradition of Greek painted pottery, in the Protogeometric style of the tenth century B.C., one can detect a tendency to analyze forms into their component parts, and to clarify the interrelationship of these parts, that is an essential characteristic of later Greek art. Parallel bands and decorative patterns such as precisely drawn concentric circles were applied to the surface of a vessel in a way that emphasized the structural components of its shape. Figural representation in Protogeometric is virtually absent—only a few simple black silhouettes of horses—but in the succeeding Geometric period (*ca.* 900–700 B.C.), which expanded the structural principles of the Protogeometric style on a grand scale, complex figural scenes became common. The basic aesthetic effect of the Geometric style was achieved by combining a wide repertoire of abstract motifs—meanders, chevrons, crosses—into a complex "symphonic" design. The human and animal figures that were created for the style were carefully fitted into the tapestrylike effect of geometric decoration. They consist of all but unarticulated black silhouettes (occasionally an eye or the pattern of a woman's skirt is indicated) that focus on the basic geometrical forms underlying the structure of the body and complement the surrounding abstract motifs. The masterpieces of the genre are the great Dipylon amphoras and kraters shown in figure 1 (*ca.* 750–700 B.C., named after the cemetery near the Dipylon gate in Athens, from which many of them come), which often measure several feet in height and seem to have served as grave monuments in public cemeteries. These are frequently decorated with funeral and battle scenes (the latter possibly influenced by epic poetry, although this is debated), as well as friezes of animals. The way in which the designs of these two types of vessels were composed from stock motifs and ornamental formulas has reminded some scholars of the way epic poems, particularly the *Iliad,* were built up from stock epithets, metrical patterns, and conventional scenes. Since both seem to have reached their peak in the late eighth century, the similarity of their principles may reflect a fundamental aesthetic predilection of the time and be more than a matter of simple coincidence.

Although the products of Athens are best known, the Geometric style existed in most areas of Greece, and while there were clearly regional variations, the homogeneity of the style, when compared to what followed in the next century, is remarkable. Beginning in the late eighth century and with accelerating intensity in the seventh, Greek culture began to expand through colonial settlements and increasing trade into other areas of the Mediterranean. One result of this expansion was that contact with the culture and art of the ancient Near East, which had been attenuated during the centuries following the collapse of Mycenaean civilization, was revived. In painting this led to a phase usually known as the "Orientalizing period" (*ca.* 700–625 B.C.) during which a flood of new subjects and designs (partly influenced by the art of the Near East) swept away the orderly Geometric style and produced a series of ambitious and experimental, if at times also ungainly, regional styles. It was during this phase that many of the familiar subjects and mythological personalities of later Greek art—the exploits of Herakles, the blinding of the Cyclops, Perseus beheading Medusa—first appear. Painted inscriptions also began at this time, some of them identifying subjects and others providing the first artists' signatures (for example, Aristonothos, whose signed krater, now in Rome, depicting Odysseus blinding the Cyclops Polyphemos on one side and a naval battle, perhaps between Greeks and Etrus-

Figure 1. Dipylon krater, detail showing a funeral procession, Geometric style, *ca.* 750–700 B.C. Overall height of vase: 123 cm. ATHENS, NATIONAL ARCHAE-OLOGICAL MUSEUM INV. NR. 990. *HIRMER FOTOARCHIV, MUNICH*

cans, on the other, can serve as something like a symbol of the age).

The two most prominent styles of the Orientalizing period are those of Corinth and its colonies, known as Protocorinthian and that of Attica and Aegina, known as Protoattic. These are supplemented by a host of regional styles, notably the "wild goat" styles (named after their most common decorative motif) of Rhodes and Chios. Of these, all, except Protocorinthian, are distinguished by outline drawing (rather than silhouettes), often applied to large, enthusiastic, and somewhat clumsy mythological scenes set in a matrix of curving vines, rosettes, and other floral motifs, and complemented by friezes of oriental animals (lions, panthers) and composite monsters (griffins, sphinxes). Well-known and typical pieces are the Protoattic amphora from Eleusis with Perseus pursued by the sisters of Medusa and the blinding of Polyphemos, and the amphora in the Metropolitan Museum of Art in New York City illustrating the story of Herakles and Nessos.

Protocorinthian in its mature phase (*ca.*

650–640 B.C.) developed in a different direction and became by far the most sophisticated of the Orientalizing styles. Corinthian potters specialized in miniature vessels, particularly the aryballos, which seem to have held a widely exported scented oil. To decorate the small surfaces of these pots a technique was developed that involved incising fine decorative details on dark painted silhouettes and then adding various colors, mainly reds and whites, to the finished design. The masterpiece of the style is the Chigi Vase (fig. 2), a small wine pitcher now in the Villa Giulia in Rome. The famous scene of a hoplite (infantry) battle on the uppermost of its two friezes combines great elegance of execution and design with a martial spirit that echoes the elegiac poetry of Tyrtaios and Kallinos. It was probably the encouragement and patronage of the tyrant Kypselos (traditionally 657–625 B.C.) that made possible the creation of works of such refinement.

Toward the end of the seventh century B.C. political changes in both Athens and Corinth stimulated the development of the

Figure 2. The Chigi Vase, detail of upper frieze depicting the hoplites being played into battle by a flutist, Protocorinthian olpe, *ca.* 650–640 B.C. Overall height of vase: 26.2 cm. ROME, MUSEO NAZIONALE DI VILLA GIULIA INV. NR. 22679. *HIRMER FOTOARCHIV, MUNICH*

next great tradition of Greek vase painting. In Athens one of a series of social reforms, which tradition ascribes to Solon, encouraged the immigration of foreign artisans, while in Corinth a series of economically restrictive measures instituted by the tyrant Periander seems to have encouraged some businessmen to emigrate. In any case, it is clear that a number of Corinthian vase painters set up shop in Athens and began to apply the Corinthian technique of incised silhouettes to the larger shapes and compositions that had been favored in Protoattic. The result was Attic black-figure, a style which in the course of the sixth century B.C. supplanted all significant competition and became the dominant form of vase painting in the Greek world. One of the earliest and finest examples of the fusion of Corinthian refinement and Attic monumentality is the large amphora in the National Archaeological Museum in Athens by the Nessos Painter illustrating the combat of Herakles and the centaur Nessos on its neck and Gorgons on its main body.

In the first half of the sixth century B.C. the most impressive works of Attic black-figure tend to be large vessels decorated with a complex assemblage of friezes (an inheritance from the Corinthian tradition) and illustrating a variety of mythological subjects. The outstanding work of the period is the François Vase (fig. 3) in the Archaeological Museum in Florence, a large krater, by the potter Ergotimos and the painter Kleitias, which combines a love of exquisite miniaturist detail with a complexity of narrative previously unparalleled. This miniaturist frieze tradition continued into the second half of the century on smaller vessels like wine cups, but around 550 B.C. a new interest in decorating larger vessels with panel-like scenes consisting of fewer and larger figures becomes apparent. The painter Lydos was an innovator in this type of design, and it was brought to perfection around 550–530 B.C. by the greatest of the black-figure painters, Exekias, one of the finest Greek artists of any era. His famous amphora (now in the Vatican Museum) with Achilles and Ajax hunched over a game board (fig. 4), the cup in the Staatliche Antikensammlungen in Munich showing Dionysos sailing on the Aegean, and an amphora in the Museum of Fine Arts and Archaeology in Boulogne depicting the suicide of Ajax have a psychological depth and dramatic tension that, when added to Exekias' skill as a draftsman, make them perhaps the most perfect of all Greek vases.

By the time of Exekias Athens had all but usurped the market for painted pottery. In the first half of the sixth century a few other regions continued to maintain moderately successful potting industries, notably Corinth, which made a specialty of vases decorated with multicolored animal friezes (see fig. 10 in CRAFTS AND CRAFTSMEN), and Lakonia, which emphasized black-figure cups. The best-known work of the latter tradition is the cup in the Bibliothèque Nationale in Paris illustrating King Arkesilas II of Cyrene supervising the work of local tradesmen.

Figure 3. The François Vase, Attic black-figure volute krater made by Ergotimos and painted by Kleitias, *ca.* 570 B.C. Height 66 cm. FLORENCE, MUSEO ARCHEOLOGICO INV. NR. 4209. *ALINARI/ART RESOURCE*

Toward the end of the century, however, these workshops too succumbed to Athenian competition.

The formal perfection that Exekias and gifted contemporaries like the Amasis Painter had brought to black-figure by the beginning of the last quarter of the sixth century B.C. would seem to have left no room for improvement, and it was probably an appreciation of their skill among the next generation of vase painters that led to an important technical change in the production of Athenian pottery and, with it, a new, experimental style. Black-figure had been produced by painting figures in a clay-base paint, which, when fired in a complicated three-stage process, resulted in glossy black designs on a reddish clay ground. These were enhanced not only by incision but also by the use of red and white paint for details. Around 525 B.C. an innovative artist known

as the Andokides Painter introduced what was essentially a reversal of this process in which the background was painted black and the figures were reserved in the reddish color of the clay. Details of the figures were then painted, rather than incised, with a quill-like instrument and a light brush. The resulting "red-figure" style is quite different in its effect from that of black-figure. One's attention is drawn more to individual figures and their internal structure rather than to the tapestrylike effect that is produced by a series of black silhouettes.

Within a short time, apparently not more than a decade or two, after the invention of red-figure took place, the concentration on the internal structure of figures that red-figure seemed to demand contributed to a major revolution in the history of painting. For millennia, both in the art of the ancient Near East and in Greece, painters had em-

Figure 4. Attic black-figure amphora by Exekias, detail depicting Achilles and Ajax playing draughts in the camp before Troy, *ca.* 550–530 B.C. Overall height of vase: 67 cm. VATICAN, MUSEO GREGORIANO ETRUSCO INV. NR. 16757. *ALINARI/ART RESOURCE*

ployed a set of conventional formulas—for example, frontal eyes on a profile face or a frontal torso on hips and legs seen in profile —in order to represent the human body. What they painted was in effect an idea or symbol as much as a representation. Toward the end of the sixth century B.C. Greek painters broke away from these ancient conventions and set out to record more of their actual optical experience of how forms were altered and even distorted as they moved in space. They invented, in other words, what is usually called "foreshortening." In order to

facilitate their studies of the human body in movement the great pioneers of red-figure in the last quarter of the sixth century, such as Euphronios, Euthymides, and Phintias, extended their repertoire of subjects beyond familiar scenes from myth and heroic legend to include scenes from the daily life of the ordinary citizen. Athletes exercising in the gymnasium, revelers at symposia, competitors in musical contests, or school scenes now became common subjects. This revolution in both the style and subject matter of Attic vase painting was not stimulated only by technical considerations. It seems also to have reflected a major change in outlook among Athenians during the time when the Peisistratid tyranny was overthrown and the new Kleisthenean democracy was being formed (510/509 B.C.). The work of late archaic vase painters seems to imply that the ordinary citizen had come to be as important in his own way as the heroes of the epic tradition.

The period between about 520 and 480 B.C. is the great age of red-figure and produced a host of very fine painters. The power and originality of the pioneers is perhaps best summed up in the great krater by Euphronios, now in the Metropolitan Museum of Art in New York City, representing the death of the epic hero Sarpedon on one side and ordinary soldiers arming on the other side. In the late archaic phase, around 500–480 B.C., the experimental achievements of the pioneers came to seem normal and became less of an end in themselves. Painters of this period apparently felt less prone to compete (as an inscription on a vase in the Staatliche Antikensammlungen und Glyptothek in Munich tells us that Euthymides and Euphronios did) and more content to follow their personal aesthetic predilections. Notable among them was the Berlin Painter, who specialized in single figures, largely or totally devoid of surrounding ornament, radiating out of a glossy black void; the Kleophrades Painter, some of whose scenes, like the sack of Troy (fig. 5) on a hydria (water jar) in the Museo Archeologico Nazionale in Naples, have a power and pathos that may reflect the atmosphere of the Persian Wars; the Brygos Painter, who specialized in lively and lusty scenes from both myth and daily life; and Douris, a prolific cup painter with a penchant for unusual subjects and a poetic touch that particularly graced his figures of women.

In the early classical period when a profound change in the temperament of Greek art becomes apparent in sculpture, and paint-

Figure 5. Attic red-figure hydria by the Kleophrades Painter, detail depicting the death of Priam and the sack of Troy, *ca.* 490–480 B.C. Overall height of vase: 42 CM. NAPLES, MUSEO ARCHEOLOGICO NAZIONALE INV. NR. 2422. *HIRMER FOTOARCHIV, MUNICH*

ing came to be dominated by great cycles of murals, one senses the first indications that vase painters were having, and would continue to have, difficulty in keeping up with technical and stylistic developments in monumental painting. Before turning to this phase of the history of vase painting, it will be useful to review what ancient literary sources tell us about the personalities, interests, and achievement of classical Greek painters.

MONUMENTAL PAINTING IN THE CLASSICAL PERIOD (*ca.* 480–323 B.C.)

The principal source of information about painters of the classical period is the thirty-fifth book of the elder Pliny's *Natural History,* written in the second half of the first century A.D., and Pausanias' *Description of Greece,* which contains descriptions of works that could still be seen in Greece in the later second century A.D. These basic documents are supplemented by important passing observations contained in the works of many other Greek and Roman writers. Pliny acknowledges many sources for his information, the chief of which seems to have been an artist named Xenokrates, who, in the later fourth or early third century B.C., wrote what was probably the first treatise that could be classified as a history of art.

Pliny ascribes a few inventions to artists of the archaic period, the most interesting of which are the *katagrapha,* or *obliquae imagines,* of the painter Kimon of Kleonai. These were in all likelihood "foreshortened views" similar to those found in the vase painting of Euphronios and others. It is with the great mural painter of the early classical period, Polygnotos of Thasos, however, that the Plinian-Xenokratean history of painting seems to have begun in earnest. In the 470s B.C. Polygnotos won the favor of the leading Athenian political leader of the time, Kimon the son of Miltiades, and was commissioned to paint murals in several important public buildings in Athens. He seems to have collaborated on some or all of these projects with two other painters, Mikon and Panainos (the brother of the great sculptor Pheidias), and the literary sources are often unclear or in contradiction about exactly which artist did which painting. The most renowned products of their work were the paintings in the Stoa Poikile in the agora, which contained the *Battle of Greeks and Amazons,* the *Sack of Troy,* and historical battle scenes, the most renowned of which represented Marathon. Pliny's assessment of Polygnotos, supplemented by what Aristotle and Pausanias say about him, make it clear that one of his major achievements was the portrayal of character (*ethos*) and emotion (*pathos*) through facial expression and gesture. Pausanias' lengthy descriptions of two Polygnotan paintings at Delphi, *The Sack of Troy* and *The Underworld,* also suggest that he experimented with the representation of space by distributing the figures in his paintings over a series of superimposed terrain lines, thus creating a landscape of sorts.

Polygnotos' interest in spatial settings was part of a broader movement in the art of the early classical period aimed at extending the range of natural experience (for instance, historical change or movement in space) that could be treated in Greek art. Shortly after his time another painter working in Athens, Agatharchos of Samos, first developed a system for the representation of perspectival diminution in painting. Vitruvius, who is the source for this information, implies that Agatharchos developed his system while preparing scene paintings for a performance of one of the dramas of Aeschylus, and the fact that the term that was used for "perspective" in later times was *skenographia* (literally, scene painting) suggests that the Vitruvian anecdote may well be true. The evidence for Agatharchos' career suggests a date somewhere between 450 and 420 B.C. The lower end of this range of years also witnessed another great technical revolution in the art of painting—the invention of shading: the modulation of light and shade to suggest mass. This achievement is attributed by various sources to yet another painter working in Athens, Apollodoros, who was known as the "the shade painter" (*skiagraphos*).

Apollodoros' invention is said to have been carried forward with particular virtuosity by one of the most famous classical painters, Zeuxis of Herakleia (in Lucania [Policoro], southern Italy), active in the late fifth and early fourth centuries B.C. In addition to being remembered for his achievements in creating illusionistic effects, Zeuxis was also remembered for his strong, flamboyant, and contentious personality. He is said, for example, to have given away some of his paintings because, in his view, no price could equal their value, and to have composed a number of barbed epigrams celebrating the superiority of his own work over that of his rivals. The foremost of these rivals, Parrhasios of Ephesus, also remembered for his lack of humility (he liked to refer to himself as the "prince of painters"), was especially famed for his subtle use of line and contours rather than shading.

The fourth century B.C. seems to have been the golden age of Greek painting, and many famous artists of this period are recorded in the literary sources. As time went on most painters seem to have allied themselves with one of three schools, the Sikyonian, the Attic, and the Ionic. The prestige of the school of Sikyon was such that, under the influence of Pamphilos, a pupil of Eupompos who founded the school, drawing was incorporated into the normal curriculum of Greek education. The most renowned artist of the school was Pamphilos' pupil Apelles, who became court painter for Alexander the Great and whose work was said to have been characterized by a certain inimitable "grace" (*charis*) that set it apart from that of other artists. Prominent in the Attic school were Nikomachos, who was famed for the rapidity with which he worked; Philoxenos, who may have painted the great battle scene that was the prototype for the Alexander Mosaic from Pompeii; Aristeides the Younger, who continued the exploration of character and emotion; and Euphranor, who was prominent both as a painter and as a sculptor and who seems to have been the most influential artist in Athens during the time of the refurbishing of the city under the administration of the conservative statesman Lykourgos. Euphranor continued in the footsteps of Polygnotos and his contemporaries by decorating the inner walls of a prominent building in Athens, the Stoa of Zeus Eleutherios, with large compositions depicting historical (the *Battle of Mantineia*) and political (*Theseus and Democracy*) subjects. The chief artist of the Ionic school was Apelles' rival Protogenes, who worked mainly on Rhodes and whose paintings were famed for their amazing painstaking attention to detail.

Xenokrates' history seems to have ended with Apelles, whose work was thought to have culminated and perfected Greek painting. (Undoubtedly there were influential and admired painters in the subsequent Hellenistic period, but the literary tradition preserves scarcely any information about them.) While the literary sources about classical painters obviously do not help us very much in visualizing what actual works by the great artists of the time looked like, they are valuable because they preserve a record not only of who the prominent painters were and what their major achievements were but also of what the atmosphere of the artistic community was like. In addition to documenting an obvious spirit of rivalry among painters, and attesting that some of them were able to achieve considerable social prominence (as, for example, Polygnotos and Apelles), the sources also make it clear that there was a self-conscious and serious intellectual tradition among classical painters that emphasized both artistic theory and criticism. A number of artists are known to have written treatises about their art and to have developed an elaborate technical and critical terminology. Agatharchos, for example, wrote a book on perspective; Euphranor wrote works on colors and on commensurability of parts, or proportion (*symmetria*); Parrhasios, Apelles, Melanthios, and Asklepiodoros are also among the painters listed by Pliny in his bibliography of sources. These writings were probably quite technical works composed for the benefit of other artists, but the intellectual tradition that they represented apparently had an eventual effect on Greek society as a whole, when, as already noted, the art of drawing was made a standard, respectable subject in the Greek educational system in the later fourth century B.C.

CLASSICAL VASE PAINTING

The majority of the red-figure vase painters of the Early Classical period (*ca.* 480–450 B.C.) seem to have wanted to capture something of the monumental style of Polygnotos and Mikon. Tall, stately figures arranged in increasingly standardized heroic postures and projecting a contemplative, serious atmosphere tend to replace the more lively, gesticulating figures of the late archaic period. One of the most successful practitioners of the new style was the Penthesileia Painter. His masterpieces, the tondos (paintings within circular frames) on two large cups, now in Munich, depicting Achilles slaying Penthesileia (fig. 6) and Apollo destroying Tityos, are probably the most successful expressions in vase painting of the *ethos* and *pathos* that typified the monumental art of the period. Another artist whose work is very uneven but who at his best appears to have been a spiritual disciple and imitator of Polygnotos was the Niobid Painter. His well-known krater in the Louvre depicting the death of the children of Niobe on one side and Herakles and Athena in the presence of a group of heroes on the other, provides an echo of what Polygnotos' experiments in spatial composition were like and may even preserve figures that were directly copied from the famous murals in Athens and Delphi.

Figure 6. Attic red-figure kylix by the Penthesileia Painter, tondo depicting Achilles slaying Penthesileia, *ca.* 460 B.C. Diameter 43 cm. MUNICH, STAATLICHE AN-TIKENSAMMLUNGEN UND GLYPTOTHEK INV. NR. 2688. *HIRMER FOTOARCHIV, MUNICH*

A quite different, but equally interesting, painter of this period was the Pan Painter. He seems to have sensed that the grandeur and new technical effects of the monumental art of the time did not suit, or could not be conveyed in, vase painting, which was essentially concerned with decorating the surface of utilitarian objects, not with creating illusionistic "windows." Rather than attempting to come to terms with the new style, he took the remarkable step of turning the stylistic clock back to the previous generation by reviving mannerisms of late archaic vase painting. His style of drawing, fondness for certain gestures, and choice of composition evoke, but do not precisely imitate, the style of the Berlin Painter, the Brygos Painter, and others. A typical example is his "name piece," a bell krater in the Museum of Fine Arts in Boston showing Pan pursuing a shepherd and Artemis slaying Aktaion (fig. 7). Although the question is disputed, the Pan Painter probably deserves to be recognized as the first artist in the Western tradition whose style was consciously archaistic. One of the distinguishing features of the art and thought of the early classical period, as already noted, is their awareness of and interest in historical change, and the Pan Painter's sensitivity to the historical character of style thus marks him as a true product of his time, even though, outwardly, he seemed to be out of step with it.

In the second half of the fifth century B.C. the best vase painters seem to have come even more strongly under the influence of monumental art, especially of the relief sculpture that adorned the Periclean buildings on the Athenian Acropolis. In the period from 450–430 B.C., for example, the Achilles Painter and the Kleophon Painter echo the serene, balanced style of the Parthenon frieze. Later in the century artists like the Dinos Painter, the Eretria Painter, and, in the last decade or so, the Meidias Painter take up and develop the elegant

Figure 7. Attic red-figure bell krater by the Pan Painter depicting Artemis slaying Aktaion, *ca.* 470 B.C. Height 37 cm. BOSTON, MUSEUM OF FINE ARTS, JAMES FUND AND BY SPECIAL CONTRIBUTION, INV. NR. 10.185

"flying drapery" style, best exemplified by the sculptures on the parapet of the temple of Athena Nike, now in the Acropolis Museum, Athens. The work of the Meidias Painter (fig. 8) in particular, with its emphases on romance, genteel eroticism, and cosmetic elegance, seems to represent a withdrawal, perhaps out of exhaustion, from the great themes and atmosphere of the art of the high classical in Athens and to point the way toward the more purely sensuous and personal art of the fourth century B.C.

While the currents of Attic red-figure between 400 and 330 B.C. are diverse, the dominant and most symptomatic development of the period was the "Kerch" style, named after the area in the Crimea (the ancient Tauric Chersonesus) to which many of the vases were exported. Its languorous, indrawn, sensuous figures are modeled with short, sketchy strokes that create a more massive effect than the elegant lines of the

Meidias Painter, but the vases themselves have the same cosmetic ornateness, now enhanced by the copious addition of extra colors, including a gold paint that gives the effect of gilding. This gilding may have reflected a growing taste for metalwork and cheap imitations of metalwork in pottery that ultimately contributed to the abandonment of red-figure in the last quarter of the fourth century and to its replacement by mold-made wares.

An offshoot of the style of classical red-figure in the second half of the fifth century B.C. that is of greater interest for the general history of Greek painting than later red-figure itself is the painting on white-ground lekythoi. A lekythos is a narrow jug that usually held scented oil and was frequently used in funeral rites. Because they were intended to be used for only a short period and then left at a tomb, these lekythoi did not require as durable a surface as red-figure vases, and

1759

Figure 8. Attic red-figure hydria by the Meidias Painter, detail depicting the Dioskouroi abducting the daughters of Leukippos in the sanctuary of Aphrodite, *ca.* 410 B.C. Overall height of vase: 521 cm. BY COURTESY OF THE TRUSTEES OF THE BRITISH MUSEUM, INV. NR. E224

Figure 9. Attic white-ground lekythos by the Achilles Painter, detail depicting a seated muse playing the kithara on Mount Helikon, *ca.* 450–440 B.C. Overall height of vase: 36.7 cm. MUNICH, STAATLICHE ANTIKENSAMMLUNGEN UND GLYPTOTHEK INV. NR. 80. *HIRMER FOTOARCHIV, MUNICH*

vase painters were thus able to cover them with a white slip and to draw and paint on them as they would on plaster, papyrus, or whitened boards. They thus provide us with examples of delicate freehand drawing colored with thin washes in a variety of hues, including blues, greens, and yellows, that could not be used in the red-figure technique. Like a Renaissance or baroque drawing, they seem to bring us very near to the artist's immediate inspiration. The subjects painted on the lekythoi are various, but most of them are related to death and funeral rites. The symbolic confrontation of the deceased and mourners at the site of a tomb is one of the most common. In the period from around 450–430 B.C., the most impressive painter in this medium is the Achilles Painter (fig. 9), who, as in his red-figure work, echoes the quiet, dignified style of the Parthenon frieze. Toward the end of the century a group of artists who follow the Reed Painter and are collectively known as "Group R" created a nervous, sketchy style that conveys a sense of mass through fluid, quick lines and may owe something to the art of Parrhasios.

Outside of Athens there was a second tra-dition of red-figure among the Greek cities of southern Italy and Sicily. Local production of red-figure vases, clearly in imitation of Attic imports, began in Italy as early 440 B.C. Herakleia in Lucania (Policoro), Taras (Taranto), and perhaps the colony of Thurii (near Sybaris, on the Gulf of Taranto, founded in 443 B.C.) were important early centers. By the beginning of the fourth century five schools or areas of production are recognized: Lucanian and Apulian, which derive from the work of the first workshops in southern Italy; and Campanian, Paestan (named after Posidonia, the Roman Paestum), and Sicilian, which may derive from a late-fifth-century workshop in Sicily. Production lasted until near the end of the fourth century B.C. The Lucanian school is best known for the relatively high quality of its early work, particularly that of artists like the Dolon Painter (*ca.* 390–380 B.C.). Apulian began auspiciously with the work of the Sisyphos Painter and eventually diverged into "plain" and "ornate" styles. Ornate Apulian, which preserves the style of drawing of Attic artists like the Meidias Painter, adds color and floral ornament in the tradition of the Kerch style, and specializes in big, multitiered scenes, is perhaps the most familiar style of south Italian red-figure. Large volute kraters with epic and theatrical subjects, like those by the Darius Painter in the Museo Nazionale in Naples, are its most impressive products (*ca.* 350–330 B.C.). Theatrical subjects, particularly scenes from a local type of farce called the *phlyax,* were also important in the work of artists in the Paestan workshops, notably Asteas and Python (*ca.* 350–320 B.C.).

In general, most south Italian red-figure seems carelessly drawn and composed when compared to Attic, but the evidence that it supplies for the influence of the theater on Greek art, and for experiments among Greek painters in rendering perspectival views of objects, particularly buildings, makes it of considerable interest even to the nonspecialist.

In the Hellenistic period there are a few interesting classes of painted pottery even after the demise of the red-figure technique. Hadra ware, named after pottery found in Alexandrian tombs of the third century B.C., for example, occasionally depicts "still life" scenes of everyday objects; and Centuripe ware, named after Centuripe in Sicily and variously dated from the third to the first centuries B.C., bears polychromatic scenes

(mainly nuptial scenes with elegantly dressed women) that anticipate or emulate monumental wall paintings of the late Hellenistic period.

ARCHAEOLOGICAL EVIDENCE FOR MONUMENTAL PAINTING

There seem to have been three types of monumental painting in Greece: (1) wall paintings, on stucco, and perhaps at times on wooden panels, adorning public buildings and private dwellings (the latter apparently very rare); (2) painted votive panels, on wood and probably also on stone (such as the archaic plaque from Pitsa mentioned earlier), set up in sanctuaries of the gods; and (3) funeral paintings, at first on stone grave stelae and later on the exterior and interior of tombs. The evidence for the first category, as already noted, is almost entirely literary, and for the second, evidence is very rare. Hence it is from funeral paintings that we derive most of what we know about monumental Greek painting.

Aside from a few very badly faded grave stelae, the evidence for funeral painting in the archaic and classical periods comes from peripheral areas—Etruria and Lucania in Italy and Lycia in southern Asia Minor—where Greek artists worked but where Greek cultural traditions were fused with those of other peoples. The underground, rock-cut tombs of the Etruscans had no parallel in Greece prior to the Hellenistic period, but the style of their wall paintings is strongly influenced by Greek art. It seems likely that many Etruscan tombs, particularly those with symposium scenes, like the Tomb of the Leopards at Tarquinii (Tarquinia; *ca.* 480–470 B.C.), were painted by itinerant, or even resident, Greek artists, but the iconography of the paintings was clearly prescribed, for the most part, by the Etruscan patrons who built and were buried in the tombs. The same mixture of Greek style and non-Greek iconography applies to the late archaic stone chamber tombs of Lycia, designed for the ruling class of the local oriental population. The cultural background of the small underground chamber tombs of Lucania, the most famous of which is the Tomb of the Diver at Posidonia (Paestum; *ca.* 480 B.C.), is more problematical. The earliest of them may have been intended for and painted by Greek colonists of the region, in which case they must be considered examples of Greek art in the strictest sense. The symposium scenes and the diving scene that decorate the walls of the Tomb of the Diver have had recondite meanings connected with Pythagorean philosophy read into them, and these interpretations have been held to confirm the Greekness of the paintings; but the scenes also have close connections with Etruscan painting and may really belong within the Etruscan cultural orbit in southern Italy. The later painted tombs of Lucania (mostly late fourth and third centuries B.C.) are humbler in quality and were clearly designed for the local Italic population.

When looked at from the perspective of Greek vase painting, the style of the archaic and classical tomb paintings contains no surprises. Their figure drawing consists of dark outlines filled in with flat, unmodulated planes of color, to which details are added. They have, of course, a wider range of color than that which is normally found in vase painting, but they in no way controvert the picture of the technical evolution of Greek painting that vase painting provides.

The evidence for monumental tomb painting of the early Hellenistic period has been dramatically augmented in recent years by the discoveries at Lefkadia and Vergina (the ancient Aigai) in Macedonia. At Lefkadia, in addition to illusionistically painted metopes and a frieze, the tomb facade has four panels, placed between engaged columns at its lower level, which depict the deceased facing the

judges of the dead. Their rich coloration, skillful shading, and dramatic expression make them one of the finest extant examples of mature Greek painting. The same is true of the scene depicting the abduction of Persephone (fig. 10) painted on one of the inside walls of the smaller of two tombs discovered in the "great tumulus" at Vergina. Here rapid, impressionistic brushwork contributes to the sense of agitation in the dramatic subject and creates effects that anticipate and call to mind frescoes of later European baroque painting. The second tomb at Vergina (containing an unplundered royal burial associated either with Philip II, the father of Alexander the Great, or Philip III Arrhidaeus, Alexander's half brother) has a hunt scene painted on its facade that belongs in the mainstream of the development of Hellenistic royal iconography. It shows an interest in elements of landscape (the hunters are shown in a grove of trees) that continued to grow throughout the Hellenistic period. The Vergina paintings belong to the last third of the fourth century B.C.; those at Lefkadia to about 300 B.C.

Another painted tomb of about the same period has been found near Kazanluk (ancient Seuthopolis) in Bulgaria (ancient Thrace). It consists of an entrance corridor painted with battle scenes and a vaulted burial chamber with a frieze showing a seated couple dining in the presence of a retinue of servants. The heavy dark outlines of the Kazanluk paintings and the simple form of hatching used to create shading constitute a technique that is less sophisticated than that of the Macedonian tombs, but whether this is because the tomb is provincial or old-fashioned or both is difficult to say.

Painted tombs of the Hellenistic period have also been found in the cemeteries of Alexandria. The finest of them, although poorly preserved, is a frieze of riders from a tomb in the Mustafa Pasha cemetery (*ca.* 250–200 B.C.). Etruscan tombs of the Hellenistic period, notably the Tomb of Typhon

Figure 10. Hades' Abduction of Persephone, detail of wall painting from Tomb I at Vergina in Macedonia, *ca.* 340–330 B.C. *In situ.* Height approx. 100 cm. *PHOTO COURTESY OF PROFESSOR M. ANDRONICOS*

and the later chambers of the Tomb of Orcus at Tarquinii (variously dated, perhaps mid second century B.C.), also document a high degree of technical sophistication.

The most impressive painted grave stelae of the Hellenistic period come from Demetrias-Pagasai (near modern Volos) in Thessaly and date from the late third and early second centuries B.C. Most of them represent the conventional sort of figures known from earlier sculptured stone grave monuments, but there is one remarkable exception, the stela of Hediste, which shows a poignant scene inside a bedchamber in which a bereaved husband contemplates the body of his wife, who has died in childbirth. Painted stelae and painted stone slabs that were used to close burial niches in tombs have also been found in Alexandria, but their state of preservation is so poor that it is difficult to draw firm conclusions about their style and development. Most seem to belong to the third and early second centuries B.C.

In the first century B.C. there is an impressive series of nonfuneral wall paintings from Rome and Campania that document the last stage of Hellenistic art, when Greek artists were working for Roman patrons. For the most part these murals, like the mystery frieze from the Villa of the Mysteries at Pompeii and the scene from the Villa of Publius Fannius Synistor at Boscoreale, as shown in figure 4 of ROMAN PAINTING AND MOSAIC (both *ca.* 50 B.C.) follow familiar canons of the classical tradition in Greek painting, in which massive, carefully delineated human figures dominate a minimal spatial setting. One startling exception, however, is the cycle known as the "Odyssey landscapes" (fig. 11) (*ca.* 50–40 B.C.), found in a house in Rome and now in the Vatican. Here for the first time in ancient painting nature comes to dominate the human figure, which is

Figure 11. Odysseus in the Land of the Laestrygonians, second panel of the fresco cycle known as the "Odyssey landscapes" found in a house on the Esquiline Hill in Rome, *ca.* 50–40 B.C. (116 × 152 cm). VATICAN, MUSEO PROFANO. *ALINARI/ART RESOURCE*

dwarfed by hills, trees, the sea, and the atmosphere. Some scholars have argued that these paintings should be classed as "Roman" because they anticipate later landscapes found at Pompeii; others insist that they are Greek and postulate prototypes in the second century B.C. Most probably, however, they are a native product of the Greco-Roman phase of the late Hellenistic period and are an invention of Greek painters working in Italy in the first century B.C.

MOSAICS

The earliest Greek mosaics are pebble mosaics, that is, mosaics made of naturally rounded stone pebbles set in a layer of fine cement. Apparently all Greek mosaics, at least until very late in the Hellenistic period and possibly not until the Roman period, were floor (as opposed to wall) mosaics. Their function was always in part utilitarian (to provide a water-resistant, smooth, cool floor, especially for dining rooms), but with the flowering of figural pebble mosaics in the late fifth century B.C. floor mosaics also became an art form.

Because early examples (eighth century B.C.) of pebble mosaics have been found at Gordion in Phrygia (western Asia Minor) and because motifs derived from the art of the Near East frequently appear in later Greek pebble mosaics, some scholars have concluded that the technique originated in the East and was imported to Greece in the archaic period. Nonfigural pebble floors, however, are known to have existed in the Greek Bronze Age (for example, in the palace at Tiryns), and there are sporadic examples dating from the early first millennium B.C. in Greece. Thus it is equally possible that the examples from Gordion were influenced by Greek mosaics, rather than vice versa, and that Greek pebble mosaics were a homegrown product.

Examples of pebble mosaic floors with figural decoration have been found in many parts of Greece as well as in Asia Minor and Sicily, but the most extensive corpus of them dating from before the Hellenistic period has been found at the city of Olynthos in Chalcidice (Macedonia), which flourished in the late fifth and the first half of the fourth century B.C. All the mosaics from Olynthos were found in private houses, most commonly on the floors of large dining rooms situated adjacent to small courtyards. The most common design among the Olynthos mosaics consists of a central rectangular, or occasionally circular, panel depicting a scene from Greek mythology (Bellerophon and the Chimera, Achilles and the Nereids, Dionysos, as shown in figure 12, with maenads and satyrs) surrounded by a floral border. The borders sometimes also contain figural friezes consisting of animals and of orientalizing motifs such as griffins and

Figure 12. Dionysos driving a chariot drawn by panthers and attended by a winged Eros, satyrs, a Pan, and dancing maenads, pebble mosaic pavement from the *andron* of the Villa of Good Fortune at Olynthos in Macedonia, fourth century B.C. *In situ.* (390 × 320 cm). *PHOTO: DAVID M. ROBINSON*

Figure 13. The Stag Hunt by Gnosis, pebble mosaic pavement found at Pella in Macedonia, *ca.* 330–300 B.C. *In situ.* Size of figured panel: 310 × 310 cm. *PHOTO: CHARALAMPOS MAKARONAS*

sphinxes. The latter also frequently appear on small entranceway mosaics, attached to the main compositions.

As pebble mosaics developed, both at Olynthos and elsewhere in the fourth century B.C., the size of the pebbles employed became smaller and a greater diversity of colors was used in an effort, apparently, to approximate the effects of polychromy and shading that were characteristic of contemporary painting. A notable example of this increasing sophistication of technique applied to designs that are essentially similar to those from Olynthos are the floors from the House of the Mosaics at Eretria in Euboia (*ca.* 350 B.C.). Equally impressive, and illustrating a form not well documented at Olynthos, are the large-scale purely floral designs found at several sites, but most remarkably in beautiful examples from Sikyon (*ca.* 350 B.C.). It has been suggested

that these may be related to the famous flower paintings, praised by ancient literary sources, of the painter Pausias of Sikyon. In addition to their appeal as consummately elegant works of graphic design, these floral mosaics are of particular importance because their forms can be paralleled to similar designs on architectural moldings and in south Italian vase painting, and these parallels help to establish the date of the mosaics.

The culmination of the pebble technique in Greek mosaics is found in the great series of floors in two large palacelike structures at Pella, the capital of Macedonia. These are datable to the last third of the fourth century B.C. and depict, in addition to traditional subjects from Greek mythology, subjects that seem to have developed as part of Macedonian royal iconography in the time of Alexander—a lion hunt and a stag hunt. The Stag Hunt scene (fig. 13), signed by an otherwise unknown mosaicist named Gnosis, is a masterpiece, astonishing both for its complexity of design and for its technical virtuosity. It represents, among other things, the high point of the attempt by Greek mosaicists working in the pebble technique to achieve the illusionism, realism, and dramatic expression that were characteristic of Greek painting in the later fourth century B.C. After this high point mosaicists seem to have felt that the challenge of capturing all the complexities of the painter's technique through the medium of pebbles was too great, and they turned to a more purely ornamental style that emphasized elegance of outline and increasingly complex borders. The beginning of this later style can be detected in some of the mosaics from Pella, but its fullest development is represented by a group of mosaics of the early third century B.C. found on Rhodes.

It was perhaps a desire to recapture some of the subtleties of the painter's technique that led, sometime in the third century B.C., to the invention of tessellated mosaics (from the Latin *tessella,* small cube, a diminutive of *tessera,* cube), mosaics composed from small cubes made of stone, glass, and terra-cotta. This is, of course, the technique that is most commonly associated with the art of the mosaicist today. By the second century B.C., it reached an amazing degree of refinement, particularly in the technique known as *opus vermiculatum,* which employed tiny tesserae (so small that as many as thirty could be fitted into a square centimeter) to achieve illusionistic effects.

The precise date of the introduction of tessellated mosaics, and the place where their invention may have taken place, are matters of dispute. Ptolemaic Alexandria, where two mosaics have been found that may document the transition from pebbles to tesserae, and Sicily in the time of King Hieron II have both been suggested. The importance of Sicily in the early develop-

ment of the tessellated technique is supported by literary sources (Athenaios' description of a large ship sent by King Hieron II to one of the Ptolemies seems to imply that the vessel had floors decorated with mosaics) and by the discovery of an early tessellated mosaic (suggested dates range from middle to late third century B.C.) in the House of Ganymede at Morgantina. There is, however, a form of mosaic pavement made of irregular flat polygonal stone chips, or of a mixture of polygonal chips and pebbles, found at a number of sites in Greece in the later fourth and third centuries B.C., and it may be that this technique represents a transitional stage between the pebble and tessellated techniques. If this is the case, tessellated mosaics most probably originated in Greece itself.

In any case, once the new technique was fully developed toward the end of the third century B.C., it spread rapidly, and by the second century B.C. appeared in a sophisticated form in many areas of the Hellenistic world. The sites from which the most plentiful and varied examples of tessellated mosaics have been preserved are the island of Delos, during the period after 166 B.C. when the Romans made it a free port under Athenian control, and Pompeii, which, during its "tufa period" in the second and early first centuries B.C., was a refined Italo-Hellenistic (rather than Roman) city. Important, although more limited, examples have also been found at Pergamon and in Ptolemaic Egypt.

Probably because Hellenistic tessellated mosaics were used most often for domestic decoration, particularly in dining rooms, their subject matter tends to be pleasant and entertaining rather than intellectually demanding or provocative. There are basically five types of subjects. Most common are (1) generic decoration featuring animals, fish, birds, cupids, and composite, imaginary creatures, such as griffins and

Figure 14. Dionysos riding on a leopard, tessellated mosaic pavement *(opus vermiculatum)* from the House of the Masks on Delos, *ca.* 166–100 B.C. *In situ.* (129 × 157 cm). *PHOTO: ÉCOLE FRANÇAISE D'ARCHÉOLOGIE, ATHENS*

centaurs; (2) subjects connected with the theater, such as masks, actors in costume, and scenes from plays. Less frequent are (3) purely mythological subjects; rarer still are examples of (4) royal iconography, like the great Alexander Mosaic from Pompeii (now in Naples) and the personification of Alexandria signed by Sophilos (now in the Greco-Roman Museum in Alexandria). Rarest of all are (5) landscape scenes, the most impressive of which is the great mosaic with scenes along the Nile from the temple of Fortuna Primigenia at Praeneste (Palestrina) (*ca.* 80 B.C.). The two monuments that most effectively preserve the effect of a total program of mosaics are the House of the Masks on Delos, in which a variety of theatrical motifs lead up to a large floor in the principal dining room with a splendid representation of Dionysos riding a leopard (fig. 14), and the House of the Faun at Pompeii, where generic, theatrical, and even landscape scenes lead to the great mosaic depicting the confrontation of

Figure 15. The Battle of Issus from the so-called Alexander Mosaic, tessellated pavement from the *oecus* of the House of the Faun at Pompeii, late second century B.C. (342 × 582 cm). NAPLES, MUSEO ARCHEOLOGICO NAZIONALE INV. NR. 10020. *ALINARI/ART RESOURCE*

Alexander and Darius III Codomannus with their respective armies (fig. 15). The technical virtuosity and dramatic effect of the Alexander Mosaic, commonly supposed to be based on, if not exactly copied from, a painting of the late fourth century, make it the masterpiece among Greek tessellated mosaics.

Although a few artists' signatures, as already noted, survive, most Greek mosaicists seem to have worked in relative obscurity. One apparently quite imaginative designer, however, Sosos of Pergamon, transcended the general anonymity of his contemporaries and was remembered in ancient literature. The elder Pliny (*Natural History* 36.184) cites two works by Sosos, one representing doves sunning themselves, preening, and drinking on the edge of a large water vessel, and the other representing an unswept room (*asarotos oikos*) covered with debris from a banquet, which were copied, or at least imitated, in Roman times. The surviving remains of the mosaics that decorated Palaces IV and V at Pergamon (built *ca.* 197–159 B.C.) consist only of borders, but the skillful polychromy and illusionism of their flowers, birds, and masks give a hint of what the technique of Sosos may have been like.

There is no hard-and-fast distinction between Hellenistic and Roman mosaic work. At sites like Pompeii the former merged smoothly into the latter, and much of the mosaic art of the Roman Empire involves an elaboration on motifs and techniques first developed in the Hellenistic world.

BIBLIOGRAPHY

GENERAL

Martin Robertson, *Greek Painting* (1959), and *A History of Greek Art* (1975); Andreas Rumpf, *Malerei und Zeichnung der klassischen Antike* (1953).

On Technique

Vincent Bruno, *Form and Color in Greek Painting* (1977).

VASE PAINTING

General

Robert M. Cook, *Greek Painted Pottery* (2d ed. 1972).

Attic

John Davidson Beazley, *The Development of Attic Black-figure* (1951), and *Attic Red-figured Vase-Painters* (rev. ed. 1964); John Boardman, *Athenian Black Figure Vases* (1974), and *Athenian Red Figure Vases: The Archaic Period* (1975); Gisela M. A. Richter, *Attic Red-figured Vases, A Survey* (rev. ed. 1958).

South Italian

Margaret E. Mayo, ed., *The Art of South Italy: Vases from Magna Graecia* (1982); Arthur Dale Trendall, *South Italian Vase Painting* (1966).

LITERARY SOURCES

Johannes Overbeck, *Die antiken Schriftquellen zur Geschichte der bildenden Künste bei den Griechen* (1868; repr. 1959); Jerome J. Pollitt, *The Art of Greece: 1400–31 B.C.: Sources and Documents* (1965), and *The Ancient View of Greek Art* (1974); Adolphe Reinach, ed. and trans., *Textes grecs et latins relatifs à l'histoire de la peinture ancienne* (1921; repr. 1981); Eugenie Strong, ed., K. Jex-Blake, trans., *The Elder Pliny's Chapters on the History of Art* (1896; repr. 1968).

MACEDONIAN TOMB PAINTING

Manolis Andronikos, "Regal Treasures from a Macedonian Tomb," in *National Geographic Magazine*, **154** (1978), and *The Royal Graves at Vergina* (1980); Photios Petsas, *Ho Taphos ton Leukadion* [*The Tomb at Lefkadia*] (1966).

MOSAICS

Pebble Mosaics

Martin Robertson, "Greek Mosaics," in *Journal of Hellenic Studies*, **85** (1965); Dieter Salzmann, *Untersuchungen zu den antiken Kieselmosaiken* (1982).

Tessellated Mosaics: Alexandria

Blanche R. Brown, *Ptolemaic Paintings and Mosaics and the Alexandrian Style* (1957).

Delos

Philippe Bruneau, *Exploration archéologique de Délos XXIX: Les mosaïques* (1972).

Pergamon

Georg Kawerau and Theodor Wiegand, *Die Pälaste de Hochburg,* in *Altertümer von Pergamon,* **5**.1 (1930).

Pompeii

Erich Pernice, *Die hellenistische Kunst in Pompeji, 6: Pavimente und figürliche Mosaiken* (1938).

Roman Painting and Mosaic

ROGER LING

INTRODUCTION

Roman painting and mosaic emerged, like Roman architecture, out of the "provincial" Italian strand of the Hellenistic tradition. In the case of painting we are dealing with an art form that had enjoyed major standing in classical Greece and this tradition was still producing works for which Roman collectors paid a fortune at the time of Julius Caesar. These works were, however, portable panel paintings, a genre for which there is virtually no surviving evidence, and which in imperial times seems rapidly to have declined into sterility, being concerned chiefly with the production of replicas and pastiches of "old masters." From then on the creative tradition was wall painting, and the contemporary painters of note—men such as Studius, Famulus (or Fabullus), Cornelius Pinus, and Attius Priscus—were all mural painters. Mosaic, unlike painting, had never been regarded as a frontline art. Its relative lack of prestige in Roman times is indicated by the pay scales fixed for craftsmen by Diocletian's Edict on Maximum Prices at the beginning of the fourth century A.D., which put mosaicists at a lower level than painters. Along with the third main medium of interior decoration, stucco reliefs, the mosaic art never had an existence as an art form independent of architectural surfaces: even when mosaic panels were made in workshops, it was always in order to be set in pavements or walls.

Given this decorative role, one should not think of Roman paintings and mosaics in isolation. They must be considered in relation to the architectural settings in which they were intended to be seen, and they must be considered in relation to each other, as complementary aspects of single decorative ensembles. In the same context we must not forget the other forms of interior decoration—not only stuccowork (used primarily on ceilings), but also marble inlay and wall veneer, and paving in specially shaped pieces of colored stone (*opus sectile*). All these forms of interior decoration will be referred to, when appropriate, in the following account.

One major problem involved in studying Roman interior decoration is the imbalance of the evidence. Mosaics, or at least floor

1771

mosaics, are disproportionately well represented in the archaeological record, partly because it was not worth the effort of the Romans or their successors to remove them for reuse, but mainly because pavements are inevitably sealed and protected when a building collapses. *Opus sectile* and wall veneer, though admittedly less common anyway, have a poor survival rate because they were liable to be salvaged and reused by later builders. Painting and stuccowork have suffered from the intrinsic fragility of the materials and from the fact that they were applied to the superstructures of buildings, those parts that rarely remained standing for long: it is significant that much of the best-preserved stuccowork, in particular, comes from underground structures such as tomb chambers.

For painting, the most important branch of interior decoration, the evidence is unbalanced by a special factor: the exceptional state of preservation of the remains of Pompeii and Herculaneum, buried by the eruption of Mount Vesuvius in A.D. 79. Here we have hundreds of complete or near-complete wall decorations, all datable to the last two centuries B.C. and the first century A.D. This abundance of evidence for the early part of the period under review has enabled the identification of a sequence of four manners, or "styles"—a sequence into which can be fitted further material in Rome, often of much higher quality, including the decorations of imperial residences such as Augustus' house on the Palatine and the fabulous Golden House of Nero, sealed beneath Trajan's Baths. After A.D. 79, however, we are dependent on scattered material that is not always easy to date. Apart from a number of decorations in Rome itself, the most complete series comes from Ostia, the port of Rome, where dating is sometimes assisted by the presence of stamped bricks in the structures; here the problem is one of quality—most of the paintings are dreary and second-rate. Farther afield there are isolated examples in central and northern Italy and the provinces. Here much of the best work again falls within the Pompeian period, but an important series of middle and late imperial date has been found at Ephesus in western Asia Minor.

One special genus of painting apart from wall decoration may be briefly mentioned: the mummy portraits of Roman Egypt. These panels applied over the heads of the deceased provide a rare opportunity to examine the techniques of ancient painting on wood and canvas and to appreciate the mastery of portraiture achieved by painters of the imperial age; but in themselves they are of minor importance—an art for the dead rather than for the living.

THE REPUBLICAN PERIOD

The first interior decorations of any artistic pretension in the Roman age belong to the so-called first Pompeian style, in which the plaster of the walls was worked in relief to imitate drafted masonry or, in the later, more ornate forms, marble veneer. The origins of the style go back to fourth-century Greece, but its maturity was achieved in the Hellenistic age, when it became the worldwide fashion. Fine examples have survived in Aegean centers such as Pergamum, Priene, Cnidus, and Delos, while further evidence comes from southern Russia, the Levant, and Alexandria. The style had reached Sicily and Italy by the third century B.C., though most of the specimens in Pompeii and Herculaneum seem to belong to the second century.

In its Aegean form this type of decoration is referred to as the "masonry" style, a term that indicates the basic differences between the eastern and western versions. In the East the syntax of the schemes remained close to that of monumental masonry as represented in particular by the walls of Hellenistic buildings in Asia Minor: tall panels at the bottom of the wall (the "orthostates") crowned by a capping or string course, above which the main part of the surface was occupied by regular courses of blocks, all of equal height ("isodomic"). These systems were richly colored, but colored in such a way as to reinforce the structural logic: thus the orthostates were all in one color, while the isodomic blockwork too tended to show uniformity of coloring, or at least a rhythmic alternation of colors, one for each course. Only the string course or courses (they were frequently doubled) carried richer variations of color and ornament. The western versions, however, as represented primarily by the material at Pompeii and Herculaneum (fig. 1), broke away from the formula of real masonry: a plain socle was inserted at the foot of the wall, pushing the orthostates up nearer to the middle, while the string courses were reduced in importance or even omitted. More strikingly, the coloring was less consistent and logical: blocks in the same course could be painted in different colors, often apparently in quite random sequence, while the variegated effects of colored marble or alabaster, confined in eastern versions principally to the string courses, were dispersed through all levels of the decoration. There was also a tendency to articulate the surface with vertical divisions such as pilasters, creating a rhythmic structure alien to the original masonry style.

The wall decorations of Italy therefore display a freer and more experimental approach to the vocabulary shared with the Aegean area. In neither East nor West, however, was there yet much scope for figure representations. The orthodox place for such subjects was on the string courses, where the scale was inevitably tiny; among the many examples found at Delos there are little friezes of cupids hunting, racing, or disporting themselves amid foliage, theatrical scenes, ath-

Figure 1. First style wall decoration in the entrance passage of the Samnite House at Herculaneum, second century B.C. *PHOTO: R. J. LING*

letic contests, and so forth. In the West there is no evidence for figure subjects in this position, apart from some fragments from a house at Cosa (Ansedonia), on the coast of Etruria; but vegetal scrolls populated by birds are attested at Pompeii. One predominantly western peculiarity, again perhaps indicative of the independent spirit of the region, is the shaping of figures from the veins of painted marbling on blocks in the upper part of the decoration: the pools of a yellow marble may take the form of a bird, or those of a purple one simulate a winged figure. Sometimes there is little pretense of a natural play of veins, and figures stand out in one color against a background of another.

More ambitious figure representations were set within pavements. It was a favorite device of the Hellenistic age, both in the eastern Mediterranean and in Italy, to create mosaic replicas of famous paintings to be inserted as centerpieces in the floor, surrounded by bands of floral and geometric ornament or by plain surfaces on which couches and other furnishings could be set. These inserted panels (emblemata) often achieved extraordinarily sophisticated effects, using tiny cubes of stone as small as one or two millimeters square to imitate the highlights, shadows, and subtle gradations of color in the painted prototypes. They provide a tantalizing insight into the quality of the masterpieces of Greek painting that are lost to us. Of the examples in Italy some may have been made in Aegean workshops and exported to the West—for example, the two delightful little scenes from the plays of Menander laid in a villa outside the walls of Pompeii and signed by a Samian craftsman, Dioscurides (fig. 2). They were set in marble trays for ease of transport. But the larger pictorial mosaics must have been worked, or at least assembled, on the spot. Such were the two great pavements found in buildings on either side of the Basilica in Praeneste (Palestrina), one showing the marine fauna of the Mediterranean and the other the topography of the Nile from its source to its delta, the details in each case spread out in maplike perspective. Another example, dated like the Palestrina mosaics to the end of the second century B.C., is the so-called Alexander Mosaic from the House of the Faun at Pompeii, which represents a scene from one of Alexander the Great's battles against the Persians (see fig. 15 in GREEK PAINTING AND MOSAIC). Here, in a composi-

tion almost worthy of Delacroix, a melee of figures and horses is depicted with a masterly use of highlights and foreshortening, all rendered in the restricted color palette characteristic of Apelles and other Greek painters of the late fourth century B.C.

By the early first century B.C., with increased wealth and patronage in the hands of the Roman nobility, Italy was moving from the shadow of Hellenism into a position of artistic leadership. One of the chief manifestations of this development was the emergence of the Second style of wall painting, in which the imitation of architectural forms was achieved by purely pictorial means. The so-called House of the Griffins on the Palatine Hill in Rome shows an early stage: the architecture is confined to two planes, a screen of columns indicated in trompe l'oeil in front of a marbled wall. This develops in decorations such as those of the Villa of the Mysteries at Pompeii into a complex play of advancing and receding forms, opened in the upper part of the wall to suggest a glimpse of an outside world, and ultimately (as in the villas at Oplontis [Torre Annunziata] and Boscoreale, respectively west and north of Pompeii) to the illusion of a more or less completely open wall, with a view through pilasters to panoramas of buildings and landscapes (fig. 3). Hints of architectural illusionism had already appeared in paintings of Hellenistic times. In the Tomb of Lyson and Callicles at Lefkadia in Macedonia (second century B.C.), for example, the walls were articulated with shaded pilasters and contained other features foretokening the Second style—garlands hanging between pilasters, the use of a single pilaster to straddle the angle of a room, and the characteristic threefold vertical and horizontal division of the scheme. But the evolution of an elaborate and fully illusionistic architectural style belongs to Roman Italy and to the first century.

Many influences contributed to this style. From the real architecture of Hellenistic pal-

Figure 2. Scene from New Comedy depicting street musicians in comic masks, mosaic panel *(emblemata)* by Dioscurides of Samos, from the so-called Villa of Cicero at Pompeii, *ca.* 100 B.C. Height 48 cm. NAPLES, MUSEO ARCHEOLOGICO NAZIONALE INV. NR. 9985. *PHOTO: ARCHAEOLOGICAL SUPERINTENDENCY, NAPLES*

aces came motifs such as exotic stones, columns decorated with gilded vine tendrils, and baroque conceits perhaps pioneered in Alexandria (arches carried on columns, broken pediments, and the like). Stage painting was certainly a source of inspiration, as Vitruvius makes clear, and as is implied by the frequent occurrence of theatrical masks amid the architecture: the Greek word for stage painting *(skenographia)* was also the technical term for linear perspective, the basis of Second style composition. There may even have been some borrowings from contemporary Italian architecture. But the combination of these strands to form an architectural manner of mural painting in which the whole wall was opened by means of a systematic and optically convincing illusion of spatial recession was an essentially new development and one of some importance in the history of western art. The anonymous Greco-Roman wall painters of late republican Italy were the spiritual ancestors of Masaccio and his imitators in the Renaissance.

Within the context of the Second style figured and other representational art became prominent in wall decoration. The famous mural that gives the Villa of the Mysteries its name shows a pageant of twenty-eight or twenty-nine figures, a little under life-size, acting out a series of Dionysiac rituals and allegories against a background of red panels. At Boscoreale a somewhat similar decoration included excerpts from Hellenistic court paintings. A frieze from a house in Rome shows episodes from the voyage of Odysseus (see fig. 11 in GREEK PAINTING AND

Figure 3. Second style wall painting from the bedroom of the Villa of Publius Fannius Sinistor at Boscoreale, mid first century B.C. NEW YORK, METROPOLITAN MUSEUM OF ART, ROGERS FUND INV. NR. 03.14.13

MOSAIC), with small figures set in vast landscapes of twisted trees and beetling crags.

As wall paintings acquired ever greater visual and artistic interest, the nature of pavements changed. Figurative themes in general, and pictorial *emblemata* in particular, became less common, and the plainer, nonrepresentational types of floor decoration almost totally supplanted them. One of these, already long established in Italy and the western Mediterranean, was *opus signinum,* a mortar containing crushed potsherds and tiles (which improved its damp-proof qualities). *Signinum* pavements were frequently decorated with inset chips of stone or lines of tesserae (the "little cubes" that compose a mosaic) arranged in geometric patterns, and these became more varied during the first century, with the addition of pieces of colored marble. Other types of flooring included patchworks of marble fragments set in backgrounds of (generally black) tesserae and patterns of oblong tesserae arranged to produce a basket-weave effect. To offset the polychromy of the walls, black-and-white designs were especially favored. These were generally carried out in conventional tessellated mosaic—either plain white, with perhaps a black border and a regular sprinkling of black tesserae, or in the form of black linear patterns (hexagonal networks, lozenges set in rectangles, or a starlike arrangement of lozenges within a circle) on a white ground.

Another important trend of the time was the emergence of stuccowork as an independent decorative medium. In the House of the Griffins in Rome, in addition to the heraldic pair of monsters that gives the house its name, executed in high relief on a red background above the cornice of a Second style wall, we find stuccoed vaults worked in imitation of the wooden coffering and paneling of Hellenistic ceilings. The curvature of vaults acted as a liberating factor upon such pseudoarchitectural forms, and during the following years stucco coffers first acquired framing enrichments and ornamental reliefs (plant motifs and armor), then began to be diversified into a variety of shapes reminiscent of those now appearing in mosaic pavements. In the House of the Cryptoportico (or underground corridor) at Pompeii (*ca.*

4⌐–30 B.C.) the full gamut of patterns and motifs was employed, and the play of light and shade across the all-white vaults served, like the black and white of contemporary floor decorations, as a perfect foil to the richly painted walls.

THE EARLY PRINCIPATE: FROM AUGUSTUS TO THE FLAVIANS

In the early imperial period artists working in Rome and Italy continued to lead the way in the development of interior decoration. The main creative area remained wall painting, in which new flights of fancy enriched the decorative repertory, new genres such as the paradise garden and the everyday landscape with figures and buildings came to prominence, and above all the concept of the picture gallery, with centralized mythological panels, invaded the home. Alongside painting, stuccowork reached maturity as an independent art form in Augustan times, then gradually entered into a closer partnership with painting, color and relief working together to produce more animated and garish effects. Pavements, in the meantime, continued to play a less prominent role. This was the great age of black-and-white geometric mosaics, and the reign of Augustus saw the invention of the most popular of all mosaic patterns, an allover network of alternating squares and eight-lozenge stars.

In painting, the seventy or so years from the rise of Augustus to the death of Tiberius (A.D. 37) have justly been regarded as a high-water mark, the period of the late Second style and the greatest achievements of the Third. They started, in the 30s and 20s B.C., with a gradual reaction against perspectival architecture. Illusionistic openings were relegated to the upper part of the scheme once more, apart from a central "window" containing a mythological or landscape scene which was set in a pavilion structure; the side wings of the characteristic tripartite compositions were occupied by imitation paintings with figures on a white ground. The architectural elements, hitherto realistic and convincing, became less solid and acquired the trimmings of fantasy: columns were sheathed with vegetal calyxes, and half-plant, half-animal forms perched upon the cornices. This trend was regarded by the traditionalist Vitruvius, writing in the 20s, as newfangled nonsense, but his patron Augustus admitted the fashion to his various properties on the Palatine, where fine examples have survived in the so-called House of Livia, in a recently excavated complex on the southwestern slope, and in the "Hall of Isis" (Aula Isiaca). The last-named chamber contains much detail in the fashionable Egyptianizing style and combines it with an extraordinarily baroque painted vault dominated by organic forms and by a snaking ribbon in blue, gold, and pink. A slightly later stage (ca. 20 B.C.) is represented by a suburban villa found across the Tiber in the grounds of the Villa Farnesina, also perhaps a property of the imperial family. Here some of the walls were articulated by candelabra in lieu of columns, while another contained classicizing pictures supported by animal-pawed Sirens.

All this led into the Third style, which rejected illusionism in favor of surface effects and fantastic ornament. While the "projecting" podium of the Second style gave way to a flat black dado with linear decoration, the architectural structures that had rested upon it were largely replaced by bands of delicate polychrome motifs; only the central pavilion retained its architectural form, but with columns too tall and spindly to be credible as supports, with all suggestion of depth and volume reduced to the minimum, and with the "window" within the pavilion turned into a framed picture. Hints of perspective lingered in the upper zone, generally on a white background, but the forms were now of a matchstick thinness and totally unreal. Among the finest decorations in this manner are the paintings from the villa at Boscotrecase (near Pompeii), decorated in the last years of the first century B.C., and those from the House of Marcus Spurius Mesor at Pompeii, now in the National Museum, Naples. In both the effect is restrained and elegant, with solid areas of red, black, and white predominant; while the marvelous richness of the ornamental detail, rendered with miniaturist precision, is carefully subordinated to the overall design. The figure paintings of this period were equally restrained. A favorite device was to put a mythological scene in a landscape setting that dwarfed the protagonists, but in which the effects of space and distance were blunted by the classical grace of the figures and by their tendency to be confined to a shallow "stage" within the picture field, with rocks or trees blotting out the horizon behind them. In the masterly paintings from Boscotrecase (fig. 4) the ambivalence of the environment, in which sea and sky were inseparably mixed, and distinctions in time and space imperceptibly blurred, was used to produce a subtle and mysterious mood rarely equaled in the history of western art.

The time of Augustus and Tiberius also saw the triumph of figure work in stucco vault decoration. Where figures had previously been rare and strictly subordinate to the pattern, they now became the main focus of interest, dictating the pattern of fields into which the surface was divided. The masterpieces of the style are the stuccoed vaults from the house at the Villa Farnesina, Rome (fig. 5), in which a tracery of shallow moldings frames a variety of decorative and representational reliefs, including busts, arabesques, scenes from Dionysiac ritual, and idyllic landscapes, all rendered with deft and delicate touches that indicate a superb control of the me-

Figure 4. Mythological landscape depicting Perseus and Andromeda, Third style wall painting from the villa at Boscotrecase near Pompeii, *ca.* 31 B.C.–A.D. 50 (161 × 120 cm). NEW YORK, METROPOLITAN MUSEUM OF ART, ROGERS FUND INV. NR. 20.192.16

dium. Forty or fifty years later the so-called Underground Basilica outside the Porta Maggiore in Rome, probably an elaborate funerary monument, shows a Third style patterning of forms, with the figures and motifs of representational scenes tending to be ranged along groundlines and the plant ornaments that occupied the subsidiary panels now stiff and isolated in a cushion of empty space. In this monument there are also signs of the developing role of stucco as a medium of wall decoration and as an adjunct of painting. The main hall, which had no direct natural lighting, was entirely decorated in white stuccowork, not only on its vaults but also on the walls, where the motifs included landscape vignettes, portrait busts, and tables carrying prizes for athletics (here perhaps symbolic of the well-spent life or of success in the hereafter). The anteroom, directly illuminated through a central skylight, combined stuccos with color. Reliefs on colored grounds, reliefs on white grounds, painted ornaments on colored grounds, painted motifs on white grounds—the whole range of possibilities was present. Although the liaison between painting and stuccowork was not new, as the discoveries in Augustus' house have strikingly confirmed, the two media now worked in closer collaboration than before.

Further examples in the late Tiberian period are known from the burial chamber in Rome of the family of Lucius Arruntius, the consul of A.D. 6, and from the baths of the House of the Labyrinth in Pompeii.

In these decorations the potential richness of the technique was held in check by the craftsmen's delicacy of touch and by the miniaturism of the detail, but as we pass from the reign of Tiberius to that of Claudius we find a new restlessness appearing in Third style decors. This was true even where painting worked alone. Ornamental detail grew more complex, color schemes became heavier and less simply structured, and hints of perspectival recession crept back into the wall. The paintings of the *ta-*

Figure 5. Stucco reliefs, detail of vault decoration from the *cubiculum* of the house at the Villa Farnesina in Rome, *ca.* 20 B.C. ROME, MUSEO NAZIONALE DELLE TERME. *ALINARI*

blinum (the central room of an atrium house) in the House of Marcus Lucretius Fronto (fig. 6) in Pompeii (mid first century A.D.) illustrate this phase, with their bands of precise but florid polychrome ornament, their intricate rhythm of red, black, and yellow backgrounds, and their subtle play of perspectival pavilions in the upper zone. To complicate the effect still further, the black dado was adorned with a representation of a formal garden. Within this scheme the central picture panel remained preeminent, though smaller and squarer than before, and with larger figures. In the side wings little paintings of contemporary villas were mounted on ornamental candelabra.

By the middle of the century the Fourth style was emerging. Its most striking feature is the return of architectural illusionism—an illusionism rendered, however, in unreal

Figure 6. Third style decoration in the *tablinum* of the House of Marcus Lucretius Fronto at Pompeii, *ca.* A.D. 40–50. *ALINARI/ART RESOURCE*

and fantastic forms. The most popular scheme, foreshadowed in the House of Lucretius Fronto, consists of broad fields alternating with narrow intervals, the former carrying picture panels or free-floating figures, the latter containing flimsy pavilions often two or three stories high. Generally the fields are colored, while the architectural forms, themselves painted in yellows and browns, are shown on a white ground suggestive of space. Sometimes this white-ground architecture reappears above the colored fields so as to give them the appearance of tapestries pinned to a continuous scaffolding—an effect reinforced when the "tapestries" are incurved at the edges to suggest billowing. Another scheme, represented in the House of Apollo and the House of Pinarius Cerialis at Pompeii (fig. 7), opens the whole wall in an elaborate play of lofty columnar structures slung with garlands and populated by little centaurs and other mythical creatures, within which human figures are set, as if in a real environment. A good example is a decoration that shows the story of *Iphigenia in Tauris* (told by Euripides): here an "old master" known from other Pompeian versions has been broken into its component figure groups, which are distributed amid the architecture like actors in a theatrical set—Iphigenia and her companions in the central opening, King Thoas and a retainer at the left, Orestes and Pylades at the right.

Not all Fourth style decorations were equally complex and illusionistic. Some schemes were monochrome, the whole room unified by a continuous ground color (red, white, or black). Some imitated or improvised upon the manner of the Third style, though with freer brushwork and a less sensitive handling of color. And, as at all times, simple, unambitious linear decorations coexisted with the elaborate ones, which were invariably reserved for "show" rooms.

In the Neronian period the Fourth style

Figure 7. Iphigenia among the Taurians, Fourth style decoration in the House of Pinarius Cerialis at Pompeii, *ca.* A.D. 70. *ALINARI/ART RESOURCE*

often displayed great exuberance and delicacy. Its finest achievements were the decorations of Nero's palaces in Rome, renowned for the marvelously rich vegetal forms hybridized with animals, which became the source of the "grotesques" of Renaissance painting. These were combined with marble veneers, gilded stuccowork, and inset "gems" of colored glass. For all the consummate skill of the emperor's artists, the overall effect is a little too fussy and florid for modern taste, and the diminutive scale of the ornament is remarkably ill-suited to the height of the rooms: much of the detail on the upper parts of walls and on the vaults would have been lost

on the viewer below. At Pompeii the most splendid examples are found in the House of the Vettii (fig. 8). They include the red-and-black banquet hall with its frieze of cupids engaged in trades and scenes from Roman life, and the twin dining rooms east of the peristyle, each with a picture gallery of reproductions (the Death of Pentheus, Dionysus discovering Ariadne, the infant Hercules strangling snakes, and so forth) set in a scheme of dazzling color and exquisitely painted detail.

In the Flavian period (A.D. 69–96) the style tended to lose its vitality and delicacy, and to become somewhat tired and overblown. The architectural frameworks were often

Figure 8. Fourth style wall paintings (including the infant Hercules strangling snakes) in the Pentheus Room of the House of the Vettii at Pompeii, *ca.* A.D. 62–79. *ALINARI/ART RESOURCE*

carried out in stucco relief, and the resulting integration of real volume and pictorial illusion, accompanied by bright coloring and by both modeled and painted figure work, as in the Stabian Baths at Pompeii and in the Domitianic rooms along the northeast edge of the Palatine Hill in Rome, produced an overwhelmingly baroque ensemble. Even where stuccowork was used in isolation, as in the Suburban Baths at Herculaneum, there was an overloading of detail and a loss in freshness that frequently palls on the senses.

In vault decoration the emphasis now passed from figures to patterns. The figures in fact tended to become fillers— single creatures (animals, birds, cupids, satyrs, bacchantes, and so on) set in individual panels of the decorative scheme. The patterns meanwhile were predominantly rhythmic networks of various shapes, all elaborately framed with vegetal ornaments in painting or reduplicated enrichments in stucco. Among these shapes, in addition to squares, there were new categories such as octagons and circles, the latter both contiguous and intersecting; a particularly complex curvilinear scheme, interpreted in a garish display of relief and color, occurs in the vestibule of the Stabian Baths, where medallions alternate with concave-sided octagons, and interweaving ribbons occupy the interstices. Similar curvilinear patterns, sometimes carried out in *opus sectile,* now made an appearance in floor decoration.

THE MIDDLE EMPIRE: FROM TRAJAN TO THE SEVERANS

With the second century A.D. a new chapter opens in the history of Roman interior decoration. Hitherto the pace had been set by wall painting, ably assisted by stuccowork, while mosaic pavements played a subdued and subordinate role. At the same time Italy had remained in the forefront of progress. The Hellenistic provinces seem to have been conservative, retaining wall decorations based on imitation veneer, albeit now rendered pictorially rather than in relief, and keeping alive the tradition of mosaic *emblemata* set in the floor. The northern and western provinces on the other hand had accepted the trends initiated in Italy. The Second and Third styles of painting had been transmitted to Gaul and the Alpine provinces (fine examples of fragmentary Third style remains are known from the Magdalensberg [probably the ancient Noreia], near Klagenfurt in Austria, and from Commugny, near Genava [Geneva] in Switzerland); and black-and-white geometric mosaics spread with them, appearing as far afield as Emporiae (Ampurias) in Spain, Augusta Treverorum (Trier) in Gallia Belgica and Fishbourne, near Noviomagus Regnorum (Chichester) in Britain. By the second century, however, the great creative thrust of Roman-Italian wall painting was largely exhausted; from now on painters were backward-looking and eclectic, ringing the changes on motifs and ideas explored in earlier times. Decorative emphasis began to return to pavements, where the more inventive and interesting developments are to be observed; and in these developments the western and northern provinces were destined to play an important part.

In wall painting some of the most attractive work of the middle imperial period rejected architectural forms altogether. From the time of Hadrian we have neat and precise paintings with delicate linear detail and nonspatial effects somewhat reminiscent of the Third style, for instance, in certain tombs of the necropolis under St. Peter's in Rome and in Hadrian's Villa at Tibur (Tivoli). In the northern provinces the favorite scheme of the early second century consisted of large red fields alternating with vegetal candelabra on a black ground; the candelabra, as in a fine decoration recovered in recent excavations at Colonia Agrippinensis (Cologne) were sometimes enlivened with swans, Sirens, sphinxes, cupids, Dionysiac figures, and the like.

Architectural wall paintings are best represented by the material from Rome and Ostia, where the general fashion was for brightly colored surfaces with architectural structures inserted or tacked on in a rather incoherent manner. Paintings from a house in Via Merulana in Rome, dated about the middle of the second century, contain relatively solid and realistic architectural forms, but the emphasis is on the harmonic combination of colored surfaces (red, maroon, and yellow), while some of the figure motifs within the schemes are set illogically at the bottoms of panels, thus appearing neither as decorative emblems in the field nor as living fauna standing on the architectural surfaces. The result is a lack of any real effect of depth. At Ostia decorators favored schemes of red and yellow, the two colors receiving almost equal emphasis, with figures standing or floating in the fields. From the comparative simplicity of the Hadrianic House of the Muses we pass to decorations in the Antonine and Severan periods that are so incoherent as to be perplexing or positively jarring. The *tablinum* of the House of Jupiter and Ganymede (fig. 9) is a case in point, reminiscent of the Fourth style but less balanced and rhythmic: the scheme is focused not on a central pavilion but on a kind of window with receding architecture on a red ground, in front of which is imposed a painted picture; while the decoration of the upper zone, despite its use of the same basic color scheme, has no organic relationship with the painted structures below. The keynote is one of deliberate and unbridled complexity. The restlessness is accentuated by

the scale of the figures on the colored fields, formerly small but now large and dominant. Against this Ostian indiscipline we may set some simpler and more consistent architectural schemes in the provinces, such as those of the House of the Consul Attalus at Pergamum (Bergama, in western Asia Minor), where a low parapet wall is painted in perspective in front of garden shrubs, and those of the "Painted House" in Dubris Portus (Dover, in Britain), where white panels are framed by short spur walls on a projecting podium. Both are probably datable to Severan times.

In vault decoration the preponderance of groined cross vaults encouraged schemes, whether painted or in stucco relief, that were symmetrical about, or even placed emphasis

Figure 9. Wall paintings in the *tablinum* of the House of Jupiter and Ganymede at Ostia, second century A.D. *PHOTO: ARCHAEOLOGICAL SUPERINTENDENCY, OSTIA*

upon, the diagonals. One such was the stucco decoration of which fragments survive in the lofty undressing room (*apodyterium*) of the Large Baths in Hadrian's Villa at Tibur; others are the vault paintings of the Vatican cemetery, which, by Antonine times, were combining polychromy with stucco enrichments to achieve a new phase of baroque resplendence. A particularly well-preserved specimen dated about the 160s occurs in the so-called Tomb of the Pancratii, or "Colored Tomb," on the Via Latina south of Rome, where mythological figure reliefs on a white ground, decorative reliefs on red, blue, and purple grounds, and paintings of landscapes, still lifes, and birds pecking fruit were blended in a rich but well-balanced play of chiaroscuro and color. Other systems included painted imitations of stone or stucco coffering (as in Hadrian's Villa or in a villa at Gadebridge, near Hemel Hempstead, in Britain) and stuccowork medallions linked by short axial strips. The most attractive example of this last type is the vault of the "White Tomb," or "Tomb of the Valerii" as shown in figure 10, again on the Via Latina (A.D. 159/160), where the stuccoist, working entirely without the aid of color, has employed a draftsmanlike style with subtle modulations and sharp incisions to produce a decoration of great elegance; the medallions contain sea nymphs and swans, the intervening spaces have cupids and arabesques.

While painters were to some extent "losing their way," mosaicists showed a greater sense of purpose and, in the West at least, a better control over the aesthetic possibilities and limitations of their medium. The *emblema* tradition continued in the eastern Mediterranean. It is best represented by the long series of pavements in Antioch (Antakya in southeast Turkey) and its vicinity, a series that runs from the beginning of the second to the sixth century A.D. and includes numerous mythological pictures in architec-

tural and landscape settings, all rendered in a fully illusionistic pictorial style. A well-known example is the panel showing the Judgment of Paris, with Hermes, Paris, and the three divine entrants in the beauty contest sitting amidst rocks and trees; around the panel runs a luxuriant vine scroll containing birds and masks, a framing motif inherited from Hellenistic times. In Italy the only true examples of pictorial panels in the Hellenistic manner are those from Hadrian's Villa at Tibur: a replica of the "Doves at a Bowl" by Sosos of Pergamum and a series of still lifes and landscapes, including a scene with centaurs and wild animals that may have owed its inspiration to a cycle of paintings by the classical artist Zeuxis. It has been suggested that these panels were salvaged from a republican villa on the site, but Hadrian's philhellene tastes and his known patronage of contemporary Greek artists make it more likely that they were commissioned or imported from Aegean workshops.

Such pictorial panels are not entirely apt for floor decorations (especially when, as in a couple of later pavements from Antioch, the picture is represented as if in a columnar niche): they normally impose a single viewpoint on the spectator and, more serious, create an uncomfortable effect of recession within the surface that above all others should appear solid and stable. In Italy and the western provinces, therefore, decorators favored representational styles that played down the three-dimensional factor and above all tried to spread the visual interest more evenly over the pavement, with the orientation of subjects varied according to their position within the room. The characteristic Italian or rather central-Italian fashion, known principally from the pavements of Ostia, was a free composition of figures in black silhouette on a white ground. This style had already been announced in some of the later mosaics at Pompeii and Her-

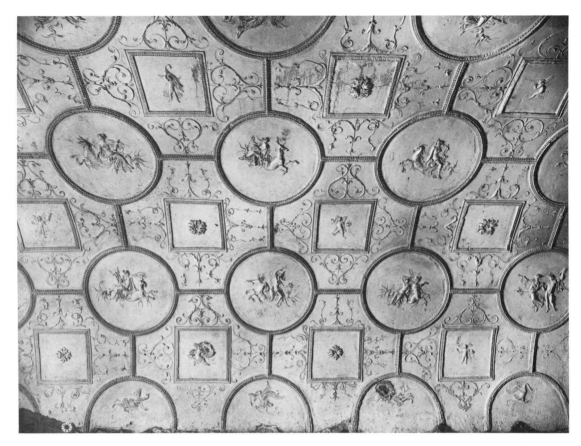

Figure 10. Stuccowork vault decoration in the "Tomb of the Valerii" on the Via Latina south of Rome, A.D. 159/160. *ALINARI/ART RESOURCE*

culaneum, but compositions as ambitious as that of the Baths of Neptune at Ostia shown in figure 11 (*ca.* A.D. 139), in which the sea god drives a team of four sea horses, surrounded by cupids riding dolphins, swimming youths, Tritons, and various other marine creatures—the whole pageant covering a floor 59 feet (18.1 m) long by 34 feet (10.4 m) wide—are unknown before the second century. Though skillfully rendered in three-quarter views, with white lines for internal detail, the figures convey no real impression of volume: the silhouette technique and the neutral white background respect the inviolability of the surface. At the same time the even distribution of the figures and the changes of orientation ensure that no one element or viewpoint receives undue at-

tention. A similar mosaic in a comparatively well-preserved tomb in the Vatican cemetery, representing the Rape of Persephone (Proserpina), shows how ably the black-and-white style complemented the bright coloring of Antonine wall paintings.

In North Africa and the provinces of northwestern Europe, however, mosaicists moved over to polychrome styles, to which they remained faithful until the end of the Roman period. Some of the most successful surviving pavements, including those of the Rhône school in Lugdunum (Lyons) and Vienna (Vienne), founded perhaps by craftsmen from Venetia in northern Italy, relied largely or wholly upon geometric patterns and motifs. Where figures were employed, they tended to be distributed in a number of

Figure 11. The Triumph of Neptune, black-and-white mosaic pavement in the Baths of Neptune at Ostia, *ca.* A.D. 140 (18.1 × 10.4 m). *ALINARI/ART RESOURCE*

more or less equally important panels within the design. Gaul, Germany, and Britain favored square, octagonal, and circular fields formed by tight borders with the characteristic braid motifs in black, red, yellow, and white; sometimes there were five or nine identical panels, and sometimes (especially from the third century onward) more elaborate arrangements of panels of varying shape and size. In Africa, perhaps the most prolific center of mosaic production in imperial times, the remarkable range of polychrome "carpet" mosaics included many with a framework of interweaving tendrils or arabesques and some with complex curvilinear patterns based upon elliptical and "cushion" shapes. One or two African mosaics bring the pictorial element into greater prominence, though the background remains largely neutral and the figures are spaced freely in the field: a good example is a representation of the Triumph of Dionysus in Hadrumetum (Sousse, in Tunisia), where the god in his tiger-drawn chariot is accompanied by his followers and animals, set at different levels in such a way as to leave their spatial relationship ill-defined. In a famous Dionysiac pavement at Cuicul (Djemila, in Algeria) a central group of Lycurgus and Ambrosia is surrounded by four allegorical or mythical scenes, each facing outward so that the viewer has to pass around the margin of the floor to "read" the action. This outward-looking presentation was later adopted by some fourth-century pavements, notably the hunting mosaic from Daphne, near Antioch, now in the Louvre, and the mosaic of Dido and Aeneas from Low Ham in Britain. Another feature of the Djemila pavement is its emphasis upon the diagonals, here occupied by winged caryatids (female supporting figures); the motif, more explicitly stated later, when such corner figures seem to strain against the weight of the central panel frame, implies the influence of decorated cross vaults and domes.

When figures were distributed in series through a pavement design, there was a natural tendency for them to be linked by a common theme. The Djemila pavement just mentioned, with its Dionysiac program, is an excellent example, and another is the Dionysiac mosaic near the cathedral in Colonia Agrippinensis (Cologne), in which a central group of Dionysus and a satyr is combined with panels containing satyrs and bacchantes, birds, wild animals, and fruits—representatives of the world of nature over which the god held sway. Favorite themes are the great names of philosophy, literature, and the arts (for example, in Augusta Treverorum [Trier]), the Muses as shown in figure 12 (again at Augusta Treverorum and elsewhere), legends associated with water (Uthina, [Oudna, in Tunisia]), the four seasons (ubiquitous) and the calendar months, often represented by scenes of agricultural operations (Saint Romain-en-Gal [across the Rhône from Vienne] and various sites in North Africa). The choice of theme was commonly bound up with the number of fields available: the number nine lent itself to the Muses, seven to the planetary deities, twelve to the months, and of course four to the seasons, probably the single most popular subject for the corners of both mosaic floors and painted ceilings.

THE LATE EMPIRE: FROM THE PERIOD OF ANARCHY TO CONSTANTINE I

In the period from the end of the Severan dynasty (A.D. 235) onward the care bestowed

Figure 12. The Muses mosaic from Neustrasse at Trier, ca. A.D. 250. TRIER, RHEINISCHES LANDESMUSEUM. *PHOTO: R. J. LING*

on wall painting was much reduced and, with the occasional exception, frescoes were technically and artistically inferior to work in mosaic and *opus sectile*, which were now preeminent in the decoration of major public buildings, not only on floors but also on walls and vaults. These cut-stone techniques were ideally suited to the two-dimensional quality of late antique art, whereas the paintbrush lent itself more readily to an illusionistic style that was now less frequently in demand. Stuccowork, with its use of relief and its generally more subtle treatment, seems to have passed largely out of fashion.

One of the symptoms of the changing tastes in interior decoration was the increased use of painting to simulate marble veneer. This "pseudo-veneer," obviously a cheap substitute for the real thing, enjoyed a heyday from the time of the Tetrarchy (A.D. 293–286), when whole walls (as in certain rooms of the house under the church of SS. Giovanni e Paolo in Rome) were divided into brightly colored panels, rectangular, diamond-shaped and circular, painted in imitation of various marbles and breccias. Elsewhere one of the most characteristic late imperial forms of painted decoration, especially popular in the third century, is the so-called red-and-green linear style. As its name implies, this consisted in the division of plain white surfaces by means of simple red and green lines or stripes; the fields so created were occupied by figures and animals, generally painted as isolated motifs with only the barest hint of an environment. On the walls the linear frameworks were entirely rectangular, but on the vaults they formed radiating and concentric systems based upon a focal medallion. This cheap and economical style, of which one of the earliest examples is the Severan decoration of the underground burial place of the Aurelii in Rome (fig. 13), became particularly associated with the Christian catacombs, where the workmanship was often rough and ready in the extreme, frames being uneven and of varying thickness, and figures gauche and irregular in scale. The chief interest of such paintings rests in the light they shed on early Christian iconography.

More important artistically are large-scale figured murals that occupy much of the wall surface. Allover paintings of peopled landscapes, animals in the wild, or seascapes populated with fishing cupids and marine fauna had appeared during the first and second centuries A.D., but only in the third century did this format become common for mythological compositions. One of the best known is a seascape on the wall of a fountain court in the house under the church of SS. Giovanni e Paolo in Rome (fig. 14). At the center, on an island, are two reclining female figures, one clothed and the other largely naked, with a male in attendance; while all

Figure 13. The so-called red-and-green linear style of painted decoration on the vault of the Hypogeum of the Aurelii in Rome, *ca.* A.D. 235. *PHOTO: PONTIFICIA COMMISSIONE DI ARCHEOLOGIA SACRA, ROME*

around are anecdotal groups of cupids in the water or in boats. Large-scale figure compositions continued into the fourth century, usually with a neutral background or at the most a rudimentary ground surface at the bottom. One of the latest survivors, dated to the second half of the century, is a painting of the old Greek theme of Perseus and Andromeda found in a niche on the western slope of the Capitoline Hill in Rome. For all its classical pedigree, this picture demonstrates a hardening and a stiffening characteristic of late antique art, with the figures turned uncomfortably into almost frontal postures (that of Perseus evidently misunderstood) and with strong emphasis being placed upon the contours. As the last known mythological painting in the metropolis, it provides an interesting comment on the continuance of the old traditions and their transformation to new artistic standards.

The sole paintings of first-rate quality to have survived from this period are those of

Figure 14. Fresco depicting a mythological seascape (possibly representing Thetis, Venus, and Adonis), in the *nyphaeum* of the house under the church of SS. Giovanni e Paolo in Rome, third century A.D. (170 × 450 cm).
PHOTO: DEUTSCHES ARCHÄOLOGISCHES INSTITUT, ROME

a room in the Constantinian palace at Augusta Treverorum. Here nine panels of a ceiling decoration have been reconstructed, four containing busts of nimbed female figures, three busts of bearded men, and the others pairs of dancing cupids. Not only are the forms and draperies fully modeled by shading, but the overlapping movement of the cupids imparts a sense of spatial recession, and the panels are all framed with trompe l'oeil enrichments giving the illusion that they are in relief. The wall too was painted with illusionistic elements, here "plastic" pilasters. This remarkably competent yet stylistically conservative decoration, carried out to an imperial commission, gives a glimpse both of the capabilities of the better artists of the time and of the classicizing taste that prevailed at court.

In floor mosaics the late third and fourth centuries saw vigorous developments in various parts of the empire. In Italy, for example, a preference for polychrome mosaics began to overtake the black-and-white style, leading eventually to the brightly colored "carpet-style" pavements of the early Christian churches in Aquileia and Ad Aquas Gradatas (Grado). In Britain new workshops emerged, one of which specialized in a peculiar type of Orpheus pavement in which the captivated birds and animals formed processions in concentric rings around the musical enchanter. No region was more influential, however, than North Africa, and no development more important than that of the large-scale compositions depicting scenes from hunting, the amphitheater, the circus, and rural life that became popular there during the third century. These were laid out, like a tapestry, in a series of polychrome figures and groups distributed in registers against a white ground. The finest examples, datable to the first half of the fourth century, are not in Africa itself but in the luxurious villa near Philosophiana (and modern Piazza Armerina) in Sicily, which has yielded no less than 3,500 square meters of mosaic pavements, all probably laid by a firm from the Carthage region. Particularly impressive is the Great Hunt, a composition 15 feet (4.5 m) wide and 197 feet (60 m) long, which shows the hunting and capture of wild animals for transhipment to the arenas of Italy; among its many memorable details are a lion turning in triumph over its prey, a leopard sinking its teeth into the neck of a gazelle, and another leopard being lured into a cage. More conventional hunting is shown in the Small Hunt pavement (fig. 15), which includes a wild boar being speared, quarry being corralled in netting, and hunters taking part in a picnic—all motifs from the African repertory—while other mosaics at Piazza Armerina feature a grand chariot race, cupids carrying out the vintage and fishing, the exploits of Hercules, and Odysseus offering wine to Polyphemus. The African style enjoyed a wide success during the fourth and fifth centuries, influencing mosaics in Spain and Italy and ultimately spreading, in modified form, even to Syria and Palestine, traditional strongholds of the *emblema*-type panel. Its adoption in the East marks the final victory of the western two-dimensional approach over the old Greek pictorial style with its logical one-view treatment of space.

While the provinces made major contributions to the history of imperial floor mosaic, it seems that the other main branch of the mosaic art owed its genesis and subsequent development primarily to the decorators of Italy and Rome. Wall and vault mosaics appeared first in the late republic and

Figure 15. Detail from the Small Hunt mosaic in the villa near Piazza Armerina in Sicily, *ca.* A.D. 300–330. *SCALA/ART RESOURCE*

early empire, inspired partly by the pumice- and shell-encrusted grottos dedicated by Roman nobles in their villas to the nymphs or Muses, and partly by the desire to adapt veneering in colored marble and glass to the curvature of vaults. Among the earliest manifestations of the technique, which was known as *opus musivum* and regarded as a distinct craft from *opus tessellatum* (floor mosaic), were the mosaic decorated fountain niches (fig. 16) in the gardens of Pompeii and Herculaneum, all datable to the first century A.D. They were characterized by their bright coloring, including blues, golds, greens, and reds, and by their pictorial treatment (of which the Poseidon and Amphitrite in the house of that name at Herculaneum is an excellent example). Glass tesserae, rare in pavements, were predominant; but openings and decorative fields were framed with rows of shells, and the rear of the niche was frequently lined with pumice. In a similar style were panels of mosaic designed to be inset into normal plastered walls, such as a plaque depicting a couple of heraldic griffins at the entrance of the Tomb of Pomponius

Figure 16. Mosaic decorated fountain niche *(opus musivum)* in the atrium of the House of Neptune and Amphitrite at Herculaneum, *ca.* A.D. 62–79. *ALINARI/ART RESOURCE*

Hylas in Rome, and a version of a well-known painting of Achilles on Skyros found in the House of Apollo at Pompeii.

The monumental equivalent of such domestic essays in *opus musivum* were the mosaic vaults of the great public baths of Rome. Almost no trace of these has survived, but literary evidence implies that they were first devised for Nero's Baths; and no doubt they reappeared in all the later complexes in the series, from Titus and Trajan to Caracalla and Diocletian: decorators would have been only too well aware of the scintillating effect

of thousands of colorful and reflective glass tesserae (all inevitably set at fractionally varying angles) above pools of water.

It is unfortunate that the best-preserved vault mosaics of the third and fourth centuries are on a very small scale or are not certainly typical of their kind. One is that of Mausoleum M of the Julii, dated to the first half of the third century, in the Vatican cemetery under St. Peter's. Though in two respects (its Christian themes and its use of a gold background) offering an interesting foretaste of the art of the Byzantine Empire, this is a tiny piece of work that gives little inkling of the effect of the soaring vault mosaics of contemporary thermal halls. Similarly with the annular vault of the ambulatory in the mausoleum of Constantine's daughters, Constantina and Helena, now the church of S. Costanza in Rome. In this case the backgrounds are white and the patterns and subjects seem to be those of contemporary pavements rather than of vaults —among them African-style allover designs with vintaging cupids and a miscellany of birds, vases, and springs of fruit derived ultimately from Hellenistic prototypes. Perhaps more typical of vault mosaics was the lost decoration of S. Costanza's dome, known from old drawings. This, like the roughly contemporary fragmentary mosaics of a domed mausoleum at Centum Cellae (Centcelles), near Tarraco (Tarragona) in Spain, incorporated numerous features alien to floor mosaics—notably a degree of illusionistic recession and a series of imitation supports (caryatids in S. Costanza, columns at Centcelles). The subject matter was partly Christian and partly pagan.

One of the essential characteristics of vault and wall mosaics, found in both the domes just mentioned, was the preference for colored backgrounds. In this connection we may compare the mural pictures in another medium, *opus sectile,* from two fourth-century monuments, the Basilica of Junius Bassus in Rome and a building outside the Marine Gate at Ostia. Those of Junius Bassus include depictions of the Rape of Hylas, a tiger killing a calf, and a consular triumph, all executed in pieces of colored marble and opaque glass on a background of dark-green serpentine. In the Ostian building there were predatory lions and a head of Christ on a background of porphyry.

It was the tradition of vault and wall mosaics that was to have the greatest artistic importance in early Christian and Byzantine decoration. The great series of mosaics, generally with backgrounds of dark blue and gold, which are the crowning glory of the fifth- and sixth-century churches of Ravenna, Rome, Mediolanum (Milan), and Thessalonica (Salonica) are the legatees of the techniques of "painting in stone" devised during the Roman period. Their permanence, the brilliance of their colors, their shimmering effect, their suitability for producing the hard unmodulated style favored in late antiquity —all commended them, rather than frescoes, to the early church builders. Not that fresco painting went out of fashion; it continued as the standard form of mural decoration, especially in the less opulent and ambitious buildings. But much of the technical competence and artistic virtuosity of the best Roman work was lost, not to be recovered until the great classical revival of the late fifteenth and early sixteenth centuries.

BIBLIOGRAPHY

SOURCES

Vitruvius Pollio, *On Architecture,* Book 7; Pliny the Elder, *Natural History,* books 35–36; Jerome J. Pollitt, *The Art of Rome ca. 753 B.C.–337 A.D.: Sources and Documents* (1966).

STUDIES

General

Bernard Andreae, *The Art of Rome* (1977); Ranuccio Bianchi Bandinelli, *Rome, the Center of Power* (1970), and *Rome, the Late Empire* (1971); Hetty Joyce, *The Decoration of Walls, Ceilings, and Floors in Italy in the Second and Third Centuries A.D.* (1981); Donald Strong, *Roman Art* (1976); Donald Strong and David Brown, eds., *Roman Crafts* (1976); Hildegard Temporini and Wolfgang Hanse, eds., *Aufstieg und Niedergang der römischen Welt,* II.12.2 (1981); Jocelyn M. C. Toynbee, *The*

Art of the Romans (1965); Fausto Zevi, ed., *Pompei 79: raccolta di studi per il decimonono centenario dell' eruzione vesuviana* (1979, 1984).

Painting

Frédéric L. Bastet and Mariette de Vos, *Proposta per una classificazione del terzo stile pompeiano,* Arnold de Vos, trans. (1979); Hendrik G. Beyen, *Die pompejanische Wanddekoration vom zweiten bis zum vierten Stil,* 2 vols. in 4 (1938–1960); Maurizio Borda, *La pittura romana* (1958); Gilbert Charles-Picard, *Roman Painting* (1970); Wladimiro Dorigo, *Late Roman Painting,* James Cleugh and John Warrington, trans. (1971); Amedeo Maiuri, *Roman Painting,* Stuart Gilbert, trans. (1953); Karl Schefold, *Vergessenes Pompeji* (1962), and *La peinture pompéienne: essai sur l'évolution de sa signification,* J.-M. Croisille, trans. (1972); Arthur F. Shore, *Portrait Painting from Roman Egypt* (1972); Arturo Stenico, *Roman and Etruscan Painting,* Angus Malcolm, trans. (1963); Rolf Winkes, "Zum Illusionismus römischer Wandmalerei der Republik," in Hildegard Temporini, ed., *Aufstieg und Niedergang der römischen Welt,* I.4 (1973); Fritz Wirth, *Römische Wandmalerei vom Untergang Pompejis bis ans Ende des dritten Jahrhunderts* (1934).

Stuccowork

Roger J. Ling, "Stucco Decoration in Pre-Augustan Italy," in *Papers of the British School at Rome,* **40** (1972); Harald Mielsch, *Römische Stuckreliefs* (1975); Emily L. Wadsworth, "Stucco Reliefs of the First and Second Centuries Still Extant in Rome," in *Memoirs of the American Academy in Rome,* **4** (1924).

Mosaic

Marion E. Blake, "The Pavements of the Roman Buildings of the Republic and Early Empire," in *Memoirs of the American Academy in Rome,* **8** (1930), "Roman Mosaics of the Second Century in Italy," in *Memoirs of the American Academy in Rome,* **13** (1936), and "Mosaics of the Late Empire in Rome and Vicinity," in *Memoirs of the American Academy in Rome,* **17** (1940); Andrea Carandini, Andreina Ricci, and Mariette de Vos, *Filosofiana: The Villa of Piazza Armerina* (1982); John R. Clarke, *Roman Black-and-White Figural Mosaics* (1978); Katherine M. D. Dunbabin, *The Mosaics of Roman North Africa* (1978); Doro Levi, *Antioch Mosaic Pavements,* 2 vols. (1947); Hans P. L'Orange and P. J. Nordhagen, *Mosaics,* Ann E. Keep, trans. (1966); *La mosaïque gréco-romaine: colloques internationaux du Centre National de la Recherche Scientifique, Paris 1963* (1965); *La mosaïque gréco-romaine, II: Deuxième colloque international pour l'étude de la mosaïque antique, Vienne 1971* (1975); Erich Pernice, *Die hellenistische Kunst in Pompeii, 6: Pavimente und figürliche Mosaiken* (1938); Frank B. Sear, *Roman Wall and Vault Mosaics* (1977); David J. Smith, "Mosaics," in Martin Henig, ed., *A Handbook of Roman Art* (1983).

Coins

R. A. G. CARSON

COINS OF GREECE

Archaic period (ca. 650–480 B.C.)

In earlier civilizations such as those of Egypt and Mesopotamia trade was carried on by means of barter or exchange based on such units of value as cattle or weighed silver, and it is as an extension of this last that coins made their first appearance around the Mediterranean. Essentially, coin is differentiated from a piece of bullion by being of a standard weight and by having a pattern or design which identifies the issuing authority and carries a guarantee. Herodotus' story that the Lydians in Asia Minor were the first to use coinage has been borne out by modern research. The earliest coins, found in the substructure of the temple of Artemis at Ephesus, were made of electrum, a natural alloy of gold and silver found in the river Pactolus on which stood the Lydian capital, Sardis. The very earliest pieces, which are dated to the mid seventh century B.C., were probably those with simply a rough striated (grooved) surface on one side and an incuse punch mark bearing the coin's impression on the other, but these were soon succeeded by pieces with a design or guarantee, such as the forepart of a lion, which was the device of the Lydian kings (fig. 1). A coin with the device of a stag bears the earliest coin inscription Φαννος εμι σεμα (I am the badge of Phanes), perhaps the merchant or banker who issued the coin (fig. 2). Electrum coinage of staters, or standard units minted locally, as well as more common subdivisions down to one-ninety-sixth, were produced by other city-states in Asia Minor, and they were identified by their types, or designs, such as the seal at Phocaea (Foca), a pun on the Greek word for seal, or the tunny fish identifying Cyzicus. In Lydia itself, King Croesus (560–546 B.C.) replaced electrum coinage with the first bimetallic coinage in gold and silver with, as types, the head of a lion confronting the head of a bull (fig. 3). Following the conquest of the Lydian kingdom by the Persians, the coinage of Croesus was eventually replaced by a Persian bimetallic coinage of gold darics and silver sigloi (equal to one-twentieth of a daric and weighing 5.35 grams), carrying as badge an archer with a spear, traditionally regarded as a representation of the Great King (Darius II) himself (fig. 4).

In mainland Greece and the islands, where silver was the preferred coinage metal, Aegina was the first to issue coins in about 610 B.C., using a technique very like that used in the early Lydian coins, with a rough punch incuse on one side and the badge of a turtle on the other (fig. 5). Almost as early in the archaic coinage came the first issues of Athens, well provided as she was with silver from the mines of Laurium. Since they bear a series of heraldic devices related to the cult of Athena, the Athenian coins of the sixth century have long been referred to by the term *Wappenmünzen* (heraldic issues). It was probably only after the death of the tyrant Peisistratus in 527 B.C. that the well-known coinage types of Athens made their first appearance. These new double-sided coins mark an important stage in the evolution of coinage both artistically and economically. On the obverse the helmeted head of Athena is of sculptural quality and in high relief, while on the reverse the sacred owl of Athena, as well as the city's name and an olive branch, form a contrasting composition (fig. 6). Hoards of these Athenian "owls" from almost every land bordering the eastern Mediterranean show how this coinage became one of the great international currencies of the ancient world. Almost equally famous was the coinage of silver staters of Corinth with its initial letter, the archaic koppa, and its type of Pegasus whose stamping hoof had opened the spring Peirene on the rock of Acrocorinthos (the citadel of Corinth). This coinage, begun about 575 B.C., was transformed in the later sixth century into double-sided coins with the head of Athena in a Corinthian helmet on the reverse (fig. 7). The silver coinage of city-states in northern Greece owed its abundance to the prolific mines of the area, and many of the tribal coins are exceptionally large, such as the octadrachm (eight-drachma piece) of the Orrescii, showing a herdsman with two huge bulls (fig. 8). The weight of a coin like this would be about 28.5 grams.

The use of silver coinage spread to the city-states colonized by the Greeks in south Italy and Sicily. In Italy, coinage in the later sixth century was of unusual fabric, a thin metal flan, or disk, on which the main design was impressed on one side in relief with the identical type in intaglio on the other, as at Metapontum where the barley-ear type is indicative of its agricultural wealth (fig. 9). More usual two-sided coins took over in south Italy and were adopted also in Sicily, where cities such as Syracuse, Naxos, and Gela coined from the later sixth century. The artistic quality is well exemplified by the silver didrachm (two-drachma piece, weighing about 17.25 grams) of Gela with its forepart of man-headed bull and horseman brandishing spear (fig. 10).

Classical Period (ca. 480–336 B.C.)

In the classical period of coinage, which can be taken as extending from the period of the Persian wars in the early fifth century to the time of Alexander the Great, coins in general terms frequently took the form of double-sided objects with the head of a deity on one side and a contrasting but thematically related design on the reverse. In the central Greek world the leading role was played by the widespread and copious coinage of Athens. The flowering of art in architecture and sculpture is not reflected in the coinage, which here kept much of its archaic style with only small variations of design, including a small crescent moon on the reverse which, it has been suggested, may be an allusion to the battle of Salamis during the Persian Wars, fought in the last quarter of the moon. For domestic use the Athenian coinage possessed a great range of denominations down to the obol, hemiobol, and

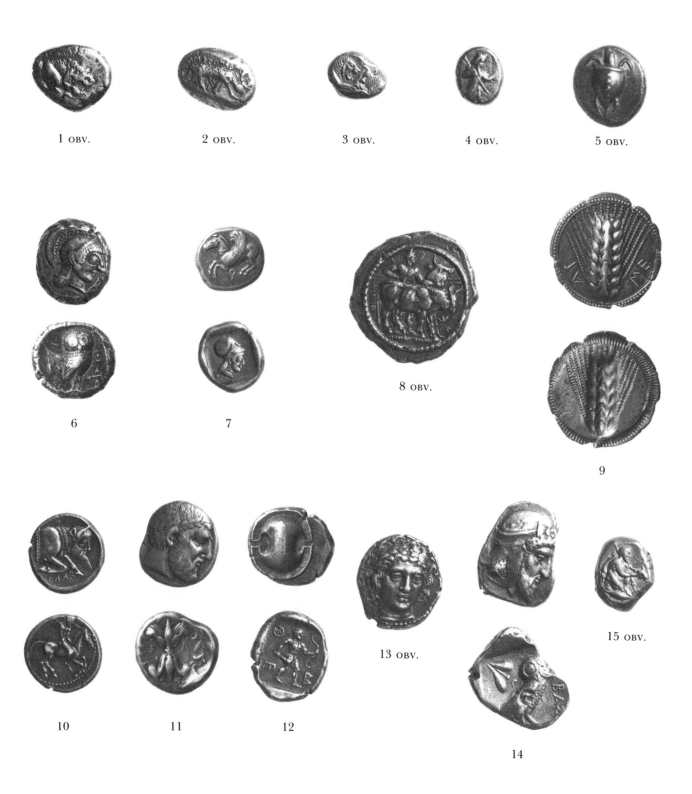

1 OBV. 2 OBV. 3 OBV. 4 OBV. 5 OBV.

6   7

8 OBV.

9

10   11   12

13 OBV.

14

15 OBV.

NOTE: All coins photographed at actual size by R. A. Gardner from the British Museum collection. Where both sides of a coin are shown, the obverse always appears above the reverse.

(*1*) Electrum stater, Ionia, *ca.* 600 B.C.; (*2*) Inscribed electrum stater, Ionia, *ca.* 600 B.C.; (*3*) Croesus, gold stater, 560–546 B.C.; (*4*) Persia, gold daric, 500–490 B.C.; (*5*) Aegina, silver stater, 600–550 B.C.; (*6*) Athens, silver tetradrachm, *ca.* 500 B.C.; (*7*) Corinth, silver stater, 525–500 B.C.; (*8*) Orrescii, Thrace, silver octadrachm, 520–500 B.C.; (*9*) Metapontum, silver stater, 530–510 B.C.; (*10*) Gela, silver didrachm, 495–485 B.C.; (*11*) Elis, silver stater, *ca.* 420 B.C.; (*12*) Thebes, silver stater, 446–426 B.C. (*13*) Amphipolis, silver tetradrachm, *ca.* 400 B.C.; (*14*) Tissaphernes, silver tetradrachm, Miletus, 411 B.C.; (*15*) Cyzicus, electrum stater, 440–420 B.C.

even tetartemorion (a quarter-obol), so waferlike that it could be carried without difficulty under the tongue, as Aristophanes amusingly relates in the *Wasps*.

In about 449 B.C. Athens issued a decree forbidding her allies to strike silver coins of their own, and among the consequences was the temporary disappearance of the rival coinage of Aegina, which had a wide circulation among the Aegean islands. Other coinages in mainland Greece, however, continued to flourish in the fifth century. The copious coinage of Corinth, whose silver staters bearing Pegasus and Athena's head were popularly known as "colts," circulated as far as the western Mediterranean, while in the Peloponnese one of the major mints was that of Elis, whose coin types refer to the worship of Zeus and Hera at Olympia, and to the Olympic festival, which the Eleans had acquired the right to celebrate (fig. 11). At Thebes, especially after its defeat of Athens at Coronea in 447 B.C., there was a rich silver coinage with traditional types of Boeotian shield and figure of Heracles, regarded as the special local hero (fig. 12). The wealth of silver in northern Greece in the fifth century as in the previous century finds expression in many splendid city coinages. One of the most brilliant is that from Amphipolis, with the remarkable head of Apollo in semifrontal pose on the tetradrachm (fourdrachma piece) series (fig. 13). The late fifth century also saw the beginning of coinage with portraits of real people. One of the earliest may be the bearded head labeled Pythagoras on tetradrachms of Abdera. It may be only the mintmaster of that name who is portrayed, but it could possibly be his namesake, the famous sixth-century philosopher and mathematician. An undoubted early portrait is found on a tetradrachm minted at Miletus in 411 B.C. It has been identified as the Persian satrap, Tissaphernes, and it is interesting that the reverse has been adapted from the Athenian tetradrachm

with the Athenian names replaced here by the word *bas* (for *basileos*), used in reference to Darius II (fig. 14). Elsewhere in Asia Minor important coinages continued to be minted in electrum, at Phocaea and Lesbos, mostly in the smaller *hektai* (sixths) denomination, and also notably at Lampsacus (Lapseki) and Cyzicus, the latter supplying the main commercial coinage for the Black Sea area. On coins of Cyzicus the local emblem of the tunny fish is always present, accompanying a great variety of types such as a kneeling Poseidon holding a dolphin (fig. 15).

At the end of the fifth century the long war with Sparta ended in the defeat of Athens, and in a last desperate measure the treasures of the Acropolis were melted to produce an emergency issue of gold coins. When the Athenian silver coinage was revived in 393 B.C., it kept its traditional types, except that now Athena's eye was drawn properly in profile. Corinth, too, preserved its earlier coinage designs, but elsewhere this century saw a rich flowering of new creative designs. One of the predilections was for a facing portrait on coin obverses, such as the striking Apollo as the sun-god on coins of Rhodes, or the delicately modeled Apollo at Clazomenae (Klazümen), where he had a shrine, and a swan on the reverse, commonly found in the delta of the nearby Hermus (Gediz) River (fig. 16). The local reference of many types is clear; at Ephesus, the stag and bee refer to the worship of Artemis, while on coins of Cnossus the labyrinth of Minoan Crete is an obvious choice (fig. 17). Local influence makes its mark, too, as on the coins of Phoenician cities, instanced on the double shekel of Byblos (Jubayl) about 350 B.C. showing a galley and hippocampus on the obverse and an archaic-seeming reverse of a lion attacking a bull with the name of King Adramelek in Phoenician script (fig. 18). In Asia Minor Cyzicus still issued its electrum staters, some with seemingly realistic portraits of elderly men, and Lampsacus produced a coinage of gold staters that had a widespread distribution, having a range of elaborate compositions, such as Nike (Victory) sacrificing a ram (fig. 19). A rich gold coinage was produced for the Black Sea area by Panticapaeum (Kerch) in Tauris (the Crimea), its griffin and barley-ear reverse indicating the source of its wealth and the head of Pan on the obverse presenting a punning device on the city's name (fig. 20). In Macedonia, as individual cities fell to Philip II, their coinage ceased. Drawing on the resources of the Pangaean mines, Philip issued an extensive coinage of silver tetradrachms with Zeus' head and racehorse reverse and of gold staters with Apollo's head and two-horse chariot reverse (fig. 21). These latter, finding their way along the Danube into western Europe, were widely and often bizarrely copied to furnish the Celtic coinage of Gaul and Britain in the first century B.C.

The coinage of the western Greeks in Sicily and Italy in the fifth and early fourth centuries achieved a brilliance of design and an aesthetic level of execution that have led them to be regarded by many as the finest examples of Greek coinage. The climate for this artistic development was provided by the courts of such tyrants as Gelon, his brother Hieron I, and later Dionysius I of Syracuse. This new style found expression at Syracuse in a special issue of silver deca-drachms (ten-drachma pieces) with a delicately modeled head of the water nymph Arethusa, encircled by dolphins, and on the other side a four-horse chariot in active movement (fig. 22). This coin has been traditionally termed "Damarateion," as it was supposed to have been struck from bullion derived from gifts from the Carthaginians to Damarete, Gelon's queen, who intervened on their behalf after their defeat at Himera in 480 B.C. Other coins of exceptional quality were produced at Aetna (Etna), as the city of Catana was named during its occupation

by Hieron I, including one featuring a powerful head of Silenus and an enthroned Zeus and, from Naxos, a magnificent series with a Dionysus head and a squatting Silenus (fig. 23). Many Sicilian cities produced coins that are sculptural masterpieces in miniature, but the series mainly of four-horse chariots at Syracuse, many dating to the last quarter of the fifth century, and signed by the artists, hold pride of place. Perhaps the most famous of these are the series of silver deca-drachms signed by Kimon and Euainetus. The obverse shows a chariot in active but smooth movement with Nike flying above and is matched by an expressive head of Arethusa on the reverse. Kimon's signature is found in the nymph's hairband. Below the chariot, a collection of pieces of armor accompanied by the word ἀθλα (arms) possibly represent trophies of war and can thus be associated with the defeat of the Athenians in 413 B.C. (fig. 24). Even more attractive were the silver decadrachms struck in the city of Acragas (Agrigento), with the chariot of Helios, the sun-god, sweeping through the air, and on the reverse two eagles perched on their prey, celebrating most probably the triumphant return of the Acragantine Exainetos, victor in the Olympic Games in 412 B.C. (fig. 25). In 406 B.C. the successful occupation of western Sicily by Carthage brought an end to many city coinages, although some mints continued to issue traditional types but with the mint name now in Punic script. Among coins of Carthaginian Sicily in the late fourth century were unusual tetradrachms with a portrait once thought to be Dido but now realized to be of the Semitic goddess Tanit. In Punic script is the legend OMMACHANAT, meaning "in the camp" (fig. 26). In 345 B.C., with the advent of Timoleon of Corinth, the liberator, the mint of Syracuse produced a coinage of Corinthian-type staters.

In Italy the coinage of the classical period rivals in artistic quality that of Sicily. Out-

(*16*) Clazomenae, silver tetradrachm, 370–360 B.C.; (*17*) Cnossus, silver stater, *ca.* 370 B.C.; (*18*) Byblos, silver double shekel, *ca.* 350 B.C.; (*19*) Lampsacus, gold stater, 350–340 B.C.; (*20*) Panticapaeum, gold stater, *ca.* 350 B.C.; (*21*) Philip II, gold stater, 359–336 B.C.; (*22*) Syracuse, silver decadrachm ("Damareteion"), *ca.* 480 B.C.; (*23*) Naxos, silver tetradrachm, *ca.* 460 B.C.; (*24*) Syracuse, silver decadrachm, 405–400 B.C.; (*25*) Acragas, silver decadrachm, 412 B.C.; (*26*) Carthage, silver tetradrachm, *ca.* 320 B.C.; (*27*) Rhegium, silver tetradrachm, *ca.* 435 B.C.; (*28*) Tarentum, silver stater, 380–345 B.C.

17 REV.

19 OBV.

20 OBV.

16

18

21

22

23

24

25

26

27

28

standing were the silver tetradrachms of Rhegium (Reggio di Calabria) of about 435 B.C. with a lion-mask badge on the obverse and the seated figure, probably of Iokastos, mythical founder of the city, on the reverse (fig. 27). More typical of the delicate and detailed style of the coins of the Italiote cities were the silver staters of Tarentum (Taranto) with the well-known design of horseman and Taras, a son of Neptune and builder of the city, riding on a dolphin (fig. 28). Quite different in characteristics and style were the coins of Etruria, typified by a silver coin of Populonia with its odd-facing Gorgon head and underneath the mark XX indicating its value (fig. 29). In the western Mediterranean the prosperity of the powerful mercantile state of Carthage found expression in a profuse coinage of gold and electrum as well as silver. The obverse normally carried the head of Tanit, assimiliated to the Greek Persephone, and the reverse commonly a horse or horsehead, an allusion to the carving said to have been found in digging the foundations of Carthage, or a palm tree, a pun on the words for palm and Phoenician (fig. 30). In Italy and Sicily the coinage of the Greek cities eventually gave way to the coinage of the expanding power of Rome.

Hellenistic period (ca. 336 B.C. onward)

The conquests of Alexander the Great transformed the Greek world from a series of small city-states and their colonies into a vast empire stretching from Macedonia and mainland Greece to Egypt in the south and India in the east, an empire that subsequently split into smaller but still extensive kingdoms. These political changes were reflected in the coinage, which henceforth tended to consist of major series that were current over large areas. The coinage of Alexander the Great, in effect the first world coinage, in its uniform construction and ex-

tensive distribution can be compared only with the issues of the later Roman Empire. Coinage was struck for Alexander in all three metals. The unit in gold was the stater with rare double pieces and occasional smaller pieces. The obverse showed the head of Athena in a decorated Corinthian helmet, and the reverse depicted Nike as copied from a monument in Athens. The major silver piece was a tetradrachm bearing, on the obverse, young Heracles' head, sometimes thought to be a likeness of Alexander himself, and on the reverse an enthroned Zeus (fig. 31). Token bronze coins also had Heracles' head and, in addition, club and bow symbols. As Alexander's conquests extended, a chain of mints was set up throughout the empire to produce his coins. Even after Alexander's death (323 B.C.) his monolithic coinage system continued, and only toward the end of the century did the kingdoms into which his successors divided his empire begin to produce their individual coinages.

Some exceptional pieces produced the first portrait coins of Alexander. Perhaps the earliest was the silver tetradrachm struck at Alexandria, depicting Alexander in an elephant-skin headdress on the obverse; and about 297 B.C. Lysimachus, for a time one of the most powerful of the successors, on his silver tetradrachms represented Alexander wearing the ram's horn of Zeus Ammon, proclaiming the divinity of which Alexander had been assured by the oracle at Siwa oasis (fig. 32). Alexander was also pictured on rare silver decadrachms, probably struck at Babylon shortly after his death. He is shown as a horseman attacking an Indian king who rides an elephant, and on the other side he is depicted holding the thunderbolt of Zeus (fig. 33). Some of the early coins of the successors were more individual, and one of the most striking tetradrachms of this period was issued by Demetrius I (Poliorcetes) of Macedonia during his fairly short exercise of power. His naval victory over Ptolemy in 306 B.C. was celebrated by the types on this coin, the commanding figure of Poseidon wielding his trident and Nike alighting on the prow of a war galley, a motif recalling the famous Nike of Samothrace (fig. 34).

In the regal coinage of Macedonia after Alexander, Alexander-type gold staters continued to be minted during most reigns, but in the main coinage of the silver tetradrachms there was a greater variety. Of special interest is a head of Pan on a Macedonian shield on coins of Antigonus I, "Gonatas," and there are magnificent portraits of Philip V and his son Perseus (fig. 35), the last king of Macedonia before its subjection by Rome.

In the satrapy of Egypt which Ptolemy took as his share of empire in 323 B.C., Alexander-type coinage was at first continued. Change came with the adoption of the title *basileus* by Ptolemy I in 305 B.C. On gold coins appeared the portrait of Ptolemy himself, one of the earliest regal issues to carry the portrait of a living man, and on the reverse the deified Alexander in a quadriga of elephants. The royal portrait appeared also on silver tetradrachms with a new reverse, an eagle on a thunderbolt, which was to become the standard type throughout the Ptolemaic coinage (fig. 36). Large gold octadrachms in the coinage of Ptolemy II have double portraits on both sides: Ptolemy II and Arsinoë II on one side and the deified Ptolemy I and his queen Berenice on the other. The deification of Arsinoë in 272 B.C. was marked by extensive issues both of silver tetradrachms and large gold pieces bearing the veiled head of Arsinoë and a double horn of plenty (cornucopia) (fig. 37). Since silver was not readily available in Egypt, gold was often used in coinage of large denomination. For ordinary transactions, the Ptolemies issued massive numbers of bronze coins of various denominations with Zeus' head on the obverse and the traditional

eagle on thunderbolt on the reverse (fig. 38). The types of Ptolemaic coinage in all metals remained fairly standard to the end, and the debased silver tetradrachms of Cleopatra VII, the last Ptolemaic ruler, still show her portrait and an eagle reverse (fig. 39).

In the division of Alexander's empire allotted to Seleucus, Alexander-type coins were initially minted until Seleucus I assumed the title of king (*basileus*) in 305 B.C. New coinage included silver tetradrachms with the head of Seleucus in a helmet ornamented with a bull's horn and Nike crowning a trophy of arms, types commemorating his victory at the battle of Ipsus in 301 B.C. (fig. 40). The main innovation in the coinage of Antiochus I, the next Seleucid ruler, was a series of tetradrachms with his portrait and a reverse of Apollo seated on the omphalos ("navel of the world," at Delphi), holding bow and arrow (fig. 41), types that persisted through much of the Seleucid coinage. They were repeated on an exceptional series of large gold octadrachms issued during the reign of Antiochus III, but a novel type was used on a series of silver tetradrachms, also issued by Antiochus III, in which the Indian elephant on the reverse is associated with his eastern campaigns (212–206 B.C.). Another variety of reverse, a seated Zeus holding Nike on an outstretched hand, added by Antiochus IV, became another of the staples of the Seleucid coinage. Very distinctive types were used on the tetradrachms of Tigranes I of Armenia, invited to occupy the Syrian throne in 83 B.C. when the Seleucid power was declining. His portrait shows him wearing a tall Armenian headdress, and on the reverse is seated the Tyche of Antioch with the god of the river Orontes at her feet (fig. 42).

A number of other smaller kingdoms, including some established as breakaway portions of the Seleucid Empire, have coinage notable for their series of splendid regal portraits, especially on silver tetradrachms. In the series for the kingdom of Pontus, the

29 OBV.

30

31

32

33

34

35

36

37

38

39

40

(*29*) Populonia, silver, *ca.* 300 B.C.; (*30*) Carthage, silver didrachm, early third century B.C.; (*31*) Alexander the Great, silver tetradrachm, 336–323 B.C.; (*32*) Lysimachus, silver tetradrachm, 297–281 B.C.; (*33*) Alexander the Great, silver decadrachm, 323–300 B.C.; (*34*) Demetrius I (Poliorcetes), silver tetradrachm, 300–295 B.C.; (*35*) Perseus, silver tetradrachm, 179–168 B.C.; (*36*) Ptolemy I, silver tetradrachm, 300–285 B.C.; (*37*) Arsinoë II, gold octadrachm, 270–250 B.C.; (*38*) Ptolemy III, bronze, 247–222 B.C.; (*39*) Cleopatra VII, silver tetradrachm, 51–30 B.C.; (*40*) Seleucus I, silver tetradrachm, *ca.* 301 B.C.

most extensive coinage was minted during the reign of Mithridates VI the Great who established suzerainty over much of Asia Minor until his defeat by Rome in 63 B.C. The handsome portrait represents him with wildly flying hair, and on the reverse grazes a graceful stag, set between the royal names and titles (fig. 43). On the coinage of another Hellenistic state, the kingdom of Pergamum, the portrait of Philetaerus, the first ruler of the Attalid dynasty, realistically depicts his flabby eunuch features (fig. 44). Under the kings of Pergamum the coinage of cistophori made its first appearance. These coins, silver tetradrachms, are among the most stylistically pedestrian Greek coins of this denomination. They have been given this name from the obverse type, the sacred chest or *kiste* used in the mysteries of Bacchus (fig. 45). Even after the creation of the Roman province of Asia this cistophoric coinage continued, carrying the names of Roman proconsuls and later of emperors. Another early kingdom to break away from the Seleucid Empire was the satrapy of Bactria (northwest India) about 250 B.C. The coinage of the Bactrian kings presents a series of unusually vivid and interesting portraits of which one impressive example, dating to the middle of the second century, shows King Eucratides wearing a crested helmet that is adorned with the ear and horn of a bull, symbols of divinity (fig. 46).

During the late Hellenistic period decline in the power of the kingdoms gave opportunity for the revival of some cities and their coinages. In Greece itself, Athens initiated in the early second century a new coinage of broad-flanned tetradrachms in a new style, a classicizing re-creation of the traditional types of Athena head and owl (fig. 47). In the western Mediterranean, the main silver coinage of Carthage was minted in Sicily, but from the later fourth century it produced not only silver but a plentiful coinage of gold and electrum at Carthage itself, the

gold most probably procured from West Africa. The types were the traditional Tanit head and horse, which persisted also on a series of electrum triple-staters struck at a Sicilian mint during the First Punic War against Rome. An unusual series of coins in silver of values up to triple shekels was struck by Hamilcar Barca and his family in Spain. In place of Tanit is a head of the Semitic god Melkart, sometimes bearded, sometimes beardless, and the traditional horse type is replaced by an African war elephant, occasionally with its mahout (fig. 48). An attractive but unproven suggestion is that the bearded portrait is Hamilcar and the beardless head, his son Hannibal, Rome's enemy in the Second Punic War.

Some coinage of city-states continued alongside the great regal coinages, but from the second century onward these were gradually eliminated as Rome's power grew to dominate the Mediterranean and as her conquests multiplied. Greek-type coinage disappeared first in Italy and Sicily, then in North Africa and Spain, and finally on mainland Greece and in Asia Minor, although even under Roman dominion some vestiges of coinage persisted that can still be described as Greek. Silver cistophoric coinage went on being produced in the province of Asia in the last decades of the Roman Republic under Augustus and by a few of his successors down to Hadrian; and at Caesarea (Kayseri) in Cappadocia (eastern Asia Minor) a coinage of silver drachms and multiples, with imperial portraits and most commonly a representation of Mount Argaeus (Erciyeş) on the reverse and inscriptions in Greek, lasted into the third century A.D. Many cities in the eastern provinces of the Roman Empire maintained their own local bronze coinage well into the third century also. The reverses very commonly allude to and illustrate local religious cults, temples and shrines, such as the famous altar of Zeus at Pergamum on bronze coins of Septimius

41   42   43   45

44 obv.

46 obv.   49 rev.

48

47

50   51   52   53

(*41*) Antiochus I, silver tetradrachm, 281–261 B.C.; (*42*) Tigranes I, silver tetradrachm, 83–69 B.C.; (*43*) Mithridates VI, silver tetradrachm, 120–63 B.C.; (*44*) Philetaerus, silver tetradrachm, 282–263 B.C.; (*45*) Pergamum, silver cistophorus, *ca.* 200 B.C.; (*46*) Eucratides, silver tetradrachm, 180–150 B.C.; (*47*) Athens, silver tetradrachm, *ca.* 175 B.C.; (*48*) Carthage, silver double shekel, 237–218 B.C.; (*49*) Pergamum, Septimius Severus, A.D. 193–211; (*50*) Alexandria, Nero, billon tetradrachm, A.D. 64; (*51*) Rome, silver didrachm, *ca.* 269 B.C.; (*52*) Rome, gold stater, *ca.* 216 B.C.; (*53*) Rome, denarius, *ca.* 211 B.C.

Severus (fig. 49). The most prolific and consistent "Greek" coinage under the empire was that issued at Alexandria in Egypt. This was essentially a coinage of tetradrachms struck in poor silver and increasingly debased until the final issues for the emperors of the First Tetrarchy in A.D. 294 were simply of bronze. A special feature was the recording on the reverse of the imperial regnal year. Many of the reverse personifications are similar to those on Roman coins, but some have unusual portraits such as that of Nero's empress, Poppaea (fig. 50).

COINS OF ROME

The Republic (ca. 290–31 B.C.)

The coinage of Rome is late in making its appearance, and the first coins to be associated with Rome are of an unusual kind. The first currency is in bronze only in the form of large rectangular bricks or bars, described as *aes signatum,* with a type on either side and weighing about five pounds. This coinage is dated to the early third century B.C., and although few of the types have any explicit reference, one bar with an elephant on one side and a sow on the other may be associated with Rome's first encounter with the war elephant in the war against King Pyrrhus of Epirus about 280 B.C. Before long, these bars were replaced by *aes grave,* heavy bronze coins cast in circular shape and initially produced at a standard weight of one libra or pound for the unit, the as. Janus, the god of beginnings, occupied the obverse and the prow of a galley was found on the reverse of all denominations of asses (the obverses of lower denominations carried the heads of lesser gods). Associated with this coinage, begun about 269 B.C., were issues of struck silver didrachms, similar in fabric and style to the coinage of Greek cities of south Italy but inscribed with the legend

ROMANO. Among a variety of types are found a Heracles head and the she-wolf and twins representing Rome's legendary foundation (fig. 51). Such was the coinage of Rome during the First Punic War, but it was replaced about 235 B.C. by a new series of silver didrachms now inscribed ROMA and bronze coins of reduced weight. One of these didrachms, with types showing a head of a young Janus and a quadriga, was still in issue at the outbreak of the Second Punic War in 218 B.C., and a similar young Janus head was used in Rome's first gold coinage of staters about 216 B.C. The reverse shows Rome and her Latin allies swearing an oath of common fealty (fig. 52).

Later in the Second Punic War Rome introduced about 211 B.C. a new silver coin, the denarius, which remained the staple silver denomination well into the third century A.D. The types of the first denarius were the helmeted head of Roma and the heavenly twins Castor and Pollux. According to legend, they had earlier come to the aid of Rome at the battle of Lake Regillus against the Latins about 496 B.C. and thus now formed an apt type for the new coinage in the crisis posed by Hannibal (fig. 53). The weight of the bronze as had been steadily reduced until, at the date of the introduction of the denarius, it had fallen to one-sixth the weight of the original issue and equaled the sextan. The Janus head and ship's prow type remained the same (fig. 54).

A second silver coin of slightly lower weight than the denarius, the victoriate, circulated for a time; it was so termed because it bore the figures of a Jupiter head and Victory crowning a trophy of arms. In the course of the second century the denarius, originally anonymous, was additionally adorned by a symbol or monogram which later expanded to include the full name of the magistrate (state official) responsible for issuing the coinage. Gradually, the initial designs also gave way to types alluding to events, real or legendary, in the earlier history of the moneyers' families. The reverse, for instance, of the denarius of the moneyer Sextus Pompeius Fostlus about 137 B.C. depicts his legendary ancestor, the shepherd Faustulus, discovering the twins Romulus and Remus being suckled by the she-wolf (fig. 55).

In the early second century B.C. a rare series of gold coins was struck, not in Rome or elsewhere in Italy as previous coinage had been but in Greece. This coinage honored the Roman general T. Quinctius Flamininus after his defeat of Philip V of Macedon at Cynoscephalae in 197 B.C. The types, adapted from the Macedonian gold stater, carry the portrait of Flamininus on the obverse, while his name accompanies the figure of Victory on the reverse (fig. 56). This is the earliest portrait of a living Roman on coins—such portraiture was normally eschewed and only became a regular feature on late republican coinage and then on imperial coins. Throughout the second century the only regular precious metal coin was the denarius, and coinage in bronze became less frequent. The so-called Social War, the revolt of Rome's Italian allies which began in 91 B.C., gave rise to a coinage of denarii issued by the rebels (the Marsic Confederation). Such issues featured a head of Italia on the obverse, and the reverses were those commonly used on Roman coins. Inscriptions in Oscan script recorded the name of Italia and sometimes the names of Marsic leaders such as General Gaius Papius Mutilus (fig. 57). The war coinage of Rome gave rise to very prolific issues of denarii, many of them marked with an elaborate series of control marks in the form of symbols, letters, or numerals, as on the coinage of L. Piso Frugi about 90 B.C. (fig. 58). After the end of this war the struggle that followed between senatorial and democratic parties in Rome made little impact on coin typology until Sulla's return to Italy, and the defeat of his Roman enemies, the followers of the late Gaius Marius at the Colline Gate in 82 B.C. brought the first coinage issued not on the authority of the senate but of a general's *imperium*. This included a substantial coinage in gold of which one issue struck by Sulla's subordinate (proquaestor), L. Manlius Torquatus, portrayed Sulla in a triumphal quadriga (fig. 59).

In the first century the bulk of the coinage continued to be produced by the mint of Rome, but political rivalry and the ensuing civil war between Pompey the Great and Julius Caesar brought an increase in military issues by generals elsewhere. A very large denarius coinage struck for Julius Caesar in 49 B.C., possibly somewhere in Cisalpine Gaul (northern Italy), with types depicting an elephant trampling a dragon and the emblems of Caesar's chief priesthood, records his recent victories over the Gauls (fig. 60). There is reference, too, to the Gallic wars on a denarius by the moneyer L. Hostilius Saserna in 49 B.C. showing a portrait, possibly of the Gallic chieftain Vercingetorix, and a Celtic war chariot. Pompey the Great was never portrayed on coinage in his lifetime, but on denarii issued shortly after his death by his sons, who continued the struggle in Spain against Caesar, the obverse carries Pompey's portrait (fig. 61). With the defeat of the Pompeians, Caesar was left supreme, and on the coinage in the first months of 44 B.C. Caesar's portrait appeared on the obverse, the first instance of a coin portrait of a living man since that of Flamininus (fig. 62).

After the assassination of Julius Caesar on the Ides of March 44 B.C., the contenders for succession, Mark Antony, Caesar's lieutenant, Lepidus, his master of horse (dictator's deputy), and Octavian (the future Augustus), his grandnephew and heir, formed the Second Triumvirate, and the checkered history of this compact until the final victory of Octavian can be followed on the coinage.

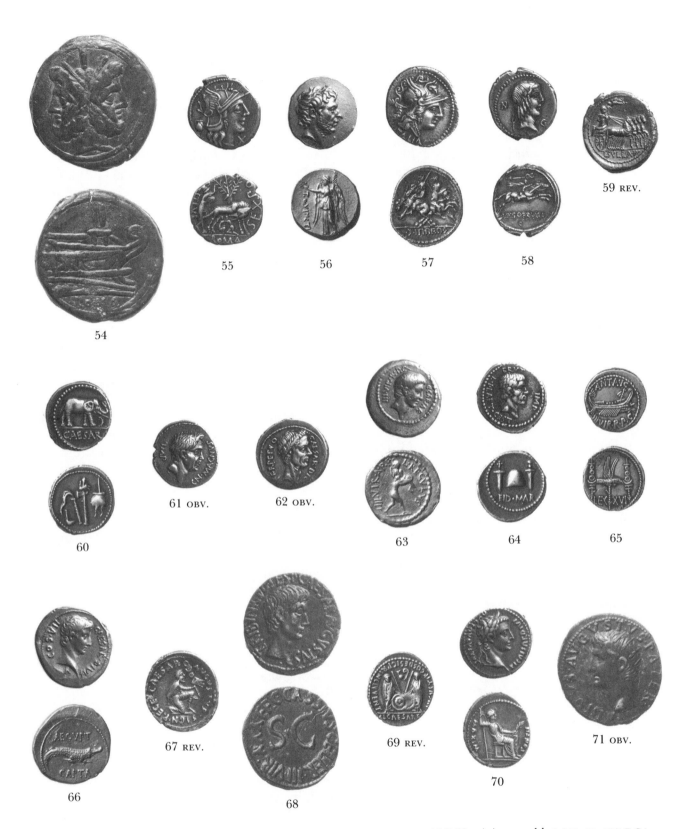

(54) Rome, bronze as, *ca.* 211 B.C.; (55) Rome, denarius, *ca.* 137 B.C.; (56) Flamininus, gold stater, *ca.* 197 B.C.; (57) Social War, denarius, 90–88 B.C.; (58) Rome, denarius, 90–89 B.C.; (59) Sulla, aureus, *ca.* 82 B.C.; (60) Julius Caesar, denarius, *ca.* 49 B.C.; (61) Pompey the Great, denarius, *ca.* 46 B.C.; (62) Julius Caesar, denarius, 44 B.C.; (63) Octavian, aureus, 42 B.C.; (64) Brutus, denarius, 42 B.C.; (65) Mark Antony, denarius, 31 B.C.; (66) Augustus, aureus, 27 B.C.; (67) Augustus, denarius, 19 B.C.; (68) Augustus, as, 22 B.C.; (69) Gaius and Lucius Caesares, denarius, 2 B.C.–A.D. 4; (70) Tiberius, denarius, A.D. 14–37; (71) Divus Augustus, as, A.D. 22–30.

There was a growing trend for the staple series of denarii to be supplemented by frequent gold issues (aurei) and occasional bronze coinage. Similarly, the tendency for the obverse to have a portrait and title after the fashion initiated by the last Caesar coinage became almost a rule. This is well illustrated by the series of aurei struck for the triumvirate by the moneyer Regulus in 42 B.C. on which each member's portrait on the obverse is accompanied by a reverse relating to his family history. In the case of Octavian, the reverse depicts Aeneas (the legendary ancestor of the Julian house into which he had been adopted), carrying his father Anchises as they escape from captured Troy (fig. 63). Even the tyrannicides followed the new fashion. Denarii of Brutus show his portrait and present a striking reverse alluding to the assassination of Caesar: the liberty cap, flanked by two daggers, with the inscription EID MAR (the Ides of March, the date on which the deed was done) (fig. 64). One of the last issues of republican coinage, the war coinage of Mark Antony, did not bear his portrait but had types of galley and a legionary eagle with standards, honoring both his fleet and the legions with which he and Cleopatra confronted Octavian in the last battle at Actium in 31 B.C. (fig. 65).

The Principate (31 B.C.–A.D. 294)

After the defeat of Antony, Octavian, or Augustus as he became entitled in 27 B.C., undertook a remodeling of coinage into a more coherent system than in the last years of the republic. In addition to the gold unit, the aureus, comprising 25 silver denarii, new denominations were introduced; in orichalcum, the ancient form of brass (an alloy of copper with zinc), the sestertius and its half, the dupondius; in copper, the as together with its half, the semis, and quarter, the quadrans. The emperor controlled the precious-metal coinage, but some role was

left to the senate in the production of the brass and copper (token) coinage, which was normally marked SC (senatus consulto). As in the late republican coinage so in the imperial issues the obverse generally carried a portrait, though at first this was not a regular feature on the lower denominational pieces. A great change, however, took place in the vocabulary of the coin reverses. Personifications such as Roma and Victory on republican coins continued and many more were added as well as representations of many deities, but many reverses were now devoted to recording an emperor's achievements, aims, and policies.

Augustus produced his first coinage at the mint of Rome, but subsequently he moved the striking of precious-metal coinage to mints in Spain and later in Gaul at Lugdunum (Lyons). His main nonprecious coinage continued to be struck at Rome; later in the reign a somewhat less common bronze coinage was also produced at Lugdunum. Only a few examples and illustrations of the new imperial denominational system and the informative nature of the reverses can be noted. An aureus struck at an eastern mint in 27 B.C. early in Augustus' reign records with its type of crocodile (the symbol of Egypt) and inscription the defeat of Cleopatra and the seizure of her country (fig. 66). A denarius struck at Rome in 19 B.C. still carried the name of the moneying magistrate, but its reverse records Augustus' diplomatic success in securing the return from Parthia of Roman military standards lost in earlier defeats (fig. 67). The new copper as with its prominent SC on the reverse was the only Augustan small denomination coin to carry the imperial portrait (fig. 68). One of Augustus' concerns was to secure a dynastic succession, and a prolific precious-metal coinage from the Lugdunum mint was devoted to making familiar his intended heirs, his grandsons Gaius and Lucius (fig. 69). The Lugdunum mint was also used to issue nonprecious coinage which had its own special reverse type, an altar, recording the establishment in Gaul of an altar to the new cult of Roma and Augustus.

Augustus' grandsons predeceased him, and his stepson Tiberius was adopted as heir, succeeding as emperor in A.D. 14. Tiberius made little change in the mint and monetary systems inherited from Augustus, and so conservative was most of his coinage that throughout his long reign virtually only one reverse type was used on his gold and silver. This was a seated female figure and is generally taken to represent his mother, the empress Livia (fig. 70). Augustus, deified after his death, received widespread commemoration on the coinage of Tiberius, especially on the copper asses (fig. 71). In the brief four-year reign of Gaius (Caligula) one of the themes of the coinage is the imperial family, and issues honored the emperor's parents, Germanicus and Agrippina the Elder, and his three sisters, Agrippina the Younger, Drusilla, and Julia (found on a sestertius) (fig. 72). As this coin shows, the sestertius obverse carried for the first time the imperial portrait. Under Gaius it seems that the issue of precious-metal coinage was moved from Lugdunum back to Rome.

The coinage of the next emperor, Claudius, shows how events were given swift commemoration. The part played by the Praetorian Guard in the proclamation of Claudius in A.D. 41 is pictured on aurei with a reverse showing the Praetorian camp and the explanatory legend IMPER[ator] RECEPT[vs] (fig. 73). Similarly the extension of the empire with the successful conquest of the new province of Britain received repeated commemoration on Claudius' coinage, and coins were struck bearing on the reverse a triumphal arch inscribed on the architrave DE BRITANN (fig. 74). The first ten years of Nero's coinage was in gold and silver only, and the use of the formula EX SC on the reverse is evidence of a brief resurgence of senatorial influence. A coinage reform in A.D. 64 removed this formula, lowered the weight standard of gold and silver coins, and instituted again a plentiful nonprecious metal coinage. The dominant influence of the emperor's mother, Agrippina the Younger, at the beginning of the reign is apparent from the appearance of her portrait along with that of the emperor on the coin obverses (fig. 75). On the resumption of lower-denominational coinage, an unusual feature for a short time was the use of orichalcum for all denominations with a mark of value on the reverse of the smaller denominations. The artistic quality of the portraiture found excellent scope for display on the large flan of the sestertius, frequently combined with interesting reverses such as that marking the closure of the temple of Janus to indicate peace throughout the Roman world, as the inscription also spells out (fig. 76).

The revolts in the western provinces against Nero's rule, which ended with his suicide in A.D. 68, had as a result a series of independent coinages. The earliest, under Gaius Julius Vindex, governor of Lugdunensis, was mainly of denarii with rare issues in gold and did not promote any individual cause; rather his choice of types recalled the coinage of Augustus and the republic. L. Clodius Macer, legionary commander (*legatus*) of Numidia, invaded the province of Africa and issued a coinage of denarii at Carthage; although he placed his portrait on his coins, he made no claim to empire. The coinage issued by Servius Sulpicius Galba (later Emperor Galba), who revolted in Spain and whose coinage was probably minted at Tarraco (Tarragona), exhibited simply the title "imperator," but following his recognition by the senate coinage in all three metals was struck for him both at the mint of Lugdunum and at Rome itself. The coinage included particularly handsome sestertii, as reflected in the portraiture that ap-

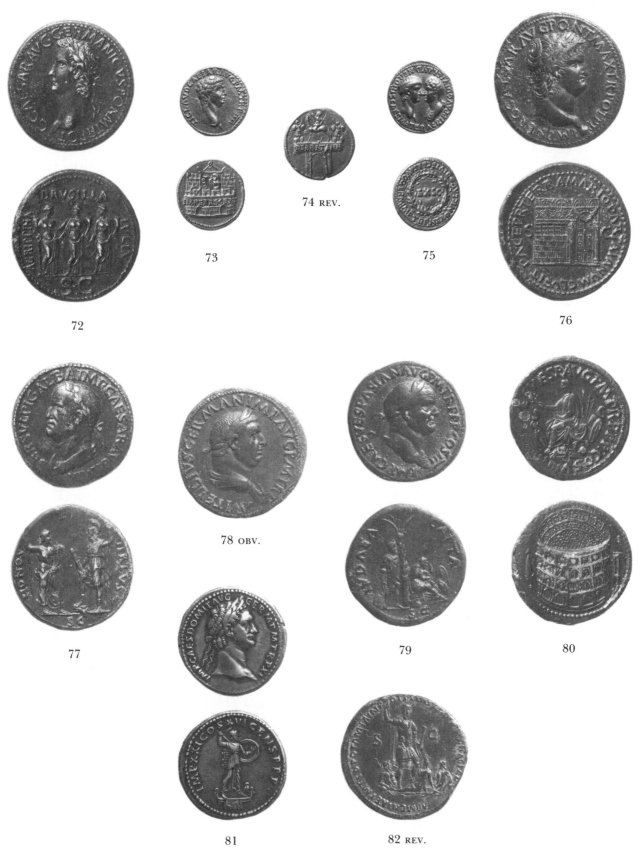

74 REV.

73

75

72

76

78 OBV.

77

79

80

81

82 REV.

(*72*) Gaius, sestertius, A.D. 37–41; (*73*) Claudius, aureus, A.D. 41; (*74*) Claudius, aureus, A.D. 46–47; (*75*) Nero and Agrippina, aureus, A.D. 54; (*76*) Nero, sestertius, A.D. 64–66; (*77*) Galba, sestertius, A.D. 68–69; (*78*) Vitellius, sestertius, A.D. 69; (*79*) Vespasian, sestertius, A.D. 71; (*80*) Titus, sestertius, A.D. 81; (*81*) Domitian, medallion, A.D. 92; (*82*) Trajan, sestertius, A.D. 116–117.

peared on obverses and in such reverse compositions as the deities Honos and Virtus, who were shown as a signal compliment to the military forces (fig. 77). The Praetorian Guard murdered Galba in January A.D. 69 and proclaimed its commander, Otho, as emperor. No token coinage was struck during his brief three-month reign, and Otho's portrait on gold and silver shows him with a strangely ridged hair style. Otho in turn was ousted by a new claimant, Vitellius, who was proclaimed by his legions in Germany. Coinage was struck for him during his advance on Italy by mints in the western provinces and ultimately in Rome itself, where the standard of portraiture, particularly on the bronze coinage, maintained a high level (fig. 78).

The civil war of A.D. 69 ended with the victory at the end of the year of Vespasian, declared emperor by the eastern legions, and the establishment of the new Flavian dynasty. The coinage of the Julio-Claudian period continued essentially unchanged, and after some issues by eastern provincial mints at the outset of Vespasian's reign, coinage was again chiefly produced at the Rome mint. In the early coinage one of the main events extensively commemorated was Vespasian's suppression of the Jewish revolt (A.D. 66–70), successfully completed by Titus (fig. 79). Coinage was issued by Vespasian also in the names of his sons, Titus and Domitian. Of the coinage of their own reigns one of the most pictorial sestertii is that of Titus commemorating the completion of the building of the Colosseum in A.D. 80 (fig. 80). A feature of the coins of the third Flavian emperor, Domitian, is the emphasis given to the cult of Minerva, whose representation provides the reverse of many coinage issues and is seen to good advantage on a silver medallion of five-denarius weight (fig. 81).

Another civil war following the assassination of Domitian in A.D. 96 was averted by the senate's nomination as emperor of the respected, elderly but childless Nerva, who secured his position among the military forces by adopting as his heir the able general Trajan. Under Trajan, who came to power in A.D. 98, the empire reached its greatest territorial extension, and his coinage provides a notable record of his achievements as a builder who greatly embellished the city of Rome and as a general who added new provinces. The acquisition of Armenia and Mesopotamia, for instance, is recorded on sestertii that show Trajan standing between reclining river gods representing the Euphrates and the Tigris (fig. 82). Under Emperor Hadrian, who succeeded in A.D. 117, the interest he took in the provinces and the army and his frequent journeys of inspection received notice in the coinage struck in all metals during his reign. The personification of Britannia made her first appearance in this coinage, most probably recording Hadrian's visit to the province in A.D. 122, which was followed by the building of the great frontier wall between the Tyne and the Solway (fig. 83).

In the relative serenity of the reign of Antoninus Pius (A.D. 138–161) there is little military reference in the coin types, one series of which early in the reign is devoted to recalling Rome's legendary past. A feature of his coinage was its emphasis on coins bearing the name of Empress Faustina I, even after her death and deification. On one particular issue her veiled portrait is accompanied by a reverse showing Antoninus Pius granting a charter to the guild of orphan girls, the Puellae Faustinianae, named in honor of Faustina (fig. 84). It is ironic that in the reign of the philosopher emperor Marcus Aurelius (A.D. 161–180) his military exploits received notice on the coins, which recorded the wars in Armenia and against the Marcomanni (a West German tribe). Throughout the second century nearly all imperial coinage was produced by the Rome mint, and the monetary system scarcely changed. Under Marcus Aurelius, however, and even more so under his son Commodus (A.D. 180–192), the weight of the silver denarius fell, its fineness declining steadily to about 65 percent.

The assassination of Commodus was followed by the brief reigns of Pertinax and Didius Julianus in A.D. 193 and then by a period of civil war between the contenders Pescennius Niger in the East, Clodius Albinus in the West, and Septimius Severus, the ultimate victor. The wars resulted in the establishment of a number of provincial mints, some of which in the East were retained for a time by Severus along with the mint of Rome. The coinage was much used to publicize the new Severan dynasty. An aureus, for instance, bore Severus' own portrait and on the reverse the portrait of his empress, Julia Domna, together with his sons, Aurelius Antoninus (Caracalla) and Geta (fig. 85). Fairly plentiful coinage issues were made in the names of all members of the Severan family, especially during the campaigns in Britain, which they conducted in person, and for the victory coinage there the emperors added the honorific title "Britannicus" to their titulature (fig. 86). Caracalla in his sole reign made the first major change in the denominational system of the imperial coinage by introducing the antoninianus or double denarius, larger in flan than the denarius and marked as a double piece by the radiate crown worn by the emperor. One of the principal reverse types of this new coin shows the sun-god in his chariot (fig. 87). When struck for an empress, the antoninianus showed her portrait set on a crescent. One of the most extraordinary emperors of the Severan dynasty was the young Elagabalus, who, at his proclamation, was the high priest of the sun-god El-Gabal (Baal) at Emesa (Homs) in Syria. The reverse of one his gold coins depicts the triumphal entry to Rome of this god in the form

of a conical stone or baetyl on the occasion of the emperor's arrival from Syria (fig. 88).

During the remainder of the third century a succession of brief-lived emperors or claimants to the office followed the end of the Severan dynasty, and some form of coinage was issued for all of them. In the coinage system the antoninianus, which from A.D. 238 virtually ousted the old denarius, was increasingly debased until by the late third century its silver fineness had fallen to less than 10 percent. The use of orichalcum and copper to distinguish the various denominations of the base-metal coinage had ceased by the end of the second century, and all denominations were struck in heavily leaded bronze; by about A.D. 260 this coinage ceased altogether. A system of branch mints in the provinces supplemented the output of Rome and gradually spread across the empire. Initially the product of these mints can be distinguished only by style, but gradually the coinage of each came to carry on the reverse the initial or abbreviated name of the mint.

One of the most interesting coinages of the mid third century was that produced for Philip I and his family to celebrate in A.D. 248 the thousandth anniversary of the foundation of Rome. One series of the antoniniani of this coinage had as types the animals that featured in the celebratory games on this occasion. For the first time, these coins carried a numeral or letter distinguishing the work of the various *officinae* (workshops) of the mint, a practice that was to remain a feature on most Roman coins (fig. 89). In A.D. 260 the western provinces revolted under Postumus, the first of the Gallic emperors, and a separate empire with its own coinage was set up comprising the provinces of Gaul, Spain, and Britain. The gold coinage especially achieved a much higher artistic standard than prevailed in the central empire, and an especially fine example coined for Postumus has an unusual pre-

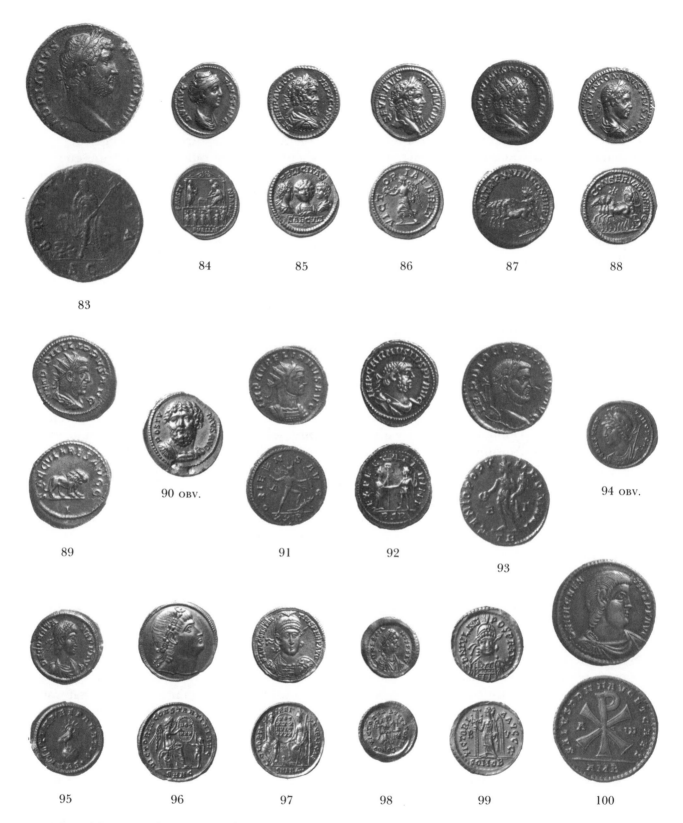

(*83*) Hadrian, sestertius, *ca.* A.D. 136; (*84*) Faustina I, aureus, *ca.* A.D. 141; (*85*) Septimius Severus, aureus, A.D. 201; (*86*) Septimius Severus, aureus, A.D. 210–211; (*87*) Aurelius Antoninus, antoninianus, A.D. 215; (*88*) Elagabalus, aureus, A.D. 219; (*89*) Philip I, antoninianus, A.D. 248; (*90*) Postumus, aureus, A.D. 263; (*91*) Aurelian, antoninianus, A.D. 274; (*92*) Carausius, denarius, A.D. 287; (*93*) Diocletian, follis, A.D. 294; (*94*) Constantinopolis, follis, *ca.* A.D. 330; (*95*) Constantius II, follis, A.D. 348; (*96*) Constantine the Great, solidus, A.D. 320; (*97*) Constantius II, solidus, A.D. 355; (*98*) Marcian, tremissis, A.D. 450–457; (*99*) Julius Nepos, solidus, A.D. 475–476; (*100*) Magnentius, bronze, A.D. 350–353.

sentation of his facing portrait (fig. 90). The empire was reunified by the emperor Aurelian, who also attempted to improve the now much-debased antoninianus. His new antoninianus, of somewhat higher silver fineness and generally of better fabric, was given a mark of value XXI, probably indicating that it was a double denarius. In his coinage and that of many of the subsequent emperors the cult of Sol, the sun-god, received prominent notice (fig. 91). Britain also later broke away under the emperors Carausius and Allectus to form a separate empire between A.D. 287 and 296. The coinage struck during their reigns at mints in Londinium (London) and Camulodunum (Colchester) followed the pattern of central empire coinage except that the rather small coinage in gold was supplemented by coinage in good silver. The reverse of one of these issues shows Carausius being welcomed by Britannia with the words EXPECTATE VENI (O come, awaited one), possibly an adaptation of a Vergilian tag from the second book of the Aeneid (fig. 92).

The Dominate (A.D. 294–498)

Toward the end of the third century a new imperial system was established by Diocletian, the tetrarchy, rule by a college of four emperors, two Augusti and two Caesars. In A.D. 294 came a reform of the coinage, which provided a gold aureus struck at a standard of 60 to the pound, its value often marked by the appropriate Greek numeral, a new silver coin at a standard of 96 to the pound and so marked XCVI, and new denominations in bronze with a small admixture of silver, the largest by tradition known as a follis (a word meaning "moneybag"). This coinage was struck by a whole chain of mints across the empire, each of which placed its name in abbreviated form on its product. The range of designs, especially on the follis, became

now largely reduced to stereotypes, such as the Genius Populi Romani (Genius of the Roman People), which can be seen on the first coinage of the tetrarchic follis (fig. 93). Under the tetrarchies and throughout the following Constantinian period the follis steadily declined in weight until in A.D. 330 it weighed only about three grams. This was the weight standard of two very common series of small folles, one with the bust of Constantinopolis (Constantine I the Great), celebrating the foundation of the new capital (fig. 94), the other honoring the old capital with a bust of Urbs Roma and the wolf and twins of legend. Eventually a new series made its appearance in A.D. 348, celebrating the eleventh centenary of Rome's foundation with a variety of types accompanied by the inscription FEL[icium] TEMP[orum] REPARATIO (the restoration of happy times) (fig. 95). In gold, a new denomination, the solidus, introduced by Constantine the Great in A.D. 310, was to remain the standard denomination to the end of the empire (fig. 96).

Throughout the imperial coinage the imperial portrait, with only occasional exceptions, had been shown in profile, but about A.D. 355 a new style of portrait was begun by Constantius II. The emperor was represented by a facing bust, helmeted and armored, a portrait type that remained almost exclusively the imperial representation on gold coins and was continued on Byzantine coinage. On this particular issue the reverse shows Rome and Constantinople holding a shield recording the imperial *vota,* the vows performed, in this case, upon the completion of thirty years of rule and the hope for a further ten (fig. 97). Toward the end of the fourth century the gold solidus was supplemented by the gold tremissis, or third of a solidus, issued with increasing frequency and most commonly with a Victory-type reverse (fig. 98). Silver coinage consisted of two denominations, a larger miliarensis and a smaller and much more common siliqua.

They played a less important part in imperial coinage, except in the West, where especially the siliqua appears to have been produced and treasured in some quantity. The coinage of the closing decades of the empire consisted essentially of gold along with small bronze pieces.

The coinage of the late empire was much less varied in its designs and much less concerned with recording events and publicizing imperial policy. If any conscious aim now informed the choice of coin types, it was directed to giving prominence to the state and the emperor who represented it. Some stereotyped representation that had long lost meaning persisted to the end. On a gold solidus of Julius Nepos, restored for a second reign and in fact the very last of the emperors of the crumbling western half of the empire, the reverse still carries the figure of Victory, though by this time she holds a long cross and has been transformed into a Christian angel (fig. 99). Though Christianity had become the official religion of the empire from the time of Constantine the Great, it had remarkably little effect on coinage design. It was only on the bronze coinage of the usurping emperor Magnentius in Gaul (A.D. 350–353) that the first indisputable Christian design appeared: a prominent chi-rho (the first two letters of "Christ" in Greek) is flanked by the letters alpha and omega (I am the alpha and the omega, the beginning and the end) (fig. 100).

By the end of the fifth century the western provinces of Britain, Gaul, Spain, Africa, and even Italy had fallen to the control of barbarian invaders, and their coinages, though influenced by that of Rome, form the beginnings of medieval coinage. In the East, the empire centered on Constantinople lived on, but its coinage, as reformed by Anastasius I in A.D. 498, belongs to another history.

BIBLIOGRAPHY

GREEK COINS

E. Babelon, *Traité des monnaies grecques et romaines*, 3 vols. in 8 (1901–1933); Barclay V. Head, *Historia numorum, a Manual of Greek Numismatics* (rev. ed. 1911; repr. 1967); George F. Hill, *A Guide to the Principal Coins of the Greeks* (1932; 2d ed. 1959); G. Kenneth Jenkins, *Ancient Greek Coins* (1972); Colin M. Kraay, *Greek Coins* (1966), and *Archaic and Classical Greek Coins* (1976); Charles T. Seltman, *Greek Coins: A History of Metallic Currency and Coinage Down to the Fall of the Hellenistic Kingdoms* (1933; 2d ed. 1955).

ROMAN COINS

Robert A. G. Carson, *Principal Coins of the Romans: I, The Republic* (1978), II, *The Principate* (1980), III, *The Dominate* (1981); John Philip C. Kent, *Roman Coins* (rev. ed. 1978); Harold Mattingly, *Roman Coins from the Earliest Times to the Fall of the Western Empire* (1928; 2d. rev. ed. 1967); Carol Humphrey V. Sutherland, *Roman Coins* (1974).

EPILOGUE

The Progress of Classical Scholarship

R. R. BOLGAR

STRICTLY SPEAKING, we ought not to talk of classical scholarship before the fifteenth century, since only then did scholars come to regard the Greek and Roman traditions as a unit. It is true however that the study of their own literature by the Greeks and the study of Greek and Latin authors by the Romans reach back well into antiquity; for it should not be forgotten that ancient Greece was the first society that kept written records other than records of laws or great public events with a view to ensuring their permanence. Initially the practice of keeping such records served the needs of administrators and professional speech writers, but then the possibility of giving permanence to other forms of composition was realized and speedily exploited. By the beginning of the fourth century B.C. not only orators, but also historians, philosophers, and poets came to see a promise of immortality in the written word, and the passing of another century established written records as a political instrument. Without them the Hellenistic effort to spread Greek culture to the nations conquered by Alexander would have had little hope of success.

If we define "scholarship" as the practice of giving careful study to written records and in particular to those which are non-utilitarian, its beginnings will go back perhaps to the debate on Homer's picture of the gods, to Plato's philosophical criticisms of poetry, and to the study of rhetoric that was in full swing by the fourth century B.C. But the most effective and widespread impulse to acquire knowledge about the Greek tradition came with the Hellenistic effort to persuade foreign peoples to understand and value that tradition.

Hellenistic scholarship, centered on the novel book collections of Alexandria and Pergamum, occupied itself with the classification of genres, lexicography, the structure of grammar, textual and literary criticism, and commentary elucidating obscure references or antiquarian detail. Scholars had as yet no clear conception of the divisions of their field. How could they have had? But all the work they did had the ultimate purpose of illuminating the heritage of the Greek past. Soon, however, Rome appeared on the scene, and the field of scholarship widened.

At first the Romans' main concern was to

create in Rome a culture equal to the Greek. They sought to rival Greek literature in all important genres: epic, tragedy, comedy, pastoral, elegy, satire, history, oratory, and even literary criticism. Here the pioneers were writers of great talent: Plautus and Terence, Catullus, Vergil, Horace, Ovid, and Livy. And while this process of imitation was still going on, they set themselves to transfer into Latin Greek knowledge on such subjects as philosophy, rhetoric, natural history, astronomy, and mathematics. Thanks to the energetic concurrence of Lucretius, Varro, Cicero, and the elder Pliny, this work did not take too long, and by the middle of the first century A.D. attention could shift to applying to Latin grammar, lexicography, metrics, and Latin literary history the techniques of analysis and commentary that had been worked out for Greek. The period of imitation in which Latin writers looked to Greece for help was succeeded by a period of chauvinistic self-regard. If Fronto and Gellius are any guide, the study of early Latin was the subject that preoccupied Romans at the end of the second century A.D.

With the next hundred years, we enter upon the age of the epitomes: Solinus scored a signal success summarizing the elder Pliny, Censorinus summarized a lost work by Suetonius, Aquila Romanus one by the Pythagorean Alexander Numenius. Civil conflict led to a drop in educational standards and to a call for simplifications. But the reforms of Diocletian (A.D. 284–305) secured the Roman Empire a further two and a half centuries of comparative peace. Admittedly, there were vast changes. Christianity was attracting many of the best talents by this time, and the Greek East, after its florescence during the Second Sophistic, settled down to a cultural life that produced an admirable philosophy in Neoplatonism, two distinguished prose writers in Julian and Libanius, epic poems of reasonable merit by Quintus Smyrnaeus and Nonnus, and numerous excellent

epigrams that were to find a home in the *Greek Anthology,* all this apart from much excellent Christian writing. The scholarship of the age was, however, unexciting. Flavius Philostratus wrote the lives of the Sophists, Diogenes Laertius wrote those of the philosophers, and Athenaeus of Naucratis produced his vast encyclopedia in the form of a dialogue. Otherwise Greek scholarship was primarily verbal, concerned with grammar and lexicography. In the West, on the other hand, we see two trends: the one concerned with the general furtherance of knowledge, the other with simplification. Servius' commentary and Macrobius' *Saturnalia,* both of which were concerned with Vergil, Donatus' grammar, and the Neoplatonist commentary on the *Dream of Scipio* (*Somnium Scipionis*) in Cicero's *On the Republic* (by the same Macrobius?) represented scholarship at a high level. But it seems likely that St. Augustine's lost *On Disciplines* (*De Disciplinis*) was an attempt to summarize useful knowledge from a Christian point of view. It is true that Varro had also written such a book. But he presumably had been concerned to pass on to his fellow Romans Greek knowledge about the seven liberal arts. Augustine in A.D. 387, the date of his baptism, had no reason to turn to Greek sources, nor did he do so. His purpose must have been to furnish his contemporaries with a simple and more accessible account of material that was already available to them.

The same is true of his successor, Martianus Capella, though his book, *The Marriage of Mercury and Philology* (*ca.* 420) is not just a digest of earlier learning. It is a digest with frills. Mercury wants to marry and consults Apollo, who recommends a learned virgin called Philologia. He accepts, and the bride is accordingly raised to divine status, after she has been persuaded to reject learning—bluestockings it would appear were not welcome in heaven. She is transported to Olympus where she finds Homer, Vergil, and Orpheus with his lute, while philosophers engage in pastimes appropriate to their philosophies. Democritus, for example, walks around in a cloud of atoms. Philologia's reception into Olympus reminds us strongly of the initiation ceremonies described by Apuleius in the final book of *The Golden Ass* (*Metamorphoses*). To avoid getting scorched by the spheres as she passes through them, Philologia anoints herself with an herb grown by the Neopythagoreans. She wears the white garments of a neophyte, takes an emetic to purge her of all her existing knowledge, and finally eats the Orphic egg (a feature of the cosmogony of the Orphic religion), which transfigures her. Having brought his heroine to Olympus, Capella changes his tune and devotes the remaining seven books to her bridesmaids, each of whom is described in terms of one of the seven arts that she represents. Here Capella becomes straightforwardly didactic. He uses a Latin summary of Euclid, Aquila's summary of the Greek Numenius, and Solinus' summary of the elder Pliny, who had consulted Greek works.

The next writer who played an important part in the transmission of Greco-Roman knowledge to the Middle Ages followed a pattern that fell between serious scholarship and simplification. Born in about 480, Boethius set himself in his twenties the task of making useful information available to his contemporaries in free translations from the Greek. He began with Nicomachus' treatise on mathematics, and followed this by one on music and one on geometry based on Euclid. He then moved to logic, but the work he did on Aristotle's *Categories*—lightheartedly as part of an encyclopedia—so gripped his imagination that he went on to translate the whole of the *Organon* with commentaries, and by the time he was thirty-five seems to have formed the grand design of putting into Latin the whole of Aristotle and Plato. Unfortunately, his execution by Theodoric the Os-

trogoth in 524 prevented him from carrying out this plan. But if Boethius was tempted from simplification to serious scholarship, his contemporary Cassiodorus, head of Theodoric's civil service, who managed to avoid his master's displeasure, was a deliberate popularizer. His *Introduction to Divine and Human Readings* (*Institutiones Divinarum et Secularium Litterarum*) was compiled for the instruction of the monks in the monastery he had founded. The first half is simply a guide to the study of the Scriptures, but the second is a compendium describing the seven liberal arts. It is a strange work that does little more than outline the structure of each art. A teacher who used it would need to supply all the relevant detail himself. Cassiodorus just provided an introduction to the texts which were his sources—Donatus for grammar, the fourth-century Fortunatianus for rhetoric, Boethius and Varro for dialectic, arithmetic, geometry, and astronomy, and Mutianus for music.

The last of the writers who were influential in transmitting Greco-Roman culture to later ages was Isidore of Seville (*ca.* 570–636). His *Etymologies* cover the same ground as Cassiodorus, but reveal in their arrangement the medieval tendency to regard names as a clue to the nature of things. His definitions are helpful at times, but are often wildly incorrect. A pyramid (he says) is a solid figure, which from a broad base narrows to a point like fire: for fire in Greek is called *pyr*. *Nox* (night) is from *nocere* (to injure) because it injures the eyes.

These transmitters were responsible for the character of many classical survivals, but what effectively set the pattern for the future was the retention in daily use of the ancient languages. In the East, in what became the Byzantine Empire, this retention was a result of the way the state was organized. A small group of mandarins ran the empire, and the aim of restricting its numbers—a common feature of elitist rule—was achieved by an educational demand. Members of the top civil service, and that included many high-ranking clerics, were expected to read and write a form of Attic Greek. They received an education that comprehended the study of ancient authors. A larger group, which included the bulk of the lesser clergy and the monks, could in many cases understand Attic Greek, but feeling themselves often hostile to the higher civil service and its traditions, seem as a body to have neglected pagan literature. And below these two educated classes, there was only the mass of the people whose demotic speech had little in common with its Attic predecessor. The study of ancient authors survived in the East because it was in the interest of the holders of power that it should do so, but by the same token the spread of this knowledge was restricted to a small number in each generation.

In the West, a different situation existed. Here it was the Catholic church that was responsible for the maintenance of Latin. Clerics were distinguished from the laity by their knowledge of that language, generally far divorced from their own. They had acquired this learning as a result of an education that could not help introducing them to at least some classical writers. Initially, in the fifth and sixth centuries, the romanized population made up everywhere the majority of the faithful, and to cling to Latin was for the church to secure their loyalty. Moreover the Germanic or Hun overlords of that time may have despised their Roman subjects, but they seem to have had a respect for Latin culture and were often prepared to be romanized. Rome was an asset to the Western church, which would incidentally have been threatened with fragmentation had the Scriptures and the liturgy been translated into the idioms of the ruling Germanic tribes and used in translation. But while members of the Byzantine bureaucracy benefited from remaining small and so restricted access to that special form of education that linked them to the past, the Western church was likely to improve its position by increasing the number of its clergy. It was prepared therefore to educate as many as possible.

As to why the education offered by the Christian church included pagan authors there is no simple answer. The most distinguished educator of the early Middle Ages, Charlemagne's protégé, Alcuin (ca. 730–804), did indeed attempt to promote a Latin based on Christian models: on the prose of Gregory the Great and the verses of poets like Fortunatus and Sedulius. He did not however succeed, and that was due perhaps to Irish and Italian influence.

The Irish whom the Roman Empire had not absorbed had been the first to feel the ill effects of a lack of knowledge of Latin among their clergy, and the first therefore to try to teach that language to novices drawn from a population that had not been romanized. Since they had not been in contact with paganism, they tended to accept all that was Latin with respect as belonging to the church. The education their missionaries brought first to Britain and then to Europe did not ban imitation of pagan authors, and the copying they initiated in the monasteries they founded embraced pagan as well as Christian works.

If the Irish shifted the emphasis of Alcuin's educational system toward a freer use of pagan texts, the Italians did likewise. Rome stood for their country's past, and to have rejected pagan literature would have meant rejecting their own history. There were pagan authors among the books Benedict Biscop brought from Italy a generation before Alcuin, some of which found their way into libraries in Jarrow and York; and there were Italian teachers—Peter of Pisa and Paul the Deacon—at Charlemagne's palace school. Alcuin could not have excluded, and did not try to exclude, pagan authors from monastic libraries. (They provided incidentally the finest models for verse, the writing of which was part of the curriculum.) Nor could he have muzzled such of his contemporaries who found pagan authors worth imitating: Einhard, for example, whose excellent *Life of Charlemagne* took Suetonius for its model. By the time the Middle Ages had organized educational activities in the ninth century, the reading of pagan authors and the copying of pagan manuscripts were too widespread to be barred.

The energy expended in copying was not matched in the ninth century by scholarly activity in correcting and collating manuscripts, composing commentaries, or producing grammars and books on rhetoric, if we disregard Alcuin's own contributions. Dungal, the Irish scholar, has been identified as the corrector of a famous Lucretius codex, and in the middle of the century, Sedulius Scottus compiled an anthology which betrays a remarkable range of classical reading. But a contemporary, Walafrid Strabo (808–849), abbot and tutor of the Carolingian king and emperor Charles II the Bald (843–877), who composed a similar anthology, restricted his classical excerpts to Seneca the Younger's *Letters* and Columella's *On Agriculture* (*De Re Rustica*).

One scholar, however, stands out from the rest. Lupus, Abbot of Ferrières (*ca.* 805–862), not only sent letters far and wide in the hope of increasing his monastery's holdings, but was also eager to procure further examples of texts he already possessed in order to be able to improve his copy through collation. His critical acumen was not exceptional, but in establishing lacunae, marking corruptions, and recording variants he was honest and systematic, and more than a dozen manuscripts of classical authors reveal traces of his activity. He should also be remembered as the teacher of Heiric of Auxerre (*ca.* 841–876), who continued Lupus' work copying and excerpting some rare manuscripts.

It should not surprise us—given the activity of the Irish and the Italians—that the century after the death of Alcuin was marked by an upsurge of interest in classical literature. But the succeeding period, 900–1050, is often described as one of decline, and this stricture is perhaps undeserved. It is true that classical texts were not copied with the eagerness manifested earlier, that the commentaries we come across at St. Gall (northeast Switzerland) and elsewhere are concerned primarily with putting a medieval dress on classical material (calling a Vestal Virgin an abbess, for example), and that few new grammars and glossaries were produced, but we meet with many widely read men of learning: Ratherius of Verona (*ca.* 887–974), the Greek-speaking Liudprand of Cremona (920–972), and above all Gerbert of Reims (*ca.* 950–1003), a mathematician who was reputedly skilled in magic and who became Pope Silvester II. The Ottonian dynasty (936–1002) of Holy Roman emperors presided over a revival of classical learning in which Gerbert played a leading role. We also see the rise of the school of Chartres. The period was one in which imitation was favored by the schools, and some remarkable works were produced: the epic *Waltharius*, which is rich in classical allusions, the *Annals* of Lambert of Hersfeld (*d. ca.* 1088), who combined the styles of Livy and Sallust, and Liudprand's lively reports on his visits to Constantinople in 950 and 968. Classical learning advanced, even if scholarship in the strict sense of the word lost momentum.

These years show us in fact a steady advance toward the colorful period generally known as the twelfth-century Renaissance. It was a period of cultural development nearly as complex as the High Renaissance that was to follow four hundred years later and was accompanied by a number of developments that had a direct bearing on scholarship. An important revival of interest in the copying of ancient authors occurred at Monte Cassino under Abbot Desiderius (1058–1087), which saved for us several indispensable texts including Tacitus' later *Annals* and his *Histories,* Apuleius' *The Golden Ass,* and the younger Seneca's *Dialogues.* There was a marked improvement in techniques of commentary, though for the moment this was restricted to nonliterary works on philosophy, theology, and rhetoric. Translators became active, turning into Latin Hippocrates and Galen, Ptolemy's *Almagest,* and some of Aristotle's logical works that had been translated into Arabic. But what makes the age remembered is the emergence of a Latin literature that could fairly claim to equal anything written in that language since the Silver Age (A.D. 14–192). Language, figures of speech, methods of composition were borrowed from the ancients, but they were used to present subjects that reflected the problems of a fresh and different age and admitted, in some cases at least, elements of romance and mystery.

The flowering of this literature was the product of those techniques of imitation that had been taught in the monastic schools. But the significance of the contribution these institutions had made has been underrated since, at the very moment of their triumph, they began to fall into a decline. Logic and to a lesser extent law and medicine promised an enlightenment that gripped the imagination of the young in what was now a flourishing urbanized society, and young men flocked in great numbers not to the monasteries, but to the cathedral schools where these subjects were taught. There was a change in the pattern of education, which by 1160 was producing a literate public, trained primarily in dialectic, that felt all intellectual problems could be swept away by the application of logical thought.

We think of the thirteenth century as the age of the great scholastic systematizers. It is the century of Vincent of Beauvais (*d. ca.* 1264), whose monumental encyclopedia aimed to cover the whole of knowledge, of St. Bonaventure, Albertus Magnus, St.

Thomas Aquinas, and Duns Scotus. But the poetry that had graced its predecessor—the lyrics of the wandering scholars, the colorful epics, the philosophical verses of Bernard of Cluny and Alan of Lille—that flowering of Latin which for the first time in a millennium added substantially to the achievements of the classical past—had vanished. Apart from the hymn writers, some of whom like Philippe de Grève (*d.* 1237) possessed a lyrical gift, the century produced no Latin verse fit to rank above a school exercise; nor was its prose much better. The great scholastics wrote lucidly at best, never elegantly; and into the official correspondence of the time there had crept a new overornate style, popularized, it would seem, by Frederick II's chancellor, Pietro della Vigna (*ca.* 1190–1249) and inspired by the rhetoric treatise *To Herennius* (written in the early first century B.C.), a style full of figures of speech and thought calculated to obscure a writer's meaning. But as if the love of fiction were a river which, blocked at one outlet, finds some alternative issue, the effort that in the twelfth century had gone into the production of a somewhat romanticized Latin literature now switched to the vernacular. It did so with the greatest effect taking place in France. Here emerged what we know as the Arthurian romances. The practice of composing poetry in French went back to the eleventh century, and the first decades of the twelfth saw a number of translations of Latin epics and histories into French verse, but it was from 1160 onward that original works in French began to appear with a wealth of expression and content that translations and summaries had been far from achieving.

The way was cleared for the transference of fictional and poetic material from Latin to a modern language, which represented an immense cultural gain; but neither the twelfth century nor the thirteenth made notable strides in scholarship. It is true that copyists were more active perhaps than ever before, but they simply reproduced earlier copies, and their transcripts have generally proved unhelpful. Commentaries were plentiful too, but as one might expect in an age that aimed to subordinate literature to its central theological interests, a strong tendency to allegorize distorted the explanations offered. The old translations of Aristotle from the Arabic were now outmoded, and a number of scholars were at work producing versions from the Greek. Many of these were available to Aquinas who was further instrumental in persuading William of Moerbeke, who had studied the language in Greece, to translate a whole group of Aristotle's works into Latin in 1273.

The end of the thirteenth century (like the beginning of the ninth) provides proof of the fact that where classical writings were accessible, they found eager readers. Dante Alighieri (1265–1321) was acquainted with an amazingly wide range of classical works, and he was not alone in this; nor was he the first to interest himself passionately in classical literature, in spite of having received a scholastic education. The work of the Paduan judge Lovato Lovati (1241–1309) contains echoes of Lucretius, Catullus, Tibullus, Propertius, and Martial, authors scarcely known at the time. He also made use of a codex of the tragedies of Seneca. Quotations from Catullus and Martial occur in an anthology compiled about the same time by another judge, a friend of Lovato, Geremia da Montagnone (*ca.* 1255–1321). Other classicizing members of Lovato's circle were Albertino Mussato, who wrote the first tragedy since antiquity that was in classical meters, and Giovanni di Matociis, who wrote the *Historia Imperialis* and was inspired by the *Historia Augusta,* the great collection of biographies of Roman emperors from Hadrian to Numerian (A.D. 117–284).

What needs to be made clear is that the enthusiasms manifested by this small group were an indication of a general revolt against the aridity of an education dominated by the study of logic, which had promised so much but was losing itself in a maze of impractical subtleties. Teachers of grammar and rhetoric, two parts of the tripartite liberal arts course, were restricted to instructing the very young and were ill paid in comparison with professors of logic; they were prominent in criticizing this third and dominant part of the course and they had some reason for it. Already merchants who had sons to educate were withdrawing them from school and university as soon as they had learned to read and write Latin and were placing them in the family counting house on the ground that the training given there would be more useful to them than the logic-chopping they would otherwise have had to master. It was against this background that Petrarch (Francesco Petrarca, 1303–1374), who had the advantage of having achieved through his lyric poems fame as an Italian poet, began his campaign for a reform of style. The Latin used in his day was marred in the writings of the Scholastics by excessive attention to logical distinctions and was marred in the official language of the chanceries by an overuse of ornament. It should, he claimed, be replaced by correct Latin based on ancient usage. This demand pleased amateurs of classical literature, pleased grammar masters, and had its appeal even for practical men who valued lucidity. But what was even more important than his reform of style was Petrarch's successful attempt to alter the public's attitude to literary achievement. Great writers, he argued, deserved admiration as much as statesmen and generals, and they shed luster on the country that produced them. For this reason, the ancients should have a unique place in our esteem. And these beliefs, for which he gained acceptance, were to open the way for great advances in classical scholarship.

Since the copying of manuscripts during the Middle Ages had not been adequately backed by any comprehensive system of cataloging, and since the neglect of classical works had been painfully common, the first task that faced Petrarch and his disciples was to discover what had survived in Latin and, as we shall see, in Greek. Petrarch himself assembled a classical library unequaled in his day. In addition to works that were to some extent in common circulation, his famous copy of Livy brought together thirty books of that historian's *History of Rome*. He found Cicero's speech *In Defense of Archias* (*Pro Archia*), letters to Atticus, Quintus, and Brutus, and he possessed a copy of Propertius' *Elegies*. A friend of his, Zanobi da Strada, who had access to the library of Monte Cassino, seems to have been instrumental in making available—to Boccaccio among others—Tacitus' *Annals* and *Histories,* Apuleius' *The Golden Ass,* Cicero's *In Defense of Cluentius* (*Pro Cluentio*) and Ovid's *Ibis.* Between 1333, when Petrarch discovered *In Defense of Archias,* and 1435, most of the "lost" works of Latin literature were recovered.

But the humanists were not merely book collectors. Petrarch recorded variants, corrected, and annotated his texts. Boccaccio was a collector of facts about classical mythology, biography, and geography. Coluccio Salutati (1331–1406) composed a defense of classical studies. Poggio Bracciolini (1380–1459) and Cyriacus of Ancona (1391–1452) collected inscriptions. Flavio Biondo (1392–1463) wrote extensively on Roman antiquities. A century after Petrarch had proclaimed the supreme value of ancient literature men's interest spread to the whole of ancient life.

One effect of Petrarch's championship of the past was to arouse interest in Greece. He possessed a collection of Platonic dialogues he could not read, and the line-by-line translation of the *Iliad* he paid a Greek to compile proved a disappointment. Nevertheless he left behind him a firmly held belief that Greek literature ought to be studied. Earlier in history this belief might not have borne fruit, but now it was fostered by the Byzantines themselves. Once they had prided themselves on being "Romans," but the experience of foreign western rule had taught them to think of themselves as Greek; and by the fourteenth century, desperate for help from the West, they were delighted to discover that influential Italians were prepared to value them as the heirs of ancient Greece. Manuel Chrysoloras (*ca.* 1355–1415), who came to Italy as an ambassador in 1393, was persuaded to stay and teach Greek in Florence where a number of important humanists became his pupils. Others—Scarparia, Guarino Veronese, Francesco Filelfo, Giovanni Aurispa—went to Constantinople to study or to purchase classical texts, so that by the time the city fell to the Ottomans in 1453 there was a sufficient interest in Greek for Byzantine exiles to feel that they could earn a living as teachers in the West.

It is a commonplace that these men brought Byzantine scholarship to the West. But what were the traditions of that scholarship? Conditions in the East were until 1204 notably different from those prevailing in the West. There was no prospect of a shortage of texts and no great burst of copying such as occurred in Carolingian times. The main concern of Byzantine scholarship was to impart a knowledge of Attic usage and rhetoric, so that commentary (in the sense of explanation) was considered necessary only for Homer and other early poets or for the recondite Aristophanes, and the energy of scholars went into the composition of grammars, lexicons, and rhetorical exercises. But after the recovery of Constantinople in 1261, conditions changed. Thanks to the mindless destruction in which the Latins had indulged, texts were relatively scarce, and there was a good deal of copying which involved some rash emendation by Manuel Moschopoulos (*ca.* late-thirteenth/early-fourteenth century) and others. Scholars spent their time promoting contacts with the West, working out the relations between ancient philosophy and Christianity, and even, at this late stage, in maintaining Atticist standards. Their main contribution to cultural progress in the West was to be in the field of philosophy and in helping the development of Ciceronianism, a service which was to have its uses, but in an unexpected way.

Perhaps the most important product of humanism was neo-Latin literature, which was born out of the desire to rival the ancients in all the major genres, the desire which had prompted Petrarch to write his *Africa*. During the next two hundred years, not only epics, but pastorals, elegies, tragedies, comedies, histories, and satires were composed in great numbers. With a few exceptions, such as Erasmus' *Praise of Folly* and Thomas More's *Utopia,* these are no longer read, but at the time they had an important function in that they proved easier to imitate in the vernacular than the classical originals would have been. They provided a halfway stage in the process by which the heritage of antiquity became embodied in our modern culture.

Ciceronianism damaged neo-Latin's chances of survival and therefore helped the emergence of the vernaculars. The wish to write correct Latin had been Petrarch's, but he had lacked the knowledge to do so. It was the Byzantines who revealed to the West what was required for effective, linguistic imitation: grammars, dictionaries, lists of idioms, identity of subject matter. The generation taught by Manuel Chrysoloras set itself to provide these requisites, and their successors, principally Lorenzo Valla (*ca.* 1407–1457), and later Desiderius Erasmus (*ca.* 1466–1536), completed their work. By the sixteenth century, any intelligent man could write Ciceronian Latin. Unfortunately, soon after the publication in 1471 of Valla's *On the Elegance of the Latin Language*

(*De Elegantia Linguae Latinae*) the learned world was torn apart by a great debate on what constituted correct Latin. In Greece this problem had not surfaced as no Greek prose writer held the dominant position attained by Cicero in Latin, so that the Atticists could take the whole body of Golden Age (fifth and fourth centuries B.C.) prose for their model. But in the West, once the idea of writing good Latin gained popularity, the idea that modern writers ought to imitate Cicero and only Cicero was immediately suggested. Angelo Poliziano (1454–1494), known as Politian, opposed this, and so did Erasmus, but Ciceronianism survived, restricting the scope of Latin and thereby encouraging its rivals.

Another way in which scholarship affected the flowering of the vernaculars was over the matter of translation. This was no longer the crude business it had been in the twelfth century when the translator of the *Aeneid* altered the story in the retelling. Nor were translators content by the end of the fifteenth century with elegant paraphrases. Readers of the vernacular wanted an accurate version, which meant that translators had to enlarge the scope of their medium by borrowing from Latin and even Greek. Respect for accuracy led to the enrichment of modern languages and what did most to set a high value on scholarly accuracy was the invention of printing. During the Middle Ages few people had been in a position to judge the accuracy with which a scholar recorded variant readings or the merit of his emendations, but printing, which ensured that any edition produced circulated in a number of copies, had the effect of publicizing every defect, and this happened in a world where scholarship was now tied to monetary recompense. Publishers looked for financial gain, and successful editors were rewarded by more and better contracts. In the fourteenth century, humanists had been men of power, chancellors, or papal secretaries holding high positions, so that by the sixteenth, ambitious men of humble birth tended to look on learning as a road to success. Competition was keen, and if a rival could be brought low by proving that he had been inaccurate, brought low he was. But if the invention of printing indirectly encouraged accuracy, it was also responsible for perpetuating inaccuracy. Once a text came into print, the printed version tended to be treated as sacrosanct, it became the *lectio recepta* (established text). In sixteenth-century Europe, where travel was slow and dangerous (and photography had not yet been invented), the systematic collation of the major manuscripts of any particular work was not possible. The theory of emendation *ex librorum auctoritate* (from the record of the text) was not unfamiliar, as we see from Francesco Robortello's brief manual of textual criticism of 1557, even if the characteristics of scribal hands at different periods were incompletely understood. Practice however did not live up to theory, and although scholarly method did improve during the two and a half centuries that followed Robortello, it was not until Karl Lachmann's time (nineteenth century) that there was adequate access to the manuscripts for a theory of critical revision to be applied.

The fame of the Renaissance does not rest however on the advances it made in textual criticism. It is remembered above all as the period when men gained a rich insight into antiquity. The philosophical ideas drawn from Aristotle which the Middle Ages had made its own were by the sixteenth century replaced on a popular level by beliefs derived from Plato and his successors. Plotinus, Porphyry, and Iamblichus entered into the intellectual universe of European man, bringing in their train convictions about magic, astrology, and occult sympathies that were fascinating, if hardly rational. But if these partisans of Neoplatonism were not rational, they were at least systematic, and

the seventeenth century was marked by enthusiasm for the production of encyclopedias, on the part of scholars—Johann Valentin Andreäe (1586–1654), Johann Alsted (1588–1638), Athanasius Kircher (*ca.* 1601–1680), and Johann Comenius (1592–1671)—many of whom took a lively interest in esoteric learning and mixed fact and fancy in equal proportions. But the progression of Neoplatonism from a philosophy to a belief that could serve as a basis for the production of vast reference books illustrates what was happening to the classical heritage in general. Thanks to the multiplication of books and the sudden expansion of vernacular writing, the emergent cultures of Europe had at their disposal most of the intellectual material available to the ancients in the second and third centuries A.D., and were set to move on from that point. In crude terms, the task of the humanists was complete, and if Latin and Greek were to survive in education, their study had to find fresh purposes.

Schools being conservative institutions, the classical languages continued to be taught, but with a changed emphasis. Free composition in Latin prose, which had been favored as preparing the young for controversy, fell out of use. In England, in the great public schools, verse composition took its place, but there were also schools run by private enthusiasts where interest shifted to Greek. Samuel Parr (1747–1825), who conducted a school at Stanmore for five years, went so far as to produce Sophocles' *The Women of Trachis* (*Trachiniae*), in Greek, for his pupils and their parents. On the Continent, the Jesuits persisted with the teaching of Latin, justified in their eyes as the language of the church. But Greek was neglected. Writing in the mid eighteenth century, Grimm complained that nobody in France now knew that language.

All the same, a distinction must be made at this stage between Greek and Greece. At no other period in history was so much attention paid to Greek antiquities. Collectors vied with each other to lay their hands on statues, inscriptions, and coins; and scholars had begun the great work of describing these systematically in sumptuous volumes. Societies of amateurs financed travelers to the Levant who brought back drawings of neglected ancient remains. At the moment when the ability to read Greek was in serious decline—except in Germany where intending parsons were made to study the New Testament in that language—Greece featured as an ideal world where men found the society they dreamed about. How this happened is well illustrated in the case of Homer. His role as the greatest of poets had been attested by the Romans. But humanists trained on Vergil's sophisticated formality found the Homeric picture of the gods trivial, the style of the *Iliad* flat and prolix, its similes vulgar. As they read the poem in dull interlinear translations or in the Vergilian hexameters of Helius Eobanus Hessus (1488–1540), this adverse judgment was not wholly surprising. At the end of the seventeenth century, however, a conscientious scholar, Anne Dacier (1647–1720), produced a French translation of the *Iliad* in prose, which one of the vocal champions of contemporary taste, Antoine Houdard de La Motte (1672–1731), decided to adapt to what he considered eighteenth-century needs. He tried to produce what Homer would have written if Homer had lived in 1714. Mme. Dacier was justly incensed, but admitted in her confutation that Homer was a primitive poet, and she claimed that this was a virtue: he gave us a glimpse of the childhood of the world. Stoics, whose influence was dominant at the end of the sixteenth century, had made no distinction between the primitive and the hardy, simple life, which they themselves admired, and figuring in Fénelon's *Télémaque* (1699), this confusion had persisted. It was now to be dispelled. Mme. Dacier's claim that we ought to value Homer because he mirrored a civilization different from our own gave a twist to the argument that was to have notable results. In his notes to his translation, Alexander Pope had talked of a quality in Homer which he called "fire." He seems to have meant a free flow of creative impulse. But the work whose influence proved decisive for the development of a new view of the primitive was Thomas Blackwell's *Enquiry into the Life and Writings of Homer* (1735). Blackwell acknowledged Homer's genius but stressed the favorable nature of his environment, which had allowed that genius to develop, and by the time we reach James Macpherson (1736–1796) and his "Ossian" (a collection of poems written by Macpherson but attributed to the legendary Gaelic poet), the idea that a primitive society represented a state of perfection from which refinement spelled a decline was firmly established. Johann Gottfried von Herder (1744–1803) linked the primitive with national origins, thereby securing for it a popularity that was to last long.

Homer provided a focus from which threads ran to the popular interest in the "noble savage," then to anthropology, the origins of language, and nationalism. Other points of contact with antiquity were furnished by aspirations for freedom, a taste for hedonism, and most important by an admiration for ancient art. The opposition of the age to absolutism found expression eventually in the revolt of the American colonies and in the French Revolution. The American Founding Fathers looked for inspiration to the heroes of the Roman Republic, seeing them as farmers turned statesmen. Some years later the Jacobins in Paris coupled the Spartans, whose simplicity they admired, with the heroes of republican Rome. It was this outburst of political enthusiasm, together with the idea prevalent already earlier in the century that the Greeks had lived pleasured lives, devoted to wine and love, that led during the revolutionary years to the fashion of wearing Grecian dress (which must have been remarkably chilly in the northern climate of Paris).

However, the most important development occurred in the field of the fine arts. Already at the beginning of the eighteenth century artists were losing their taste for the baroque. The virtues of simplicity were under discussion in many studios and the notion was picked up by an ambitious self-educated scholar, Joachim Winckelmann (1717–1768), who embodied it in a pamphlet glorifying the simplicity and nobility of Hellenic sculpture. This concept was elaborated in his *History of Art Among the Ancients* (1764) and proved surprisingly influential; perhaps its contrast to the fashionable mood of "storm and stress" seemed to offer a solution to life's problems. The Greeks had been passionate and violent, but in their art they had subordinated these qualities to beauty. Why could not the Germans imitate them? A finer genius than Winckelmann, Goethe (1749–1832) wrote *Iphigenia in Tauris,* and Schiller (1759–1805) struggled desperately with the idea of a superiority he could not hope to equal.

That the idealizing interest in antiquity during the eighteenth century should have led to a revival of classical studies is not in itself unexpected. But the further fact that this revival resulted in the emergence of a curriculum that dominated European education for over a century requires explanation. The Industrial Revolution, which brought money and power to its fortunate entrepreneurs, also brought a demand for education. Admittedly, the education that newly prosperous industrialists might have been expected to favor was a practical one, providing professional skills, but all that was offered was the traditional course in Greek and Latin. Since they were not only practical men but also socially ambitious, wanting for their sons "the education of a gentleman,"

the industrialists were prepared to accept this. Moreover one result of the French Revolution and the Napoleonic Age was the growth of a belief in France and Germany that it was the duty of the state to take an interest in education, so that to a greater extent than ever before universities and learned enterprises could command support both from private and public sources, a phenomenon from which classical scholarship was to benefit.

Since Greek and Latin did not offer exactly the education that practical men and utilitarian administrators could be expected to endorse, the support they received might not have lasted long but for one odd circumstance. The character of classics teaching had changed during the eighteenth century. A teacher's primary aim was no longer to train people to write Latin for use in learned works. Translation from and into the ancient languages took the place of honor. Now to translate a passage of English prose into the style of Cicero or Thucydides requires a fair intelligence, a good memory, and many years of patient industry as a biddable pupil carrying out instructions. (It required in short the very qualities one hoped to find in civil servants and other professional men.) Success in a classical course, with the demands it made of industry and accuracy, was a good indication of success later in professional life, so that the course acted as a selection test. It is also worth remarking that a school and university course that centered its attention on language and style was an excellent preparation for the practice of textual criticism, which, thanks to easier communications, could be pursued effectively for the first time since the Renaissance. Thus, because it was socially useful as a professional selection technique and because it served the needs of scholarly enthusiasm, classical education survived.

Could it be regarded as an education?

The debate that raged throughout the nineteenth century ought to have settled the point, but as we read the articles that were exchanged, it becomes rapidly evident that the contending parties were not agreed on what they wanted to discuss. The critics, scientists like Thomas H. Huxley and scientific popularizers like H. G. Wells, aimed their shafts at the teaching that was carried on in the classroom: the grammar and vocabulary drills, the painstaking memorizing of phrases for mechanical reproduction in exercises, the preoccupation in reading with problems of syntax. The defense on the other hand, led by Matthew Arnold, based its arguments on the value of the classics as literature, the supreme excellence of Homer and Aeschylus. It is not surprising that the two sides in the debate failed to find common ground.

Since it served the limited aims we have described, the classics course did not exercise the wide appeal that Arnold ascribed to it. Inevitably, minds with a mathematical bent and those dominated by curiosity about the nature of things turned to the study of the natural sciences. That in itself was not a fatal blow to the predominant position of classical studies. What proved a more important threat was the multiplication of other disciplines in the liberal arts: history, modern languages, political science, and moral philosophy, all of which attracted the very students who would have done well in classics.

In the mid nineteenth century classical studies had to all appearances stood at the beginning of a "golden age." When a systematic treatment of manuscript traditions became possible, Germany led the way. The method associated with Karl Lachmann seemed to herald a new dawn in textual criticism that would enable correct texts to be produced for every author. But the manuscript tradition of some authors such as Persius resisted ordering into a manuscript genealogy (*stemma*). The critical revision of texts (*recensio*) was supplemented more and more by recourse to improvements by critical editing (*emendatio*) until that fell from favor in its turn, evoking a conservative reaction that banned all conjecture. But in spite of these disagreements a zeal for editing kept its hold on the higher ranges of scholarship well into the twentieth century. At the same time the amassing of knowledge about antiquity which appeared to have such a golden future when August Böckh started work on his *Collection of Greek Inscriptions* (*Corpus Inscriptionum Graecarum*) in 1825 began to disintegrate as an academic subject. The systematic study of language, once a branch of classical studies, extended its scope far beyond Greek and Latin. So did the science that was to burgeon as anthropology. Ancient history and ancient philosophy also achieved independence to the degree that those committed to them wondered whether they were primarily classicists or historians and philosophers.

Faced with such pressures, classical studies lost ground, which they tried to regain in the twentieth century by imitating methods that had proved popular in kindred, more modern studies. In the 1920s, the decade in which popular biographical "reassessments" by Lytton Strachey and André Maurois were published, we come across a number of biographies of Vergil, Terence, and others. Then, as the pioneering work of Leo Spitzer (1887–1960) and Jules Marouzeau (1878–1964) began to exercise an influence, Vergil and Catullus became the center of interest in stylistic scholarship. Since that time, if the number of students of Greek and Latin has diminished, the number of works produced on the subject has almost certainly increased.

But the development that brought classical themes most obviously to public notice had little to do with scholarship. To the generation of writers that came to the fore in the interwar period, the suggestions advanced by Sir James Frazer and Sigmund Freud seemed to hold great promise. If ancient themes, such as the Oedipus legend, corresponded to suppressed human desires, the use of them in a modern form seemed likely to ensure the success of any work in which they appeared. Various devices were employed. A classical story could be transferred to a modern setting. George Bernard Shaw did this with *Pygmalion* (1915) and Eugene O'Neill with *Mourning Becomes Electra* (1929–1931), which he further complicated by giving a Freudian twist to the Orestes legend. Or alternatively, an ancient theme could be worked out in its original setting, but embellished with modern references as in Jean Cocteau's *The Infernal Machine* (*La machine infernale* [1934]), Jean-Paul Sartre's *The Flies* (*Les mouches* [1943]), and Jean Anouilh's *Antigone* (1944). Cocteau, like O'Neill, based his plot on Freud, and Sartre used the *Oresteia* to expound existentialism. More effective perhaps than either of these was Jean Giraudoux's *Tiger at the Gates* (*La guerre de Troie n'aura pas lieu* [1935]), which, using Homeric characters in a situation Homer had not explored, attacked the unreasonableness of war. The success of these plays fulfilled their authors' expectations, but it is noteworthy that the ideas they expressed were all modern. The ancient stories did no more than provide decorative wrapping.

The story of classical scholarship falls into two halves. Seventeenth-century Europe learned from the past, making its own the facts and techniques which had survived from antiquity. By 1700, however, all that could be easily learned from the classical tradition had been learned, and men were building on the foundations antiquity had provided. During the next two hundred years, the achievements and institutions of Greece and Rome, which still commanded great admiration, were pillaged by would-be reformers to provide idealized examples of political organization, moral behavior, and art; but whereas in the past it was the reading of classical authors that inspired reforms, now it was a contemporary interest that acted as inspiration. With the present century we enter however on yet another phase. Scholarship has advanced, but the added knowledge it has brought us of the classical world has not been utilitarian, and its relevance in a world of computers remains problematic. No one can have serious doubts that to immerse ourselves in the life of a complex civilization remote from our own will contribute to our development, but what the nature of that contribution will be in the setting of our particular society cannot be easily foretold.

MAPS

MAP 1

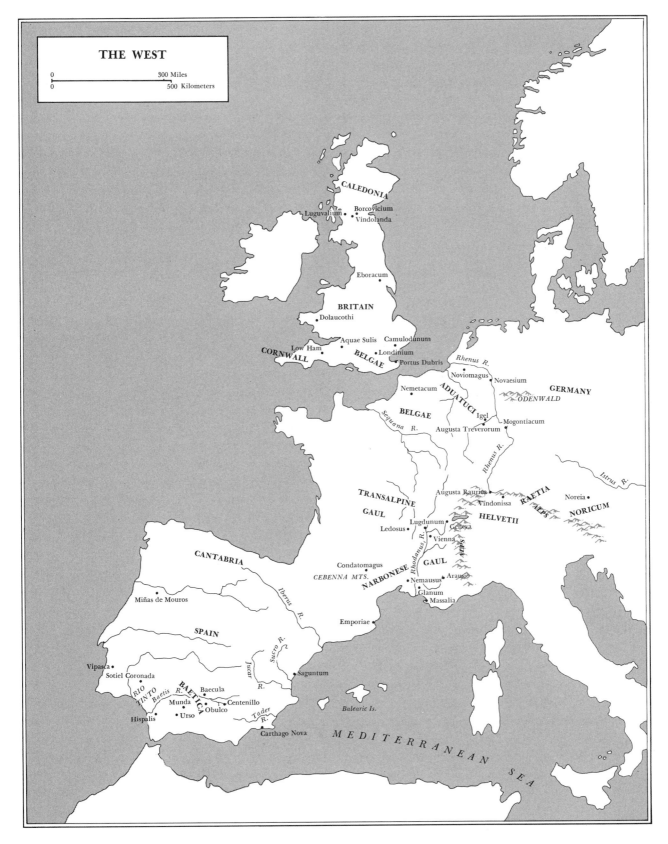

THE WEST

0   300 Miles

0   500 Kilometers

CALEDONIA

Luguvalium •   Borcovicium
         Vindolanda

Eboracum

BRITAIN

Dolaucothi

Aquae Sulis   Camulodunum
Low Ham   Londinium
CORNWALL   BELGAE   Portus Dubris

Rhenus R.

Noviomagus   Novaesium   GERMANY
Nemetacum   ADUATUCI   ODENWALD
BELGAE   Igel
Sequana R.   Augusta Treverorum   Mogontiacum

Rhenus R.

Istrus R.

TRANSALPINE   Augusta Raurica   RAETIA   Noreia
     Vindonissa   ALPS   NORICUM
GAUL   HELVETII
Ledosus •   Lugdunum   Geneva

CANTABRIA   Vienna

Miñas de Mouros   Condatomagus
CEBENNA MTS.   NARBONESE   GAUL
     Nemausus   Arausio
Iberus R.   Glanum
SPAIN   Massalia

Emporiae

Vipasca •   Sucro R.
Sotiel Coronada   Jucar   Saguntum
RIO   BAETICA   Baecula
TINTO   Baetis R.   Munda   Centenillo
     Obulco
Hispalis   Urso   Tader R.
     Carthago Nova   Balearic Is.

MEDITERRANEAN SEA

1835

ITALY AND SICILY

| 0 | 100 Miles |
| 0 | 160 Kilometers |

ROME AND VICINITY

Orgala • Blera
Tarquinii • SABINI
Centumcellae L. Sabatinus
Pyrgi Caere • Veii • Fidenae
LATIUM ROME
Digentia R. • Tiora
Tiber R.
Anio R.
Castrimoenium Gabii Praeneste Liris R.
Politorium Tusculum HERNICI
Ostia L. Albanus ▲ Mt. Albanus
Lanuvium LATIUM Velitrae
Norba • Satricum

| 0 | 40 Miles |
| 0 | 60 Kilometers |

Comum
Eporedia • L. Benacus Grado
Verona
CISALPINE GAUL Atesis R.
Trebia R. Padus R. Spina Pola
Mutina
Genua Bononia (Felsina) Ravenna
LIGURIA Misa
Luna

Novilara
ETRURIA
ADRIATIC SEA
Vetulonia L. Trasimene Hispellum PICENUM
ILVA Rusellae • Clusium
(AITHALIA) L. Volsiniensis Volsinii SABINI
Telamon VESTINI
CORSICA Cosa • Capestrano
PAELIGNI
See inset C. Garganus
ROME AND VICINITY Mt. Casinus
Liris R. SAMNIUM DAUNI PEUCETII
Fundi VOLSCI IAPYGIA
Formiae See inset Taras (Tarentum) CALABRIA
CAMPANIA Lupiae
Silarus R.
SARDINIA TYRRHENIAN SEA LUCANIA
Poseidonia (Paestum) Herakleia

Sybaris

Kroton

CAMPANIA
| 0 | 40 Miles |
| 0 | 60 Kilometers |
Beneventum
Volturnus R. Caudine Forks
Phlegraean Acerrae CAMPANIA Strongyle
Fields Cumae Neapolis BRUTTII Riace Marina
L. Avernus Herculaneum Sarnus R. Lipara Is. IONIAN
L. Lucrinus Pompeii Thermessa
Pithekousai Misenum Boscoreale Mylai Lokroi Epizephyrioi
Oplontis Stabiae Silarus R. Zankle Rhegion SEA
Mt. Vesuvius Sicilian Strait
Himera Mt. Aitna Tauromenium
Motya Kenturipe Naxos
SICILY Morgantina Katane
Henna Philosophiana
Akragas (Agrigentum) Leontinoi
Syracuse
Anapos R.

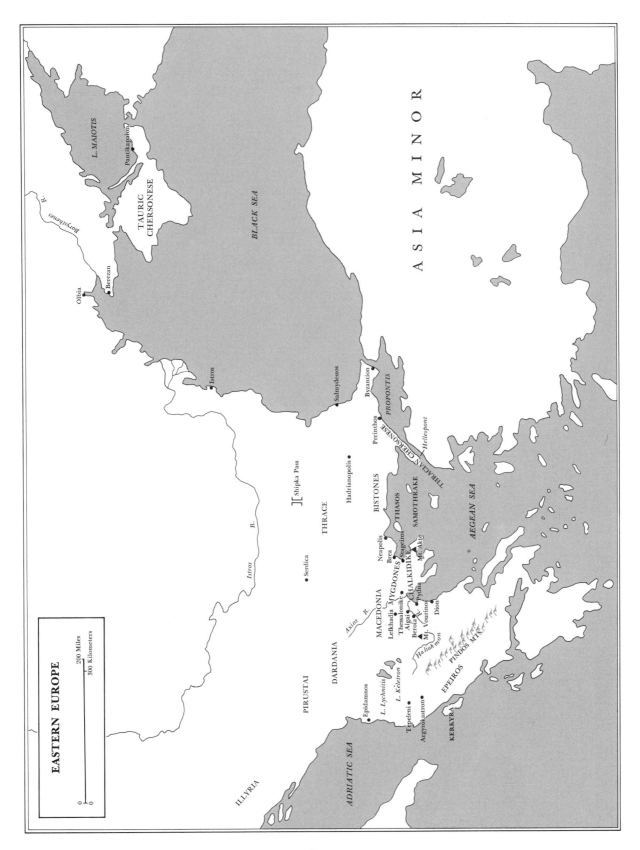

EASTERN EUROPE

200 Miles

300 Kilometers

L. MAIOTIS

Pantikapaion

TAURIC
CHERSONESE

Borysthenes R.

BLACK SEA

Berezan

Olbia

A S I A   M I N O R

Istros

Salmydessos

Byzantion

PROPONTIS

Perinthos

THRACIAN CHERSONESE

Hellespont

Shipka Pass

Hadrianopolis

BISTONES

THRACE

THASOS

SAMOTHRAKE

AEGEAN SEA

Istros R.

Neapolis

Brea

Stageiros

Mt. Akte

Serdica

MYGDONES

CHALKIDIKE

MACEDONIA

Lefkhadia

Thessalonike

Pydna

Axios R.

Aigai

Dion

Beroia

Mt. Vourinos

DARDANIA

Haliakmon

PINDOS MTS.

PIRUSTAI

L. Lychnitis

EPEIROS

L. Keletron

Epidamnos

KERKYRA

Tepeleni

Argyrokastron

ADRIATIC SEA

ILLYRIA

MAP 4

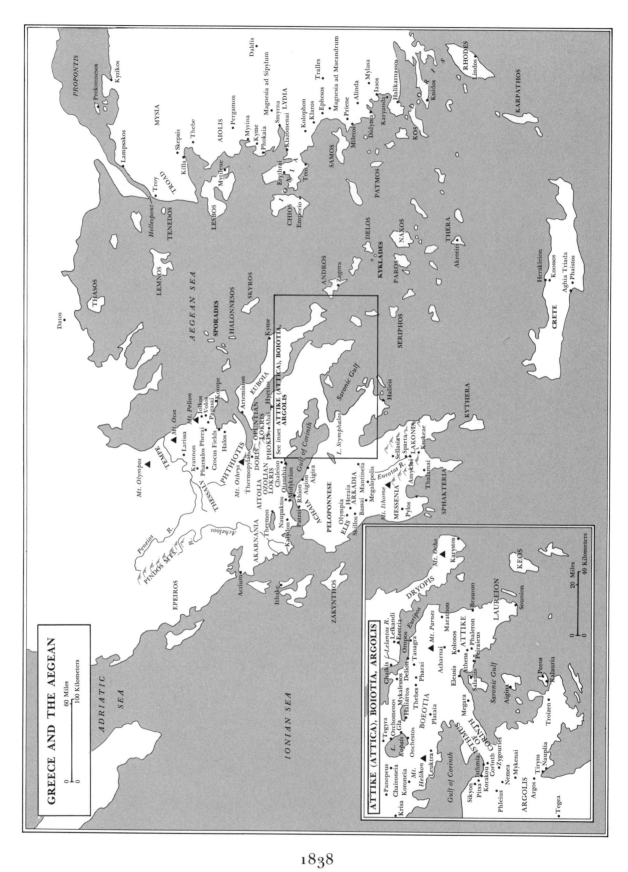

GREECE AND THE AEGEAN

ATTIKE (ATTICA), BOIOTIA, ARGOLIS

MAP 5

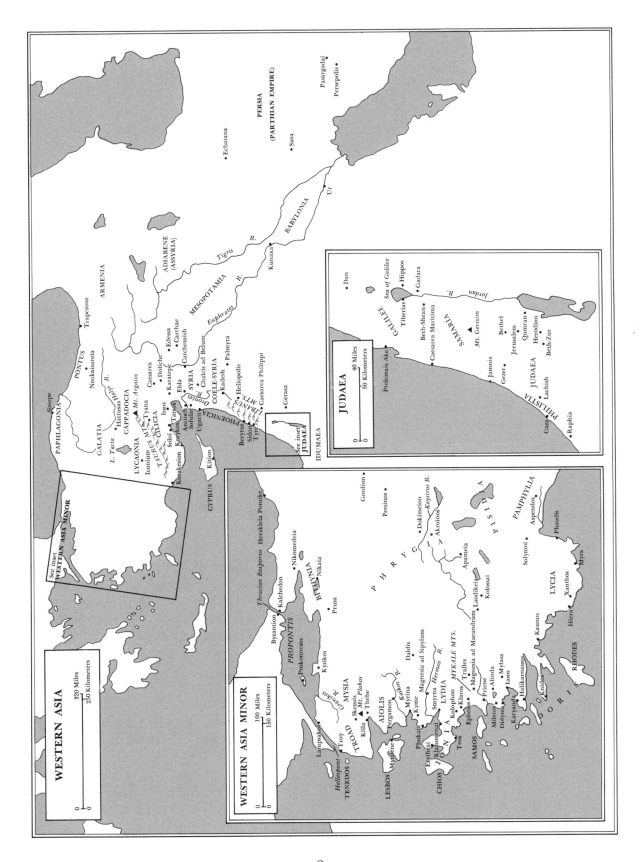

WESTERN ASIA

320 Miles
250 Kilometers

WESTERN ASIA MINOR

100 Miles
150 Kilometers

See inset
WESTERN ASIA MINOR

See inset
JUDAEA

JUDAEA

40 Miles
50 Kilometers

PERSIA
(PARTHIAN EMPIRE)

Pasargadai
Persepolis

Ecbatana

Susa

Ur

BABYLONIA

Tigris R.

Euphrates R.

Kunaxa

MESOPOTAMIA

ADIABENE
(ASSYRIA)

ARMENIA

Trapezous

PONTUS

Neokaisareia

Sinope

PAPHLAGONIA

GALATIA

L. Tatta

Halys R.

Hattusas

CAPPADOCIA

Tyana

Mt. Argaios

Caesarea

Karatepe

Edessa

Carrhae

Carchemish

Doliche

Ebla

Chalcis ad Belum

Palmyra

SYRIA

COELE-SYRIA

Heliopolis

Kadesh

Caesarea Philippi

Gerasa

Iconium

LYCAONIA

TAURUS MTS.

CILICIA

Soloi

Tarsos

Korykos

Antioch

Seleukeia

Ugarit

Orontes R.

LIBANUS MTS.

Berytus

Sidon

Tyre

PHOENICIA

IDUMAEA

CYPRUS

Kition

Korakesion

ISos

JUDAEA inset

Dan

Sea of Galilee

Hippos

GALILEE

Tiberias

Gadara

Beth-Shean

Jordan R.

SAMARIA

Mt. Gerizim

Bethel

Qumran

Herodion

Beth-Zur

Caesarea Maritima

Jamnia

Gezer

Jerusalem

JUDAEA

Lachish

PHILISTIA

Gaza

Raphia

Ptolemais Ake

WESTERN ASIA MINOR inset

Gordion

Pessinos

Dokimeion

Kaystros R.

Akroinos

Apameia

PHRYGIA

PISIDIA

PAMPHYLIA

Aspendos

Phaselis

Solymoi

LYCIA

Myra

Xanthos

Hiera

Kaunos

Knidos

RHODES

DORIS

Halikarnassos

Karyanda

Didyma

Mylasa

Iasos

Miletos

Alinda

Priene

SAMOS

Ephesos

Magnesia ad Maeandrum

Laodikeia

Kolossai

Tralles

MYKALE MTS.

Magnesia ad Sipylum

Klaros

Kolophon

Teos

Erythrai

CHIOS

Klazomenai

Phokaia

Smyrna

Hermos R.

IONIA

LYDIA

Daldis

Kyme

Myrina

Kaïkos R.

Pergamon

AIOLIS

Mytilene

LESBOS

Thebe

Mt. Plakos

Skepsis

MYSIA

Granikos R.

Killa

Troy

TROAD

Lampsakos

Hellespont

TENEDOS

Kyzikos

Prokonnesos

PROPONTIS

Byzantion

Thracian Bosporus

Kalchedon

Prusa

BITHYNIA

Nikaia

Nikomedeia

Herakleia Pontike

1839

MAP 6

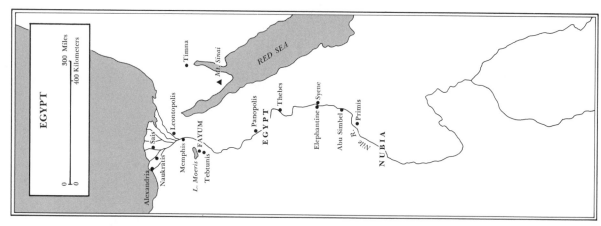

EGYPT

Timna
Mt. Sinai
RED SEA
Leontopolis
Sais
Naukratis
Alexandria
Memphis
FAYUM
L. Moeris
Tebtunis
Panopolis
Thebes
EGYPT
Elephantine Syene
Abu Simbel
Primis
Nile R.
NUBIA

300 Miles
400 Kilometers
0
0

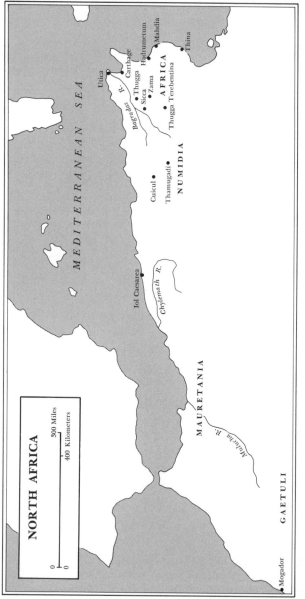

NORTH AFRICA

MEDITERRANEAN SEA

Utica
Carthage
Bagradas R.
Thugga
Sicca
Hadrumetum
Zama
Mahdia
Thina
AFRICA
Thugga Terebentina
Cuicul
Thamugadi
NUMIDIA
Iol Caesarea
Chylemath R.
MAURETANIA
Mulucha R.
GAETULI
Mogador

300 Miles
400 Kilometers
0
0

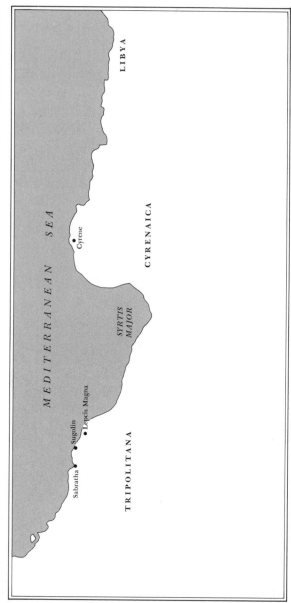

LIBYA
MEDITERRANEAN SEA
Cyrene
CYRENAICA
SYRTIS MAJOR
Sugolin
Lepcis Magna
Sabratha
TRIPOLITANA

MAP 7

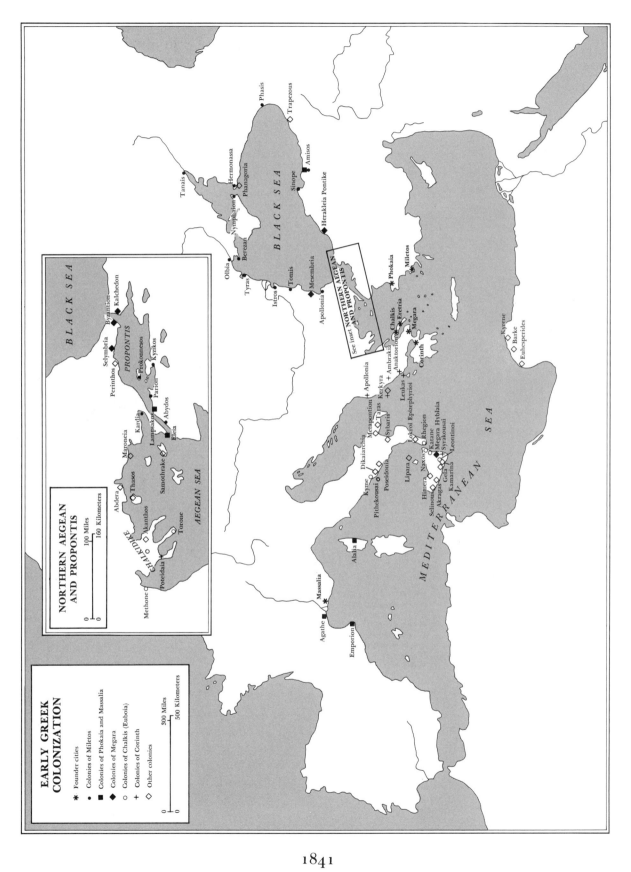

EARLY GREEK COLONIZATION

* Founder cities
• Colonies of Miletos
■ Colonies of Phokaia and Massalia
◆ Colonies of Megara
○ Colonies of Chalkis (Euboia)
+ Colonies of Corinth
◇ Other colonies

300 Miles
500 Kilometers

NORTHERN AEGEAN AND PROPONTIS

100 Miles
160 Kilometers

BLACK SEA

PROPONTIS

AEGEAN SEA

Byzantion
Kalchedon
Selymbria
Perinthos
Prokonnesos
Kyzikos
Parion
Abydos
Lampsakos
Eleia
Kardia
Maroneia
Abdera
Thasos
Akanthos
Samothrake
Torone
Proteidaia
Methone
CHALKIDIKE

Tanais
Hermonassa
Phanagoria
Nymphaion
Berezan
Olbia
Tyras
Istros
Tomis
Mesembria
Apollonia
Phasis
Trapezous
Amisos
Sinope
Herakleia Pontike

BLACK SEA

Phokaia
Miletos
Chalkis
Eretria
Ambrakia
Anaktorion
Megara
Corinth
Kerkyra
Apollonia
Leukas
Epizephyrioi
Metapontion
Taras
Sybaris
Lokroi
Rhegion
Dikaiarchia
Poseidonia
Kyme
Pithekousai
Naxos
Lipara
Himera
Selinous
Akragas
Gela
Katane
Megara Hyblaia
Syrakousai
Leontinoi
Kamarina

Kyrene
Barke
Euhesperides

MEDITERRANEAN SEA

Alalia
Massalia
Agathe
Emporion

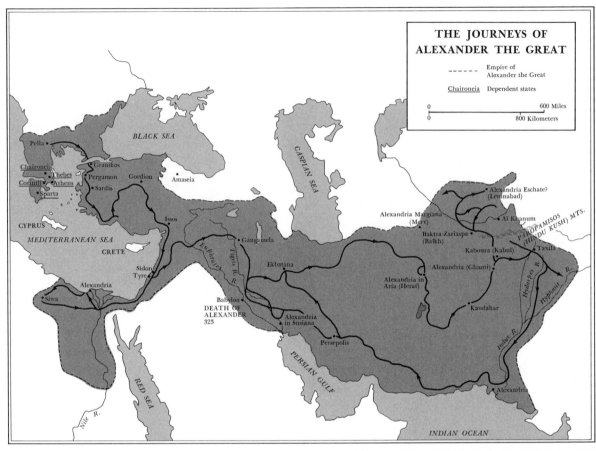

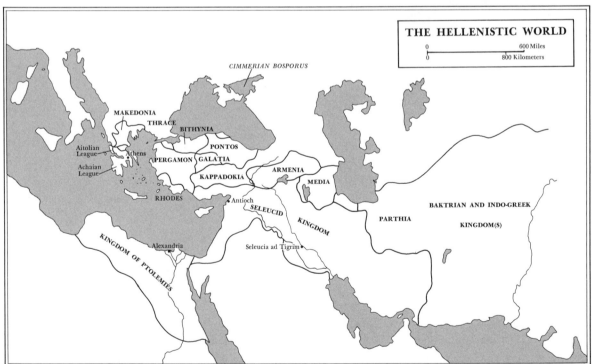

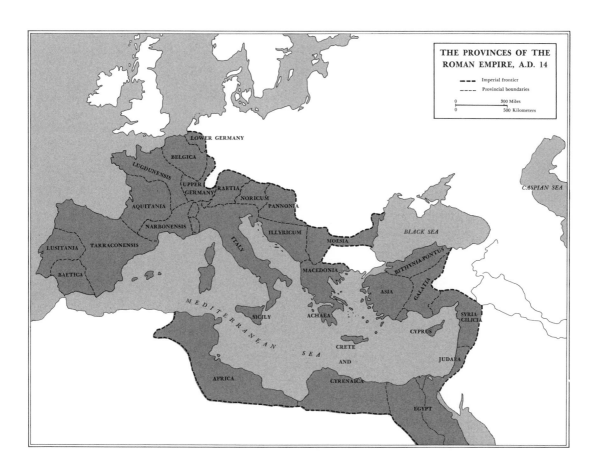

**THE PROVINCES OF THE
ROMAN EMPIRE, A.D. 14**

- - - Imperial frontier
- · - Provincial boundaries

0   300 Miles
0   500 Kilometers

LOWER GERMANY

BELGICA

LUGDUNENSIS

UPPER GERMANY   RAETIA

AQUITANIA   NORICUM

NARBONENSIS   PANNONIA

LUSITANIA   TARRACONENSIS

BAETICA

ITALY

ILLYRICUM

MOESIA

MACEDONIA

SICILY

ACHAEA

CRETE

AND

AFRICA   CYRENAICA

MEDITERRANEAN SEA

BLACK SEA

BITHYNIA-PONTUS

ASIA   GALATIA

SYRIA-CILICIA

CYPRUS

JUDAEA

EGYPT

CASPIAN SEA

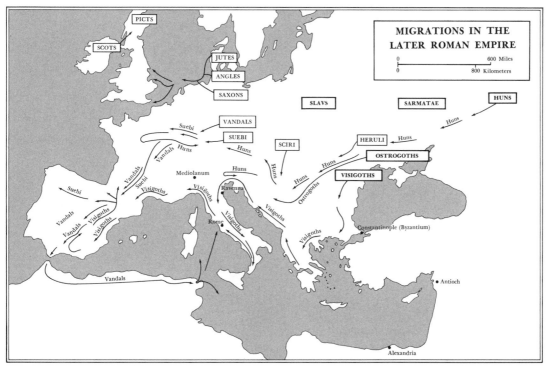

**MIGRATIONS IN THE
LATER ROMAN EMPIRE**

0   600 Miles
0   800 Kilometers

PICTS

SCOTS

JUTES

ANGLES

SAXONS

SLAVS   SARMATAE   HUNS

VANDALS

SUEBI   SCIRI   HERULI

OSTROGOTHS

VISIGOTHS

Mediolanum

Ravenna

Rome

Constantinople (Byzantium)

Antioch

Alexandria

Suebi   Vandals   Huns   Visigoths   Ostrogoths

LIST OF
CONTRIBUTORS

List of Contributors

J. K. ANDERSON
University of California, Berkeley
Wars and Military Science: Greece

PETER D. ARNOTT
Tufts University
Drama

ELIZABETH ASMIS
University of Chicago
Roman Philosophical Movements

M. M. AUSTIN
University of St. Andrews
Greek Trade, Industry, and Labor

MARY BEARD
Newnham College, Cambridge University
Roman Priesthoods

R. R. BOLGAR
Formerly of King's College, Cambridge University
The Progress of Classical Scholarship

LARISSA BONFANTE
New York University
Clothing and Ornament

EDWARD KERR BORTHWICK
University of Edinburgh
Music and Dance

THOMAS D. BOYD
University of Texas at Austin
Urban Planning

RICHARD BRILLIANT
Columbia University
Roman Sculpture and Gems

DON R. BROTHWELL
Institute of Archaeology, University of London
Foodstuffs, Cooking, and Drugs

ALISON BURFORD
University of North Carolina at Asheville
Crafts and Craftsmen

A. R. BURN
Formerly of the University of Glasgow
Historical Summary of Greece

STANLEY M. BURSTEIN
California State University, Los Angeles
Greek Class Structures and Relations

R. A. G. CARSON
Formerly of the British Museum
Coins

LIONEL CASSON
New York University, *emeritus*
Piracy; Transportation

1847

SUSAN GUETTEL COLE
University of Illinois at Chicago
Greek Cults

J. J. COULTON
Ashmolean Museum, Oxford
Greek Architecture; Greek Building Techniques

RONALD A. CROSSLAND
Formerly of the University of Sheffield
Early Greek Migrations

CAROLYN DEWALD
University of Southern California
Greek Education and Rhetoric

SHEILA K. DICKISON
University of Florida
Women in Rome

J. RUFUS FEARS
Boston University
Ruler Worship

JOHN FERGUSON
Formerly of Selly Oaks Colleges, Birmingham
Divination and Oracles: Rome; Divinities; Magic; Roman Administration; Roman Cults

ARTHER FERRILL
University of Washington
Historical Summary of Rome

NICHOLAS R. E. FISHER
University College, Cardiff
Greek Associations, Symposia, and Clubs; Roman Associations, Dinner Parties, and Clubs

HELENE P. FOLEY
Barnard College
Women in Greece

VALERIE FRENCH
American University
Birth Control, Childbirth, and Early Childhood

ROBERT GARLAND
Colgate University
Greek Spectacles and Festivals

MICHAEL GRANT
Formerly of Queen's University of Belfast
Alternative Paths: Greek Monarchy and Federalism

FREDERICK T. GRIFFITHS
Amherst College
Literary Criticism

BRYAN HAINSWORTH
New College, Oxford University
Epic Poetry

JUDITH P. HALLETT
University of Maryland
Roman Attitudes Toward Sex

DAVID M. HALPERIN
Massachusetts Institute of Technology
Bucolic Poetry

WILLIAM F. HANSEN
Folklore Institute, Indiana University
Folklore

JOHN F. HEALY
Royal Holloway and Bedford New College, University of London
Mines and Quarries

PEYTON RANDOLPH HELM
University of Pennsylvania
Races and Physical Types in the Classical World

JEFFREY HENDERSON
University of Southern California
Greek Attitudes Toward Sex

KEITH HOPKINS
King's College, Cambridge University
Roman Trade, Industry, and Labor

J. DONALD HUGHES
University of Denver
Land and Sea

JOHN H. HUMPHREY
University of Michigan
Roman Games

MICHAEL H. JAMESON
Stanford University
Sacrifice and Ritual: Greece

EVA JAUNZEMS
Clothing and Ornament

RACHEL KITZINGER
Vassar College
Alphabets and Writing

HELMUT KOESTER
Harvard University
Christianity

WERNER A. KRENKEL
Institut für Fremdsprachen, Wilhelm-Pieck-Universität Rostock
Prostitution

JOHN G. LANDELS
University of Reading
Engineering

DAVID LANGSLOW
Wolfson College, Oxford University
Languages and Dialects

VASILIKI LIMBERIS
Haverford College
Christianity

ROGER LING
University of Manchester
Roman Architecture; Roman Painting and Mosaic

ROBERT J. LITTMAN
University of Hawaii at Manoa
Greek Taxation

G. E. R. LLOYD
King's College, Cambridge University
Greek Philosophy; Theories of Progress and Evolution

DOUGLAS M. MACDOWELL
University of Glasgow
Greek Law

ALEXANDER GORDON MCKAY
McMaster University
Houses

RONALD MELLOR
University of California, Los Angeles
Roman Historiography and Biography

OSWYN MURRAY
Balliol College, Oxford University
Greek Forms of Government

JOHN A. NORTH
University College, London
Sacrifice and Ritual: Rome; The Afterlife: Rome

JAMES E. PACKER
Northwestern University
Roman Building Techniques

SHALOM PERLMAN
University of Tel-Aviv
Interstate Relations

JOHN POLLARD
Formerly of University College of North Wales
Divination and Oracles: Greece

JEROME J. POLLITT
Yale University
Greek Painting and Mosaic; Greek Sculpture and Gems

SARAH B. POMEROY
Hunter College
Greek Marriage

JOSEPH RUSSO
Haverford College
Greek Lyric and Elegiac Poetry

RICHARD P. SALLER
University of Chicago
Roman Class Structures and Relations

ALAN E. SAMUEL
University of Toronto
Calendars and Time-Telling

JOHN SCARBOROUGH
University of Wisconsin–Madison
Medicine

SETH SCHWARTZ
Harvard University
Judaism

BRENT D. SHAW
University of Lethbridge
Roman Taxation

MICHAEL SIMPSON
University of Texas at Dallas
Myths and Cosmologies

CHESTER G. STARR
University of Michigan, *emeritus*
Greek Administration

E. STUART STAVELEY
Formerly of Royal Holloway and Bedford New
College, University of London
Roman Forms of Government

SUSAN A. STEPHENS
Stanford University
Book Production

J. P. SULLIVAN
University of California, Santa Barbara
Epigrams and Satire

E. A. THOMPSON
Formerly of University of Nottingham
Late Roman Migrations

WESLEY E. THOMPSON
University of California, Davis
Insurance and Banking

SUSAN TREGGIARI
Stanford University
Roman Marriage

JUDY ANN TURNER
California Polytechnic State University
Greek Priesthoods

STEPHEN USHER
Royal Holloway and Bedford New College, University
of London
Greek Historiography and Biography

ROBERT GLENN USSHER
University of Adelaide
Letter Writing

EMILY VERMEULE
Harvard University
The Afterlife: Greece

PETER WALCOT
University College, Cardiff
Images of the Individual

ALAN WATSON
University of Pennsylvania
Roman Law

GRAHAM WEBSTER
Formerly of the University of Birmingham
Wars and Military Science: Rome

K. D. WHITE
University College, London
Farming and Animal Husbandry

THOMAS E. J. WIEDEMANN
University of Bristol
Slavery

GORDON WILLIAMS
Yale University
Roman Lyric and Elegiac Poetry

JOHN J. WINKLER
Stanford University
The Novel

CECIL W. WOOTEN
University of North Carolina
at Chapel Hill
Roman Education and Rhetoric

DAVID C. YOUNG
University of California, Santa Barbara
Athletics

INDEX

Index

A

Abai, map 4
Abdera, map 7
  founding of, 14
Abortion, 1356
Ab Urbe Condita. See Livius, Titus (Livy)
Abu Simbel, map 6
  Greek soldiers' graffiti, 15
Abydos, map 7
Accursius
  Great Gloss, 628
Acerrae, map 2
Achaea (Achaia), map 4, map 10
Achaea (Achaia), confederacy of, map 9
  abolition, 40
  under Aratos of Sikyon, 493
  constitutional structure, 493
  demiourgoi (deputies), 493
  dissolution under Philopoimen, 493
  federal state, 38
  voting, 493
  war with Sparta, 39
Achaians (Achaeans)
  colonized southern Italy, 12
Acharnai, map 4
Acharneis. See Aristophanes
Acheloos River, map 4
Achilleid. See Statius, Publius Papinius

Achilles
  shield decoration 217, 444
Achilles Painter, 1760 *illus.*
Achilles Tatius, 1566
  Leukippe and Kleitophon, 1570
  noble characters, criminal situations and motives,
    1570
Acoustics, Greek
  Aristoxenus, 1625
Acrophony, 404, 405
Acropolis
  in Greek cities, 1691
Acropolis, Athenian, 1662 *illus.,* 1663–1664, 1707,
    1734, 1758
  atypical nature, 1691
  Hekatompedon pediments, 1708
  Roman architecture, 1676
  temple of Athena Nike, 1715 *illus.*
  See also Erechtheum, Parthenon
Acrotiri
  wall paintings from West House, 697
Actium, map 4
  battle of, 63
Actors
  Greek guilds of, 1150
  income and status of Greek, 1481–1482, 1487
  requirements for, 1482
  Roman, 1159, 1488
Acts of John, 1050

Acts of Thomas, 1061
Adiabene (Assyria), map 5
Administration, Greek
 in archaic period, 631–635
 in classical period, 635–641
 community services, 634–635
 in Hellenistic period, 641–647
 military, 633–634, 636
 mnemones (memory clerks), 634
 Ptolemaic Egypt, 642–645
 record-keeping, 634–635, 638, 641
 sacred functions of, 632–633, 636
 Seleukid Empire, 645
 sources of revenue, 634–635, 640, 645
 taxation, 795–807
 wages, 634–635
 See also Magistrates, Greek
Administration, Roman
 administrative purpose of tribes, 654
 aristocratic nature, 50
 under Augustus, 65–66
 censors, 651–652
 census, 659
 changes after Republican revolution, 650–651
 civil service, 658
 classes of landowners, 650
 Comitia Curiata, 653
 of conquered peoples, 669
 cursus honorum (proper succession of offices), 653
 expansion of executive branch, 48
 in the fourth century, 652
 growth of after Roman expansion, 653–654
 ius Latii (Latin rights), 652
 under Julio-Claudian emperors, 659–660
 legacy of, 663–664
 local government, 660
 merging of settlements into Rome, 649
 military influence, 55
 minor officials and clerks (*apparitores*), 653
 municipal, 820
 municipia (municipalities), 652
 Polybius on states and orders, 655
 praetorian prefects, 663
 in provinces, 654
 under Republican constitution, 652–653
 Severan reorganizations, 76
 and structure of Roman Catholic Church, 664
 taxation by, 809–825
 See also particular emperors
Adonis
 rites of, 1187

Adoption
 Greek laws governing, 596
 Roman legal forms for, 615
Adriatic Sea, map 2, map 3, map 4, 88 *illus.*
 piracy in, 838
Aduatuci, map 1
Adultery
 Augustan laws, 1353
 consequences for wife, 1351
 double standard for husband, 1351
 fear of among Greeks, 1310–1311
 Roman attitudes, 1276
 Roman law against, 67
 Roman preoccupation with, 1328
Aedile, 503, 523
 duties under Republican constitution, 652–653
Aegean islands
 volcanism, 95
Aegean Sea, map 3, map 4, map 7, 88 *illus.*
 piracy in, 839
Aegidas of Crete, 1135
Aegina (Aigina), map 4
 coinage of, 1796, 1798
 temple of Aphaea (Aphaia), 1659, 1661, 1708
Aeneas Tacticus
 class tension in fourth century B.C., 543
 military handbook, 696
Aeneid. See Vergilius Maro, Publius (Vergil)
Aeolian (Lipari) Islands
 volcanism, 94
Aeolis, map 5
 architecture of, 1658
Aerarium militare (military treasury), 811
Aerarium Saturni (Treasury of Saturn), 810
Aerial photography
 of Roman city plan, 1697
Aeschines
 Against Ctesiphon, 1096
 oversimplification in speeches, 1096
Aeschylus
 Agamemnon, 1304, 1313, 1315
 Danaid trilogy, 1305
 eastern dirge music (*Persians*), 1508
 elaborate symphonic odes (*Oresteia*), 1508
 Eumenides, 1305, 1315–1316
 man's emergence from a primitive past, 268
 Oresteia, 1315, 1483
 Oresteia and Athenian democracy, 468
 The Persians, 1479
 preference for trilogy structure, 1483
 Prometheus Bound, 397

Seven against Thebes, 1305
  slavery and religion, 584
Aesop
  adaptations of Aesopic fables, 1122–1123
  use of fables in daily life, 1122
Aetius, Flavius
  defeat of Attila, 82
Afranius, Lucius
  contemporary sexual themes in comedies, 1271
Africa, map 6, map 10
  large-scale mosaic style, 1790–1791
  Roman "carpet" mosaics in, 1787–1788
Africa, northwest
  geography, 92, map 6, map 10
  physical description of people, 149
  pygmies, 149
Afterlife, Greece, 987–995
  belief in better, 991
  concept of, 990
  variety of thoughts about, 987
Afterlife, Rome, 997–1007
  concept of, 998
  Greek influence on concept of, 999
  literary texts and, 1000
  and new Eastern cults, 1002
  speculation rather than belief, 1002
Against Apion. See Josephus, Flavius
Against Ctesiphon. See Aeschines
Agamemnon. See Aeschylus
Agatharchos of Samos, 1756
Agathe, map 7
Agathias Scholasticus of Myrina
  collection of epigrams in *Cyclus,* 1498
Agesilaus, king of Sparta
  use of mercenaries, 692
Agesilaus. See Xenophon
Aghia Triada, map 4
Agis IV, king of Sparta, 39, 546
Agora
  in Bronze Age society, 445
  in Greek architecture, 1660–1661 *illus.,*
    1665–1666 *illus.,* 1668 *illus.*
  in Greek city plans, 1691, 1693–1694, 1698–1699
  at Priene, 296
  as trading and commercial center, 727
Agora, Athenian
  in fifth century, 470
  Roman destruction of, 41
  sacred areas of, 888
Agorakritos
  statue of Nemesis, 1713

Agricultural festivals, 1145–1146
Agricultural tools, Greek, 213
  seed drill, 217
  symmetrical ard plow, 216
Agricultural tools, Roman
  plow types, 222–223
  symmetrical ard plow, 221
Agriculture
  irrigation engineering, 345, 346, 347 *illus.*
Agriculture, Greek
  agronomy as a science, 212
  in archaeological sources, 213
  basis of wealth and power, 9
  calendar, 216–218
  in classical literature, 212–213
  climate and growing season, 214
  definition of an agriculturalist, 212
  depicted in classical art, 213
  harvest, 217
  land use, 214–216
  rainfall pattern and distribution, 214
  rural-urban interdependence, 211–212
  soil conditions, 215–216
  sowing, 216–217
  weeding, 217
  See also particular crops
Agriculture, Roman
  decline of in literature, 218–219, 220
  decline of small farmers, 56
  deep plowing, 221
  distribution of crops and animals, 220–221
  fallowing, 222
  importance of grain cultivation, 218
  partial rotation of crops, 222
  plowing, 221–222
  population decline and agricultural productivity,
    127
  relationship between theory and practice, 218,
    219, 220
  slavery and decline of, 218–219
  soil and crop selection, 220–221, 222
  use of legumes in crop rotation, 222
  See also particular crops
Agrigentum. *See* Akragas
Agrippa I, king of Judah, 1039
Agrippina, Julia (the Younger)
  claims to political power, 1322
Agrippina, Vipsania (the Elder)
  coinage portraiture of, 1820
Aigai, map 3
Aigina. *See* Aegina

Volume One: 1–720; Volume Two: 721–1298; Volume Three: 1299–1832

Aigion, map 4

Aigira, map 4

Ai Khanum, map 8

Aiolis, map 4

Aischrologia (women's jokes), 1146

Aithalia. *See* Ilva

Aitolia (Aetolia), map 4
    alliance with Rome, 39
    independence, 38
    piracy in Aegean, 39

Aitolia (Aetolia), confederacy of, map 9
    apokletoi (committee), 493
    constitutional structure, 492–493
    defense of Delphi against Gauls, 493
    federal state, 38

Akanthos, map 7

Akarnania, map 4

Akragas (Agrigentum), map 2, map 7
    siege by Rome, 53
    zenith of power under Theron, 489

Akroinos, map 5

Akrotiri, map 4

Alalia, map 7

Alans
    entering of Gaul, 174
    settlement in Lusitania, 175, map 10

Alaric I, king of the Visigoths
    relations with Rome, 178
    sack of Rome, 410 A.D., 82

Alaric II, king of the Visigoths
    Lex Romana Visigothorum, 627

Albanus, Lake, map 2

Alcaeus (Alkaios)
    Alcaic stanza, favorite meter, 1446
    drinking songs, 1444–1445
    exile from Mytilene, 17
    poems of political conflict, 1444
    poems sung to lyre, 1507
    political biography of, 1444
    on power of wealth, 534
    on seventh-century turmoil in Mytilene,
        1176
    skilled use of metaphor, 1445
    on symposia, 1171
    sympotic songs, 1445
    on tyrants of Mytilene, 449
    use of mythological themes, 1445

Alcibiades
    decoration of his house, 1369–1370
    life style, 1185
    removal from Sicilian command, 1185

Alcinous
    household of, 1392

Alcman
    composer of *partheneia* (maiden songs), 1507
    early Greek choral poet, 1447–1448
    partheneia (maiden songs), 1448
    Spartan nationality, 1447–1448
    surviving fragments, 1448

Alcuin
    reform of Latin prose style, 1822

Alexander of Abonutichus
    fraudulent oracle, 956–957

Alexander III, king of Macedonia (the Great)
    adoption of barbarian customs, 1398–1399
    architectural influences under, 296
    banquets and drinking parties, 1190
    character and achievements, 35–36
    courts of the Successors, 1190
    cult of, 1012
    death at Babylon, 35, map 8
    defeats Persians, 34–35
    disaffection of officers, 35
    empire of, 34–37, map 8
    images by Lysippos, 1718
    Indian campaigns, 35
    invasion of Asia Minor, 34
    journeys of, map 8
    mercenaries of, 543
    monolithic world coinage under, 1801–1804
    navy of, 841
    as prototype of posthumous cults of charismatic
        rulers, 1012
    siege of Tyre, 696
    successors, 36, 331, 1150
    youthful exile, 33

Alexander Jannaeus (Yannai), 1033

Alexander sarcophagus, 1702

Alexandria, map 6, map 8, map 9, map 11, 88 *illus.*
    Alexandrian schemes of literary classification,
        1468
    court fashions, 1398
    Deinokrates' city plan, 1695
    general administration, 643
    Greek coinage of, 1806
    Jews of, 1042
    lighthouse at, 362
    Museum and Library, 415, 643, 1091, 1101,
        1195, 1233, 1425, 1519, 1537, 1554, 1555,
        1819
    papyrus industry in, 423
    port of, 362–363

scholar-poets of, 1194
as trade center, 770
Alexandria Eschate? (Leninabad), map 8
Alexandria (Ghazni), map 8
Alexandria in Aria (Herat), map 8
Alexandria in Susiana, map 8
Alexandria Margiana (Merv), map 8
Alinda, map 4, map 5
Alkamenes
architectural sculptures, 1713
Alkiphron
Letters from Courtesans, 1581
Alliances, Greek, 672–675
Al-Mina
ancient settlement at, 401
evidence for Greek trade, 737
Alphabet
development of, 402 *illus.*
Etruscan, 416
Alphabet, Greek
development of, 400–401, 404–406
epichoric, 401
Alphabet, Phoenician
adaptation by Greeks, 398–406
introduction into Greece, 10
Alphabet, Roman
adopted from Etruscans, 47
development of, 416–417
Alpheus River
geology, 108
Alps, map 1, 88 *illus.*
Altar
importance to Greek sanctuary, 1660
used to communicate with supernatural, 968
Altar of Domitius Ahenobarbus, 1732 *illus.*
relief from, 1730–1731
Altar miniature
automated, 350 *illus.*
Altar of Pity, 1676
Alxenor, 386
marble relief by, 387 *illus.*
Amaseia, map 8
Ambarvalia
Arval Brethren in, 915
main prayer to Mars, 915
purification of land, 915
sacrificial procession, 915
Ambassadors. *See* Envoys
Ambrakia, map 7
Amelung's Goddess type, 1711
Amisos, map 7

Ammianus Marcellinus
attention to detail, 1550
political and administrative history, 1550
Amores. See Ovidius Naso, Publius (Ovid)
Amphictyonies (Greek religious leagues), 668–669
Amphitheater
Roman, 300, 1159–1160, 1675, 1678–1679, 1681 *illus.*
Amphitheatrum Flavium (Colosseum), 1160
coinage commemoration of, 1812
purpose of, 1489
in Roman architecture, 1675, 1678–1679, 1681 *illus.*
Amunos
cult of, 1186
Amyklai, map 4
Anabasis (The March Up Country). See Xenophon
Anacreon
contrasted to Sappho and Alcaeus, 1446
detachment, 1446
last major monodist, 1447
middle-aged perspective, 1446
poet as traveling professional, 1447
precursor of Hellenistic style, 1447
skillful word arrangement, 1446
wit, 1447
Anaktorion, map 7
Anapos River, map 2
Anaxagoras
contrasted to Empedocles, 1595
man the most intelligent of creatures, 268
postulated an original plurality, 1595
Anaximander, 409
Boundless the first principle, 1588
chief concern with origins, 1588
on human adaptation for survival, 267
indeterminate nature of the Boundless, 1588
on the natural world, 1525
rational criticism of Thales, 1589
Anaximenes, 409
Air the first principle, 1589
condensation and rarefaction, 1589
notion of underlying physical element, 1589
Andocides (Andokides)
on Athenian law, 479
laws governing heiresses, 596
On the Peace with Sparta, 1095
speeches in self-defense, 1093–1094
Andokides Painter, 1753
Andros, map 4

Anecdotes
  apothegms, 1123
  compilation of, 1123
  definition of, 1123
  khreia, 1124
  philosophical, 1123
Angles, map 11
Animal hunts, 1162–1163
Animal husbandry
  cattle in post-Mycenaean Greece and Rome, 257
  erosion and deforestation caused by, 117, 126
  goats, 258
  pigs, 257–258
  sheep, 258
Animal husbandry, Greek
  cattle, 218
  constraints of fodder supply, 218
  pigs, 218
Animal husbandry, Roman
  breaking in of plow oxen, 235
  constraints of fodder supply, 234
  cows, 234
  economic considerations, 234
  effects of overgrazing, 235
  goats, 235
  mules, 235
  pigs, 234
  sheep, 234, 235
Animals
  arena performance using, 1163
  killing of, 1164
Anio River, map 2
Anio (Aniene) valley
  aqueduct siting, 341
Annales maximi (annual lists)
  important early records, 1542
Annals. See Tacitus, Cornelius, 1280
Annona, 823
Anonymous Iamblichi
  discussion of *eunomia* in, 467
Antakya. *See* Antioch
Anthesteria (festival of Dionysus), 893, 1145–1146
Anthologia Latina
  Latin epigrams in, 1496–1497
  modern, 1497
Antigone. See Sophocles
Antigonos (Antigonus) II, king of Macedonia,
    37–38
  bawdy activities of, 1190
Antigonos (Antigonus) III, king of Macedonia, 546
  forms Hellenic League, 39

Antikythera mechanism, 326, 347, 348 *illus.,*
    349 *illus.*
Antimachus of Colophon
  critiques of, 1424
  literary artist as epicist, 1423–1424
Antioch (Antakya), map 5, map 9, map 11, 88 *illus.*
  city plan using colonnaded streets, 1699
  famine in fourth century, 762
  Judgment of Paris, 1785
  mosaic *emblemata* series, 1785
Antiochos (Antiochus) II, Seleukid ruler
  conquest of Palestine, 1031–1032
Antiochos (Antiochus) III, Seleukid ruler
  conquest of Judaea, 1031
  relations with Rome, 675
  war with Rome, 40, 54
Antiochos (Antiochus) IV, Seleukid ruler
  procession of at Daphne, 1192
  social behavior of, 1190
Antioch, Church of
  center of Christian expansion, 1048
Antipater
  imposed oligarchic government on Athens,
    545
Antiphanes
  The Soldier or Tychon, 807
Antiphon
  hypothetical murder cases, 1093
  Sophist orator, 1598
Antoninus Pius, 73
Antonius, Marcus (Mark Antony)
  affair with Cleopatra, 63
  conflict with Octavian, 62, 63
  after death of Caesar, 62
  in Second Triumvirate, 62
  war coinage of, 1809
Antonius Diogenes
  Marvels Beyond Thule, 1567
Antony, Saint
  founder of Egyptian monasticism, 1067
Aoide (Greek art of song), 1418
Apameia, map 5
Aparchai (first fruits), 966
Apartment houses
  cenacula, 1378
  height limitations, 1380
  life-style mandated by, 1380–1381
  in Ostia, 1378–1381 *illus.*
  Ostia, block of the Charioteers, 1380
  Ostia, House of Diana, 1380
  and Roman city crowding, 1700

Roman fire codes, 1379–1380
See also Tenement (*insula*)
Apatouria, 1146
    festival of Apollo, 893
Apelles
    Greek painter, 1749, 1757, 1774
Apennines, 88 *illus.*
Aphesimoi hemerai (days of release), 1149
Aphrodite
    birth of, 865
    origin of, 850
    Roman followers of Greek cult of, 1270
    romanization of, 1270
Apicius, Marcus Gavius
    cookbook of, 250
    uses of olives, 255
Apocolocyntosis. See Seneca, Lucius Annaeus (Seneca
    the Younger)
Apocryphon of John, 1050, 1053
Apollo
    associations, 849
    attributes, 868
    birth of, 868
    chief oracular god, 949
    cult centers, 849
    double origin of, 849
    god of poetry, 868
    image on Temple of Zeus at Olympia, 849
    oracle at Delphi, 868
    source of order in the community, 868
Apollo, cult of
    taxes for, 639
Apollodorus of Alexandria
    toxicology tracts, 1236
Apollodorus of Athens, fifth century B.C.
    Greek painter, 1756
Apollodorus of Athens, second century B.C.
    origins of the universe (*Library*), 863
Apollodorus of Damascus
    architect of Forum Traianum (Trajan's Forum),
        308–311, 1698
    narrative representation on Trajan's column,
        1741–1742
Apollonia, map 7
Apollonios of Tyre
    popular folk book, 1568
Apollonius
    diocetes under Ptolemy II, 643
Apollonius of Rhodes
    Argonautica, 1425
    librarian at Alexandria, 1425

Apollonius of Tyana
    Cappadocian writings, 201
Apology. See Plato
Apology. See Tertullianus, Quintus Septimius Florens
    (Tertullian)
Appian of Alexandria
    History of Rome, 1534–1535
Appius Claudius, 506
Apprenticeships
    to craftsmen, 375, 376
Apse
    in Greek architecture, 278, 1657, 1679
    in Roman architecture, 1674, 1677, 1688, 1689
Apuleius
    cult of Isis, 858
    The Golden Ass, 1569–1570
    Lucius (hero-narrator), 1570
    tale of Cupid and Psyche, 1125
Aquae Sulis, map 1
Aqua Marcia (Roman aqueduct), 340, 341 *illus.,*
        341 *table,* 342
    comparison with Aqua Claudia, 341 *table*
Aqueducts
    Aqua Serino, 1374–1375
    cost of building, 823
    evolving technology of, 340–343, 341 *illus.,*
        342 *illus.*
    in Roman architecture, 1672, 1676–1677
    surveying and siting of, 340–342
Aquitania, map 10
Arabia
    annexed by Trajan, 72
Ara Pacis Augustae (Altar of Augustan Peace),
        1410 *illus.,* 1734, 1737, 1740
    monumental altar, 1676
Aratos of Sikyon
    military successes, 38
Arausio, map 1
Arbitration
    Greek interstate, 673
Arcesilaus
    adopted form of skepticism, 1619
    head of Plato's Academy, 1619
Arch
    commemorative or triumphal, 309–310, 1677,
        1684
    in Greek architecture, 296 *illus.,* 297
    in Roman architecture, 296–297, 302, 1674,
        1681–1683, 1687–1688
    Syrian, 1681–1682
    See also Dome; Vault

Arch, corbeled
  in Greek architecture, 295 *illus.*, 296
Archaic Period, Greek
  funeral paintings, 1761–1762, 1763 *illus.*, 1764
  monumental painting, 1756
  vase painting, 1750 *illus.*, 1751, 1752
Arch at Beneventum, 1740
Arch of Constantine, 1744–1745 *illus.*
  reliefs on, 1744–1745 *illus.*, 1748
Arche (principle)
  Anaximander's term, 1587
Archidamus, king of Sparta
  xenia relationship with Pericles, 671
Archilochos (Archilochus) of Paros, 17
  archaic Greek monodic poet, 1439–1440
  dominant themes, 1439–1440
  favored meters, 1439
  on King Gyges of Lydia, 488
  use of sarcastic iambics in satire, 1500
Archimedes
  advancement of mathematical knowledge, 274
  deductive work in hydrostatics, 1625
  fortress of Euryalus, 696
  on levers, 323
  Method, 1623
  On the Equilibrium of Planes, 1626
  On Floating Bodies, 1625
  On the Quadrature of the Parabola, 1623
  reported results and methods of discovery, 1623
  rigorous deductive proof of basic statics
    propositions, 1626
  used reductio and method of exhaustion, 1623
Architecton (master craftsman), 377
Architects
  family connections among, 375
  Roman, 306, 308–312
  social role of, 385
  working techniques of, 308, 310–312
  See also names of specific individuals
Architectural dating
  using trademarked Roman bricks, 307
Architectural forms, Roman
  influence, 320
  integrated diversity of, 1671, 1675, 1679–1681,
    1684–1685, 1687–1689
  legacy of, 1688–1689
  precursor of, 1671
  See also Construction materials and techniques
Architectural innovations, Roman
  integration of rectilinear and domed shaped,
    1680–1681

vaulting with concrete, 316–319, 1672–1674,
    1676, 1686–1687, 1689
  in windows and lighting, 1682 *illus.*, 1686, 1689
Architectural interior decoration. *See* Interior
    decoration, Roman; Rome; Tomb decoration
Architectural orders
  Aeolic, 1658
  Corinthian, 1653–1654, 1655, 1668, 1675, 1689
  Doric, 1653–1659, 1663, 1668–1669, 1689
  Ionic, 1653–1660, 1663–1665, 1667–1668, 1670,
    1689
  Roman Corinthian, 305, 310–311 *illus.*, 313, 317
  Roman Ionic, 317
  Roman usage of Greek, 1671, 1673–1676, 1679,
    1681, 1683, 1689
  Tuscan, 319
Architectural sculpture, Greek
  Acropolis applied, 1663–1664, 1753–1759
  Ionic, 1655, 1658, 1663–1665, 1670, 1719,
    1720 *illus.*
Architectural sculpture, Roman, 309, 313–314
  Arch of Constantine, 1684, 1744 *illus.*
  See also Ara Pacis Augustae (Altar of Augustan
    Peace)
Architecture, Byzantine, 1688–1689
  Hagia Sophia (Constantinople), 1689
Architecture, early Christian
  Basilica of St. Paul's Outside the Walls (Rome),
    301
Architecture, Etruscan
  construction of, 299, 301
Architecture, Greek
  archaic architectural sculpture, 1708
  See also Scale and proportion
Architecture, Hellenistic, 1667–1670
  coffered ceilings, 1776
  Roman imitation of coffered ceilings, 1776
Architecture, Roman
  Christian influence, 82
  construction durability of, 300, 302, 320
  styling details of, 309–310
  See also Scale and proportion
Archons, Athenian
  dates designated by names of, 392, 393
  origins of office, 8–9
  powers of, 9
Arch of Titus, 1156, 1738–1739, 1740 *illus.*
Areopagus, Athenian, 9
  eligibility for, 22, 24
  murder trials, 597
  myths of foundation, 867, 868

powers, 22, 28
reform in fifth century, 468
Ares
　origin, 850
Arete (excellence), 1012, 1308
　and cooperative ethic, 448
　in Homeric society, 443
　identified by Stoics as the only good, 1617–1618
Argolis, map 4
Argos, map 4
　agriculture of, 215
　chariot racing, 1139
　Dark Age settlements, 7
Argyrokastron, map 3
Aristarchus
　criticized by Stoic philosopher Cleanthes, 1630
　heliocentric hypothesis, 1629
　On the Sizes and Distances of the Sun and Moon, 1628
Aristeides of Miletos
　collection of novellas in *Milesian Tales,* 1126
Aristides, Aelius
　Sacred Teachings, 945
　on shrine of Asclepius at Pergamon, 945
Aristides Quintilianus
　deplores cultural degeneracy of age, 1513
　therapeutic value of music, 1513
Aristobulus
　Alexandrian Jewish philosopher, 1037
　Judaism a philosophical school, 1037
Aristobulus II, king of Judah, 1033
Aristocracy, Greek
　and *basileus,* 442
　overthrow at Corinth, 448
Aristonothos, 1750–1751
Aristophanes
　Assemblywomen, 1309
　Birds, 944
　comedy about jurors (*Wasps*), 600
　commentary on slave police, 583
　on demagoguery (*Knights*), 472
　derided avant-garde composers, 1509
　economic hardship in *Lysistrata,* 542
　Euripides as special target in *Frogs,* 1517
　Frogs, 1509
　invocation to Pallas Athena in *Equites* (*Knights*), 850
　on lower-class sympotic behavior in *Wasps,* 1181
　Lysistrata, 542, 1304, 1309, 1314
　pacifist rebellion in *Lysistrata,* 1187
　parody of Assembly proceedings (*Thesmophoriazusae*), 470

pattern in comedies, 1484
peltasts in *Acharnians,* 692
Philokleon on tongue kissing in *Wasps,* 1251
pokes fun at Athenian credulity, 944
portrayal of aristocratic wife in *Clouds,* 1285
revival of comedies, 1491
vinedresser in *Eirene* (*The Peace*), 217
vineyards in *Acharneis* (*Acharnians*), 217
Wealth, 1485
Women at the Thesmophoria, 583, 1509
Aristotle, 1607–1614
　accomplishments of, 1607
　adopting a trade, 535
　analysis of perception, 1613
　arguments for sphericity of earth, 1624
　avoids dualism between soul and body, 1613
　on balancing budgets, 641
　on the Boundless, 1588
　Categories, 1611
　on changes in Athenian constitution, 637
　on the city-state, 271
　class basis of government, 530
　compared and contrasted to Plato, 1608
　compares men's and women's lives, 1303, 1306–1308
　complaint about atomists, 1596
　comprehensive political history studies, 1609
　concept of active reason, 1608
　concept of catharsis, 1290
　Constitution of Athens, 455, 477, 480, 637, 1609
　on Cretan and Spartan social customs, 1177
　decay of Spartan system, 544
　defined moral excellence, 1611
　development of jurisprudence, 597
　difference between history and poetry, 1280
　disagreed with Plato's transcendent Forms, 1611
　discussion of predecessors, 1586
　doctrine of categories, 1610
　doctrine of substances, 1611
　duties of *astynomoi,* 637
　on early childhood, 1359–1360, 1361
　emphasized individual members of species, 1611
　epic an innately flawed genre, 1424
　exploitation of audience psychology by rhetoricians, 1280
　father of folklore studies, 1128
　hero's fall results from *hamartia* (error), 1518
　on Hippodamos, 1695–1696
　household vs. polis, 1303
　on human reproductive system, 1306
　immortality of the active reason, 1608, 1613

Aristotle (continued)
  importance of gifts, 975
  inclusion of philosophy in rhetoric, 1092
  on increasing revenues, 638–639
  interdependence of character and judgment, 1612
  inventor of formal logic, 1607
  katharsis, 1518
  levels of political organization, 462
  on liturgies, 801
  on man as political animal, 795
  man as a social creature, 1612
  medical applications in zoological tracts, 1233
  member of Plato's Academy, 1607
  Metaphysics, 1585–1586, 1611
  military service and political rights in early polis, 447
  mimesis, 1518
  mythos (plot) mechanisms, 1518
  Nicomachean Ethics, 1609
  notion of a supreme being, 1613–1614
  Oeconomica (*Financial Management*), 638–639, 724
  On the Heavens, 1624
  On the Parts of Animals, 1609
  On the Soul, 1613
  personality extremes in *Republic*, 1289
  on Pheidon of Argos, 488
  phratriai in politics, 464
  on physicians, 1232
  Physics, 1588
  Physiognomy, 1285
  Platonist who criticized Plato, 1608
  Poetics, 861, 1424, 1492, 1518–1519
  political theory, 440
  Politics, 444, 1510
  possibilities of progress, 271–272
  preeminence of group over individual, 1280
  on primitive human society, 270–271
  psychological bases of rhetoric, 1092
  on racial superiority, 1281
  recorded first calculation of earth's size, 1624
  rediscovery of, 1519
  rejected moral relativism, 1608
  rejected Plato's theory of forms, 271
  respect for his predecessors, 1609
  respect for ordinary opinions, 1609
  Rhetoric, 1091–1092
  selecting jurors, 600
  on social groupings, 1179
  society divided into rich and poor, 529
  Solonian reforms, 453
  soul and body are interdependent, 1613

  on Spartan system of government, 456, 461
  stasis in *Politics*, 478
  stress on technical excellence, 1424
  teleologist, 1608
  on Thales' principle of water, 1586
  theoria (contemplation) is man's highest excellence, 1612
  theory of causes (four questions), 1609–1610
  theory of the four humors, 1281
  theory of four simple bodies, 1610
  three kinds of speech, 1092
  translations into Latin, 1821, 1825
  unity of action in drama, 1518
  virtues of style, 1092
  on young men in symposia, 1171–1172
  zoological studies, 1608–1609
Aristotle, Lyceum of
  cult functions of, 1188
  organization of library, 1090
  Peripatetics, 1090
  political considerations, 1090–1091
  as research institute, 1090
  teaching of rhetoric, 1090
  theoretical model, 1090
Aristoxenus of Tarentum
  biographer of philosophers, 1537
  study of acoustics, 1625
  systematized modal scales, 1510
Arius
  theology of, 1068–1069
Arkadia, map 4
  confederacy of equals, 492
  demiourgoi (federal board), 492
Arkesilaos
  cult statue of Venus Genetrix, 1728
Arkteia
  female puberty ritual, 895
Armenia, map 5, map 9
Arms race
  among successors of Alexander the Great, 331
Army, Roman
  adaptability and military achievement, 704
  alae (wings of the army), 715
  annual enrollment, 705
  auxilia, 712, 713, 715
  Auxilium of Constantine, 718
  basis of imperial power, 71
  camp setup, 705
  cavalry, 705, 718
  Christianity in, 1068
  coinage issued by, 1807, 1810, 1812

comitatenses (mobile armies), 718
control of by Augustus, 66
creation of professional army, 705, 707–708
cunei (cavalry wedges), 715
development of independent provincial armies, 526
distribution of legions at accession of, 660
in early empire, 713
effect of expansion on military recruitment, 708
enlistment of barbarians, 716
establishment of permanent peacetime force, 713
Etruscan legacy, 703
financial support in third century, 717
hastati (first ranks), 705
influence on government, 514–515
land-military manpower nexus, 558
military tactics, 51
naval, 704
numeri (numbers of men), 715
organization and discipline, 705
origins, 703–704
overseas service, 705
political influence in late empire, 716
principes (second ranks), 705
punishment and rewards, 705
recruitment of barbarian mercenaries, 80
recruitment of *capita censi*, 709
reforms under Constantine, 80
reforms of Marius, 56–57
retirement bonuses for soldiers, 811
sacramentum (oath of loyalty), 705
service and social mobility, 569
under Severan emperors, 76
soldiers' diet, 242
triarii (third ranks), 705
velites, 705
veterans' resettlement and social unrest, 559, 561, 562–563
vexillationes (mobile field armies), 715, 717
wages of, 810, 812
in writings of Livy and Polybius, 704–705
See also particular emperors; Weapons, Roman
Arnobius of Sicca
critical of sacrifice, 985
Arno River
geology, 101, 104
Arretium (Arezzo)
pottery of and Roman trade routes, 763
Arrhephoria
annual festival of Athens, 894
Arrhichion, 1139

Arria
supreme example of marital devotion, 1326–1327
Arrianus, Flavius (Arrian)
account of Alexander the Great's expedition, 1534
admirer of Xenophon, 1534
critical spirit, 1534
on Indian races, 147
Arringatore (Orator). *See* Metellus, Aulus
Arrows catapult. *See* Catapults
Ars Amatoria (*Art of Love*). *See* Ovidius Naso, Publius (Ovid)
Arsinoë
census and list of occupations, 772
Art, Hellenistic
mosaic subject types, 1767 *illus.*, 1768 *illus.*, 1769
and *Trompe l'oeil* Roman painting, 1772, 1773, 1785
Artapanus
on Judaism, 1037
Artemidorus of Daldis
significance of dreams, 944
Artemis
cult statue of, 850
origin and associations, 850
relation with hunters, 123
Artemision, map 4
Striding God, 1711, 1712 *illus.*
Artemon
editor of Aristotle's letters, 1573
invention of engines, 695
Articulation (Roman wall). *See* Wall painting, Roman
Artist
personal pride in work, 386
See also Craftsmen
Artists, Greek. *See* specific artists' names; Painters; Potters; Mosaicists; Sculptors; Vase Painters
Art of Love (*Ars Amatoria*). *See* Ovidius Naso, Publius (Ovid)
Art of Poetry (*Ars Poetica*). *See* Horatius Flaccus, Quintus (Horace)
Arval Brethren
ritual records, 981
Asclepiades of Bithynia
Greek doctor practicing in Rome, 1236
Asclepius (Asklepios)
Blacas head, 1716
cult images, 1716
cult of, 1186
cures by, 902–903

Volume One: 1–720; Volume Two: 721–1298; Volume Three: 1299–1832

Asclepius (continued)
  Epidauria at Athens, 904
  introduction by Romans to Tiber, 857
  origin and associations, 852
  paeans honoring, 904
  votive offerings to, 903–904
Asclepius, sanctuaries of
  at Epidaurus, 902, 945, 1715
  miraculous cures at, 945
  at Pergamon, 945
  rites at, 902, 904
Asia, map 10
  depiction of people in art and literature, 146–147
  western, map 5
Asia Minor, map 3, 88 *illus.*
  architecture of, 1658, 1683 *illus.*, 1684
  becomes Roman province, 40
  coinage of, 1795, 1798
  Colchians, 146
  conquest by Rome, 54–55
  diverse Iron Age population, 146
  engineering in, 329, 339
  geography, 92
  geology of lakes, 107
  geology of plains, 101
  geology of rivers, 105
  highly developed bureaucracies, 641–642
  oracles of Apollo, 956
  Protogeometric pottery, 7
  wall paintings at Ephesus, 1772, 1773
  western, 88 *illus.*
Aspasia
  encouraged women's education, 1294
Aspasia type, 1711
Aspendos, map 5
Assemblywomen. See Aristophanes
Assimilationism, Jewish
  adoption of Greek lifestyle, 1030
  different factions of, 1032
  expressed in literary works, 1029–1030
  of the Jerusalem priesthood, 1029
  in local coinage and pottery, 1030
Assyria
  lost control of Egypt, 15
  use of road network, 353
  writing system of, 399
Astrological calculator
  Antikythera mechanism, 326, 347, 348 *illus.*,
    349 *illus.*
Astrology, 953

Astrology, Greek
  practiced by Ptolemy and Hipparchus, 1633
  science overlaps philosophy, 1633
Astronomical cycles, 389, 391
Astronomy, Greek, 1626–1633
  and ancient Near East, 1626
  Antikythera mechanism, 347, 348 *illus.*, 349 *illus.*
  aspects important to daily life, 1633
  and attempt to regulate the calendar, 1633
  construction of geometrical models, 1626
  reduced complexity of heavenly movements to
    simple motions, 1628
  theory kept alive by astrology, 1633
Astylos, 1140
Ataraxia (peace of mind)
  skeptics sought by suspending judgment, 1620
Atesis River, map 2
Athanadoros, 1728
Athanasius, bishop of Alexandria
  ejection by Arians and Melitians, 1069
  exile by Constantine II, 1069
  Life of St. Antony, 1067
Athena
  birth of, 867
  origin and associations, 850
  Parthenon built in her honor, 867
  patron of Athens, 867
  patron of Odysseus, 867–868
  power over the mind, 868
Athena, cult of
  administration, 636
  financial documents of, 639
Athenaeus
  on bread, 240
  Deipnosophistai (The Learned Banquet), 1167, 1511
  on social value of symposia and dinners, 1180
  on wine drinking in archaic Rome, 1201–1202
Athenaion Politeia (Constitution of Athens). See Aristotle
Athena Polias, festival of, 1397
Athenian law, 479–480
Athenians
  use of writing, 411–412
Athenion, 1725
  cameo by, 1724 *illus.*
Athens, map 4, map 8, map 9, 88 *illus.*
  agora, 1660–1661 *illus.*, 1668 *illus.*
  agoranomoi (market commissioners), 637–638
  agora waterwheel, 329–330
  Altar of the Twelve, 849
  alternative ideologies in, 484

appointment of public officials, 637
archaic constitution of, 8–9
architecture after Persian sack of, 1662
aristocratic oligarchy, 9
athletes in, 1140
attack by Dorians, 6–7
city plan of, 1660, 1662–1665
civic buildings, construction of, 285 *illus.*, 286, 289, 291, 292, 293, 296, 1668 *illus.*
civil war of 404 B.C., 478
in classical period, 466
Cleisthenic reforms, 467, 468
coinage of, 1796–1798, 1804
concept of equality in, 467–468
conflict in fourth century, 542
conquest of Boeotia, 23, 29
control of piracy by, 840–841
control of trade by naval power, 731
Council of 500, 470–471, 637
decision making in, 470–471
defeat of Persians, 24, 27
defeat by Philip II of Macedonia, 33
defeat at siege of Syracuse, 695
demagogues, 541, 637
demes and demarchs, 638
democratic ideology in fifth century, 475–476
democratic reforms, 23, 24
dioecetes (manager of finances), 641, 643, 644
division between military and political leadership, 474, 475, 482
dokimasia, 637
dramatic festivals, 1481
ecclesia (assembly), 637
effect of empire building on, 539
election by lot, 474
equality vs. merit in, 540
execution of decisions in, 474
expansion in Attica, 21
expansion of hoplite force, 690
Festival of Peace, 669
festivals in, 1145–1149
in fifth century, 468–470
financial administration, 483, 638–641
financial records, 639–640
fortification wall construction, 291
governing boards, 637–638
hegemonial league of, 674
hegemony in Aegean, 27
imperialism, 6
import of laborers, 538

informing the citizen body, 635–636
isonomia in, 467
knights and cavalry in sixth century, 690
laws protecting slaves, 581
loss of land empire, 29–30
magistrates responsible for festivals, 1148
as manufacturing center, 378
marriage laws and customs, 1337–1341
masonry styles of, 292, 293 *illus.*
metics (resident foreigners), 151, 543, 799, 800
military and naval administration, 636, 637, 640
military service, 598
monetary economy of, 741
navy, 25, 31, 698–699, 700, 840–841
oligarchic rule of, 540
open diplomacy of, 667
open social structure, 1179
ostracism, 468
Periclean architecture, 1662–1665
peristiarchus, 636
Persian sack of, 291
philosophy schools closed by Justinian, 43
political theory and, 540
private subordinated to public life, 1311–1312
public banquets and feasts, 1179–1181
public meetings, 475
public political discourse in, 469, 472, 473–474
Pylian refugees in, 6
pyramidal social structure, 530
record-keeping, 638, 641
regulation of trade, 636–637
reorganization of social structure, 539
revenue sources, 798–800
revision of laws in fourth century, 479–480
revision of Solon's code, 479–480
revolt against Alexander's successors, 38
revolts against, 27, 29–30
rhetor (orator), 482–483
role of private groups in administration, 638
Roman buildings in, 41
Roman students of philosophy at, 41
sack of, A.D. 267, 42
Scythian archers as police, 689, 798
Sicilian expedition, 29–30
slavery in, 746
social conflict, 538, 539
social mobility in classical period, 541
Social War (357–355 B.C.), 483
Solon, laws of, 479
Solon's census groups, 530, 531

Athens (continued)
 Solon's constitution, 22
 Solon's reforms, 538–539
 state control over cults, 636
 status divisions, 538, 541
 strategoi (board of ten generals), 467, 471, 474, 637
 symmoriai (tax groups), 800
 taxation in, 640, 797–803
 temple of Hephaestus, 850
 Thirty Tyrants oligarchy, 477, 479
 Thirty Years' peace with Sparta, 673
 Tower of the Winds, 109–110
 treason of aristocracy in fifth century, 469
 trierarch, 640
 unplanned city growth of, 1694–1695
 vase painting of, 1751–1755, 1759
 wages and social structure in, 541, 542
 war with Corinth and Aegina, 28
 war with Sparta, 28–29
 See also Ecclesia (assembly), Athenian; Law, Athenian; particular Athenian buildings
Athla (athletic festival), 1133
Athletic contests, Greek
 competitiveness in purest form, 1451
 honor in victory, 1451
 at Olympia, Delphi, Nemea, and Isthmia, 1450–1451
 pankration (boxing and wrestling combined), 1451
 simple wreath as prize, 1451
 type of competitions, 1451
 victory odes composed for, 1450–1452
Athletic contests, Roman
 and painting, 1773
 See also Games, Roman
Athletics, Greek, 1131–1141
 attitude toward, 1133
 events of, 1134–1139
 festivals, 1131–1134
 nakedness in, 1152
 origins of, 1131–1132
 prizes for, 1131, 1138, 1140–1141, 1144
 respect for athletes, 1141
 spectators at, 1134
 stadium architecture for, 1666
 typical events, 1153
 unpopular in Rome, 1153
 See also Festivals, Greek; names of specific games
Athlothetai, 1148
Atlantic Ocean, 88 *illus.*
Atomic theory, 1596

Atotas the Paphlagonian, 384, 386
Atrium
 Etruscan innovation, 1372
 impluvium (central basin), 1373
Attalos (Attalus) I, king of Pergamon
 victory monuments, 1718
Attalos (Attalus) III, king of Pergamon
 wills kingdom to Rome, 40, 56
Attic alphabet, 401
Attic pottery
 black-figure vase painting, 1752–1753 *illus.*
 Kleophrades Painter hydria, 1755 *illus.*
 red-figure vase painting, 1757–1761, 1758 *illus.*, 1759 *illus.*
 white-ground vase painting, 1760 *illus.*
Attike (Attica), map 4
 festivals in, 1149
 grain exports, 22
 sixth-century economic crisis, 22
Auditorium
 in Roman architecture, 1673
Augurs
 in charge of Sibylline Books, 911
 concerned with signs from the gods, 935
Augury, 941
 attempt to codify laws of, 944
 dextral and sinistral omens, 943
 divination by observing actions of birds, 953
 in Greek and Roman religion, 123–124
 two kinds of signs, 953
August
 month renamed in honor of Augustus, 917
 Roman festivals in, 917
Augustan Constitution
 consistency with *mos maiorum*, 521
 consularis potestas (consular power), 520
 elections, 522
 electoral canvass, 522
 imperium maius, 519, 520
 inclusion of equestrian order, 522, 521
 life tenure of Princeps, 519
 power sharing between Senate and Princeps, 521
 powers of Princeps, 520
 restructuring of legislative bodies, 521
 tribunicia potestas (tribunician power), 520
Augusta Raurica, map 1
Augusta Treverorum (Trier), map 1
 The Muses mosaic, 1788 *illus.*
Augustinus, Aurelius (St. Augustine)
 De Disciplinis (On Disciplines), 1820
 on early childhood, 1359, 1360

on mother's love for him in *Confessions,* 1289

native language, 196–197

six ages of mankind in *On Genesis against the Manichees,* 1289

Augustus, Caesar Octavianus

absolutism of, 67

achieves supreme power in Rome, 63

alliance with Mark Antony, 62, 63

appointment of procurators for Spanish mines, 788

architecture under, 1675–1676

assumption of provincial command, 519

authority of jurists under, 610

basis of his authority, 658

building program, 1211, 1212

census, 659

champion of ancient Roman traditions, 65

character, 65

clothing styles, 1409–1410

coinage under, 1807, 1809–1810

creation of Roman navy, 843

creation of Rome cohorts, 712

cuirass statue of from Prima Porta, 1734, 1735 *illus.*

development of civil service, 658

dictatorial *imperium,* 518, 519

dinner parties, 1212–1213

diplomatic skills of, 713

disparity between policy and life style, 1212

duplicity of sexual views, 1276

effort to raise the birthrate, 1276

encouraged traditional household crafts, 1401–1402

establishment of permanent peacetime force, 713

family disappointments, 67, 1214

financial reform, 659

Forum of Augustus, 1734

governmental reforms, 518–519, 524

heir of Julius Caesar, 62

imperial administration, 64, 65–66

imperium of, 712

imperium maius, 659

institution of *consilium principis* (Committee of Senate), 658

laws governing slavery, 582

legal authority, 65

legislation through Comitia Tributa, 610

legislation regulating sexual conduct, 1456

marriage and inheritance laws, 1352–1353

military reforms, 66, 712

monarchy cloaked in republicanism, 65

naval fleets, 712

patronage of architecture, 305

as patron of literature, 1457

Pax Romana, 669

peaceful coexistence with Parthians, 713

personal habits, 1210–1211

political skills, 64

popularity of cults, 1015

power delegated in Augustan Constitution, 520

praetorian guard, 658

problem of succession, 66–67

reforms of, 563–564

restoration of Republic, 658

restrictions upon manumission (*Lex Aelia Sentia*), 579

ruler-worship of, 858–859

in Second Triumvirate, 62

securing of communication routes, 713

securing of frontiers, 658

sumptuary laws of, 1211

taxation system, 659

transfer of power, 525

Via Labicana statue of, 1736

Aurelianus, Lucius Domitius (Aurelian)

administrative reforms, 716

defensive walls built by, 716–717

installation of Unconquered Sun as supreme god, 859

Aurelius, Marcus

cancellation of tribute payments, 821

commemorative column, 1741

fiscal difficulties, 822

frontier problems, 73

highly introspective writings, 1647

Meditations, 42, 73, 1647

persecution of Christians, 1055

restoration of filial succession, 660

Stoic views, 1647

value of the human spirit, 1647

vanity of human existence, 1647–1648

Aurelius Antoninus, Marcus (Caracalla), 76

architecture under, 1685 *illus.*

coinage of, 1813

grant of Latin status, 661

Autobiography, Roman

Caesar's *Commentaries,* 1558

Cicero's letters to Atticus, 1559

imperial (*Res Gestae* of Augustus), 1558

Auxerre, Goddess of, 1706 *illus.*

Avernus, Lake, map 2

Axios River, map 3

Volume One: 1–720; Volume Two: 721–1298; Volume Three: 1299–1832

B

Babyloniaka. See Iamblichus
Babylonia, map 5
Babylonians
  writing system of, 399
Babylon, map 8
Bacchae. See Euripides
Bacchylides
  compared to Pindar, 1452
  composer of *epinicia* for Greek games, 1450,
    1452
  manuscript of poems, 429
Bactria
  Alexandrian kingdom, 36
Baecula, map 1
Baetica, map 1, map 10
Baetis River, map 1, 88 *illus.*
Bagradas (Medjerda) River, map 6
  geology, 106
Baiae (Baia)
  architecture of, 1676
Bakchios, 386
Baker's Monument, 1731
Baktra-Zariaspa (Balkh), map 8
Baktrian Kingdom, map 9
Balearic Is., map 1
Balkan Peninsula, 88 *illus.*
  geography, 91
  geology of lakes, 106–107
Balkans, 88 *illus.*
Banking
  argentarii (dealers in silver), 829
  bank royal in Ptolemaic Egypt, 833
  deposits in temple banks, 832
  emergency loans, 831
  exchange of domestic coins, 829–830
  exchange of foreign currency, 829
  importance of in Greek and Roman economies,
    833
  importance of private bankers in commerce,
    831
  loans in classical literature, 830
  municipal bank of Temnos, 646
  private-party financing, 833–834
  public banks in Hellenistic era, 833
  resident aliens as private bankers, 829
  sources of information on, 829
  syndicates, 834
  temple banks, 831–832
  testing of coins, 830

trapezites (banker), 829
  types of deposits, 830
  value for merchants, 830
Barbarian invasions
  significance of, 83
  See also particular tribes
Barbarians
  Greek view of, 150, 204
Barbegal near Arles
  waterwheel, 329
Bar-Deisan (Bardesanes)
  freedom from fate in *Book of the Laws of the
    Country,* 1061–1062
Barges
  for river transport, 360, 363
Barke, map 7
Bar Kokhba (Simeon ben Kosiba)
  revolt against Rome, 1040
Barleycorns
  purificatory function, 970
  use in animal sacrifice, 966
Baroque architecture
  Roman precursors of, 1681–1683, 1687
  St. Peter's, 1689
Baroque art
  Greek precursor of, 1762, 1763 *illus.*
  Roman precursors of, 1775, 1777, 1781, 1782,
    1785
Basil, Saint
  letter as image of the soul, 1574
Basil of Caesarea
  trinitarian theology of, 1071
Basileus (kingship)
  archon for religious affairs, 906
  aristocracy and, 442
  in colonial cities, 450
  and *eunomia,* 450
  in Homeric poems, 532
  in Homeric society, 442
  megaron (hall) of as center of power, 442
Basilica
  early Christian churches, 1684, 1688
  of Julia, 1676
  of Maxentius (Basilica Nova), 1686–1687 *illus.*
  in Roman architecture, 1674, 1676–1677, 1679,
    1684, 1686 *illus.*–1687
Basilica, The Underground (Rome)
  wall decoration, 1778–1779
Basilica. See Leo VI, the Wise
Basilica of St. Paul's Outside the Walls (Rome),
  301, 315 *illus.*

Basilica Ulpia (Roman lawcourt)
  construction of, 304, 306 *illus.*, 309–310, 312–316
  interior design of, 316–317 *illus.*
  revenues from, 798
Bassai, map 4
  temple of Apollo, 1664–1665
Baths, Roman. *See* Thermal baths
Battering ram
  vs. tower cranes, 332
Bay of Naples. *See* Gulf of Cumae
Beam construction. *See* Roof construction systems
Bedroom, 1378
Belgae, map 1
Belgica, map 10
Belisarius
  defeat of Ostrogoths by, 176, 177, 179
Bellum Punicum. See Naevius, Gnaeus
Belts
  Greek, 1390, 1393, 1394
  Roman, 1407
Belvedere Torso, 1727
Benacus, Lake, map 2
Bendis
  cults of, 1186
Beneficia (imperial benefactions), 820–821
Beneventum (Benevento), map 2
  Arch of Trajan, 1740
Benignus, Quintus Candidus, 385
Ben Sira
  assimilationist ethos, 1034
  The Wisdom of Jesus ben Sira, 1034
Berezan, map 3, map 7
Berlin Painter, 1755, 1758
Beroia, map 3
Berytus, map 5
Bethel, map 5
Beth-Shean, map 5
Beth-Zur, map 5
Bible
  manuscripts of, 432–433
  See also Scripture
Biblion (book), 425
Bidding associations, Roman, 816–819
Biography
  defined, 1535
  as encomium (Isocrates and Xenophon), 1536, 1537
  fifth-century writers, 1535
  of literary figures, 1537
  as political publicity, 1537
  precursors of, 1535

Biography, Greek, 1554–1555
Biography, Roman
  Greek background, 1554
  tradition of funeral orations, 1555
Bion the Borysthenite
  use of *diatribe,* 1500
Birds
  domestication of in Mediterranean, 259
  in Greek and Roman diets, 258–259
  as omens, 123–125, 942, 943, 944, 953
Birds. See Aristophanes
Birth
  Amphidromia, key birth ritual, 893
  announced differently for girls and boys, 892–893
  celebrations for, 893
  Roman rituals of, 921
Birth control. *See* Contraception; Family planning
Bistones, map 3
Bithynia, map 5, map 9
  annexation by Rome, 41
Bithynia-Pontus, map 10
Bitter Lakes (Egypt)
  geology, 107
Black-figure vase painting. *See* Vase Painting; Attic pottery
Black Sea, map 3, map 7, map 8, map 10, 88 *illus.*
  economic importance to Greeks, 15
  fisheries, 14
  water budget, 104
Blacksmiths, 373 *illus.*
Blackwell, Thomas
  Enquiry into the Life and Writings of Homer, 1829
Blera, map 2
Blood in the Arteries. See Galen of Pergamon
Boats
  for river transport, 363–364
Boeotia (Boiotia), map 4
  oligarchic constitutions, 477
Boeotian League, 477
  development of, 491
  under Theban leadership, 492
Boethius, Anicius Manlius Severinus
  execution by Theodoric, 177
  preservation of Greek musical theory, 1513
  translations from Greek, 1821
Bona Dea
  Roman goddess worshipped by women, 1321
  Roman women's festival in December, 918
Bononia (Felsina), map 2
Book (codex), 430–434
Book of the Laws of the Country. See Bar-Deisan

Book production, 421–434
Book rolls, 423, 426–430, 431
    See also Writing
Borcovicium, map 1
Borysthenes River, map 3, 88 *illus.*
Boscoreale, map 2
    wall painting of, 1764, 1774–1776 *illus.*
Boscotrecase
    wall painting of, 1778 *illus.*
Bosphorus, Thracian, map 5
Bouphonia (ox-murder) ritual, 978
Boustrophedon style of writing, 412
Boxing, 1131, 1132, 1128–1139
Boys' rites, Greek, 893–894
Brassiere (*strophium*), 1404
Brauron, map 4
    cult of Artemis, 1338
Brauronia, 1146
    festival honoring Artemis, 895
Bread. *See* Grains and bread
Breakwaters, 364
Brea, map 3
Brickworks, 376
Bridges, Roman, 1672, 1677
    by Apollodorus of Damascus, 308, 309
    aqueduct type, 341–342 *illus.*
    construction of, 296, 355
Britain, map 1
    collapse of imperial power, 180
    conquest by Rome, 68, 69
    disappearance of British culture and language, 180
    Irish migration to Scotland, 181
    migration to Brittany, 180–181
    mosaic art of, 1783, 1784, 1787
    mosaic Orpheus pavement, 1790
    raiding by Scots and Picts, 180
    Roman coinage of, 1812–1813, 1815
    Roman expansion under Vespasian, 70
    Saxon invasions, 180
    wall and ceiling painting of, 1783, 1784, 1785
Britannia
    coinage personification of, 1812
Britons
    mixed Iron Age population, 144
    physical description, 143–144
Bronze, Roman
    architectural and hardware, 304–305
Bronze Age, Greek, 3
    architecture of, 277, 296

athletics in, 1131–1132
clothing production, 1392
destruction of Mycenaean culture, 679–680
dialects, 156, 163, 164
end of Mycenaean civilization, 6
government in, 796
Mycenaean culture, 531
Mycenaean government, 441
naval warfare, 697
public finance in, 796–797
slavery, 531
social structure, 531–532
taxation in, 796
writing systems, 10
    See also Mycenae
Bronze horse, Geometric style, 1705 *illus.*
Bronzeworking, 371, 372 *illus.*
Brothels
    established by Solon in Athens, 1293
    run for profit, 1294
    serviced by foreign-born, 1293
Bruttii, map 2
Brutus, Marcus Junius
    lending of money to Salamis, 817
Bryaxis, 1717
Brygos Painter, 1755
Bublos (papyrus), 425
Bucolic poetry
    cast of low characters, 1470–1472
    compared to epic, 1469–1470
    herdsman as protagonist of, 1470
    invented by Theocritus, 1467
    landscapes of, 1471–1472
    lesser Greek poets, 1467
    meter, 1468
    resemblance to Hellenistic mime, 1469–1470
    Roman, 1472–1474
    Vergil composed in Latin, 1467
    See also Vergilius Maro, Publius (Vergil)
Building hardware
    Roman bronze, 304
Building materials and construction, Etruscan
    tufa masonry, 1371
Building materials and techniques. *See* Construction materials and techniques
Building projects, Roman
    financing of, 823
Burgundians
    in Sabaudia, 174–175
    settlement in Roman Empire, 174

Burial, Greek, 993
    improper, 987
    See also Funerals
Burial, Roman
    development of tradition of, 1001
    elaborate sarcophagi, 1001, 1102, 1743
    See also Funerals
Burning
    to consecrate sacrificial animal, 968
    ritual purposes, 969
Byzantine art
    Roman mosaic precursors of, 1792–1793
Byzantium (Byzantion, Istanbul), map 3, map 5,
        map 7, map 11, 88 *illus.*
    architecture of, 1688–1689
    Church of the Holy Wisdom (Hagia Sophia),
        1689
    imperial dress, 1411
    new capital built by Constantine, 1068
    silk trade in, 1402
    transfer of Roman capital to, 663

C

Caere (Cerveteri), map 2
    Etruscan tomb interiors, 1372
    Etruscan underground tomb forms, 1371
    Tomb of the Painted Stuccoes, 1373
Caesar, Gaius Julius
    against collegia, 1210
    ambitions of, 61
    appointment to governorship of Gaul, 711
    architecture under, 1675–1676
    assassination, 563
    Civil War, 1558
    coinage commemoration of, 1807, 1809
    created new literary genre, 1558
    crossing of Rubicon, 562
    deification of, 62, 1014, 1736
    dictatorship of, 62
    encounter with pirates, 842–843
    established *Acta Senatus* (minutes of the Senate),
        1551
    first triumvirate with Pompey and Crassus, 60
    Gallic War, 1558
    governmental reforms, 518
    land bill of, 561
    legislation and reforms, 657

    military abilities, 60
    military strategies, 712
    murder of, 62
    racial prejudice in *Gallic War,* 152
    reform of calendar, 61, 392
    reforms of, 563–564
    rise to political prominence, 59, 60
    seizes control of Italy and Rome, 61
    settlement of veterans, 562–563
    struggle with Pompey, 562
    used *commentarii* as effective propaganda, 1558
Caesarea (Kayseri), map 5
    famine in fourth century, 762
Caesarea Maritima, map 5
Caesarea Philippi, map 5
Calabria, map 2
Calchas
    famous augur in *Iliad,* 942
Calchedon. *See* Kalchedon
Calculator, analog mechanical
    Antikythera mechanism, 326, 347, 348 *illus.*,
        349 *illus.*
Caledonia, map 1
Calendar, Roman
    compiled by priests, 912
    source of knowledge about religious rituals, 983
    standard markings, 912
    three fixed points in month, 912
Calendar cycles
    and miniature engineering, 348 *illus.*, 349 *illus.*
Calendars, 389–395
    festival or religious, 1145
    Gregorian, 394
    Julian, 392, 393–394
Caligula. *See* Gaius Julius Caesar Germanicus
Calligraphy, 426
Callimachus of Cyrene
    criticized Antimachus, 1424
    effect on Roman literature, 1497
Callimachus (sculptor). *See* Kallimachos
Callippus, 391
Callistus
    excommunication of Hippolytus, 1058
Camargue Delta
    ecology, 104
    geology, 107
Camarina. *See* Kamarina
Camels, 356
Cameos
    Blacas Cameo, 1737

Cameos (continued)
Britannic Triumph Cameo,1737 *illus.*
Gemma Augustea, 1737
Grand Camée de France, 1737
Triumph of Licinius, 1747 *illus.*
"Vienna cameo," 1724 *illus.*, 1725
Camillus, Marcus Furius, 50, 51
Camillus, P. Longidienus
grave stele, 370 *illus.*
Campania, map 2
Camulodunum, map 1
Candelabrum
motif in Roman wall painting, 1777, 1780, 1783
Cantabria, map 1
Canuleian Law
plebeian-patrician intermarriage, 651
Canvas, 374
Capestrano, map 2
Capitoline Brutus, 1729
Capitoline temple
first in Rome, 1672 *illus.*
Cappadocia. *See* Kappadokia
Capstan, 326
Caracalla. *See* Aurelius Antoninus, Marcus
(Caracalla)
Carchemish, map 5
Cardia. *See* Kardia
Cargo
of sailing ships, 360–361
Carinus, Marcus Aurelius
celebratory games with music, 1512
Carmen Saeculare. See Horatius Flaccus, Quintus
(Horace)
Carpathus. *See* Karpathos
Carpenters, Greek
roof woodwork of, 286
Carpentry, 369–370
Roman construction techniques, 313, 315–316,
319
Carpentry, ship
automated model of, 351–352 *illus.*
Carpet mosaics of Africa. *See* Africa;
Mosaic art, Roman
Carrhae, map 5
Carriages
Carpentum, 356
carruca dormitoria (sleeping wagon), 356
Carthage, map 6, 88 *illus.*
capture of by Vandals, 175
defeat in 480 B.C., 1662
loss of empire to Rome, 54

naval power, 53
Roman invasion of, 53
wars with Rome, 52–54
Carthaginians
dress of, 1407
Carthaginian War, First (264–241 B.C.)
causes of, 52
Sicily brought into Roman orbit, 40
war of attrition, 53
Carthaginian War, Second (218–201 B.C.)
early Roman defeats, 54
and social changes, 554
Carthago Nova, map 1
Carts and wagons
cisium (open cart), 356
four-wheeled, 355, 356
Greek, 280–281
two-wheeled, 355, 356
Carystus. *See* Karystos
Casina. See Plautus
Caspian Sea, map 8, map 10
Cassandra
dangers of female independence, 1315
Cassandra peninsula
excavated mine workings (stopes), 782
Cassiodorus, Flavius Magnus Aurelius
popularizer of classical knowledge, 1821
Castella (water tanks), 342
Castrimoenium, map 2
Catana. *See* Katane
Catapults, Greek, 333–338, 335 *illus.*, 336 *illus.*,
337 *illus.*
crossbow (*gastraphetes*), 333, 334 *illus.*
literary documentation, 333
Categories. See Aristotle
Catharsis. *See* Katharsis
Cato, Marcus Porcius (Cato the Elder)
accuracy of information in *De Agricultura* (*On
Agriculture*), 219–220
began tradition of political autobiography, 1544,
1557
contribution to Roman medicine, 1236
on decline of Republic, 512
discrediting of Scipio Africanus, 708
equipment and labor lists for animal husbandry,
234–235
expulsion of Flamininus from the Senate, 1203
on extramarital affairs in "On the Dowry," 1269
magic charms, 884
Origines (*Origins*), 1544
partisan support of plebeians, 1544

purposes in writing his history, 1544
relied on Greek sources, 1544
sexual attitudes of, 1273
Cato Uticensis, Marcus Porcius (Cato the Younger)
remarriage to ex-wife, 1350
Catullus, Gaius Valerius
contradiction between desire and dislike,
1457–1458
demands reader's imaginative sympathy, 1458
epigrammatic style and influence, 1497
intensely personal tone, 1457
invectives against sexual misbehavior, 1274–1275
invented love elegy, 1457
literary achievements, 64
love as affliction, 1458
marriage hymns, 1322
outstanding lyric poet of antiquity, 1462
technique of indirection, 1458
themes of poetry, 1457–1458
Caudine Forks, map 2
battle of, 51
Cebenna Mountains, map 1
Ceilings, Greek
Hellenistic, 1776
marble, 288, 1659, 1663–1664
Ceilings, Roman
compluvium (skylight), 1372, 1373
Celer
Roman architect (Nero's Golden House), 308
Cella
in Greek architecture, 280 *illus.*, 285
in Greek temples, 1653
Celsus, Aulus Cornelius
medical practices of, 1237
on Roman medical practices in *On Medicine*,
1237
Celts
cranial morphology, 143
depiction in classical art, 143
early migration, 142–143
physical description, 143, 152
Roman descriptions of, 1407
Censor, 48, 502, 523
Censorship, Roman
under Augustus, 1457
imperial suppression of critical writings,
1559–1560
Lex maiestatis, 1559
nonexistent during Roman Republic, 1559
trial of Aulus Cremutius Cordus, 1559
writers prosecuted under Tiberius, 1559

Census, Roman, 811–812, 813–814
Census classifications, Roman
centuriae, 557
Census relief, 1731–1732 *illus.*
Centenillo, map 1
Centumcellae, map 2
Centuria (land unit), 815
Centuriate
role of *populus* in, 505–506
Centuriate assembly
conferring *imperium* on consuls, 499
establishment, 499
group vote in, 499
loss of power under Augustan Constitution, 521
timocratic nature of, 499, 500
Centuriation, 815
Roman city land allocation system, 1697
Centuripae. *See* Kenturipe
Ceos. *See* Keos
Cerberus, hound of death, 989
Cerealia
Roman Festival of Ceres, 914
Certum aes (tribute), 822
Cerveteri. *See* Caere
Chaireas and Kallirhoe. See Chariton
Chaironeia, map 4, map 8
battle of, 33
Chalcis ad Belum, map 5
Chaleion, map 4
Chalkidike, map 3, map 7
Greek colonies, 14
league of cities of, 492
Chalkis, map 4, map 7
becomes Athenian dependency, 23
colonies of, 12, map 7
war with Eretria, 12–13
Chaos (void), 864
Characters. See Theophrastus
Charioteers, 1157
Chariot races
Greek, 1131, 1133, 1139
Roman, 1155–1157
Chariton, 1566
Chaireas and Kallirhoe, 1567–1568
Charon, boatman of underworld, 989
Chartes (charta; book rolls), 423
Chastity
impudicitia (lack of chastity), 1328–1329
Roman ideal, 1326
Chattel-slavery. *See* Slavery
Cheiron. See Pherecrates

Cherchel
  wall mosaic showing grape cultivation, 228
Chersonese, Tauric, map 3
Chersonese, Thracian, map 3
Chigi Vase, 1751–1752 *illus.*
Child
  afterlife of in Greek literature, 993
  early developmental stages of, 1359–1360
  importance of nurturing treatment, 1359–1360
  protective deities, 1361
  special characteristics of, 1359
Child abuse, 1362
Childbirth
  mortality rates, 1357
  role of midwife, 1358
  Soranus on, 1357–1358
  use of birthing chair, 1358
Child care
  decreased parental involvement, 1361
  effects of reliance on outsiders, 1361–1362
  father's role in, 1359
Chion of Heraklea. *See* "Khion of Herakleia"
Chios, map 4, map 5
  law of, 454–455
Chiton
  Alexandrian style, 1398
  in archaic period, 1395
  in classical period, 1396
  Etruscan styles, 1399
  Homeric references, 1392, 1393
  Ionic, 1391 *illus.*, 1394
  man's, 1390
  woman's, 1390, 1391 *illus.*, 1394
Chlamys, 1390, 1391, 1398
Choes, 893, 1146
Choral lyric, Greek, 1447–1450
  in Athenian drama, 1452
Chorus
  disappearance in Roman theater, 1488
  functions of, 1477–1478
  members, 1481
  peripheral nature in fourth century, 1486
Christian church
  basilica churches, 1684, 1688
  church of Antioch, 1048
  church in Jerusalem, 1047–1048
  congregations, 1052–1053
  early architecture, 1684, 1688–1689
  early codices, 432–434
  early organizational history, 1052–1053
  ecclesiae (assemblies), 1048

persecution of, 77, 79, 1023
prostasis (president of congregation), 1052
readmission of lapsed Christians, 1060
rejection of civic religions, 1003
resident officers, 1052
Roman garb as liturgical vestments, 1404–1405,
  1410, 1411
at Rome, 1058–1059, 1060
in Syria, Mesopotamia, and Persia, 1060–1062
Christian epistolary tradition
  didactic function, 1577
  distinctive features, 1577
  Saint Basil, 1578
  Saint Jerome, 1578
Christianity
  African, 1059–1061
  anchorite, 1067
  apologetic literature, 1056
  Apostles' Council, 1048
  Apostles' Creed, 1054
  asceticism, 1061, 1067
  baptism, 1048
  Book of Revelation, 1053
  charismata (religious gifts), 1052
  Christian schools, 1053
  under Constantine, 1067–1068
  conversion of Ostrogoths to, 176
  conversion of Vandals to, 175
  conversion of Visigoths to, 172
  Diocletian's edicts against, 1064
  diversity of movements in second century, 1058
  Donatist controversy, 1066
  early messianism of, 1048
  early missions, 1048, 1052
  Enkratite (abstaining) group, 1061
  eschatological proclamations, 1053
  first literature, 1048
  Great Persecution, 1062–1065
  growth in third century, 1062–1063
  integration in Roman society, 1063
  Marcionites, 1053–1054
  under Marcus Aurelius, 1055
  martyrdoms by Jews, 1054–1055
  Modalism, 1058
  monarchical episcopate, 1052–1053
  monasticism, 1066–1067
  Montanism, 1053
  New Testament, 1049, 1054
  Novatianists, 1060
  Old Testament, 1053, 1054
  and paganism in Roman Empire, 937

Pauline corpus, 1053
persecution in early empire, 1054–1056
persecution in Eastern Empire, 1065
persecutions under Valerian, 1055–1056
as philosphy, 1056–1058
prophets and teachers, 1053
Quartodeciman controversy, 1058
reconciliation of Hellenic tradition with, 1056–1057
in Roman associations, 1054
Roman church, 1058–1059
and Roman coinage, 1816
social services of, 1067
Syrian, 1049, 1061, 1067
Trinitarian controversy, 1068–1072
Christianity, Arian
Antiochian Creed, 1069
Constantinopolitan Creed, 1071
Fourth Sirmium Council, 1070
Nicene Creed, 1069, 1071
opposition to Athanasius, 1069
precepts of, 1068–1069
radical under Constantius II, 1069–1070
rejection of by Constantine I, 1069
Christianity, Jewish
Elkasaites, 1049
emphasis on words of Jesus, 1049–1050
Gospel According to the Hebrews, 1051
Greek-speaking, 1049
Judaizers, 1049
movement to Pella, 1049
use of Aramaic, 1049
Christian wall painting and mosaic art. See Early Christian art
Chrysippus
developed Stoic logic, 1618
invented propositional logic, 1618
Chrysoloras, Manuel
Greek scholar in Italy, 1826
Chylemath River, map 6
Chytroi, 1146
Cicero, Marcus Tullius
Academica, 1642
addresses College of Priests, 910–911
on advantages of broad general education, 1119
agriculture the most worthy occupation, 564
aim to combine philosophy with rhetoric, 1641
attempt to revive sophistic tradition, 1119
on ballot law, 555
categories of letters defined, 1578
child as symbol of innocence, 1362

concordia ordinum, 657
on Cornelia (mother of the Gracchi), 1323
corpus of philosophical writings, 1641
on craftsmen, 368
critiques of democracy, 549
defined genre of moral historiography, 1545
De Legibus (On Laws), 1642
De Natura Deorum (On the Nature of the Gods), 1643
De Officiis (On Duty), 1643
De Oratore (On the Orator), 1641
De Republica (On the Republic), 1642
difficulties of dowry payments, 1348–1349
on dinner parties, 1205–1206, 1207
discredits woman in court, 1328
disdain for Epicureanism, 1642–1643
on divination, 942
"Dream of Scipio," 1000
epic poems of, 1428
ethics as main interest, 1641
execution by Octavian, 62
first Western philosophical essayist, 1643–1644
Gracchan reforms and class division, 556
great historical theorist, 1544–1545
Herodotus the father of history, 1525
on the ideal state, 1641, 1642
imitation of in Renaissance, 1827
influence of wife Terentia on, 1320–1321
Letters to Atticus, 1324
letters cover history of late Roman Republic, 1578
letters of recommendation (epistulae commendaticiae), 1579
literary achievements, 64
literary education for the orator, 1520
name of slave, 579
Paradoxa Stoicorum (Paradoxes of the Stoics), 1642
philosophical beliefs, 1640–1644
political role, 59
Pro Caelio (In Defense of Caelius), 1328
rationality as aspect of divinity, 1642
reconciles Stoic and Peripatetic ethics, 1643
Servilia's influence, 1324
on skepticism, 1642
on Stoic philosophy, 1643
student in Athens, 1640–1641
on tax revenues, 809
on technical tradition of rhetorical training, 1118
three types of rhetorical style, 1115
translates and adapts Greek philosophy, 1641
Tusculan Disputations, 1643
two types of divination, 952

Cicero (continued)
  on upper-class luxuries, 1208
  on vineyards, 227
  wealth of, 63
  worship of politically advantageous god, 857
Cicero, Quintus Tullius
  on electioneering, 1209–1210
Ciceronianism, 1827
Cilicia, map 5
  pirates of, 842
Cimmerian Bosphorus, kingdom of, map 9
  foundations of state, 489–490
  grain export from, 732
Cimon of Athens. *See* Kimon (Cimon) of Athens
Cimon of Syracuse. *See* Kimon (Cimon) of Syracuse
Circus, Roman, 1155–1157
  factions, 1156–1157
  in Roman floor mosaics, 1790
Circus Flaminius, 1156
Circus Maximus, 1155–1156
  euripus, 1156
Cistern, Pelasgic
  near Mesolongi, 295 *illus.*
Citium. *See* Kition
Citizenship, Greek
  in Athens, 469, 480, 481–482, 1337
  under confederacies, 675
  equality of citizenship rights, 674–675
  and ethnic prejudice, 151
  loss of in Spartan law, 593
  for membership in ruling elite, 545
  participation in the polis, 1691
  reforms of Kleisthenes, 464–465
  regulation of civil disputes with foreigners, 673
  rights of citizens, 1251–1252
  sexual behavior and, 1259
  in Sparta, 456
Citizenship, Roman
  civitas sine suffragio (citizenship without vote), 652
  of conquered populations, 670
  edict of Caracalla, 76
  and ethnic prejudice, 151
  extended to all inhabitants of Empire, 611
  for Latins and other Italians, 57, 58, 556, 558, 656, 661
  privileges and responsibilities, 566, 811
City, Greek
  laying out of, 1692–1693
  modular components of, 1692–1693
  terraced city, 1669 *illus.*, 1695
  typical facilities, 1691, 1693–1695

  typical Hellenistic buildings, 294
  See also City plans
City, Roman
  laying out of, 1696–1698
  marking the boundary, 1697
  modular components of, 1697–1698
  typical facilities, 1698–1700
  See also City plans
City planners, Greek, 1692–1693, 1695–1696
City planners, Roman, 1697
City plans
  of Augustan colonies, 1676
  axial orientation plans, 1697–1698
  controlled hierarchy of vistas, 1699
  of Greek colonies, 1660
  on Greek mainland, 1660–1665, 1668–1669, 1691–1696
  Hellenistic, 1693–1694, 1695, 1669 *illus.*
  ideal urban life and zoning, 1696
  integrated plan and landscape, 1669 *illus.*, 1695
  Ionian developments in, 1665–1667
  military encampment, 1698–1699 *illus.*
  orthogonal (gridlike) plan, 1692–1693, 1695
  Pergamum, 1669 *illus.*, 1670
  Priene, 1665, 1666 *illus.*
  Roman, 1696–1700
City-states, Greek
  decline of under ruler worship, 1018
  diplomacy of, 667–669
  taxation in, 797–803
  treaties and agreements, 672–675, 676
Civic buildings
  Greek, 1644–1670
  See also specific building types
Civil engineering, Greek
  corbeled arch, 295 *illus.*, 296
Civil service, Byzantine
  education of, 1822
Civil wars, Roman, 558–562
  Caesar and Pompey, 60–61
  and coinage, 1812
  after death of Caesar, 712
  after death of Commodus, 75
  after death of Nero, 70
  Marius and Sulla, 57–59, 711
Civil War. See Caesar, Gaius Julius
Claros. *See* Klaros
Classical Period (Golden Age)
  funeral paintings, 1761–1762, 1763 *illus.*, 1764
  monumental painting, 1755–1757, 1769
  vase painting, 1757–1761

Class structures, Greek, 529–546
  under Alexander the Great, 543, 544–545
  apetairoi, 537, 538
  in archaic period, 533–539
  aristocracy under Roman rule, 546
  class divisions, 529, 531, 536, 543, 544, 546
  in classical period, 539–544
  development of luxury crafts, 534
  discrimination against noncitizens, 545
  and elective financial offices, 545
  ethnicity in status determination, 544
  Greek inheritance law, 535
  in Hellenistic period, 544–546
  influence of Spartan revolution on, 546
  kinship in archaic period, 535
  land ownership, 530, 535, 544
  membership in status groups, 529
  nonnoble rich, 534
  "shipboard mobility," 535, 542
  social mobility, 531, 532, 533, 541, 543
  social terminology, 530
  status divisions, 537, 538
Class structures, Roman, 549–573
  under Augustan Principate, 563–564, 570–571
  during civil wars, 558–562
  cohesion of upper orders, 557–558
  curial class, 565–566
  definition of social categories, 550
  equestrian order, 565
  expansion and growth of wealth, 554–555
  Imperial social order, 564–569, 571
  patrician-plebeian division, 551
  racial mixture of, 579
  in the Republic, 550–558
  senatorial class, 564–565, 570
  separation of Orders, 566
  slaves, 568–569
  social mobility, 569
  sumptuary legislation, 554
  working class, free, 566–568
  See also Equestrian Order; Patrician Order;
    Plebeian Order
Claudianus, Claudius (Claudian)
  De Raptu Proserpinae (*Rape of Proserpine*),
    1434
  hexameter satires, 1503
  historical epicist, 1434
  panegyrist, 1434
  tableaux rather than narrative, 1434
Claudius (Tiberius Claudius Nero Germanicus)
  cameo of Britannic triumph, 1737 *illus.*, 1748

character and achievements, 68
conquest of Britain, 713
extension of Roman citizenship, 661
extravagant behavior of, 1216
financial and civil service reforms, 661
granting of citizenship, 661
legislation through Council of Plebs, 610
military reforms, 713–714
Clay pottery, 373–374
Clay tablets, 422
Clazomenae. *See* Klazomenai
Cledomancy, 946
Cleisthenes. *See* Kleisthenes
Cleitias
  Francois vase, 694
Clement of Alexandria
  reconciliation of Hellenic tradition and
    Christianity, 1056–1057
Cleomedes
  hero-worship of, 853
Cleomenes. *See* Kleomenes
Cleon
  ambitions, 475
  and Athenian polis, 469
Cleopatra VII, queen of Egypt, 36–37
  and Caesar, 61
  coinage portraiture of, 1802, 1809
  death, 41
  and Mark Antony, 63
Cleromancy
  divination by lots (*kleros*), 945
  in *Iliad*, 945
  omen in a chance saying, 946
  at oracle of Hermes at Pharae, 948
Cleruchic land, 804
Climate, Mediterranean
  effect on culture, 112–113
  historic changes in, 111–112
  influence of topography, 111
  Mediterranean climatic zone, 108
  "Mediterranean Light," 112
  Piora Oscillation, 111
  precipitation, 109
  seasons, 109
  temperatures, 109
  winds and weather, 109–111
  Würm Glaciation, 111
Cloak
  Greek, 1393, 1397
  Roman, 1402, 1405
Clocks, 395

Clodius Pulcher, Publius
  blasphemy of, 953
  murder, 562
  political use of collegia, 1210
  populist tribune, 561–562
  sacrilege at Bona Dea festival, 918
Clothing
  archaeological evidence, 1385
  artistic evidence, 1386
  of barbarians, 1395–1396
  change from ancient to modern forms, 1386
  children's, 1397, 1405, 1409
  as gifts, 1385, 1392–1393
  of gods and goddesses, 1396
  literary evidence, 1385, 1386
  making of, 374
  as political statement, 1411
Clothing, Etruscan, 1399–1400
  accessories, 1400
  archaic period, 1385
  classical period, 1385
  Greek influences, 1399
  Hellenistic period, 1385
  influence on Roman styles, 1406
  Orientalizing period, 1385, 1399
  tebenna, 1399
  woman's, 1399
Clothing, Greek, 1386–1391
  accessories for, 1390–1391, 1398
  archaic period, 1385, 1390, 1394–1396
  artistic evidence, 1390, 1394
  basic items of, 1389–1392
  ceremonial costumes, 1397
  classical period, 1385, 1390–1391, 1396–
    1398
  differentiated by age and occupation, 1397
  Eastern influences, 1391–1392, 1398–1399
  fashion changes, 1390, 1395
  fitting of, 1389
  Geometric period, 1394
  Hellenistic period, 1385, 1391, 1398–1399
  Homeric dress, 1392–1394
  materials and fabrics, 1386–1387
  metal ornaments, 1394
  Orientalizing period, 1385, 1390, 1394–1396
  priests' robes, 1397
  Scythian styles, 1396
  Severe style, 1396
  theatrical costumes, 1397
  undergarments, 1393
  wide variety of, 1397–1398
  woman's, 1393, 1398
  woman's veil, 1393–1394, 1394–1395
Clothing, Roman, 1401–1412
  artistic evidence, 1405
  Byzantine period, 1410–1411
  colors, 1402
  conservatism of religious dress, 1405
  differences from Greek dress, 1401
  early Roman period, 1385
  Etruscan influences, 1399, 1406
  fashion changes, 1405
  forms of, 1403–1405
  imperial family garb, 1410 illus.
  Iron Age styles, 1406
  later Empire, 1385, 1410
  legislative restrictions on, 1408–1409, 1411
  materials and fabrics, 1401
  metal ornaments, 1403
  military, 1402, 1405, 1406, 1407
  priests', 1402, 1406, 1409–1410
  reflected social class, 1401
  religious, 1408
  Republican, 1385, 1405, 1407–1408
  soldier's dress, 1404
  symbolic nature of decoration, 1401, 1402–1403
  theatrical clothing, 1405
  trabea, 1406
  triumph of barbarian styles, 1412
  tunic, 1402, 1403–1404
  undergarments, 1403, 1404
  woman's, 1404, 1409
  woman's veil, 1405
Clouds. See Aristophanes
Clusium, map 2
Clytemnestra, 1303, 1313
  destructive actions, 1315
Cnidus. See Knidos
Cnossus. See Knossos
Codex, 430–433
  Christian, 432–434
  papyrus, 434
Codex Sinaiticus, 429, 433
Codex Theodosianus, 611
Coele-Syria, map 5
Coffers (architectural)
  imitation of in art, 1776, 1785
  in Roman architecture, 1673 illus.
  temple of Artemis at Ephesus, 304
Cogwheel, 337, 338 illus.
Coin
  definition of, 1795

Coinage, Carthaginian, 1802
Coinage, Celtic, 1799
Coinage, Etruscan, 1801
Coinage, Greek
  archaic, 533, 1795–1796
  artistry, 734
  in Athenian monetary economy, 741
  banks, 741
  bronze, 741
  as bullion, 739
  classical period, 1796–1801
  coin issue and availability of precious metals, 741
  credit practices, 740–742
  as first worldwide, 1801
  Hellenistic period, 1801–1806
  international status of, 741
  invention of, 797
  issuing of for state-related payments, 734
  large denominations of, 739
  mints, 635
  monetary foundations in Hellenistic period, 741
  moneylending, 741
  as political symbol, 734
  sculptural references on, 1801–1802
  in Spartan society, 537
  spread of Greek styles, 733–734
  for trade purposes, 739–740
  for troop payment, 729
  use of silver in, 97
Coinage, Roman, 1801, 1806–1816
  debasement under Severans, 77
  devaluation of, 824
  Diocletian's reforms, 663
  growth of trade and money supply, 759
  high quality under Nero, 70
  for military and trade purposes, 758
  during Second Triumvirate, 1807–1809
  solidus issued by Constantine, 80
  value of money, 758–759
  See also specific periods and rulers names
Coinage, Roman imperial
  Augustan innovations in, 1807–1810
  Caracallan changes in, 1813
  commemorative purpose, 1810
  dynastic succession themes, 1809–1810
  facing bust portraiture, 1815
  See also specific names of rulers
Coinage artists
  of signed coins, 1799
Coinage innovations
  bimetallic coinage, 1795

  double-sided coins, 1796
  facing bust portraiture, 1815
  first Christian design, 1816
  first Roman Military issue, 1807
  imperial commemoration, 1809
  military issue, 1810, 1812
  moneyer magistrate issue, 1806–1807
  portraits of the living, 1807
Coin denomination types, Greek, 1785–1806
  Athenian owls, 1796, 1804
  Corinthian colts, 1796, 1798
  Damarateion, 1799
  electrum, 1795
  range of, 1796–1797
  use of under Romans, 1804–1805
  See also specific period or city names
Coin denomination types, Roman, 1806–1816
  aes signatum and as (bronze bricks and coins), 1806
  antoninianus, 1813
  Augustan imperial system of, 1809
  aurei (gold issue), 1809
  denarius, 1806
  follis, 1815
  introduction of mint marks, 1813
  sestertius with imperial portrait, 1810
  silver cistophoric coinage, 1804
  solidus, 1815
  tremissis, 1815
  victoriate, 1806
College of Pontiffs
  legal interpretations of, 609–610
Colleges of priests, Roman. See Priesthood, Roman: Quattuor amplissima collegia
Collegia (voluntary associations)
  of apparitores, 1220
  Arval Brethren, 1219
  augustales, 1220
  Augustan restrictions on, 1220, 1221
  Bacchic mystery cults, 1204
  burial concerns, 1223
  conviviality of, 1223
  of Diana and Antinous, 1221, 1223
  early Christian, 1222
  in early empire, 1219–1224
  electioneering, 1209–1210
  government restrictions on, 1204
  imperial restrictions on, 1224
  laws against, 1204, 1210
  lower class, 1222
  of poets, 1219–1220

Collegia (continued)
  priestly, 1219
  promiscuity associated with, 1223–1224
  regional variations in, 1221–1222
  relations with government, 1222
  riots at Pompeii, 1221
  in Roman Republic, 1204
  social status of members, 1223
  unofficial, 1221
  vici, 1210
  wall portraits of the sages in Ostian wine bar, 1224
  of young men, 1220–1221
Colonies, Greek, map 7
  colonization distinguished from migration, 6
  in Cyrenaica, 16
  duties of the *oikist* (leader), 1692
  Italian attacks, 39
  in Italy and Sicily, 11
  north of Danube, 14–15
  in northern Aegean, 13–14
  Roman military control of, 52
  in southern Italy, 13
  spurred by land scarcity, 11–12
  transformed Greek world, 16–17
  and urban planning, 1691–1692, 1696
Colonies, Roman
  architectural developments in, 1683 *illus.*, 1684, 1687, 1688 *illus.*, 1689
  policy of Gaius Gracchus, 557
  urban planning, 1696–1698
  See also Provinces, Roman
Colonnades
  color in Greek architecture, 283, 1655–1665
  color in Roman architecture, 300, 1676–1677, 1679–1680, 1684, 1686, 1689
  in Greek architecture, 1657–1659, 1663–1665, 1667–1668, 1670
  in Greek interiors, 285–286 *illus.*
  incompatibility with true arch, 297
  in Roman architecture, 1676–1677, 1682, 1684, 1687, 1689
  Roman construction of, 313–314 *illus.*, 316, 317
Colonus. *See* Kolonos
Colophon. *See* Kolophon
Color
  in Greek architecture, 283
  the palette of marbles, 301
  in Roman architecture, 300
Colossae. *See* Kolossai
Colosseum. *See* Amphitheatrum Flavium
  (Colosseum)

Colts (Corinthian coins), 1796, 1798
Columella, Lucius Junius
  breaking in of plow oxen, 235–236
  causes of environmental deterioration, 126
  decline of agriculture, 220
  on kitchen garden, 232
  on plowing, 221
  six grafting techniques, 233–234
  on soil exhaustion, 219
  trench measuring device, 229
  on vinedresser's knife, 228
Column, Greek
  construction of, 281–283, 289–290, 291 *illus.*, 294, 324, 325
Column, Roman
  construction of, 301, 307, 309, 310, 311, 313
Columnar orders, classical. *See* Architectural orders
Comedy, Greek
  agon (contest), 1484
  aspects of Athenian condition in, 1484–1485
  changes after Peloponnesian War, 1485
  contemporary nature of, 1484
  focus from state to family, 1485
  Lenaea festival devoted to, 1484
  nature worship, 1483
  New Comedy, 1485–1487
  plot material, 1483–1484
  realism in fourth century, 1486
  situation, 1485
  sterotyped characters, 1485
  structure of, 1484
  See also Aristophanes
Comedy, Roman
  authors' lack of control over, 1488
  influence on later genres, 1492
  lack of political commentary in, 1487
Comitia Centuriata, 650, 653
  army recruitment, 703
  establishment and structure, 48–49
  military significance, 49
Comitia Curiata
  moribund by end of monarchy, 48
Comitia Tributa
  establishment of, 651
Commemorative arch
  in Roman architecture, 1677, 1684
Commemorative column, Roman, 1679
  to Antoninus Pius, 1745
  to Marcus Aurelius, 1741
  to Trajan, 309, 1741, 1743
  See also Trajan, column of

Commentarius (memoir)
  of Cicero, 1557
  of Julius Caesar, 1557–1558
Commerce
  social stigma attached to, 564, 565
Commodus (Marcus Aurelius Commodus
  Antoninus)
  bust of as Hercules, 1745 *illus.,* 1746
  cruel and tyrannical spendthrift, 75
Common Peace Treaties (*koine eirene*), 674
Communication. *See* Language; Writing
Communications
  via courier, 353–354
Competition. *See* Athletics
Comum, map 2
Concilium plebis (Council of the Plebs)
  abandonment of under Principate, 523
  absorption into official government, 501, 502
  policy of compromise, 501
  private legislation enacted by, 609, 610
  voting methods, 501
Concordia, shrine to
  as reinforcer of Augustan policies, 1211
Concrete
  brick-faced, 303, 304
  hydraulic, 363, 364
  reticulate-faced, 302 *illus.,* 303
  in Roman construction, 297
  wall and vault construction with, 317, 318, 319
Concubinage, 1353
Condatomagus (La Graufesenque), map 1
  pottery and Roman trade routes, 763
Conductores (tribute leaseholders), 820
Confederacy (*sympoliteia*), 675
Confessions. See Augustinus, Aurelius (St. Augustine)
Conscription, military, 49, 56
  of rural poor, 558
Consecration, Greek modes of, 967–969
Conspiracy of Catiline. See Sallust (Gaius Sallustius
  Crispus)
Constantinople. *See* Byzantium (Byzantion, Istanbul)
Constantinus, Flavius Claudius (Constantine III)
  repelled Vandal invasion, 175, 180
Constantinus, Flavius Valerius (Constantine I)
  acceptance of Christianity, 1067–1068
  agent of reform and stability, 80
  ambiguity of personal life, 1068
  Arch of, 1683–1684, 1744 *illus.*
  architecture under, 1683–1684, 1687, 1790
  cessation of emperor worship under, 1018
  changes in senatorial power, 663

coinage of, 1815, 1816
  conversion to Christianity, 79
  divorce laws, 614
  Donatist controversy, 1066
  economic policies, 80
  edict of toleration, 1065
  frontier fortifications, 718
  military reforms, 718
  monarchy under, 527
  organization of imperial court under, 663
  priority of Eastern over Western Empire, 80
  rejection of Arianism at Nicene Council, 1069
  Second Rome (Constantinople), 1068
  transfer of capital to Byzantium, 663
  worship of Unconquered Sun, 859
Constantius, Flavius Julius (Constantius II)
  radical Arianism of, 1069–1070
Constitution of Athens, 540, 541
  criticism of democratic reforms in, 540
  leadership in, 541
  wages for public service, 542
  See also Aristotle
Constitution of Crete, 591
Construction industry, Roman, 306–308, 320
  supply and inventory management, 307–308
Construction materials and techniques, Greek,
  1655–1656, 1658
  Archaic period, 286–289
  ashlar masonry, 287, 1671, 1675, 1677–1678,
    1680
  classical period, 289–294
  column drums joinery, 281–283, 289–290,
    291 *illus.,* 294
  economies of quantity, 294–295
  Egyptian similarities to, 287–288
  Hellenistic development, 294–297
  innovations in, 287–288
  limestone, 1663
  marble, 283, 288, 1659, 1663–1664
  masonry hoisting, 282–283, 287–288, 289 *illus.,*
    294, 327 *illus.*
  monumental masonry, 281 *illus.,* 282–283
  mud-brick walls, 277–278
  relationship to transportation, 280–281
  roof woodwork and terra-cotta tiling, 283,
    284 *illus.,* 285 *illus.,* 286 *illus.,* 287
  transport, 356
  vernacular, 277–278, 279 *illus.,* 282, 291
Construction materials and techniques, Roman
  for aqueducts, 340–343, 341 *illus.,* 342 *illus.*
  architectural terra-cottas, 303–304 *illus.*

Construction materials and techniques (continued)
ashlar masonry, 1671, 1675, 1677–1678, 1680
brickwork, 307, 1677–1678, 1680, 1685, 1687, 1689
bronze, 304–305, 317
concrete work, 297, 301–302 *illus.*, 303, 304, 312, 317, 318, 319, 340, 1671–1673, 1676–1678, 1680–1681, 1685–1687, 1689
Iron Age, 299
local tufa and travertine stone, 300
marble and granite, 300–301, 307, 309, 313–314, 319–320, 1675
marble masonry, 1675, 1678–1679
mud-brick, 299
pise (aggregate masonry), 1672
prefabrication, 1679
public and private buildings, 320
reticulate masonry, 1676, 1678
stone dressing, 312
stonewood, 1657–1658, 1663
stucco, 300, 313–314, 319–320
transport, 360
wattle-and-daub, 299
wood, 303–304
See also Masonry construction; specific places and building names
Consuls, Roman
authority, 508
imperium given, 499
plebeian consul required, 500
reliance on senatorial backing, 510–511
status under Principate, 523
transfer of power to centuriate, 508
Contraception
methods of prostitutes, 1295
and sexual practices, 1276–1277
techniques, 1356
Contract, law of
acceptilatio (act of extinction), 622
actio de dolo (action for fraud), 621
actio negotiorum gestorum, 625
arra (earnest money), 623
buyer's obligations, 624
commodatum, 622
condictio, 622, 625
consensual, 623–625
dotis dictio, 622
errors in, 623
guarantees, 624
innominate contracts, 625
iusiurandum liberti, 622
literal, 622

loans, 622
locatio conductio (hire), 624
mandatum (mandate), 625
metus (extortion), 621
price, 623
real, 622–623
rights of conquered populations, 670
seller's obligations, 624
senatus consultum macedonianum, 622
societas (partnership), 624–625
stipulatio, 621–622
verbal, 621–622
Conubium (marriage right), 670
Convivia (dinner parties)
adoption of Etruscan customs, 1201
cenae rectae (large-scale formal dinners), 1214–1215
courses of, 1205
customs, 1201
differences from Greek, 1199–1200
drinking parties in love poetry, 1213–1214
in early empire, 1212–1214, 1214–1219
emperor's informal, 1215
entertainments, 1209, 1219
etiquette and conversation, 1207
in Etruscan art, 1201
food served, 1206
formal, of Augustus, 1212–1213
gladiatorial banquets, 1161
Greek writers on, 217–1218
Hellenization of, 1202–1204
invitations to, 1206–1207
repudiation of Hellenistic practices by later emperors, 1216
sexual and romantic activity, 1208–1209
social and political functions, 1200, 1205, 1217
sportula (food or money handouts), 1214
status distinctions at, 1205–1206, 1213, 1215, 1217–1218
sumptuary laws, 1215
triclinia, 1208, 1216
wine drinking, 1201–1202, 1209
Copais, Lake. *See* Kopais, Lake
Copts
symbols, 434
wore classical Roman clothing, 1410
Copying
of biblical manuscripts, 433
of scrolls, 428–429
Coracesium (Alanya)
slave market near, 842
Coracles (*quffa*), 363–364

Corax
  originator of formal rhetoric, 1081, 1085
Corcyra (Corfu, Kerkyra), map 3, map 7
  oligarchic coup at, 543
  temple of Artemis, 1658, 1708
Corinth, map 4, map 7, map 8
  attack on Megara, 28
  bronzes from, 1733
  coinage of, 1796, 1798
  colonies of, map 7
  craftsmen of, 378
  kings of, 18
  oligarchic rule, 18–19
  razed by Romans, 40
  vase painting of, 1751–1753, 1752 illus.
Corinth, Gulf of, map 4
Corinth, Isthmus of, map 4
  slipway, 634
Cornwall, map 1
Coronea. See Koroneia
Corruption
  in Roman tribute system, 818–819
Corsica, map 2
Corvée, 825
Cosa, map 2
Cosmogonies, Greek, 863
Cos. See Kos (Cos)
Cotton, 374
  in Roman clothing, 1401
Courier system
  Persian, 353–354
Coursed masonry. See Masonry construction;
  Wall construction
Craft associations
  collegia, 384–385
Crafts, 367–387
  Greek influence on, 369
  Roman influence on, 369
  techniques used in, 368–369
  titles for, 381
  workshops for, 375–378
Craftsmanship
  pride in, 386–387
  specialization of, 380–381
Craftsmen, 367–387
  apprenticeship to, 375, 376
  competitiveness of, 386
  dedication to deities by, 383–384, 384 illus.
  and the economy, 378–383
  family connections among, 375–376
  individual achievement by, 386–387
  knowledge required of, 377

migration of, 382
military, 379, 385
professional solidarity among, 384–385
social role of, 385–386
and society, 383–386
superstitions of, 377–378
training of, 375–378
versatility of, 377
wages of, 382, 1771
wall painting scenes of, 1781
Craftsmen, Greek
  bards characterized by Homer as, 1515
  Corinthian painters in Athens, 1752
  social status of, 743
Craftsmen, Roman
  in construction trades, 307–308
  as an effective work force, 320
Cranes
  siege engines against, 326, 332–333
  technological development of, 324, 325, 326 illus.
Crannon. See Krannon
Crassus, Marcus Licinius
  death at Carrhae, 60
  in First Triumvirate, 59, 60
  military victories, 59
Cremation
  in Greek history, 993
  Roman tradition of, 1001
Cremutius Cordus, Aulus
  reported by Tacitus, 1559–1560
  rhetorical civil war history, 1547
  tried for treason on basis of histories, 1559
Crete, map 4, map 8, map 10
  agnatic succession in, 537
  athletes of, 1135
  collective training, 1177
  Dorian militaristic society of, 21
  Greek dialects, 157–158, 159
  male deity, 847
  male rites of passage, 1178
  pirates from, 839
  social organizations in archaic period, 1177–1179
  social structure, 537
  as source of Greek law, 450
  supremacy of great goddess in second
    millennium, 847
Crimea
  Thracian settlements, 14–15
Criminal fiction
  elements in, 1569–1570
Criminal law, Roman. See Delict, law of
Crisa. See Krisa

Crocus Fields, map 4
Croesus, king of Lydia
  bi-metallic coinage of, 1795
Cronos
  castrates his father, 864
  son of Earth and Sky, 864
Cronos, Age of. *See* Golden Age
Cross, ansate, 434
Crossbow (*gastraphetes*), 333, 334 *illus.*
Croton. *See* Kroton (Croton)
Ctesibius. *See* Ktesibios
Cuicul (Djemila), map 6
  Dionysiac mosaic pavement, 1787–1788
Cults, Greek
  civic, 896–900
  of the family, 891–896
  of heroes, 994–995, 1010
  life and death, 900–907
  objects of worship, 1014
  sacred areas, 887–888
  types of ritual, 889–891
Cults, Roman, 1003
  calendar, 912–913
  festivals, 913–920
  forms of, 910
  military calendar, 920–921
  priests, 910–912
  private, 921–923
  recorded on coins, 1810, 1812
Culture, Greek
  admiration for in modern Europe, 1828–1829
  archaic period, 1707
  classical period, 1717
  Dark Age, 1704
  fourth century, 1714
  Geometric period, 1704
  Hellenistic effort to spread, 1819
  influence on Judaism, 1031, 1034–1038, 1044
  Roman period, 1711
  Rome as preserver and transmitter, 45
Culture, Roman
  Augustan Golden Age, 66
  brutality, 1163
  Greek influences, 55, 64
  impact of political absolutism, 69
  in later Empire, 74
  in later Republic, 63–64
  Silver Age, 69–70
Cult worship
  propriety between divine and human orders, 1021
  propriety between men, 1021

Cumae (Cuma). *See* Kyme
Cunaxa. *See* Kunaxa
Cuneiform, 399
Cupids motif
  in Roman painting and mosaics, 1781, 1782, 1783, 1786, 1789, 1790, 1791, 1793
Curial Order, 565–566
  as councillors (*decuriones*), 565–566
  relationship with government, 565
  requirement of, 565
  three aristocratic qualities of, 565
Curse
  hostile prayer, 963
Curule aediles
  legal responsibilities, 609
Customs duties, 799, 810
Cybele (Magna Mater)
  black baetyl (sacred stone), 855, 857, 858
  cult of, 938, 1270
  Megalensia, 1270
Cyclades (Kyklades), 1702, map 4
  island gems, 1722, 1723
  marble ceiling architecture of, 1659, 1663–1664
  Protogeometric style, 8
Cyclus. See Agathius Scholasticus of Myrina
Cyprian, bishop of Carthage
  literary work, 1060
  martyrdom, 1060–1061
  readmission of lapsed Christians, 1060
Cyprus, map 5, map 8, map 10
  survival of Mycenaean culture, 8, 10
  writing system of, 401
Cypselus. *See* Kypselos
Cyrenaica, map 6, map 10
Cyrene. *See* Kyrene
Cyrus II, king of Persia
  relations with Jews, 1028
Cythera. *See* Kythera
Cyzicus. *See* Kyzikos

D

Dacia
  loss of, 77
  Trajan's conquest of, 72, 308, 309, 314 *illus.*, 714
Dacians
  Trajan's Forum sculptures of, 309, 314 *illus.*
Dacier, Anne
  translation of Homer, 1829

Daedalus, 368 *illus.*, 1705
　　as craftsman, 367
Daldis, map 4, map 5
Damasus, Pope
　　latinization of Roman liturgy, 187
Damon
　　conservative views on music, 1509–1510
Dance, Greek
　　Corybantes (maenads), 1508
　　Cretan acrobatic dancing, 1508
　　dithyramb, 1507
　　geranos, 1508
　　male province, 1508
　　ritual, 1146, 1152
Dance, Roman, 1512
　　pantomimi (solo dancing), 1512
Daniel, Book of, 1035
Dan, map 5
Dante Alighieri
　　wide classical knowledge, 1825
Danube River
　　geology, 106
Daphnis and Chloe. See Longus
Dardania, map 3
Darius II, king of Persia
　　coinage of, 1796
Darius III, king of Persia
　　defeat by Alexander, 34–35
Dark Age, Greek, 3–7
　　city government, 8
　　eleventh-century recovery, 7
Dating
　　difficulties of, 392–394
Datos, map 4
Dauni, map 2
Days of the month
　　naming of, 390, 392
Dead
　　barrier between worlds of dead and living,
　　　987
　　closed society of, 989
　　cult of, 994–995
　　festivals of, 1146–1147
　　king and queen of, 990–991
　　not allowed within walls of Rome, 998
　　offerings to, 998
　　passage of to another world, 995
　　possible communication with, 995
　　potential to harm the living, 998
　　Roman festivals for, 997
　　separation of from society, 995

Dead Sea
　　geology, 107
Dead Sea Scrolls, 421, 424, 431
Dead Sea Sect
　　characteristics, 1036
　　Damascus Covenant, 1036
　　identity of (Essenes?), 1035
　　pesharim (commentaries), 1036
　　Rule of the Community, 1036
　　Temple Scroll, 1036
　　War Scroll, 1036
De Agricultura. See Cato, Marcus Porcius (Cato the
　　Elder)
De Architectura. See Vitruvius Pollio
Death
　　in archaic period, 991
　　incomplete, 988
　　judgment and punishment after, 990
　　Lucretius on fear of, 1640
　　Roman rituals of, 921–922, 923
　　Thanatos, agent of, 991
De Bello Civili. See Lucanus, Marcus Annaeus
　　(Lucan)
Debt, Greek
　　and social conflict, 535, 538, 541, 546
Debt, Roman
　　Caesar's reforms, 562
　　laws governing, 553
　　manus iniectio, 552
　　nexum, 552–553, 615
　　for peasant farmers, 552, 567
　　security for, 619
Debt bondage
　　in Near East, 553
　　in Roman Republic, 552–553
　　in Solonian Athens, 553
December
　　Roman festivals in, 918
Decemviri
　　early Roman legal codes, 608
Decius (Publius Decius Mus)
　　persecution of Christians, 1055–1060
　　self-sacrifice in battle, 910
Declamations
　　controversia, 1115–1116
　　as entertainment in imperial period, 1115
　　examples of, 1116
　　influence on Roman literature in Silver Age, 1118
　　opportunities for success in, 1118
　　suasoria, 1116
　　types of, 1115–1116

Decuriones (town councillors), 820
Decursio, 1745
Dedications to deities
    by craftsmen, 383–384, 384 *illus.*
Defense of Palamedes. See Gorgias
Deianira, 1303
    virtuous wife misled, 1309
Deification
    of imperial family members, 1017
    of living Romans, 1010, 1022
    of Roman emperor, 1015
Deinokrates of Rhodes
    Greek city planner, 1695
Deipnosophistai. See Athenaeus
Delian League
    dominance by Athens, 492
    tribute to Athens, 798–799, 800, 803
Delict, law of
    actio de pauperie, 627
    assessments, 626
    damnum iniuria datum (wrongful damage to
        property), 626
    furtum (theft), 625
    involuntary delict, 627
    limited liability, 627
    os fractum (broken bone), 626
    personal injury, 626
    rapina (robbery with violence), 626
Delion, map 4
Delium
    battle of, 690
    Boeotian siege of, 331
Delos, map 4
    banking activities at Shrine of Apollo, 832
    as free port, 841
    harbor at, 362
    Hill House, 1369 *illus.*
    House of the Diadumenos, 1369 *illus.*
    House of the Inopus, 1369 *illus.*
    House of the Masks mosaic, 1767 *illus.,* 1769
    House of the Sacred Lake, 1369 *illus.*
    House of the Trident, 1369 *illus.*
    Ionian festivals, 17
    Roman free port, 41
    sacking of, 842
    as slave market, 839
Delphi
    amphictyony of, 491, 668, 1144
    Athenian treasury, 1708
    athletic and music festivals, 17
    Charioteer, 1704

decline of oracle, 956
    fifth temple of Apollo, 1704
    Naxian sphinx, 1708
    omphalos, 946
    oracle of Apollo, 868
    Pythia (prophetess), 946
    Roman contacts with oracle, 955–956
    Sikyonian treasury, 1708
    Siphnian treasury, 1709 *illus.*
Delphic oracle
    ambiguity of, 947
    most influential Apolline oracle, 948
    power of, 947
Delphinion
    in Athenian homicide trials, 597
Deltos (wooden tablet), 430
Dema Wall, 693
Deme festivals, 1149
Demes
    organization of by Kleisthenes of Athens,
        463–464
Demeter
    and Eleusinian Mysteries, 867
    festivals in honor of, 1145, 1146
    festival of the Skira, 849
    origin and associations, 849
    separation from Persephone, 867
    worshiped in Eleusinian Mysteries, 849, 906–907
    See also Thesmophoria
Demeter and Persephone myth
    basis for Eleusinian Mysteries, 1316
    Homeric *Hymn to Demeter,* 1316
Demetrios (Demetrius) I, king of Macedonia
    attack on Rhodes, 332
    presentation of Parthenon as palace to, 853
    siege of Rome, 839
    symposium of, 1190
Demetrios (Demetrius) of Phaleron
    Aristotle's pupil, 1090
    classified types of letters, 1573–1574
    compilation of Aesopic fables, 1123
    founder of Alexandria's Museum, 1091
    Greek epistolographer, 1574
    manual on letter writing, 1573
    On Style, 1573, 1574
    Typoi Epistolikoi (*Forms of the Letter*), 1573
Demetrius, Jewish chronographer, 1037
Democracy (*demokratia*)
    absolute equality vs. need for leadership,
        475–476
    Athenian ideology, 469, 475–476, 478–484

and Greek painting subjects, 1754–1755
  shift in political values, 478–479
  supremacy of law in, 479
  transition to written rules, 479
Democritus
  elaborated atomic theory, 1596
  mind derives data from senses, 1596
Demodocus
  bard of *Odyssey*, 1419
  style of composition, 1419
Demos (people)
  and citizenship, 465
  cults of, 1013
  isonomia and, 465
Demosthenes
  campaign against Philip, 1095–1096
  deliberative rhetoric as educational tool, 1095
  lawcourt speeches, 594
  laws on assault, 597
  on naval finances, 640
  Olynthiacs, 1095
  On the Crown, 1095
  On the False Legation, 427
  Philippics, 1095
  speeches of, 428
  text of maritime loan, 740
  use of language in speeches, 1095
  on wives, concubines, and prostitutes, 1312
De Rerum Natura. See Lucretius (Titus Lucretius Carus)
Description of Greece. See Pausanias
Desiderius, Abbot of Monte Cassino
  copying of ancient manuscripts, 1823–1824
Deus ex machina
  crane-assisted Greek theatrical effect, 326
Dexamenos of Chios, 1723
  scaraboid, 1724 *illus.*
Diagoras, 1138–1139
Dialectic
  in Plato's thought, 1604
Dialects, Greek
  bilingualism, 164
  "class" dialect in Mycenaean states, 164
  development of classical dialects, 163–164
  effect of Dorian migration on, 163
  fifth through third century dialect groups, 156
  groups in Bronze Age, 163
  Linear B texts, 157–158, 163, 164
  Mycenaean Greek, 156, 164
  spread of Indo-European, 157
Dialogue with Trypho. See Justin Martyr

Diaulos, 1134
Dicaearchus
  decline of mankind, 272
Dictation, 429
Dictator
  powers of, 48
Dictatorship, Roman
  of Caesar, 518
  first dictator, 502
  imperium, 502, 518, 519–520
  under Octavian, 518–522
  of Sulla, 516–517
  tenure of office, 502
Didactic poetry
  moral admonition and practical instruction, 1422
Didyma, map 4, map 5
Diet and food production
  birds, 258–259
  bread in Greek diet, 240
  cereal grains, 247–249
  famine food substitutes, 242–243
  fish and seafood, 259–260
  food grain preferences, 241
  food shortages, 242–243
  free food distribution, 248–249
  fruit, 242, 252–254
  herbs and condiments, 252
  honey, 260
  legumes (pulses), 249
  meat, 242, 257–258
  nutritional value of cereal diet, 236
  nuts, 251–252
  spoilage, 242
  three parts of Roman dinner, 247
  use of condiments, 236–237
  vegetables and salad plants, 242, 250–251
  wild animal species, 258
  See also Fruit-growing; Vegetables and salad plants; Wine production
Digentia River, map 2
Dikaiarchia, map 7
Dinaric Alps
  geology, 108
Dining couches
  arrangement in *andron*, 1365
Dinner parties, Roman. *See* Convivia
Dio Cassius
  on Equestrian Order, 565
  History of Rome, 1535
  history sacrificed to narrative momentum, 1535

Dio Chrysostom
  on Ephesian money in temple of Artemus,
    832–833
Diocles, Gaius Apuleius, 1157
Diocles of Carystos
  drugs and surgical techniques, 1233
Diocletianus, Gaius Aurelius Valerius (Diocletian)
  abdication, 79
  concept of theocracy, 526
  economic and military reforms, 1063
  edict against Christians, 1063–1064
  Edict on Prices, 79, 382, 770, 1771
  financial reforms, 662–663
  military dynast, 78
  military reforms of, 717–718
  palace near Salonae, 1687–1688 illus.
  price controls, 770, 1411–1412
  reform of provincial administration, 662
  reorganization of provincial government, 78–79
  restores imperial stability and power, 78
  tax reorganizations, 79
  tetrarchy, 78, 526, 662, 717, 1063
  textile prices, 765
Diodorus Siculus
  on Athenian colonial city planning, 1693
  on conditions in Spanish mines, 757–758
  early stages of human development, 270
  Library of History, 1534
  on mining reef gold in Egypt, 783
  Pentekontaetia (Fifty Years) 1534
  Stoic doctrine of the brotherhood of man, 1534
  on tin mining, 784
  on underground water hazard in Spanish mines,
    785
  working conditions of Nubian miners, 788
Diogenes Laertius
  Aristippos on anecdotes, 1124
Diognetos
  military engineer of Rhodes, 332
Dion, map 3
Dionysia
  City, 1147, 1148
  Rural, 1145, 1149
Dionysiaca. See Nonnus of Panopolis
Dionysiac cults
  women stereotyped as irrational, 1305
Dionysiac figures
  in Roman painting and mosaic, 1764, 1755, 1778,
    1781, 1783, 1787
Dionysios (Dionysius) (Skytobrachion) of Alexandria
  The Argonauts, 1566

Phrygian Composition, 1567
  rapid-firing catapult inventor, 338
Dionysius, bishop of Alexandria
  Modalist dispute, 1063
Dionysius (Dionysios) of Halicarnassus
  Antiquitates Romanae (Roman Antiquities), 1533
  elements of dramatic plot, 1564
  on Isocrates' contribution to education, 1088
  letter as medium for literary criticism, 1577
  noted rhetorician, 1574
  promotion of Atticism, 1105
  rhetorical history, 1533–1534
  rhetoric as literary criticism, 1105
Dionysius (Dionysios) I, tyrant of Syracuse, 39, 489
  fortress of Euryalus, 696
  military dictatorship of Syracuse, 695
  siege of Motya, 696
  war against Carthage, 728–729
Dionysos (Dionysus)
  in Aristophanes' Frogs, 869
  associated with Orpheus, 901
  associations, 850–851
  birth of, 851, 869
  in Euripides' The Bacchants, 869
  festival of at Athens, 1254
  god of wine and theater, 901
  important topic of later Greek epicists, 1433
  major festivals, 901
  marriage to Ariadne, 851
  mythical conquest of India, 1433
  oracles cured sickness, 948
  orgiastic rites, 869
  origin of, 851
  patron god of drama, 1481
  protection after death, 901
  rites of, 1187
  spread of mystery cults in Rome, 1204
  technitai (artists) of, 1194
  worshippers of, 901
Diorthotes (corrector), 427
Dioscorides
  book on plants, 252
  pharmacology in Materia Medica, 1236
Dioscurides of Samos, 1774–1775 illus.
Diplomacy
  ad hoc nature of Greek and Roman, 667
  advisory office in Roman empire, 667
  diplomatic representatives. See Envoys; Fetiales;
    Heralds; Proxenia
  diplomatic service, 672, 675
  Greek concepts of particularism, 668

open and secret, 667–668
Roman, 669–672, 675–678
unspecialized vocabularies for, 667
Diplomatic immunity, 672, 676
Dipylon krater (detail), 1750–1751 *illus.*
Discus throwing, 1137
Disiecta membra, 421
Divination
artificial, 952–953
Cicero's contempt for, 1643
Etruscan, 951–952
Greek, 941–946
importance of good omens, 971
natural–dreams and prophecy, 952
Divinities
attitude of worshippers to same god under
different titles, 857
Celtic adoption of Roman gods, 856
cult titles, 856–857, 857
deification of abstract principles, 855
exclusiveness of Jewish gods, 858
Greek pantheon, 849–850
of Minoan Crete, 847–848
Numina, 853–854
personifications, 852
powers of nature, 851
river-gods, 851
Roman expansion and growth of pantheon,
854–855
sacred marriage of sky and earth, 848
spread of Egyptian cults in Hellenistic period,
858
triad of Roman deities, 854
of the underworld, 851
use of Roman divine names for local deities,
856
See also Religion, Greek; Religion, Roman
Divorce
in case of rape, 1339
double standard for husbands, 1340
in Gortyn, 1337
Hellenistic law, 1342
Julian law formalized, 1352
by verbal declaration, 1352
Divorce, Roman. *See* Marriage laws, Roman
Dodona
oracle of Zeus, 942
Dokimeion, map 5
Dolaucothi, map 1
Doliche, map 5
Dolichos, 1135

Dome
construction of, 319
in Roman architecture, 1676, 1680, 1682 *illus.,*
1688–1689
Domitianus, Titus Flavius (Domitian)
administrative achievements, 71
architectural patronage of, 308
architecture under, 1679–1680
assassination of, 308
commissioned Arch of Titus, 1738–1739
palace of, 1680
public banquets of, 1214–1215
relations with Senate, 661
tyranny, 71
war with Dacia, 714
Domus (home)
woman's domain, 1322
Domus Aurea. *See* Nero
Donatus
conversion of Africans to Christianity, 1066
Donkeys, 355
Doors
miniature automatic, 350, 351 *illus.*
Roman bronze, 305
Dorians
in Crete and Rhodes, 169
invasion of Greece, 4–5
invasion of Peloponnese, 159–162
migration of, 168
origins, 4–5, 161
overseas migrations, 168
pastoralists, 4–5
phylai, 5
"return of the *Herakleidai,*" 160–161
Doris, map 4, map 5
Douris, 1755
Dowry
in Athens, 1338
compulsory for *epikleros thessa,* 1340
Greek, 1333, 1334
in Hellenistic world, 1341–1342
in invalid marriages, 1347–1349
payment, 1348
sources of information about, 1348
See also Epikleros
Drakon
Athenian laws published, 22, 595
code of law, 452
homicide law, 464, 479
Drama, Greek, 413–414
Artists of Dionysus, 1486–1487

Drama, Greek (continued)
  attendance, 1482
  audience, 1482
  author's responsibilities in fifth century, 1482
  battle between sexes a common theme, 1314
  Charition, 1566
  competitions in, 1148
  competitive performances of, 1517
  copying of texts, 1491
  crowd-pleasing devices, 1482–1483
  dancing and movement, 1478
  dramatists and the works of others, 1517
  financing of, 1481
  as forum for political discourse, 473–474
  functions of chorus, 1477–1478
  influence of Homeric poems, 1477
  instrumentation, 1478
  introduction of actors, 1477, 1478
  The Jealous Mistress, 1566
  literary influence of, 1491
  masks, 1482, 1485
  monodramas, 1478
  music, 1478
  myths in, 874
  new comedy, 1485
  origins of, 1477–1479
  pattern of tragedy, 1478
  performance of, 1479–1483
  popular plays, 1555, 1566
  prizes for, 1482
  public discourse in, 473–474
  realism in Hellenistic period, 1486
  reliance on language, 1480
  at religious festivals, 1481
  revivals of, 1491
  rhetorical style of, 1480–1481
  satyr play, 1481
  source of popular narrative, 1565
  subject matter, 1479
  thematic interest in human abilities, 268
  touring after Alexandrian conquests, 1485
  trilogies, 1481
  underwriting of, 801
  writers of tragedy, 1483
  See also Actors; Comedy; Theater; Tragedy;
    particular writers
Drama, Roman, 1158–1159
  aquacades, 1489
  balletic extravaganzas, 1490
  borrowing from Greeks and Etruscans, 1487
  disappearance of in sixth century, 1490
  dominance of mime and farce, 1158–1159
  effect of Christianity on, 1490
  failure to achieve Greek status, 1487
  festivals for, 1487
  financing of, 1487
  gladiatorial contests, 1489
  Greek plays in translation, 1487
  masks, 1488
  mimi (mimes), 1490
  pantomimi (solo dance recitals), 1490
  revival of, 1491
  tragedy in early empire, 1489
Dreams
  appearance of soul of departed in, 987
  interpretation of, 952
  and rite of incubation, 944
  significance of, 944
Drill, running, 1702
Drugs. *See* Medicines and drugs
Dryopis, map 4
Dungal
  Irish classical scholar, 1823
Dura-Europos
  papyri and parchments from, 421, 425
Duris of Samos
  historian as dramatist, 1531
Duties. *See* Customs duties; Excise duties
Dyes and dyeing, 1387
  Tyrian purple, 1402, 1409
Dyiskolos. See Menander

E

Early Christan art
  and Roman painting and mosaic, 1789 *illus.,*
    1790, 1792–1793
Eastern Europe, map 3
Ebla, map 5
Eboracum, map 1
Ebro River. *See* Iberus (Ebro) River
Ecbatana. *See* Ekbatana
Ecclesia (assembly), Athenian, 637
  agendas of, 472, 481
  efficiency of, 473
  limitations on decision-making, 472
  membership of, 471
  oratory in, 472
  paid attendance at, 481
  Pnyx (meeting place), 471, 480–481

prytaneis, 470
small interest groups in, 473
Ecclesiastes
conformity to Judaism, 1030
Ecology
attitude of ancient cultures toward, 129–130
deforestation and erosion, 117, 126
development of ecological science, 130
effect of mines and smelting, 128
effects of ancient wars on, 127, 130
garbage and sewage disposal, 129
hunting and disturbance of ecosystems, 127
industrial pollution, 128
lead poisoning, 128
natural law in classical literature, 125–126
salinization and agricultural productivity, 126–127
simplification of ecosystems, 127
and survival of ancient civilizations, 125–130
urban pollution, 128–129
Economy, Greek
absence of economic analysis, 724
application of modern theory to, 724–725
commercial function, 727
consequences of urbanization, 726–727
contrast between wealth and poverty, 725
derivation of "economy," 724
effect of territorial expansion on, 725
export bans, 731
factors influencing development, 725–727
functions of gift-giving, 736–737
lack of investment, 742
monopolies, 735
ownership of mines, 730
in political literature, 724
political and social causes of urbanization, 726
public vs. private ownership and trade, 729–730
role of state in, 729–734
sources of information, 723–725
taxation and, 795–807
territorial expansion and population increase, 725–726
See also Agriculture; Trade
Economy, Roman
agricultural nature of, 753, 771
agricultural production, 755
development of in western provinces, 757
factors determining structure, 753–754
income differentiation among peasants, 771
low productivity of agricultural population, 755
luxury items in archaeological finds, 771
population factors influencing, 754–755

prosperity in first and second centuries, 771
road-building and repair, 759–761
taxation and, 809–825
technological innovations, 755, 757
See also Agriculture; Trade
Edessa, map 5
Edicts, imperial
constitutio Antoniniana, 611
decreta, 611
epistulae (rescripts), 611
mandata (instructions to governors), 611
Editor (games-giver), 1160, 1161
Education
classical curriculum in modern Europe,
1830–1831
pagan authors in Christian curriculum, 1822
Education, Roman
adapted for Christian purposes, 1120
advent of schools, 1112
criticism of in antiquity, 1118
declining standards in later Empire, 1820
in early Rome, 1110
effect of second-century expansion on, 1111
government support of, 1112
grammar and language, 1112, 1113
importance of example in, 1111
influence of peasant virtues on, 1109
limitations of, 1119–1120
literary education, 1112–1113
in provinces, 1113
restricted to rhetoric at higher levels, 1114
secondary, 1112–1113
in second century, 1119
spread of Greek culture through, 1113
Education of Children, The. See Plutarchus, L.(?)
Mestrius (Plutarch)
Education of Cyrus. See Xenophon
Education of an Orator. See Quintilianus, Marcus
Fabius (Quintilian)
Education and rhetoric, Greek, 1077–1106
Athenian judicial and deliberative speechmaking,
1086
in Byzantium, 1822
change from *mythos* to *logos,* 1081
and class division, 545–546
contribution of sophists, 1081–1086
definition of cultural heritage, 1086
and drawings, 1757
education of citizen body, 1080
elementary, 1111–1112
emergence of city-state, 1080

Education and rhetoric, Greek (continued)
  emulation of Greek practices, 1111–1112
  four-part theory of judicial speech, 1081
  in fourth century, 1086–1092
  function of in city-state, 1597–1598
  grammatistes (teacher of letters), 1080
  handbooks of technical rhetoric, 1086
  in Homeric poems, 1077–1079
  imitation of literary models, 1520
  importance of epic poetry in, 1080
  inappropriate speaking in Homeric poems, 1077–1078
  mentors and apprenticeships, 1078–1079
  military leadership and formal speech, 1079
  origin of formal rhetoric, 1081
  pattern after second century, 1111
  prescriptive requirements for speechmaking, 1086
  professional schools and curricula in fourth century, 1086
  professional teachers of, 1598
  in Sparta, 457, 461
  of Spartan males, 20–21
  speechmaking skill as gift of Gods, 1078
  teaching methods, 1112
  teaching patterns in archaic period, 1078–1079
  women's, 1302–1303, 1308
  writing and development of philosophy, 1080–1081
  youth training in fourth century Athens, 482
Education and rhetoric, Hellenistic and Greco-Roman
  Alexandrian art of rhetoric, 1099–1100
  classical literature, 1098
  effect of Eastern expansion on, 1097
  euergetism, 1100
  higher education, 1100
  language, 1098
  mathematics and science, 1100
  meletai (practice declamations), 1100, 1102
  philosophical schools, 1101
  progymnasmata, 1099
  reading, 1098
  research institutions and libraries, 1101
  structure and curriculum, 1098
  teaching methods, 1098
Egypt, map 6, map 10, 88 *illus.*
  Alexander the Great crowned pharaoh, 34
  architectural building techniques, 287–288, 296
  Athenians defeated by Persians, 29

  chariot-fighting, 683
  evidence for Roman taxes, 810
  geography, 92
  Greek mercenaries in, 15–16
  influence on Greek sculpture, 1701
  influence upon Greeks, 15
  Jews of under Roman rule, 1042
  languages and dialects, 197
  Nile irrigation pumps, 347
  oracles, 957
  Ptolemaic calendar, 391
  Ptolemies, 1736
  Roman coinage of, 1809
  Roman mummy portraits, 1772
  worship of pharaoh's statues, 1009
Egypt, Ptolemaic
  coinage, 1802
  corruption in second century, 644
  dynastic cult, 1012
  dynasty, 36–37, 41
  economic control of dynasty, 734–736
  economic policies, 734–736
  exploitation of natural resources, 735
  financial administration, 643–644
  foreign possessions, 644
  Kingdom of Ptolemies, map 9
  monopolies, 644
  nome administration, 643
  overseas trade by, 735
  peasant sabotage of system, 645
  relations with Rome, 55
  under Roman Republic, 645
  royal bank, 833
  status of native labor, 735
  taxation, 804–805
  temple administration, 642
  use of Greek professional administrators, 642
  village administration, 643
  See also Ptolemy
Egyptians
  depiction in classical art, 147
  physical description, 147–148
  physical variation among, 147
  use of papyrus, 422
  writing system of, 398–399
Einhard
  Life of Charlemagne, 1823
Eirene. See Aristophanes
Eisphora (tax on wealth), 800
Ekbatana (Ecbatana), map 5, map 8

Elagabalus, 76
Electra. See Euripides
Electrum coins
 definition of, 1795
Elegiac poetry, Greek, 1437, 1438–1439
 archaic elegiac poets, 1440
 elegiac couplet, 1438–1439
 and epic, 1439
 uses for, 1439
 and vase painting, 1751
Elegy
 definition of, 1457
Eleia, map 7
Elements. See Euclid
Elephantine, map 6
 Judahite colony, 1029
Elephants
 in coinage, 1801, 1804, 1806, 1807
 killing of, 1164
Eleusinian Mysteries, 900, 904–907, 1143, 1151
 anaktoron housed sacred images, 906
 Athenian archon's authority over, 906
 based on Demeter-Persephone myth, 1316
 duration, 930
 economic benefits to priestess, 930
 epimeletai (administrators), 927
 fertility rite, 867
 focus on afterlife, 867
 Greater and Lesser Mysteries, 906
 Hierophant, 1145
 Hymn to Demeter, 1145
 initiation, 1145
 most widespread rite, 867
 murderers excluded, 906
 open to all Greek speakers, 906, 1304
 political aspects, 449
 public aspect, 1144
 revelations in, 906
 rites at Eleusis, 905
 symbolism of grain and reproduction, 906
Eleusis, map 4
 control of Athens over, 1152
 record of expenditures, 641
 rusticated tower wall at, 293 *illus.*
 union with Athens, 21
Eleutheria (Festival of Liberty), 1152
Elis, map 4
 administration of Olympic Games, 1144
 settlement of by Dorians, 5
Elkasai, 1049, 1061

Elysium
 place of eternal happiness, 1000
Emblemata. See Mosaic art, Roman
Emigration, Greek
 to raise social status, 535
Empedocles
 change interpreted as mixing of the four
  elements, 1594
 cosmic cycles, 267
 On Nature, 1595
 Purifications, 1595
 role of two principles, 1595
 source of early Pythagoreanism, 1594
 two principles, Philia and Strife, 1594
Emperor, Roman
 beneficence and social and political integration,
  1021
 as gods' vicegerent on earth, 1009, 1018
 as intercessor with gods, 1020
 posthumous cults of, 1014
Empire, Roman
 Arab expansion and defeat of Eastern Empire,
  181
 artistic styles under the tetrarchs, 1748
 barbarian invasions, 82, 715–716
 Barracks Emperors, 77
 coinage, 1807–1816
 cosmopolitan nature, 73–74
 decline, 75, 77, 80–81, 83
 division of, 82, 83
 duration of Pax Romana, 64
 dynastic principle, 75
 Eastern Empire, 75, 82, 84
 eastern oracles, 955–956
 end of Western Empire, 718–719
 expression of in architecture, 309, 320
 fiscal powers, 820–821
 "Five Good Emperors," 71–73
 under Flavian emperors, 70–71
 frontiers under Hadrian, 72
 imperial frontiers, map 10
 "Indian Summer" under Antoninus Pius, 73
 under Julio-Claudian emperors, 69
 Mediterranean cultural unity, 64
 military power, 660
 northern frontiers under Augustus, 66
 paternal absolute monarchy, 74
 priority of Eastern Empire, 80
 provinces, map 10
 provincial influence increases, 76

Empire, Roman (continued)
  public welfare programs, 74
  reorganization by Diocletian, 78–79
  ruler worship in Christian empire, 1018
  rural rebellion and fall of, 560, 587
  under Severan emperors, 76
  stabilization under Justinian, 719
  taxation by, 819–821
  Western Empire, 75, 82, 84
Empire-states, Greek
  land holdings, 803
  treasuries, 803
  See also Egypt, Ptolemaic; Seleukid Empire
Emporiae (Emporion), map 1, map 7
Emporio, map 4
Encomium of Helen. See Gorgias
Engineering
  documentation, 323, 340, 341, 342
  hydraulic, 338–352
  mechanical, 323–330
  military, 330–338
  miniature, 347–352
  See also Construction materials and techniques;
    Mechanical engineering; Mechanics, principles
    of
Engye (betrothal), 1338
Ennius, Quintus
  enhancement of Latin language, 188–189
  epic of Rome, 1427
  father of Latin literature, 1427
  originator of satura, 1499
  satirized by Gaius Lucilius, 1427
Entablature, Roman, construction of, 314 illus.
Entertainers, professional, 1150
Envoys
  definitions of, 667
  Greek, 671–672
  Roman, 667, 671–672
Epaminondas (Epameinondas)
  fortification of Messene and Mantinea, 696
  military tactics, 691
  Theban general, 30–31
Epeiros, map 3, map 4
Ephebeia, 1100
  in archaic Sparta, 1178
  changes in after Cleisthenes, 1180
  in fourth-century Athens, 482
  gymnasiarches, 1100
  in Hellenistic period, 1193
  in hoplite military education, 687
  military and citizenship training, 894

  oath of, 894
  transformation of institution, 546
Ephesus (Ephesos), map 4, map 5
  banking activities at temple of Artemis, 832
  coinage of, 1795, 1798
  Library of Celsus, 1683–1684 illus.
  temple of Artemis, 281, 304, 850, 1795
Ephetai
  in Athenian homicide trials, 597
Ephialtes
  Athenian democrat, 28
Ephoros
  on Cretan social life, 1177
Ephorus of Cyme
  Histories, 1530
  widely read historian, 1531
Epic, 1417–1435
  apolitical genre, 1430
  attempts of historical epicists, 1431–1432
  audience for, 1425
  composition of, 1419
  dactylic hexameter meter of, 1468
  distinction between early narrative verse and,
    1417–1418
  distinguishing characteristics of heroic narrative,
    1418
  early Roman, 1426–1427
  effects of rhetoric on, 1430–1431
  elaborate verbal formulae, 1419
  Greek primary epic and offshoots, 1419–1423
  Greek revival of, 1432–1434
  Hellenistic literary epic, 1423–1426
  narrative, 407
  Neoteric and Augustan, 1427–1430
  origin of term, 1417
  parataxis, 1419
  prehistoric origins, 1417–1419
  problematic relation to history, 1431
  rhapsodoi (reciters), 1421
  Roman rhetorical, 1430–1432
  and vase painting, 1750
  See also Homeric epic
Epichoric alphabets, 401
Epictetus
  dedicated teacher, 1647
  Stoic philosopher, 1647
Epicureanism, 1615–1617
  afterlife in, 1001
  chief aim, 1616
  contrasted with Stoics, 272
  degree of social involvement advocated, 1617

effect on divinity of traditional gods, 1020
influence on Roman life, 1644
Lucretius as Roman exponent of, 1637–1640
pleasure as primary good, 1616
Epicurus
  atomic theory as presented by Lucretius, 1639
  on avoiding pain and anxiety, 1616
  doctrine of atomic swerve, 1616
  formation of worlds, 1616
  free will, 1616
  importance of friendship, partnership, 1617
  Letter to Menoeceus, 1617
  modified atomic theory, 1615–1616
  notion of the divine, 1617
  On Nature, 1615
  perception the ultimate basis of knowledge, 1615
  pleasure and pain, 1615, 1616
  Principal Doctrines, 1616
  prolepsis (preconception), 1615
  Seneca on, 1646
  two main sources of his work, 1615
Epicycle-eccentric theory
  first proposed by Apollonius, 1630
  flexible model, 1632
  Hipparchus, 1630
  movement of sun, moon, and planets, 1631
  Ptolemy, 1630
Epidamnos, map 3
Epidaurus (Epidauros)
  temple of Asklepios, 1715
  temple building in, 378
  theater of, 1480, 1491
  theater by Polykleitos, 1666–1667 *illus.*
Epideixis (demonstration lecture)
  how Sophists publicized teaching skills, 1598
  source of Hippocratic treatises, 1598
Epidoseis, 802
Epigrams, 1495–1499
  in Alexandrian period, 1495
  in *Anthologia Latina,* 1496
  Catullan circle, 1497
  Christian and Byzantine innovations, 1496
  classical successors to Martial, 1498–1499
  development as separate genre, 1496
  elegiac couplet, 1496
  Garland of Meleager, 1497
  for grave and dedicatory inscriptions in Byzantine period, 1498
  Greek, under Justinian, 1498
  influences on Hellenistic, 1495–1496
  modern definition, 1496

origin of, 1495
paegnia (play things), 1495
in Renaissance, 1499
satiric in early empire, 1497
subdivisions of in *Greek Anthology,* 1496
Epikleros (heiress), 596, 926, 1311, 1336, 1340
  epikleros thessa (woman of lowest property class), 1338
Epiktetos, 1749
Epimenes, 1723
  scaraboid, 1724 *illus.*
Epinomis
  human reciprocity with nature in, 126
Epistle to the Pisones (Ars Poetica). See Horatius Flaccus, Quintus (Horace)
Epistles. See Horatius Flaccus, Quintus (Horace)
Epistulae ex Ponto. See Ovidius Naso, Publius (Ovid)
Epoche (suspension of judgment)
  Skeptic's practice, 1619
Epodoseis, 805
Eponia (excise duties), 799–800
Epopoios (epic poet), 1417
Eporedia, map 2
Epulones
  in charge of sacred banquets, 911
Epyllia (epic fragments)
  freed poet from demands of epic form, 1425
  Hecale by Callimachus, 1425
  in Hellenistic age, 1426
  Idylls of Theocritus, 1425
Equant
  attacked by Copernicus, 1631
  center of uniform motion, 1631
Equestrian competitions, 1133, 1139
Equestrian Order
  administrative responsibilities under Hadrian and Trajan, 661
  appointment to administrative posts, 564
  under Augustus, 685
  elevation under Augustan Constitution, 521–522, 523–524
  internal stratification, 565
  powers gained under Gracchan reforms, 656
  as procurators, 820
  as *publicani,* 816
  reestablishment of by Augustus, 563–564
  relation with imperial government, 570
  replacement of senatorial order by, 570
  after Servian reforms, 650
  under Severus, 76
  status under Gracchan reforms, 557–558

Equestrian Order (continued)
  Sulla's confiscation of property, 559
  taxation, 571
  wooed by Gaius Gracchus, 56
Equites (Knights). See Aristophanes
Era, used in dating, 393
Erasistratus
  complexity of human cortex, 1235
  Hellenistic biologist, 1621
  neura and *synastomoses,* 1235
  pathology, 1235
  pneuma (life force), 1234–1235
  respiration and vascular function, 1235
  studies on human physiology, 1234
Eratosthenes
  calculated earth's size, 1624
Erechtheum (Erechtheion), 1662 *illus.,* 1664, 1676
  construction labor for, 743
  Roman restoration of, 1676
  sculpture of *Athena Polias,* 1664
  tile roofing system of, 285 *illus.,* 289
Eretria, map 4, map 7
  public building in, 444
  war with Chalkis, 12–13
Ergoteles of Crete, 1135
Erinna
  loss of a lover, 1311
Erinyes (Furies), 1305, 1315–1316
  associations, 852
Erotimos
  François Vase, 1752, 1753 *illus.*
Erythrai, map 4, map 5
Esther, Book of, 1034
  in Greek, 1036
Ethical theory, Aristotelian
  definition of moral excellence, 1611
  not an exact science, 1611
Ethiopians
  physical description, 148
Ethnic prejudice
  in citizenship laws, 151
  in classical ethnography and geography, 150–151
  in classical Europe and Africa, 152
  color prejudice in classical world, 152–153
  Greek-Roman antipathy, 151–152
  between Greeks and barbarians, 150
  between Greeks and Jews, 152
  official attitudes toward, 151
  physical variations and climatic difference, 150
  popular prejudice, 151–153

racial chauvinism, 150
  Roman ethnic slurs, 152
  theories of racial differentiation, 150–151
Ethos, 1710
Etna
  volcanism, 94
Etruria, map 2
  city states, 47
  economic decline, 497
  eroticism in Etruscan art, 1267
  marital bond depicted on sarcophagi, 1267
  political impact on Rome, 47
  Roman views of eroticism, 1267–1268
Etruscan League
  military reverses of, 497
Etruscans
  civilizers of central Italy, 46–47
  commercial network, 47
  decline, 50
  language, 46
  leisure activities, 1201
  military legacy, 703
  origins, 46
  writing system of, 416
Etruscus, Claudius, 823
Euagoras (Evagoras). See Isocrates
Euainetus
  coin artist of Syracuse, 1799
Euboia, map 4
  colonies, 11, 12
  Levantine trade of, 8
  war in, 12–13
Eubulus
  political power through financial control, 483
Euclid
  argument by reductio ad absurdum, 1622
  asserted starting points, 1621
  Elements, 1621
  influenced studies of optics, statics, hydrostatics, 1625
  introduction of the parallel postulate, 1622
  method of exhaustion, 1622
Eudaimonia (being blessed or fortunate), 1602
Eudoxus of Cnidos
  nature of his theory, 1628
  solution to irregular planetary movements, 1627
  sources for his system, 1627
  system of concentric spheres, 1627
Euergesia (beneficence)
  in Greek society, 443

Euhesperides, map 7
Eumenes II, king of Pergamon, 329
Eumenides. See Aeschylus
Eunomia
  ancient poem, 451
  in archaic polis, 465,466
  in archaic Sparta, 455–456
  in classical period, 467
  in Greek government, 449–450
  Hesiod's view, 450
  replacement by *isonomia,* 467
  in Solonian code, 453,454,455
Euphranor, 1716, 1749, 1757
Euphrates River, map 5, map 8
  transport on, 363
Euphronios, 1754–1756
Eupolemus
  assimilationist Jerusalem priest, 1034
Euripides
  Bacchae (*The Bacchants*), 1305, 1316, 1508
  closeness to popular narrative, 1565
  Helen, 1309
  Hippolytos (*Hippolytus*), 414
  on inconstancy of human nature, 1282
  on inequality of wife and husband (*Medea*), 1340
  on innate good or evil, 1282
  insight into human motivation in *Electra,*
    1285–1286
  Iphigenia in Tauris, 1316, 1780–1781 *illus.*
  library of, 413
  Medea, 1308, 1309
  Phaedra's revenge motive in *Hippolytus,* 1286
  Phoenician Women, 1309, 1314
  questioning of traditional values in plays, 1483
  questions masculine ideal of women, 1309
  tribulations of wife in *Medea,* 1286–1287
Euripos, map 4
Eurotas River, map 4
Euryalus
  fortress of, 696
Eusebius of Caesarea
  Life of Constantine, 1068
Euthymides, 386
Eutychides
  statue of the Fortune of Antioch, 852
Evolution
  classical theories of, 265–275
  no concept of biological evolution, 267
Excise duties, 799–800
  See also Taxation

Exekias, 1752–1753, 1754 *illus.*
Exhaustion, method of
  Euclid's form of reductio ad absurdum, 1622
  originated by Eudoxus of Cnidos, 1622
Expenditures, public, 795, 806
  in archaic and classical Greece, 797
  in classical Athens, 798
  by Roman state, 810, 822–823
Export duties, 799, 804
Extispicy
  divination from entrails, 946
Extortion court, Roman
  focus of tension between elite orders, 557
Ezekiel
  Exagoge, Hellenistic tragedy, 1037
Ezra, governor of Judah
  imposed Deuteronomic law code, 1028

F

Fabius Pictor, Quintus
  first Roman to write prose history, 1543
  invocation of *numina* by priest of Ceres, 853
Fables
  Aesopic, 1122–1123
  ainos, 1122
  in ancient Hebrew literature, 1122
  climax of, 1125
  literary use of, 1123
  Mesopotamian, 1123
Fabrics. *See* Textiles
Facade and surface elaboration
  in Roman architecture, 1674, 1676, 1679,
    1683–1684 *illus.,* 1687–1689
Facta et Dicta Memorabilia. See Valerius Maximus
Family, Greek
  domestic religious duties, 892
  household divinities, 892
  See also Women, Greek
Family businesses, Roman
  construction (Haterii), 326
  trademarked bricks, 307
Family planning
  methods of, 1356–1357
  tendency to limit size, 1355
Famine
  in ancient world, 242–243
  chestnuts as bread substitute, 243
  lupine as bread substitute, 243

Farce, Atellan, 1159

Fasti (*The Roman Calendar*). *See* Ovidius Naso, Publius (Ovid)

Fauna
  animal combats (*venationes*), 123, 125
  birds, 120
  depicted in classical art and literature, 124
  exhibitions of exotic, 123
  extinction of, 124–125
  fish and other sea life, 121–122
  human uses of, 122–125
  insects, land mollusks, and worms, 121
  large mammals, 119–120
  reptiles and amphibians, 120

Fayum, map 6

Feasters
  arranged ritual meals (*epula*)for the gods, 935

Feasts, Greek
  in classical Athens, 1179–1181
  exclusivity of membership, 1169
  hestiaseis (public feasts), 1180
  in Homeric poems, 1169
  homosexuality at, 1169
  initiation into adulthood, 1169
  marriage, 1180
  reciprocal, 1170
  state-sponsored, 1180–1181
  tribal associations, 1180
  values of shared feast, 1170
  women at, 1170

February
  Roman festivals in, 920

Federalism, Greek
  Achaian confederacy, 493
  Aitolian confederacy, 492–493
  Amphictyones (dwellers around), 491
  Arkadian League, 492
  Boeotian League, 491–492
  confederacy of Thessalian tribal states, 491
  definition of, 491
  Delian League, 492
  league of cities of Chalkidike, 492
  Panhellenic League of Corinth, 492
  Peloponnesian League, 492
  religious character of, 491
  tagos (military leader), 491
  See also particular confederacies

Feltmaking, 1388

Festivals, Greek, 896–900, 1143–1152
  adaptations to changes in political climate, 899
  administration of, 1148–1149

  agricultural, 1145–1146
  annual, 1145
  Athenian, 896–897, 1145–1149
  athletic, 1133–1134, 1144, 1150
  costs of, 727
  cultural functions of, 1151–1152
  deme, 1149
  festival assemblies (*panegyreis*), 669
  funding of, 1148
  in Hellenistic world, 1149–1150
  international, 1150
  and interstate relations, 669
  monthly, 1145
  only interruption of civic and business affairs, 897
  origins of, 1151–1152
  Panhellenic, 1144–1145
  periodos, 1134, 1144
  political functions of, 1148
  Posthellenic, 1151
  purpose of, 898
  religious, 1132, 1145
  restrictions on attendance, 897
  as social occasion, 897
  Spartan, 1149
  tickets for, 1148

Festivals, Roman, 913–921
  epulones (collegium of priests), 1203
  games at, 1154

Fetiales, Roman, 675
  responsibilities of, 667, 670

Fidenae, map 2

Fighting
  boxing, 1131, 1132, 1138–1139
  pancration, 1133, 1139
  wrestling, 1132, 1135–1136
  See also Gladiatorial games

Finance, public, 795
  See also Expenditures, public; Taxation

Financial organization
  types of, 803

Fire-fighting pump apparatus, 343

Fire hazards, 1379
  Juvenal on, 1379–1380

Fires
  and rebuilding projects in Rome, 305–306

First fruits
  as votive offering, 977

First Triumvirate, 561

Fiscus (treasury), 810, 820

Fish and other sea animals
  biotic zones, 121

of the continental shelf, 121
crustaceans and mollusks, 122
in diet and economy, 121–122
ecology and lack of diversity, 121
freshwater species, 122
mammals, 122
Fish and seafood
archaelogical evidence of in diet, 259–260
fish dishes, 260
in Greek diet, 259
in Roman diet, 260
shellfish, squid, and octopus, 260
Five Theological Orations. See Gregory of Nazianzus
Flaccus, Aulus Persius (Persius)
literary qualities of satire, 1501–1502·
Flaccus, Fulvius
citizenship bill, 558
Flaccus, Valerius
Argonautica, 1432
mythological epicist, 1432
Flamethrowers, 331, 332 *illus.*
Flamines
distinctive restrictions and features, 936
priests of fifteen gods and goddesses, 936
taboos surrounding, 911
Flamininus, Titus Quinctius, 54
coinage portrait of, 1807
Flood myth
Deucalion and Pyrrha, 870
Floor pavements, Roman. *See* Mosaic art, Roman
Floralia
spring festival of Flora, 914
Flowers and branches
Daphnephoria, 964
eiresione (olive branch), 964
in rituals, 964
Flute playing, 1139–1140
Folklore
anecdote, 1123–1124
definition of, 1121
element of supernatural in legends, 1126
fables, 1122–1123
functions of, 1128
generic types of jokes, 1124
influence on literature and scholarship, 1128
jokes told at social occasions, 1124–1125
legends, 1126–1127
magic tales, 1125
novellas, 1126
origin of term, 1121
proverbs and riddles, 1127–1128

sources of information on, 1121–1122
women's stories, 1125
Folk medicine, Roman, 1236
Folktales
collections of, 1564
Food
in rituals, 965–967
Footrace, 1131, 1134–1135
Force pump (Ktesibian machine), 343–345,
344 *illus.,* 351
Fordicidia
Roman festival for fertility of land, 914
Forestry
erosion and deforestation, 117–118
logging in classical literature, 117
for military and diplomatic purposes, 116–117
uses for timber, 116
Forma censoria (tribute property), 812
Formiae, map 2
Forms, Platonic theory of
and domain of politics, 1604
Forms as paradigms, 1606
functions of, 1604
implications for moral philosophy, 1603–1604
relationship with particulars, 1605–1606
Fortifications
Eastern city walls, 694
financing of, 798
Fortifications, Greek
field, 693
permanent, 696
Forum, Roman
in architecture, 1674–1677, 1679–1680
contrasted with Greek agora, 1698–1699
restoration of, 1734
urban planning importance of, 309–310 *illus.,*
1698
Forum of Caesar, 1728
Forums, imperial, 300, 305, 306 *illus.,* 310 *illus.*
axial plan of, 1698
Forum of Augustus, 301, 305, 306 *illus.,* 310 *illus.*
Forum-of-Transit (Forum of Nerva), 306 *illus.,*
308, 310 *illus.*
Forum of Trajan (Forum Traianum), 306,
308–320, 310 *illus.,* 311 *illus.,* 314 *illus.,*
317 *illus.,* 318 *illus.,* 319 *illus.,* 1698
repetition of styling details, 309–310
Fountain niche decoration, Roman, 1791–1792 *illus.*
Fountains
Hero's Fountain, 345 *illus.*
water supply of, 342–345

Franchise, Roman, 57
François Vase, 1752–1753 *illus.*
Fresco painting, Roman. *See* Wall painting,
    Roman
Frieze, continuous running, 1708
Frieze (painted wall), Roman. *See* Stucco relief art,
    Roman; Wall painting, Roman
Friezes and reliefs, narrative
    Arch of Constantine, 1744–1745 *illus.*
    Baker's Monument, 1731
    Trajan's Column, 1741 *illus.*
Friezes and reliefs, portrait, 1730
Frogs. See Aristophanes
Frontier policy, Roman, 713
    under Constantine, 718
    limitanei (frontier armies), 718
Frontinus, Sextus Julius
    Roman water commissioner and technical writer,
    340, 342
Fronto, Marcus Cornelius
    aimed at modern style (*elocutio novella*), 1580
    archaism of, 1522
    correspondence with his pupil Marcus Aurelius,
    1580
Fruit-growing
    apples, 253
    cherries, 234
    citron in Jewish religious practices, 254
    citrus, 254
    dates, 253
    figs, 232, 253
    orchards, 233–234
    peaches, 234
    pears, 253
    Prunus species, 253
Fulling, 374, 375 *illus.*
Fulvia (wife of Mark Antony)
    military role in Perusine War, 1322, 1325
    as political force, 1324
Fundi, map 2
Funeral games, 1131, 1132, 1134
Funerals, Greek
    archaic and classical paintings of, 1761–1762,
    1763 *illus.*, 1764
    Dipylon krater painting of, 1750–1751 *illus.*
    grave stelae painting, 1763–1764
    in Hellenistic painting, 1762–1763 *illus.*
    mourning song (*goos*), 994
    rites, 993–994
    vigil wake of dead (*prothesis*), 994
    women's role, 1305, 1307

Funerals, Roman
    prohibitions of elaborate, 998
Funerary sculpture, 1708
Furnituremaking and joinery
    Greek, 286

G

Gabii, map 2
Gadara, map 5
Gaetuli, map 6
Gaiseric, king of the Vandals
    occupation of North Africa under, 175
Gaius (second century A.D.)
    comments on types of Roman marriage, 1344
    Institutes, 610–611, 627, 1344
Gaius Julius Caesar Germanicus (Caligula), 68
    extravagant behavior of, 1215, 1216
    taxes decreed by, 820
Galatia, map 5, map 9, map 10
Galba, Servius Sulpicius, 70
Galen of Pergamon
    concept of *pneumata*, 1239
    demonstration of arterial blood in *Blood in the
    Arteries*, 1240
    dissecting technique in *On Anatomical Procedures*,
    1238
    dynameis (powers) and humors, 1238, 1240
    influence on later medical theory, 1241
    on innate heat, 1231, 1240–1241
    krasis (blending of elements) and humors, 1239
    medical terminology, 1241
    medical writings, 1238–1239
    On Habits, 1633
    On the Usefulness of the Parts of the Body, 1633
    organization of concepts, 1241
    personal background, 1238
    pneuma, 1240
    refinements of Platonic doctrines, 1239
    structural anatomy in *On the Usefulness of the Parts
    of the Body*, 1238
Galerius Valerius Maximianus, Gaius
    edict of toleration, 1065
    persecution of Christians, 1064, 1065
    rebuilding of pagan cults, 1065
Galilee, map 5
    geology, 107
Galley, 358, 841, 843
    used by pirates, 840

Galley, Liburnian, 843
Gallia Narbonensis (Provence). *See* Gaul, Narbonese
Gallic War. See Caesar, Gaius Julius
Gallienus, Publius Licinius Egnatius
  awarded military command to equestrians, 524
  murder by troops, 716
Gallus, Gaius Cornelius
  manuscript fragment, 428
Gallus, Quintus Roscius, 1159
Games, Greek
  draughts game (in vase painting), 1752,
    1754 *illus.*
  See also Athletics; Festivals, Greek; particular
    games
Games, Roman, 1153–1164
  in amphitheaters, 1159–1162
  attraction of, 1154
  at circuses, 1155–1157
  gladiatorial, 1159–1162
  killing in, 1163–1164
  morality of, 1163–1164
  occasions for, 1154
  participants in, 1153, 1161, 1162
  spectators at, 1154, 1160, 1163
  sponsors of, 1160, 1161
  in theaters, 1157–1159
Games courts (*palaestrae*)
  in Roman architecture, 1686
Gamoroi (landsharers)
  in Greek archaic period, 535
Ganosis, 1702
Garden house complexes
  for upper-class residents, 1378 *illus.*, 1379
Gardens
  described by Pliny the Younger, 1376
  House of Gaius Julius Polybius (Pompeii),
    1376–1377
  town houses, 1367–1377
  villas, 1376
Garganus, C., map 2
Garland of Meleager
  collection of epigrams in, 1497
Garland. See Philippus of Thessalonica
Gaugamela, map 8
  battle of, 34
Gaul, 88 *illus.*
  conquest by Caesar, 60
  Roman conquest of Cisalpine Gaul, 53
Gaul, Cisalpine, map 2
Gaul, Narbonese (Gallia Narbonensis) (Provence),
  map 1

geography, 91
  Tomb of Julii, 1732
Gaul, Transalpine, map 1
Gauls
  sack of Rome, 387 B.C., 50–51
Gaza, map 5
Gela, map 7
  dominance over Sicily, 489
Gellius, Aulus
  archaism of, 1522
  on dinner party etiquette, 1207
Gelon, tyrant of Syracuse, 489
Gem cutters, 386
Gems, Greek, 1721–1725
  baroque style, 1725
  Bronze Age engraving skills, 1721
  carnelian quartz, 1722
  Hellenistic style changes, 1723–1724
  sixth-century styles, 1723
  skills lost in Dark Age, 1721
  uses of, 1721, 1722
Gender roles
  associations in myth and literature, 1253–1254
  division of labor (Xenophon), 1302–1303, 1306
  Greek competitions and male character
    development, 1251
  in Hellenistic literature, 1309
  in Homeric epics, 1302, 1305–1306, 1310, 1312
  ideal male and female characteristics, 1253
  in marriage, 1350
  mutual exclusivity of, 1252, 1253
  noncitizens and women, 1251–1252
  sexual behavior and social status, 1251
  women.limited to domestic sphere, 1302–1303,
    1305–1306
  women's duties in *oikos,* 1252
Genealogiai. See Hecataeus of Miletus
Genesia, 1146
Geneva, map 1
Genius
  power of fertility in paterfamilias, 921
Genius Augusti, cult of, 1015
Genua, map 2
Geocentricity
  absence of visible stellar parallax argued for,
    1630
  astronomical considerations for, 1630
  models of Hipparchus and Ptolemy, 1632
Geography, Mediterranean
  area defined, 91
  boundaries and major·provinces, 91–92

Geography. See Ptolemy (Claudius Ptolemaeus)
Geology, Mediterranean
  aquifers, 108
  Karst topography, 108
  lakes, 106–107
  limestone formation, 95–96
  marshes, 107–108
  mineralization, 96–98
  mountain-folding in Paleozoic, 95
  mountains, 99–100
  ophiolites, 96
  plateaus, plains, and lowlands, 100–101
  plate tectonics, 92–94
  rivers, 104–106
  rock origins and characteristics, 95–96
  soils, 98–99
  volcanoes, 94–95
Geometric period
  pottery, 1704
  solid-cast bronze statuettes, 1704
Geophysics, Greek theoretical
  Aristotle's arguments for earth's sphericity, 1624
  attempts to determine earth's size, 1624
  origins, 1624
Gerasa (Jerash), map 5
  colonnaded streets, 1699
Gerbert of Reims
  classical learning, 1823
Germans
  destruction of Western Empire, 718–719
  etymology, 144
  invasion of Italy, 57, 73
  physical description, 144, 152
  physical remains, 144
  racial integrity of, 144
  Roman diplomacy with, 672
Germany, map 1
Germany, Lower, map 10
Germany, Upper, map 10
Gezer, map 5
Ghosts
  precautions against, 1146
  Roman festivals concerning, 923
Gier aqueduct
  to Lyons (France), 342
Gift-giving
  importance of in Greek society, 975
Gildas
  on raiding of Britain in *The Destruction of Britain,* 180–181
Girls' rites, Greek, 894–895

Gladiatorial games
  amphitheaters for, 1159–1160
  elements in, 1161
  missio, 1161
  organization of, 1160–1161
  origin of, 1159
Gladiators
  lives of, 1162
  schools for, 1162
Gla, map 4
Glanum, map 1
Glass, 374
Glassblowing, 374
Glazier Codex, 434
Gluemaking, 374
Gnosis
  Greek mosaicist, 1766 *illus.,* 1767
Gnosticism
  Basilidians, 1051
  beginnings of, 1050
  Carpocratians, 1051
  festival of the Epiphany, 1051
  fragmentation of, 1051
  hymns, 1050–1051
  Odes of Solomon, 1051
  in second-century Roman Empire, 1051
  sects and schools, 1051–1052
  Sethian, 1051
  use of sacraments, 1051–1052
Gods
  Athenian comic poets on, 976
  conquest of the Titans, 865
  foreign gifts to, 632
  immortal, but not eternal, 866
  influence on destiny, 866
  offspring of Cronos and Rhea, 865
  pantheon, 865
  provided for all human needs, 887
  Roman attitude toward, 982–983
  statues as omens, 945–946
  temples and memorials for, 632
Gold, 373
  Macedonian mines, 819
  mining, Greek, 779–780
Golden Age
  Hesiod's myth of the metals, 265–266
  multiple versions of myth, 265
  pastoral idyll, 265
  Plato's version, 266
  rhetorical device to stress present miseries, 266
Golden Ass. See Apuleius

Gordion, map 5, map 8
Gorgias
  Defense of Palamedes, 1084
  Encomium of Helen, 1084, 1085
  Sophist challenge, 1599–1600
  On What is Not, 1599
Gortyn
  Law Code, 537, 580, 591–592, 1336–1337
  temple of Apollo, 1706
  See also Adoption; Homicide; Theft; Inheritance
Goths
  origin, 172
  sea raids by, 844
Government, Greek forms of, 439–486
  in archaic polis, 465–466
  assembly, 446
  in classical polis, 466–478
  collective consciousness and, 465–466
  concept of equality, 467–468
  concept of good order, 446–447
  concept of justice, 452
  decision-making in, 440, 445, 446, 451, 458
  effect of population size on, 439
  executive power and, 446
  Greek law and, 445
  and Greek political theory, 440
  impact of literacy on, 450–451
  importance of community (*koinonia*), 440
  inability to cope with evil, 477–478
  mixed constitutions in Hellenistic period, 461, 478
  oligarchy in late fifth century, 476–477
  origins of political organization, 441–462
  parallel with Phoenician society, 440
  patrician state, 499–500
  plebeian institutions, 500–502
  political theory, 440
  political vocabulary, 440
  rationality and, 466
  rise of demagogues in fifth century, 469
  social composition and, 439
  stasis in late fifth century, 477–478
  voting by lot, 468
  written law codes and, 450
  See also particular states and institutions
Government, Roman, 495–528, 508
  abandonment of popular sovereignty, 521
  administrative bureaucracy develops, 523
  Augustan Constitution, 519–522
  Caesar's reforms, 518
  changes with urban-based assembly, 514

collapse of monarchy, 497
corporate benefits of patronage, 507
during decline of Republic, 511–518
decline of Senate under Principate, 524–525
dictatorship, 502–503
Diocletian's concepts of tetrarchy and theocracy, 526
group vote, 506
impact of economic recession on, 497
under last Roman king, 496–497
military influences on, 514–515, 526
monarchy, 495–497
in overseas provinces, 503
popular supremacy in second century B.C., 513
power divorced from office, 504
Principate, 518–527
promagistracy, 523
representative principle, 506
restructuring under Augustus, 518–519, 524
structure of Republican state, 498–500
Sullan reforms, 516–517
third-century monarchies, 526
transition to statute-based government, 516
See also Senate, Roman; particular offices and institutions
Gracchus, Gaius Sempronius
  attacks on senatorial privileges, 656
  franchise bill, 558
  grain supply for urban poor, 557
  land reforms of, 557–558
  overseas colonization, 656
  reform of the orders, 557
  reforms of, 56, 516, 708–709
Gracchus, Tiberius Sempronius
  challenge to senatorial authority, 513
  land reforms of, 55–56, 556–558, 656
  opposition to, 708
  tribunate of, 511
Grado, map 2
Grain
  free distribution of, 824
  Greek trade in, 727, 731
  law to ensure Athenian supply, 732
  public funding of purchases, 805
  Samian grain law, 732
  sitonai (grain commissioners), 732
  state control of on own territory, 733
Grains and bread
  barley, 237, 238
  breadmaking, 238–242, 249
  bread ovens, 240

Grains and bread (continued)
  brewer's yeast, 239
  emmer, 237, 238, 241
  grain importation, 248
  grains, 236–237
  grain shortages in Rome, 248
  handmilling, 239
  leavening, 239–240
  milling, 236, 237, 249
  preference for wheat or barley, 248
  processing of different food grains, 237–238
  quality of bread, 241
  quality of Roman bread, 240–241
  sieves, 238, 239
  Triticum vulgare, 237
  whole meal and flour production, 237
Granikos, map 8
Granikos River, map 5
Grapevine
  growing of, 227–229
  See also Wine production
Gratianus, Flavius (Gratian)
  rejected position as *pontifex maximus,* 937
Great Panathenaia, 1147, 1148
Greece, map 4, 88 *illus.*
  lakes, 107
  races and physical types in Iron Age, 142–143
  rivers, 105
Greek
  Attic dialect among Byzantine elite, 1821–1822
  demotic speech, 1822
  introduction in Peloponnese, 158
  modern neglect of, 1828
  phonetic changes in prehistoric period, 158
  reading and writing of classical, 1098
  regains literary primacy in later Empire, 74
  Roman philosophers' use of, 1646
  translation of Jewish literary works, 1037–1038
Greek Anthology, 1820
  epigrams, 1496
Green open space
  lack of in Greek cities, 1693
Gregory of Nazianzus
  trinitarian theology of (*Five Theological Orations*),
    1071
Gregory of Nyssa
  on concerns of merchant ship financiers, 770
Gregory of Nyssa
  trinitarian theology of, 1071
Gregory of Tours
  on first century of Frankish rule, 174

Griffins
  in Roman art, 1791
  Roman sources of motifs, 1781
Grove, sacred (*temene, templa*), 118
Guardianship, Roman
  actio tutelae, 616
  appointment of tutor, 615
  Atilian Law, 615
  curators, 616
  infans, 615
  lunatics, 616
Guilds, Roman
  construction trade, 307
Gulf of Cumae (Bay of Naples)
  economic prosperity of, 1220
  resort for wealthy Romans, 63
  volcanism, 95
Gundobad, king of Burgundy
  Lex Romana Burgundionum, 627
Gyges, king of Lydia
  tyranny of, 488
Gymnasium
  at Pergamon, 296 *illus.,* 297

H

Hades, god of the dead, 990
Hadrianopolis, map 3
Hadrianus, Publius Aelius (Hadrian)
  aqueduct construction under, 340, 342
  architecture under, 1680
  cancellation of tribute payments, 821
  conflict with Senate, 72
  development of frontier zones, 714
  dynastic problems, 73
  frontier strategy, 72
  Latin and Greek imperial correspondence, 661
  Lex Metalli Vipascensis (Aljustrel Tables), 788
  military reforms, 714–715
  Philhellene, 72
  philhellenic taste of in art, 1744
  Villa at Tibur (Tivoli), 1783, 1785
  visit to Britain, 1812
  wall of in Britain, 714
Hadrumetum, map 6
Hagesandros, 1728
Hairstyles
  blonde hair favored, 1409
  Etruscan, 1399, 1400

Greek, 1395, 1396
Hellenistic, 1398
wigs, 1409
Haliakmon River, map 3
Haliartos, map 4
Halicarnassus, Mausoleum of, 1704
Halieis (Porto Kheli), map 4
planned city layout of, 1695–1696 *illus.*
Halikarnassos, map 4, map 5
Haloa, 1145
Halonnesos, map 4
Halos, map 4
Halteres, 1136–1137
Halys River, map 5, 88 *illus.*
Hamilcar, 53
Handwriting style, 433
Hannibal
coinage under, 1804, 1806
defeat at Zama, 54, 707
invasion of Italy, 39, 54, 706
in Spain, 53
Harbors, 362–363
at Delos, 841
fees, 799
at Rhodes, 841
Harma (chariot race), 1133
Harmenopoulos
Hexabiblos, 627
Harmoniai (modal scales)
Dorian, 1510
Ionian, 1510
Lydian, 1510
Phrygian, 1510
Harness, 355
Haruspices
sacrificial priests, 985
Haruspicy, 971
changing fortunes of, 952
divination from entrails, 946, 952
Hasdrubal
defeat by Rome, 54
Hasmoneans, 1032
legitimacy of, 1035
See also Maccabees
Haterii, tomb of, 326, 1742, 1743 *illus.*
Hats, 1398
Greek, 1394
Macedonian *kausia,* 1399
Phrygian, 1396
Hattusas, map 5
destruction of, 166

Head tax, 799, 813
Healing cults, 901–904
Healing shrines
cures effected through dreams, 945
at Epidaurus, 945
Hecataeus (Hekataios) of Miletus
Genealogiai, 1525
logographer, 1525
Periegesis (*Journey Around the World*), 138–139, 1525
Hegesianax of Alexandria
lost novel about Trojan War, 1566–1567
Heiric of Auxerre
classical scholar, 1823
Helen. See Euripides
Heliocentricity
astronomical arguments against, 1630
Seleucus of Seleucia, 1629
unanimous rejection of, 1629–1630
Heliodoros
Aithiopika, 1568–1569
Heliopolis (Baalbek), map 5
transport of columns for temples, 360
Helios
worship of, 851
Hellanodikai, 1144
Hellenica. See Theopompus
Hellespont, map 3, map 4, map 5
Athenian campaigns at, 15
Helots. *See* Sparta: Helots
Helvetii, map 1
Hemerologia (lists of months), 384
Hemiola (galley), 840
Henna, map 2
Hephaestus
marriage to Aphrodite, 850
origin of, 850
Hephaisteion, 1654 *illus.,* 1664
Hera
sacred marriage to Zeus, 849
Heracles
ambiguity of name, 1287
founded the Olympic Games, 873
Near Eastern origin of myth, 875
three cycles of myths, 873
twelve labors of, 852
Heraclitus
appearances are deceptive, 1591
challenged accepted human judgments, 1591
connected diverse entities, 1590
contrasted with the Milesians, 1591
divergences contain moral, 1590

Heraclitus (continued)
   famous for obscurity, 1589–1590
   harmony in the cosmos, 1510
   inadequacy of human language to discriminate,
      1590
   puzzling oracular pronouncements, 1591
   universality of process of change, 1591
Heraia festival, 1140
Heraia, map 4
Herakleia, map 2
Herakleia Pontike (Ereğli), map 5, map 7
   oligarchic rule of, 543
Herakleids, 5
   return of, 160
Herakleion, map 4
Herakles. *See* Heracles
Herald (*keryx*)
   diplomatic immunity of, 672, 676
Herbs and condiments
   liquamen (fish sauce), 252, 260
   salt and vinegar, 252
   Silphium, 252
Herculaneum, map 2
   black and white mosaics, 1785–1786
   evidence of interior decoration styles, 1772
   House of Neptune and Amphitrite,
      1791–1792 *illus.*
   House of the Wooden Frame tenement, 303–304
   Isis-Fortuna, bronze statuette, 1732, 1733 *illus.*
   new-style housing, 1375
   papyri from, 421
   Samnite House, 1773 *illus.*
   Villa dei Papiri (Malibu reconstruction of), 307
   See also Pompeii
Hercules, Pillars of, 88 *illus.*
Hermagoras of Temnos
   stasis theory, 1103
Hermes
   origin and associations, 850
Hermippus of Smyrna
   biographer of Seven Wise Men, 1537
Hermogenes
   Greek architect, 1667–1668
Hermogenes of Tarsus
   handbook of *progymnasmata*, 1105
   stasis theory, 1105
   treatise on rhetorical style, 1105
Hermonassa, map 7
Hermos River, map 5
Herms, 892
Hernici, map 2

Hero of Alexandria
   on catapult design, 333–334
   on engineering, 323
   on force pumps, 343
   fountain of, 343–344, 345 *illus.*
   on miniature engineering, 349–352
   on screws, 326–327
   steam engine (*pneumatica*) of, 350 *illus.*
Herod, king of Judaea
   client king of Rome, 1038
   rise of, 1033
Herodes Atticus
   tutor to Marcus Aurelius, 42
Herodion, map 5
Herodotus
   admiration for Eastern cultures, 269
   aim of his researches, 1526, 1527
   on book rolls, 425
   climate and racial differentiation, 150
   on coinage, 1795
   collector of folktales, 1564
   compared to Thucydides, 1526–1529
   dependence on oral style in *Histories*, 410
   on Ethiopians, 148
   ethnographic digressions, 139
   Greek consciousness of, 156
   Greeks and barbarians in irreconcilable worlds,
      1527
   Histories, 1526
   hubris and human action, 1528
   man's subjection to divine will and fate, 1528
   opportunities for wealth in archaic period,
      534
   on Persian courier system, 353–354
   on priestly duties, 929
   prostitution in Babylonia, 1292, 1293
   reports on Thales of Miletus, 1586
   on royal genealogies, 156
   on sex-role reversals in Egypt, 1314–1315
   on source of Greek alphabet, 398
   traditional religious view, 1528
   women's positive influence on society, 1303
Heroes, Greek
   cults of, 994–995
   distinguished from gods, 1010
   reward of in afterlife, 993
   sources for myths of, 872
   worship of, 852–853
Heroines (*Heroides*). *See* Ovidius Naso, Publius (Ovid)
Herophilus
   human anatomy in *On Dissections*, 1234

medical terminology, 1234
theory of pulses, 1234
Heruli, map 11
Hesiod
  agricultural catalog in *Works and Days,* 216
  ambiguous relations of gods and men, 976
  archaic misogynist, 1303–1304, 1310–1311, 1313
  on augury, 942
  on Boeotian society, 532
  and concept of *eunomia,* 450
  on debts, 534
  didactic poetry as separate genre, 1422
  disapproval of technological change, 267
  fable of nightingale and hawk, 1123
  on farming, 21
  genealogical catalog of, 863
  Golden Age, 870
  and Greek social order, 447
  heroic age in, 870
  human decline not unilinear, 266
  human life charged with divinity, 863
  king's judgments in Greek law, 590
  later attitude to, 409
  magic and religion, 883
  myth of five ages of man, 870
  myth of the metals, 265–266
  notions of human betterment, 267
  orientalizing influence on, 1422
  origins and uniqueness, 11
  on Pandora, 1284, 1335
  prescription for finding a good wife, 1334
  Prometheus' deception of Zeus, 970
  Theogony, 863, 1422
  won singing contest, 1515–1516
  Works and Days, 864, 1422
Hestia
  associations, 850
  goddess of the hearth, 892
Hetaira (courtesan), 1172, 1175, 1292, 1294
  only female performers, 1508
Hetaireiai (bands or clubs)
  in archaic period, 1176–1176
  Cleisthenes' reforms, 1177
  failure of Peisistratos' sons to control, 1177
  Pittakos' reforms in Mytilene, 1176
  political, in Athens, 1184–1185
  and political change, 1176
  Solon's reforms, 1176–1177
  and tyranny in fourth century, 1185
Hexabiblos. See Harmenopoulos
Hides. *See* Skins

Hiera, map 5
Hieroglyphics, 398
Hieron (filled with divine power), 889
Hieron I
  successful racehorse owner, 1139
  tyranny of, 489
Hieronymus of Cardia
  upheld tradition of sober historiography, 1531
Highways
  Mesopotamian, 353
  Roman, 354
  See also Roads
Hilarion, Tiberius Flavius, 385
Himation, 1390, 1397, 1399, 1404
Himera, map 2, map 7
Hipparchus
  discovered precession of the equinoxes, 1632
  first comprehensive star catalog, 1632
  outstanding observational astronomer, 1632
Hippias of Elis
  advances in the arts, 270
Hippocrates of Cos
  on agriculture and human nutrition, 1230
  on black bile, 1230–1231
  case history of Tychon, 1227–1228
  effect of climate on culture, 112
  Hippocratic corpus in Greek medicine, 1228
  on humors, 1230
  on innate heat, 1231
Hippocratic writers
  on the advance of medicine, 270
  women's health, 1306
Hippodamos (Hippodamus) of Miletos
  city planner, 1660, 1695–1696
Hippokrates (Hippocrates), tyrant of Gela, 489
Hippolochos
  sympotic letters, 1191
Hippolytos (Hippolytus). See Euripides
Hippolytus
  Apostolic Tradition, 1058–1059
  excommunication by Callistus, 1058
Hipponax of Ephesus
  realism in satire, 1500
Hippos, map 5
Hispalis, map 1
Hispellum, map 2
Historia Augusta
  forgery in style of Suetonius, 1556–1557
Historiae Philippicae. See Trogus, Pompeius
Historians, Greek, 410–411
Histories. See Polybius

Histories. See Sallust (Gaius Sallustius Crispus)
Historiography, Greek, 1525–1540
    change of direction as free city-state dies, 1531
    comparative role of Thucydides and Herodotus, 1526–1529
    dramatic function, 1531
Historiography, Roman
    Cicero on function of history, 1541
    compared to Greek historiography, 1543
    corrupting effect of power, 1561
    decline of republican Rome, 1560
    focused on public life of Roman people, 1560
    freedom vs. tyranny, 1561
    high social status of historians, 1542, 1554
    methods, 1551
    moral dimension of political issues, 1541, 1560
    nostalgia for lost Golden Age, 1560
    speeches as political acts, 1561
    unreliable early annalists, 1544
    use of Greek models, 1543
History of Plants. See Theophrastus
History of Rome. See Dio Cassius
History of Sicily. See Philistus of Syracuse
Hoist
    technological development of, 324–326
Hoists, Greek
    and building techniques, 282–283, 287–288, 289 *illus.*, 294, 327 *illus.*
Hoists, Roman
    heavy crane, 326 *illus.*
    simple crane, 312–313 *illus.*
    winches, 317
Hollow casting, 1702
Home
    evidence for taxation in archaic times, 796–797
Homer
    Achilles' teachers, 1078
    Agamemnon a mediocre speaker, 1078
    Agamemnon's test of his troops, 445–446
    Athene as mentor of Telemachus, 1079
    athletic contests (*Odyssey*), 1132
    audience evaluation of songs, 1515–1516
    authenticity of warfare in, 682
    basis of ancient Greek education, 872
    boar's tusk helmet of Meriones, 681
    catalog of ships, 3, 681, 697
    Chryses' sacrifice (*Iliad*), 961
    contrasts of warrior and coward in *Iliad*, 1283
    on craftsmanship, 367
    duties of the *oikist*, 1692
    on feasting, 1169, 1170
    funeral games (*Iliad*), 1132
    god's share of sacrifice, 976
    helmet of Damasos, 681
    heroes in epic poetry, 680, 682
    historical events in, 155
    Iliad, 406, 407
    influential portrait of gods, 3–4
    land of Phaeacians, 444
    marriage of Hephaestus and Aphrodite, 850
    military weapons, 680–681
    modern study of, 1829
    Nestor's sacrifice (*Odyssey*), 969
    not highly regarded in Renaissance, 1829
    oath-taking test in *Iliad*, 445
    Odysseus' speech to Nausicaa, 1078
    Odysseus' tale to Eumaios, 1122
    Odyssey, 406, 407, 408, 417
    patterns of education, 1078–1079
    pirates in the *Odyssey*, 837–838
    quarrel between Achilles and Agamemnon, 1079
    raids on the Nile Delta in *Odyssey*, 697
    recited at Panathenaic Festival, 872
    ships, 697
    single combat in, 680–681, 682
    speech and deception in poems, 1079
    on supremacy of Zeus in *Iliad*, 848
    Telemachus' complaint to the Ithacan assembly, 446
    Thersites' right to use formal speech, 1078
    treatment of legal offenses, 590
    treatment of prisoners and slain, 684, 693, 694
    use of chariots, 680, 682
    use of simile in *Odyssey* 1283
    warriors' code, 679, 684
Homeric epic, 531–533, 872
    alternative socioeconomic roles, 532
    amalgam of dialects for metrical convenience, 1469
    bardic anonymity, 1516
    basileus, 442
    cast in didactic role, 1422
    dating of events in, 531
    feasting as social ritual in, 443
    genre canonized, 1423
    gift-giving and status in, 442–443
    Greek, 872
    heros (elite warrior class), 532
    ideas of afterlife in, 988
    Iliad, 1420–1421
    indispensable devices listed, 1421
    kleos (heroic fame) in, 1516
    marriage by capture in, 1334
    marriage patterns in, 1333–1334

matrilineal and patrilineal succession in, 1333
metrical form, 1420–1421
models of political behavior in, 441
monumental scale, 1420
mutual gift exchange, 533
Mycenaean palace society, 531
nonagricultural services, 532
Odyssey, 1420–1421
oikos (household), 532
oral composition, 1469
prenuptial contests in, 1333–1334
preservation of, 1421
reflection of Bronze Age society, 10
role of Muses, 1515
social mobility, 533
status divisions, 532–533
strong formal sense, 1420
temene (land allotments), 532
thetes, 532, 533
traditional ornaments and devices, 1420
use of extended simile, 1421
utilized direct speech, 1421
written down in Ionia, 10
Homeric Hymns
short narratives about gods, 1423
Homicide
Greek laws governing, 590, 597, 603
Homosexuality
behaviors of pursuer and pursued, 1259, 1260
common among adolescents, 1295–1296
competitive aspects of, 1258–1259
double standard in, 1296–1297
eromenos and *erastes*, 1258, 1259, 1261
female, 1261–1263
in fourth century and later, 1260
and male gender roles, 1258
between master and slave, 1296
penetration, 1260
among prostitutes, 1295
restricted by law and custom, 1258
Spartan, 1260–1261
at symposium, 1175
in transition to adulthood, 1255
Homosexuality, Roman, 1266, 1272
charges of as political weapon, 1274
"Greek" sex, 1272
tolerated but never glorified, 1277
Hoplites (race in armor), 1134–1135
in archaic period, 533, 535
hippeis (cavalry), 689
hoplite phalanx, 685–687, 688
military education of, 687

new political class, 447
social class of, 686, 687
Horatius Flaccus, Quintus (Horace)
addressed urgent political issues, 1463–1464
Ars Poetica, 1430, 1472–1473, 1521, 1580
Carmen Saeculare (*Centenary Hymn*), 1464
characterization of a witch, 885
in circle of Maecenas, 1463
comments on the epic, 1430
contribution to satire, 1501
controlled poetic distance, 1463
defense of his work in "Apologia pro Opere suo," 1501
Epistles, 1580
Epodes, 1463
Greek poets as models, 1463, 1464
importance of *convivia* and symposia in poetry, 1213
invocation of gods for secular games in *Ludi saeculares*, 855
Odes, 1326, 1463–1464
on poetic method, 1521
poet as *vates* (prophet, seer), 1463
Sabine farm, 1375
technique of indirection, 1463
unchaste behavior linked to Rome's decline, 1326
use of stereotypes in *Art of Poetry*, 1289
verse letters, 1580
versified *Epistles*, 1521
Horse races, 1133, 1139
Horses
for chariot racing, 1157
for pulling wagons, 355
for riding, 356
Horticulture, Roman
Gallic auger, 233
grafting techniques, 233–234
herbs, 233
kitchen garden, 232–233
Hours of the day, 395
House construction, Roman
mud-brick, 299
repetition of styling details, 309–310
wattle-and-daub, 299
wood-frame and concrete tenement, 303–304
See also Forums
Household, Greek, 1301–1303
vs. polis, 1303
Household, Roman
principal gods, 922
scene of key rites of passage, 922

Houses, Etruscan, 1371–1373
  ash urn models of, 1372
  atrium plan, 1372
  decoration and furnishings, 1372–1373
  Marzabotto residences, 1371–1372
  paved central courtyard with well, 1371–1372
Houses, Greek, 1656–1657, 1661, 1666–1669
  adobe (sun-dried brick), 1365
  andron (men's dining room), 1363
  archaic tiled roof, 287
  bathing facilities, 1369
  bathroom facilities, 1365
  Dema country house, 1363, 1364 *illus.*
  development of peristyle, 1367
  early styles, 1363–1365
  heating, 1365–1366
  horizontal emphasis of structural forms, 1364
  importance of privacy, 1370
  interior decoration and furnishing, 1369–1371
  modular pattern, 1365
  at Olynthus, 1365–1367
  pastas (veranda element) on ground level, 1364, 1365, 1368
  peristyle, 1669
  peristyle mansions, 1368–1369
  of Priene, Morgantina, and Delos, 1367–1369
  scale of, 1369
  size, 1363, 1365, 1366
  typical construction of, 277–278, 283, 294
  typically two stories, 1365
  urban dwellings, 1363
  and Vitruvian prescriptions, 1367–1368 *illus.*
Houses, Roman
  Ostian apartments, 1378–1381
  Ostian town, 1381–1382
  villa, 1677, 1680–1681, 1687
  water supplies to, 342
  See also Apartments; Tenement (*insula*)
Houses, Roman town, 1373
  design elements, 1373–1375
  Herculaneum, Samnite House, 1373
  House of the Nymphaeum, 1381
  Ostia, House of Cupid and Psyche, 1381
  Pompeii, House of the Faun, 1374 *illus.*
  Pompeii, House of the Surgeon, 1373
  Pompeii, House of the Vettii, 1375
House wall decoration. *See* Wall painting
Housing, city
  Greek modular, 1692–1694
  Roman apartment crowding, 1700
Hubris (*hybris*)
  characteristic forms of, 1177

  laws concerning, 601–602, 1184
  at symposium, 1174
Human anatomy
  Greek view of reproduction, 1306
Humanists
  classical scholarship of, 1826
Humor
  and personality in *Problems,* 1281
Humors, theory of
  balancing of, 1229
  black bile, 1230–1231
  connection with qualities, seasons and elements
    of Empedocles, 1231
  effect of atmospheric conditions on 1230
  expelling of, 1232
  Galen's theories, 1239
  plethora or *plerosis* (accumulation) of, 1230
  predictions of diseases by, 1231
  reduced to four, 1230
  treatment with drugs, 1231
  water not a true humor, 1230
Huns, map 11
  arrival in Europe, 171–172, 176
  attack on Rome, 82
  battle of Châlons, 173
  horse-oriented life-style, 178–179
Hunting, 1162–1163
  in classical literature, 123
  effects on ecosystems, 127
  and extinction of animal species, 124, 125
  in Pella mosaic, 1766 *illus.,* 1767
  as preparation for fighting, 690
  spiritual nature of, 122–123
  as subject of Roman art, 1787, 1790,
    1791 *illus.*
  subsistence, 122
Hunts, animal, 1162–1163
Hyacinthia, 1149, 1151
Hydaspes River, map 8
Hydraulics. *See* Water engineering
Hyettos, map 4
Hyginus (land surveyor), 814
Hyle (matter)
  term coined by Aristotle, 1587
Hymenaios (marriage song), 1334, 1339, 1438
Hymn to Apollo, 534, 868, 1438
Hymn to Demeter, 1145, 1316
  early evidence of Eleusinian Mysteries, 905
  loss of daughter, 1335
  marriage from a bride's perspective, 1335
Hymn to Hermes
  Apollo's warning to would-be seers, 942

Hymns, Greek
  prayers set to music, 890
  regular feature of communal worship, 890
Hyperides
  purchase of slave boy by client, 830
Hyphasis River, map 8

I

Iambic poetry
  uses for, 1439
Iamblichos
  Babyloniaka, 1570
Iapygia, map 2
Iasos, map 4, map 5
Iberian Peninsula, map 1, 88 *illus.*
  geography, 91
Iberians
  Greek and Roman contacts, 142
  physical description, 142
Iberus (Ebro) River, 100, map 1, 88 *illus.*
  geology, 104
  geology of valley, 100–101
Ibycus
  epic and mythic themes, 1449
  erotic poetry, 1449
  Greek lyricist, 1449
Icarus, 367, 368 *illus.*
Iconium, map 5
Ictinus
  temple of Apollo at Bassai, 1664–1665
Ideograms, 400
Idumaea, map 5
Igel, map 1
Ignatius of Antioch
  establishment of monarchical episcopate, 1052
Ikkos of Tarentum, 1138
Iliad. See Homer
Illustration, book
  color in, 434
  origins of medieval miniatures, 434
Illyria, map 3
  pirates from, 838, 839
Illyricum, map 10
Ilva (Aithalia), map 2
Imitation paintings. *See* Trompe l'oeil Roman
    painting
Immolatio
  sanctification of sacrificial victim, 984
Immortality
  belief in, 1006

kleos (undying fame), 991
  possibility of, 988
Immunity, diplomatic
  for envoys and heralds, 672, 676
Imperial forums. *See* Forums
Imperium
  censor's lack of, 502
  consul's extended, 499, 503
  and decline of Republic, 515–516
  dictator's, 502
  expansion of, 503
  graded, 502, 503
  infinitum, 515
  maius of Octavian, 520
  military tribunes, 503
  of Princeps, 524
  of Roman senators, 509, 510
  used by Augustus, 518, 519–520
Import duties, 799, 804
Incense
  burning of, 964
  fuel for miniature machines, 350, 351 *illus.*
Incest, 1250–1251
  laws concerning, 1337
  restrictions, 1345, 1346
Incubation, rite of, 944
India
  Alexander's campaigns, 35, 36
  Roman trade with, 770
Indian Ocean, map 8
Indians
  physical description, 147
Indictiones (surtaxes), 822–823
Individualism
  development of biography in fourth century,
    1282
  Greek, 1018
  growth of in fourth century, 1282
Indo-Greek Kingdom, map 9
Indus River, map 8
Industry, Greek
  craftsmen's associations, 743
  decline in fourth century, 213–214
  fragmented nature of, 743–744
  limitations of technology, 742
  predominance of handmade goods, 742
  Ptolemaic monopolies, 735
  techne (skill), 742
Infanticide (exposure), 1338, 1356–1357
  Roman laws, 1276
Inflation
  under Diocletian, 79

Inheritance
    Greek law governing, 592, 596–597
    restrictions, 1349
Ink
    carbon, 425
    iron-tannin, 426
Inns, Roman, 354
Insanity
    guardianship of the insane, 616
Inscriptions
    on crafts, 403
    monumental, 411–412, 413, 418
Insurance
    burial associations, 835
    decree of Miletus, 835
    maritime commercial loans, 834
    real estate, 834–835
Intercalation, 390, 391, 392, 394
Interior decoration, Greek
    lavish Hellenistic, 1370–1371
    model Athenian, 1369–1370
    wall paintings, 1364
    walls, floors, and ceilings, 1749–1770
Interior decoration, Roman
    Early Principate, 1777–1783
    survival of, 1771–1772
    themes of, 1771, 1785, 1788 *illus.*
    of Trajan's Forum buildings, 316–317, 319–
        320
    walls, floors, and ceilings, 1771–1794
    See also Mosaic art; Stucco relief art; Tomb
        decoration; Wall painting
Interior space
    in Greek architecture, 286, 1653, 1657,
        1659–1661, 1663 *illus.*, 1664, 1668 *illus.*
    in Roman architecture, 1674–1675, 1677,
        1680–1682 *illus.*, 1685 *illus.*, 1686–1689
International law. *See* Law of Nations
International organizations
    arbitration, 673
    Greek amphictyonies (religious leagues), 668–
        669
    hegemonial leagues, 674
    Panhellenic festivals and games, 669
Inventory management, Roman
    of construction materials, 307
Iol Caesarea, map 6
Iolkos, map 4
Ion of Chios
    on Greek society, 1182
    on symposia, 1182

Ionia, map 4, map 5
    city plans in, 1665–1667
Ionians
    migrations to Asia Minor, 6
    revolt against Persian rule, 23–24
Ionian Sea, map 2, 88 *illus.*
Iphicrates
    use of peltasts in Corinthian War, 692
Iphigenia in Tauris. See Euripides
Irenaeus of Smyrna
    establishment of Christian Bible, 1054
Irish
    role of church in preserving classical knowledge,
        1822
Irnerius
    glossators, 628
    school of at Bologna, 627–628
Iron
    wrought, 371
Irrigation
    water pumps and wheels, 329–330, 345, 346,
        347 *illus.*
Irrigation engineering, 329–330
Isaeus
    on women at symposia, 1172
Ischia
    Greek colony, 11, 193
Isidore of Seville
    transmission of classical knowledge, 1821
Isis, cult of, 938, 1003, 1004
    in Rome, 858
Island gems, 1722
    "Serpent Master" amygdaloid, 1724 *illus.*
Island League
    recognizes Ptolemaia, 1150
Isle of Blessed, 993
Isocrates
    academic program, 1087
    Antidosis (Exchange of Property), 542
    connection between personal and civic morality,
        1087, 1088
    didacticism of extant speeches, 1088
    Euagoras (Evagoras), importance of, 1536
    Gorgianic approach of, 1087–1088
    influence on fourth century rhetorical education,
        1086–1087
    on the Panhellenic festivals, 669
    rhetorical works, 1536
    on social conflict, 542
    speeches of, 428
    teacher of fourth-century historians, 1530

teaching style, 1087
use of epideictic speech, 1094
vision of achievable excellence, 1087
Isonomia
in classical Athens, 467
Cleisthenic reforms and, 467
in fifth century Athens, 469
replacement by *demokratia,* 469
Isopoliteia treaties
and equality of citizen rights, 674–675
Issos, map 5, map 8
Istanbul. *See* Byzantium (Byzantion, Istanbul)
Isthmia, map 4
Isthmian Games, 1133, 1134, 1144
Isthmus of Corinth, 162
Istros, map 3, map 7
Istros (Istrus, Danube) River, map 1, map 3, 88 *illus.*
Italy, map 2, map 10, 88 *illus.*
classical Greek coinage of, 1799–1801
conquest by Rome, 50–51
geography, 91
loss of favored status under Diocletian, 78
oracles of, 954–955
pirates from southern Italy, 839
Ithake (Ithaca), map 4
Iuvenalis, Decimus Iunius (Juvenal)
climax of Roman satiric tradition, 1502
cynical treatment of gods, 855–856
exaggerated satirical effects, 1502
female behavior signals society's decline, 1329
fire hazards of tenements, 1379–1380
misbehavior of upper-class wives, 1328–1329
requirements for a teacher, 1113
Satire Six, 1328–1329
techniques, 1502
on urban ills, 129
Izmir. *See* Smyrna (Izmir)
Izmit. *See* Nicomedia

J

Jacket, Persian (*kandys*), 1396, 1398
Jack-of-all-trades, 381
James (brother of Jesus of Nazareth)
assassination of, 1049
role in Apostles' Council, 1048
Jamnia, map 5
January
Roman festivals in, 909–910

Jars, clay, 360–361
Jason of Cyrene
source of 1 Maccabees, 1036
Javelin throwing, 1137
ankyle (mechanical aid), 1137
Jerome, Saint
Latin Christian epistolographer, 1578
Jerusalem, map 5
becomes Roman colony, 73
Christians in, 1049
temple in, 1027, 1039, 1040
Jesus of Nazareth
gospel of, 1047
Jew (*Yehudi* or *Ioudaiso*)
identity of, 1028
Jewelry, 373
Carthaginian, 1407
Celtic torque, 1400
Etruscan, 1399, 1400
pendant (*bulla*), 1400
Jewish Antiquities. See Josephus, Flavius
Jews
intermarriage with Gentiles, 1027–1028
revolt against Hadrian suppressed, 73
revolt against Trajan, 72
taxation of, 811
Job, Book of
nature of God and problems of evil, 1030
John
Gospel of, 1050
John Hyrcanus I
spread of Judaism by, 1033
Jordan River, map 5
Josephus, Flavius (Joseph ben Matthias)
Against Apion, 1041
Jewish Antiquities, 1041
Jewish histories, 74
The Jewish War, 1041
on siege of Jerusalem, 714
Jucar River, map 1
Judaea, map 5, map 10, 88 *illus.*
becomes Roman province, 1039
expansion of , 1033
Hellenistic, 1030–1038
kingdom of, 1033
Judah ha-Nasi, patriarch of Palestine, 1043
Judah (Maccabee), son of Mattathias
advocate of Jewish independence, 1032
alliance with Rome, 1032
Judaism, 1027–1045
ambiguous ethnic and religious identities, 1028

Judaism (continued)
  apologetics for, 1037
  attacks on in seventh century Spain, 174
  Hellenistic Period, 1030–1038
  high priests of, 1031
  intermarriage controversy, 1027–1028
  outlawed by Antiochus IV, 1032
  Persian Period, 1028–1030
  ritual observances, 1028
  Roman Period, 1038–1042
  separatism, 1031, 1034, 1035, 1043
  temples of, 1027
  worship of Yahweh alone, 1027
  See also Assimilationism, Jewish; Rebellions,
    Jewish
Judaism, Rabbinic
  differences, 1043
  extent of, 1044
  Mishnah, earliest document of, 1040
  rituals and standards, 1043–1044
  separatism, 1043
Judaization
  of overseas Judahite colonies, 1029
  policy of Alexander Jannaeus, 1033
Jugurtha, king of Numidia
  capture by Sulla, 709–710
  defeat of Romans in 109 B.C., 709
  war with Rome, 57
Jugurthine War. See Sallust (Gaius Sallustius Crispus)
Julianus, Flavius Claudius (Julian the Apostate)
  administrative ability, 81
  attempts to restore Olympian religion, 43, 81
  paganism of, 1070
  social unrest under, 1070
  war policy, 1070–1071
Julianus, Salvius
  codification of praetors' edicts, 662
  consolidation of praetor's edicts, 610
Julian year, 392
July
  month renamed in honor of Julius Caesar, 916
  Roman festivals in, 916
Juno
  variety of epithets for, 857
Jupiter
  goddesses associated with on Capitol, 854
  supremacy of, 854
Jurists, Roman
  books by, 610
  in *consilium principis*, 662
  opinions of, 609, 610

Jury courts (*heliaia*)
  in Solonian code, 453–454
Jury trial
  by the Areopagos, 599
  by arkhon, 599, 600
  chairmen of, 600
  defense procedures, 600
  method of voting, 600
  penalties, 600–601
  predecessor of (*heliaia*), 599
  procedures of, 600
  selecting jurors, 600
  witnesses, 600
Justice
  Greek concept of (*dike*), 445, 452
  Plato's myth in *Protagoras*, 476
Justinianus, Flavius Petrus Sabbatius (Justinian I)
  annihilation of Ostrogoths, 177
  Code of, 612
  Corpus Juris Civilis, 612
  divorce laws, 614
  Fifty Decisions, 612
  restoration of Roman Empire, 176, 177
  survival of Eastern Empire under, 719
Justin Martyr
  acceptance of Platonic metaphysics and Stoic
    ethics, 1056
  Christian apologies of, 1056
  Dialogue with Trypho, 1056
  founded school in Rome, 1058
Jutes, map 11

K

Kaboura (Kabul), map 8
Kadesh, map 5
Kaikos River, map 5
Kalami (reed pens), 426
Kalamis, 1711
Kalauria (Kalaureia, Poros), map 4
  union of Saronic Gulf cities and Orchomenos
    (Boiotia), 491
Kalchedon (Calchedon), map 5, map 7
Kallias
  military engineer of Rhodes, 332
Kallimachos (Callimachus), 1702
  flying drapery style of sculpture, 1714
Kalydon, map 4
Kamarina (Camarina), map 7

Kandahar, map 8
Kappadokia (Cappadocia), map 5, map 9
Karanis
    tax list from second century, 771
Karanos, feast of, 1191
Karatepe, map 5
Kardia (Cardia), map 7
Karneia, 1143, 1149
Karpathos (Carpathus), map 4
Karyanda, map 4, map 5
Karystos (Carystus), map 4
Katane (Catana), map 2, map 7
Katharsis (catharsis) (purgation or purification),
    1518
Kathekonta (duties)
    social obligations recognized by Stoics, 1618
Kaunos, map 5
Kayseri. *See* Caesarea
Kaystros River, map 5
Keles (horse race), 1133
Keletron, Lake, map 3
Kenturipe (Centuripae), map 2
Keos (Ceos), map 4
Kerkyra. *See* Corcyra (Corfu, Kerkyra)
"Khion of Herakleia" (Chion of Heraklea)
    epistolary novel, 1567, 1581
Khreia (*Anecdotes*), 1123
Kibotos (capsa, book boxes), 428
Killa, map 4, map 5
Killing
    in Roman games, 1163–1164
Kimon (Cimon) of Athens
    ostracism of, 468
    tenure as *strategos,* 474
Kimon (Cimon) of Syracuse
    coin artist, 1799
Kin groups
    in archaic and classical Greece, 797
Kithara, 1139
Kition (Citium), map 5
Klaros (Claros), map 4, map 5
Klazomenai (Clazomenae), map 4, map 5
Klearchos
    tyranny of, 543
Kleisthenes (Cleisthenes)
    democratic reforms in Athens, 23
    laws regarding exile, 24–25
    reforms of, 539,540
    reorganization of government, 463–465
    reorganization of traditional forms of association,
        463–464

Kleitias, 1752, 1753 *illus.*
Kleitomachos of Thebes, 1139
Kleomenes (Cleomenes) I, king of Sparta, 27
    massacre of Argives, 693
Kleomenes (Cleomenes) III, king of Sparta
    aimed to restore former Spartan glories, 546
    land reforms, 39
Kleon, 541
Kleophon, 541
Kleophrades Painter
    Attic red-figure hydria, 1755 *illus.*
Klepsydra, 394
Knidos (Cnidus), map 4, map 5
Knitting, 1388
Knossos (Cnossus), map 4
Knowing, Greek concepts of, 1602
Kokytos, river of underworld, 989
Kollemata (papyrus sheets), 422
Kolonos (Colonus), map 4
Kolophon (Colophon), map 4, map 5
Kolossai (Colossae), map 5
Kopais (Copais), Lake, map 4
Korai, 1706
    clothing worn by, 1390, 1394–1395
    hairstyles, 1395
    Nikandre statue, 1394
Korakesion, map 5
Korakou, map 4
Koroneia (Coronea), map 4
Korope, map 4
Korykos, map 5
    list of occupations from, 772
Kos (Cos), map 4
    Dark Age settlements, 6
    silk industry, 1387
Koureion
    celebrates formal entry of son into phratry,
        893
Koureotis
    boy's puberty rite, 893, 1146
Kouros, 1702, 1706
    from Anavyssos, 1707
    clothing worn by, 1390, 1395
    on Delos, 1706
    at Delphi, 1707
    evidence of aristocratic lifestyle, 534
    from Peiraeus, 1701
    Sounion group, 1707 *illus.*
Krannon (Crannon), map 4
Kresilas, 1713
Krisa (Crisa), map 4

Kritios, 1710
Tyrant Slayers, 1710
Kritios boy, 1710
Krokeae (Krokeai), map 4
Kroton (Croton), map 2
athletic domination of, 1140
Ktesibios (Ctesibius)
Alexandrian Greek inventor of the force pump,
343
inventor of hydraulus, 1511
Kunaxa (Cunaxa), map 5
Pythian Games at, 1133
Kyklades (Cyclades). *See* Cyclades
Kylon
failed coup in Athens, 22
Kyme (Cumae, Cuma), map 4, map 5
first Greek colony in West, 11
source of Etruscan alphabet, 416
Kyme (Cumae, Cuma), 954, map 2, map 7
Kyniska of Sparta, 1140
Kypselos (Cypselus)
tyrant of Corinth, 18–19
Kyrene (Cyrene), map 6, map 7
foundation of, 16
monarchy of, 487
trade of, 16
Kyrios (guardian of the bride), 1338
Kythera (Cythera), map 4
Kyzikos (Cyzicus), map 4, map 5, map 7

L

Labor
armaments manufacture, 378
availability of skilled, 379
availability of slave labor vs. technological
progress, 328–329
in building construction, 288
control of wealthy minority over, 744
dependent labor, 745, 748, 749
division of, 380–381
engineering projects, 324, 347, 352
Greek architectural, 1662–1663
limited development of wage labor, 745
in mining, 758
occupational diversity, 772
overlapping occupations of freedmen and slaves,
744
Roman architectural traveling, 1679, 1684

Roman specialization and guilds, 307–308
for shipbuilding, 768
skilled slaves, 379
slavery and status of free citizens, 772
Spartan-Helot form of dependence, 748–749
subjection of one community by another, 748
supply of, 379
use of in roadbuilding, 759–760
Lacedaemon. *See* Sparta
Lacer, Julius, 383
Lachish, map 5
Laconia (Lakonia), map 4
conquest of, 162
status distinctions among residents, 593
Lactantius
polemic against the tetrachy, 1064
La Graufesenque. *See* Condatomagus (La
Graufesenque)
Lakes, Mediterranean, 106–107
Lamps
made from molds, 379, 380 *illus.*
Lampsakos, map 4, map 5, map 7
Land
allocation in Greek city, 1692–1693
allocation in Roman city, 1697–1698
classes of, 804
measurement of, 815
private ownership in Greece, 729–730
royal, 804
rural land division and city planning, 1693, 1696
survey, Roman, 814–815
taxes on, 803–804, 823
Land dispossession, Roman, 554, 555, 559, 566
of peasant-soldiers, 554
as result of veterans' settlement, 559, 561,
562–563
of senators and equestrians, 559
of small landowners, 554
Land ownership
in Hellenistic world, 803–804
in Roman provinces, 813
Land reform
in archaic Greece, 535, 536, 538
under Augustus, 563
in classical Greece, 539, 541
failure of Licinian-Sextian legislation, 560
under Gracchus, 556–557
in Hellenistic period, 546
Landscape
in Roman painting and mosaic, 1774–1775 *illus.*,
1777, 1778, 1785

Land use, Greek
  criteria for settlement, 215
  fallow, 216
  grain farming, 215–216
  horse raising, 215
  pasture area, 215
Land use, Roman
  changes in and political effects, 219
  suitability of different types, 221
  terracing, 221
Language
  Phoenician, 404–406
  Semitic, 399
  spoken vs. written, 407–408
Languages and dialects, Asia Minor
  Cappadocian, 201
  Carian, 201
  Galatian, 201–202
  Greek as colloquial language, 200
  Latin never a colloquial language, 202
  Luwian-related, 201
  Lycaonian, 201
  Lycian, 200
  Lydian, 200
  Mysian, 200
  Old Phrygian, 199
  Pisidian, 201
  relation of Phrygian to other languages, 199–200
  Sidetic, 201
Languages and dialects, Balkan
  Daco-Mysian, 202
  Epirote, 203
  Illyrian, 202–203
  Macedonian, 203–204
  Paeonian, 203
  Thracian, 202
Languages and dialects, France
  Celtic, 194–195
  Gaulish (Gallic), 194
  Greek, 194
  Lepontic, 194
  Ligurian, 194–195
Languages and dialects, Greek
  Atticist movement, 186–187
  decline of classical dialects, 186
  decline after third century, 187–188
  dialects of the first millennium, 185
  Doric dialects, 185
  in early to middle Helladic cultures, 184
  in eastern Roman Empire, 187
  ethnocentrism of Greek speakers, 204

koine glossa (common tongue), 185–186
  lack of interest in other languages, 204
  learned by educated Roman, 187
  Linear B script, 184–185
  literary dialects, 185
  Mycenaean dialect, 184–185
  in Palestine and Syria, 198–199
  Pelasgian, 184
  pre-Greek, 184
  restructuring of in fourth century, 186
Languages and dialects, Indo-European, 183
  in Italy, 193
  pre-Indo-European substrate, 183
Languages and dialects, Italy
  Celtic, 195
  Etruscan, 193–194
  Faliscan, 192
  Greek, 193
  Messapian, 192–193
  Osco-Umbrian, 191–192
  Phoenician and Punic, 193
  Sabellian dialects of central Italy, 191–192
  Sicanian, 193
  Venetic, 192
Languages and dialects, North Africa
  Coptic, 197
  Demotic, 197
  early Phoenician contact, 196
  Egyptian, 197
  Greek, 197
  hieratic, 197
  hieroglyphic, 197
  Massylian, 196
  Old Egyptian, 197
  Punic, 196–197
Languages and dialects, Palestine and Syria
  Aramaic, 198
  Aramaic-Greek bilingualism, 199
  Canaanite, 198
  Hebrew, 198
  Latin in military and law, 199
  Phoenician, 198
  Safaitic, 198
  Syriac, 198
Languages and dialects, Spain
  Basque, 195
  Celtiberian, 195
  Iberian, 195
Lanuvium, map 2
Laocoön and His Sons, statue of
  rediscovery, 1728

Laodikeia, map 5
Lararium (private shrine), 921
Lares
  powers of the farmland, 921
Larissa, map 4
Last Decree (*senatus consultum ultimum*)
  martial law, 57
Latin
  archaic, 188
  in Charlemagne's palace school, 1822
  distinction between language of prose and
    poetry, 189
  in early Christian church, 1822
  Greek analytic techniques applied, 1820
  Greek views of, 204–205
  historical factors in development, 190
  increasing literary sophistication, 64
  influence of foreign cultures on, 188
  as language for philosophy, 1646
  legal and administrative language, 48
  literary language, 188–189, 205
  in plays and literature, 189
  provincial dialects, 190
  Scholastic faults of style, 1825
  spread of in ancient world, 188
  teaching of in modern England, 1828–1829
  translation of Christian testaments into, 1059
  translation of Greek philosophy, 1638–1639
  as universal language, 205
  vulgar Latin, 189–190
Latin League
  defeated by Rome, 51
  treaty with Rome, 50
Latium, map 2
  defense of, 50
  vortex of cultural conflict, 46
Laudatio Turiae
  funerary inscription praising good wife, 1320
Laurium (Laurion), map 4
  mine labor practices, 744
  revenue from mines at, 635, 639
  silver mines of, 25, 744, 780, 1796
Law, Athenian, 479–480
  adoption, 596
  child legitimacy, 595–596
  concerning metics, 595
  disenfranchisement, 595
  divorce, 595
  homicide, 597
  importance of, 604
  individual citizen's public duties, 598

inheritance, 596
liturgies, 598–599
lying in the assembly (ekklesia), 599
on marriage, 595
naturalization, 595
property rights, 596–597
and public affairs, 598
religious offenses, 599
on slavery, 595
treason, 599
trial by jury, 599–601
tyranny, 599
Law, Cretan
  concerning family property, 592
  council of elders, 592
  law of Minos, 591, 593
  legal status of individuals, 592, 596
  rape laws, 592
Law, divine
  Roman definition of, 617
  Roman rituals, 909
Law, Greek
  agraphoi nomoi (unwritten laws), 450
  apagoge, 602
  apographe, 602
  blackmail and sycophancy, 601
  Boeotian laws, 590
  changes in fourth century, 603–604
  civil status, 595
  codes of, 409, 411
  damage (*blabe*), 598
  development of jurisprudence, 597
  diadikasia, 603
  diamartyria, 603
  dokimasia, 602
  eisangelia, 599, 602
  endeixis, 602
  ephegesis, 602
  euthyna, 602
  family rights, 592, 594, 596
  graphe, 602
  guilt by motive, 597–598
  in the Homeric Age, 590–591
  hybris, 601,602
  hyleris, 597
  importance of written codes, 450
  in independent states, 589
  inheritance, 596
  initiating proceedings, 601
  king's judgment in deciding disputes, 590
Law Code of Gortyn. *See* Gortyn

lawgivers (*nomothetai*) and, 449–451
legislation restricting women, 1311
magistrates' power, 601
mercantile cases (*dike emporike*), 603
nomos, 450, 480
obligations to state, 598–599
offenses against persons and properties, 597
paragraphe, 603
phasis, 602
private cases, 601, 601, 603
probole, 599, 602
property laws, 596–597
property rights, 592, 594, 598
prosecution of cases, 601
public arbitrators, 603
public cases, 601, 602–603
public opinion and, 591
separation from government, 480
thesmos, 450
trial by elders or leading men, 590–591
trial by jury, 599–601
Law, Roman
    actions, 612–613
    alimenta (nutritional subsidies for poor children),
        1356
    Aquilian, 609, 626
    Atilian, 609, 615
    Atinian, 609
    Augustan legislation, 1343, 1352–1353
    Byzantine codifications, 627
    Canuleian, 608
    categorization of, 607
    of censorship (*Lex maiestatis*), 1559
    Cincian, 609
    of contract, 608, 621–625
    customary in early Republic, 608–609
    of delict, 626–627
    demand for codification of, 608
    effects on later law, 627–628
    forbade legal marriage of slaves, 1353
    formulary procedures, 612
    among Germanic tribes of Western Empire, 627
    honestiores/humiliores distinctions, 566
    influence on modern Greek civil code, 627
    jurists' opinions, 609
    legal authority over women, 1330
    legislation on fire safety, 1379
    Lex Oppia, 1320, 1321, 1330
    Lex Papia Poppaea (Papian and Poppaean law) (to
        increase family size), 1349, 1355–1356
    on marriage, 1344, 1345–1347

Minucian law, 1347
model for European civil codes, 628
Napoleonic Code, 628
patria potestas, 614–615, 1344
peculium, 614–615, 616
of persons, 613–617
Plaetorian, 609, 616
private, 609
religious, 617
revival of local law, 628
slavery code, 580,581
source of in the Republic, 608–610
sources of in early empire, 610–611
sources of postclassical, 611
spread by colonization, 628
of succession, 619–621
sui iuris, 1330
Twelve Tables, 49, 417, 550, 551, 552, 550, 552,
    580–581, 608, 651, 703
See also particular offices and individuals; and
    legal areas; Contract, law of; Delict, law of
Law, Spartan
    concerning women, 593
    infanticide in, 593
    laws of Lykourgos, 593, 594
    military obligation of males, 593
    origins, 593
    on property, 593
Lawcourts. *See* Basilica Ulpia
Law of Moses
    continued observation of by Jewish Christians,
        1049
Law of Nations (*ius gentium*), 670
Laws, Jewish, 1028, 1029
Laws. *See* Plato
League of Korinth, 543
Leap year, 394
Leather
    book rolls, 425, 431
    See also Hides
Leatherworking, 374, 1388
Lebadeia (Libadia)
    oracle of Trophonius, 944
Lecanomancy
    divination by peering into water, 945
Ledosus (Lezoux), map 1
    pottery and Roman trade routes, 764
Lefkadia (Lefkhadia), map 3
    tomb paintings at, 1762
Lefkandi, map 4
    architecture of, 1657, 1679, 1685

Lefkandi (continued)
  Dark Age settlement of, 7–8
  and excavations at, 532
  Geometric pottery, 1704
  tenth-century tomb excavations, 1394
Leges Sacrae (sacred laws)
  about cult matters, 960
  rules governing sacrifice, 972
Legumes (pulses)
  broad bean (*Vicia faba*), 249
  favism and lathyrism, 249
  lentils, 249
  pea (*Pisum sativum*), 249
Lelantos River, map 4
Lembos (galley), 840
Lemnos, map 4
Lemuria, 997
  Festival of the Dead, 914
  role of paterfamilias, 914
Lenaia, 1148
Leochares, 1716
Leochares (attributed to)
  Apollo Belvedere, 1727
Leonidas, king of Sparta, 26
Leonidas of Rhodes, 1135
Leontinoi, map 2, map 7
Leontopolis, map 6
Leo VI, the Wise
  Basilica, 627
Lepcis (Leptis) Magna, map 6
  Severan Basilica, 1747
Lepidus, Marcus Aemilius
  in Second Triumvirate, 62
Lepidus, Marcus Aemilius
  uprising of dispossessed farmers (77 B.C.), 559
Lesbianism. *See* Homosexuality
Lesbos, map 4, map 5
  musical and lyric tradition, 1507
  settlement of, 6
"Letter of Aristeas"
  Greco-Jewish philosophical text, 1037
Letters of Chion of Heraklea. See "Khion of Herakleia"
Letters. *See* Alphabet
Letters. See Plinius Caecilius Secundus, Gaius (Pliny the Younger)
Letter writing, 1573–1582
  basic requirement of friendship, 1573–1574
  Christian epistolary tradition, 1577–1578
  content of, 1577
  defined by purpose, 1573–1574
  formulas of, 1576–1577
  fourth-century A.D. Greek, 1574

  history and practice, 1575–1581
  as literary art form, 1573–1574
  papyrus, 1575
  purposes of, 1573–1574
  real vs. imaginary, 1581
  Roman, 1574–1575
  Roman classical tradition, 1578–1580
  sent by private messenger, 1576
  on tablets, of wood or metal, 1575
  theory, 1573–1575
  in verse, 1580–1581
Leucippus
  propounded atomic theory, 1596
Leukas, map 7
Leukippe and Kleitophon. See Achilles Tatius
Leuktra, map 4
  battle of, 459, 460, 544, 577, 691
Lever, 323, 324 *illus.*
Lex Domitia
  provisions of for priestly colleges, 934
Lex Oppia
  debate on repeal of, 1320
  female demonstration against, 1321
  repeal, 1408
Lex Romana Burgundionum, 627
Lex Romana Recesvindiana, 627
Lex Romana Visigothorum, 627
Lezoux. *See* Ledosus
Libadia. *See* Lebadeia
Libanus Mountains, map 5
Libations
  Choai, 965
  of liquids, 964–965
  participation of gods in, 965
  phiale, 965
  spondai, 965
  used at critical moments, 965
Liberalia
  Roman spring fertility festival, 913
Libraries, Greek, 413, 415
  See also Alexandria; Pergamon
Libraries, Roman, 1674, 1679, 1683, 1685 *illus.*
Libraries of Trajan, 309, 317 *illus.*, 318 *illus.*, 319–320
Library. See Apollodorus
Library of History. See Diodorus Siculus
Libya, map 6, 88 *illus.*
Libyan Desert, map 6, 88 *illus.*
  geography, 92
  geology, 101
Libyans
  physical description, 148–149

Life of Aesop
    folk-book-based moral tales, 1568
Life of Alexander
    unknown author impersonates older historian,
      1567
Life of Charlemagne. See Einhard
Life of Constantine. See Eusebius, 1068
Life of St. Antony. See Athanasius, 1067
Lighthouses, 362–363
Liguria, map 2
Limbo
    Roman concept of, 1000
Linares
    miners on bas-relief near, 786
Lindos, map 4
Linear A, 401
Linear B, 400
Linen, 374
    Bronze Age industry, 1392
    in Greek clothing, 1387, 1398
    in Roman clothing, 1401
Lipara, map 2, map 7
Liris River, map 2
Literacy
    in Greece, 406, 411–413
    in Rome, 417–418, 1554
Literary scholarship, Hellenistic, 1519–1520
Literature. *See* Book production
Literature, Greek
    determinants of attitudes toward women,
      1312–1313
    and development of writing system, 406–409,
      413, 414–415, 416
    Hellenistic audience, 1313
    Humanist interest in, 1826
    modern study of, 1828–1829
    study of, 1819–1832
    translation in Renaissance, 1827
Literature, Jewish, 1029–1030
Literature, medieval
    classical themes in vernacular, 1824
    French vernacular, 1824
    Latin, 1824
Literature, modern
    classical themes in, 1832
Literature, oral
    Greek tradition of, 406–409
    Roman tradition of, 417
Literature, Roman
    decline in later Empire, 75
    fourteenth-century rediscovery of "lost" works,
      1826

    imitation of Greek models, 1820
    influence of Greek literature on, 417–418
    medieval manuscript copying, 1823
    modern study of, 1828–1829
    predominance of Ciceronian style, 1827
    study of, 1819–1832
    translation in Renaissance, 1827
Litters
    for traveling, 357
Liturgies, 640, 797, 805, 806
    agoranomia, 805
    antidosis (exchange), 598–599, 802
    architheoria, 801
    choregia, 801
    gymnasiarchiai, 801
    hestiasis, 801
    hippotrophia, 801
    sitonia, 805
    synchoregia, 801
    trierarchy, 801–802
Lives of the Famous Men. See Nepos, Cornelius
Lives of the Twelve Caesars. See Suetonius Tranquillus,
    Gaius (Suetonius)
Livia's Portico, 1211
Livius, Titus (Livy)
    Ab Urbe Condita (*History of Rome*), 1546
    accession of Numa Pompilius, 953
    augury procedures followed, 953
    Augustan historian, 1546–1547
    Ciceronian in style and political approach, 1546
    criticism of Roman vices, 66
    dependence on literary sources, 1546–1547
    destruction of Roman Republic, 1546
    distinction between male and female worlds, 1320
    on Hellenistic symposia, 1202
    improvements in annalistic historiography, 1547
    Lex Oppia, 1320
    Lucretia's suicide, 1265
    on military career of Spurius Ligustinus, 706
    natural conservative, 1546
    praises of *pudicitia,* 1325–1326
    Rome's rise to world domination, 1546
    sexual misconduct of Tarquinius Superbus and
      Tullia, 1267
    on state contracts, 818
    stories as exempla of republican values, 1547
    stories of Verginia and Lucretia, 1325–1326
    story of Aeneas, 877
    story of Verginius, 1268
    writings on Roman warfare, 704
Livius Andronicus, Lucius, 417
    Greek plays in Latin, 1487

Livius Andronicus (continued)
  translated *Odyssey* into Latin, 1427
  used native Latin verse form, 1427
Logographers, Greek, 409
Logos (reasoned argument)
Lokris, Opuntian, map 4
Lokris, Ozolian, map 4
Lokroi Epizephyrioi, map 2, map 7
Lollianos
  Phoinikika, 1569
Lombards
  invasion of Italy, 177
Londinium, map 1
Longinus
  De Sublimitate (*On the Sublime*) (*Peri Hypsous*),
    1429–1430, 1521
  on rhetorical style in *On the Sublime,* 1105
Long jump, 1136–1137
  See also Halteres
Longus
  Daphnis and Chloe, 1568–1569
  teenage love, 1568
Loom
  Roman types, 1402
  two-beam, 1388
  upright, 1387–1388
Lost wax technique, 1702
Lots
  oracles given by, 955
Lovati, Lovato
  classical knowledge, 1825
Love
  as affliction, in poems of Catullus, 1458
  Hellenistic novelty, 1570–1571
  and marriage, 1570–1571, 1571
  motive in bucolic poetry, 1468
  one element of early novels, 1571
  as play, in Ovid's poetry, 1460
  Theocritus' treatment of, 1471
Love letters
  Alkiphron's *Letters from Courtesans,* 1581
  Ovid (*Art of Love*), 1581
Low Ham, map 1
Lucania, map 2
Lucanus, Marcus Annaeus (Lucan)
  De Bello Civili (*Civil War*) (*Pharsalia*), 69, 1431
  literary weaknesses, 1431
Lucaria
  Roman festival of the grove, 916
Lucian
  on prostitution, 1292, 1293

satire on rhetorical education, 1104
social indignities suffered by Greek intellectuals,
  1217
Lucian of Samosata
  prose satire of, 1501
Lucilius, Gaius
  contemporary sexual themes in writing, 1272
  founder of satire, 1499
  influence on satirical form, 1499–1500
  invented genre of satire, 1455
  made poetry writing respectable, 1455
  satirical realism, 1501
  slander of Scipio Aemilianus, 1272
Lucretia
  rape by Sextus Tarquinius, 878, 1201
  woman's virtue more precious than life, 1326
Lucretius (Titus Lucretius Carus)
  corruption caused by material advance, 272–273
  cycle of birth and death, 1640
  educational aims, 1639
  Epicurean philosophy the salvation of man, 273
  ethical message of physics, 1638
  gradual advance of man, 272–273
  happiness defined, 1638
  on human soul, 1640
  indifference of gods to man, 1640
  life of, 1637
  opposition to traditional religion, 1638
  philosophy, 1637–1640
  poetic form to Epicurean physics, 1637
  refashions Epicurean argument, 1639
  rhetorical methods, 1640
  scientific knowledge defined, 1639
  structure of *De Rerum Natura,* 1638
  two basic propositions, 1639–1640
Lucrinus, Lake, map 2
Lucrum (profit), 817
Ludi, 1153,1154, 1157
  See also Games, Roman
Ludi Apollinares
  popular Roman festival, 916
Ludi Plebeii
  Plebeian games festival in November, 918
Ludi Romani, 1154
  account of procession by Dionysius of
    Halicarnassus, 917
  games festival honoring Jupiter, 917
  lusus Troiae (war dance on horseback), 918
Ludovisi Battle sarcophagus, 1746 *illus.,* 1747
Ludus Magnus, gladiatorial school, 1162
Lugdunensis, map 10

Lugdunum (Lyons), map 1
  Roman mint at, 1809–1810
Luguvalium, map 1
Luna, map 2
  marble quarries at, 1729
Lunar calendars, 389–390
Lupa Romona, 1729
Lupercalia
  adaptive capacity, 984
  innovations of Caesar, 984
  multiple purposes of, 983
  Roman festival run by Luperci, 920
  sacrifices, 983
Luperci
  Roman association of priests, 920
Lupiae, map 2
Lupus, Abbot of Ferrières
  classical scholar and manuscript editor, 1823
Lusitania, map 10
Lustration (purification ceremony), 910
Luxuria (tendency to excess)
  causes perversion of traditional religion, 1329
  theme in Juvenal's Satire Six, 1329
Lycaonia, map 5
Lychnitis, Lake, map 3
Lycia, map 5
Lycurgus (Lykourgos) of Athens
  control over city finances, 483
Lydia, map 4, map 5
  origination of coinage, 1795
Lydos, 1752
Lykourgos (Lycurgus) of Sparta
  equality of landholding, 593
  and hoplite polis, 455
  identity, 21
  laws of, 451, 458, 460, 593, 594
  Spartan constitution, 20
Lynkeus
  sympotic letters, 1191
Lyric and elegiac poetry, Roman
  affected by rise of adultery, 1456
  autobiographical component of, 1455–1456
  early Roman attitude to, 1455
  five great masters of, 1455
  influences on, 1455–1457
  politics as subject of, 1456
  technique of indirection, 1457
Lyric poetry, Greek
  flowering of, 1441–1447
  forms of, 1437
  Lyric Age of Greece, 1437

  monody or choral song, 1438
  poetry sung to the lyre, 1437
Lyric poets, Greek
  inspiration for, 1516
  manipulation of traditional song form, 409
  multiplicity of audiences, 1516–1517
  subjectivism of, 1516
Lysander
  and collective purpose of polis, 1018
  compelled worship of, 1011
  cult honors viewed as excess, 1011
  defeat of Athenian fleet at Aegospotami, 693, 700
  deification of, 1011
Lysias
  prose style as model of Attic purity, 1094
Lysippos (Lysippus) of Sikyon
  Apoxyomenos (Youth Scraping Himself with a
    Strigil), 1717 *illus.*
  Granikos monument, 1718
  Hellenistic iconography and baroque style, 1718
  new canon of proportions, 1717
Lysistrata. See Aristophanes

M

Maccabees
  successful revolt, 1032
Maccabees, Books of, 1035–1036
Macedonia (Makedonia), map 3, map 9, map 10
  under Antigonid dynasty, 490
  becomes Roman province, 55
  coinage of, 1802
  control of king over timber export, 731–732
  destruction by Rome, 40
  disorders after death of Alexander, 37–38
  fifth-century monarchy, 490
  gold mines of, 819
  Greek customs, 1189
  Lefkadia tomb paintings, 1762
  Olynthos pebble mosaic pavement, 1765 *illus.*,
    1766
  Pella pebble mosaic pavement, 1766 *illus.*, 1767
  rivalry for throne, 31
  royal courts of, 1189
  secret diplomacy of, 668
  Vergina tomb paintings, 1762, 1763 *illus.*
  wars with Rome, 54
  See also Alexander III, king of Macedonia; Philip
    II, king of Macedonia

Machine engineering
  crane, 324
  winch, 323–324 *illus.*, 333, 335 *illus.*
  See also Mechanics, principles of
Machines, Greek
  double (compound) winch, 294, 325 *illus.*
  multiple-pulley hoist, 288–289 *illus.*, 294,
    327 *illus.*
  treadmill (treadwheel), 294, 326 *illus.*
Machines, Roman
  hoists and cranes, 312–313 *illus.*, 317,
    326 *illus.*
  lathe, 313
  stone dressing, 312
  winch, 317
Macmillan Painter
  phalanx on vases of, 686–687
Macrobius, Ambrosius Theodosius
  claims for sun-god in *Saturnalia*, 859
  on Roman dinner parties, 1206
Maecenas, Gaius
  mansion and gardens of, 1211
  patronage of poets, 1429
Magic
  across societal levels, 882
  amulets in disease protection, 884–885
  contagious, 881–882
  curses, 882
  definition of, 881
  destructive, 882
  evil eye, 885
  in Greece, 883
  for healing and protection, 884
  historical examples of, 885–886
  in literature, 885
  objects of magical power, 882–883
  productive, 882
  protective, 882
  religious connections, 881, 883
  in Rome, 884–886
  scapegoat ceremonies, 883
  sympathetic, 881
Magistrates, Greek
  evaluation of performance, 641
  liturgical, 800–802, 805
Magistrates, Roman
  election of, 652
  legal powers of, 609
Magnesia ad Maeandrum. *See* Magnesia on the
  Maeander (Ortaklar)

Magnesia ad Sipylum, map 4, map 5
Magnesia on the Maeander (Ortaklar), map 4,
  map 5
  city plan of, 1694
Mahdia, map 6
Maiotis, Lake, map 3
Majuscule, 433
Makedonia. *See* Macedonia (Makedonia)
Mamuralia
  Roman scapegoat festival, 913
Mani
  community of the elect (monks), 1062
  founder of syncretic religion, 1062
Manichaeism, 1062
Mannes, 386
Mantinea (Mantineia), map 4
  battle of, 688
Mantis (seer)
  at sacrifices, 900, 971
Manus (how wife enters her husband's control)
  usus (use), 1344
Manuscripts
  ancient, 429
  biblical, 433
  medieval, 428
Marathon, map 4
  battle of, 24
Marble
  ceilings, 288, 1659, 1663–1664
  cutting techniques, 792
  in Cycladic sculptures, 789
  for decorative purpose in empire, 790
  different types, 789, 791
  geochemical identification, 789–790
  main sources of, 789
  Marmorata (marble yards), 301, 307
  masonry techniques for repair of, 313–314
  Naxian tiles, 288
  painted simulations of, 1773–1774, 1788–1789
  in Periclean Athens, 1663
  production and inventory of, 307, 1675,
    1678–1679
  quarrying and dressing of, 283
  sources and colors of, 301, 1678–1679, 1685
  use by Romans, 301
  veneer, 319–320
  See also Quarries
March Up Country, The. See Xenophon
Marcion
  ecclesiastical organization of, 1054, 1058

edition of Pauline letters and Gospel of Luke, 1053–1054
Margites, 1423
  use of satire in, 1500
Marine fauna
  in mosaics, 1774
Marius Gaius, 559
  admission of *proletarii* in army, 657
  appointment as consul, 709, 710
  battle tactics, 710
  conflict with Sulla, 710–711
  consulship of, 656–657
  defense of Italy against barbarians, 710
  enlistment of rural poor, 558
  military reforms of, 57–58, 711
  political incompetence, 58
  recruitment of *capite censi,* 709
  social origins, 57
  war command of, 516
Market
  for craftsmen's goods, 381–382
Market gardening, 217–218
  Munich bas-relief, 217–218
Marketplace, Greek
  urban planning important of, 1691
Markets of Trajan, Rome
  construction of, 317, 319 *illus.,* 1680
Market taxes, 799
Maroneia, map 7
Marriage
  international, 670, 675
Marriage, Greek
  age of, 1336, 1338
  in archaic poetry, 1334–1335
  between aristocracy and nonnobles, 534
  endogamous patterns, 1311, 1334
  exogamous patterns, 1310, 1334
  gift-giving in, 134
  Hellenistic changes, 1341, 1341–1342
  in Homeric epic, 1333–1334
  laws governing, 589, 595, 596
  matrilocal, 1333
  patrilocal, 1333
  as pictured in *Medea,* 1287
  in Plato's *Republic,* 1341
  purpose of, 1339
  romanticized in Homeric epic, 1310
  sex roles in, 1334, 1340
  as source of male anxiety, 1311
  symbolic death for women, 1311

  unequal age of partners, 1311
  in vase paintings, 1338
  wedding ceremony, 1338–1339
  See also Dowry; particular states
Marriage, Roman, 670, 675
  Augustan legislation, 1352
  betrothal customs, 1347
  capacity, 1345–1347
  consent, 1345
  conubium right and Roman citizenship, 670
  divorce, 1352
  dowry, 1347–1349
  duty of citizens to marry, produce children, 1343
  engagement customs, 1347
  forbidden to slaves, 1353
  growth of free marriage, 1344–1345
  manus, 1344–1345
  property, 1349
  remarriage, 1350–1351
  rituals of, 921
  sex roles, 1350–1351
  weddings, 1349–1350
  women's traditional costume, 1402
  See also Divorce
Marriage laws, Greek
  Athenian, 1337, 1339
  Hellenistic, 1341–1342
  Spartan, 1335
Marriage laws, Roman
  between classes, 613–614
  concerning slaves, 614
  consent, 614
  divorce, 614
  dowries and gifts, 613
  impact on status, 614
  incest, 614
  legal age, 614
Marriage of Mercury and Philology. See Martianus Capella
Mars
  agricultural function of, 854
  cult titles in Celtic West, 856
Marshes, Mediterranean, 107–108
Marsic Confederation
  coinage of, 1807
Martialis, Marcus Valerius (Martial)
  Epigrams, 74
  later influence, 1499
  metropolitan tenement life, 1380
  obscenity of, 1498

Martialis (continued)
short "gift" couplets, 1498
subjects of epigrams, 1498
Martianus Capella
Marriage of Mercury and Philology, 1820–1821
Masada, 1039
Masonry. *See* Construction materials and techniques
Masonry construction, Greek
ashlar, 287, 1671, 1675, 1677–1678, 1680
clamps, dowels, and tenon fittings, 282, 288, 289, 290 *illus.,* 294, 295
column drums, 282–283
foundation, 281 *illus.,* 282
Hellenistic, 295–297
hoisting for blocks, 282–283, 287, 289 *illus.*
monumental dry-laid stone, 288, 297
rubble stonework, 277–278
rustification effects, 293 *illus.*
stone and tile aqueducts, 339
stone dressing, 281 *illus.,* 282–283, 283
tools of, 282
use of concrete, 297
vernacular, 277–278, 279 *illus.*
See also Wall construction
Masonry construction, Roman
ashlar, 1671, 1675, 1677–1678, 1680
clamps, dowels, and tenon fittings, 312
marble, 300–301, 307, 309, 319–320, 1675, 1678–1679
marble repair technique, 313–314
stone dressing, 313, 1657–1658, 1663
stone and tile aqueducts, 340, 341 *illus.*
types of, 301–302 *illus.*
See also Construction materials and techniques; Wall construction
Masons, Roman
tools of, 312
Massalia, map 1, map 7
colonies of, map 7
Mass production, Roman, 379–381, 380 *illus.*
of marble building components, 307, 1679
Materia Medica. See Dioscorides
Mathematics, Greek, 1621–1626
and ancient Near East, 1621
demonstration by deductive argument from identified premises, 1621
provided model of demonstration for exact sciences, 1623
Mathematics and science, Hellenistic, 1620–1634
Matociis, Giovanni di
history written on classical models, 1825

Matralia
festival of Italian mother goddess, 915
Matrona (married woman)
position of responsibility in household, 1350
role in public worship, 1350
Matronalia
Roman festival of June, 923
Mauretania, map 6
Mausoleum
in Roman architecture, 1687–1688
Maximus of Rome (housebuilder), 386
Measurements, Roman
of water channel and pipe sizes, 342–343 *table*
Measurement units
Greek city surveying (Doric foot and Ionic foot), 1692–1693
Roman city surveying (*actus, centuria, heredium,* and *ingerus*), 1697
Roman construction, 303–304, 307, 309–314, 316, 318
Mechanical engineering, 323–330
Mechanical engineering literature
Archimedes' lost, 323
by Hero of Alexandria, 323
by Thucydides, 331
by Vitruvius Pollio, 332
Mechanics, principles of
cam and lever, 351–352 *illus.*
cylinder and piston, 351
gears and gear ratios, 326, 330, 331 *illus.,* 347, 348 *illus.*
jet propulsion, 350 *illus.*
lever, 323
pulleys, 326 *illus.,* 333
ratchet, 333
reduction ratios and cogwheel, 327, 328 *illus.*
screw, 326–327, 328 *illus.,* 329 *illus.,* 351
steam power, 349, 350 *illus.*
strain energy, 334
torsion spring, 334–335 *illus.,* 336 *illus.,* 337
vernier principle, 337
See also Machine engineering
Medallions. *See* Stucco relief art, Roman
Medea. See Euripides
Media, map 9
Medianum (corridor room), 1378
assimilated to luxury-style living, 1381–1382
different functions, 1380
Medicine, Greek
contributions of fifth-century philosophers to, 1229

education of physicians, 1232
Hippocratic approach, 1228–1232
Hippocratic obstetric tradition, 1357–1358
human reproduction explained, 1306
humors, 1229–1231, 1232
impact of Plato and Aristotle on, 1233
influence of Socratic nature-philosophers, 1229
innate heat, 1231–1332, 1240
interactions with natural philosophy, 1620
medical writers' aims, 1313
Methodism, 1237
origins of, 1229
post-Hippocratic and Hellenistic, 1232–1236
rational discipline (*techne*), 1620
studies at Alexandria, 1233, 1235–1236
Medicine, Roman
Cato's contributions to, 1236
Galen's contribution, 1237–1241
Greek prominence in, 1236, 1237
medical philosophical sects in early empire, 1237
Roman encyclopedists, 1236–1237
Medicines and drugs, 252
Mediolanum (Milan), map 11
church mosaics and Roman influence, 1793
Meditations. See Aurelius, Marcus
Mediterranean Sea, map 1, map 6, map 7, map 8, map 10, 88 *illus.*
characteristics of inland sea, 1–2
currents, 103–104
geography, 101–102
harbors of, 362–363
naming of, 102
piracy in, 837–844
prevailing winds, 359–360
salinity and evaporation, 103
source of waters, 103
Straits of Gibraltar, 103
subdivisions of, 102
tides, 102–103
transport across, 353, 357–362
Medjerda River. *See* Bagradas River
Megalesia
games honoring Great Mother Cybele in Rome, 913
Megalopolis, map 4
Megara, map 4, map 7
attacked by Corinth, 28
colonies, 14
founded by Dorians, 7
Megara Hyblaea (Megara Hyblaia), map 7
city plan, 1660

Meidias Painter, 1758, 1759, 1760 *illus.*
Meion (sacrifice)
at Apatouria, 893
Melesias, 1138
Melissus of Samos
developed Parmenides' monism, 1594
Melitius, bishop of Lycopolis
church of the martyrs, 1068
Membranae (parchment), 430
Memorabilia of Socrates. See Xenophon
Memorials
of craftsmen, 383–384
Memphis, map 6
Menander
Dyskolos (*The Grouch*), 1486
Sikyonios, 427
Menippus of Gadara
use of diatribe in *Saturae Menippeae*, 1500
Meno
history of medicine, 1233
Menstruation
Greek medical view, 1306
seen as polluting, 1307
symbol of woman as sacrifice, 1314
Mercenaries
in city-state, 798
Merchantmen. *See* Sailing ships
Mercury (liquid silver)
availability of, 351
Mesembria, map 7
Meseta (Spanish plateau)
geology, 100
Mesopotamia, map 5
highways in, 353
narrative tradition in service of religion, 1418
Messana (Messina)
attacked by Hiero of Syracuse, 52
Messenia, map 4
conquest by Sparta, 536
Spartan Helots, 456
Messianism, Jewish, 1040–1041
Jesus of Nazareth, 1039
Messina. *See* Messana
Metals
mining for, 371, 376
Metalworking, 371–373, 372 *illus.*
Metamorphoses. See Ovidius Naso, Publius (Ovid)
Metaphysics. See Aristotle
Metapontion, map 7
Metellus, Aulus
statue of *Arringatore* (Orator), 1408 *illus.*

Metempsychosis
    Roman concept of, 999
    in writing of Orpheus, 992
    in writing of Pythagoras, 991
Method. See Archimedes
Methone, map 7
Metoikion (head tax), 799
Meton of Athens, 391
    calendar cycles discovery, 348
Midrashim, legal
    rabbinic laws, 1043
Midwife
    role in childbirth and postnatal care, 1358
    status of, 1357–1358
Migrations, early Greek, 3–6, 155–169
    across Aegean, 168–169
    Aegean pottery in Palestine, 165
    Aetolian pottery in Peloponnese, 167
    appearance of Minyan pottery styles, 158, 159
    archaeological evidence , 167–168, 156
    Boeotian, 161, 162
    changes in pottery styles in twelfth century, 162
    in classical literature, 159–162
    to Crete, 169
    development of Mycenaean states, 159
    Dorian, 159–162, 168
    Early Helladic cultural change, 158
    effect on political development, 169
    evidence of dialect, 163–165, 156, 157–158
    of Greek-speaking people, 158, 159
    Hellenes in classical literature, 155–156
    in historical tradition, 155–159
    Ionian overseas, 168
    Isthmus of Corinth, 162, map 4
    in late prehistoric period, 157
    Mycenaean movement into Knossos, 158
    from northern Greece after Trojan War, 156
    in royal genealogies, 156
    Sea Peoples, 165–167
Migrations, late Roman, map 11
    beginnings of, 171–174
    change from infantry to cavalry during, 178–179
    collusion of Romans and barbarians, 178
    conversion of tribes to Christianity, 176, 179
    Germanic positions in the mid-fourth century, 171
    second phase of, 174–176
    third phase of, 176–177
    See also particular tribes and regions
Milesian Tales. See Aristeides of Miletos
Milestones (*militaria*), 355

Miletus (Miletos), map 4, map 5, map 7
    Black Sea colonies, 14
    clothing styles, 1394–1395
    colonies of, map 7
    foundation of, 6
    philosophers from, 1585–1589
    revenue-raising decree, 835
    sixth-century siege of, 686
Military calendar
    dominated by imperial cult, 921
Military encampments, Roman
    and city plans (Thamugadi), 1698–1699 *illus.*
Military engineering
    cranes vs. siege engines, 326
    crossbow (*gastraphetes*), 333, 334 *illus.*
    Greek, 330–338
    literary sources, 331–332
    missile projectors (catapults), 333–338, 335 *illus.*, 336 *illus.*, 337 *illus.*
    need for inventors and artisans, 330
    Roman, 338
    siege engines vs. tower cranes, 332–333
Military expenditures, 798
Mills
    crane treadmill, 326 *illus.*
    grain, 328, 330, 331 *illus.*
Milo, Titus Annius, 562
Milo of Croton, 1136
Mime plays, Roman, 1158–1159
Minas de Mouros, map 1
Minerals, Mediterranean
    fossil fuels, 97–98
    gold, 96–97
    iron, 97
    lead, 97
    silver, 97
    tin, 97
Miniature engineering, 327–352
    Antikythera mechanism, 326, 347, 348 *illus.*, 349 *illus.*
    automated miniature altar, 350 *illus.*
    automatic temple doors, 350, 351 illus.
    automaton theater, 351–352 *illus.*
Miniaturism
    in Roman wall and mosaic images, 1776, 1778, 1779, 1781
Mining
    dangers of, 376
    slave labor in, 586–587
    as source of Roman revenue, 815
    and water pumps, 345

Mining, Greek, 371
  administration of, 787
  categories of mines, 781
  contracts and leases, 787
  drainage, 782
  ergasteria (processing plant), 781
  fire setting, 783
  hauling ore, 783
  labor force, 788
  lighting, 782
  mesokrineis (supporting rock pillars), 782
  open cut method, 780
  Pangaean silver, 1799
  placer method, 779–780
  poletai (mining officials), 787
  prospecting by mineral identification, 780
  roof shoring, 781–782
  shafts, 781
  size of galleries, 781
  underground, 780
  ventilation, 782
  working conditions, 788
  See also Tools, mining
Mining, Roman, 757–759
  administration, 787–788
  Archimedean screw, 785
  contracted freeborn miners, 788–789
  contracted to *publicani* (tax farmers), 787–788
  drainage , 785
  ergasteria (processing plant), 786
  galleries, 784–785
  hauling ore, 786
  helicoidal washeries, 787
  hushing (hydraulicking), 783
  of iron, 757
  labor force, 788
  laws governing, 788
  methods of draining, 785
  mining disasters, 788
  opencast, 784
  ore processing, 786–787
  plynterios (washery), 787
  procurator metallorum (procurator), 788
  prospecting, 784
  Rio Tinto mine, 757–758
  scale of Roman operations, 758
  segellum, 784
  shafts, 784
  of silver and lead in Spain, 757–758
  in Spanish provinces, 783
  state control of, 783

technology of, 758
  tools, 786
  ventilation and lighting, 785
  weight separation, 787
  working conditions, 788–789
Minos, king of Knossos
  Cretan lawgiver, 591
  and Greek written law, 450
Mints, 373, 380, 635
  Alexander the Great's, 1801
  Camulodunum (Colchester), 1815
  Greek, administration of, 635
  Londinium (London), 1815
  Lugdunum (Lyons), 1808–1810
  Roman provincial, 1813, 1815
  Rome, 1807, 1809, 1810, 1812
  Sicily, 1804
  Spain, 1809
  Syracuse, 1799
  use of marks by the Roman Empire, 1813, 1815
Misa, map 2
Misenum, map 2
Mishnah, 1043
Misogyny, Greek
  in archaic poetry, 1335
  countered by Euripides (*Captive Melanippe*), 1304
  extent debated, 1312
  in Hellenistic world, 1342
  Hesiod, 1284, 1303–1304, 1310–1311, 1313
  myth of woman's separate origin, 1306–1307
  Semonides, 1284–1285, 1303, 1307–1308, 1310
Missio, 1161
Mithraism, 858
Mithras, cult of, 1003
Mithridates VI, king of Pontus, 41
  defeat by Pompey, 59
  massacre of Romans in Asia Minor, 58
Models, automated. *See* Miniature engineering
Modestinus
  definition of marriage, 1343
Moeris, Lake (Birket Qārūn), map 6
  geology, 107
Moesia, map 10
Mogador, map 6
Mogontiacum, map 1
Moldings
  in Greek architecture, 1656–1657 *illus.*
Molds
  for pottery, 380
Molykrion, map 4

Monarchy, Greek
  arete and *eunomia* of aristocratic regimes, 488
  in Asia Minor, 490
  basileis, 487
  Cimmerian Bosphorus, 489–490
  in Corinth, 18
  Dark Ages, 487
  decline of under ruler worship, 1018
  distinction between king and god, 1020
  end of, 8–9
  fifth-century, 489–490
  Greek theories of, 484
  Hellenistic, 490
  Hellenistic administration, 646–647
  ideal theories of Isokrates and Plato, 489
  Macedonian, 490
  in Mycenaean culture, 442
  Ptolemaic kingdom, 490
  Seleucid dynasty, 490
  in Sicily, 489
  Sparta, 20
  succeeded by aristocracy, 488
  and *tyrannos,* 448
  See also Tyrants, Greek
Monarchy, Roman
  administration under, 649–650
  chronology, 46
  collapse of in sixth century, 497
  election of kings, 47, 495
  parallels with Greek tyrannies, 496
  scope of royal power, 495
  seven early kings, 46
  in third century, 526
Monasteries
  contribution to classical scholarship, 1824
Monasticism
  in Egypt, 1066–1067
Moneyers, Roman
  coinage of, 1806–1807, 1809
Moneylending, 817
  cash basis of, 741
  commercial loans, 741
  expression of social relations, 742
  in Greek trade, 739
  institutionalized, 741
  personal character of, 742
  usury, 742
Monody, Greek
  compared to choral lyric, 1438, 1439
  for decline of genre, 1452–1453
  early monodic poetry, 1439–1441

elegiac verse, 1438–1439
  expresses personal point of view, 1439
  iambic verse, 1438–1439
  later monodic poets, 1452
  lyric, 1438
Montanus of Phrygia, 1053
Month
  days of, 390, 392
  length of, 391, 392
  lunar, 389, 1145
  naming of, 390
  Roman, 391
Monumental and commemorative architecture. *See*
    specific building and commemorative structure
    types
Monumental construction, Greek, 279–285, 288,
    297
  See also Construction materials and techniques
Monumental painting, Greek, 1749, 1761
  Archaic Period, 1756
  Classical Period (Golden Age), 1755–1757,
    1769
  funeral paintings, 1761–1762, 1763 *illus.,* 1764
  grave stelae, 1763–1764
  under Roman patronage, 1764 *illus.,* 1765,
    1778 *illus.*
  and theater, 1756, 1761
  See also Painters; Vase painting, Greek
Moon-zodiac calculator. *See* Antikythera mechanism
Moral Essays. See Seneca, Lucius Annaeus (Seneca
    the Younger)
Moral Letters. See Seneca, Lucius Annaeus (Seneca
    the Younger)
Moretum (*The Country Salad*)
  milling in, 239
Morgantina, map 2
  House of the Arched Cistern, 1368
  House of the Office, 1368
Mosaic art, Byzantine, 1792–1793
Mosaic art, Greek
  floral design, 1766
  Hellenistic subjects, 1767 *illus.,* 1768 *illus.,* 1769
  pebble mosaics in Pella, 1370–1371
  pebble pavements, 1765 *illus., 1766 illus.,* 1767
  tessellated mosaics, 1767 *illus.,* 1768 *illus.,* 1769
  and theater, 1768–1769
Mosaic art, Roman, 1689, 1771–1772
  aesthetic possibilities and limitations of, 1785
  African carpet-style, 1787–1788, 1790
  black and white style, 1776, 1777, 1783, 1786,
    1790

Volume One: 1–720; Volume Two: 721–1298; Volume Three: 1299–1832

in the colonies and provinces, 1786–1788, 1790–1791 *illus.*

dominance over late antique painting, 1788

emblemata tradition, 1774–1775 *illus.*, 1783, 1785, 1786

influence of dome and vault ceiling decoration on, 1788

Late Empire, 1788, 1790, 1791 *illus.*, 1792 *illus.*

legacy of, 1689

Middle Empire, 1785–1786, 1787 *illus.*, 1788 *illus.*

opus musivum (wall and vault decoration), 1791, 1792 *illus.*, 1793

opus signinum (mosaic pavement), 1776–1777

opus tessellatum (floor mosaics), 1776, 1791, 1793

"painting in stone" with colored backgrounds, 1793

subject themes and series in, 1785, 1788 *illus.*

in thermal baths, 1686, 1786–1787 *illus.*, 1792–1793

Mosaicists, Greek, 371, 1766–1767, 1769
See also specific names of individuals

Mosaicists, Roman, 307

Moses, Law of
attack on validity, 1048

Mos maiorum, 1541
limited women's activities, 1322, 1330

Motherhood
chief wifely virtue, 1351

Motya, map 2

Mountains
Alps, 100
Black Sea area, 100
eastern Mediterranean basin, 99–100
western Mediterranean basin, 99

Mount Aitna, map 2

Mount Akte, map 3

Mount Albanus, map 2

Mount Argaios, map 5

Mount Casinus, map 2

Mount Gerizim, map 5

Mount Helikon, map 4

Mount Ithome, map 4

Mount Ocha, map 4

Mount Olympos, map 4

Mount Ossa, map 4

Mount Othrys, map 4

Mount Parnes, map 4

Mount Parnon, map 4

Mount Pelion, map 4

Mount Plakos, map 5

Mount Sinai, map 6

Mount Taygetos, map 4

Mount Vesuvius, map 2

Mount Vourinos, map 3

Mousike (music), 1505

Mules, 355

Mulucha River, map 6

Mummy portraits
of Roman Egypt, 1772

Munda, map 1

Munera, 1153, 1154, 1159–1162, 1163–1164
See also Games, Roman

Municipal government
tax responsibilities, 820

Mural painting. *See* Wall painting, Roman

Music, Greek
patronage of artists in city-state, 1507

Music, Roman
no prominent public role, 1511
in theater, 1511

Musical competitions, 1139–1140, 1148

Musical instruments, Greek
aulos (double-reed wind instrument), 1505
kithara, 1506
lyre, 1505
salpinx (double-reed wind instrument), 1505
syrinx (Pan pipes), 1506

Musical instruments, Roman
cornu (horn), 1511
hydraulus (water organ), 1511
tibia (reed-blown pipe), 1511
trumpets (*tuba, lituus*), 1511

Musicians
mosaic panel of in Pompeii, 1775 *illus.*

Musicians, Greek
Chigi Vase painting flutist, 1752 *illus.*, 1760 *illus.*

Musonius Rufus, Gaius
equality of women, 1646–1647

Mutina, map 2

Mycenae
architecture of, 1656
conquest of Knossos, 158 (map 4)
Greek migration, 159
influences on Greek architecture, 1656
pottery at Thrace, 159 (map 3, map 9)
signs of raiding of, 162
in thirteenth century, 159

Mygdones, map 3

Mykale Mountains, map 5

Mykalessos, map 4

Mykenai, map 4

Mylae (Mylai), map 2
  battle of, 53
Mylasa, map 4, map 5
Myoparo (galley), 840
Myra, map 5
Myrina, map 4, map 5
Myron, 1711
  Discus Thrower, 1711
Mysia, map 4, map 5
Mystai (initiates), 901
Mystery cults, 1003
  doctrines of immortality in, 1004
Mythological themes in art
  Greek themes in Roman painting,, 1789
  in house mosaics, 1765 *illus.*-1766
  Iphigenia in Tauris wall painting, 1780–1781 *illus.*
  Judgment of Paris mosaic, 1785
  Jupiter and Ganymede wall painting, 1784 *illus.*
  Lycurgus and Ambrosia mosaic, 1787
  the *Muses* mosaic, 1788 *illus.*
  Orpheus mosaics in Britain, 1790
  Perseus and Andromeda wall painting (Capitoline Hill), 1789
  Rape of Persephone (Proserpina) tomb mosaic, 1786
  in Roman home picture galleries, 1777, 1778
Mythos (plot), 1564
Myths, Greek
  birth and development of the gods, 865–869
  defined, 861
  early history of man, 867–874
  Hesiod's *Theogony*, major primary source, 864
  muthos defined by Aristotle, 861
  Near Eastern influence on, 874–876
  oral traditions, 862
  origin of the universe, 864–865
  relation to ritual, 862–863
  role in tragedy, 874
  and Roman myths, 876
Myths, Near Eastern
  concept of underworld, 875
  flood, 875
  Heracles myth, 875
  parallels to Greek mythic themes, 875
Myths, Roman
  absence of mythical tradition, 876
  compared to Greek myth, 876
  creation of national literature, 876
  effect of literacy on, 876
  Hellenizing of Roman gods, 876
Mytilene, map 4, map 5
  archaic female organizations, 1176

colonies, 14
  seventh-century turmoil in, 1176
  tyranny of Pittakos, 17–18
  tyrants of, 449

N

Nabis, king of Sparta, 546
Naevius, Gnaeus
  Bellum Punicum (*Punic War*), 877, 1427
  Rome's first epic poet, 877
  use of sexual allusions in comedies, 1271
Nag Hammadi
  papyrus codices, 434
Naoi. See Temples, Greek
Narbonensis, map 10
Narrative, epic, 407
Nature
  divine force to Lucretius, 1638
Naukratis, map 6
  Greek trading port in Egypt, 16
Naupaktos, map 4
Nauplia, map 4
Naval engineering, 324, 326, 331–333
Naval power
  of Athens, 840–841
  in Carthaginian Wars, 53
  financing of, 801
  piracy and, 840–844
  of Rhodes, 841
  Roman development of, 52
  Rome as, 843–844
Naxos, map 2
  Dark Age settlements, 6
  invention of marble tiles, 288
Naxos, Sicily, map 4, map 7
  first Greek colony, 12
Neapolis, map 2, map 3
Nearchos, 383, 384 *illus.*
Necromancy
  uncommon in Greece, 946
Nehemiah, governor of Judah
  extreme separatist, 1029
  policies and practices, 1029
Nemausus (Nîmes), map 1
  Maison Carrée, 1734
  Maison Carrée temple, 1676–1677
Nemea, map 4
Nemean. See Pindar

Nemean Games, 1133, 1134, 1144

Nemeseia, 1147

Nemetacum, map 1

Neokaisareia, map 5

Neoplatonism
  influence on Christian thought, 1648
  mystical movement, 1648
  in Renaissance, 1828

Nepos, Cornelius
  how Roman wives lived, 1319
  Lives of the Famous Men, 1555
  wrote first surviving Latin biographies, 1555

Nero (Lucius Domitius Ahenobarbus)
  architectural achievements, 70
  architecture under, 1677–1678 *illus.,* 1772,
    1780–1781
  artistic interests, 68–69
  Domus Aurea (Golden House), 308, 1217, 1376,
    1677–1678 *illus.,* 1772
  execution of Christians, 1055
  extravagant behavior of, 1216
  first on coinage wearing divine attribute, 1017
  painting styles under, 1780–1781
  passion for music, 1512
  patronage of architecture, 308
  Seneca's relationship with, 1645
  stage appearance by, 1159

Nerva, Marcus Cocceius, 72

Nesiotes, 1710
  Tyrant Slayers, 1710

New Testament, 432, 433

Nexum
  abolishment of, 553
  effect on Plebeian Order, 552

Nicaea, Council of, 80

Nicander of Colophon
  works bridge Hellenistic and Roman texts,
    1236

Nichoria
  excavations at, 7

Nicias
  relinquishes victory to recover dead, 689

Nicolaus of Damascus
  panegyrical life of Augustus, 1537

Nicomachean Ethics. See Aristotle

Nicomachus
  revision of Athenian political institutions, 479,
    480

Nicomedia (Nikomedeia, İzmit), map 5
  demolition of church in, 1064

Nikaia, map 5

Nike of Samothrace
  on coinage, 1802

Nile Delta
  geology and history, 101, 107–108

Nile River, map 6, map 8, 88 *illus.*
  annual flood, 105
  geology, 105–106
  transport on, 363

Niobid Painter, 1758

Nomothetes (lawgiver)
  in seventh century, 450
  Solon as, 452, 453

Nonaggression treaties. *See* Treaties and
    international agreements

Nonnus of Panopolis
  Dionysiaca (Epic of Dionysus), 1433
  last great epic of antiquity, 1433

Norba, map 2

Noreia, map 1

Noricum, map 1, map 10

North Africa, map 6

Notebooks
  papyrus, 430–431

Notitia Dignitatum, 717–718

Noumenia, 1145

Novaesium, map 1

Novel
  criminal and immoral tales, 1569
  as "discovered" ancient document, 1566–1567
  early forms, 1566–1570
  and historiography, 1565
  important cultural form after Alexander, 1563
  origins, 1564–1566
  redefined, 1563
  storytelling skills, 1564, 1565

Novilara, map 2

Noviomagus, map 1

Nubia, map 6

Nudity
  of Greek athletes, 1152

Numen Augusti, cult of
  Augustus established, 1016

Numidia, map 6

Numina
  ambivalence of gender, 854
  birth functions of, 853
  limited functions of, 854

Nuts
  almond, 251
  chestnuts, 251–252
  walnuts and hazelnuts, 251

Nymphaeum (fountain house), 1381–1382
Nymphaion, map 7
Nymphe (bride)
   childless bride, 896

O

Oaths
   important role in Greek society, 891
   occasions for, 891
   punishments for breaking, 891, 1000
Obscenity
   in art, poetry, and festivals, 1255–1256
   and degree of sexual repression, 1256
   Greek four-letter words, 1256
   magical powers of, 1256
   metaphorical and symbolic expressions, 1256
   as release from sexual inhibitions, 1255–1256
Obstetric practices
   folk traditions, 1357
   medical, 1357–1358
   role of midwife, 1357–1358
Obulco, map 1
Octavian. *See* Augustus, Caesar Octavianus
October
   "October Horse" chariot race, 918
   Roman festivals to Mars and Liber, 918
Odenwald, map 1
Odes. See Horatius Flaccus, Quintus (Horace)
Odoacer
   forces abdication of last Roman emperor in Italy, 83
   peaceful rule, 176
Odysseus
   piracy of, 837–838
Odyssey. See Homer
Oeconomica (Financial Management). See Aristotle;
   Pseudo-Aristotle
Oeconomicus (Household Management). See Xenophon
Oianthia, map 4
Oikeiosis
   Stoic doctrine of, 1617–1618
Oikist (Greek colony leader), 1692
Oikos (household), 1336, 1339, 1340, 1341
   in Homeric epics, 532
Oikos (household)
   importance in Olynthian houses, 1365
   management of by women, 1252
   Xenophon's view of, 1301–1303

Olbia, map 3, map 7
Old Testament, 432
Olive oil
   shipping of, 361
Olives
   archaeological evidence of, 255
   Cato's orchard, 234
   olive oil, 254–255
   processing of, 255
   production of, 231–232
   spread of in ancient Greece, 255
   uses in foods, 255
Olive wreaths, 1144
Olympia, map 4
   temple of Hera, construction of, 284 *illus.*, 287
   temple of Zeus, 96, 848, 849, 1661–1662, 1709,
     1710, 1711 *illus.*
   temple of Zeus, tile roofing system, 284 *illus.*
Olympias
   cause of Alexander's exile, 33
   influence on Alexander, 36
Olympic Council, 1144
Olympic Games, 1144
   administration of, 1144
   age divisions, 1140
   beginnings of, 1132
   coinage commemoration of, 1799
   dating on basis of, 393
   eligibility to compete, 1153
   end of, 1151
   events of, 1134–1139
   first, 1131
   judges for, 1144
   nationality of contestants, 1133
   prizes for, 1140–1141, 1144
   women barred from, 17
Olynthiacs. See Demosthenes
Olynthus (Olynthos)
   Greek houses excavated, 1365–1367
   House of the Comedian, 1367
   Villa of Good Fortune, 1367, 1765 *illus.*-1766
Omens
   birds, 942, 943, 944
   sneeze, 944
   from statues of gods, 945–946
Omphalos Apollo style, 1711
On Anatomical Procedures. See Galen of Pergamon
On Ancient Medicine
   possibility of future improvements, 270
On Architecture. See Vitruvius Pollio
Onasiteles, 1150

Onchestos, map 4
On Dissections. See Herophilus
Onesimos, 1723
On Floating Bodies. See Archimedes
On Habits. See Galen of Pergamon
On Mechanics, 272
On Medicine. See Celsus, Aulus Cornelius
On Music. See Plutarchus, L.(?) Mestrius (Plutarch)
On Nature. See Empedocles
On Nature. See Epicurus
On Stones. See Theophrastus
On the Crown. See Demosthenes
On the Equilibrium of Planes. See Archimedes
On the False Legation. See Demosthenes
On the Heavens. See Aristotle
On the Parts of Animals. See Aristotle
On the Peace with Sparta. See Andocides (Andokides)
On the Soul. See Aristotle
On the Usefulness of the Parts of the Body. See Galen of Pergamon
On What is Not. See Gorgias
Ophiteia (Snaketown)
    legend of, 1126
Opisthographs, 428
Oplontis, map 2
Optimates
    opposition to Caesar, 60
    Roman political party, 58, 59
Opus musivum, opus signinum, opus tessellatum. See Mosaic art, Roman
Opus sectile. See Wall painting, Roman
Oracle of Faunus
    indigenous Italian oracle, 954
    ritual at Tibur, 954–955
Oracles, Greek, 946–949
    most prestigious method of divination, 946
    See also particular oracles
Oral tradition, 1564
    in Greece, 406–409, 414
    in Rome, 417
Orantes River, 88 *illus.*
Orators, Greek
    Demosthenes-Aeschines debate, 482–483
    in fourth century Athens, 482–483
    legal control of, 483
Oratory, Greek, 411, 413, 413
    antithetical mode of, 473
    argument in, 473
    in Athens, 469, 472, 473–474, 479
    definition of Greek culture and tradition in, 1097
    deliberative speech, 1094–1097

demagogic style in, 469, 472
at end of Greek city-state, 1096
epideictic speech, 1094
in fourth century, 1092–1097
funeral, 1094
judicial speech, 1093–1094
logographer (paid speechwriter), 1093
reported by Herodotus, 1527
reported by Thucydides, 1527
and rise of demagoguery in fourth-century politics, 1096
Second Sophistic, 1101
Sophists' use of display speech, 1094
as stylistic model for later prose, 1097
traveling orators, 1101
written records of speeches, 428
Oratory, Roman
    Cicero's views on, 1641
    funeral orations (*encomia*), 1542
    in history, 1553, 1558
    as political acts, 1553
    use of in autocracy, 1553
    use of in Roman historiography, 1553
    value of, 1553
    See also Cicero, Marcus Tullius; Quintilianus, Marcus Fabius (Quintilian)
Orchomenos, map 4
Order
    in Roman social structure, 550
Orders (decorative architectural). *See* Architectural orders
Ores
    mining of, 371
Oresteia. See Aeschylus
Orestes
    three treatments of in Greek tragedy, 1479
Orestes. See Euripides
Orgala, map 2
Orgeones (worshipper associations), 927
Orgia (rites or mysteries), 905
Oribasius
    disciple of Galen, 1241
Origenes Adamantius (Origen)
    Against Celsus, 1057
    asceticism of, 1066
    biblical theology of, 1057
    On First Principles, 1057
    followers of, 1057, 1063
    Hexapla (Greek translation of Old Testament), 1057
    Platonism, 1057–1058

Orontes River, map 5
Oropos, map 4
Orpheus
  cult of salvation, 852
  image in Christian art, 852–853
  origin and associations, 852
  religious influence of in Rome, 999
Orthogonal layout. *See* City plans
Oschophoria, 1145, 1151
Osiris, cult of, 1004
Ostia, map 2
  apartment houses, 1380
  apartment houses for middle- and upper-class
    citizens, 1378
  Baths of Neptune mosaic pavement,
    1786–1787 *illus.*
  cost of port facilities, 823
  decline of, 1381–1382
  House of Cupid and Psyche, 1381
  House of Jupiter and Ganymede paintings,
    1783–1784 *illus.*
  House of the Nymphaeum, 1381
  housing revolution (third century B.C.), 1378
  town houses, 1381
  wall painting of, 1772
Ostracism, 412
  in Athens, 468
  as political weapon, 25
Ostrogoths, map 11
  annihilation of by Belisarius, 177
  attack on Odoacer, 176
  collusion with Romans and Byzantines, 178
  conversion to Arian Christianity, 176
  settlement in Pannonia, 176
  under Theodoric, 176–177
Ovidius Naso, Publius (Ovid)
  adaptation of epic form to love elegy, 1461
  Amores (*Loves*), 1460–1461
  Ars Amatoria (*Art of Love*), 1266, 1461
  created love letter in verse, 1580
  on drinking parties, 1214
  Epistulae ex Ponto (*Letters from the Black Sea*)
    (*Epistles*), 1461
  exiled by Augustus to the Black Sea, 67, 1461
  four stages of childhood, 1289
  Heroides (*Heroines*), 1461
  on illegitimacy of Romulus in *The Roman Calendar,*
    1268
  imaginary letters (*Heroines* [*Heroides*]), 1580
  ironic treatment of Augustus' lifestyle, 1212
  love as play, 1460

  Metamorphoses, 878, 1430
  plays against predecessor's conventions, 1460
  public recitations and compositional style,
    1460–1461
  Roman Calendar, The (*Fasti*), 914, 981
  Tristia, 1461
  verse letters, 1461
  on witchcraft, 885
Owls (Athenian coins), 1796, 1798
Oxen, 355, 356
Oxylos, king of Aetolia
  Dorian invasion of Peloponnese, 161–162
Oxyrhynchus papyri, 1569

P

Pack animals, 356
Padus River, map 2
Paean. See Paian
Paeligni, map 2
Paestum. *See* Poseidonia
Paetus, Sextus Aelius
  Tripertita, 610
Pagasai, map 4
Pagondas
  defeat of Athenian army by, 690
Paian (*paean*) (hymn to Apollo), 1438
Painters, Greek, 371
  documentation of, 1755–1757, 1761, 1769
  innovations of, 1754–1756, 1761
  professional activities of, 1752, 1756–1757, 1769
  Roman patronage of, 1764 *illus.,* 1765, 1778 *illus.*
  See also Monumental painting, Greek; Vase
    painting; specific individuals
Painters, Roman, 1771
  See also specific individuals
Painting, Greek
  Roman mosaic *emblemata* replicas of, 1774
  See also Funerals, Greek; Monumental painting;
    Vase painting
Painting, Roman
  foreshortening, 1774
  linear perspective (*skenographia*), 1775
  map-like perspective, 1774
  and monumental architecture, 1683
  pictorial perspective in mosaic flooring,
    1785–1786
  spatial recession, 1790
  techniques, 1778, 1779

Painting in stone. *See* Mosaic art, Roman
Paionios, 1714
   Nike at Olympia, 1714
Palaces, imperial Roman, 1677–1678 *illus.*, 1679,
    1680, 1687–1688 *illus.*
   See also specific emperors
Palaestra, 1135
Pale (wrestling), 1135
Palimpsest, 425–426
Palladion
   in Athenian homicide trials, 597
Palladius
   on harvesting methods, 226
Palmyra, map 5
Pamphaios (potter), 383
Pamphylia, map 5
Panathenaia, 1147–1148
   Great, 898, 899
   presentation to Athena of new peplos,
    897
Panathenaic Games, 1133
Pancration, 1133, 1139
Pandora myth
   ambiguity of human existence, 871
   in Hesiod, 1284, 1306–1307
   moral of the bad wife, 1335
   woman as evil gift from the gods, 871
Panegyrics, 1150
Pangaean silver mines, 1799
Panhellenic Games, 1144
Panhellenic League of Corinth
   domination by Philip II, 492
Panionion
   Amphictyones, 491
   sanctuary of Poseidon Helikonios, 491
Pannini, Giovanni Paolo
   Interior of the Pantheon painting, 1682 *illus.*
Pannonia, map 10
Panopeus, map 4
Panopolis, map 6
Pan Painter, 1758 *illus.*
Pantheon, 1680, 1682 *illus.*, 1689, 1734
   transport of columns for, 360
Pantikapaion, map 3
Pantomime, 1159
Papacy, Roman
   preserver of ancient culture, 84
Paper, 422
Paphlagonia, map 5
Papyrus, 422–424, 425
   Cyperus papyrus, 422

export of from Egypt, 425
   Greek use of, 425
   rolls, 423, 426–430
Paradise, 993
Paragraphus, 427
   See also Punctuation
Parallel Lives. See Plutarchus, L.(?) Mestrius
   (Plutarch)
Parapet
   in Roman architecture, 314
Paraphrase. See Theophilus
Parchment, 424–425, 430, 431
Parentalia, 997
   Roman Festival of the Dead, 920
   simple offerings, 920
Parilia
   country festival described by Ovid, 914
Parion, map 7
Parmenides
   compared to Heraclitus, 1591
   cosmological thought, 1592–1593
   denied plurality and change, 1593
   followers of, 1593–1594
   natural philosophers opposed, 1594
   rejected creation from nothing, 1593
   trusts only reasoned argument (*logos*), 1592
   two modes of inquiry, 1592
   Way of Seeming, 1592
   Way of Truth, 1592
Parmenides. See Plato
Paropamisos (Hindu Kush) Mountains, map 8
Paros, map 4
Parrhasios of Ephesus, 1756–1757
Parthenon, 1662 *illus.*, 1663 *illus.*, 1664, 1704
   built in honor of Athena, 867
   construction of, 286, 292, 325, 639
   Pheidian sculptures, 1711–1713
   procession of maidens, 1713 *illus.*
   sculpture of Athena Parthenos, 1663 *illus.*
Parthia, map 9
   negotiated return of Roman standards, 672,
    1809 *illus.*
   treaty with Augustus, 66
Particularism, Greek, 668
Pasargadai, map 5
Pasion
   banking activities of, 830–831
   financial success, 831
   military loans to Timotheus, 831
Pasiteles
   guidebook to Greek art, 1728

Pastoral poetry
  distinguished from bucolic genre, 1470
  in fifteenth-century Italy, 1470
  Vergil founder of tradition, 1470
  See also Bucolic poetry
Pathos, 1710
Patimos, map 4
Patrai, map 4
Patrician Order
  conspicuous consumption of, 551
  control of government offices, 49
  decline of in fourth century, 652
  definition of, 551
  effect of Gracchan reforms on, 556
  hereditary aristocracy, 47
  struggle of the Orders, 553
Patriciate
  auctoritas patrum (right of veto), 499
  in centuriate assembly, 497
  chain of magistracy, 500
  control of interregnum, 499
  origins of, 499
Patroklos
  funeral of, 993
  funeral games of, 1131, 1134
  psyche of, 988
Patronage, Roman, 49
  of historians, 1554
  patron-client relationship, 549, 551, 555, 569,
    570
  of poets, 1457
Patronage of architecture, Greek, 1668–1669
  under Pericles, 1662–1665
Patronage of architecture, Roman
  under Augustus, 305, 1675–1677
  under Caesar, 1675–1676
  under Caracalla, 1685 *Illus.*
  under Constantine, 1683–1684, 1687,
    1744 *illus.*
  construction industry and, 306–308, 320
  under Diocletian, 1687–1688 *illus.*
  under Domitian, 306, 308, 1679–1680
  under Hadrian, 1680
  imported marble, 300–301
  under Nero, 305, 1677–1678 *illus.,* 1772,
    1780–1781
  under Septimius Severus, 1684–1685
  under Trajan, 306, 308–320, 1698
  under Vespasian, 305
Patronage of art, Greek
  political motives, 449

Patronage of art, Roman
  under Constantine, 1789–1790
  of Greek painting, 1764 *illus.,* 1765, 1778 *illus.*
  under Hadrian, 1783, 1785
  under Nero, 1780–1781
Paul, bishop of Samosata
  Antiochene school, 1063
  relationship with Queen Zenobia of Palmyra,
    1063
Paul, Saint
  eastern missionary work, 1048
  letters in New Testament, 1048–1049
  sea travel by, 361
Pausanias
  collector of folktales, 1564
  Description of Greece, 1755
  on Olympic Games, 1132
Pavement, decorated, 371
Paving, of roads, 354, 355
Pax deorum (favor of the gods)
  sought by Romans, 951
Pax Romana, 669
  and Roman interstate relations, 669–670
Peace
  Common Peace (*koine eirene*), 674
  definitions of, *eirene,* 669
Pediatrics, 1360
  Aulus Cornelius Celsus, 1360
  Hippocratic writers, 1360
  Soranus, 1360
Peiraieus (Piraeus), map 4
  city plan of, 1695–1696
  establishment of by Themistocles, 468
  market for international exchange, 733
Peisistratos (Pisistratus)
  and Panathenaic festival, 1148
  patron of music and poetry, 1507
  tyranny of, 455, 539
  tyrant of Athens, 23
Pelanos
  ritual offering, 966
Pella, map 8
  pebble mosaic floors, 1370–1371
  pebble mosaic pavement, 1766 *illus.,* 1767
Peloponnese, map 4
  architecture of, 1656, 1665
  dependence on Italian grain, 12
Peloponnesian League
  Spartan dominance of, 492
Peloponnesian War, 29–30
  and Athenian foreign policy, 469, 471

cost of, 798
exacerbates class tensions, 543
slavery during, 541,542
Penates
spirits of pantry or larder, 921
Peneios River, map 4
Pens, 426
Pentateuch
literary qualities, 1029
product of committee, 1029
work of compromise, 1029
Pentathlon, 1132, 1136–1137
Pentekontaetia. See Diodorus Siculus
Pentelicus
marble quarries at, 1663, 1684
Penthesileia Painter, 1758 *illus.*
Peplos
in archaic period, 1395
ceremonial, 1147
in classical period, 1396
gift to Athena, 1393
Homeric references, 1392
varied meanings of term, 1386, 1397
woman's, 1389 *illus.*, 1393, 1394
Perachora
vernacular building model, 278, 279 *illus.*
Pergamon (Pergamum, Bergama), map 4, map 5,
map 8, map 9
Acropolis of, 1669 *illus.*, 1670
Altar of Zeus, 1670, 1719, 1720 *illus.*, 1804–1805
city plan integrated with landscape, 1669 *illus.*,
1695
court fashions, 1398
Greek coinage of, 1802
gymnasium, 296 *illus.*, 297
Hellenistic administration, 646
Hellenistic baroque sculpture, 37, 1718
royal library at, 1537, 1819
Temple of Asclepius, 1687
Temple of Trajan, 1679
water pipeline of, 339 *illus.*
Periandros (Periander)
tyrant of Corinth, 19
Pericles (Perikles)
abandonment of Attica to Peloponnesian Army,
690
architecture under, 1662–1665
building program in Athens, 1711
citizenship law, 151
citizenship reforms of, 541
democracy under, 468–469

Megarian decree, 733
portrait by Kresilas, 1713
public building program of, 468
supporter of Themistocles, 27
tenure as *strategos*, 474, 475
wages for civil servants under, 469
on woman's proper role, 1303
xenia relationship with Archidamus of Sparta,
671
Periegesis. See Hecataeus (Hekataios) of Miletus
Peri Hypsous. See Longinus
Perinthos, map 3, map 7
Periodonikes, 1134, 1136
Peripatetic school
emphasis on character types, 1554
Perirrhanteria (lustral basins), 888
Peristylium (peristyle court)
in Greek architecture, 1667–1669
in private house, 1367, 1373
Persephone, queen of the dead and wife of Hades,
990
Persepolis, map 5, map 8
Persia (Parthian Empire), map 5
Persian Empire
administration of, 642
breakup of, 37
clothing, 1395–1396
coinage of, 1795–1796
courier system of, 353–354
different official languages, 200
reborn under Sasanian dynasty, 77
Roman diplomacy with, 672
trilingual inscriptions, 200
Persian Gulf, map 8
Persians. See Aeschylus
Persian Wars, 23–27
effect on Greek architecture, 1662
effect on Greek art, 1709
Personality
animal analogies, 1284–1285
childhood experience and adult personality,
1282–1283, 1287
contrast and comparison in analysis of, 1283
Electra complex, 1285
heredity vs. environment in classical literature,
1281–1283
honor and good birth in Greek and Roman
cultures, 1283
individual case studies by ancient writers, 1283
individual vs. type in classical literature,
1279–1281

Personality (continued)
  insight on human motivation in Euripides'
      tragedies, 1286
  mother and son relations, 1286–1289
  physiognomy, 1285
  Socratic theory and modern analysis, 1289
  theory of the four humors, 1281
  timocratic man in Plato's *Republic*, 1287–1288
  triumph of nature over culture in Greek
      tragedies, 1282
  use of character types by classical historians, 1280
  weakness of ancient attempts to explain, 1289
Pessinos, map 5
Petrarca, Francesco (Petrarch)
  campaign for reform of Latin style, 1825
  unrivaled classical library, 1826
Petronius Arbiter
  classical hexameter satire in *Satyricon*, 1500
  criticism of declamation, 1117
  "Dinner with Trimalchio" in *Satyricon*, 1218–1219
  example of *suasoria* in *Satyricon*, 1116
  on problem of poet and historical themes, 1431
  Satyrika (*Satyricon*), 1569–1570
  sexual promiscuity in *Satyricon*, 1266
  story of Eumolpus, 1126
Peucetii, map 2
Phaedo. See Plato
Phaedrus
  collection of Aesopic fables, 1123
Phaedrus. See Plato
Phaistos, map 4
Phaleron, map 4
Phallus
  public representations of, 1254
Phanagoria, map 7
Phantasiai kataleptikai (apprehensible presentations)
  Stoic chief criteria of truth, 1618
Pharae (Pharai), map 4
  oracle of Hermes, 948
Pharisees, 1035
Pharmakoi (human scapegoats), 974
Pharsalos, map 4
Phaselis, map 5
Phasis, map 7
Phayllos, 1138
Pheidias (Phidias), 1756
  Athena Parthenos (Parthenon Athena sculpture),
      1663 *illus.*
  earnings of, 382
  Parthenon sculptures, 1711–1713
  statue of Zeus at Olympia, 848, 1711
  workshop of, 377–378

Pheidon of Argos
  tyranny of, 488
Pherai, map 4
Pherecrates
  Cheiron, 1509
  derided avant-garde composers, 1509
Phidias. *See* Pheidias
Philhellenes
  in Rome, 55
Philia
  Empedocles' principle of Love, 1594
Philip II, king of Macedonia
  admiration for Athenian culture, 32
  coinage under, 1799
  diplomatic successes, 31
  Macedonian phalanx, 691
  military genius, 31
  military tactics, 33
  murder of, 33–34
  organized siege train, 696
  and Pythian Games, 1144
  securing of army's economic base, 691
  transformation from pastoral to agricultural
      economy, 691
  use of Greek hegemonial alliances, 674
  victory at Chaironeia, 33
Philip V, king of Macedonia
  alliance with Carthage, 54
  defeat by Rome, 54
  use of pirates, 839
Philippi, battle of, 62
Philippica. See Theopompus
Philippics. See Demosthenes
Philippus of Thessalonica
  collection of epigrams in *Garland*, 1497
Philistia, map 5
Philistus of Syracuse
  History of Sicily, 1531
Philo, 818
  commentaries on the Pentateuch, 1042
  discrimination in Hellenistic Greece, 545
  on spirituality of Jewish ascetic community, 1194
Philocrates, Peace of
  open trade treaty, 733
Philodemus
  On Music, 1510
  treatise on rhetoric, 1103
Philogelos (*Lover of Laughter*)
  compilation of Greek jokes, 1124
Philosopher-kings
  education of, 1604
  in Plato's *Republic*, 1604

Philosophers, Greek
 attitude toward craftsmen, 367–368
 characteristic dress of, 1397
 in Rome, 1637
 See also particular philosophers
Philosophers, Roman. *See* particular philosophers
Philosophiana, map 2
Philosophy, Greek, 1585–1636
 adaptation by Christian writers, 1056–1057
 Byzantine role in transmission, 1827
 Cicero's writings on, 1640–1644
 Hellenistic mathematics and science, 1620–1634
 Hellenistic philosophy, 1614–1620
 origins and sources, 1585–1589
 sophists, mathematicians, doctors, scientists,
  1596–1614
 theories of change and knowledge, 1585–1596
 translation into Latin, 1637–1638
Philosophy, Hellenistic
 applicability of philosophy to life's problems,
  1614
 ataraxia (freedom from fear and anxiety), 1614
 internationalist perspective, 1614
 practical orientation in philosophy and science,
  1614
 specialization trend in sciences, 1614
 three main philosophical schools, 1615
Philosophy, Roman, 1637–1649
 merged with Greek philosophy, 1648
Philostratos
 epistolary guidelines, 1574
Phlegraean Fields, map 2
Phleius, map 4
Phocaea. *See* Phokaia
Phocis. *See* Phokis
Phoenicia, map 5
 influence of traders on Greece, 737
Phoenicians
 alphabet of, 398, 401, 404–405
 coinage of, 1798
 language of, 404–406
 writing system of, 398, 404–405
Phoenician Women. See Euripides
Phokaia (Phocaea), map 4, map 5, map 7
 colonies of, map 7
Phokis (Phocis), map 4
 defeat by Philip of Macedonia, 31–32
Phonetics, 398, 399
Phratries
 adolescent rites of passage, 1175, 1180
 Apatouria festival, 1146
 feasting of in classical Athens, 1180

 organization of in archaic period, 1168
 organization of in classical period, 464
 organizations of male kin groups, 893
 rituals of, 464
Phronesis (practical intelligence), 1612
Phrygia, map 5
Phryne
 accusations of impiety, 1188
Phthiotis, map 4
Phylai
 Dorian, 462–463
 Ionian, 463–464
 and organization of Greek polis, 462–463
Phylarchus of Athens
 historian as dramatist, 1531
Physics
 Seneca on, 1646
Physiognomy. See Aristotle
Piaculum (act of atonement), 910
Piazza Armerina
 Roman villa, 1377 *illus.*, 1687–1688
 Small Hunt mosaic pavement, 1791 *illus.*
Picenum, map 2
Picts, map 11
Piety
 Greek conception of, 889
Pinax (wooden tablet), 430
Pindar
 on athletes, 1138–1139
 celebrated athletes at four great festivals, 872
 conservative view of political order, 467
 elaborate choral compositions, 1507
 epinician odes, 872
 Heracles myth (*Nemean*), 873–874
 honored victorious athletes, 1450
 on initiates of Eleusinian Mysteries, 906
 language and imagery, 1451–1452
 master of *epinicia* (victory odes), 1450
 poet as international, well-paid professional, 1450
 recurring themes, 1450
 upheld aristocratic values, 1451
Pindos
 Dorian settlement of, 160–161
Pindos Mountains, map 3, map 4, 88 *illus.*
Pins and brooches, 1393
Piraeus. *See* Peiraieus
Pirates
 booty, 839
 Cilician, 842
 Cretan, 839
 holding for ransom, 839, 842
 Illyrian, 838, 839

Pirates (continued)
  punishment of, 839–840
  Roman suppression in Adriatic, 53
  ships of, 840
  suppression by Pompey, 561
  Tyrrhenian, 839
Pirustai, map 3
Pisé (aggregate)
  Roman innovation of, 1672
Pisidia, map 5
Pisistratus. *See* Peisistratos
Pithekousai, map 2, map 7
Pitsa, map 4
Pittakos (Pittacus)
  tyrant of Mytilene, 17–18
Plague
  in Italy, 166 A.D., 73
Planetary Hypotheses. See Ptolemy (Claudius
    Ptolemaeus)
Planetary week, 394
Plataia (Plataea), map 4
  battle of, 27
  siege of, 695
Plato, 1600–1607
  analogies between human soul and state in
    Republic, 1287, 1289
  Apology, account of Socrates' trial, 1601
  and *arete,* 1012
  art of fencing, 688
  attitudes toward music, 1509–1510
  banished poets from his ideal state, 1518
  benevolent craftsmanlike deity, 1607
  communication depends on definition, 1606
  cosmos running in reverse, 266
  on craftsmen, 367
  on creativity and inspiration, 1518
  on Cretan and Spartan social customs, 1177
  criticism of sophistic movement, 1088
  danger of *mimesis,* 1518
  defense of democracy in *Protagoras,* 476
  development of mathematical and scientific
    courses, 1089
  dualism of mind and body, 1605
  on early childhood, 1359–1360, 1361
  educational theory, 1088–1089
  eschewed literary criticism and theory, 1517
  founded Academy, 1600
  Golden Age myth, 266
  and Greek political theory, 440
  Heraclitus' influence, 1600
  hostility toward tragedy, 414
  ideal state, 1604

influenced by Pythagoreanism, 1600–1601
influence on medical theory, 1233
interrelations of Forms themselves, 1606
Laws, 271
on luxuries, 1183
marriage in the utopian society, 1341
master of literary dialogue form, 1600
military purpose of Cretan law in *Laws,* 591
moral issues of Socratic dialogues, 1601–1602
moral and political recommendations in *Republic,*
    271
objective realities underpin thought, 1606
Parmenides, 1605
Phaedo, 1603
Phaedrus, 414–415
philosopher-kings, 1604
on physicians, 1232
on *proxenia* (*Laws*), 671
remedy for class strife (*Republic*), 540
Republic, 415, 1604
on ruler worship, posthumous, 1012
slavery vs. serfdom in *Laws,* 577
Socrates' influence on, 1601
on the Sophists, 1517–1518
Spartan model in *Republic,* 462
static ideal of society, 271
Symposium, 1182–1183, 1603
theory of Forms, 1603–1605
theory of Ideas, 415
Timaeus, cosmological work, 1606
on the timocratic man, 1287–1288
tripartite soul, 1605
universe product of intelligent design, 1606
use of dialogue form, 415
wars in Greek archaic period, 633
women's abilities, 1308
written vs. spoken language, 414–415
See also Forms, Platonic theory of
Plato, Academy of
  cult functions of, 1188
  curriculum of, 1089
  focus of education, 1089
  as forerunner of modern schools, 1088
  teaching of rhetoric in, 1089
  training for government leadership, 1089
Plautus, Titus Maccius
  Amphitryon, 1327
  comedies of, 1488, 1491
  male homosexuality in *Casina,* 1271
  sexual metaphor in comedies, 1271
  virtues of *pudor* as dowry, 1327
Plays, Hellenistic. *See* Drama, Greek

Plays, Roman. *See* Drama, Roman
Plebeian Assembly (*concilium plebis*), 517
  legislative powers of, 501
  loss of power under Augustan Constitution, 521
  loss of power under Sulla, 517
  tribunician rights, 500
Plebeian Order
  absence of unifying ideology, 560, 570
  access to office, 553
  acts of succession, 651
  ban on intermarriage, 551
  clients of powerful patricians, 47
  Comitia Tributa, 651, 653
  concilium plebis (popular assembly), 651, 653
  definition of, 551
  emergence of, 551
  Licinian and Sextian reforms, 552, 652
  political interests of, 551–552
  right of veto, 704
  struggle of the Orders, 553
  struggle for political power, 49, 50
  Tacitus' class divisions, 570
  tribunes, 651
Plinius Caecilius Secundus, Gaius (Pliny the Younger)
  correspondence as literary genre, 1579
  critiques of democracy, 549
  defense of epigrammatic genre in *Letters*, 1497
  on dining styles, 1217
  epistolary anthology, 1579
  on his wife, Calpurnia, 1327
  Letters, 74
  letter to Trajan on spread of Christianity, 1055
  practical and cultural correspondence, 1579
  on simplicity of Trajan's dinner, 1216
  wealth of, 564
Plinius Secundus, Gaius (Pliny the Elder), 1357, 1358
  on baling water from the Baebelo mines, 785
  book rolls of, 428
  on breadmaking, 238–239
  contributions to Roman medicine in *Natural History*, 1237
  dictation by, 430
  on emmer in Roman diet, 238
  environmental consequences of quarrying, 790
  Etruscan system of divination, 951
  five types of plows, 222–223
  folklore in *Natural History*, 884
  Greek painters, 1755–1757, 1769
  on husked wheat bread, 241
  on invention of parchment, 425
  lapis specularis (selinite) mining, 791
  on mining techniques, 786
  Natural History, 74
  omens in everyday life, 957
  on papyrus manufacture, 422, 423
  on prospecting for gold and tin, 784
  on stone-cutting techniques, 791, 792
  technical developments in grape pressing, 230
  varieties of marble, 791
Pliny the Elder. *See* Plinius Secundus, Gaius
Pliny the Younger. *See* Plinius Caecilius Secundus, Gaius
Plotinus
  goal of the individual, 1648
  philosophical creed, 78
  three entities or hypostases, 1648
Plowing ritual
  Roman city boundary, 1697
Plutarchus, L.(?) Mestrius (Plutarch)
  advice on marital infidelity, 1342
  advocates marriage based on love, 1342
  on aesthetic quality of roads, 760
  biography of Coriolanus, 1282
  Caesar's divorce of Pompeia, 1265
  on Cato's attitude toward education, 1110
  Cato's proposition to restore morality, 1269
  childhood of his subjects, 1361
  on childhood of Lycurgus, 1360
  on decline of Greece, 42
  Fulvia's drive for public power, 1325
  on importance of good birth in *The Education of Children*, 1282–1283
  on land reform and indebtedness, 546
  letter on his daughter's death, 1362
  on Lucullus' gastronomic extravagances, 1206
  Moralia, 1538
  On Music, 1509
  only historical source of popular opinions, 1539
  Parallel Lives, 1538–1539
  philosophical and moralistic biographies, 74
  purpose of biographical writings, 1538
  on social status of craftsman, 743
  on Spartan military training, 1178
  "Symposium of the Seven Wise Men," 1224
  women's status in, 1338
Pluto
  carving of on Velletri sarcophagus, 1744
Pneumatica (Hero of Alexandria's steam engine), 350 *illus.*
Poblicius, Lucius
  funerary statue, 1737–1738 *illus.*

Poet
  important role in ancient world, 1438
Poetics. See Aristotle
Poetry
  presentation of on scrolls, 427
Poetry, Greek
  commemorating athletes' feats, 1141
  community values in, 448
  competitions, 1148
  contests in Homeric tradition, 1515–1516
  and development of alphabet, 404
  early development, 17
  lyric, 1437–1439
  meter and genre, 1468
  narrator of, 409
  recitation of, 407–409
  three major classes, 1437
  transmission of community values, 1515
  and vase painting parallels, 1750–1751
  written versions, 427
  See also Bucolic poetry; Elegiac poetry; Lyric
    poetry
Poetry, Roman
  under Augustus, 66
  genres, 1521
  influence of Greek poetry on, 417–418
  Neoterics ("New Poets"), 1428–1429
  pagan authors as models in early church,
    1822–1823
  Saturnian verse, 417–418
  See also Bucolic poetry
Pola, map 2
Police
  in Athens, 798
Polis, Greek
  absence of privileged class, 446
  in archaic period, 465–466, 533, 797
  in classical period, 466–478, 797
  coinage, 533
  colonizing movement and, 445
  concept of good order, 447
  decline of collective purpose of, 1018
  definition of, 631–632
  historical development of, 444–446
  hoplite, 455
  law and justice in, 445
  meaning of, 1691
  organization of, 443, 462
  phylai in, 462–463
  physical characteristics of, 444
  political decision-making, 451

Spartan system of government, 461
  transformation of pre-state forms, 462–465
  use of public space in, 444–445
  writing and orality in, 411–414
Polites of Caria, 1135
Politorium, map 2
Pollio, Gaius Asinius
  eyewitness history of civil war, 1547
Pollio, Vedius
  reprimand of by Augustus, 1211
Poll tax, 811, 813
Pollution, ritual
  childbirth, 888
  contact with corpse, 888
  polluted person barred from sanctuary, 888
Pollux
  distinguished types of hymns, 890
  dithyramb (to Dionysus), 890
  paean (*paian*) (to Apollo), 890
  processional hymn, 890
Polybius
  aimed to record Roman dominion, 1532
  Black Sea trade of Greece, 740
  on Byzantine freedom-of-trade policy, 733
  on Cato the Elder, 1273–1274
  critical of sensationalism, 1532
  on extravagances of Hellenistic Romans, 1202
  on generosity to Rhodes after earthquake, 737
  greatest Greek historian after Thucydides, 1532
  human decline not inevitable, 270
  on human technological progress, 269
  on interdependence of orders, 655
  on prevalence of youthful licentiousness, 1274
  role of chance in human affairs, 1533
  on Roman constitution, 505
  on Roman Republic, 269
  on Roman warfare, 704–705
  Spartan revolution and oligarchies, 546
  on three kinds of Roman states, 655
Polyclitus. *See* Polykleitos of Argos
Polycrates of Samos
  water supply scheme, 338
Polydoros, 1728
Polyeuktos
  Demosthenes, 1719 *illus.*
  realistic portraits by, 1718
Polygnotos of Thasos, 1756–1758
Polykleitos (Polyclitus) of Argos, 1703, 1705, 1713
  Canon of anatomical symmetry, 1713
  Doryphoros (Spear Bearer), 1713, 1714 *illus.,* 1734
Polynices, Camillus, 385

Pompeii, map 2
  Alexander mosaic, 1757, 1768 *illus.*, 1769, 1774
  amphitheater, 1159
  architecture of, 1674
  black and white mosaics, 1785–1786
  delivering wine on terra-cotta relief, 231
  evidence of interior decoration styles, 1772
  Greek painting at, 1757, 1764–1765, 1778 *illus.*
  House of Cryptoportico, 1776–1777
  House of the Faun, 1374 *illus.*
  House of Marcus Lucretius Fronto paintings,
    1779–1780 *illus.*
  House of Pinarius Cerialis paintings,
    1780–1781 *illus.*
  House of the Vettii, 1375, 1781–1782 *illus.*
  list of first-century occupations, 772
  paintings of architecture, 1683
  Stabian Baths wall decoration, 1782
  Villa of Cicero wall paintings by Dioscurides,
    1764, 1774–1775 *illus.*
  Villa of the Mysteries, 1774, 1775
  Villa of the Mysteries wall painting, 1764
  See also Herculaneum
Pompeius, Gnaeus (Pompey)
  alliance with Caesar, 60–61
  coinage portraiture of, 1807
  eastern victories, 41
  expansion and provincial reorganization under,
    657
  in First Triumvirate, 59, 60, 657
  opposition to, 561
  restores power to tribunes, 59
  settlement of veterans, 561
  and Spartacus' rebellion, 560
  struggle with Caesar, 562
  success against piracy, 561, 843
  suppression of Lepidus' uprising, 560
  theater of, 1489
Pompeius, Sextus, 61
Pont du Gard
  Roman bridge, 1677
Pontifex maximus, 910
  competed for in popular election, 935
  emperor as, 937
  powers of, 935
Pontine (Pomptine) Marshes
  geology and history, 107
Pontius Pilatus, 1039
Pontos (Pontus), map 5, map 9
Poppaea
  coinage portraiture of, 1086

Population, Roman
  characteristics of, 754–755
  fluctuations, 754
  life expectancy, 754
  limits on production and consumption, 754
  slave import and growth of, 754
Populus, Roman
  kinship (curiae), 496
  legislative powers, 505
  limitations on authority, 505
  role in centuriate, 505–506
  in tribal assemblies, 506
  voting rights and methods, 506
Porches
  in Greek temple architecture, 1653
Po River
  geology and history, 101, 104–105
Pornikos telos (prostitution tax), 800
Poros, map 4
Portico
  in Roman architecture, 294
  Suetonius comments on safety features, 1379
  See also Stoa
Portoria (transit tolls), 809–810
Portrait coinage
  facing bust, 1815
  profile, 1798
Portraits, panel
  Egyptian mummy, 1772
Ports. *See* Harbors
Portus Dubris, map 1
Poseidon
  domain and associations, 849
Poseidonia (Paestum), map 2, map 7
  city plan of, 1693
  Temple of Poseidon, roof construction, 286 *illus.*
Posidonius (Poseidonios) of Apamea, 1533
  calculated earth's size, 1624
  on technological advance, 273
Postal service, Roman
  use of couriers, 354
Postumus, Marcus Cassianius
  coinage of, 1813–1815
Poteidaia, map 7
Potters, 373–374
  family connections among, 376
Potters' Hymn, 378
Pottery, 373–374 *illus.*
  mass production of, 380
  mold for, 380
  workshops for making, 376, 377 *illus.*

Pottery, Greek
appearance of Minyan styles, 158, 159
evidence of early Greek migrations, 167
Late Helladic to Geometric development, 167
Mycenaean at Thrace, 159
in Peloponnese, 167
Protogeometric, 7
twelfth-century Greece, 162
Pottery, Roman
Arretine vases, 763
implications for trade of other goods, 764
as indicator of Roman trade patterns, 762–763
marketing of, 763
Power sources
gears, 331 *illus.*
harnessed animal, 328, 347
manpower, 324, 328–329, 347, 352
slave labor, 328–329
steam, 349, 350 *illus.*, 351
water, 329–330
Praefectus praetorio, 523
responsibility for in-kind taxes, 824
Praefectus urbi (prefect of the city), 523
Praeneste (Palestrina), map 2
Basilica mosaics, 1774
Sanctuary of Fortuna Primigenia, 1673 *illus.*,
1674, 1687–1688
Praetor, 503, 523
administration of provinces, 653–654
formulae, 609
imperium of, 650
legal authority, 609
praetor peregrinus (responsible for foreign visitors),
671
praetor urbanus, 652
types of edicts, 609
when established, 48
Praxagoras of Cos
studies of pulse, 1233
Praxiteles, 1701, 1703
Aphrodite of Knidos, 1715, 1716 *illus.*
urbane style, 1715
Prayer
embodied in poetry, 963–964
Homeric example, 889–890
nature of Greek, 963
occasions for, 890
paean (*paian*) to Apollo, 963
Prefabrication, Roman
of building components, 303, 304, 307, 312, 313,
1679
See also Mass production

Pre-Socratic philosophers
writing in prose, 409
Priene (Turunçlar), map 4, map 5
agora gateway arch, 296
city plan of, 1666 *illus.*, 1693
Greek houses at, 1367–1368 *illus.*
temple of Athena Polias, 1665
Priesthood, Greek
acquisition of, 926–928
appointment of, 927
benefits and rewards of, 930
duties and functions, 929
economic status, 930
election to, 927
gender of, 926
hereditary, 926
importance of religious role, 925
inheritance of, 926–927
legal status of, 929–930
purchase of, 927
qualifications for, 928–929
rights of, 930
social status of, 929
tenure in office, 929
Priesthood, Jewish
assimilationist and conservative factions, 1031
prominence in Judaea, 1031
Priesthood, Roman
administrative and religious functions of pontiffs,
935
augurs (diviners), 911, 934, 981
College of Priests, 910–911
colleges of, 981
under the Empire, 937–938
fetials, 911, 981
flamines, 911
influence of foreign cults, 938
pontifices (pontiffs), 934, 981
provincial, 938
Quattuor amplissima collegia (four major colleges),
934, 981
quindecimviri sacris faciundis (priesthood of fifteen),
934, 935
recruitment by popular election, 934
under the Republic, 934–937
septemviri epulones (seven feasters), 934
sodales (associates), 911–912
Vestal Virgins, 911
Primis, map 6
Principal Doctrines. See Epicurus
Principate
Augustan constitution, 519–522

under Caesar, 518
Constantine I's monarchy, 527
control of Princeps over appointments, 524
decline of Senate, 524–525
Diocletian's concepts of theocracy and tetrarchy, 526
dynasticism of early Principate, 525
freedmen in administrative positions, 523
instability in third century A.D., 526
power of provincial armies, 526
proliferation of consuls and praetors, 523
restructuring by Augustus, 518–519
stability of, 525–526
transfer of power to nonelected officials, 523
Prinias
temple of Apollo, 1706
Printing
importance for classical scholarship, 1827–1828
Priscus of Panium
account of Huns under Attila, 176
Prisoners of war, Greek
commercial value of, 693, 694
treatment of, 693
Private cult, Roman
defined by Festus, 921
principal deities of, 921
Privateers, 839
See also Pirates
Prizes
in Greek athletics, 1131, 1138, 1140–1141, 1144
in Roman games, 1154
Proairesis (deliberate choice), 1612
Problems, 1281
Pro Caelio. See Cicero, Marcus Tullius
Processions
festival, 1147, 1150, 1152
at gladiatorial games, 1161
Procopius
famine in besieged Rome, 243
History of the Wars of Justinian, 179
Procurator (imperial provincial official), 820
Prodigia (prodigies)
defined, 982
and ritual, 982
Proeisphora, 800, 801
Professio (census declaration), 812, 814
Progress
classical theories of, 265–275
fifth-century Greek theories, 267–268
Greco-Roman cyclic ideas of time, 267
idea of scientific advance, 273
intellectual, 266–267

moral, 267
scientific writers' view of, 270
technological, 266, 274
Proklos
Epistolimaioi Kharakteres (Styles for Letters), 1573
types of letters, 1573–1574
Prokonnesos, map 4, map 5, map 7
Promagistracy, Roman
development in second century B.C., 504
under Principate, 523
weaknesses of, 515–516
Prometheus
Aeschylus' Prometheus Bound, 871
art and science of augury, 943, 971
defines the status of man, 871
gifts to mankind, 397
theft of fire from the gods, 870
Prometheus Bound. See Aeschylus
Propertius, Sextus
on Augustus' lifestyle, 1212
close link between love and death, 1458
differences between male and female worlds, 1330–1331
funeral elegy, 1330–1331
love as slavery, 1458–1459
lover as soldier, 1458–1459
patronage of Augustus and Maecenas, 1459
techniques, 1459
Property
gifts between husband and wife, 1349
woman's property rights, 1349
Property, law of
in iure cessio, 617
interdicts, 618
mancipatio, 617
ownership vs. possession, 618
private things, 617
public things, 617
security for debt, 619
servitudes, 619
transfer of, 617–618
usucapio, 618
Property taxes, 804
Propontis, map 3, map 4, map 5, map 7, 88 illus.
Propylon (Greek monumental gateway), 1660
Prose writing
development of, 409–410
Prostitution
candidates for, 1291, 1293, 1295
condemnation of, 1293, 1294, 1296
economic basis for, 1292–1294
effect on society, 1294, 1296, 1297

Prostitution (continued)
  fees, 1293–1294, 1296
  female, 1291–1295
  Greek, 1257
  legal control of, 1294, 1295–1296
  male, 1295–1297
  politics and, 1296
  religious origins, 1291–1292
  Roman, 1328
  tax on, 800, 820, 1294
  temple prostitution, 1292, 1293
  viewed as necessary institution, 1295
  See also Hetaira
Protagoras
  four kinds of speech, 1085
  needs of society, 268–269
  progress from a primitive state, 268
  regulation of the city-state, 269
Protocollon, 423
Protomai (bronze caldron attachments), 1705
Proverbs
  assimilationist work, 1030
Provinces, Roman
  architecture, 1675–1677, 1683 *illus.*, 1684
  boundaries, map 10
  coinage of rebellious generals, 1810–1812
  mosaic styles of, 1786–1788, 1790–1791 *illus.*
  painting in, 1783–1785
  spread of mints, 1813, 1815
  taxation of, 812–814
  taxation and agricultural production, 776
Proxenia (guest-friendship), 490
  responsibilities of, 667, 670–671
Prusa, map 5
Prusias II, king of Bithynia
  submission to Rome, 1407–1408
Psalms of Solomon
  explicitly anti-Hasmonean, 1036
Psamatik (Psammetichos) I, pharaoh of Egypt
  Greeks in service of, 15, 1701
Pseudo-Aristotle
  Oeconomica (*Financial Management*), 803
  on supremacy of Zeus in *On the Cosmos*, 848
Pseudo-Demosthenes
  purpose of wives, 1339
Pseudo-veneer marble. *See Trompe l'oeil* Roman
    painting
Ptolemaia, 1150
  ceremonies of, 1192
  institution of, 1192
Ptolemais Ake, map 5

Ptolemy (Claudius Ptolemaeus)
  advance of astronomy, 274
  Geography, 1625
  on Hipparchus, 274
  introduced notion of equant, 1631
  Optics, 1625
  physical account of heavenly dynamics, 1632
  Planetary Hypotheses, 1632
  rejected heliocentricity, 1629
  star catalog, 1636
  Syntaxis (Arabic *Almagest*), 1629
  treatise on astrology, *Tetrabiblos*, 1633
Ptolemy I, king of Egypt
  administration of, 642
  first in Egyptian dynastic cult, 1012
Ptolemy II, king of Egypt
  Great Procession, 1150
  Gymnopaedia, 1149, 1151
  library and temple at Alexandria, 1233
  Ptolemaia, 1150
Publicanus ("government man"), 558, 816–819
Public lavatories
  baths and wells, 342, 343
Public service
  payment for performance of, 798
Public services, Greek
  taxation to pay for, 795–807
Public works
  craftsmen involved in, 378, 379
Publius Servilius Rullus
  land distribution bill, 560
Pudicitia (chaste behavior)
  equivalence to *fides* (fidelity), 1326
  lack of, 1328
  Roman ideal for women, 1325
Pudor (decency, propriety)
  Pliny's description of his wife Calpurnia, 1327
Pugillares (codices), 430
Pulleys, 326, 333, 352
  multiple (*polyspaston*), 325 *illus.*, 333
Pump. *See* Force pump; Screw pump
Punctuation, 427
Punning
  in coinage, 1795, 1799, 1801
Purification rites, Greek
  emergency, 974
  marked important transitions, 974
  materials used, 974
  role of *pharmakoi*, 974
  routine, 974
Purification. *See* Lustration

Purifications. See Empedocles
Pyanopsia, 1146
Pydna, map 3
  victory of new over old military tactics, 707
Pylos, map 4
  capture by Athenian fleet, 699
  sack by Dorians, 5
Pyrgi, map 2
Pyrgoteles, 1725
Pyrrhic War, 51–52
Pyrrho of Elis
  first Hellenistic skeptic, 1619
Pyrrhus, king of Epeiros
  invasion of Italy, 52
Pythagoras
  death of, 1136
  doctrine of soul's immortality, 1594
  music of the spheres, 1510
  precepts of, 883
  religious influence of in Rome, 999
  taught a way of life, 1594
Pythagoreans
  table of opposites, 1314
  views on hunting, 123
  on woman's role, 1305
Pythian Games, 1133, 1134, 1144

Q

Quadrireme, 841
Quaestor, 502, 503
  administration of provinces, 653, 654
  responsibilities of, 651
  when established, 48
Quarries, Greek
  limestone (*lithos porinos*), 789
  marble, 789
  Pentelicus marble, 1663
  poros, 789
  techniques, 277–278, 279–281, 791
Quarries, Roman, 1678–1679, 1685
  basalt, 790
  marble, 790
  non-Italian sources, 791
  porphyry and hornblende granite in Egypt, 791
  sources and techniques, 300–301, 791
  travertine (calcareous limestone), 790
  tufa and peperino, 790
  water-driven saws in fourth century, 791–792

Quarrymen. *See* Stonemasons
Quintilianus, Marcus Fabius (Quintilian)
  considered Vergil the Roman Homer, 1432
  criticism of Afranius' plays, 1271–1272
  on draping the toga, 1409
  on early childhood, 1359, 1360
  Education of an Orator, 74
  on study of speeches, 1117
  on teaching of declamation, 1118
  on training of orator, 1115
  on writing materials, 430
Quirinus
  associations, 854
Qumran, map 5

R

Rabirius
  Roman architect (Domitian's palace plan), 306,
    308–309
Race
  in classical literature, 137–138
  concept of, 137–138
  establishing criteria, 137, 138
  in historical and geographical literature, 138–139
  See also Races and physical types
Races
  chariot, 1131, 1133, 1139, 1155–1157
  foot, 1131, 1134–1135
  horse, 1133, 1139
Races and physical types
  in ancient art, 139
  Asia Minor (Anatolia), 146
  Balkan Peninsula, 142
  Britain, 143–144
  cranial morphology, 140–141
  Egypt, 147–148
  Ethiopia and east Africa, 148
  fantastic peoples in classical literature, 149
  Gaul, 142–143
  Germany, 144–145
  Greeks and Romans, 141–142
  Iberian Peninsula, 142
  India, 147
  Libya and northwest Africa, 148–149
  major physical types in prehistory, 140
  from physical remains, 138, 140–141
  Scythia, 145
  Thrace, 145

Races and physical types (continued)
    western and central Asia, 146–147
    See also Race
Racetrack, Roman. *See* Circus, Roman
Racism. *See* Ethnic prejudice
Raetia, map 1, map 10
Rafts (*kelek*), 363
Rampin Rider, 1708
Rape, 1260
Raphia, map 5
Ravenna, map 2, map 11
    architecture of, 1689
    church mosaics and Roman influence, 1793
Reading, 413
    See also Literacy; Writing, Greek
Rebellions, Jewish
    against Antiochus IV, 1032
    coinage commemoration of, 1812
    in Egypt and Cyprus, 1042
    in Judaea, 1038–1040
Recitation, 407
Red-figure vase painting. *See* Vase Painting, Greek
Red Sea, map 6, map 8, 88 *illus.*
    trade in, 770
Reincarnation, 999
    See also Metempsychosis; Orpheus; Pythagoras
Religion
    distinguished from politics, 1018
    social control through, 1006
Religion, Greek
    anthropomorphism in, 1019
    Athenian festival calendar, 1145
    citizens' participation in, 892
    crucial role of priesthoods, 925–926
    differences from Roman, 999
    economic effects of, 727–728
    Homer's portrait of gods, 3–4
    polytheism, 1010
    under Romans, 930
    sacred places, 887–888, 889
    and slavery, 584
    state cults, 925
    women's role, 1304–1305
Religion, Roman
    adaptation of Greek priesthoods to, 930
    adoption of Greek gods and myths, 855
    adoption of sun-god in third century, 859
    concept of heaven, 1000
    concept of hell, 999
    cult of the people (*genius populi*), 1014
    happiness after death, 1000
    importance of cult rather than belief, 909
    importation of new gods in republican period, 857
    influence of Stoicism, 1648
    Lucretius' opposition to, 1638
    of peasants, 999
    Rex sacrorum (king of the ceremonies), 910, 936
    shift from paganism to Christianity, 937
    third-century cults, 77–78
    women's public role, 1321
Religious festivals
    athletics in, 1132
Religious leagues (amphictyonies), 668–669
Renaissance
    influence of Roman building styles, 1689
Renaissance, twelfth-century
    revival of interest in pagan authors, 1823
    translations of pagan authors, 1824
Renaissance painting
    Roman precursors of, 1775, 1781
Republic, Roman
    agrarian makeup of electorate, 507
    annuality, 498
    centuriate assembly, 497
    coinage of, 1806–1809
    collapse of, 655–657
    composition of the ruling class, 654–655
    conflict of the orders, 651
    consuls, 508, 523
    decline of, 511–518
    depopulation of rural areas, 514
    development of proletarian army, 515
    dictatorship, 502
    disaffection of urban masses, 562
    dual magistracy, 498, 503
    elections, 510–511
    enlargement of magisterial colleges, 503
    height of, 505–511
    imperialism, 812–813
    inspiration for eighteenth-century revolutionists, 1829
    interior decoration developments, 1772–1777
    interrex, 497, 499
    lack of continuity in, 503–504
    later history, 55–64
    Licinian-Sextian law, 500
    magistrate's *imperium*, 498, 499, 503
    military influences, 515–516
    overseas provinces, 503
    patrician state, 499
    plebeian institutions, 500–502

populus, 505–507
principles of popular sovereignty, 516, 517
after revolution, 497–498
rise, 497–511
Roman code of political ethics, 511
shared *imperium,* 511
structure of state, 498–500
Sullan reforms, 571
territorial expansion, 511
timocratic principle in assembly, 500
traditional priesthoods, 934–937
wealth of late Republic, 63
See also Senate, Roman; particular offices
Republic. See Plato
Revenues, public
in Greek city-state, 798–800
of Roman state, 809, 810, 813, 821–822
See also Taxation
Rhegion, map 2, map 7
Rhenus River, map 1, 88 *illus.*
Rhetoric
awareness of audience psychology, 1280–1281
in Greek education, 413
influence on early historians, 1527
three types, 1527
See also Education and rhetoric
Rhetoric. See Aristotle
Rhetoric, Greco-Roman
Atticism, 1104–1105
attitude of philosophers toward, 1103–1104
domination of education in late Republic and
early empire, 1104
in Latin, 1104
as part of social structure, 1106
prescriptive rules for in late antique period, 1106
Rhetoric, Hellenistic
"Asianic," 1101–11021
ceremonial, 1102
deliberative speech, 1102
from oratorical to literary discipline, 1103
Peripatetics, 1102
psychology in persuasion, 1102
schemata (figures), 1102
Stoics' influence on style, 1103
technical developments, 1102
Rhetoric, Roman
arrangement of model speech, 1114
declamations, 1115–1118
decline of republican style under Principate, 1115
functions of orator, 1115
Latin theory, 1114

modeled on Greek, 1113
practical benefits of, 1114
progymnasmata, 1118
speechmaking, 1114
studied in Greek, 1114
style, 1114
treatises on, 1118–1119
Rhetoric, schools of
epistolary skills taught, 1574
Rhion, map 4
Rhodanus (Rhone) River, map 1, 88 *illus.*
geology and history, 101, 104
Rhodes, map 4, map 5, map 9
actions against piracy, 841
Dorian occupation of, 168–169
merchant marine of, 841
merchant oligarchy, 39
navy, 646, 841
orthogonal city plan by Hippodamos, 1695
Rhodian school of sculptors, 1728
siege of by Demetrios I, 332
social aid, 646
Rhodopis
memorial sent to Delphi, 632
Rhoikos of Samos, 1703
Rhone River. *See* Rhodanus River
Rhythmoi, 1710
Riace
bronze warriors, 1710
Riace Marina, map 2
Right of Appeal, 558
Rio Tinto, map 1
Cerro San Dionisio lode, 784
main ore bodies along, 784
mine drainage wheel from, 785–786
two periods of mineralization, 784
Rites of passage, 1146
Ritual, Greek, 959–979, 1151, 1152
"bear-girls" of Artemis, 928
elements of, 963–967
Enagizein, 973
festal meals, 966, 972
giftgiving, 967
honors gods, 959
Odysseus' ritual at edge of underworld, 973–974
powerful actions, 973–975
priests of Herakles, 928
for war, 900
Ritual, Jewish
Passover, 1028
purity laws, 1028

Ritual (continued)
  Sabbath, 1028
  Tabernacles, 1028
Ritual, Roman
  calendar, 983
  College of Priests, 981
  compared with Greek rituals, 981
  errors in carrying out, 982
  instauratio, 982
  literary evidence, 983
  prodigia, 982
Rivers
  transport on, 363–364
Rivers and springs
  worship of, 851
Roads, Roman, 1672
  aesthetic considerations, 759–760
  building of, 354–355
  compass orientation of, 1697
  construction of, 759, 760
  costs of repair and maintenance, 760–761
  organization required for building and repair,
    761
  and trade expansion, 759
Road system
  in Mesopotamia, 353
Romaia, 1151
Roman Calendar, The (Fasti). See Ovidius Naso,
    Publius (Ovid)
Romanitas, 1021
Roman numerals, 417
Rome, map 2, map 11, 88 *illus.*
  air pollution in, 128
  Amphitheatrum Flavium (Colosseum), 300,
    305–306, 1678–1679, 1681 *illus.*
  Basilica of St. Paul's Outside the Walls, 301
  Basilica Ulpia, 304, 306 *illus.,* 309–310,
    312–317 *illus.*
  coinage commemorating founding, 1806, 1813
  column of war (*columna bellica*) in, 670
  critical geographic location, 48
  defensive walls of Aurelian, 716–717
  Domus Aurea (Nero's Golden House), 305, 308,
    1667–1678 *illus.,* 1772
  of early church, 1793
  fall of, 82
  filled power vacuum left by Etruscan decline, 50
  founding of, 46, 1697
  Greek philosophers in, 1637
  Hypogeum of the Aurelii wall painting, 1789 *illus.*

imperial forums of, 300, 305, 306 *illus.,* 310 *illus.,*
    1698
imperial trade and growth of, 775
importance to Christian church, 1822
last known mythological painting, 1789
legendary origins, 877–878
Marmorata (marble yards), 301, 307
military domination of Italy, 51
Milvian (Mulvian) Bridge, 296
mints of, 1807, 1809, 1810, 1812
"Odyssey landscapes" (Greek painting cycle),
    1764 *illus.,* 1765, 1775–1776
Pantheon, 305, 320
port of, 361
S.S. Giovanni e Paolo, Roman house fresco
    under, 1789–1790 *illus.*
Tomb of the Valerii stuccowork, 1785–1786 *illus.*
Trajan's Forum (Forum Traianum), 306,
    308–320, 310 *illus.,* 311 *illus.,* 314 *illus.,* 317,
    317 *illus.,* 318 *illus.,* 319 *illus.,* 1680, 1698
Underground Basilica wall decoration, 1778–
    1779
Vatican cemetery mosaics and paintings, 1783,
    1785, 1786, 1792
Villa Farnesina stucco reliefs, 1778–1779 *illus.*
wall painting of, 1772, 1778–1779, 1781, 1785,
    1791–1793
water supply of, 340, 343
See also Aqueducts
Rome, architecture in
  Amphitheatrum Flavium (Colosseum),
    1678–1679, 1681 *illus.,* 1812
  Arch of Constantine, 1684, 1744 *illus.*
  Basilica Julia in the Forum Romanum, 1676
  Basilica of Maxentius, 1686 *illus.,* 1687
  Baths of Caracalla, 1685 *illus.,* 1686
  Capitoline temple, 1672 *illus.*
  Church of Santa Costanza (Constantina's
    mausoleum), 1688
  Domus Aurea (Nero's Golden House),
    1677–1678 *illus.,* 1772
  forum (piazza), 1679–1680, 306 *illus.,* 310 *illus.*
  imperial palaces, 1677–1679
  Pantheon, 1680, 1682 *illus.*. 1689
  Servian Wall, 1672, 1684
  St. Peter's Cathedral, 1689
  Tabularium (state archives), 1674
  Thermae Agrippae (bath building), 1676
  Trajan markets, 1680
  See also Rotunda and octagon forms

Rome, Etruscan
dominant city state in Latium, 47
Latin official language, 48
Romulus
appointment of Senate, 649
civic structure of tribes, 649
Romulus and Remus
in Livy's history of Rome, 877
Roof construction, Greek
flat clay, 278
terra-cotta tiling and woodwork, 283, 284 *illus.*,
285 *illus.*, 286 *illus.*, 287
thatch, 278, 279 *illus.*
Roof construction, Roman
bronze gilt tiling, 304–305
installation of, 314, 315 *illus.*, 316, 317
under Republic, 299
terra-cotta tiling, 303–304 *illus.*
timber truss, 286, 294–295, 314 *illus.*, 315 *illus.*,
317
Rope manufacture, 374
Rope technology, 324
hair, 336
sinew (neuron), 335–336
Rotunda and octagon forms
in Roman architecture, 1680, 1682 *illus.*, 1688
Rufus, Publius Rutilius, 557
Rufus, Publius Sulpicius
and Roman civil wars, 559
Rufus, Quintus Curtius
biographical history of Alexander, 1555
Ruler worship
ability to inspire deep religious piety, 1021
actively fostered by Roman emperors, 1017
alien to traditional Roman religion, 1014
Augustus and, 1015
Augustus' destruction of self-government and,
1014
beneficence and, 1011
cessation of, 1017, 1018
character and significance of, 1018–1024
characteristic features of, 1011
Christianity inherited Jewish abhorrence of, 1023
as a coinage subject, 1801, 1802, 1810, 1812
criticism of, 1021
culmination of in Greco-Roman world, 1017
decline in importance of, 1017
defined, 1009
deification of community, 1014
effect of Stoicism on, 1020

in Egypt, 1009
Egyptian or Eastern influence on, 1011, 1017
of the Emperor Trajan, 309
as extension of Greco-Roman paganism, 1023
first Greek instance of, 1011
fusion of patriotism and religion, 1021
gradual development of in Roman world, 1017
Greek, 1009–1014
as Hellenistic institution, 1013
indication of decline of city-state, 1018
Jewish abhorrence of, 1023
justification by inadequacy of gods, 1019
in Mesopotamia, 1009
most important form of in Rome, 1014
municipal cults of living rulers, 1012
by municipalities, groups and individuals, 1016
opposition to, 1011, 1022
prayer for emperor to gods, 1020
precedents for, 853
prepared men to accept savior both God and
man, 1023
by provincials, not Roman citizens, 1016
reasons for, 1011
Roman distinction between divinity and person,
1015
Roman emperors, 858–859
seminal development of polytheism, 1009
as standard debate theme, 1021
Rullus, Publius Servilius
land distribution bill, 560
Running contests, 1131, 1134–1135
Rusellae, map 2
Rustification, 293 *illus.*
See also Masonry construction

S

Sabas
martyrdom in *Passion of St. Sabas*, 172–173
Sabatinus, Lake, map 2
Sabazios (Phrygian god)
rituals of, 1187
Sabine women
role of rape in building Rome, 1268
Sabini, map 2
Sabratha, map 6
Sacadas of Argos, 1507
Sacred Teachings. See Aristides, Aelius

Sacrifice, Greek, 959–979
  acceptance of, 977
  ancient views on, 975–977
  appropriateness, 973
  characterizes civilized man, 978
  distinctions among, 962
  explained by practices of hunting cultures, 977
  in Homer's *Iliad*, 961
  meaning of, 960–963
  not represented in art or drama, 970
  persistence of as major rite, 961
  procedures, 969–973
  shares to cult officials, 972–973 ·
  sources of information, 959–960
Sacrifice, human, 975
Sacrifice, Roman
  animal victims or bloodless, 910
  central ritual, 984–985
  commonest Roman ritual, 910
  effects of ruler cult, 985
  litatio, 985
  at Lupercalia, 983
  perlitatio, 985
  sculptural evidence, 986
  significance of, 985
Sadducees, 1035
Saguntum, map 1
Sailing ships, 357–362
  amenities on, 361–362
  building of, 358
  capacity of, 358–359
  cargo of, 360–361
  passengers on, 361–362
  preying of pirates on, 837–844
  rigging of, 359–360
Sailmaking, 374
Saint Peter's Cathedral, Rome, 1689
Saints, cult of
  contribution of hero worship, 1023
Sais, map 6
Salamis, map 4
Salamis, battle of, 26
Salaries. *See* Wages
Sales tax, 799, 807, 821–822
Sallust (Gaius Sallustius Crispus)
  on animal sacrifices, 977
  biting prose style, 1545
  Conspiracy of Catiline, The, 1545
  descriptions of Caesar and Cato, 1283
  discredits Sempronia, 1328
  Histories, 1545

Jugurthine War, The, 1545
  Neoplatonic pagan philosopher, 976
  saw Rome's decline as a moral problem, 1545
  sought to unmask political reality, 1545
Salmydessos, map 3
Salonae (Split)
  palace of Diocletian, 1687–1688 *illus.*
Salonika. *See* Thessalonica
Saltpeter, 331
Salt tax, 804
Samaria, map 5
Samnites
  Roman war of attrition against, 51
Samnium, map 2
Samos, map 4, map 5
  clothing styles, 1394–1395
  Ionic temple of Hera, 1658–1659
  oligarchic coup at, 543
  settlement of, 6
  siege of, 798
  statue of Hera, 1707
  water tunnel of Polycrates, 338
Samothrace (Samothrake), map 3, map 7
  Nike of, 1719
Samothracian Mysteries, 901
Sanctuary
  funding of as a civic activity, 1662, 1663
  in Greek architecture, 1660, 1662–1664
Sanitation
  public baths and lavatories, 342
Sappho
  associates, 1442–1443
  on the beloved, 1443
  called tenth muse, 1304
  cultivation of Aphroditic arts, 1442–1443
  epithalamia, 1335, 1443
  exile from Lesbos, 17
  greatest lyric monodist, 1444
  homosexuality, 1442
  homosexual love in poetry, 1262–1263
  illustrated on vase painting, 426
  on loss of a lover, 1311
  love poems written for a cult association, 1176
  "Ode to Aphrodite," 1443
  poet as subject of poetry, 408
  pursuit of the beautiful, 1309
  Sapphic meter, 1443
  special relation to her audience, 1441
Sardinia, map 2
Sardis, map 8
Sarmatae, map 11

Sarnus River, map 2
Saronic Gulf, map 4
Sasanian Empire
  expansion of, 715
Satire
  Attic Old Comedy, 1500
  classical hexameter, 1500
  development of by Romans, 1499
  diatribe, 1500
  fourth-to fifth-century Christian writers, 1502
  Hellenistic contribution to Roman satire, 1500
  as literary genre, 1501
  literary techniques, 1501
  origins of *satura*, 1499
  political, in fifth-century Athens, 1500
  satiric epigram, 1502
  spoudogeloion, 1500
Satricum, map 2
Saturae Menippeae. See Menippus of Gadara
Saturnalia
  popular Roman winter festival, 919
Saturnalia. See Macrobius, 859
Saturninus, Lucius Appuleius, 558
Satyricon. See Petronius Arbiter
Saxons, map 11
Scaevola, Quintus Mucius
  commentary on civil law, 610
Scale and proportion
  in Greek architecture, 1658, 1661, 1667, 1679
  in Roman architecture, 1679–1680, 1682 *illus.*,
    1683, 1685 *illus.*, 1686
  in Roman art, 1789, 1790–1791, 1790 *illus.*,
    1791
  See also Miniaturism
Scales. *See* Harmoniai
Scamander River
  associations, 851
Scapegoat, human, 974
Scarabs and scaraboids, 1724 *illus.*
Scholarship, classical, 1819–1832
  advances in textual criticism, 1828
  eighteenth-century revival, 1830
  nineteenth-century developments, 1831
  Petrarch's role in advancing, 1825
Scholarship, Greek
  in Eastern Empire, 1820
  Hellenistic, 1819
  main concerns of Byzantine scholars, 1826–1827
Scholarship, Roman
  nature of, 1819–1820
  in Western Empire, 1820

Scholasticism
  and classical authors, 1824
  in Hellenistic period, 415
Science, Greek
  Galen quotes biologist Erasistratus, 1634
  rigorous demands of research, 1633–1634
Sciences, natural
  idea of progress, 273–274
Scipio, Publius Cornelius (Scipio Africanus the
    Elder)
  attack on Carthage, 707
  defeat of Hannibal at Zama, 707
  defeat of Hasdrubal at Ilipa, 707
  destruction of Carthaginian army in Spain, 707
  given *imperium*, 707
  invasion of North Africa, 54
  patron-client relationship with troops, 708
Scipio Aemilianus Africanus Numantinus, Publius
    Cornelius (the Younger)
  attacked sexual behavior taught in dancing
    schools, 1274
  sexual slander of by Lucilius, 1274
Sciri, map 11
Scots, map 11
Scottus, Sedulius
  compiled classical anthology, 1823
Screw principle and applications, 326–327,
    328 *illus.*
  screw manufacturing device, 329 *illus.*
Screw pump, 345, 346 *illus.*, 346 *table*, 347 *table*
Scribes, 398, 427, 428–429, 432
Scriptures
  Jewish law regarding, 432
Sculptors, Greek
  family connections among, 375
  major employers of, 1720
  status and role of, 1719–1721
Sculptors, Roman
  of architectural elements, 313–314
Sculpture, Greek, 1701–1721
  acrolithic, 1703
  anticlassical style in, 1715
  archaic style, 1707, 1708
  bronze, 1701, 1702, 1703
  canons of proportion for, 1702, 1706
  character, emotion, and morality in, 1711
  chronology of, 1703–1704
  chryselephantine statues, 1703
  classical period, 1711
  clay sculptures, 1703
  coinage references to, 1801–1802

Sculpture (continued)
  Daedalic style, 1706
  Egyptian influence, 17
  elegant or flying drapery style, 1714
  first manifestations of classicism, 1715
  hollow casting, 1702
  human emotion in, 1714
  lost wax technique, 1702
  maquettes used, 1703
  marble, 1701, 1702
  Pheidian style, 1702, 1711
  polychrome in, 1702
  Pythagorean aesthetic vision, 1711
  realism in, 1718, 1719
  relief sculpture in architecture, 1708
  revived archaic and classical styles, 1719
  rococo style, 1719
  Roman copies, 1703, 1711
  Roman period, 1711
  Roman preference for, 1727–1728
  sculptural elements in vase painting, 1758–1759
  sensuousness in, 1716
  Severe style, 1709
  stylistic and iconological history, 1704–1719
  techniques and materials, 1701–1703
  terra-cotta, 1703
  tools for, 1702
  in wealthier Hellenistic homes, 1371
Sculpture, Italian and Etruscan, 1729
Sculpture, Roman, 1727–1748
  allegorical themes, 1732
  Antonine period in, 1746
  Augustan, 1730, 1733–1737
  bronze, 1729, 1733
  eclectic imagery in, 1742–1744
  eclecticism of, 1728,1733
  expressionism, 1746
  figurative tradition, 1742–1743
  Flavian period, 1738–1739
  funerary, 1738 *illus.*, 1742 *illus.*, 1743 *illus.*,
    1746 *illus.*
  Greco-Roman works, 1728, 1732
  Greek heritage of, 1727–1729
  Hellenistic tradition in, 1728, 1730, 1731, 1732,
    1736, 1737
  iconography of military victory in, 1732
  as imperial propaganda, 1736
  Julio-Claudian period, 1737–1738
  limestone, 1729, 1730
  marble, 1729
  materials as determinants of style, 1729

  narrative representations in, 1740–1741
  native tradition in, 1729, 1730, 1731
  portraiture in, 1730
  problems in differentiating from Greek,
    1727–1728
  in provinces, 1732, 1738
  realism in, 1741
  republican revival under Trajan, 1739–1741
  retreat from Greek naturalism, 1747
  Roman subjects and Greek models, 1733–1734
  Severan period, 1746
  stylistic developments in Republic, 1729–1733
  techniques of, 1746
  terra-cotta, 1729
  tufa, 1729
  See also Friezes and reliefs
Scylax. *See* Skylax
Scythians
  depiction in classical art, 145
  physical description, 145
  trade with Greeks, 14
Sea of Galilee, map 5
Sea Peoples
  destruction of Hattusas, 166
  invasions of Egypt, 165, map 6, map 10, 88 *illus.*
  names and origin of, 165–166
  Phrygian immigration to Anatolia, 166
Seaports, Greek, 362
Seaports, Roman, 363
Seasons
  relation to calendar, 391, 393
Sea transport, 357–364
  effect of weather on, 357
  prevailing winds and, 359–360
  seasonal, 357
  speed of, 359
Sea voyages, 357–362
Secret diplomacy, 667
Sejanus, Lucius Aelius
  influence under Tiberius, 67
Seleucia ad Tigrim, map 9
Seleucid Era, dating mechanism, 393
Seleukid (Seleucid) Empire, 36, 37, map 9
  administrative system of *strategiae*, 645
  coinage of, 1802–1803
  defeat by Rome, 54–55
  dynastic cult, 1012
  taxation in, 803–804
  See also Antiochos
Seleukos (Seleucus) I
  territories ruled by, 645

Selinus (Selinous), map 7
  temple of, 1708
Sellasia, map 4
Selymbria, map 7
Semonides of Amorgos
  archaic Greek misogynist, 1441
  denunciation of aristocratic women, 534
  on grain processing, 238
  iambic diatribe, 1441
  ten types of female personalities, 1284, 1285
  woman's separate origins, 1307
Semonides of Samos
  use of sardonic rage in satire, 1500
Senate, Roman, 495, 508–511
  advisory council to early kings, 47
  basis of power, 508–509
  Caesar's reforms, 61
  challenges to authority, 513, 514, 516
  changes under Augustan Constitution, 521–522, 525
  coinage issue, power of, 1807, 1809, 1810
  commercial activity prohibited, 56, 564
  composition of membership, 509
  corruption, 512
  decline of influence on policy, 512–513
  and deification of emperor, 1015
  in early Republic, 48
  envoys of, 672
  equestrians' encroachment on, 524
  ethnic prejudice in membership requirements, 151
  foreign policy powers of, 670
  ignored by later emperors, 661
  imperium, 509, 510
  loss of control to Princeps, 524–525
  mos maiorum (ancestral custom), 510, 518
  Ovinian law, 509
  patres conscripti, 496
  power over appointments, 509
  power over magistrates, 510
  powers curtailed under Diocletian, 78
  powers under Augustus, 658, 659
  ratification of treaties, 675
  reforms under Caesar, 518
  regulatory decrees, 510
  relations with "Five Good Emperors," 71
  reorganized by Flavian emperors, 71
  restructuring under Sulla, 516–517
  role in foreign policy, 509
  selection of kings by, 495–496
  senatus consulta (decrees), 611

senatus consultum ultimum, 516
  Sulla increases power of, 58–59
  veto rights, 508
Senatorial Order, 564–565
  accumulation of wealth, 564
  alienation from imperial government, 570
  income from trade and industry, 564
  internal stratification, 565
  reestablishment of by Augustus, 563
  status under Gracchan reforms, 557–558
  Sulla's confiscation of property, 559
  three aristocratic qualities of, 564–565
Seneca, Lucius Annaeus (seneca the Elder)
  on declamations, 1116, 1117
Seneca, Lucius Annaeus (Seneca the Younger)
  biography, 1644
  character and reputation, 1644–1645
  classical hexameter satire in *Apocolocyntosis,* 1500
  corpus of philosophical writings, 1644
  defines happiness, 1645
  educational purpose, 1645
  highly personal nature of writings, 1645–1646
  humanity a key ethical concept, 1644
  letter to his mother, Helvia, 1280, 1323
  Letters to Lucilius (*Moral Letters*), 273, 1645–1646
  literary achievements, 69
  Moral Essays, 1645
  Naturales Quaestiones (*Natural Questions*), 273, 1646
  noise pollution, 1379
  On Anger, 1645
  On Clemency, 1645
  On the Happy Life, 1645
  On Leisure, 1645
  On the Shortness of Life, 1645
  practical application of philosophy, 1646
  reconciles Stoic and Epicurean views, 1646
  retirement from politics, 1646
  rooming-house hazards, 1379
  Stoic views, 1644
  tragedies of, 1489
  on true wisdom, 273
  use of epistolary form in *Moral Letters,* 1579
  wealth of, 564
Septuagint
  Greek translation of Pentateuch, 1037
  source for later historians, 1037
Sequana River, map 1
Serdica, map 3
Serfdom
  among noncitizens in Greece and Rome, 577–578
  and slavery in economic system, 577, 585, 588

Serial subjects and themes
    in Roman painting and mosaic, 1771, 1777, 1778,
        1785, 1788 *illus.*
Seriphos, map 4
Servian Wall (Rome), 1672, 1684
Servilia (mother of Brutus)
    informal political power, 1323, 1324
Servius Tullius
    adminstrative innovations, 496
    centuriate assembly, 497
    development of hoplite army, 703
    tribal reforms of, 650
Seven against Thebes. See Aeschylus
Seven Wise Men of antiquity, 1535
Severus
    Roman architect, 308
Severus, Septimius
    achievements, 76
    architecture under, 1684–1685
    coinage of, 1813
    origins, 76
Severus Alexander, Marcus Aurelius, 76
    military reforms, 715
    murder of, 715, 716
Sewage system, city
    Roman engineering of, 1700
Sextus Empiricus
    most important Skeptic, 1619
    took Pyrrhonist practice of suspending judgment,
        1619
Sexual attitudes
    double standard, 1293, 1296–1297, 1340, 1351
    monogamy as ideal, 1351
Sexual attitudes, Greek
    anteran (to reciprocate eros), 1259
    Athenian laws governing, 1339
    definition of sexuality, 1250
    distinguishing *pais* (citizen male child) from *pais*
        (slave), 1260
    eros (desire) as external force, 1257
    extramarital sex, 1257–1258
    in festivals and cults, 1254
    gender and status roles, 1256
    general roles, 1251–1253
    homosexuality, 1258–1263
    idealization of youth, 1259
    inhibitions on sexual expression, 1255
    male transition to adulthood, 1260
    masturbation, 1260
    obscenity and sexual repression, 1255–1256
    penetration, 1260

phallic representation, 1254–1255
    philia (love) vs. lust, 1257
    pursuit of sexual object, 1256–1257
    religious and philosophical considerations,
        1250
    sexual activities of gods in Greek poetry, 1254
    sexuality and changes in cultural norms, 1250
    sexuality as divine force, 1254
    sexual vocabulary in Greek language, 1254
    See also Homosexuality; Women, Greek
Sexual attitudes, Roman
    ambivalence of in classical literature, 1265–1266
    Augustan legislation on, 1275
    beginnings of sexual self-expression in second
        century, 1270
    cultural background, 1276–1278
    defamation of powerful through sexual slander,
        1274
    distinguishing fact from fiction in literature,
        1275–1276
    early concepts of sexuality, 1268
    in early Latin literature, 1270–1272
    evidence of extramarital and homosexual
        relationships, 1275
    female sexual behavior, 1266–1267
    hellenization of Roman life, 1275
    hypocrisy of leaders advocating sexual
        restrictions, 1276
    lack of marital intimacy, 1276
    lack of sexual alternatives for women, 1266
    paternal responsibility, 1266
    permissive outlook in imperial Rome, 1276
    procreative aspects of sex, 1268
    reliance of literature on Greek models, 1271
    restraints on Bacchic worship, 1269
    romanization of sexual terms in classical period,
        1273
    in second century, 1269–1270
    sex and religion, 1270
    sexual artifacts, 1266
    sexual desire as danger to state, 1268
    sexual innuendo in literature, 1275
    stuprum (sexual disgrace), 1268
    See also Homosexuality, Roman
Sexuality, female
    misogynists' view, 1310–1311
    self-control as highest virtue, 1308
Shipbuilding, 358, 370 *illus.*
Shipbuilding, Roman
    comparison with modern vessels, 767
    costs of construction, 767–768

number of voyages made, 768
return on investment, 768
size of Roman merchant ships, 766–767
Shipka Pass, map 3
Shipping
of Greek masonry, 281
Shipping jars, 360–361
Ships
and bilge pumps, 345
crane unloading of, 326
miniature construction model, 351–352 *illus.*
pirate, 840
Rhodian, 841
See also specific types of ships
Shirt (*camisia*), 1386
Shoemakers, 381 *illus.*
Shoes
Etruscan, 1399, 1406–1407
Greek, 1394
Roman, 1404, 1406
Shops
lodging for lower classes, 1378
in private houses, 1365
Sibylline Books, 953–954
consultations of, 954
priests responsible for, 935
responsibility of the augurs, 911
sale to Tarquinius Priscus, 954
Sicca, map 6
Sicilian Strait, map 2
Sicily, map 2, map 10
coinage of, 1799, 1804
Greek colonization of, 11–12, 13
origin of formal rhetoric in, 1081
Roman-Carthaginian conflict over, 52–53
Rome's first province, 53
Sidon, map 5, map 8
Siege engines
cranes against, 326, 332–333
flamethrowers, 331, 332 *illus.*
See also Catapults
Siege warfare, Greek, 694–696
compared to Assyrian, 694
siege mound, 695
Sikyon, map 4
tyrants of, 19
Sikyonios. See Menander
Silarus River, map 2
Silk, 374
in Greek clothing, 1387
in Roman clothing, 1401, 1410

Silver, 371, 373
coinage supply, 1798
mines, 797
Simeon
expansionist policies, 1032
independence for Judaea, 1032
Simeon, son of Gamaliel, 1043
Simeon II
protégé of Antiochus III, 1031–1032
Simonides of Keos (Ceos)
epigrams, 1449
epitaph for Spartans, 1495
first ancient poet to charge fees, 1449
international career, 1449
transitional figure, 1449
wide range of genres and meters, 1449
Simplicius
commentary on Aristotle's *Physics,* 1588
Sinope, map 5, map 7
Siphnos
gold and silver mines on, 780
treasury at Delphi, 1704, 1708
Siwa, map 8
Skenographia. See Stage set concepts
Skepsis, map 4, map 5
Skepticism, 1619–1620
Cicero on, 1642
moral implications of, 1620
radical challenge to dogmatic philosophy, 1620
route to peace of mind, 1620
Skeptron
symbol of authority, 445–446
Skillos, map 4
Skins
as writing surface, 424–425, 431
Skira, 849
Skopas of Paros, 1715
head in style of, 1716 *illus.*
Skylax (Scylax) of Caryanda
Periplus (*Sea Journey*), 148
Skyros, map 4
Slave markets, 839, 842
Slavery
after abolition of debt bondage, 587
abolitionist movement, 576
advantages to owner, 746–747
in Athenian law, 538, 581
in Athenian silver mines, 586
chattel-slavery, 575
in classical Athens, 541
in classical period, 586

Slavery (continued)
common elements of in different societies, 576
compensation for injuries, 579–580
concentrations of slaveholdings, 774
conditions of agricultural and mine employment, 773
in Cretan society, 537
definitions of, 575
diet, 238, 241
in Egyptian households, 774
in Emperor's household, 583–584
enslavement of debtors, 578
as form of economic exploitation, 576–577
freedman/patron relationship, 579
freedom for in Roman Empire, 774
freeing of slaves (manumission), 578–579, 580, 747
functions of in Roman economy, 774–775
in Greece and Western Empire, 774
Greek sexual attitudes toward slaves, 1251, 1253, 1256–1257, 1260
Greek view of, 745–746, 747
Greek warfare and growth of, 729
growth of agricultural, 775–776
in Homeric period, 585, 586
humanizing by Christians, 576
import of by aristocracy, 738
jobs shared with freemen, 586
laws governing, 585
legal rights of slave, 581, 585
marriage of slaves, 579, 1353
membership in collegia, 1223
as method of integration into household economy, 578
in municipal capacity, 583
in Mycenaean palace society, 531
in Mycenaean period, 585
naming of slaves, 579–580
owner's legal responsibility, 581
owners' rights and expectations, 579
as part of social system, 576
pastoralism and agricultural uses, 586
peculium, 579
plantation, 218
positive economic effect of, 747
public slaves, 730
reciprocal flow of slaves and exported peasant soldiers, 774
religion and spiritual societies, 584
resentment and rebellion of, 747

and rights in society, 578
and rising status of free citizen, 746
role in Roman education, 1111, 1112
after Roman wars of conflict, 554
sanctions against brutality, 582–583, 585
sanctuaries and asylum, 584–585
Scythian archers as police, 583
selling into, by pirates, 839
Seneca on, 1644
as sign of political and social progress, 746
in skilled occupations, 773
slave artisans, 569
slave/free polarity in Greek thinking, 577
slave rebellions, 587
slaves as article of property, 745
slaves as index of wealth, 586
slave trading, 746
Spartacus' rebellion, 560, 587
state ownership of slaves, 730
status divisions, 568
and status of free Roman citizens, 773
testifying against owner, 581–582
transfer of ownership, 581, 585
treatment of Roman domestic, 773
use in Greek manufacturing, 743–744
use of in Roman theater, 1488
variety of functions and statuses, 747
war captives, 746
Slavery laws, 578, 580, 581–582
acquiring slaves, 616
freed persons, 617
noxal surrender, 616
ownership of property, 616
senatus consultum Claudianum, 616
ways of freeing slaves, 616–617
Slaves
in crafts, 376, 370
as gladiators, 1162
as prostitutes, 1293, 1295–1296
in Roman construction guilds, 307–308
as skilled laborers, 379
Slavs, map 11
Smith, Adam
premodern philosophy of taxation, 796
Smiths, 371, 373 *illus.*
safety threats to, 376
Smyrna (Izmir), map 4, map 5
capture of by Lydian king Alyattes, 695
fortifications of, 686
public building in, 444

Snakes
  associated with famous seers, 942
Sneeze
  omen of good luck, 944
Social organizations, Greek
  admission to in Hellenistic period, 1193
  in archaic period, 1168–1169
  archaic and pseudoarchaic in Crete and Sparta,
    1177–1179
  benevolent acts of, 1188, 1191–1192
  burial of members, 1188
  in classical Athens, 1179–1189
  class intermingling in, 1195
  clubs of specialized workers, 1195
  complexity of, 1168
  cult basis of, 1186
  dependence of cities on benefactions, 1193
  economic interests, 1195
  education and physical services, 1193
  foreign cults, 1186–1187, 1188
  Greek-Roman imitation, 1192–1193
  gymnasium, 1193–1194
  in Hellenistic courts, 1190
  in Hellenistic period, 1189–1195
  organized by tribes, 1168
  orgeones, 1186
  philosophical schools, 1188
  private associations in Hellenistic period,
    1194–1195
  professional associations, 1194
  pseudokinship groupings, 1168–1169
  public sacrifices and banquets, 1193
  records of, 1185–1186
  royal sponsorship of festivals, 1192
  Solon's law on, 1175
  symposium in Hellenistic period, 1194
  theater, 1194
  thiasoi, 1195
  women in, 1187, 1195
  of younger aristocrats, 1169
Social organizations, Roman
  apparel and hairstyles, 1208
  in archaic period, 1200–1202
  Augustan reforms, 1211
  baths, 1205
  benefactions, 1215
  in early empire, 1210–1224
  extravagances in second century, 1202
  festivals and shows, 1203–1204
  laws concerning, 1200, 1203

luxuries of leisured classes, 1204–1205,
    1207–1208
  patron-client relationships, 1220, 1201
  raiding activities of gens groups, 1200
  response of to outside influences, 1201
  status distinctions, 1204
  typical day, 1205
  variety of, 1200
Social War, 58, 559, 708
  rebel coinage, 1807
Societas (bidding association), 816–817
  associates, 817
  offices of, 817
  profits, 817
Socrates
  advocates censorship of some styles of music,
    1510
  on Athenian symposia, 1182
  chief concerns of the Dialogues, 1601–1603
  and collective purpose of polis, 1018
  dialogue with Euthyphro, 1601–1602
  equates male and female virtue, 1308
  nature-philosophers and Greek medicine, 1229
  practice of the good life, 1601
  theory of recollection, 1289–1290
  trial of, 1601
  verdict of Delphic oracle, 1602
Sodalitates (sodalities or associations), 936
Sofular, map 5
Soils, Mediterranean
  calcareous, 98
  chernozems, 98
  deltas, 99
  desert topography, 98–99
  mountain, 98
  terra fusca, 98
  terra rosa, 98
Soldier or Tychon. See Antiphanes
Solinus, Gaius Julius
  coined term *Mare Mediterraneum,* 102
Soloi, map 5
Solon, 411
  adoption laws of, 596
  code of laws, 453, 477, 479–480
  debt reforms, 586
  in Egypt, 15
  eunomia, 453
  failure of political reforms, 455
  laws of, 479
  new Athenian constitution, 22

Volume One: 1–720; Volume Two: 721–1298; Volume Three: 1299–1832

Solon (continued)
  as *nomothetes,* 452, 453
  people's council formed by, 454
  property codes of, 453–454
  social reforms of, 536, 538, 539, 540
  themes in poetry, 452–453
Solymoi, map 5
Sophilos
  athletics contest depicted, 1134
Sophists
  application of reason to problem-solving, 1085
  argumentation, 1083
  development of philology, 1085
  distinguishing justice from tradition, 1080
  doxa (opinion), 1084, 1083
  effect on education, 1084
  effect on Greek rhetorical style, 1082, 1084–1085, 1085
  experiments in rhetorical style, 1085
  in fifth-century Athens, 469, 476
  as first professional educators, 1082
  individualistic approach of, 1082
  instruction related to interest of philosophy, 1599
  intellectual importance of, 1598
  Plato's attack on, 1597–1598
  program of study under, 1084
  Second Sophistic, 1101
  taught rhetoric for a fee, 1597
  use of epideictic speech, 1094
  views on language, 414
  work in philosophy and social sciences, 1082–1083
Sophocles
  Antigone, 1304, 1313–1314
  argument in Greek oratory (*Antigone*), 473
  focus on human issues in plays, 1483
  on human ingenuity, 268
  Women of Trachis, 1309
Sophrosyne (self-restraint), 1308, 1709
Soranus
  biography of Hippocrates, 1237
  obstetrical writings, 1356, 1357–1358, 1360
  principles of Methodism, 1237
Sosos of Pergamon, 1769, 1785
  Roman mosaic replica of his painting, 1785
Sossios, Loukios, 386
Sotades of Crete, 1135
Soteiria (Festival of Deliverance), 1152
Sotiel Coronada, map 1
Soul (*psyche*)
  body (*soma*) distinguished from, 987

body as prison of soul, 992
  condition after death, 988
  difficult to recall by prayer, 987
  endowment of with temporary body, 989
  guide (*psychopompos*), 987
  immortality of, 999
  Lucretius on, 1640
  purification through suffering, 1000
  and self (*autos*), 988
Sounion, map 4
Spain, map 1, 88 *illus.*
  brief Byzantine occupation, 174
  Roman-Carthaginian rivalry, 53–54
  Roman mint in, 1809
  Roman mosaics in, 1783, 1793
  Vandal invasion, 175
  Vandals establish state, 82
Sparta, map 4, map 8
  and Athens, 673, 674
  attempt to suppress Athenian democracy, 23
  battle of Leuktra, 459, 460, 544, 577, 691
  battle at Nemea River, 691
  categories of free noncitizens, 593
  citizenship in, 456
  class conflict, 544
  communal aspects, 1261
  conquest and land distribution, 536
  constitution, 20
  control of family life, 1177, 1179
  council of elders (gerousia), 536
  Dark Age, 7
  decay of social system, 544
  defeat by Thebes, 30–31
  dominance of Peloponnesian League, 492
  double kingship, 458
  educational system, 20–21, 457, 460, 461, 537, 593
  education of young, 1261
  erastes and *eromenoi,* 1261
  expansion on land, 19–20
  fails to unite Greece, 30
  falling birthrate, 30
  festivals in, 1149
  Great Rhetra of, 451,454
  hegemonial league of, 674
  Helots, 19, 456, 460, 577, 593, 730
  homosexuality, 1260–1261
  lack of manpower, 459–460
  land apportionment in, 456, 460
  law codes of, 451, 454
  male social life, 20

manpower decline, 544
marriage customs, 460
marriage laws, 1335–1336
military training in, 687, 1178
origin of monarchy, 487–488
at Panhellenic Congress of 481 B.C., 492
Peloponnesian conquests, 21
problems of leadership, 459
proxenia of, 671
reverence for age, 1261
revolts against, 20, 28
revolution at, 39
revolution in Hellenistic period, 546
role of *apella*, 458–459
role of noncitizen communities, 457–458
in Roman times, 42
secret diplomacy of, 667–668
secret youth organizations (*krypteia*), 458
sharing of women, 1261
social aims, 461
social organizations in, 1177–1179
social reorganization in, 536
status divisions in, 537
status of women in, 457, 462
sumptuary rules in, 537
syssitia (formal messes), 1178–1179
treatment of conquered Messenians, 577
war with Athens, 27–28
warrior class of, 456
wealth of, 20
women's freedom in, 1303, 1308, 1310
Sparta, political institutions
assemblies, 458, 459
in classical period, 461
collapse of, 459–462
commensality, 462
council of elders (*gerousia*), 458, 459
ephoroi (elected board), 459
eunomia, 455–456
hoplite polis, 455, 461
influence on fourth-century political theory, 461
organization of, 455–459
and utopian political thought, 461
Spartacus
slave uprising under, 560, 587
Spartikos I, 489
Spear-throwing, 1137
Spectator sports, 1134, 1154
Speech
and oral tradition, 407–408
vs. written language, 407–408, 415–417

Sphagia (blood-lettings)
Agamemnon's oath sacrifice (*Iliad*), 974
before battle, 975
at a boundary crossing, 975
in powerful actions, 974
Sphakteria, map 4
Spina, map 2
Spinster tax, 806, 811
Splanchna
eating of expressed sense of community, 972
organs of sacrificial animal, 971
significance of, 972
Spondephoroi, 1144
Sporades, map 4
Sports and diversions, 1133
See also Athletics
Stabiae, map 2
Stade (footrace), 1134, 1140
Stadium (racetrack)
in Greek architecture, 1666
Stageiros, map 3
Stage set concepts
in Roman art, 1773, 1778–1780
Skenographia (linear perspective), 1775
Standard of living
Roman, 1700
Staphylodromoi, 1149
Stasis, 440, 477–478
defined, 531
State-friend. *See* Proxenia
Stater (coin)
definition of, 1795
Statius, Publius Papinius
Achilleid, 1432
declamatory mythological epicist, 1432
Thebaid, 1432
Statue niches
in Roman architecture, 1685–1686
Steam engineering, 349, 350 *illus.*, 351
Stelae, grave
Greek funeral paintings, 1763–1764
Stephen, bishop of Rome
admission of Novatianists into church, 1060
Stesichorus
early Greek choral poet, 1448–1449
narratives in lyric meters, 1449
preference for epic and mythological material, 1449
Stevedores, 361
Stichometrics, 427
Stilicho, Flavius, 82

Stipendiary towns, 812
Stipendium (tribute), 810
Stoa (freestanding portico), 1660, 1665, 1668 *illus.*
   construction of, 278, 285, 296, 1668 *illus.*
   dominance of the agora, 1694
Stoa of Attalos, 296, 329–330, 1668 *illus.*
Stoichedon style of writing, 412
Stoicism, 1617–1619
   active and passive principles defined, 1618–1619
   Cicero on, 1642, 1643
   continuum theory, 1618
   defined the good as *arete* (excellence), 1617
   developed by Chrysippus, 1617
   dominant philosophy in Rome, 1644
   effect on ruler worship, 1020
   founded by Zeno of Citium, 1617
   influence on Roman religion, 1648
   moral doctrine, 1618, 1619
   positive, dogmatic philosophical system, 1617
Stoics
   contrasted with Epicureans, 272
   divine providence, 1619
   influence on rhetorical style, 1103
   pneuma (vital spirit), 1618
   possibilities for moral improvement, 273
   rhetorical handbooks of, 1103
Stone, decorative, 371
Stone dressing. *See* Masonry construction
Stonemasons, 370
   dedications to deities by, 383–384
   family connections among, 375–376
   tools of, 376 *illus.*
Strabo
   description of Celts, 143
   on Greek trade, 740
   on Iberian Peninsula, 142
   on Luna marble quarries, 790
   on physical environment in first century, 139
   recorded Cinderella tale, 1564
Strategoi (board of ten generals), 637
   and Athenian Council, 471, 474
   continuity of tenure, 474
Streets, city
   colonnaded, 1698–1699
   Greek rhythm of (*stenopoi* and *plateiai*), 1693
   Roman compass orientation of (*decumanus* and *cardo*), 1697
   See also Roads
Strongyle (Stromboli), map 2
   volcanism, 94

Structural principles, Greek
   arch, 295 *illus.*, 296 *illus.*, 297
Structural principles, Roman
   arch, 296–297, 302, 309–310
   cantilever, 314
   dome, 319
   tie-beam truss, 286, 294–295, 315 *illus.*,
Struggle of the Orders, 553
Stucco
   on Greek architectural facades, 283
Stucco relief art, Roman, 1771–1772, 1776–1777, 1778–1779 *illus.*
   decline of, 1788
   First Pompeian (masonry) style, 1722, 1773 *illus.*, 1774
   integration of painting and stuccowork, 1779
   Middle Empire, 1784–1785, 1786 *illus.*
   monochrome medallions, 1785–1786 *illus.*
   Second Pompeian (architectural illusionism) style, 1774–1776 *illus.*
   Third Style vaults, 1779–1778 *illus.*
Stucco work, Roman
   for the repair of marble, 313–314
   Trajan's Forum interiors, 319–320
   on tufa and travertine facades, 300
Stylus, 430
Stymphalos
   orthogonal city plan of, 1693–1694 *illus.*
Stymphalos, Lake, map 4
Subversion
   in foreign states, 674
Succession, law of
   classification of heirs, 619–620
   for freeborn, 620
   responsibility for *sacra,* 620
Sucro River, map 1
Suebi, map 11
   entering of Gaul, 174
   Spanish migration of, 175
Suetonius Tranquillus, Gaius (Suetonius)
   access to archives, 1556
   Augustus' sexual activities, 1276
   Augustus' views on literature, 1429
   on Caesar's sexual views, 1276
   effect of childhood experiences, 1361
   Lives of the Twelve Caesars, 1556
   model for later biographers, 1556
   organization by topics, 1556
   Roman biographer, 74
   sexual misconduct of the emperors, 1266
Sugolin, map 6

Volume One: 1–720; Volume Two: 721–1298; Volume Three: 1299–1832

Sui iuris (in her own power), 1321
Sulla, Lucius Cornelius
  adherent of Optimates, 58
  administrative reforms, 59
  appointment as consul, 711
  attempt to restore old system, 657
  capture of Jugurtha, 709–710
  conflict with Marius, 710–711
  dictatorship, 58–59
  introduction of non-Roman Italians to Senate, 657
  new form of dictatorship, 526
  reforms of, 516–517, 559–561
  and Roman civil wars, 559
  siege of Athens, 41
Sundials, 395
Surtaxes, 822–823
Surveying
  of aqueducts, 340–341
Surveyors, building
  Roman, 312
Surveyors, land
  Greek *geometrai*, 1692–1693
  Roman *agrimensores*, 1697–1698
Susa, map 5
Switzerland
  Roman mosaics in, 1783
Sybaris, map 2, map 7
Syene, map 6
Symbola (legal procedures for civil disputes with foreigners), 673
Symbols in writing, 399, 400, 406
  See also Alphabets
Symmetria, 1705, 1717
Sympoliteia (confederacy of states), 675
Symposium. See Plato
Symposium. See Xenophon
Symposium, Greek
  andron (men's room), 1172
  in archaic literature, 1171–1172
  in archaic period, 1170–1179
  Athenian, in classical literature, 1182–1183
  in classical art, 1175
  in classical period, 1183
  contests at, 1174
  in Hellenistic period, 1189–1191
  and housing design, 1172
  hubris and, 1174
  komos (drunken procession), 1175
  literary and philosophical discussions at, 1190–1191

  main features of, 1171
  membership as sign of manhood, 1171–1172
  moral concepts associated with, 1173
  physical circumstances of, 1172
  political consequences of luxuries at, 1183–1184
  private, 1181–1183
  role of women, 1172
  rules for, 1173
  sexual rivalries, 1174–1175
  sympotic behavior of lower classes, 1181–1182
  sympotic letters, 1191
  uninvited guests, 1183
  wine drinking, 1173
Symposium, Roman
  in Greek literature, 1218
  idealized in Horace's poetry, 1213
Syracuse (Syrakousai), map 2, map 7
  autocracy of Agathocles, 490
  limestone quarries of, 789
  mint of, 1799
  naval battle in Great Harbor of, 699
  rebellion against Rome, 54
  siege of, 695
Syria, map 5, 88 *illus.*
  becomes Roman province, 59
Syria-Cilicia, map 10
Syrian arch, 1681–1682
Syries, 1723
Syrtis Major, map 6

T

Tabellae (wood tablets), 430
Tablets
  clay, 422
  wax, 430, 432
  wooden, 430
Tablinum (principal salon), 1373
Tabularium (public record office), 1551
Tacitus, Cornelius
  Agricola, 1549, 1555
  Annals, 1549
  biographical elements in histories, 1555
  class division of urban plebs, 570
  criticized Agrippina the Younger, 1325, 1328
  Dialogue on Orators, 1548
  early German slavery, 578
  focuses on imperial court, 1550
  Germania, 1549

Tacitus (continued)
  Histories, 1549
  history of political life and loss of liberty, 1549
  mother's proper influence on children, 1323
  physical description of Iberians, 142
  prose style, 74
  purpose of his writings, 1549
  rise of municipal and provincial classes, 1216
  on training for public speaking, 1110
  transformed annalistic genre, 1549
  use of character types in *Annals,* 1280
Tader River, map 1
Tages
  taught divination to Etruscans, 951
Taj Mahal
  and Roman architecture, 1689
Tanagra, map 4
Tanagra statuettes, 1398
Tanais, map 7
Tanais River, 88 *illus.*
Tanning, of skins for writing, 424
Tapestries, imitation. *See Trompe l'oeil* Roman
    painting
Taphai, 1147
Taras (Tarentum, Taranto), map 2, map 7
  war with Rome, 51–52
  wool production, 1401
Tarquinii (Tarquinia), map 2
  fresco of the Tomb of the bulls, 1267
Tarquinius Priscus
  undermines senatorial powers, 496
Tarquinius Superbus, king of Rome
  dynastic claim, 496
  legend of his deposition, 878
Tarraconensis, map 10
Tarsos, map 5
Tartaros
  prison of rebellious immortals, 990
Tatian
  Diatessaron, 1061
  Enkratite (abstaining) group, 1061
Tatta, Lake, map 5
Tauromenium, map 2
Taurus Mountains, map 5
Taxatio, 809
Taxation, Greek, 795–807
  in archaic and classical periods, 797–803
  collection and distribution, 640
  direct, 799
  in Hellenistic period, 803–805

  in Homeric period, 796–797, 799
  indirect, 799–800
  military expenditures, 798
  modern taxation compared, 805–807
  purpose of, 807
  See also Liturgies
Taxation, Roman, 809–825
  under Augustus, 659
  capita, 825
  control of rural mobility, 571
  direct, 811
  effect on trade, 775–776
  exemption from, 811, 820–821
  under the Principate, 819–821
  of provinces, 812–814
  provincial taxes, 654
  standard units of calculation, 825
  status of taxpayers, 811–812
  tax rates, 822
  See also Tribute
Tax collection
  in Athens, 800, 802–803
  corruption in, 818–819
  in Ptolemaic Egypt, 805
  Roman, 815–819
Tax farming, 802–803, 805
  fiftieths, 802
Taxila, map 8
Tax outlaws, 818
Tebtunis, map 6
  tax list from first century, 771–772
Technological innovation
  missed inventions, 324, 331, 342, 347, 350, 352
  slow spread of, 329
  See also Mechanics, principles of
Technology, Roman
  agricultural, 756
  cultural barriers to progress, 756
  engineering achievements of road-building, 761
  inventions, 756
  reliance on human energy, 755
  use of draft animals, 755–756
Tegea, map 4
  temple of Athena Alea, 1715
Tegrya, map 4
Teisamenos
  decree on lawgivers, 479
Telamon, map 2
Teleology
  main link between science and philosophy, 1633

Telesterion in Eleusinian Mysteries, 1145
Tempe, map 4
Temples, Greek, 1653, 1654 *illus.*, 1655–1660
  administration of, 632–633
  as banks, 832
  buildings at larger sanctuaries, 888
  built in sacred areas, 888
  construction of, 285, 324, 325, 727
  Doric, 1653–1659, 1661–1664, 1669
  Hellenistic, 1667–1668
  Ionic, 1653–1655, 1658–1659, 1667–1668, 1670
  miniature automatic, 350, 351 *illus.*
  physical layout of, 888
  priests, 632, 633, 636
  worship outside at nearby altars, 888
  See also Naoi
Temples, Roman
  architecture, 1672 *illus.*, 1675–1677, 1683 *illus.*,
    1687
  construction of, 299
  divinatory section, 951–952
  Maison Carrée at Nemausus, 1676–1677
Ten Books on Architecture. See Vitruvius Pollio
Tenedos, map 4, map 5
Tenement (*insula*), 303–304, 1377
  squalid living conditions, 1378
Teochares, 1727
Teos, map 4, map 5
Tepelini, map 3
Terence (Publius Terentius Afer)
  comedies of, 1488, 1491
Terentia (wife of Cicero)
  managed her own financial empire, 1320–1321
Termessos
  architecture of, 1683 *illus.*
Terpander, 1505
  nomos (solo song with kithara accompaniment),
    1507
Terra-cotta. *See* Construction materials and
  techniques
Terra-cotta goods, 373–374 *illus.*
Tertullianus, Quintus Septimius Florens (Tertullian)
  on Christian obedience, 1059
  on clothing styles, 1409, 1410
  concern for public order, 1222
  formulation of Trinitarian doctrine, 1059–1060
  On the Robe, 1405
  Tertullianists, 1060
  use of language, 1059
Tessellatum. See Mosaic art, Roman

Tetrabiblos. See Ptolemy (Claudius Ptolemaeus)
Teuta, queen of Illyria, 838
Textiles
  Carthaginian, 1407
  demand for in Roman Empire, 764
  different types of, 765
  Eastern sources of, 1387
  embroidery, Phrygian, 1402
  government factories, 765
  home manufacture of, 1387
  prestige of textile crafts, 1392
  production of, 374, 1402
  professional weavers, 764
  regional competition for markets, 765
  Roman commercial production, 1389, 1401–1402
  See also Cotton; Linen; Silk; Wool
Thalamai, map 4
Thales of Miletus
  father of philosophy, 1585
  first investigated material causes, 1585
  and origin tales in Hesiod's *Theogony,* 1587
  primary concern with origins, 1588
  relationship to earlier thought, 1587
  water principle of all things, 1585
Thamugadi (Timgad), map 6
  military city plan, 1698–1699 *illus.*
Thargelia, 1146
Thasos, map 3, map 4, map 7
  Greek colony, 14
  Phoenician silver mines on, 780
Theater
  of Balbus, 1158
  at Epidaurus, by Polykleitos, 1666, 1667 *illus.*
  in Greek architecture, 1666–1667 *illus.*
  Greek and Roman compared, 1674–1675
  of Marcellus, 1158
  miniature automated, 351–352 *illus.*
  of Pompey, 1158
  in Roman architecture, 1671, 1674–1675, 1677
Theaters, Greek
  acoustics, 1480
  competitions in, 1148
  deus ex machina special effect, 326
  ekkyklema (small platform), 1480
  fifth century, 1479–1485
  Hellenistic, 1486
  mechane (crane), 1480
  mechanical effects, 1480
  and mosaic art, 1768–1769
  orchestra, 1479, 1486

Theaters (continued)
  and painting, 1756, 1761
  public discourse in, 473–474
  revivals of fifth-century plays, 1485
  shape of, 1479
  size of, 1480
  skene (hut or tent), 1479, 1486
  theater-in-the-round, 1479
  touring companies, 1485
  See also Drama, Greek
Theaters, Roman
  building of in early empire, 148
  design of, 1158
  events in, 1157–1159
  first permanent, 1489
  and mosaic art, 1774–1775 *illus.*
  and painting, 1773, 1775, 1778, 1780
  portable, 1488
  See also Drama, Roman; Stage set concepts
Thebaid. See Statius, Publius Papinius
Thebe, map 4, map 5
Thebes, map 4, map 6, map 8
  conquest of northern Greece, 31
  defeat by Philip of Macedonia, 33
  qualifications for political participation, 543
  revolt against Alexander, 34
  war with Sparta, 30
Theft
  Greek law governing, 598
Themistocles
  exile from Athens, 28
  founder of Piraeus, 468
  military strategy, 24
  opposition to in Athens, 25
  origins, 24
Theocritus
  Alexandrian poet personified, 1472
  comic irony, 1469
  linguistic inventiveness, 1469
  on love in poetry, 1194
  love spell of injured girl, 884
  on middle class life, 545
  self-reflexive dimension of his pastoralism, 1472
  tone of amused detachment, 1469
  use of low-mimetic subjects, 1471
Theodoric, king of the Ostrogoths
  execution of Boethius, 177
  rule with Odoacer, 176
  sixth-century government of, 176–177
Theodoric I, king of the Visigoths
  resistance to Huns, 173

Theodoros of Samos, 1703, 1723
Theodosius I
  last ruler of whole Roman Empire, 81
  prohibits pagan festivals, 1151
  rule of Visigoths, 172, 173, 178
Theodosius II
  Law of Citations, 611
Theogenes of Thasos, 1139
Theognis of Megara
  prolific Greek elegiac poet, 1440
  on social order, 543
Theogonies, Greek, 863
Theogony. See Hesiod
Theon of Antioch, 386
Theophanes of Mytilene
  lauded Pompey, 1537
Theophilus
  Paraphrase, 627
Theophrastus (Theophrastos)
  advocated vegetarian offerings, 977
  best offering a pure mind, 977
  evaluation of medicinal plants, 252
  fig cultivation, 232
  first treatise on medical botany, 1236
  four virtues of style in *On Style,* 1102
  hope for advances in knowledge, 272
  leadership of philosophical schools, 1188–1189
  motive of sacrifice, 975
  On Stones, 272
  standards for botany in *History of Plants,* 1233
  Superstitious Man in *Characters,* 883
  on technical advances in agriculture, 212
Theopompus (Theopompos)
  biographical content in histories, 1536
  on performance of religious duties, 892
  Philippica, 1531
  on self-indulgence of Philip II in *Philippica,* 1189
  taste for censure, 1531
Theoria (contemplation)
  Aristotle's view of man's highest excellence, 1612
  exercise of reason in theoretical domains, 1612
  Nicomachean Ethics, 1612
Theorikon, 1148
Theoroi, 1144
Thera (Thira), map 4
  eruption of in Bronze Age, 95
Thermal baths
  automatic doors of, 351
  House of the Faun, 1374
  mosaic decoration of, 1792–1793
  at Pompeii, 1374

in Roman architecture, 1675–1677, 1680, 1685 *illus.*, 1686, 1782–1783, 1792–1793
  Stabian Baths (Pompeii) stucco relief and painting, 1782
  urban planning importance of, 1700
  water supply for, 342
Thermessa, map 2
Thermopylae (Thermopylai), map 4
  battle of, 26
Thermum (Thermon), map 4
  temple of Apollo, 1658
Thesmophoria, 840, 849, 1143, 1145, 1187
  activities of, 899–900
  Aristophanes (*Women at the Thesmophoria*), 1305
  devoted to Demeter, 899
  excluded slaves and resident foreigners, 900
  fertility cult, 1305
  restricted to married women, 899
Thesmophoriazusae. See Aristophanes
Thespis
  introduction of first actor, 1477
Thessalonica (Thessalonike, Salonika), map 3
  church mosaics and Roman influence, 1793
Thessaly, map 4
  confederacy of tribal states, 491
Thetes
  in Homeric poems, 532, 533
  opportunities for in classical period, 541
Thina, map 6
Thirty Years' Peace, 673
  preliminaries to Peloponnesian War, 668
Thorikos
  adits (mine passages), 781
  pit mining of, 780
Thourioi
  city plan of, 1693, 1695
Thrace, map 3, map 9
  mercenaries from, 692
  physical description of Thracians, 145
Threnos (ritual lament for a death), 1438
Thucydides
  on age of Pericles, 469
  and Athenian debate, 473
  battle of Mantinea, 688
  beginning of Greek naval warfare, 698
  on the Boeotian migration, 161
  on ceremony for war dead, 1147
  compared to Herodotus, 1526–1529
  concept of *stasis*, 477–478
  contemporary history the only serious history, 1526

delineated long-term and immediate causes, 1528
  difficult style, 1527
  on the Dorian migration, 160
  early Greek nomadism, 531
  evacuation of Attic countryside, 211
  History of the Peloponnesian War, 411, 1526
  on human nature, 1281–1282
  ignorance of catapult, 333
  importance of religion as state institution, 1528
  interest in machines, 331
  man as measure of all things, 1528
  no clear sense of human progress, 269
  nomadism, 531
  oligarchic coups at Kerkyra, 543
  Pericles on democracy, 475–476
  on piracy, 838
  political upheaval and moral degeneration, 269
  rise of Greek demogogues, 469
  rural backgrounds of Athenians, 212
  siege of Plataea, 695
  and Spartan *eunomia,* 455
  stasis and fifth-century migration, 160
  two mainsprings of human motivation, 1528
  writing style, 410–411
Thugga, map 6
Thugga Terebentina, map 6
Thusia. See Sacrifice
Tiberias, map 5
Tiberius Julius Caesar Augustus
  dining at Spelunca, 1216
  dynastic problems, 67
  effective administrator, 68
  election of magistrates, 661
  heir to Augustus, 67
  personal flaws, 68
  reign of terror, 67
  retirement to Capri, 67
Tiber (Tevere) River, map 2
  geology and history, 104
Tibullus, Albius
  technique, 1460
  themes, 1460
Tibur (Tivoli), map 2
  Hadrian's Villa wall painting, 1783, 1785
Tigranus, M. Perennius, 374 *illus.*
Tigris River, map 5, map 8
  transport on, 363
Tiling, Greek
  marble ceiling, 288
  terra-cotta. *See* Construction materials
Timaeus. See Plato

Timaeus of Tauromenium
  first Greek historian of Rome, 1531–1532
Time
  measurement of, 389–395
  units of, 389
Timna, map 6
Timotheus (Timotheos), 1716
  avant-garde composer, 1509
  Persians, 1509
  sculptor, 1716
Tin
  mining of, 783–784
Tiora, map 2
Tiresias
  renowned Theban seer, 942
Tiryns, map 4
Tisias
  originator of formal rhetoric, 1081, 1085
Toga, Roman, 1404 *illus.*
  Etruscan origin, 1400
  forms of, 1401, 1402, 1404
  imperial symbol, 1411
  mark of Roman citizenship, 1404, 1406
  prescribed dress of magistrates, 1409
  short toga, 1408 *illus.*
  style changes, 1409, 1411
Toletum (Toledo)
  Visigoth capital at, 174
Tolls, 799, 809–810
Tomb
  cakes and oil offerings at, 994
  graveside meals, 998
  gravestone inscriptions, Roman, 1002
  objects buried in, 998
  wreaths on, 994
Tomb, Greek, 994
  importance of grave marker, 994
  tumbos (grave mound), 991
  visits to, 994
Tomb decoration
  black-and-white-style mosaic, 1786
  Hypogeum of the Aurelii (Rome) wall painting,
    1789 *illus.*
  Tomb of the Pancratii wall painting (Rome), 1785
  Tomb of the Valerii stuccowork (Rome),
    1785–1786 *illus.*
  Vatican necropolis, 1783, 1785, 1786, 1792
Tomb painting, Greek. *See* Monumental painting
Tomis, map 7
Tools
  carpentry, 352

of land surveyors, 1692, 1697
  stoneworking, 370
  wrench or spanner, 337
Tools, mining
  battering device for gold quartz mining, 786
  Roman use of Greek and Egyptian, 783
  skalis (shovel), 783
  tykos (pick), 782–783
  typis or *tykos* (hammer), 782
  xois (gad), 782
Torone, map 7
Torsion spring, 334–335 *illus.*
  frame, 336 *illus.*, 337
  sinew (*neuron*) spring cord, 335–336
Tosefta, 1043
Towboats, 364
Toys, 1361
Track events, 1132, 1134–1135
Trade, 382
  and international economic relations, 673–674,
    676
  naval control of trade routes, 731
  and needs of craftsmen, 378
  transport of goods, 353–364
Trade, Greek
  access to markets, 732–733
  aristocratic demand for slaves and luxury items,
    738
  Athenian pottery, 740
  branches of local trading, 737
  control of international routes, 733
  in craftsmen's wares, 381–382
  and development of Greek writing system,
    403
  establishment of long-distance, 737
  financing of, 739
  foreign traders, 732–733, 735
  functional locations for in cities, 737
  grain trade, 727, 731
  importance of in Greek Iron Age, 9–10
  influences on Greek city planning, 1691
  international centers of, 727, 733
  maritime, 730–731, 737, 738
  moneylending, 739
  partnerships, 738
  policing of markets, 732–733
  to serve import, not export, needs, 737–738
  social status of traders, 738
  state control of markets, 732
  taxes and tolls, 733
  vessels for, 730

wartime necessities, 729
wine trade, 740
Trade, Roman
in building materials, 1679
entrepots, 770
implications of pottery finds, 762–763, 764
investment in merchant vessels, 769, 775
labor specialization and volume of, 769
large-scale in provincial cities, 769
maritime expansion, 765–769
military conquest and spread of, 756–757
profits on luxury items, 770
and Roman road system, 759
splitting risks of, 769
in textiles, 764–765
volume within Roman Empire, 771
Trademarks, Roman
on dated bricks, 307
Tragedy, Greek, 413–414
choral and musical parts prominent, 1508
and myths, 873
Trajan, column of, 309, 1698
invasion of Dacia on, 714
numeri on, 715
Trajanus, Marcus Ulpius (Trajan)
campaign against Parthia, 714
circular medallion of, 1739 *illus.*
coinage of, 1812
commemorative column, 1740, 1741, 1743, 1741,
1743
domestic policies, 72
eastern campaigns, 72
forum of, 1741
invasion of Dacia, 714
military achievements, 72
permission for *eranoi* (benefit societies) in Amisus,
1222
popularity, 72
rejection of Hellenistic practices, 1216
restrictions on collegia at Nicomedia, 1222
role in institutionalizing imperial cult, 1017
Roman expansion under, 660
treatment of Christians, 1055
Tralles, map 4, map 5
Transit tolls, 809–810
Translation
from Greek to Roman, 417–418
Transportation, 353–365
dependence on maritime, 755
expense of overland, 762
by land, 281, 353–357

of masonry, 280–281
modes of, 353–364
by sea, 281, 301, 357–364
Trapezous, map 5, map 7
Trasimene, Lake, map 2
Travel
via roads, 354–357
via ships, 361–362
Travel narratives, 1565–1566
Treadmill, Greek (treadwheel), 294, 326 *illus.*
Treasury
in Greek architecture, 290
See also Delphi
Treasury, Greek
in architecture, 1660
Treasury, Roman
military, 811
provincial, 820
surplus in, 822
Treaties and international agreements, 672–675
conclusion of, 670
types of Roman, 675–676
Trebia River, map 2
Tribal Assembly
democratic composition, 49
Tribune
appointment of, 500
election of, 49
legal authority, 501
military, 503
right of veto, 500
role in later Republic, 501
Tribute
collection of, 815–819, 820
exemption from, 811, 812, 813, 820–821
payment in kind, 823, 825
phoros, 813
remission of, 821
as Roman form of taxation, 810–811, 812–814
tributum, 810, 813
vectigal, 810, 813
Tributum capitis (head tax), 813
Tributum solis (land tax), 813
Triconch (trefoil hall)
in Roman architecture, 1687–1688
Triemiolia (galley), 841
Trier. *See* Augusta Treverorum
Trinitarian doctrine
Arianism, 1068–1069
Cappadocian Fathers, 1071
controversy over, 1068–1070, 1071–1072

Trinitarian doctrine (continued)
  Council of Constantinople, 1071–1072
  formulation of, 1059–1060
  homoousios, 1069
  Melitians, 1068, 1069
Tripertita. See Paetus, Sextus Aelius
Tripolitana, map 6
Trireme, 841
Tristia. See Ovidius Naso, Publius (Ovid)
Triumph, Roman
  triumphing general's garb, 1407, 1408
Troad, map 4, map 5
Trogus, Pompeius
  universal history (*Historiae Philippicae*), 1547
Troizen, map 4
Trojan War
  as historical marker, 156
  See also Homer; Troy
Trompe l'oeil Roman painting, 1790
  architectural illusionism, 1774–1775
  Hellenistic worldwide fashion for, 1772, 1773,
    1785
  imitation coffering, 1785
  imitation framed paintings, 1777
  imitation marbling, 1773–1774, 1783, 1788–
    1789
  imitation tapestries, 1780
  reaction against, 1777
Trophonius, oracle of (Lebadeia), 944
Trousers
  bracae, 1386
  Etruscan styles, 1399
  in later Roman Empire, 1405
  prohibited by Honorius Flavius, 1412
  Roman soldiers' use of, 1404
  worn by Greeks' neighbors, 1395–1396
Troy, map 4, map 5
  gates of, 694–695
  siege of in epic poetry, 680
  wooden horse of, 694
Truce, 672
  definitions of, 667, 669
  Greek, 668
  Roman, 675
Tugboats, 362
Tunis
  Artemis on mosaic panel, 235
Turin Papyrus
  map of shaft-and-tunnel mining complex (Sudan),
    779
Tusculum, map 2

Tuz Gölü
  geology, 107
Twelve Tables
  furtum (theft) in, 625
  Law of, 703–704
  law of succession, 620
  in Paetus' *Tripertita*, 610
  ritual search for stolen property, 626
  See also Law, Roman
Tyche (Fortune)
  in Greek literature, 852
Tyrants, Greek, 488–489
  activities to increase power, 489
  aristocracy and, 449
  centralization of Greek artistic patronage under,
    449
  centralization of power, 449
  and development of polis, 449
  economic causes of tyranny, 536
  importance of, 19
  in Ionia, 488
  origin and definition of, 488
  public works, 634
  revolutionary despots, 18
  second-generation, 489
  in seventh century, 448–449
  Sicilian, 448
Tyras, map 7
Tyre, map 5, map 8
Tyrrhenian Sea, map 2, 88 *illus.*
Tyrtaeus of Sparta
  and hoplite values, 448

U

Ugarit, map 5
Ulfilas
  conversion of Visigoths to Christianity, 172, 179
  translation of bible into Gothic, 172
Underworld
  escape from, 992
  judges and judgments in, 992
  topography of, 989–990
  visit to, 992–993
Urbanization
  economic consequences in Greece, 726–727
Urban life
  Roman regulation of, 1700
  See also City plans

Urine, tax on, 821
Ur, map 5
Urso, map 1
Utica, map 6
Utopian political thought
  in fourth-century Athens, 484
  Spartan system of government, 461
Utopian societies
  mythical settings for, 266
  and Spartan social structure, 546

V

Valens
  battle of Hadrianopolis, 718
Valentinianus, Flavius (Valentinian I), 81
  use of tribal kings in military, 718
Valentinus, 1058
  tripartite cosmological system, 1051
Valerianus, Publius Licinius (Valerian)
  persecution of Christians, 1055–1056
Valerius Maximus
  compilation of anecdotes, 1548
  ethnic stereotypes, 152
  Facta et Dicta Memorabilia (*Memorable Deeds and Sayings*), 1548
  marital severity, 1319–1320
  women as public speakers, 1321–1322
Vale of Tempe
  land use, 215
Vandals, map 11
  conversion to Arian Christianity, 175
  destruction of Western Empire, 718–719
  entering of Gaul, 174
  northwestward migration, 175
  occupation of North Africa under, 175–176
  occupation of Spain and Gaul, 82, 175
Varro, Marcus Terentius
  decline of agriculture, 220
  herdsman's life, 235
  mule production, 235
  on planting kitchen garden, 232
  production of table luxuries, 235
  transmission of Greek knowledge, 1820
Vase painters, Greek
  travel of, 1752
Vase painting, Greek
  Archaic geometric, 1750, 1751 *illus.*
  Archaic orientalizing, 1750–1752 *illus.*

athletic scenes, 1133–1134
  Attic black-figure, 1751–1752, 1753 *illus.*
  Attic white-ground drawing, 1759, 1760 *illus.*
  classical period, 1757, 1758 *illus.*, 1759 *illus.*, 1760 *illus.*, 1761
  depicts details of rituals, 960
  Italian and Sicilian schools of, 1760–1761
  limitations of medium, 1749
  red-figure, 1753–1754, 1755 *illus.*
  sculptural influences on, 1758–1759
  See also Monumental painting; specific painters
Vatican
  Cancelleria Reliefs, 1739
  Roman cemetery vault paintings under, 1783, 1785, 1786, 1792
Vault, Greek, 296–297
Vault, Roman, 296
  architectural innovations of, 1672–1674, 1676, 1686–1687, 1689
  barrel type, 1673
  cloister type, 1674
  construction of, 316–319
Vectigalia. See Xenophon
Vegetables and salad plants
  artichoke, 251
  cabbages (*Brassica oleracea*), 250–251
  cucumber, 251
  different uses of, 250
  lettuce, 250
  onions and leeks, 250
  radishes, 250
  turnips, 250
  white mustard, 251
  as wild food resource, 250
Vegetarian offerings
  approved by ancient critics, 976
Vegetation
  Alpine tundra, 115
  deciduous forest belt, 115
  deforestation and erosion, 117–118
  desert, 115–116
  ecosystems and life zone, 113–116
  effects of grazing on, 117, 126, 235
  evergreen forest life zone, 113–114
  forestry and timber, 116–117
  garigue, 114
  introduction of foreign species, 119
  maquis, 114
  Mediterranean mountain zone, 115
  plant diversity and Ice Age glacial sheet, 113
  sacred groves, 118–119

Vegetation (continued)
  seasonal adaptations, 114,116
  steppes, 115
  wild plant species, 112
Vehicles, 355–356
Veii, map 2
  war with Rome, 50, 811
Velitrae, map 2
Velleius Paterculus
  history devoted to Tiberius, 1547–1548
  popularity of Augustus, 564
  racial prejudice in writings, 152
Velletri sarcophagus, 1743–1744, 1743 *illus.*
Vellum, 424
Venantius Honorius Clementianus Fortunatus
  approach to epigram, 1499
Venationes (animal hunts), 1161, 1162
Veneralia
  Roman festival of Venus, 913
Venice
  Mori Tetrarchs, 1747 *illus.*, 1748
Venus
  festival of, 1270
  merging with Greek Aphrodite, 1270
Venus Genetrix, temple of, 1728
Vergilius Maro, Publius (Vergil)
  adoption of epic genre, 1429–1430
  Aeneid, 877, 1430
  Aeneid quoted on coins, 1815
  allegorical uses of myth, 1520
  Bucolics, 1467, 1472–1474
  confiscation of land, 563
  on Dido's magic, 885
  epic devices used to glorify Roman cause, 1430
  manifest destiny of Rome, 66, 877
  pastoral metaphor for the creative imagination,
    1472
Vergina
  tomb painting at, 1762, 1763 *illus.*
Verginia
  example of behavior to unmarried girl, 1326
Verona, map 2
Verus, Lucius
  eastern victories, 73
Vespasian (Titus Flavius Vespasianus), 70–71
  building program, 70
  fiscal difficulties, 822
  grant of Latin status to provincial magistrates,
    661
  lex data (general order) for mine exploitation, 788
  origins and character, 70

patronage of architecture, 305
  role in institutionalizing imperial cult, 1017
  sea travel by, 362
  slavery laws, 581
  tax on urine, 821
Vessels
  river, 363–364
  seagoing, 357–362
  See also Coracles; Rafts; Sailing ships; Ships
Vestalia
  Festival of Vesta, 915
Vestal Virgins, 1321
  distinctive features, 936
  duties and restrictions, 911, 935
  prestige and power, 935
  symbolic sexual value of fire, 1268
Vestibulum (entrance hall), 1373
Vestini, map 2
Vesuvius
  eruption of, 94–95, 303
Vetulonia, map 2
Via Appia, 354
Via Flaminia, 355
Victor, Bishop
  first Latin leader of Roman church, 1058
Victor, Gaius Julius
  Latin epistolographer, 1574–1575
Victoria (Victory)
  origin of cult, 855
  temple of on Palatine, 855
Victory Odes (*epinikia*), 1438
  composed for Olympic victors, 1516
  later Greek choral works, 1450–1452
  poetic form of, 1451
  sudden decline of genre, 1451
Vienna, map 1
Vienne
  mosaic panel showing grape pressing, 230
Villa, Roman, 1375–1378, 1677, 1680–1681, 1687
  oil producing, 1376
  reconstruction of, 307
  wine making, 1376
  working farm, 1376
Vinalia
  Roman spring wine festival, 914
Vindolanda, map 1
  wooden writing tablets from, 421
Vindonissa, map 1
Violence, human
  and sacrifice, 978
  and throat-cutting *sphagia,* 978

Vipasca, map 1
Virginity
   as qualification for priesthood, 928
Virtus, 1322
   aristocratic ideal for men, 1325
Visigoths, map 11
   battle of Chalons, 173
   conversion to Christianity, 172, 174
   kingdom of Tolosa, 173–174
   migration under Alaric I, 173
   migration to lower Danube provinces, 172
   northward migrations under Ataulf, 173
   overthrow of Tolosa by Franks, 173, 174
   persecution of orthodox Christians, 172–173
   Romans as administrators for, 173
   settlement within Roman Empire, 81
   Spanish migration of, 174
   under Theodosius I, 172, 173
   victory at Hadrianopolis, 172
Visual refinement
   in Greek architecture, 1654–1655, 1663–1664,
      1679
Vitruvius Pollio
   on the architectural profession, 308
   on architecture, 1657, 1667–1668, 1674, 1689
   on concrete, 302
   on construction woods, 304
   Ctesibius' force pump in *On Architecture,* 786
   on engineering, 323
   Hellenistic house styles, 1367–1368
   on hoists and cranes, 312
   on painting and interior decoration, 1755, 1756,
      1777, 1793
   propriety of housing for different classes,
      1373–1374
   on pulleys, 325
   on pumps, 343, 345
   on rustic huts, 299
   on siege engines, 332
   The Ten Books on Architecture, 1373
   Vitruvian proportions (architectural), 310–311
   on water engineering, 339–340
   on the waterwheel, 329
Void
   atomic theory of, 1596
Volero, Lucius Publilus
   plebeian movement, 500
Volos, map 4
Volsci, map 2
Volsiniensis, Lake, map 2
Volsinii, map 2

Volturnus River, map 2
Votive offerings
   marked important life transitions, 891
   token gifts for favors received, 890
   types offered by Greeks, 890–891
Votum (vow)
   devotio (self-sacrifice) in battle, 910
   ver sacrum (vow of spring), 910

W

Wages
   of craftsmen, 382
   of government officials, 798
Wagons. *See* Carts and wagons
Wall, Hadrian's
   commemorated in coinage, 1812
Wall construction, Greek
   classical period, 290–294
   coursed, 291, 292 *illus.,* 293 *illus.,* 294
   fortification, 291, 292, 293 *illus.*
   foundation, 281 *illus.,* 282
   joint systems, 290–291, 292 *illus.,* 293 *illus.*
   monumental dry-laid stone, 281 *illus.,* 282–283
   mud-brick, 277–278, 287, 291
   polygonal, 292, 293 *illus.*
   rubble, 282, 291
   rustification, 293 *illus.*
   surface dressing, 281 *illus.,* 293 *illus.,* 294
Wall construction, Roman
   foundation and rusticated, 312
   terra-cotta framed concrete, 318
   in the Trajan Forum, 312, 313, 314, 316–317,
      318
   types of, 301–302 *illus.,* 312, 318
   See also Masonry construction
Wall painting, Greek, 370–371
   panel pictures, 1370
   Roman mosaic replicas of, 1774
   See also Funeral painting; Monumental painting
Wall painting, Roman
   architectural context of, 1771–1772
   Candelabra articulation motif, 1777, 1780, 1783
   in the colonies and provinces, 1783–1785
   Egyptianizing style, 1777
   Fourth style, 1780–1781 *illus.,* 1782 *illus.,* 1783,
      1784
   late empire, 1788, 1789 *illus.,* 1790 *illus.*
   middle empire, 1783, 1784 *illus.,* 1785

Wall painting, Roman (continued)
   opus sectile and wall veneer, 1771–1772, 1783,
     1788, 1793
   picture gallery concept, 1777
   preservation by eruption of Vesuvius, 1772
   red-and-green linear style, 1789 *illus.*
   Renaissance revival of techniques, 1793
   surface articulation devices, 1773, 1777, 1780,
     1783
   Third style, 1777–1778 *illus.*, 1779–1780 *illus.*,
     1783
Wall veneer, art, Roman, 1771–1772, 1773–1774,
   1783, 1788–1789
   See also Marble; Wall painting
Wanax (king), 531
   in Homeric society, 442
   in Mycenaean culture, 441
Wappenmünzen
   heraldic coinage, 1796
War
   definitions of, unheralded (*akeryktos*), 669
   financing of, 798, 802
   formal declaration of, 670
Warehouse architecture, Roman
   Porticus Aemilia, 1672, 1673
Warfare
   cost of, 812
   financing of, 812–813, 822
Warfare, Greek
   behavior in victory, 689
   economic effects of, 728–729
   in historic period, 684–694
   in Homeric poems, 679–684
   military administration, 633–634
   preparation for fighting, 690
   rules of, 668–669
Warfare, Greek land
   Asiatic criticisms of, 685
   cavalry, 689–690, 690
   defense of city state, 685–686
   end of the phalanx, 707–708
   frontier guards, 685
   hoplite phalanx, 685–687, 688
   Macedonian phalanx, 691
   mercenaries in Hellenistic period, 692
   objectives of hoplite army, 685–686, 688–689,
     693
   peltasts, 692–693
   Theban column, 691
Warfare, Greek naval, 696–700
   against Persian warships, 698

Bronze Age, 697
   developments in Geometric period, 698
   diekplous, 699
   expenditures, 633–634
   fleets of Alexander's successors, 700
   Liburnians (small warships), 700
   naucraries, 634
   naval crews, 699
   periplous, 699
   quadrireme and quinquereme, 700
   rowers, 698, 700
   superdreadnoughts, 700
   trierarchs, 699, 700
   trireme, 698
   war galley, 697
Warships, 358
Washing
   as symbolic act of purification, 964
Wasps. See Aristophanes
Water engineering, Greek, 338–340
   Pergamon pipeline, 339 *illus.*
   Samos tunnel, 338
Water engineering, Roman
   open-channel method, 340
   technology of aqueducts, 340–343, 341 *illus.*,
     342 *illus.*
Water lifting
   animal labor, 328
   bucket wheel, 346–347 *illus.*
   with gears, 331 *illus.*
   waterwheel, 329–330 *illus*
Water management systems, Roman
   gutters, 314
   tile pipes and drains, 303
Water pump. *See* Force pump; Screw pump
Water supply, Greek
   construction of, 295 *illus.*, 296
Water supply, Roman, 1700
   See also Aqueducts
Water supply systems, city
   aqueducts, running water and wells, 338–343
   distribution, 342–343
Water supply systems, country
   waterwheels, pumps, and wells, 343, 345, 346,
     347 *illus.*
Water transport, 357–364
Waterwheels, 329–330 *illus.*, 352
   possible cam and lever application, 352
Wax tablets, 430, 432
Wealth
   Greek view of, 723–724

and political power in fourth-century Athens, 483–484

Solon's view of, 452–453, 454

tax on, 800, 810

Wealth. See Aristophanes

Weapons

crossbow (*gastraphetes*), 333, 334 *illus.*

See also Military engineering

Weapons, Greek

bow, 680, 683, 689

catapults, 695–696

chariot, 680, 682, 682, 683

dating of Bronze Age, 681

defensive armor, 681

helmets, 681

sarissa (pike), 691

shield, 688

spear, 680, 688

stone-throwers, 696

sword, 680

Weapons, Roman

ballista, 717

breastplate, 705

hasta (spears), 705

lancea, 718

martiobarbulus (barbed darts), 718

pilum, 705, 711

plumed helmet, 705

scutum (shield), 705

Weaving

as metaphor for poetry, 1302

noblewomen's craft, 1392

patterns, 1388

tapestry, 1388, 1402, 1410–1411

woman's art, 1302–1303

Wedding, Greek, 895–896

bride's procession to husband's home, 896

ritual bathing of bride, 896

Wedding ceremony

components of, 1349–1350

Week, planetary, 394

Wells, 343

White-ground vase painting. *See* Vase painting

William of Moerbeke

translation of Aristotle, 1825

Wills

appointing heirs, 620

before Comitia Calata, 620

fideicommissa (trusts), 620–621

legacies, 620

par aes et libram, 620

power to make, 620

in procinctu, 620

Voconian law, 620

Winch, 323–324 *illus.,* 325 *illus.*

Greek double (compound winch), 294, 325 *illus.*

Roman, 317

See also Hoist

Window lighting, Roman

alabaster glazed, 301

Basilica of Maxentius, 1686 *illus.,* 1687

influence of, 1689

Pantheon oculus, 1680, 1682 *illus.*

skylight, 1799

Winds, prevailing, 359–360

on Nile River, 363

Winds and weather

bora, 110

etesian, 111

jet stream, 110

mistral, 110

pressure centers, 110

sirocco, 110

Wine

as common Roman drink, 256

in Greek religion and culture, 256

mixing of, 256

shipping of, 361

to sustain Roman armies, 256–257

Wine production, 217

drainage and aspect of vines, 227–228

fermentation process, 230–231

grape pips in archaeological digs, 256

grapes and grape products, 255–257

grape treading, 229–230

importance of soils, 227

lever or screw press, 229, 230

must (unfermented grape juice) in food production, 256

planting and spacing of vines, 228–229

propping system for vines, 228

storage, 231

transportation and delivery, 231

vinedresser, 227

vinedressing tools, 228

westward domestication of the grape, 256

Women

as church officers, 1052

in Marcionite church, 1054

Women, Etruscan

at banquets, 1201

Women, Greek
  Adonis ritual, 1187
  afterlives of in literature, 993
  allegiance to natal household, 1311
  in athletics, 1140
  in crafts, 375
  cults of Artemis, 1338
  cultural stereotypes, 1309, 1315
  diminished status after archaic times, 1312
  disparity between literary and real roles,
    1313–1316
  drinking at symposium, 1173
  education of, 1308
  fear of female sexuality in classic literature, 1286,
    1284–1285
  female stereotypes criticized, 1309
  festivals celebrated by, 1146
  freedom of movement and social status, 1252
  in Hellenistic social organizations, 1194, 1195
  Hellenistic women's role improves, 1304, 1312
  Homeric view of, 1310
  homosexuality, 1262–1263
  images of women in classic literature, 1283–
    1286
  laws governing marriage, 596
  legal status in Athens, 595
  legislative restrictions on, 1311
  literary use of sex-role reversal, 1309
  male fear of women's mysteries, 1305
  management of oikos, 1252
  moral capabilities, 1302, 1307–1309
  mourning customs, 1394
  Musonius on equality of, 1646–1647
  mysterious and polluting aspects, 1254
  personality types in classic literature, 1283–1286
  physical ideal of, 1259–1260
  polis vs. household, 1311–1312
  political influence, 1304
  in priesthood, 926, 929
  property rights in Sparta, 594
  religious activities, 1252–1253
  religious role, 1301, 1304–1305, 1307
  ritual functions of, 1187
  ritual role in Athens, 1187
  role at feast, 1170
  role in grain processing, 238
  role at symposium, 1172, 1175
  seen as temptation, 1258
  segregation of, 1252, 1257
  sexual attitudes, 1257
  sexual attitude toward servile or foreign, 1257

  social organizations in Mytilene, 1176
  social seclusion of, 1302, 1303, 1311
  Spartan freedom, 1303, 1308, 1310
  See also Prostitution
Women, Roman, 1319–1332
  age at marriage, 1266
  denied roles in public and military service, 1322
  at dinner parties, 1201
  education in early Rome, 1110
  fides (fidelity), 1326–1327
  freedom of movement after marriage, 1329–
    1330
  homosexual activity, 1266
  ideals of behavior, 1325–1331
  membership in collegia, 1223
  in mime performances, 1490
  pietas (devotion to family), 1331
  as priests, 935
  public role in state religion, 1321
  pudicitia as restraint on women's lives, 1329
  pudor (decency, propriety), 1327
  restrictions, 1329–1330
  Roman stereotypes of, 1329–1330
  sexual attitudes, 1266–1267
  source of fama (glory or reputation), 1331
  spheres of activity, 1319–1322
  spheres of influence, 1322–1325
  wine drinking in archaic Rome, 1201–1202
Women of Trachis. See Sophocles
Wood
  varieties of Roman construction, 303–304
Wool, 374
  in Greek clothing, 1386–1387
  preparation of, 1387
  in Roman clothing, 1401
  spinning of, 1387
  weaving of, 1387–1388
Working class, free (humiliores), 566–568
  citizenship, 567–568
  classes of, 566
  debt, 567
  dispossession of, 566
  effect of slavery on, 567
  ex-slaves among, 568
  funerary monuments and social status, 568
  property ownership and status divisions, 566
  social mobility of, 568
  tenant farmers, 566–567
  urban, 568
Works and Days. See Hesiod
Workshops, 375–378

Volume One: 1–720; Volume Two: 721–1298; Volume Three: 1299–1832

Wrestling, 1132, 1135–1136
Writing
  with a pen, 426
  and spread of Greek culture, 1819
  style for biblical manuscripts, 433
Writing, Greek
  development of, 398–406
  effect on government, 451–452, 453
  importance of, 397, 408, 409–416
  and intellectual change, 409–411
  Mycenaean clay tablets, 441
  Mycenaean syllabic writing system, 450
  from Phoenician script, 450
  relation to language, 404–406
Writing materials
  inks, 425–426
  pens, 426
  stylus, 430
  surfaces, 422–425, 430–431
Writing systems
  Assyrian, 399
  Babylonian, 399
  Cypriot, 401
  Egyptian, 398–399
  Greek, 400–401, 404–406
  Phoenician, 398, 404–405
  Roman, 416–417
  Semitic, 399–400, 404–405
  syllabic, 400

X

Xanthippos (the shoemaker), 384
  grave stele, 385 *illus.*
Xanthos, map 5
  Nereid monument, 1715
Xenias of Elis
  as Spartan *proxenos,* 671
Xenokrates
  artist and author, 1756
Xenophanes of Colophon
  discoveries depend on human endeavor, 267
  on symposia, 1171, 1173–1174
  theological satire, 1500
Xenophon
  advises husband to teach wife liberal arts, 1342
  Agesilaus as model for later biographers, 1536
  Agesilaus'victory at Coronea, 688–689
  Anabasis (*The March up Country*), 444, 692, 1530, 1536
  army as polis, 444
  on artisans' social status, 743
  attempts to relate character to environment, 1536
  attitude to Zeus, 857
  belief in omens, 943
  as biographer and autobiographer, 1530
  civil war of 404 B.C., 478
  Cyropaedeia (*Education of Cyrus*), 1536
  description of typical residence, 1364
  on early childhood in Sparta, 1360
  on economic consequences of urbanization, 726
  on farmers as soldiers, 687
  on festivals, 1143–1144
  on financial management, 724
  games of the mercenaries, 1132
  Hellenica (*History of Greece*), 1529
  hunting and weapons practice, 690
  on increasing state revenues, 638
  on the laws of Lykourgos, 593
  link to epideictic literature, 1536
  on nationalization of mines, 787
  Oeconomicus (*Household Management*), 1301–1303, 1364
  rebellion of Kinadon, 1179
  on sexual intercourse, 1339
  social benefits of sacrificial generosity, 975
  on Sparta, 456
  on status of artisans, 535
  Symposium, 1183
  on sympotic customs, 1174
  Theramenes' anecdote, 1124
  use of character types in *The March Up Country,* 1280
  Vectigalia (*On Taxation*), 797
  on wife-lending in Sparta, 1336
Xerxes, king of Persia
  invasion of Greece, 25–26

Y

Yahweh
  identification with other gods, 858
Year
  designation of, 392–393
  Julian, 392
  length of, '389–390
  lunar, 390

Z

Zagora, map 4
Zakynthos, map 4
Zama, map 6
Zankle, map 2
Zenobia, queen of Palmyra
    defeat by Aurelian, 1063
Zeno of Citium
    founded Stoicism, 1617
Zeno of Elea
    attacked pluralism, 1593
Zeus
    associations, 848
    manifestations of his power, 866

myths of, 865
offspring, 865
oracle at Dodona, 948
oracle of Zeus-Ammon, 948
origin of, 848
supremacy of as precursor to monotheism,
    848
Zeuxis of Herakleia, 1749, 1756
Zodiac-moon calendar
    Antikythera mechanism, 326, 347, 348 *illus.*,
        349 *illus.*
Zoning, Greek
    for ideal city life, 1696
Zosimus, Marcus Canuleius, 386
Zygouries, map 4